MODERN GENOCIDE

MODERN GENOCIDE

The Definitive Resource and
Document Collection

VOLUME 4: RWANDAN GENOCIDE, OTHER
ATROCITIES, AND INTERNATIONAL LAW

Paul R. Bartrop and Steven Leonard Jacobs

Editors

 ABC-CLIO

Santa Barbara, California • Denver, Colorado • Oxford, England

Library of Congress Cataloging-in-Publication Data

Modern genocide : the definitive resource and document collection / Paul R. Bartrop and Steven Leonard Jacobs, editors.
   volumes cm
Includes bibliographical references and index.
ISBN 978-1-61069-363-9 (hard copy : alk. paper) — ISBN 978-1-61069-364-6 (ebook)
1. Genocide—History. I. Bartrop, Paul R. (Paul Robert), 1955–   II. Jacobs, Steven L., 1947–
   HV6322.7.M63   2015
   364.15'1—dc23   2014019716

ISBN: 978-1-61069-363-9
EISBN: 978-1-61069-364-6

19 18 17 16 15   1 2 3 4 5

This book is also available on the World Wide Web as an eBook.
Visit www.abc-clio.com for details.

ABC-CLIO, LLC
130 Cremona Drive, P.O. Box 1911
Santa Barbara, California 93116-1911

This book is printed on acid-free paper ∞
Manufactured in the United States of America

To Our Grandchildren

In the hope, and with the prayer,
that their world will become one that is freed
from the scourge of genocide

PAUL R. BARTROP
Jacob, Madeline, Mila, Asher, Max

STEVEN LEONARD JACOBS
Laun, Jacob, Greer, Drew, Liam

Contents

Entry List

RWANDAN GENOCIDE

Maps List

Preface

Genocide is a global problem of the first magnitude. It has been for hundreds, if not thousands, of years, but in the 20th century it assumed hitherto unparalleled dimensions. Numerically, more people were murdered at the hands of others, as part of deliberate policies, than at any other time in recorded history.

While the 20th century was the century of total war—two global conflicts that began in Europe in 1914 and 1939 testify to that—it was also, concurrently, the century of genocide. The destruction of entire human groups, *as policy*, saw mass annihilation on a scale much greater than that of military deaths in wartime. And not only that: frequently, war (whether international or civil conflict is immaterial) served as a mask for genocide, even though the nature of genocidal destruction is such that war need not be present in order for genocide to take place.

While whole libraries of studies have been written attempting to analyze the actions of governments, responses of bystanders, and failures to rescue the victims, collections laying out both the key reference entries and the major primary source documents of genocide are relatively rare. The purpose behind a collection of this kind is itself singular: to provide, in an easy-to-read format, the most important reference entries and documents about the century of genocide. It is intended that this will be of particular benefit to teachers and students, as well as to those not engaged in the formal study of genocide but who are interested in learning more. Much thought was put into the selection of primary source material; not only have we provided important official statements, acts, memoranda, reports, and the like, we have also included a number of personal accounts from those who were in some way involved in the genocides under examination. These range from those who were victims to those who were witnesses—and, in some cases, even to those who actually perpetrated the genocide. It is hoped, by doing so, that we have managed to retain something of the very necessary human dimension of what genocide really is: a thoroughly antihuman activity that is, in its essence, all too human is its execution.

When considering what content to include in this encyclopedia, it was decided from an early date that we would adhere to the widely accepted UN definition of genocide, as embodied in the UN Convention. The definition, located at Article 2, is as follows:

> In the present Convention, genocide means any of the following acts committed with intent to destroy, in whole or in part, a national, ethnical, racial or religious group, as such:
>
> (a) Killing members of the group;
> (b) Causing serious bodily or mental harm to members of the group;

(c) Deliberately inflicting on the group conditions of life calculated to bring about its physical destruction in whole or in part;

(d) Imposing measures intended to prevent births within the group;

(e) Forcibly transferring children of the group to another group.

Based on this definition, the encyclopedia includes the following genocides, in alphabetical order: Armenia (1915–1923), Bosnia (1992–1995), Cambodia (1975–1979), Darfur (2003–2006), East Timor (1975–1999), Guatemala (1981–1983), Herero (Namibia) (1904–1907), the Holocaust (1941–1945), Kurdistan (1988), and Rwanda (1994).

Despite our use of the term, it must be pointed out that the UN definition of genocide is imperfect, and has been interpreted in various ways by politicians to rationalize their own agendas. There is tremendous debate over what constitutes genocide. At least one scholar has argued that there are only three historical case studies that can truly be termed genocide: Armenia, the Holocaust, and Rwanda. Critics might argue that there is no justification for including Bosnia, Cambodia, Darfur, East Timor, Guatemala, Kurdistan, or Namibia in this encyclopedia. For these latter cases, the applicability of the UN Convention can be debated or questioned, but we should certainly not discount them. We also should not dismiss other events that some consider genocide. For that reason, we have included in Appendix I over one hundred reference entries on other atrocities, massacres, and war crimes that do not neatly fit the UN definition of genocide.

Some scholars place the issue of "intentionality" at the forefront of their genocide definitions. In other words, they believe that an event only qualifies as genocide if there is proven *intent* to destroy a national, ethnic, racial, or religious group. Unfortunately, there is often no "smoking gun" that leads back to the government or groups responsible for genocidal violence, making it difficult to prove that a perpetrator possesses the requisite intention to destroy a victim group based on his or her nationality, race, ethnicity, and/or religion. However, in criminal law a repeated pattern of actions resulting in the same outcome is frequently adjudged to infer intent on the part of a perpetrator, regardless of an expressed statement of intent. It is therefore our judgment that the events covered in this encyclopedia all conform, in one way or another, to the UN definition of what constitutes genocide.

In assembling this work, two people have provided particular assistance that it is our pleasure to acknowledge. Padraic (Pat) Carlin, our editor at ABC-CLIO, has at all times been professional while keeping a benevolent eye on the time and personal demands that can sometimes draw professors' attention away from deadlines and other publishing obligations. We are indeed grateful to Pat for all his support and his gentle (though necessary) prodding.

At a time when help was sorely needed, Paul Bartrop's graduate student at Florida Gulf Coast University, Sara Gottwalles, stood up and provided invaluable assistance in tracking down some hard-to-come-by documents, as well as helping to supplement the list on her own initiative. We are both personally grateful to Sara for adding to her workload, while holding down two jobs and writing her thesis, in order to help us with this project.

The entries and documents included here provide some of the most horrible reading conceivable. Horrible because of its content, yes; but also horrible because it not only happened, but isn't science fiction. The entries and documents point to events that were all too real, took place within living memory, and—tragically—are still with us today. It is in the hope that such reference material and primary source documents will one day only be historical rather than contemporary, that we dedicate this volume to our grandchildren. May they, and their generation, not know a world in which genocide is a fact of their daily lives, as it has been in ours.

Introduction

Genocide is a new word for an ancient practice, and has taken many forms in the far distant and too recent past. Death and destruction, in which innocent people were killed (often in large numbers), had always occurred during wartime. Massacres and other violations of human rights on a massive scale also frequently occurred, in which non-combatants were often deliberately targeted. But war was not, and is not, the same as genocide. This must be understood clearly. Even World War I, the greatest conflict in history up to that time—a war which resulted in the death of nearly 10 million combatants—hit civilians to the extent of 5 percent of all those who died. While this was to rise enormously as the 20th century proceeded (World War II, e.g. saw a 60 percent death rate of all casualties), it should be borne in mind that death on such a scale was essentially a phenomenon of the modern era. Genocide, though while occurring often throughout history, reached its zenith during the 20th century.

This new word—genocide—was coined by Polish-Jewish-American lawyer Raphael Lemkin (1900–1959), who has, together with his voluminous writings (much of which went unpublished during his lifetime), become the subject of renewed scholarly and popular interest. Now recognized as the "father" of the United Nations Convention on the Prevention and Punishment of the Crime of Genocide 1948, awards have been given in his name, biographical accounts of his fascinating life have been published,

and edited and commented upon texts of his writings on genocide have now appeared in print.

With regard to the specific genocides included in these volumes, we offer the following overviews. It is important to note that all of them have been—and remain—the subject of much scholarly and other investigation, and continue to generate both controversy and fresh insights.

The Herero of German South-West Africa

The German assault against the Herero people in 1904–1907, in Germany's colonial possession of South-West Africa (now Namibia), was the 20th century's first true instance of genocide. During this time, the destruction of up to 80 percent of the total population took place. The devastation was not isolated, as at least 50 percent of the Nama, or "Hottentot," population, were also wiped out at this time.

In January 1904, the Hereros rebelled with the intention of driving the Germans out of their historic lands. At this time, according to the best estimates, the Hereros numbered some 80,000. After a German counterattack, reinforcement, and a widespread campaign of annihilation and displacement that forced huge numbers of Hereros of both sexes and all ages into the Omaheke (Kalahari) Desert, tens of thousands perished. The situation was exacerbated by the policy of German General Lothar von Trotha

(1848–1920), who arrived on June 11, 1904, with more than 14,000 troops, and ordered that all waterholes be located and poisoned in advance of the arrival of those Herero who might have survived the desert. Von Trotha saw the only military solution as one of extermination and annihilation, as his infamous *Vernichtungsbefehl* ("Extermination Order"), issued on October 1, 1904, demonstrated.

Before his return to Germany, initially in disgrace but rather quickly rehabilitated, von Trotha was also responsible for the death of thousands of Nama people, with over half the population destroyed during that year alone.

The second stage of the genocide saw the introduction and implementation of so-called concentration camps and work camps under his successors. Together, these might more appropriately be termed "death camps," as diseases such as typhoid were rampant, together with other debilitating conditions such as malnutrition, extreme overwork, and constant brutality to men, women, and children.

By the time the uprising was over, the Herero and Nama populations had been destroyed by military action, starvation and thirst, disease, and by overwork in the concentration and labor camps. Evidence exists of medical experiments having been carried out as well, and of sexual crimes committed against Herero women. In 1911, when a count was made of the surviving Herero, only about 15,000 could be found. The vast majority of the rest had been killed, either directly or indirectly, by German forces over the preceding half-dozen years, though the majority of the killing had taken place during the years 1904–1905. Though somewhat contested, scholars remain divided on the issue of whether or not the behavior of the Germans in South-West Africa later set the stage for the Nazi assault on the Jews and others.

The Ottoman Genocide of Christians

Genocide was committed against the Armenian, Greek, and Assyrian populations of the Ottoman Empire by the regime of the Committee of Union and Progress (*Ittihad ve Terakki Jemyeti*), also known as the Young Turks, in the period following April 24, 1915. According to most accounts, closer to 1.5 million Armenians were slaughtered as a direct result of deliberate Turkish policies seeking the Armenians' permanent eradication.

Massacres of Armenians had already been carried out by different regimes within the Ottoman Empire during two time-frames, between 1894–1896, and 1909. In the

first, Sultan Abdulhamid II carried out a series of pogroms, the worst occurring in 1895. Estimates of those killed range widely, from anywhere between 100,000 and 300,000, with thousands more maimed and rendered homeless.

The massacre of 1909, by contrast, which occurred in the region surrounding the city of Adana, was largely the result of civil strife between supporters of the Sultan and the Young Turk reformers, in which the Armenians appeared to be scapegoats for both sides. The Adana Massacres claimed possibly up to 30,000 victims.

The reasons for these persecutions are varied. As the size of the Ottoman Empire shrank during the 19th century, conditions deteriorated for the Christian minority populations as well, who became scapegoats blamed for the deterioration of the empire. With the weakening of the Sultan's authority and respectability, a militant group of Turkish nationalists, the Young Turks, launched a revolution in 1908. Their goal was to create a modern, revitalized and pan-Turkic empire that would stretch all the way to Central Asia. The revivified Turkish state would thus need to be modernized: to achieve this, the Young Turks saw that the state would have to become militarized, industrialized, and much more nationalistic. Led by the triumvirate of Minister of Interior Mehmet Talaat Pasha (1874–1921), Minister of War Ismail Enver Bey (1881–1922), and Minister of the Navy Ahmed Djemal Pasha (1872–1922), the new regime instituted a plan that would transform the multicultural Ottoman society into a much more homogeneous Turkish and Islamic one.

The year 1915 saw a massive military defeat for Turkey at the hands of the Russians at the Battle of Sarikamish (December 22, 1914, to January 17, 1915) in the Caucasus Mountains, and further defeats in Egypt and Sinai in February. On April 20, an Armenian revolt occurred in the city of Van, and on April 25, 1915, British, French, Indian, Australian, and New Zealand (ANZAC), and Newfoundland troops landed on the Gallipoli Peninsula. The Young Turk leadership considered the regime—indeed, the Empire—to be in a state of dire peril.

Looking for a scapegoat, the Young Turk government responded swiftly and forcefully. They implemented confidential plans that had been formulated in secret party meetings several months earlier. On the night of April 24, 1915, some 250 Armenian leaders in Constantinople were arrested, in an action that precipitated the genocide to follow. Scarce military resources were then diverted to the campaign of murdering the Armenian and other Christian populations. These measures saw all the relevant agencies of government directed toward the singular aim of totally destroying the Armenian population.

At the same time as the Armenian Genocide, the Young Turks also carried out genocides against the empire's Assyrians, and the Pontic and Anatolian Greeks.

In all cases, most fatalities occurred as a result of death marches into the Syrian desert. These were the victims of heat, starvation and thirst, exposure, and incessant brutality at the hands of their captors.

The eventual result was a loss of life—in a relatively short space of time—of what had hitherto been unimagined proportions. The worst of the killing was over within about 18 months, but this did not stop the killing, and Armenian and other communities in various parts of the empire, where they were found, continued to be attacked up through the early 1920s. Today—a century later—the modern Turkish state refuses to acknowledge that what transpired at the hands of its predecessors was, in truth, genocide.

The Nazi Holocaust of the Jews

The Holocaust is the term in English most closely identified with the attempt by Germany's National Socialist regime, together with its European allies, to exterminate the Jews of Europe during World War II. While an exact number of those murdered is impossible to determine, the best estimates settle at a figure approximating 6 million Jews, 1 million of whom were children under the age of 12 and 0.5 million of whom were aged between 12 and 18.

On March 20, 1933, *Reichsführer-SS* Heinrich Himmler (1900–1945) announced the establishment of the regime's first concentration camp, Dachau, while others quickly followed. These were places of political imprisonment. Jews started being victimized from 1935 onward, due largely to the effects of the so-called Nuremberg Laws on Citizenship and Race, according to which the formal status of Jews was defined and put into practice.

The first large-scale arrests of Jews were made after November 9, 1938, in an event that has gone down in history as *Kristallnacht*, the "Night of Broken Glass." The pogrom resulted in greater concentrated destruction than any previous anti-Jewish measure under the Nazis, and spelled out to those Jews who had up to now thought the regime was a passing phenomenon that this was not the case.

Henceforth, Jews were targeted for the sole reason of their Jewishness: not what they did, but who they were. From now on, physical acts of an antisemitic nature became state policy.

The outbreak of war on September 1, 1939, saw the establishment of a system of ghettos in occupied Poland from October 1939 onward. Here, Jews were persecuted and terrorized, starved, and deprived of all medical care. From the summer of 1942 onward the ghettos began to be liquidated, with the Jews sent to one of six death camps located throughout occupied Poland.

Prior to this, however, mobile killing squads known as *Einsatzgruppen* ("Special Action Groups"), accompanying the German military during the Nazi assault on the Soviet Union beginning in June 1941, had been at work murdering all Jews found within their areas of control. The *Einsatzgruppen* would round up their captive Jewish populations—men, women, and children—take them outside of village and town areas, force the victims to dig their own mass graves, and then shoot them to death. When the repetition of that activity provided psychologically troublesome, mobile gas vans using carbon monoxide poisoning were brought in both to remove the intimacy of contact and to sanitize the process. It is estimated that between 1941 and 1943 the *Einsatzgruppen* were responsible for the death of more than 1 million Jews.

It is not known precisely when the decision to exterminate the Jews of Europe was made, though best estimates settle on sometime in the late spring or early summer of 1941, commensurate with Germany's invasion of the Soviet Union ("Operation BARBAROSSA," June 22, 1941). At a conference convened by SS General Reinhard Heydrich (1904–1942) held at Villa Wannsee, Berlin, on January 20, 1942, the process was systematized and coordinated among Nazi Germany's relevant government departments, and, in the months following, a number of camps were established in Poland by the Nazis for the express purpose of killing large numbers of Jews. These six camps—Auschwitz-Birkenau, Bełżec, Chełmno, Majdanek, Sobibór, and Treblinka—were a departure from anything previously visualized, in both their design and character. These were the *Vernichtungslager*, the death (or extermination) camps.

These camps were institutions designed to methodically and efficiently murder Europe's entire Jewish population. Mass murder took place in specially designed gas chambers, employing either carbon monoxide from diesel engines (in fixed installations or mobile vans) or crystallized hydrogen cyanide ("Zyklon B") which on contact with air oxidized to become hydrocyanic (or prussic) acid gas.

As the Nazi armies on the eastern front began to retreat before the advancing Soviet forces (and later from American and British troops in the west), renewed efforts were made to annihilate Jews while there was still time. Then, in March 1944, a shock of cataclysmic proportions then fell upon the Jews of Hungary, the last great center of Jewish population still untouched by the killing. Over 500,000 Jews were annihilated in the space of four months, in the fastest-killing operation of any of the Nazi campaigns against Jewish populations in occupied Europe.

With the Soviet armies advancing toward Germany through the second half of 1944, the evacuation of Auschwitz, the largest of these killing centers, was ordered for January 17, 1945. The earliest date of free contact with Soviet forces was January 22, 1945; when the site was formally occupied two days later, there were only 2,819 survivors left. Most of the prisoners had already been evacuated so as not to fall into Russian hands.

The evacuations have properly been called death marches, as vast numbers of prisoners died or were killed while *en route*. When the prisoners arrived at their new destination their trials were hardly eased, as they faced massive overcrowding in the camps to which they had been evacuated.

Painfully slowly, as German units both west and east surrendered, the camps were liberated, and with their liberation—and the end of the war—the objectives of those who shaped the post-1945 became dominated by the call for "Never Again." As time wore on, however, this became more and more muted owing to the onset of the Cold War. The traumatic effects of the Holocaust reverberate in Jewish communities today around the world, but most especially in the state of Israel and the United States, Jewry's two largest population centers.

The Cambodian Genocide

In April 1975, a Communist tyrant named Pol Pot won a bloody civil war in Cambodia, and began one of the most radical and dramatic attempts at remodelling an existing society the world had ever seen. In taking the Cambodian people back to the Year Zero, as he put it, at least 1.7 million (and possibly up to 2 million) people lost their lives. This would appear to be a clear-cut case of genocidal mass murder, though for some, there is a major difficulty associated with appreciating the massive human destruction that took place, based around the question of whether or not the events of that terrible time can be described as genocide according to the definition embedded in the United Nations Convention on Genocide. Some scholars, however, have chosen to label it a case of either "auto-genocide" or "self-genocide."

The difficulty lies in the fact that the majority of the deaths that took place at the hands of Pol Pot's Khmer Rouge were perpetrated against his own Khmer (Cambodian) people. Most of the victims were not targeted for reason of their membership of any of the groups identified under the United Nations definition, but were instead killed for social or political reasons. We are therefore confronted with a primary definitional issue: under what circumstances may we depart from the UN definition in order to apply the classification of genocide to an event of massive human destruction, and what are the implications of our doing so? Under international law, of course, no charge could stick, particularly in a case where those killed came from a political or social group. The task would be made harder again if there was any doubt as to the perpetrator's intention. Pol Pot intended to create a new type of communist utopia, to be sure; but did he intend to annihilate millions of his own people in order to do so—and were his victims targeted for the sole reason of their existence? The answer for Cambodia is, sometimes, yes, and at other times no. The issues of target group and of intent are key points of difficulty militating against a satisfactory blanket application of the UN Convention.

The East Timor Genocide

While the cataclysm of Cambodia was being played out, another Cold War genocide was taking place elsewhere in Asia, in the former Portuguese territory of East Timor. In 1975, one of the political factions jockeying for power in the aftermath of Portuguese decolonization, FRETILIN (*Frente Revolucionária de Timor-Leste Independente*, or Revolutionary Front for an Independent East Timor), declared the territory's independence. Within weeks Indonesian military forces invaded, declared East Timor to be that country's 27th state, and began a systematic campaign of human rights abuses which resulted in the death of up to 200,000 people—about a third of the pre-invasion population.

For many years the international response to what was happening in East Timor was one of indifference. Indonesia's neighbor, Australia, was especially keen not to antagonize the large nation to its north. United Nations resolutions calling on Indonesia to withdraw were ignored, and the United States, anxious lest a hard-line approach be seen by the Indonesians as a reason to look elsewhere for support, trod softly on the whole issue. Only in 1999, after a long period of Indonesian oppression and the threat of another outbreak of genocidal violence, was East Timor freed. In 2002 the first parliament, elected by universal suffrage and guaranteed by the United Nations, took its place in the community of nations.

The Guatemala Genocide

Throughout the late 1970s, the 1980s, and into the early 1990s, government death squads and government-supported militias in the Central American country of Guatemala killed up to 200,000 people, primarily impoverished Maya residing in tiny countryside villages. They were victims of terror, extrajudicial killings, hundreds of massacres, and, ultimately, genocide.

During the 1960s and 1970s Guatemala experienced a period of almost unbroken military rule. By way of response, political activism, in the form of Catholic "liberation theology," emerged. This emphasized solidarity with the poor, employed Marxist analysis to critique capitalist exploitation, and organized local development projects. The movement spread throughout the Guatemalan highlands, and at the same time opposition guerrilla organizations extended their reach into the Mayan regions.

On March 23, 1982, following a disputed presidential election, General José Efraín Ríos Montt (b. 1926) seized power in a coup d'état. A military *junta* immediately suspended the constitution, shut down the legislature, set up secret tribunals, and began a campaign against political dissidents that included kidnapping, torture, and extrajudicial assassinations. At first, many welcomed Ríos Montt's tough approach, as it portended an end to corruption. Moreover, he appeared to have a vision for Guatemala that included education, nationalism, an end to want and hunger, and a sense of civic pride that until now seemed to have been lacking.

However, a number of guerrilla factions that predated his ascent to power united as a group called the Guatemalan National Revolutionary Unity organization (URNG). They denounced the *junta* and intensified their attacks against the central government.

On April 20, 1982, the military high command officially launched Operation "*VICTORIA 82*" ("Victory 82"), a campaign designed to destroy the support base of the guerrillas. The slaughter that followed was aimed directly at those of Mayan descent who eked out an impoverished existence in the highlands where the insurgency was being carried out, and civilian villages were attacked in large numbers.

Little or no distinction was made, inducing widespread terror. Ríos Montt's regime saw the bloodiest single period in Guatemala's independent history. Maya suspected of sympathizing with the leftist antigovernment guerrillas were killed en masse and subjected to atrocities that included mutilation, torture, and rape. Hundreds of villages were destroyed by government troops, and up to a million Maya were displaced from their homes. It is estimated that more than 600 individual massacres took place in the Mayan highlands, including the widespread killing of women, children, and the elderly. And this, it should be pointed out, was but a part of a much larger civil war that plagued Guatemala between 1960 and 1996, during which time at least 200,000 people were killed.

The Kurdistan Genocide in Iraq

The Kurds are the largest national entity in the world without a sovereign state of their own. Comprising anywhere between 25 million and 35 million people living primarily in four nation-states—Iran, Iraq, Syria, and Turkey—they are a Muslim people who do not see themselves as Arabs and are united by language, culture, and history.

Iraqi dictator Saddam Hussein (1937–2006) possessed what can only be described as an outright hatred of the Kurds. Ali Hassan al-Majid (1941–2010) commonly known as "Chemical Ali" was minister of defense in Saddam's Ba'ath Party regime and, in addition to being Saddam's cousin, was one of his senior advisers and a brutally tough "enforcer" for the regime.

In March 1987, al-Majid was given the post of secretary-general of the Northern Bureau, the location of Iraqi Kurdistan. He issued orders for the Kurds to vacate their ancestral villages and homes, and to move into camps where they could be controlled by the Iraqi government. Those who refused to move from the "prohibited zones" were deemed traitors and targeted for annihilation. The Iraqi attack, when it came, included gassing and machine-gunning Kurds after they had been captured and taken to remote locations. The campaign, which began in 1987, was code-named *al-Anfal*, the title of one of Saddam's favorite chapters (Sura) from the Qur'an, referring to the "bounties of war."

The campaign continued through 1988, and saw Iraqi troops, military police, and reserve forces of the National Defense Battalions destroy a thousand or more Iraqi Kurdish villages and kill nearly 200,000 people, most of whom were unarmed and many of whom were defenseless women and children. Those who survived were, generally, forced into areas bereft of water, food, housing, or medical care. The genocide took place within the space of just six months. For international observers, there was little doubt that the Iraqi campaign was systematic, state-driven, and genocidal in nature.

It was here that al-Majid earned his nickname of "Chemical Ali," from the crime for which he was finally convicted: attacks in which he ordered the indiscriminate use of chemical weapons such as mustard gas, sarin, tabun, and VX against Kurdish targets.

Included among those killed were some 5,000 who died on March 16, 1988, when the town of Halabja was saturated with chemical weapons. The attack on Halabja was the largest chemical weapons assault directed against a civilian-populated area in history. For many people, the attack on Halabja is considered to be separate event from the al-Anfal genocide, though the destruction took place simultaneously with the broader campaign.

By 1988, up to 4,000 villages had been destroyed, at least 180,000 Kurds had been killed and some 1.5 million had been deported to the south of Iraq.

The Bosnian Genocide

The disaster of Bosnia-Herzegovina, in the former Yugoslavia, dominated international news for much of the 1990s. It was the first outbreak of genocide taking place in Europe since the Holocaust, and involved the killing and displacement of Bosnia's Muslims (Bosniaks) by both local Serbs and Serbian forces from the Yugoslav National Army. These actions were justified by the perpetrators on the grounds of ethnoreligious ideology and the need to acquire (or retain) territory seen as sacred by the Serbs. The questions thrown up by the genocide were many, but of greater concern was the position of the bystanders. In a world climate, especially among Western nations including the United States, which pledged after the Holocaust that such a phenomenon would never again be permitted to happen, efforts to stop the genocide while it was in progress were neither effective nor quick to emerge.

The genocide in Bosnia, between April 1992 and December 1995, was yet another case of international inaction in the face of massive human rights violations. The Western powers, led by the UN, the European Community, and NATO (and preeminently, the USA and Britain), failed consistently both to resolve the war and to stop the killing. Diplomatic efforts were subjected to ridicule, and military efforts reached their lowest ebb with what was effectively the surrender, by Dutch peacekeepers acting as part of the United Nations Protection Force (UNPROFOR), of the so-called safe haven of Srebrenica in July 1995. In the days following this surrender, nearly 8,000 Bosniak men and boys were hunted down and killed; it was the greatest massacre on European soil since World War II.

The Rwandan Genocide

The international community's guilty conscience, if indeed one existed, did not help the Tutsi population of the tiny African country of Rwanda between April and July 1994. All it took was one little spark for an intricate machinery of death to swing into operation, and this happened on April 6, 1994, with the assassination of Rwanda's authoritarian president, Juvénal Habyarimana (1937–1994).

Once in train, the genocide could only have been stopped by outside intervention—but this, when it came, did not arrive from the West, but rather from an army of Tutsi rebels known as the Rwandan Patriotic Front, who had grown up outside the country, the legacy of earlier anti-Tutsi pogroms.

In the space of 100 days, perhaps as many as 1 million people were killed in a genocide that shocked the world. Dumbfounded, the United Nations did practically nothing to stop the killing until the two peoples involved—extremist Hutu killers on the one side, and innocent Tutsi and moderate Hutu victims on the other—had exhausted the killing machine. The killings were for the most part done by hand, with the murderers using machetes (*pangus*) or nail-studded clubs (*masus*). There was nothing sophisticated or "clean" about these murders, though the genocide was carefully planned in advance, to such a degree that death lists of names marked for murder had already been prepared long before the killing actually began.

The Genocide in Darfur

In the first years of the 21st century, the Government of Sudan (GOS), aided by Arab militias known as *Janjaweed* ("devils on horseback"), carried out a campaign of terror, economic destruction, rape, and murder against the non-Arab "black Africans" of Sudan's Darfur region.

Roughly the size of France, Darfur is located in the western part of Sudan. Prior to the outbreak of violence in 2003, the population of some 6 million people consisted of dozens of different tribal groups, of which 39 percent were considered "Arab" and 61 percent were considered "non-Arab" or "black African." Due to intermarriage, distinctions owe more to lifestyle differences and cultural affiliation than race. Darfuri Arabs tend to lead nomadic lives, herding cattle and camels throughout the region, while non-Arabs tend to be sedentary farmers.

Beginning in 2003, the regime of Omar Hassan Ahmad al-Bashir engaged in a scorched earth campaign against the black Africans of Darfur. For years, the Fur, Masalit, and Zaghawa ethnic groups had been calling on the government in Khartoum to help them develop the region through the building of roads, schools, and hospitals. They were also aggrieved that Arabs were given preferential treatment over black Africans.

A rebel group, the Sudanese Liberation Army, was formed, and in early 2003 began carrying out attacks against government and military installations. Al-Bashir recruited nomadic Arabs to join forces with GOS troops to fight the rebels, but instead the army and the *Janjaweed* militias carried out a scorched earth policy against all black Africans, which saw the indiscriminate killing of men, women, and children. Young girls and women were raped. Plunder was widespread prior to hundreds of entire villages being torched. By 2006, estimates of those killed ranged upward to 400,000, with over 2 million Darfuris internally displaced and another 250,000 in refugee camps in Chad.

Eyewitness accounts describe how Sudanese government forces and *Janjaweed* would sweep into villages on horse or camel back, wielding automatic weapons and firing indiscriminately at civilians. Homes, grain stores, and crops were destroyed, while women, children, and the elderly were whipped, raped, tortured, and, frequently, murdered. These tactics were designed to terrorize victims, forcing them to flee their homelands. Once gone, Arab populations would resettle the land, effectively eradicating the rebels' power base. Even today the United Nations has been reluctant to declare—and therefore, act upon—this tragedy as genocide, with far too many individual nations following suit.

The Century of Genocide?

It would seem as though the century between 1904 and 2004 was a century in which genocide characterized world events. Indeed, the cases reflected in these volumes, as well as in the massive scholarly and popular literature related to the field (including films both documentary and fiction), all testify and provide concrete evidences of this reality.

More disturbing, however, is that contemporary nation-states appear to have learned little if anything in a preventative sense from previous genocides; if anything, the opposite appears to be the case. It might well be that successful genocides appear to inspire later iterations, almost as if only the *génocidaires* do their homework in a truly significant and meaningful way. Furthermore, political gridlock on an international level (i.e., the ongoing reluctance of nation-states to label these events as what they truly are—genocides) appears to manifest itself continuously by a failure to intervene during the worst excesses of mass slaughter; it seems as if state actors only to flex their political and military muscle after the fact when the greatest numbers of casualties have already taken place.

Then, too, while the work of such scholars as Israel W. Charny (b. 1931) in Israel and Franklin H. Littell (1917–2009) in the United States vigorously pursued the idea of a Genocide Early Warning System, neither the United Nations collectively nor individual nation-states have seriously sought to adopt such instruments. Much scholarly work has been done since the latter half of the 20th century to isolate those recurring factors which, when actualized, would lead and have led to these various genocides. More controversial, however, have been the questions of both prevention and intervention. Questions such as the following have dominated discourse: At what point in the genocidal process do the surrounding nation-states intervene to prevent further slaughter? What of those further away? What other options (e.g., economic boycotts, trade embargos, bank account freezes) are available to halt the process of genocide? Regarding intervention: At what point does knowledge of what is about to transpire and/or is transpiring early on energize others to act?

Finally, there is the question of humanitarian aid during a given genocide—despite the horror stories of repeated failures to get the aid of those most in need (specifically food, water, and medical supplies) and corruption of government workers at all levels siphoning off such good for their personal and familial use. Coupled with this is the ongoing (the keyword here being "ongoing") support on all levels once the genocide is over. What obligations and roles do the various nation-states of world assume in respect of rebuilding efforts? And for how long? Are those most responsible for bringing about the cessation of a given genocide also responsible for the judicial system of punishments? And for how long?

Questions such as these and others reflect the seriousness with which these volumes and the publisher, editors, and contributors have attempted to address these tragedies and their ongoing blights on any sense of civilization's progress. Our hope is that by educating a new generation to what has transpired in the century just concluded we can break this cycle of violence, death, and destruction and move humanity forward positively.

RWANDAN GENOCIDE

Essays

Rwandan Genocide Overview

The 1994 Rwandan Genocide, which occurred amidst a civil war between the Hutu and Tutsi, resulted in the deaths of hundreds of thousands of Tutsi. Rwanda's small size (at 10,169 square miles) belies the enormity of the bloodletting it suffered in the course of one of the largest genocides of the last century. Beginning in early April 1994, and continuing relentlessly over the next 1,000 days, an estimated 650,000 Tutsi civilians were killed at the hands of Hutu elements identified with the incumbent regime, headed by President Juvénal Habyarimana. To these must be added tens of thousands of Hutu victims, mostly from the southern parts of the country, and largely identified with opposition parties. Assessing the causes and individual responsibilities for the killings is no easy task. Few other comparable dramas have generated as much discord and controversy among local actors and outside observers.

The country's environmental constraints, social structure, and basic facts of its history have had a profound impact on the destinies of its people. Landlocked, overpopulated, and overwhelmingly dependent on agriculture, Rwanda stands as one of the poorest countries in Africa. With one of the highest population densities in the continent, the shortage of cultivable land has remained a major source of social tension in the countryside. No attempt to grasp the roots of genocidal violence, or assess the long-term viability the present regime, can overlook the implications of Rwanda's demographic explosion. From 2.5 million in 1960 Rwanda's population today is estimated at 10 million, of whom more than half live below the poverty level.

A former German colony later entrusted to Belgium—first as a Mandate under the League of Nations, and then as a Trust Territory under the United Nations—through much of the colonial era, Rwanda stood a classic example of "indirect rule." While the king (*mwami*) and his chiefs served as the legitimate instruments of colonial domination, the Tutsi as a whole saw their privileges substantially enhanced. As the main recipients of a Western education, their status as an elite group seemed firmly established—until challenged by the rise of a Hutu revolutionary movement in the mid-1950s. The postwar years saw a major shift in Belgian policies, owing in part to the rising influence of Christian Democracy among the missionary community, and UN pressures for hastening the pace of democratization. The publication in 1956 of a mildly reformist pro-Hutu manifesto, known as *Le manifeste des Bahutu,* must be seen as the first significant challenge to Tutsi hegemony, culminating in 1959 with the outbreak of widespread anti-Tutsi violence. Acting hand in hand with the Catholic clergy and the Belgian tutelle, the newly created Parmehutu party—*Parti de l'émancipation du peuple Hutu*—served as a vehicle for the defense of the Hutu masses against the elitist claims of the "feudo-hamitic" monarchists. In response, Tutsi politicians sought to

Rwanda Genocide, 1994

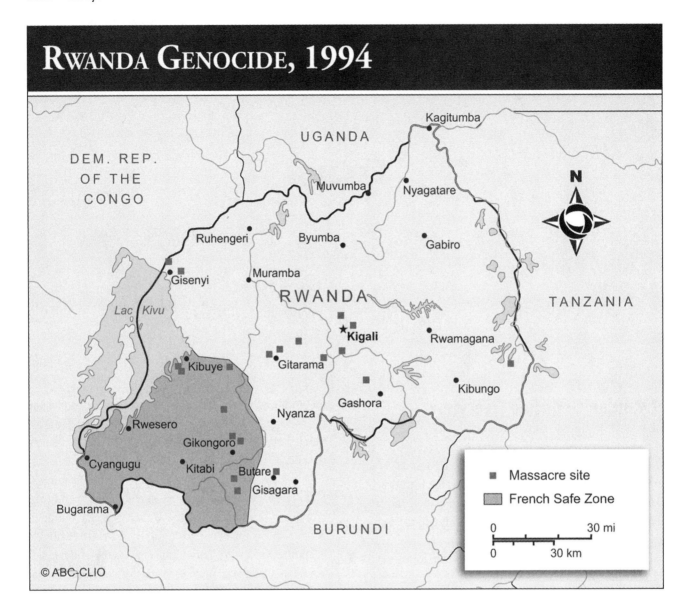

mobilize support through the *Union nationale rwandaise* (Unar), a left-leaning monarchical party formally headed by a Hutu.

The peasant uprisings that broke out in November 1959 eventually morphed into a full-fledged revolution, actively supported and encouraged by the Belgian authorities. As the country crossed the threshold of independence on July 1, 1962, as a Hutu-dominated republic, some 200,000 Tutsi had been forced into exile, mostly in Uganda, Burundi, and the Congo. Not until 32 years and a million deaths later would the country's destinies be once again be entrusted to Tutsi hands.

On October 1, 1990, some 6,000 refugee warriors of predominantly Tutsi origins marched across the border

from Uganda into Rwanda and proceeded to fight their way to the capital, Kigali. Most of them belonged to the Rwandan Patriotic Front (RPF), a politico-military organization created in 1979 by Tutsi exiles. Thus began a 30-month civil war accompanied by untold atrocities by both sides, and culminating with the pivotal event that triggered the bloodbath: the shooting down of President Habyarimana's plane on April 6, 1994, on a return flight from Dar es Salaam.

The killings began moments after the crash. The first to be targeted were Hutu officials identified with opposition parties and therefore of pro-RPF sympathies. Opposition figures, Hutu and Tutsi, were disposed of in a matter of hours. Doing away with hundreds of thousands of Tutsi civilians proved a more difficult undertaking, especially

Children who fled the fighting in Rwanda rest in Ndosha camp in Goma, Democratic Republic of the Congo, July 1994. (UN Photo/John Isaac)

in the southern region, where mixed marriages were more frequent. Nonetheless, the scale and swiftness of the massacre leaves no doubt about the determination of the machete-wielding militias. After setting up roadblocks and checkpoints, the death squads sprang into action. An estimated 20,000 people were killed in Kigali and its environs in the three weeks following the crash.

For weeks and months, from one locality after another, hundreds and thousands of Tutsi civilians (and Hutu civilians who looked like Tutsi), men, women and children, were shot, speared, clubbed, or hacked to pieces in their homes, church compounds, and courtyards. That a carnage of this magnitude could have been going on day after day, week after week, without interference from the international community speaks volumes for its lack of resolve in dealing with such massive human rights violations.

After weeks of vicious fighting in and around Kigali on July 4, the RPF effectively took control of the capital. The RPF victory and the new government were promptly recognized by the international community. On July 19,

Pasteur Bizimungu, a Hutu member of the RPF was proclaimed president of the republic for a five-year mandate, and Faustin Twagiramungu, also a Hutu, prime minister of a national unity government. But there was little doubt about who was in charge: from now on the man who led his ragtag army of refugee warriors to victory, Major General and now Vice-President Paul Kagame, would quickly assert himself as the central figure in the new Rwanda.

RENÉ LEMARCHAND

Further Reading

Barnett, Michael. *Eyewitness to a Genocide: The United Nations and Rwanda.* Ithaca, NY: Cornell University Press, 2002.

Dallaire, Roméo. *Shake Hands with the Devil: The Failure of Humanity in Rwanda.* Toronto: Random House, 2004.

Malvern, Linda. *Conspiracy to Murder: The Rwanda Genocide.* Rev. ed. London: Verso, 2006.

Prunier, Gérard. *The Rwanda Crisis, 1959–1994: History of a Genocide.* Kampala: Fountain Publishers, 1995.

Rittner, Carol. *Genocide in Rwanda: Complicity of the Churches.* St. Paul, MN: Paragon House, 2004.

Straus, Scott. *The Order of Genocide: Race, Power, and War in Rwanda.* Ithaca, NY: Cornell University Press, 2008.

Rwandan Genocide Causes

No particular event or set of circumstances can be singled out as the cause of the genocide. A multiplicity of underlying factors lies behind the tragic outcome. That there are proximate and remote causes is not at issue. Where disagreements arise is on the question of responsibility in the chain of events leading to the apocalypse.

While there is broad consensus about the determining impact of the crash of President Juvénal Habyarimana's plane on subsequent events, there are basic differences of opinion as to who was responsible for shooting the SA-6 missiles (of Ugandan provenance) that brought the plane down. Some observers—among them Philip Gourevitch in the United States and Jean-Pierre Chrétien and Gérard Prunier in France—insist that the "dastardly deed" was the work of Hutu extremists associated with the presidential entourage, the so-called akazu in Kinyarwanda, or "little hut"; perceived as too moderate in dealing with the Rwandan Patriotic Front (RPF), only by eliminating the president could the country be reset on the right path. Such is also the official version endorsed by the new Rwandan authorities.

Others take a radically different view, pinning full responsibility on Paul Kagame. They point to the fragility of the argument in support of an akazu plot given that the crash of the presidential aircraft took the lives some of its key members; they draw attention to the massive body of circumstantial evidence available from the testimonies of ex-RPF defectors, including the devastating accusations made by Lieutenant Abdul Joshua Ruzibiza in his *Rwanda: L'histoire secrète* (2005); they show that only the RPF could have had access to SA-6 missiles from a Ugandan arsenal, and furthermore go on to point to the well-grounded fear on the part of Kagame that if elections were to be held three years down the road, as had been agreed at the Arusha conference in 1993, the Hutu would most certainly come out on the winning side. This, by and -large, is the position endorsed by a number of experts on Rwanda, most notably Filip Reyntjens in Belgium and André Guichaoua in France. The counterargument most frequently advanced, that "there is no smoking gun," loses much of its force when confronted with the growing amount of evidence suggesting otherwise.

Regardless of such differences, for the vast majority of Hutu observers there could be no question that the RPF was behind the crash of the presidential plane. This fact alone played a critical role in mobilizing the militias. But the context in which it happened is no less significant.

From the beginning of the RPF invasion on October 1, 1990, Hutu and Tutsi lived in a climate of extreme fear and uncertainty. The country was awash in anti-Tutsi propaganda; the wildest rumors spread about the infiltration of Tutsi spies (*ibyetso*) within the government and opposition parties; while the civil war exacted a mounting toll among civilians, anti-Tutsi sentiment gathered momentum; the assassination of a number of moderate Hutu politicians further contributed to raise intense fears within and outside the Hutu community. In such highly charged political climate it is easy to see why hard-liners were able to channel anti-Tutsi feelings into mass killings. What is involved here has little to do with what some refer to as Rwanda's "culture of obedience"; the critical factor must be found in the capacity of Hutu extremists to manipulate ethnic fears to their advantage.

Tempting though it is to dismiss the importance of history as a predisposing factor, to do so is to make unduly short shrift of the broader context in which genocide occurred. The first point to stress is that the seeds of the RPF invasion were sown during the 1959–1962 Hutu revolution. The first and second generation of Tutsi refugees living in Uganda shared intense longings to return to their beloved homeland, a sentiment reinforced by the growing economic and political constraints they faced in the host country. The same applies to most exiles living in the Democratic Republic of the Congo (DRC) and Burundi: they needed little prodding to join the RPF crusade. As for the million or so Tutsi living in Rwanda they were generally considered as potential allies. Few had forgotten the anti-Tutsi pogroms unleashed in Rwanda in December 1963, under the presidency of Grégoire Kayibanda, when, in the wake of an aborted raid by refugees coming from Burundi, thousands were killed. Kayibanda's overthrow by a northern army man, Juvénal Habyarimana, in July 1975, resulted in a major power shift among Hutu politicians: as northern Hutu elements—a culturally distinct subgroup also known as Kiga—became more influential, their anti-Tutsi dispositions, rooted in history and culture, came into sharper focus.

The regional context played a major role. While there is reason to believe that there would have been no genocide in the absence of the RPF invasion, the invasion would have never succeeded without the full support—military, logistical, and political—of Uganda's President Yoweri Museveni. This is not to minimize Kagame's impressive military skills, but to stress the importance of external safe havens in facilitating the recruitment of

RPF combatants. If support from Uganda proved critical for the RPF, political events in Burundi were equally important in sharpening the edge of ethnic conflict in Rwanda. The assassination on October 21, 1993, of the first popularly elected Hutu president, Melchior Ndadaye, by a phalanx of hardcore Tutsi elements within the Burundi army, meant that for the foreseeable future the Tutsi-dominated military would reign supreme, allowing the free passage of Rwandan refugees to join the ranks of the RPF. In Rwanda, furthermore, the news of Ndadaye's death was received with consternation and anger; Hutu suspicions that "you just cannot trust the Tutsi" seemed amply confirmed. When five months later came the announcement that the newly appointed president of Burundi, Cyprien Ntaramyira, was among those on board when Habyarimana's plane exploded in midair, suspicion became certainty. By then few Hutu could ignore let alone forgive the fact that in five months three Hutu presidents had been killed at the hands of Tutsi elements.

To emphasize the significance of contextual factors is not to deny the contribution of environmental forces, of which the most obvious is population pressure on the land. This dimension has been ably analyzed by Jared Diamond in his chapter on Rwanda in his best-selling book, *Collapse: How Societies Choose to Fail or Succeed* (2005). There is no question that the Malthusian equation cannot be left out of the accounting in any attempt to explain not just Hutu-Tutsi hostility but intra-Hutu violence as well. Land hunger, and more generally the desire of perpetrators to acquire the property belonging to their victims, is indeed an important element in the background of the genocide. Equally plain, however, is that a tragedy of this magnitude is not reducible to a Malthusian prophecy.

RENÉ LEMARCHAND

Further Reading

Barnett, Michael. *Eyewitness to a Genocide: The United Nations and Rwanda.* Ithaca, NY: Cornell University Press, 2002.

Dallaire, Roméo. *Shake Hands with the Devil: The Failure of Humanity in Rwanda.* Toronto: Random House, 2004.

Rwandan Genocide Consequences

The depth and extensiveness of the transformations ushered by the new rulers are difficult to overestimate. No sector of society remained untouched. While the country's rate of economic growth surpassed all expectations, the degree of coercion exercised by the new regime in suppressing the opposition dispelled all hopes for a genuine transition to multiparty democracy.

The process of political consolidation orchestrated by Paul Kagame began immediately after seizing control of the capital, with the appointment of a government of national unity comprising a number of opposition politicians, a move in keeping with the political overture announced by the Rwandan Patriotic Front (RPF). Approximately half of the cabinet ministers were of Hutu origins, including the Mouvement Révolutionnaire National Pour le Développement (MDR) prime minister, Faustin Twagiramungu. Along with power-sharing at the top, however, every effort was made to remove most of the local officials appointed by the previous regime. Many simply disappeared. Meanwhile, the revenge killings reported by Alison Des Forges in her definitive inquest into the genocide, *Leave None to Tell the Story* (1999), went on unabated, causing tens of thousands of deaths among Hutu civilians.

The arrests taking place in the countryside soon took on dramatic proportions. From 30,000 in November 1994, the number of Hutu suspected of participating in the genocide jumped to 80,000 a year later, eventually reaching twice that number in the late 1990s. The brutality of the regime came in full light during the so-called Kibeho incident, in 1995, when an estimated 5,000 Hutu IDPs (internally displaced persons), fleeing the war zone, were killed in cold blood. In the face of this rapidly deteriorating situation power-sharing proved impossible to sustain. By 1995 the ministers representing the opposition had no choice but to resign. Another major crisis erupted in early 2000 when three high ranking officials, two of them Hutu, resigned from their positions as speaker of the National Assembly (Joseph Sebarenzi), prime minister (Pierre-Célestin Rwigema), and president of the republic (Pasteur Bizimungu). On April 17, 2000, General Kagame was formally elected president of the republic in a joint session of the government and the National Assembly.

The trend toward dictatorial control was made clear during the 2003 presidential and legislative elections, the first to be held since the regime change. In view of newly adopted constitutional provisions giving the government a blank check to sanction anyone or any organization suspected of encouraging "divisionism"—a move clearly intended to eventually disqualify Hutu parties and candidates from running for office—it is no surprise that Kagame ran virtually unopposed in the 2003 presidential elections, winning 95 percent of the vote. The RPF, meanwhile, gained unfettered control of both houses. Much the same scenario unfolded during the 2008 elections, when Kagame was reelected with 98 percent of the vote. Both in 2003 and 2008 Hutu candidates were systematically discouraged or prevented from campaigning or running for the presidency. In April 2003 the MDR, until then the only significant opposition party, was dissolved on the grounds of being "divisionist"; the same fate befell the leading human rights organization, *Ligue pour la promotion des droits de l'homme au Rwanda* (LIPRODHOR); a similar accusation was used to discredit and arrest independent journalists, notably those associated with the newspapers *Le Partisan* and *Umuseso*. The most celebrated case of a candidate to the presidency disqualified and then arrested and brought to trial on the grounds of "divisionism" is that of Victoire Ingabire, president of the United Democratic Forces-Inkingi (FDU-Inkingi); on October 30, 2012, she was found guilty on six counts, including genocide ideology and divisionism, and sentenced to eight years in jail.

With the banning of all references to Hutu and Tutsi, ethnic identities have been drastically reshaped. Starting from the premise that ethnicity was the root cause of the genocide, the regime found in the banishment of ethnic labels the best guarantee of social harmony. Since Hutu and Tutsi have been legislated out of existence, Rwanda has officially become the land of the *Banyarwanda* ("the people of Rwanda"). Such drastic alteration of the country's ethnic map required drastic means. Only through a constitutional amendment, accompanied by extensive legal sanctions, could "divisionism" become an effective political tool to disqualify, harass, arrest, or expel Hutu opposition candidates.

Profound as the consequences have been domestically, the fallout from the genocide went far beyond Rwanda's borders. Beginning in July 1994 widespread fear of an impending countergenocide caused a huge outflow of Hutu refugees into the Democratic Republic of the Congo (DRC). Over 2 million, including civilians, army men, politicians, and civil servants, sought asylum in eastern DRC. Soon countless cross-border raids were launched against Rwanda by remnants of the Forces Armées Rwandaises (FAR) and génocidaires. In November 1996, in response to mounting threats to the country's security, Kagame sent units of the Rwandan Patriotic Army (RPA) into eastern DRC with instructions to destroy every refugee camp along the border with Rwanda and Burundi. In a matter of days some 20 camps were reduced to rubble.

Countless refugees perished and over a million ran for their lives. Except for the half a million or so who went back to Rwanda, thousands died of exhaustion, disease, and hunger. A considerable number of those reported missing were killed by the Rwandan army. Having made the Congo borderland safe for Rwanda, Kagame now proceeded to make sure his control would extend to the entire country.

By then an entirely new ball game came into view, with Rwanda and Uganda joining hands with the anti-Mobutist Congolese rebellion led by Laurent Kabila. While his newly created movement, the Alliance of Democratic for the Liberation of the Congo (ADFL) received much of the credit for its victorious march on Kinshasa, the Rwandan army, as is now acknowledged, did much of the heavy lifting. In May 1997 Mobuto Sese Mobutu was overthrown and replaced by Kabila as the new "king" of the Congo, but the Rwandan kingmakers continued to yield considerable influence in the affairs of the state. So much so that in August 1998 Kabila felt he had no choice but to get rid of his Rwandan advisers, a move that turned his former allies into bitterest enemies and led straight to the catastrophic second Congo civil war (1998–2003).

With the world's attention fixated on regime change in Kinshasa, little attention was paid to the 1996–1997 wholesale massacre of Hutu refugees in eastern DRC at the hands of Rwandan soldiers assisted by elements of ADFL. Although hints of the atrocities committed by Kagame's army had transpired in Western media long before, not until July 2010, with the publication of the *UN Mapping Report*, was the magnitude of the carnage disclosed to the outside world. As many as 300,000 Hutu civilians may have lost their lives between November 1996 and July 1997. Just how many génocidaires were able to survive the extensive "search-and-destroy" operations conducted jointly by the RPA and the AFDL is unknown; what is beyond doubt is that among them are many of the Hutu extremists responsible for the violence now sweeping across eastern DCR.

RENÉ LEMARCHAND

Further Reading

Prunier, Gérard. *The Rwanda Crisis, 1959–1994: History of a Genocide.* Kampala: Fountain Publishers, 1995.

Rwandan Genocide Perpetrators

The vast majority of perpetrators were ordinary citizens, mostly young men, many with a secondary education; they were fathers and husbands, school teachers and farmers, with no record of previous involvement in violence. As Scott Straus has convincingly demonstrated in *The Order of Genocide* (2006) far fewer were involved than suggested by the Paul Kagame government: between 175,000 and 210,000 is the overall figure cited by Straus, representing 7–8 percent of the active adult Hutu population, or 14–17 percent of the adult male Hutu population. Approximately 50 percent of the killers were between the ages of 15 and 29; 70 percent were farmers; many belonged to party youths, with the Mouvement Révolutionnaire National Pour le Développement (MRND, National Revolutionary Movement for Development) youth wing, the *Interahamwe* ("those who fight together"), playing a central role. Given that the MRND recruited the bulk of its members from the north, it is hardly surprising that the militias of northern origins were at the forefront of the anti-Tutsi violence. Every party had a youth wing, including opposition parties. Where the Interahamwe stand out as a particularly dangerous organization is that their members were militarily trained, relatively well rewarded for their dirty work, and consistently egged on by radical elements to take a lead role in the genocide.

The perpetrators consisted of different social categories. At the core of the genocide stood the hard-liners who manned the killing machine, drawn from the *akazu*, the army, high-ranking members of the MNRD, and a handful in charge of running the media. They were the orchestrators of the violence carried out in the lower echelons, prefectures, and communes. Here a rough division of labor emerged between two distinctive groups: on the one hand the prefectoral and communal elites, including prefects, communal councilors, communal secretaries and burgomasters, heads of NGOs, and in some instances local church officials; and on the other the grassroots "thugs," the jetsam and flotsam who formed the bulk of the militias, that is, unemployed youths, delinquents, demobilized soldiers, and police officers. They are perhaps best described as the foot soldiers of the killing machine.

Although this pattern applies broadly to the country as a whole, the dynamics of violence were by no means the same everywhere. Depending on the personalities holding office, and the geographical context, the perpetrators met significant resistance in some places—as in the Butare commune, where the incumbent prefect and his administrators courageously stood his ground against Hutu militias for three weeks after the start of the killings in Kigali. Perhaps the most striking feature of the violence

that took place at the communal level has been the trial of strength between moderates and hard-liners among local Hutu elites. This has been well described by Scott Straus: he shows how, after Juvenal Habyarimana's assassination and the resumption of the war, a number of communes became the theater for a play for power among Hutu; in this "space of opportunity" a premium was placed on extremism, since compliance with incitements from the top served as a basis of legitimacy for aspiring Hutu politicians. Only in one commune (Giti) did the scenario fail to materialize: the only people killed were those Hutu who fell under the bullets of the "liberating" Rwandan Patriotic Army (RPA).

In a sense the killings became a strategy for gaining power. But such calculations cannot be imputed globally to all perpetrators. Nor can the killings be reduced to a premise of blind obedience built into Rwanda's cultural matrix, or simply to greed, even though this may well have been the case in a number of cases. Although there is little question about the core group's visceral hatred of the Tutsi as a group, widely seen as the enemy, it is equally true that a majority of those who killed did so because they feared retribution if they did not. Many felt that their only option was to kill or be killed. Even when confronted with the choice of killing their Tutsi wives or relatives or being killed many chose to save their own lives.

Tempting as it is to invoke the legacy of a strong state—the hallmark of the political system since precolonial times—as the normative framework for explaining compliance with orders from above, the argument raises further questions. As we now realize, as the killings got under way, bitter disagreements emerged among representatives of the state, casting doubts about its coherence. In his most recent book, *Rwanda: De la Guerre au Génocide* (2010), based on a close examination of the testimonies before the Arusha-based International Criminal Tribunal for Rwanda (ICTR), André Guichaoua shows how the genocide, so far from resulting from a long-standing state-sponsored master plan, came about as the consequence of a bitter fight for supremacy between the moderates associated with the interim government headed by Prime Minister Jean Kambanda and the three notorious hard-liners who stand as the architects of the killings: Colonel Théoneste Bagosora, Joseph Nzirorera, and Mathieu Ngirumpatse, respectively, adviser to the minister of defense, secretary-general, and chair of the MNRD. In addition to having access to substantial financial resources, all three enjoyed wide-ranging connections within and outside the government; they stood out among the biggest of the big men (*bagaragu*) surrounding the presidency, and as such could reshape and reactivate the strategic patron-client ties that have always formed the axis around which much of Rwandan politics revolved.

RENÉ LEMARCHAND

Further Reading

Dallaire, Roméo. *Shake Hands with the Devil: The Failure of Humanity in Rwanda*. Toronto: Random House, 2004.

Rwandan Genocide Victims

How many died at the hands of the perpetrators is impossible to tell. The most plausible figure is 650,000, overwhelmingly Tutsi. But this leaves out the accounting the tens of thousands of Hutu killed by other Hutu in the course of the genocide, because of their affiliation to opposition parties, or because they tried to protect their Tutsi friends and relatives. Again, when the tens of thousands of Hutu civilians killed by Paul Kagame's troops during and after the invasion are added to the wholesale murder of Hutu refugees in eastern Democratic Republic of Congo (DRC) in 1996 and 1997, the total number of Hutu victims may well exceed the number of Tutsi losses.

Above and beyond such macabre accounting certain facts are well established. For one thing, the killing of Tutsi civilians by the Forces Rwandaises de Défense (FAR, Rwanda Defense Forces) and the militias began long before Juvénal Habyarimana's assassination. Scores if not hundreds of Bagogwe—a Tutsi-related minority living in the northeast—were massacred by FAR soldiers in the wake of the January 23, 1991, surprise attack on Ruhengeri by the Rwandan Patriotic Front (RPF), leading to the liberation of a number of prisoners. In March 1992 in the Bugesera region, east of Kigali, for the first time the authorities called upon groups of Interahamwe to kill Tutsi as part of their communal work (*umuganda*). When it became clear that the killings could not be denied, the argument put forth by the authorities was that they could not control outbursts of popular anger. This became a standard argument in the arsenal of those officials who denied responsibility in the massacre.

All cabinet ministers belonging to opposition parties, irrespective of ethnic identities, were killed the day following Habyarimana's assassination. This was essentially the work of the presidential guard. Their prime target

were moderate Hutu elements affiliated to the Mouvement Démocratique Républicain (MDR, Democratic Republican Movement); the Parti Social Democrate (PSD), Social Democratic Party; and the Parti Liberal (PL, Liberal Party); including its president, Lando Ndasingwa. Forty hours after the crash roadblocks were set up throughout the capital, manned by *Interahamwe*. The carnage then began to spread to rural areas and provincial towns, causing thousands of panic-stricken Tutsi civilians to flee their homes. While some were sheltered by Hutu neighbors, others tried to flee to RPF-controlled areas, and still others sought refuge in churches or went into hiding in neighboring swamps. The worst massacres took place in mission churches and mission compounds, as in Nyamata, Musha, Karubamba. Throughout the carnage the media, including notoriously murderous Radio-Télévision Libre des Mille Collines, played a major role in whipping up anti-Tutsi hatred. Through caricatures and historical narratives newspapers such as *Kangura, La Médaille-Nyiramacibiri,* or *Power* never missed an opportunity to remind their readers of the evil-mindedness of the Tutsi, in keeping with the image of the Hamites conveyed by Hutu pundits and commentators. The Hutu-Tutsi cleavage became the omnipresent frame of reference for distinguishing between friend and foe. When doubts arose about the victims' ethnic identity, a look at their identity cards was enough to spell the difference between life and death, yet cases were reported of Tutsi-looking Hutu being killed for no reason other than their body maps.

The methods employed by the génocidaires have been described with clinical precision in a number of reports, notably by Human Rights Watch and Physicians for Human Rights. Their weapons of choice included machetes, massues (clubs studded with nails), axes, knives, fragmentation grenades; many victims were beaten to death; others were amputated and left bleeding; some were drowned or buried alive; women were routinely raped before being killed. The use of firearms became increasingly frequent after the debacle of the FAR, when soldiers and militias joined hands in their cleansing operations. The metaphors used to conceal the horror left few doubts to the imagination: killings were generally referred to as "collective work" (*umuganda*); cutting limbs was "bush clearing"; murdering women and children was "pulling out the roots of the bad weeds."

It bears repeating that not all victims were Tutsi; nor were the perpetrators invariably Hutu. It is now widely believed that many of the moderate Hutu killed before and after the crash were dispatched by RPF elements, as a strategy designed to deepen the rifts between extremists and moderates. Again, there is now substantial evidence available from impartial observers to suggest that many horrendous crimes were committed by the RPF in the course of its campaign. Nor is there any doubt that a large number of Tutsi could have been saved if, instead of making a run for the capital city, the FPR had attended to the urgency of saving endangered lives. Capturing power was all that mattered, even if it meant turning a blind eye to scenes of mayhem in the countryside.

RENÉ LEMARCHAND

Further Reading

Straus, Scott. *The Order of Genocide: Race, Power, and War in Rwanda.* Ithaca, NY: Cornell University Press, 2008.

Rwandan Genocide Bystanders

The United Nations Assistance Mission for Rwanda (UN-AMIR) was the UN peacekeeping operation established by Security Council Resolution 872 to help implement the Arusha Peace Accords, the latter of which was signed by various parties (the Rwandan Patriotic Front [RPF] and the Government of Rwanda) on August 4, 1993. UNAMIR's mandate was, in part, to monitor the cease-fire agreement (the two factions had been engaged in combat off and on since October 1990); establish and expand the demilitarized zone and demobilization procedures; provide security for the Rwandan capital city of Kigali; monitor the security situation during the final period of the transitional government's mandate leading up to elections; and assist in the coordination of humanitarian assistance activities in conjunction with relief operations.

In actuality, UNAMIR's mandate and strength were revised on a number of occasions throughout the duration of its operation, mostly as a result of the genocide in Rwanda between April and July 1994. After the start of the genocide in April 1994, UNAMIR attempted to broker a cease-fire between the RPF and various extremist Hutu forces but to no avail, acting as an intermediary between the killers and the victims and assisting in humanitarian activities. With this change, however (as a result of Security Council Resolution 912), the number of troops composing UNAMIR was reduced from 2,548 to 270. As the killing intensified,

the United Nations altered the mandate of UNAMIR once again, and under Security Council Resolution 918 of May 17, 1994, it imposed an arms embargo against Rwanda, called for urgent international action, and increased UN-AMIR's strength to 5,500 troops. (Despite this, it took nearly six months before member states of the United Nations donated troops.)

UNAMIR was on a Chapter VI (or traditional peace-keeping) mandate that was untenable in light of the circumstances, which was exacerbated by the fact that the force was undermanned, under-resourced, and provided with poorly equipped and poorly trained troops from a variety of small and impoverished nations. Despite UN-AMIR's force commander Major-General Romeo Dallaire's repeated pleas to the United Nations for a stronger mandate (Chapter VII or a peace enforcement mandate) and more troops and arms that would have allowed the force to engage the génocidaires in combat, the United Nations retained its totally inadequate Chapter VI mandate and refused to provide him with additional troops. As a result, he and his troops were more or less forced to observe, up-close, the unfolding of the horror of the genocide.

In one of his last cables to UN headquarters toward the end of the genocide, Dallaire was scathing about the UN's failure to upgrade UNAMIR's mandate at the time it was most needed to save lives. Summing up, Dallaire wrote that the international community and UN member states, with only a few exceptions, "have done nothing substantive to help the situation." Debate has since raged about how effective UNAMIR could have been with a more wide-ranging mandate and the capacity to use force to end the genocide in Rwanda. In the absence of clear-cut answers, such debate is likely to continue far into the future.

With the capture of Kigali by rebel Rwandan Patriotic Front troops in mid-July 1994, UNAMIR resumed its efforts to ensure security and stability and support humanitarian assistance and refugee relief. At the request of the new, postgenocide Rwandan government of Paul Kagame, UNAMIR was withdrawn in March 1996.

RENÉ LEMARCHAND

Further Reading

Kuperman, Alan. *The Limits of Humanitarian Intervention: Genocide in Rwanda.* New York: Brookings Institution Press, 2001.

Rwandan Genocide International Reaction

The lack of effective response from the international community became dramatically clear on April 21 when the United Nations (UN) voted to reduce the United Nations Assistance Mission for Rwanda (UNAMIR) presence by nearly 90 percent, to 270 men. The pullout of UNAMIR troops, precisely when the killing frenzy reached a new pitch of intensity, had disastrous consequences. Besides being readily interpreted as a sign of weakness by the Hutu extremists, it sent the wrong message to those countries that had contributed troops. The move was emblematic of the sense of confusion and impotence displayed by the permanent members of the UN Security Council after the killing of 10 Belgian soldiers by the FAR on April 7. Although the UN Security Council reversed itself on May 6, when it adopted a new resolution providing for a 5,500-man deployment operating under Chapter 7 of the UN Charter, thus allowing the potential use of force when the circumstances required, by then the crisis had already spinned out of control.

Among the countries with close ties with Rwanda, Belgium was too traumatized by the death of its Blue Helmets to react constructively to the crisis. The United States, still smarting from its disastrous intervention in Somalia, showed little inclination to get involved in another messy situation in a country where it had no vital interests at stake. France, on the other hand, under rising domestic pressures, decided to launch what became known as "Operation Turquoise," designed to provide protection and humanitarian assistance. Thus, beginning on June 23, immediately after the Security Council gave France the green light to intervene under Chapter 7, some 2,500 men, accompanied by impressive fire power and equipment, fanned out of Goma (Democratic Republic of Congo) into eastern Rwanda where they carved out a Safe Humanitarian Zone (SHZ).

Gérard Prunier, who was closely associated with the planning of the operation, openly admits in his book *The Rwanda Crisis* (1995), that the French intervention delivered far less than it promised. While it may have saved hundreds of Tutsi lives, it failed to prevent the massacre of thousands of others, while at the same time giving ammunition to critics who blamed the French for allowing the génocidaires to evade capture. A more devastating criticism points to the early failure of the French to rein in the murderous activities of the Forces Rwandaises de Défense (FAR, Rwanda Defence Forces): although they worked hand in hand with the Juvénal Habyarimana government in the training of its army, and in providing military assistance in the weeks immediately following the Rwandan Patriotic Front (RPF) invasion, nothing was done to halt the killings, even though hundreds of French troops were on the ground at the time the crisis erupted.

The French were not alone in laying themselves open to criticisms. While the French finally recognized the existence of a genocide in May 1994, the representative of the U.S. State Department consistently refused to use the g-word, instead referring to "acts of genocide." By refusing to label the ongoing massacre as a genocide, the United States felt it was under no obligation to intervene. Not until 1998 would President Bill Clinton express regrets in Kigali, but conspicuously avoided taking personal responsibility.

The sense of shame and embarrassment felt by Western nations for their inaction goes far in explaining the vast quantities of financial and economic assistance to the new authorities, which also helps account for Kigali's impressive economic performance over the years. Aid flows steadily increased over the years, growing by over 45 percent between 2006 and 2009 (reaching $711 million in official development assistance [ODA] in 2007). But as recent research by An Ansom and Donatelle Rostagno shows, inequality remains a major problem, and so also the rising levels of poverty: between 2000 and 2005 the absolute number of poor individuals increased by 560,000, while the number of those living in extreme poverty rose to 190,000. Nor did development aid from the West prevent the Paul Kagame government from intervening in the domestic politics of the DRC. Only in 2012, after a UN report disclosed the military support given by Kigali to insurgents in eastern DRC, did donors, including the United States, finally agree to suspend their economic and/or military assistance. Hence the paradox noted by Eugenia Zorbas: while the sense of guilt shared by the West translates into high levels of aid dependence, the government of Rwanda remains blissfully indifferent to Western proddings in terms of its policy options. That this situation is becoming highly counterproductive in terms of U.S. interests in Central Africa is all too clear; how long it may endure is anybody's guess.

RENÉ LEMARCHAND

Further Reading

Kuperman, Alan. *The Limits of Humanitarian Intervention: Genocide in Rwanda.* New York: Brookings Institution Press, 2001.

Timeline

March 24, 1957
The Bahutu Manifesto is published.

1985
The Rwandan Patriotic Front is established by Paul Kagame and Fred Rwigyema.

1990
The Interahamwe is formed.

May 1990
The first issue of Kangura newspaper is first published.

October 1, 1990
Civil war begins in Rwanda.

1992
The Impuzamugambi is formed.

1992
Pauline Nyiramasuhuko is made the minister of family welfare and women's affairs.

February 1992
The Coalition pour la Défense de la République (CDR) is founded.

June 12, 1992
Peace talks begin in Arusha.

1993
Jean Paul Akayesu becomes the mayor of Taba.

July 8, 1993
Radio-Télévision Libre des Mille Collines begins broad casting.

August 4, 1993
The Arusha Accords are signed.

October 3, 1993
Twenty-four UN peacekeepers and 18 U.S. soldiers are killed in Somalia.

October 5, 1993
The United Nations Assistance Mission for Rwanda (UNAMIR) is created.

October 21, 1993
Burundi president Melchior Ndadye is assassinated. During the coup, 10,000 are murdered, and approximately 375,000 flee to Rwanda.

October 22, 1993
UNAMIR Force Commander Romeo Dallaire arrives in Kigali.

November 1993
Jacques-Roger Booh-Booh becomes head of UNAMIR.

December 30, 1993
Sixty civilians are reported dead near Ruhengeri during November 1993 in a UN report.

January 11, 1994
Dallaire requests protection for an Interahamwe military informant providing information on weapons caches and planned attacks of RPF and Belgian soldiers and to pursue a reconnaissance mission to verify the intelligence.

February 1994
Political figures Felicien Gatabazi and Martin Bucyana are assassinated.

February 1994
The final issue of Kangura is published.

February 22, 1994
Thirty-seven are killed during an outbreak of political violence.

March 1994
Kabuga reportedly imports 50,000 machetes from Kenya. It is believed that these were purchased to be used as weapons in the massacres to follow.

April 6, 1994
The plane carrying Juvénal Habyarimana and Cyprien Ntaryamira is shot down.

April 7, 1994
Amnesty International reports government officials Faustin Rucogoza, Landoald Ndasingwa, Frédéric Nzamurambano, and human rights activist Charles Shamukiga have been taken prisoner by the presidential guard.

April 7, 1994
Prime Minister Agathe Uwilingiyimana is assassinated. UN military observer Mbaye Diagne rescues her five children from a nearby compound.

April 7, 1994
Minister for Labor and Social Affairs Landoald Ndasingwa and his family are murdered by members of the presidential guard.

April 7, 1994
Ten Belgian UN officers are killed.

April 7, 1994
Those seeking shelter at the parish of Mushubi are killed.

April 8, 1994
The evacuation of foreigners in Rwanda begins.

April 8, 1994
The interim government is established.

April 9, 1994
Agathe Habyarimana is evacuated to France.

April 9, 1994
Interahamwe forces attack a church at Gikondo, in Kigali. Approximately 100 die.

April 9, 1994
The RPF proposes a join force with UNAMIR and the Rwandan army to end the slaughter of civilians. The proposal is rejected.

April 9, 1994
RPF soldiers reportedly kill Sylvestre Bariyanga.

April 10, 1994
Belgian Operation SILVER BACK begins.

April 11, 1994
Ex-patriates and Belgian soldiers are evacuated from the Ecole Technique Officielle (ETO), in a suburb of Kigali. Civilians at ETO under UNAMIR protection are massacred following the departure.

April 11, 1994
Eight hundred are killed by government supporters in Murambi.

April 12, 1994
The Nyange parish is surrounded by Hutu soldiers and Interhamwe militiamen. Attacks on the parish last until April 16, when the church is bulldozed and all survivors are killed.

April 13, 1994
RPF murders in Murambi, Byumba, begin.

April 15, 1994
The Adventist compound of Mugonero is surrounded by Hutu extremists. Three thousand die following the attack begun the next morning.

April 15, 1994
Hundreds of Interahamwe militiamen and civilians fleeing from Sake, Kibungo, following the mass murder

of Tutsis there are attacked by RPF forces. Only three survive.

April 15, 1994
RPF forces arrive at Ntarama, ending the killing of 5,000 Tutsis in the area.

April 15, 1994
Patients being carried by a Red Cross Ambulance are killed at a roadblock.

April 16, 1994
Augustin Bizimungu is promoted to major general and made head of the Rwandan army.

April 17, 1994
Over 100 Tutsis are killed by soldiers and militiamen in Nyanza.

April 18, 1994
Following a meeting with Rwanda's interim government, Akayesu stops protecting Tutsis in Taba and promoted citizens to participate in the killings.

April 18, 1994
The Mabirizi Roman Catholic church is attacked by local militiamen armed with grenades and machine guns. Of the 2,000 seeking refuge there, only an estimated 200 survive.

April 19, 1994
UN Belgian units leave Rwanda.

April 21, 1994
The UN Security Council reduces UN forces from 2,548 to 270. A number of additional personnel remained against Security Council orders.

April 21, 1994
Felicitas Niyitegeka is executed.

April 23, 1994
Government troops attack Butare hospital, killing nearly 170 patients.

April 25, 1994
Félicien Kabuga heads the newly created Comité Provisoire du Fonds de Défense Nationale (National Defence Funds Acting Committee, or FDN).

April 25, 1994
Militias attack Tutsis misled into believing Red Cross aid was being provided at the Butare football stadium.

April 25, 1994
The RPF begins evacuating civilians to Byumba and Rutare.

April 28, 1994
Five hundred are killed in an attempt to escape from a stadium in Cyangugu.

May 17, 1994
UNAMIR II is established.

May 31, 1994
Diagne is killed in an RPF attack on a Hutu extremist checkpoint.

June 2, 1994
Some 40 people are killed by RPF forces near Runda.

June 5, 1994
Archbishop Vincent Nsengiyumva and other clergymen are killed in Kabgayi, allegedly by advancing RPF soldiers.

June 13, 1994
UN forces successfully evacuate 300 from the Saint Famille church complex.

June 14, 1994
Forty Tutsi boys are taken from the Saint Famille church complex and killed.

June 19, 1994
RPF soldiers fire on crowds gathered in Mukingi killing over 100 individuals.

June 22, 1994
Operation TURQUOISE begins.

June 25, 1994
RPF soldiers kill Josias Mwongereza and his family.

June 27, 1994
The Bisesero Hill massacre occurs.

July 1, 1994
Shahryar Khan replaces Booh-Booh as the head of UNAMIR.

July 3, 1994
Radio-Télévision Libre des Mille Collines is shut down by RPF forces.

July 4, 1994
RPF forces capture Kigali.

July 14, 1994
RPF forces capture Rehengeri.

July 17, 1994
Goma, Zaire, is bombed. The UN Emergency Rwandan Aid Office in Goma reports that more than 1 million Rwandans sought refugee in Zaire.

July 17, 1994
Gisenyi is captured by RPF forces.

July 18, 1994
The RPF gains control over Rwanda. A cease-fire is declared. It is estimated that 800,000 have been killed prior to the cease-fire.

July 19, 1994
Pasteur Bizimungu is sworn in as president.

July 22, 1994
Operation SUPPORT HOPE begins.

July 31, 1994
France's Operation TURQUOISE troops begin to withdraw.

August 18, 1994
Kabuga and his family are expelled from Switzerland.

September 20, 1994
UN soldiers find 8,000 bodies in Gafunzi.

October 17, 1994
Claude Simard is assassinated.

November 9, 1994
The International Criminal Tribunal for Rwanda is established.

January 15, 1995
The Association of Genocide Widows (AVEGA) is founded.

April 22, 1995
Internally displaced persons are killed in Southwest Rwanda.

October 10, 1995
Akayesu is arrested.

February 13, 1996
Georges Rutaganda is arrested.

March 9, 1996
Théoneste Bagosora is arrested.

Fall 1996
The African Crisis Response Initiative, later renamed the African Contingency Operations Training and Assistance Program, is founded.

January 20, 1997
Three Spanish aid workers are murdered in northwestern Rwanda.

February 2, 1997
Guy Pinard is murdered by Hutu terrorists.

February 4, 1997
Five human rights observes are killed in Cyangugu.

February 14, 1997
Vincent Nkezazaganwa is assassinated.

February 14, 1997
Froduald Karamira is sentenced to death.

February 28, 1997
Virginia Mukankusi is sentenced to death.

July 18, 1997
Jean Kambanda and Nyiramasuhuko are arrested.

1998
Jerry Kajua is sentenced to life imprisonment by the Rwandan national court.

1998
Philip Gourevitch publishes *We Wish to Inform You That Tomorrow We Will Be Killed with Our Families.*

January 31, 1998
Vjekoslav Curic is shot.

April 28, 1998
Karamira, Mukankusi, Bizimana, and Gatanazi are publically executed.

September 2, 1998
Akayesu is found guilty of genocide and crimes against humanity. He is later sentenced to life in prison.

September 4, 1998
Kambanda is sentenced to life in prison.

1999
Alison Des Forges publishes *Leave None to Tell the Story: Genocide in Rwanda.*

December 16, 1999
The UN "Report of Independent Inquiry into the Actions of the United Nations During the 1994 Genocide in Rwanda," also known as the Carlsson Report, is released.

January 9, 2000
Augustin Ndindiliyimana is arrested.

April 7, 2000
Belgian prime minister Guy Verhofstadt issues an apology for Belgian withdrawal during the Rwandan genocide.

June 1, 2000
Georges Ruggiu is found guilty of inciting genocide and crimes against humanity.

October 2000
The Media Trail, with defendants Jean-Bosco Barayagwiza, Ferdinand Nahimana, and Hassan Ngeze, begins. All were found guilty and sentenced to jail time.

October 19, 2000
Kambanda's appeal is dismissed.

March 2001
Rwanda adopts *gacaca* law.

February 14, 2002
A Rwandan census reveals that approximately one seventh of the population had been murdered, and 94 percent of victims were Tutsis.

August 21, 2002
Augustin Bizimungu appears initially in ICTR court, pleading not guilty to the nine charges against him.

September 12, 2003
Kagame is sworn in as president.

December 3, 2003
Jean-Bosco Barayagwiza is found guilty and sentenced to 35 years in prison.

2004
Patrick de Saint-Exupéry publishes *L'inavouable: La France au Rwanda.*

September 20, 2004
Military Trial 2, which includes Augustin Bizimungu, opens.

December 22, 2004
Hotel Rwanda is first released in the United States.

April 2006
An Ordinary Man, an autobiography by Paul Rusesabagina, is published.

October 2, 2006
The trial of singer Simon Bikindi begins. He is later sentenced to seven years in prison, and his music is banned from national radio stations.

November 2006
Rwanda ends diplomatic relations with France.

December 13, 2006
Athanase Seromba is found guilty of aiding genocide and crimes against humanity and is sentenced to 15 years' imprisonment.

2007
Rwanda abolishes the death penalty.

January 4, 2007
Political asylum is denied to Agathe Hayarimana in France.

November 28, 2007
Barayagwiza's sentence is reduced to 32 years.

December 18, 2008
Bagosora, Ntabakuze, and Nsengiyumva are found guilty of war crimes, genocide, and crimes against humanity.

December 11, 2009
De Saint-Exupéry is acquitted of defamation in the Paris Criminal Court.

March 2, 2010
Agathe Habyarimana is arrested.

April 25, 2010
Barayagwiza dies.

June 24, 2010
Presidential candidate Bernard Ntaganda is arrested on charges of divisionism.

August 9, 2010
Kagame is reelected as president.

September 30, 2011
Former minister of foreign affairs Jérôme Bicamumpaka is acquitted.

May 17, 2011
Augustin Bizimungu is sentenced to 30 years in prison.

June 24, 2011
Nyiramasuhuko and the rest of the Butare Six are found guilty. Nyiramasuhuko is sentenced to life in prison.

2010
Dallaire publishes *They Fight Like Soldiers, They Die Like Children.*

January 23, 2012
Léon Mugesera is deported from Canada.

June 2012
Rwanda's *gacaca* courts are closed.

Topical List of Entries

BOOKS AND FILMS

Hotel Rwanda (Film, 2004)
Leave None to Tell the Story: Genocide in Rwanda
Rwanda: Death, Despair and Defiance
Rwanda: The Preventable Genocide
We Wish to Inform You That Tomorrow We Will Be Killed with Our Families

DOCUMENTATION

Arusha Accords
Bahutu Manifesto
Carlsson Report

EVENTS

Burundi, Genocide in
Day of Remembrance of the Victims of the Rwanda Genocide
Kamuhanda Trial
Kayishema Trial
Media Trial in Rwanda
Munyenyezi, Beatrice, Trial of
Rutaganda Trial
Rwanda Civil War

Operation SUPPORT HOPE
Operation TURQUOISE

GROUPS

Hutus
Tutsis
Twas

INDIVIDUALS

Akayesu, Jean-Paul
Allen, Susan
Anyidoho, Henry Kwami
Bagosora, Théoneste
Barayagwiza, Jean-Bosco
Barril, Paul
Beardsley, Brent
Bicamumpaka, Jérôme
Bikindi, Simon
Bisengimana, Paul
Bizimungu, Augustin
Booh-Booh, Jacques-Roger
Bushnell, Prudence
Carlsson, Ingvar
Curic, Vjekoslav
Dallaire, Roméo
de Saint-Exupéry, Patrick

Des Forges, Alison
Diagne, Mbaye
Gaillard, Philippe
Gisimba, Damas
Habyarimana, Juvénal
Kabuga, Félicien
Kagame, Paul
Kajuga, Jerry
Kambanda, Jean
Karamira, Froduald
Kovanda, Karel
Lane, Laura
Micombero, Michel
Mugesera, Léon
Nahimana, Ferdinand
Ndadaye, Melchior
Ndindiliyimana, Augustin
Ngeze, Hassan
Ntaganda, Bosco
Ntakirutimana, Elizaphan
Nyirabayovu, Thérèse
Nyiramasuhuko, Pauline
Prosper, Pierre-Richard
Ruggiu, Georges
Rusesabagina, Paul
Rutaganda, Georges
Uwilingiyimana, Agathe
Wallace, Gretchen Steidle
Wilkens, Carl

MOVEMENTS
Denial of the Rwandan Genocide
Hamitic Hypothesis
Identity Cards, Rwanda
Rape
Rwandan Genocide, French Response to the
Rwandan Genocide, Role of Propaganda in the
Rwandan Genocide, U.S. Response to the

ORGANIZATIONS
African Crisis Response Initiative
AVEGA-AGAHOZO
Coalition Pour la Défense de la Rèpublique
Forces Armées Rwandaises
Interahamwe
International Criminal Tribunal for Rwanda
Kangura
Radio-Télévision Libre des Mille Collines
Roman Catholic Church
Rwandan Patriotic Army
Rwandan Patriotic Front
United Nations Assistance Mission for Rwanda

PLACES
Burundi
Congo, Democratic Republic of
Rwanda

A

African Crisis Response Initiative

The African Crisis Response Initiative was a U.S. government-sponsored program designed to train African armed forces to conduct humanitarian and peacekeeping missions on the African continent. The African Crisis Response Initiative (ACRI), which was renamed the African Contingency Operations Training and Assistance Program (ACOTA) in 2004, was established by U.S. secretary of state Warren Christopher in the autumn of 1996. The ACRI began operations in 1997. The immediate catalyst for the ACRI was the 1994 Rwandan Genocide, in which some 800,000 Rwandans were systematically killed in the span of only three months.

The ACRI and its successor agency (ACOTA) were intended to offer training to African national armies so that they could be mobilized rapidly in times of crisis to provide humanitarian relief operations in the event of natural and man-made disasters and to mount peacekeeping missions in the event of war or civil unrest. The training period for each army is 70 days and is conducted by 70–100 U.S. military specialists. Thereafter, the U.S. training team pays a follow-up visit every six months. The program is paid for entirely by the U.S. government.

The African national armies who have been trained in the American-led effort include Senegal, Uganda, Malawi, Mali, Ethiopia, Kenya, and Rwanda, among others. Initially, some in Congress were concerned that Rwandan troops who had participated in the genocide were receiving American training, but that has not proven to be a significant problem. A number of African leaders feared that the ACRI was an attempt on the part of the Americans to disengage from Africa, while others viewed it as a veiled attempt to advance U.S. interests there. The ACRI and ACOTA have worked closely with the United Nations Department of Peacekeeping Operations as well as the Organization of African Unity and other African-based groups to ensure that the training is being utilized properly.

PAUL G. PIERPAOLI JR.

See also: Rwanda; Rwanda Civil War

Further Reading

Kamukama, Dixon. *Rwanda Conflict: Its Roots and Regional Implications.* 2nd ed. Kampala, Uganda: Fountain Publishers, 1998.

Akayesu, Jean-Paul

Jean-Paul Akayesu was the first person to be convicted of the crime of genocide in an international tribunal. Born in 1953 in Taba commune in Rwanda, he had been a school teacher, an active member of the local football team, and then a school district inspector, prior to his election to the office of *bourgmestre,* or mayor, of the town of Taba in April 1993. He served as mayor from then until June 1994, when he fled Rwanda. A member of the Mouvement

Démocratique Républicain (Democratic Republican Movement, or MDR), a Hutu political party he joined in 1991, he soon rose through the party ranks and eventually became the local branch president.

In his capacity as mayor of Taba, Akayesu had formal control of the communal police, and was responsible for the maintenance of order, subject only to the district prefect. His authority, however, extended beyond these formal limits. In Rwanda, a considerable degree of informal dominion devolved upon the role of mayor, who acted as a kind of "father figure" within the commune. As a communal leader he was respected, widely considered to be a man of high morals, intelligence, and integrity. A family man, he was the father of five children.

Initially, Akayesu kept Taba out of the mass killing after the Rwandan genocide began on April 6, 1994. He refused to let Interahamwe militia operate there, and struggled with them to protect the local Tutsi population. On April 18, however, a meeting of *bourgmestres* with leaders of Rwanda's interim government saw a fundamental change take place—both in Taba and in Akayesu himself. Conscious that his political and social future depended on joining those carrying out the genocide, Akayesu began collaborating directly with the extremists, and from this point started to incite his citizens to join in the killing.

During the genocide, it has been estimated that some 2,000 Tutsis were massacred in Taba, many of whom had sought refuge in the Bureau Communale (approximating a city hall and a community center)—the heart of Akayesu's domain. It has been alleged that Akayesu did not provide support or succor for those his position had entrusted him to protect; not only this, but he actively encouraged the Interahamwe militias who had come to Taba, as well as the local Hutu population, to participate in the mass murder and torture of the Tutsis.

In addition, numerous Tutsi women were the victims of sexual violence in the Bureau Communale. They were mutilated and systematically raped, often by more than one attacker and in public. Armed police, as well as Akayesu himself, were reportedly present when some of these acts took place. Akayesu was also suspected of having ordered several murders, and to have stood by while they were carried out. In addition, he allegedly gave a death list to Hutu extremists, and ordered house-to-house searches to locate Tutsis. It was later concluded that his actions in Taba amounted to direct participation in the crime of genocide.

In the aftermath of the conquest of Rwanda in July 1994 by the forces of the Tutsi-led Rwandan Patriotic Front

(RPF), Akayesu fled the country, first escaping to Zaire (now the Democratic Republic of the Congo), then to Lusaka, Zambia, where he was arrested on October 10, 1995. Zambia thereby became the first African nation to extradite an alleged *génocidaire* to the International Criminal Tribunal for Rwanda (ICTR) in Arusha, Tanzania. He was formally indicted on February 13, 1996, and transferred to ICTR jurisdiction on May 15, 1996. The trial got underway on January 9, 1997.

Akayesu's was the first genocide trial in history. (Many are under the misconception that the Nuremberg Tribunal at the end of World War II conducted the first trials of genocide, but this, in fact, tried the defendants on charges of crimes against humanity and war crimes, not genocide.) Initially, Akayesu was charged with encouraging the killing of Tutsis, directly ordering the killing of numerous individuals, and supervising the interrogation, beating, and execution of people from Taba. Richard Goldstone, the chief prosecutor for the ICTR, charged Akayesu with 12 counts of genocide, crimes against humanity, and violations of Article II of the 1949 Geneva Conventions. Ultimately, three additional counts of genocide and crimes against humanity were added to the charges, alleging that he had ordered and condoned the rape and sexual mutilation—and then, the murder—of hundreds of Tutsi women. The prosecutor for the Akayesu trial was an American attorney, Pierre-Richard Prosper.

Akayesu pleaded not guilty on all counts. His primary defense was that he had played no part in the killings, and that he had been powerless to stop them. His essential position was that at the time of the genocide he had not been in a position of authority, and his attorneys argued that Akayesu was being made a scapegoat for the crimes of the people of Taba.

The trial judges found that, in his role as mayor, Jean-Paul Akayesu *did* have the responsibility for maintaining public order and executing the law in the municipality of Taba and that, in this function, he had effective authority over the police. His criminal responsibility was based on his direct participation in acts of genocide and on his position as hierarchical superior. Article 6, section 3, of the statute setting up the ICTR states that a superior can be responsible if he knew or had reason to know that a subordinate was about to commit criminal acts or had done so, and that the superior had failed to take the necessary measures to prevent such acts or punish the perpetrators.

On September 2, 1998, Akayesu was found guilty on 9 of the 15 counts with which he was charged regarding genocide and crimes against humanity (extermination, murder [3 counts], torture, rape, and other inhuman acts). This made him the first person convicted of the specific crime of genocide in an internationally accredited courtroom, and thus the first occasion on which the 1948 UN Convention on Genocide was upheld as law. It was a landmark decision also in that it recognized the crime of rape as a form of genocide, and made the legal definition of rape more precise.

On October 2, 1998, Akayesu was sentenced to life imprisonment for each of the nine counts, the sentences to run concurrently. He immediately appealed, but this was rejected by the Appeal Chamber on June 1, 2001. On December 9, 2001, Akayesu was transferred to Bamako Central Prison, Mali, to serve out his life sentence.

PAUL R. BARTROP

See also: Interahamwe; International Criminal Tribunal for Rwanda; Rape; Rwandan Patriotic Front

Further Reading

Bodnarchuk, Kari. *Rwanda: A Country Torn Apart.* Minneapolis, MN: Lerner Publishing Group, 1998.

Friedrichs, David O., ed. *State Crime.* Brookfield, VT: Ashgate/Dartmouth, 1998.

Allen, Susan

Susan Allen is an American medical doctor who was engaged in research into HIV/AIDS in Rwanda both before and after the genocide of 1994. She was born in 1958 in Caracas, Venezuela, to Irish American parents, and grew up in Brazil and Lebanon. Her education was in French schools, her parents reasoning that regardless of where they might be located, the curriculum would be more or less the same everywhere. As a result, Allen's school experience left her fluent in French—a major asset to her survival in Rwanda later.

In 1980 she graduated in chemistry from Duke University, from where she would obtain her degree in medicine in 1984. During her residency at the University of California in San Francisco (UCSF), where she specialized in pathology, she undertook autopsies on gay men dying of unusual disease combinations that would soon be linked to the AIDS virus. While a resident doctor she also completed her Masters of Public Health degree at UC Berkeley.

In 1984, a Belgian guest speaker then passing through San Francisco, Dr. Nathan Clumeck, addressed a group at Allen's hospital. From his address, she learned that

heterosexual African AIDS patients were also dying from typically treatable diseases. Approaching Clumeck later, she suggested that his hospital needed a pathology laboratory to diagnose the nature of the infections that were doing so much damage. He offered to write her a letter of introduction to the Rwandan Ministry of Health if she could obtain funding to set up such a laboratory in Kigali. In response, Allen wrote 150 grant applications, netting U.S. $30,000 to go to Kigali in order to test pregnant women for HIV antibodies. She moved to Rwanda in 1986 with seed money from UCSF and the State of California. Her initiative created the first mobile HIV testing laboratory on the African continent.

In 1988 her research took a startling turn. While tracking HIV in pregnant Rwandan women, she found that 14 percent of her 1,500 research subjects did not share the same HIV status as their partners. To Allen, this discordance made these women and their partners an ideal cohort both to understand the factors that determine virus transmission and to identify strategies to prevent it. She began a program in which both partners received counseling about prevention strategies, and were routinely tested as a result. It was soon shown that HIV incidence among counseled couples could be as much as 50–70 percent lower than among those who were not counseled.

As a researcher engaging in a new and unknown area of medicine that could have fatal consequences for its victims, living in the Rwanda of President Juvénal Habyarimana was not easy. The Rwandan government was wary about any discussion of HIV, fearful of its potential to kill off foreign investment and scare away tourists who came to see the country's mountain gorillas. Allen was forbidden to publish any of her research results from 1986 until 1991, which placed pressure on her from her funding agencies in the United States who demanded to see her results. Partly in order to deflect Rwandan government attention, she began giving her work the official-sounding name of "Project San Francisco," cutting out any reference to Africa. The ploy worked, but only up to a point. She recalls having her phone tapped and her mail opened, and being shadowed by government agents spying on her activities. And, all too often, she could hear gunfire, as the Hutu Power campaign of hatred against the country's Tutsi population intensified throughout the early 1990s.

In April 1994 she traveled to Zambia to set up another research project, but returned to Kigali immediately after she learned that President Habyarimana's plane had been shot down and that interethnic violence had begun. Allen, her son, and his father were evacuated out of the country along with the convoys organized through Laura Lane of the U.S. embassy.

The Rwandan Genocide brought Allen's research to an abrupt halt. She and her team had been making good progress in terms of recruiting and educating people for the project, until the genocide forced Allen to flee and the project to shut down. Hundreds of those involved in her study were murdered, together with about half of the staff of 70 assisting in the project. In August 1994, Allen returned alone to Kigali to learn the fate of her colleagues. The project was in tatters, and many of those who had survived were in mourning for lost family members. Allen herself concluded that she was suffering from the syndrome known as survivor guilt, as a result of which she required counseling back in San Francisco.

After a period of rest in the United States, she redeployed research funds that had previously been earmarked for Rwanda in order to develop a similar program in Zambia, where she had been when the genocide broke out in April 1994. Zambia, however, did not afford her the security she now craved. In Lusaka she received death threats from Rwandan exiles who had been involved in the genocide, forcing her to carry a gun for her own protection.

In 1996 Allen joined the University of Alabama at Birmingham to continue her work, and in 2004 moved to Emory University in Atlanta, Georgia, where she became a professor of global health at the Rollins School of Public Health, with a joint appointment in epidemiology. The project she directs, known around the world as the Rwanda Zambia HIV Research Group (www.rzhrg.org), includes the largest and longest-standing cohort of HIV-discordant couples in the world. It has helped to identify strategies that reduce HIV transmission and to uncover the effects of the host's genotype and immune response on the evolution of the virus.

In addition to her medical work, Susan Allen is also active in genocide prevention and broadening awareness about Rwanda's genocidal past. One of her primary concerns is that the genocide of 1994 remains a wound that can only be healed by bringing those who led it to justice. While this is taking place progressively through such courts as the International Criminal Tribunal for Rwanda, the Rwandan national courts, and the gacaca tribunals within Rwanda, much more needs to be done to flush out perpetrators who have thus far not been captured or who have evaded detection. In pursuit of this, Allen has directed her attention to raising consciousness to the fact that many of the organizers of the genocide are now living free in the United States and elsewhere, and that as a matter of social concern the perpetrators be identified and brought to justice. She has noted that if the opportunity of bringing Rwandan *génocidaires* to justice is passed by, it will render much more complex situations, such as Darfur, next to impossible to resolve.

PAUL R. BARTROP

See also: Habyarimana, Juvénal; International Criminal Tribunal for Rwanda; Lane, Laura

Further Reading

Bodnarchuk, Kari. *Rwanda: A Country Torn Apart*. Minneapolis, MN: Lerner Publishing Group, 1998.

Evans, Glynne. *Responding to Crises in the African Great Lakes*. Oxford: Oxford University Press, 1997.

Anyidoho, Henry Kwami

Major General Henry Kwami Anyidoho was born in Tanyigbe, in the Volta Region of Ghana, on July 13, 1940, and is arguably Ghana's most distinguished and well-known military officer. A career soldier, he is a graduate of the Ghana Military Academy and the U.S. Marine Staff College, Quantico, Virginia. He received his commission with the Ghanaian army's Signal Corps in 1965, and served in various military capacities including commanding officer of the Army Signal Regiment, commandant of the Ghana Military Academy and Training Schools, director general Logistics, Joint Operations and Plans at the General Headquarters of the Ghana Armed Forces, and general officer commanding Northern Command.

Anyidoho is probably best known internationally as a leader and participant in a number of important United Nations peacekeeping missions, particularly in Rwanda in 1994 and Darfur since 2005. Prior to these deployments, Anyidoho had already served with the United Nations Emergency Force (UNEF) in Sinai; with the United Nations Interim Force in Lebanon (UNIFIL) as chief military press and information officer; with the Economic Community of West African States Monitoring Group (ECOMOG) in Liberia in 1990; and with the United Nations Transitional Authority in Cambodia (UNTAC). Appointed in December 1993 to serve as deputy force commander and chief of staff of the United Nations Assistance Mission for Rwanda (UNAMIR), under the overall command of Lieutenant General Roméo Dallaire, he arrived in Kigali on January 15, 1994. He also commanded the Ghanaian contingent of the UNAMIR forces.

Anyidoho's experiences in previous peacekeeping missions did not provide him with a template of how to respond to the carnage that descended on Rwanda in April 1994, but he was quick to adapt himself to the situation as it developed. Organizing the Ghanaian troops under his command, and liaising closely with Dallaire, he found himself pulled in a dozen different directions at once, with calls to station soldiers at the homes of prominent moderate Hutu politicians, or to rescue others and bring them to safety. The forces under his command were very quickly overwhelmed by circumstances, yet he continued to try to fulfill his commitments at the highest level of professionalism and with the key aim of saving lives.

As the genocide developed in the first days of April 1994, however, the initial peacekeeping/monitoring mandate of UNAMIR was rapidly brought to an end by the UN in New York. States that had originally contributed troops began to withdraw them, and on April 21 the UN Security Council passed Resolution 912, which called for a reduction of the UNAMIR force from 2,548 to just 270. Anyidoho was the first senior officer in Kigali to receive the news on the phone, as Dallaire was at that time away from the office attempting to negotiate a ceasefire. His immediate reaction was to resist the reduction order, and defy the UN command to withdraw. He advised Dallaire along these lines; Dallaire, in turn, had received the news from his chief of staff, Major Brent Beardsley, and had already reached more or less the same conclusion as Anyidoho. Pleading with New York to not close down the mission, Dallaire achieved a reprieve of sorts that allowed UNAMIR to remain but only with the reduced force of 270 troops. Ultimately this figure settled at 456, 78 percent of whom were Anyidoho's Ghanaian battalion. The higher figure was not endorsed by the Security Council; it was simply adhered to by the personnel on the ground in Rwanda who refused to leave.

Anyidoho's decision to stay in Rwanda to try to save lives was his alone. He communicated the decision to his government in Accra as a *fait accompli,* and the government agreed to it retrospectively. With this commitment forming the backbone of his force, Dallaire was henceforth able to husband his resources, in an effort to maximize whatever efforts he could mount. As a result, it has been estimated, up to 30,000 people were saved from the gruesome fate intended by the Hutu Power government and the militias acting in its name.

After leaving Rwanda in 1994, Anyidoho was reassigned to become special assistant to Ghana's minister of defense. He then embarked on a number of different appointments: as a member of the Organization of African Unity (OAU; later reconstituted as the African Union, AU) task force on the Mechanism for Conflict Prevention Management and Resolution; as the UN expert who wrote the major discussion document at the initial meeting of the Heads of the Armed Forces of the OAU in Addis Ababa in June 1996; and, in 2004, as the team leader of UN observers for the Cameroon-Nigeria Mixed Commission. Soon after this, Anyidoho was made team leader of another UN mission, an Assistance Cell providing strategic advice to the African Union on Darfur, following which he became coordinator of UN Support to the AU Mission in Sudan, or AMIS. This gave him a unique qualification for his next post; in 2005 he was appointed by the secretary-general of the African Union and the United Nations secretary-general as the joint special representative for the AU-UN Hybrid Operation in Darfur, UNAMID.

In 1999, Anyidoho published his memoir of his time in Rwanda during the genocide, *Guns over Kigali.* Roméo Dallaire's own book on Rwanda, *Shake Hands with the Devil,* appeared in 2003, and corroborated much of what Anyidoho had recalled earlier. The conclusion to be drawn from both works is that the courage and resourcefulness of Anyidoho and his Ghanaian troops did a lot to keep the residual UNAMIR force in place in Rwanda, maintaining a UN presence in the country when the preference from New York was otherwise one of closing down that presence altogether. Anyidoho, who was later decorated with the Distinguished Service Order for Gallantry, must thus be considered a major force behind the protection of tens of thousands of Rwandan Tutsis and moderate Hutus, who, through his actions, were saved from certain death.

Paul R. Bartrop

See also: Dallaire, Roméo; United Nations Assistance Mission for Rwanda

Further Reading

Evans, Glynne. *Responding to Crises in the African Great Lakes.* Oxford: Oxford University Press, 1997.

Klinghoffer, Arthur Jay. *The International Dimension of Genocide in Rwanda.* New York: New York University Press, 1998.

Arusha Accords

The Arusha Accords was a set of comprehensive protocols signed in Arusha, Tanzania, on August 4, 1993, intended to end the three-year-long Rwandan Civil War and to institute a governmental power-sharing arrangement in Rwanda. The accords were also designed to foster the formation of a popularly elected democratic regime in Rwanda. The talks took place chiefly between the sitting Rwandan government and the Rwandan Patriotic Front (RPF), whose rebel forces had been engaged in the civil war. Unfortunately, most of the terms of the Arusha agreements, which were cosponsored by the Organization of African Unity, France, and the United States, were never carried out.

The main negotiations at Arusha commenced on July 12, 1992, and lasted until June 24, 1993. From July 19 to July 25, 1993, concluding talks were conducted in Rwanda. Although the resulting accords covered a host of issues, including refugee resettlement and the makeup of the Rwandan military, the main focus was on neutralizing President Juvénal Habyarimana's dictatorial rule, cobbling together a broad-based transitional government, and preparing Rwanda for the transition to a permanent, popularly elected, multiparty, multiethnic national government.

The RPF was to be included in the national assembly, and the Rwandan military was to be divided so that 60 percent of its forces came from the established government's army, and 40 percent from the RPF. Of the 21 cabinet posts in the proposed transitional government, the ruling party was granted 5; the RPF was also to receive 5; the remaining positions were to be divided among the four other major parties. The transitional government was to be in place within 37 days of the signing of the accord, and that regime would last no longer than 22 months, after which elections had to be held. As the negotiators attempted to implement the accords, which required numerous meetings in Arusha, it was clear that Habyarimana and the Hutu-dominated government intended to delay their implementation as long as possible. Indeed, no transitional government was formed.

On April 6, 1994, as Habyarimana and Burundian president Cyprien Ntaryamira (a Hutu) were returning to Kigali from a meeting in Arusha, a missile shot down their plane, killing all of the occupants. Who fired the missile remains unknown, but Rwanda's Hutu-dominated government nevertheless blamed the Tutsis and the RPF. The incident sparked the Rwanda Genocide in which as many as 1 million Tutsis and moderate Hutus were killed in little more than three months.

PAUL G. PIERPAOLI JR.

See also: Habyarimana, Juvénal; Rwandan Genocide, French Response to the; Rwandan Genocide, U.S. Response to the; Rwandan Patriotic Front

Further Reading

Ali, Taisier M., and Robert O. Matthews. *Civil Wars in Africa: Roots and Resolution.* Toronto: McGill-Queen's University Press, 1999.

Shaw, Martin. *War and Genocide: Organized Killing in Modern Society.* Cambridge, UK: Polity, 2003.

Smith, M. James, ed. *A Time to Remember. Rwanda: Ten Years after Genocide.* Retford, UK: The Aegis Institute, 2004.

AVEGA-AGAHOZO

AVEGA-AGAHOZO is a nonprofit Rwandan organization formed in January 1995 to help survivors of the 1994 Rwandan Genocide. The name AVEGA-AGAHOZO is partly an acronym for *L'Association des Veuves du Génocide,* or Genocide Widows' Association. Founded by 50 Rwandan widows who lost their spouses during the genocide, the organization's initial mission was to help the many thousands of widows and orphans in the aftermath of the mass killings by extending financial, material, and moral support to them. AVEGA-AGAHOZO was formally recognized by the Rwandan government on October 30, 1995. In 1997, the organization began decentralizing its operations by establishing regional and local offices, which enabled it to aid individuals faster and more effectively. The headquarters remains in Kigali.

In more recent years, AVEGA-AGAHOZO has broadened its mission, which now includes aid to children who lost parents and became the heads of households. It also seeks to bring together AVEGA-AGAHOZO members so that they may engage in mutual support and encouragement, to foster closer cooperation with similar groups who are helping genocide survivors, to memorialize the events and victims of the genocide, to seek justice for perpetrators and victims alike, and to pursue reconciliation and reconstruction efforts within Rwanda. In 2012, AVEGA-AGAHOZO's membership stood at some 25,000 widows and more than 71,000 orphans and dependents.

AVEGA-AGAHOZO sponsors a number of specific programs aimed at helping genocide victims. These include medical care, psychological counseling, education, vocational training, legal aid, and housing and shelter. Medical care and counseling have been especially important for the many thousands of women who were raped or abused during the genocide. At least 47,000 women are currently receiving medical services through AVEGA-AGAHOZO. These same medical facilities have also been critical in testing for HIV and treating patients with AIDS.

The organization helps and encourages victims to testify in trials against genocide perpetrators, and so far some 800,000 perpetrators have been convicted. AVEGA-AGAHOZO has also successfully lobbied the Rwandan legislature to update and reform inheritance laws so that women may now inherit land and other assets. Until 1999, Rwandan women had been legally unable to inherit such things. In 2009, the Rwandan government enacted the country's first gender-based antiviolence law, which was accomplished largely through the efforts of AVEGA-AGAHOZO.

Paul G. Pierpaoli Jr.

See also: Rape; Rwanda

Further Reading

Smith, M. James, ed. *A Time to Remember. Rwanda: Ten Years after Genocide.* Retford, UK: The Aegis Institute, 2004.

Waller, James. *Becoming Evil: How Ordinary People Commit Genocide and Mass Killing.* Oxford: Oxford University Press, 2002.

B

Bagosora, Théoneste

During the period of the 1994 Rwandan Genocide, Colonel Théoneste Bagosora was Rwandan defense minister. A Hutu, Bagosora was born on August 16, 1941, in the Giciye commune of the Gisenyi prefecture, an area from which Rwandan president Juvénal Habyarimana also originated. From this background he became linked to the Akazu, the so-called Little Hut—the inner circle of Habyarimana's associates, dominated by the president's wife, Agathe Habyarimana.

The son of a school teacher, Bagosora spent his whole career in the Rwandan army, the Forces Armées Rwandaises (FAR). In 1964, he graduated from Kigali's École des officiers (Officers' School), with the rank of second lieutenant. He then continued his studies in France, where he obtained a diploma in Advanced Military Studies from the French Military School. He was later appointed second-in-command of the École supérieure militaire (Higher Military School) in Kigali, after which he received promotion to the rank of colonel, with command over the important Kanombe military camp. He remained there until June 1992, when he was appointed as *directeur du cabinet* (director of the cabinet) in Rwanda's Ministry of Defense. Despite his official retirement from the military on September 23, 1993, he retained this position until fleeing the country in July 1994.

Bagosora was considered to be the mastermind of the genocide and had, by 1990, reportedly developed a plan to exterminate Rwanda's Tutsis. He was a vehement opponent of the Arusha Accords of 1993 (even though he was present at the negotiations on behalf of the government), as he wanted nothing to do with the Rwandan Patriotic Front (RPF) or, for that matter, shared governance of Rwanda with the Tutsis—let alone any measure of coexistence. Sounding much like Adolf Hitler, who warned the Jews on January 30, 1939, that if Germany's treatment of them resulted in a war being waged against Germany they would face total annihilation, Bagosora publicly stated that the Tutsis would be wiped out if the RPF continued its fight against Rwanda and/or if the Arusha Accords were enforced.

On December 4, 1991, President Habyarimana set up a military commission whose task was to find a reply to the question: "What must be done to defeat the enemy in military, propaganda and political terms?" Bagosora was appointed to coordinate an appropriate response. The resultant report was nothing other than an incitement to hatred employed by high ranking officers who encouraged and facilitated revulsion and ethnic violence.

As early as 1992, Bagosora reportedly had the Rwandan army's general staff draw up lists of all those who were thought to be associated with the RPF. Ultimately, such lists were used by the military and the Interahamwe militias to locate, capture, and kill Tutsis and moderate Hutus during the period of the genocide. Beginning in early 1993,

Bagosora is known to have had weapons distributed to militias and other extremist Hutus.

Assuming effective control of Rwanda after April 6, 1994, most accounts consider Bagosora as being the man responsible for coordinating the genocide of Rwanda's Tutsi population following Habyarimana's assassination on that date. He is said to have given the order on April 7, 1994, for the military to begin the killing, and to have issued the order that roadblocks be set up across Rwanda to capture and kill fleeing Tutsis and moderate Hutus.

Immediately after Habyarimana's assassination, Bagosora and a few other officers established a "Crisis Committee" to work out what to do next. The head of the United Nations Assistance Mission for Rwanda (UNAMIR), Canadian general Roméo Dallaire, contacted Bagosora in the hope of providing some direction and oversight for the country at this time of crisis. Bagosora proposed having the military take control of the political situation until they could hand it over to the politicians, but Dallaire rejected this, emphasizing that Rwanda still had a working government led by the next in line to the succession, the prime minister, Agathe Uwilingiyimana. Within hours, however, Uwilingiyimana was murdered, one of the first casualties of the genocide. Bagosora and his associates then set up an interim government comprised of extremist Hutus dedicated to one essential objective—the elimination of the Tutsis and any Hutus who stood in their way.

With the end of the genocide and the victory of the Rwandan Patriotic Front in July 1994, Bagosora disappeared. It was later learned that he fled initially to neighboring Zaire (now the Democratic Republic of Congo), after which he moved to Yaoundé, Cameroon, where he lived from July 1995 until his arrest on March 9, 1996.

The International Criminal Tribunal for Rwanda (ICTR), based in Arusha, Tanzania, had long been interested in Bagosora, and indicted him soon after its inception in 1994. Upon being located and arrested in Cameroon, Bagosora was transferred to the United Nations prison quarters in Arusha on January 23, 1997, to face 13 counts of 11 different international crimes relating to genocide, crimes against humanity, and war crimes. At his first appearance before the Tribunal, he entered a plea of not guilty. The trial itself began on April 2, 2002, simultaneously with three others—Brigadier General Gratien Kabiligi, former chief of military operations in the FAR; Lieutenant Colonel Anatole Nsengiyumva, former military commander of Gisenyi Military Camp; and Major Aloys Ntabakuze, former commander of the Kanombe Paracommando Battalion, Kigali. The joint proceedings became known as the "Military Trial 1."

Preparation for the trial took up an enormous amount of the Tribunal's time before finally getting underway. It was only on October 14, 2004, that the prosecution's case concluded, with the trial finally wrapped up on June 1, 2007. On December 18, 2008, the ICTR found Bagosora, Ntabakuze, and Nsengiyumva guilty of genocide, crimes against humanity, and war crimes. Overall, Bagosora was convicted of 10 counts of 8 different crimes, including genocide, murder, extermination, rape, persecution, other inhumane acts, 2 counts of violence to life, and outrages upon personal dignity.

Bagosora was sentenced to life imprisonment. His trial was the most important heard before the Tribunal, and was especially significant in that it addressed such points as to how the genocide was planned and carried out at the highest levels of the Rwandan military, as well as the relationship between the army and extremist Hutu politicians.

On December 14, 2011, Bagosora's life sentence was reduced to 35 years.

PAUL R. BARTROP

See also: Forces Armées Rwandaises; Habyarimana, Juvénal; Interahamwe; International Criminal Tribunal for Rwanda; Rwandan Patriotic Front; Uwilingiyimana, Agathe

Further Reading

Melvern, Linda. *Conspiracy to Murder: The Rwandan Genocide.* London: Verso, 2006.

Off, Carol. *The Lion, the Fox and the Eagle: A Story of Generals and Justice in Rwanda and Yugoslavia.* Toronto: Random House, 2000.

Bahutu Manifesto

The *Bahuto Manifesto* was a sociopolitical declaration issued on March 24, 1957, in Rwanda, which was then under Belgian rule. The ten-page manifesto was the work of nine Hutu intellectuals, including Catholic archbishop André Perraudin, and played a key role in fomenting anti-Tutsi sentiment among Rwanda's Hutu majority. The declaration had a number of decrees and goals. First, it denounced the Tutsis' historic domination over the Hutus, which had begun in earnest under German rule, which began in the 1880s. Second, it demanded the liberation of the Hutus from both white, colonial European rule and Tutsi rule. Third, it called for the disenfranchisement of the Tutsis and a ban on intermarriage between Hutus and Tutsis. Fourth, it sought the imposition of racial quotas in all aspects of public life, including employment and education, which were to be advantageous to the Hutus. Fifth, it demanded the exclusion of Tutsis from the Rwandan military. Finally, and perhaps most troubling, it argued that Hutus were socially, culturally, and morally superior to Tutsis. This argument was based upon faulty and outmoded thinking concerning racial differences and placed the blame for Rwanda's problems exclusively on the Tutsis.

The *Bahutu Manifesto* certainly did not espouse many new ideas. In fact, it largely codified the thinking among many Hutus that had its origins dating back at least to the late 19th century. Both German and Belgian colonizers had historically favored the minority Tutsis, often ruling through the Tutsi-dominated monarchy. The Europeans tended to see the Hutus as "inferior" to the Tutsis because they generally had darker skin. This favoritism toward the Tutsis created much distrust among the Hutus and only deepened their antipathy toward the Tutsis.

Growing anger and frustration among the Hutus ultimately led to the *Bahutu Manifesto.* That document would become the ideological underpinning of the Hutus' drive to seize control in Rwanda and to eradicate the Tutsis and their influence. That effort began in earnest in 1959, when Hutu leaders ousted the Tutsi monarchy, a move that the Belgians tacitly supported. This precipitated the mass killings of Tutsis and the forced exodus of at least 130,000 Tutsis from Rwanda. It also brought to power a Hutu-dominated government. In July 1962, the Belgians left the Rwandans to their own devices, freeing the nation of almost 80 years of colonial domination.

For decades thereafter, the Hutus dominated Rwandan politics and created an increasingly hostile environment for the minority Tutsis. This turn of events radicalized a segment of Tutsis by the late 1980s, and in 1990 the Tutsi-led Rwandan Patriotic Front (RPF) launched a civil war against the Hutus and the Hutu-led government. The Hutus fought back, often times brutally, creating a powder keg of racial tensions within the country. In April 1994, radicalized Hutus, employing the attitudes and language of the *Bahutu Manifesto,* commenced a mass genocide against Rwanda's Tutsis and moderate Hutus. In less than three months, a million or more people had been killed.

PAUL G. PIERPAOLI JR.

See also: Hutus; Rwandan Genocide, Role of Propaganda in the; Rwandan Patriotic Front; Tutsis

Further Reading
Kamukama, Dixon. *Rwanda Conflict: Its Roots and Regional Implications.* 2nd ed. Kampala, Uganda: Fountain Publishers, 1998.
Newbury, Catherine. *The Cohesion of Oppression: Clientship and Ethnicity in Rwanda, 1860–1960.* New York: Columbia University Press, 1988.
Straus, Scott. *The Order of Genocide: Race, Power, and War in Rwanda.* Ithaca, NY: Cornell University Press, 2008.

Barayagwiza, Jean-Bosco

Jean Bosco Barayagwiza was an anti-Tutsi media executive in Rwanda, active before and during the genocide of 1994. He was born in 1950 in Mutura commune, in Gisenyi, western Rwanda. A lawyer by training who studied in the Soviet Union, he held the office of director of political affairs in Rwanda's Foreign Ministry. He was a cofounder, with Ferdinand Nahimana, of the *"Comité d'initiative,"* which in turn established the anti-Tutsi radio station Radio-Télévision Libre des Mille Collines (RTLM). This was to be largely responsible for sustaining the Hutu public's focus on the annihilation of the Tutsis both before and after the start of the genocide on April 6, 1994.

It has been alleged that between 1990 and July 1994 Barayagwiza and others conspired to exterminate the civilian Tutsi population and eliminate members of the Hutu opposition. The components of their plan included the broadcasting of messages of ethnic hatred and incitements to violence, the training of militias, the distribution of weapons to anti-Tutsi militias, and the preparation and distribution of lists of people to be killed. Within his own district of Gisenyi, Barayagwiza allegedly presided over several meetings to plan these activities, and delivered weapons and money to help with the murders.

Barayagwiza's political party, the Coalition pour la Défense de la République (CDR), was established in February 1992. He set it up with two other extreme anti-Tutsi Hutu ideologues: a former member of the Tutsi-led Rwandan Patriotic Front (RPF) who had defected, Jean Shyirambere Barahinura, and the founder-owner of the radical newspaper *Kangura,* Hassan Ngeze. The party was exclusively Hutu, to the extent that a person with even one Tutsi grandparent was denied membership. It was also extremely violent; a party militia movement, the Impuzamugambi ("those with a single purpose"), was established expressly for the purpose of harassing, assaulting, and, ultimately, murdering Tutsis wherever they could be found. The CDR was fervently opposed to President Juvénal Habyarimana's rapprochement with the RPF during 1993 and early 1994, and was in the forefront of those undermining his authority after the signing of the Arusha peace accords on August 4, 1993. Unsurprisingly, after Habyarimana's assassination on April 6, 1994, the CDR entered into a coalition with the hastily formed interim government that was formed to deal with the emergency that had, it was claimed, been instigated by the Tutsis. Through the Impuzamugambi, the CDR was thus a major participant in the Rwandan tragedy, a criminal organization that played a key role in the fastest genocide of the 20th century.

According to the later prosecution of Barayagwiza by the International Criminal Tribunal for Rwanda (ICTR), he knew that members of the CDR killed Tutsis and moderate Hutus in Gisenyi, where he presided over the CDR from February 6, 1994. Further, he allegedly conspired with Nahimana, Félicien Kabuga, and others to set up RTLM in order to promote the Hutu Power extremist ideology.

As Rwanda was progressively overrun by troops of the Rwandan Patriotic Front during June and July, 1994, Barayagwiza, along with most other high-ranking *génocidaires,* fled the country. Upon the request of the new, postgenocide Rwandan government he was arrested in Yaoundé, Cameroon, on March 27, 1996, and—after incarceration for 330 days without being informed of the charges against him—was transferred to the jurisdiction of the ICTR in Arusha, Tanzania, on November 19, 1997. The delay was contrary to ICTR standing orders, which stipulate that charges must be laid within 90 days of an arrest being made. Because of this breach of procedure, the ICTR was obliged to release him. He pleaded not guilty to all counts on February 23, 1998.

However, on March 31, 2000, the ICTR Appeals Chamber overturned its earlier decision, and directed that he stand trial. This, in turn, was consolidated into a larger proceeding, along with two other media executives involved in the genocide, Hassan Ngeze, former editor of the newspaper *Kangura,* and his cofounder of RTLM, Ferdinand Nahimana (who was also the former director of the Rwandan National Information Office, ORINFOR). Collectively known as the "Media Trial," the three were found responsible for creating a climate that implanted the idea of Tutsi annihilation onto the Hutu worldview long before the killing actually began.

All three were alleged to have conspired to set up Radio-Télévision Libre des Mille Collines in order to promote Hutu extremism and ethnic division, and to incite the murder and persecution of persons of Tutsi origin. They were charged with several counts of genocide, public incitement to commit genocide, complicity in genocide, and crimes against humanity. According to the ICTR indictment, Barayagwiza allegedly presided over several meetings to plan the murder of Tutsis and moderate Hutus in Mutura commune, Gisenyi prefecture. He is also alleged to have assisted in the distribution of weapons and funds to the Interahamwe militia, and ordered murders and violent acts against Tutsis. Further, it was stated that he knew or had reason to know that members of the CDR party had participated in the killings of Tutsi and moderate Hutu in Gisenyi prefecture. In spite of his position and responsibilities in the CDR, he allegedly did nothing to prevent those acts or to punish their authors.

Barayagwiza refused to participate in the trial, claiming that the judges were not impartial. On December 3, 2003, the trial chamber of the ICTR found him guilty on nine counts, and sentenced him to 35 years' imprisonment. The Appeals Chamber affirmed his guilt on November 28, 2007, but only for the counts of instigating the perpetration of acts of genocide, for planning, ordering, or instigating the commission of a crime against humanity (extermination), and for instigating the perpetration of a crime against humanity (persecution). For this, his original sentence was reduced from 35 years in prison to 32 years, and on June 27, 2009, he was transferred to Akpro Missérété Prison in the Republic of Benin to serve out his sentence.

He immediately appealed the sentence, and in subsequent years others were made, as well. His last formal appeal was rejected by the ICTR on June 22, 2009. Early on the morning of Sunday April 25, 2010, Jean-Bosco Barayagwiza died at the Centre Hospitalier Départemental de l'Ouémé, in Porto Novo, Benin. Earlier, on March 5, 2010, he had been admitted with an advanced case of Hepatitis C. His family subsequently reported that he was denied adequate treatment, though this has yet to be verified.

Paul R. Bartrop

See also: International Criminal Tribunal for Rwanda; Media Trial in Rwanda; Nahimana, Ferdinand; Ngeze, Hassan; Radio-Télévision Libre des Mille Collines

Further Reading

Barnett, Michael. *Eyewitness to a Genocide: The United Nations and Rwanda.* Ithaca, NY: Cornell University Press, 2002.

Beigbeder, Yves. *Judging War Criminals: The Politics of International Justice.* New York: St. Martin's Press, 1999.

Barril, Paul

Paul Barril is an expert in international security issues and special operations and worked for a number of years in the French Gendarmerie Nationale (French national police force), during which he was involved in a number of clandestine and sometimes controversial operations. A shadowy figure, he was allegedly involved in the 1994 Rwandan Genocide, although the precise extent of his involvement remains shrouded in mystery.

Paul Barril was born on April 13, 1946, in Vinay, Isère, France and earned a law degree from the University of Paris (Sorbonne). By the early 1970s, he had joined the Gendarmerie; later, he helped establish the Groupement d'Intervention de la Gendarmerie Nationale (GIGN), which is a special-forces unit usually involved in clandestine activities. From approximately 1974 until 1982, he served as the second officer of the GIGN, under Christian Prouteau, who commanded the outfit. In 1982, Barril was tapped to establish and supervise a counterterrorist unit under orders of French president François Mitterand. He remained in this post until the early 1990s and left the Gendarmerie in 1995. In 1979, he helped the Saudi Arabian government quash an uprising by fundamentalist Muslims at the Grand Mosque in Mecca, the holiest site in all of Islam.

In the meantime, Barril established several private security firms, beginning in 1984, through which he worked for several world leaders and foreign governments, including the Ivory Coast. Sometime in the late 1980s, Barril formed the Société d'Études de Conception et de Réalisation d'Equipements Techniques de Sécurité (known by its acronym SECRETS), which provided security consultations: for foreign nations; many of these took the form of covert armed intervention, special operations, and mercenary equipage and training.

Perhaps Barril's most controversial actions involved Rwanda and the Rwandan Genocide, which began in 1994. In 1989, his company was reportedly retained to reorganize Rwanda's intelligence service; some sources claim that his company was enlisted to provide an efficiency audit of Rwanda's army in 1990. Barril allegedly worked as a high-level military and security advisor to Juvénal Habyarimana, Rwanda's Hutu president from 1973 to 1994. At the same time, it has been suggested that Barril and other French agents were arming and training extremist Hutus who would commence the Rwandan Genocide. Some of these Hutus likely set up the assassination of President Habyarimana, which provided the catalyst for the mass killings of Tutsis and moderate Hutus beginning in April 1994.

After Habyarimana's plane was shot down as it neared the airport in Kigali on April 6, 1994, the president's widow, Agathe, supposedly retained the services of Barril's company, SECRETS, to find the perpetrators of her husband's assassination. Barril claimed publicly that he believed Rwandan Patriotic Front operatives, led by Tutsi Paul Kagame, took the plane down with shoulder-fired missiles. That helped stir Hutu outrage and sparked the genocide that would follow. After the genocide, Barril continued to work for the temporary Hutu-led government. Much of Barril's involvement in the events in Rwanda remains sketchy and fragmentary, and some reports were based on Barril's own claims, which should be viewed with some skepticism.

Barril continues to head his private security concerns and advise foreign governments.

PAUL G. PIERPAOLI JR.

See also: Habyarimana, Juvénal; Hutus; Kagame, Paul; Rwanda; Rwandan Patriotic Front; Tutsis

Further Reading

Des Forges, Alison. *Leave None to Tell the Story: Genocide in Rwanda.* New York: Human Rights Watch, 1999.

Straus, Scott. *The Order of Genocide: Race, Power, and War in Rwanda.* Ithaca, NY: Cornell University Press, 2008.

Beardsley, Brent

Major Brent Beardsley is a Canadian infantry officer who served as chief of staff to General Roméo Dallaire in Rwanda before and during that country's 1994 genocide. Born in Ottawa on November 25, 1954, he was raised in Montreal. He graduated from a pre-Arts program at Sir George Williams University in 1974, completed a BA in history from Concordia University in 1977, and undertook a postgraduate Diploma in Education at McGill University in 1978. In the same year, he joined the Canadian army. As an officer in the Royal Canadian Regiment he has held a wide range of command, staff, and training positions, and has served four tours of duty in Norway, Germany, and Cyprus. He has been employed as an instructor on the Basic Officer Training Course, as a doctrine author responsible for the first draft of the first Canadian Forces Peacekeeping Manual, and as the chief instructor of the Canadian Forces Peacekeeping Training Centre. He is currently a research officer at the Canadian Forces Leadership Institute of the Canadian Defence Academy at the Royal Military College, Kingston, Ontario.

During the 1990s he served with the Canadian delegation to the United Nations in New York, prior to being sent in 1993 as operations manager (effectively chief of staff and personal assistant) to Dallaire, the force commander of the United Nations Assistance Mission for Rwanda, or UNAMIR. He was thus ideally placed as an eyewitness to the genocide in Rwanda, both as an observer and as a participant who tried to mitigate the suffering of those around him and stop the killing.

Beardsley saw on a daily basis how Rwanda was viewed as essentially insignificant to the world's powers while the genocide was taking place, and was disgusted as the UNAMIR force was reduced, by a unanimous vote in the Security Council on April 21, 1994, from 2,500 troops to just 270. Together with Dallaire and his second-in-command, General Henry Anyidoho of Ghana, Beardsley watched with increasing frustration and anger as the United Nations Department of Peacekeeping Operations in New York consistently refused to see the genocide as anything other than a civil war into which the UN could not intrude. At a later time, Beardsley would be quoted as saying "It was almost to the point where you know you want to get on the phone and just yell in to it 'Is there anybody alive out there?' The world just didn't care and it made no difference what you said or how you said it to them."

Many of the issues facing Beardsley and Dallaire were later committed to paper in an award-winning memoir of the experience the two co-authored, *Shake Hands with the Devil: The Failure of Humanity in Rwanda* (2003). Beardsley is also active in promoting Rwanda awareness through speaking at universities and in other public forums, and has taken part in numerous documentaries as well as writing articles and participating in commemorative events relating to the Rwandan Genocide. In February 2004 Beardsley testified at the International Criminal Tribunal for Rwanda (ICTR) in Arusha, Tanzania, in the trial of Théoneste Bagosora, the alleged architect of the Rwandan Genocide, for genocide and crimes against humanity.

Building on his experiences in Rwanda and elsewhere, Beardsley holds today that Canadians urgently need to reexamine the way they view national security. Addressing issues of international aid and security, his view is that Canada should view environmental and humanitarian crises as issues having a profound effect on national security, as it is these types of issues, which, if left unchecked, can become a source of conflict in the future. People living without hope or an opportunity to improve their lives, for whom survival is a day-to-day struggle, can become so frustrated that eventually violent rage builds that can spill over into major physical conflict. Beardsley has put the question as to whether it is by then too late to intervene with any hope of success. While these issues are not of themselves a threat to comfortable middle-class security in the West, a failure to prevent or stop them can lead to escalation—and then humanitarian crises become security threats. An immediate solution would be to begin the promotion of democracy in developing nations, so that people have a stake in seeing to it that their societies do not descend into situations that threaten their own lives.

On July 18, 1995, Brent Beardsley was awarded the Meritorious Service Cross (MSC), presented by the governor-general of Canada, for his heroic personal actions in Rwanda. He is also a recipient of the Canadian Forces Decoration (CD) with bar, for his many years of military service. In September 2006, Beardsley was named as a fellow of the Montréal Institute of Genocide and Human Rights Studies, at Concordia University.

PAUL R. BARTROP

See also: Anyidoho, Henry Kwami; Dallaire, Roméo; International Criminal Tribunal for Rwanda; United Nations Assistance Mission for Rwanda

Further Reading

Anyidoho, Henry Kwami. *Guns over Kigali: The Rwandese Civil War, 1994. A Personal Account.* Accra: Woeli Publishing Services, 1997.

Dallaire, Roméo. *Shake Hands with the Devil: The Failure of Humanity in Rwanda.* Toronto: Random House, 2004.

Bicamumpaka, Jérôme

Jérôme Bicamumpaka was the minister of Foreign Affairs and Cooperation in Rwanda's interim government between April 9 and mid-July 1994. The interim government was directed by Hutu extremists close to the so-called Akazu clique, an informal organization of relatives and close friends of the Habyarimana clan. As foreign minister, Bicamumpaka was responsible for, and exercised authority over, all government policy on foreign affairs. In this position he attended cabinet meetings where he was informed about the sociopolitical situation in the country, and where he was apprised of Hutu extremist policy.

Bicamumpaka, a Hutu, was born in 1957 in Mukono, Ruhondo commune, in Ruhengeri district. From late 1990 until July 1994, he is said to have joined and become wholly dedicated to the elaboration and execution of a plan to exterminate Rwanda's Tutsi population. In the execution of this plan, Bicamumpaka allegedly organized, ordered, and participated in the massacres that took place after April 6, 1994. He has been accused of conspiring with other senior figures in Rwanda, notably Théoneste Bagosora, to establish and execute this genocidal plan.

It is alleged by the International Criminal Tribunal for Rwanda (ICTR) that Bicamumpaka knew—or from his position of power, should have known—that those in his Department had committed, or were about to commit, crimes involving the massacre of Tutsis and moderate Hutus. Between April 8 and July 14, 1994, a wide variety of public officials, from ministers to civil servants and the police, ordered, encouraged, committed, and helped to commit these massacres, in such districts as Butare, Kibuye, Kigali, Gitarama, and Gisenyi, and did nothing to prevent them or punish the perpetrators. The ICTR has further alleged that between April 11 and July 14, 1994, Bicamumpaka and other ministers traveled to several of these same districts in order to supervise the implementation of the interim government's orders, particularly in matters of civil defense and security. The inescapable conclusion arrived at by the ICTR is that Bicamumpaka knowingly failed in his duty to ensure the security of the population of Rwanda, and consciously participated in the massacres from a command position.

By mid-July 1994 the forces of the interim government were in full retreat before the advance of General Paul Kagame's Rwandan Patriotic Front. Bicamumpaka fled Rwanda, and sought sanctuary in Cameroon. It was here that he was arrested, at the request of the ICTR prosecutor, on April 6, 1999. On July 31, 1999, he was transferred to the United Nations prison complex in Arusha, Tanzania.

Bicamumpaka was indicted on May 7, 1999. The charges were conspiracy to commit genocide, genocide, complicity in genocide, direct and public incitement to commit genocide, murder as a crime against humanity, extermination as a crime against humanity, rape as a crime against humanity, and war crimes. At his first court appearance, on August 17, 1999, he refused to plead either guilty or not guilty to any of the charges, and so, in accordance with the ICTR statute, the judges concluded that he had pleaded not guilty.

At the request of the prosecutor, Bicamumpaka's case was joined with those of three other members of the interim government: Casimir Bizimungu, the minister of health; Justin Mugenzi, the minister of trade and industry; and Prosper Mugiraneza, the minister of the civil service. The joint proceedings, referred to as the "Government II Trial," opened in Arusha on November 6, 2003, before the second trial chamber of the ICTR. By June 23, 2005, the prosecution had presented, and closed, its case.

Then, on October 31, 2005, with the trial still underway, Jérôme Bicamumpaka was partially acquitted of various counts in the indictment, namely, rape as a crime against humanity, outrages upon personal dignity as a war crime, and conspiracy to commit genocide insofar as his superior responsibility was concerned.

On June 12, 2008, the evidence phase of the trial was closed and on November 22, 2008, the defense filed its closing brief. The case was completed in December 2008. The prosecutor called for the maximum penalty available to the ICTR—life imprisonment—against Bicamumpaka. On September 30, 2011, in a verdict that surprised many, the tribunal acquitted Jérôme Bicamumpaka of all charges. He was immediately released from custody, and reunited with his family.

PAUL R. BARTROP

See also: Bagosora, Théoneste; International Criminal Tribunal for Rwanda

Further Reading

Boot, Machteld. *Genocide, Crimes against Humanity, War Crimes: Nullum Crimen Sine Lege and the Subject Matter Jurisdiction of the International Criminal Court.* Antwerp: Intersentia, 2002.

Melvern, Linda. *Conspiracy to Murder: The Rwandan Genocide.* London: Verso, 2006.

Bikindi, Simon

Simon Bikindi was a well-known composer, director, and singer of popular music in Rwanda before and during the Rwandan Genocide of 1994. Born on September 28, 1954, to farmers in a village in the commune of Rwerere, northwestern Rwanda, Bikindi is an ethnic Hutu. After the genocide, when on trial, he recounted how he inherited his love of music from his parents: his mother, who was a singer, dancer, and narrator invited to perform at popular festivals; and his father, a blacksmith, who played the Rwandan sitar in his free time. At school, Bikindi made a name for himself among his peers by playing a combination of modern and regional music from his home province.

As a popular recording artist, Bikindi was in effect a propagandist for the extremist Hutu cause against the country's Tutsis. His songs included the following:

- *Twasezereye Ingoma Ya Cyami* (*We Said Good-Bye to the Monarchy*), which was performed for the first time in 1987 during the celebrations for the 25th anniversary of independence. Here, Bikindi criticized the monarchy that was overthrown in 1959, celebrating instead the end of feudalism and colonization that came with independence in 1962. This song, which was played constantly on Radio Rwanda and Radio Télévision Libre des Mille Collines (RTLM) in 1992 and 1993, was a public appeal for Hutus to band together to oppose the Arusha Accords, the power-sharing agreement signed in August 1993 between the Hutu Power president of Rwanda, Juvénal Habyarimana and the Tutsi-led Rwandan Patriotic Front (RPF).
- *Akabyutso* (*The Little Awakening*) was a song expressing Bikindi's hatred of those Hutus who did not live up to the highest standards of proper behavior expected of a Hutu—those who did not look out for their fellow Hutus, who were mean with money, who forgot the old days of the Tutsi hegemony, or who were disparaging of other Hutus.
- *Bene Sebahinzi* (*The Descendants of Sebahinzi*) praised the significance and value of the 1959 Hutu revolution.
- *Impuruza* (*Warning*), composed in 1993.

Bikindi's songs were comprised of popular and catchy tunes that mixed Kinyawanda lyrics with French and English words in a style that combined rap and folk melodies, and through this he became Rwanda's most famous popular singer. Prior to the genocide he directed the famous Irindo ballet, and was also a civil service official in the Ministry of Youth and Sport, as well as a member of Habyarimana's ruling Mouvement Républicain National pour le Développement et la Démocratie (National Republican Movement for Development and Democracy, or MNRDD) party.

When the war broke out in October 1990 between the government and the Tutsi rebels of the RPF, Bikindi was already the most popular singer in Rwanda. It has been alleged that from then on Bikindi contributed to a government-run media campaign designed to stir up anti-Tutsi hatred. In particular, he was said to have composed and performed songs aimed at the Interahamwe and the civilian population, in order to encourage them to kill Tutsis. He recorded songs with anti-Tutsi lyrics that were in turn broadcast repeatedly across the radio. It has been further alleged that in the months prior to the genocide Bikindi consulted with President Habyarimana, Minister of Youth and Sports Callixte Nzabonimana, and officers from Rwanda's military forces about the lyrics of certain anti-Tutsi songs.

Although Bikindi left the country a few days before the start of the killing in April 1994, it was well known that throughout the genocide Hutu killers sang Bikindi's songs as they slaughtered Tutsis. When groups of extremist Hutus went searching for Tutsis to kill, they often sang the songs they had heard on RTLM, and radio appeals to attack the Tutsis were often preceded or followed by Bikindi's music. His songs were therefore a crucial part of the genocidal project, as they incited the ethnic hatred of Tutsis and further incited people to the task of annihilation.

Bikindi returned to Rwanda later in June 1994, and it has been alleged that he participated actively in massacres of Tutsis, reportedly recruiting, training, and supervising the Interahamwe militia in Gisenyi. He was also said to have personally ordered the execution of some victims. With the advance of the RPF he fled to Zaire (the Democratic Republic of Congo), alongside most of Rwanda's Hutu Power militias, military, and government officials. There, he continued singing and playing to Hutu groups.

On July 12, 2001, Bikindi was arrested in a center for asylum seekers in Leiden, Holland. He fought calls from Rwanda for his extradition and requested asylum, but on March 27, 2002, he was transferred instead to the jurisdiction of the International Criminal Tribunal for Rwanda (ICTR) in Arusha, Tanzania. The ICTR indicted him with conspiracy to commit genocide; genocide, or alternatively complicity in genocide; direct and public incitement to commit genocide; and murder and persecution as crimes against humanity. On April 4, 2002, he appeared before the ICTR and pleaded not guilty on all counts.

The trial began on October 2, 2006, and took 61 days. Closing arguments were heard on May 26, 2008, when the prosecution demanded a sentence of life imprisonment, arguing that Bikindi should be convicted on the basis of his personal participation in planning and instigating acts of genocide and the murder of Tutsi civilians. The defense used the argument of Bikindi exercising his right of freedom of expression, but the judges rejected this argument. On December 2, 2008, Bikindi was found guilty on the count of direct and public incitement to commit genocide, and sentenced to 15 years' imprisonment, with credit for the 7 years he had already served in custody. This was the only count among the six for which he had been charged that could stick. The judges held that all the songs under discussion had been written before 1994, and thus before the period covered in the ICTR statute. They also found that there was not enough evidence to prove that Bikindi had played a role in the dissemination of the songs via RTLM, even though that radio station had played the songs throughout the genocide.

Bikindi appealed, arguing that he had never killed anyone and that he could not stop the *génocidaires* from singing his songs. The appeals chamber of the ICTR rejected Bikindi's appeal in its entirety on March 18, 2010, affirming the Trial Chamber's decision regarding his guilt in directing and publicly inciting the Hutu population to commit genocide, and upheld the original conviction and sentence.

Simon Bikindi was the first performing artist to have been brought before an international court and charged with using his creativity to incite genocide. For some legal and human rights commentators, this presented problematic elements of humanitarian justice, given that artistic expression and its influence is an extremely broad field leading to a variety of interpretations. It came as something of a relief, therefore, that judgment was not able to be rendered in this area, and that Bikindi was found guilty on other grounds.

In postgenocide Rwanda since 1994, his songs have been banned from national radio stations.

PAUL R. BARTROP

See also: Arusha Accords; Habyarimana, Juvénal; Interahamwe; International Criminal Tribunal for Rwanda; Radio-Télévision Libre des Mille Collines

Further Reading

Jokic, Aleksandar, ed. *War Crimes and Collective Wrongdoing: A Reader.* Malden, MA: Blackwell Publishers, 2001.

Kressel, Neil Jeffrey. *Mass Hate: The Global Rise of Genocide and Terror.* New York: Plenum Press, 1996.

Bisengimana, Paul

Paul Bisengimana was mayor of Rwanda's Gikoro Commune (in the Kigali-rural Prefecture) who was indicted and found guilty by the International Criminal Tribunal (ICTR) for his role in the Rwandan Genocide of 1994. Paul Bisengimana was born circa 1945 in the Gikoro Commune. By the early 1990s, he had become mayor of the commune and was allied with the Interahamwe, a Hutu paramilitary organization with strong ties to the Hutu-dominated government in Rwanda. This organization was a decentralized militia force that operated throughout the country, especially in provincial towns and the rural countryside.

As the mayor of the Gikoro Commune, Bisengimana was tasked with carrying out orders from the central government; he therefore exercised complete control over administrative subordinates as well as the local police force. Between late 1990 and mid 1994, he took part in the planning and implementation of policies designed to harass, persecute, and murder scores of Tutsis living in the area under his control. He helped arm local elements of the Interahamwe, established lists of those to be displaced or killed, and personally took part in atrocities against local Tutsis, including rape, mutilation, and mass murder.

Between January 1 and April 30, 1994, Bisengimana met repeatedly with other individuals implicated in the genocide, even holding some of the meetings at his home. At the same time, he helped procure arms for the Interahamwe and incited its members to kill Tutsis and others who opposed the national government. On or about April 8, 1994, Bisengimana reportedly raped a Tutsi woman who worked in the commune's administrative offices. That same day, he exhorted Interahamwe members to rape and kill Tutsi women. Some two days later, he gave the order to kill at least 200 Tutsi refugees. Three days later, he led a group of Tutsi refugees to a church, assuring them that their safety would be guaranteed. Soon thereafter, he ordered their mass executions; the women were first mutilated, then raped, and finally killed. Bisengimana, who reportedly took part in the killings, then ordered the bodies buried in a mass grave.

In June or July of 1994, as Tutsi opposition forces began closing in on the commune, Bisengimana fled the country, eventually settling in Mali, where he was arrested on December 4, 2001. At his trial, he pled guilty to the charges and was sentenced to 15 years in prison.

PAUL G. PIERPAOLI JR.

See also: Interahamwe; International Criminal Tribunal for Rwanda

Further Reading

Malvern, Linda. *Conspiracy to Murder: The Rwanda Genocide.* Rev. ed. London: Verso, 2006.

Straus, Scott. *The Order of Genocide: Race, Power, and War in Rwanda.* Ithaca, NY: Cornell University Press, 2008.

Bizimungu, Augustin

Augustin Bizimungu was the chief of staff of the Rwandan armed forces (Forces Armées Rwandaises, or FAR) before and during the Rwandan Genocide of 1994. An ethnic Hutu, Bizimungu was born in Nyange, Byumba prefecture, in northern Rwanda on August 28, 1952, and was a career soldier. His climb through the Rwandan military was a steady one, and by April 6, 1994, he held the rank of lieutenant colonel, with the responsibility for military operations in the Ruhengeri prefecture.

Facing trial before the International Criminal Tribunal for Rwanda (ICTR) in Arusha, Tanzania, from 2004 onward, it was alleged that from late 1990 onward Bizimungu conspired with other radical Hutus in working out a plan intended to exterminate the civilian Tutsi population and eliminate members of the opposition. The indictment against him alleged that this plan consisted of such things as encouraging hatred and ethnic violence among the Hutu population toward Tutsis; organizing the training and distribution of weapons to extremist militiamen; and the preparation of lists of people to be murdered. In executing the plan, Bizimungu was said to have organized, ordered, and participated in massacres of the Tutsi population.

Bizimungu was reputedly one of a number of senior officers opposed to the Arusha Peace Accords signed between the government of Rwanda and the Rwandan Patriotic Front (RPF) in August 1993. Allegedly, his view was that any attack on Rwanda by the RPF, or an implementation of the Arusha Accords, would result in the extermination of the Tutsi population in his area of operations. In February 1994 Bizimungu is said to have stated that if the RPF attacked again, he did not want to see one Tutsi left alive in his sector. According to the ICTR indictment, the training of the soldiers and militia groups (in particular the Interahamwe) carrying out the genocide was supervised by Bizimungu. Such training was conducted simultaneously in several prefectures around the country, including Bizimungu's zone of operations in Ruhengeri prefecture. Bizimungu was alleged to have distributed weapons to militiamen either by giving them directly or through his subordinates, mayors, and district councilors.

On April 16, 1994—10 days after the beginning of the genocide—Bizimungu was promoted to major general and appointed as head of the army. The former army chief of staff, Déogratias Nsabimana, died in the same plane crash as the Rwandan president, Juvénal Habyarimana, on April 6, 1994, necessitating not just a new appointment, but one from the ranks of the radical Hutus who now formed the interim government. This promotion, which he retained until July 1994, crowned Bizimungu's military career. From this position, he was the leading military figure involved in negotiations with the United Nations Assistance Mission for Rwanda (UNAMIR), and particularly its force commander, Lieutenant General Roméo Dallaire.

From April to July 1994, officers of the army general staff, one of whom was Bizimungu, allegedly participated in daily briefings at which they were informed of the massacres of the civilian Tutsi population and of moderate Hutus. It has been further alleged that these higher echelon officers ordered, encouraged, and backed the massacres. On or about May 18, 1994, during a meeting at which Bizimungu was present, these officers were reported to be very pleased with the performance of the Interahamwe in the killing process, while at the same time underlining the need to provide them with better arms.

Within his own locality of Ruhengeri, Bizimungu was allegedly aware that his subordinates were about to commit (or had already committed) crimes, but did nothing to prevent them or punish the perpetrators. Between April 10 and 15, 1994, several Tutsis sought refuge in the Ruhengeri prefecture. On orders from Bizimungu, certain of these refugees were killed by armed civilians. To cover up the massacre—as if such a measure was needed—Bizimungu allegedly issued an order that a message be aired over the radio indicating that it was an attack by the RPF which was responsible for the death of the refugees.

The postgenocide government of Rwanda, furthermore, accused Bizimungu of various anti-Tutsi activities after the genocide had ended. The most damning charge was that as the former head of the FAR and *de facto* head of the Interahamwe he orchestrated various and sundry attacks against Rwanda while in exile in the Democratic Republic of Congo after 1994.

In July 1994, faced with the advance of the RPF, Bizimungu fled Rwanda and found sanctuary in Angola among the Angolan rebel movement UNITA. On April 12, 2002, the ICTR issued an arrest warrant for Bizimungu, who was finally uncovered among demobilized UNITA militants. He was arrested by the Angolan government in Luena, northeastern Angola, on August 12, 2002, and on August 14 transferred to the prison quarters of the United Nations in Arusha, Tanzania. The charges he faced were conspiracy to commit genocide, genocide or alternatively complicity in genocide, three counts of crimes against humanity, and war crimes. He was also charged with specific additional crimes and command responsibility for crimes committed by his subordinates. The acts covered within Bizimungu's indictment include murder, extermination, and rape; he is also charged with directly ordering acts to be committed against Tutsis and, by way of his omissions, in failing to halt the acts of his subordinates. At his initial court appearance on August 21, 2002, Bizimungu pleaded not guilty to all of the nine counts with which he was charged.

At the request of the chief prosecutor, the ICTR then ordered a combined trial for Bizimungu and three other senior officers of the FAR on the same counts. They were: Augustin Ndindiliyimana, chief of staff of the National Gendarmerie; François-Xavier Nzuwoneyeme, commander of the Reconnaissance Battalion of the Rwandan army; and Innocent Sagahutu, second-in-command of the Reconnaissance Battalion. According to a new indictment dated August 23, 2004, Bizimungu was also accused of having participated in a plan conceived in the early 1990s to exterminate the Tutsi population through acts including the training of the Interahamwe.

The trial of Augustin Bizimungu and his co-accused, known as "Military Trial 2," opened on September 20, 2004, before the Second Trial Chamber of the ICTR. At the beginning of the trial, he once more pleaded not guilty to all charges. The trial was completed on June 29, 2009. On May 17, 2011, Bizimungu was sentenced to 30 years' imprisonment by the ICTR for his part in the genocide.

PAUL R. BARTROP

See also: Forces Armées Rwandaises; Interahamwe; International Criminal Tribunal for Rwanda; United Nations Assistance Mission for Rwanda

Further Reading

Kressel, Neil Jeffrey. *Mass Hate: The Global Rise of Genocide and Terror.* New York: Plenum Press, 1996.

Neier, Aryeh. *War Crimes: Brutality, Genocide, Terror, and the Struggle for Justice.* New York: Times Books, 1998.

Booh-Booh, Jacques-Roger

Jacques-Roger Booh-Booh is a former foreign minister of Cameroon and special representative of the secretary-general of the United Nations (SRSG) in Rwanda between November 1993 and June 1994. In the latter capacity, he was the senior UN civilian official in Rwanda during the time of the Rwandan Genocide.

Booh-Booh was born on February 5, 1938, in Manak, Cameroon, when the country was still a French colony. After Cameroon's independence on January 1, 1960, the country sought to develop an autonomous foreign policy within the Western bloc. In this context, Booh-Booh chose a career as a diplomat in the Ministry of External Relations. He rose to become head of the Department of African Affairs, director for Asia and Africa, and deputy permanent representative to the United Nations. As a foreign representative, he was ambassador to Morocco, Greece, and UNESCO, before his most prestigious postings as ambassador to the Soviet Union (1981–1983) and France (1983–1988). On May 16, 1988, he became Cameroon's minister of external relations.

In November 1993 Booh-Booh took up his position as the head of the United Nations Assistance Mission for Rwanda (UNAMIR). This had been established on October 5, 1993, by UN Security Council Resolution 872 for the express purpose of helping to implement the Arusha Peace Agreement signed in Arusha, Tanzania, on August 4, 1993, by the primarily Hutu government of Rwanda and the Tutsi-led Rwandan Patriotic Front (RPF). The Arusha Accords were a set of five agreements intended to end the civil war between the two parties. The talks leading to Arusha had been cosponsored by the United States, France, and the Organization of African Unity, and ranged over a wide variety of topics: refugee resettlement, power-sharing between Hutu and Tutsi, the introduction of an all-embracing democratic regime, the dismantling of the military dictatorship of President Juvénal Habyarimana, and the encouragement of a transparent rule of law throughout Rwanda.

In monitoring the Accords, UNAMIR's mandate was to supervise the cease-fire, establish and expand the demilitarized zone and demobilization procedures, provide security for the Rwandan capital city of Kigali, monitor the security situation during the final period of the transitional government's mandate leading up to elections, and assist in the coordination of humanitarian assistance activities in conjunction with relief operations. UNAMIR was on a Chapter VI mandate that was untenable in light of the fact that it was undermanned, under-resourced, and provided with poorly equipped and trained troops from a variety of small and impoverished nations. UNAMIR had a huge job to do, but only a small force of approximately 2,548 military personnel with which to do it.

As SRSG, Booh-Booh's role was to act as chief executive officer of the mission, reporting directly to

Secretary-General Boutros Boutros-Ghali. His relationship with UNAMIR's force commander, General Roméo Dallaire, was far from effective. Handpicked by Boutros-Ghali, with whom Booh-Booh was a personal friend, the SRSG's role was supposedly to report back to New York jointly with Dallaire. It has been widely alleged, however, that Booh-Booh regularly undervalued and miscalculated the implications of Dallaire's reports that were in some instances based directly on intelligence gathered directly from Hutu informers. Other accusations have been that Booh-Booh refused to acknowledge the lethal nature of the Hutu Power threat, or how organized and centralized the killing arrangements were, and that he rarely showed up at UN headquarters in Kigali. After the genocide began in earnest, moreover, accusations have been made that he became less and less available to provide appropriate leadership when the military leadership was calling for it. Also, according to RPF claims based on secret message intercepts, Booh-Booh allegedly held close ties to the Hutu militant leadership.

Despite Dallaire's attempts to minimize deaths and participate actively as a peacekeeper during the genocide, he and Booh-Booh appeared to be working at cross-purposes. In the aftermath of a series of murders of Tutsis in late February 1994, Booh-Booh reported to UN headquarters that there was no evidence that the killings had been "ethnically motivated," notwithstanding advice from Dallaire (operating on a tip-off from a former key member of the Interahamwe militia in January) that this was precisely what it was.

Booh-Booh considered that both the military and the civilian branches of UNAMIR were under the orders of the SRSG, and he did not see himself as being accountable to Dallaire. One of the points of the Arusha Accords was that neither side should rearm, but Booh-Booh held that Dallaire was not impartial when it came to the rearmament of the RPF. He informed Boutros-Ghali of problems such as this, and criticized Dallaire for never having passed any intelligence files to him since he took command. He noted, correctly, that Dallaire's relationship with Habyarimana was strained, and held the force commander responsible for the diplomatic breakdown between UNAMIR and the Rwandan president.

Many in the international community voiced concern about just how impartial Booh-Booh really was for someone in his position. Not only were he and Habyarimana close friends, he was also close with the leadership of the extremist Hutu-dominated MRNDD (Mouvement Républicain National pour Démocratie et le Développement, the Republican Movement for National Democracy and Development), and was associated with some who became the most notorious leaders of the 1994 Rwandan Genocide, including Théoneste Bagosora.

In April 2005, Booh-Booh hit back at these claims, in a book published in Paris entitled *Le Patron de Dallaire Parle* (*Dallaire's Boss Speaks*). He strongly criticized all previous accounts, and denounced Dallaire's actions before and during the genocide. He accused Dallaire of aiding the RPF, and claimed that Dallaire did not report to him the events of the night April 6, 1994, when the plane carrying Habyarimana and the president of Burundi, Cyprien Ntaryamira, was shot down. It was this act that triggered the genocide of Rwanda's Tutsi population and the death of the Hutu liberal middle class over the next three months. Among the other accusations he made was the claim that Dallaire also did not inform him of the brutal murder and mutilation of 10 Belgian officers under his command on April 7, precipitating a wholesale pullout of UN military contributions to UNAMIR.

Booh-Booh's role in Rwanda as SRSG has been the subject of harsh criticism from Dallaire and many of his senior staff officers, foremost amongst whom have been Major Brent Beardsley and General Henry Anyidoho, who have contended that he played an instrumental role in forestalling preventive action against the Hutu *génocidaires* even before the plane was shot down. Booh-Booh was eventually dismissed as SRSG to Rwanda, ostensibly because he left the country in May 1994 without UN permission. He was replaced as SRSG on July 1, 1994, by Shahryar Khan of Pakistan, who remained in this role until 1996.

PAUL R. BARTROP

See also: Dallaire, Roméo; Habyarimana, Juvénal; United Nations Assistance Mission for Rwanda

Further Reading

Booh-Booh, Jacques-Roger. *Le Patron de Dallaire Parle: révélations sur les dérives d'un général de l'ONU au Rwanda.* Paris: Duboiris, 2005.

Dallaire, Roméo. *Shake Hands with the Devil: The Failure of Humanity in Rwanda.* Toronto: Random House, 2004.

Burundi

The earliest inhabitants of Burundi are believed to have been Twa Pygmies. They were followed by the Bantu-speaking Hutus, who arrived between 500 BCE and 1000

CE and soon outnumbered the Twa peoples. The Nilotic Tutsi people migrated into the area from the northeast during the 1400s–1600s and in the 1700s established a Tutsi kingdom and several states. The Tutsi king governed other Tutsis and the more-numerous Hutus in a feudal system.

Germany took possession of Burundi (Urundi) in 1890, incorporating it and neighboring Rwanda (Ruanda) into German East Africa. At the time, Germany did not even have an outpost in the territory and it governed primarily through indirect rule. During World War I, Germany's few troops in the region were easily routed by Belgian Army forces stationed in what is now the Democratic Republic of Congo. Belgium was given a League of Nations mandate over Urundi-Ruanda in 1919.

At the end of World War II, Urundi-Ruanda became a United Nations (UN) Trust Territory, with Belgium continuing as its administrator. In UN-supervised elections held in September 1961, the Union for National Progress (UPRONA)—a party formed several years earlier by the son of the ruling Tutsi king—emerged victorious. The son, Louis Rwagasore, served as prime minister for two weeks before being assassinated; his brother-in-law, Andre Muhirwa, succeeded him. Full independence came on July 1, 1962, following the granting of internal self-government and the establishment of Burundi and Rwanda as two separate states. The Tutsi king, Mwami Mwambutsa IV, took over the leadership of the new nation.

Hutu-Tutsi tensions grew during the first years of independence. Despite overall Tutsi political dominance, Hutu candidates captured a majority of seats in 1965 parliamentary elections. The king, however, appointed a Tutsi to serve as prime minister and a group of Hutu police responded by staging a coup attempt. Loyalist police put down the rebellion, but the king fled the country and was declared deposed the following year by his son, Charles. (Charles then became Mwami Ntare V.) In the wake of the coup attempt, almost all of the country's Hutu political elite were executed and most of the army's Hutu officers were purged.

In November 1966, Ntare's prime minister, Captain Michel Micombero, ousted the king and declared Burundi a republic, with himself as president. Hutus staged another rebellion in 1972, again provoking a swift and harsh reaction from the Tutsi government, which proceeded to execute virtually all Hutus with higher education, as well as all remaining Hutu army officers. An estimated 100,000–200,000 people were killed in the massacres, which prompted thousands of Hutus to flee the country. (Ntare V was also killed during the unrest.) The following year,

Micombero formed a seven-member presidential bureau with himself as president and premier. In 1974, the government adopted a new constitution that declared UPRONA to be the sole governing party. Micombero became secretary-general of UPRONA and was reelected president.

Micombero was overthrown in a 1976 military coup led by Colonel Jean-Baptiste Bagaza. Bagaza formed a Supreme Revolutionary Council that governed until January 1980, when it was replaced by an UPRONA central committee headed by Bagaza. A new constitution adopted in November 1981 reconfirmed Burundi's one-party system and also provided for the formation of a popularly elected National Assembly. Legislative elections were held in October 1982 and presidential elections, won by Bagaza, in July 1984. Three years later, Major Pierre Buyoya took control of the country while Bagaza was abroad, accusing the president of corruption. Buyoya suspended the constitution, dissolved the legislature, and formed a ruling Military Committee for National Salvation.

Ethnic violence flared again in August 1988, when Hutus killed several hundred Tutsis in two northern towns, claiming they had been provoked. The government deployed soldiers of the Tutsi-dominated army to the region and widespread massacres of Hutus followed. (Estimates of the number of Hutus killed range from 5,000 to 20,000.) Several months later, Buyoya took steps to encourage national unity by appointing a majority of Hutus to the Council of Ministers, including a Hutu prime minister. He also authorized an investigation into the August massacres, pledged to eliminate discrimination against Hutus, and announced new measures to give Hutus equal educational and employment opportunities.

Over the next few years, progress toward a more democratic political system continued, culminating in the adoption of a new multiparty Burundi Constitution in March 1992 and democratic presidential elections in June 1993. The winner of those elections, Melchior Ndadaye, became the nation's first Hutu president. Strongly committed to ethnic reconciliation, Ndadaye appointed a Tutsi prime minister and named Tutsis to several other cabinet posts. Just three-and-a-half months after his inauguration, however, Ndadaye and a number of his government ministers were killed in a military coup led by Tutsi army officers. The coup collapsed within several days—with army leaders asking remaining government members to resume control—but not before setting off a new wave of ethnic violence that left as many as 100,000–200,000 people dead.

Foreign Affairs Minister Sylvestre Ntibantunganya, a Hutu and a close friend of Ndadaye's, was chosen to serve as interim president for several months before the legislature elected Cyprien Ntaryamira as president in January 1994. Three months later, Ntaryamira and Rwandan president Juvénal Habyarimana were killed in a suspicious plane crash and Ntibantunganya again assumed control. The legislature elected him to fill the post of president on a permanent basis in October 1994, not long after the nation's various political factions had signed a new power-sharing agreement. The power-sharing agreement did little to resolve the ongoing ethnic conflict, however, and killings on both sides have been a constant in recent years.

The fighting reached a new peak in March 1995, when Tutsi extremists—allegedly backed by army troops—went on a rampage in the capital, killing hundreds of Hutus as Ntibantunganya proved unable to rein in the Tutsi-dominated army. Escalating violence throughout 1995 and into 1996 prompted fears of widespread massacres, similar to the ones in neighboring Rwanda during April–June 1994. Domestic and international observers expressed little hope about the chances of breaking the cycle of violence, but representatives of the Hutu-based Front for Democracy in Burundi and UPRONA opened talks on the issue in late April 1996.

In late July 1996, the Tutsi-dominated army staged a coup, ousting Ntibantunganya's government and naming Pierre Buyoya as president. Buyoya claimed that he accepted the position because he wanted to halt the escalating ethnic violence. The international community strongly condemned the coup, however, and several neighboring nations imposed an economic blockade.

In the following years, representatives of Hutu rebels and Buyoya's military government held talks, but the Hutu-Tutsi conflict proved intractable. Both sides took steps toward peace after former South African president Nelson Mandela took charge of peace negotiations in December 2000, but violence continued to plague the country. In July 2001, Buyoya and most of Burundi's political parties signed a power-sharing agreement that established a transitional government in which he would remain head of state for 18 months, after which a Hutu would assume the office. However, the country's two main rebel groups rejected the agreement, and fighting intensified just days after the transitional government was sworn in November 2001.

After a Hutu, Domitien Ndayizeye, assumed the office of president in a peaceful transfer of power in April 2003,

the rebel Forces for the Defense of Democracy (FDD) began negotiating with Ndayizeye's government. However, the other main Hutu rebel group, the National Liberation Forces (FNL), maintained that Ndayizeye's presidency made little difference as long as the military was still dominated by Tutsis. As a result of peace talks, FDD rebels joined Ndayizeye's government in November 2003, but the FNL continued to fight the government.

PAUL R. BARTROP

See also: Burundi, Genocide in; Habyarimana, Juvénal; Hutus; Rwanda; Tutsis

Further Reading

Webster, John B. *The Political Development of Rwanda and Burundi.* Syracuse, NY: Maxwell Graduate School of Citizenship and Public Affairs, Syracuse University, 1966.

Weinstein, Warren, and Robert Schrire. *Political Conflict and Ethnic Strategies: A Case Study of Burundi.* Syracuse, NY: Syracuse University Press, 1976.

Burundi, Genocide in

Sometimes referred to as Rwanda's "false twin," Burundi has a great deal in common with its neighbor to the south, including its small size (28,000 square kilometers), high population density (180 per square kilometers), traditional political systems (both were monarchies), colonial heritage, and ethnic map. Of a population of some 8 million, 15 percent are Tutsi, and 74 percent Hutu. And both have experienced bloodshed on a genocidal scale. The case of Burundi is by no means a carbon copy of the Rwandan Genocide: there are notable differences in the magnitude of the bloodshed, and unlike what happened in Rwanda, the victims were Hutu. Nonetheless, though largely forgotten by the outside world, the killing of anywhere from 200,000 to 300,000 Hutu in 1972 at the hands of a predominantly Tutsi army remains deeply etched in the collective memory of the Barundi.

The roots of the genocide are inscribed in part in the particularities of the country's ethnic configurations, in part in its history. Its social structure, though strikingly similar of that of Rwanda, was more complex. The power-holders were the princes of the blood, known as *ganwa*, who stood as an ethnically distinct group. The Tutsi minority, moreover, was sharply divided into two separate subcategories, the high-ranking Banyaruguru, and the lowly Hima. Among Hutu, rank and privilege had a great deal to do with family origins. All this meant that the political system had none of the sharply defined fractures typical of Rwanda, ensuring a relatively smooth transition to self-government. With considerable support from both Hutu and Tutsi the nationalist party Union pour le Progrès National (Uprona), led by Prince Rwagasore, king (*mwami*) Mwambutsa's eldest son, easily won a majority of the seats in parliament. The assassination of Rwagasore by a Greek gunman in the pay of the opposition party, Parti Démocrate Chrétien (PDC), in 1961 only enhanced the legitimacy of his party.

With the advent of independence (1962) the social landscape underwent a radical change. With the emergence in Rwanda of a Hutu-dominated republic, the Rwandan model served as a powerful pole of attraction for the Hutu of Burundi—and of repulsion for the Tutsi. As their efforts to gain a meaningful share of power proved unavailing, Hutu leaders felt their only option was the use of force. On October 18, 1965, Hutu anger broke out in an abortive coup directed at the king's palace, followed by sporadic attacks against Tutsi elements in the interior. In reprisal Tutsi units of the army arrested and shot 86 leading Hutu politicians and army officers, many affiliated to the pro-Hutu Parti du Peuple (PP). Allegations by the government of a Hutu plot in 1969, led to the arrest of another 70 Hutu personalities, civilian and military, followed by the execution of 19 of them. After the king's decision to leave country in 1965, the Burundi National Army (BNA), led by Colonel Michel Micombero, a Tutsi, emerged as the key player.

The turning point came in April 1972 with the outbreak of a local peasant uprising in the southern region of Rumonge and Nyanza-Lac, causing hundreds and possibly thousands of deaths among Tutsi civilians. In a matter of hours, terror was unleashed by Hutu upon Tutsi. The response of the Micombero government was immediate and unforgiving. Following a brutal repression in rebel-held localities, the army, assisted by the pro-Uprona youth group, the Jeunesses Révolutionnaires Rwagasore (JRR), proceeded to launch a nationwide manhunt, arresting and killing almost every Hutu male in sight. What began as a repression quickly morphed into a genocide. Some of the most gruesome scenes took place on the premises of the university in the capital, Bujumbura, and in secondary and technical schools. In a scenario that would repeat itself again and again groups of soldiers and members of the JRR would suddenly appear in classroom, call students by name and take them away. Few ever returned. The Church, the civil service, the army were systematically purged of

Hutu elements. Exactly how many died is impossible to determine. If the figure of 300,000 cited by Kiraranganiya, a Tutsi observer, may seem excessive, most informed observers would agree that at least 200,000 perished.

Although there is widespread agreement that the Hutu insurgents represented a tiny minority, and included a sprinkling of non-Hutu elements from eastern Congo, their underlying motives are a matter of controversy. The commonly accepted view that the insurrection can best be described as a local peasant rebellion with limited aims, that is, the removal of specific grievances, such as bringing an end to Tutsi exactions and privileges, has been challenged by two well-known experts, the French historian Jean-Pierre Chrétien and the Belgian journalist Jean-Francois Dupaquier. In their co-authored volume on the events of 1972, *Burundi 1972: Au bord des génocides,* they make the argument that the insurrection had as its ultimate objective the physical elimination of the Tutsi community. Put differently what has been abusively described as a genocide of Hutu was really designed to avert a genocide of Tutsi. On the strength of the limited evidence offered by the authors the least that can be said is that their argument is less than compelling.

Just as the Hutu as a group cannot be held responsible for the killings of Tutsi, the genocidal response of the army and youth groups cannot be imputed collectively to all Tutsi. Only a small number of extremists in the government, the army and the JRR were actively involved in the decision to carry out the carnage. Much of the planning was the work of the Minister of Foreign Affairs at the time, Artémon Simbabaniye, assisted in this gruesome task by the Minister of Interior and Justice, Albert Shibura, and the executive secretary of the ruling Uprona party André Yanda, the latter two holding key positions in the BNA. As the social profile of the victims makes clear, the aim was to systematically kill all educated Hutu elements, including civil servants, teachers, agronomists, university students and schoolchildren, so as to eliminate for the foreseeable future any serious challenge to Tutsi domination.

One of the most puzzling questions raised by the Burundi bloodbath relates to the silence of the international community. Although the horrors sweeping across the country were accurately relayed to Washington by the U.S. Embassy Deputy Chief of Mission (DCM) Michael Hoyt, soon confirmed by a devastating report by The Carnegie Endowment for International Peace, *Passing-By: The United States and Genocide in Burundi* (1972), the reaction of the U.S. State Department was conspicuously low-key, reflecting Henry Kissinger's view at the time that, however regrettable, the mass killings of Hutu did not pose a major threat to the U.S. national interests. Hardly more edifying was the response of the UN Secretary General, Kurt Waldheim, who blandly expressed his fervent hopes that peace, harmony, and stability can be restored successfully and speedily. Even more astounding was the official statement released by the Organization of African Unity (OAU), through its Secretary General Diallo Telli, who said that he and the OAU stood in total solidarity behind the government and the fraternal people of Burundi. Behind the silence of the international community lies the obvious fact that very little was known at the time about the circumstances of slaughter (not unlike what happened in Rwanda 21 years later), or for that matter about Burundi. Equally important to bear in mind is that human rights issues had yet to acquire the saliency they have today. Again, at a time when the international concerns of Western nations were largely centered on Cold War issues, what was at stake in this human tragedy had little to do with their vital interests.

Nor did they feel especially concerned by the aftermath of the crisis. What emerged from the carnage was a state utterly dominated by Tutsi elements. It would take another 16 years before a localized Hutu revolt again erupted in the north, in turn setting in motion a process of democratization that led to multiparty presidential and parliamentary elections in July 1993, and to the election of the first popularly elected Hutu president, Melchior Ndadaye. The sense of elation felt by the Hutu masses proved short-lived, however. On October 21, 1993, Ndadaye was assassinated by Tutsi extremists in the army acting hand in hand with their civilian counterparts. After years of unfettered control of the institutions of the state, a surrender of power to representatives of the Hutu majority is what the hardcore Tutsi politicians and army men were unwilling to accept. It is at this juncture that, in retrospect, a significant connection emerges between the genocides in Burundi and in Rwanda. For if the mass killing of Hutu in Burundi created the chain of circumstances that led to the death of Ndadaye 21 years later, his assassination by Tutsi soldiers is what unleashed the rise of the militantly anti-Tutsi Hutu Power movement in Rwanda. If any event helps account for the radicalization of anti-Tutsi sentiment in Rwanda, it is the death of Ndadaye, but his death cannot be fully explained unless we take into account the murderous legacy of 1972.

RENÉ LEMARCHAND

See also: Burundi; Rwanda

Further Reading

Brown, Michael, Gary Freeman, and Kay Miller. *Passing-By: The United States and Genocide in Burundi, 1972.* New York: The Carnegie Endowment for International Peace, 1973.

Lemarchand, René, ed. *Forgotten Genocides: Oblivion, Denial and Memory.* Philadelphia: University of Pennsylvania Press, 2011.

Totten, Samuel, William S. Parsons, and Israel W. Charny, eds. *Century of Genocide: Eyewitness Accounts and Critical Views.* New York: Garland Publishing, 1997.

Bushnell, Prudence

Prudence Bushnell was a senior American administrator and diplomat who took a prominent role in attempting to keep the Rwandan Genocide of 1994 at the forefront of her government's attention whilst it was in progress. Born in 1946 in Washington, D.C., the daughter of American diplomat Gerald Bushnell, as a child she experienced life in a range of diverse countries and cultures as a result of her father's many overseas postings. These included periods growing up in Iran, Germany, France, and Pakistan. She was educated at the University of Maryland and Russell Sage College (a women's college located in Troy, New York). Upon graduating she worked as a management consultant in Texas, prior to joining the U.S. Foreign Service in 1981 as an administrative track officer. Her first assignment was in Mumbai, India, prior to serving as deputy chief of mission under Ambassador George Moose at the U.S. embassy in Dakar, Senegal.

In 1993, Moose was appointed assistant secretary of state for African Affairs by President Bill Clinton, and Bushnell joined him as deputy assistant secretary at the Africa Desk. Ultimately, she rose to the position of principal deputy assistant secretary of state, at a time marked by heightening tension in Africa. In one country, Rwanda, attempts had been made at resolving violence between hardline Hutu nationalists espousing a culture of ethnic purity, and Rwandan Tutsi *émigrés* based in Uganda. The result was a set of five agreements signed by the Hutu-dominated government of Rwanda and the Tutsi-led Rwandan Patriotic Front (RPF) in Arusha, Tanzania, on August 4, 1993. The Arusha Accords, so-called, had been cosponsored by the United States, France, and the Organization of African Unity, and it was intended that they would end the civil war raging between the two sides. They ranged over a wide variety of topics: refugee resettlement, power-sharing between

Hutu and Tutsi, the introduction of democracy throughout Rwanda, the dismantling of the military dictatorship of President Juvénal Habyarimana, and the encouragement of a transparent rule of law throughout the country. In the months that followed the signing of the Accords, a number of subsequent meetings took place for the purpose of negotiating their implementation. This involved the parties traveling to and from Arusha, sometimes by road and at other times by plane. It was after one of these meetings, on April 6, 1994, that the plane carrying Habyarimana and the president of Burundi, Cyprien Ntaryamira, was shot down by a missile as the plane neared Kigali airport. All on board were killed, triggering the genocide of Rwanda's Tutsi population and the death of the Hutu liberal middle class over the next three months.

In early 1994 Bushnell was sent to Rwanda to try to impress upon President Habyarimana the importance of seeing the Arusha Accords implemented successfully. She cautioned him that failure to follow through on Arusha could cost Rwanda U.S. support in the future. Then, on the same day as the president's assassination, Bushnell was the first U.S. official to alert the State Department of the likelihood of widespread violence and a military takeover of the country once word got out that Habyarimana's death had been deliberate. The next day, April 7, the first phase of the Rwandan Genocide began with the assassination of moderate Hutu politicians and the prime minister (and head of state presumptive in an interim government), Agathe Uwilingiyimana.

During the crisis weeks that followed, Bushnell was the U.S. State Department official most closely connected to developments in Rwanda. As news of the killings came across her desk she began calling Rwandan military officials to try to persuade them to stop the carnage. She was for the most part either ignored, or her pleas were treated with contempt. On a number of occasions she spoke directly by phone to the chief of staff of the Rwandan Armed Forces (Forces Armées Rwandaises, or FAR), Major General Augustin Bizimungu, warning him that President Clinton was holding him personally responsible for the killings then taking place. On April 28, Bushnell rang the head of the interim Hutu Power government, Théoneste Bagosora, warning him that the State Department was fully apprised of what was happening in Rwanda and ordering him on behalf of the United States to stop the killing and immediately arrange a ceasefire. While Bushnell's action was clearly a case of foreign intervention in the domestic affairs of a sovereign state, she was unrepentant about exceeding her authority in this instance. Elsewhere, Bushnell proposed reducing the effectiveness of the Hutu killers by jamming their major anti-Tutsi propaganda arm, Radio-Télévision Libre des Mille Collines (RTLM), but permission to do this was denied on the grounds that it was both too expensive and contrary to international (as well as American) law.

Throughout and after the genocide, Bushnell remained at her post as deputy assistant secretary. In 1996 she was nominated by President Clinton to serve as U.S. ambassador to Kenya. In this role, she and her embassy were targeted on August 7, 1998, when a car bomb was detonated next to the embassy by Al Qaeda terrorists. Twelve embassy staff and 212 Kenyan civilians were killed, and Bushnell was cut by flying glass. Then, in 1999, Bushnell was appointed as U.S. ambassador to Guatemala, where she served until July 2002 prior to becoming dean of the Leadership and Management School at the Foreign Service Institute (the U.S. government's main training institution for officers and support personnel of the U.S. foreign affairs community, located in Arlington, Virginia).

In 2005, Bushnell was portrayed in a made-for-television movie about the Rwandan Genocide, *Sometimes in April,* directed by Haitian-born filmmaker Raoul Peck. In this film, three-time Academy Award–nominated American actress Debra Winger explored Bushnell's daily dilemmas as she agonized over the inaction of U.S. policy toward Rwanda despite her constant pleas and attempts to stop the killing.

Overall, Prudence Bushnell was the only high-ranking American official to keep attention focused on the killing in Rwanda throughout the genocide. At the time, she was derided for this by many in the U.S. government, but she has since been applauded for her efforts, both in and outside the corridors of government in the United States.

PAUL R. BARTROP

See also: Bisengimana, Paul; Radio-Télévision Libre des Mille Collines

Further Reading

Gribbin, Robert E. *In the Aftermath of Genocide: The US Role in Rwanda.* New York: I Universe, 2005.

Ronayne, Peter. *Never Again? The United States and the Prevention and Punishment of Genocide since the Holocaust.* Lanham, MD: Rowman & Littlefield Publishers, 2001.

C

Carlsson, Ingvar

Ingvar Carlsson is a Swedish politician. A former leader of the Swedish Social Democratic Party and prime minister, he was born the son of a warehouse worker in Boras, Sweden, on November 9, 1934. He studied social sciences at Lund University, graduating in 1958. In 1965, after completing higher degree studies in economics at Northwestern University, Illinois, he was elected as a member of the Swedish parliament.

His political star rose relatively quickly, and his portfolios accumulated: minister of Education, 1969–1973; minister of Housing, 1973–1976; deputy prime minister, 1982–1986; and, following the assassination of Olof Palme in 1986, prime minister. In 1990 Carlsson resigned after failing to gain political endorsement for his economic reforms, but his cabinet was immediately reinstated upon amending its program. The Social Democrats lost the 1991 elections, but Carlsson returned to office after new elections in 1994. He was succeeded by Goran Persson as prime minister and party leader in 1996, and retired from politics.

In March 1999 he was approached by UN secretary-general Kofi Annan with an invitation to chair an inquiry into the actions of the United Nations during the 1994 genocide in Rwanda. Carlsson accepted the invitation, and eventually established an inquiry composed of himself, former foreign minister of the Republic of Korea Han Sung-Joo, and Lieutenant General Rufus M. Kupolati of Nigeria.

After an exhaustive consultation and research process, the final report, dated December 15, 1999, and comprising more than 150 pages, was handed down. Officially entitled "Report of the Independent Inquiry into the Actions of the United Nations During the 1994 Genocide in Rwanda," it was divided into five parts and analyzed the key events associated with the genocide (e.g., the Arusha Peace Agreement, the establishment of the United Nations Assistance Mission for Rwanda (UNAMIR), the fax of January 11, 1994, sent by General Roméo Dallaire to UN Headquarters in New York), and provided a lengthy list of conclusions citing failures on the part of the United Nations. These included the inadequacy of UNAMIR's mandate, confusions and failures to respond to the genocide, the effect of earlier events in Somalia, the lack of political will on the part of UN member-states, failures in protection and evacuation, and impediments to the flow of information. Most importantly, with an eye to the future, 14 strongly worded recommendations were included. These were:

1. an action plan to prevent genocide
2. improving the capacity of the UN to conduct peacekeeping operations
3. military preparation on the part of contributing member-states to "prevent acts of genocide or

gross violations of human rights wherever they may take place"

4. improving the early warning capacity of the UN
5. improving protection of civilians
6. improving protection of UN personnel and staff
7. improving cooperation of UN personnel
8. improving the flow of information in the United Nations system
9. improving the flow of information in and to the Security Council
10. improving the flow of information on human rights issues
11. improving coordinating evacuation operations
12. re-addressing what membership in the Security Council means (in this regard, it may be noted that Rwanda itself was a member of the Security Council during the period of the genocide)
13. supporting efforts to rebuild Rwanda
14. UN acknowledgement of its own responsibility (i.e., failure) for not having done more to prevent or stop the genocide.

A lengthy "Chronology of Events," detailing happenings between October 1993 and July 1994, was annexed to the report.

Carlsson's own view was that the Security Council had the power to have prevented at least some of the Rwandan tragedy, and was in a position to ensure such a tragedy did not happen again. The Security Council's decision to reduce the strength of UNAMIR after the genocide started—in spite of its knowledge of the atrocities—was, he concluded, the cause of much current bitterness in Rwanda toward the UN. Further general conclusions he drew were that in future the UN Secretariat must tell the Security Council exactly what is needed to bring about effective action, and that the Council must ensure that short-term financial constraints do not prevent its realization. The Council, moreover, must give missions the mandate they need, mobilize the necessary troops and resources, and accept its responsibility irrespective of where problems occur.

Upon its release, Kofi Annan declared that he fully accepted the Inquiry's conclusions. He argued that its recommendations merited very serious attention, and urged member states to engage in reflection and analysis aimed at improving the capacity of the UN to respond to various forms of conflict.

As a fitting extension to his involvement with the United Nations through the Inquiry, in 1995 Carlsson and Sir Shridath ("Sonny") Ramphal, the former secretary-general of the Commonwealth, co-chaired a United Nations Commission on Global Governance. The commission was established with the full endorsement of UN secretary-general Boutros Boutros-Ghali. The commission's report, *Our Global Governance,* caused a controversy in some quarters, as it called for increased UN control over areas currently the preserve of sovereign states, namely international development, international security, globalization and, of course, global governance.

The Carlsson Report on Rwanda suggested that serious attention would be given in the future to United Nations involvement in peacekeeping and humanitarian intervention activities. In light of a new report in January 2005, however, entitled "Report of the International Commission of Inquiry on Darfur to the United Nations Secretary-General," the lessons of the earlier tragedy would seem not to have been learned. A decade further on from Rwanda, there was still a reluctance to label Darfur as a true genocide, rendering Carlsson's strong recommendations ultimately meaningless so far as future action was concerned.

PAUL R. BARTROP

See also: Carlsson Report; United Nations Assistance Mission for Rwanda

Further Reading

Eltringham, Nigel. *Accounting for Horror: Post-Genocide Debates in Rwanda.* London: Pluto Press, 2004.

Scherrer, P. Christian. *Genocide and Crisis in Central Africa: Conflict Roots, Mass Violence, and Regional War.* Westport, CT: Praeger, 2002.

Carlsson Report

The Carlsson Report was officially released on December 16, 1999, and was the product of an independent commission of inquiry established by United Nations (UN) secretary-general Kofi Annan that investigated the 1994 Rwandan Genocide. The commission was chaired by Ingvar Carlsson, former prime minister of Sweden. Also on the commission were Lieutenant General Rufus M. Kupolati of Nigeria and Hang Sung-Joo, former foreign minister of South Korea. The report, officially entitled "Report of the Independent Inquiry into the Actions of the United

Nations during the 1994 Genocide in Rwanda," accomplished several things: it provided a detailed chronology of the genocide; analyzed the failings of the international community and the UN in preventing or stopping the genocide; and made a long list of recommendations so that future genocides could be averted.

The report begins by giving a detailed history of events, commencing with the 1993 Arusha Peace Agreement, which ended the Rwandan Civil War. It then details the establishment of the UN Assistance Mission for Rwanda (UNAMIR), the downing of the Rwandan president's aircraft on January 11, 1994, which served as the immediate catalyst to the genocide, and the actual major events during the genocide.

Next, the report cites a number of failures on the part of the UN and international community that permitted the genocide to proceed, unabated. These include the UN's inability to act on pregenocide intelligence that strongly suggested that a genocide was about to occur; the lack of will to intervene in the genocide; weak and conflicting UNAMIR policies and rules of engagement; and a lack of communication among various UN departments and its offices in the field.

The most important—and illuminating—section of the Carlsson Report detailed recommendations to prevent or stop future genocides. A number of these have now been formally adopted by the UN. They include: drafting formal plans to prevent genocide; improving UN peacekeeping missions; preparing member states' militaries to deal more effectively with genocide or mass human rights abuses; fine-tuning the UN's ability to foresee impending genocides; bolstering protections for civilian populations and UN peacekeepers; improving inter-UN communications; enhancing UN-supervised evacuation operations; clarifying UN Security Council membership; supporting reconciliation and reconstruction in Rwanda; and formally acknowledging the UN's failures in preventing and halting the Rwandan Genocide.

PAUL G. PIERPAOLI JR.

See also: Arusha Accords; Carlsson, Ingvar; Dallaire, Roméo; Habyarimana, Juvénal; United Nations Assistance Mission for Rwanda

Further Reading

Eltringham, Nigel. *Accounting for Horror: Post-Genocide Debates in Rwanda.* London: Pluto Press, 2004.

Scherrer, P. Christian. *Genocide and Crisis in Central Africa: Conflict Roots, Mass Violence, and Regional War.* Westport, CT: Praeger, 2002.

Coalition Pour la Défense de la République

The Coalition Pour le Défense de la République (CDR) was a radical, right-wing Hutu political party formed in February 1992 that played a key role in the 1994 Rwandan Genocide. The CDR was founded and first led by Martin Bucyana; after his 1994 assassination the party leadership was taken over by three rabid, anti-Tutsi ideologues: Jean-Bosco Barayagwiza, Hassan Ngeze, and Jean Shyirambere Barahinura. Barayagwiza was a high-ranking official with *Radio-Télevision Libre des Milles Collines,* a virulent propaganda vehicle and anti-Tutsi media outlet; Ngeze owned and edited the anti-Tutsi *Kangura* newspaper. Prior to the genocide, the CDR was loosely allied with the *Mouvement Révolutionnaire National Pour le Développement* (MRND). After the genocide ended, the CDR was permanently banned. Several CDR leaders were also indicted and convicted by the International Criminal Tribunal for Rwanda as perpetrators of the Rwandan Genocide. They included Barayagwize, Ngeze, and Ferdinand Nahimana.

The CDR refused to admit any members who were Tutsi or had close Tutsi relatives. It was a major purveyor of hatred and intolerance toward the Tutsis and openly encouraged its membership to oppress, harass, intimidate, assault, and kill Tutsis. The party's slogan, "Watch Out!" was meant to intimidate Tutsis into submission. The CDR called for Hutu cultural supremacy, complete Hutu domination of the Rwandan government and other national institutions, and strict segregation between Tutsis and Hutus. It condemned any intermarriage between the two people and branded Hutu women who married Tutsi men as "traitors." The CDR also forbade its members from doing any business with Tutsi establishments and threatened banishment from the party for anyone caught doing so. In short, the CDR labeled all Tutsis as "the enemy."

Initially, the CDR had supported Rwandan president Juvénal Habyarimana, but by 1993, it withdrew its support because the party flatly rejected the president's attempts to seek compromise and to accommodate the Rwandan Patriotic Front (RPF). After Habyarimana signed the August 4, 1993 Arusha Accords, which was an attempt to end the ongoing Rwandan Civil War, the CDR actively attempted to undermine the president's regime and broke ties with the MRND, which had agreed to the Arusha Accords. The CDR was now entirely divorced from Rwanda's main political landscape and was shut out of the transitional government. About the same time, it formed its own anti-Tutsi militia, the *Impuzamugambi,* which carried out many Tutsi killings during the subsequent genocide and harassed or killed Tutsis prior to that time.

After Habyarimana was assassinated on April 6, 1994, however, the CDR again allied itself with the MRND and was given power in the shaky transitional government. The two parties now conspired to perpetrate a genocide by blaming the Tutsis for the president's death and by alleging that the Tutsis had deliberately provoked a nationwide confrontation with the Hutus. The *Impuzamugambi,* along with the *Interahamwe* militia, were major perpetrators of the Rwandan Genocide.

PAUL G. PIERPAOLI JR.

See also: Arusha Accords; Barayagwiza, Jean-Bosco; Habyarimana, Juvénal; Hutus; Interahamwe; International Criminal Tribunal for Rwanda; Media Trial in Rwanda; Nahimana, Ferdinand; Ngeze, Hassan; Radio-Télévision Libre des Mille Collines; Rwanda; Tutsis

Further Reading

Kressel, Neil Jeffrey. *Mass Hate: The Global Rise of Genocide and Terror.* New York: Plenum Press, 1996.

Valentino, Benjamin A. *Final Solutions: Mass Killing and Genocide in the Twentieth Century.* Ithaca, NY: Cornell University Press, 2004.

Waller, James. *Becoming Evil: How Ordinary People Commit Genocide and Mass Killing.* Oxford: Oxford University Press, 2002.

Congo, Democratic Republic of

No other event in the history of the Democratic Republic of the Congo (DRC) has had a more profoundly destabilizing impact than the 1994 genocide in Rwanda. Besides triggering the rebellion that led to the violent overthrow of President Mobutu Sese Seko's 30-year dictatorship, and then to the assassination of his successor, Laurent Kabila, in January 2001, the Rwanda carnage is the central element behind two of the most devastating

Hutu refugees receive water at a relief center near Doma, Zaire (now Democratic Republic of Congo), as they prepare for their return journey to Rwanda, 1994. (Department of Defense)

wars experienced by the DRC. No less critical have been the aftereffects of these deadly conflicts. Much of the violence sweeping across the eastern provinces of North and South Kivu is indeed traceable to the priorities and policies set by Rwanda's President Paul Kagame in the wake of the genocide.

The dynamics of violence in DRC are inscribed in its ethnic map. Contrary to a widespread belief, Rwanda and Burundi are not the only states in the continent to claim Hutu and Tutsi populations. Tens of thousands of them are also found in eastern DRC. Even before the 1994 bloodbath the civil war in Rwanda drove a deep wedge between the two communities across the border. As the Tutsi-dominated Rwandan Patriotic Front (RPF) fought its way into Rwanda in the early 1990s, thousands of Tutsi exiles joined its ranks, many from the DRC. Conscious of the threat posed to his long-time friend, President Juvénal Habyarimana of Rwanda, and indeed to his own security, Mobutu gave his local allies in the east a free hand to turn against ethnic Tutsi. Despite the fact that a large number of them traced their roots in eastern Congo to pre-colonial days, such as the so-called Banyamulenge ("the people of Mulenge") of South Kivu, their imputed foreign origins were often perceived as proof their pro-FPR sympathies. For many self-styled "authentic" Congolese their alienness made it imperative to send them back to Rwanda, by force if needed. Countless outbreaks of anti-Tutsi violence were reported in the months preceding and following the seizure of power by the RPF in Rwanda in July 1994. Meanwhile, with the outpouring of some 2 million Rwandan Hutu across the border to eastern DRC, including many perpetrators, it was not long before eastern DRC served as a jumping off point for armed raids against Rwanda.

Kagame sensed with growing concern the danger thus posed to Rwanda's security, and in November 1996 the Rwandan Patriotic Army (RPA), assisted by ethnic Tutsi from DRC, launched a deadly strike at the refugee camps strung along the border, killing thousands and sending an untold number running for their lives. Perhaps as many as 300,000 Hutu civilians were systematically killed by the PRA and its Congolese allies in the course of one of the most extensive exercise in ethnic cleansing recorded in the history of the Congo. Most of the young men who were able to survive the onslaught later joined the militant pro-Hutu militia, Forces Démocratiques pour la Libération du Rwanda (FDLR), now the principal target of the Congolese army in eastern DRC.

The first Congo war (1996–1997) thus had as its immediate objective to destroy the camps sheltering the Hutu perpetrators and their families, and then to move on to the next order of business, the overthrow of the Mobutist state. Both were accomplished with remarkable speed. Spearheaded by a Congolese rebel movement consisting largely of ethnic Tutsi, the Alliance des Forces Démocratiques pour la Libération du Congo (AFDL), headed by Laurent Kabila, the rebellion enjoyed the military and logistical support of several regional players, among them Uganda, Angola, Zimbabwe, Namibia, and Eritrea. Although it took months before Kagame finally conceded his leading role in waging the war, the RPA was the backbone of the anti-Mobutist crusade. Predictably, once Kabila had been anointed the new king of the Congo, the kingmakers insisted on keeping a close watch on their client state. But having Tutsi advisors dictating to him what course of action to take is what Kabila categorically refused to accept—but not without creating a major crisis of confidence between himself and his former allies.

Thus began the second Congo war (1998–2000), which proved even more costly in human lives than the first. Added to the fragmentation of the Congolese arena, the involvement of seven states in the conflict—with the key protagonists on opposite sides—made for an extremely complicated and fluid picture. What emerged in effect was a triangular conflict among three factions: against the Kabila government, supported by Angola and Zimbabwe, were arrayed the northern-based Mouvement pour la Libération du Congo (MLC), headed by Jean-Pierre Bemba, and the Tutsi-dominated Rassemblement Congolais pour la Démocratie (RDC), respectively in thrall to Uganda and Rwanda—until they, too, came to blows over access to the country's mineral wealth. Not until 2003, when the warring factions agreed to the terms of the so-called Global and Inclusive Accord (GIA), did a glimmer of peace loom on the horizon. Subsequent events showed just how fragile the peace deal turned out to be.

In view of the wide array of domestic and international players, the nature of the stakes involved in the country's mineral wealth, the inadequacy of the peacekeeping operations undertaken by the United Nations (UN), and the reluctance of the international community, particularly Britain and the United States, to rein in Kagame's attempts to intervene in the internal affairs of the Congo, it is hardly surprising that the conflict lasted as long as it did, and with such horrendous consequences. According to the International Rescue Committee (IRC) the death toll in DRC between 1998 and 2008 is estimated at 5.4 million. Although subsequent estimates by the Canadian Human Security Report would downsize that figure by 50 percent, there can be no doubt about the appalling human losses. Nor is there any question about the responsibility of Kagame's army in contributing to the carnage, a fact made painfully clear in the 2010 UN Mapping Report which provides a detailed description of the killings of Hutu civilians in eastern DRC, going as far as to suggest a possible genocide.

Rwanda's extensive and unceasing support of pro-Tutsi secessionist militias in eastern Congo is one of the most dramatic of the many unanticipated consequences of the Rwandan Genocide. Kagame's "imperial" ambitions in eastern DRC have been remarkably consistent over the years. First by providing extensive military and political assistance to the RCD, until its gradual collapse after the 2005 Congolese elections, then by throwing his weight behind Laurent Nkunda's Conseil National pour la Défense du Peuple (CNDP), until a deal was made to bring it into the fold of the Congolese army, and finally, after the deal went sour, by giving military and logistical aid to the newly created militia, the so-called M23, Kagame has consistently demonstrated his determination to control the rich Congo borderlands. Protecting the lives of the Tutsi minority is not his only motive; access to the Congo's mineral wealth, directly or through proxies, is the key imperative. Thus if the past is anything to go by, there is every reason to believe that the spinoffs of the Rwandan Genocide will be felt in eastern Congo for many years to come.

RENÉ LEMARCHAND

See also: Burundi; Rwanda; Rwanda Civil War

Further Reading

Lemarchand, René. *The Dynamics of Violence in Central Africa.* Philadelphia: University of Pennsylvania Press, 2009.

Prunier, Gérard. *Africa's World War: Congo, the Rwandan Genocide, and the Making of a Continental Catastrophe.* New York: Oxford University Press, 2009.

Reyntjens, Filip. *The Great African War: Congo and Regional Geopolitics, 1996–2006.* Cambridge: Cambridge University Press, 2009.

Stearns, Jason. *Dancing in the Glory of Monsters: The Collapse of the Congo and the Great War of Africa.* New York: Public Affairs, 2011.

Turner, Thomas. *The Congo Wars: Conflict, Myth and Reality.* London and New York: Zed Books, 2007.

Curic, Vjekoslav

Vjekoslav "Vjeko" Curic was a Bosnian Croat Franciscan priest and humanitarian, best known for his role in helping to save Rwandan Tutsis threatened with annihilation during the Rwandan Genocide of 1994. Born in Lupoglava, Bosnia-Herzegovina, on April 26, 1957, he studied in Visoko, central Bosnia, and in Sarajevo. He entered the Franciscan order on July 15, 1976, and was ordained to the priesthood on June 21, 1982, in Sarajevo. Later in 1982 he went to Paris to train as a missionary, and on August 18, 1983, he began his missionary work in Rwanda. He was one of the first volunteers of the Franciscan Africa Project.

It was in Rwanda, during and after the genocide of 1994, that Curic's service was at its most intense. Reportedly one of only two non-African Catholic priests to stay in Rwanda throughout the duration of the genocide, his own actions saved hundreds of lives. He revealed later that he had sheltered many Tutsis from the Interahamwe and Impuzamugambi militias, and had secretly ferried them out of the country in the bottom of his truck. At the beginning of the genocide, he similarly saved the lives of numerous white clergy—many of them Belgian priests, monks, and nuns—whose lives were in danger. He allegedly received an order direct from the Vatican to leave the country, but refused to do so, claiming that while his flock was in danger he could not abandon them.

By 1994 Curic was a long-term resident of Gitarama, working to help develop his neighborhood. He was well-known and liked by those in his parish of Kivumu, and when the killing got underway in April and May the local people looked to him as one who would offer them rescue. Curic decided to remain at a time when many expatriates were leaving. True to his ideal that he had come to Rwanda to serve the people, he made a stand with the people of Kivumu. He threw himself into the work of providing assistance to all who reached him, as well as helping others to escape. He also continued to preach the Gospel, condemning the violence and calling for peace.

Among those he encountered were a BBC television news crew fronted by David Belton, a director, writer, and film producer. In early May 1994 Belton had arrived in Rwanda to cover the genocide for the current affairs program, *Newsnight.* He traveled throughout the country, witnessing the horror and reporting it for British television. At one point, the violence became so bad that Belton and his team had to seek shelter, and it was to Curic that they turned. On several occasions, Curic protected the *Newsnight* team from extremist violence, as the Hutu Power authorities became increasingly suspicious of their presence. This experience would later bring Curic's story to a much broader audience through the popular media.

After the genocide, Curic continued his work in Kivumu parish. He helped to resettle widows and re-establish their shattered lives, and established educational projects for children. He remained impartial throughout, helping both Hutus and Tutsis rebuild their communities, blind to the differences that had so divided them just a few weeks and months earlier. He worked selflessly to help the victims of both groups equally.

For this, his efforts were not universally appreciated. He was viewed by many Hutus as a collaborator with the Tutsis who had come in with the Rwandan Patriotic Front in July 1994 to stop the genocide, and subsequently established a Tutsi-led government. In 1996, Curic escaped an attempt on his life, but still refused to leave, against the advice of many of those around him. His attitude was that he had stayed with this congregation during the genocide, and would not abandon them now that peace had come. Then, on January 31, 1998, he was shot in his car, murdered in the heart of downtown Kigali. The perpetrators of the crime are not known to this day. The Catholic Church immediately declared that he had gone to a martyr's death after devoting himself to the rescue others for the glory of God and love of his neighbors. He was buried in Kivumu, the community he had served without interruption for 15 years, in a church which he and his congregation had built together. His funeral was attended by the prime minister of Rwanda, Pierre-Célestin Rwigema, and other members of the government, along with a vast number of Catholics and other Christians, as well as representatives from the Jewish and Islamic communities.

Several years later, the British director David Belton learned that Curic had been murdered. It forced him to revisit a period of his life that he had, in effect, put aside, and as a result he wrote down his recollections of his time in Rwanda during the genocide. In 2005 Belton's account of Curic formed the backdrop of a movie about Rwanda, *Shooting Dogs* (dir. Michael Caton-Jones), which was released in the United States as *Beyond the Gates.* Belton cowrote the original story and was the movie's producer; the screenwriter, David Wolsencroft, also knew Curic in Rwanda in 1994, and both men employed their memories of Curic as the inspiration for one of the film's leading characters, Father Christopher, played by John Hurt.

Paul R. Bartrop

See also: Rwandan Patriotic Front; Tutsis

Further Reading

Bodnarchuk, Kari. *Rwanda: A Country Torn Apart.* Minneapolis, MN: Lerner Publishing Group, 1998.

Eltringham, Nigel. *Accounting for Horror: Post-Genocide Debates in Rwanda.* London: Pluto Press, 2004.

D

Dallaire, Roméo

Lieutenant General Roméo Dallaire was the force commander of the United Nations Assistance Mission for Rwanda (UNAMIR) prior to, during, and after the 1994 Rwandan Genocide. He was born in June 25, 1946, in Denekamp, Holland, to a French Canadian soldier and a Dutch nurse he met while on active service. Later that year the family left Holland and returned to Canada. Raised in Montreal, in 1963 Dallaire joined the Canadian army. He studied at the Royal Military College Saint-Jean (Le Collège militaire royal de Saint-Jean) in Quebec, and graduated as an artillery officer in 1970 with a Bachelor of Science degree. Rising over succeeding years, on July 3, 1989, he was promoted to brigadier general.

On October 5, 1993, the UN Security Council, by Resolution 872, established UNAMIR, for the express purpose of helping to implement the Arusha Peace Accords signed on August 4, 1993, by the primarily Hutu government of Rwanda and the Tutsi-led rebel Rwandan Patriotic Front (RPF). In late 1993 Dallaire was nominated as UNAMIR force commander. His mission's mandate included monitoring the cease-fire agreement; establishing and expanding the demilitarized zone and demobilization procedures; providing security for the Rwandan capital city of Kigali; monitoring the security situation during the final period of the transitional government's mandate leading up to elections; and assisting in the coordination of humanitarian assistance activities in conjunction with relief operations.

It was Dallaire's first UN command, and for most of those involved it was anticipated that this would be a relatively straightforward mission.

A reality to which Dallaire was not alerted prior to his posting was that the extremist Hutus were intent on annihilating the Tutsis and had said as much in media broadcasts, newspaper articles, and declarations. Dallaire's first major test—apart from trying to ensure that his force was equipped and ready to carry out its mission despite an appalling lag time in the transfer of matériel from donor countries—came in early 1994. On January 10, Dallaire received intelligence that a radical Hutu, codenamed "Jean-Pierre," was prepared to disclose information regarding a planned genocide of Tutsis. Jean-Pierre had been an officer in Rwanda's presidential guard, but had left to become one of the key men in the Interahamwe militia. It transpired that Jean-Pierre had much to say. He described in detail how the Interahamwe were trained, by whom, and where, adding that the militia was in a state of permanent readiness sufficient to kill 1,000 Tutsis in Kigali within 20 minutes of receiving an order to do so. As a sign of his goodwill and reliability, Jean-Pierre offered to reveal the location of a large stockpile of weapons somewhere in central Kigali. Dallaire, operating within the terms of his mandate, assessed that these arms had to be confiscated. He decided to order an arms raid, and faxed the UN Department of Peacekeeping Operations (DPKO) in New York, headed at that time by Kofi

Annan, for authorization. This cable outlined in detail Jean-Pierre's revelations.

Dallaire's fax was received negatively in New York. DPKO ordered him not to carry out the raid for fear of exacerbating the situation. Under no circumstances was he authorized to conduct arms raids. He was taken to task for suggesting that he exceed his Chapter VI peacekeeping mandate, and was ordered to turn over what Jean-Pierre had disclosed to Rwanda's president, Juvénal Habyarimana—the very man whose anti-Tutsi cause the Interahamwe was enforcing. The DPKO, together with the office of the then secretary-general, Boutros Boutros-Ghali, decided that process was more important, on this occasion, than action; not only this, but they were concerned for the image of the UN in light of an earlier failed arms raid that took place with heavy loss of life in Mogadishu, Somalia, in October 1993. Dallaire protested the decision insistently, but New York would not budge, with catastrophic consequences three months later.

As the crisis in Rwanda worsened, particularly in early 1994, Dallaire came to the conclusion that the constant stream of murders he and his soldiers were discovering and witnessing was not a result of warfare between two combatants, but, rather, crimes against humanity by one group (Hutus) against another (Tutsis). Initially he referred to such killing as "ethnic cleansing," and continued to fire one urgent message after another to UN headquarters requesting more forces and supplies, and the broadening of his mandate to quell the violence perpetrated by the Hutu extremists, but it was all to no avail.

On April 6, 1994, Habriymana's plane was shot down by two missiles as it was about to land in Kigali. Fighting between the Hutus and Tutsis broke out immediately, and genocidal mass murder began against the Tutsis and any Hutus who opposed the killers. Within a day, 10 of Dallaire's peacekeepers from Belgium had been murdered while trying to protect the interim head of state in Habyarimana's stead, Prime Minister Agathe Uwilingiyimana, but she, too, was murdered by the presidential guard. Dallaire attempted to broker a cease-fire between the RPF and the extremist Hutus, but to no avail. His immediate conclusion was that UNAMIR's mandate was untenable in light of the changed circumstances, but despite his repeated pleas for a stronger Chapter VII mandate and more troops and arms that would have allowed the force to engage the *génocidaires* in combat, the UN retained its totally inadequate Chapter VI mandate and refused to provide him with additional troops.

Dallaire pleaded for additional logistical support, and for UNAMIR to be immediately reinforced with 2,000 more troops. He put forth a plan arguing that with an overall command of 5,000 well-equipped and highly trained troops he could stop the killing and reimpose peace. The Security Council refused, and then dropped a bombshell of its own. On April 21, some two weeks into the killing, the Council voted to reduce UNAMIR to a force of just 270 peacekeepers, justifying its decision by saying that the mission to monitor the peace was now redundant. The peace had not held. UNAMIR was reduced, and Dallaire was ordered home. He, together with his deputy force commander, General Henry Kwami Anyidoho of Ghana, and ably supported by his chief of staff, Major Brent Beardsley, refused to obey this order.

Stripped of authority, manpower, resources, and logistical support, Dallaire came to the conclusion that he was witnessing genocide. He and what was left of UNAMIR did what they could to help people, Dallaire's command alone saving the lives of an estimated 30,000 Tutsis and moderate Hutus in safe areas established by UNAMIR, such as the Amahoro Stadium and the Mille Collines Hotel.

The killing continued, however. Ultimately, the Security Council revised its earlier decision and, too late, voted to establish a revamped mission, UNAMIR II, with a troop complement of 5,500. It did not arrive until early July, however, after the genocide had ended with the victory of the Rwandan Patriotic Front under General Paul Kagame. Estimates range between 800,000 and one million murdered in the space of 100 days.

Dallaire returned to Canada in August 1994, and was appointed to different commands in Quebec and Ottawa. His experiences in Rwanda had taken a terrible personal toll on him, however, and he nearly lost his sanity as a result of what he witnessed and his frustration at not being able to stop the killing. He viewed his mission as a failure that had appalling consequences, concluding that his efforts at convincing his superiors in New York and Ottawa as to the gravity of the situation were inadequate, and that this cost many hundreds of thousands of lives.

In 1996, two years after his return to Canada, Dallaire was made an Officer of the United States Legion of Merit, the highest military decoration awarded to foreigners, but, diagnosed with post-traumatic stress disorder, his health had suffered severely by this stage. He began to drink heavily, trying to blot out his memories of the genocide, and attempted suicide on more than one occasion. On January 24, 2000, he commenced a period of extended sick leave. By mid-2000, he took early retirement from the Canadian army, and a few months later he combined alcohol with his antidepressant medication in another attempt to kill himself. He was found comatose under a park bench in Hull, Quebec. Having reached rock bottom, a slow process of recovery then began.

In 2004, 10 years after the start of the UNAMIR mission to Rwanda, Dallaire and Brent Beardsley published a book of memoirs of the genocide entitled *Shake Hands with the Devil: The Failure of Humanity in Rwanda.* Given his trauma following the experience, it had taken this long for Dallaire to be able to gather his thoughts and reflect clearly on his understanding of what had happened and why. Awarded the Governor-General's Literary Award for Non-Fiction in 2004, the book became a bestseller in Canada and several other parts of the world.

In the 10th anniversary year of the genocide, a documentary film, *Shake Hands with the Devil: The Journey of Roméo Dallaire* (dir. Peter Raymont, 2004), was produced showing Dallaire's return to Rwanda. The same year saw the appearance of the first major motion picture on the genocide, *Hotel Rwanda* (director/writer/producer, Terry George). The film starred Don Cheadle in a celebration of the actions of the manager of Kigali's Hotel Mille Collines, Paul Rusesabagina, and offered a controversial portrayal of the head of the UN peacekeeping forces, a Canadian officer named "Colonel Oliver," played by Nick Nolte. It showed a character very much at variance with the reality of who Dallaire was and what he had been able to achieve. He was also portrayed—much more empathetically—in a Canadian movie that took its title from Dallaire's book. *Shake Hands with the Devil* (dir. Roger Spottiswoode, 2007) starred Canadian actor Roy Dupuis in the role of Dallaire, who helped in the project and even offered a line-by-line review of the script.

Dallaire has become a national hero for Canadians, despite his own views about his inadequacy in Rwanda. On October 10, 2002, he was made an Officer in the Order of Canada (OC), and in 2005 a Grand Officer of the National Order of Quebec (GOQ). On March 24, 2005, he was appointed to the Canadian Senate by Prime Minister Paul Martin, representing Quebec.

Since his retirement from the military, Dallaire has become increasingly involved in the world of education and academia. In 2004–2005, he served as a Fellow at the Carr Center for Human Rights Policy at Harvard University's John F. Kennedy School of Government, and on September 8, 2006, he joined the Montreal Institute for Genocide and Human Rights Studies (MIGS) at Concordia University as a senior fellow and codirector of the MIGS "Will to Intervene" project. This is a research initiative that seeks to find ways to set in practice the UN-endorsed set of principles known as Responsibility to Protect. As part of this, Dallaire and the MIGS Director, Professor Frank Chalk, were among the authors of a study in 2010, *Mobilizing the Will to Intervene: Leadership to Prevent Mass Atrocities.*

In 2010 Dallaire, pursuing an additional humanitarian interest of his own, published a work in his own right, *They Fight Like Soldiers, They Die Like Children,* a passionate study of the use made by militias and governments of children to serve their purposes as "child soldiers."

Throughout the entire period since Rwanda, Roméo Dallaire has sought to draw the world's attention to the dangers of genocide, describing Darfur as "Rwanda in slow motion," and calling on NATO to intervene in Sudan. A featured speaker wherever he goes, he will long be remembered for a maxim that has come to characterize his humanitarian vision in light of his experiences in Rwanda: "All humans are human, and there are no humans more human than others."

Paul R. Bartrop

See also: Anyidoho, Henry Kwami; Arusha Accords; Beardsley, Brent; Habyarimana, Juvénal; United Nations Assistance Mission for Rwanda

Further Reading

Dallaire, Roméo. *Shake Hands with the Devil: The Failure of Humanity in Rwanda.* Toronto: Random House, 2004.

Smith, M. James, ed. *A Time to Remember. Rwanda: Ten Years after Genocide.* Retford, UK: The Aegis Institute, 2004.

Day of Remembrance of the Victims of the Rwanda Genocide

April 7 marks the Day of Remembrance of the Victims of the Rwanda Genocide, which has been observed each year since 2004. The day of remembrance was declared by the United Nations (UN) General Assembly, to coincide with the 10th anniversary of the beginning of the Rwandan Genocide. On April 6, 1994, a plane carrying Rwandan president Juvenal Habyarimana was shot down and crashed as it attempted to land in the Rwandan capital of Kigali. Many Hutus (who essentially controlled the Rwandan government) blamed the assassination on Tutsis. This incident ended up being the immediate catalyst for the Rwanda Genocide, and the mass killings of Tutsis and moderate Hutus commenced on April 7. The orgy of violence that followed was also the result of decades-long tension between the two chief ethnic groups in Rwanda, and by the time the genocide ended only weeks later, some 800,000–1,000,000 people had been killed.

The outside world did little to stop the killing, and the UN proved particularly ineffective during the crisis. In 1995, less than a year after the genocide, the UN called for an outreach program to help the survivors and victims of the Rwandan catastrophe. It also called for educational efforts to prevent such occurrences in the future. The day of remembrance is observed in varying ways around the world. Observances usually take the form of material/historical exhibitions, scholarly or student conferences, or ceremonies honoring the dead. The UN outreach program and remembrance activities are organized and sponsored by the UN Department of Public Information.

PAUL G. PIERPAOLI JR.

See also: Habyarimana, Juvénal; Rwanda; Rwanda Civil War

Further Reading

Melvern, Linda. *Conspiracy to Murder: The Rwandan Genocide.* London: Verso, 2006.

---

de Saint-Exupéry, Patrick

Patrick de Saint-Exupéry is a French journalist who has spent much of his career covering major stories in various parts of Africa (Liberia, South Africa, Rwanda), the Middle East (the Gulf War, Iran, Libya, Saudi Arabia), as well as Cambodia, Canada, and the Soviet Union. He was born in 1962, the son of Count Jacques de Saint-Exupéry and his wife, the Countess Martine Anglejan. The writer Antoine de Saint-Exupery was his grandfather's cousin.

De Saint-Exupéry began his career as a journalist at the age of 19 after winning a competition for young reporters. In 1983 he joined *France Soir* magazine, moving to its foreign desk in 1987. In 1988 he freelanced for *L'Express* and *Grands Reportages,* prior to becoming a foreign reporter with *Le Figaro* in 1989. Between 2000 and 2004 he was *Le Figaro*'s permanent correspondent in Moscow.

During the 1994 Rwandan Genocide, de Saint-Exupéry was one of the few journalists who managed to send reports out of the country while the killing was in progress. In particular, his articles on Operation TURQUOISE and the Bisesero resistance and massacres cast immense doubt on the role played by the French military, leading to an intense reaction on the part of the French government.

Operation TURQUOISE was the name given to UN Security Council Resolution 929 of June 22, 1994, in which France set in motion an intervention in Rwanda with an initial deployment of 2,500 French and Senegalese troops. They set up a block of so-called Safe Areas in the southwest of Rwanda, claiming that this was the best way to prevent vast numbers of refugees moving into northern Zaire (now the Democratic Republic of Congo), while at the same time safeguarding the refugees' lives. Much speculation has taken place regarding the possible ulterior motives of the French in setting up the safe areas where they did, given that nearly all of those who fled to them were Hutus rather than Tutsis, and that among these were substantial numbers of genocidal killers. It has also been suggested that France decided to defend these Hutus from the advance of the army of the Rwandan Patriotic Front (RPF), a force that was largely English-speaking in a Francophone country. An important consequence of Operation TURQUOISE was that the Hutus were not disarmed satisfactorily by the French troops. Extremists still possessing arms were able to operate effectively within the safe area, continuing to kill any Tutsis they could find, unhindered by any fears of being caught by the RPF. French troops did step in between Hutu killers and Tutsi victims whenever contact was obvious, but this was infrequent.

In his newspaper columns, de Saint-Exupéry left little room for doubt as to his view that Operation TURQUOISE was helping the Hutu killers rather than acting impartially or assisting the Tutsi victims. He was in Rwanda when the French troops arrived, and witnessed the deployment in person. But the general observations he had on Operation TURQUOISE were enhanced by his witnessing of the French behavior over the Tutsi resistance at Bisesero in late June 1994.

Bisesero was located in the Kibuye district of western Rwanda, in an area with the highest proportion of Tutsis in Rwanda. Soon after the genocide began, Tutsis from the surrounding area numbering up to 50,000 converged on Bisesero for refuge. They sought safety in numbers, making the most of the few weapons they had with which to defend themselves. For the most part, they possessed only farm tools and stones, as against the Hutus' grenades and guns. Nonetheless, the people of Bisesero managed to stave off Hutu assaults until mid-May, killing a number of their attackers and repulsing others. But it was bitterly cold in the hills and raining heavily, and they were short of food. Each Hutu attack claimed hundreds of Tutsis.

On May 13 the attackers returned in full force, armed with weapons the Tutsis could not match. Although the struggle continued throughout May and into early June, the remaining Tutsis became steadily weaker from wounds, hunger, and exposure. After many days of further resistance, Hutu reinforcements from the Republican Guard and Interahamwe militiamen, armed with modern powerful weapons, organized a serious attack against the Tutsis. Under this new assault, the people of Bisesero could not resist for very long.

The final assault, known by some today as the Bisesero Hill Massacre, took place on June 27, 1994. The Tutsis' last stand saw them throwing rocks and fighting hand to hand against powerfully armed army and Interahamwe forces who had been sent to finish them off. French soldiers from Operation TURQUOISE had been to Bisesero a few days before the final massacre and talked many of the Tutsis into coming down from the hills, saying the genocide was over and that additional French forces would provide humanitarian aid. Before the French arrived in force, however, Hutu military and Interahamwe moved in and thousands more Tutsis were killed. In the end, those too weak to resist could only attempt to hide and hope not to be discovered, or, in a last desperate encounter with the *génocidaires,* try to rush toward those with guns to at least secure a swifter end. By the time the French forces returned to impose order on whatever population was left, only around 1,300 of the 50,000 Tutsis were still alive.

De Saint-Exupéry witnessed these events directly, and in his reports did not hold back from describing what he saw. This included the arrival of French Special Forces and an air deployment of troops to Bisesero on June 27, 1994. At no stage did he see the French troops helping the survivors—though he did observe them fighting against the RPF.

In covering the genocide, he stirred up a hornet's nest within the French political and military establishment, as well as in the media. Having been a witness to the genocide—having seen the machetes, the mass graves and massacre sites, the survivors and the killers—he also accompanied the first convoy of French soldiers of Operation TURQUOISE on June 26, 1994.

His articles in *Le Figaro* had an enormous impact on opinion at home, and these, followed by a series of follow-up pieces in 1998, triggered the establishment of a Parliamentary Commission of Inquiry on Rwanda chaired by Paul Quiles, the then-president of the National Assembly's Commission of National Defense and the Armed Forces.

The Commission delivered its report in December 1998. It found that France was not responsible for the genocide, and did not bear liability for the annihilation of the Tutsis. The Commission did not come to a conclusion as to who actually was responsible, but was careful to emphasize that, whoever it was, it was not France.

After the genocide and his return to other duties, de Saint-Exupéry decided to pursue a fuller account of what had happened, and led an investigation to unravel just how far his impressions at the time were matched by the historical record. His main interest was to try to discover the extent to which the French government and military went in assisting the Hutu killers, and how extensive their responsibility in the genocide actually was. Ten years after the genocide, in 2004, he published his findings in a book, *L'inavouable: La France au Rwanda* (*The Unspeakable: France in Rwanda*) published by Editions Les Arènes. It was reissued in April 2009, with a new preface in which he provided a fresh assessment of the record of France in Rwanda. To date, these works have not yet appeared in English.

It was a matter of conjecture as to whom he considered to be "the unspeakable"; it could have been the Hutu killers, but it could just as easily have been the French politicians. He specifically singled out Foreign Minister Dominique de Villepin, and began with a powerful indictment of Villepin's rhetoric in which he framed France's intervention in Operation TURQUOISE in terms of the Rwandan "genocides," pointedly using the plural and thus indicting the RPF in some sort of equation of moral equivalence between Hutu Power and the RPF. De Saint-Exupéry's book was a courageous indictment of French foreign policy in Rwanda, in which he also argued that France armed and trained those who were guilty of committing the genocide. He named a number of political leaders, military figures, and institutions as accomplices in the genocide, prompting law suits against both himself and his publisher for defamation. In one key case, where former Foreign Legion commander Colonel Jacques Hogard sued de Saint-Exupéry, the Paris Criminal Court acquitted the journalist on December 11, 2009, taking much of the sting out of his opponents' hostility.

In January 2008, Patrick de Saint-Exupéry took extended leave without pay from *Le Figaro.* He used this time to establish a new newsmagazine, *XXI,* with his colleague Laurent Beccaria. De Saint-Exupéry currently serves as the magazine's editor-in-chief.

PAUL R. BARTROP

See also: Operation TURQUOISE Rwandan Genocide, French Response to the; Rwandan Patriotic Front;

Further Reading

Eltringham, Nigel. *Accounting for Horror: Post-Genocide Debates in Rwanda.* London: Pluto Press, 2004.

Smith, M. James, ed. *A Time to Remember. Rwanda: Ten Years after Genocide.* Retford, UK: The Aegis Institute, 2004.

Denial of the Rwandan Genocide

No genocide is immune to denial. Rwanda is no exception. But because of the many unanswered questions surrounding the circumstances of the bloodshed—to what extent are the Tutsi invaders directly or indirectly responsible for the massive retribution exacted by the Hutu extremists? Who is responsible for the crash of President Juvénal Habyarimana's plane? How do the crimes committed by the Rwandan Patriotic Front (RPF) measure up to those attributed to the Hutu perpetrators?—the temptation to deny the genocidal quality of the carnage has been particularly difficult to resist.

In his ground breaking analysis, *States of Denial* (2001), Stanley Cohen draws a distinction among three types: literal ("nothing is happening"), interpretive ("what is happening is really something else") and implicatory denial ("what is happening is justified"). The first has little to do with the case at hand; the evidence is too massive to be shoved under the rug. Literal and interpretive denial is where the Rwanda bloodbath has generated its richest harvest of disavowals.

Interpretive denial in Rwanda hinges on the notion that the term genocide is a misnomer to describe what actually happened. Rather than a calculated attempt to physically eliminate the Tutsi community as a whole, the killings can best be described as a spontaneous outburst of popular anger. The argument draws attention to the collective fear generated by the invasion of the country by the Tutsi-dominated Rwandan Patriotic Front (RPF) on October 1, 1990, later brought to a paroxysm of ethnic anger by the death of President Habyarimana, on April 6, 1994. Widely perceived by Hutu leaders as the outcome of a plot by the RPF to shoot his plane down on a return trip from Dar-es-Salaam (Tanzania), the assassination of their president is what triggered the killings of Tutsi by Hutu. From this perspective the Rwanda tragedy is the direct consequence of the mortal threats posed by the FPR to the security of the state and its people.

Implicatory denial is an attempt to justify the genocide of Tutsi by blaming the FPR for the genocidal crimes committed against the Hutu community. Here attention shifts to the "double genocide thesis," with the emphasis placed on the equivalence, in terms of numbers killed, between the horrors committed by the Hutu génocidaires and those attributed to the RPF in the course of the civil war. The thrust of the argument is that the Tutsi are themselves too morally compromised by their human rights violations to accuse the Hutu of having committed a genocide. Since the RPF leaders, too, have genocidal blood on their hands, they have no right to level accusations of genocide against Hutu leaders.

The first type of denial is frequently set forth by domestic and international actors wishing to exonerate Hutu perpetrators. Among Rwandan politicians and intellectuals it finds its clearest expression in the statements issued by the refugee-based party Republican Rally for Democracy in Rwanda (RDR), well known for its efforts to spread genocide revisionism and denial. The contention that the Tutsi bear much of the onus of responsibility for the Rwanda tragedy is a frequent theme of its propaganda, along with references to "a civil war," "tragedy," "crisis" to designate what others call genocide. What Tom Ndahiro, a Rwandan journalist and human rights activist, calls "genocide laundering" recurs time and again the political discourse of the RDR; the aim is to deflect attention from the g-word by making the Rwanda tragedy appear as the unfortunate by-product of the FPR aggression. As the French historian Jean-Pierre Chrétien has shown, this is also a central theme in the commentaries offered by a number of French and Belgian human rights activists, journalists, and missionary milieux.

Implicatory denial, best illustrated by the "double genocide" thesis, is typical of the attitude displayed by representatives of Rwandan opposition parties in the months following the seizure of power by the RPF. In 1996, a coalition of opposition members in exile identified with the Resistance Forces for Democracy (FRD), issued a political platform with an entire section devoted to "le double génocide." The same theme finds a powerful echo in the statements made by a number of Western human rights activists, including missionaries and journalists. Its most authoritative formulation came from the late French president Francois Mitterrand, in 1995, when he famously corrected his interlocutor to pluralize the Rwandan Genocide.

Regardless of the arguments mustered to defend one type of denial or another, the Rwandan Genocide will continue to generate considerable controversy. Too many facets of this tragedy have yet to be fully investigated, actors to be interrogated, events to be explored and responsibilities to be established, before a broader consensus of opinion can be reached. Once all is said and done, and on the basis of the substantial body evidence available, no serious observer can deny that what has happened in Rwanda in a 100 days, in the spring and summer of 1994, cannot be described otherwise than as one of the largest genocides of the last century.

RENÉ LEMARCHAND

See also: Hutus; Rwanda Civil War; Rwandan Patriotic Front; Tutsis

Further Reading

Cohen, Stanley. *States of Denial: Knowing about Atrocities and Suffering.* Cambridge: Polity Press, 2001.

Ndahiro, Tom. "Genocide-Laundering: Historical Revisionism, Genocide Denial and the Rassemblement Républicain pour la Démocratie au Rwanda." In *After Genocide: Transitional Justice, Post-Conflict Reconstruction and Reconciliation in Rwanda and Beyond.* Edited by Phil Clark and Zachary Kaufman. London: Hurst Publishers, 2008.

Shaw, Martin. *What Is Genocide?* Cambridge: Polity Press, 2007.

Des Forges, Alison

Alison Des Forges was a human rights researcher and historian, and the leading American voice for human rights in Rwanda. She was born in Schenectady, New York, on August 20, 1942, and educated at Radcliffe College (Massachusetts) and Yale University (MA, 1966; PhD, 1972). Both her MA and her PhD were examinations of aspects of the history of Rwanda under German and Belgian colonial rule. She was drawn into human rights work when colleagues and friends in Rwanda and Burundi began suffering discrimination, harassment, and in some cases, death at the hands of repressive governments.

Having begun working on Rwanda as a student, she then dedicated her life's work to understanding the country, to exposing the serial abuses suffered by its people, and to helping to bring about positive change that could help establish a peaceful and prosperous future for the country. She spent most of her adult life working on Africa's Great Lakes region, despite a short period in China with her husband, Roger, a professor of Chinese history at the University of Buffalo.

In the 1980s Des Forges began working as a volunteer for the New York–based nongovernmental organization Human Rights Watch (HRW), and from the early 1990s onward she was HRW's senior adviser on Africa. Where Rwanda was concerned, she worked almost exclusively at trying to draw attention to what she saw as genocide in the making. She cochaired an international commission looking at the rise of ethnic violence in the region, and was part of a group convened by Human Rights Watch and other organizations examining human rights abuses, including killings and attacks and kidnappings of civilians, in Rwanda from 1990 to 1993. The inquiry published a report of its findings several months before the genocide.

Prior to April 1994 she tried hard to warn the world that Rwanda was sliding into genocide, but when the killing began she was still in the United States. Unable to do anything directly for the people she knew in Rwanda, she lobbied diplomats in the U.S. to at least try to give some form of succor to those most directly threatened. Thus, on the first day of the genocide, she spent long hours on the phone calling her friend Monique Mujawamariya, a human rights associate in Kigali, as the first actions of the *génocidaires* were being carried out. Mujawamariya managed to escape by crossing the border, and she received sanctuary partly through Des Forges's efforts. Upon her arrival in the United States, Mujawamariya then lobbied the White House, albeit unsuccessfully, to intervene during the early weeks of the genocide.

In April 1994 Des Forges was one of the first foreigners to claim that genocide was under way in Rwanda, and a month later, in May, she called for the killings to be officially declared as such. By then, about 200,000 people had been killed.

Once the genocide was over, Des Forges set herself the task of documenting the events as extensively as possible in order to establish the definitive account of what had happened. She spent four years interviewing both the organizers and the victims of the genocide, her research also encompassing government documents. In 1999 this work resulted in the book *Leave None to Tell the Story: Genocide in Rwanda,* a meticulously detailed description of the methods by which the anti-Tutsi campaign by the Hutu Power killers took place. The book also analyzed the failure of the international community to intervene. Des Forges offered extensive analysis and narrative on the many warnings preceding the genocide, the redistribution of the victims' property, the Hutus who tried to resist participation in the slaughter, and—importantly and controversially—the killings that took place in retaliation by the Tutsi-led Rwandan Patriotic Front (RPF). Her insistence that RPF forces should also be held to account for their crimes, including the murder of 30,000 people during and immediately after the genocide, placed her at odds with the new RPF-led government, and in 2008 she was banned from the country after Human Rights Watch published an extensive analysis of judicial reform there that drew attention to problems of inappropriate prosecution and external influence on the judiciary resulting in trials and verdicts that in several cases failed to conform to facts of the cases.

After publishing *Leave None to Tell the Story*, the Mac-Arthur Foundation recognized her work with a "Genius Grant," in which Des Forges won U.S. $375,000 to enable her to continue her research on the Great Lakes region.

With a commitment to postgenocide justice for the victims, Des Forges appeared as an expert witness in 11 genocide trials at the International Criminal Tribunal for Rwanda, 3 trials in Belgium, and at trials in Switzerland, the Netherlands, and Canada. She also provided documents and other assistance in judicial proceedings involving genocide in four other national jurisdictions, including the United States. Her expertise was sought on numerous occasions, and she provided assistance to investigations undertaken by the French National Assembly, the Belgian Senate, the United States Congress, the Organization of African Unity, and the United Nations.

After the Rwandan Genocide, Des Forges turned her attention to the killings then known to be taking place in the eastern region of Democratic Republic of Congo (DRC), and she was among a number of critics who accused the RPF government of killing civilians and refugees in the eastern Congo in 1996 and 1997. Des Forges then began working on a Human Rights Watch report about these killings, and in doing so she became an authority on DRC human rights violations.

On February 12, 2009, Alison Des Forges was killed in an air crash, when Continental Connection flight 3407, flying from Newark, New Jersey, crashed into a home near Buffalo, New York (where Des Forges lived). She was among the 50 passengers who died in the crash.

PAUL R. BARTROP

See also: *Leave None to Tell the Story: Genocide in Rwanda;* Rwandan Patriotic Front

Further Reading

Des Forges, Alison. *Leave None to Tell the Story: Genocide in Rwanda.* New York: Human Rights Watch, 1999.

Gribbin, Robert E. *In the Aftermath of Genocide: The US Role in Rwanda.* New York: I Universe, 2005.

Diagne, Mbaye

Mbaye Diagne was an army officer from the African country of Senegal, who worked as a United Nations Military Observer in Rwanda before and during the 1994 genocide. One of nine children, he studied at the University of Dakar before joining the Senegalese army. In 1993, as a young captain, he was assigned to the United Nations Assistance Mission for Rwanda (UNAMIR) as a military observer (MILOB) covering the implementation of the Arusha Accords. He was stationed at the Hôtel des Mille Collines, one of Kigali's luxury hotels and the scene of a major sustained rescue of Tutsis throughout the genocide.

Within hours of the start of the genocide on April 6, 1994, Diagne decided that his orders not to intervene were unacceptable given the lives that were at stake. The morning after the assassination of President Juvénal Habyarimana, the next in line of succession, the moderate Hutu prime minister Agathe Uwilingiyimana, was herself assassinated, with her husband, by presidential guards. Learning of Uwilingiyimana's murder, Diagne decided to investigate by going to the scene of where he had been told the murder took place. He instead found the prime minister's five children hiding in the adjoining housing compound of the United Nations Development Program. After a fruitless wait for UN evacuation vehicles that never arrived, he finally decided to put the children into his own vehicle, hide them with blankets, and then return to the relative safety of the Mille Collines. He then faced the problem of finding a way to evacuate them to the airport, by crossing the various checkpoints established by the Interahamwe militias undetected, and, once there, to obtain a passage for them out of the country. He was able to achieve all this, and the children were removed safely on a Canadian transport that took them to Nairobi, Kenya.

It was a reckless and risky move, but it was only the first of many occasions on which the young officer would ignore the standing orders from UN headquarters to remain neutral and not get involved. As a MILOB, his job was to try to find ways to prevent conflict and report on what he had seen. It was essentially a liaison and investigation role, in which the military observer could find himself involved in a variety of situations designed to facilitate a peaceful outcome. This was not what Diagne did. In the weeks following the start of the genocide, Diagne worked hard to save the lives of hundreds of Rwandans, charming his way past roadblocks, smiling, joking, sharing cigarettes with the murderers, and over and over again talking his way through the checkpoints. In this way he personally saved hundreds of lives. His solo rescue missions, nearly always at great peril to himself, attained legendary status among the UN forces in Kigali.

Diagne's strength lay in his ability to persuade others of his friendliness and comradeship. His disposition helped him to obtain the confidence of families, groups, and leaders of all parties in the conflict. It was calculated that he had to pass through 23 Interahamwe checkpoints in order to get to most of the people he was trying to save. The Interahamwe, who, depending on the time of day, could be drunk or drugged, had to be convinced on each occasion that he was not harboring Tutsis. Diagne would find Tutsis who were hiding, drive them back through the same checkpoints, and then hide them—often in the Amahoro Stadium, from which he would then ferry them to some other place of refuge. He engaged in countless such missions, as he could only carry three to four (or sometimes, five, though this was extremely hazardous) at a time. On one occasion he spent an entire day operating in precisely this format after he came across a group of 25 Tutsis hiding in a house in Nyamirambo, Kigali. On each occasion he bluffed his way through the roadblocks. He relied on his extensive contacts among the Hutu military and militias; his ability to defuse tense situations owing to a sharp sense of humor; and, from time to time, bribery in the form of cigarettes or money. His dynamism saw him seemingly everywhere at once.

It certainly helped that in his position as a MILOB he had access to most of the city, and was known widely by all sides of the conflict. But in engaging in his acts of selfless bravery, he was repeatedly forced to flout his operational orders—which were, put simply, not to intervene in the conflict. UNAMIR's commander, General Roméo Dallaire, was aware of what Diagne was doing, but neither stopped him nor reprimanded him for disobedience. While everyone in the UN establishment seemed to know of Diagne's actions, some believed that Dallaire would not discipline him owing to him undertaking a role that Dallaire himself would have preferred to be doing.

On May 31, 1994, Diagne was driving alone, back to UN headquarters in Kigali with a message for Dallaire from the chief of staff of the Rwandan Armed Forces, Augustin Bizimungu. At this time the rebel Rwandan Patriotic Front (RPF) was closing in on Kigali, and engaged in fierce fighting with the Rwandan army. A random mortar shell, fired by the RPF toward a Hutu extremist checkpoint, accidentally landed behind his jeep. Shrapnel entered through the rear window and hit Diagne in the back of the head, killing him instantly.

Mbaye Diagne was universally recognized as a real-life hero of the Rwandan Genocide. Upon learning of his death, UNAMIR Force Headquarters held a minute of silence in his honor, and a small parade took place at Kigali airport on June 1. A devout Muslim, he was buried in Senegal with full military honors. Later, his wife and two small children accepted on his behalf the UMURINZI award, Rwanda's Campaign against Genocide Medal.

Paul R. Bartrop

See also: Dallaire, Roméo; United Nations Assistance Mission for Rwanda; Uwilingiyimana, Agathe

Further Reading

Barnett, Michael. *Eyewitness to a Genocide: The United Nations and Rwanda.* Ithaca, NY: Cornell University Press, 2002.

Dallaire, Roméo. *Shake Hands with the Devil: The Failure of Humanity in Rwanda.* Toronto: Random House, 2004.

F

Forces Armées Rwandaises

The Forces Armées Rwandaises (Rwandan Armed Forces, FAR) constituted the national military establishment of Rwanda from its founding in 1962 until its dissolution and reformation in 1994, in the immediate aftermath of the 1994 Rwandan Genocide. The FAR in fact played a major role in the genocide. At the time of the genocide, the FAR numbered some 40,000–50,000 men, many of whom were Hutus. The force was administered by the ministry of defense but reported solely to the Rwandan president. The FAR included a small air force as well as an elite Presidential Guard Reserve Force, a National Guard, the Armée Rwandaise (AR), which was the main body of ground troops, and the Gendarmerie Nationale (GN), which functioned as a police and internal security force. The AR and GN were heavily involved in the killings that constituted the Rwandan Genocide.

The size of the FAR increased exponentially beginning in the early 1990s, when the Rwandan government began fighting the Rwandan Patriotic Front (RPF). The RPF had been formed by the Tutsi diaspora in Uganda during the late 1980s. The FAR received much help and training from the French government, which dispatched as many as 1,200 troops to Rwanda after 1990.

When the Rwandan Genocide began in April 1994, the RAF was a principal perpetrator of mass murder against Rwanda's Tutsi minority and moderate Hutus who either objected to the killing of Tutsis or tried to protect them. Although the brunt of the genocide lasted for only 100 days, as least 800,000 people died in the bloody calamity, and 75 percent of the Tutsi population was wiped out.

When a new Tutsi-led RPF government was installed in Rwanda in July 1994, the FAR was substantially recast, reduced in size, and renamed the Rwandan Defense Forces (RDF), which continues to this day as Rwanda's military establishment. Thousands of Hutus who had been in the FAR fled from Rwanda in the aftermath of the genocide, fearing arrest or revenge by Tutsis or the RPF government. Most went to the Democratic Republic of the Congo (DRC), from which they have staged raids against Rwanda. It should be noted, however, that RPF was not guilt-free in the Rwandan Genocide, because it perpetrated atrocities against Hutus. It is also responsible for the deaths of as many as 200,000 Hutu refugees in the DRC after the genocide ended.

A number of FAR officers and soldiers have been indicted and tried by the International Criminal Tribunal for Rwanda (ICTR), based in Arusha, Tanzania. To date, the ICTR has completed 50 trials, 29 of which resulted in convictions. A sizable number of the defendants were soldiers or FAR officers. The trials are ongoing.

PAUL G. PIERPAOLI JR.

See also: Congo, Democratic Republic of; Hutus; International Criminal Tribunal for Rwanda; Rwanda Civil War; Rwandan Genocide; Rwandan Patriotic Front; Tutsis

Further Reading

Ali, Taisier M., and Robert O. Matthews. *Civil Wars in Africa: Roots and Resolution.* Toronto: McGill-Queen's University Press, 1999.

Dallaire, Roméo. *Shake Hands with the Devil: The Failure of Humanity in Rwanda.* Toronto: Random House, 2004.

G

Gaillard, Philippe

Philippe Gaillard is a Swiss Red Cross worker who headed the mission of the International Committee of the Red Cross (ICRC) in Rwanda during the 1994 Rwandan Genocide. Born in Valais, Switzerland, on July 6, 1956, Gaillard studied literature at the universities of Geneva, Freiburg-in-Breisgau, and Salamanca. Joining the ICRC in 1982, he worked for more than 10 years in Latin America and 2 in the Middle East, as well as a year spent at ICRC headquarters in Geneva.

The ICRC opened a delegation in Rwanda in 1990, prior to which it covered the country from a larger regional headquarters in Kinshasa, Zaire. In mid-July 1993 Gaillard went to Rwanda at his own request, just as the Arusha Agreement was being signed between the Hutu Power government of President Juvénal Habyarimana and the rebel Rwandan Patriotic Front (RPF), led by General Paul Kagame. He was appointed head of the ICRC's Rwanda delegation, a post he was to hold for a year. On July 20, 1993, Gaillard met Habyarimana as part of a larger ICRC delegation to Rwanda. At this time people around the country were nervous as to what the future might hold, and despite the Arusha Accords being signed on August 4, there were signs that the situation was not going to be easily remedied.

Soon after Gaillard's arrival the United Nations Assistance Mission for Rwanda (UNAMIR) was established with Canadian general Roméo Dallaire as force commander. Within weeks, more than 50 people were killed in the so-called demilitarized zone between the government forces and those of the RPF. Radio and television propaganda, encouraging Hutus to kill Tutsis with machetes, was broadcast daily. In January 1994 Gaillard was invited by Dallaire to the residence of UN special representative of the secretary-general Jacques-Roger Booh-Booh. Dallaire told Gaillard at this time of the news he had received about the impending genocide, and that he had sent a fax to UN headquarters in New York seeking permission to go on a raid against Interahamwe arms caches. With the raid forbidden by New York, it was from here onward that Gaillard realized that the so-called peace process was not feasible.

Once the genocide began in April 1994, Gaillard worked hard to facilitate both safety and medical support for thousands of sick and wounded Rwandans, regardless of their ethnicity. At the outset of the massacres he called Geneva to explain what was happening, and after discussing the pros and cons of going public with the story it was decided that the ICRC would go against its past record of confidentiality in order to let the world know. Gaillard sent out a very short press release of about five lines regarding a single incident involving the treatment of ICRC wounded, and the next day the story was news around the world. After this, with the support of the ICRC in Geneva, Gaillard was tireless in his efforts to get the word out to the international media about the ongoing slaughter. Gaillard felt he had to speak out in the context of such horror. His attitude was that by remaining silent he would be complicit in the genocide, and that he had a responsibility to make his views known, even if only so that the international community could not say that it didn't know what was happening. This was probably the first occasion in the 20th century when the Red Cross had made a public announcement of atrocities taking place while its delegates were still in the field.

While many of the other nongovernmental organizations and expatriate communities were evacuating, there was little hesitation about staying as far as the ICRC was concerned. Gaillard was later to comment that the main reason the ICRC decided to stay was on account of its local staff. He reduced the expatriates to six key workers (mainly doctors), but owing to the respect paid by all sides to the Red Cross only 1 person out of the 120 local staff who remained at their posts was killed during the genocide. Gaillard received a lot of support for his efforts from Geneva, and spoke with headquarters every day. Needing more and more help with the medical side of the crisis, he found that all he had to do was ask, and within days there would be more surgeons, nurses, and other specialized staff on their way to Kigali.

Toward the end of April 1994, the UN sent the recently appointed High Commissioner for Human Rights José Ayala Lasso to Rwanda. On May 12 he met with Gaillard and Dallaire to obtain an appreciation of the situation. Upon being asked approximately how many people had been killed to date, Gaillard replied that his best estimate would be at least 250,000. Dallaire did not think the figure was as high as that, but Gaillard later concluded that he in fact had better intelligence sources that Dallaire owing to the ICRC's reach throughout the whole country.

One of the major challenges in providing humanitarian aid is to help victims without also helping their murderers. The ICRC gave the militias fuel to remove the corpses of their victims, and rarely named killers publicly in order to be able to continue its humanitarian activities. During the genocide, however, Gaillard found himself talking to and dealing with the killers all the time. He would visit the Ministry of Defense twice and sometimes three times a week to discuss the situation, and one day even confronted the mastermind of the genocide, Colonel Théoneste Bagosora, and demanded that something be done to stop the killing.

At an early date in the genocide—around April 10 or 11—Gaillard went to the Ministry of Defense to speak directly with the minister, Augustin Bizimana, with whom Gaillard had previously been in close touch. He asked for a government-appointed liaison officer, the better to be able to coordinate contact between the ICRC and the Rwandan Armed Forces. Later that same day Bizimana appointed Colonel François Munyengango, a Hutu colonel affected by HIV/AIDS. By all accounts, in his new role Colonel Munyengango helped to save hundreds of defenseless civilians. He assisted ICRC delegates and medical workers to cross the checkpoints, and would browbeat the Interahamwe into giving way. On one occasion he learned that an orphanage in Butare with Tutsi children was being threatened by Interahamwe. Colonel Munyengango immediately drove to Butare, alone, and organized the evacuation of 1,619 orphans from Butare to Burundi. Sadly, by the end of 1994 his illness took his life.

Despite Gaillard's own life being threatened on numerous occasions by the Interahamwe, he has concluded that the Red Cross saved somewhere between 60,000 and 70,000 people. Ten thousand people were taken care of in Gaillard's hospital alone. Perhaps thousands more orphans were saved, either directly by the Red Cross or through its initiatives.

Throughout the time of the genocide, Gaillard maintained his psychological balance through poetry. He had with him *A Season in Hell* by the French poet Arthur Rimbaud, and before having dinner every evening, around seven o'clock, he would read a poem from the collection to his colleagues, who listened in silence.

After the genocide, he remained with the ICRC, but he found himself to be somewhat inured to horror. For Gaillard today, his advice is that simple beauty should be enjoyed more. And while he and his wife had previously decided not to have children, after the genocide both wanted to create life. Now, as a father, senior humanitarian aid worker, and—it must be said—genocide survivor, he is attracted to beauty in all its forms.

PAUL R. BARTROP

See also: Dallaire, Roméo; Rwanda

Further Reading

Eltringham, Nigel. *Accounting for Horror: Post-Genocide Debates in Rwanda.* London: Pluto Press, 2004.

Evans, Glynne. *Responding to Crises in the African Great Lakes.* Oxford: Oxford University Press, 1997.

Gisimba, Damas

Damas Gisimba is the director of an orphanage in Kigali, Rwanda who hid more than 400 mostly Tutsi adults and children during the 1994 Rwandan Genocide.

Damas Gisimba was born in Rwanda in 1950. In 1980, Gisimba's father and mother founded the orphanage, and Damas and his brother Jean-François both worked to serve the children there. In 1986, after his father's death, Damas Gisimba became director of the facility. The orphanage was well-run and well-respected within Rwanda.

By the time of the Rwandan Genocide, which began in April 1994, the orphanage was known as the Gisimba Memorial Center and housed about 65 orphaned children. It was supported by the larger community in Kigali by way of donations and staffing support. When the carnage began in April, Gisimba, a Hutu, was determined to shield as many Tutsis as he could. Gisimba later stated in interviews that his parents had taught him not to focus on ethnicity, to respect all people equally, and to help them in times of need. Over the proceeding 100 days, encouraged by the Hutu-dominated government, the Interahamwe militia, a de facto mass killing organization, massacred hundreds of thousands of people—mainly Tutsis and moderate Hutus—in cities, villages, and the countryside within Rwanda. Hutu civilians also heeded their government's call, and a sizable number became caught up in the violence; Hutu neighbors killed Tutsi neighbors and friends, and some hardline Hutus even murdered members of their own family, if they happened to be moderate Hutus or Tutsis.

It was amid this shocking cataclysm that Gisimba and his brother Jean-François decided to hide as many people as they could at the orphanage, knowing full well that their discovery would inevitably lead to their own deaths. Within a week or so after the genocide began, more than 400 children and adults had flooded into the orphanage. They were all Tutsis or moderate Hutus. The huge influx taxed Gisimba's already meager food supplies, but he managed to scavenge what he could without raising undue suspicions. Several times, Interahamwe fighters threatened the orphanage, but the Gisimba brothers managed to keep them at bay, using a combination of bribes and threats. In the end, all those who had sought refuge with Gisimba survived the terrible ordeal.

Damas and his brother have since received numerous accolades, awards, and honors for their selfless courage. They have come from the postgenocide Rwandan government as well as a wide variety of international organizations and individual nations. Today, the orphanage continues to be directed by Gisimba and houses some 150 children. Until about a decade ago, nearly all the facility's children were victims and/or survivors of the genocide. In recent years, that profile has shifted to children orphaned because of poverty or disease, especially AIDS. Meanwhile, Gisimba continues to instill in his children the importance of not judging people because of their ethnicity or other outward appearances.

PAUL G. PIERPAOLI JR.

See also: Interahamwe; Rwanda; Hutus; Tutsis

Further Reading

Des Forges, Alison. *Leave None to Tell the Story: Genocide in Rwanda.* New York: Human Rights Watch, 1999.

Melvern, Linda. *Conspiracy to Murder: The Rwandan Genocide.* London: Verso, 2006.

H

Habyarimana, Juvénal

Juvénal Habyarimana was president of Rwanda from 1973 until his death by assassination on April 6, 1994. He was born into an aristocratic Hutu family on March 8, 1937, in Gasiza, Gisenyi, the son of a landowner, Jean-Baptiste Ntibazilikana, and his wife Suzanne Nyirazuba. He was educated in Zaire, and studied medicine before entering Rwanda's Officer Training School in Kigali in 1960. Graduating in 1961, he rose to become chief of staff in the Rwandan military forces (Forces Armées Rwandaises, or FAR) in 1963. In 1965, at the age of 28, he was made minister for the armed forces and police in the government of his cousin, Gregoire Kayibanda. In 1973 he was promoted to major general, and then overthrew Kayibanda in a military coup on July 5, 1973.

Habyarimana's military regime remained in office until 1978, when a referendum established a new constitution. Habyarimana, setting himself up as the only candidate, was elected to a five-year term as president, which was renewed in subsequent sham elections. Under Habyarimana, the quality of life for most Rwandans improved: there was political stability, and the economy recovered to reach unprecedented levels. This "golden age" came at a price, however. Every Rwandan citizen, including babies and the elderly, had to be a member of Habyarimana's political party (the only one permitted), the Mouvement Révolutionnaire National pour le Développement (National Revolutionary Movement for Development, or MRND). This

was a party of Hutu exclusivism, and through it Habyarimana was able to build what was, in essence, an apartheid-like state in which the Tutsi minority was discriminated against institutionally.

Throughout this time, Habyarimana relied heavily on an inner clique of the MRND, the so-called Akazu (Kinyarwanda, "Little Hut"), a euphemism given to an informal but tightly knit (and highly corrupt) network of Habyarimana's closest family members, friends, and party associates. It was said to be so thoroughly dominated by Habyarimana's wife Agathe (née Kanziga) that, at times, even her husband could be frozen out of the decision-making process. The name Akazu was originally, in precolonial times, a term given to the inner circle of courtiers to the royal family; under the MRND regime, and particularly Agathe Habyarimana's dominance, it developed such awesome power that it even instituted its own death squad, recruited from members of the presidential guard The Akazu was an oligarchy that not only held back any possibility of Rwanda returning to democracy, but also worked assiduously to promote the interests of northern Rwanda (the Akazu base) over those of the south. This further destabilized the position of the minority Tutsis throughout the country, and, through its extensive network of supporters in the bureaucracy, the financial sector, and society generally, the Akazu skimmed off vast amounts of public money for the greater good of the extended Habyarimana family.

The late 1980s saw Rwanda experience an economic downturn, as world coffee prices—upon which the Rwandan economy relied heavily—dropped sharply. This destabilized Habyarimana's regime, forcing him to introduce an economic austerity program that led to widespread unrest. In hopes of curbing unprecedented antigovernment sentiment, he convened a national commission to study how best to implement a multiparty democracy in Rwanda. Whilst army control ensured that he still held the country in an iron grip, forced budget cuts in 1989—accompanied by a drought in 1988–1989 and a plea for financial assistance to the World Bank—saw pressure brought against Habyarimana to begin a process of liberalization for Rwanda's political system.

Despite this, Habyarimana was and remained a Hutu supremacist. While portraying an image of one who would not be averse to a liberalization of his government, in reality he also armed and encouraged the activities of extremist Hutu militias such as the Interahamwe ("those who attack together") and the Impuzamugambi ("those with a common purpose").

In late 1990 a large and well-equipped rebel Tutsi army located in nearby Uganda, the Rwandan Patriotic Front (RPF), invaded the country. This émigré force engaged the Rwandan army in heavy fighting that came close to Kigali, and threatened Habyarimana's grip. Only the intervention of French paratroopers, units of which stood physically between the RPF and the government forces, stopped the invasion. The civil war continued intermittently for another three years, further damaging Rwanda's already vulnerable economy, and led Habyarimana inevitably to the conclusion that he would have to open some form of negotiation process if his administration was to survive. This began in 1992, when the country held its first multiparty elections, and changes in the legislation provided for both a prime minister and a president.

By August 4, 1993, delegates from the RPF met with officials of the Habyarimana administration and representatives of the United States, France, and the Organization of African Unity, to negotiate a settlement. The resulting settlement, signed at Arusha, Tanzania, saw a set of five accords agreed to between the two parties. These ranged over a wide variety of topics: refugee resettlement, power-sharing between Hutu and Tutsi, the introduction of an all-embracing democratic regime, the dismantling of Habyarimana's dictatorship, and the encouragement of a transparent rule of law throughout Rwanda. Arusha guaranteed the RPF half of the officer corps and 40 percent of the enlisted men in a reorganized Rwandan army, as well as Tutsi representation in key government posts.

In the months that followed, a number of subsequent meetings took place for the purpose of negotiating their implementation. This involved the parties traveling to and from Arusha, sometimes by road and at other times by plane. Some observers considered that Habyarimana purposely allowed these negotiations to drag on in order to buy time and thereby reinforce his position at home, the more so as Hutu extremist elements were becoming increasingly frustrated at Habyarimana's "capitulation" to the rebel forces by even entering negotiations in the first place.

On April 6, 1994, while returning to Kigali from one of the negotiation rounds in Arusha, Habyarimana's Falcon 50 jet, carrying the president as well as the president of Burundi, Cyprien Ntaryamira, the chief of staff of the Rwandan military, and numerous others, was shot down by two missiles fired from just outside the Kigali airport perimeter. The plane crashed into the grounds of the presidential palace, with all on board killed. Within hours, as if the assassination had sounded a tocsin to the Hutu extremists in Rwanda, the killing of all Tutsis and the Hutu liberal middle class began.

It has never been proven conclusively who was responsible for the missile attack. A French investigating team blamed the RPF, in particular its leader (and later president of Rwanda), General Paul Kagame. Others have argued that it was Hutu extremists, believing Habyarimana far too moderate, who decided to use his death as a necessary sacrifice to force a final reckoning with the RPF and the Tutsis. Yet others have even suggested that it was members of the Akazu—and thus, Habyarimana's own family—who arranged for the plane to be shot down.

Whatever the case, the assassination certainly served as an opportunity for extremist Hutus to unleash unprecedented ethnic violence in Rwanda. Within hours, the militias, the FAR, the presidential guard and the Gendarmerie Nationale (the national police force) unleashed wholesale carnage against Rwanda's Tutsis. At least 800,000 people—though by several estimates, nearly a million—were killed over the next three months, in one of the fastest genocides in recorded history.

Three days after the assassination, French forces escorted the slain president's widow, Agathe Habyarimana, out of the country, evacuating her to France. Reports of her living a life of luxury in Paris surfaced frequently over the next several years, rubbing salt into the wounds of the RPF-dominated government that came to power in

Rwanda after the genocide. As one of the leading members of the Akazu (also known in some circles as the "Clan de Madame"), Agathe Habyarimana was alleged by the RPF to have been one the genocide's masterminds. After many years in exile, "Madame Agathe" as denied political asylum in France on January 4, 2007 (though incongruously, she was permitted to remain in the country).

Then, on March 2, 2010, she was arrested by the government of French president Nicolas Sarkozy on suspicion of her involvement in the genocide. The move against her followed a visit to Rwanda by Sarkozy during which he promised that "those responsible for the genocide must be found and punished." She was detained at her home in the southern Paris suburbs by police executing a Rwandan-issued international arrest warrant released in October 2009. Immediately, the Rwandan government urged Paris to extradite her for trial, though it is considered that France will never actually do so. French judges have consistently refused to extradite genocide suspects to Kigali on the grounds that they would not receive a fair trial, and it is certain that Agathe Habyarimana would find it extremely difficult to obtain this.

PAUL R. BARTROP

See also: Arusha Accords; Forces Armées Rwandaises; Interahamwe; Rwandan Patriotic Front

Further Reading

Jokic, Aleksandar, ed. *War Crimes and Collective Wrongdoing: A Reader.* Malden, MA: Blackwell Publishers, 2001.

Melvern, Linda. *Conspiracy to Murder: The Rwandan Genocide.* London: Verso, 2006.

Hamitic Hypothesis

Stock-in-trade of early colonial historians, the Hamitic Hypothesis lies at the core of racist theories purporting to show the innate superiority of the Tutsi people as the ideal embodiment of the Hamitic race. According to historian David Newbury, it is founded on the following assumptions: that ethnic categories are defined by biological criteria, that the origin of each group is traceable to a distinct geographical area, that they each possess a specific corporate history, and that the history of the region can best be explained in terms of the conquest of one race by another.

Such ideas can be found in germ, as it were, in the writings of early European explorers who saw in the somatic traits of Tutsi and Hima people unmistakable proof of their Ethiopian origins. After coming in contact with the people of Uganda in the 1850s, John Henning Speke was one of the first to air the notion that people of Hamitic descent were racially superior to lesser breeds of Africans. His views were later echoed in Count Gustav Adolf von Goetzen's description of the Tutsi of Rwanda, in 1894, as being exceptionally gifted, physically and culturally distinct from the great mass of Hutu agriculturalists, and must have migrated with their long-horned cattle from Abyssinia to Rwanda. Father A. Pagès gave further respectability to the term in the title of his book, *Au Rwanda: Un royaume hamite au centre de l'Afrique* (1933). Writing in the 1920s, the British anthropologist C.G. Seligman captured the gist of the myth in his book on *The Races of Africa* (1922) when he referred to the Hamites as "pastoral Europeans." For all the critical responses voiced by more serious observers, the Hamitic hypothesis showed a surprising capacity to survive in one form or another throughout the colonial period and after.

The Hamitic frame seemed ideally suited to legitimize the Belgian version of indirect rule. Though later appropriated by Rwandan historians of Tutsi origins, most notably Alexis Kagame, to reclaim self-rule, on the eve of independence Hamitic references became a familiar theme in the discourse of Hutu politicians anxious to discredit the monarchy and its feudal supporters. It eventually surfaced as a notoriously noxious ideology during the genocide, when it was used as a tool in the hands of Hutu extremists to insist on sending the Tutsi back to their "original homeland," Ethiopia.

As a hypothesis, a myth or an ideology the Hamitic frame of reference has had a profound influence on the destinies of Africans. It has added a strongly racist coloration to the writings of early historians; it has shaped the ideas and practices of colonial administrators and missionaries in many parts of Central Africa, including Rwanda and Burundi; and, most importantly, it has given a spurious halo of respectability to the proponents of genocidal ideas during the Rwandan carnage.

RENÉ LEMARCHAND

See also: Rwandan Genocide, Role of Propaganda in the; Tutsis

Further Reading

Chrétien, Jean-Pierre. *The Great Lakes of Africa: Two Thousand Years of History.* Translated by Scott Strauss, New York: Zone Books, 2003.

Newbury, David. *The Land beyond the Mists: Essays on Identity and Authority in Precolonial Congo and Rwanda.* Athens: Ohio University Press, 2011.

Prunier, Gérard. *The Rwanda Crisis, 1959–1994: History of a Genocide.* Kampala: Fountain Publishers, 1995.

Sanders, Edith. "The Hamitic Hypothesis: Its Origins and Functions," *Journal of African History* 10, no. 4 (1960): 521–532.

Hotel Rwanda (Film, 2004)

Hotel Rwanda was a critically acclaimed U.S.-made movie released in 2004 based on real events that occurred during the spring of 1994 during the Rwandan Genocide. The film is based on the real-life actions of Paul Rusesabagina (played by Don Cheadle), who managed a small hotel in the Rwandan capital of Kigali, and his family. *Hotel Rwanda* also stars Sophie Okonedo, Joaquin Phoenix, Nick Nolte, and Jean Reno. As the Rwandan genocide begins, Rusesabagina, who is a Hutu, and his wife Tatiana, who is a Tutsi, are increasingly horrified by the violence they see unfolding around them. To complicate matters, their mixed marriage is frowned upon by the Hutu-led Interahamwe militia. Despite their increasing fears that one or both of them will be killed, Rusesabagina negotiates with and bribes local officials to leave the hotel alone, and before long it becomes a refuge for nearly 1,300 Rwandan refugees, mostly Tutsis. Many critics have called *Hotel Rwanda* an African-based version of *Schindler's List,* a 1993 movie about the Jewish Holocaust.

Like *Schindler's List, Hotel Rwanda* deals with the causes and results of mass violence and genocide, societal and political corruption, hypocrisy, and the redeeming value of human kindness even in the midst of unspeakable human suffering. An independent film, the movie had a limited release in December 2004 but was more widely released in February 2005. *Hotel Rwanda* was a modest success financially, but received many accolades. It received awards at the Toronto Film Festival and the Berlin Film festival, among others.

In a subtle way, *Hotel Rwanda* also deals with the unwillingness—or inability—of the international community to stop the bloodshed. United Nations (UN) peacekeeping troops are portrayed as being deeply concerned about the mass killings, but essentially unable to take any offensive action against the Hutus or the Interahamwe because the UN had forbidden them from intervening in the genocide. The film ends with Rusesabagina's family, along with the refugees he shielded, successfully leaving the hotel after joining a UN convoy and reaching Tutsi rebel protection.

PAUL G. PIERPAOLI JR.

See also: Dallaire, Roméo; Interahamwe; Rusesabagina, Paul

Further Reading

Dallaire, Roméo. *Shake Hands with the Devil: The Failure of Humanity in Rwanda.* Toronto: Random House, 2004.

Melvern, Linda. *Conspiracy to Murder: The Rwandan Genocide.* London: Verso, 2006.

Hutus

The term "Hutu" refers to the majority of citizens occupying the region of Rwanda-Burundi. The Rwandan government, dominated by the Hutus, perpetrated genocide against the Tutsis of Rwanda in 1994.

The Hutus and Tutsi are descended from ancestors sharing a common language, Kinyerwanda, who settled the Rwanda-Burundi area of east central Africa more than 1,000 years ago. Two forms of subsistence developed among these people. One group relied strictly on cultivation and farming. The other relied on cattle raising. Over time, the farmers came to be known as Hutus and the pastoralists as Tutsis. In this culture, cattle were a marker of wealth. With time, Hutu and Tutsi became class markers with the pastoral Tutsi as the wealthier members of the society.

At the time of the German conquest in the 1880s, Rwandan society had begun to polarize. The majority Hutu occupied the peasant, or subject, position to the Tutsi minority holding the tribal leadership positions. The German colonizers did little to interfere with the social makeup of the indigenous people. When Belgium assumed control over Rwanda at the close of World War I, the situation changed. The Belgians relied heavily on indigenous Tutsi leaders to govern the colony. This served to reinforce Tutsi control and provided apparatus to repress the masses of the people. Belgian leaders excluded Hutus from government service and from higher education.

During the 1950s, the Hutus began a resurgence back into public life, using the decolonization programs of the United Nations to gain access to education and public office. Hutu leaders were successful in exploiting the decolonization process to gain power throughout Rwanda. When Rwanda revolted against Belgium and secured its independence in 1961, the class roles were reversed, and the Hutus held the positions of power.

Tutsi rebels challenged Hutu rule immediately. In response to cross-border rebel incursions, the Hutu government massacred some 20,000 Rwandan Tutsis and forced

300,000 to flee. In the aftermath, a military dictatorship solidified its power in Rwanda. Over the next two decades, the standard of living in Rwanda declined steadily.

As the economic decline in Rwanda continued, the power base of the military leadership eroded. Rebel groups, most notably the Rwandan Patriotic Front, began to challenge the government from camps in neighboring states. Tutsi participation with the rebels gave justification for further repression of the Tutsis. The government began planning the genocide of the Tutsis as a way of repolarizing the population.

The assassination of President Juvenal Habyarimana on April 6, 1994, provided the catalyst for action against the Tutsis. During the next 13 weeks, military forces compelled the Hutu population of Rwanda to massacre the Tutsis. More than 800,000 Tutsis and perhaps 20,000 Hutus were killed. Three-quarters of the Tutsi population were exterminated.

The Hutus maintain leadership in Rwanda, which remains one of the world's poorest nations.

ROB COYLE

See also: Arusha Accords; Habyarimana, Juvénal; Radio-Télévision Libre des Mille Collines; Rwandan Patriotic Front; Tutsis

Further Reading

Adelman, Howard, and Astri Suhrke, eds. *The Path of a Genocide: The Rwanda Crisis from Uganda to Zaire.* New Brunswick, NJ: Transaction Publishers, 1999.

Webster, John B. *The Political Development of Rwanda and Burundi.* Syracuse, NY: Maxwell Graduate School of Citizenship and Public Affairs, Syracuse University, 1966.

I

Identity Cards, Rwanda

Identification cards resembling passports were issued to all Rwandans beginning in the early 1930s. They were mandated by Belgian authorities, who had been ruling the country since World War I. The identity cards indicated an individual's ethnicity—Tutsi, Hutu, or Twa—and also contained the bearer's address or place of residence and other personal information. All Rwandans were required to carry their cards with them at all times and present them to authorities when asked. The cards helped the Belgians and their Tutsi allies, who then dominated Rwanda, to control the movement of people within the country. Indeed, no Rwandan could move to a new address or location without seeking permission from the government ahead of time. If the move was approved, a new identity card would be promptly issued.

The identity cards were a major bone of contention among Rwandans, especially the majority Hutu, whom the Belgians relegated to second-class citizenship. Indeed, most Hutus were barred from government service, had separate educational institutions that were patently inferior to those for Tutsis, and were routinely discriminated against in most public venues, including employment and housing. The identity cards only served to drive a larger wedge between the Tutsis and Hutus and created a corrosive atmosphere of mutual distrust and dislike among Rwanda's two principal ethnic groups. This atmosphere was reinforced by Belgian policies that clearly favored the minority Tutsis.

Amid this environment, the Hutus rebelled against the Tutsi monarchy and Tutsi elites in 1959. Thousands of Tutsis died in the violence, and at least 130,000 were forced to flee the country. By 1961, the Hutus had formed their own government, which shut out the Tutsis completely. In 1962, the Belgians left and Rwanda became an independent nation under a Hutu-dominated government. Thereafter, race relations in the country remained poor, and the government continued to mandate the identity cards, but now the tables were turned and they were used chiefly to single out, ostracize, or repress the Tutsis. When the Rwandan Genocide commenced in April 1994, the Hutu government and allied militia groups like the *Interahamwe,* used the cards to single out Tutsis for murder. Thus, the cards made the process of mass killing based on ethnicity much faster and simpler. Some have argued that the identity cards also helped some Hutus distance themselves psychologically from the genocide by reinforcing long-ingrained but faulty ideas about ethnic superiority and ethnic vilification.

PAUL G. PIERPAOLI JR.

See also: Habyarimana, Juvénal; Hutus; Interahamwe; Rwanda; Twas

Further Reading

Melvern, Linda. *Conspiracy to Murder: The Rwandan Genocide.* London: Verso, 2006.

Prunier, Gérard. *The Rwanda Crisis, 1959–1994: History of a Genocide*. Kampala: Fountain Publishers, 1995.

Straus, Scott. *The Order of Genocide: Race, Power, and War in Rwanda*. Ithaca, NY: Cornell University Press, 2008.

Interahamwe

The Interahamwe was the largest and most potent of the anti-Tutsi paramilitary groups in Rwanda and played a central in the 1994 Rwandan Genocide, which killed an estimated 800,000–1,000,000 Tutsis and moderate Hutus. The Interahamwe (the word is derived from the Rwandan word that means to "stand, fight, or work together") worked closely with the Hutu-dominated Rwandan army, which provided training and weapons to Interahamwe members. The group grew out of a youth-oriented soccer club during the early 1990s, under the tutelage of Robert "Jerry" Kajuga, who turned the club into a brutal killing machine; he served as its president during the Rwandan Genocide. Ironically, Kajuga was an ethnic Tutsi whose father had illegally acquired Hutu identification papers. The Interahamwe cultivated a deep hatred of Tutsis, and often recruited its members at gunpoint from among the Hutu peasantry. The group referred to Tutsis in subhuman terms, even employing the term "cockroaches" to describe them. By 1994, the Interahamwe had a membership approaching 6,500 well-armed men.

Many Interahamwe fighters were trained by French forces under the direction of President Juvenal Habyarimana between 1991 and 1994. Not surprisingly, the Interahamwe vigorously opposed the 1993 Arusha Accords, which witnessed Habyarimana's reluctant accommodation with the Rwandan Patriotic Front (RPF), a Tutsi group. From 1992 until the outbreak of the genocide in April 1994, the Interahamwe, in conjunction with other anti-Tutsi militias like the Impuzamugambi, with which it was closely allied, waged a virtual guerilla-style war designed to rally Hutus against the Tutsis and to force Tutsis to flee Rwanda. This activity was supported by the Rwandan government and armed forces, and Rwandan vice president Georges Rutaganda directed many of the group's attacks.

The downing of Habyarimana's presidential plane in Kigali on April 6, 1994, provided the Interahamwe, along with other like-minded groups and the Rwandan military, a pretext to launch a campaign of genocide against Tutsis, who were blamed for the president's death. The killing occurred on a scale nearly unthinkable, and in just 100 days, as many as 800,000 Tutsis and Hutu sympathizers were dead.

Once the bloodletting was over, many Interahamwe members fled to the Democratic Republic of the Congo; some then made their way to other neighboring countries, including Burundi and Uganda. From there they launched raids against Rwanda, now governed by the Tutsi-dominated RPF. In 1999, Interahamwe refugees in Uganda were responsible for the murders of 14 foreign tourists in Uganda's Bwindi National Park.

Since the RPF takeover of the Rwandan government, a number of Interahamwe senior cadre have been tried and convicted by the International Criminal Tribunal for Rwanda (ICTR), based in Arusha, Tanzania. Some Interahamwe leaders have also been tried in Rwanda, including under the *Gacaca* Law. The ICTR has indicted at least 20 Interahamwe leaders since 1995. The Interahamwe was a principal instigator of the Rwandan Genocide because it stirred up anti-Tutsi hatred long before Habyarimana's April 1994 assassination.

PAUL G. PIERPAOLI JR.

See also: Arusha Accords; Habyarimana, Juvénal; Hutus; International Criminal Tribunal for Rwanda; Kajuga, Jerry; Rutaganda, Georges; Rwandan Patriotic Front; Tutsis

Further Reading

Valentino, Benjamin A. *Final Solutions: Mass Killing and Genocide in the Twentieth Century*. Ithaca, NY: Cornell University Press, 2004.

Waller, James. *Becoming Evil: How Ordinary People Commit Genocide and Mass Killing*. Oxford: Oxford University Press, 2002.

International Criminal Tribunal for Rwanda

The International Criminal Tribunal for Rwanda (ICTR) was created by the United Nations (UN) Security Council in 1994 to prosecute the people responsible for the 1994 genocide in Rwanda. The UN hoped that the tribunal would facilitate the process of national reconciliation between warring ethnic groups and maintain peace in the region.

The Tribunal takes its structure from Security Council Resolution 955. This statute creates a three-part judicial system, consisting of three trial chambers and an appeals chamber, which function as courts; the Office of the Prosecutor, which is in charge of investigating and prosecuting alleged crimes; and the Registry, which handles administrative matters. The 16 judges in the chambers are elected to four-year terms by the General Assembly from a list submitted by the Security Council. No two judges may come from the same country. The Tribunal's jurisdiction is clearly defined. It can prosecute genocide, crimes against humanity, and other crimes defined in Article 3 of the Geneva Convention and its Additional Protocol II. It can only prosecute crimes committed between January 1 and December 31, 1994. The crimes must have been committed by Rwandans within Rwanda or its neighboring states or by non-Rwandans who committed crimes in Rwanda. The Tribunal also has a Witness and Victims Support Section to protect the anonymity of Rwandans who testify against those accused of genocide.

Accused individuals are detained by the tribunal before and during their trials; they may communicate with family and friends and receive visits. They are also allowed to mingle with one another and have full access to legal counsel. People who are convicted by the trial chambers may appeal their convictions to the appeals chamber.

The maximum sentence meted out by the Tribunal is life imprisonment.

The Tribunal's first trial was that of Jean-Paul Akayesu, who was convicted of genocide in 1998. By 2012, 50 cases had been completed, and 29 individuals had been convicted. Eleven more trials were in progress, and 14 individuals were awaiting trial. Thirteen others remained at large, some presumed dead. The Tribunal posts daily updates on its Web site, including a daily journal and case minutes. The records of all trials are also available.

Amy Hackney Blackwell

See also: Akayesu, Jean-Paul; Barayagwiza, Jean-Bosco; Coalition for International Justice; Kamuhanda Trial; *Kangura;* Kayishema Trial; Media Trial in Rwanda; Nahimana, Ferdinand; Ngeze, Hassan; Radio-Télévision Libre des Mille Collines

Further Reading

Boot, Machteld. *Genocide, Crimes against Humanity, War Crimes: Nullum Crimen Sine Lege and the Subject Matter Jurisdiction of the International Criminal Court.* Antwerp: Intersentia, 2002.

Schabas, William A. *Genocide in International Law: The Crime of Crimes.* Cambridge, UK: Cambridge University Press, 2000.

K

Kabuga, Félicien

Félicien Kabuga is a multimillionaire Rwandan business-man alleged to have been the chief financier of the Rwandan Genocide of 1994. On the run since 1994, he is one of the most wanted men in Africa.

Kabuga was born in 1935 in Muniga, in the commune of Mukarange, Byumba, and had close ties to the long-serving president of Rwanda, Juvénal Habyarimana, and his ruling party, the Mouvement Révolutionnaire National pour le Développement (National Revolutionary Movement for Development, or MRND). He was one of the main financial contributors to MRND, and to the Coalition pour la Défense de la Republique (Coalition for the Defense of the Republic, or CDR), an extremist anti-Tutsi Hutu party emerging from within the MRND.

It has been alleged that from the end of 1990 until July 1994 Kabuga played an important role in the preparation and execution of a plan aimed at the extermination of the Tutsis. This plan encouraged hatred and ethnic violence, trained and armed anti-Tutsi militias, and drafted lists of people to be murdered.

Kabuga also became president of the ruling committee of the rabidly anti-Tutsi radio station Radio-Télévision Libre des Mille Collines (RTLM), helping to indoctrinate the Rwandan people with extremist Hutu ideologies. In November 1993, and again in February 1994, the Habyarimana government, which was at that time attempting to project to the world an image of pluralism and tolerance, publicly urged Kabuga to stop the distribution of messages aiming at inciting interracial hatred, but instead Kabuga countered by declaring that RTLM should become the official voice of the Hutu Power regime. Throughout the genocide, in the spring of 1994, RTLM subsequently played a vital propaganda and directing role to help facilitate the killing.

Kabuga also wielded considerable influence as a result of his wealth. On April 25, 1994, it is reported that Kabuga and others met in Gisenyi in order to create the Comité Provisoire du Fonds de Défense Nationale (National Defence Funds Acting Committee, or FDN), of which he became president. The FDN was created for the purpose of providing assistance to the radical Hutu-dominated interim government to help destroy Tutsis and moderate Hutus. The purpose of the FDN was to buy weapons, vehicles, and uniforms for the Interahamwe militia and the national army. Kabuga was granted signatory power over the fund's bank accounts. It was in this capacity that he became known as the chief paymaster of the Interahamwe militias that undertook the task of carrying out and directing the Rwandan Genocide.

It is alleged that he exercised authority over organizations aligned with Hutu Power, enabling him to organize, order, and even participate in the mass murders. Certainly, he employed his wealth to outfit the Interahamwe. Before and during the genocide, Kabuga is alleged to have participated in the provision of weapons to the militia, purchasing vast quantities of machetes, hoes, and other agricultural tools for Interahamwe use. From 1992, one of Kabuga's companies, ETS, was reported to have bought massive stocks of machetes, hoes, and other farm tools, in the belief that they would be used as weapons during the massacres. In March 1994, just before the genocide began, Kabuga was reported to have imported 50,000 machetes from Kenya. Kabuga has also been accused of continuing to supply machetes and other weapons during the four months of the genocide itself. Additionally it has been alleged that he supplied uniforms and transportation to the Interahamwe through his company-owned vehicles.

Kabuga has always claimed he is innocent of the accusations leveled against him.

In June 1994, as troops from the Rwandan Patriotic Front (RPF) advanced on Kigali and then took over most of the country, Kabuga fled Rwanda. On July 22, 1994, he sought asylum in Switzerland on a valid visa. He was expelled, at Swiss government expense (with his wife and seven children), on August 18, 1994, and flew immediately to Kinshasa in the Democratic Republic of Congo (DRC). Before leaving Switzerland, it is alleged, he withdrew funds from his Swiss bank account with UBS at the Geneva international airport. He then spent a period of time in DRC, arranging sanctuary in a third country, widely believed to be Kenya. He took up residence in Nairobi, where he allegedly found protection from senior government officials of then-president Daniel Arap Moi. This protection enabled him to evade a number of attempts at arrest by Kenyan police and international bodies.

In 1995, when the International Criminal Tribunal for Rwanda (ICTR) was established, Kabuga was one of the first of those for whom the Tribunal began an investigation. In August 1998 he was indicted by the ICTR on 11 counts that included genocide, conspiracy to commit genocide, complicity in genocide, and violations of the laws and customs of war. One year later, in August 1999, an international arrest warrant for his arrest was issued.

Despite these efforts, as of this writing Kabuga has still not been arrested. He is said to be a frequent traveler to various African nations where he buys protection. A 1999 report of a United Nations commission of inquiry into arms purchases by the former militia of the Rwandan government reported that Kabuga had been seen in Southeast Asia in September 1998, and in 2000 he was said to have transited through Belgium, where his wife at that time lived.

From this time on, concerted efforts were made to capture Kabuga. On June 11, 2002, the United States offered a reward of up to U.S. $5,000,000 for any information leading to his capture, and later that year the United States formally accused Kenyan security authorities of having given sanctuary to Kabuga and of using governmental infrastructures to prevent him from being arrested. On August 28, 2003, in Security Council Resolution 1503, the UN urged all member states (and Kenya in particular) to intensify their cooperation to find Kabuga and bring him to justice. The ICTR also arranged to have Kabuga's financial assets confiscated, and to block access to his bank accounts in France, Switzerland, and Belgium.

In November 2009 the United States ambassador for war crimes issues, Stephen Rapp, told reporters in Nairobi that he was convinced Kabuga was still currently in Kenya, and that he had seen pictures of Kabuga in Kenyan neighborhoods. By way of response, Kenyan prime minister Raila Odinga declared his belief that Kabuga was not in the country. Then, on a visit to the ICTR in Arusha, Tanzania, in February 2010, Rapp once more announced that Kabuga was still in Kenya, notwithstanding government declarations to the contrary.

As of this writing, Félicien Kabuga remains on the run. The Kenyan government continues to deny he is in the country, but has reaffirmed its pledge to arrest him if he is located.

PAUL R. BARTROP

See also: Coalition Pour la Défense de la Rèpublique; Habyarimana, Juvénal; Interahamwe; International Criminal Tribunal for Rwanda; Radio-Télévision Libre des Mille Collines

Further Reading

Friedrichs, David O., ed. *State Crime.* Brookfield, VT: Ashgate/Dartmouth, 1998.

Neier, Aryeh. *War Crimes: Brutality, Genocide, Terror, and the Struggle for Justice.* New York: Times Books, 1998.

Kagame, Paul

Paul Kagame is a Rwandan politician, who, as the leader of the Tutsi-led Rwandan Patriotic Army (RPA), the military arm of the Rwandan Patriotic Front (RPF), defeated Hutu extremist forces to end the 1994 Rwandan Genocide. In 2000 he became president of Rwanda, a position he holds to this day.

A Tutsi, Kagame was born in Gitarama on October 23, 1957, and as a child became a refugee as his family (among

Major General Paul Kagame became Rwanda's first Tutsi president since independence in 1961 when the National Assembly elected him to the post in April 2000. Kagame also serves as the commander of the Rwandan Patriotic Front. (Government of Rwanda)

tens of thousands of other Rwandan Tutsis) fled to Uganda in 1960 in the face of Hutu attacks on Tutsis. In 1962 they settled into a Ugandan refugee camp, where Kagame spent the rest of his childhood years. He was educated in the Ugandan education system, was taught in English rather than French (as spoken in Rwanda), and studied for a time at Makerere University in Kampala. For the next 30 years after 1960, he lived his life as an exile.

Determined to resist oppressive regimes, as a young man Kagame decided on a rebel military career, and he joined with a Ugandan dissident leader, Yoweri Museveni, who had formed his own National Resistance Army (NRA). Together, the two spent five years fighting as guerrillas against the government of Milton Obote. When Museveni took power in 1986, he sent Kagame to Cuba for training with several other intelligence officers then under Kagame's command. Then, in 1989, Museveni sent Kagame on a training course at the U.S. Army Command and Staff College at Fort Leavenworth, Kansas.

In 1985, as a young, English-speaking Tutsi refugee burning to return to Rwanda, Kagame and his best friend, Fred Rwigyema, established the Rwandan Patriotic Front (RPF), a political organization with an armed wing named the Rwandan Patriotic Army composed mostly of Tutsis who had fought in Uganda with Museveni's NRA in the overthrow of President Idi Amin in 1979. By October 1990 the movement was strong enough to launch an invasion of Rwanda from Uganda, supported by Museveni. Rwigyema was killed during the invasion, which failed after a French-led intervention force stopped its advance after an appeal for help from Rwandan president Juvénal Habyarimana. After Rwigyema's death, Kagame became the head of the RPF. Kagame's role in negotiations with the Habyarimana regime throughout the 1990s was important, and certainly contributed to the signing of the Arusha Accords, a peace settlement between the RPF and the Rwandan government signed on August 4, 1993. Habyarimana's assassination on April 6, 1994, however, destroyed any possibility that these accords would be implemented.

Controversy has since dogged Kagame over Habyarimana's assassination, with several accusations made against him for his alleged responsibility for having shot down Habyarimana's plane—an event which killed not only the president, but also the president of Burundi, Cyprien Ntaryamira, and the plane's French pilot and crew. In January 2000, three Tutsi informants told United Nations investigators that they were part of an elite hit squad that had assassinated Habyarimana. Their confession implicated Kagame in his capacity as overall commander, though nothing was proven and no official allegations were made. According to Lieutenant Aloys Ruyenzi, a member of the RPA, Kagame was primarily responsible for shooting down the plane, while the French government launched its own investigation, leading to a conclusion by Judge Jean-Louis Bruguière that Kagame in fact ordered the shooting. In response, in November 2006, Rwanda severed all diplomatic ties with France and ordered its entire diplomatic staff out of Rwanda within 24 hours. Relations between the two countries remained strained for several years after this, but in an attempt to establish better relations with France Kagame visited Paris in mid-September 2011, reciprocating a visit to Rwanda by French president Nicolas Sarkozy in February 2010.

All accusations against Kagame have been met consistently with vigorous denials by Kagame and his supporters, who have argued that the plane was shot down by Hutu extremists furious with Habyarimana for arranging a peace settlement with the detested Tutsis, and who exploited the events in order to commence the already well-planned genocide. In 2007 the Rwandan government launched a formal investigation into the plane crash. The results were released in 2010, concluding that Hutu extremists were responsible for shooting down the plane in an effort to derail Habyarimana's peace negotiations with Kagame and the Tutsi rebels.

With the onset of the genocide in April 1994, Kagame and the RPF renewed their civil war against the government, and by the end of May they controlled most of Rwanda. Kigali was captured on July 4, 1994, and the remnants of the extremist Hutu Power government of Jean Kambanda fled. Once the conflict was over, Kagame became vice president and defense minister under Pasteur Bizimungu, but many believed that Kagame was the real power behind the presidency. Bizimungu, who was a deputy commander of the RPF and an ethnic Hutu, eventually came into conflict with Kagame over the direction of postgenocide policy-making. He resigned in March 2000, and Kagame became caretaker president. He was then elected in a landslide on August 25, 2003, in the first national elections since the genocide. Kagame won 95.5 percent of all votes cast, and was sworn in for a seven-year term on September 12, 2003. Then, on August 9, 2010, Kagame was reelected for a second seven-year term as president. In an outcome questioned by many observers from around the world as thoroughly unimaginable for a free and fair election, Kagame received 93.08 percent of the vote.

After the genocide, many of the Hutus responsible for the killing fled to neighboring Zaire (later called the Democratic Republic of the Congo, or DRC) using the country as a base from which to continue attacking Rwanda. Kagame sent Rwandan troops into the country in late 1996 in order to pursue these Hutus, in what was a clear violation of the larger country's sovereignty. Kagame now found himself embroiled in a confusing conflict in which a Congolese civil war involving forces either supporting or opposing Zairean president Mobutu Sese Seko and his adversary Laurent Kabila—and all these forces were inconsistent in which side they championed—had fragmented into a series of smaller conflicts involving competing local warlords and the government. Into this mix came the Rwandan Hutu exiles, the invading Rwandan forces, as well as an army from Museveni's Uganda. Some parts of the DRC were then occupied by Rwandan troops for the next five years. In the course of the war, the Rwandan army financed its invasion through an illegal trade in the Congo's natural resources.

Kagame's invasion of DRC has been severely criticized in several quarters, as the army was known to have committed a series of brutal (and often systematic) massacres against fleeing, unarmed Hutus. Also, in order to finance the campaign, the Rwandan military allegedly plundered vast amounts of precious minerals from the areas in eastern Congo it occupied. Kagame was known to support the rebel forces in DRC until 2002, when he signed a peace accord and agreed to remove Rwandan troops in exchange for the disarmament and repatriation of Hutu forces. This notwithstanding, a Rwandan presence—sometimes quite active and violent—remained throughout the next few years, further confusing an already confused and disastrous situation which some estimates claim have cost up to 5 million lives overall.

In the aftermath of the genocide and the 34 years of exile that preceded it, a major focus of Kagame's presidency has been to build Rwandan national unity. Accordingly, his preference for postgenocide Rwanda is for the nation's citizens to downplay all references to their separate ethnic identities. During the 2003 presidential campaign he portrayed himself as a Rwandan rather than a Tutsi, and has since made it illegal for any politician or citizen to make statements encouraging ethnic animosity or expressing ethnic solidarity. Some have seen this as the tip of an antidemocratic iceberg that suppresses human rights, and Kagame has been criticized as an authoritarian leader who often disregards and stifles public opinion. The international humanitarian monitoring organization Human Rights Watch has accused Rwandan police of several instances of extrajudicial killings and deaths in custody, and Kagame has been accused of being a ruthless and repressive leader intolerant of criticism. Some have pointed out that he favors Tutsis over Hutus in senior positions.

On the other hand, Kagame's leadership style has enabled him to devote much of his attention to issues of postgenocide justice, peace building, and reconciliation, often without dissent. Other areas of priority have included economic development, good governance, women's empowerment, and advancement of education. Kagame has received international recognition for his leadership of what was a broken country, and he is considered by many to be one of the most dynamic and effective leaders in Africa in the early 21st century.

PAUL R. BARTROP

See also: Arusha Accords; Habyarimana, Juvénal; Kambanda, Jean; Rwandan Patriotic Front

Further Reading

Bodnarchuk, Kari. *Rwanda: A Country Torn Apart.* Minneapolis, MN: Lerner Publishing Group, 1998.

Eltringham, Nigel. *Accounting for Horror: Post-Genocide Debates in Rwanda.* London: Pluto Press, 2004.

Kajuga, Jerry

Jerry Robert Kajuga was the founder and national president of the Rwandan youth militia known as Interahamwe ("those who stick together"). Born in 1960, Kajuga was the child of a mixed Hutu-Tutsi marriage. His father was a highly respected Episcopal priest of Tutsi background who had married a Hutu woman, and it is believed that the family at first disguised their official identity as Tutsi and "passed" as Hutus.

The genesis of the Interahamwe movement, which Kajuga founded and of which he was president, can be located in a number of junior soccer clubs, one of which, the *Loisirs* ("Leisure") club, Kajuga coached. Under his direction, Interahamwe was transformed from a youth organization when it was founded in 1990, to a radical Hutu killing machine, as the anti-Tutsi campaign of hatred fostered by Rwandan president Juvénal Habyarimana intensified throughout 1992 and 1993. After Habyarimana was killed in a plane crash as the result of a missile attack on April 6, 1994, it was Interahamwe, together with the Rwandan army and the presidential guard, which took the lead in the massacre of Tutsis throughout the country.

The Interahamwe was comprised of young males who were connected with the youth wing of Habyarimana's Mouvement Révolutionnaire National pour le Développement (the National Revolutionary Movement for Development, or MRND) party. They were among the most active killers during the 1994 Rwandan genocide. As a paramilitary unit, Interahamwe was fundamental to the Rwandan Genocide, and the most important of the anti-Tutsi militias prevailing throughout the country.

Originally trained by the French at Habyarimana's request, the Interahamwe formed the shock troops of the Hutu war of extermination. They were the most radical of the many factions opposed to the Arusha peace process of 1992. In the years prior to the genocide, the Interahamwe engaged in lethal street fights hoping to upset the social order. Their source of weapons was provided through the army, allowing them to engage in daily murder sprees employing machetes and other implements. On January 26, 1994, MRND leaders, including Kajuga, reportedly met to discuss ways to create conflict between the Interahamwe and Belgian soldiers serving with the United Nations Assistance Mission for Rwanda (UNAMIR). The militias were ordered to never obey orders from the Belgians, to call for support from surrounding areas whenever confronted by Belgians, and to get as many people as possible from the surrounding area to witness the confrontation. Then, on February 25, 1994, Kajuga presided over a meeting of Interahamwe leaders that recommended greater vigilance against Tutsis in Kigali; this resulted in lists of Tutsis in the city being drawn up, presumably for any future action that might be taken. The leaders decided on a system of communications using telephones, whistles, runners, and public criers. They ordered militia members to be ready to act at any moment using traditional weapons and firearms. The meeting ordered the Interahamwe to be ready to come to the aid of members of the militias of other radical Hutu political parties such as the Impuzamugambi of the extremist Coalition pour la Défense de la République, or CDR.

To keep the Interahamwe in check, there were periodic purges of the most zealous members, who wished to proceed at a pace faster than that preferred by their political leaders; thus, when the call for action finally came after Habyarimana's assassination on April 6, 1994, none were more bloodthirsty than the Interahamwe. From this time on, Interahamwe killing units were left largely to their own devices. They knew their instructions, and required little further prompting.

Right up to the end of the genocide, all members and cells of the Interahamwe were carefully monitored by Joseph Nzirorera (b. 1950), the secretary-general of the MRND, even though the day-to-day affairs of the Interahamwe were coordinated by its vice president, Georges Rutaganda. The Interahamwe forcefully recruited peasants in order to "popularize" their role as mass killers. When the killing ceased, many of the Interahamwe members managed to escape to eastern Congo. What is most significant about the existence of the Interahamwe and its actions is that they demonstrate that the genocide was far from spontaneous but, instead, a carefully planned campaign of extermination which had its executioners prepared and waiting to go into action long before the trigger on the night of April 6, 1994.

Kajuga justified the role of the organization of which he was national president on the grounds that Rwanda's Tutsis were waging a concerted offensive, through the Tutsi-led Rwandan Patriotic Front (RPF), to destroy the Hutus. A fanatic of the most extreme caliber, Kajuga was active throughout the genocide not only in running the Interahamwe, but also in his dealings with Rwanda's Hutu Power interim government and with the UNAMIR forces under General Roméo Dallaire who were trying desperately to save lives.

During the genocide, Kajuga kept his brother Wyclif at the Hotel des Mille Collines in Kigali, as a safeguard due to the family's hidden Tutsi identity. This may have contributed to the success of the Mille Collines in remaining safe from the genocide. The Mille Collines stood as an island of refuge for a select few Tutsis threatened with extermination, largely at the initiative of the hotel manager, a Hutu named Paul Rusesabagina. Throughout the genocide, the hotel, in a garden setting at the intersection of the Avenue de la République and the Avenue de l'Armée, in central Kigali, was protected by a constant United Nations presence through UNAMIR troops.

In July 1994, as the forces of the Rwandan Patriotic Front conquered more and more of Rwanda and began to close in on Kigali, the Interahamwe fled in advance of their arrival. Kajuga fled along with many thousands of his militia members. He escaped capture within Rwanda until 1996, and then slipped into Zaire, where he lived for another two years. In 1998 he was arrested by UN security forces, and was taken to Kigali, where he stood trial before a Rwandan national court. He was sentenced to life imprisonment for war crimes.

PAUL R. BARTROP

See also: Coalition Pour la Défense de la Règublique; Interahamwe; United Nations Assistance Mission for Rwanda

Further Reading

Dallaire, Roméo. *Shake Hands with the Devil: The Failure of Humanity in Rwanda.* Toronto: Random House, 2004.

Shaw, Martin. *War and Genocide: Organized Killing in Modern Society.* Cambridge, UK: Polity, 2003.

Kambanda, Jean

Jean Kambanda was the prime minister of Rwanda during the genocide that took place between April and July 1994. After President Juvénal Habyarimana and Prime Minister Agathe Uwilingiyimana had been assassinated—the former as the result of a missile attack on his plane by unknown attackers on April 6; the latter, a Hutu moderate, murdered by Hutu extremists a day later—Kambanda was sworn in as head of an interim government on April 9.

A member of the Mouvement démocratique républicain (Democratic Republican Movement, or MDR), Kambanda remained prime minister throughout the period of the genocide, directing general government policy with regard to the genocide of Rwanda's Tutsi population. He broadcast messages on Radio Télévision Libre des Mille Collines (RTLM) inciting Hutus to kill Tutsis, and urged Hutus to construct roadblocks throughout Rwanda in order to prevent Tutsis fleeing the country. He also traveled throughout Rwanda for the express purpose of rousing the Hutu population to undertake genocide, while at the same time providing weapons and ammunition to Hutu militia movements such as the Interahamwe and the Impuzamugambi. As the head of the government he also contributed indirectly to the killing by failing—or rather, refusing—to condemn the militias when they broke the law by killing Tutsis and destroying vast amounts of property.

Jean Kambanda, prime minister of Rwanda (1994), pleads guilty to genocide before the United Nations' International Criminal Tribunal for Rwanda on September 3, 1998. (Alessandro Abbonizio/AFP/Getty Images)

Born on October 19, 1955, Jean Kambanda was an educated member of Rwanda's dominant Hutu middle class, with a degree in commercial engineering. He was director of the Union of Popular Banks of Rwanda from May 1989 to April 1994, and, with an interest in politics, had become vice president of the Butare section of the MDR by the time the genocide broke out in April 1994. The MDR had earlier been promised the position of prime minister in the negotiations that led to the signing of the Arusha Accords of August 4, 1993. This was a series of agreements made between Habyarimana's government of Rwanda and the rebel Rwandan Patriotic Front (RPF), and was designed to end the country's civil strife and help bring about a regime based on democratic principles. In the transitional government that would follow, the MDC and other parties were guaranteed certain compromises, one of which involved earmarking specific positions in any future administration. Owing to a series of internal party intrigues, however, the party's first choice, Faustin Twagiramungu, was bypassed for the job by Kambanda, who then remained prime minister throughout the hundred days of the genocide. (Ironically, Twagiramungu became prime minister after Kambanda at the end of the genocide. He retained that position until his resignation in 1995.) When the forces of the RPF defeated the army of the interim government on July 19, 1994, Kambanda fled Rwanda and his government collapsed.

He was on the run for three years, until arrested in Nairobi, Kenya, on July 18, 1997, after a seven-week stakeout by a multinational team of police investigators. He was transferred immediately to the jurisdiction of the International Criminal Tribunal for Rwanda (ICTR) in Arusha, Tanzania, and was arraigned on a variety of charges relating directly to genocide and crimes against humanity. These were: genocide, and conspiracy to commit genocide; public and direct incitation to commit genocide; aiding and abetting genocide; failing in his duty to prevent the genocide which occurred while he was prime minister; and two counts of crimes against humanity. Acknowledging his responsibility, on May 1, 1998, he pleaded guilty on all counts. The court sentenced him to life imprisonment, the maximum penalty that can be imposed by the ICTR, on September 4, 1998.

After this, however, he rescinded his confession and appealed against his conviction. His defense was that his original confession had been in error, and that his legal counsel had misrepresented him. Indeed, there was no little controversy surrounding the appointment of Kambanda's counsel, who was chosen by the ICTR Registrar from a limited list that excluded French and Canadian Francophone lawyers. This forced Kambanda to defend himself for four months, effectively denying him the same access to legal process available to all other accused. Allegations began to be made that the trial was thus for show—to make the ICTR look good—rather than for the purpose of pursuing justice. After then receiving competent legal counsel, his attorneys argued that Kambanda had in fact been a sham figurehead, a puppet in the hands of a genocidal military led by such figures as Colonel Théoneste Bagosora, who used Kambanda for the purpose of legitimizing their own control of the country by cloaking it in the mantle of constitutional respectability. The Tribunal was petitioned to reduce Kambanda's sentence to two years' imprisonment owing to his having been forced to act "under duress with limited responsibility." The ICTR, for its part, concluded that this defense against a charge of genocide was irrelevant, and dismissed the appeal on October 19, 2000. The original verdict was upheld on all counts, and he was transferred to Bamako Central Prison, Bamako, Mali, where he is currently serving his sentence.

The significance of the Kambanda verdict is that it was the first occasion on which a head of government had pleaded guilty to committing genocide, and the first such conviction. As the highest-ranking political leader in the custody of the ICTR, Kambanda's verdict has further enhanced the legal principle that refuses to recognize state immunity as a legitimate defense against genocide. This principle, first set down as one of the "Nuremberg Principles" adopted by the United Nations International Law Commission in 1950, accepts that every person is responsible for their own actions, and that, as a result, no one stands above international law. The defense of "following superior orders" is nullified by these principles, and in the specific case of Kambanda the third principle prevails: "being a Head of State or a government official does not absolve a person from the responsibility of having committed a criminal act, if the act committed is criminal within international law."

PAUL R. BARTROP

See also: Arusha Accords; Habyarimana, Juvénal; Interahamwe; International Criminal Tribunal for Rwanda; Radio-Télévision Libre des Mille Collines; Uwilingiyimana, Agathe

Further Reading

Melvern, Linda. *Conspiracy to Murder: The Rwandan Genocide*. London: Verso, 2006.

Prunier, Gérard. *The Rwanda Crisis, 1959–1994: History of a Genocide*. Kampala: Fountain Publishers, 1995.

Kamuhanda Trial

In April 2001, Jean de Dieu Kamuhanda, former minister of higher education and scientific research in the Rwandan interim government of 1994, was placed on trial in the International Criminal Tribunal for Rwanda (ICTR) on nine counts of genocide and crimes against humanity. Kamuhanda was accused of leading the massacre of 800 Tutsis at a church in Gikomero commune, Kigali-Rural Prefecture, in April 1994. He was also charged because the interim government in which he held high office either directed or failed to stop many of the 1994 massacres during the Rwandan genocide. Kamuhanda was arrested on November 26, 1999, in France. He fought extradition, but was soon sent to the ICTR.

The trial witnessed numerous delays: first, two of the presiding judges had to be replaced because one died and another was promoted. Subsequently, scheduling conflicts arose with other trials that were sharing the same court space. After almost two years, the trial had met in session for only 73 days. Initially, the prosecution hoped to try Kamuhanda along with seven other former government officials, but the ICTR rejected the idea of a joint trial. Some critics argued that Kamuhanda's prosecution was less important than other government officials and that his prosecution was being driven by a political pressures. The prosecution portrayed Kamuhanda as the instigator of the events at Gikomero, as well as an influential member of the Movement of the Republic for National Development (MRND). He was reportedly promoted to minister in May 1994 because of his support for the ongoing massacres. The defense countered that Kamuhanda had been in Kigali at the time of the Gikomero attacks and could not possibly have traveled there given the fighting in the region. The defense also argued that he was never influential in the government and that, base on previous legal precedents; he could not be convicted simply for being part of an organization engaged in killings.

Kamuhanda was tried in the reconstituted Trial Chamber II, with Judge William Sekule of Tanzania presiding; Winston Matazima Maqutu of Lesotho and Arlette Ramaroson of Madagascar also served on the judicial panel. Douglas Moore of Ireland led the prosecution team, while Aicha Conde of Guinea directed Kamuhanda's defense. In August 2002, as the defense opened its case, it successfully argued that the count of conspiracy to commit genocide should be dropped for lack of evidence, so Kamuhanda now faced a total of eight counts.

In presenting its case, the prosecution called 27 witnesses. Most testified about events that took place in Gikomero in mid-April 1994. According to their accounts, Kamuhanda delivered weapons to local Hutu gendarmes and members of the Interahamwe. He then visited the church compound where many Tutsis were seeking refuge and told officials "to begin work." Hours later, hundreds were killed in the compound. The prosecution portrayed Kamuhanda as an influential party official who had been a presidential adviser even before his appointment as minister. This claim of previous advising was crucial because Kamuhanda did not become minister until May 25, 1994, almost two months after large-scale killings had begun.

The defense did not deny that a genocide had occurred, but questioned the reliability of the witnesses that placed Kamuhanda in Gikomero. Several of the witnesses reported only what they had heard from others. Such hearsay evidence was allowed by the Tribunal, but was considered weak. Other witnesses stated that they saw a man at Gikomero, but only later identified him as Kamuhanda. The defense questioned these identifications. Some witnesses identified Kamuhanda in court, but he was the only male on his side of the courtroom. The defense also presented Kamuhanda's testimony, supported by that of some two dozen friends and relatives, that he was in Kigali from April 6 until April 18 and thus could not have been responsible for events that took place in Gikomero during that time. To answer the question of whether he might have briefly visited Gikomero, the defense presented witnesses who testified that fighting in the area made it impossible to travel between Kigali and Gikomero. The defense also tried to counter the portrayal of Kamuhanda as a key party figure. In their accounts, Kamuhanda never had close ties to the interim president or other high-ranking officials. Defense lawyers claimed that he had risen quickly in the government because of his talent and efficiency, not as a reward for his support of massacres. Furthermore, the defense argued, he accepted the promotion to minister because he feared for his life and was never more than a figurehead leader.

Kamuhanda was ultimately convicted of genocide and of extermination as a crime against humanity, but was acquitted of conspiracy to commit genocide, rape as a crime against humanity, and war crimes and other inhumane acts. He was sentenced to life imprisonment. Following an appeal, his sentence was affirmed in 2005 and on December 7, 2008, he was transferred to Mali to serve his sentence.

JOHN DIETRICH

See also: International Criminal Tribunal for Rwanda; Rwanda

Further Reading

Cruvellier, Thierry. *Court of Remorse: Inside the International Criminal Court for Rwanda.* Madison: University of Wisconsin Press, 2010.

Des Forges, Alison, and Longman, Timothy. "Legal Responses to Genocide in Rwanda." In *My Neighbor, My Enemy: Justice and Community in the Aftermath of Mass Atrocity.* Edited by Eric Stover and Harvey M. Weinstein, 49–63. Cambridge: Cambridge University Press, 2004.

Kangura

Kangura was a virulent anti-Tutsi newspaper and pro-Hutu propaganda vehicle that played a major role in laying the ideological and social foundations of the 1994 Rwandan Genocide. Kangura, which translates from Kinyarwanda (Rwandan) as "Wake Them Up," was edited by Hutu businessman and journalist Hassan Ngeze. The paper's first edition came out in May 1990, to coincide with the start of the Rwandan Civil War and the full flowering of the Hutu Power Movement; the last published newspaper came out in February 1994, less than two months prior to the beginning of the genocide. As the title implies, the publication was intended to "educate" and "inform" the Hutu majority about the alleged dangers posed by the minority Tutsi population. It was also intended to expose moderate, pro-Tutsi Hutus, who were branded as enemies of the Hutus.

In December 1990, *Kangura* published what was perhaps its most inflammatory and controversial material—the "Hutu Ten Commandments." Many of the so-called commandments echoed long-standing policies and attitudes toward the Tutsis, but they certainly helped galvanize Hutu public opinion against the Tutsis, and the material was frequently re-published. These commandments forbade marriage or friendship with or support to Tutsi women; extolled the superiority of Hutu women; exhorted Hutus to abandon Tutsi spouses or relatives; asserted that Tutsis could not hold any positions in government or the military; argued that education should be dominated by Hutus; instructed all Hutus to show no mercy toward the Tutsis; ordered Hutus to band together to fight the "Tutsi menace"; and encouraged educators to instruct all Hutus in "Hutu ideology" and the revolution Hutus began in 1959.

Through the constant repetition of the commandments and the virulently anti-Tutsi articles and editorials, *Kangura* served to dehumanize the Tutsis while giving Hutu readers the impression that oppressing and hurting Tutsis was acceptable. The newspaper frequently referred to the Tutsis as Inyenzi (cockroaches), with the implication that like cockroaches, the Tutsis were dirty vermin who had to be exterminated. The paper also issued frequent (and entirely unfounded) warnings that the Tutsis were out to enslave or eradicate the Hutus. Because of its clever manipulations and the fact that Hutus significantly outnumbered Tutsis, *Kangura* enjoyed a wide readership, and there were no Tutsi publications that could compete with it.

Not surprisingly, the newspaper vilified the Tutsi-dominated Rwandan Patriotic Front (RPF) and exhorted Hutus to support the government in the ongoing civil war with the RPF. It refused to support President Juvénal Habyarimana's efforts to bring an end to the conflict or to seek any accommodation with the RPF. Kangura bitterly denounced the August 1993 Arusha Accords as a traitorous sell-out to the RPF and the minority Tutsis. The newspaper worked closely with other pro-Hutu propaganda media outlets, especially Radio-Télévision Libre des Mille Collines (RTLM), with whom it frequently coordinated its propaganda and sensationalist reporting. Ngeze was in fact one of the main program directors of RTLM.

After the United Nations Assistance Mission for Rwanda (UNAMIR) was dispatched to Rwanda to help the country implement the terms of the Arusha Accords and to prevent a flare-up in violence, *Kangura* savagely attacked the UN mission. These attacks included spurious claims that the UNAMIR was a tool of the Tutsis and was sent to Rwanda to aid in a Tutsi takeover of the government. By early 1994, the newspaper was openly advocating the mass extermination of Tutsis, especially those in the RPF, to avoid having Rwanda overrun by Tutsis and their Hutu supporters. *Kangura* also published the names of Hutus whose "loyalty" to their ethnicity was questionable. Later, when the genocide began in April 1994, many of these Hutus were murdered as "traitors."

Although *Kangura* ceased publication in February 1994, there is no doubt that it contributed greatly to the anti-Tutsi hatred and hysteria that ultimately manifested itself in the Rwandan Genocide. In December 2003, the International Criminal Tribunal for Rwanda (ICTR) convicted Ngeze of various crimes associated with the genocide. He was given a life sentence, which in 2008 was reduced to 35 years in prison.

PAUL G. PIERPAOLI JR.

See also: Arusha Accords; Hutus; International Criminal Tribunal for Rwanda; Media Trial in Rwanda; Ngeze, Hassan; Radio-Télévision Libre des Mille Collines; Rwanda; Rwandan Genocide, Role of Propaganda in the; Rwandan Patriotic Front; Tutsis

Further Reading

Kressel, Neil Jeffrey. *Mass Hate: The Global Rise of Genocide and Terror.* New York: Plenum Press, 1996.

Valentino, Benjamin A. *Final Solutions: Mass Killing and Genocide in the Twentieth Century.* Ithaca, NY: Cornell University Press, 2004.

Karamira, Froduald

Froduald Karamira was a radical Rwandan politician prior to and during the genocide of 1994. Born on August 14, 1947, in Mushubati, central Rwanda, to a mixed Tutsi-Hutu family, he could have claimed either identity. He began life as a Tutsi, but started to identify as a Hutu as he grew older. As an adult he was accepted as such by other Hutus. Entering Hutu society provided him with opportunities to gain in importance both politically and economically, and he advanced himself to such an extent that by the late 1980s he was the owner of several properties in downtown Kigali.

As a member of the Mouvement Démocratique Républicain (MDR) party, Karamira became vice president and was a leader in the party's extremist wing, MDR-Power. He represented a faction that was hostile to any cooperation with the rebel Rwandan Patriotic Front (RPF), and was vehemently opposed to the Arusha Accords, the peace settlement between the Rwandan government and the RPF signed on August 4, 1993.

Already in July 1993, as the negotiations leading to Arusha were taking place, Karamira engineered a split in the party over the extent to which it had become radicalized. Karamira's perspective was that the party was not sufficiently pro-Hutu, and that any form of negotiation with the RPF was an intolerable ethnic betrayal. On October 23, 1993, he made a highly inflammatory speech at the Nyamirambo Stadium in Kigali, in which he called on the Hutus to "look within ourselves for the enemy which is amongst us," and rise up to "take the necessary measures" to target that enemy. In this speech he first introduced the concept of "Hutu Power," which, from then on, designated the coalition of the Hutu extremists and became their slogan. Karamira was now recognized as the principal ideologue of the Hutu Power idea.

After the death of Hutu president Juvénal Habyarimana on April 6, 1994, Karamira participated in the creation of Rwanda's interim government, a regime that quickly became radicalized along pure ethnic Hutu lines. Karamira's party, MDR-Power, participated actively in the genocide of Rwanda's Tutsis that began almost immediately. Karamira went on the air daily on Radio-Télévision Libre des Mille Collines, the rabidly anti-Tutsi private radio station, delivering messages that were hate-filled incitements to commit mass murder against the Tutsis.

It has been alleged that he was personally responsible for hundreds of murders, and directly answerable for the deaths of at least 13 Tutsi members of his own family. He was, indeed, well placed to commit such atrocities as a local leader of the anti-Tutsi Interahamwe militia. As the rebel forces of the RPF closed in on the interim government in June and July 1994, Karamira fled, disappearing from view. In June 1996 he was arrested in Mumbai, India, and extradited, via Addis Ababa, to Rwanda.

While he was on the run, the newly installed RPF Rwandan government indicted Karamira for genocide, murder, conspiracy, and nonassistance to people in danger. On January 13, 1997, with Karamira now confined, his trial got underway in a Special Trial Chamber in Kigali. The indictment was amended by this stage to also include crimes against humanity and inciting genocide through his daily radio speeches, as well as playing a key role in the creation and arming of the Interahamwe and in providing them with arms. Karamira's defense attorney asked for a deferment of the hearing, stating that he had not had the possibility of meeting with Karamira before the start of the trial. The trial judge granted this request, and postponed the start of the trial for a few days until January 28, 1997.

The trial, when it did come, was short. On February 14, 1997, Froduald Karamira was found guilty of the crimes of genocide, murder, conspiracy, and nonassistance to people in danger, and in organizing the implementation of the 1994 genocide. He was sentenced to death. He appealed to the Kigali Appeals Court, but on September 12, 1997, the court rejected the appeal.

On April 24, 1998, in a public event at the same Nyamirambo Stadium in Kigali where he had made his most inflammatory public speeches, Karamira was publicly executed by firing squad. The event was carefully stage-managed before thousands of cheering spectators, and was met with considerable protest from human rights groups around the globe. Karamira was not alone when facing the execution squad; a number of other *génocidaires* convicted of involvement in the genocide were also shot on or around April 24, in similar circumstances. On the same day as Karamira's execution, for example, a schoolteacher, Virginie Mukankusi (the first woman to be executed for the Rwandan Genocide), a former medical assistant, Déogratias Bizimana, and a farmer, Egide Gatanazi, were also publicly executed.

The trials and executions took place pursuant to a new postgenocide Rwandan law, Organic Law no. 08/96, dated August 30, 1996. Special Trial chambers, such as that which tried Karamira, were set up specifically for the purpose of dealing with alleged *génocidaires,* as it was felt that existing courts that existed before the genocide did not have the legal competence to try cases related to genocide and crimes against humanity. Karamira was thus subjected to a new and special form of justice, with the death penalty on the table. This can be contrasted with the UN-established International Criminal Tribunal for Rwanda, which tries major cases in Arusha, Tanzania, but does not have the death penalty as the ultimate sanction.

For its part, Rwanda abolished the death penalty in 2007. Those executed in 1998, including Karamira, were among the very last to have been executed in Rwanda in accordance with Rwandan courtroom procedures.

PAUL R. BARTROP

See also: Interahamwe; International Criminal Tribunal for Rwanda; Radio-Télévision Libre des Mille Collines

Further Reading

Melvern, Linda. *Conspiracy to Murder: The Rwandan Genocide.* London: Verso, 2006.

Prunier, Gérard. *The Rwanda Crisis, 1959–1994: History of a Genocide.* Kampala: Fountain Publishers, 1995.

Kayishema Trial

The 1997–1999 trial of Clement Kayishema, the former prefect of Kibuye in Rwanda, by the International Criminal Tribunal for Rwanda (ICTR). Kayishema was indicted on 24 counts of genocide and crimes against humanity. The charges were based on four separate incidents, three occurrences in which Kayishema reportedly led attacks on Tutsis who had sought refuge in churches and other communal locations, and one incident of a more sustained effort to kill Tutsis in the hills of Bisesero. On the latter charge, businessman Obed Ruzindana was tried along with Kayishema. The trial was one of the first conducted by the

ICTR and was therefore watched carefully for legal precedents. It was also hoped that indicting and convicting local officials would serve as a stepping stone to convictions of higher-level Rwandan officials. Kayishema based his defense on claims that he was not physically at some of the massacre sites and that, given the chaos of the period, the prefect and government was powerless to stop local mobs. The judges rejected Kayishema's account and found him guilty of genocide in each of the four incidents. Kayishema was given a life sentence. Ruzindana was also found guilty of genocide, but was given a 25-year sentence. The judges, however, dealt the prosecution a severe blow by ruling, for various legal reasons, that Kayishema could not be found guilty on any of the 24 counts of crimes against humanity. Both sides appealed the case. While the genocide rulings were upheld, the prosecution was embarrassed by having its appeal on the crimes against humanity charges thrown after missing a filing deadline.

Kayishema had been a physician who became prefect of Kibuye in 1992. As prefect, he was the top government official in the region and had command of several law enforcement groups. He also reportedly had some influence over the Interahamwe, an unofficial paramilitary group of extremist Hutus. When ethnic tensions and killings mounted in April 1994, many Tutsis sought refuge in churches and other communal locations. Kayishema reportedly ordered and led attacks on three of the major refuges, the local catholic church, Home St. Jean, a local stadium, and a church in Mubuga. Additionally, Kayishema, along with Ruzindana, reportedly helped organize and direct a major effort to kill tens of thousands of Tutsis who had fled into the hills of Bisesero.

In December 1995, Kayishema became one of the first Rwandans indicted by the Tribunal. For each of the three refuge attacks and the fighting in Bisesero, he was indicted for genocide, crimes against humanity (murder, extermination, and other inhumane acts) and violations of the Geneva Conventions. The trial began on April 11, 1997, in trial chamber II. Judge William Sekule of Tanzania presided and was joined by Judge Yakov Ostrovsky of the Russian Federation and Tafazzal Hossain Khan of Bangladesh. There were three prosecutors, including Brenda Sue Thornton, who made many of the key arguments. Kayishema was defended by Andre Ferran, who many regarded as the rhetorical star of the trial.

The prosecution employed more than 50 witnesses, 400 pieces of physical evidence, and 3,400 pages of files in an attempt to establish Kayishema's knowledge of and direct control over the massacres. The prosecution also relied heavily on forensic evidence from the sites. Ferran tried to win sympathy for his client by pointing out the extreme disparity of available resources for the prosecution and defense. He also argued that Kayishema was not even at the sites of the massacres. Kayishema's wife and others stated that Kayishema had gone into hiding between April 16th and 20th, and thus could not possibly have been involved. The prosecution countered with several witnesses who reported seeing Kayishema at the sites discussing plans, signaling the start of the attacks, and participating in the attacks. The defense also tried to portray Kayishema as a man under threat from extremists and powerless to stop the violence. The highlight of the trial was Kayishema's six days of testimony, during which he vigorously rejected the prosecution's contentions.

The trial reached its conclusion on May 21, 1999. In its judgment, the ICTR judges largely echoed the prosecution's view of events. They rejected Kayishema's alibi and ruled that there was clear evidence that he had led a systematic effort to destroy the Tutsi people. Therefore, they found him guilty on all four counts of genocide. They then ruled that the prosecution had not shown a direct link between the specific crimes and the existing armed conflict in Rwanda, so the Geneva Convention did not apply. Next, they ruled that the indictment for "other inhumane acts" did not stipulate the crimes the prosecution intended to prosecute, so they found Kayishema not guilty on those counts. Finally, in a controversial split decision, they ruled that, because the genocide counts and the crimes against humanity counts for murder and extermination were based on the same incidents and same evidence, finding Kayishema guilty on all counts would mean sentencing him twice for the same crime. They therefore rejected the crimes against humanity counts on a vote of two to one. On appeal, the judgments were upheld and Kayishema began serving his life sentence.

JOHN DIETRICH

See also: International Criminal Tribunal for Rwanda; Rwanda

Further Reading

Cruvellier, Thierry. *Court of Remorse: Inside the International Criminal Court for Rwanda*. Madison: University of Wisconsin Press, 2010.

Des Forges, Alison, and Timothy Longman. "Legal Responses to Genocide in Rwanda." In *My Neighbor, My Enemy: Justice and Community in the Aftermath of Mass Atrocity*. Edited by Eric Stover and Harvey M. Weinstein, 49–63. Cambridge: Cambridge University Press, 2004.

Kovanda, Karel

Karel Kovanda is a Czech diplomat who served as the permanent representative of the Czech Republic to the United Nations. At the UN Security Council in 1994, during the Rwandan Genocide, he worked tirelessly to bring the attention of the world to the genocide as it was taking place.

Kovanda was born on October 5, 1944, in the northern English village of Gilsland, Cumbria. Active in the Czech student movement opposed to the communist regime between 1964 and 1969, he studied as an undergraduate at the Prague School of Agriculture and became president of the National Students' Union. In November 1968, during the period of government liberalization known as the Prague Spring, he was chairman of the student strike organized by the Action Committee. In the spring of 1969 he was elected chairman of the Association of University Students of Bohemia and Moravia, but in the communist clampdown after the Prague Spring his position became untenable, such that in 1970 he left Czechoslovakia as a political exile and moved to the United States. Here, he earned a PhD in political science at the Massachusetts Institute of Technology in 1975, a subject he taught at a number of southern California colleges between 1975 and 1977. From 1977 to 1979 he worked in China as a consultant to Radio Beijing, and from 1980 to 1990, back in the United States, he worked in private business as a manager with international responsibilities. He also worked as a freelance journalist and translator (he is fluent in Czech, English, Slovak, Spanish, and French, and is conversant in German and Russian). In 1985 he completed an MBA at Pepperdine University, Los Angeles.

In November 1989 the communist government of Czechoslovakia fell, and by 1990 Kovanda had returned from exile. Joining the civil service, between 1991 and 1993 he headed the administration section at the Ministry of Foreign Affairs, and in 1993 became a political director at the ministry with responsibility for European and North American affairs. In June 1993 he was appointed the Czech Republic's ambassador to the United Nations, aligning with his country's membership of the Security Council in 1994–1995.

In January 1994 the Czech Republic assumed the presidency of the Security Council, with Kovanda in the chair. In this capacity, he received a visit from one Claude De Saide, representing the Rwandan Patriotic Front (RPF). It was the first connection Kovanda had had with any problems in the tiny African country. Later that month, the Department of Peacekeeping Operations, led by Kofi Annan, received the so-called Genocide Fax from the UN force commander in Rwanda, General Roméo Dallaire. In subsequent comments, Kovanda wrote that the secretary-general, Boutros Boutros-Ghali, did not share the information received from Dallaire with the Security Council. This was a prelude of things to come, as succeeding weeks and months were to show. Kovanda later recalled that the Secretariat constantly refused to pass information on to the Security Council, severely inhibiting the Council's capacity to act to stop the crisis. After the genocide exploded, Kovanda later wrote, there was a long time during which events in Rwanda were far from clear.

The Security Council was constantly frustrated about the lack of information coming from the Secretariat, information on which it depended in order to be able to assess the situation. Moreover, Rwanda, governed by the Hutu Power administration of Juvénal Habiyarimana and the interim government that followed his death on April 6, 1994, was, ironically, also a serving member on the Security Council at the same time as the genocide. Overall, factors such as these led to a real lack of understanding being conveyed to the Council as to what was happening in Rwanda and how it should be handled.

While it was very difficult for Kovanda and the Security Council (and in particular, the states that were not permanent members, such as the Czech Republic) to obtain full or accurate information, that did not stop some from trying to do so. At one point, Kovanda invited an expert from Human Rights Watch, Alison Des Forges, to meet with the Czech delegation to share with his colleagues from the Security Council what she knew about Rwanda.

Kovanda was motivated to try to do something to stop the killing in Rwanda for personal as well as international reasons. With the memory of many members of father's family having been murdered in the Holocaust, Kovanda at one point told the Security Council that the suggestion that the RPF should negotiate a cease-fire with the Hutu Power government was akin to asking Hitler to reach a ceasefire with the Jews.

His frustration at having to sit in Security Council meetings to discuss Rwanda, where no action was ever contemplated to help the Tutsis, was intense. All around him, he saw evidence from nonofficial sources of the immensity of the killing that was taking place in Rwanda. In an interview for the 1999 *Frontline* documentary *The Triumph of Evil* (prod. Mike Robinson and Ben Loeterman), he was asked by reporter Steve Bradshaw whether he felt that UN inaction was leading to lives being at stake in the Security Council chamber. Kovanda's emotional response was unequivocal: "Oh, heaven—heaven knows, yes. Yes! There were lives at stake! Lives which were just like sand disappearing through our hands day after day. You've got 10,000 today, 12,000 tomorrow, and if you don't do something today, then tomorrow there will be more. If you don't do something this week, then next week there will be more, with no end in sight at the time. No end in sight."

Moreover, he was personally informed by his superiors in Prague not to call what was happening in Rwanda by the name "genocide." From where this order originated he was not sure, but he recalled being informed that it was the United States that had approached the Czech government with the request that Kovanda "lay off pushing Rwanda," and especially referring to "genocide." Kovanda was not sure whether the pressure was coming from the U.S. representatives in Prague or from the State Department in Washington, but he was certain the United States had communicated this to the Czech leadership.

Kovanda was bitterly disappointed that his own small country, with its history of having been abandoned by the international community in 1938, should be prepared to do so with regard to another small country, this time in the centre of Africa. Despite the instructions he received from Prague, he did what he could to disseminate the information being received from the nongovernmental organizations operating in Africa, and led the Czech delegation in being the first to articulate the word genocide publicly at a Security Council meeting concerning Mozambique on May 5, 1994. At the same meeting, he expressed shock that neither the Security Council nor the Secretariat had so far used the word describing the events that were taking place. Taking a leadership role in the absence of one, he then directed the sessions which resulted not only in the Council adopting a statement using the UN Genocide Convention to describe what was happening in Rwanda as genocide, but led to the eventual deployment of a reinforced "UNAMIR II" force that would have much more authority than Dallaire's United Nations Assistance Mission for Rwanda (UNAMIR) possessed originally.

After Kovanda left the United Nations in February 1997, he held a number of other important positions in the Czech Foreign Ministry, including deputy minister of foreign affairs (1997–1998) and ambassador to NATO (1998–2005). In April 2005 he went to Brussels to become deputy director general for external relations of the European Commission. From then until he left the post in 2010, he was responsible for the Common and Foreign Security

Policy (CFSP), multilateral relations and human rights, and relations with North America, East Asia, Australia, New Zealand and (non-EU) Western Europe, and the European Free Trade Association (EFTA).

On July 4, 2010, Kovanda received Rwanda's Campaign against Genocide Medal, the UMURINZI award, in recognition of his efforts to bring the world's attention to the genocide during 1994.

PAUL R. BARTROP

See also: Des Forges, Alison; Rwandan Genocide, U.S. Response to the; United Nations Assistance Mission for Rwanda

Further Reading

Des Forges, Alison. *Leave None to Tell the Story: Genocide in Rwanda.* New York: Human Rights Watch, 1999.

Klinghoffer, Arthur Jay. *The International Dimension of Genocide in Rwanda.* New York: New York University Press, 1998.

L

Lane, Laura

Laura Lane was a Foreign Service officer in the U.S. embassy in Kigali, Rwanda, prior to and during the earliest days of the Rwandan Genocide of 1994. Born in Evanston, Illinois, on February 1, 1967, she attended Loyola University, Chicago, where she graduated summa cum laude in political science and history, and then received a Masters degree in foreign service and international economics at Georgetown University, Washington, D.C. This strong Jesuit education assisted in providing her with a strong moral compass to guide her in her future work, and in many ways influenced her decisions during the fateful early days of the crisis in Kigali in 1994.

One of the youngest women in the Foreign Service when she went to Rwanda, she was also one of the youngest women to have passed the Foreign Service examination. Her first posting as a consular officer was to Bogotá, Colombia (1990–1992), at a time when the drug culture, violence, and corruption were making the lives of average Colombians difficult and dangerous. Lane volunteered to go to that country believing that often in the worst of situations the greatest good can be achieved through persistent effort and determination.

At the age of 26, in the fall of 1993, she undertook her second posting, to Kigali. She had requested to go to Rwanda to learn French and have a larger role in a small embassy. She was also conscious that the country was going through some momentous times, with the Arusha Agreement having just been signed between the Hutu Power government of Juvénal Habyarimana and the rebel Rwandan Patriotic Front (RPF) led by General Paul Kagame. In view of the political situation, Lane saw the possibility of helping the people in their transition through what was going to be a difficult—though hopefully, uplifting—period.

The mission in Kigali was quite small and Lane found herself to be one of only six full-time Foreign Service staff, including the ambassador. She became, in her own words, the "everything else" officer, responsible for issues relating to economics and trade, visas and passports, military security assistance and training, and many other areas. As her strength was in economic reporting, she had a huge learning curve in the other technical areas, even participating in military security assistance training and studying all she could about military command and control functions. The embassy, being a Special Embassy Program post, was not protected by U.S. Marines, though her husband, Greg, was a former U.S. Marine, so as an added measure of personal protection they both carried weapons in Kigali when they thought the situation required it.

In her military assistance role, Lane's task was to liaise with the various military parties to the Arusha Agreement, as a consequence of which she spent many hours traveling to and from Kigali and the RPF headquarters in Mulindi in northern Rwanda, making the hazardous trip crossing the demilitarized zone to see Kagame. Her task required building trust between the parties, with the United States as an impartial but friendly presence. Americans were generally viewed as being trustworthy and neutral by all sides, unlike the Belgians and French, who, it was believed, were closely aligned with the Hutu Power government and/or the RPF.

Within the embassy, almost everyone was aware that Arusha could collapse at any moment, and that just one small incident could destabilize the fragile emerging peace. The precarious situation was felt especially keenly by the deputy chief of mission, Joyce Leader, who was intimately involved with the negotiations involving the major actors.

Beginning in February 1994, the situation began visibly to deteriorate, and the cable traffic between the embassy in Kigali and the State Department in Washington flowed thick and fast. The embassy staff tried hard to explain the situation at ground level in Rwanda, and the cables sent from Kigali played a very important role in informing the UN and U.S. government of what was happening. They flagged to State that Arusha might be unraveling. The ambassador, deputy chief of mission, and Lane were fully aware that there were strong factions within the Hutu Power government that were more than just anti-Tutsi; they were opposed to anyone in favor of the peace process. The embassy staff knew a number of moderate Hutus who were likely to run up against these strong factions within the Hutu Power government, and it was recommended that a high-level response should be made from Washington and the UN to the Habyarimana government to step in and quell the poisonous atmosphere that was making deep inroads on the political culture of the country. Unfortunately, too little action followed on from these reports to prevent the cycle of violence spiraling out of control.

After Habyarimana's plane was shot down on the night of April 6, 1994, and the genocide plan began swiftly to be executed, Lane took over responsibility for coordinating the evacuation of all Americans from Rwanda. She had already done a great deal of work in the lead-up to that day in identifying where all Americans were located throughout the country, and, if at all possible, photographing them to assist with identification in the event of such an evacuation. She sincerely felt that she had a responsibility for every single American in Rwanda (which at the start of the crisis numbered 257 but ended with 258—with the birth of an American along the evacuation route), and she was determined that she would be the one to supervise their safe passage out of the country.

Examples of killing or destruction were everywhere, with the eerie sounds of piped-in classical music over the city's public speaker system as the Interahamwe and presidential guard pulled moderate Hutus and Tutsis from their homes and hiding places and killed them. At first most of the violence was in Kigali, and the terror was obvious just by looking out the window or stepping onto a sidewalk.

Washington's response to the mounting violence forced an early decision at the State Department to close the embassy.

Lane then made an extraordinary request: to keep the embassy open, even if she and her husband were the only ones there, so as to maintain an American presence that could serve as a safe haven to those who could get through the lines of fighting to the embassy and thereby be protected from the killing. Never thinking about her own personal safety, she only thought about the prospect of keeping alive whoever could make it to the embassy. Every waking minute was spent trying to work out how to help. For as long as there was an official American presence in the country prior to the evacuation of the embassy itself, she didn't sleep. She wanted to use the embassy as a base of operations not only for the evacuation of the American community, but for anyone in need. Her attitude was that if just one life could be saved, that was one life worth saving. Yet despite her pleas, Lane was forced to obey the order to leave, and begin the process of closing down the embassy. The Americans were to evacuate overland to Bujumbura, the capital of Burundi.

Before the embassy shutdown was complete and the evacuation convoys launched, Lane drafted personal, handwritten notes and left them on the desks of each one of the Foreign Service nationals (FSNs)—local Rwandan employees at the embassy—to the effect that she would do all in her power to ensure they were looked after and that she would return to Kigali as soon as possible. Tragically, only one of Lane's FSN staff would survive the genocide.

Lane helped organize multiple American evacuation convoys over the next couple of days. The last was the longest, with some 100 vehicles carrying over 600 people, only 9 of whom were American. The rest included Kenyans, Tanzanians, Germans, Belgians, and French. Lane had been in touch with the other embassies, and many of their nationals came forward for protection under the aegis of the American evacuation. The convoy also included Rwandans. Not all were Tutsis; some of them were of mixed Hutu/Tutsi background. The question of who could be saved was largely ad hoc; there was little time to plan for anything in detail, and it was difficult enough for anyone to reach the embassy in any case. Attempts were made to accommodate all who could reach the embassy compound seeking sanctuary.

The embassy had requested that the U.S. government not send in protection from the Marines stationed in Burundi and Kenya, as this could have been seen as a hostile act and/or drawn fire on the convoys and made a complicated support mission even more challenging. Instead, unarmed UN escorts were provided that could do little when the presidential guard stopped and tried to pull people out of their cars. One convoy coming to the embassy to fuel up cars included the wife of Ambassador David Rawson. A car in her convoy was stopped, and attempts were made to force out a visiting African American aid officer who was mistaken Interahamwe and for a Tutsi. Lane heard the commotion over the radio network and sprinted several blocks through the city streets of Kigali to intervene. Dressed in red track pants and a Mickey Mouse sweatshirt, she was visible and identifiable to all from a long distance away. When she arrived on the scene, she faced down the Interahamwe and presidential guards, asserting that this was the convoy of the wife of the U.S. ambassador, that every vehicle in it had diplomatic immunity, and that they were not to be stopped again. Stunned in many ways at this young white woman's effrontery, they gave way to her orders and never stopped any other cars coming to the embassy again if they carried the American flag or a white flag of neutrality (be it a ripped up sheet or t-shirt), agreed on as the indentifying symbols for the American convoys.

And as each of the convoys were being assembled and headed to the embassy for fuel, there were some Rwandans who were given "honorary American" status in the convoys with travel papers indicating that they were on official U.S. business. Lane's position was a simple one: if people could make it through the roadblocks and to the American embassy, she would find a way to help get them safe passage out of Kigali. While this was hardly proper procedure, Lane stretched the bounds of legality a long way in order to ensure that the people could be granted sanctuary. She knew that with travel documents in hand, the Rwandans would be able to enter Burundi with the rest of the convoy, as the Burundian authorities, suspicious of anyone who was undocumented, respected documents of this kind. The possession of travel documents thus gave desperate people more hope than if they had nothing at all. Lane did not claim they were Americans, but the protection she provided nonetheless

vouched for them sufficiently to guarantee their safe passage across the border. In this way, she was able to arrange for the survival of several innocent Rwandans caught in the crossfire who otherwise would have had next to no chance of staying alive (in some cases, she even hid them in car trunks in order to get them through the checkpoints).

The road trip between Kigali and Bujumbura normally should have taken about five hours, but given the length of the final convoy, the constant stopping, the roadblocks, and the checkpoints, the evacuation took closer to 18–20 hours. Laura Lane and her husband were the last Americans out, in the last car in the last convoy. She had insisted that they would be the last out, as she wanted to be sure that no one who wanted to leave was left behind.

Once in Bujumbura, Lane and the others provided an on-the-ground assessment of the situation for the State Department. They stayed there for almost a week, and were then flown back to Washington, D.C., where Lane joined a task force established to field calls from Rwanda regarding the situation and find ways to assist those who were able to establish contact. While in Washington, Lane worked closely with Deputy Assistant Secretary for Africa Prudence Bushnell, who was herself striving to raise consciousness within the administration about the Rwandan situation. Lane did all she could to help both in providing information for the government, and in establishing and maintaining contact with any of the FSNs back in Rwanda whose phone numbers she still had. The calls, however, were far from encouraging, and over time, fewer and fewer came.

By mid-summer—with more than a million Rwandans dead and the RPF having won control of the country—the State Department decided the embassy should be reopened, and that people were needed to go back to Kigali. Without hesitation, Lane immediately jumped at the offer, wanting to make good on her promise to her Rwandan staff and friends. She flew back to Kigali at the end of July 1994, and during August acted as a political adviser to U.S. forces providing humanitarian relief. The evidence of killing and destruction was everywhere. Returning to her former home, Lane saw that the house had taken several hits during the fighting, and that the destruction throughout the city had been massive and wanton, with ransacking of homes and commercial establishments in a highly personal—and vicious—manner.

To her dismay, Lane was not allowed to stay long in Kigali, as new Foreign Service officers had been commissioned to resume the embassy's daily functions. She stayed long enough to provide for the few survivors among the Rwanda staff, ensuring that they received the benefits and support to which they were entitled. She then closed this chapter in her life and returned to Washington, where she worked in the Trade Policy and Programs office in the Bureau of Economic and Business Affairs at the U.S. Department of State (1995–1997) and subsequently moved to the U.S. Trade Representative's office and then on to the private sector.

As the years passed, however, Lane kept an active interest in Rwanda, most importantly through her support of Emory University professor of public health Susan Allen, who set up a foundation to raise awareness that the criminals responsible for the genocide are still at large. The foundation's focus has been on collecting evidence about their activities, and meeting with the Departments of Justice and State to try to find ways to ensure that *génocidaires* are not allowed to travel, can be extradited from the United States when found, and made to stand trial for their crimes. Lane also worked on a documentary with the United States Holocaust Memorial Museum to ensure that no one ever forgot what happened in Rwanda and how the world watched passively as a million people were killed in the space of three months.

Looking back, Laura Lane's reflections on her time in Rwanda have been that more of a difference could have been made if more people took the decision to make that difference. Instead, politics intruded on a situation where lives were at stake, crippling the human dimension from the start. Of her experiences, her feelings are mixed. On one hand, she regrets the closure of the U.S. embassy at a time when it was needed more than ever to stay open as a refuge for those escaping the violence and evil. On the other hand, she knows that her actions at least saved some lives—even though she wishes every day since then that it could have been more.

PAUL R. BARTROP

See also: Allen, Susan; Bushnell, Prudence; Habyarimana, Juvénal; Interahamwe; Kagame, Paul; Rwandan Genocide, U.S. Response to the; Rwandan Patriotic Front

Further Reading

Barnett, Michael. *Eyewitness to a Genocide: The United Nations and Rwanda.* Ithaca, NY: Cornell University Press, 2002.

Melvern, Linda. *Conspiracy to Murder: The Rwandan Genocide.* London: Verso, 2006.

Leave None to Tell the Story: Genocide in Rwanda

Leave None to Tell the Story: Genocide in Rwanda was a comprehensive report on the 1994 Rwandan Genocide published by Human Rights Watch in 1999 and authored principally by the American historian Alison Liebhafsky Des Forges. Des Forges was among the first individuals outside Rwanda to recognize that a genocide in Rwanda was occurring; after the mass killing was over, she went to Rwanda with a group of researchers to document the events that occurred in 1994. She used Rwandan government documents, United Nations documents, local news reports, interviews, and other elements to assemble the meticulously detailed book. Des Forges also testified 11 times at the International Criminal Tribunal for Rwanda and presented evidence to the United Nations, the Organization of African Unity, and the national legislatures of Belgium, France, and the United States, among others.

Both *The New York Times* and *The Economist* termed *Leave None to Tell the Story* the "definitive account" of the Rwandan tragedy. While the book does not focus much attention on the meaning and interpretation of the genocide, it does offer unparalleled narratives of the killings, and is unabashed in assigning blame to various players. The genocide was not simply an ad hoc explosion of tribal conflicts, argues Des Forges; rather, it was a well-orchestrated plan conceived and carried out by Rwanda's Hutu-led government. She also points out that the Tutsi-dominated Rwandan Patriotic Front (RPF) shares blame because it engaged in retaliatory killings once the genocide was underway. The United Nations Security Council is excoriated for its limp reaction to the crisis, as are the governments of France, Belgium, and the United States. The book offers new insights on the warning signs that preceded the crisis, and also offers a detailed treatment of the plight of Hutus who attempted to resist participation in the genocide.

PAUL G. PIERPAOLI JR.

See also: Des Forges, Alison; International Criminal Tribunal for Rwanda; Rwandan Genocide, U.S. Response to the; Rwandan Patriotic Front

Further Reading

Des Forges, Alison. *Leave None to Tell the Story: Genocide in Rwanda.* New York: Human Rights Watch, 1999.

M

Media Trial in Rwanda

The Media Trial took place between October 23, 2000, and December 9, 2003, and was conducted by the International Criminal Tribunal for Rwanda (ICTR), based in Arusha, Tanzania. The trial was so named because it involved three Rwandan defendants who had been involved in media outlets in Rwanda both before and during the Rwanda Genocide of 1994. Although they were indicted separately, the ICTR decided to try them together because they had interconnected roles in the genocide. The presiding judge was Navanethem Pillay. The charges against the defendants included crimes against humanity, complicity to commit genocide, incitement to commit genocide, and conspiracy to commit genocide.

The first defendant, Ferdinand Nahimana, had co-founded the Radio-Télévision Libre des Mille Collines (RTLM), a virulently anti-Tutsi Rwandan radio/television station that incited hatred toward Tutsis, and supervised RTLM's radio programming. The second defendant, Jean-Bosco Barayagwiza, belonged to the radical Coalition pour la Défense de la Republique (CDR), a Hutu-dominated, anti-Tutsi political party and was the director of RTLM radio. The third defendant, Hassan Ngeze, had co-founded the anti-Tutsi newspaper *Kangura* and the CDR and was a principal investor in RTLM.

The ICTR indicted the three men under the provisions of the 1948 United Nations Convention on the Prevention and Punishment of the Crime of Genocide (UNCG).

The Rwanda Media Trial was the first of its type to indict and try defendants who had not taken part in mass killing themselves, but instead had encouraged genocide through their positions as media personnel. The defense team argued that convicting the men based solely on messages they had devised for print and media broadcasts was a fundamental violation of free speech. The prosecution, however, successfully countered that the men's actions went far beyond free expression or even hate speech, and that they had in fact helped incite a genocide in which at least 800,000 people died. This was accomplished by rabid anti-Tutsi rhetoric and propaganda as well as actual directives to a mass audience encouraging Hutus to kill Tutsis and moderate Hutus.

The verdict, rendered on December 9, 2003, was unambiguous. It found the three defendants responsible for the deaths of thousands of Rwandans, and that the RTLM had indeed directly compelled listeners to engage in the mass killing of Tutsis and Hutu sympathizers. The court also determined that Ngeze's *Kangura* newspaper had created an atmosphere toward the Tutsis that was so toxic that it was a de facto incitement to genocide, even though the paper had ceased publication several months before the start of the genocide.

Ngeze and Nahimana were given life-long prison sentences, while Barayagwiza was given a 35-year prison term. Lawyers for the three men appealed both the verdicts and sentences, but on November 28, 2007, the ICTR affirmed the verdicts as valid. The court did, however, alter the sentences. Ngeze's sentence was reduced to 35 years to life, while Nahimana's sentence was reduced to 30 years to life. Barayagwiza's sentence was reduced to 32 years.

PAUL G. PIERPAOLI JR.

See also: Barayagwiza, Jean-Bosco; Hutus; International Criminal Tribunal for Rwanda; *Kangura;* Nahimana, Ferdinand; Ngeze, Hassan; Radio-Télévision Libre des Mille Collines

Further Reading

Valentino, Benjamin A. *Final Solutions: Mass Killing and Genocide in the Twentieth Century.* Ithaca, NY: Cornell University Press, 2004.

Waller, James. *Becoming Evil: How Ordinary People Commit Genocide and Mass Killing.* Oxford: Oxford University Press, 2002.

Micombero, Michel

Michel Micombero was the first president of the central African state of Burundi, serving in that role between 1966 and 1976. A Tutsi, he was born in Rutovu, Bururi province, southern Burundi, in 1940, and educated in local Catholic schools. In 1960 he joined the Belgian colonial army, and was sent to Brussels for officer training. In 1962, he returned to Burundi with a commission as captain, and took up a position in the armed forces of what had by then become an independent state.

Burundi at this time had a population mix dominated by a large Hutu majority (85 percent), with a much smaller Tutsi minority. At independence from Belgium in 1962, the Tutsis, who had been the traditional rulers before and during Belgian colonialism, retained their ascendancy—largely by force of arms and a tightly controlled bureaucracy. Upon his return from Belgium, Micombero joined the National Progress and Unity Party (UPRONA), the ruling party dominated by the Tutsi elite, and rose quickly to become secretary of state for defense (1963). The country, however, was about to enter a period of anarchy. In 1965, legislative elections gave Hutu parties a resounding victory, winning 23 out of 33 seats in the National Assembly. This victory was overthrown, however, when the Tutsi *mwaami* (King), Mwambutsa IV, appointed a Tutsi from the royal family as prime minister. Soon thereafter, on October 19, 1965, an attempted coup was suppressed ruthlessly, but this served only to intensify Hutu anger at their second-class status, and in some parts of the country massacres of Tutsis began to take place.

In mid-1966 Micombero conspired with others in arranging for a palace coup that saw the crown prince,

Charles Ntare V Ndizeye, take the throne. On July 11, 1966, Micombero formed a government, with himself as prime minister. Then, on November 28, 1966, he overthrew the monarchy, declared Burundi a republic, and placed himself at its head as president.

Micombero now became an advocate of what became known as African socialism. This was a vague ideology asserting that economic resources should be shared in what he called a "traditional African" manner. Within the Cold War context, both the Soviet Union and communist China courted African states professing African socialism, and Micombero's Burundi fell under the patronage of China as a result. Micombero imposed a tight law and order regime throughout the country, and did all he could to repress any possibility of a Hutu ascendancy. He also cracked down on Hutu militancy.

It was against this background that on April 29, 1972, Hutu radicals in the southern provinces of Burundi launched an uprising against Micombero's military government, massacring several thousand Tutsi civilians. They were supported (and in some instances, organized) by Hutu refugees outside Burundi itself. This was viewed as a final challenge for supremacy by many Tutsi leaders, in particular Micombero. On the same day as the Hutu rising, he dissolved the government.

It was now that the country began to descend into disorder. Ethnic hostility between Hutus and Tutsis appeared more overtly than beforehand, and regional factionalism between Tutsi politicians and other members of the elite started to divide the government. Micombero adopted harsh measures to bring the country to heel, beginning with the brutal repression of Hutu suspects in Bururi, the physical elimination of all Hutu troops in the army, and the transformation of regionally based measures into country-wide repression. A number of public sector purges were also carried out. Hutu hopes looked to the now-exiled ex-king Ntare to return and overthrow Micombero; he did return, but was killed soon thereafter while in government custody. It is widely believed that it was Micombero himself who personally ordered Ntare's assassination.

Micombero was now unchallenged in the measures he could adopt to suppress the Hutus, and he began to institute a series of deliberately targeted campaigns that can only be described as genocide. The intention of these killings was the elimination of all Hutu political aspirations, once and for all. A series of deliberate campaigns took place against specific categories of Hutus, such as those in government employ, intellectuals (who could include any Hutu with a university education, whether completed or current; secondary school students; and teachers), and the Hutu middle and upper classes. Estimates of the number killed between April and October 1972 vary, but most settle at somewhere between 100,000 and 150,000. Hundreds of thousands more fled abroad, with Micombero unquestionably playing a leading role in the campaign.

The overall impact of these events took a personal toll on Micombero. Although he could claim to have saved the country (or at least, the Tutsi ascendancy within it), it was reported that he began drinking heavily and slipped into a psychological nether world, paranoid and delusional. His administration henceforth became increasingly corrupt and inefficient. By November 1976, some members of the army, anxious to restore order to Burundi (though without necessarily seeking to come to the aid of the Hutus), staged a coup d'état led by the chief of staff (and Micombero's distant cousin and clan member), Jean-Baptiste Bagaza. Micombero was arrested. After a short period of imprisonment in the capital, Bujumbura, he went into exile in Somalia, where he died of a heart attack in 1983.

The killing, however, did not end there. Subsequent large-scale massacres of Hutus by Tutsi government forces took place in 1988 and by Hutus against Tutsis in 1993. Accompanying these savage assaults was the wholesale exodus of scores of thousands of refugees to neighboring countries, leading to an intensifying destabilization of the Great Lakes region which culminated in the Rwandan Genocide of April–July 1994. Until the early 1990s, however, successive Burundian governments refused to acknowledge that genocide had even taken place in the country—a situation with which many in the international community seemed content to follow.

PAUL R. BARTROP

See also: Congo, Democratic Republic of; Hutus; Tutsis

Further Reading

Jennings, Christian. *Across the Red River: Rwanda, Burundi and the Heart of Darkness.* London: Phoenix, 2000.

Scherrer, P. Christian. *Genocide and Crisis in Central Africa: Conflict Roots, Mass Violence, and Regional War.* Westport, CT: Praeger, 2002.

Mugesera, Léon

Léon Mugesera is a former Rwandan Hutu Power politician and ideologue, recently resident in Canada and facing deportation as a suspect accused of inciting the 1994 Rwandan Genocide. Born in 1952 in Kibirira Commune, Gisenyi, Mugesera studied under Canadian missionaries

in Rwanda in the 1970s and at Laval University in Quebec City in the 1980s. At that time he completed internships with the Canadian and Quebec governments, and later became a professor at the University of Rwanda. He was a member of the ruling Hutu party, the Mouvement républicain national pour la démocratie et le développement (National Republican Movement for Democracy and Development, or MRNDD), and was MRNDD vice chairman for Gisenyi prefecture in 1992.

On November 22 of that year, Mugesera made a 15-minute speech to a thousand party members at a political meeting in Kabaya, in which he allegedly said that Rwandan law permitted the death penalty for traitors, and that if the judicial system did not carry out this punishment against the Tutsi *inyenzi* ("cockroaches"), the people must do it themselves. "Know that the person whose neck you do not cut," he exclaimed, "is the one who will cut yours." He stated that "we the people are obliged to take responsibility ourselves and wipe out this scum," and that Hutus should kill Tutsis and "dump their bodies into the rivers of Rwanda" and send them back to Ethiopia. The speech was recorded and widely replayed.

In the eyes of many, this speech helped to form the ideological rationalization for the genocide that would follow in 1994.

The Rwandan minister of justice, Stanislas Mbonampeka, at that time a human rights activist and member of the Liberal Party opposed to the regime of President Juvénal Habyarimana studied Mugesera's speech and issued an arrest warrant against him for inciting racial hatred. Mugesera was hidden by the army, and then spirited out of the country. He first went to Congo, then Spain, before he was granted refugee status in Canada in 1993. (Mbonampeka was soon forced to resign from his post as minister of justice. In 1993 he joined with Hutu Power, and sought to resume his political career. He became a wanted fugitive after the genocide, and as of this writing is still yet to be apprehended.) Mugesera and his family were quickly granted permanent resident status, which critics allege was made possible by political connections between the Quebec establishment and Rwanda's Hutu ruling elite. Mugesera secured a job teaching at Laval University, where he began postdoctoral work.

In 1995, the government of Rwanda sought Mugesera's extradition. The Canadian government commenced deportation proceedings against him for having lied about his background in his refugee application, along with the war crimes allegations. Article 318 of the Canadian Criminal Code, dealing with those who advocate genocide, provides for five years' imprisonment for anyone who "advocates or promotes genocide," and Section 7 of the Code provides for universal jurisdiction over crimes against humanity or war crimes committed by non-Canadians found in Canada for acts undertaken outside of Canada. The preference on this occasion, however, was to deport Mugesera rather than prosecute him, and in 1996 it was ordered that he be deported from Canada.

Upon appeal, Mugesera denied the accusations against him, despite the evidence shown in a video of him making his speech in November 1992.

In a surprise ruling on April 12, 2001, after Mugesera was ordered deported by two Immigration Board tribunals, the Canadian Federal Court of Appeal overturned these verdicts. Federal Court justices Marc Nadon and Robert Décary concluded there was no proof linking the November 1992 speech to genocide in the spring of 1994. Nadon requested that the Immigration Board tribunal review its claim that Mugesera incited racial hatred and thereby helped to foment genocide, and asked the board's appeals tribunal to re-examine the conclusions it had drawn about Mugesera's culpability. Nadon also ordered that deportation proceedings against Mugesera's wife and five children be halted immediately. Then, on August 1, 2001, Mugesera requested a trial under Canada's new Crimes against Humanity and War Crimes Act.

In 2003 the Federal Court of Appeal again found that the allegations against Mugesera were without foundation, winning him a further reprieve.

On June 28, 2005, the Supreme Court of Canada overturned the Federal Court of Appeal's decision by an 8–0 decision, upholding the original deportation order. The Supreme Court ordered Mugesera out of the country, but the government in Ottawa showed reluctance to enforce the order on the grounds that he would likely be subjected to mistreatment from a regime whose judicial system might not meet international standards. Also, Canada had a long record of reluctance to deport persons to places carrying the death penalty.

In 2007, however, Rwanda abolished the death penalty, removing this long-standing Canadian legal concern over Mugesera's deportation. In 2009, Ottawa agreed to restart deportation proceedings, though the federal government also said it needed more time to review Mugesera's case. While it does so, Mugesera remains in the country on appeal. In mid-2010 the Rwandan government filed hundreds of pages of previously unseen documents to the Canada Border Services Agency, responsible for enforcing decisions of the Immigration and Refugee Board, to make its case in favor of Mugesera's deportation. Mugasera was deported on January 23, 2012.

In early February 2012, Mugesera was formally charged with planning genocide, inciting participation in genocide, and the distribution of arms. Since returning from adjournment in April, a number of appeals delaying the start date of the trial have been made. As of this writing, there is no date set.

PAUL R. BARTROP

See also: Habyarimana, Juvénal; Rwanda

Further Reading

Kressel, Neil Jeffrey. *Mass Hate: The Global Rise of Genocide and Terror.* New York: Plenum Press, 1996.

Schabas, William A. *Genocide in International Law: The Crime of Crimes.* Cambridge, UK: Cambridge University Press, 2000.

Munyenyezi, Beatrice, Trial of

On February 21, 2013, a jury in a U.S. federal court in Concord, New Hampshire, found Beatrice Munyenyezi, a Hutu who had fled Rwanda in the aftermath of the Rwandan Genocide, guilty of having lied about her actions in that tragedy when she applied for U.S. citizenship. In 1998, Munyenyezi and her three daughters settled in Manchester, New Hampshire, where she secured a job with the Manchester Housing Authority. Munyenyezi had initially sought refugee status, claiming that she would be persecuted if she were to return to Rwanda. She subsequently applied for permanent resident status (a green card), which was granted, and in 2003, she was granted full citizenship.

In June 2011, Munyenyezi's husband and mother-in-law, both alleged members of the Hutu Interahamwe militia responsible for prosecuting much of the Rwandan Genocide, were sentenced to life imprisonment for war crimes, crimes against humanity, and genocide. The sentences were handed down by the International Criminal Tribunal for Rwanda. Those trials brought to light Munyenyezi's activities in 1994, and federal prosecutors decided to investigate her role in the genocide. At approximately the same time, Munyenyezi's sister, Prudence Kantengwa, stood trial for having lied about her political affiliations in Rwanda before emigrating to the United States in the 1990s. Found guilty in 2012, she was given a 21-month prison sentence and will likely be deported at the end of her incarceration.

Federal prosecutors brought two charges against Munyenyezi. The first alleged that she had lied about her role in the genocide and her involvement in a radical Hutu political party; the second claimed that she had entered the United States illegally by making false statements on her refugee and green card applications. Her first trial ended with a deadlocked jury in March 2012. The second trial, which saw her convicted of both charges in February 2013, witnessed new prosecutorial tactics and witnesses, which proved more convincing. Several witnesses testified that Munyenyezi had been stationed at a roadblock during the 1994 genocide where she singled out Tutsis to be murdered; others claimed that she had worn the uniform of an extremist Hutu group implicated in its involvement in the mass killings. Munyenyezi vehemently denied these claims, but chose not to testify in either of her trials. She did, however, testify in defense of her husband and mother-in-law, which likely did not aid her own case. She now faces up to 10 years in a U.S. prison and deportation when she is sentenced in June 2013.

Attorneys for Munyenyezi are filing an appeal with the 1st Circuit of Appeals. They also argue that forcing their client to return to Rwanda would be a virtual death sentence, as the country is now controlled by Tutsis who would likely take a dim view of Munyenyezi and her alleged activities in 1994.

Paul G. Pierpaoli Jr.

See also: Hutus; Interahamwe; International Criminal Tribunal for Rwanda; Tutsis

Further Reading

Huffington Post. "Beatrice Munyenyezi Lied about Her Role in Rwanda Genocide; Faces Deportation From New Hampshire," February 22, 2013.

Melvern, Linda. *Conspiracy to Murder: The Rwandan Genocide.* London: Verso, 2006.

N

Nahimana, Ferdinand

Ferdinand Nahimana is a former Rwandan professor of history, and was a leading propagandist for the radical Hutu cause against the Tutsi minority prior to and during the Rwandan Genocide of 1994. He was born on July 15, 1950, in the commune of Gatonde, Ruhengeri Prefecture. He obtained a PhD in history from the University of Paris VII, and taught at the National University of Rwanda while at the same time becoming involved in Hutu supremacist politics. He developed a number of theories concerning the racial origins of the Rwandan population—theories he was later to popularize when promoting the cause of ethnic Hutu superiority over the Rwandan airwaves. Between 1979 and 1994 he allegedly wrote and published articles aimed at encouraging the population to rise up against the Tutsis and moderate Hutus.

In late 1990 Nahimana became director of the Rwandan National Information Office (ORINFOR), and served as the overseer of the state-owned Radio Rwanda, the newspaper press, and all other media related activities. He left this position in February 1992, but in 1993 he and some of his colleagues—most of whom were members of the then ruling party, the Mouvement Révolutionnaire National pour le Développement, or MRND—the party of Rwandan president Juvénal Habyarimana—established the first approved private radio station in Rwanda, Radio-Télévision Libre des Mille Collines (RTLM).

As a senior executive of this anti-Tutsi radio station, Nahimana was largely responsible for the propagandistic content of the station's programming. He performed a vital role as an anti-Tutsi ideologue and Hutu apologist. Nahimana was also a cofounder of a radical breakaway from the MRND, the Coalition pour la Defense de la République (Coalition for the Defence of the Republic, or CDR) an openly genocide Hutu Party.

Soon after the genocide began in April 1994, Nahimana was given sanctuary in the French embassy, escaping the fighting in Kigali between units of the Tutsi-led Rwandan Patriotic Front (RPF) and the government forces. On April 12, 1994, the French subsequently allowed him to escape to Bujumbura, Burundi. During Operation TURQUOISE, a French military operation under the auspices of the United Nations, he returned to Rwanda, and into the "safe zone" created by the French that acted as a sanctuary for Hutus escaping the advance of the RPF through Rwanda. He left again after the RPF had taken over the whole country in July. By August 30, 1994, Nahimana arrived in Cameroon, where he settled into a semipermanent exile.

On March 26, 1996, he was arrested there, pursuant to a request for extradition issued by Rwanda's RPF government. On April 15, 1994, the prosecutor of the International Criminal Tribunal for Rwanda (ICTR) requested the Cameroonian government not to proceed with the extradition—though still holding Nahimana in custody—while a formal indictment was prepared against him. On July 22, 1996, the indictment was produced. Nahimana was charged with genocide, conspiracy to commit genocide, direct and public incitement to commit genocide, and crimes against humanity. He was transferred from Cameroon to the ICTR in Arusha, Tanzania, in January 1997, and his initial court appearance took place on February 19, 1997. At his first appearance, he pleaded not guilty.

Nahimana's trial was quickly consolidated into that of two other anti-Tutsi propagandists, Jean-Bosco Barayagwiza, the former director of political affairs at the Ministry of Foreign Affairs and a member of the board at RTLM, and Hassan Ngeze, the former editor of the hate newspaper *Kangura*. It commenced on October 21, 2001. Collectively known as the "Media Trial," the three were held responsible for creating a climate that implanted the idea of Tutsi annihilation onto the Hutu worldview long before the genocidal killing actually began. In addition, Nahimana was accused of chairing meetings at which MRND leaders discussed how to go about annihilating the Tutsis and moderate Hutus. He also allegedly gave direct orders to murder Tutsis, and helped to distribute weapons to the anti-Tutsi Interahamwe militia.

After three years of testimony, the trial culminated in August 2003 when the tribunal retired to consider its verdict. The prosecutor demanded the maximum sentence, life imprisonment, for Nahimana, Barayagwiza, and Ngeze. On December 3, 2003, the Trial Chamber announced its verdict. Nahimana was sentenced to life imprisonment for genocide; conspiracy to commit genocide; incitement, directly and publicly, to commit genocide; complicity in genocide; and persecution and extermination as crimes against humanity.

Nahimana appealed his sentence, and the trial before the ICTR Appeals Chamber opened on January 16, 2007. On November 28, 2007, the Appeals Court affirmed his guilt, but only for the counts of direct and public incitement to commit genocide and persecution as a crime against humanity. It overturned several charges, notably those which touched on facts taking place or articles he had written before 1994. It also overturned the conclusion of the initial trial judges that there had been a conspiracy between the RTLM, the CDR, and *Kangura* with a view to committing genocide. Accordingly, his sentence was reduced from life imprisonment to 30 years.

On December 3, 2008, Nahimana was transferred from Arusha to Bamako Central Prison, Mali, where it was directed that he would serve out his sentence.

PAUL R. BARTROP

See also: Barayagwiza, Jean-Bosco; International Criminal Tribunal for Rwanda; *Kangura;* Ngeze, Hassan; Radio-Télévision Libre des Mille Collines; Rwandan Patriotic Front

Further Reading

Midlarsky, Manus I. *The Killing Trap: Genocide in the Twentieth Century.* Cambridge, MA: Cambridge University Press, 2005.

Neier, Aryeh. *War Crimes: Brutality, Genocide, Terror, and the Struggle for Justice.* New York: Times Books, 1998.

Ndadaye, Melchior

Melchior Ndadaye was elected president of Burundi in June 1993, defeating then-president Pierre Buyoya and becoming the first democratically elected head of state and the first from the majority Hutu ethnic group. He was killed on October 21, 1993, during an unsuccessful coup attempt by units of the Tutsi-dominated military.

Ndadaye was born on March 28, 1953, and was still in secondary school when he fled the country for Rwanda in 1972 to escape a round of ethnic massacres by the army. He sought refuge in Butare, in the south of Rwanda, where he attended the Group Scolaire before going to France to study banking. He was active in political affairs in Rwanda's refugee community and was one of the founding members of a student movement, as well as the Labor Party of Burundi. He was a lecturer in Rwanda from 1980 to 1983.

Ndadaye returned to Burundi in 1983 and entered the banking sector, heading up a credit organization from 1983 to 1988. Following further ethnic massacres in 1988, Ndadaye called for the nomination of a Hutu prime minister, a democratic charter, and the restructuring of the army; he was subsequently imprisoned for close to three months. The following year, as the country made strides toward democracy and ethnic reconciliation, Ndadaye joined the rural development ministry as a counselor. He later was named to a constitutional commission but resigned from that body in 1991. Ndadaye's Front for Democracy in Burundi was legalized in 1992 and Ndadaye went on to win the June 1993 presidential elections with approximately 65 percent of the vote. He assumed office on July 10, 1993, and was assassinated, along with a number of his cabinet members, three-and-a-half months later.

LYNN JURGENSEN

See also: Burundi; Rwanda

Further Reading

Africa South of the Sahara 1994. London: Europa, 1993.

Ndindiliyimana, Augustin

Augustin Ndindiliyimana was the chief of staff of the Rwandan Gendarmerie Nationale, the national police force, during the Rwandan Genocide of 1994. As chief of staff from September 2, 1992, he was responsible for the maintenance of peace and public order, and ensuring the observance of law, throughout Rwanda. Ndindiliyimana was born in Nyaruhengeri commune, Butare prefecture, in 1943. A career soldier in the Rwandan Armed Forces (FAR), at the time of the genocide he held the rank of major general.

Sometime prior to his appointment as chief of staff of the Gendarmerie Nationale, it is alleged in his indictment by the International Criminal Tribunal for Rwanda (ICTR) that he conspired with other high-level FAR officers to plan the logistics of what would become the annihilation of the Tutsi minority in Rwanda at the hands of the Hutu Power government.

On the night of April 6, 1994, Rwandan president Juvénal Habyarimana was assassinated when his plane was shot from the sky upon its approach to Kigali airport. A Crisis Committee was immediately set up, comprised of senior FAR officers led by Colonel Théoneste Bagosora, Tharcisse Renzaho, the governor of Kigali prefecture and president of the Civil Defense Committee for Kigali, and Ndindiliyimana in his capacity as chief of staff of the Gendarmerie Nationale. This Committee was a grab for power by the military forces. The force commander of the United Nations Assistance Mission for Rwanda (UNAMIR), General Roméo Dallaire, was invited to the initial meeting of the Crisis Committee, and arrived to find only senior military and paramilitary figures present. None of the civilian leadership was there. Dallaire rejected Bagosora's proposal of having the military take control of the political situation until they could hand it over to the politicians, reminding him that Rwanda still had a government headed by Prime Minister Agathe Uwilingiyimana. Bagosora responded that she was incapable of governing the nation. A few hours later, Uwilingiyimana was murdered with her husband by members of the presidential guard.

In his capacity as head of Rwanda's paramilitary police, Ndindiliyimana has also been accused of tipping off the leaders of the Interahamwe militias that Dallaire was about to embark upon an arms raid of Interahamwe weapons caches. If carried out, this would have gone directly against Dallaire's instructions from UN Headquarters in New York. These weapons, hidden away as a result of the tip-off, were then used in the genocide. According to the ICTR prosecutor, Ndindiliyimana thus bears responsibility not only for the atrocities committed by the forces under his control, but also indirectly for making these weapons available to the militias.

Ndindiliyimana has been accused of sexual violence and rape of Tutsi women, and has been charged with participating in the murder of 10 Belgian UNAMIR peacekeepers that were guarding Prime Minister Uwingiliyimana at the time of her assassination on April 7, 1994. The death of the Belgian soldiers precipitated the withdrawal of all Belgian troops from UNAMIR.

There are some, despite this, who have found Ndindiliyimana's behavior during the genocide to be something less than fanatical, like so many of those around him were. Dallaire was of the view that he might have been initially a moderate voice in the Crisis Committee, while others share this view. For example, Ndindiliyimana was known to be responsible for dismantling a potentially disastrous roadblock in front of the Hôtel des Mille Collines, at a time when the hotel manager, Paul Rusesabagina, employed the hotel as a United Nations–protected safe zone. Some have suggested that Ndindiliyimana was ambivalent toward the extreme measures being taken by the interim government.

After the end of the genocide in July 1994, Ndindiliyimana fled Rwanda for Belgium, where he was granted the status of a political refugee. On January 29, 2000, however, he was apprehended in the Belgian town of Termonde and extradited to the custody of the ICTR in Arusha, Tanzania, to face charges of conspiracy to commit genocide, genocide or complicity in genocide in the alternative, crimes against humanity, and war crimes. The ICTR had earlier issued an indictment against Ndindiliyimana and three other former FAR officers. Ndindiliyimana has, from the outset, pleaded not guilty to all charges against him. Known as the "Military II" trial, the indictment also groups together the former chief of staff of the FAR, General Augustin Bizimungu, and two commanding officers in the reconnaissance battalion, Major François Xavier Nzuwonemeye and Captain Innocent Sagahutu. According to the indictment of August 23, 2004, Augustin Ndindiliyimana is alleged to have conspired with his co-accused in the planning and commission of a plan to exterminate Tutsis in Rwanda. He was charged with 10 counts of genocide, crimes against humanity, and violations of the Geneva Conventions on the treatment of combatants and civilians in wartime. Proceedings against Ndindiliyimana began on September 20, 2004.

Ndindiliyimana's defense attorney is a Canadian lawyer, Christopher Black, who has for a long time argued that the foundation upon which the ICTR was established is questionable, at best. Black has argued that the ICTR's interpretation of the events in Rwanda in 1994 as genocide is not a correct reading of what really transpired, and that there was no genocide of the country's Tutsis at the hands of the government. The case against Ndindiliyimana was completed on June 29, 2009. On May 17, 2011, Ndindiliyimana was sentenced by the ICTR to 11 years, 3 months, and 19 days' imprisonment, the equivalent of his time served since his arrest. The Tribunal found that Ndindiliyimana had limited control over the men he commanded and was personally opposed to the killings.

PAUL R. BARTROP

See also: Bagosora, Théoneste; Bizimungu, Augustin; Dallaire, Roméo; United Nations Assistance Mission for Rwanda; Uwilingiyimana, Agathe

Further Reading

Dallaire, Roméo. *Shake Hands with the Devil: The Failure of Humanity in Rwanda*. Toronto: Random House, 2004.

Strozier, Charles B. and Michael Flynn, eds. *Genocide, War, and Human Survival*. Lanham, MD: Rowman & Littlefield Publishers, 1996.

Ngeze, Hassan

Hassan Ngeze was a Rwandan journalist responsible for writing, publishing, and spreading anti-Tutsi propaganda prior to the Rwandan Genocide of 1994. Born on December 25, 1957, in Rubavu commune, Gisenyi, Ngeze is a Muslim and Hutu supremacist. His early life history is difficult to track down. His education seems to have been restricted only to primary school, after which he scratched out a living as a shoe shine boy and then a bus conductor. It does not appear that Ngeze had any formal apprenticeship or education as a journalist, though it is known that he worked as a columnist for different Rwandan newspapers from 1978 onward. Prior to 1990 he was a correspondent and distributor in Gisenyi for *Kanguka*, a newspaper critical of the ruling regime of President Juvénal Hayarimana, especially of the military.

In 1990, Ngeze and other radical Hutus from the family entourage of the Hayarimana clan (a clique known as the "Akazu," or "Little Hut") founded *Kangura* (*Wake Them Up*), an anti-Tutsi, pro-Hutu popular newspaper intended as a counterweight to *Kanguka*. The first issue was entirely financed by the Information Bureau of the Presidency. It continued publication with ongoing financial assistance from high-level members of Hayarimana's ruling MRNDD (Mouvement républicain national pour la démocratie et le développement) party, and, later, from the extremist CDR (Coalition pour la Défense de la République) party, of which Ngeze was a cofounder.

The creation of *Kangura*, for which Ngeze was made the chief editor, was part of a much wider strategy on the part of the State. Its first issue appeared in May 1990, and its last in February 1994—two months before the start of the genocide—and it became a primary instrument in the preparation of the Hutu population for the actions against the Tutsi population that took place after April 6, 1994.

Ngeze has always asserted that he was a businessman and entrepreneur rather than a Hutu Power ideologue, but the pages of *Kangura* constantly showed him to be much more than what he claimed to be. Perhaps the most infamous piece he authored for *Kangura* was a catalogue of 10 admonitory instructions—the "Hutu Ten Commandments"—that were to be followed by every Hutu in order to destroy Tutsi influence in Rwandan society, and guarantee Hutu hegemony. Their repetition through the pages of *Kangura* served as an important conditioning agent for the Hutus. Published in issue number 6 of *Kangura*, in December 1990, Ngeze claimed later that the list had been circulating for some years before, and was not in fact composed by him alone. The "Ten Commandments," in their essence, could in many respects have been adapted directly out of the Nazi Nuremberg Laws.

Kangura also published material that referred constantly to Tutsis as *Inyenzi*—cockroaches—and drove home the message that these *Inyenzi* (including those from outside, the *Inkotanyi*, or rebels, from the Rwandan Patriotic Front) were about to enslave all the Hutus and/or exterminate them. The answer to this "problem," it put rhetorically (and frequently), was to wipe out the Tutsis. Prior to ceasing publication, *Kangura* also published the names of Hutus deemed to be politically suspect—with the insinuation that they should suffer the same fate as the Tutsis—and exhorted "true" Hutus to take all measures to ensure that they would predominate now and into the future. Employing sensationalism at every turn, and with a readership many times greater than its circulation figures suggested, *Kangura* was a crucial instrument in developing a consciousness for genocide, notwithstanding that it had ceased publication by the time the genocide actually began.

Ntaganda, Bosco   1777

Along with Jean-Bosco Barayagwiza and Jean Shyirambere Barahinura, Ngeze co-founded the extremist CDR party, and in 1993 became a founder, shareholder, correspondent, and leading director of the anti-Tutsi radio station Radio-Télévision Libre des Mille Collines (RTLM), which was to some extent a radio equivalent of *Kangura*. Although *Kangura* did not play any direct role in the genocide while it was in progress (having ceased publication in February 1994), Ngeze played a very active role in the genocide nonetheless.

As a former member of the MRND and one of the founders of the CDR, Ngeze also exercised political control over the Interahamwe militias, and was an organizer of the CDR's Impuzamugambi militia. During the genocide he provided RTLM with the names of people to be killed in his prefecture of Gisenyi, which were broadcast on air. He is also alleged to have personally supervised and taken part in torture, mass rape, and killings within the prefecture.

In June 1994, Ngeze fled Rwanda in advance of the opposition Rwandan Patriotic Front forces, and on July 18, 1997, upon the demand of the prosecutor of the International Criminal Tribunal for Rwanda (ICTR), he was arrested in Mombasa, Kenya. He was transferred to the United Nations penitentiary in Arusha, Tanzania, the same day.

The ICTR charged Ngeze with several counts of genocide, public incitement to commit genocide, complicity in genocide, and crimes against humanity. His trial, which opened on October 23, 2000, was consolidated into that of two other anti-Tutsi propagandists, Barayagwiza and Ferdinand Nahimana; collectively known as the "Media Trial," the three were found responsible for creating a climate that implanted the idea of Tutsi annihilation onto the Hutu worldview long before the killing actually began.

From the beginning, Ngeze boycotted the trial for several days, protesting at the way in which his newspaper articles had been translated for the ICTR. He also demanded a complete translation of 71 issues of *Kangura* from Kinyarwanda into English and French. He then pleaded not guilty to all counts in the indictment against him.

When the trial got underway, his lawyer argued that it was not Ngeze himself who was on trial, but, rather, freedom of the press. The trial thereby assumed a special importance, since it was the first time since the trial of Hitler's propagandists at Nuremberg that journalists were appearing in the dock of an international tribunal—and, no less,

for the crime of genocide. While the main elements of the trial were conducted on this important democratic principle, the Tribunal judges were ultimately not moved by such arguments. All three defendants were found guilty in December 2003. Ngeze was found guilty on the counts of genocide; conspiracy to commit genocide; direct and public incitement to commit genocide; and crimes against humanity (persecution and extermination). He was acquitted on the charges of complicity to commit genocide and of crimes against humanity (murder). He was sentenced to the maximum permitted the ICTR by the United Nations, life imprisonment.

Ngeze appealed his conviction, and a further trial before the Appeals Chamber opened on January 16, 2007. On November 28, 2007, the Appeals Chamber affirmed his guilt, but only for the counts of aiding and abetting the commission of genocide, for direct and public incitement to commit genocide through publication, and for aiding and abetting crimes against humanity (extermination). His sentence was reduced to 35 years' imprisonment. On December 3, 2008, he was transferred to Bamako Central Prison, Mali, to serve out his sentence.

PAUL R. BARTROP

See also: Barayagwiza, Jean-Bosco; Coalition Pour la Défense de la Règpublique; Habyarimana, Juvénal; Interahamwe; International Criminal Tribunal for Rwanda; *Kangura;* Nahimana, Ferdinand; Radio-Télévision Libre des Mille Collines; Rwandan Patriotic Front

Further Reading

Friedrichs, David O., ed. *State Crime.* Brookfield, VT: Ashgate/Dartmouth, 1998.

Valentino, Benjamin A. *Final Solutions: Mass Killing and Genocide in the Twentieth Century.* Ithaca, NY: Cornell University Press, 2004.

Ntaganda, Bosco

Bosco Ntaganda is a Congolese military leader who is under indictment by the International Criminal Court (ICC) for war crimes and crimes against humanity for acts he committed or condoned between July 2002 and December 2003. Ntaganda, a Tutsi, was born in 1973 in the Rwandan village of Kiningi. As a teenager, he went to Ngungu, in the eastern portion of the Democratic Republic of the Congo (DRC), to escape the persecution of Tutsis then taking place in Rwanda. In 1990 he joined the leftist Tutsi Rwandan Patriotic Front, which was operating in southern Uganda. He saw action with the armed wing of that group during the 1990s, and following the 1994 Rwandan Genocide, he participated in the movement that ousted the Hutu-dominated government.

Later, Ntaganda became a member of the Patriotic Forces for the Liberation of Congo, which was the military wing of the Union of Congolese Patriots (UPC). He soon became chief of military affairs. Later still, he joined the National Congress for the Defense of the People (CNDP), a militia force active in the DRC, serving as its chief of staff. In recent years, Ntaganda and the UPC have controlled several lucrative mines in the eastern part of the DRC. It has been reported that Ntaganda has personally profited from these operations and has repeatedly engaged in illicit trade. Some have likened his control over eastern Congo to that of a Mafia kingpin. Most recently, he led the M23 Group, an armed militia movement that tried unsuccessfully to seize the city of Goma, DRC, adjacent to the Rwandan border.

In August 2006, the ICC issued an arrest warrant for Ntaganda, based upon his actions during 2002–2003. The specific charges included: employment of child soldiers; murder; rape; sexual slavery; and ethnic-based persecution. In April 2012, Congolese president Joseph Kabila called for the arrest of Ntaganda, citing his virtual war against the DRC's government.

In a stunning turn of events, Ntaganda surrendered himself to the U.S. Embassy in Kigali, Rwanda on March 18, 2013. He then requested that he be transferred to the ICC. It remains unclear why Ntaganda would surrender to an authority that in all likelihood will sentence him to many years of imprisonment. Some have surmised that pressure by former allies in Rwanda or the DRC urged him to do so. Others have opined that with the recent split in the M23 Group and Kabila's demand for his arrest, Ntaganda saw surrender to the ICC as a more palatable alternative to being a hunted fugitive. Still others have suggested that Ntaganda arranged some sort of deal with the ICC whereby self surrender would yield more sympathetic treatment during a trial. As of this writing, no trial date has been set.

Paul G. Pierpaoli Jr.

See also: Congo, Democratic Republic of; Rwandan Patriotic Front

Further Reading

"Rebel Leader in the Congo Is Flown to The Hague," *The New York Times,* March 22, 2013.

"Why Did Infamous War Criminal Bosco Ntaganda Just Surrender at a U.S. Embassy?," *Washington Post,* March 18, 2013.

Ntakirutimana, Elizaphan

Elizaphan Ntakirutimana was a Rwandan minister who was convicted of genocide in 2003. Elizaphan Ntakirutimana, a Hutu, was born in Kibuye Prefecture, Rwanda in 1924. He eventually became a minister in the Seventh-day Adventist Church in Rwanda and then a pastor at the Mugonero church located in Ngoma. In mid-April 1994, at the height of the Rwanda Genocide, several Seventh-day Adventist ministers sent a letter to Ntakirutimana in which they relayed the plight of the hundreds of Tutsi refugees under their care. The following day, well-armed Hutu militiamen converged on the refugees, murdering several hundred of them.

Ntakirutimana apparently was complicit in the massacre of the refugees because he had transported and aided the militia. His crime was first brought to international attention in 1998 in Philip Gourevitch's book *We Wish to Inform You That Tomorrow We Will Be Killed with Our Families.* Indeed, the title was taken from the letter written to Ntakirutimana by the besieged ministers at Mugonero. Prior to the publication of that book, however, Ntakirutimana had fled Rwanda, knowing that he had already been implicated in the massacre and that Rwandan and international law enforcement officials were in pursuit of him.

Ntakirutimana ultimately found his way to the United States, via Mexico, and was apprehended in Laredo, Texas, in 1996. Already wanted for trial by the International Criminal Tribunal for Rwanda (ICTR), he was detained in a federal penal facility while he fought extradition. In January 2000, the U.S. Supreme Court ruled that Ntakirutimana had exhausted all legal avenues to fight extradition. This permitted his transfer to a detention facility run by the ICTR in Arusha, Tanzania.

The ICTR's Trial 1 charged Ntakirutimana with genocide, conspiracy to commit genocide, three counts of crimes against humanity, and one count of violating Common Article 3 of the Geneva Conventions. Meanwhile, his son Gérard, a physician, was also put on trial for his role in the Rwandan Genocide. Ntakirutimana the elder was found guilty of genocide but not guilty of the other charges. On February 19, 2003, he became the first clergyman to be convicted for his role in the genocide. He appealed the decision, but the genocide charge remained and he was imprisoned until December 6, 2006, when he was released. All told, Ntakirutimana spent 10 years detained or imprisoned. He died in Arusha, Tanzania, on January 22, 2007.

Paul G. Pierpaoli Jr.

See also: International Criminal Tribunal for Rwanda; Rwanda; *We Wish to Inform You That Tomorrow We Will Be Killed with Our Families*

Further Reading

Gourevitch, Philip. *We Wish to Inform You That Tomorrow We Will Be Killed with Our Families: Stories from Rwanda.* New York: Picador, 1999.

Straus, Scott. *The Order of Genocide: Race, Power, and War in Rwanda.* Ithaca, NY: Cornell University Press, 2008.

Nyirabayovu, Thérèse

Thérèse Nyirabayovu is a widowed Hutu Rwandan who hid as many as 18–20 people in her modest home during the 1994 Rwandan Genocide.

Nyirabayovu was born sometime in 1927 in Kigali, the capital city of Rwanda. Little is known of her life before or after the awful events of 1994. As a young woman, she became a midwife, and was well respected in the Nyarugenge neighborhood of Kigali. Sometime prior to the start of the genocide, her husband died, leaving her to raise four children on her own (she had several other children, who had died in childhood) with meager resources. Although Nyirabayou was not as poor as some Rwandans, she certainly lived a very frugal and circumscribed life.

On April 4, 1994, a plane carrying Rwandan President Juvenal Habyarimana, a Hutu, was shot down by a missile as it approached Kigali's airport. This event proved to be the tipping point following the 1990–1993 civil war and mounting ethnic tensions in Rwanda. The Rwandan government, controlled by the Hutus, blamed the president's assassination on the Rwandan Patriotic Front (RPF), which was a Tutsi organization. Habyarimana's death provided the government with the perfect pretext for encouraging the mass killing of Tutsis all across Rwanda. Within weeks, the genocide began, aided in large measure by the Interahamwe, a Hutu-dominated militia group that became a de facto mass killing machine. Tutis and moderate Hutus were killed by the hundreds of thousands, and in the mere 100 days that encompassed the Rwandan Genocide, as many as 900,000–1,000,000 people died. Those not massacred by the Interahamwe were often murdered by their neighbors, friends, and even family members.

Amid this horrifying spectacle, Nyirabayovu decided to hide Tutsis in her modest home, knowing full well that doing so could result in her death and the deaths of her family members. With the help of her children, she sheltered as many as 20 people and fed them as best she could. Local members of the Interahamwe suspected her of hiding Tutsis, but they did not unduly bother her because she was elderly and was one of the most well-respected people in the neighborhood. Still, however, her home was searched multiple times, and someone threw a grenade at it, which fortunately caused no damage.

Nyirabayovu stated later that she did what she did because she always believed in helping other people who were in danger. During the genocide, she also provided food to refugees who had sought refuge in a nearby church, Ste. Famille. After the killing ended, Nyirabayovu volunteered in refugee camps in Zaire (now Democratic Republic of the Congo), even though several militiamen there had known about her actions in Kigali and did not approve of them.

PAUL G. PIERPAOLI JR.

See also: Habyarimana, Juvénal; Interahamwe; Rwandan Patriotic Front

Further Reading

Des Forges, Alison. *Leave None to Tell the Story: Genocide in Rwanda.* New York: Human Rights Watch, 1999.

Melvern, Linda. *Conspiracy to Murder: The Rwandan Genocide.* London: Verso, 2006.

Nyiramasuhuko, Pauline

Pauline Nyiramasuhuko was the minister of family welfare and women's affairs in Rwanda before and during the genocide of 1994. A Hutu, she was born in 1946 in the commune of Ndora, Butare prefecture, into a poor farming family which produced just enough to stay above subsistence level. A bright student, she managed in spite of her poverty to attend the Karubanda School of Social Studies, where she became friends with Agathe Kanziga, who later would marry Juvénal Habyarimana, and thus become the wife of the president.

After completing her studies, Nyiramasuhuko became a social worker and took up a post in the Ministry for Social Affairs in Kigali. As a result of her connections with Agathe Kanziga, Nyiramasuhuko, at the age of just 22, rose quickly in the civil service. In 1968, she married Maurice Ntahobali, who later went on to become a government minister, president of the National Assembly, and finally rector of the National University of Rwanda (Université Nationale du Rwanda, or UNR), Butare. The couple had four children, one of whom, Arsène Shalom Ntahobali, would himself be indicted on crimes against humanity and genocide charges arising from his role as an Interahamwe commander during 1994. After working in social services for many years, in 1986 Pauline Nyiramasuhuko became one of the rare women to take up law studies at the UNR, and in 1990 she graduated with a law degree.

In 1992 she was appointed minister of family welfare and women's affairs in Rwanda's first multiparty government. Her appointment was a bolt from the blue so far as the public was concerned, yet she retained her post until July 1994, when she fled Rwanda in the aftermath of the genocide. From the end of 1990 until July 1994, Nyiramasuhuko was said to have adhered to—and then participated in—the detailed development of a plan aimed at exterminating Rwanda's Tutsis. Then, when the genocide began, Nyiramasuhuko allegedly publicly incited the Hutu population to annihilate the Tutsi population.

Between April 9 and July 14, 1994, during various meetings of the Council of Ministers, Nyiramasuhuko and other ministers made requests for arms for distribution within their home prefectures in order to perpetrate massacres. Nyiramasuhuko was given responsibility for Butare. Ministers were instructed to foment hatred and ethnic violence, and to facilitate the training of anti-Tutsi militias and provide them with arms. They were also to assist in drafting lists of those to be eliminated.

In pursuit of this, Nyiramasuhuko reportedly planned, ordered, and participated in massacres in Butare. Here, she allegedly orchestrated a trap for the Tutsi population as word got out that food and shelter were being provided for the Tutsis by the Red Cross at the Butare football stadium. On April 25, the trap was sprung, and large numbers were instead raped, tortured, and killed by militias lying in wait. In a much-quoted incident, Nyiramasuhuko is said to have told the Interahamwe, "before you kill the women, you need to rape them." Soon afterward, Nyiramasuhuko reportedly went to a camp where a group of Interahamwe were holding some 70 Tutsi women and young girls as prisoners. It was later alleged that she then ordered the Interahamwe to rape the women before dousing them with gasoline and burning them to death. This was among a number of occasions when Nyiramasuhuko was reported to have encouraged (and sometimes ordered) the Interahamwe to rape the women to be murdered.

Between April 19 and the end of June 1994, Nyiramasuhuko supervised the Interahamwe as they searched for Tutsi victims in the University district within Butare. When located, they would often be removed to different places within the prefecture for their execution. It was said that there were occasions when the victims were forced to strip off their clothes before being transported, at which point Nyiramasuhuko is said to have selected which Tutsi women would be raped.

The ferocity with which she allegedly urged the Interahamwe to slaughter Tutsis extended also to old women and unborn babies. It was said that she was sometimes seen dressed in military fatigues and boots, and carrying a rifle over her shoulder.

In July 1994, as the forces of the Rwandan Patriotic Front advanced on Kigali and the grip of the Hutu Power government became more and more tenuous, Nyiramasuhuko fled Rwanda for Zaire (now the Democratic Republic of Congo). After first going into hiding in a refugee camp run by the Catholic charity Caritas, she made her way to Kenya, where she lived for the next three years. On July 18, 1997, she was arrested in Nairobi at the request of the chief prosecutor of the International Criminal Tribunal for Rwanda (ICTR). She was transferred the same day to the jurisdiction of the ICTR in Arusha, Tanzania, and charged with conspiracy to commit genocide, genocide (or, alternatively, complicity in genocide), public and direct incitement to commit genocide, and crimes against humanity including murder, extermination, rape, persecutions on political, racial, and religious grounds, other inhumane acts, and war crimes. At her initial court appearance on September 3, 1997, Nyiramasuhuko pleaded not guilty to the five charges with which she was indicted.

She was not only the first woman to be indicted by the ICTR; she was the first woman to be brought to trial by any international tribunal. She also became the first woman ever to be indicted for rape as a crime against humanity, and the first woman to face genocide charges before an international tribunal. Moreover, she is the first woman ever charged with encouraging rape as an instrument of genocide.

On October 6, 1999, the ICTR, on request of the prosecutor, ordered a combined trial for Nyiramasuhuko and five other persons accused of crimes committed in the Butare prefecture in 1994. They were: Nyiramasuhuko's son Arsène Shalom Ntahobali; Joseph Kanyabashi, the Hutu Power mayor of Ngoma; Sylvain Nsabimana, the *préfet* of Butare; Elie Ndayambaje, the mayor of Muganza;

and Alphonse Nteziryayo, the *préfet* of Butare during the genocide.

The "Butare Six" trial, so called, became the longest and most costly trial in the history of international criminal justice. It opened on June 12, 2001, and closing arguments finished only on April 30, 2009, with the prosecutor seeking life imprisonment for all the accused. Judgment was delivered on June 24, 2011, with Nyiramasuhuko found guilty by the ICTR of genocide, conspiracy to commit genocide, crimes against humanity (extermination, rape, and persecution) and several serious violations of the Geneva Conventions. She was sentenced to life imprisonment.

Nyiramasuhuko's son Arsène Shalom Ntahobali and four others of the "Butare Six" were also found guilty, with Ntahobali also sentenced to life imprisonment.

Paul R. Bartrop

See also: Habyarimana, Juvénal; Interahamwe; International Criminal Tribunal for Rwanda; Rape

Further Reading

Eller, Jack David. *From Culture to Ethnicity to Conflict: An Anthropological Perspective on International Ethnic Conflict.* Ann Arbor: University of Michigan Press, 1999.

Kressel, Neil Jeffrey. *Mass Hate: The Global Rise of Genocide and Terror.* New York: Plenum Press, 1996.

O

Operation SUPPORT HOPE

Operation SUPPORT HOPE was a U.S. humanitarian mission to aid refugees in the aftermath of the April–June 1994 Rwandan Genocide. Operation SUPPORT HOPE began on July 22, 1994, and ended on September 27. It was launched in coordination with aid efforts undertaken by the United Nations (UN) High Commissioner for Refugees (UNHCR). The UNHCR took over humanitarian relief programs after the U.S. mission ended. The Rwandan Genocide, perpetrated by Hutus against the minority Tutsis and their moderate Hutu supporters, resulted in nearly 1 million deaths in a matter of weeks. Once the carnage was over, as many as 2 million (mainly) Hutus fled the country, flooding neighboring Tanzania, Burundi, and the Democratic Republic of the Congo (DRC). This mass exodus resulted in a major humanitarian crisis, as refugee camps witnessed starvation and rampant disease and sickness.

President Bill Clinton authorized SUPPORT HOPE on July 22, and within two days U.S. military personnel were being put in place in Goma, DRC, Entebbe, Uganda, and the Rwandan capital of Kigali. At the same time, U.S. Air Force C-5 and C-141 transport aircraft were ferrying into the area massive quantities of food, water, medicine, and other badly needed supplies. In all, the Air Force flew in excess of 1,200 sorties carrying a total of 15,000 tons of humanitarian relief supplies. By the end of July, the death rate in the refugee camps had dropped markedly. The American relief effort was designed chiefly to bring immediate relief to the refugees and to allow time for the UNHCR to ramp up its operations in the region.

On August 14, the UNHCR requested that direct humanitarian shipments be halted so that the relief effort could be managed entirely by the UN agency. Thereafter, American relief flights tapered off, and on September 27 President Clinton announced an end to Operation SUPPORT HOPE. At its peak, the U.S. operation involved 2,350 military personnel.

Operation SUPPORT HOPE was a successful and worthwhile humanitarian mission, but it had done nothing to prevent the Rwandan Genocide, or to stop it once it had begun. The world community, including the UN, proved unwilling and/or incapable of intervening when aid was the most critical—that is, as the killing was underway. President Clinton has since stated that the failure to act prior to SUPPORT HOPE was one the biggest regrets of his entire presidency. SUPPORT HOPE did have at least one negative impact, however. By aiding the Hutu refugees, the relief effort was also aiding many genocide perpetrators, who would go unpunished. Hutu guerillas also launched a number of attacks on Rwanda from refugee camps in Uganda and the DRC.

PAUL G. PIERPAOLI JR.

See also: Hutus; Rwandan Genocide, U.S. Response to the; Tutsis

Further Reading

Gribbin, Robert E. *In the Aftermath of Genocide: The US Role in Rwanda.* New York: I Universe, 2005.

Power, Samantha. *"A Problem from Hell": America and the Age of Genocide.* New York: Harper Perennial, 2007.

Operation TURQUOISE

Operation TURQUOISE was a French-led military operation designed to establish a safe haven for Tutsis and moderate Hutus in the late stages of the April–July 1994 Rwandan Genocide, which resulted in the deaths of 800,000–1,000,000 people. The operation began on June 22 and ended on August 22; the safe haven was located in the southern quarter of Rwanda. In May 1994, as the genocide reached the zenith of its destruction, the United Nations Security Council (UNSC) enacted Resolution 918, which called for a larger and more potent force to augment the United Nations Assistance Mission for Rwanda (UNAMIR), which was already on the ground in Rwanda. The French government strongly supported this effort, and offered to deploy its own troops to Rwanda. UNSC Resolution 929 empowered the French to undertake that mission on June 22, and within days French forces had begun deploying to Rwanda.

The French dispatched 2,550 troops, who served with approximately 500 troops from neighboring African countries. This force established a safe zone (known as the "Turquoise Zone") in the southern part of Rwanda (comprising about one-fifth of the country), where embattled Tutsi and moderate Hutus could seek refuge, ostensibly free from danger. Operation TURQUOISE included a battery of 120 mm mortars, ten armed helicopters, four French Jaguar fighter-bombers, two reconnaissance planes, and about 100 armored personnel vehicles.

Operation TURQUOISE proved highly problematic, however. First, the numerous roadblocks in areas not controlled by the French operation meant that many Tutsis could not make their way to safety; many died en route. Second, in July the operators of Radio-Télévision Libre des Mille Collines (RTLM), a radical Hutu media outlet that was exhorting Hutus to kill Tutsis, relocated their transmitters to the Turquoise Zone. The French made no immediate moves to seize them or silence them. Third, most of the refugees who fled to the French safe zone were in fact Hutus rather than Tutsis; some of them had been involved in perpetrating the genocide, and they continued to kill Tutsis even within the safe zone. The French were unable to prevent many of these killings. Fourth, the French troops did a poor job of disarming those who sought refuge in the Turquoise Zone (especially Hutus), which endangered Tutsis within the zone. Finally, the commander of the UNAMIR opposed the deployment of French troops, arguing that having two UN-mandated operations in the same country but with different missions was a recipe for confusion and ineffectiveness.

Other controversies also bedeviled the French operation. Some Tutsis in Rwanda and others in the international community accused the French of having undertaken the mission to prop up the Hutu regime responsible for starting the genocide. France had previously backed the Hutu government of President Juvénal Habyarimana and provided it with financial and military aid. Others alleged that the French were more interested in protecting Hutus from the Tutsi-dominated Rwandan Patriotic Army (RPA) instead of protecting Tutsis from the Hutu. Still others argued that by permitting so many Hutus into the Turquoise Zone, France permitted many genocide perpetrators to escape justice in Rwanda, or to flee the country entirely. That in turn enabled exiled Hutus to engage in warfare against the postgenocide Rwandan government from places like Congo and Uganda.

The French government has steadfastly denied these claims and allegations, insisting that it deployed troops to Rwanda in June 1994 based solely on humanitarian considerations. The last French troops were withdrawn on August 22, at which time UNAMIR II began its formal operations in Rwanda.

PAUL G. PIERPAOLI JR.

See also: de Saint-Exupéry, Patrick; Habyarimana, Juvénal; Hutu; Rwanda; Rwandan Genocide, French Response to the; Rwandan Patriotic Army; Rwandan Patriotic Front; Tutsis; United Nations Assistance Mission for Rwanda

Further Reading

Dallaire, Roméo. *Shake Hands with the Devil: The Failure of Humanity in Rwanda.* Toronto: Random House, 2004.

Melvern, Linda. *Conspiracy to Murder: The Rwandan Genocide.* London: Verso, 2006.

P

Prosper, Pierre-Richard

Pierre-Richard Prosper is a U.S. attorney and former ambassador-at-large within the Office of War Crimes Issues. He attracted worldwide attention when he successfully prosecuted the first case at the International Criminal Tribunal for Rwanda (ICTR) to bring in a guilty verdict for the crime of genocide. Born in Denver, Colorado, in 1963, Prosper is the son of two medical doctors who were refugees from Haiti. Raised in New York State, he was educated at Boston College (BA, 1985) and Pepperdine University Law School (JD, 1989).

Upon graduation in 1989, Prosper became a deputy district attorney for Los Angeles County, California, where he remained until 1994. He then entered service with the Federal government as an assistant U.S. attorney for the Central District of California in Los Angeles, where he investigated and prosecuted major international drug cartels while assigned to the Narcotics Section of the Drug Enforcement Task Force.

It was a colleague in the U.S. Attorney's office, Steve Mansfield, who was to draw Prosper's attention to Rwanda. Returning from a trip to that country, Mansfield briefed the staff about the 1994 genocide, and motivating Prosper to want to know more—and to want to help. From this moment on, he saw that he could make a difference in the broken society Rwanda had become, though he was aware of the pitfalls involved and the good

life as an assistant U.S. attorney he might well have to give up. Throwing off his concerns, he first went to Rwanda in April 1995 as part of a fact-finding mission to examine the national justice system. He was appointed as a special legal consultant of the United States government mission in Kigali, where he assessed the postgenocide Rwandan justice system and assisted in developing an action plan to reinstate some form of judicial operation in a country that had been stripped of its legal infrastructure. To do so he consulted with Rwandan, United Nations, and donor country representatives, coordinating activities in order to maximize international efforts. He remained in this position until May 1995.

Building on this experience, and given that he was then working and living in Rwanda, he was offered a position by the United Nations to be one of two American prosecutors at the ICTR, sitting in Arusha, Tanzania. The more he learned, the more he came to regard the horrors committed in Rwanda as not just a crime against Rwandans but against all humanity. It was while in this position that he successfully prosecuted the ICTR case against the former mayor of the town of Taba, Jean-Paul Akayesu. For Prosper, serving as lead prosecutor became a life-transforming experience. He and the judges on the Tribunal were confronted with the task of having to determine, for the very first time, what constitutes genocide in a legal sense. Reviewing the language of the 1948 Genocide Convention and half a century of legal scholarship, Prosper and his team had to establish how the concept of genocide applies in the contemporary context. They studied legal precedent, investigated the astonishing circumstances not only of the situation in Rwanda, but also with regard to the specific case being tried, met with victims and survivors, and stood before mass graves—all prior to even starting the trial process.

The result saw a powerful prosecution that resulted in the first-ever conviction in any courtroom specifically for the crime of genocide, with Akayesu sentenced to life imprisonment. The trial was also the first-ever case of genocide under the 1948 Convention on the Prevention and Punishment of the Crime of Genocide. An important part of the judgment saw the further development of genocide case-law, as the three trial judges—Laity Kama from Senegal presiding; Navanethem Pillay from South Africa; and Lennart Aspegren from Sweden—ruled that rape could henceforth be considered within a general legal definition of genocide and crimes against humanity. In the 14-month trial, Prosper won additional life-sentence convictions against Akayesu for crimes against humanity. In developing his case, Prosper traveled widely, supervising investigations throughout Africa, Europe, and North America.

Reflecting on his Rwanda experience later, Prosper said it both altered his professional life and challenged his fundamental assumptions about human nature. It changed his views concerning the nature of human evil, and of how important it is that all people contribute to making the world a better place.

Prosper remained a trial attorney with the ICTR until October 1998. In January and February 1999 he became a special assistant to the assistant U.S. attorney general (where he helped with the development of international justice initiatives), prior to a secondment to the State Department as special counsel and policy adviser to the Office of War Crimes Issues within the Office of the Secretary of State. Here, he worked directly with the first U.S. ambassador-at-large for war crimes issues David Scheffer, developing policy and assisting in formulating U.S. responses to serious violations of international humanitarian law around the world. He traveled to affected areas in Europe, Africa, and Asia to promote initiatives and build coalitions, as well as engaging in negotiations in support of U.S. government positions.

On May 16, 2001, Prosper was nominated by President George W. Bush to succeed Scheffer as ambassador-at-large for war crimes issues. After being confirmed by the U.S. Senate, he was sworn in on July 13, 2001, thereby becoming an official who served in high office in the administrations of both a Democrat (Bill Clinton) and a Republican (George W. Bush). He would serve in this capacity until October 2005, and, as such, was responsible to two secretaries of state—Colin Powell and Condoleezza Rice—on all matters relating to violations of international humanitarian law around the world. His role was important in that he advised not only the secretary of state, but also the president of the United States, secretary of defense, attorney general, national security adviser, chairman of the Joint Chiefs of Staff, director of the Central Intelligence Agency, White House counsel, and other senior U.S. government officials.

The human rights violations that formed the centerpiece of Prosper's brief included genocide, crimes against humanity, and war crimes. Prosper was often required to speak publicly on behalf of the United States, as the face of U.S. war crimes, genocide, and crimes against humanity policies around the world. As with his earlier appointments, Prosper traveled extensively, conducting diplomatic negotiations and consultations with heads of state, foreign ministers, and senior government officials from over sixty different countries. He regularly visited conflict zones in efforts to secure peace, stability, and the rule of law. After September 11, 2001, Prosper played a key role in helping to develop antiterrorism policies, within a legal human rights framework.

In October 2005 Prosper resigned his position in order to run for the Republican nomination for attorney general of California in the 2006 primaries. He withdrew his candidacy in February 2006, and did not proceed with his campaign.

In November 2006 and April 2007 he headed an International Republican Institute Election Observation Mission to observe and monitor the 2007 Nigerian presidential and National Assembly elections. He led a team of 59 international observers, meeting and consulting with candidates, political leaders, voters, and international observers. In February 2007 he was elected by the United Nations General Assembly to serve as an independent expert to the UN Committee on the Elimination of Racial Discrimination, a human rights treaty body located in Geneva, Switzerland. This monitors compliance by state parties to the Convention on the Elimination of All Forms of Racial Discrimination. Then, in April 2008, he was appointed by President Bush to serve as a member of the United States Holocaust Memorial Council.

As of this writing, Prosper is an attorney in the Los Angeles office of the California law firm Arent Fox LLP, having joined on January 1, 2007, after his time in public service.

PAUL R. BARTROP

See also: Akayesu, Jean-Paul; International Criminal Tribunal for Rwanda

Further Reading

Jokic, Aleksandar, ed. *War Crimes and Collective Wrongdoing: A Reader.* Malden, MA: Blackwell Publishers, 2001.

Neier, Aryeh. *War Crimes: Brutality, Genocide, Terror, and the Struggle for Justice.* New York: Times Books, 1998.

R

Radio-Télévision Libre des Mille Collines

Radio-Télévision Libre des Mille Collines (RTLM), meaning "One Thousand Hills Free Radio and Television" in French, was an independent Rwandan radio station that operated with the tacit approval and support of the Hutu-dominated Rwandan government prior to and during the 1994 Rwandan Genocide. RTLM played a central role in the genocide because it broadcast rabidly anti-Tutsi propaganda that condoned and even encouraged mass violence against Rwanda's Tutsi minority and Hutus who were sympathetic to the Tutsis.

The radio station began operations on July 8, 1993, in Kigali, the Rwandan capital. It was organized and operated by supporters of President Juvenal Habyarimana, who were trying to sabotage ongoing talks between the Rwandan government and the Tutsi Rwandan Patriotic Front (RPF). Although the station was supposedly independent, it received clandestine support from Habyarimana's government and utilized transmitting equipment owned by Radio Rwanda, the official state-operated radio station. RTLM quickly became very popular, particularly among Hutu youths, who were drawn to the station by its popular music selections and other youth-oriented programming. Interspersed with that programming was virulent anti-Tutsi rhetoric and propaganda that demonized the minority group as subhuman and "cock roaches." The station was said to have had a major impact on members of the Interahamwe, a rabid anti-Tutsi militia group that played a major role in the Rwandan Genocide.

RTLM worked closely with the virulently anti-Tutsi newspaper known as *Kangura,* and the paper's head, Hassan Ngeze, was also a major shareholder in RTLM. RTLM had a broad listenership that grew by the month. Although some members of the international community, including the United States, contemplated jamming RTLM's signals or destroying its transmitting towers, none took any action because it was feared that such action would be construed as abrogating free speech and expression. Meanwhile, anti-Tutsi hate speech and propaganda intensified, and after Habyarimana's assassination on April 6, 1994, RTLM took a central role in the ensuing genocide of Tutsis and moderate Hutus by actively encouraging Hutus to murder Tutsis. The station also broadcast the location of Tutsis and sympathetic Hutus as the genocide unfolded.

On July 3, 1994, advancing RPF troops raided RTLM's Kigali studios, but the station continued to broadcast sporadically until the end of the month, using mobile transmitters. In 2000, nearly six years after the genocide ended, RTLM's major players and supporters, including Ngeze, Jean-Bosco Barayagwize, and Ferdinand Nahimana, were tried for war crimes, crimes against humanity, and genocide in conjunction with their work with RTLM and their anti-Tutsi propaganda campaigns. In December 2003, all three men were found guilty and eventually given lengthy prison sentences by the International Criminal Tribunal for Rwanda (ICTR).

PAUL G. PIERPAOLI JR.

See also: Akazu; Habyarimana, Juvénal; International Criminal Tribunal for Rwanda; *Kangura;* Media Trial in Rwanda; Nahimana, Ferdinand; Ngeze, Hassan; Ruggiu, Georges; Rwandan Patriotic Front

Further Reading

Eller, Jack David. *From Culture to Ethnicity to Conflict: An Anthropological Perspective on International Ethnic Conflict.* Ann Arbor: University of Michigan Press, 1999.

Kressel, Neil Jeffrey. *Mass Hate: The Global Rise of Genocide and Terror.* New York: Plenum Press, 1996.

Valentino, Benjamin A. *Final Solutions: Mass Killing and Genocide in the Twentieth Century.* Ithaca, NY: Cornell University Press, 2004.

Waller, James. *Becoming Evil: How Ordinary People Commit Genocide and Mass Killing.* Oxford: Oxford University Press, 2002.

Rape

Rape was used as a weapon of genocide by the Hutu ethnic majority of Rwanda against the Tutsi ethnic minority during the Rwandan Genocide. Common estimates of 250,000 to 500,000 of mostly Tutsi women and girls were raped in a systematic fashion and often in a public or group setting during the genocide, many being raped hundreds of times each. Hutu women who resisted the genocide or were married to Tutsi men were also targeted, as were some men.

The genocide was inspired by and occurred with the organized support of the government of the central African state of Rwanda from April 6, 1994, to mid-July, 1994. Government propaganda and racist newspapers specifically targeted the sexuality of Tutsi women as a means to enflame anti-Tutsi hatred and promoted sexual violence against Tutsi women. Jean Kambanda was the Prime Minister for the interim government of Rwanda that orchestrated the genocide.

From the start of the genocide, Tutsi women were often raped and mutilated or raped and murdered after being forced to watch family members being tortured to death. More frequently, Tutsi women were not murdered but held as sexual slaves and raped many times a day by groups of Hutu or individuals. In addition to participating in the mass murders, Hutu women participated in the mass rapes. Approximately five weeks after the start of the genocide in mid-May 1994, a centralized command went out from the government to begin murdering Tutsi women in addition to the men, increasing the frequency of deaths amongst rape victims. The mostly Tutsi Rwandan Patriotic Army that won the civil war, ending the genocide, also raped and enslaved some Tutsi women who had been taken by the Hutu. Rape victims who remained alive at the end of the civil war suffered economic deprivation, extreme psychological trauma, physical mutilations, and permanent health problems, including an extremely high rate of HIV/AIDS. Rape victims were also often ostracized by their families and communities. Several thousand children were born from the genocidal rape victims.

Rape has long been considered a war crime by the international community, but it is only rarely punished. Rape was already a common war crime in the Rwandan Civil War. Genocidal rape is done with the intent to shame and terrorize a group and destroy the cohesion of the community, thus destroying the community. Rape as a constitutive element of genocide through sexual violence against a targeted group was first legally recognized by the international community on September 2, 1998, when the International Criminal Tribunal for Rwanda (ICTR) convicted Burgomaster (Mayor) Jean-Paul Akayesu of ordering genocidal rape in the Taba Commune of Rwanda. Taba Commune is a small village located west of Kigali, the capital of Rwanda. The ICTR was created by the United Nations Security Council on November 8, 1994. Akayesu was also found guilty of eight other genocidal crimes and crimes against humanity. The conviction was the first conviction of genocide by an international tribunal trial under the 1948 UN Convention on the Prevention and Punishment of the Crime of Genocide. Local prosecutions for rape during the genocide have been limited.

BRIAN G. SMITH

See also: Hutus; Rwanda; Tutsis

Further Reading

Nowrojee, Binaifer. *Shattered Lives: Sexual Violence during the Rwandan Genocide and Its Aftermath.* New York: Human Rights Watch, 1996.

United Nations Security Council, 53rd Session. "Agenda Item 50: Report of the International Criminal Tribunal for Rwanda," Annexes, Official Record. New York, 1998.

Roman Catholic Church

The Roman Catholic Church has for many decades played a sizable role in Rwandan society and politics. Indeed, since the days of European colonization in Africa, the Church was afforded a preferential position within Rwanda; after Rwandan independence, it continued to enjoy this position by supporting the Hutu-dominated government, particularly after 1959. A number of Catholic clergy—both nuns and priests—have more recently been successfully prosecuted for their roles in the 1994 Rwandan Genocide. These trials have occurred in Belgian courts as well as the International Criminal Tribunal in Rwanda. The Church recognizes that a genocide took place in Rwanda, but officially it denies any direct responsibility for it, arguing that those clergy who were involved were acting on their own initiative and not on orders from the Vatican. Claiming that it had no advance knowledge of the activities of some of its personnel, the Vatican so far has not issued an apology for the Church's role in the killings, despite international pressure to do so. On the other hand, some Catholic clergy went out of their way to forestall the genocide and help those who were targets.

For much of the 20th century, Catholic prelates and religious personnel played a pivotal role in Rwandan society. Indeed, by mid-century, the majority of Rwandans—both Hutus and Tutsis—were Roman Catholic. The Church operated numerous schools, where teachers instilled in their students the faulty premise that the Tutsis and Hutus were racially separate, which encouraged racial segregation, mutual misunderstanding and mistrust, and even hatred. Similar messages emanated from many Catholic pulpits throughout Rwanda. In the colonial era, the Church supported the Tutsis, who dominated society even though they were in the minority. When a Hutu-led government emerged after 1959, however, the Church switched allegiances and began to support the Hutus, even though many ruling Hutus hinted darkly that they might rid themselves of the Tutsis when the opportunity arose.

This Church support came from archbishops and bishops within Rwanda, so it is hard to comprehend how leaders in the Vatican did not know about the Church's activities. Archbishop Vincent Nsengiyumva was a member of the Rwandan government's central committee for 15 years and publicly championed the iron-fisted rule of President Juvénal Habyarimana. In the 1950s, Archbishop André Perraudin helped establish the concept of "Hutu Power," a blatantly racist idea that called for the subjugation of the Tutsis. Even well after the genocide, Kigali's Catholic archbishop claimed that the Church had no power to stop the tragedy; he also denied that any clergy

had been willing or active participants in the killings, despite considerable evidence to the contrary.

In the years since the genocide, physical evidence and eyewitness testimony have shown clearly that hundreds—perhaps thousands—of Rwandans died inside Catholic Churches or other alleged Catholic facilities, where some priests and nuns participated in the killings, encouraged them, or refused to intervene to stop them. Catholic churches at Nyange, Nyarubuye, Nyamata, Nyange, Ntarama, Saint Famille, and Cyahinda were all sites of various massacres in 1994. Father Athanese Seromba, the pastor at Nyange, was convicted by the International Criminal Tribunal for Rwanda in 2006 and sentenced to 15 years in prison. In April 1994, Seromba convinced some 2,000 men, women, and children to take refuge in his church. He then ordered local militiamen to set fire to the structure. To make sure that all the refugees were dead, and to hide his involvement, the priest then ordered the building bulldozed to the ground. In late 2006, the same court found a Rwandan nun guilty of aiding genocide and sentenced her to 30 years in prison. She had participated in the mass killing of civilians who had been hiding in a hospital. Two other nuns were convicted for their roles in the genocide by a Belgian court in 2001. There are numerous other Catholic clergy wanted for crimes related to the genocide but who have not yet been apprehended.

Since 1994, there have been numerous reports that clergy involved in the genocide have sought and received refuge in Catholic churches in other parts of the world, including Europe. The Church's role in the genocide has resulted in a marked drop off in attendance at Catholic churches in Rwanda, and in fact there has been a major upswing in the number of Rwandans who have converted to Islam. During the genocide, many Muslims provided aid and refuge to the victims. Although Protestant churches in Rwanda also share responsibility for the tragedy, the power, size, and centrality of the Catholic Church in Rwanda means that it shares the lion's share of the blame. Nevertheless, the black marks on the Church must not negate the many good works provided by moral and conscientious Catholic clergy, many of whom risked their own lives to aid the victims. For example, Sister Felicitas Niyitegeka, a nun in Gisenyi, smuggled hundreds of Tutsis to relative safety in Zaire before she was killed by Rwandan government militiamen.

PAUL G. PIERPAOLI JR.

See also: International Criminal Tribunal for Rwanda; Rwanda

Further Reading

Prunier, Gérard. *Africa's World War.* Oxford, UK: Oxford University Press, 2009.

Rittner, Carol. *Genocide in Rwanda: Complicity of the Churches.* St. Paul, MN: Paragon House, 2004.

Straus, Scott. *The Order of Genocide: Race, Power, and War in Rwanda.* Ithaca, NY: Cornell University Press, 2008.

Ruggiu, Georges

Georges Ruggiu was a journalist and radio broadcaster instrumental in presenting anti-Tutsi programs prior to and during the Rwandan Genocide of 1994. He was born to a Belgian mother and an Italian father on October 12, 1957, in Verviers, Belgium. Ruggiu had previously worked as a state civil servant in Belgium's social security department, but in 1993 he moved to Rwanda, in part because of boredom in Belgium, and in part because of the prospect of work through an acquaintance, Ferdinand Nahimana, a founder of the private anti-Tutsi radio station, Radio-Télévision Libre des Mille Collines (RTLM). With no previous experience in the media, Ruggiu began work as a journalist with RTLM on January 6, 1994. Between then and the following July, he was based in Kigali, writing, producing, and broadcasting programs that incited Hutus to attack and kill Tutsis and any Hutus who stood against them. His programs consistently incited his listeners to commit murder or serious attacks against the physical or mental well-being of the Tutsis, and constituted acts of persecution against Tutsis, moderate Hutus, and Belgian citizens. Like all the RTLM broadcasters, Ruggiu incited violence against Tutsis over the air. Radio-Télévision Libre des Mille Collines consistently broadcast anti-Tutsi propaganda before the genocide, and called on Hutus to kill their fellow Tutsis during its course. His broadcasts incited the public to kill and cause seriously bodily and mental harm to the Tutsi population, two of the categories of crime constituting genocide according to the United Nations Convention on the Prevention and Punishment of the Crime of Genocide 1948.

There were anomalies with Ruggiu, however. He was not Rwandan, neither Hutu nor Tutsi, and had no previous experience in journalism. He did not speak Kinyarwanda. Within the Rwandan Hutu Power hierarchy, he held no official position. When charged by the International Criminal Tribunal for Rwanda (ICTR) in 1997, he was the only non-Rwandan charged with involvement in the genocide.

After the collapse of the radical Hutu regime in July 1994, and its flight before the forces of the Rwandan Patriotic Front, Ruggiu fled the country—first to refugee camps in Zaire (now the Democratic Republic of Congo), then to Tanzania, and finally to Kenya. Here, he converted to Islam, adopted the name Omar, and joined a Somali Muslim community in Mombasa.

While on the run he was indicted by the ICTR, sitting in Arusha, Tanzania, on two counts of incitement to commit genocide and incitement to commit crimes against humanity. He was arrested in Mombasa on July 23, 1997, and transferred for trial to Arusha shortly thereafter. His indictment stated that Ruggiu played a key part in RTLM's campaign to spread extremist Hutu ideology. In October 1997 he pleaded not guilty, but changed his plea in May 2000, stating that he both affirmed that what happened in Rwanda was indeed genocide, and that he participated in it. On May 12, 2000, he pleaded guilty to the two charges in the indictment, admitting that he had incited murders of members of the Tutsi population with the intention of destroying, in whole or in part, the Tutsi ethnic group in Rwanda. He demonstrated remorse for his actions, admitting that he had incited mass murder and the other crimes for which he had been charged.

He was found guilty of incitement to commit genocide and to crimes against humanity (persecution), and on June 1, 2000, was sentenced to 12 years' imprisonment on each of the charges, to be served concurrently. The Tribunal ruled that Ruggiu's time in custody since his arrest was also to be taken into account, and counted toward his imprisonment. The government of Rwanda protested the sentence as inadequate, as the prosecutor had asked for a sentence of 20 years. Ruggiu did not appeal his sentence. In reaching its verdict, the Tribunal took note of a number of mitigating circumstances, namely, the fact that he pleaded guilty, his cooperation throughout the proceedings, the absence of any criminal record, his malleable character, his regrets and remorse, the fact that he had played a hand in saving a few Tutsi children, the fact that he neither belonged to the Rwandan ruling elite nor to the decision-making body of the RTLM, and finally the fact that he had not participated directly in the massacres. His sentence was also influenced by his having agreed to testify against a number of other members of RTLM then awaiting or undergoing trial. Ruggiu was the third defendant to plead guilty at the ICTR, the first two being former prime minister Jean Kambanda and former militia leader Omar Serushago.

In February 2008 the ICTR decided to transfer Ruggiu to Italy, to serve out the remainder of his sentence. The transfer followed an agreement between the United Nations and the Italian government, after a Rome court had ruled that ICTR sentences could henceforth be enforced in that country. Then, on April 21, 2009, Ruggiu was granted an early release by the Italian authorities, a violation of Article 27 of the ICTR Statute which states that only the president of the ICTR may decide on the early release of those convicted, no matter where the sentence is being served.

Georges Ruggiu remains the only non-Rwandan to be convicted by the ICTR for involvement in the genocide, and was the fourth person convicted by the ICTR to be released after serving out a sentence.

PAUL R. BARTROP

See also: International Criminal Tribunal for Rwanda; Nahimana, Ferdinand; Radio-Télévision Libre des Mille Collines

Further Reading

Kressel, Neil Jeffrey. *Mass Hate: The Global Rise of Genocide and Terror.* New York: Plenum Press, 1996.

Schabas, William A. *Genocide in International Law: The Crime of Crimes.* Cambridge, UK: Cambridge University Press, 2000.

Rusesabagina, Paul

Paul Rusesabagina is a much-honored former Rwandan, best known as a rescuer of Tutsis during the Rwandan Genocide between April and July 1994. He was born in Murama-Gitarama in the Central-South of Rwanda, about 50 miles from Kigali, on June 15, 1954. Of mixed Hutu-Tutsi background—his father was Hutu and his mother Tutsi—his parents and their nine children pursued the traditional vocation of many rural Hutus as farmers. Rusesabagina was educated at a local Seventh Day Adventist Missionary School in Gitwe, and spent three years as a theology student in Cameroon. He then studied in the Hotel Management Program at Utalii College in Nairobi, Kenya, and continued his studies in Switzerland. After graduating, he was hired as the assistant general manager of the Mille Collines Hotel in Kigali, a luxury property owned by the Belgian airline SABENA. He remained in this position from October 1984 until November 1992, when he was promoted to general manager of the nearby Hotel Diplomates, an equally prestigious property. On April 12, 1994, Rusesabagina returned to the Mille Collines as general manager.

In the 11 weeks that followed—he was managing both hotels, as the Belgian owners of the Mille Collines had appointed him temporary manager after the white managers had been ordered back to Belgium—Rusesabagina managed to shelter no fewer than 1,268 people, mostly Tutsis, from the Hutu militias bent on their destruction.

At first, troops from the United Nations Assistance Mission for Rwanda (UNAMIR), under the command of General Roméo Dallaire, provided protection for the hotel and those within, but this did not last indefinitely—nor could Dallaire's hard-pressed and tiny force have offered much resistance if it came to a showdown with the Interahamwe or Impuzamugambi militias or the Rwandan armed forces. About halfway into the genocide the protection detail of UNAMIR was largely withdrawn, and Rusesabagina was forced to rely on other means to protect the hotel and those he was sheltering inside, who included among their number both refugees and orphans.

Not only did the Hutu Power killers continually threaten imminent death; they blockaded the hotel so that foodstuffs, water, electricity, and communication with the outside world were cut off. One phone/fax line, however, was missed and remained operative, and through this the people at the Mille Collines were able to make desperate calls to international agencies to let the world know what was happening and to seek some form of intervention to save their lives. After the water supply was cut off, only the water in the hotel pool was available as a reservoir that could be tapped into for basic needs. Beyond this, all Rusesabagina had available to keep the militias at bay were a combination of diplomacy, flattery, and deception—and the hotel's well-supplied wine cellar, which was attractive to those besieging the hotel and its occupants.

At first he enjoyed a relatively favorable position, despite his mixed parentage and the fact that he had married a Tutsi woman. His business and personal connections with important Hutus such as Georges Rutaganda and Colonel Augustin Bizimungu led to a measure of protection, the more so after Rusesabagina found ways of paying them off with bribes funded through those the hotel was haboring.

Eventually, at the end of the genocide in July 1994, Rusesabagina and his family managed to escape to Tanzania, but soon afterward he returned to Rwanda and to hotel management. He remained in Kigali running the Mille Collines for another two years, but his position became increasingly untenable owing to continued ethnic tensions and the controversy over his role during the genocide. He even faced death threats. In September 1996 he sought asylum in Belgium, and moved to Brussels. He found work as a taxi driver, but later developed a trucking company which he now operates out of Zambia, shipping goods within Europe and Africa. He did not leave Rwanda behind him, however, and in 2005 he started the Hotel Rwanda Rusesabagina Foundation (HRRF), an organization that works to prevent future genocides and raise awareness of the need for a new truth and reconciliation process in Rwanda and Africa's Great Lakes region.

For his efforts, Rusesabagina has since been referred to by some as "the Oskar Schindler of Rwanda," yet this is a title he plays down, preferring to offer the view that saving people from murder is nothing special, just the right thing to do. Others have not been so flattering. Many of those who remember the conditions at the Mille Collines during the genocide have recalled how Rusesabagina would charge for the water drawn from the pool; would only accept people who could pay cash to stay in the hotel; and would evict people who could no longer pay—their fate to be decided by the militias waiting outside. Criticism of Rusesabagina has become something of a cottage industry in Rwanda, with Rwandan president Paul Kagame suggesting that Rusesabagina has built his reputation on a falsehood, and that he is in fact not the hero that has been portrayed. In 2005 François Xavier Ngarambe, the president of the peak association of genocide survivors, Ibuka ("Remember"), dismissed claims to heroism for Rusesabagina, saying that he was more interested in making money out of the chaos in 1994 than in saving lives. The relationship between Rusesabagina and many in Rwanda, particularly the Kagame regime, continues to smolder. On June 23, 2011, Belgian police, on the advice of the Rwandan government, questioned Rusesabagina over his possible involvement with the Forces démocratiques de libération du Rwanda (Democratic Forces for the Liberation of Rwanda, or FLDR), a Hutu rebel group operating out of the Democratic Republic of Congo. It includes several key perpetrators of the 1994 genocide who have so far evaded capture.

Rusesabagina's story has been told to high acclaim in the West, particularly the United States. In 2000, he was awarded the Immortal Chaplains Foundation (Minnesota) Prize for Humanity. Early in 2005 he received a National Civil Rights Museum Freedom Award, and in October the same year was awarded the prestigious Wallenberg Medal from the University of Michigan in recognition of his

rescue work during the genocide. Finally, on November 9, 2005, Rusesabagina received the U.S. Presidential Medal of Freedom from President George W. Bush.

In 2004 Rusesabagina and the story of the Hotel Mille Collines during the genocide was the subject of the first major Hollywood motion picture on the genocide, *Hotel Rwanda* (director/writer/producer, Terry George, United Artists, 2004), an Academy Award–nominated movie starring Don Cheadle in the starring role. Rusesabagina told his own story in an autobiography, *An Ordinary Man*, published in April 2006.

PAUL R. BARTROP

See also: Bizimungu, Augustin; Dallaire, Roméo; *Hotel Rwanda* (Film, 2004); Rutaganda, Georges; United Nations Assistance Mission for Rwanda

Further Reading

Eltringham, Nigel. *Accounting for Horror: Post-Genocide Debates in Rwanda*. London: Pluto Press, 2004.

Rusesabagina, Paul. *An Ordinary Man: An Autobiography*. New York: Viking, 2006.

Rutaganda, Georges

Georges Rutaganda was the first defendant to be convicted of war crimes by the International Criminal Tribunal for Rwanda (ICTR). The vice president of the Rwandan Interahamwe Hutu militia, he was born on November 28, 1958, in Ngoma, Kibuye prefecture. A man of some wealth, Rutaganda was an agricultural engineer and businessman, and chairman of his own limited liability company importing food and beverages and other commodities into Rwanda prior to the genocide of 1994.

Rutaganda was a member of the national and regional committees of the Mouvement Républicain National pour le Développement et la Démocratie (MRNDD), the political arm of the authoritarian regime of Rwandan president Juvénal Habyarimana. An anti-Tutsi militant, he was also a shareholder in the Hutu Power radio propaganda arm, Radio-Télévision Libre des Mille Collines (RTLM), and during the period of the genocide he appeared on RTLM in Kigali. In April 1994 Rutaganda was instrumental in directing, encouraging, and participating in the killing of vast numbers of Tutsis by the Interahamwe, as well as any Hutus who opposed the murders. It was alleged that he also participated in several killings of civilians, and led house-to-house searches during which Tutsis were captured and executed. His alleged crimes also included the distribution of guns and other weapons to the Interahamwe, and ordering and participating in the deaths of 18 Tutsis at a roadblock near his office. Allegations were also made to the effect that he participated in the attack on the École Technique Officielle (Official Technical School) in Kicuckiro commune after the withdrawal of Belgian United Nations forces, where unarmed people had found refuge. Rutaganda reportedly ordered and participated in the slaughter of men, women, and children at the school, and directed the forcible transfer of the survivors. It has been further alleged that Rutaganda captured, raped, and tortured Tutsi women in Interahamwe strongholds in Kigali. Throughout this time, it was said that Rutaganda's Interahamwe forces were supplied with weapons and other items stolen from the Rwandan military.

For all his activities, Rutaganda was known to be a leading figure involved in the genocide, highly sought-after by the ICTR.

With the defeat of the Hutu Power government by the Tutsi-led Rwandan Patriotic Front army, Rutaganda fled the country with tens of thousands of others in July 1994. He was tracked down and arrested in Lusaka, Zambia, on October 10, 1995, and indicted by the ICTR on February 13, 1996, charged on eight counts including genocide, crimes against humanity, and violations of the common article 3 of the Geneva Conventions. In his defense, Rutaganda's attorneys argued that he had in fact attempted to save lives, and that he had no influence over the roadblocks where victims were stopped and singled out for immediate execution. He pleaded not guilty to all charges in the indictment.

He was transferred to the custody of the ICTR in Arusha, Tanzania, on May 26, 1996, and, on December 6 the court found him guilty on three counts in his indictment: count 1 (genocide), count 2 (crimes against humanity: extermination) and count 7 (crimes against humanity: murder). He was sentenced to life imprisonment.

Both Rutaganda and the ICTR prosecutor appealed the decision, respectively on January 5 and 6, 2000. The Appeal Chamber's decision was handed down on May 26, 2003. The five judges unanimously found Rutaganda guilty on four counts: genocide, crimes against humanity (extermination), and two counts of murder related to war crimes (violations of article 3 common to the Geneva Conventions). The Chamber confirmed the convictions relating to counts 1 and 2, but acquitted Rutaganda of count 7 due to a lack

of coherence in statements from various witnesses. It further found Rutaganda guilty on two new counts of wilful killing in violation of the common article 3 of the Geneva Conventions, making this the first time a defendant before the ICTR had been convicted of war crimes. The Appeal Chamber considered that the revised verdict with respect to both the acquittal and the two new counts did not affect the validity of the facts on which the Trial Chamber's original decision had been based. Rutaganda's life sentence was thereby confirmed. He was the sixth Rwandan to be convicted of genocide by the ICTR, and the fourth to be sentenced to life in prison. On June 27, 2009, he was transferred to Cotonou, Benin, to serve out the remainder of his life sentence. On October 22, 2010, he died in jail following what was termed a "sudden complication" after a long illness.

In 2004, Rutaganda was controversially portrayed in an Academy Award–winning movie about the Rwandan genocide, *Hotel Rwanda,* directed by Irish filmmaker Terry George. In the film, the part of Rutaganda was played by Nigerian-born British actor Hakeem Kae-Kazim. Rutaganda was represented in the movie as an unscrupulous anti-Tutsi fanatic and war profiteer, prepared to go to any lengths to kill Tutsis, elevate Hutus (and co-opt them into the genocidal project), and make as much money for himself as he could along the way. In the film he had the most contact with the hero, Paul Rusesabagina, who was in reality an old friend of Rutaganda from the days before the genocide. The reasons behind the controversy came in the film's aftermath, as many who were witness to Rutaganda's actions during the genocide claimed that the movie misrepresented his efforts to lessen anti-Tutsi actions at roadblocks and elsewhere, in order to make the film's main characters—Rusesabagina and the UN commander, Colonel Vincent (a mask for the real-life leader of the UN forces, General Roméo Dallaire)—look more saintly. While the filmmakers took dramatic license for the sake of the plot, however, Rutaganda's indictment, trial, and verdict all showed that assertions claiming his virtuousness were at least exaggerated, if not altogether false.

PAUL R. BARTROP

See also: Habyarimana, Juvénal; *Hotel Rwanda* (Film, 2004); Interahamwe; International Criminal Tribunal for Rwanda; Radio-Télévision Libre des Mille Collines; Rutaganda Trial

Further Reading

Melvern, Linda. *Conspiracy to Murder: The Rwandan Genocide.* London: Verso, 2006.

Prunier, Gérard. *The Rwanda Crisis, 1959–1994: History of a Genocide*. Kampala: Fountain Publishers, 1995.

Rutaganda Trial

Between March 1997 and December 1999, Georges Rutaganda, former second vice president of the national committee of the Rwandan (Hutu) Interahamwe militia, was tried by the International Criminal Tribunal for Rwanda (ICTR) on eight counts of genocide and crimes against humanity. The trial was delayed many times, primarily because of the defendant's health. Throughout the trial, the prosecution and defense presented near polar opposite accounts of Rutaganda's life, both in the years before the 1994 Rwandan genocide and in the crucial month of April 1994, when most of the killings of Tutsis occurred.

The prosecution argued that, between 1991 and 1994, Rutaganda had risen to be a party leader and that the Interahamwe was a well-organized movement within the party. Rutaganda argued that during this time he was an overworked businessman with little time for, or interest in, party affairs. He also argued that the Interahamwe was never formally organized. The accounts became increasingly divergent in describing the April events. The prosecution argued that the Interahamwe had transformed itself into a militia responsible for thousands of deaths. It claimed that Rutaganda, as a group leader, organized roadblocks separating out Tutsis, distributed weapons, and led several massacres in Kigali and the Masango commune. Rutaganda countered by saying that the Interahamwe had ceased to exist by the time of the April chaos. Furthermore, he portrayed himself as a man protecting his business interests, fearing for his own life, and helping many Tutsis flee. The Tribunal found Rutaganda guilty of genocide and two counts of crimes against humanity. He was found not guilty on two overlapping crimes against humanity counts and three counts of violating the Geneva Convention. Both sides appealed the ruling, but the appeals were even more drawn out than the original trial.

Rutaganda was arrested in Zambia in October 1995. He was indicted by the Tribunal the following spring; many expected his trial would be one of the first completed, because he was in custody at the time of the indictment. The trial was held in Chamber 1, with Laity Kama presiding along with Lennart Aspergen and Navanethem Pillay. James Stewart led the prosecution. Twenty-seven prosecution witnesses were called to support the allegations that Rutaganda was a key leader and was personally responsible for the killings. Tiphaine Dickson led the defense. She was generally considered to have presented a strong defense.

Rutaganda was from a well-known and politically influential family. He worked as a government agricultural engineer, but later went into private business. His main concern was an import company that specialized in beer. He was also a minority owner of the company that owned Radio-Télévision Libre des Mille Collines, which later became known for broadcasting provocative anti-Tutsi propaganda. In 1991, he joined the Movement of the Republic for National Development (MRND) and soon became a leader of its youth group, the Interahamwe. The prosecution argued that these affiliations proved that he was a key party figure. In his defense, Rutaganda testified that he had joined the party only because of a businessman's need for political connections and that he had never played a major party role.

The specific charges against Rutaganda were based on a series of incidents in April 1994. Around April 10, Rutaganda reportedly organized the Interahamwe to establish roadblocks in Kigali. Those with Tutsi identification cards were separated out, interrogated by Rutaganda and later killed. On April 11, he reportedly led a massacre of hundreds who had taken refuge at the École Technique Officielle (ETO). Those who survived the ETO attack were taken to a gravel pit where the remaining Tutsi victims were killed. Rutaganda was also accused of leading house-to-house searches for Tutsis in Masango and then forcing those captured into a river. Finally, Rutaganda reportedly pursued and killed with a machete a man who was fleeing another roadblock.

The defense called witnesses who asserted that Rutaganda had not been at the locations in question. The defense also questioned the reliability of prosecution witnesses. The key to the defense, however, was Rutaganda's testimony. He sharply disputed the contention that the Interahamwe had become an organized militia. Instead, he portrayed the killings as a series of isolated events. He also described how he feared that his businesses would be looted or destroyed and that he feared for his own safety and that of his family should the shifting political landscape bring new people to power. Furthermore, he argued that rather than leading attacks on Tutsis, he made several efforts to shelter them or help people through the roadblocks. The prosecution argued that these comments in fact demonstrated that he did have influence over the

Interahamwe, but Rutaganda denied this and concluded by arguing that he had been buoyed by the prospect of inquiries into the April events because he believed they would lead to his recognition as a humanitarian.

Almost two years after the trial began; Rutaganda was found guilty on three counts and sentenced to life in prison. He was found not guilty on two counts of crimes against humanity for murder, because the judges ruled that he was guilty of extermination in these cases, but should not be convicted twice for the same event. The court also found him not guilty of violations of the Geneva Convention, because the Interahamwe was not an organized combat force. The prosecution appealed in hopes of convicting him on more crimes against humanities counts. The defense also appealed, claiming the Tribunal had been biased against Rutaganda and that his punishment was influenced by pressure from the Rwandan government after the Tribunal had released another defendant on technical grounds.

Rutaganda died in prison in Benin on October 11, 2010.

JOHN DIETRICH

See also: Interahamwe; International Criminal Tribunal for Rwanda; Radio-Télévision Libre des Mille Collines; Rutaganda, Georges

Further Reading

Cruvellier, Thierry. *Court of Remorse: Inside the International Criminal Court for Rwanda.* Madison: University of Wisconsin Press, 2010.

Des Forges, Alison, and Timothy Longman. "Legal Responses to Genocide in Rwanda." In My Neighbor, *My Enemy: Justice and Community in the Aftermath of Mass Atrocity.* Edited by Eric Stover and Harvey M. Weinstein, 49–63. Cambridge: Cambridge University Press, 2004.

Rwanda

The first known inhabitants of Rwanda were the Twa, or Pygmies, but they were eventually displaced by the Hutu peoples, who migrated from the Congo River basin during the 7th to 10th centuries. The Hutu agriculturists were well established by the time the Tutsi peoples arrived from the north in the 15th century. The Tutsis conquered the Hutus and ruled through an elaborate feudal system. Tutsi kings, or *mwamis,* governed with the Tutsi elite, who served as chiefs and subchiefs. The Hutu majority became serfs. The caste system was strictly enforced, with little intermarriage or mingling of cultures. The remaining Twa

existed on the very bottom of the social hierarchy. By the late 18th century, a single Tutsi-ruled state dominated most of what is now present-day Rwanda. The king had the ultimate power over his regional Tutsi vassals, who in turn ruled over the Hutu. The kingdom enjoyed its peak in the middle to late 19th century under the *mwami* Kigeri IV Rwabugiri, who had a standing army equipped with guns obtained from traders on the east African coast.

The first Europeans arrived in Rwanda in 1858, and in the 1880s, German explorers arrived. In 1890, the *mwami* of Rwanda agreed—without a fight—to accept German rule and join German East Africa. However, in practice, the Germans had no real influence over the region and devoted few resources to the development of their new holding. Not until 1907 did Germany have an administrative center in Rwanda. After World War I, Belgian forces occupied the region, along with present-day Burundi, as the Territory of Ruanda-Urundi, as directed by the League of Nations. The Belgians held Rwanda as a United Nations (UN) trust territory after World War II. Under Belgian rule, the traditional governing system remained intact. The Belgians forced the Tutsi aristocracy to phase out the unequal social caste system, but the Tutsis held on to their political power and the economic opportunities that came with it. That power emphasized class divisions and intensified the ethnic tensions that had been in place for centuries.

During the 1950s, the Hutus became increasingly vocal regarding their grievances about the inequalities of Rwanda's political and social system. They published a manifesto calling for more Hutu influence in the region's affairs and demanded a change to the Tutsi-dominated feudal structure. When King Muratara III died and Kigeri V succeeded him in 1959, the Hutus rebelled and claimed that the new leader was inappropriately chosen. Fighting erupted, and the Hutus won the battle. Hundreds of thousands of Tutsis fled, including King Kigeri V, and the Hutus took political control. Elections were held in 1960, and Grégoire Kayibanda of the Hutu Emancipation Movement (Parmehutu) became prime minister. A year later, the government proclaimed Ruanda a republic and abolished the Tutsi monarchy. Under pressure from the UN, Belgium granted the country independence on July 1, 1962. The country changed its name to Rwanda, while Parmehutu became the Democratic Republican Movement (MDR). When a Rwandan Constitution was adopted a few months later, Kayibanda became the nation's first president. He was reelected in 1965 and 1969. For the first time in the region's history since the Tutsis arrived, the

Hutus—who remembered the bitter taste of hundreds of years of serfdom—were in charge.

In 1964, the exiled Tutsis, who had fled when the Hutus revolted in 1959, returned to Rwanda as a rebel army and invaded from Burundi. The invasion was a failure and provoked a formidable retaliation by the Hutu Army, which began a large-scale massacre of Tutsis. Although the two sides reached an agreement in 1965, the peace was uneasy, and sporadic ethnic violence continued. Just before the 1973 elections, Kayibanda was ousted in a bloodless military coup led by General Juvénal Habyarimana. Habyarimana dissolved the National Assembly and suspended the MDR, which by then had become the only legal party. He founded the National Revolutionary Movement for Development (MRND) as the new ruling party. A new constitution in 1978 officially reconfirmed the country as a single-party state, now with the MRND as the sole legal party. Habyarimana became president, and in 1983 and 1988, he was reelected unopposed. During the 1980s, an intense drought devastated agriculture, and an influx of thousands of Burundi refugees added pressure to the already-declining economy. International aid donors, weary of pouring money into a mismanaged economy, pressured the government to make political and economic reforms. In 1990, opposition parties were legalized, but the move did not bring political peace.

The Rwandan Patriotic Front (FPR), made up of Tutsis and Hutu moderates and led by Paul Kagame, rose up against the government in 1990. Belgium and southwestern African countries sent forces to help the government put down the rebellion. After sustaining a strong blow to its forces, the FPR changed its tactics to guerrilla warfare and conducted intense, violent attacks from Ugandan bases. The Hutus used that to justify large-scale exterminations of Tutsis. However, the uprising did accelerate political reform. In 1991, a new constitution provided for multipartyism and other democratic reforms, and a prime minister was appointed to head a transitional MDR-led coalition government until 1995 elections. The UN sponsored a peace accord between the Rwandan government and the FPR in 1993 and dispatched peacekeeping forces to the country.

In early April 1994, Habyarimana was killed in a suspicious plane crash. Hutu forces, who credited Tutsi rebels with shooting down the president's aircraft, then began a series of large-scale massacres of Tutsis and Hutu moderates. (Many analysts believe the plane was actually shot down by Hutu hard-liners opposed to Habyarimana's steps toward implementing power-sharing arrangements with the Tutsis.) Without a mandate to stop the ethnic violence, the UN troops did nothing while the Hutu government sponsored the systematic massacre of at least 500,000 people. That massacre fueled an all-out civil war as the FPR began a concentrated offensive and moved toward Kigali. The FPR captured the capital in May 1994, and the government fled. By July, FPR forces had established control over most of the country. More than 1 million people—most of them Hutus fearful of Tutsi revenge for the massacres—fled from the victorious FPR troops. One-quarter of the prewar population was either killed or fled the country during the conflict.

The FPR installed a new government led by Pasteur Bizimungu, a moderate Hutu. The MRNDD (the MRND became the National Republican Movement for Democracy and Development in 1991) was forbidden to participate in the new administration. Meanwhile, hundreds of thousands of Hutu refugees in neighboring countries refused to go home because they feared Tutsi retaliation should they return. Toward the end of 1996, however, a rebellion launched by Tutsi rebels in Zaire and backed by Rwanda's Tutsi-dominated government led to the displacement of more than a million Rwandan Hutu refugees who had fled to Zaire in 1994. Hundreds of thousands of them returned home, although some fled west into Zaire's dense jungle areas. Many of the latter refugees died of disease and starvation during their trek across the country as the rebels swept to victory. The Zairian rebel forces, allegedly aided by Rwandan soldiers, were also accused of slaughtering tens of thousands of the Hutu refugees. (Rebel leader Laurent Kabila, who became president of Zaire in May 1997 and renamed it the Democratic Republic of Congo, denied the allegations.)

The UN had completed the withdrawal of its troops in Rwanda in early 1996 at the request of the Rwandan government, which blamed the UN for failing to stop the 1994 massacres. An international war crimes tribunal for Rwanda was installed at The Hague in June 1995 and began hearing its first case in 1996, but more than 50,000 people were still being held in seriously overcrowded jails in 2003, prompting the government to release 40,000 people in January of that year. Most played minor roles in the genocide and had already served more time than they would have received if convicted, and the government pledged that all would eventually be tried. The slow pace of prosecution by the war crimes tribunal has led the government to shift many cases to local *gacaca* courts, where suspects will be tried directly in front of their communities.

Before the Zairian rebellion that led to the return of hundreds of thousands of refugees, remnants of the former Hutu government army and the Hutu militias that carried out most of the 1994 killings had already begun making incursions into Rwandan territory from their bases at the refugee camps in neighboring nations. The violence within Rwanda grew worse after the return of the refugees, which included in their number Hutu militants. Human rights groups have also accused Rwandan Army soldiers of carrying out indiscriminate killings of civilians as part of their conflict with the Hutu militants.

Those attacks and violent clashes between ethnic groups continued through the late 1990s, but beginning in 1999, a series of government reform measures stabilized the country somewhat. In March 1999, local elections were held for the first time since the genocide, partly reestablishing precolonial systems of smaller, autonomous local governments. The government signed peace agreements with neighboring Uganda and the Democratic Republic of Congo in 2001 and 2002, respectively, extracting its troops from spillover wars with those countries. In a decisive step toward overcoming ethnic rivalries, 93 percent of Rwandan voters approved a new constitution in May 2003. The constitution outlaws dominance by one party in the government and incitement of ethnic hatred; it also paved the way for national elections in August 2003, in which Kagame won a landslide victory, getting 95 percent of the vote. Although he was accused by both opposition leaders and an international human rights group of suppressing opposition campaigning, including arresting at least 10 opposition leaders in the lead-up to the elections, international observers said they saw relatively few problems during polling. In 2004, the government allowed private radio stations to operate for the first time since the genocide. (Some broadcasters have been found guilty of inciting ethnic hatred during the genocide.)

There is both an international court and a series of local *gacaca* courts trying those accused of participating in the 1994 ethnic killings. However, the International Criminal Tribunal for Rwanda had been criticized for working too slowly, and several genocide witnesses were killed before they could testify in the *gacaca* courts, leading to suspicions of a backlash by those who carried out the genocide. In 2003, the government began to release large numbers of prisoners in an attempt to ease overcrowding in the prisons. In 2005, during the third phase of the process, 36,000 prisoners were released, most of whom had confessed to involvement in the 1994 genocide.

Paul R. Bartrop

See also: Arusha Accords; *Bahutu Manifesto*; Congo, Democratic Republic of; Dallaire, Roméo; Forces Armées Rwandaises; Habyarimana, Juvénal; Interahamwe; International Criminal Tribunal for Rwanda; Kagame, Paul; Media Trial in Rwanda; Radio-Télévision Libre des Mille Collines; Rwandan Patriotic Front; United Nations Assistance Mission for Rwanda

Further Reading

Adelman, Howard, and Astri Suhrke, eds. *The Path of a Genocide: The Rwanda Crisis from Uganda to Zaire.* New Brunswick, NJ: Transaction Publishers, 1999.

Dorsey, Learthen. *Historical Dictionary of Rwanda.* Metuchen, NJ: Scarecrow Press, 1994.

Kamukama, Dixon. *Rwanda Conflict: Its Roots and Regional Implications.* 2nd ed. Kampala, Uganda: Fountain Publishers, 1998.

Prunier, Gérard. *The Rwanda Crisis, 1959–1994: History of a Genocide.* Kampala: Fountain Publishers, 1995.

Rwanda Civil War

The Rwanda Civil War took place in Rwanda between October 1, 1990, and August 4, 1993. The conflict pitted the Rwandan government of Juvénal Habyarimana, which was dominated by the Hutus, against rebel forces (the Rwandan Patriotic Army), the armed component of the Rwandan Patriotic Front (RPF), which was a Tutsi organization. The Rwandan Civil War played a significant role in precipitating the Rwandan Genocide of 1994, which began only months after the civil war ended in a tenuous and shaky settlement.

The civil war in Rwanda had multiple causes besides the decades-old tension and hostility between the majority Tutsis and minority Hutus. The economy of Rwanda began to slip badly during 1989–1990, while inclement weather had produced low crop yields and food shortages. Meanwhile, a prodemocracy movement had been building in parts of Rwanda, which had received support from the French. This led to increased political agitation toward the Hutu-led government. At the same time, thousands of Tutsis who had earlier fled Rwanda, many of them residing in appalling conditions in Uganda, had begun to coalesce around the RPF. That group was advocating a mass return to Rwanda, where it hoped to reclaim former Tutsi lands and sought political and social recognition. A number of

Tutsis were also now serving in the Ugandan military. The Ugandan government, in the meantime, had begun to forbid non-Ugandans from owning land, which discriminated against Tutsi refugees living in Uganda. This made the refugees even more anxious to return to Rwanda.

The Rwandan Patriotic Army, some 4,000–6,000-men strong, launched an invasion of northern Rwanda from Uganda on October 1, 1990, setting off the three-year conflict. Many were dressed in Ugandan military uniforms and carried Ugandan weapons. The RPF rebels struck while both the Ugandan and Rwandan presidents were out of their countries attending a United Nations summit in New York. The RPF demanded an immediate end to ethnic segregation and discrimination in Rwanda and a host of other prodemocracy changes to the Rwandan government. Within days, both Zaire and France intervened in the hostilities, both supporting the Rwandan government forces.

On the evening of October 4, Rwandan government forces launched an offensive in the capital of Kigali, chiefly to intimidate the city's residents and convince them to support the government. At least 10,000 Rwandans were also arrested for allegedly supporting the RPF rebels. By early 1991, the RPF decided to down-play the conventional aspects of their insurgency and instead focus on a guerilla-style war, principally in northern Rwanda. The guerilla war was a classic hit-and-run affair, which Rwandan troops found very difficult to defend against. Villages were often targeted, with many civilians killed or wounded.

Meanwhile, there were numerous attempts to broker a cease-fire, some by the international community. On June 12, 1992, truce talks finally commenced at Arusha, Tanzania, but those negotiations would drag on until August 4, 1993, when the Arusha Accords created a new power-sharing arrangement in Rwanda. A tenuous cease-fire had begun on July 31, 1992, although there was continued lower-level fighting for months thereafter. Within Rwanda, the civil war greatly increased already-high ethnic tensions between the Hutus and Tutsis. Many Hutus were now bent on destroying the Tutsis, whom they feared would re-create the Rwanda of old, which was ruled with an iron hand by the Tutsi minority. The results of the civil war clearly helped create the conditions within which the Rwandan Genocide would occur. That bloody conflagration began in April 1994, just eight months after the conclusion of the Arusha Accords.

PAUL G. PIERPAOLI JR.

See also: Forces Armées Rwandaises; Habyarimana, Juvénal; Hutus; Rwanda; Rwandan Patriotic Army; Rwandan Patriotic Front; Tutsis

Further Reading

Ali, Taisier M., and Robert O. Matthews. *Civil Wars in Africa: Roots and Resolution.* Toronto: McGill-Queen's University Press, 1999.

Prunier, Gérard. *Africa's World War.* Oxford, UK: Oxford University Press, 2009.

Rwanda: Death, Despair and Defiance

Rwanda: Death, Despair and Defiance is a written report on the Rwandan Genocide first issued by the London-based human rights group African Rights in 1994. In 1995, a second edition was published and made available to the public for purchase. *Rwanda: Death, Despair and Defiance* was the first detailed account of the 1994 genocide in Rwanda. The report begins with a brief history of Rwanda and an analysis of how that history contributed to the mass bloodletting. Much of the work is based upon actual accounts of the events by survivors. The stories are unembellished and translated into English virtually verbatim. The report also examines the various institutions in Rwandan society and the role they played in the genocide. Thus, the genocide is examined at varying levels—from the personal, to the local, to the regional, to the national. The report also analyzes the ideology that underwrote Hutu extremism.

The survivors' accounts document the graphic and psychological horrors of the killing, and they also describe the betrayal of friends, neighbors, and even family during the ordeal. As well, the survivors describe flashes of brightness amid the dark terror, including the compassion and kindness of those who tried to help or shield them, as well as the resilience of the human spirit.

The report also details the Rwandan government's attempts to stifle and then liquidate Hutus who opposed the regime, as well as the propensity of genocide perpetrators to engage in violence against women and children. While the authors of the work reveal that a number of well-educated Hutus became willing participants in the genocide, they are not wholly successful in explaining why. Finally, the report examines world reaction to the events in Rwanda and how the international community failed to stop the carnage. Some critics of the report have asserted that the authors failed to assign adequate blame to the Rwandan Patriotic Front (RPF), arguing that its questionable activities went largely unexamined. Although the report has since been eclipsed by more recent literature, it remains a useful guide to understanding the Rwandan Genocide.

PAUL G. PIERPAOLI JR.

See also: Rwanda; Rwandan Patriotic Front

Further Reading

African Rights. *Rwanda: Death, Despair and Defiance.* 2nd rev. ed. London: African Rights, 1995.

Rwanda: The Preventable Genocide

Rwanda: The Preventable Genocide is a comprehensive report on the 1994 Rwandan Genocide sponsored by the Organization of African Unity and released in July 2000. An international panel of experts studied the issue and compiled the report. That panel included individuals from Africa, India, Canada, and Sweden. *Rwanda: The Preventable Genocide* consists of an introduction in addition to 24 chapters, the last of which includes recommendations on how to avert future genocides. The report gives a summary of the causes, course, and results of the Rwandan Genocide, but its main focus is clearly one of assigning blame to various players and bystanders who either helped precipitate the genocide or who did nothing to stop the killing once it began.

The report is highly critical of the United Nations (UN), particularly then-Secretary General Boutros Boutros-Ghali and the UN Security Council, for their failure to take sufficient action to prevent or limit the scope of the killings. The Security Council, the authors make clear, was slow to respond, and once it finally settled on the deployment of a peacekeeping mission, it hamstrung its efforts by forbidding UN forces from directly intervening in the genocide and by limiting the number of troops sent to Rwanda. The United States also shares responsibility in the disaster, so the report argues, because it did not exercise its clout within the UN and actually hindered the deployment of an adequate and effective peacekeeping force.

The French government is also taken to task for its policies in the region before and during the carnage in Rwanda, and the work also made clear France's alleged role in permitting thousands of genocide perpetrators to flee Rwanda

for nearby Zaire. The Catholic Church is also faulted for its inaction during the genocide. The report concludes that the genocide was entirely preventable, and further that it was possible only because of the international community's failure to intervene. The Rwanda Genocide was not, the report's authors argue, precipitated by poverty; rather, it was caused by long-standing racial hatred that had been stoked and even encouraged by colonial policies and the foreign policies of certain Western nations, including the United States, France, and Belgium. Finally, the report recommends the payment of reparations to the genocide survivors by those nations and institutions who stood by and did nothing to stop the bloodletting. That recommendation has, to date, not been realized.

PAUL G. PIERPAOLI JR.

See also: Boutros; Rwanda; United Nations Assistance Mission for Rwanda

Further Reading

Straus, Scott. *The Order of Genocide: Race, Power, and War in Rwanda.* Ithaca, NY: Cornell University Press, 2008.

Rwandan Genocide, French Response to the

France's longstanding involvement in Rwanda's affairs prior to, during, and after the Rwandan Genocide has led many to believe that the country was complicit in that catastrophe. As early as the early 1960s—when Rwanda was granted independence from Belgium—French leaders and policymakers sought to provide aid and support to the Rwandan government's Hutu leaders. This support increased substantially after François Mitterrand became the French president in 1981. He hoped to maintain the French language in Rwanda (French was the official language there until 2007) and expand French influence in Africa. He also cultivated an especially close relationship with Rwandan president Juvénal Habyarimana.

After the Tutsi-led Rwandan Patriotic Front (RPF) commenced open warfare with Habyarimana's regime, which in turn precipitated the 1990–1993 Rwandan Civil War, France stepped up its aid to Rwanda significantly. This aid, known as Opération NOIROT, came in the form of military equipment and ammunition of all types as well as advice from French military advisers and other experts who were dispatched to Rwanda. These advisers helped Habyarimana to expand his army from some 9,000 soldiers in late

1990 to more than 30,000 by 1991. French military personnel also helped train Rwandan army units, including Habyarimana's presidential guard. However, some of the French aid ended up going to anti-Tutsi militias, including the infamous *Interahamwe,* which played a key role in the Rwandan Genocide.

The genocide began after Habyarimana's presidential aircraft (which the French had loaned to him for his personal use) was shot down over Kigali on April 6, 1994. Habyarimana died in the attack. The Rwandan government blamed Tutsis and the RPF for the assassination, and almost immediately began to carry out its plans to exterminate Rwanda's minority Tutsi population, along with Hutus who tried to protect them. To this day, however, there is no conclusive evidence to indicate who was behind Habyarimana's death.

On April 8, 1994, as evidence of a mounting genocide was becoming clear, the French government implemented Opération AMARYLLIS, which evacuated some 1,500 individuals, most of them Europeans, from Rwanda. The operation also helped evacuate officials within the Habyramana government from the country. The mission ended on April 14. Later, the French were criticized for evacuating Europeans and government officials from Rwanda while they did nothing to evacuate Rwandans threatened by genocide. Indeed, the operation did not even extend to Rwandans who had been working for French military advisers and technical experts. Meanwhile, a commander of the United Nations Assistance Mission for Rwanda (UN-AMIR), which had been in Rwanda since the summer of 1993, reported that one of the French aircraft involved in the operation had unloaded some 5 tons of ammunition. The French vehemently denied this claim.

Despite its checkered involvement in the genocide, during May and June 1994, while the international community fretted over—but did nothing—to stop the genocide, French officials at the UN supported a strengthened UN-AMIR. It also suggested another aid operation to Rwanda, Operation TURQUOISE. Under French leadership, the operation established a "safe haven" in southeastern Rwanda, where embattled Tutsis and moderate Hutus could seek refuge. The UN approved the operation, which began on June 22 and lasted until August 22. Unfortunately, by then, the genocide had subsided and the operation occurred too late to save many lives. To make matters worse, many Hutu perpetrators sought refuge in the safe haven, which rendered them virtually immune to prosecution.

Since 1994, Franco-Rwandan relations have been on the skids, especially after Tutsi president Paul Kagame took power in 2000. His government has been highly critical of France's role in the genocide and believes that it must share the blame for it. The French government has engaged in several inquiries and commissions designed to gauge French complicity in the genocide, but none found any overt wrongdoing on the part of the French government.

In April 2004, Kagame publicly chastised the French for their failure to apologize for their complicity in the Rwandan Genocide. The French, in turn, accused Kagame of having orchestrated Habyarimana's death and therefore setting off the mass killings. Kagame categorically denies any such involvement. In August 2008, an independent Rwandan commission concluded that France had helped train and equip Hutu militias. The commission's report went on to name 33 senior French government and military leaders who were responsible—directly or indirectly—for the genocide, including Mitterrand as well as France's prime minister and foreign minister. The French government continues its official denials, although there are many Frenchmen, both civilians and government officials, who are suspect of the French government's position. In 2007, the Kagame regime made English the official language of his country and sought membership in the British Commonwealth, a sure sign that it is trying to purge Rwanda of its ties to France. Not surprisingly, Franco-Rwandan relations' remain very poor.

PAUL G. PIERPAOLI JR.

See also: Habyarimana, Juvénal; Kagame, Paul; Operation TURQUOISE; Rwanda; Rwandan Patriotic Front; United Nations Assistance Mission for Rwanda

Further Reading

Dallaire, Roméo. *Shake Hands with the Devil: The Failure of Humanity in Rwanda.* Toronto: Random House, 2004.
Melvern, Linda. *Conspiracy to Murder: The Rwandan Genocide.* London: Verso, 2006.

Rwandan Genocide, Role of Propaganda in the

Propaganda played a critical role in the implementation and execution of the 1994 Rwandan Genocide. Hutu extremists used propaganda to breed ethnic tension within Rwanda and to mobilize Hutus to participate in the killing. In the weeks preceding the genocide and continuing throughout the massacre, anti-Tutsi propaganda dominated Rwandan radio, television, newspaper, and all other forms of media. Galvanized by the messaging of the

Machetes and bullets near the border in Gisenyi, Rwanda, July 1994. (UN Photo/John Isaac)

propaganda, almost 85 percent of the Hutu population, including government officials, soldiers and police, political leaders, religious figures, and various militia members, acted to exterminate more than 800,000 of their Tutsi family members, friends and neighbors, as well as moderate Hutus, primarily using machetes, in just 100 days.

Propaganda was directed toward several successive purposes: first, to cast Tutsis as the enemy; second, to dehumanize the enemy; and third, to convince the Hutu population that killing the enemy was the only option for survival. To achieve the first purpose, propaganda portrayed Tutsis as scapegoats for historical inequities between Hutus and Tutsis, drawing heavily on stereotypes that had survived since the Hutu and Tutsi identities were first constructed by Belgian colonizers. Messaging was strategically intended to make Hutus fearful for their lives and livelihoods, warning that the Tutsi Rwandan Patriotic Front (RPF) and Tutsi civilians were working to assure "RPF victory and death to Hutu." Toward the second purpose, propaganda used imagery aimed at dehumanizing Tutsis, depicting them as cockroaches or "*inyenzi*" that must be killed. Anti-Tutsi propaganda even specified the machete as the weapon of choice for killing. To achieve the third purpose, propaganda delineated two groups of the population: the killers and the victims, with no middle ground. "Kill or die," the Hutu saying went. When the official call to action sounded, and as a directly result of the sustained and pervasive propaganda campaign, many

Hutus believed that they had no other option; survival dictated they participate in the genocide.

The use of propaganda to carry out acts of genocide and to incite its commission in Rwanda was confirmed in a 2003 judgment by the International Criminal Tribunal for Rwanda (ICTR) in the so-called Media Case. The ICTR was established in 1994 by the United Nations Security Council for the prosecution of persons responsible for genocide and other serious violations of international humanitarian law in Rwanda between January 1, 1994, and December 31, 1994. The three defendants in the Media Case all held influential roles within the Rwandan media: one was the founder and editor-in-chief of the Kangura newspaper, another, a founding member of the *Radio Television Libre des Mille Collines,* and the third the Director of the Rwandan Office of Information. Based on their involvement in the anti-Tutsi propaganda campaign, all three defendants were found guilty of conspiracy to commit genocide, genocide, and direct and public incitement to commit genocide. The judgment was one of the first of its kind to find that the use of propaganda to incite and commit genocide entailed criminal responsibility, highlighting the significant role that propaganda played in the Rwandan Genocide.

ELINOR O. STEVENSON

See also: Hutus; Rwanda; Rwanda Civil War; Tutsis

Further Reading

Des Forges, Alison, and Timothy Longman. "Legal Responses to Genocide in Rwanda." In *My Neighbor, My Enemy: Justice and Community in the Aftermath of Mass Atrocity.* Edited by Eric Stover and Harvey M. Weinstein, 49–63. Cambridge: Cambridge University Press, 2004.

Hatzfield, Jean. *Machete Season: The Killers in Rwanda Speak.* Translated by Linda Coverdale. New York: Farrar, Straus and Giroux, 2005.

International Criminal Tribunal for Rwanda, Prosecutor v. Ferdinand Nahimana, Jean-Bosco Barayagwiza, and Hassan Ngeze, Judgment and Sentence, Case No. ICTR-99–52-T (Trial Chamber 1, December 3, 2003).

Power, Samantha. *"A Problem from Hell": America and the Age of Genocide.* New York: Harper Perennial, 2007.

Rwandan Genocide, U.S. Response to the

Mirroring sentiments within the larger international community, the U.S. government chose not to intervene in the 1994 Rwandan Genocide, which resulted in the deaths of as many as 1 million Tutsis and moderate Hutus. After the carnage began on April 6, 1994, many of the world's leading powers refused to become involved in the genocide, terming it an internal Rwandan problem. France, China, and Russia all opposed intervention, and the United Nations (UN) was powerless to act, even though it had peacekeeping troops on the ground in Rwanda as part of the United Nations Assistance Mission for Rwanda (UNAMIR). That mission had been dispatched in October 1993 to implement a peace arrangement between the Hutu-led Rwandan government and the Tutsi-dominated Rwandan Patriotic Front (RPF). Without a broad-based mandate to stop the killing, it was highly unlikely that the Bill Clinton administration would have intervened unilaterally.

The Clinton administration was also reluctant to act because of the disastrous 1992–1993 Somalia intervention, an operation that Clinton had inherited from his predecessor, George H. W. Bush. After the humanitarian mission morphed into a program designed to disarm rival warlords in 1993, U.S. troops suffered a humiliating defeat in the October 3–4 Battle of Mogadishu. That engagement resulted in the deaths of 18 American soldiers and the wounding of 73 others. As cameras rolled, one soldier's body was dragged through the streets by an angry mob. The incident was a deep embarrassment for the young, new president and drew much criticism from Republicans and Democrats alike. Clinton soon withdrew all troops from Somalia, convinced that unilateral military interventions were not worth the inherent risks involved with them.

As news of the Rwandan tragedy unfolded, Clinton came under increasing pressure to do something to stop the killing. But fearing another Somalia debacle, and unwilling to act without UN authority or intervene unilaterally, the U.S. government chose inaction. Furthermore, Clinton's main advisers and military commanders cautioned against an intervention in an unstable place, where the United States had few strategic interests. Hoping to tamp down any public criticism, Clinton ordered administration officials not to term the events in Rwanda as a genocide, although documents released more recently indicate that in private administration officials were referring to the killings as a genocide only two weeks after the cataclysm began. U.S. ambassador to the UN, Madeleine Albright also refused to term the conflict as a genocide.

In addition, the United States refused to denounce the Rwandan government, did nothing to jam anti-Tutsi radio and television stations, and hesitated to send military supplies to the UNAMIR II mission, which was being mobilized before the genocide had even ended. Despite this great prevarication, documents show that the U.S. government was cognizant of the extent of the carnage in Rwanda only a week into the conflict, and that Clinton and his cabinet almost certainly knew that the Hutu Rwandan government was bent on exterminating the Tutsis within Rwanda.

Clinton's failure to respond to the Rwandan Genocide deeply troubled him. He later expressed much regret over his government's inaction and has stated that it was one of low points of his eight-year presidency. He has visited Rwanda several times, and in 1998, while still president, he apologized for his "personal failure" to prevent the genocide. To help make amends, his Clinton Foundation has been heavily involved in reconstruction and humanitarian efforts in Rwanda. While the U.S. refusal to intervene in the Rwandan crisis was certainly a great humanitarian failure, it is important to remember that this failure is shared by the entire world.

PAUL G. PIERPAOLI JR.

See also: Bushnell, Prudence; Hutus; Operation SUPPORT HOPE; Rwandan Patriotic Front; Tutsis; United Nations Assistance Mission for Rwanda

Further Reading

Gribbin, Robert E. *In the Aftermath of Genocide: The US Role in Rwanda.* New York: I Universe, 2005.

Power, Samantha. *"A Problem from Hell": America and the Age of Genocide.* New York: Harper Perennial, 2007.

Rwandan Patriotic Army

The Rwandan Patriotic Army (RPA) was the armed wing of the Rwandan Patriotic Front (RPF), a Tutsi rebel group established in 1987 by Tutsi refugees living in Uganda. For the most part, at least until 1994, when the RPA was absorbed into Rwanda's national defense establishment (now known as the Rwandan Defense Forces [RDF]) the RPA's history mirrored that of the RPF. By the late 1980s, the RPF was determined to destabilize the Hutu-dominated government of Juvénal Habyarimana in order to oust it from power or force it into a power-sharing arrangement with the RPF. Either way, the ultimate goal was to permit the 200,000-plus Hutu refugees living in Uganda to return to Rwanda. These refugees had been living in squalid conditions since the early 1960s and were routinely oppressed and harassed by the Ugandan government.

In 1989–1990, the RPA numbered only about 5,000 troops, and many had formerly served in the Ugandan military. Some of them were not well-trained, and most did not have access to the latest weaponry. In 1990, the RPF, using the RPA, decided to commence a military campaign against the Rwandan government. This entailed engaging Rwandan government troops (Forces Armées Rwandaises, FAR) as well as launching raids against civilian Hutus. The RPA's operations resulted in mounting deaths within Rwanda, which compelled the Rwandan government to seek military and financial help from the French. They supplied the FAR with arms and ammunition, helped train its soldiers, and significantly enlarged the size of the army, which numbered 40,000–50,000 men by 1994. The RPA's campaign resulted in the deaths of three of its original commanders—Fred Rwigyema, Peter Bayinga, and Chris Bunyenyezi—between 1990 and 1994.

By 1994, the command of the RPA had passed to Paul Kagame, who worked mightily to secure more and better weapons and to recruit more soldiers. In the spring of 1994, when the Rwandan Genocide began, the RPA numbered 25,000 men. This, however, meant that the army was only half the size of the FAR. The chaos that resulted in the April 6, 1994, assassination of Habyarimana and the genocide that followed permitted the RPA to overpower the FAR, and by August 1994, the RPA had secured most of the country and had stopped the killing. At that point, the RPF assumed control of the Rwandan government. Soon thereafter, the RPA was integrated into a new national military establishment, the RDF.

The RPA committed its own atrocities during and immediately after the 1994 genocide. RPA soldiers killed thousands of Hutus as they tried to flee Rwanda, and they killed many thousands more in refugee camps within Rwanda and in neighboring countries. It is estimated that as many as 200,000 Hutus died at the hands of the RPA. For this reason, the RPF, which now governed Rwanda, dissolved its army, and the RDF was constituted using soldiers from the RPA as well as some soldiers who had served in the extinct FAR. This arrangement was also part of the 1993 Arusha Accords. Today, the RDF is composed of the High Command Council, the General Staff, and the Rwandan Land Force. There are now four divisions divided by region; each division contains three brigades.

PAUL G. PIERPAOLI JR.

See also: Arusha Accords; Forces Armées Rwandaises; Habyarimana, Juvénal; Hutus; Kagame, Paul; Rwandan Patriotic Front; Tutsis

Further Reading

Ali, Taisier M., and Robert O. Matthews. *Civil Wars in Africa: Roots and Resolution.* Toronto: McGill-Queen's University Press, 1999.

Dallaire, Roméo. *Shake Hands with the Devil: The Failure of Humanity in Rwanda.* Toronto: Random House, 2004.

Rwandan Patriotic Front

The Rwandan Patriotic Front (RPF) was a Tutsi rebel refugee group established in Uganda in 1987, and which since 1994 has been the predominant political party in Rwanda. The Rwandan Patriotic Front (RPF) was created by exiled Tutsis who had begun to flee Rwanda in 1959, when the Hutus overthrew the Tutsi monarchy and systematically installed a Hutu-dominated regime there. Over time, the number of refugees ballooned, reaching some 200,000 in Uganda alone by 1990. Unfortunately, the Tutsi refugees in Uganda were treated abhorrently, especially after Uganda president Milton Obote's dictatorial government began enacting harsh and repressive antirefugee legislation in the 1960s. Obote was ousted in 1985, with the help of disgruntled Tutsi refugees.

Ugandan politics remained quite unstable during the 1980s, and the Tutsis living there continued to be treated as third-class citizens. Some Tutis who had joined the Ugandan military opted out by the mid-1980s, now determined to regain their access to Rwanda, using military means if necessary. This proved to be the genesis of the RPF, which in most of its pregoverning years was more of a militia rather than a political party.

The RPF had gained considerable traction by 1990, when it numbered roughly 5,000 armed militiamen, but it grew exponentially under the leadership of Paul Kagame. By 1994, the RPF numbered some 25,000 troops, which was known as the Rwandan Patriotic Army (RPA). At the same time, the RPF stepped up its destabilization efforts aimed at Rwanda's Hutu government. Kagame's goal was to threaten Rwandan president Juvénal Habyarimana's regime to such an extent that he would be forced to enter into a power-sharing arrangement with the RPF. Increasingly deadly raids carried out by the RPF accomplished that goal in June 1993, when the RPF and other rebel Tutsi groups compelled Habyarimana to reach a comprehensive peace settlement. That permitted many Tutsi refugees to return to Rwanda and allowed for the RPF to begin sharing power in Rwandan governance.

United Nations soldier (right) from Malawi talks to soldiers of the Rwanda Patriotic Front (RPF) in Gisenyi, Rwanda, July 1994. (UN Photo/John Isaac)

This shaky peace was shattered on April 6, 1994, when Habyarimana's plane was shot down over Kigali, resulting in the president's death. The Hutu government blamed the Tutsis for the assassination, while the Tutsis accused radical Hutus of having orchestrated the killing as a pretext for genocide against the Tutsis. This event triggered the Rwanda Genocide, in which as many as 800,000–1,000,000 Tutsis and moderate Hutus were slaughtered. The RPF used the tragedy to oust the Hutus from power and end the genocide, and by August 1994 the RPF had taken form control of the country. Sadly, however, the RPF was accused of having unleashed its own genocide against Rwandan Hutus fleeing the country during and after the genocide. Perhaps as many as 200,000 Hutu refugees died.

In March 2000, RPF leader and current Rwandan president Paul Kagame took office in Rwanda. Under his guidance, the RPF became a mainstream political organization and divested itself of the RPA, which was absorbed by the Rwandan Defense Forces (RDF). The RDF continues today as Rwanda's formal military establishment. Although Kagame and the RPF now rule in a coalition with other smaller parties, the RPF had held a majority of seats in the Rwandan parliament for well over a decade. The Kagame government has attempted to move beyond the Rwandan Genocide by virtually outlawing the classification of Rwandans by race; all Rwandans are now simply Rwandans rather than Hutus, Tutsis, or Twas. The RPF's governing philosophy may best be classified as leftist nationalism.

Paul G. Pierpaoli Jr.

See also: Arusha Accords; Forces Armées Rwandaises; Habyarimana, Juvénal; Hutus; Kagame, Paul; Rwandan Patriotic Army; Tutsis; Twas

Further Reading

Dallaire, Roméo. *Shake Hands with the Devil: The Failure of Humanity in Rwanda.* Toronto: Random House, 2004.

Des Forges, Alison. *Leave None to Tell the Story: Genocide in Rwanda.* New York: Human Rights Watch, 1999.

T

Tutsis

The Tutsis are the minority class of citizens that occupy the region of Rwanda-Burundi. Centuries of Tutsi rule in Rwanda ended in 1961. The Tutsis were the victims of genocide at the hands of the Hutu majority in 1994.

The Hutu and Tutsi are descended from ancestors sharing a common language, Kinyerwanda, who settled the Rwanda-Burundi area of east central Africa more than a thousand years ago. Two forms of subsistence developed among these people. One group relied strictly on cultivation and farming. The other relied on cattle raising. Over time, the farmers came to be known as Hutus and the pastoralists as Tutsis. In this culture, cattle were a marker of wealth. With time, Hutu and Tutsi became class markers with the pastoral Tutsi as the wealthier members of the society.

By the time of the German conquest in the 1880s, Rwandan society had begun to polarize, with the majority Hutu occupying the peasant, or subject, position to the Tutsi minority holding the tribal leadership positions. The German colonizers did little to interfere with the social makeup of the indigenous people. When Belgium assumed control over Rwanda at the close of World War I, the situation changed. The Belgians relied heavily on indigenous Tutsi leaders to govern the colony. This served to reinforce Tutsi control and provided apparatus to repress the masses of the people. Backed by the Belgian leadership, the Tutsi drove the Hutus from public life.

During the 1950s, Tutsi control over Rwanda began to erode as the United Nations supervised decolonization. Hutus were successful in exploiting the decolonization process to gain power throughout Rwanda. When Rwanda revolted against Belgium and secured its independence in 1961, the class roles were reversed, and the Hutus held the positions of power.

Tutsi rebels challenged Hutu rule immediately. In response to cross-border rebel incursions, the Hutu government massacred some 20,000 Rwandan Tutsis and forced 300,000 to flee. In the aftermath, a military dictatorship solidified its power in Rwanda. Over the next two decades, the standard of living in Rwanda declined steadily. With the long-term economic decline, the power base of the military leadership eroded. Rebel groups, most notably the Rwandan Patriotic Front, began to challenge the government from camps in neighboring states. Tutsi participation with the rebels gave justification for further repression of the Tutsi. The government began planning the genocide of the Tutsi as a way of repolarizing the population.

The assassination of President Juvenal Habyarimana on April 6, 1994, initiated the action against the Tutsis. During the next 13 weeks, military forces compelled the Hutu population of Rwanda to massacre the Tutsis. More than 800,000 Tutsis were exterminated. In 1998, the International Criminal Tribunal for Rwanda determined that the massacre was a genocide and was the first tribunal to convict on those grounds. Today, most Tutsis live as refugees in nations bordering Rwanda.

ROB COYLE

See also: Habyarimana, Juvénal; Hutus; International Criminal Tribunal for Rwanda; Rwanda; Rwandan Patriotic Front

Further Reading

Adelman, Howard, and Astri Suhrke, eds. *The Path of a Genocide: The Rwanda Crisis from Uganda to Zaire.* New Brunswick, NJ: Transaction Publishers, 1999.

Webster, John B. *The Political Development of Rwanda and Burundi.* Syracuse, NY: Maxwell Graduate School of Citizenship and Public Affairs, Syracuse University, 1966.

Twas

The Twas, or BaTwas, are pygmy peoples who live in the forests and savannah plains stretching from Uganda in the north down along the Lakes Region of Central Africa to Rwanda, Burundi, and the Democratic Republic of Congo. In addition, there are Twa populations scattered in Botswana, Angola, Zambia, and Namibia, where they have adopted to living conditions in deserts and swamps as well as their more familiar forests. In 2000, Twa numbered around 80,000 in total and in some of these countries they represent significant minorities.

Like other pygmy peoples, the Twa have been dominated by their Bantu and Cushitic neighbors and speak their languages. Most Twas speak Kirundi and Kinyarwanda, the languages of the Hutus and Tutsis. In Rwanda and Burundi, the Twa make up 1 percent of the population in each country and, due to the heavy demands for farming and grazing lands, much of the natural forest habitat has been lost over the last several centuries. Like other pygmies, little of their own culture still exists.

The Twas are thought to be among the oldest living groups connected to the Tschitolian culture dating back some 25,000 years. They seem to have lived in a widespread area before the Bantu expansions starting in the second millennium BCE and lasting, with different waves and patterns, into the first century CE. The Twas, as hunters and gatherers, helped provide meat and honey to the Bantus in trade for iron goods and agricultural products. In some situations, the two were able to develop a symbiotic relationship and the Kubas of Angola and southern Democratic Republic of Congo have brought Twas into their mask societies. That is, among the masks made and worn at special occasions are those that represent Twas with a noticeably large head, large, bulging forehead, and wide nose. Called a *bwoon* mask, they are worn at funerals of important men who belonged to the initiation societies.

In the colonial period, Twa society began to unravel in a number of places. Their hunting and gathering skills were less and less needed and their natural habitat was quickly cut down. Twas began to gather on the outskirts of Bantu towns and villages and became a source of menial labor, in often very abusive terms. They were generally ignored in the postcolonial developments, and their communities still today suffer from the lack of schools, electricity, water, and medical treatment. Missions did not seek them out and today it is estimated that only some 7 percent of Twas are Christians. The largest number of them adheres to syncretic Apostolic forms that combine Christian belief with indigenous systems of belief or still follow indigenous (mainly Bantu) forms of belief. Twas have been able to preserve some of their specific cultural practices such as dances and songs during social gatherings. Hunting was banned in the 1970s, and though Twa men still know how to make bows and arrows, they have been persecuted and jailed for continued hunting.

In the fighting between the Hutus and Tutsis in Rwanda in 1994, the Twas suffered greatly and some 30 percent of the Twas in Rwanda died at the hands of the Hutu Interahamwe militias. According to the Unrepresented Nations and Peoples Organization (UNPO), some 10,000 Twas were killed in the Rwandan Genocide and another 8,000 to 10,000 fled to nearby countries.

Twa communities suffer from problems of alcoholism and are treated with contempt by their countrymen. In 2007, it was reported that with no source of income, over 40 percent of the Twas in Rwanda earned a living through begging. The majority are illiterate and many Twa children drop out of school due to harassment by other students. UNPO states that 91 percent of Twas have no formal education. Twa women are subject to harassment, including sexual harassment from Bantu men. A source of income and of cultural identity is pottery making; however, the swamp lands where the Twas have enjoyed joint land rights for centuries with Hutu farmers came into danger starting in 2005 with plans to develop rice plantations. In both Rwanda and Burundi, the Twas are not legally recognized, have no representation in government, and have no land rights. In 2009, Burundi began the process of bringing the Twas into the government in an attempt to finally deal with the situation. In addition, a number of different organizations have taken up the cause of not only the Twas, but other pygmy peoples in Africa.

JOHN A. SHOUP

See also: Interahamwe; Rwanda

Further Reading

Adekunle, Julius O. *Culture and Customs of Rwanda.* Westport, CT: Greenwood, 2007.

Oyebade, Adebayo. *Culture and Customs of Angola.* Westport, CT: Greenwood, 2006.

U

United Nations Assistance Mission for Rwanda

The United Nations Assistance Mission for Rwanda (UNAMIR) was chiefly a humanitarian mission sent to Rwanda to help implement the August 1993 Arusha Accords, which ended the Rwandan Civil War. The UNAMIR was officially established by UN Security Council Resolution 872 on October 5, 1993. It took almost five months for the mission to achieve its authorized strength of 2,500 personnel, however. Designed to encourage the peace process between the Rwandan government dominated by the Hutus and the Tutsi-dominated Rwandan Patriotic Front (RPF), the UN mission was also tasked with expanding the demilitarized zone, monitoring Rwanda's internal security situation, and providing humanitarian and relief aid to refugees and others affected by the civil war. Unfortunately, the UNAMIR was entirely unprepared for the outbreak of the Rwandan Genocide, which began in April 1994 and claimed the lives of 800,000–1,000,000 people.

The institution of a new, transitional government, as called for in the Arusha Accords, was significantly delayed, and when it was finally brought to fruition in January 1994, violence and political assassinations wracked Kigali. On April 5, 1994, ironically one day before Rwandan president Juvénal Habyarimana's assassination, which triggered the genocide, the UN extended the UNAMIR's mandate to July 29, 1994. The UN accompanied its extension with a statement expressing its "deep concern" with the worsening security situation in Rwanda.

When the mass killing began on April 6, the UNAMIR was in no position to intervene. The mission was understaffed with poorly trained and equipped troops, was in a strictly defensive position, and was not authorized to employ arms to stop the genocide. Although it was able to save the lives of several thousand Tutsis and moderate Hutus who fled to its base near Kigali, the UNAMIR was largely a passive bystander to the genocide. The UNAMIR commander, Canadian general Roméo Dallaire, almost immediately asked for an additional 5,000 troops, but the UN turned him down. Instead, on April 21 the UN Security Council passed Resolution 912, which dramatically reduced the size of the UNAMIR, citing its concern for the mission's personnel. It also instructed Dallaire to help negotiate an immediate ceasefire. Dallaire was flabbergasted by this, and repeatedly asked for more troops, which the UN consistently denied.

Finally, on May 17, the UN passed Security Council Resolution 918, which would enlarge the UNAMIR presence to 5,500 troops and provide other badly needed military equipment. This, however, took almost six months to implement. Meanwhile, the genocide continued into the summer of 1994, as UNAMIR personnel watched in hopeless horror as hundreds of thousands of Rwandans died. Almost no additional UNAMIR troops entered Rwanda

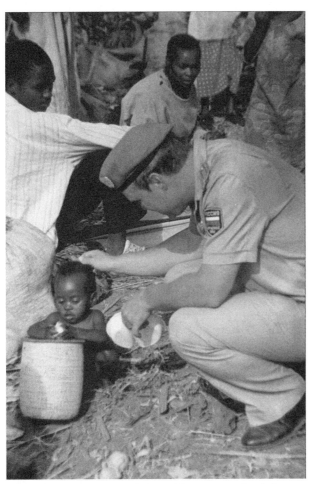

A Russian United Nations (UN) soldier visits with a baby in a Rwandan refugee camp. The United Nations Assistance Mission for Rwanda (UNAMIR) was established in 1993 to help implement a peace agreement between warring ethnic groups. (Corel)

until after the Tutsi-led Rwandan Patriotic Army (RPA) had secured most of the country, overthrown the Hutu government, and stopped the slaughter. With the gradual insertion of these additional troops, UNAMIR became known as UNAMIR II, which helped administer post-genocide Rwanda. UN peacekeeping troops were also unable to prevent the murders of some 200,000 Hutus at the hands of the RPA.

Dallaire, citing extreme frustration and exhaustion, left his post as UNAMIR commander in August 1994, after the killing had stopped. Before departing, he lambasted the UN for not doing more to stop the carnage and for taking far too long to approve a troop surge which he had requested within days of Habyarimana's assassination. UNAMIR II was tasked with stabilizing the Rwandan government, policing the fragile armistice,

promoting long-term peace, and, most critically, tending to the monumental humanitarian crisis that followed by the genocide. Indeed, by the fall of 1994, at least 4 million Rwandans were in refugee camps in Rwanda, Zaire, Tanzania, Uganda, and Burundi.

The UNAMIR II remained in Rwanda until March 8, 1996, when the mission was withdrawn upon the request of the Rwandan government, which had by then begun to criticize the mission for its failure to prevent or stop the genocide. Between 1993 and 1996, 40 UN member states provided troops or civilian support personnel to the UNAMIR. During that time, 22 soldiers, three military observers, one security officer, and one civilian staffer died while on duty.

PAUL G. PIERPAOLI JR.

See also: Arusha Accords; Dallaire, Roméo; Habyarimana, Juvénal; Rwanda; Rwandan Patriotic Army; Rwandan Patriotic Front; Tutsis

Further Reading

Barnett, Michael. *Eyewitness to a Genocide: The United Nations and Rwanda.* Ithaca, NY: Cornell University Press, 2002.

Dallaire, Roméo. *Shake Hands with the Devil: The Failure of Humanity in Rwanda.* Toronto: Random House, 2004.

Uwilingiyimana, Agathe

Agathe Uwilingiyimana was Rwanda's first female prime minister, and one of the earliest victims of the Rwandan Genocide of 1994. A Hutu, she was born on May 23, 1953, in the village of Nyaruhengeri, some 140 kilometers southeast of the Rwandan capital, Kigali. She was educated at Notre Dame des Citeaux High School, and at the age of 20 qualified as a teacher of humanities. In 1976 her qualifications were extended and she became a teacher of mathematics and chemistry. Also in 1976 she married Ignace Barahira, a fellow student from her village, and they settled down to a family life that would eventually produce five children.

In 1983 Uwilingiyimana became a teacher of chemistry at the National University of Rwanda, Butare. She received a bachelor's degree in science in 1985, and taught chemistry for four more years in the Butare area. During this time she began her public life, first through helping to establish a Savings and Credit Cooperative Society for the faculty at Butare, then, having attracted the notice of the central government, through her appointment in 1989 as a senior official in the Ministry of Commerce. In 1992 she joined the Mouvément Démocratique et Republicain (Republican and Democratic Movement, or MDR), and before the year was out she had been elevated to the position of minister of education in the government of Dr. Dismas Nsengiyaremye. The MDR was an opposition party, and Nsengiyaremye became the first opposition prime minister under a power-sharing scheme negotiated between President Juvénal Habyarimana and a grouping of opposition parties.

In her capacity as minister of education, Uwilingiyimana abolished the system of ethnic quotas established by the Habyarimana regime as a means to positively discriminate in favor of Hutus against Tutsis. Accordingly, public school places and scholarships would henceforth be awarded in accordance with a merit principle and competitive examinations throughout the country. Politically, this was an unwise move on Uwilingiyimana's part; while it was admirable on moral grounds, it alienated her from the government and Hutu nationalists, who saw her as a Hutu willing to compromise on issues of ethnic supremacy—and thus an adversary to be watched.

Nsengiyaremye's tenure as prime minister lasted from April 2, 1992, to July 17, 1993. On the day of his political downfall, Uwilingiyimana became prime minister after a meeting between Habyarimana and leaders of the other major political parties in the new pluralistic system. She was viewed as a "lame-duck" prime minister by all concerned, able to be controlled at a whim by both the president and the other political parties. Now out of office, Nsengiyareme even suspended Uwilingiyimana's MDR membership upon her accession to the premiership. Habyarimana himself doubted his choice once he saw the discord the promotion had generated, and dismissed her as prime minister less than three weeks after her appointment. Despite this, he allowed her to remain in office in a caretaker capacity, which she did until both his and her deaths resolved the issue in April 1994.

She became prime minister at a critical juncture in Rwanda's history, when a rapprochement was being attempted by the Hutu-dominated government of Habyarimana and the Tutsi-dominated rebel force, the Rwandan Patriotic Front (RPF). This was a period when it was hoped by many (though certainly not all) that as a result of the Arusha Accords signed on August 4, 1993, between the government, its supporting parties and the RPF, a multiparty democracy and a pluralistic political culture would be established. Peace and stability would finally come to Rwanda—an arrangement in which both Hutus and Tutsis

were welcome and treated fairly. Faustin Twagiramungu would now lead the MDR in the new arrangement, as the party had already suspended Uwilingiyimana. A new interim government was to have been set in place on March 25, 1994, at which time Uwilingiyimana would officially step down in favor of Twagiramungu. This was postponed, however, owing to the failure of the RPF to turn up to the swearing-in ceremony, and Uwilingiyimana remained in office in a temporary capacity until the handover ceremony could take place.

Following the shooting down of Habyarimana's plane on April 6, 1994, the genocide began. At this time, Uwilingiyimana became Rwanda's temporary head of state, and the commander of the United Nations forces in the country overseeing the Arusha agreement, General Roméo Dallaire, immediately dispatched Belgian and Ghanaian troops to her home in order to secure her safety and escort her to Radio Rwanda in order to enable her to make a broadcast to the Rwandan people and thus avoid a national crisis. Early the following morning, however, units of Rwanda's presidential guard—a corps that had been radicalized by Habyarimana's Hutu nationalists—forced the Belgian soldiers to stand aside and lay down their weapons. Led by Major Bernard Ntuyahaga, the presidential guard troops then slaughtered the Belgians and mutilated their bodies. These troops became the first UN casualties, ultimately leading the government of Belgium to abandon the Rwandan mission altogether.

In desperation, Uwilingiyimana and her family, still in their pajamas, fled their house, and sought refuge in the compound of the UN Development Programme. Presidential guards reached the compound before reinforcements, who were held up by Hutu militia roadblocks, could arrive from Dallaire's headquarters. Uwilingiyimana and her husband, fearing for the lives of their five children, surrendered to the presidential guard, and were shot immediately at point-blank range. When Uwilingiyimana's body was found it had been horribly mutilated, left half-naked, and with a beer bottle shoved in her vagina. (The children remained in hiding, were smuggled by a Senegalese UN soldier, Captain Mbaye Diagne into the Hôtel des Mille Collines, and eventually took refuge in Switzerland. Captain Diagne was to lose his own life to RPF shelling several weeks later.)

Agathe Uwilingiyimana was succeeded as prime minister of the interim government by an extremist Hutu hardliner, Jean Kambanda. During her prime ministership she showed that a vision for Rwanda that was not steeped in ethnic exclusion and hatred did exist and was something worth working toward. She set a standard to which other women in Africa could aspire, as one of only a very few women in the world to that stage (and the only one in Africa) to have attained the highest reaches of government office. Her life, as much as her death, marks her as a major figure in a troubled time.

PAUL R. BARTROP

See also: Dallaire, Roméo; Diagne, Mbaye; Habyarimana, Juvénal; Kambanda, Jean; Rwandan Patriotic Front; United Nations Assistance Mission for Rwanda

Further Reading

Dallaire, Roméo. *Shake Hands with the Devil: The Failure of Humanity in Rwanda.* Toronto: Random House, 2004.

Scherrer, P. Christian. *Genocide and Crisis in Central Africa: Conflict Roots, Mass Violence, and Regional War.* Westport, CT: Praeger, 2002.

W

Wallace, Gretchen Steidle

Gretchen Steidle Wallace is an American humanitarian campaigner dedicated to advancing women's rights and well-being in Rwanda and other countries affected by genocide. Born in 1974 as the daughter of a U.S. Navy admiral, she grew up in a variety of settings around the world. Living in the Philippines for a time as a child, she saw the effect that desperate poverty can have on a community, and she has since worked hard to address the injustices and disparities that poverty can bring. She attended the University of Virginia (from which she graduated with a BA in foreign affairs in 1996) and Tuck School of Business at Dartmouth College, where she obtained an MBA in 2001. Between 1996 and 1999, she worked in international project finance for PMD International, Inc., a boutique investment banking firm specializing in infrastructure development in poor countries.

In 2004, Wallace went to South Africa to help with the HIV/AIDS epidemic. Studying the AIDS initiatives of major multinational corporations, she learned of the financial consequences of AIDS with regard to health care costs and lost production. She also began to study the extent to which various companies developed and applied efficient solutions to these problems. She learned that many solutions were in fact flawed, due largely to a poor understanding of health care and the stigma attached to HIV/AIDS. It became apparent that many employees were reluctant to undergo AIDS testing or to seek assistance if

they knew they were infected. Culturally, women faced the problem of not being empowered to insist on their partners using condoms. Wallace came to the realization that some form of social initiative was needed to promote the rights of women regarding sexual freedom and HIV/AIDS prevention. She knew that some women in South Africa were already employing enterprising techniques at the grassroots level and realized that they were determined to address critical issues facing women and girls, although struggling without the training and resources necessary to ensure their success. Wallace decided to dedicate her work to supporting these emerging agents of change and their ideas.

As a result, later the same year Wallace established Global Grassroots, a nonprofit organization supporting conscious social change for women in postconflict and developing countries, particularly in Africa. Through personal transformation work and social entrepreneurship training, Global Grassroots helps marginalized women and genocide survivors reclaim their lives and discover their value to society through the development of their own ideas for social change. Global Grassroots offers seed funding grants and 12 months of advisory support to launch those projects that advance the well-being and rights of women. Global Grassroots also engages in creative campaigns to raise awareness of critical women's issues globally.

With Global Grassroots established, Wallace saw an enormous amount of work awaiting her. Her first initiative, in 2005, connected her interests with those of her brother, Brian Steidle, who had already been doing significant work in raising awareness around the world about the on-going genocide in Darfur, Sudan. Steidle and Wallace took their respective campaigns to the refugee camps of eastern Chad, where they worked on issues overlooked by aid organizations, such as establishing a human rights library and providing education about refugee rights, domestic and sexual violence, and female genital mutilation. Wallace also provided on-site training to try to ensure her projects would be sustained in the long-term.

Returning to the United States, Wallace began to develop her new social entrepreneurship program but saw a great need to return to Africa in order to work with genocide survivors in Rwanda, where mass rape during the 1994 genocide had led to a huge spread of victims of HIV/AIDS. In 2006, she trained 180 Rwandan women, many of them widows raising several children, and many of them rape victims, in the development of social projects in Kigali.

Dealing with the aftermath of rape is one of the issues for which Global Grassroots soon became best known. In Africa, as elsewhere, mass rape is a common problem, especially in situations of war and civil strife. The promotion of dialogue about rape is an important, although difficult, first step in raising awareness and addressing the issue. Again, knowledge of mass rape was brought home to Wallace through the observations of her brother Brian in Darfur, where the Janjaweed militias engaged in the practice of raping female genocide survivors, often en masse.

Since 2006, Global Grassroots has trained 250 "change leaders," managing to fund several important locally designed projects serving thousands of vulnerable women and girls. These initiatives deal with issues relating to domestic violence, water access, child rape, prostitution, property rights, HIV/AIDS, discrimination, and illiteracy. Most of these are in postgenocide Rwanda, which has become the main field of operations for Global Grassroots, but projects among Darfur refugees in eastern Chad are also now underway. Global Grassroots is one of the major providers of assistance to female genocide survivors and focuses almost exclusively on the promotion of what Wallace calls "conscious social change" driven by and on behalf of marginalized women in postconflict Africa.

In early 2007, Global Grassroots and Wallace were also heavily involved in producing an Emmy-nominated documentary film about the Darfur genocide, *The Devil Came on Horseback* (directed by Ricki Stern and Anne Sundberg). Based on Brian Steidle's memoir of the same title (which Wallace co-authored), *The Devil Came on Horseback* tells the story of Steidle's direct encounter with genocide in Darfur.

As a social entrepreneur, Wallace has always believed in inner-driven change, holding that decisions made with the greatest level of awareness will ensure the wisest response and most potent, effective results. This was one of the key motivators behind the establishment of Global Grassroots in 2004. Wallace's interests lay in looking for gaps in existing systems and fostering ideas of what to do about them, but the greatest measure of success at Global Grassroots is the impact that locally chosen projects can have in transforming communities for the better. There is a focus on training and project design, and each project has built into it social impact goals and evaluation metrics. Monitoring of a project's progress, and the provision of high-engagement advisory support, takes place for a minimum of 12 months after it begins. Global Grassroots assists local project teams in developing their baseline study and working with their target population to assess the issue and their progress over time, the real measure of success at the end of the day being that of how many lives are touched.

In recognition of her contribution to the betterment of the human condition through management and entrepreneurship strategies, in 2007 Wallace was honored by *World Business* magazine and Shell as one of the top International 35 Women under 35. By the end of the 21st century's first decade, the antigenocide enterprise created by one woman's vision had become an inspiration to communities throughout many parts of Africa, and a model for others to follow.

PAUL R. BARTROP

See also: Rape; Steidle, Brian

Further Reading

Cheadle, Don, and John Prendergast. *Not on Our Watch: The Mission to End Genocide in Darfur and Beyond.* New York: Hyperion, 2007.

Steidle, Brian, and Gretchen Steidle Wallace. *The Devil Came on Horseback: Bearing Witness to the Genocide in Darfur.* New York: PublicAffairs Books, 2008.

We Wish to Inform You That Tomorrow We Will Be Killed with Our Families

We Wish to Inform You That Tomorrow We Will Be Killed with Our Families: Stories from Rwanda was a book written by Philip Gourevitch and published by Farrar, Straus, and Giroux in 1998 that details the Rwandan Genocide of 1994. Gourevitch is a respected journalist and writer who has long been affiliated with *The New Yorker* magazine and who once edited the *Paris Review. We Wish to Inform You That Tomorrow We Will Be Killed with Our Families* is based upon the author's extensive travels in Rwanda after the genocide, during which he interviewed scores of witnesses and survivors, talked to government officials, and gathered documentary materials for his book.

The book's title was taken from a letter, written in April 1994, by several Seventh-day Adventist ministers (Tutsis), to Adventist pastor Elizaphan Ntakirutimana. The ministers had taken refuge in an Adventist-run hospital in the Kibuye Prefecture, along with other besieged Tutsis, and were writing to tell the pastor of their plight. The very next day, hundreds of refugees at the hospital were slain by Hutu rebels. Gourevitch asserted that it was Ntakirutimana who had given away the refugees' position and had given support to the force that committed the massacre. Ntakirutimana was later convicted of war crimes by the International Criminal Tribunal for Rwanda, largely on the evidence produced in Gourevitch's book.

Gourevitch's work focuses largely on stories of the genocide and the aftereffects it has had on the survivors and Rwanda as a whole. While it offers a brief history of events prior to 1994, it is not enough to explain fully how and why the genocide occurred. Readers will have to look elsewhere for that. Nevertheless, the book was awarded several prestigious awards in 1998.

PAUL G. PIERPAOLI JR.

See also: International Criminal Tribunal for Rwanda; Ntakirutimana, Elizaphan; Rwanda

Further Reading

Gourevitch, Philip. *We Wish to Inform You That Tomorrow We Will Be Killed with Our Families: Stories from Rwanda*. New York: Picador, 1999.

Lemarchand, René. *The Dynamics of Violence in Central Africa*. Philadelphia: University of Pennsylvania Press, 2009.

Wilkens, Carl

Carl Wilkens is the former head of the Adventist Development and Relief Agency (ADRA) International in Rwanda, and, during the genocide in 1994 was the only American to remain in the country. Born in 1957, in 1978 he first went to Africa as part of a college volunteer program in Transkei, South Africa. He returned to the United States to complete his university undergraduate degree in industrial education, and then returned to Africa with his wife Theresa in 1981. At first they settled in Zimbabwe, before moving to Zambia. Returning once more to the United States in 1987, Wilkens undertook an MBA course at the University of Baltimore. In 1990 he and Theresa and their three children moved to Rwanda, where Wilkens became country director of ADRA assisting in building schools and operating health centers around the country.

In the summer of 1993 the Wilkens family were on home leave in the United States, and they returned to Rwanda with high hopes for the country's future. The optimism continued through December 1993 and into January 1994, but things began to sour from then on. By February, there was fighting in Kigali, and Wilkens could feel the growing tension. All of a sudden, Adventist missionaries were being evacuated, and the question of whether to stay or leave began to be asked throughout the community.

At the U.S. embassy, there had previously been meetings with the expatriate community about evacuation in the event of a crisis, and how it would take place. Always in the back of Wilkens's mind, however, was the prospect that there would still remain a core group who would keep the embassy open should there be strife. Immediately after the genocide began on April 6, 1994, Wilkens called the embassy, and found that already there was talk about establishing evacuation assembly points. The embassy's Laura Lane was at this time Wilkens's main contact person. When the embassy had the evacuation plans in place, Wilkens was told that the first group was going to be taken over the next few days, driving by road to Burundi. The Adventist American missionaries said they would wait until the Sunday of that first week before they left. Wilkens was in the thick of organizing the details of their evacuation, but he and his wife Theresa had already decided that he would himself stay. Conveying this information to Laura Lane, he invoked the right of a private citizen to choose his own path without the interference of the U.S. government. All Lane could do in the circumstances was to insist that Wilkens sign a statement to the effect that he had refused the help of the U.S. government to evacuate. Theresa and the children were eventually relocated to Nairobi, Kenya, where they managed to stay in touch with Wilkens by radio.

Wilkens chose to stay so as to be able to deliver aid to children in need despite the ongoing violence. His choice to remain would result in preventing the massacre of hundreds of children over the course of the genocide. One example related to the Gisimba Orphanage, which was secretly providing a safe haven for 400 people threatened by the genocide. When Wilkens arrived at Gisimba he saw up to 50 armed militiamen looking for an opportunity to close in and kill the orphans, but they appeared hesitant owing to Wilkens's presence as a witness. As a deterrent, Wilkens decided to sleep that night at the orphanage. He stayed there until there was some hope for a more prolonged protection for the orphans, and then drove out to try to find the local provincial governor and plead for their salvation. Amazingly, Wilkens made contact with the prime minister of Rwanda's interim Hutu extremist government, Jean Kambanda, and in a brazen act of nerve he simply asked him for his help in saving the orphans. Equally amazingly, Kambanda agreed to give assurances that the militias would be called off and those at the orphanage would be saved. Wilkens decided to move the orphans to a safer location, the Saint Michel Cathedral. Within a few days he had organized two buses and a military escort to help them through the roadblocks, ensuring their security in this most insecure of situations. He was able to replicate this success in a number of other cases, and save hundreds of people as a result.

The complexity of living through the genocide and trying to be an effective agent of rescue found Wilkens often working at the fringes of compromise. Frequently, he found himself in situations that could have been interpreted as collaboration with the killers—just to save lives. Yet any ally in the process of human salvation was welcome, and sometimes Wilkens even found help among members of the Interahamwe. Personal contacts with the killers enabled him to obtain a freer passage through the roadblocks, for example, providing him with the means to travel to places where he knew vulnerable people were hiding—people he managed in one way or another to smuggle to safety.

Not all of his contacts were with the killers. Before the onset of the genocide, Wilkens had known the Frenchman Philippe Gaillard of the International Committee of the Red Cross, and during the crisis the two met at every opportunity. For Wilkens, this connection served as an important emotional support, as here he found someone equally committed to staying in Rwanda and helping as many people as he could. Another avenue of support came from ADRA director David Syme, who actually went into Rwanda as the genocide was in progress, and spent several

days with Wilkens in his home. Syme provided valuable items that enabled Wilkens to continue his work: handheld radios, license plates bearing the ADRA mark that could be affixed to Wikens's vehicles, a UN flak jacket, and other supplies.

After the victory of the Rwandan Patriotic Front in July 1994, Wilkens remained in Rwanda to assist with the distribution of water, food, and equipment for the hardpressed inhabitants of Kigali. Reunited with his family, they returned to the United States for a period but in 1995 they were back in Rwanda where they stayed for another 18 months, working for the Adventist Church in reconstruction activities.

Since 1996, the Wilkens family has been living in the U.S. Carl Wilkens became an Adventist pastor in Oregon, and began speaking about his Rwanda experiences. As an initiative to confront the forces that can bring about a genocidal situation, and foster an appropriate response to genocide today, Wilkens has created *World outside My Shoes,* a nonprofit educational and professional development organization committed to inspiring and equipping people to enter the world of "The Other." He invites people to "Take a moment to try and put yourself in the shoes of the family members and friends who had loved ones taken from them," and to learn from Rwanda in order to equip and inspire oneself to enter the world of the "Other." The "Other," he shows, "may be under our own roof or on the other side of the globe." Through *World outside My Shoes,* Wilkens seeks to inspire and equip people to stand up against genocide, racism, and intolerance, through the promotion of values such as integrity, dignity, community, simplicity, and what he calls "respond-ability." The motto of *World outside My Shoes* is as straightforward as it is challenging: "One person really can ignite change when they discover the power of choice!"

Carl Wilkens's story, which he published as a short memoir (*I'm Not Leaving*) in 2011, is a constant reminder of the profound connection between history and the moral choices everyone faces each day. Staying in Rwanda even as others fled, Wilkens decided to remain at his post and help wherever he could. Today, he tours the United States to speak to students, teachers, parents, policymakers, and communities about his experience in Rwanda. Through telling the story of how the genocide unfolded, mostly his preference is to focus on the courage and resilience he witnessed as people faced impossible choices relating to life and death, and what this can mean for everyone as they confront the challenges of the 21st century.

Paul R. Bartrop

See also: Gaillard, Philippe; Interahamwe; Kambanda, Jean; Lane, Laura; Rwandan Patriotic Front

Further Reading

Bodnarchuk, Kari. *Rwanda: A Country Torn Apart.* Minneapolis, MN: Lerner Publishing Group, 1998.

Wilkens, Carl. *I'm Not Leaving.* United States: C. Wilkens, 2011.

Historical Dilemmas

The Historical Dilemma section introduces students and researchers to debates and controversies in the study of certain genocides and atrocities. It presents a historical question with different perspectives on the issue, showing users not only how scholars utilize evidence to present their respective arguments, but how certain topics in genocide studies continue to be debated.

Could the United Nations Have Done More to Stop the Genocide in Rwanda?

Introduction

In 1994, over the course of 100 days, an estimated 800,000 Rwandans were killed in a genocide that pitted the majority Hutus against the minority Tutsi population. The genocide came at the end of a short civil war between a small band of Tutsi refugees, the Rwanda Patriotic Front (RPF), and the Rwandan government's Hutu military. The conflict drew the attention of the international community, and both the Organization of African Unity, in 1992, and the United Nations (UN), in 1993, sent observation and peacekeeping missions to the region to help implement a cease-fire and power-sharing agreement signed in Arusha, Tanzania. Despite these efforts, tension within the small nation remained high, with Hutu militias determined to maintain power and spreading a violent anti-Tutsi message throughout the country.

On April 6, 1994, a missile shot down a plane carrying Juvénal Habyarimana, the Rwandan Hutu president, as it approached the Rwandan capital. Who was responsible for the plane crash is still debated, but the event triggered an immediate outbreak in violence that became the Rwanda genocide. Over the 100 days that followed, Hutus throughout the country, civilian and military, murdered Tutsis because of their ethnicity. Moderate Hutus were also targeted, and the RPF continued to wage its war in hopes of capturing the capital. An estimated 800,000 people—and according to some claims as many as 1.1 million people—were brutally killed in just over three months. When the genocide began, the UN already had a small peacekeeping force in place in Rwanda, but these troops were not given the support, funding, or mandate to effectively stop the violence. More than 16 years later, the UN and the international community are still trying to learn from this mistake in order to find a way to truly prevent genocide and other crimes against humanity. Could the UN have done more to stop the genocide in Rwanda?

In early 1994, a small group of United Nations (UN) peacekeeping forces tasked with monitoring the implementation of the Arusha Accords between Rawanda's Hutu government and a Tutsi rebel group stood by helplessly as evidence of an impending humanitarian disaster mounted in front of them—which they communicated to the UN. Ever since the genocide ended in the summer of 1994, the failure of the UN to take stronger action to prevent or stop the massacre has been the subject of analysis and debate.

This debate continues in the following essays. In the first essay, international studies scholar Isabelle Lagarde argues that the UN was hampered by a lack of will among the international community to act more forcefully. The United States in particular was instrumental in preventing UN involvement, she argues, and U.S. leaders and citizens were not enthusiastic about spending money or putting lives in danger to intervene in little-known countries. Alanna Pardee, also an international studies expert, argues in the second essay that UN authorities could and should have responded much more quickly and forcefully to the situation by strengthening the terms of the mandate and more effectively communicating with commanders on the ground in Rwanda. She argues that those failures played a major role in eroding international support for forceful intervention.

Pro/Con 1: The UN Could Not Have Stopped the Genocide

In 1994, the international community stood back and watched as the Rwandan genocide claimed almost 1 million lives. Despite specific information and intelligence from sources on the ground, both leading up to and during the genocide, the United Nations failed to send a substantial peacekeeping force that could have worked to stop the mass violence. Indeed, when the killings were under way, the United Nations (UN) Security Council voted to abandon their mission rather than reinforce it. The UN was created to maintain peace and to prevent exactly this kind of horrendous event, but it failed to stop the genocide in Rwanda. The UN could not have stopped the genocide because it lacked support from the international community.

The United Nations was established after World War II as an international organization designed to preserve peace and security, promote social development, and foster friendly relations among states. Currently there are 192 member states, each weighted equally in the General Assembly. However, the victors of the war reserved a special leadership role for themselves in the form of the five permanent seats (P5) on the Security Council. The Security Council is one of the six main branches of the UN and

is charged with maintaining peace and security around the world. The P5 countries are the United States, United Kingdom, China, Russia, and France, and these countries alone have the power to veto any resolution that comes through the Security Council. They also boast a great deal of influence due to their status and their large financial contributions to the organization.

The United States, in its position as a world superpower, holds a great deal of sway over decisions by the Security Council, and was instrumental in preventing the UN from getting involved in the Rwanda conflict. U.S. involvement in the UN is highly influenced by domestic politics, and foreign aid and intervention is often a low priority for Americans, so involvement in unknown countries with no direct ties to U.S. interests can be unpopular among the American population.

In 1992, the Security Council sent a peacekeeping mission to the East African nation of Somalia, with the support of the United States, in order to oversee a ceasefire and help deliver humanitarian aid. In 1993, during the Battle of Mogadishu, Somali militia killed 18 U.S. soldiers, and a 19th was killed shortly after. These events shocked the American population and severely diminished support for international humanitarian involvement. One year later the Security Council began to discuss a peacekeeping mission to Rwanda, and accordingly U.S. support for and commitment to such a mission was negligible. President Bill Clinton, not wishing to become involved in another ethnic conflict, presented the violence as an internal civil war and refused to let Americans, or the UN, become involved in any significant way.

Before the genocide began, several countries did provide troops to the original UN Assistance Mission to Rwanda (UNAMIR) in 1993, among them Rwanda's former colonial power, Belgium. These troops were on the ground at the start of the genocide, but were quickly targeted by the Hutu militias. During the first few days of the genocide, 10 Belgian peacekeepers were tortured and murdered, putting the UN on high alert and prompting the Security Council to reconvene. With international support dwindling, and many seeing a repeat of the debacle on Somalia, the UN Security Council unanimously voted to reduce the UN peacekeeping mission to a skeleton force of barely 200 soldiers. Cables from the U.S. State Department to the U.S. mission to the UN show how American policy was set against intervention, and pushed the UN to withdraw troops and prevent a stronger mandate. It is also important to note that at this time Rwanda held one of the 10 rotating seats on the Security Council, and the Hutu government's representative did his part to discourage action and diminish fears of a genocide.

In international law, language is extremely important, and the international community's failure to apply the term "genocide" to Rwanda shows a clear decision to ignore the events happening on the ground and remain uninvolved. The term genocide was defined in 1948 in the UN's Convention on the Prevention and Punishment of the Crime of Genocide. This document also recognized genocide as a crime under international law and obligated its signatories to prevent and punish genocide anywhere in the world. Today there are 140 states that have ratified or acceded to the convention, including each of the P5, which are therefore legally required to act when a genocide is determined to be taking place. In August 1993, the UN human rights investigator in Rwanda first raised the possibility of a genocide, and in January 1994, Lieutenant General Roméo Dallaire, head of UNAMIR, sent a letter warning of the risk of genocide. Once the violence erupted, Clinton and the members of the Security Council had access to irrefutable evidence of genocide through embassy staff, nongovernmental organization staff, Dallaire, and journalists on the ground. Despite these warnings and information, the UN Security Council failed to use the term genocide to describe the conflict until late June, a few weeks shy of the end of the conflict, thereby shielding themselves from any obligation to intervene.

The UN is only as strong as its members make it, especially the P5 members. International law lacks real enforcement measures, and one powerful member state can decide how or if the UN becomes involved in an international incident. The UN and the international community have since recognized their negligence and abandonment of Rwanda in 1994, and after a damning report, the UN even admitted to failing to prevent the genocide. The combination of the peacekeeping failure in Somalia and a lack of strategic or political interests in Rwanda made members of the international community, especially the United States, unwilling to become involved. This atmosphere of fear and denial led to a failure to acknowledge the atrocities being committed as genocide. In the end, the collective lack of will, and the pressure from the United States, prevented the UN from intervening in Rwanda until it was already too late.

Isabelle Lagarde

Pro/Con 2: The UN Could Have Stopped the Genocide with a Stronger Mandate

The United Nations (UN) was created in 1945 to promote the universal values of international peace, security, and human rights—concepts that are believed to be supranational ideals. Although these are admirable goals, many argue that the UN lacks the power to resolve pressing international conflicts because it lacks sufficient support from its member states. However, in the case of the Rwandan genocide, the UN, although admittedly poorly supported, could have done more to stop the genocide. In not issuing a stronger peacekeeping mandate, the UN allowed the mass killings to continue for 100 days, and nearly 1 million Rwandans perished.

The first mistake in Rwanda was that the UN did not give a strong enough mandate to the United Nations Assistance Mission for Rwanda (UNAMIR), which was deployed to Rwanda to aid in carrying out the Arusha Accords, a peace agreement signed by the Rwandan government and the Rwandan Patriotic Front (RPF) in Arusha, Tanzania, in August 1993. Under the UN Security Council Resolution 872, UNAMIR was initially given 2,548 troops and a Chapter VI Mandate, which extended into April 1994 when the atrocities began. Under the UN Charter, a Chapter VI mandate does not allow UN peacekeepers to use force or implement the will of the UN; they can facilitate and oversee but not engage.

The Chapter VI Mandate advised UNAMIR that their mission was strictly to monitor the Arusha Accords and ease the transition to a new power-sharing government that incorporated the RPF. The UN personnel were present to ensure security in Kigali, the capital, and monitor the armistice: this was a mission with limited troops, and almost no legal power to protect the Rwandan people. As the violence began to unfold, UNAMIR continued to follow and was legally bound to their Chapter VI mandate. UNAMIR was so restricted by the mandate that the troops literally had to stand and watch as the massacre of Tutsis continued.

The lowest point for UNAMIR came early in April 1994 when the Rwandan army killed 10 Belgian commandos. Under the Chapter VI monitoring mandate, the UN troops were unsure of whether or not they could use force to defend themselves or Rwandan civilians. After handing over their weapons to government soldiers, as advised by their commander, they were killed with their own weapons. Belgium, knowing that the mission would now be unpopular with its citizens at home, immediately withdrew its other troops in reaction to the deaths. Three weeks into the genocide other countries also horrified by the attacks began to withdraw their troops, and UNAMIR's peacekeepers dwindled to only 270 military personnel. If the United Nations had clearly outlined the details of the mandate and communicated better with their troops and commanders, the course of the genocide in Rwanda could have been drastically different.

UNAMIR's weak and unclear Chapter VI Mandate led to the failure of the UN in Rwanda and lost important international support for the mission. Furthermore, it allowed the genocide to proceed at a rapidly destructive pace. As the violence escalated and it became clear that the Arusha peace agreement was no longer a viable mission in Rwanda, the UN should have acted quickly to change UNAMIR's mandate to a Chapter VII mandate, which allows for the possibility of enforcement. A Chapter VII mandate would have allowed the UN Security Council to establish the threat to peace and security and take military or nonmilitary action to deter any potential threats. Although this eventually did happen, it took months for it to be approved and even longer for countries to commit troops to the mission. This was not consistent with UNAMIR commander Roméo Dallaire's request for 5,000 troops to arrive immediately. The mission was still unclear on whether or not they could use force to stop the mass killings, even with the Chapter VII mandate. By the time increased troops arrived, the genocide was basically over. Had UNAMIR been more strongly supported by the UN, and General Dallaire's request for more troops been filled, UNAMIR would not have been considered a failure.

The UN could have done more in Rwanda if it had acted swiftly and had established mechanisms in place to deal with international conflicts. The UN, like many other international organizations, is only as strong as its member countries allow it to be. The UN depends on the financial and political support of its members. For these reasons, UN actions are rarely consistent and are subject to the fluctuations of member-state politics, which are often in disagreement. For example, in 1994, the idea of resolving conflicts in faraway places, and risking troops in the process, was not popular in the United States. The country had just been involved in a failed mission in Somalia, which both humiliated and infuriated the American populace. For this reason, the United States was hesitant to give full support to the mission in Rwanda. As a result, other countries were hesitant to commit troops and necessary military equipment to the mission. The UN needs to be especially aware of how the results of other political and humanitarian missions affect each other, to ensure that a proper mandate is given. The UN should be faulted for not realizing how the mission in Somalia would affect UNAMIR and for not changing strategies when they realized the failures of the Somalian peacekeeping force.

Even though its members limit its power, there are certain aspects of the UN within the organization's control that must be properly established in order to both increase the efficacy of UN peacekeeping missions and ensure international security. Troops must be properly informed of their mission and their right to take military and/or nonmilitary action. Missions, especially failed ones like in Somalia, should be thoroughly reviewed and used to inform future missions. The bureaucracy and lack of speed with which the UN responded to the Rwandan genocide was unacceptable. The UN's identity crisis, whether it is solely a peacekeeping or intervening organization, also prolonged the genocide in Rwanda.

ALANNA PARDEE

Documents

---

1. President Bill Clinton's Remarks to the People of Rwanda, March 25, 1998

Spoken upon his arrival at Kigali Airport, Rwanda, President Clinton came "to pay the respects of my Nation to all who suffered and all who perished in the Rwandan genocide," and acknowledging that "the international community, together with the nations of Africa, must bear its share of responsibility for this tragedy, as well." After detailing somewhat the 90 days of the genocide, he also challenged the world community both to prevent and to stop genocide and called upon the United States and others to develop a genocide early warning system (which remains unfunded by his successors). He also called upon the nations of Africa to work with the United States to establish a coalition to prevent regional genocide, and committing the United States to $2,000,000 in relief efforts for 1998, and further committing itself to support the work of the International Criminal Tribunal for Rwanda. While applauding its overall positivity, critics of this speech were quick to point out that President Clinton never used the word "I'm sorry" or "We're sorry" anywhere in his comments.

THE PRESIDENT: Thank you, Mr. President. First, let me thank you, Mr. President, and Vice President Kasame, and your wives for making Hillary and me and our delegation feel so welcome. I'd also like to thank the young students who met us and the musicians, the dancers who were outside. I thank especially the survivors of the genocide and those who are working to rebuild your country for spending a little time with us before we came in here.

I have a great delegation of Americans with me, leaders of our government, leaders of our Congress, distinguished American citizens. We're all very grateful to be here. We thank the Diplomatic Corps for being here, and the members of the Rwandan government, and especially the citizens.

I have come today to pay the respects of my nation to all who suffered and all who perished in the Rwandan genocide. It is my hope that through this trip, in every corner of the world today and tomorrow, their story will be told; that four years ago in this beautiful, green, lovely land, a clear and conscious decision was made by those then in power that the peoples of this country would not live side by side in peace.

During the 90 days that began on April 6 in 1994, Rwanda experienced the most extensive slaughter in this blood-filled century we are about to leave. Families murdered in their homes, people hunted down as they fled by soldiers and militia, through farmland and woods as if they were animals.

From Kibuye in the west to Kibungo in the east, people gathered seeking refuge in churches by the thousands, in hospitals, in schools. And when they were found, the old and the sick, the women and children alike, they were killed—killed because their identity card said they were Tutsi or because they had a Tutsi parent, or because someone thought they looked like a Tutsi, or slain like thousands of Hutus because they protected Tutsis or would not countenance a policy that sought to wipe out people who just the day before, and for years before, had been their friends and neighbors.

The government-led effort to exterminate Rwanda's Tutsi and moderate Hutus, as you know better than me, took at least a million lives. Scholars of these sorts of events say that the killers, armed mostly with machetes and clubs, nonetheless did their work five times as fast as the mechanized gas chambers used by the Nazis.

It is important that the world know that these killings were not spontaneous or accidental. It is important that the world hear what your President just said—they were most certainly no the result of ancient tribal struggles. Indeed, these people had lived together for centuries before the events the President described began to unfold.

These events grew from a policy aimed at the systematic destruction of a people. The ground for violence was carefully prepared, the airwaves poisoned with hate, casting the Tutsis as scapegoats for the problems of Rwanda, denying their humanity. All of this was done, clearly, to make it easy for otherwise reluctant people to participate in wholesale slaughter.

Lists of victims, name by name, were actually drawn up in advance. Today the images of all that haunt us all: the dead choking the Kigara River, floating to Lake Victoria. In their fate, we are reminded of the capacity for people everywhere—not just in Rwanda, and certainly not just in Africa—but the capacity for people everywhere to slip into pure evil. We cannot abolish that capacity, but we must never accept it. And we know it can be overcome.

The international community, together with nations in Africa, must bear its share of responsibility for this tragedy, as well. We did not act quickly enough after the killing began. We should not have allowed the refugee camps to become safe haven for the killers. We did not immediately call these crimes by their rightful name: genocide. We cannot change the past. But we can and must do everything in our power to help you build a future without fear, and full of hope.

We owe to those who died and to those who survived who loved them, our every effort to increase our vigilance and strengthen our stand against those who would commit such atrocities in the future—here or elsewhere. Indeed, we owe to all the peoples of the world who are at risk—because each bloodletting hastens the next as the value of human life is degraded and violence becomes tolerated, the unimaginable becomes more conceivable—we owe to all the people in the world our best efforts to organize ourselves so that we can maximize the chances of preventing these events. And where they cannot be prevented, we can move more quickly to minimize the horror.

So let us challenge ourselves to build a world in which no branch of humanity, because of national, racial, ethnic, or religious origin, is again threatened with destruction because of those characteristics, of which people should rightly be proud. Let us work together as a community of civilized nations to strengthen our ability to prevent and, if necessary, to stop genocide.

To that end, I am directing my administration to improve, with the international community, our system for identifying and spotlighting nations in danger of genocidal violence, so that we can assure worldwide awareness of impending threats. It may seem strange to you here, especially the many of you who lost members of your family, but all over the world there were people like me sitting in offices, day after day after day, who did not fully appreciate the depth and the speed with which you were being engulfed by this unimaginable terror.

We have seen, too—and I want to say again—that genocide can occur anywhere. It is not an African phenomenon and must never be viewed as such. We have seen it in industrialized Europe; we have seen it in Asia. We must have global vigilance. And never again must we be shy in the face of the evidence.

Secondly, we must as an international community have the ability to act when genocide threatens. We are working to create that capacity herein the Great Lakes region, where the memory is still fresh. This afternoon in Entebbe leaders from central and eastern Africa will meet with me to launch an effort to build a coalition to prevent genocide in this region. I thank the leaders who have stepped forward to make this commitment. We hope the effort can be a model for all the world, because our sacred task is to work to banish this greatest crime against humanity.

Events here show how urgent the work is. In the northwest part of your country, attacks by those responsible for the slaughter in 1994continue today. We must work as partners with Rwanda to end this violence and allow your people to go on rebuilding your lives and your nation.

Third, we must work now to remedy the consequences of genocide. The United States has provided assistance to Rwanda to settle the uprooted and restart its economy, but we must do more. I am pleased that America will become the first nation to contribute to the new Genocide Survivors Fund. We will contribute this year $2 million, continue our support in the years to come, and urge other nations to do the same, so that survivors and their communities can find the care they need and the help they must have.

Mr. President, to you, and to you, Mr. Vice President, you have shown great vision in your efforts to create a single nation in which all citizens can live freely and securely. As you pointed out, Rwanda was a single nation before the European powers met in Berlin to carve up Africa. America stands with you, and will continue helping the people of Rwanda to rebuild their lives and society.

You spoke passionately this morning in our private meeting about the need for grass-roots efforts, for the development projects which are bridging divisions and clearing a path to a better future. We will join with you to strengthen democratic institutions, to broaden participation, to give all Rwandans a greater voice in their own governance. The challenges you face are great, but your commitment to lasting reconciliation and inclusion is firm.

Fourth, to help ensure that those who survived in the generations to come never again suffer genocidal violence, nothing is more vital than establishing the rule of law. There can be no place in Rwanda that lasts without a justice system that is recognized as such.

We applaud the efforts of the Rwandan government to strengthen civilian and military justice systems. I am pleased that our Great Lakes Justice Initiative will invest $30 million to help create throughout the region judicial systems that are impartial, credible, and effective. In Rwanda these funds will help to support courts, prosecutors, and police, military justice and cooperation at the local level.

We will also continue to pursue justice through our strong backing for the International Criminal tribunal for Rwanda. The United States is the largest contributor to this tribunal. We are frustrated, as you are, by the delays in the tribunal's work. As we know, we must do better. Now that administrative improvements have begun, however, the tribunal should expedite cases through group trials, and fulfill its historic mission.

We are prepared to help, among other things, with witness relocation, so that those who still fear can speak the truth in safety. And we will support the War Crimes tribunal for as long as it is needed to do its work, until the truth is clear and justice is rendered.

Fifth, we must make it clear to all those who would commit such acts in the future that they too must answer for their acts, and they will. In Rwanda, we must hold accountable all those who may abuse human rights, whether insurgents or soldiers. Internationally, as we meet here, talks are underway at the United Nations to establish a permanent international criminal court. Rwanda and the difficulties we have had with this special tribunal underscores the need for such a court. And the United States will work to see that it is created.

I know that in the face of all you have endured, optimism cannot come easily to any of you. Yet I have just spoken, as I said, with several Rwandans who survived the atrocities, and just listening to them gave me reason for hope. You see countless stories of courage around you every day as you go about your business here—men and women who survived and go on, children who recover the light in their eyes remind us that at the dawn of a new millennium there is only one crucial division among the peoples of the Earth. And believe me, after over five years of dealing with these problems I know it is not the divisions between Hutu and Tutsi, or Serb or Croat and Muslim and Bosnian, or Arab and Jew, or Catholic and Protestant in Ireland, or black and white. It is really the line between those who embrace the common humanity we all share and those who reject it.

It is the line between those who find meaning in life through respect and cooperation and who, therefore, embrace peace, and those who can only find meaning in life if they have someone to look down on, someone to trample, someone to punish and, therefore, embrace war. It is the line between those who look to the future and those who cling to the past. It is the line between those who give up their resentment and those who believe they will absolutely die if they have to release one bit grievance. It is the line between those who confront every day with a clenched fist and those who confront every day with an open hand. That is the only line that really counts when all is said and done.

To those who believe that God made each of us in His own image, how could we choose the darker road? When you look at those children who greeted us as we got off that plane today, how could anyone say they did not want those children to have a chance to have their own children? To experience the joy of another morning sunrise? To learn the normal lessons of life? To give something back to their people?

When you strip it all away, whether we're talking about Rwanda or some other distant troubled spot, the world is divided according to how people believe they draw meaning from life.

And so I say to you, though the road is hard and uncertain, and there are many difficulties ahead, and like every other person who wishes to help, I doubtless will not be able to do everything I would like to do, there are things we can do. And if we set about the business of doing them together, you can overcome the awful burden that you have endured. You can put a smile on the face of every child in this country, and you can make people once again believe that they should live as people were living who were singing to us and dancing for us today.

That's what we have to believe. That is what I came here to say. And that is what I wish for you.

Thank you and God bless you.

Source: Public Papers of the Presidents of the United States: William J. Clinton, 1998, Book I, pp. 431–434.

2. The Akayesu Verdict and Sentence, September 2, 1998 and October 2, 1998

The trial of Jean-Paul Akayesu at the International Criminal Court for Rwanda was the first genocide trial in history. On September 2, 1998, he was found guilty on 9 of the 15 counts (including crimes against humanity and genocide) with which he was charged. It was a landmark decision in that it constituted the first international conviction of genocide, and it also embedded into the definition of genocide crimes against humanity based on rape. Following his conviction, Akayesu was sentenced to life in imprisonment.

VERDICT: having considered all of the evidence and the arguments, the Chamber unanimously finds as follows:

Count 1: Guilty of Genocide

Count 2: Not guilty of Complicity in Genocide

Count 3: Guilty of Crime against Humanity (Extermination)

Count 4: Guilty of Direct and Public Incitement to Commit Genocide

Count 5: Guilty of Crime against Humanity (Murder)

Count 6: Not guilty of Violation of Article 3 common to the Geneva Conventions (Murder)

Count 7: Guilty of Crime against Humanity (Murder)

Count 8: Not guilty of Violation of Article 3 common to the Geneva Conventions (Murder)

Count 9: Guilty of Crime against Humanity (Murder)

Count 10: Not guilty of Violation of Article 3 common to the Geneva Conventions (Murder)

Count 11: Guilty of Crime against Humanity (Torture)

Count 12: Not guilty of Violation of Article 3 common to the Geneva Conventions (Cruel Treatment)

Count 13: Guilty of Crime against Humanity (Rape)

Count 14: Guilty of Crime against Humanity (Other Inhumane Acts)

Count 15: Not guilty of Violation of Article 3 common to the Geneva Conventions and of Article 4(2)(e) of Additional Protocol II (Outrage upon personal dignity, in particular Rape, Degrading and Humiliating Treatment and Indecent Assault)

Signed in Arusha, 2 September 1998,

Laïty Kama (Presiding Judge), Lennart Aspegren (Judge), Navanethem Pillay (Judge)

SENTENCE, OCTOBER 2, 1998

Trial Chamber I, . . . noting that Akayesu was convicted on Counts 1, 3, 4, 5, 7, 9, 11, 13 and 14 of the indictment in the judgement delivered by this Chamber on 2nd September 1998, noting the brief submitted by the prosecutor, having heard the prosecutor and Akayesu in punishment of the above mentioned crimes, sentences Jean Paul Akayesu . . .

For Count 1, life imprisonment for the crime of genocide.

Count 3 of the indictment, life in imprisonment for the crime—for crimes against humanity, extermination.

Count 4, life imprisonment for direct and public incitement to commit genocide.

Count 5, 15 years of imprisonment for crimes against humanity, murder.

For Count 7, 15 years of imprisonment for crimes against humanity, murder.

For Count 9, 15 years of imprisonment for crimes against humanity, murder.

For Count 11, 10 years of imprisonment for crimes against humanity, torture.

Count 13, 15 years imprisonment for crimes against humanity, rape.

Count 14, 10 years of imprisonment for crimes against humanity, other inhumane acts.

The Chamber decides that the above sentences shall be served concurrently and therefore sentences Akayesu to a single sentence of life imprisonment.

Source: Prosecutor V. Akayesu, Case No. ICTR-96–4, Verdict (Sept 2, 1998) and Sentence (Oct 2, 1998). Used by permission of the United Nations. Available online: Verdict: http://www.unictr.org/Portals/0/Case/English/Akayesu/judgement/akay001.pdf; Sentence: http://www1.umn.edu/humanrts/instree/ICTR/AKAYESU_ICTR-96–4/Sentence_ICTR-96-4-T.html

3. The Courtroom Testimony of "Witness JJ" before the ICTR

In 1997 the trial of Jean-Paul Akayesu (b. 1953) commenced at the International Criminal Tribunal for Rwanda (ICTR). At one point in the trial of this former mayor of the village of Taba, a so-called secret witness, known only by the initials JJ, appeared. Her testimony was one of the accounts that led to his being sentenced to life imprisonment for genocide. A Tutsi from Taba, JJ lived with her husband, sister, and four children before the genocide. After April 1994, the farm on which she lived was attacked and three of her children fled. Her sister was severely wounded by machete cuts and became lost: in the confusion, JJ managed to escape with her baby son. She fled to the bureau communale, where she sought protection from Akayesu, but this had been taken over by the Interahamwe. Over the following days she and other Tutsi women were subjected to repeated beatings and systematic rapes. Part of her shocking testimony before the ICTR is produced here.

418. Following the amendment of the Indictment, Witness JJ, a Tutsi woman, testified about the events which took place in Taba after the plane crash. She [testified] that she was driven away from her home, which was destroyed by her Hutu neighbours who attacked her and her family after a man came to the hill near where she lived and said that the bourgmestre had sent him so that no Tutsi would remain on the hill that night. Witness JJ saw her Tutsi neighbours killed and she fled, seeking refuge in a nearby forest with her baby on her back and her younger sister, who had been wounded in the attack by a blow with an axe and two machete cuts. As she was being chased everywhere she went, Witness JJ said she went to the bureau communal. There she found more than sixty refugees down the road and on the field nearby. She testified that most of the refugees were women and children.

419. Witness JJ testified that the refugees at the bureau communal had been beaten by the Interahamwe and were lying on the ground when she arrived. Witness JJ encountered four Interahamwe outside the bureau communal, armed with knives, clubs, small axes and small hoes. That afternoon, she said, approximately forty more Interahamwe came and beat the refugees, including Witness JJ. At this time she said she saw the Accused, standing in the courtyard of the communal office, with two communal police officers who were armed with guns, one of whom was called Mushumba. Witness JJ said she was beaten on the head, the ribs and the right leg, which left her disabled. That evening, she said, the Accused came with a policeman to look for refugees and ordered the Interahamwe to beat them up, calling them "wicked, wicked people" and saying they "no longer had a right to shelter." The refugees were then beaten and chased away. Witness JJ said she was beaten by the policeman Mushumna, who hit her with the butt of his gun just behind her ear.

420. Witness JJ testified that she spent the night in the rain in a field. The next day she said she returned to the bureau communal and went to the Accused, in a group of ten people representing the refugees, who asked that they be killed as the others had been because they were so tired of it all. She said the Accused told them that there were no more bullets and that he had gone to look for more in Gitarama but they had not yet been made available. He asked his police officers to chase them away and said that even if there were bullets they would not waste them on the refugees. As the refugees saw that death would be waiting for them anywhere else, Witness JJ testified they stayed at the bureau communal.

421. Witness JJ testified that often the Interahamwe came to beat the refugees during the day, and that the policemen came to beat them at night. She also testified that the Interahamwe took young girls and women from their site of refuge near the bureau communal into a forest in the area and raped them. Witness JJ testified that this happened to her—that she was stripped of her clothing and raped in front of other people. At the request of the Prosecutor and with great embarrassment, she explicitly specified that the rapist, a young man armed with an axe and a long knife, penetrated her vagina with his penis. She stated that on this occasion she was raped twice. Subsequently, she told the Chamber, on a day when it was

raining, she was taken by force from near the bureau communal into the cultural center within the compound of the bureau communal, in a group of approximately fifteen girls and women. In the cultural center, according to Witness JJ, they were raped. She was raped twice by one man. Then another man came to where she was lying and he also raped her. A third man then raped her, she said, at which point she described herself as feeling near dead. Witness JJ testified that she was at a later time dragged back to the cultural center in a group of approximately ten girls and women and they were raped. She was raped again, two times. Witness JJ testified that she could not count the total number of times she was raped. She said, "each time you encountered attackers they would rape you,"—in the forest, in the sorghum fields. Witness JJ related to the Chamber the experience of finding her sister before she died, having been raped and cut with a machete.

422. Witness JJ testified that when they arrived at the bureau communal the women were hoping the authorities would defend them but she was surprised to the contrary. In her testimony she recalled lying in the cultural center, having been raped repeatedly by Interahamwe, and hearing the cries of young girls around her, girls as young as twelve or thirteen years old. On the way to the cultural center the first time she was raped there, Witness JJ said that she and the others were taken past the Accused and that he was looking at them. The second time she was taken to the cultural center to be raped, Witness JJ recalled seeing the Accused standing at the entrance of the cultural center and hearing him say loudly to the Interahamwe, "Never ask me again what a Tutsi woman tastes like," and "Tomorrow they will be killed" (Ntihazagire umbaza uko umututsikazi yari ameze, ngo kandi mumenye ko ejo ngo nibabica nta kintu muzambaza. Ngo ejo bazabica). According to Witness JJ, most of the girls and women were subsequently killed, either brought to the river and killed there, after having returned to their houses, or killed at the bureau communal. Witness JJ testified that she never saw the Accused rape anyone, but she, like Witness H, believed that he had the means to prevent the rapes from taking place and never even tried to do so. In describing the Accused and the statement he made regarding the taste of Tutsi women, she said he was "talking as if someone were encouraging a player" (Yavugaga nk'ubwiriza umukinnyi) and suggested that he was the one "supervising" the acts of rape. Witness JJ said she did not witness any killings at the bureau communal, although she saw dead bodies there.

423. When Witness JJ fled from the bureau communal, she left her one year-old child with a Hutu man and woman, who said they had milk for the child and subsequently killed him. Witness JJ spoke of the heavy sorrow the war had caused her. She testified to the humiliation she felt as a mother, by the public nudity and being raped in the presence of children by young men. She said that just thinking about it made the war come alive inside of her. Witness JJ told the Chamber that she had remarried but that her life had never been the same because of the beatings and rapes she suffered. She said the pain in her ribs prevents her from farming because she can no longer use a hoe, and she used to live on the food that she could grow.

Source: International Criminal Tribunal for Rwanda. Decision of 2 September 1998. Available at http://www.unictr.org/Portals/0/Case/English/Akayesu/judgement/akay001.pdf. Used by permission of the United Nations.

4. Fergal Keane at Nyarubuye

Fergal Keane (b. 1961) is an Irish writer and broadcaster, highly decorated within his profession. In 1990 he was appointed as the BBC's correspondent in Southern Africa, leading him to cover the collapse of Apartheid in South Africa as well as the Rwandan Genocide on 1994. In Season of Blood, his observations of the post-genocide situation in Rwanda after the journalists were permitted to return, he relates how he and his colleagues reported on a society that had been completely shredded by genocide. This document is a riveting account from his journal, in which he describes his emotions on being confronted with the carnage at the church of Nyarubuye, where an estimated 20,000 people were murdered on April 15–17, 1994.

This was always going to be the hardest part, this remembrance of what lay ahead in the dusk on that night in early June. My dreams are the fruit of this journey down the dirt road to Nyarubuye. How do I write this, how do I do justice to what awaits at the end of this road? As simply as possible. This is not a subject for fine words. We bounce and jolt along the rutted track on an evening of soft, golden light. The air is sweet with the smell of warm savannah grass. Clouds of midges hover around the cars, dancing through the windows. Although I can sense the nervousness of everybody in the car, we are exhausted and hungry from the long day's travelling, and we are too tired to bother fighting off the insects. Moses shifts down into first gear as we face into a long climb. The wheels begin to lose their grip and they spin in the loose sand of the incline.

"Oh, shit," mutters Moses. We climb out and begin to shove and push, but the car rolls back down the hill and we have to jump out of the way. The countryside is vastly different to the deep green hills around Byumba. From the top of the hill we can see a great expanse of yellow savannah grass, dotted here and there with thornbush and acacia. Glenn says it reminds him of home. He is right. This could be the bushveld around Louis Trichardt in the far Northern Transvaal. After about fifteen minutes of manoeuvring Moses eventually gets the car going again and we move off. Frank has become very quiet and he is fingering the stock of his assault rifle. After about another fifteen minutes we come to a straight stretch of track, wider than before and with a line of tall trees on either side. Up ahead is the façade of a church built from red sandstone. "This is Nyarubuye," says Frank. Moses begins to slow the car down and Glenn is preparing his camera to film. As we drive closer the front porch of the church comes into view. There is a white marble statue of Christ above the door with hands outstretched. Below it is a banner proclaiming the celebration of Easter, and below that there is the body of a man lying across the steps, his knees buckled underneath his body and his arms cast behind his head. Moses stops the car but he stays hunched over the wheel and I notice that he is looking down at his feet.

I get out and start to follow Frank across the open ground in front of the church. Weeds and summer grasses have begun to cover the gravel. Immediately in front of us is a set of classrooms and next to that a gateway leading into the garden of the church complex. As I walk towards the gate, I must make a detour to avoid the bodies of several people. There is a child who has been decapitated and there are three other corpses splayed on the ground. Closer to the gate Frank lifts a handkerchief to his nose because there is smell unlike anything I have ever experienced. I stop for a moment and pull out my own piece of cloth, pressing it to my face. Inside the gate the trail continues. The dead lie on either side of the pathway. A woman on her side, an expression of surprise on her face, her mouth open and a deep gash in her head. She is wearing a red cardigan and a blue dress but the clothes have begun to rot away, revealing the decaying body underneath. I must walk on, stepping over the corpse of a tall man who lies directly across the path, and, feeling the grass brush against my legs, I look down to my left and see a child who has been hacked almost into two pieces. The body is in a state of advanced decay and I cannot tell if it is a girl or a boy. I begin to pray to myself. "Our Father who art in heaven . . ." These are prayers I have not said since my childhood but I need them now. We come to an area of wildly overgrown vegetation where there are many flies in the air. The smell is unbearable here. I feel my stomach heave and my throat is completely dry. And then in front of me I see a group of corpses. They are young and old, men and women, and they are gathered in front of the door of the church offices. How many are there? I think perhaps a hundred, but it is hard to tell. The bodies seem to be melting away. Such terrible faces. Horror, fear, pain, abandonment. I cannot think of prayers now. Here the dead have no dignity. They are twisted and turned into grotesque shapes, and the rains have left pools of stagnant, stinking water all around them. They must have fled here in a group, crowded in next to the doorway, an easy target for the machetes and the grenades. I look around at my colleagues and there are tears in Tony's eyes. Glenn is filming, but he stops every few seconds to cough. Frank and Valence have wandered away from us into a clump of trees and the older man is explaining something to the boy. I do not know what he is saying, but Valence is looking at him intensely. I stay close to David because at this moment I need his age and strength and wisdom. He is very calm, whispering into Glenn's ear from time to time with suggestions, and moving quietly. The dead are everywhere. We pass a classroom and inside a mother is lying in the corner surrounded by four children. The chalk marks from the last lesson in mathematics are still on the board. But the desks have been upturned by the killers. It looks as if the woman and her children had tried to hide underneath the desks. We pass around the corner and I step over the remains of a small boy. Again he has been decapitated. To my immediate left is a large room filled with bodies. There is blood, rust coloured now with the passing weeks, smeared on the walls. I do not know what else to say about the bodies because I have already seen too much. As we pass back across the open ground in front of the church I notice Moses and Edward standing by the cars and I motion to them to switch on the headlights because it is growing dark. The sound of insects grows louder now filling in the churchyard silence. David and the crew have gone into the church and I follow them inside, passing a pile of bones and rags. There are other bodies between the pews and another pile of bones at the foot of the statue of the Virgin Mary. In a cloister, next to the holy water fountain, a man lies with his arms over his head. He must have died shielding himself from the machete blows. "This is fucking unbelievable," whispers Tony into my ear. We are all whispering, as if somehow we might wake the dead with our voices. "It is just fucking unbelievable. Can you imagine what these poor bastards went through?" he continues. And I answer that no, I cannot imagine it because my powers of visualization cannot possibly imagine the magnitude of the terror. David and Glenn say nothing at all and Frank has also lapsed into silence.

Valence has gone to join the drivers. I do not know the things Valence has seen before this and he will not talk about them. I imagine that the sight of these bodies is bringing back unwelcome memories. Outside the church the night has come down thick and heavy. Tony shines a camera light to guide our way. Even with this and the car lights I nearly trip on the corpse of a woman that is lying in the grass. Moths are dancing around the lights as I reach the sanctuary of the car. While we are waiting for Glenn and Tony to pack the equipment away, we hear a noise coming from one of the rooms of the dead. I turn to Moses and Edward. "What is that? Did you hear that?" I ask. Edward notices the edge of fear in my voice and strains his ear to listen. But there is no more sound. "It is only rats, only rats," says Moses. As we turn to go I look back and in the darkness see the form of the marble Christ gazing down on the dead. The rats scuttle in the classrooms again.

Source: Fergal Keane, *Season of Blood: A Rwandan Journey,* London: Penguin Viking, 1995, pp. 76–81. Used by permission.

5. Arusha Accords, August 1993

The signing of these Accords brought to an end the genocidal conflict between the Government of the Republic of Rwanda and the Rwandan Patriotic Front. In reality, the Accords consisted of several documents: (1) the Peace Agreement; (2) the N'sele Cease-Fire Agreement; (3) Protocol of Agreement on the Rule of Law; (4) Protocol of Agreement on Power-Sharing; (5) Protocol of Agreement on Power-Sharing within the Framework of the Transitional Government; (6) Protocol of Agreement on the Repatriation of Refugees and Resettlement of Displaced Persons; (7) Protocol of Agreement on the Integration of the Armed Forces; (8) Protocol of Agreement on Miscellaneous Issues and Final Provisions.

Peace Agreement between the Government of the Republic of Rwanda and the Rwandese Patriotic Front

The Government of the Republic of Rwanda on the one hand, and the Rwandese Patriotic Front on the other;

Firmly resolved to find a political negotiated solution to the war situation confronting the Rwandese people since 1st October, 1990;

Considering and appreciating the efforts deployed by the countries of the Sub-region with a view to helping the Rwandese people to recover peace;

Referring to the numerous high-level meetings held respectively at Mwanza, United Republic of Tanzania, on 17th October, 1990, in Gbadolite, Republic of Zaire, on 26th October, 1990, in Goma, Republic of Zaire, on 20th November, 1990 in Zanzibar, United Republic of Tanzania, on 17th February, 1991, in Dar-es-Salaam, United Republic of Tanzania, on 19th February, 1991 and from 5th to 7th March, 1993;

Considering that all these meetings aimed first and foremost at establishing a ceasefire so as to enable the two parties to look for a solution to the war throughdirect negotiations;

Noting the N'SELE Ceasefire Agreement, of 29th March, 1991 as amended in GBADOLITE on 16th September, 1991 and at ARUSHA on 12th July, 1992;

Reaffirming their unwavering determination to respect principles underlying the Rule of Law which include democracy, national unity, pluralism, the respect of fundamental freedoms and rights of the individual;

Considering that these principles constitute the basis and consistency of a lasting peace awaited by the Rwandese people for the benefit of the present and future generations;

Noting the Protocol of Agreement on the Rule of Law signed at Arusha on 18th August, 1992;

Considering that the two parties accepted the principle of power-sharing within the framework of a Broad-Based Transitional Government;

Noting the Protocols of Agreement on Power-Sharing signed at ARUSHA respectively on 30th October, 1992, and on 9th January, 1993;

Considering that the conflictual situation between the two parties can only be brought to an end through the formation of one and single National Army and a new National Gendarmerie from forces of the two warring parties;

Noting of the Protocol of Agreement on the integration of Armed Forces of both Parties, signed at Arusha on 3rd August, 1993;

Recognizing that the unity of the Rwandese people cannot be achieved until a definitive solution to the problem of Rwandese refugees is found and that the return of Rwandese refugees to their country is an inalienable right and constitutes a factor for peace and national unity and reconciliation;

Noting the Protocol of Agreement on the repatriation of Rwandese refugees and the Resettlement of Displaced Persons, signed at ARUSHA on 9th June, 1993;

Resolved to eradicate and put a definite end to all the root causes which gave rise to the war;

Have, at the conclusion of the Peace Talks held in Arusha, United Republic of Tanzania, between 10th July, 1992 and 24th June, 1993 as well as Kinihira, Republic of Rwanda from 19th to 25th July, 1993 under the aegis of the Facilitator, His Excellency Ali Hassan MWINY1, President of the United Republic of Tanzania, in the presence of the Representative of the Mediator, His Excellency, MOBUTU SESE SEKO, President of the Republic of Zaire as well as Representatives of the Current Chairmen of the OAU, His Excellency Abdou DIOUF, President of the Republic of Senegal, and Hosni MUBARAK, President of the Arab Republic of Egypt, the Secretary General of the OAU, Dr. Salim Ahmed SALIM, the Secretary General of the United Nations, Dr. Boutros Boutros GHAU and Observers representing the Federal Republic of Germany, Belgium, Burundi, the United States of America, France, Nigeria, Uganda and Zimbabwe;

Calling the International Community to witness;

Hereby agree on the following provisions.

Article 1: The war between the Government of the Republic of Rwanda and the Rwandese Patriotic Front is hereby brought to an end.

Article 2: The following documents are an integral part of the present Peace Agreement concluded between the Government of the Republic of Rwanda and the Rwandese Patriotic Front:

I. The N'SELE Ceasefire Agreement of 29th March, 1991 between the Government of the Republic of Rwanda and the Rwandese Patriotic Front, as amended in GBADOUTE on 16th September, 1991 and at ARUSHA on 12th July, 1992;

II. The Protocol of Agreement between the Government of the Republic of Rwanda and the Rwandese Patriotic Front on the Rule of Law, signed at ARUSHA on 18th September, 1992;

III. The Protocols of Agreement between the Government of the Republic of Rwanda and the Rwandese Patriotic Front on Power-Sharing within the Framework of a Broad-Based Transitional Government, signed at ARUSHA respectively on 30th October, 1992 and on 9th January, 1993;

IV. The Protocol of Agreement between the Government of the Republic of Rwanda and the Rwandese Patriotic Front on the Repatriation of Refugees and the Resettlement of Displaced Persons, signed at Arusha on 9th June, 1993;

V. The Protocol Agreement between the Government of the Republic of Rwanda and the Rwandese Patriotic Front on the integration of Armed Forces of the two parties, signed at ARUSHA on, 3rd August 1993;

VI. The Protocol of Agreement between the Government of the Republic of Rwanda and the Rwandese Patriotic Front on Miscellaneous Issues and Final Provisions signed at Arusha on 3rd August, 1993.

These entire documents are attached as Annex.

Article 3: The two parties also agree that the Constitution of 10th June, 1991 and the Arusha Peace Agreement shall constitute indissolubly the Fundamental Law that shall govern the Country during the Transition period, taking into account the following provisions:

1. The following articles of the Constitution shall be replaced by the provisions of the Peace Agreement relating to the same matters. The Articles in question are: 34, 35, 38, 39, 40, 41, 42, 43, 44, 45, 46, 47, 48, 49, 50, 51, 52, 54, 55, 56, 57, 58, 59, 60, 63, 65, 66, 67, 68, 70, 71, 73, 74, 75 paragraph 2, 77 paragraphs 3 and 4, 81, 82, 83, 84, 85, 86, 87, 88 paragraph 1, 90, 96, 99, 101.

2. In case of conflict between the other provisions of the Constitution and those of the Peace Agreement, the provisions of the Peace Agreement shall prevail.

3. The Constitutional Court shall verify the conformity of Laws and Orders in Council with the Fundamental Law thus defined. Pending the enactment of the law on the Supreme Court, the existing Constitutional Court shall remain

composed of both the Court of Cassation and the State of Council. The Presiding Judge of the Constitutional Court shall assume the presidency.

Article 4: In case of conflict between the provisions of the Fundamental Law and those of other Laws and Regulations, the provisions of the Fundamental Law shall prevail.

Article 5: The Government of the Republic of Rwanda and the Rwandese Patriotic Front undertake to make every possible effort to ensure that the present Peace Agreement is respected and implemented.

They further undertake to spare no effort to promote National Unity and Reconciliation.

Article 6: The two parties agree on the appointment of Mr. TWAGIRAMUNGU Faustin as Prime Minister of the Broad-Based Transitional Government, in accordance with Articles 6 and 51 of the Protocol of Agreement between the Government of the Republic of Rwanda and the Rwandese Patriotic Front on Power-Sharing within the framework of a Broad-Based Transitional Government.

Article 7: The Transitional Institutions shall be set up within thirty seven (37) days following the signing of the Peace Agreement.

Article 8: The current Government shall remain in Office until the Broad-Based Transitional Government is established. The maintenance of that Government does not mean that it can encroach on the mandate of the Broad-Based Transitional Government being established.

The current Government shall, in no case, take decisions which may be detrimental to the implementation of the Broad-Based Transitional programme.

Article 9: The "Conseil National de Developpment" (CND) shall remain in Office until the Transitional National Assembly is established. However, as from the date of signing the Peace Agreement, it shall not enact laws.

Article 10: The present Peace Agreement is signed by the President of the Republic Rwanda and the Chairman of the Rwandese Patriotic Front, in the presence of:

- The Facilitator, His Excellency, Ali Hassan MWINYI, President of the United Republic of Tanzania,
- His Excellency, Yoweri Kaguta MUSEVENI, President of the Republic of Uganda; Observer country;
- His Excellency Melchior NDADAYE, President of the Republic of Burundi, Observer country;
- The Representative of the Mediator, His Excellency Faustin BIRINDWA, Prime Minister of Zaire;
- Dr. Salim Ahmed SALIM, Secretary General of the OAU;
- The Representative of the Secretary General of the United Nations;
- The Representative of the Current Chairman of the OAU;
- The Representatives of other Observer countries: Germany, Belgium, United States of America, France, Nigeria and Zimbabwe;
- The delegations of the two parties.

Article 11: The present Peace Agreement shall come into force upon its signing by the parties.

Done at Arusha, on the 4th day of the month of August, 1993 both in French and English languages, the original text being in French.

Protocol of Agreement Between the Government of the Republic of Rwanda and the Rwandese Patriotic Front on the Rule of Law

PREAMBLE:

The Government of the Republic of Rwanda and the Rwandese Patriotic Front.

Reaffirming that the Rule of Law, the principle of the establishment of which was agreed upon by the signatories of the present Protocol of Agreement, in accordance with Article V of the N'sele Agreement, as amended in Gbadolite, on the 16th of September, 1991 and in Arusha on the 12th of July, 1992, shall characterize the political life in our country.

Considering that the Rule of Law implies that nobody, including the authorities, is above the law and that the laws must respect the fundamental rights of the citizens;

Reaffirming that the Rule of Law does not mean merely a formal legality which assures regularity and consistency in the achievement and enforcement of democratic order, and which is first and foremost and fundamentally characterised by Justice based on the recognition and full acceptance of the supreme value of the human personality and guaranteed by institutions providing a framework for its fullest expression;

Convinced that the Rule of Law:

- is the best guarantee of national unity, the respect of the fundamental freedoms and rights of the individual;
- is a concrete manifestation of democracy;
- hinges on National Unity. Democracy, Pluralism and Respect for human rights:

Have agreed as follows:

Chapter I. National unity

Article 1: National unity must be based on equality of all citizens before the law, equal opportunities in all fields including the economic field and respect for fundamental rights as stipulated, notably, in the Universal Declaration of Human Rights and in the African Charter on Human and Peoples' Rights.

Article 2: National unity implies that the Rwandese people, as constituent elements of the Rwandese nation, are one and indivisible. It also implies the necessity to fight all obstacles to national unity, notably, ethnicism, regionalism, integrism and intolerance which subordinate the national interest to ethnic, regional, religious and personal interest.

Article 3: National unity entails the rejection of all exclusions and any form of discrimination based notably, on ethnicity, region, sex and religion. It also entails that all citizens have equal opportunity of access to all the political, economic and other advantages, which access must be guaranteed by the State.

Article 4: The two parties acknowledge that the national unity of the people of Rwanda cannot be achieved without a definitive solution to the problem of Rwandese refugees. They recognize that the return of the Rwandese refugees to their country is an inalienable right and represents a factor of peace, unity and national reconciliation. They undertake not to hinder the free exercise of this right by the refugees.

Chapter II: Democracy

Article 5: Democracy is founded on the idea that sovereignty belongs to the people. It is expressed, notably, through regular, free, transparent and fair elections. Popular representation must be the authentic expression of the will of citizens.

Article 6: The two parties accept the universality as well as the implications of the following fundamental principles of democracy:

- sovereignty of the people;
- government based on the consent of the people expressed through regular, free, transparent and fair elections;
- separation of the legislative, the executive and the Judiciary powers;
- independence of the Judiciary:
- guarantee for the fundamental rights of the individual as provided for in the Universal Declaration of Human Rights as well as in the African Charter on Human and Peoples' Rights, among others, freedom of speech, enterprise and of political, social and economic association;
- laws and regulations based on the respect of fundamental human rights;
- equality before the law;
- respect of laws and regulations by all;
- Constitution which respects the principles enunciated above, organises the State powers and defines the powers and limitations of the institutions of the Republic;
- multipartism, social and economic pluralism.

Article 7: The two parties recognize that multipartism entails the legitimate existence of a democratic opposition and consider, as legitimate, the aspiration of any Rwandese citizen to accede to power through democratic process.

Article 8: The two parties resolutely reject and undertake to fight:

- political ideologies based on ethnicity, region, religion and intolerance which subordinate national Interest to the ethnic, regional, religious or personal interest:
- any form of coup d'etat as being contrary to the democratic system as described above.

Article 9: In order to promote and consolidate the democratic system as described above, the two parties undertake to work for social, economic and cultural development of the country and to fight hunger, ignorance, poverty and disease.

Article 10: Elections shall be organised in such a way that transparency is guaranteed and fraud eliminated through the establishment of efficient supervision mechanisms including, if the need arises, enlisting the assistance of International Observers.

The prior and full explanation of the citizens' rights and civic duties including the issues at stake in the elections is their inalienable right as a way of avoiding any form of political manipulation.

Article 11: The two parties accept to promote, in national political life, a democratic culture based on the principles enunciated above.

Article 12: The broad-based transitional government provided for in Article V of the N'sele Agreement, as amended in Gbadolite, on 16th September, 1991 and in Arusha on 12th July, 1992, shall lead the country to a democratic system as defined above.

To this end, the two parties note that a political process has been initiated by the Rwandese people to ensure the progress of democracy and reaffirm the need to build together a society founded on the Rule of Law as stipulated in the present Protocol.

Chapter III: Pluralism

Article 13: The two parties recognise that a democratic society is also founded on pluralism which is the expression of individual freedoms and must respect national unity and the fundamental rights of the citizen.

Chapter IV: Human Rights

Article 14: The two parties recognise the universal nature of human rights and should express concern when these rights are violated anywhere and by anybody.

They also recognise that the International Community would be justified in expressing concern in the event that these rights are violated by anybody on Rwandese territory. These rights should be guaranteed by the Constitution and the laws of the Republic of Rwanda.

Article 15: The two parties agree that a National Commission on Human Rights shall be established. This institution shall be independent and shall investigate human right violations committed by anybody on Rwandese territory. in particular, by organs of the State and individuals in their capacity as agents of the State or of various organisations.

The Investigation work of the Commission shall not be limited in time.

The Commission shall be provided with the necessary means, especially legal means, to efficiently accomplish its mission. It shall utilise its findings to:

a) sensitize and educate the population about human rights;
b) institute legal proceedings, where necessary.

Article 16: The two parties also agree to establish an International Commission of Enquiry to investigate human rights violations committed during the war.

Conclusion

Article 17: The two parties concur that national unity, democracy and peace are invaluable and solemnly undertake to do everything possible so as to preserve these values In the interest of the present and future Rwandese generations.

Done at Arusha, the 18th day of August, 1992 in French and English, the French version being the original.

Protocol of Agreement on Power-Sharing Within the Framework of a Broad-Based Transitional Government Between the Government of the Republic of Rwanda and the Rwandese Patriotic Front

The Government of the Republic of Rwanda and the Rwandese Patriotic Front;

Agree on the following provisions which are an integral part of the Protocol of Agreement on Power-sharing:

Chapter I: General Principles

ARTICLE 1:

The two parties reaffirm the acceptance of the principle of powersharing within the framework of a Broad-Based Transitional Government, in conformity with Article V.3. of the N'sele Ceasefire Agreement, as amended at GBADOLITE on 16th September. 1991 and at ARUSHA on 12th July, 1992. The modalities of implementation of this principle are the object of the present Protocol of Agreement on Power-sharing.

ARTICLE 2:

The two parties agree that those modalities shall consist of:

(a) the maintenance of the current structure of the Coalition Government with appropriate adjustments to be mutually agreed upon In this Protocol, with a view to making room for the participation of the RPF and other political forces in the country,

(b) appropriate adjustments to be mutually agreed upon in this Protocol, to be made at the level of the State powers with a view to enabling the RPF and other political forces in the country to participate in and make for the efficient management of the transition, in compliance with the principle of separation of powers.

Chapter II: Transitional Institutions

ARTICLE 3: During the Transitional Period, the State institutions shall be:

(I) The Presidency of the Republic;
(ii) The Broad-Based Transitional Government:
(iii) The Transitional National Assembly;
(iv) The Institutions of the Judiciary.

Source: Available online at http://peacemaker.un.org/sites/peacemaker.un.org/files/RW_930804_PeaceAgreementRwanda-RwandesePatrioticFront.pdf; http://peacemaker.un.org/sites/peacemaker.un.org/files/RW_920818_ProtocolOnRuleOfLLaw.pdf; and http://peacemaker.un.org/sites/peacemaker.un.org/files/RW_930109_ProtocolOnPowerSharing.pdf.

6. The "Genocide Fax," January 1994

On January 10, 1994, Lieutenant-General Roméo Dallaire (b. 1946), the Canadian Force Commander of UNAMIR (the United Nations Assistance Mission for Rwanda), received intelligence that a radical Hutu, codenamed "Jean-Pierre," was prepared to disclose information regarding a planned genocide of Tutsis. "Jean-Pierre" had been an officer in Rwanda's Presidential Guard, but had left in order to become one of the key men in the Interahamwe militia. Upon closer inquiries, he described in detail how the Interahamwe were trained, by whom, and where; he added that the militia was in a state of permanent readiness sufficient to kill one thousand Tutsis in the capital, Kigali, within 20 minutes of receiving an order to commence the genocide. As a sign of his goodwill and reliability, "Jean-Pierre" offered to reveal the location of a large stockpile of weapons somewhere in central Kigali. Dallaire, realizing that these arms had to be confiscated, decided to order an arms raid, and faxed the UN Department of Peacekeeping Operations in New York, headed at that time by Kofi Annan (b. 1938), for authorization. This cable outlined in detail "Jean-Pierre's" revelations. Dallaire's fax was responded to negatively, however. Under no circumstances was he authorized to conduct arms raids; he was taken to task for suggesting that he exceed his Chapter VI peacekeeping mandate; and he was ordered to turn over "Jean-Pierre's" revelations to the president of Rwanda, Juvénal Habyarimana (1937–1994)—the very man whose anti-Tutsi cause the Interahamwe was enforcing. The UN's Department of Peacekeeping Operations, together with the Office of the then secretary general, Boutros Boutros-Ghali (b. 1922), decided that legality and process was more important, on this occasion, than action; not only this, but they were concerned for the image of the UN in light of an earlier failed arms raid that took place with heavy loss of life in Mogadishu, Somalia, in October, 1993. Dallaire protested the decision insistently, but New York would not budge, with catastrophic consequences. The "genocide fax" of January 10, 1994, represents a missed opportunity on the UN's part to nip the nascent génocidaires in the bud; it was a mistake whose price was the Rwanda genocide three months later.

1. Force commander put in contact with informant by very very important government politician. Informant is a top level trainer in the cadre of interhamwe-armed militia of MRND.

2. He informed us he was in charge of last Saturdays demonstrations which aims were to target deputies of opposition parties coming to ceremonies and Belgian soldiers. They hoped to provoke the RPF BN to engage (being fired upon) the demonstrators and provoke a civil war. Deputies were to be assassinated upon entry or exit from Parliament. Belgian troops were to be provoked and if Belgians soldiers restored to force a number of them were to be killed and thus guarantee Belgian withdrawal from Rwanda.

3. Informant confirmed 48 RGF PARA CDO and a few members of the gendarmerie participated in demonstrations in plain clothes. Also at least one Minister of the MRND and the sous-prefect of Kigali were in the demonstration. RGF and Interhamwe provided radio communications.

4. Informant is a former security member of the president. He also stated he is paid RF150,000 per month by the MRND party to train Interhamwe. Direct link is to chief of staff RGF and president of the MRND for financial and material support.

5. Interhamwe has trained 1700 men in RGF military camps outside the capital. The 1700 are scattered in groups of 40 throughout Kigali. Since UNAMIR deployed he has trained 300 personnel in three week training sessions at RGF camps. Training focus was discipline, weapons, explosives, close combat and tactics.

6. Principal aim of Interhamwe in the past was to protect Kigali from RPF. Since UNAMIR mandate he has been ordered to register all Tutsi in Kigali. He suspects it is for their extermination. Example he gave was that in 20 minutes his personnel could kill up to 1000 Tutsis.

7. Informant states he disagrees with anti-Tutsi extermination. He supports opposition to RPF but cannot support killing of innocent persons. He also stated that he believes the president does not have full control over all elements of his old party/faction.

8. Informant is prepared to provide location of major weapons cache with at least 135 weapons. He already has distributed 110 weapons including 35 with ammunition and can give us details of their location. Type of weapons are G3 and AK47 provided by RGF. He was ready to go to the arms cache tonight-if we gave him the following guarantee. He requests that he and his family (his wife and four children) be placed under our protection.

9. It is our intention to take action within the next 36 hours with a possible H HR of Wednesday at dawn (local). Informant states that hostilities may commence again if political deadlock ends. Violence could take place day of the ceremonies or the day after. Therefore Wednesday will give greatest chance of success and also be most timely to provide significant input to on-going political negotiations.

10. It is recommended that informant be granted protection and evacuated out of Rwanda. This HQ does not have previous UN experience in such matters and urgently requests guidance. No contact has as yet been made to

any embassy in order to inquire if they are prepared to protect him for a period of time by granting diplomatic immunity in their embassy in Kigali before moving him and his family out of the country.

11. Force commander will be meeting with the very very important political person tomorrow morning in order to ensure that this individual is conscious of all parameters of his involvement. Force commander does have certain reservations on the suddenness of the change of heart of the informant to come clean with this information. Recce of armed cache and detailed planning of raid to go on late tomorrow. Possibility of a trap not fully excluded, as this may be a set-up against this very very important political person. Force commander to inform SRSG first thing in morning to ensure his support.

13. Peux Ce Que Veux. Allons-y.

Source: National Security Archive.

7. "The Hutu Ten Commandments"

The so-called Hutu Ten Commandments was a catalogue of 10 admonitory instructions that were to be followed by Hutus in order to destroy Tutsi influence over Rwandan society, and guarantee Hutu hegemony. Published in issue number 6 of the anti-Tutsi newspaper Kangura, *in December, 1990, the "Ten Commandments of the Hutu" were written by the magazine's editor, Hassan Ngeze (b. 1961)—though in his trial testimony before the International Criminal Tribunal for Rwanda (ICTR), Ngeze claimed that the list had been circulating for years before, and was not in fact composed by him alone. The "Ten Commandments" could in many respects have been adapted directly out of the Nazi Nuremberg Laws.*

1. Every Hutu male should know that Tutsi women, wherever they may be, work for the interest of their Tutsi ethnic group. As a result, a Hutu who marries a Tutsi woman, befriends a Tutsi woman, or employs a Tutsi woman as a secretary or concubine, shall be considered a traitor;

2. Every Hutu should know that our daughters are more suitable and conscientious in their role as woman, wife and mother. Are they not beautiful, good secretaries, and more honest?

3. Hutu women, be vigilant, and try to bring your husbands, brothers and sons back to reason;

4. Every Hutu should know that all Tutsis are dishonest in their business dealings. They are only seeking the supremacy of their own ethnic group. Any Hutu who engages in business dealings or partnerships with the Tutsis is a traitor;

5. All strategic positions—political, administrative, economic, military, and security—should be entrusted to the Hutus;

6. The education sector should be majority Hutu;

7. The Rwandan armed forces must be exclusively Hutu;

8. The Hutus should stop having mercy on the Tutsis;

9. Hutus, wherever they may be, must have unity and solidarity, and be concerned about the fate of their Hutu brothers;

10. The 1959 revolution, the 1961 revolution, and the Hutu ideology must be taught to Hutus at all levels. Every Hutu must spread this ideology widely. Any Hutu who persecutes his brother Hutu for having read, spread and taught this ideology, is a traitor.

Source: *Kangura,* No. 6 (December 1990). Available online at http://www.trumanwebdesign.com/~catalina/commandments.htm.

Bibliography

Adekunle, Julius O. *Culture and Customs of Rwanda.* Westport, CT: Greenwood Press, 2007.

Adelman, Howard, and Astri Suhrke, eds. *The Path of a Genocide: The Rwanda Crisis from Uganda to Zaire.* New Brunswick, NJ: Transaction Publishers, 1999.

Africa South of the Sahara 1994. London: Europa, 1993.

African Rights. *Rwanda: Death, Despair and Defiance.* 2nd rev. ed. London: African Rights, 1995.

Ali, Taisier M., and Robert O. Matthews. *Civil Wars in Africa: Roots and Resolution.* Toronto: McGill-Queen's University Press, 1999.

Anyidoho, Henry Kwami. *Guns Over Kigali: The Rwandese Civil War, 1994. A Personal Account.* Accra: Woeli Publishing Services, 1997.

Barnett, Michael. *Eyewitness to a Genocide: The United Nations and Rwanda.* Ithaca, NY: Cornell University Press, 2002.

Bell-Fialkoff, Andrew. *Ethnic Cleansing.* Sydney, Australia: Palgrave Macmillan, 1999.

Bodnarchuk, Kari. *Rwanda: A Country Torn Apart.* Minneapolis, MN: Lerner Publishing Group, 1998.

Boutros-Ghali, Boutros. *An Agenda for Peace: Preventive Diplomacy, Peacemaking and Peace-Keeping.* New York: United Nations, 1992.

Bowden, Mark. *Black Hawk Down: A Story of Modern War.* New York: Atlantic Monthly Press, 1999.

Brown, Michael, Gary Freeman and Kay Miller. *Passing-By: The United States and Genocide in Burundi, 1972.* New York: The Carnegie Endowment for International Peace, 1973.

Chrétien, Jean-Pierre. *The Great Lakes of Africa: Two Thousand Years of History.* Translated by Scott Strauss, New York: Zone Books, 2003.

Cohen, Stanley. *States of Denial: Knowing about Atrocities and Suffering.* Cambridge: Polity Press, 2001.

Cook, Susan E., ed. *Genocide in Cambodia and Rwanda: New Perspectives.* New Brunswick, NJ: Transaction Publishers, 2006.

Cruvellier, Thierry. *Court of Remorse: Inside the International Criminal Court for Rwanda.* Madison: University of Wisconsin Press, 2010.

Dallaire, Roméo. *Shake Hands with the Devil: The Failure of Humanity in Rwanda.* Toronto: Random House, 2004.

Del Ponte, Carla, and Chuck Sudetic. *Madame Prosecutor: Confrontations with Humanity's Worst Criminals and the Culture of Impunity.* New York: Other Press, 2009.

Des Forges, Alison. *Leave None to Tell the Story: Genocide in Rwanda.* New York: Human Rights Watch, 1999.

Des Forges, Alison, and Longman, Timothy. "Legal Responses to Genocide in Rwanda." In *My Neighbor, My Enemy: Justice and Community in the Aftermath of Mass Atrocity.* Edited by Eric Stover and Harvey M. Weinstein, 49–63. Cambridge: Cambridge University Press, 2004.

Dorsey, Learthen. *Historical Dictionary of Rwanda.* Metuchen, NJ: Scarecrow Press, 1994.

Edgerton, Robert. *The Troubled Heart of Africa: A History of the Congo.* New York, St. Martin's Press, 2002.

Eller, Jack David. *From Culture to Ethnicity to Conflict: An Anthropological Perspective on International Ethnic Conflict.* Ann Arbor: University of Michigan Press, 1999.

Eltringham, Nigel. *Accounting for Horror: Post-Genocide Debates in Rwanda.* London: Pluto Press, 2004.

Evans, Glynne. *Responding to Crises in the African Great Lakes.* Oxford: Oxford University Press, 1997.

Facing History and Ourselves. *Decision-Making in Times of Injustice.* Brookline, MA: Facing History and Ourselves National Foundation, 2009.

Friedrichs, David O., ed. *State Crime*. Brookfield, VT: Ashgate/Dartmouth, 1998.

Gourevitch, Philip. *We Wish to Inform You That Tomorrow We Will Be Killed with Our Families: Stories from Rwanda*. New York: Picador, 1999.

Gribbin, Robert E. *In the Aftermath of Genocide: The US Role in Rwanda*. New York: I Universe, 2005.

Hatzfield, Jean. *Machete Season: The Killers in Rwanda Speak*. Translated by Linda Coverdale. New York: Farrar, Straus and Giroux, 2005.

Huffington Post. "Beatrice Munyenyezi Lied about Her Role in Rwanda Genocide; Faces Deportation from New Hampshire," February 22, 2013.

Hurd, Douglas. *The Search for Peace*. New York: Little, Brown, 1997.

International Criminal Tribunal for Rwanda, Prosecutor v. Ferdinand Nahimana, Jean-Bosco Barayagwiza, and Hassan Ngeze, Judgment and Sentence, Case No. ICTR-99–52-T (Trial Chamber 1, December 3, 2003).

Jennings, Christian. *Across the Red River: Rwanda, Burundi and the Heart of Darkness*. London: Phoenix, 2000.

Jokic, Aleksandar, ed. *War Crimes and Collective Wrongdoing: A Reader*. Malden, MA: Blackwell Publishers, 2001.

Kamukama, Dixon. *Rwanda Conflict: Its Roots and Regional Implications*. 2nd ed. Kampala, Uganda: Fountain Publishers, 1998.

Kiernan, Ben. *Blood and Soil: A World History of Genocide and Extermination from Sparta to Darfur*. New Haven, CT: Yale University Press, 2007.

Klinghoffer, Arthur Jay. *The International Dimension of Genocide in Rwanda*. New York: New York University Press, 1998.

Kressel, Neil Jeffrey. *Mass Hate: The Global Rise of Genocide and Terror*. New York: Plenum Press, 1996.

Kuperman, Alan. *The Limits of Humanitarian Intervention: Genocide in Rwanda*. New York: Brookings Institution Press, 2001.

LeBor, Adam. *"Complicity with Evil": The United Nations in the Age of Modern Genocide*. New Haven, CT: Yale University Press, 2008.

Lemarchand, René. *The Dynamics of Violence in Central Africa*. Philadelphia: University of Pennsylvania Press, 2009.

Lemarchand, René, ed. *Forgotten Genocides: Oblivion, Denial and Memory*. Philadelphia: University of Pennsylvania Press, 2011.

Meisler, Stanley. *Kofi Annan: A Man of Peace in a World of War*. New York: Wiley, 2008.

Melvern, Linda. *Conspiracy to Murder: The Rwandan Genocide*. London: Verso, 2006.

Meredith, Martin. *The State of Africa*. London: Free Press, 2005.

Midlarsky, Manus I. *The Killing Trap: Genocide in the Twentieth Century*. Cambridge, MA: Cambridge University Press, 2005.

Ndahiro, Tom. "Genocide-Laundering: Historical Revisionism, Genocide Denial and the Rassemblement Républicain pour la Démocratie au Rwanda." In *After Genocide: Transitional Justice, Post-Conflict Reconstruction and Reconciliation in Rwanda and Beyond*. Edited by Phil Clark and Zachary Kaufman. London: Hurst Publishers, 2008.

Neier, Aryeh. *War Crimes: Brutality, Genocide, Terror, and the Struggle for Justice*. New York: Times Books, 1998.

Newbury, Catherine. *The Cohesion of Oppression: Clientship and Ethnicity in Rwanda, 1860–1960*. New York: Columbia University Press, 1988.

Newbury, David. *The Land beyond the Mists: Essays on Identity and Authority in Precolonial Congo and Rwanda*. Athens: Ohio University Press, 2011.

Nowrojee, Binaifer. *Shattered Lives: Sexual Violence during the Rwandan Genocide and its Aftermath*. New York: Human Rights Watch, 1996.

Nzongola-Ntalaja, Georges. *The Congo: From Leopold to Kabila: A People's History*. London: Zed Books, 2002.

Off, Carol. *The Lion, the Fox and the Eagle: A Story of Generals and Justice in Rwanda and Yugoslavia*. Toronto: Random House, Canada, 2000.

Oyebade, Adebayo. *Culture and Customs of Angola*. Westport, CT: Greenwood, 2006.

Power, Samantha. *"A Problem from Hell": America and the Age of Genocide*. New York: Harper Perennial, 2007.

Prunier, Gérard. *Africa's World War*. Oxford, UK: Oxford University Press, 2009.

Prunier, Gérard. *Africa's World War: Congo, the Rwandan Genocide, and the Making of a Continental Catastrophe*. New York: Oxford University Press, 2009.

Prunier, Gérard. *The Rwanda Crisis, 1959–1994: History of a Genocide*. Kampala: Fountain Publishers, 1995.

"Rebel Leader in the Congo Is Flown to The Hague." *The New York Times*, March 22, 2013.

Reyntjens, Filip. *The Great African War: Congo and Regional Geopolitics, 1996–2006*. Cambridge: Cambridge University Press, 2009.

Rittner, Carol. *Genocide in Rwanda: Complicity of the Churches*. St. Paul, MN: Paragon House, 2004.

Ronayne, Peter. *Never Again? The United States and the Prevention and Punishment of Genocide since the Holocaust*. Lanham, MD: Rowman & Littlefield Publishers, 2001.

Rusesabagina, Paul. *An Ordinary Man: An Autobiography*. New York: Viking, 2006.

Sanders, Edith. "The Hamitic Hypothesis: Its Origins and Functions." *Journal of African History* Vol. 10, no. 4, (1960): 521–532.

Schabas, William A. *Genocide in International Law: The Crime of Crimes*. Cambridge, UK: Cambridge University Press, 2000.

Scherrer, P. Christian. *Genocide and Crisis in Central Africa: Conflict Roots, Mass Violence, and Regional War*. Westport, CT: Praeger, 2002.

Shattuck, John. *Freedom on Fire: Human Rights Wars and America's Response*. Cambridge, MA: Harvard University Press, 2003.

Shaw, Martin. *War and Genocide: Organized Killing in Modern Society*. Cambridge, UK: Polity, 2003.

Shaw, Martin. *What Is Genocide?*. Cambridge: Polity Press, 2007.

Smith, M. James, ed. *A Time to Remember. Rwanda: Ten Years after Genocide.* Retford, UK: The Aegis Institute, 2004.

Stearns, Jason. *Dancing in the Glory of Monsters: The Collapse of the Congo and the Great War of Africa.* New York: Public Affairs, 2011.

Straus, Scott. *The Order of Genocide: Race, Power, and War in Rwanda.* Ithaca, NY: Cornell University Press, 2008.

Strozier, Charles B. and Michael Flynn, eds. *Genocide, War, and Human Survival.* Lanham, MD: Rowman & Littlefield Publishers, 1996.

Totten, Samuel, William S. Parsons, and Israel W. Charny, eds. *Century of Genocide: Eyewitness Accounts and Critical Views.* New York: Garland Publishing, 1997.

Turner, Thomas. *The Congo Wars: Conflict, Myth and Reality.* London and New York: Zed Books, 2007.

United Nations. *Atrocities and International Accountability: Beyond Transitional Justice.* New York: United Nations, 2008.

United Nations Security Council, 53rd Session. "Agenda Item 50: Report of the International Criminal Tribunal for Rwanda," Annexes, Official Record. New York, 1998.

Valentino, Benjamin A. *Final Solutions: Mass Killing and Genocide in the Twentieth Century.* Ithaca, NY: Cornell University Press, 2004.

Waller, James. *Becoming Evil: How Ordinary People Commit Genocide and Mass Killing.* Oxford: Oxford University Press, 2002.

Webster, John B. *The Political Development of Rwanda and Burundi.* Syracuse, NY: Maxwell Graduate School of Citizenship and Public Affairs, Syracuse University, 1966.

Weinstein, Warren, and Robert Schrire. *Political Conflict and Ethnic Strategies: A Case Study of Burundi.* Syracuse, New York: Syracuse University Press, 1976.

"Why Did Infamous War Criminal Bosco Ntaganda Just Surrender at a U.S. Embassy?" *Washington Post,* March 18, 2013.

Wilkens, Carl. *I'm Not Leaving.* Spokane (WA): United States: C. Wilkens, 2011.

Contributors

Dr. Paul R. Bartrop
Professor of History
Director of the Center for Judaic,
    Holocaust, and Genocide
    Studies
Florida Gulf Coast University

Amy Hackney Blackwell
Independent Scholar

Rob Coyle
Independent Scholar

John Dietrich
Associate Professor of Political Science
Bryant University

Lynn Jurgensen
Independent Scholar

Isabelle Lagarde
Independent Scholar

Dr. René Lemarchand
Emeritus Professor of Political Science
University of Florida

Alanna Pardee
Independent Scholar

Dr. Paul G. Pierpaoli Jr.
Fellow
Military History, ABC-CLIO, Inc.

Dr. John A. Shoup
Professor of Anthropology
Al Akhawayn University, Morroco

Dr. Brian G. Smith
Associate Professor of Political Science
Georgia Southwestern State University

Elinor O. Stevenson
Attorney
Public International Law and Policy Group

APPENDICES

Appendix I: Atrocities, War Crimes, and Crimes against Humanity

Since the 19th century, there have been many major incidences of mass murder that do not fit neatly into the 1948 Convention on the Prevention and Punishment of the Crime of Genocide (UNCG) definition of what constitutes the crime of genocide. However, while some of these episodes continue to be debated among scholars as to whether they do constitute genocide, they do fit the broader categories of atrocities, war crimes, and crimes against humanity. This section includes concepts, individuals, places, events, and organizations that showcase incidents of mass murder in modern history. These incidents, while not considered genocide according to the UNCG, are still important to consider in terms of their historical impact as major atrocities, war crimes, and crimes against humanity.

Topical List of Entries

EVENTS

Argentine Dirty War
Baga Massacre
Bangladesh Massacres (1971)
Bataan Death March
Cannibalism in the Holodomor
Congo Mass Rapes
Cultural Revolution
Dresden Bombing
First Five Year Plan
Great Leap Forward
Great Purges
Hama Massacre
Hamburg Raids
Harukei Isayama Trial
Hiroshima, Bombing of
Houla Massacre
Hue Massacre
Indian Removal Act
Indonesian Killings (1965)
Irish Potato Famine
Japanese Bacteriological Weapons Trial
Katyn Forest Massacre
Kesselring Trial
Kharkov Trial
Kochang Incident
Korean War Atrocities
Krasnodar Trial
Lidice Massacre

Louvain, Destruction of
Maillé Massacre
Malmédy Massacre
Manila Massacre
My Lai Massacre
Nagasaki, Bombing of
Nogun-ri Railroad Bridge Incident
Oradour-sur-Glane Massacre
Rape of Nanjing
Sook Ching Massacre
Spanish-American War, War Crimes
Syrian Civil War
Tiananmen Square Incident
Tiger Force Killings
Tokyo Bombing
Ukrainian Starvation (Holodomor)
Vietnam War Atrocities
Volhynian Poles Massacres
World War I Atrocities
World War II Atrocities, European Theater
World War II Atrocities, Pacific Theater
Wounded Knee Massacre
Yamashita Trial

GROUPS

Australian Aborigines
Comfort Women
Death Squads

Somalia
South Africa
Soviet Union
Spain
Sri Lanka

Syria
Turkey
Uganda
United States
Yemen

A

Afghanistan

Afghanistan has been the site of ongoing and brutal conflict since 1978. During this time there have been numerous accusations of war crimes against all participants, including allegations of massacres, summary executions, torture, rape, indiscriminate bombing, targeting of civilians, and other atrocities. To date, however, there have been no large-scale prosecutions of the perpetrators of these crimes, although human rights groups continue to collect evidence and identify suspects.

Accusations of war crimes began after the April 1978 coup in which the People's Democratic Party of Afghanistan (PDPA), a Marxist group, overthrew the existing Afghan government and tried to transform Afghanistan forcibly into a socialist state through purges, mass arrests, secret detentions, and executions of its opponents. Resistance to this regime spurred the Soviet Union to invade Afghanistan in 1979; during and after the invasion, the Soviets were accused of engaging in widespread war crimes, especially indiscriminate bombing and reprisals against civilians that caused some 5 million Afghans to flee the country. The Soviets also helped create a repressive secret police force that routinely tortured prisoners to obtain information. The mujahideen (resistance) fighters also committed criminal acts, including the torture and summary execution of their captives.

In 1984, the United Nations Commission on Human Rights appointed a special rapporteur to monitor and report on human rights violations in Afghanistan. In a series of reports, the special rapporteur described reports of mass arrests, disappearances, summary executions, and indiscriminate bombing of civilian targets.

When the Soviets withdrew from Afghanistan in 1992, the conflict continued as the government of Mohammed Najibullah tried to maintain power through the use of militias. These government-backed militias were accused of engaging in widespread looting and indiscriminate attacks on civilians. Their mujahideen opponents continued to engage in systematic torture and the summary execution of detainees; one of the more notorious of these groups, Hizb-i Islami, was headed by Gulbuddin Hekmatyar, who would later serve briefly as Afghan prime minister. Hizb-i Islami reportedly maintained a prison near Peshawar in which Afghan refugees reported being tortured with the complicity of Pakistani intelligence services.

In April 1992, the Najibullah government collapsed and the country descended into civil war, largely along ethnic lines. Both sides employed rape as a weapon and committed other serious human rights abuses. For three years, fighting raged through Kabul, the capital of Afghanistan, with all sides engaging in indiscriminate bombing and rocket attacks on civilians. The city was virtually leveled and thousands of civilians were killed.

With the backing of Pakistan, the Taliban, a militant fundamentalist Islamic group, eventually emerged as the dominant force, taking control of Kabul in 1996. The

Taliban drew their support primarily from the Pashtun ethnic group. As the Taliban moved into non-Pashtun areas, they burned villages and massacred civilians, sometimes in revenge for massacres that they had suffered earlier, including a 1997 massacre at Mazar-i Sharif that is thought to be the largest prisoner massacre of the entire conflict. The Taliban also engaged in the destruction of sacred objects of other faiths. In one especially notorious incident in early 2001, the Taliban dynamited the famed Buddhas of Bamyan, huge statues that had been carved into nearby cliffs some 1500 years earlier, and had been designated a "world heritage site" by the United Nations Educational, Scientific, and Cultural Organization (UNESCO). The Taliban also severely restricted the education and employment of women and girls; beat and executed those civilians who resisted its authority; and frequently carried out collective punishment, including the destruction of crops, food supplies, and houses.

In response to the terrorist attacks of September 11, 2001, the United States and some of its NATO partners committed combat forces to Afghanistan to overthrow the Taliban and capture Al Qaeda fighters. Major combat ended in late 2001, but remnants of the Taliban fled into the rugged countryside and to Pakistani border areas, where they eventually regrouped. During the intense fighting preceding the fall of the Taliban, there were numerous allegations that U.S. allies had committed war crimes, particularly against captured Taliban forces. In one of the most notorious incidents, hundreds of Taliban fighters held in a prison in Mazar-i-Sharif were reportedly slaughtered by U.S.-backed members of the Northern Alliance. In another incident, Afghan forces commanded by U.S. ally Rashid Dostum held surrendered Taliban prisoners in sealed cargo containers in the vicinity of Konduz, where hundreds allegedly died of asphyxiation and dehydration. Later, the U.S. was accused of committing war crimes itself, as revelations concerning the torture of prisoners held in Afghanistan came to light.

Following the fall of the Taliban and the installation of a new Afghan government, human rights groups continue to complain that the United States and its allies have turned a blind eye to the presence of known war criminals in positions of power. In 2007, the upper and lower houses of the Afghanistan parliament approved a war crimes amnesty that would have exempted certain Afghan warlords from war crimes prosecutions arising from incidents during the Soviet resistance era and the civil war. These warlords had now become powerful members of the new government of Afghanistan, and it was thought to be impossible as a practical matter to prosecute them. Afghan President Hamid Karzai refused to sign the bill, however, and it has not yet become law. The Supreme Soviet of the former Soviet Union had previously granted amnesty to Soviet soldiers accused of committing war crimes in Afghanistan during the Soviet invasion era.

Afghans continue to debate whether past war criminals should be brought to justice as part of a transitional justice agenda, or whether the focus should be on fact-finding, compensation of victims, and the rehabilitation and integration into society of those accused of past war crimes.

ALEXANDER MIKABERIDZE

See also: Soviet Union; United States

Further Reading

Dupree, Louis. *Afghanistan.* Princeton, NJ: Princeton University Press, 1980.

Maley, William. *The Afghanistan Wars.* New York: Palgrave Macmillan, 2002.

Amin, Idi

Military president of Uganda from 1971 to 1979, Idi Amin commanded a brutal and lawless regime, the violent effects of which destabilized the East African republic for years.

Born in 1924 or 1925 in Koboko, British Uganda, an area remarkable for its fiercely combative culture and high homicide rate, Idi Amin Dada had a rugged upbringing among the Kakwa tribe with no formal education. This background made him an ideal recruit for the King's African Rifles, the British colonial army. He joined in 1946, and his physical prowess made him popular with the troops and his superiors (he was the heavyweight boxing champion of Uganda for nine years). More importantly, Amin saw action in Burma fighting for the Allies during World War II and helped the British put down the Mau Mau insurgency in Kenya between 1952 and 1956. By 1960, he had been promoted to effendi, a newly created rank that signified the highest position an African soldier could attain in British East Africa.

Two years after Uganda achieved independence in 1962, Amin became a colonel and deputy commander of the army and air force; as such, he developed close ties to Dr. Milton Obote, then prime minister of the new nation. In 1966, Obote and Amin overthrew the president and King Edward Mutesa II, the figurehead of the royalist Baganda tribe. From that year until 1970, Amin was head of the armed forces. He later exploited the resentment between the Baganda and the Langi tribes to prepare the way for the coup he staged in 1971. Not content simply to oust Obote, Amin was responsible for the slaughter of soldiers from Langi (Obote's homeland). These events demonstrated Amin's talent for exacerbating tribal conflict.

Amin's eight-year reign was marked by ethnic bloodshed, administrative breakdown, economic collapse, and the large-scale migration of Ugandan professionals. Amin was a difficult master to serve because his moods altered quickly from playful to savage. Fierce nationalism characterized his thought, and in 1972 he deported most of the Asian community of middle-class professionals who had managed the country's bureaucracy, causing irreparable damage to the economy. During his reign, roughly a quarter of a million people were killed, including intellectuals, Christians, and those loyal to the former government. A Muslim, Amin courted the revolutionary Arabs of Libya and Palestine, involving himself personally with the Palestinian hijacking of a French airliner to Entebbe in 1976. By 1977, when Amin severed ties with Great Britain and Israel in favor of Arab support, his army was composed mostly of foreign recruits with no ethnic or religious relation to the indigenous population. In 1979, with revolts against his rule on the rise, Amin escaped to Saudi Arabia, as Tanzanian troops and Ugandan exile forces invaded from neighboring Tanzania and secured control of the country with little resistance.

In 1989, Amin was caught trying to reenter Africa using a fake passport, perhaps with the idea of attempting a military-backed return to power. In March 1998, Saudi authorities were reported to have confined the former dictator to Mecca after Amin tried to ship weapons to rebels in northern Uganda. In July 2003, after Amin slipped into a coma, his family asked the Ugandan government to allow him to die in his homeland and be buried there. The issue caused much controversy, and Ugandan President Yoweri Museveni at first stated that Amin would be arrested for crimes against human rights if he returned. However, Museveni relented after even the party that Amin had overthrown called on the government to grant the request of Amin's family.

Amin never returned to Uganda, however, as his health continued to decline, primarily because of kidney failure. On August 16, 2003, Amin died in a Saudi Arabian hospital. Following his death, a number of the Ugandan Asians whom he had persecuted and expelled, as well as at least one human rights group, said they were saddened that

Amin had escaped justice for the massive human rights violations he committed during his rule.

PAUL R. BARTROP

See also: Obote, Milton; Uganda

Further Reading

Avirgan, Toni, and Martha Honey. *War in Uganda: The Legacy of Idi Amin.* Westport, CT: L. Hill, 1982.

Bwengye, Francis Aloysius Wazarwahi. *The Agony of Uganda, from Idi Amin to Obote: Repressive Rule and Bloodshed: Causes, Effects, and the Cure.* New York: Regency Press, 1985.

Argentine Dirty War

Campaign launched by the Argentine military against its political opponents during 1974–1983. The roots of the Dirty War (Guerra Sucia) stretch back to the early 1930s, when the military became active in Argentine politics. Ultraconservative elements within the Argentine Army argued that the political process was beyond redemption and that elections and political pluralism threatened to move Argentina in the wrong direction. General José Félix Uriburu's dictatorship (1930–1932), which openly embraced such antidemocratic viewpoints, appears to have foreshadowed the Dirty War.

The Perónist movement, led by President Juan Perón, emerged out of a military dictatorship beginning in 1946 and helped polarize Argentine politics and society. After a military coup forced Perón from power in 1955, his supporters fought successfully to limit the ability of any party, group, or force to rule effectively in Argentina. Anti-Perónist factions within the military became increasingly frustrated with decades of struggle against the Perónist forces, which dominated labor unions.

As the military became more involved in Argentine politics, the political scene became increasingly violent and unstable. Student groups, Catholic reform groups connected to working-class and rural communities, and factions within the Perónist movement became radicalized. Influenced by successful guerrilla strategies in other settings—most notably the 1959 Cuban Revolution as assessed by Ernesto "Che" Guevara—opponents of the Argentine military armed themselves and trained for battle in the 1960s.

With the political process wholly discredited, groups on the Right and Left clashed violently beginning in 1969. On the Left a number of groups, led by the Montoneros and the Ejercito Revolucionario del Pueblo

(ERP, Revolutionary Army of the People), kidnapped business leaders and government officials, robbed banks and businesses, attacked government sites, and challenged the authority of the military and its civilian allies. On the Right, groups such as the Argentine Anti-Communist Alliance, with ties to the military, police force, and conservative factions within the Perónist movement, also emerged.

The political chaos and violence had reached a crucial point by 1972. Pressure from all sides forced government authorities to allow Perón's return from exile, as activists across the political spectrum had fought to bring the ex-president back to power. The polarization of the political process had frustrated anti-Perónist elements in the military. Having failed at their attempts to rule without the Perónists, they accepted his return and inevitable election in 1973.

Perón's return brought no solution. Political and economic mayhem continued as rival factions fought for positions within the Perónist movement after 1973. Perón's 1974 death only added to the volatile environment. Behind the scenes, the military once again moved to take control of the country.

The Dirty War began in earnest with military-sponsored campaigns against guerrilla operations in northwestern Argentina in 1974. Combining political and security operations, military commanders seized authority across provinces and systematically detained, interrogated, and killed thousands of "subversives" whom its officers had identified as "enemies of order."

By 1975, using clandestine operations against real and suspected terrorist cells, the military had neutralized guerrilla forces throughout the country. At this juncture a second phase of the Dirty War began. Commanders of the armed forces deposed María Estela Martínez de Perón's government in 1976. The army, navy, air force, and police throughout the country then deployed antisubversive units that targeted enemies of the state for detention. The ensuing kidnappings, tortures, and murders launched a wave of state-sponsored terrorism that aimed at "disciplining" the population.

It is estimated that as many as 40,000 Argentineans may have been murdered in the Dirty War during 1974–1983. Working with military officials in Brazil, Chile, Uruguay, and Paraguay, the Argentine military dictatorship shared intelligence and coordinated actions against targeted enemies who had fled across borders to avoid capture. The military junta speciously justified its abhorrent actions as a broad and just campaign against international communism and in support of Christian civilization.

Understandably, the Dirty War generated significant domestic and international opposition. Although many of the dictatorship's officers had received training at the U.S.-backed School of the Americas, U.S. president Jimmy Carter cited human rights violations as justification for limiting aid to Argentina. The Mothers of the Plaza de Mayo, an organization of mothers of victims of the regime's policies that held silent marches near the presidential palace, led a growing domestic opposition that pressured the dictatorship.

Ultimately, economic mismanagement and military blunders forced the dictatorship from power and ended its campaign of political violence in 1982. Already by 1980, its misguided fiscal policies created inflation and capital flight that had destroyed Argentina's economy. In the hopes of distracting popular attention, the armed forces launched an expedition that captured the Falkland and South Georgian Islands in 1982. Believing that the United Kingdom lacked both the will and the interest to contest this move, Argentine military commanders hoped to build national support for their evolving political ambitions.

Before the dictators could capitalize on their "liberation" of these islands, however, the British government mounted a methodical campaign to take back the Falklands. The decision by U.S. president Ronald Reagan to assist the British with logistical support for their transatlantic campaign surprised the Argentine dictatorship and demoralized the operation's commanders. The success of the British invasion both discredited the regime and forced the military to accept a return to civilian rule.

Efforts to bring those involved in the Dirty War to justice continue. In turn, the term "Dirty War" has developed a broader connotation as revelations of government actions against political opponents in other Latin American countries during the 1960s–1980s have come to light.

DANIEL LEWIS

See also: Mothers of the Plaza de Mayo; Videla, Jorge Rafael

Further Reading
Lewis, Paul. *Guerrillas and Generals.* Westport, CT: Praeger, 2002.
Rock, David. *Authoritarian Argentina.* Berkeley: University of California Press, 1993.

Assad, Bashar al-

Son of long-time Syrian President Hafez al-Assad, Bashar al-Assad was nominated at age 34 to become the country's president following the death of his father in June 2000. He was inaugurated on July 17. A member of the Alawite sect, as was his father, Assad took over minority leadership of a country that is dominated by Sunni Muslims.

Born on September 11, 1965, in Damascus, Bashar al-Assad is the third of five children of Hafez al-Assad, a career air force officer who served as defense minister before seizing power as Syria's president in 1970. Raised in Damascus, he attended the elite Al Hurriyeh high school, where he was educated in both French and Arabic. Upon graduation in 1982, he enrolled at Damascus University, where he completed his studies in general medicine six years later. Specializing in ophthalmology, Assad received advanced training at a military hospital in Damascus and later in Britain.

Known as "Doctor Bashar" among many Syrians, Assad was considered the shy young counterpart to his gregarious and outgoing older brother Basil, who was long groomed as his father's heir apparent. With the death of Basil in a 1994 car crash, however, Bashar was summoned home from Britain to acquire the necessary credentials to become the country's next ruler-in-waiting.

Over the next few years, Assad was slowly introduced to the world of international politics and diplomacy, dispatched to represent his country to the governments of Jordan, Oman, Saudi Arabia, and France, where he caused a stir by traveling through Paris without bodyguards. He also acted as Syria's liaison to Lebanon, a country over which Syria exercises broad political and military control.

Despite his limited military background, Assad was immediately promoted from colonel to lieutenant general and commander in chief of the armed forces upon the death of his father. The People's Assembly voted within hours of Hafez al-Assad's death to amend the Syrian Constitution, lowering the age requirement for the presidency from 40 to 34. Within days, Assad was named secretary-general of the ruling Baath Party and, while he has never held a government post, he was also nominated as the sole candidate to assume the presidency.

Although his father's government had moved swiftly to assure his smooth ascension to power, Assad faced his first challenge in a claim issued by his exiled uncle, Rifaat al-Assad, who asserted just days after the president's death that he himself was the rightful heir to the presidency. The younger brother of Hafez al-Assad, Rifaat al-Assad, once a member of his brother's government, had been stripped of his military and political credentials and had lived primarily in exile after attempting to unseat his brother while the president was hospitalized following a heart attack. Although the recent challenge to Bashar al-Assad was quickly dismissed by the government and the Syrian public, analysts speculated that if young Assad's leadership proves to be weak or unpopular in the future, Syrians might look to the more experienced Rifaat al-Assad to take the reins.

While Assad himself has admitted that his presidential apprenticeship was not yet complete at the time of his father's death, he has offered Syrians the prospect of economic and political reform and technological progress, while retaining the confidence of hard-liners in his father's government. Upon solidifying his hold on power in Syria, Assad joined a new generation of Arab leaders, including King Abdullah II of Jordan, King Mohammed VI of Morocco, and Sheik Hamad ibn Isa al-Khalifa of Bahrain, who all came of age after the Arab-Israeli wars and who have assumed power from their fathers despite their lack of political or military credentials.

Though many felt that Assad was likely to liberalize Syria to some extent, his rule has in many ways mirrored that of his father. The country has remained under the state of emergency declared in 1963, despite increasing calls to lift the declaration. Assad's government has suppressed prodemocracy movements as well as Islamist organizations that pose some degree of political risk to the regime. The sort of generalized paranoia common to many authoritarian governments has continued in Syria under Assad, despite periodic easing of certain restrictions. Internet access in widely used Internet cafes is subject to government monitoring, and Web site deemed subversive are routinely blocked, especially during times of increased political unrest. Dissidents and political opponents have allegedly been arrested, tortured, prevented from leaving the country, and even killed. Limited economic liberalization has taken place, but the state still closely controls most industries.

In foreign policy, Assad has allied himself closely with Iran and has continued Syrian political involvement in Lebanon. During the Iraq War, Syria was frequently at odds with the United States and was perennially accused of providing support or passage to Iraqi insurgents fighting against the American occupation forces. In 2005, the assassination of Lebanese prime minister Rafik Hariri and the subsequent demonstrations that became known as the Cedar Revolution put intense pressure on Syria to pull its military forces out of Lebanon (where they had been since the 1976 outbreak of the Lebanese Civil War). In April of that year, Assad called all Syrian forces back to Syria, ending the long occupation of Lebanon. Assad has remained generally antagonistic toward Israel, though he is said to have discussed the possibility of a peace treaty with Israeli prime minister

Ehud Olmert in 2008 via Turkish diplomats. (Turkey, unlike Syria, maintains diplomatic relations with Israel.)

In early 2011, the political unrest that had been brewing for some time in Syria began to boil over as popular uprisings in other Arab countries—most notably Tunisia and Egypt—successfully challenged long-standing dictatorial regimes. Relatively small protests began in January and seemed to diminish in February. But in mid-March, large protests erupted in cities around the country, triggering a mass movement against the Assad regime. Some believed that the Syrian government would fall, as the Egyptian and Tunisian ones did. However, unlike in Egypt and Tunisia, the loyalty of the military to the regime has been carefully cultivated and maintained by the Assads over the past four decades. The army did not side with the protesters, and when Assad charged the military with breaking the demonstrations, it complied. In late March the government began to crack down with great violence against the protesters, even as Assad offered concessions, including a proposal to lift the state of emergency. The protests and violence intensified during April and May, and the military besieged and occupied cities where protests were particularly large, arresting hundreds of dissidents and killing or injuring many others.

By the fall, armed opposition groups began to fight back, inching Syria closer to civil war and increasing the threat to Assad and his regime. Syrian opposition fighters vowed to topple Assad in the same way that Libyan rebels had ended the Muammar Qaddafi dictatorship, as Assad's violent crackdown sparked criticism from the world community.

PAUL R. BARTROP

See also: Syria; Syrian Civil War

Further Reading

Amin, Rula, "Bashar Assad Moves Closer to Ruling Syria," *CNN. com*, June 20, 2000 (http://www.cnn.com).

Sachs, Susan, "Exiled Relative Issues Challenge to Syria's Heir to Power." *The New York Times*, June 13, 2000.

Sachs, Susan, "Leaders of Syria Building Support for Son of Assad." *The New York Times*, June 12, 2000.

Sachs, Susan, "Syrians See in the Heir Possibility of Progress." *The New York Times*, June 11, 2000.

Australia

When Dutch explorers first discovered Australia in 1606, there were an estimated 500,000–1,000,000 Aboriginals (indigenous peoples) living on the huge, continent-sized island. The British claimed the eastern portion of Australia in 1770; the first permanent British settlement was founded at New South Wales in 1788. The English population grew steadily thereafter, and in 1828 the British took formal control of the western half of Australia. Early British colonists were drawn to Australia chiefly because of its ranching and agricultural potential. In 1803, the British claimed the neighboring island of Tasmania, which also had a sizable Aboriginal population. British colonization proved calamitous for Australia's Aboriginals; by 1933, the Aboriginal population stood at just 74,000; meanwhile, the Aboriginals on Tasmania were virtually wiped out. The influx of Europeans to Australia and Tasmania set the stage for continual conflict with the Aboriginals over land ownership, not unlike the conflicts between American colonists and Native Americans that began in the 1600s.

Although land encroachment, cultural insensitivity, and ill-conceived "assimilation" policies on the part of the government resulted in the deaths of thousands of Aboriginals, most Aboriginal peoples died from communicable diseases brought by the Europeans to which they had no natural immunity. The biggest killers were measles, influenza, and smallpox.

There were countless examples of atrocities and massacres perpetrated upon the Aboriginals between the 1780s and 1920s. Many were small-scale affairs that went unrecorded (and until the early 20th century, Australian courts did not often recognize violence against Aboriginals as a punishable crime). And many white colonists saw nothing wrong with killing or harassing Aboriginals if they perceived them as a threat to their person or land. Indeed, some Europeans did not even consider them as fully human. Like Native Americans, the Aboriginals were compelled to give up their ancestral lands to European colonists, with virtually no compensation. They were herded onto reservations, where the land and climate was often less than ideal for agriculture. This resulted in widespread hunger and even famine. Those who resisted were often killed.

The Aboriginal Protection Act of 1869, which was intended to "assimilate" the Aboriginals and force them into adopting European ways, proved to be nothing less than tragic for Aboriginals. A central part of this program involved the involuntary removal of Aboriginal children from their families. The children were then placed in white households and were raised as Europeans. This policy only accelerated the population loss among Aboriginals.

In May 1804, white settlers murdered 60 Aboriginals at Risdon Cove (Tasmania) because they had simply approached the colony. The so-called Black War in Tasmania (1828–1832) resulted in the practical eradication of Tasmanian aboriginals. By 1835, only about 150 such individuals were left, and by the 1850s, they had disappeared completely. In recent years, this sad affair has been labeled a genocide.

In the 1824 Bathurst Massacre in New South Wales, 16 Aboriginals were killed after seven Europeans had been killed by Aboriginals following a land dispute. The 1833–1834 Convincing Ground Massacre near Portland, Victoria, witnessed the killing of as many as 200 Aboriginals; that incident was the result of a dispute over fishing rights. In the 1838 Myall Creek Massacre, 28 Aboriginal men, women, and children were murdered for no justifiable reason. Notably, however, several perpetrators were tried and executed for the crime, the first time that a white person had ever been tried for a crime against Aboriginal peoples.

During October and November 1861, white settlers and local constables killed at least 170 Aboriginals in the central highlands of Queensland; land disputes were involved here too. In the 1884 Battle Mountain Massacre near Mount Isa, Queensland, 200 Aboriginals were killed after a local shepherd was found dead. The last significant atrocity against the Aboriginals occurred in 1928 in Coniston (Northern Territory) after two whites were attacked by Aboriginals. In retaliation, a local white resident raided an Aboriginal outpost, shooting and killing 28 people, many of them women and children. The official report of the incident ruled that the murders "were justified."

Clearly, the fate of Australia's Aboriginals was a sad one; most of the deaths that occurred over a period of some 150 years were not intentional, but were rather the result of European-spread diseases. However, purposeful actions by individuals, small groups, and the government did result in many deaths. Not until the second half of the 20th century did the Australian government come to terms with the injustices visited upon the Aboriginals. More enlightened government policies have attempted—at least in a small way—to right some of past wrongs and to restore to the Aboriginals some of their own cultural heritage. A recent census indicated that there were some 500,000 people of Aboriginal descent living in Australia, a sharp increase from the 74,000 in the 1930s.

Paul G. Pierpaoli Jr.

See also: Australian Aborigines; Black War; Stolen Generations

Further Reading

Australian Government. *Bringing Them Home: Report of the National Inquiry into the Separation of Aboriginal and Torres Strait Islander Children from Their Families.* Sydney: Human Rights and Equal Opportunity Commission, 1997.

Manne, Robert. "The Stolen Generation." *Quadrant* (January–February 1998): 53–63.

Turnbull, Clive. *Black War: The Extermination of the Tasmanian Aborigines.* Melbourne: Cheshire-Lansdowne Press, 1965.

Australian Aborigines

The Aboriginal peoples of Australia and the nearby island of Tasmania suffered catastrophic losses once Europeans began to colonize those regions in the early 1800s. In the case of Tasmania, the Aborigines were virtually exterminated, partly because of diseases carried by the Europeans to which they had no resistance, but also because of purposeful policies of forced resettlement and extermination. In Australia, the decimation of Aborigines was caused not only by communicable diseases, but also by land encroachment, forced resettlement, forced labor, murder, rape, torture, and cultural insensitivity and forced assimilation policies on the part of the government. The Aboriginal population of Australia was estimated to be between 500,000 and 1,000,000 prior to European settlement in the late 1770s. By 1933, that number had plummeted to just 74,000. In Tasmania, the death rate was even more dramatic. The Pallawah (Tasmanian Aborigines), who numbered about 4,000 in 1803, suffered at least a 50 percent reduction in their population between 1803 and 1820 alone. The so-called Black War against the Pallawah, waged between 1828 and 1832, left a Pallawah population of only 250; the rest had been killed or were resettled elsewhere.

Australia's Aborigines have a rich and varied history. In 1788, when the British established the first permanent European settlement at New South Wales, it is estimated that there some 400 distinct Aboriginal groups throughout the continent-sized island of Australia. Each group had its own customs, culture, and language or dialect, and their socio-economic circumstances varied based largely upon where they were located. The Aborigines were mainly hunter-gatherers, and their sedentary agricultural ways were largely determined by the area and climate in which they lived. The three main cultural zones of the Aborigines were in the north, south, and central part of Australia. Aborigines in the north and south, owing to the climate and soil/topography were more numerous than those in the central region, where the climate and topography made daily life more challenging. Those in the central region also did not have access to maritime endeavors. Beyond these larger cultural divisions were smaller tribal groupings.

By 1828, the British had secured most of Australia, and British settlers were soon drawn to it because of its rich agricultural and ranching potential. Meanwhile, in 1803, the British established a small penal colony near modern-day Hobart, Tasmania (then known as Van Diemen's Land). Soon thereafter, throngs of British settlers began to arrive in Tasmania, hoping to become successful farmers and sheepherders.

The first major challenge for the Aborigines in Australia and Tasmania was the onslaught of diseases carried there by European settlers. Thousands of them died within just a few years' time from illnesses like measles, influenza, smallpox, and chickenpox because they lacked natural resistance to them. In Australia, the decimation of the Aboriginal population was somewhat inadvertent and more gradual. Many of the atrocities committed against them were small-scale affairs (largely unrecorded). And until the early 20th century, white violence against Aborigines was not a punishable offense. Many Aborigines were driven from their ancestral lands and concentrated in missions or reservations, where the land and climate were often unsuited for agriculture. The result was widespread hunger and even famine. Those who resisted these forced relocations were often murdered.

In 1869, the Australian government enacted the Aboriginal Protection Act in an effort to staunch the precipitous drop in the Aboriginal population and "assimilate" them to European ways. This legislation proved disastrous, however. A central part of the program involved the involuntary removal of Aboriginal children from their families (50,000 by some estimates). The children were placed in white homes and were raised as Europeans. This policy only accelerated the population loss among Aboriginals and virtually destroyed their culture and language. Some Aboriginals were forced into indentured servitude to whites, used as sex slaves on cattle ranches, or were forcibly sterilized. Europeans justified their actions by claiming that the Aborigines were subhuman, wild beasts whose culture, language, and customs had to be subjugated by European culture. When Aborigines resisted or fought back, they were met with blunt force that rarely resulted in an Aboriginal victory. In 1896, a Royal Commission charged with preventing the complete extinction of the Aborigines resulted in Australian legislation in 1897 that was the first official statute enacted in history designed to protect a specific group of humans.

Because most atrocities against Aborigines were on a small scale and largely unreported, it is difficult to say how many died because of deliberate violence perpetrated by whites. Some of the worst atrocities on record in Australia include the 1883–1884 Convincing Ground Massacre in which more than 200 Aborigines died. Some 200 Aborigines were killed in the 1884 Battle Mountain Massacre, and 20 were killed in 1928 in Coniston (Northern Territory). The vast proportion of Aboriginal deaths occurred because of disease, famine, and ill-conceived government policies that often created more problems than they ever solved.

In Tasmania, the decimation of the Pallawah Aborigines tended to be more deliberate and dramatic. Between 1803 and 1806, white settlers engaged in wholesale murder, abduction, force labor, and mass rape. This, along with communicable diseases, caused the Aboriginal population to plummet. By the late 1820s, as colonists encroached on Aboriginal lands with near impunity, some Pallawah fought back, commencing a guerilla-style war against whites. The white government on Tasmania demanded that all Pallawah submit to colonial policies; those who refused were to be summarily shot. As the 1828–1832 Black War ensued, the government began offering bounties for Aborigines taken alive, as if they were a sport animal. By 1832, only 250 Pallawah were left on Tasmania. The remainder had been killed or resettled on small, off-shore islands.

Clearly, the fate of Australia's Aborigines was a tragic one; most of the deaths that occurred over a period of some 150 years were not intentional, but were rather the result of European-spread diseases. However, purposeful actions by individuals, small groups, and the government did result in many deaths. Not until the second half of the 20th century did the Australian governments begin to come to terms with the injustices visited upon the Aborigines. More enlightened government policies have attempted—at least in a small way—to right some of past wrongs and to restore to the Aborigines some of their own cultural heritage. A recent census indicated that there were some 500,000 people of Aboriginal descent living in Australia, a sharp increased from the 74,000 in the 1930s. By the same token, however, the Australian government has declined to offer an official apology to the Aborigines, asserting that past policies had good intentions and that past behavior cannot be judged by modern-day standards.

PAUL G. PIERPAOLI JR.

See also: Australia; Black War; Stolen Generations

Further Reading

Hernon, Ian. *Britain's Forgotten Wars: Colonial Campaigns of the 19th Century.* Stroud, Gloucestershire, UK: The History Press, 2003.

Manne, Robert. "The Stolen Generation." *Quadrant* (January–February 1998): 53–63.

Turnbull, Clive. *Black War: The Extermination of the Tasmanian Aborigines.* Melbourne: Cheshire-Lansdowne Press, 1965.

B

Baga Massacre

The Baga Massacre occurred on April 16–17, 2013, in the village of Baga, Nigeria. The event unfolded when fighting broke out between the Nigerian military and members of the Boko Haram, a rebel group that the Nigerian government has been fighting since early 2009. The most recent reports of the massacre claim that at least 200 civilians were killed, many of them children and the elderly, with several hundred more wounded. Baga is a small fishing town on the shore of Lake Chad, not far from the Niger and Chad borders. At the time of the killings, Boko Haram fighters had controlled parts of Baga and some of the surrounding countryside.

On the night of April 16, several Boko Haram insurgents fired on a small detachment of Nigerian soldiers at a military outpost on the outskirts of Baga; one of the soldiers was killed and another one was wounded. Outraged by the attack, Nigerian military officials called in heavily armed reinforcements, with some soldiers arriving in armored vehicles. The military contingent swept quickly into Baga that same night, firing indiscriminately and setting many houses and businesses on fire. The rationale for the assault was to "flush out" the rebels; however, the result instead was mass civilian casualties and much destruction of property. When the dust and smoke cleared the next day, as many as 2,000 houses and businesses had been destroyed. Villagers who attempted to escape the

blazes were often shot and killed; others sought refuge in Lake Chad, but they too were gunned down. Others escaped into the adjacent bush; a number of survivors managed to make their way to safety, but they were completely homeless.

The Nigerian military has blamed the Boko Haram rebels for the atrocity in Baga, but that is in sharp contrast to what eyewitness villagers say happened on the night of April 16–17. Indeed, this incident was not an isolated event; since the government went to war with the Boko Haram insurgents, the military has pursued a scorched-earth policy, and civilians have been routinely killed. This was, however, the worst loss of civilian life since the campaign began some four years previously. The military has attempted to keep journalists out of Baga since the massacre, and has claimed that only six civilians died in the fighting. Meanwhile, military officials claim that 30 rebels were killed, which has not yet been substantiated.

The violence in Baga has provoked outrage within Nigeria as well as in the international community. The Nigerian National Assembly plans to conduct an investigation, and the military is conducting its own inquiry, although that will undoubtedly be subject to much scrutiny. Nigerian allies have threatened to reduce or withdraw support for Nigeria's campaign against the Boko Haram, including the United States. Much more remains to be done before a completely accurate account of the events in Baga comes to light, but it seems all but certain that the Nigerian military was complicit in the massacre.

PAUL G. PIERPAOLI JR.

See also: Nigeria; Uganda

Further Reading

Dixon, Robyn. "Dozens Killed in Gun Battles in Northern Nigeria." *Los Angeles Times,* April 22, 2013.

Nossiter, Adam. "Massacre in Nigeria Spurs Outcry over Military Tactics." *New York Times,* April 29, 2013.

Bangladesh

Located in southern Asia, Bangladesh gained its independence from Pakistan in 1971. Until then, it was part of Pakistan. It is largely a Muslim nation (about 88 percent of the population); Hindus make up most of the remaining population (10–11 percent). During the nine-month war for liberation (March 25–December 16, 1971) fought between the Pakistan Army and its local militia supporters on the one hand and Bengali separatists and their supporters on the other, a full-blown genocide unfolded, resulting in the deaths of hundreds of thousands of people, the majority of whom were Hindu. After independence, Bangladesh remained desperately poor, and famine, floods, and other natural disasters only added to this misery. Political instability resulted in sporadic violence and a number of coup d'états. When democracy finally took root beginning in 1991, Bangladesh's economy and political landscape brightened, but the main political groups remain polarized, and sporadic violence against the Hindu minority continues.

As Bengali independence fighters sought to secede from Pakistan, the Pakistani government began a major offensive on March 25, 1971. The operation was initially aimed at Hindus (the perennial enemy of Pakistan) as well as political dissidents and Bengali intelligentsia; later, the scope of the offensive would be widened to include many innocent civilians in urban as well as rural areas. The Pakistani army first instructed allied militia forces to attack Dhaka University, Bangladesh's largest and most prestigious university. On the evening of March 25, and continuing over the next several days, the militias began killing or capturing hundreds of unarmed students (most of them Hindu and other minorities), faculty, and staff members. More than 100 died, while 563 young Bengali women were seized and imprisoned in various places throughout Dhaka. They were repeatedly raped by militia men and Pakistani soldiers. On March 26, meanwhile, Bengali nationalists declared their independence from Pakistan.

What followed was a major outbreak of violence. It is estimated that during the short, nine-month conflict Pakistani and allied forces murdered 990 teachers, 49 physicians, 42 attorneys, 16 writers and artists, and 13 journalists. Some estimates suggest that as many as 200,000 women were raped. Hindus were targeted the most. On April 23 at Jathibhanga, anywhere from 3,000–5,000 Hindus were murdered in their village or while attempting to escape, but the worst atrocity of the entire war occurred on May 20, during the Chuknagar Massacre, in which some 8,000–10,000 Hindus were murdered en masse. The dead included men, women, children, and the elderly. Although it is impossible to pinpoint how many Hindus died during the entirety of the war, their fatality rate was certainly much higher than any other group.

After India entered the war in early December 1971, the conflict drew to a rapid conclusion. On December 16, Pakistani military forces surrendered, making Bangladesh's independence drive a fait accompli. Just three days later, however, another massacre occurred—this time in front of foreign journalists—when a group of prisoners of war were shot to death by Bengali-allied guerillas at a repatriation ceremony. The total number of those killed during the war varies by source. The Bangladeshi government has claimed as many as 3 million dead. Other sources, however, claim 300,000–500,000 dead. Another 8 to 10 million (mostly Hindus) were forced to flee to India as refugees. Much of the international community has since labeled the conflict as a genocide.

In 2010, the Bangladeshi government finally decided to bring the perpetrators of the 1971 genocide to justice by convening the Bangladesh War Crimes Tribunal, with help from the United Nations. By the end of 2012, nine Muslim suspects and two suspects from the Bangladesh National Party had been formally indicted. The first conviction came in January 2013, when Abul Kalam Azad was sentenced to death (in absentia). The court has come under international criticism, however, from some international groups, including Human Rights Watch, which claims that the trial of Delwar Hossain Sayedee was badly compromised.

Although Bangladesh has generally moved beyond the mass killings of the 1970s, it is far from immune to sectarian violence. In early May 2012, Islamic extremists damaged or destroyed at least 1,500 Hindu homes, shops, and temples throughout Bangladesh. On May 9, 27 people died in nationwide clashes between the Islamist group Hefajet-e-Islam and Bangladeshi security forces.

PAUL G. PIERPAOLI JR.

See also: Bangladesh Massacres (1971); Bangladesh War Crimes Tribunal; Pakistan

Further Reading

Choudhury, G.W. *The Last Days of United Pakistan.* Oxford, UK: Oxford University Press, 1994.

Sisson, Richard, and Leo Rose. *War and Secession: Pakistan, India, and the Creation of Bangladesh.* Berkeley: University of California Press, 1990.

Totten, Samuel, William S. Parsons, and Israel W. Charny, eds. *Century of Genocide: Eyewitness Accounts and Critical Views.* New York: Garland Publishing, 1997.

Zaheer, Hasan. *The Separation of East Pakistan: The Rise and Realization of Bengali Muslim Nationalism.* Oxford, UK: Oxford University Press, 1994.

Bangladesh Massacres (1971)

Bangladesh's emergence as a nation in 1971 came at the cost of 3 million people dead and a quarter of a million women and girls raped. Ten million other people fled to India, and 30 million people were forced to flee their homes. East Pakistan, from which Bangladesh was created, was made up of a province on the west side of India (former Punjab et al.) and on the east side of India (former East Bengal). The army was manned and commanded by people from West Pakistan. Elections for a Constitutional Assembly were held in Pakistan in December 1970. The East Pakistan-based Awami League won an outright majority of seats in this Assembly and planned to write a constitution that would give the majority population of East Pakistan political control of the country. To prevent this, on the evening of March 25, 1971, the military and political elite of West Pakistan turned the army of West Pakistan on the Bengali population of East Pakistan. They hoped to emasculate the Awami League, to rid East Pakistan of its Hindu population of 10 million, and to terrorize the civilian population into complete and permanent submission. This plan of intimidation, brutalization, and extermination continued until the West Pakistan military capitulated on December 16, 1971.

Particularly at risk were Awami League politicians and their supporters, most of whom had gone into hiding in the countryside or escaped to India. The armed security and police forces manned by Bengalis were an early target, but many of them also escaped with their weapons to return as guerrillas. Bengali students, professors, and intellectuals were summarily executed. The West Pakistan Army was particularly intent on killing every single Hindu it could find. Slum and squatter areas of the major cities and towns were also obliterated, along with their occupants.

All able-bodied young Bengali men were considered freedom fighters. Early on, they were routinely rounded up, tortured, and killed. Very quickly, however, they fled the cities and towns for the guerrilla camps in the countryside and in India. The Army of West Pakistan now turned its fury on the women and girls left behind. Girls and women were publicly raped in front of their family members. They were also routinely abducted to special camps near army barracks to be gang-raped, brutalized, and killed, or to live with the eternal shame of their violation. Many committed suicide.

As the Bengali guerrilla campaign became more effective against the West Pakistan Army, the army undertook daily retaliatory missions to destroy as many villages as possible. In December 1971, when the Army of West Pakistan was finally forced to retreat back to its cantonments, it systematically set about killing all the influential intellectuals and professionals in each city and town that they had besieged. The genocidal campaign of the West Pakistani military elite against the Bengali population of East Pakistan stopped only when the Indian Army disarmed the Army of Pakistan to prevent the guerrilla movement from spreading to separatist elements in the Indian State of West Bengal.

Genocide as government policy failed to prevent the birth of Bangladesh. The West Pakistani military elite never recognized that Sheikh Mujibur Rahman and the Awami League had crafted a compelling vision of an independent Bangladesh arising from the blood of millions of martyrs who supported the vast guerrilla movement. West Pakistan's military authorities recruited Muslim collaborators who had emigrated to East Pakistan from other parts of India after partition in 1947, and had attracted East Pakistani political parties opposed to the Awami League, but those efforts were not enough to prevent the independence of Bangladesh. Retribution against the poorer of these collaborators was swift and brutal immediately after the surrender of the West Pakistani Army. Armed violence became and remains an accepted part of ordinary Bangladeshi life. Better situated collaborators survived, however, and by 1975 they were participating in Bangladeshi public life. To this day, however, an elemental enmity between freedom fighters and collaborators continues to cause political and social turmoil.

JOHN P. THORP

See also: Bangladesh; Bangladesh War Crimes Tribunal; Pakistan

Further Reading

Bose, Sarmila. *Dead Reckoning: Memories of the 1971 Bangladesh War.* New York: Columbia University Press, 2011.

Jahan, Rounaq. "Genocide in Bangladesh." In *Century of Genocide: Eyewitness Accounts and Critical Views.* Edited by Samuel Totten, William S. Parsons, and Israel W. Charny, 291–316. New York: Garland Publishing, 1997.

Schendel, Willem van. *A History of Bangladesh.* Cambridge, UK: Cambridge University Press, 2009.

Bangladesh War Crimes Tribunal

The Bangladeshi government established the Bangladesh War Crimes Tribunal in March 2010 to bring to justice those individuals suspected of having committed war crimes and crimes against humanity during Bangladesh's war of liberation in 1971. From the outset, the tribunal has been beset with criticism. Many view it as being politically motivated, while other assert that it is little more than a venue for show trials that are inherently unfair to the defendants. From the start, the Bangladeshi government excluded from prosecution of Pakistanis, meaning that commanders of Pakistani forces would not be brought to justice for crimes committed under their watch. Instead, the focus of the tribunal has been the two chief political opposition parties, which has raised concerns in Bangladesh and elsewhere that the Bangleshi government is using the tribunal as a political weapon.

Within months of the tribunal's creation, a number of leading oppositional leaders were arrested and detained. They included Delwar Hossain Sayedee, Golam Azam, Motiur Rahman Nizami, Ali Ashan Mujahid, Nayeb-e-Ameer, Qader Mollah, Abdul Aleem, and Salahuddin Quader Chowdhury. The men were charged with various war crimes, but the evidence connecting some of them to such alleged wrongdoings was sparse and controversial. The first to face trial was Sayedee. His trial, which is ongoing, proved highly controversial, especially in November 2012, when a key defense witness was abducted just prior to his call to testify on Sayedee's behalf. The Bangladeshi government vehemently denied that the witness had been abducted, alleging instead that the defense had staged the event.

Less than a month later, in December 2012, Bangladeshi officials accused British publication *The Economist* of having hacked emails, phone calls, and voice mails of the tribunal's leaders after it ran an article outlining alleged misconduct and improprieties on the part of the court's judges. As a result of the negative publicity, Mohammed Nizamul Huq, the chairman of the court, resigned on December 11. Only days later, Human Rights Watch called for a new trial for Sayedee, arguing that his current trial had been badly compromised. The Bangladeshi government, meanwhile, ignored the international condemnation and vowed to press forward with more trials.

Even before this controversy, there were serious allegations against the tribunal. Amnesty International and the European Parliament asserted that the court does not meet the minimum standards of the international legal community. Human Rights Watch has argued that basic defendants' rights have not been upheld. Numerous international legal scholars and lawyers have also stated their objections to the tribunal, warning that serious miscarriages of justice might result from tainted procedures and trials. Nevertheless, the Bangladeshi government continues to move forward with the proceedings.

PAUL G. PIERPAOLI JR.

See also: Bangladesh; Bangladesh Massacres (1971); Pakistan

Further Reading

Bose, Sarmila. *Dead Reckoning: Memories of the 1971 Bangladesh War.* New York: Columbia University Press, 2011.

Lewis, David. *Bangladesh: Politics, Economy and Civil Society.* Cambridge, UK: Cambridge University Press, 2011.

Schendel, Willem van. *A History of Bangladesh.* Cambridge: Cambridge University Press, 2009.

Bataan Death March

The Bataan Death March was a forced march of 12,000 U.S. soldiers and 64,000 Filipino troops after the Japanese captured the Bataan Peninsula in the Philippines in April 1942. On April 3, 1942, Japanese Gen. Masaharu Homma launched a new offensive against the Bataan defenders. The U.S. Far Eastern commander, Gen. Douglas MacArthur, had ordered the troops to continue to fight, but six days later, with his men worn down by the strain of constant combat, disease, and starvation, Maj. Gen. Edward P. King, commander of the forces on Bataan, ordered them to surrender. The troops had been on half rations since January.

Homma had decided that he would hold the prisoners at Camp O'Donnell, 100 miles away. The Japanese forced the prisoners to march 52 miles from Mariveles to San Fernando, Pampanga, in order to be transported by rail to Capas, Tarlac. They would then walk another 8 miles to Camp O'Donnell. King expressed concern about his men being able to make this trip and asked that trucks transport them to their final location. Homma rejected the request.

The trek began on April 10, 1942, and lasted for over a week. The march is remembered for its sheer brutality, but before it even began, each prisoner was searched, and anyone found to possess a Japanese souvenir was executed on the spot.

Allied soldiers were, for the most part, denied food and water by their guards until the completion of their journey. The only food that some received was a bit of rancid rice. The prisoners of war were given only a few hours of rest each night in crowded conditions. One of the worst forms of punishment inflicted on the captives was known as the sun treatment, in which the prisoner, denied any water, was forced to sit in the scalding Philippine sun without the protection of a helmet. Prisoners were beaten, kicked, and killed for falling behind or violating the smallest rule.

Between 7,000 and 10,000 of the prisoners died before reaching Camp O'Donnell. The Japanese had failed to take into consideration both the poor health of their captives and their numbers. Although a few of the prisoners escaped into the jungle, most were physically unable even to make the attempt. A number were murdered at random by their guards.

Many who survived the march died in the overcrowded, suffocating boxcars on the rail trip to Capas. In the two months after reaching the camp, 1,600 Americans and 16,000 Filipinos died of starvation, disease, and maltreatment. The cruelty of the march became well known, and U.S. commanders used the story of the Bataan Death March to motivate their troops in subsequent fighting against the Japanese.

T. Jason Soderstrum

See also: Homma, Masahura; Japan; Manila Massacre; World War II Atrocities, Pacific Theater

Further Reading

Berry, William A. *Prisoner of the Rising Sun.* Norman: University of Oklahoma Press, 1993.

Falk, Stanley Lawrence. *Bataan: The March of Death.* New York: Norton, 1962.

Hubbard, Preston. *Apocalypse Undone: My Survival of Japanese Imprisonment during World War II.* Nashville, TN: Vanderbilt University Press, 1990.

Beria, Lavrenty

Lavrenty Pavlovich Beria was born on March 29, 1899, in Merkheuli, Russia. He eventually took a post with state security and steadily advanced up the ranks of the Communist Party, serving as first secretary of the Georgian Communist Party (1934–1938). From November 1938 until January 1946, he headed the People's Commissariat for Internal Affairs (NKVD), supervising the vast system of forced labor camps in the Soviet Union. The NKVD served as the Soviet Union's internal police force for political security. Among its other duties, it operated the gulag system (Main Administration of Camps) with its expansive network of corrective labor camps, corrective labor colonies, and special settlements. It also administered a parallel structure of internment camps for prisoners of war and foreign civilian internees that was known as the Main Administration for the Affairs of Prisoners of War and Internees (GUPVI). These two camp systems employed millions of forced laborers during Beria's tenure as head of the NKVD.

In particular, Beria oversaw the expansion and transformation of the special settlement regime into a system that would not only socially isolate certain ethnic groups but would also economically integrate them into regions far removed from their homelands. Beria organized the deportation of over 3 million people to remote locations in the Soviet Union during the 1940s. More than 2 million of these people came from eight nationalities that were deported in their entirety. These included Russian Germans, Karachais, Kalmyks, Chechens, Ingush, Balkars, Crimean Tatars, and Meskhetian Turks. Confined to internal exile in Siberia, Kazakhstan, Central Asia, and the Urals, these deportees received the legal status of "special settlers." As such, they could not leave their assigned settlements without written permission from special NKVD commandants. They also lacked the freedom to choose their employment. The Soviet regime used them as a captive labor force to develop agriculture, fisheries, industry, mining, and forestry in sparsely inhabited regions of the Soviet Union.

During World War II, the Soviets mobilized nearly 400,000 of these individuals and earlier deportees belonging to suspect nationalities and placed them into forced labor battalions. This system of forced labor garnered the name "labor army" (*trudarmiia*) from the Soviet citizens conscripted into it. Beria's NKVD sent 220,000 of these men and women to work in gulag camps under conditions similar to those of convicts. The remaining 180,000 worked for civilian commissariats under NKVD supervision and lived in NKVD-guarded barracks. The ethnic composition of these forced laborers consisted of more than 315,000 Russian Germans, 14,000 Russian Koreans, 15,000 Kalmyks, and 5,000 Crimean Tatars, as well as Russian Finns, Russian Greeks, and others. They built factories, erected dams, laid railways, felled timber, mined coal, extracted oil, and manufactured munitions in Siberia, Kazakhstan, and the Urals during the 1940s. The mass induction of Russian Germans and other stigmatized nationalities into forced labor brigades mitigated the loss of labor from the reduction of gulag prisoners during World War II, many of whom were inducted into the army. Labor army conscripts suffered a high rate of mortality because of malnutrition, disease, exposure, and other causes. More than 100,000 Russian Germans may have perished as a result of their service in the labor army.

After stepping down from the NKVD, Beria retained considerable power by virtue of his post as deputy prime minister and head of state security. In June 1953, amidst the confusion and political intrigue surrounding Soviet leader Joseph Stalin's death, Beria was arrested and charged with treason and other offenses. Even before Stalin had died the previous March, Beria had been plotting to neutralize his opponents and consolidate power for himself. Overwhelmed by his adversaries, he was tried, convicted, and executed on December 23, 1953, in Moscow.

J. OTTO POHL

See also: Great Purges; Gulags; Stalin, Joseph; Soviet Union

Further Reading

Knight, Amy. *Beria: Stalin's First Lieutenant*. Princeton, NJ: Princeton University Press, 1993.

Pohl, J. Otto. *Ethnic Cleansing in the USSR, 1937–1949*. Westport, CT: Greenwood, 1999.

Biafra

Biafra was a region in eastern Nigeria that briefly became a sovereign republic (1967–1970). The Republic of Biafra came into existence on May 30, 1967, by the proclamation of Gen. Chukwuemeka Ojukwu, then military governor of Nigeria's South Eastern Region, following an edict of the Eastern Region Constituent Assembly. The new independent country was comprised of the Igbo, Efik, Ibibio, Ijaw, Kalabari, Ogoja, and Ogoni ethnic groups. The name was adopted from the ancient West African kingdom of Biafra, on the inlet of the Atlantic coastline that early Portuguese explorers called the Bight of Biafra.

Two immediate causes led to the establishment of a sovereign republic. First was the northern Nigerian military officers' countercoup of July 29, 1966, in which some 200 Igbo officers and men of the Nigerian army were killed, including the country's first military head of state, Gen. J. T. U. Aguiyi-Ironsi. Second was the May, July, and September 1966 Nigerian genocide against Igbo settlers in other parts of Nigeria, but mainly in the north. These events created a pervasive sense of insecurity among the Igbo and other eastern ethnicities in the old Nigerian nation. The growing animosity between Nigeria's political leaders only heightened the cultural and religious tensions between the south and the north.

Nigeria's first military coup d'état, on January 15, 1966, upset the delicate political balance among the country's three dominant ethnic groups: the Igbo, Yoruba, and Hausa-Fulani. Northern leaders interpreted the coup as a ploy by the Christian Igbo to usurp political power from the Arab and Muslim Hausa-Fulani. The consequences were the coup of July 29, the bloodiest in modern Africa and the first black-on-black genocide in modern history, in which an estimated 50,000 Igbo settlers in northern Nigeria were butchered in a state-sponsored wave of ethnic cleansing; meanwhile, hundreds of thousands died of starvation and other causes. Over 1 million survivors of the ensuing nationwide pogrom fled back to the Igbo traditional homeland in the east to help found Biafra as a protection against the brutality of the Nigeria government.

Yakubu Gowon, a northerner who became Nigeria's second military head of state, refused to recognize the sovereignty of Biafra. He declared a state of emergency, subdivided the existing four regions of Nigeria into twelve states, and ordered a military invasion of the Eastern Region. The 30-month civil war that broke out in July 1967 displayed Biafra's ingenuity through the technological inventiveness of its research and production unit (RAP), the efficiency of its military forces, and the perseverance of its people. As a test of its successful diplomacy, Biafra gained varying recognition from France, Gabon, Haiti, Ivory Coast, Israel, Portugal, South Africa, and Tanzania.

The Nigerian government, however, influenced by the Biafran oil and armament proliferation interests of its British and Soviet Union sponsors, unleashed further acts of genocide against Biafran civilians. Nigeria's Egyptian pilots bombed the Igbo Awgu market, and the Nigerian army wiped out an entire population of old men and male children in the Igbo town of Asaba. In spite of the protestations of the Vatican, the World Council of Churches, the International Red Cross, the United States, and others, Nigeria imposed an economic blockade against Biafra. Under the program of "starvation as a legitimate weapon of war," the Nigerian government ordered the afternoon downing of a Swedish Red Cross plane on June 5, 1969, an incident that clearly defied international law.

About 1 million Biafran children died of starvation and kwashiorkor, a debilitating disease brought on by malnutrition. Over 2 million Biafrans had died by the time of its surrender on January 12, 1970. The Nigerian-Biafran War officially ended on January 15, 1970, but the continuing agitation of the Movement for the Actualization of the Sovereign State of Biafra (MASSOB) attests to the rampant marginalization of the former Eastern Region and the failure of the Nigerian postwar governments to bring about reconstruction, rehabilitation, and reconciliation.

OBIWU IWUANYANWU

See also: Nigeria; Uganda

Further Reading

Sherman, John. *War Stories: A Memoir of Nigeria and Biafra*. Indianapolis, IN: Mesa Verde Press, 2002.

Soyinka, Wole. *The Open Sore of a Continent: A Personal Narrative of the Nigerian Crisis*. New York: Oxford University Press, 1996.

Uzokwe, Alfred Obiora. *Surviving in Biafra: The Story of the Nigerian Civil War*. New York: Writer's Advantage, 2003.

Black War

Conflict waged between British colonists and Tasmanian Aborigines (the Pallawahs) from 1828 until 1832. The Black War resulted in the near extinction of the Pallawahs on Tasmania (then still known as Van Diemen's Land) and the assertion of British control over the entirety of the mainland.

In 1642, the Dutch were thought to have been the first Europeans to visit Tasmania; thereafter, other Europeans also had contact with the Pallawahs. It was not until 1803, however, that a European nation attempted to establish a colony there. In that year, the British founded a penal colony near the modern-day city of Hobart, Tasmania. Thereafter, swarms of British began arriving, hoping to become successful farmers and sheepherders.

The arrival of so many Europeans proved catastrophic to the Aborigines. Lacking any defenses against communicable diseases carried by the Europeans, many died. Indeed, by the late 1820s, perhaps as much as 50 percent of the Pallawah population had succumbed to diseases and other problems associated with the British onslaught. As the colonists encroached on Aboriginal lands with virtual impunity, some of the Pallawahs commenced a guerilla-style war against the British. This compelled British administrators to establish policies that scholars and historians would later call a genocide.

As Pallawah raids increased, in November 1828 British governor George Arthur issued a martial law declaration covering much of the colony. The order called for the capture of all Aborigines within areas settled or controlled by the British; those who failed to cooperate would be summarily shot. At the same time, however, Arthur cautioned that the use of armed force should be employed only sparingly. Many colonists, however, did not pay heed to that caveat.

As Pallawah-colonist violence continued, Arthur offered bounties for Aborigines taken alive. The bounties, however, were only in force when an Aborigine was taken from a British-controlled area; once again, the governor warned against the use of indiscriminate violence against the Pallawah. Nevertheless, wholesale killing of the Pallawahs continued. Later that year, Arthur was determined to end the conflict, so he ordered all male colonists to form a human chain (called the "Black Line") that was to fan out into the countryside and capture the remaining Aborigines. They would then be deported to an off-shore island for resettlement. The Black Line consisted of some 1,500 civilians and British troops.

By 1832, there were only about 250 Pallawahs left in Tasmania; the rest had been exterminated or resettled. The following year, the remaining Aborigines struck a deal with the British, thereby agreeing to stop their raids and be settled on off-shore islands. By 1835, there were just 150 "peaceful" Aborigines in Tasmania. In a mere 30 years, the British had reduced the native population from some 4,000 to 150. Some modern historians, however, have questioned these statistics.

PAUL G. PIERPAOLI JR.

See also: Australia; Australian Aborigines; Stolen Generations

Further Reading

Hernon, Ian. *Britain's Forgotten Wars: Colonial Campaigns of the 19th Century.* Stroud, Gloucestershire, UK: The History Press, 2003.

Turnbull, Clive. *Black War: The Extermination of the Tasmanian Aborigines.* Melbourne: Cheshire-Lansdowne Press, 1965.

Bokassa, Jean-Bédel

Jean-Bédel Bokassa was the leader of the Central African Republic from 1966 to 1979. His bizarre behavior and violent policies made him a symbol of the corrupt leadership that afflicted many postindependence African nations.

Bokassa was born in Bobangui, in the French colony of Ubangi Chari, on February 22, 1921. He was one of 12 children of a Mbaka chief in the Lobaye province. When he was six, his father was killed in a French prefecture's office. His mother committed suicide very soon thereafter. The orphaned Bokassa was educated in Roman Catholic mission schools in Bangui and Brazzaville. He considered joining the priesthood but instead opted for a career in the military.

In 1939, Bokassa enlisted in the French colonial army in the opening days of World War II. After the fall of France in 1940, he joined the Free French Forces organized by Gen. Charles de Gaulle and was decorated for combat in France and the Congo. After the war, he served the French Army in Indochina between 1946 and 1954, becoming an officer in 1949. By the time he left the French Army in 1961, he had attained the rank of captain.

The Oubangui-Chari colony achieved its independence in 1960 and became the Central African Republic. Bokassa's family played an instrumental role in the campaign to end French rule. Bokassa's uncle, Barthelemy Boganda, led the independence movement until his death in 1959. Bokassa's cousin, David Dacko, became the nation's first president. Dacko appointed Bokassa as the commander in chief of the nation's armed forces in 1963.

The new nation faced serious economic problems, which President Dacko tried to solve through a series of austerity measures. When he proposed cuts in the budget of the armed forces, however, Bokassa overthrew him on December 31, 1965, and declared himself president. Bokassa declared his intentions to return the nation to civilian rule when the economic crisis subsided. After removing all potential threats to his authority, however, he failed to relinquish his position as the nation's dictator.

Shortly after his accession to power, Bokassa began to exhibit erratic behavior. In 1970, he outlawed all strikes and demonstrations within the country. In 1971, to commemorate Mother's Day, he released all women imprisoned in the nation's jails and executed all men accused of serious crimes against women. The following year, he had himself declared president for life. In 1976, he renamed his nation the Central African Empire and crowned himself Emperor Bokassa I. His coronation was celebrated with an elaborate ceremony that cost the impoverished country $30 million.

Bokassa cultivated relations with Western nations willing to supply economic assistance to his regime. France retained close relations with Bokassa despite his odd behavior because it was reliant on the Central African Republic as a supplier of uranium. Bokassa also sought aid from Libya and briefly converted to Islam to curry favor with Libyan leader Muammar Qaddafi. He returned to Christianity, however, when the aid was not forthcoming. Eventually, Bokassa's bizarre behavior embarrassed Western donors, who began withdrawing their assistance in the late 1970s.

In early 1979, Bokassa announced that all schoolchildren in the nation were required to wear expensive uniforms produced by a factory owned by one of his wives. The order inspired widespread protests. The army arrested many of the child protesters and placed them in prison, at which point they were massacred by Bokassa's own personal guard. Fed up with the emperor's bizarre and bloody rule, the French supported a coup against Bokassa in September 1979. Bokassa was sent into exile in Côte d'Ivoire and replaced by Dacko, the man he had ousted 14 years earlier.

Dacko's hold on power proved tenuous, and the military removed him from power six months after he took office. Bokassa returned to the Central African Republic in 1986 and stood trial for the murder of several political opponents as well as for cannibalism and grand theft. He was convicted and sentenced to death, but his sentence was commuted to life in prison. He was granted amnesty in 1993 and died on November 3, 1996.

PAUL R. BARTROP

See also: Congo, Democratic Republic of; Ethiopia; Libya; Mozambique; Uganda

Further Reading

Chirot, Daniel. *Modern Tyrants: The Power and Prevalence of Evil in Our Age.* Princeton, NJ: Princeton University Press, 1994.

Titley, Brian. *Dark Age: The Political Odyssey of Emperor Bokassa.* Montreal: McGill-Queen's University Press, 1997.

C

Cannibalism in the Holodomor

During the mass starvation (Holodomor) in Ukraine between 1932 and 1933, a relatively small number of individuals turned to cannibalism in order to survive. The famine in Ukraine began in earnest in 1932, although its antecedents came be traced back to the late 1920s. In 1928, the Soviet regime under Joseph Stalin initiated an ambitious scheme to industrialize the USSR in a short period of time. The First Five Year Plan established specific targets for nearly all industrial production, to include the mining of raw materials, the production of oil, and the generation of electricity. In 1929, the Plan was amended to include the complete collectivization of Soviet agriculture. Part of the collectivization effort meant the eradication of the kulaks (landed peasantry) throughout the Soviet Union, including Ukraine, which had a large number of kulaks.

The effort to kill, deport, or imprison the kulaks of Ukraine wrought complete chaos in Ukraine's agricultural sector, which until then had been among the most productive in all of the USSR. By 1931, there were certainly ominous signs of a potential famine in Ukraine, as agricultural production went down and the Soviet government's grain requisition quotas went up. Poor crop yields in 1932 compounded these problems, and the Soviet government turned a blind eye to the growing crisis. In fact, it stepped up its efforts to enforce collectivization by aggressively punishing individuals who were caught hoarding or stealing food. At the same time, most Ukrainians were forbidden from traveling to other regions of Ukraine or the Soviet Union where food supplies were more plentiful.

By mid-1932, the Holodomor was reaching its apex. The winter of 1932–1933 was perhaps the worst part of the catastrophe, as the winter weather made foraging off the land that much more difficult. By then, perhaps as many as 25,000 Ukrainians were dying every day (almost 25 percent of all Ukrainians living in the countryside perished between 1932 and 1933).

Amid these desperate circumstances, some people turned to cannibalism, after having consumed almost every conceivable animal, including moles, badgers, and rats. The extent of the cannibalism in the Ukraine is hard to determine, because for decades the Soviets attempted to hide or erase any evidence of the Holodomor. But the Soviet government clearly knew about it, because some Holodomor survivors recalled having seen posters that read: "Eating Your Own Children is Barbarism." One source claims that the Soviets convicted some 2,500 Ukrainians for cannibalism.

One survivor remembered that some families ate family members who had died, and even consumed corpses that had been brought to the cemetery. The death rate was so high that cemeteries could not accommodate the dead. One report documents that some corpses had large cuts in their abdomen, indicating that the livers had been removed for human consumption. Another survivor told how his neighbor killed his own elderly wife to make soup out of her bones. Others have indicated that sometimes children would simply disappear, and they had assumed that they had been killed and eaten.

While any discussion of cannibalism is extremely discomforting, and while the act of cannibalism itself is almost impossible to conceive, the sheer extent of the starvation in Ukraine during the early 1930s certainly goes a long way in explaining how people could have engaged in such activity. While estimates on the number of people who died in the Holodomor vary considerably, it is believed that at least 3.2 million perished, while some estimates claim as many as 5 million or more died. This occurred over a very short span of time. It is not, therefore, beyond comprehension that some individuals turned to truly desperate acts to survive.

PAUL G. PIERPAOLI JR.

See also: Dekulakization; Kulaks; Soviet Collectivization; Soviet Grain Requisition Policies; Soviet Union; Stalin, Joseph; Ukrainian Starvation (Holodomor)

Further Reading

Conquest, Robert. *The Harvest of Sorrow: Soviet Collectivization and the Terror-Famine.* New York: Oxford University Press, 1987.

Conquest, Robert. *Reflections on a Ravaged Century.* New York: W.W. Norton, 2000.

Kiernan, Ben. *Blood and Soil: A World History of Genocide and Extermination from Sparta to Darfur.* New Haven, CT: Yale University Press, 2007.

Chemical Weapons and Warfare

Poison gas had been utilized with considerable effect by the major belligerents in World War I. In the course of the conflict, the combatants had deployed about 113,000 tons of chemicals, and some estimates indicate over 1 million soldiers were injured by poison gas during the war, 10 percent of them fatally.

In the interwar period, the major powers discussed outlawing the use of poison gas, but they also continued to produce it. Prior to World War II, more than 40 nations signed the Geneva Protocol of 1925 banning the offensive use of chemical weapons in warfare. All of the main combatants in World War II save the United States and Japan ratified the protocol, which went into force in August 1928. Although the United States had first proposed the treaty, isolationist sentiment blocked its ratification in the Senate. Japan feared giving away any advantage in case of a conflict with the far more populous China. The signatory powers, however, reserved the right to utilize chemical weapons in a retaliatory attack and to employ them against a country that had not signed the protocol.

Chemical weapons are categorized by their effects on human beings, animals, and plants. Lung irritants, such as phosgene, make victims choke or suffocate, with symptoms usually delayed for several hours after contact. Vesicants, such as mustard gas, cause the skin to blister and the eyes to swell, sometimes with loss of sight. The symptoms of vesicants can be delayed up to 48 hours. Lacrimators are tear gases, such as chloracetophenone and brombenzylcyanide, which irritate the eyes and cause difficulty with breathing.

The warring powers also produced irritant smoke (such as sneezing gases or adamsite), screening smokes, and incendiaries. A new and very deadly chemical agent, nerve gas, was developed during the war. Nerve gases take effect quickly, producing symptoms in 10 to 30 minutes, depending on whether they are inhaled or absorbed through the skin.

Chemical weapons can be launched in a variety of forms: through shells and bombs that explode and disperse the chemicals into the air in drops or small particles, from containers with vaporized solids that infiltrate the air as a smoke, and through liquids released from airplanes as drops or mist. Chemical weapons can be more useful than conventional weapons, since their effects are longer lasting, sometimes persisting for days or weeks. The most desirable chemical agents have many of the same characteristics in common. They are effective in small concentrations, difficult to protect against, quickly and cheaply manufactured, made from easily obtainable raw materials, heavier than air, easily and safely transportable, effective against multiple parts of the body, and not easily detectable.

Three of the most common means used to deploy chemical agents by the end of World War I were the portable gas cylinder, the Livens Projector, and the chemical mortar. But these delivery systems were obsolete by the time of World War II, given the greater mobility of infantry troops. Accordingly, the size of chemical mortars was increased as was their range (to 1,400 yards), and the Livens Projector was replaced by 100 mm caliber, mobile rocket launchers. During the interwar years, governments also experimented with using airplanes to deliver chemical weapons, through cluster bombs and spraying. By the time World War II began, aerial bombardment with chemical weapons was the most common deployment mechanism. It is also possible to deploy chemical weapons, particularly mustard gas, in land mines and grenades. German leaders debated the feasibility of combining missiles and chemical weapons, but production of such mechanisms did not occur.

In stark contrast to the situation in World War I, chemical weapons were used only sparingly in World War II. The major powers were reluctant to employ them. This was, in part, because they were convinced that their opponents had extensive stockpiles of poison gases and because their own populations were not adequately prepared to withstand a retaliatory attack. They also did not wish to be the first to violate the Geneva Protocol. Several key leaders were hesitant to authorize the use of chemical weapons. German leader Adolf Hitler, who had been gassed at Ypres in 1918, had a strong aversion to the use of gas as an offensive weapon, and President Franklin D. Roosevelt also opposed the use of chemical weapons. For the European powers in particular, the threat of retribution against cities and large-scale civilian suffering was a major deterrent. The shipping of chemical weapons and equipping friendly troops for chemical attacks also presented logistical difficulties. Lastly, fighting in World War II, marked as it was by rapid movement, was dramatically different from the trench warfare of the previous conflict. Early in the war, the Axis powers scored a succession of quick victories and did not need to resort to poison gas.

The fate of the SS *John Harvey* illustrated the difficulty of shipping poison gas. The ship sailed from the United States to Italy in 1943, carrying 2,000 bombs loaded with mustard gas. Each bomb held 60 to 70 pounds of the gas. The ship docked at Bari on November 28, 1943. Four days later, German aircraft attacked the port. Their 20-minute assault sank 17 ships and badly damaged 8 others. Racked by explosions, the *John Harvey* sank, and some of the mustard gas in the bombs in its hold was released. It mixed with the oil and smoke and rolled across the water. More than 1,000 Allied soldiers and Italian civilians died as a result, and hundreds were blinded, some permanently. The death rate was particularly high because no one knew of the cargo until several weeks had passed.

Yet such difficulties did not preclude the use of poison gas. The Italians, for example, utilized mustard gas and tear gas grenades in their 1935–1936 conquest of Ethiopia. They employed it to protect their flanks by saturating the ground on either side of the advancing columns. They also targeted Ethiopian communications centers and employed mustard gas against Ethiopian military personnel. In fact, the Italians deployed more than 700 tons of gas against the local population, either as bombs (each container contained about 44 pounds) or sprayed from aircraft. Their use of chemical weapons was indiscriminate, targeting both military and civilian areas. One-third of all Ethiopian military casualties in this conflict resulted from exposure to chemical agents.

The Italian decision to employ chemical weapons on a large scale in Ethiopia prompted other nations to renew their production of such weapons and to plan for protecting their armed forces and civilian populations. France began production at a phosgene facility at Clamency in 1936. The U.S. government reopened mustard gas and phosgene plants in New Jersey the following year. The Soviet Union opened three new chemical weapons production plants. And in November 1938, after the Munich Conference, the British government issued tens of thousands of gas masks to civilians and mandated a minimum level of production of 300 tons of mustard gas per week, with 2,000 tons held in reserve.

At the beginning of World War II, Germany held a commanding lead in the stockpiling of chemical weapons, but its government officials did not know this. German stockpiles in 1939 are estimated at 10,000 tons, as compared with 500 tons in Great Britain, 1,000 tons in the United States, and 2,000 tons in Japan.

During World War II in the European Theater, chemical weapons were never deliberately employed on a large scale. In June 1940, British Prime Minister Winston Churchill discussed with his cabinet the idea of using poison gas to repel a German invasion of either Great Britain or Ireland. Although many of the senior military staff opposed this notion, the cabinet approved it. The British government also considered the use of poison gas to combat the German V-1 and V-2 rockets later in the war. By 1944, Germany's production capacity was 10,000 tons of poison gas per month; in addition, myriad delivery systems were available, including grenades filled with hydrogen cyanide and machine guns capable of firing bullets faced with tabun or sarin. The Luftwaffe had more than 480,000 gas bombs, ranging in size from 33 to 1,650 pounds.

In the Pacific Theater, the Japanese were also involved in massive production of poison gas and had been since the later portion of World War I. By 1937, Japan was daily producing up to 2 tons of lewisite, a virulent form of mustard gas. In their invasion and occupation of China from 1937 to 1945, the Japanese employed a wide variety of poison gases, including phosgene, hydrogen cyanide, mustard gas, and Lewisite. Because the Chinese population, both military and civilian, was completely unprotected against chemical warfare, the effects were devastating.

The Japanese deployed the chemicals weapons by aerial bombardment and artillery shells. They also designed rockets capable of holding 10.5 quarts of a chemical agent and traveling up to 2 miles; flamethrowers that propelled hydrogen cyanide; and a handheld antitank weapon that employed hydrogen cyanide. The Japanese also utilized gas grenades during the Imphal Campaign in 1944. The United States considered using poison gas during the invasion of Iwo Jima and the proposed invasion of the Japanese home islands, but the former was never ordered and the latter proved unnecessary.

The deadliest form of chemical warfare at that time, nerve gas, was never used in battle. A German scientist, Gerhard Schrader, employed by I.G. Farben in 1936, discovered tabun while he was trying to create a more powerful insecticide. Tabun can be absorbed directly into the body and is colorless and odorless. It stops the nervous system from producing a key enzyme, acetylcholinesterase, that allows contracting muscles to relax. If this enzyme is not active, important muscles, such as the heart, contract and begin to spasm. As all the body's muscles contract, the person suffocates. Tabun is 100 to 1,000 times more deadly than chlorine gas and 10 to 100 times more deadly than mustard or phosgene gas. Later, Schrader discovered a second and even more toxic nerve gas, which he named sarin. It is almost 10 times more lethal than tabun. In 1944, a still more deadly nerve gas, soman, was discovered, but it was never mass-produced during the war. Great Britain also manufactured sarin and soman.

Germany's leaders chose not to deploy tabun, as they lacked the ability to protect their own population against this nerve gas and no known antidote existed. The Germans did test their nerve gases on unwilling inmates of concentration and prisoner-of-war camps. At the Natzweiler concentration camp, tests with both mustard and phosgene gases were also conducted on unwilling prisoners. Germany moved its storage of nerve gas in 1944 in anticipation of Allied advances in the west, but their production facility in Silesia fell into Soviet hands.

The German government also used a poison gas, namely, Zyklon B, against prisoners in concentration camps and in its killing centers in Poland. Zyklon B was developed in the 1930s by Deesch, a subsidiary of I.G. Farben that was experimenting with more powerful insecticides. Zyklon B, also known as Prussic acid, is a powerful, toxic, volatile, and colorless liquid. In order to transport the gas, it was absorbed by wood circles or small cubes because of its great volatility.

Zyklon B was dropped into gas chambers and caused suffocation, as well as feelings of fear and dizziness and vomiting. The Germans constructed gas chambers to use Zyklon B in many of their concentration camps, including Auschwitz, Buchenwald, Sachsenhausen, Neuengamme, Majdanek, Mauthausen, Stutthof, Gross-Rosen, and Treblinka. In Auschwitz alone, more than 2.5 million people were murdered through the use of Zyklon B between May 1940 and December 1943. At other concentration camps and killing centers, prisoners were killed by carbon monoxide poisoning.

By 1945, the major combatants as a group had stockpiled more than 500,000 tons of chemical weapons, led by the United States with 110,000 tons. This amount was five times the total amount of gas employed in World War I. Although poison gases were never used in large-scale attacks during World War II, the threat was present throughout the conflict. Given their deadly nature, the updated deployment systems, and the large stockpiles, chemical weapons could have played an enormous role in World War II.

LAURA J. HILTON

See also: Unit 731

Further Reading

Harris, Robert, and Jeremy Paxman. *A Higher Form of Killing.* New York: Hill and Wang, 1982.

Price, Richard M. *The Chemical Weapons Taboo.* Ithaca, NY: Cornell University Press, 1997.

Spiers, Edward. *Chemical Warfare.* Urbana: University of Illinois Press, 1986.

Chile

Recent discussions about war crimes in Chile have focused almost exclusively on the South American country's experiences with internal armed conflicts while under military rule between 1973 and 1990. Like many other Latin American nations, Chile has a long-standing military tradition but did not participate in any large-scale external war during the 20th century. It did not have a military role in the world's major world wars, and relations with other Latin American nations have been relatively stable despite a turbulent history of border disputes with its neighbors, Peru, Bolivia, and Argentina. Since 1973, however, Chileans have seen a democratically elected government overthrown in a military coup, the establishment of an authoritarian dictatorship that lasted 17 years, and a slow and difficult transition to democracy. After 1990, as the Chilean state has returned to civilian control, questions have arisen over whether international agreements, such as the Geneva Conventions, can be applied to internal combat operations and to what extent military and intelligence officials who allegedly committed war crimes against the citizens of Chile and several other countries should be punished.

On September 11, 1973, General Augusto Pinochet led a violent military coup that overthrew Salvador Allende, a Socialist Party leader, who had won the 1970 presidential election. Pinochet immediately seized control of the media, eliminated the independence of the judiciary, exiled dissidents, banned all political opposition, and dismantled any social organization that he deemed threatening. He also sanctioned the creation of a national intelligence service, the National Intelligence Directorate (DINA), in 1974 and the National Information Center (CNI) in 1977. These intelligence organizations cultivated neighborhood informant networks, abducted and killed suspected political opponents, constructed secret camps where prisoners were tortured for information, and carried out assassination plots within Chile and in other nations.

Pinochet's government sanctioned some of the worst practices of state terrorism in the region. Chilean military and intelligence organizations led the so-called Caravan of Death, a national operation targeting political enemies throughout the country. Military commanders and landowners executed labor organizers at the local level. In 1976, Chilean intelligence agents assassinated Orlando Letelier, Allende's defense minister, in Washington D.C. The U.S. Central Intelligence Agency (CIA) also funneled millions of dollars to right-wing paramilitary groups, political organizations, and corporations. As a result, more than 3,000 people were killed or forcibly "disappeared."

International pressure to cede power to civilian leaders concerned military officials, who believed that they would later be vulnerable to charges of war crimes. Indeed, in 1978, the United Nations issued a resolution strongly condemning Pinochet's government for human rights violations. In the same year, Pinochet's regime enacted Decree 2191, which gave a broad amnesty to officers, soldiers, and intelligence officials during and after the military coup. Human rights organizations objected that this controversial law was a direct violation of international treaties that Chilean governments had signed and ratified, including the Geneva Conventions.

Pinochet eventually stepped down in 1990 after losing a plebiscite. Still, he maintained control over the military until 1998, occupied a senate seat for life, and had many supporters in key positions within the government. The first elected government since Allende established a Truth and Reconciliation Commission, known as the Rettig Commission, in 1990. A year later, it issued its first report documenting the deaths of those Chileans and foreigners who had been killed at the hands of the military government during the 1970s and 1980s.

Because of the lack of a national framework for establishing war crimes tribunals, however, these cases have been pursued through the Chilean court system. At first, this produced mixed results. Some judges, such as Juan Guzmán Tapia, were eager to initiate cases against military and intelligence officials, but Pinochet's supporters, especially within the Chilean Supreme Court, had successfully blocked these actions. In 1990, in a case implicating Manuel Contreras, the former DINA director, and others in the disappearances of 70 people between 1973 and 1977, the Supreme Court ruled that the 1978 amnesty law outweighed the Geneva Conventions and all other international agreements. However, lawyers for the victims appealed to the Inter-American Human Rights Commission and won, arguing that Chile's ratification of the American Convention on Human Rights in 1990 overturned the 1978 decree. Later, in 1995, the Chilean Supreme Court found Contreras guilty of Orlando Letelier's 1976 assassination.

Indeed, efforts to prosecute other officials gained momentum when, in 1997, Eduardo Frei Ruíz-Tagle, as president, pushed through reforms that returned more control of the country's judicial system to the hands of elected leaders. Still, members of the military and Pinochet supporters and family members have openly protested investigations of officers. In the late 1990s, civilian-led prosecutions were more successful in filing charges of financial corruption against military leaders or forcing Pinochet-era officers into retirement.

The prospect of trying Pinochet himself seemed remote until 1998 when he traveled to London for medical treatment. While there, Baltazar Garzón, a Spanish judge, filed charges against the former dictator for the deaths of 34 Spanish citizens since 1988 and requested that the British government extradite Pinochet to Spain. These actions triggered other extradition requests on behalf of exiled Chileans in French, Belgian, and Swiss courts. Pinochet's lawyers argued that the charges and extradition requests brought against him were a violation of the

Geneva Conventions and that a former head of state was immune from prosecution. These arguments failed to persuade a British court when, in late 1999, it ruled that Pinochet could be extradited to Spain. British doctors in early 2000, however, concluded that Pinochet was medically unfit to stand trial. The British government decided to send Pinochet back to Chile to face charges there. Still, Garzón's extradition request set the precedent that a former head of state accused of war crimes could be brought to trial in any country. Pinochet returned to Chile to find that the courts had successfully stripped him of immunity protections.

Pinochet's death in late 2006 may have halted national and international war crimes proceedings, but Pinochet's subordinates, followers, and family members are still under investigation. In August 2007, the former head of the CNI, Hugo Salas Wenzel, became the first senior military officer during the Pinochet years to be sentenced to a life term in prison for human rights violations.

Jesse Hingson

See also: Pinochet, Augusto

Further Reading

Constable, Pamela, and Arturo Valenzuela. *A Nation of Enemies: Chile under Pinochet.* New York: W.W. Norton and Company, 1993.

Hawkins, Darren G. *International Human Rights and Authoritarian Rule in Chile.* Lincoln: University of Nebraska Press, 2002.

China

China, the world's most population nation, has witnessed a long series of human rights abuses and atrocities, dating back to the beginning of the Chinese Civil War, which began in 1927. Over the course of the Chinese Civil War (1927–1937, 1945–1949), the Sino-Japanese War (1937–1945), and the Communist era that commenced in October 1949, tens of millions of Chinese have perished, many of them civilians. These deaths were the result of armed conflict, mass relocations, forced annexations, and government policies design to industrialize China and collectivize its agriculture during the late 1950s and early 1960s. Government efforts to "purge" Chinese society of dissidents, "capitalists," and other alleged nonconformers also resulted in many deaths, disappearances, and imprisonments during the late 1960s through the mid-1970s. Citing exact details for many of these tragedies is almost impossible because of China's insularity before the Communist takeover in 1949, and because of government propaganda and media blackouts since then.

The Chinese Civil War had its roots in the collapse of the Qing Dynasty in 1911; thereafter, China's government became hopelessly fragmented, dominated by a number of rival but powerful warlords. Sun Yixian (Sun Yat-sen), who sought to consolidate power in China, diminish the warlords, and rid his country of undue foreign influence, founded and led the Guomindang (GMD). During roughly the same period, leftist Chinese nationalists formed the Chinese Communist Party (CCP). They too sought an independent China, but one that embraced communism. A split within the GMD, meanwhile, which saw the left faction of the party defect to the CCP, caused a major uproar within the GMD. On April 12, 1927, Sun's successor, Jiang Jieshi (Chiang Kai-shek), ordered the brutal "suppression" of CPC members as well as GMD "leftists" in Shanghai. The resulting April 12 Incident, or Shanghai Massacre, resulted in the deaths of 300–500 individuals; another 4,000–5,000 simply disappeared and were likely murdered. This proved to be the opening salvo in the long-running civil war.

In the late 1920s, CCP and GMD forces fought each other, with both sides involving civilians. Thousands were reportedly killed throughout China. Jiang instituted more purges of suspected communists and leftists while CCP Mao Zedong consolidated his power in the countryside, in the process assembling an impressive force of some 200,000 soldiers by 1933. At the same time, Japan was attempting to make inroads in China in a bid to take control of the strategic region of Manchuria. By 1932, the Japanese had assumed control of Manchuria (now known as Manchukuo). In December 1936, the GMD and CCP reluctantly joined forces to fight the Japanese, who began to wage a full-scale war with the Chinese in 1937.

The fighting between the Chinese and Japanese intensified, in the process killing thousands of innocent civilians. In the infamous Nanjing massacre (Rape of Nanjing, December 13, 1937–January 22, 1938), the Japanese, frustrated that they could not defeat the Chinese insurgency or force their surrender at Nanjing, instituted a policy of destruction in the city that resulted in the deaths of as many as 300,000 soldiers and civilians. At least 20,000 women were raped and then murdered. Some Chinese soldiers were buried alive while others died as a result of poison gas that the Japanese deployed. Countless homes, buildings, and shops were wrecked. This mass destruction occurred in just six weeks' time. The Chinese fought back, which only increased brutal reprisal attacks by the Japanese. The Japanese also forced at least 100,000 Chinese women into prostitution during the occupation of China. Euphemistically known as "comfort women," they were forced to serve the Japanese army as concubines and sex slaves. It is estimated that some 3.9 million Chinese died during the Sino-Japanese War, most at the hands of the Japanese.

With the defeat of Japan in August 1945, the shaky pseudo-alliance between the GMD and CCP broke down, and before long, the civil war began anew. By then the communists controlled a large swath of the country; they also boasted 900,000 soldiers and a party membership of 1.2 million. Full-scale combat resumed in June 1946, but by then the GMD was losing ground as well as support. In October 1949, the CCP under Mao had militarily defeated the GMD and declared the existence of the People's Republic of China (PRC). Jiang and the remnants of the GMD, meanwhile, established a rival regime on Taiwan.

Human rights abuses seemed only to intensify in Mao's PRC. The 1950–1953 Korean War saw hundreds of thousands of Chinese troops intervene in that conflict; to support the troops and help pay for the war, Mao instituted iron-fisted policies that resulted in major dislocations to the vast Chinese peasantry. Many died of starvation or were killed as soldiers in the war. At the same time, the CCP carried out a program to eradicate "counterrevolutionaries" and corrupt party officials. As a result, thousands were imprisoned or simply disappeared.

The worst single atrocity in modern China occurred during the disastrous Great Leap Forward program, instituted in 1958 and designed to collectivize agriculture and turn China into a modern, industrial powerhouse. More than 20,000 farm communes were created between 1958 and the early 1960s, but the Great Leap Forward turned into a massive stumble backward. A great famine swept China, killing millions and forcing some Chinese peasants to resort to cannibalism to survive. The death toll during this period is estimated at 18–35 million people. Mao quietly abandoned his failed campaign by early 1962.

Throughout the history of the PRC, the government has often resorted to political suppression by declaring dissidents to be mentally ill; this was especially the case under Mao. Perhaps several million Chinese were incarcerated in bogus "mental facilities" because they were viewed as dissidents or troublemakers. During the Cultural Revolution of 1967–1976, countless CCP members, intellectuals, teachers, and those suspected of "antirevolutionary" sentiments were arrested, imprisoned, or killed. Some

estimates suggest that as many as 1 million people died during the Cultural Revolution, while at least 750,000 became the victims of political persecution. Mao's death in 1976 helped put an end to the ruinous revolution he had launched some nine years earlier.

The post-Mao era has seen far fewer policies that have resulted in wholesale catastrophe for the Chinese people. But human rights abuses and atrocities nevertheless persist. Religious and ethnic minorities have routinely been subjected to government-sponsored violence. After the takeover of Tibet, 6,000 monasteries were destroyed; since then, the Chinese government has brutally suppressed periodic attempts to assert Tibetan nationalism. In Inner Mongolia, anywhere from 23,000–50,000 people have died at the hands of the Chinese government. In July 1975, in what is now called the Shadian Incident, government troops massacred 1,000–1,600 Hui people, another ethnic minority within the PRC. At the same time, more than 4,400 homes were destroyed.

In more recent times, the student-led, prodemocracy movement that occurred in the late 1980s led to a heavy-handed crackdown in the Chinese capital of Beijing in June 1989. The suppression of the movement in Tiananmen Square on June 4, which was captured by international journalists as it unfolded, shocked the world community and caused Chinese relations with many of its international partners to plummet. The photograph of a lone protester standing in front of an army tank became one of the most iconic images of the late 20th century. During the Tiananmen massacre, anywhere from 250 to as many as 10,000 people died or were injured; the estimates vary wildly because the Chinese government has steadfastly refused to release any specific information about the incident. Hundreds of others were arrested and indefinitely detained. Post-Tiananmen, the Chinese government has attempted to avoid large-scale shows of force, but human-rights abuses continue in China. The country has one of the highest incarceration rates in the world, and the Chinese government executed more of its citizens during the 1990s than any other nation. Torture was not officially outlawed until 1996.

PAUL G. PIERPAOLI JR.

See also: Comfort Women; Cultural Revolution; Great Leap Forward; Mao Zedong; Rape of Nanjing; Tiananmen Square Incident; Tibet Annexation

Further Reading

Blecher, Marc J. *China against the Tides: Restructuring through Revolution, Radicalism and Reform.* London: Continuum, 2003.

Dreyer, Edward L. *China at War, 1901–1949.* New York: Longman, 1995.

Hinton, Harold C., ed. *The People's Republic of China, 1949–1979: A Documentary Survey.* 5 vols. Wilmington, DE: Scholarly Resources, 1980.

Yamamoto, Masahiro. *Nanking: Anatomy of an Atrocity.* Westport, CT: Praeger, 2000.

Class enemies

Class enemies is a somewhat generic term used to describe groups of people who were seen as antithetical to the Russian Revolution that began in 1917. The term was applied to a wide variety of individuals, and over time its definitions and inclusions shifted, mainly in response to the political motivations of Soviet officials. A number of Ukrainians—especially kulaks—were classified as enemies of the state. Most Soviet authorities believed that such groups had to be eliminated, either by murder, deportation, or imprisonment. This concept helped precipitate the great famine in Ukraine during 1932–1932, which Ukrainians refer to as the Holodomor.

Class enemies are in fact closely related to enemies of the state, a concept first employed in ancient Rome. During the French Revolution, which began in 1789, Committee of Public Safety deputy Maximilien Robespierre referred to "enemies of the people," meaning those who did not support the revolution. Russian revolutionaries began employing the term "class enemies" quite extensively. Vladimir Lenin spoke of "enemies of the people" only days after the Bolshevik Revolution commenced. After that, the concept was variously applied to the czar, his family, and supporters of the czar, as well as the bourgeoisie, anarchists, kulaks, Mensheviks, Trotskyites, and immigrants, among others.

Class enemies were to be eliminated or neutralized. Those who owned land, like the kulaks in Ukraine, were subjected to land confiscation by the Soviet government. Most class enemies, including the kulaks, were subjected to such categorization and treatment not necessarily for their attitudes or actions against the government, but rather because of their socioeconomic status, profession, or social position prior to the 1917 Revolution.

After 1929, when Soviet general secretary Joseph Stalin decided to implement the complete collectivization of Soviet agriculture, the kulaks in Ukraine, as class enemies, were subjected to land confiscation and forced into communal farming. Those who resisted—and there were many who did—were sent to gulags (hard-labor prisons), deported to distant and remote parts of the Soviet Union, or resettled on communal farms within Ukraine. This "dekulakization" greatly impeded agricultural production during the early 1930s, which was still reeling from forced collectivization. In the Ukraine, the loss of hundreds of thousands of agricultural workers and resistance on the part of many kulaks resulted in a widespread famine, the Holodomor. In the late 1930s, remaining kulaks were imprisoned or murdered during the Great Purges, which were set in motion by Stalin.

PAUL G. PIERPAOLI JR.

See also: Dekulakization; Great Purges; Gulags; Kulaks; People's Commissariat for Internal Affairs (NKVD); Soviet Union; Stalin, Joseph; Ukrainian Starvation (Holodomor)

Further Reading

Conquest, Robert. *The Harvest of Sorrow: Soviet Collectivization and the Terror-Famine.* New York: Oxford University Press, 1987.

Werth, Nicolas, Karel Bartošek, Jean-Louis Panné, Jean-Louis Margolin, Andrzej Paczkowski, and Stéphane Courtois. *The Black Book of Communism: Crimes, Terror, Repression.* Cambridge, MA: Harvard University Press, 1999.

Colombia

Atrocities and massacres have been and continue to be frequent occurrences in Colombia's on-going internal armed conflict. The armed conflict in Colombia originated during 1964–1966, when the Revolutionary Armed Forces of Colombia (FARC) and the National Liberation Army (ELN) were founded and began their guerilla insurgency campaigns against successive government administrations of the Liberal and Conservative political parties. Successive government administrations, known as the National Front, agreed to govern Colombia jointly, alternating liberal and conservative presidents every four years for 16 years. The National Front ended "la violencia" (1948–1958), a period of political violence and civil conflict in various areas of the Colombian countryside between supporters of the Colombian Liberal Party and the Colombian Conservative Party.

While the political violence between the formal political parties subsided, guerrilla groups were founded in response to the many social and political injustices that continued under the National Front. The guerilla groups were heavily influenced by Cold War doctrines and events such as the 1959 Cuban Revolution. During the late 1970s and early 1980s, powerful and violent drug cartels emerged, which exerted strong political, economic and social influence throughout the country. The drug cartels financed and influenced illegally armed groups on the right and the left. The armed conflict in Colombia consists of fighting among guerrilla groups, paramilitary groups, the Colombian army, and the National Police and Private Security Services.

The most important parties in the Colombian armed conflict, besides the army and the National Police, are: Special Vigilance and Private Security Services (Servicios de Vigilancia y Seguridad Privada, CONVIVIRs); paramilitary groups allied as the United Self-Defense Group of Colombia (Autodefensas Unidas de Colombia, AUC); and Colombia's three largest guerrilla groups, the Revolutionary Armed Forces of Colombia (Fuerzas Armadas Revolucionarias de Colombia, FARC), the National Liberation Army (Unión Camilista-Ejército de Liberación Nacional, UC-ELN), and the Popular Liberation Army (Ejército Popular de Liberación, EPL).

According to Human Rights Watch, all parties are guilty of war crimes in Colombia's armed conflict. The laws of war applicable to the armed conflict in Colombia are: Common Article 3 of the Geneva Conventions of 1949, which addresses armed confrontations between organized armed forces or armed groups occurring exclusively within the territory of a particular state; Protocol II Additional to the Geneva Conventions, which applies to noninternational armed conflict in which insurgent forces are highly organized and is meant to protect civilians and prisoners of war; and, customary international law.

While the Colombian army teaches its officers the basics of international humanitarian law and makes instructional material available to all its members, the army continues to engage in violations of the laws of war. The basis of the violations is the army's consistent failure or refusal to properly distinguish civilians from combatants. In eastern Colombia, where paramilitary groups are weak, the army has been implicated in the killing of noncombatants and fighters who have surrendered or been taken prisoner. Where paramilitaries are present and strong, the army fails to act against them and often tolerates their activities.

The National Police has also been educated in the laws of war and human rights. In general, they are more responsive than the military to reports of violations by their members and act relatively quickly to investigate abuses;

however, the National Police continue to be implicated in many war crimes. Many police officers have been found guilty of capturing suspects and executing them, and in areas where paramilitaries are present, some police officers have been directly implicated in joint army-paramilitary activity.

CONVIVIRs are groups licensed by the government and led by civilians who are supposed to engage in self-defense as a quick responder to guerrilla attacks. Many CONVIVIRs, however, have taken a direct role in hostilities by attacking guerrillas and closely coordinating operations with the army and police. In many cases, CONVIVIRs have used government-supplied weapons to commit human rights violations. There are at least seven paramilitary groups allied under the name AUC (the United Self-Defense Group of Colombia). Human rights organizations have found that AUC depends on the explicit, deliberate, and systematic violation of international humanitarian law to wage war. Many Colombian officials, of the state, church, and humanitarian aid groups, claim that AUC only pays lip service to the protections contained in Common Article 3 and Protocol II. AUC has been found guilty of committing massacres, killing civilians, engaging in torture, the mutilation of corpses, death threats, forced displacement, hostage-taking, arbitrary detention, and looting among other violations.

FARC, Colombia's largest guerrilla group, is also guilty of not conforming to international humanitarian standards and continues to commit war crimes. In addition, FARC takes in $200 million to $400 million annually from the illegal drug trade. FARC, however, often receives more international media attention than any other group, and thus often showcases an observance of international humanitarian law for public and political advantage. Documented violations committed by FARC include massacres and targeted killings of civilians, the killings of people who have surrendered, torture, hostage-taking, looting, and attacks on nonmilitary targets like ambulances.

The UC-ELN was among the first insurgent groups in Colombia to begin an internal discussion regarding international humanitarian law. When the Colombian government initially refused to adopt Protocol II, the UC-ELN called for negotiations aimed at humanizing the armed conflict. Their openness to negotiation, however, is not reflected in their behavior in the conflict. The UC-ELN is guilty of the same violations as FARC in addition to using land mines and violating the ban on attacking nonmilitary targets by bombing Colombia's oil pipelines in order to extort money from oil companies and to bring international attention to their cause. The EPL has told human rights organizations in Colombia that it respects international humanitarian law; however, it too is guilty of committing political killings. In addition, the EPL has documented violations such as the killing of family members of guerrilla deserters, hostage-taking, and attacks on non-military targets, like public buses.

In addition to the violations listed above, all parties involved in Colombia's armed conflict are guilty of recruiting children under the age of 15 to fight and forced displacement of civilians, both war crimes that are prohibited under the international laws of war.

CHARLENE T. OVERTURF

See also: Chile; Peru

Further Reading

Braun, Herbert. *Our Guerrillas, Our Sidewalks: A Journey into the Violence in Colombia.* Lanham, MD: Rowman & Littlefield Publishers, 2003.

Dudley, Steven. *Murder and Guerrilla Politics in Colombia.* London: Routledge Press, 2006.

Human Rights Watch. *War without Quarter: Colombia and International Humanitarian Law.* New York: Human Rights Watch, 1998.

Kirk, Robin. *More Terrible Than Death: Massacres, Drugs and America's War in Colombia.* New York: Public Affairs Books, 2004.

Columbian Exchange and Disease

The incidence of epidemics in world history leading to the deaths of millions of people is not unique to the early modern period. The Justinian Plague (named after the Byzantine emperor) of late antiquity and the Black Death (in its various manifestations of bubonic plague, pneumonic plague, and septicemic plague) of the late medieval period led to the destruction of large swaths of the population of the Afro-Eurasian ecumene, with recurrences of the plague lasting well until the 18th century. However, increasing contact between the Old World and the New following Christopher Columbus's "discovery" of 1492 led to the greatest incidence in demographic change in the Americas, not only due to the migration of peoples but also the related migration of pathogens. The Columbian Exchange of disease, mostly in the form of smallpox, measles, malaria, the plague, among other pathogens, and along with other contributing factors, led to the death of an estimated 100 million people in the Americas.

These catastrophic losses of the indigenous population of the Americas, over approximately 400 years, had political, economic, and social consequences for this period.

While contact with Old World diseases is a factor for the demographic depletion after 1492 in the Americas, other factors also contributed to the mass death of millions of indigenous Americans. Incidences of warfare, dispossession of property, interbreeding, and mass killings on perpetrated by Europeans against indigenous Americans also contributed to the massive demographic loss in the Americas. The introduction of pathogens into societies with no immunity in tandem with European incursions (and Africans brought as slaves) and conquest contributed to the death of millions. Outbreaks continued as diseases new to the Americas were introduced and subsequently spread through trade routes with other indigenous groups. Some scholars suggest that some indigenous American societies never actually came into contact with Europeans or Africans and yet suffered tremendous losses after the introduction of diseases into their communities.

Historians speculate that the lack of immunity to these diseases given the lack of contact that existed led to the introduction of such pathogens into long-established societies with little to no understanding of the occurrence of such diseases. Known as "virgin soil epidemics," meaning that the populations exposed to them had no immunity to them, these diseases did have historical precedents in terms of their impact on existing societies. Much like in Europe and Asia during outbreaks of the Black Death, entire communities suffered outbreaks en masse, with large swaths of the population dying. Severely weakened by disease and with segments of the productive (such as those who procure food and forage) dead or weakened, the pandemics along with other factors, illustrate how these American societies were depleted over time. Moreover, having no prior experience with such epidemics and their societal impact, their societies were severely weakened and depleted. This contributed to the collapse of the local and regional economies, political structures, and societies as a whole.

Scientists and historians have meticulously compiled lists of diseases and epidemics that were introduced in the Americas by Europeans and Africans after 1492. While some of these are based on speculation and hypotheses, others are based on empirical archeological and historical research and data. The major diseases that afflicted the New World that originated from the Old World are the following: smallpox, diphtheria, measles, whooping cough, bubonic plague, malaria, trachoma, cholera, typhoid fever, scarlet fever, yellow fever, dengue fever, influenza, and dysentery. The overwhelming amount of diseases which arrived in waves and the lack of immunity on the part of indigenous Americans illustrate the level of the impact that Columbian exchanges of pathogens had on American populations over the next 400 years. Pockets of isolated communities, once in contact with Europeans, Africans, or other Americans, were also prone to outbreaks as recently as the mid-20th century.

The relationship between the depletion of indigenous Americans and the onset of the transatlantic slave trade is also illustrative of the impact of Old World diseases on the Americas. The inability to procure sufficient amounts of labor from the Americas by Europeans, as these societies collapsed as a result of conquest and disease, was offset by the influx of millions of black African slaves forcibly brought to the Americas. Black Africans further introduced more diseases, which exacerbated the already catastrophic situation of the indigenous Americans. As African slaves were seen as amenable and resistant to tropical conditions and diseases by their European oppressors, they were coerced to work for the cultivation and production of cash crops.

While historians do not disagree that the introduction of diseases contributed to the extermination of millions of indigenous Americans and the collapse of their civilizations, there are disagreements as to the level of complicity of other factors. It is argued that by placing the onus of the collapse and conquest of the Americas on the spread of diseases, it minimizes the level of agency on the part of European conquest and warfare. This narrative, purported by many environmental historians, proposes that it was biological immunity that doomed indigenous populations to their collapse. However, other historians, such as Alfred W. Crosby, suggest that while "virgin soil epidemics" caused the destruction of millions of Americans after 1492, other factors also contributed to the collapse of these societies. As such, all these factors have to be taken into account when discussing the history of the mass death of indigenous Americans after contact with Europeans and Africans, lest it not offer a fuller perspective of the multicausal confluence of historical processes.

ABRAHAM O. MENDOZA

See also: Indigenous Populations; Native American Genocide

Further Reading

Crosby, Alfred W., Jr. *Ecological Imperialism: The Biological Expansion of Europe, 900–1900.* New York: Cambridge University Press, 1986.

Crosby, Alfred W., Jr. *The Columbian Exchange: Biological and Cultural Consequences of 1492.* Westport, CT: Greenwood Press, 1972.

McNeill, William H. *Plagues and Peoples.* New York: Anchor Books/Doubleday, 1976.

Comfort Women

In the last decade of the 20th century, the world began to learn the tragic stories of some of the forgotten victims of World War II—the "comfort women." Those were women who were forced into sexual servitude by the Japanese Imperial Army during the war. Although Japanese, Chinese, Taiwanese, Filipino, Indonesian, and Dutch women worked as comfort women, the majority, at least 80 percent, were Korean.

"Voluntary Corps"

During World War II, over 200,000 girls and women, ages 14 to 30, were conscripted from Japan's prewar colonies and occupied territories. They were sent to the front for the duration of the war, housed in brothels, and forced by the Japanese military into institutionalized sexual slavery on a massive scale. The women were originally called "voluntary corps." Later, the Japanese government coined the term "military comfort women." Historical documents found both in Washington, D.C. and Japan indicate that the procurement of comfort women was institutionalized to prevent soldiers from raping local women, which would have encouraged local opposition; to protect soldiers from the spread of venereal disease; and to safeguard military secrets.

At the beginning of World War II, the Japanese Army brought Japanese prostitutes to the front for the soldiers. (The institution of prostitution was not prohibited legally by Japan until 1957.) However, many of the women were already infected with venereal diseases and infected the soldiers, which rendered them unfit for combat. Therefore, Japanese brokers recruited Korean village girls by offering money to their impoverished families.

Toward the end of the war, the supply of women was enlarged by more indiscriminate kidnapping of women, including married women. The Military Compulsory Draft Act (1943) allowed the Japanese Imperial Army to take more women, and as many as 70,000 to 80,000 were sent as comfort women to work in "comfort stations" on the front lines in Asia. When the war was over, many of the comfort women were deserted by the Japanese Army, while others were massacred. Some women committed suicide because they were unable to overcome the shame, and others lived in silence.

A Demand for Justice

On December 6, 1991, three Korean comfort women filed suit demanding justice for the crimes against humanity committed against them. They demanded an official apology, compensatory payment, a thorough investigation of their cases, the revision of Japanese school textbooks identifying that issue as part of the colonial oppression of the Korean people, and the building of a memorial museum.

Eighteen former comfort women from the Philippines filed a class action suit in April 1992. Subsequently, four more groups did the same. In December 1992, a public hearing was held in Tokyo at which former comfort women from six countries testified. One of the plaintiffs explained that her decision to finally disclose what had happened to her was prompted by the fact that since all her close family members had died, there was no one left who would be shamed because of her past.

On April 26, 2000, the Yamaguchi district court in southwestern Japan ruled that "the Japanese government which inherited Imperial Japan has the duty to make restitution for damage done in the war, in particular for the pain and suffering of the comfort women. Its failure to do this has resulted in increased pain suffered by victims. The comfort women system was sexual and racial discrimination, violating fundamental rights of women." The court ordered the Japanese government to pay 360,000 yen ($3,540) to each of the South Korean comfort women but said they could not direct government policy regarding the apology.

As Yet, No Official Apology

For 47 years, the Japanese government denied any role in the comfort women scheme. However, in January 1992, documents from Japan's defense agency's archives surfaced that directly linked the Japanese military with the brothels. In August 1993, the Japanese government admitted that Japanese military authorities were in constant control of women who were forced to provide sex for soldiers before and during World War II.

Since then, Japanese prime ministers have made personal apologies to the women, but they have not issued an official apology or set up an official compensation plan. They maintain that the violations against the rights of the comfort women were not in violation of the Japanese legal system existing at the time they were committed and that all claims for compensation for citizens of various countries have already been settled by virtue of the various treaties of peace with Japan negotiated after the war.

PAUL R. BARTROP

See also: China; Japan; Rape

Congo, Democratic Republic of

Nation located in central Africa. The Democratic Republic of Congo (DRC), formerly known as Zaire, and before that called The Belgian Congo, has been almost continuously engulfed by war since winning its independence in 1960. The fact that scores of people who died there were victims of war crimes is why Thomas Lubanga Dyilo was convicted of war crimes by the International Criminal Court (ICC) in March 2012. Lubanga was a Congolese nationalist and military leader. The ICC is an independent judicial body loosely affiliated with the United Nations and the International Court of Justice in The Hague. It was created in 2002 and, despite the fact the United States initially opposed it out of fear that it would be used to scrutinize American military activity, it is today supported by the United States and more than 100 other nations. The tribunal is authorized to investigate and prosecute war crimes and crimes against humanity throughout the world. Lubanga was the ICC's first defendant.

Lubanga's story is just a small part of the history of violence that has plagued the Democratic Republic of Congo since 1960. Less than a year after independence, the country was shaken by the murder of its prime minister, Patrice Lumumba, by forces loyal to army chief Joseph Mobutu. After four years of wielding influence behind the scenes, Mobutu formally seized power in 1965. Renaming himself Mobuto Sese Seko, he also renamed the country Zaire. A staunch Cold War ally of the United States, Mobutu allowed Zaire to become a staging ground for military operations against Soviet-backed Angola. In return, the Americans helped stabilize Mobutu's regime, which included the suppression of antigovernment movements. After the Cold War ended in the early 1990s, Zaire and Mobutu were no longer of interest to the United States. When Rwanda invaded Zaire in 1997 in pursuit of Hutu guerillas, anti-Mobutu forces used the opportunity to rebel, capturing the capital of Kinshasa and forcing Mobuto to flee. They then installed Laurent Kabila as president. One of Kabila's first official acts was to rename Zaire the Democratic Republic of Congo.

The nation had barely a year of respite from conflict, between 1997 and 1998. In 1998, a falling out between Kabila and his former allies ignited a civil war that would claim his life in 2001. The fighting in the DRC between 1998 and 2003, although nominally referred to as a civil war, looked more like a world war. Nearly 4 million people died and another 2 million became refugees as the country was flooded with troops from Angola, Namibia, Rwanda, Uganda, and Zimbabwe. The war also brought Thomas Lubanga to the attention of the ICC. The Lubanga-led Union of Congolese Patriots (UPC), staffed in part by child soldiers, occupied the city of Bania in 2002 and killed large numbers of civilians in the process. It was his involvement in the murders of nine United Nations peacekeepers in 2005 that prompted the Congolese government, now under the leadership of Laurent Kabila's son, Joseph, to order his arrest.

The indictments against Lubanga alleged that between 1998 and 2003 he formed and led the UPC, an armed militia operating in Ituri in the northeast of the DRC. He also received assistance from Uganda. It was while head of the UPC that Lubanga was accused of ordering murders, torture, the rape of civilians, and the forced conscription of child soldiers. At one point, the indictments alleged, Lubanga had as many as 30,000 children serving in the UPC filling roles as soldiers, cooks, carriers, and, in some cases, sexual slaves. Some were as young as 10. Allegedly, many of the children were pressed into service by their parents upon demands by Lubanga that they provide either money, livestock, or children to help the UPC.

Lubanga was held by authorities in Kinshasa while representatives from the ICC conducted an investigation. In 2006, the ICC issued a warrant for Lubanga's arrest for war crimes, and he was transferred to a Dutch prison unit in The Hague. In January 2007, a judge for the ICC announced that prosecutors had supplied sufficient evidence that Lubanga was responsible for war crimes consisting of enlisting and conscripting children under the age of 15. His trial, for the war crime of "conscripting and enlisting children under the age of fifteen years and using them to participate actively in hostilities" opened on January 26, 2009. Lubanga was found guilty on March

14, 2012. On July 10, 2012, he was sentenced to a 14-year prison term, which was reduced to 8 years to compensate for the 6 years he had spent in detention between 2006 and 2012.

JOHN MORELLO

See also: Congo Mass Rapes

Further Reading

Boustany, Nora. "Court Orders Trial for Congolese Warlord Accused of Conscripting Children." *The Washington Post*, January 30, 2007, A8.

Edgerton, Robert. *The Troubled Heart of Africa: A History of the Congo.* New York, St. Martin's Press, 2002.

Congo Free State

The Congo Free State, situated in south-central Africa's Congo River Basin, existed from 1885 until 1908. During those years, the region was personally controlled by Belgian King Leopold II, who exercised complete and final authority over the area and its people. After the horrific abuses that occurred in the Congo Free State were publicized in the early years of the 20th century, Leopold's personal and solitary control of the Congo basin ended, and the area became known as the Belgian Congo on November 15, 1908. The Belgian Congo remained a Belgian colony, under the supervision of the Parliament and king, until it achieved independence in 1960. Leopold's reign of terror was driven primarily by greed, and it exacted a terrible toll on the Congolese people; estimates vary, but it is generally assumed that as many as 10 million Congolese died in the Congo Free State roughly between 1885 and 1908. Precise data concerning deaths and specific atrocities are not well documented or known because Leopold ordered the systematic destruction of most documents relating to the Congo Free State in order to cover his tracks.

What made Leopold's strangle hold on the Congo even more unsettling was the duplicitous way in which he insinuated himself into the region. By the mid-1870s, the king was well aware of the riches of raw materials that lay untapped in the Congo Basin. The area was awash in ivory and rubber, which commanded high prices in the developed world. The Congo was also rich in other commodities and minerals, such as copper. Couching his interest in strictly humanitarian terms, Leopold sponsored conferences in Brussels to attract explorers, geographers, and philanthropists, whom he hoped to attract to the Congo

Basin in order to improve the lives of its people, although his real mission was to exploit the land and its people. Before long, he had gained the financial and intellectual support of a number of governments and individuals, both in Europe and America. All along, Leopold planned on eventually seizing the region for himself.

In the early 1880s, Leopold founded the International Association of the Congo, a political front organization that would legitimize his activities and act as conduit by which he could exercise control over the Congo. During the 1884–1885 Berlin Conference, in which leading imperial nations tried to codify and rationalize African colonialism, Leopold's Association of the Congo officially became the Congo Free State on May 29, 1885, under the personal suzerainty of King Leopold.

Leopold, his bogus humanitarian goals not withstanding, soon established a sweeping colonial bureaucracy and internal defense force (Force Publique, FP) in the Congo that had but one goal: attaining maximum profits with minimal expenses. To accomplish this, he decreed that all land not currently inhabited or cultivated be turned over to his control (this was in fact the majority of the region's land). His agents, in turn, would be free to exploit the land for natural resources. By the early 1890s, the king had issued another sweeping decree, which forbade Congo's indigenous peoples from selling products they personally harvested (chiefly rubber and ivory) to any other party except his Congo Free State. Because Leopold's administration exercised complete control over the prices of such commodities, he could dictate how much money—if any—the Congolese people would get for these products. All income flowed into Leopold's coffers, and private extraction and trading companies were thus driven out of the region. In 1892, Leopold did grant partial concessions to two privately held companies, but he was able to control the land they worked, the indigenous labor force they exploited, and the amount of income they received from the harvesting or extraction of various commodities.

Because Leopold had gained complete control of the Congo Free State's economy and labor force, he, along with his colonial cronies, bureaucrats, and the two concession companies, essentially dictated the lives of the vast majority of Congolese. The system imposed on them was ghastly and inhumane. They were forced to labor at backbreaking work with miniscule pay, little to eat, and few if any medical facilities. The colonial bureaucracy, which was corrupt to the core, instilled in the population a sense of abject fear and hopelessness. Bribery was rife, and colonial officials often played favorites and encouraged the Congolese people to spy on one another to ensure that everyone was working at peak efficiency. The FP was tasked with maintaining order and, more critically, with enforcing rubber and ivory quotas, which it did quite brutally.

The FP employed white, European officers and black indigenous soldiers. Armed with firearms and the chicotte—the ubiquitous bull whip—the FP burned villages, raped women, tortured and whipped recalcitrant workers, and killed perhaps hundreds of thousands. The FP's soldiers were required to cut off the hands of their victims (sometimes while they were still alive) to prove that they had done their job and had not wasted ammunition on hunting or other activities. Rubber quotas were often measured in the number of severed hands an FP company could produce. The taking of human hands became so pervasive that some villages raided other villages just to harvest the appendages to meet the quota. Many Congolese also turned on each other in the quest to gather the most severed hands.

A junior white officer in the FP wrote about a raid on a Congolese village that had balked at the unrealistic rubber quotas. He reported that the FP entered the village, beheaded its male inhabitants, and hung their heads from a nearby palisade. The women and children, after being shot, were hung from the same palisade, in the form of a crude cross. The harvesting of rubber in the Congo was particularly harsh because it was taken from vines instead of trees. Workers would often cut the vines and coat their bodies with the liquefied rubber. When it hardened, they scraped it off their skin, resulting in skin abrasions and worse.

After considerable international scrutiny and outrage, Leopold's cruel reign ended in 1908. This by no means freed the Congolese people from colonial abuses, but the worst of the atrocities subsided. The death toll of 10 million includes those Congolese killed directly by colonial authorities, malnutrition, disease and infection, intervillage conflict, and labor. It is estimated that 20 percent of the entire Congolese population died as a result of the exploitative, forced-labor system alone. The exploitation and inhumanity of the Leopold era left an indelible imprint of the Congolese, and their nation remains a deeply troubled society today.

PAUL G. PIERPAOLI JR.

See also: Congo, Democratic Republic of

Further Reading

Edgerton, Robert. *The Troubled Heart of Africa: A History of the Congo.* New York, St. Martin's Press, 2002.

Nzongola-Ntalaja, Georges. *The Congo: From Leopold to Kabila: A People's History.* London: Zed Books, 2002.

Congo Mass Rapes

The Democratic Republic of the Congo, located in central Africa, has gained the unfortunate reputation of being the rape capital of the world. Rape has been used as a weapon of war in Congo since 1996, when Rwandan troops entered the eastern part of the region to stop attacks upon their country. Uganda and Burundi subsequently entered the fray in support of Rwanda. The forces opposed to the Rwandans include the Mai-Mai, armed groups of Rwanda Hutus, and Burundian rebels of the Forces for the Defense of Democracy (FDD) and the Front for National Liberation (FNL). By 2011, the conflict, arguably the world's largest civil war, had claimed more than 5 million lives.

All of the groups fighting in Congo have frequently and sometimes systematically raped women and girls. Men have also been the target of sexual assaults since at least 2010, but these attacks are not mass rapes. In many cases, combatants raped women and girls as part of a widespread attack against villages in which they killed and injured civilians and destroyed property. Such attacks aimed to terrorize communities into ceding control to the attackers. The assaults were also designed to punish villages for real or alleged aid to opposing forces, particularly if the attacking force had recently come under fire. The International Rescue Committee, a group formed in 1933 to assist refugees, estimates that tens of thousands of women and girls have suffered rapes, which leave them physically wounded and emotionally traumatized. The social effects of such attacks include rejection and stigmatization by families and communities. One Rwanda woman reported that she could not comfortably walk through her villages because her neighbors would taunt her with the name, "*Maman Kubakwa*" (raped woman).

The United Nations and various other nongovernmental agencies have been active in Congo to reduce tensions and speed healing and reconciliation, but they have had limited effect. North and South Kivu remain hot spots of violence. Despite peace agreements in 2003 and 2008, mass rapes continue to occur. A 2010 study of rape survivors by the Harvard Humanitarian Initiative and Oxfam revealed that almost 60 percent had been gang raped. The ages of victims ranged from 3 to 80 and spanned all ethnicities.

CARYN E. NEUMANN

See also: Congo, Democratic Republic of; Rape; United Nations

Further Reading

Csete, Joanne. *The War within the War: Sexual Violence against Women and Girls in Eastern Congo.* New York: Human Rights Watch, 2002.

Kippenberg, Juliane. *Soldiers Who Rape, Commanders Who Condone: Sexual Violence and Military Reform in the Democratic Republic of Congo.* New York: Human Rights Watch, 2009.

Cultural Revolution

The Cultural Revolution was a violent political movement launched in the People's Republic of China (PRC) by Chinese leader Mao Zedong during 1966–1969, although its influence was felt into the mid-1970s. The Cultural Revolution led to 2 million deaths, mostly the professional and educated class of Chinese people.

Mao termed the Cultural Revolution (CR) his "lifetime achievement" apart from leading the successful 1949 revolution. Some have compared its significance to the 1917 Bolshevik Revolution in Russia, but it has also been seen as a clash of personalities, ideologies, and policies between Mao and President Liu Shaoqi, the second most powerful figure in the PRC. Mao sought to use the CR to enhance his authority. High-ranking CR proponents included Mao, Premier Zhou Enlai, Foreign Minister Chen Yi, and Defense Minister Lin Biao. On the other hand, the so-called capitalists who opposed the CR dominated the Chinese Communist Party's (CCP) Politburo, Central Committee, regional bureaus, and provincial party committees, including the crucial Beijing unit. They included Liu, General Secretary of the CCP Deng Xiaoping, Beijing mayor Peng Zhen, chief of the People's Liberation Army (PLA) general staff Luo Ruiqing, and Marshal He Long.

These groups differed over the handling of contradictions inside and outside the CCP in regard to society, culture, and the economy. Among the contentious issues was whether the CCP should be revived with new socialist ideals or maintained predominantly as a bureaucratic entity. The two sides also clashed on the collectivization of agriculture, moral/material incentives, and self-reliance versus free markets. The rift also pitted the Maoist mass line model advocating a continuing class struggle against those capitalists who advocated economic development and modernization as a means to achieve superpower status.

External factors also drove the CR, including the Sino-Soviet split, the Soviet Union's revisionist peaceful coexistence with the West, and antipathy toward supporting developing nations. Liu was labeled a "Chinese Khrushchev" during the CR, in reference to Soviet leader Nikita Khrushchev's reforms of the 1950s.

The 16-point guidelines issued on August 8, 1966, initiated the CR, although the more immediate catalyst was Beijing vice-mayor Wu Han's play *Hai Rui's Dismissal from Office,* an allegory about a Ming Dynasty official's vindication after being forced from his post. The play indirectly referred to former defense minister Peng Dehuai's 1959 removal from office following the Lushan Conference, when Peng criticized Mao for the disastrous Great Leap Forward. Radicals within the Politburo, including the Gang of Four clique comprising Mao's wife Jiang Qing and Shanghai-based Communist Party members Wang Hongwen, Zhang Chunqiao, and Yao Wenyuan, responded in late 1965 with countercritiques, one by Yao to the Shanghai newspapers and a literary critique from Jiang, that rallied the opponents of Peng.

Once Mao in August and September 1966 accorded legitimacy to the CR through the medium of the big-character poster, the movement spread across the PRC. Soon, a three-in-one system was formed, comprised of the military, revolutionary cadres, and representatives of the masses. In March 1967, they were tasked with carrying forward the revolution. The CCP's Central Committee thereby lost its influence to the Central Cultural Revolution Small Group, made up of radicals loyal to Mao. The so-called Red Guards, tasked with replacing "old world with new world," were one of the main proselytizers of the CR movement.

Beginning in August 1966, the Red Guards carried out actions against the Four Olds: old ideas, old culture, old customs, and old habits. In the process, they condemned, humiliated, and often brutalized or killed Communist Party cadres and corrupt revisionist authorities accused of taking the capitalist road and criticized petit bourgeois teachers. PRC military and security forces were ordered to support the revolutionary masses of the Left and, in the latter phases of the CR, to restore order in the chaotic society and economy. In January 1967, Mao pressed the PLA to restore order in the country, and by April 1969 the CCP's Ninth Congress declared the CR at an end.

The effects of the CR were numerous. Liu, in ailing health, was imprisoned and denied medical treatment. He died in prison of diabetes in 1969. Peng, Luo, and others were purged. Many students were sent to rural outposts to learn from peasants in 1968. Thousands of households considered bourgeois were ransacked and their occupants killed. Priceless cultural artifacts, regarded as feudal or capitalist anachronisms, were smashed or otherwise destroyed. Over the long term, the CR also led to the erosion of the CCP's political authority. The CCP's June 27, 1981, Resolutions on Questions of Party History stated that the CR had imposed a "severe setback and the heaviest losses suffered by the party, state, and the people" since 1949.

SRIKANTH KONDAPALLI

See also: China; Great Leap Forward; Mao Zedong; Tibet Annexation

Further Reading

Daubier, Jean. *A History of the Chinese Cultural Revolution.* Translated by Richard Seaver. New York: Vintage, 1974.

Robinson, Thomas, ed. *The Cultural Revolution in China.* Berkeley: University of California Press, 1971.

Schoenhals, Michael, ed. *China's Cultural Revolution, 1966–1969: Not a Dinner Party.* Armonk, NY: M. E. Sharpe, 1996.

D

D'Aubuisson, Roberto

Roberto D'Aubuisson was a right-wing political and military figure in El Salvador who was linked to El Salvador's notorious right-wing death squads, who served as president of the country's Constituent Assembly from 1982 to 1983.

Roberto D'Aubuisson Arrieta was born on April 23, 1943, in Santa Tecla and entered a military academy at age 15. After graduation he joined the National Guard, specializing in intelligence and national security. He also studied abroad at private police academies in the United States, including the International Police Academy, which was subsequently closed by the U.S. Congress for teaching techniques of torture.

In the late 1970s, d'Aubuisson formed links with right-wing paramilitary organizations in El Salvador and allegedly formed the Union de Guerreros Blancos (Union of White Warriors), a death squad that openly declared responsibility for many killings. As a result of a coup in 1979, D'Aubuisson went into exile as the moderate Christian Democrats assumed power. He subsequently formed a series of political parties, most notably the Nationalist Republican Alliance in 1981, to fight the land reforms and bank nationalizations of the Christian Democrats. There is evidence that he masterminded the murder of Attorney General Mario Zamara Rivas, a Christian Democrat he labeled a communist, and Archbishop Oscar Arnulfo Romero, a champion of the poor. He also led a failed coup attempt in 1980. Two months after Romero's March 1980 assassination, D'Aubuisson and his supporters were arrested on a farm, where recovered evidence implicated D'Aubuisson in organizing and financing death squads and planning a coup d'état to depose the Revolutionary Government Junta (JRG) governing El Salvador. Denouncing the JRG, D'Aubuisson openly spoke in a 1981 interview to the *Washington Post,* "of the need to kill 200,000 to 300,000 people to restore peace to El Salvador."

Backed by the wealthy "Fourteen Families" of El Salvador and private U.S. interests, D'Aubuisson and his right-wing coalition assumed control of a newly elected Constituent Assembly in April 1982, and D'Aubuisson became its president. The Ronald Reagan administration at first supported this coalition in hopes of more moderate policies, but d'Aubuisson soon intensified his right-wing tactics and suspended his modest land reform proposals. Other government members, fearing loss of peasant support and U.S. aid, withdrew their support and pushed him out of the 1984 election, which was won by moderate Jose Napoleon Duarte.

In 1987, Duarte's government began the process of bringing D'Aubuisson to trial for his involvement in the 1980 killing of Romero, but in 1989 the case collapsed when evidence was ruled inadmissible. That same year, a right-wing government returned to power in El Salvador, and D'Aubuisson began to rebuild his influence. He died of cancer on February 20, 1992.

ALEXANDER MIKABERIDZE

See also: Death Squads; El Salvador

Further Reading

Stanley, William D. *The Protection Racket State: Elite Politics, Military Extortion, and Civil War in El Salvador.* Philadelphia: Temple University Press, 1996.

White, Christopher M. *The History of El Salvador.* Westport, CT: Greenwood Press, 2009.

Death Squads

Terror groups employed by modern states. Death squads are one of the primary instruments of state terrorism and repression. These squads, with their ability to circumvent a nation's bureaucracy and laws in order to eliminate potential internal threats, are an extension of state security by other means. Death squads can serve political purposes as well as operate on a cultural level or as a means of social control. The death squad phenomenon can arise during times of state formation, transition, or crisis to ensure political and social control under authoritarian or democratic governments.

The death squad phenomenon has arisen with the advent of the modern state. The vertical division of responsibilities within the modern state among national, regional, and local levels, and horizontally between various agencies and departments has facilitated the rise of death squads as well as their deniability by the state as various bureaucracies at all levels operate with greater autonomy. Division of state responsibilities in Weimar Germany fostered an environment in which death squads could operate. A number of government and military officials, particularly at the regional and local level, favored the existence of death squads as a supplement to Germany's weakened security forces. The Weimar paramilitary death squads acted covertly so as not to stir up public opinion; the state, meanwhile, an infant democracy, was able to plausibly deny their existence. Meanwhile, the justice system turned a blind eye to the squads' violence by not prosecuting their crimes or, when prosecuted, by handing down lenient sentences, especially when said crimes had been committed against members of the political left by those of the right.

Death squads tend to be clandestine organizations. The covert, paramilitary nature of death squads provides states with a measure of deniability and unaccountability.

The squads conduct extrajudicial acts of violence to eliminate potential enemies of the government. These enemies can range from armed insurgents, who fight against the state, political opponents and members of opposition parties, and individuals suspected of subversive activity. While death squad activities often begin with relatively specific targets, the violence may spiral out of control as the definition of subversive activity expands and death squads are used to preemptively suppress all resistance. The Ministry for State Security (Stasi) in the former German Democratic Republic (GDR, East Germany), although acting covertly, effectively created an environment of fear and uncertainty in which everyone was suspect and watched. Up to 50 percent of the GDR's citizens served in the Stasi or were informants at one time or another. The Stasi would covertly make people disappear for interrogation, arrest, imprisonment, or to be turned as informants. Some victims, however, never returned home after being held in Stasi prisons. While the Stasi tended to act clandestinely, they effectively created an environment of fear, which was intended to preemptively deter any subversive activity, whether in rhetoric or action, against the communist regime.

The means utilized by death squads included murder, rape, kidnapping, and torture. The members of the squad that conduct such acts of violence were often immune to state judicial systems. In Uganda, the government of Idi Amin sought to create a superficial appearance of legality and structure that provided its death squads with an environment in which they could operate unchecked. Military tribunals were set up that acted alongside the regular court system. While the tribunals tried both civilians and soldiers, they were not subject to civilian or constitutional oversight. Death squads were thus able to operate in a vacuum with no fear of punishment from the state.

While death squads may carry out extrajudicial violence, many of their members are closely associated with the state. Death squad members often belong to legitimate security organizations within the state, such as police forces, the military, or intelligence agencies. Although closely tied to the state, death squads make no pretense about carrying out legitimate violence. They wear no uniforms and make no indication of their leaders. The secretive, extrajudicial nature of the squads provides the state with the ability to plausibly deny the squads existence or connection to the state. In Guatemala, in order to avoid state accountability for death squad activities, victims simply disappeared.

Death squads, while instruments of domestic state terrorism, also have an international dimension. In many cases where death squad violence occurs in poor countries, a powerful country will act as a sponsor. The arms industry, the largest industry in the world, provides the arena for states and corporations such as the United States, Russia, and other Western governments to influence and support state terror throughout the world. Weapons sold to dictators or foreign security bodies provide the means for state-sponsored repression through death squads. In Northern Ireland, Britain covertly aided and colluded with Loyalist paramilitary groups and death squads in their struggle against the Irish Republican Army (IRA). British intelligence agencies supplied the Loyalists with arms and intelligence about Catholics. While Britain may no longer have been the great colonial power that it once was, collusion with the Loyalists was an extension of British colonial policy in Ireland.

In addition to being instruments of policy, whether domestic or foreign, death squads can also serve as a means of social control. During the "dirty war" in El Salvador, military officers, many of whom were also involved in death squads, thought of guerillas as a virus that was corrupting society and thus needed to be eradicated. The health of the state, as an organic body, was the first priority of the security organizations and led to the killings of not only guerillas, but also their families. Death squads may also be used to maintain the social status quo. White violence in the American South, particularly by the Ku Klux Klan, against black men and their families occurred periodically during times of social tension, such as during Reconstruction, the post-World War II period, and the Civil Rights Movement. This violence included lynching, public dismemberments, or beatings to terrorize the black community into submission so that it would not challenge the power of white elites and the social status quo.

Death squads often utilize fear as a weapon in order to maintain social control. Although death squads as organizations tend to be covert, their actions can be quite public. Headlines and publicity spread fear throughout the population. Deliberately fostering an environment of fear is a means of social control used by death squads to terrorize potential resistance into submission. In El Salvador, civil conflict throughout the 1980s led to the emergence of publicity seeking death squads. Mutilated corpses were a common sight during this time of strife. In some cases, EM, short for Escaudrón de la Muerte (or death squad), was carved into the bodies as a warning of what would happen

to those who defied the government. This was not the only incidence of the overt existence of death squads in El Salvador. Roberto D'Aubuisson's Nationalist Republican Alliance (ARENA), a legitimate political party, possessed its own security force in the form of the Secret Anticommunist Army (ESA), which became the public face of the party's death squad.

The consideration of cultural norms influences the development of death squads' tactics and makes them all the more effective in spreading fear and preventing resistance. In Argentina, disappearances occurred frequently during the civil strife between 1976 and 1982. Like in Guatemala, forced disappearances left the families and communities of the victims in a chronic state of fear and uncertainty, yet more importantly, the disappearances in Argentina also provided evidence as to how death squads operated on a cultural level. In Argentina, the corpse plays a significant role in burial rituals because of the perceived connection between ideas, spirit, and body. The void left by disappearances, rather than overt executions, left the families and communities completely terror-stricken and in a state of limbo, with no body, thus preventing them from seeking revenge.

Terrorizing people on a cultural level is not unique to Argentina's death squads. The insurgency in Kashmir, India also provides a good example of how death squads used cultural values to repress opposition. The Indian troops preyed on Muslim cultural values regarding sexuality in an attempt to so thoroughly terrorize and humiliate the Kashmiri Muslims that they would be incapable of resistance. Indian troops attacked Kashmiri men by raping their women. Serbian paramilitary units also employed this tactic during the ethnic conflicts in the former Yugoslavia as they raped Bosnian Muslim women in an effort to humiliate the men into submission.

The death squad has arisen within the modern state as a means of extrajudicial security. It is a global phenomenon funded, supplied, and tacitly supported by the modern state system. Cultural and societal norms shape death squad tactics, but the ultimate goal remains the same: using violence to retain power and maintain the social and political status quo.

Robyn Rodriguez

See also: D'Aubuisson, Roberto; El Salvador

Further Reading

Campbell, Bruce B. and Arthur D. Brenner, eds. *Death Squads in Global Perspective: Murder with Deniability.* New York: St. Martin's Press, 2000.

Menjívar, Cecilia, and Néstor Rodríguez. *When States Kill: Latin America, the U.S., and Technologies of Terror.* Austin: University of Texas Press, 2005.

Sluka, Jeffrey A., ed. *Death Squad: Anthropology of State Terror.* Philadelphia: University of Pennsylvania Press, 2000.

Dekulakization

Dekulakization was a Soviet government policy aimed at eliminating the kulaks throughout the Soviet Union and its constituent republics, roughly between 1929 and 1933. Ukraine boasted a large number of kulaks, and they suffered grievously during the forced collectivization of agriculture and the mass starvation of 1931–1933 (the Holomodor). Kulak was a term used to describe and classify relatively affluent farmers in the late Russian Empire and the early years of the Soviet Union. After the Soviets came to power in Russia in the early 1920s, they classified peasants into three large categories: bednyaks (poor farmers); serednyaks (middle-income farmers); and kulaks (high-income farmers). The early Soviets believed that only the bednyaks were capable of joining the proletariat (industrial working class) in a Leninist-inspired revolution; the kulaks, on the other hand, were viewed as "class enemies" because they owned their own land and had relatively high incomes. During the first phase of the Russian Revolution, that began in November 1917, peasants who had refused to provide the Red Army with grain and other supplies were labeled "kulaks," and were often subjected to violence and intimidation. That general view of this group carried over into the early Soviet period.

In 1929, Soviet general secretary Joseph Stalin ordered the complete collectivization of Soviet agriculture, which was part of the larger First Five Year Plan. That scheme was designed to modernize and industrialize the Soviet Union in a relatively short period of time. Collectivization meant that farmers would no longer own their own land or livestock and that agricultural policy would be established by the central government and be carried out on collective farms. By early 1930, Soviet policy embraced the concept that kulaks, were to be eliminated as a group, a concept dubbed dekulakization. Some would be sent to gulags (prisons) or executed; others would be deported to distant and isolated parts of the country (like Siberia), while the remainder would be deported within their home provinces where they would be forced to live and toil on collective farms. Soon, even farmers who owned a few livestock (but no land) were classified as kulaks. Stalin's ultimate goal was more than collectivization—he sought to assert Soviet control over the entirety of the countryside and eliminate any vestiges of capitalism and nationalism.

Ukraine had a large number of kulaks, and so the policies put in place in the early 1930s had a profound effect on all Ukrainians, whether they were farmers or not. Many Ukrainian kulaks resisted collectivization, choosing to plow under crops and slaughter their livestock rather than turn them over to the state. By 1934, the Soviet government estimated that 26.6 million head of cattle had been killed along with 63.4 million sheep. This widespread slaughter, combined with failed and plowed-under crops precipitated a major famine during 1932–1933, which hit the Ukrainians very hard.

Many kulaks were either murdered on their own land, or died after being deported or imprisoned. Between 1930 and 1937, some estimates claim that as many as 4–5 million peasants in Ukraine, many of them kulaks, perished. The enormity of these developments did not come to full light until the collapse of the Soviet Union in 1991.

Paul G. Pierpaoli Jr.

See also: Cannibalism in the Holodomor; Class enemies; First Five Year Plan; Kulaks; People's Commissariat for Internal Affairs (NKVD); Soviet Collectivization; Soviet Grain Requisition Policies; Soviet Union; Stalin, Joseph; Ukrainian Starvation (Holodomor)

Further Reading

Conquest, Robert. *The Harvest of Sorrow: Soviet Collectivization and the Terror-Famine.* New York: Oxford University Press, 1987.

Conquest, Robert. *Reflections on a Ravaged Century.* New York: W.W. Norton, 2000.

Kiernan, Ben. *Blood and Soil: A World History of Genocide and Extermination from Sparta to Darfur.* New Haven, CT: Yale University Press, 2007.

Democide

In its most inclusive form, democide refers to the murder of an individual or individuals by a government entity. Democide can encompass genocide, although not all genocides are democides, the main difference being that genocide typically involves the mass killing of people because of their specific group characteristics, such as race, ethnicity, nationality, or religion. Democide does not always or even necessarily involve the eradication of a specific group, and it may involve both intentional deaths and unintentional deaths. Thus, the government killing of political opponents can be considered democide, but so too can government indifference toward pollution, for instance, especially when a government knows about the pollution and its consequences but does nothing to stop it from killing people.

The political scientist Rudolph J. Rummel is credited with having popularized the term democide, which he defines as "the murder of any person or people by a government, including genocide, politicide, and mass murder." Rummel has argued that deaths from democide, particularly in the 20th century, have far surpassed deaths through war. He also asserts that the aggregation of concentrated political power has resulted in ever-increasing bouts of democide and the attendant increase in deaths from it. Oftentimes, democide has been used in a legal context to describe governmental killing of political opponents, or government-sponsored mass killings that may or may not rise to the level of genocide. Rummel is careful to exclude from his definition battle deaths, capital punishment, and collateral civilian deaths during wartime, namely in cases in which the principal target was not civilians but rather military installations.

Some examples of democide include North Korean government policies since the 1980s that resulted in the mass starvation of large portions of its population, Chinese leader Mao Zedong's Great Leap Forward effort of the late 1950s and early 1960s, and Soviet leader Josef Stalin's politically motivated and murderous purges of the 1930s.

PAUL G. PIERPAOLI JR.

See also: Class enemies; Ethnic Cleansing; Total War

Further Reading

Rummel, R. J. *Death by Government.* Piscataway, NJ: Transaction Publishers, 1997.

Rummel, R. J. *Democide: Nazi Genocide and Mass Murder.* Piscataway, NJ: Transaction Publishers, 1991.

Dresden Bombing

Allied strategic bombing raid against the German city of Dresden. This operation, conducted from February 13 to 15, 1945, has become the most commonly evoked image to illustrate the excesses and horror of conventional bombing of cities. The firestorm caused by Royal Air Force (RAF) Bomber Command on the night of February 13 rivaled

that of the raid on Hamburg of July 27, 1943. The immediate controversy about the raid contributed to the end of Allied strategic bombing. Cold War rhetoric and sensationalist presentations in history books and movies have clouded the facts ever since.

At the Yalta Conference on February 4, 1945, the Soviets asked for Allied air attacks on communication centers to prevent the shifting of German troops to the Eastern Front. They specifically mentioned Berlin and Leipzig, but Allied planners also identified Dresden and Chemnitz as appropriate objectives to meet Soviet needs. On February 8, Supreme Headquarters, Allied Expeditionary Forces (SHAEF) instructed RAF Bomber Command and the U.S. Strategic Air Forces to prepare an attack on Dresden because of its importance in relation to movements of military forces to the Eastern Front. Contrary to later reports, Dresden did contain many important industrial and transportation targets, and it was defended, although many of its guns had been sent east to fight the Soviets. The allocation of effort was also shaped by the prodding of British Prime Minister Winston L. S. Churchill, although he later tried to distance himself from the operation and the atmosphere engendered by the pursuit of Operation THUNDERCLAP. The latter was a British plan to break German morale with a massive Allied assault on the German capital, Berlin, and refugee centers. The attack on Berlin was conducted on February 3 over the protests of U.S. Eighth Air Force Commander James Doolittle. Other Americans in the U.S. Strategic Air Forces headquarters and in Washington were also uneasy over concentrating on cities such as Dresden, but that did not stop the operation.

The operation opened on the night of February 13 with two separate British raids. The first blow was delivered by 244 Lancasters dropping more than 800 tons of bombs. This attack was moderately successful. The inhabitants of the city were surprised with a second attack three hours later, this time by 529 Lancasters delivering a further 1,800 tons of bombs. The concentrated accuracy of the bombing against so many wooden structures and during ideal weather conditions produced a terrible conflagration. The smoke and flames made aiming very difficult the next day for the more than 300 American B-17s attempting to drop another 700 tons of bombs on the city's marshaling yards. Obscuration of the target area was even worse for a similar attack on February 15.

When news of the destruction of Dresden reached Britain, there was considerable public outcry over the destruction of such a beautiful city when the war seemed to be virtually won. American air leaders were worried by similar reactions in the United States, especially after careless remarks by a SHAEF briefing officer inspired such nationwide newspaper headlines as "Terror Bombing Gets Allied Approval as Step to Speed Victory." Secretary of War Henry Stimson ordered an investigation of the "unnecessary" destruction, but was satisfied by the resulting report explaining the background of the operation. Public reaction in the United States was muted. The controversy contributed to the Allied decision to suspend strategic bombing in April.

The casualty figures reported by German fire and police services ranged between 25,000 and 35,000 dead. However, thousands more were missing, and there were many unidentified refugees in the city. It is probable that the death total approached the 45,000 killed in the bombing of Hamburg in July-August 1943. Some careless historians, encouraged by Soviet and East German propaganda, promulgated figures as high as 250,000. Although David Irving later recanted his claim of 135,000 dead, one can still find that number cited in many history books.

Public impressions of the excesses of Dresden were reinforced by Kurt Vonnegut's novel *Slaughterhouse Five* and the movie it inspired. More than 50 years later, when critics of U.S. air operations against Iraq or Yugoslavia needed a metaphor to condemn conventional bombing attacks on cities, almost invariably they cited Dresden in 1945.

CONRAD C. CRANE

See also: Hamburg Raids; Tokyo Bombing; United States; World War II Atrocities, European Theater

Further Reading

Crane, Conrad C. *Bombs, Cities, and Civilians: American Airpower Strategy in World War II.* Lawrence: University Press of Kansas, 1993.

Irving, David. *The Destruction of Dresden.* New York: Ballantine, 1965.

Taylor, Frederick. *Dresden: Tuesday, February 13, 1945.* New York: HarperCollins, 2004.

Duranty, Walter

Walter Duranty was a controversial English-born American journalist who for years was known for his pro-Soviet sympathies and who gained widespread notoriety for his denial of the 1932–1933 Holodomor (mass Ukrainian starvation) in the Soviet Union.

Duranty was born in Liverpool, England on May 25, 1884, and attended college in England before moving to Paris to become a journalist. He reported on World War I, and first gained attention with an article he wrote on the 1919 Paris Peace Conference. In 1921, he went to the Soviet Union, beginning a long journalistic career covering events in that nation. The next year, he secured a position with the *New York Times* as that publication's bureau chief in Moscow, a post he retained for more than 13 years. His reporting from the Soviet Union was largely uncritical. Duranty arranged an exclusive interview with Soviet leader Joseph Stalin in 1929, the coverage of which brought him much attention in the United States and Europe. His reporting on the Soviet Union during the early 1930s garnered him a Pulitzer Prize in 1932 and nearly universal name recognition.

Duranty's reporting, however, left many experts perplexed concerning his interpretation of the Soviet Union and its leaders, and it continues to be controversial. He asserted that Russians were communally oriented and thus could only function under a regimented, autocratic regime. Attempts to westernize Russia, he continued, were relics of European colonialism that were doomed ultimately to fail. Vladimir Lenin, he argued, failed in his attempts to remake Russian society because his ideas contained too many Western prescriptions. Stalin, however, Duranty opined, did not regard himself as a dictator; rather, he was the guardian of Stalinism, a new way of governing the Russians that would bring them peace and prosperity. Stalin's infamous Five-Year Plans, the journalist asserted, were necessary to bring about the modernization of the Soviet Union and prosperity for its people. In June 1931, Duranty reported on the collectivization of Soviet agriculture, arguing that it was necessary for the reformation of Soviet society.

By 1933, however, Duranty had inserted himself into the growing controversy regarding mass starvation in Ukraine (the Holodomor). In an August 1933 article in the *New York Times,* he argued that "any report of a famine in Russia today is an exaggeration or malignant propaganda." After British journalist Gareth Jones reported on the famine in Ukraine, Duranty penned a sharp rebuke of Duranty's findings, terming them gross distortions fueled by the ongoing diplomatic rift between London and Moscow. Malcolm Muggeridge, of the *Manchester* (England) *Guardian,* termed Duranty "a liar." Despite this controversy, Duranty retained his position in Moscow and was held in high esteem by many mainstream journalists. Duranty returned to the United States in 1934 and remained a special correspondent for the *New York Times* until 1940.

He also wrote a number of books, most of them detailing his reporting on and travels to the Soviet Union; all were largely uncritical of the Soviet regime.

With the advent of the Cold War in the years immediately following World War II, Duranty became marginalized and was unable to secure jobs in journalism because of what many perceived to be his pro-Soviet reporting. By then, pro-Soviet journalists and writers were being labeled as communists amid the Second Red Scare. He earned money chiefly from book royalties and from lectures he frequently gave. By the early 1950s, and with the advent of McCarthyism in the United States, Duranty had jettisoned his former pro-Russian views and embraced anticommunism. After retiring to Florida, Duranty died in relative obscurity in Orlando on October 3, 1957.

Many years after his death, historians took Duranty to task for ignoring the Holodomor until it was nearly over.

Duranty never fully acknowledged the tragedy, nor did he seem to grasp its enormity or legacy. In 2003, the Ukrainian Canadian Civil Liberties Association formally appealed to the Pulitzer Board, requesting that it posthumously revoke Duranty's 1932 Pulitzer Prize. The Board refused to do so, however, noting that the prize was awarded not for Duranty's coverage of the Holodomor, but rather for his coverage of Soviet society in general.

PAUL G. PIERPAOLI JR.

See also: Jones, Gareth; Stalin, Joseph; Ukrainian Starvation (Holodomor)

Further Reading

Conquest, Robert. *The Harvest of Sorrow: Soviet Collectivization and the Terror-Famine.* New York: Oxford University Press, 1987.

Taylor, S. J. *Stalin's Apologist: Walter Duranty: The New York Times' Man in Moscow.* New York: Oxford University Press, 1990.

E

Egypt

Since Egypt cast off the last vestiges of foreign domination when King Farouk was overthrown in 1953, this ancient Middle Eastern nation has seen more than its fair share of human rights abuses and atrocities. Indeed, Farouk's ouster was preceded by massive rioting in Cairo in January 1952 that resulted in 26 deaths; another 552 were wounded. In April 1954, Gamal Abdel Nasser assumed full control over Egypt's government, becoming its first president. Nasser's regime immediately banned the Islamist Muslim Brotherhood, arresting many of its members and driving others out of the country. To modernize his country and to improve its economy, Nasser embraced state-imposed socialism. Nasser's rule was often heavy-handed, and it tolerated little in the way of opposition or criticism. The large and intrusive internal security force routinely arrested and detained citizens for long periods of time and without formal charges. Perhaps the most egregious atrocity during the Nasser era occurred on April 8, 1970, during the War of Attrition with Israel. Israeli aircraft mistook an elementary school in Bahr-el-Baqar for a military facility and bombed it. The attack killed 46 children under the age of 11.

In the wake of Nasser's death in 1970, Anwar Sadat assumed the Egyptian presidency. He moved to undue Nasser's statist economic policies, eventually embracing Intifah (Economic Opening) by the mid-1970s. For a time, he also relaxed the political climate, freeing Muslim Brotherhood prisoners and encouraging Muslim student groups to organize as counterpoints to the leftists who opposed his policies. In January 1977, however, Sadat's decision to lift subsidies on food products provoked huge riots in a number of Egyptian cities including Cairo. At least 75 people died in the so-called Bread Riots; another 500–1,000 were arrested by security forces.

After Sadat sought peace with Israel in the late 1970s, his regime came under much criticism at home. This forced him to crack down on political dissidents on both the left and right and to move against Islamist groups, who abhorred any accommodation with the Israelis. In September 1981, Sadat ordered the arrest of nearly 2,000 suspected opponents, including Jihadists, the Coptic Christian pope and many of his clergy, as well as a number of activists and intellectuals. This move proved highly unpopular, and Sadat was assassinated on October 6, 1981, by a right-wing Jihadist group that had eluded arrest.

Sadat was succeeded by Hosni Mubarak, who would lead Egypt until the Egyptian Revolution of 2011. Mubarak took a much harder line than Sadat. He reversed Sadat's earlier moves toward political liberalization and ensured that the executive branch of government would govern absolutely. He invoked emergency laws and left them in place for years, and waged a virtual war against fundamentalist and radical groups that engaged in periodic terrorism in Egypt until the late 1990s. He reacted swiftly and purged the army of "negligent" officers after an Egyptian soldier killed seven Israelis vacationing at Ras Burqa and another Egyptian soldier on October 5, 1985. In February 1986, there was a massive mutiny among the Central Security Forces. Seeking higher pay, the mutineers looted and burned sections of Cairo. Mubarak had to mobilize the army to suppress the unrest; no accurate casualty estimates are available, but it is believed dozens of people were killed or wounded in the violence.

Islamic extremism proved to be one of Mubarak's biggest headaches. In 1992, Egyptian police and army troops stormed a poor Cairo suburb to root out followers of the radical Sheik Omar Abdel-Rahman. In the process, scores were wounded and several civilians died. At least 5,000 residents were forcibly relocated. In 1993, 1,106 Egyptian civilians were killed or wounded because of Islamist terror operations; 120 police officers also died. Egyptian Islamic extremists massacred 64 tourists at Luxor, Egypt, on November 17, 1997. On July 23, 2005, an Islamic group attacked and killed some 80 tourists—mostly foreign—and wounded another 150 at a Sharm el-Sheikh resort on the Red Sea. The ongoing Israeli-Palestinian conflict has also resulted in sporadic violence within Egypt. On October 7, 2004, Palestinian terrorists killed 34 and wounded 171 in a terrorist attack on the Sinai Peninsula.

Violence against the Coptic Church has also resulted in atrocities. On January 2, 2000, a Muslim mob attacked Coptic Christians at Kosheh, killing 21 and wounding 40. On January 7, 2010, Muslim extremists gunned down and killed 11 Coptic Christians as they left a church in Nag Hammadi. Another 11 were wounded. In Alexandria on January 1, 2011, a bomb attack against the Coptics killed 23 and wounded 97. On October 9–10, 2011, in Cairo, 28 Coptics were killed and another 212 wounded when Egyptian police and army personnel attacked a congregation of Coptics who were peacefully demonstrating against the demolition of a church.

In late January 2011, protesters of all stripes gathered in Tahrir Square in downtown Cairo to demand Mubarak's resignation. Over a period of 18 days, the crowds grew larger and larger, and their protests became louder. During what has now come to be called the Egyptian Revolution of 2011, security forces and the Egyptian military tried to stem the unrest; as a result, hundreds died and many thousands more were wounded. Finally, on February 11, Mubarak resigned and power passed to the Egyptian Army, with elections to be held at an unspecified date in the near future. The death toll during the revolution stood at 846; 12,000 were arrested, and another 6,467 were injured. In April, Mubarak was detained while authorities investigated his role in the use of force against the protesters. The former president was then ordered to stand trial on charges of official negligence because he had not ordered the police and military to cease the use of force against the rebellious Egyptians. That trial is ongoing.

In 2012, Mohamed Morsi was elected president of Egypt. He took office on June 30 of that year. By November of 2012, Morsi had already begun to consolidate his power, not unlike Mubarak had done before him. Citing national security, he gave himself virtually unlimited executive powers to "protect" Egypt, and rescinded judicial review of presidential decisions. This caused major street demonstrations, and by the end of 2012, Morsi nullified his former decrees, although for all intents and purpose he continues to govern as a quasidictator. There remain serious concerns about the status of human rights in Egypt under Morsi, despite the fact that the 2011 revolution had been launched, in large measure, to stop human rights abuses under the Mubarak regime.

PAUL G. PIERPAOLI JR.

See also: Israel/Palestine; Libya

Further Reading

Abdel-Malek, Anouar. *Egypt: Military Society, the Army Regime, the Left, and Social Change under Nasser.* New York: Random House, 1968.

Beattie, Kirk J. *Egypt during the Sadat Years.* New York: Palgrave, 2000.

Kassem, Maye. *Egyptian Politics: The Dynamics of Authoritarian Rule.* Boulder, CO: Lynne Rienner, 2004.

Tripp, Charles, and Roger Owen. *Egypt under Mubarak.* London: Routledge, 1990.

El Salvador

The small Central American nation of El Salvador has historically been dominated since independence by the Fourteen Families, a small wealthy elite group of large landowners of Spanish descent controlling the lives of a largely Indian and mestizo population living in poverty. In the late 1970s, the guerilla movement Farabundo Martí Libertad Nacional (FMLN) made up of peasants, workers, and students, along with a small number of Marxists, challenged the elites and won the support of much of the population and nearly overthrew the military junta running the government.

Salvadorian elites reacted with brutal repression. They directed the national army and right-wing paramilitary death squads to target anyone with even mildly reform-ist goals. Entire villages were wiped out on even the slight-est suspicion of residents sympathizing with the guerillas. Dissidents were routinely kidnapped, tortured, raped, or murdered. Students, peasants, and Catholic priests and nuns were the main targets. The guerillas were not inno-cents, but they were nowhere near as indiscriminate in their violence; the FMLN routinely assassinated police or army officers, generally in retaliation for involvement in torture or murders. Mayors were also murdered for sup-porting the government.

The army and paramilitary death squads committed more than ninety percent of the murders. The most no-torious case of government directed violence involved the assassination of Archbishop Óscar Romero in March 1980 as he was celebrating mass. That same year, 600 peasants were massacred at Sumpul River. The case to gain the most notoriety internationally involved four American nuns who were gang-raped, tortured, and then murdered, their mutilated bodies left by the roadside. The atrocity almost led to the cutoff of American support for the dictatorship by the U.S. Congress. However, the Ronald Reagan admin-istration remained strong in its conviction that support for El Salvador's elites was vital to the struggle against Com-munism and often suppressed evidence of atrocities by the Salvadorian government. That support finally came close to being undercut by the murder of six Jesuit priests in 1989 at the University of Central America. Still, the suc-ceeding administration of George H.W. Bush continued its support. In 1990, Costa Rican President Óscar Arias negotiated a ceasefire, ending the civil war. In 1992, lead-ers of the Salvadoran government and the FMLN signed a United Nations-brokered permanent peace agreement. The FMLN was finally permitted to become a legitimate political party.

The civil war death toll officially stood at some 100,000. Salvadorian government repression and the death squads claimed at least 65,000 of those lives. In addition, one in four Salvadorians became refugees. Some 1.25 million oth-ers fled to the United States, while nearly a quarter million more fled to Mexico or other Central American countries.

The agreement ending the conflict established two commissions: a truth commission to investigate the vi-olence, and an ad hoc commission to review the human rights records of El Salvador's military. The Ad Hoc Com-mission issued its report in secret, but forced the removal of more than 100 top military officers. The Commission on the Truth for El Salvador issued another report, "From

Madness to Hope," which named some 40 other high-ranking military leaders. The report also recommended reforming the courts, expelling still more military officers, and creating a civilian police force to replace the paramili-tary. The truth commission found Roberto D'Aubuisson, founder of the National Republican Alliance (ARENA), guilty of giving the order to assassinate Archbishop Romero and reported that he had given instructions to his security service to act as a death squad; later, declassified U.S. documents confirmed this.

Five days after the truth commission's report, the Salva-doran legislature enacted a blanket amnesty for war crimes. El Salvador has continued to be dominated by ARENA, whose founder, Roberto D'Aubuisson, also founded and directed the right-wing death squads. ARENA often won elections by violent intimidation of voters, as in 1982, or by fraud as in 1989. Voters' desire for stability and U.S. sup-port for ARENA also played important roles.

Still, the commissions did make an impact in the recon-ciliatory process after a bloody civil war. Salvador's elites, and their U.S. government sponsors, had often done their best to hide evidence of the campaign of atrocities. The commissions put an end to all denials, and El Salvador be-came far less dominated by the military. Later observers have pointed to the commissions as a somewhat successful model of how to move a state beyond civil war.

Salvadorians and human rights activists continued to seek justice for victims despite the blanket amnesty. The Center for Justice and Accountability brought several suc-cessful lawsuits against war criminals. In 2002, the center won a $54 million civil suit for torture and killings or-dered by two ex-Salvadoran generals who had moved to Miami. In 2004, it won a judgment of $10 million against Alvaro Saravia for his role in the assassination of Arch-bishop Romero. In 2004, the administration of George W. Bush challenged the constitutionality of these rulings and lost. In 2005, the Organization of American States' human rights court re-opened its investigation into the 1981 mas-sacre of peasant farmers in El Mozote, one of the most in-famous atrocities of the civil war.

One of the enduring legacies of the civil war has also been a huge surge in Central American gangs like MS-13, both in their home countries and in the United States. Some of the older gang leaders and members were once members of death squads or served in the army. In recent years there have been reports of newer death squads mak-ing a comeback in order to target alleged gang members. In a bit of irony, in 2007 three ARENA party leaders were murdered, likely by gang members and, perhaps, former death squad members or soldiers.

ALTON CARROLL

See also: D'Aubuisson, Roberto; Death Squads; Hernández Martínez, Maximiliano

Further Reading

Stanley, William D. *The Protection Racket State: Elite Politics, Military Extortion, and Civil War in El Salvador.* Philadelphia: Temple University Press, 1996.

White, Christopher M. *The History of El Salvador.* Westport, CT: Greenwood Press, 2009.

Ethiopia

After seizing political control over Ethiopia, located in east Africa, on September 12, 1974, the Provisional Military Administrative Council (PMAC) instituted a policy of threats, arrests, torture, and extrajudicial killing to repress any opposition to it. Such repression only provoked greater resistance by a variety of ethnic and political factions. For example, in 1975, the Tigray People's Liberation Front began armed opposition to the military government. The new regime also faced threats from the Western Somalia Liberation Front and from the Eritrean People's Liberation Front, both of which supported the right of ethnic groups to secede from Ethiopia.

Beginning in 1975, the Ethiopian People's Revolutionary Party (EPRP) sought to integrate the diverse ethnic-based opposition in demands for a more radical socialist transformation of Ethiopia under civilian control. By February 1977, armed conflict between and among the various groups vying for control of Ethiopia escalated to the point of mutual annihilation. The EPRP began assassinating leaders of the PMAC in what came to be known as the "white terror." Government forces responded with the so-called "red terror," and by the end of 1977 they had killed, tortured, or jailed so many members and supporters of the EPRP that it was practically eliminated as a political force.

Between 1984 and 1986, the government of Ethiopia conducted a program designed to forcibly resettle hundreds of thousands of peasants from arid environments to more fertile areas. Although resettlement had been employed in Ethiopia since 1950, the revolutionary government in power during the 1980s lacked the necessary resources, including malaria prevention measures. Moreover, the government used resettlement as a political tool, placing its supporters in key areas and moving political opponents to distant or less-desirable provinces. Those who refused to move were forced to do so. Government soldiers seized people including the sick and elderly from the streets, markets, and farms and forcibly resettled them. By the end of 1986, about 700,000 people had been resettled. Conflicts between the resettled people and those indigenous to the areas, as well as government attacks against resettlement camps, added to the death toll created by diseases and hunger.

EDWARD KISSI AND ERIC MARKUSEN

See also: Somalia; Uganda

Further Reading

Giorgis, Dawit Wolde. *Red Tears: War, Famine, and Revolutions in Ethiopia.* Trenton, NJ: Red Sea Press, 1989.

Kissi, Edward. *Revolution and Genocide in Ethiopia and Cambodia.* Lanham, MD: Lexington Books, 2006.

Ethnic Cleansing

Ethnic cleansing is a broad concept that encompasses actions ranging from nonviolent pressure on a specific ethnic group or groups to the deliberate extermination of a people to effect their removal from a particular place; it is distinguished from genocide in that the ultimate goal is not the destruction of its victims, but rather their complete removal from a specific area. Ethnic cleansing can be accomplished through genocide, but not all cleansings are genocides.

Like the term "genocide," the term "ethnic cleansing" is ambiguous and has a number of different meanings ascribed to it; in fact, the term is often misused as a synonym for genocide. Although the term was popularized in the 1990s, during the conflicts in the former Yugoslavia, antecedents exist in the Nazi use of the phrase "racial cleansing." Ethnic cleansing lacks a standard legal definition as a war crime. As an activity, it is encompassed within the definition of genocide in the 1948 United Nations Convention on the Prevention and Punishment of the Crime of Genocide.

There is debate over whether or not ethnic cleansing is a strictly modern phenomenon. A number of premodern examples have been suggested: the events of the Exodus in the Old Testament, Roman and Greek enslavement of enemy peoples, the devastation of Native Americans, the expulsion of Jews and Moors from Spain, and the English conquest of Ireland. Because the formulation of the term is ethnic cleansing, however, the phenomenon is usually regarded as a result of the spread of the concept of the nation-state in the 19th century. The ethnic character of a state defined it and was synonymous with "nation." Ethnic minorities were thus seen as potentially disloyal and in need of assimilation. Some states turned to expulsion, such as the expulsion of Muslims from the newly independent Balkan states in 1831 and 1877–1878. European colonial powers also engaged in cleansing in their colonial possessions.

Technological changes allowed for greater organization and execution of ethnic cleansing in the 20th century, which facilitated greater lethality. Events in Anatolia overshadowed incidents of cleansing during the Balkan Wars of 1912–1913. The Ottoman Empire/Republic of Turkey feared that resident Armenians and Greeks were potentially disloyal, and that Greece and Russia would use their presence to advance claims on Turkish territory. The Turks thus expelled approximately 1.5 million Armenians in 1915, half of whom died during the expulsion, and 1.5 million Greeks during and after the Greco-Turkish War of 1921–1922. Quixotically, the response of the League of Nations was less to regard ethnic cleansing itself as a crime than to attempt to regulate it as a necessary evil. While creating a system for minority protection, the League of Nations oversaw compulsory population transfers in the 1920s among countries such as Turkey, Greece, and Bulgaria.

Nazi German policies of redrawing both the political and ethnic maps of Europe utilized ethnic cleansing in the 1930s and 1940s. The Nazis, for example, pressured the Jews to leave Germany after 1933; after 1939, there was discussion of deporting all Jews from Europe. Beginning in 1941, Jews were slated for extermination, and some 6 million would be killed in the Holocaust. The Nazis targeted other ethnic groups, slating Roma for extermination as well as Poles, Ukrainians, and Russians for removal from conquered territories; however, the "cleansing" of Jews was unique in its importance to Nazi ideology. Similarly, the German-allied Independent State of Croatia sought to cleanse itself of Serbs, helping to drive the 1941–1945 civil war in Yugoslavia. Other German client states engaged in cleansing on a more limited scale.

The Soviet Union engaged in ethnic cleansing before and during World War II, shifting nearly a dozen groups of potentially disloyal non-Russian nationalities away from its borders. Imperial Russia had deported Jews and Germans away from the front during World War I, but Soviet operations were more brutal. The forced resettlement of the Chechens-Ingush in 1944 killed 100,000 out of the 494,000 involved, and half the 189,000 Crimean Tatars resettled in 1944 also died.

The postwar expulsion of the Volkdeutsch, ethnic Germans living outside of Germany, proved to be the largest cleansing in history. Over 10 million were forced to relocate from Eastern Europe in 1944–1947, with perhaps a million killed in the process. The Soviets' redrawing of borders led to forced resettlements of Poles from Ukraine and Ukrainians from Poland during 1946–1947. Allied leaders regarded such cleansing as necessary to remove future German territorial claims.

Cleansing also accompanied the end of the European colonial empires. Colonial borders had not been drawn along ethnic divisions, and conflict often emerged along ethnic lines in the new states. The worst case was the transfer of Muslim and Hindu populations between India and Pakistan in 1946–1947, with millions forced to relocate. Numerous lesser incidents occurred in both postcolonial civil wars and international conflicts. Claims of ethnic cleansing accompanied the 1948 and 1967 Arab-Israeli Wars, as well as the Turkish intervention in Cyprus in 1974. Iraq relocated or destroyed Kurdish populations in sensitive border areas during the 1980–1988 Iran-Iraq War.

Ethnic cleansing in the former Yugoslavia between 1991 and 1996 attracted wide-spread international attention. The wars in Croatia and Bosnia resulted in the deaths of some 250,000 people and a million forced relocations. All sides used cleansing as a deliberate weapon to reinforce claims to specific territories by driving out rival ethnicities. Although attention focused on the Serbian use of cleansing, hundreds of thousands of Serbs also became victims. These actions were repeated in the 1999 Kosovo conflict, during which Serbian security forces cleansed Albanians during the bombing campaign; Kosovo Liberation Army (KLA) guerillas cleansed Serbs afterward.

Events in Rwanda in April 1994, which followed similar events in Burundi in 1972, are more complicated, because the Hutu and Tutsi are not "ethnicities" in the strict European sense of the term. In its effects, however, the intentions were the same: the Hutus intended to drive Tutsis out of the country. At least 500,000 Tutsis died in the massacres, and the resulting war led to hundreds of thousands of Hutus fleeing to the Congo.

Ethnic cleansing in both Yugoslavia and Rwanda was frequently portrayed as the result of "ancient hatreds." In each historical case, while ethnic tension did exist, the cleansing operations themselves were the result of deliberate manipulation and organization by political leaders. Ethnic cleansing possesses a political utility that has made it attractive in the past. It remains to be seen if international regulation will change this.

JAMES W. FRUSETTA

See also: Democide; Total War

Further Reading

Bell-Fialkoff, Andrew. *Ethnic Cleansing.* Sydney, Australia: Palgrave Macmillan, 1999.

Naimark, Norman M. *Fires of Hatred: Ethnic Cleansing in Twentieth-Century Europe.* Cambridge, MA.: Harvard University Press, 2002.

Power, Samantha. *"A Problem from Hell": America and the Age of Genocide.* New York: Harper Perennial, 2007.

F

First Five Year Plan

The First Five Year Plan was an ambitious economic policy instituted by the Soviet leadership in 1928 that sought to rapidly industrialize the USSR and collectivize its agriculture. While the First Five Year Plan (hereafter First Plan), which lasted until 1932, made significant strives in the industrial sector, it wrought havoc in the agricultural sector and helped precipitate famine in many areas of the country, including Ukraine. Soviet general secretary Joseph Stalin and other Soviet leaders believed that the First Plan would make the USSR more self sufficient by increasing its industrial, financial, and military capacity. Indeed, Stalin saw it as a way to wage economic warfare against the capitalist world, which in the long run would strengthen his regime and cement Stalinism as the credo of the Soviet Union.

The goals prescribed in the First Plan were unrealistically high, but significant progress was made within the industrial sector. The agricultural sector, however, took a giant step backward between 1929 and 1932, chiefly because of the ruinous and hastily instituted collectivization policies, continued food exports to foreign nations, and unreasonable grain requisition policies implemented by the Soviet regime.

Stalin and his bureaucrats revised the First Five Year Plan in 1929, which now included a crash program of farm collectivization. Included in this revision was the elimination of the kulaks (landed peasantry) throughout the Soviet Union (a process later dubbed dekulakization). All privately owned farms were to be turned over to the state, and peasants were expected to work on communal farms (kolkhozy) or state-owned farms (sovkhzy). Small, privately owned and operated farms would be abolished, and Soviet agriculture would be composed of huge communal agricultural compounds, completely controlled by the government.

Besides the central ideological reason for embracing collectivization (i.e., Soviet communism forbade the ownership of private property), Soviet leaders hoped that collectivization would result in larger crop yields and surplus crops, which could be used to feed the swelling ranks of industrial workers in the cities, and which could be sold to foreign countries so that more foreign machinery could be purchased. Kremlin officials also sought to modernize and mechanize Soviet agriculture.

Collectivization, however, was a short-term disaster. It created confusion and chaos among farmers, resulted in the deaths and deportation of hundreds of thousands of kulaks, and actually significantly impeded agricultural output. Indeed, Soviet agriculture did not fully recover from these dislocations until the late 1940s.

Nowhere was the agricultural problem more dire than in Ukraine. Dekulakization resulted in a shortage of experienced farmers, and many kulaks, out of protest and desperation, destroyed crops and slaughtered millions of livestock. These developments created food shortages that were only worsened by unrealistic grain requisition policies put in place by the Soviet government. Crop failures in Ukraine in 1932 added immeasurably to the growing crisis (total Soviet grain production in that year was 32 percent below average), and the government did virtually nothing to alleviate growing hunger among most of the remaining peasants. In the end, the mass starvation in the Ukraine during 1932–1933 (called the Holodomor) wrought horrific misery among Ukrainians and scarred them for at least a generation. The First Plan and Soviet collectivization played a central role in bringing about this catastrophe.

Nevertheless, the Soviet regime was so pleased with the strides made in the industrial sector that it ended the First Plan a year early, in 1932, and instituted the Second Five Year Plan. That scheme had similar goals and lasted until 1937. The agricultural sector, however, remained hobbled and weak.

PAUL G. PIERPAOLI JR.

See also: Dekulakization; Great Purges; Kolkhoz; Kulaks; People's Commissariat for Internal Affairs (NKVD); Soviet Collectivization; Soviet Grain Requisition Policies; Soviet Union; Stalin, Joseph; Ukrainian Starvation (Holodomor)

Further Reading

Conquest, Robert. *The Harvest of Sorrow: Soviet Collectivization and the Terror-Famine.* New York: Oxford University Press, 1987.

Fitzpatrick, Sheila. *The Russian Revolution.* 2nd ed. New York: Oxford University Press, 1994.

G

Great Leap Forward

During the first few years of communist rule, China experienced marked economic development. Not only had the government succeeded in halting the runaway inflation of the 1940s, but China witnessed a tremendous increase in industrial output, despite hardships brought on by the demands of the Korean War. For these reasons, many Chinese were optimistic regarding China's economic future, none more so than party leader Mao Zedong. In early 1958, the Chinese government announced a plan for an economic "Great Leap Forward." By encouraging everyone—peasants, bureaucrats, and even government officials—to participate in industrial production, Mao believed China could rapidly catch up with and even surpass the industrial giants of the West.

The Great Leap Forward set production targets for coal, electricity, and, most especially, steel. Steel, many believed, was the symbol of industrialization, and therefore steel production was the ultimate measuring stick for the Great Leap Forward. At this time, however, China was still a poor nation and lacked the capital to construct the new steel mills necessary to reach its production goals. Instead, government leaders called on the people to build backyard steel furnaces out of mud and brick. At one point, an estimated 600,000 such furnaces were functioning in China. Similar methods were implemented in other industries as well.

In order to acquire capital and free up the labor necessary for this Great Leap Forward, Mao believed China had to have a simultaneous increase in agricultural productivity. To accomplish this, he called for the creation of agricultural communes. These communes were to represent the apex of socialist living, with free hospitals, schools, nursing centers, and dining halls. Each member of the commune would be required to work on the commune farm and all private property would be eliminated. Mao believed these communes would put China at the forefront of the worldwide socialist revolution. Equally important, these communes would be much more agriculturally productive than any other system, allowing for huge increases in output. The government would then use the excess grains and vegetables to feed industrial workers or to exchange for Soviet machinery. By 1958, nearly all of China's agricultural workers were living on one of 26,000 communes.

In both the agricultural and the industrial sectors, Mao stressed voluntarism over structuralism. In other words, he believed that structural limitations (the lack of steel mills, for instance) could be overcome by sheer willpower, or voluntarism. He refused to listen to economists or scientists who claimed the Great Leap Forward was structurally impossible, labeling them capitalists or reactionaries. Instead, Mao surrounded himself with individuals who were more ideologically correct and unwilling to challenge his assumptions. During this competition between the ideologues and the scientific experts, the ideologues gained the upper hand. As a result, optimistic government planners encouraged the increased use of irrational farming and industrial techniques.

During the early months of the Great Leap Forward, the economic figures appeared impressive. These results seemed to validate Mao's voluntarism and led to even greater optimism regarding the future. Unfortunately, these early results also led to greater reliance on irrational techniques. For example, many individuals believed that in order to double wheat production, a farmer needed only to plant twice as many seeds per acre. While such methods did lead to more wheat shoots, the amount of wheat produced on these shoots did not increase twofold. Instead of interpreting this as a sign of failure, however, the proponents of the Great Leap Forward suggested that the proper course of action was to plant triple or even quadruple the number of seeds per acre.

Within a few months, the early gains of the Great Leap Forward disappeared. Owing in large part to these unscientific techniques, agricultural and industrial productivity plummeted. Dense planting led to crop failures. At best, backyard mud furnaces produced unusable pig iron. At worst, they washed away in rainstorms. By 1959, it was becoming increasingly difficult to ignore the failings of the Great Leap Forward.

Despite these failures, many government officials refused to accept the reality of the situation. Local officials oftentimes inflated production numbers, fearful to admit the truth to their superiors. Seeing these inflated numbers, central government officials increased their grain requisition quotas. When peasants refused to fill these requisitions, government agents accused them of hoarding and confiscated what little crops they were in fact producing. Such deception became endemic, with optimistic officials placing ever-increasing quotas on the backs of the farmers and industrial workers.

Many inside China were unaware of the extent of the failure. The international community was even more unaware. Historians have suggested that during the economic crisis of the late 1950s, the Chinese Communist Party was more vulnerable than at any time in its history. Fearing international criticism (or perhaps worse), Beijing refused to ask for humanitarian aid. Consequently, the outside world remained largely ignorant of the failures of the Great Leap Forward.

The results of the Great Leap Forward were devastating for China. Estimates hold that 20 million people starved to death between 1959 and 1962, the largest manmade famine in history. China's economy was devastated as the gains of the early 1950s disappeared almost overnight. The Great Leap Forward also led to a radical restructuring of the Communist Party leadership. By the early 1960s, party moderates had stripped Mao of nearly all formal government positions. They also began reversing many of his policies. It would take the so-called Cultural Revolution for Mao to reassert his leadership role in the late 1960s. By that time, the average person had irretrievably lost the optimism and ideological faith that characterized the Great Leap Forward.

DAVID L. KENLEY

See also: China; Cultural Revolution; Mao Zedong

Further Reading

Bachman, David. *Bureaucracy, Economy, and Leadership in China: The Institutional Origins of the Great Leap Forward*. New York: Cambridge University Press, 1991.

Becker, Jasper. *Hungry Ghosts: Mao's Secret Famine*. New York: The Free Press, 1996.

Chan, Alfred L. *Mao's Crusade: Politics and Policy Implementation in China Great Leap Forward*. New York: Oxford University Press, 2001.

Domenach, Jean-Luc. *The Origins of the Great Leap Forward: The Case of One Chinese Province*. Translated by A. M. Berrett. Boulder, CO: Westview, 1995.

MacFarquhar, Roderick. *The Great Leap Forward, 1958–1960. The Origins of the Cultural Revolution*. Vol. 2. New York: Columbia University Press, 1983.

Teiwes, Frederick C, and Warren Sun. *China's Road To Disaster: Mao, Central Politicians and Provincial Leaders in the Unfolding of the Great Leap Forward, 1955–1959*. Contemporary China Papers. Armonk: M.E. Sharpe, 1998.

Great Purges

Ostensibly an internal "cleansing" of the Soviet hierarchy in the middle to late 1930s, the Great Purges were in fact repressive measures taken to remove any and all potential threats to the continuance of the Communist Party and to control by Joseph Stalin.

Periodic purges were not unheard of in Soviet Russia after the Bolshevik seizure of power in November 1917. Most were directed at subordinate officials and low-ranking party members, who bore the brunt of policy failures. The Great Purges (*Yezovshchina* in Russian) were characterized by their focus on party and state elites, mass terror, and dramatic public "show trials" and "confessions" by the accused.

The Great Purges began in earnest with the assassination on December 1, 1934, of Sergei M. Kirov, Stalin's chief lieutenant in Leningrad. Kirov, it is alleged, received more votes than Stalin in the Central Committee elections during the Seventeenth Party Congress of 1934, and many party members desired Stalin's removal from his post as general secretary. Kirov's assassin, Leonid V. Nikolaev, and 13 so-called accomplices were arrested, given a sham trial, and executed on December 30. Eventually, 49 people were directly implicated in the plot and were shot. Supposedly these individuals implicated others, who implicated still others. Although never proven, it has been suggested that Stalin arranged Kirov's murder and then had those who carried out the deed executed to cover his tracks. In any case, Kirov's assassination now became the justification for the Great Purges.

Beginning in 1936, in a series of show trials held in Moscow, numerous leading Communists and old Bolsheviks, chiefly members of the former left and right oppositions, were tried, convicted, and sentenced either to execution or to hard labor in the gulags. The spillover effect on the general population was horrendous. The purge soon extended to the Red Army.

In June 1937, the secret summary arrest and trial of several Red Army leaders took place. Charged with Trotskyism and with conspiring with Germany and Japan, three of the five marshals of the Soviet Union—Michael N. Tukhachevsky, chief of the Soviet General Staff; Alexander I. Yegorov; and Vasily K. Bluecher—were summarily tried and executed. Immediately thereafter, the purges descended to the lower echelons of the Soviet armed forces. Before ending, they claimed, in addition to the marshals, 14 of 16 army commanders, all 8 admirals, 60 of 67 corps commanders, 136 of 199 division commanders, and 221 of 397 brigade commanders. All 11 vice-commissars of defense and 75 of 80 members of the Supreme Military Council, all military district commanders, and all air force commanders also were murdered.

This devastating decapitation of the Soviet armed forces eliminated more than 50 percent of the senior officer corps. Those lost included the most aggressive, outspoken, and capable. Some observers consider the purge of the officer corps the chief cause of the near-disastrous performance of the Red Army early in the 1941 German invasion of the Soviet Union. Not all were executed or died in the gulags, however. Many survived to be rehabilitated in the wartime emergency. Some, such as Konstantin Rokossovsky, later a marshal of the Soviet Union, became national heroes.

For others, the path to prominence previously closed was opened. A little-known regional commander, Georgii K. Zhukov, rose to become chief of the Soviet General Staff in three years; during the same period, Nicholas G. Kuznetsov rose from cruiser commander to chief of the Soviet navy.

At the same time that the great show trials were going forward, millions of ordinary Soviet citizens simply disappeared without benefit of trial in what became known as the "Deep Comb-Out." Approximately 8 million people were arrested; 1 million were executed, and the rest were sent to the gulags.

Arthur T. Frame

See also: Beria, Lavrenty; Class Enemies; Kulaks; People's Commissariat for Internal Affairs (NKVD); Soviet Collectivization; Soviet Union; Stalin, Joseph; Ukrainian Starvation (Holodomor)

Further Reading

Conquest, Robert. *Stalin: Breaker of Nations.* New York: Penguin, 1991.

Dziewanowski, M.K. *A History of Soviet Russia.* Englewood Cliffs, NJ: Prentice-Hall, 1979.

Medvedev, Roy A. *Let History Judge: The Origins and Consequences of Stalinism.* New York: Columbia University Press, 1989.

Gulags

Gulag is a Russian acronym for Glavnoye Upravleniye Lagerey (State Director of Camps), an agency of the Soviet secret police, which administered the Soviet system of forced labor camps where political dissenters, dissidents, and other "enemies of the state" were sent.

The first gulags were established in Czarist Russia and the early Soviet era under Vladimir Lenin. The gulags reached their zenith in the period of Joseph Stalin's rule. Unlike other labor camps before and after, people were imprisoned not just for what they had done, but also for who they were in terms of class, religion, nationality, and race. The gulag was one of the means by which to implement Stalin's political purges, which "cleansed" the Soviet Union of real and imagined enemies.

The first gulag victims were hundreds of thousands of people caught in the collectivization campaigns in the early 1930s. After the Red Army's invasion of the Baltic States and Poland in June 1941, the secret police incarcerated potential resisters. When Adolf Hitler sent German armies into the Soviet Union in June 1941, people of German ancestry in eastern Europe were incarcerated as well. Following the German defeat at Stalingrad, the Red Army advanced west, capturing and imprisoning enemy soldiers. Stalin also incarcerated partisan groups from all over eastern Europe.

Following World War II, the Allies agreed that all Russian citizens should be returned to the Soviet Union. This naturally included Soviet POWs held by the Germans. The Western allies also forced anti-Soviet émigrés, many of whom had fought with Hitler, to return to the Soviet Union. The vast majority of these were either shot or simply disappeared into a gulag. In March 1946, the Soviet secret police began incarcerating ethnic minorities, Soviet Jews, and youth groups for allegedly "anti-Stalinist" conspiracies, as well as people who were viewed as a hindrance to Sovietization campaigns in eastern Europe.

The "juridical" process for sentencing people to a gulag comprised a three-person panel, which could both try and sentence the accused, or simply rely on Article 58 of the Soviet Criminal Code. Article 58 deprived Soviet citizens suspected of "illegal" activity of any rights and permitted the authorities to send anyone to the camps for any reason, justified or not. The gulag served as an institution to punish people, but also was meant to fulfill an economic function, for Stalin sought to deploy workers in remote parts of Russia in brutal climates but with rich natural resources.

In the early 1950s, gulag authorities issued reports revealing that the camp system was unprofitable. Stalin, however, commanded further construction projects such as railways, canals, power stations, and tunnels. Thus thousands of prisoners died and maintenance costs skyrocketed. To an extent, the situation changed in the gulags after the war because the inmates had changed. These "new politicals" were well-organized and experienced fighters who often banded together and dominated the camps. Slowly, authorities lost control.

Immediately following Stalin's death in March 1953, Lavrenty Beria briefly took charge, reorganized the gulags, and abandoned most of Stalin's construction projects. He granted amnesty to all prisoners sentenced to five years or less, pregnant women, and women with children under 18. He also secretly abolished the use of physical force against detainees. In June 1953, he announced his decision to liquidate the gulags altogether. However, Beria was subsequently arrested and executed. The new Soviet leadership under Nikita Khrushchev reversed most of Beria's reforms, although it did not revoke the amnesties.

Because neither Beria nor Khrushchev rehabilitated the political prisoners, they began to fight back with their new and well-organized groups. They killed informers, staged strikes, and fomented rebellions. The biggest of these occurred in Steplag, Kazakhstan, and lasted from spring until late summer 1954. Inmates seized control, but Soviet authorities brutally quashed the revolt.

In the aftermath of the Steplag rebellion, the secret police relaxed gulag regulations, implemented an eight-hour day, and gradually began to re-examine individual cases. This process was accelerated by Krushchev's condemnation of Stalin's rule in February 1956. In the so-called Thaw Era, the gulags were officially dissolved, and the two biggest camp complexes in Norilsk and Dalstroi were dismantled. Despite "the Thaw," certain "politicals" were still incarcerated.

Under Leonid Brezhnev, "politicals" were renamed "dissidents." In the wake of the Hungarian Revolution in October 1956, the KGB used two camps in Moldovia and Perm to incarcerate dissidents. In contrast to former prisoners, these detainees consciously criticized the government and purposely invited incarceration to gain the attention of Western media. By 1966, Brezhnev, and later Yuri Andropov, then chairman of the KGB, declared these dissidents "insane" and imprisoned them in psychiatric hospitals. When Mikhail Gorbachev took power in 1985 and embarked on reform, perestroika brought a final end to the gulags in 1987, and glasnost allowed limited access to information about their history.

It is impossible to determine just how many people were imprisoned and how many died in the gulags. Conservative estimates hold that 28.7 million forced laborers passed through the gulag system. There were never more than 2 million people at a time in the system, although perhaps as many as 3 million people died during the Stalin era in the camps.

FRANK BEYERSDORF

See also: Beria, Lavrenty; Class Enemies; Kulaks; People's Commissariat for Internal Affairs (NKVD); Soviet Union; Ukrainian Starvation (Holodomor)

Further Reading

Applebaum, Anne. *Gulag: A History.* New York: Broadway Books, 2003.

Ivanova, Galina Mikhailovna, with Donald J. Raleigh. *Labor Camp Socialism: The Gulag in the Soviet Totalitarian System.* Translated from the Russian by Carol Fath. Armonk, NY: M. E. Sharpe, 2000.

Khevniuk, Oleg. *History of the Gulag.* New Haven, CT: Yale University Press, 2003.

Solzhenitsyn, Aleksandr. *The Gulag Archipelago, 1918–1956: An Experiment in Literary Investigation.* 3 vols. New York: Harper and Row, 1974–1978.

H

Haiti

Haiti is located on the western third of the Caribbean island Hispaniola, adjacent to the Dominican Republic. Haiti's history has been often punctuated by violence, tyranny, political coups, and myriad massacres and human rights abuses. Over the last 100 years or so, Haiti has also been mired in abject poverty, making it the poorest nation in the Western Hemisphere. The 20th century in Haiti began amid great political upheaval and violence. Between 1911 and 1915 alone, six different presidents ruled the country, all of whom were either forced into exile or assassinated. During the early years of the new century, peasant-based militias roamed the countryside, intimidating civilians and murdering or kidnapping those who refused to cooperate with them. In early 1915, Vibrun Guillaume established yet another dictatorship over Haiti. In July 1915, under threat of another rebellion, Guillaume ordered 167 political prisoners and opponents murdered, many of them from well-to-do Haitian families. This precipitated a massive backlash, and an angry mob lynched Guillaume in the Haitian capital.

This tumult prompted the United States to intervene in Haiti, and U.S. Marines occupied the country from 1915 until 1934. The American occupation did not end violence or political corruption, however. A revolt that began in 1919 and spearheaded by the peasant militias known as Cacos attacked the capital of Port-au-Prince in October. U.S. and Haitian forces hit back hard in an attempt to crush the rebellion, which was ended in 1920. In the process, as many as 3,250 Haitians died in the fighting (some sources claim the death toll was closer to 10,000–15,000). Meanwhile, poverty remained high in Haiti and corruption prospered, sometimes with the tacit support of American forces. The Marines also helped establish the National Guards, a paramilitary organization that was used to impose terror on Haitians for decades after.

Before American troops withdrew from Haiti in 1934, they had established a firm border with the Dominican Republic, but they had often incorporated disputed border areas, making them part of Haiti. This rankled the Dominicans, and in 1937, Rafael Trujillo, then the head of the Dominican government, unleashed on Haiti the single worst atrocity in that country's long and troubled history. Between October 2 and 8, Dominican troops massacred between 10,000 and 20,000 Haitians in an attempt to recover the disputed land areas. The mass killings were genocidal in scope and came to be known as the Parsley Massacre.

Periodic violence and political instability continued in Haiti, with coups taking place in 1946 and 1950; in 1957, six different men occupied the presidency. That same year, François "Papa Doc" Duvalier began a 29-year reign of terror over Haiti. Declaring himself "president for life" in 1964, he had political rivals or critics murdered and empowered the terroristic paramilitary organization known as the Tontons Macoutes to impose his rule—by force and violence—on the civilian population. Employing threats of "voodoo curses" against peasants and creating a cult of personality, Duvalier was probably responsible for the deaths of at least 30,000 Haitians during his rule.

When Papa Doc died in 1971, his son, Jean-Claude "Baby Doc" Duvalier assumed the presidency. He continued his father's despotic and violence ways; during his presidency thousands of Haitians were tortured, kidnapped, murdered, or simply disappeared. Political opponents and uncooperative journalists were especially targeted. Duvalier was notorious for his extravagant lifestyle, which was fueled largely by corruption, cronyism, and the international drug trade. In late 1985, however, growing protests against Duvalier's rule snowballed into a major rebellion. Duvalier fled to France in February 1986, and a new constitution was drafted the following month.

In November 1986, nation-wide elections sparked more violence, as the Tontons Macoutes and government soldiers killed dozens of peaceful protesters in Port-au-Prince and many more civilians in rural areas. On July 23, 1987, Tontons Macoutes and their allies massacred 139 civilians in Jean-Rabel (some sources claim the death toll was closer to 1,000) on the orders of a local land owner who was resistant to land reform. On September 11, 1988, 13–50 churchgoers at Saint Jean-Bosco Church in Port-au-Prince were shot and killed by masked gunmen (probably Tontons Macoutes members). The church was home to Roman Catholic priest (and future Haitian president) Jean-Bertrand Aristide, who had been sharply critical of the Haitian government. This massacre precipitated yet another coup in September 1988.

New elections in December 1990 brought Aristide to the presidency. He promised badly needed land reform and an ambitious program to invigorate Haiti's poor economy. Less than seven months after taking office, however, on September 30, 1991, a bloody coup overthrew Aristide. This ushered in yet another violence-plagued military regime, which endured until 1994. As many as 5,000 Haitians died during the three-year-long military dictatorship, and thousands of Haitians tried to flee their country. During 1991–1992 alone, the U.S. Coast Guard rescued or interdicted more than 41,000 Haitians trying to reach American shores in ramshackle boats. Hundreds of others died during the perilous journey.

With U.S. support and threats of military intervention, Aristide was returned to power in September 1994. An international peacekeeping force, led by the Americans, helped ensure short-term stability. The Aristide government soon descended into political corruption and political intimidation, however. He left office in 1995, but he and his supporters tried repeatedly to destabilize the new government under President René Preval. Aristide was reelected in December 2000 amid accusations of rigged election results. Some three years into his second term, street revolts broke out on rumors that Aristide's government had become hopelessly corrupt. The embattled president was forced to resign in February 2004, under pressure from both Haitians and the international community.

Aristide's terms certainly did not see the level of violence and repression that earlier presidencies witnessed, but Aristide's promises of reform went largely unfulfilled. Haiti has struggled since he left office, and a devastating earthquake in January 2010 killed as many as 250,000 people and made at least 3 million people homeless. Some 250,000 homes and 30,000 commercial buildings were either flattened or badly damaged. International relief poured into the small country, but the catastrophe only further delayed Haiti's economic and political rehabilitation.

PAUL G. PIERPAOLI JR.

See also: United States

Further Reading

Fatton, Robert. *Haiti's Predatory Republic: The Unending Transition to Democracy.* Boulder, CO: Lynne Rienner, 2002.

McKissick, Patricia C. *History of Haiti.* Maryknoll, NY: Henry Holt, 1998.

Hama Massacre

The Hama Massacre was the mass killing of Syrian citizens by Syrian armed forces under the control of President Hafez Assad from February 2 to February 28, 1982, at Hama.

After the end of World War II, Syria witnessed increasing tensions between conservative religious and secular nationalist ideologies. The Baath Party of Syria, which came to power in the 1960s and embraced Arab nationalism and socialism, had frequently clashed with the Muslim Brotherhood, which espoused conservative Islamism. The tensions between the two groups, however, transcended ideological fault lines. The secular and nationalist Baath Party was dominated by the minority Alawites, whom the conservative Sunni Muslims, the bulwark of the Muslim Brotherhood, considered apostates.

The Alawites consolidated their power following the rise of Assad in the early 1970s. He ruled Syria mainly through the power of the army, which was dominated by the Alawites. Although his government did contribute to economic growth in Syria, it did so while maintaining tight control over the population and using brutal force to suppress any dissent.

Beginning in the late 1970s, Sunni Islamic groups, including the Muslim Brotherhood, sought to challenge Assad's regime through a variety of methods, including hit-and-run and bomb attacks against government officials. In June 1980, President Assad himself barely survived an abortive assassination attempt on his life; he responded by unleashing a wave of violence against his opponents. He also sanctioned the massacre of several hundred political prisoners held in the infamous Tadmor Prison while government forces rampaged through the city of Aleppo, where more than 2,000 residents were killed for their opposition to Assad's regime.

The most infamous crackdown, however, occurred in February 1982, when Assad ordered a brutal crackdown in the defiant city of Hama, where the Sunni Muslim community continued to defy the regime. In the predawn hours of February 2–3, a group of insurgents attacked government forces in Hama, and the relatively small engagement soon escalated into an open rebellion against the government. The attack against Hama was carried out by some 12,000 armed men under General Rifaat al-Assad, the president's younger brother, and resulted in widespread carnage. The Syrian military's initial assault faced stiff resistance, prompting Assad to surround Hama with artillery and bombard it for some three weeks, leveling much of the city and killing thousands of civilians. The Syrian military then entered the rubble, hunting for any surviving insurgents.

Contemporary reports suggested that the military action resulted in about 1,000 killed, but as more details emerged on what transpired in Hama, subsequent estimates reported between 20,000 and 40,000 civilians (and 1,000 government troops) killed, and large parts of the old city destroyed. The brutal crackdown effectively destroyed the Islamist insurrection in Syria, and Assad's regime endured largely unchallenged until the rise of the Arab Spring in 2011–2012.

ALEXANDER MIKABERIDZE

See also: Syria; Syrian Civil War

Further Reading

Dam, Nikolaos van. *The Struggle for Power in Syria: Politics and Society under Asad and the Baath Party.* New York: I.B. Tauris, 1996.

Maoz, Moshe, and Avner Yaniv, eds. *Syria under Assad: Domestic Constraints and Regional Risks.* London: Croom Helm, 1987.

Hamburg Raids

The air battle of Hamburg consisted of a series of six raids in July and August 1943 that destroyed a large portion of the city and killed more than 45,000 people. Most of them died in the horrendous firestorm of the night of July 27, the first such conflagration induced by bombing. More than half of the residential units in the city were destroyed, and 900,000 people lost their homes. The Americans and British bombed the city many times later in the war, but none of those raids approached the results or notoriety of the July attack.

Four of the attacks were mounted at night by the British Royal Air Force (RAF), and two in daylight by the U.S. Army Air Forces (USAAF) Eighth Air Force. The initial British operation, which began the night of July 24, featured the first use of chaff, code-named window, in combat. The cloud of metallic strips blotted out large segments of enemy radar screens and provided cover for aircraft that stayed within the pattern, cloaking the bomber stream. This helped keep losses relatively low during RAF operations; only 87 British bombers were lost out of more than 3,000 sorties. The USAAF sent 252 B-17 Flying Fortresses over Hamburg on July 25 and 26 but lost 17 aircraft. In addition, the American bombing accuracy was poor, because primary targets were often obscured by smoke from the earlier RAF raid. The Americans dropped only about 300 tons of bombs on the city, whereas RAF bombers had delivered more than 8,000 tons.

The second British attack combined concentrated bombing with ideal weather conditions of high temperature and low humidity to produce an unexpected firestorm, which was further helped along because most of Hamburg's firefighters were in distant sectors of the city dealing with the results of the earlier attacks. Most of the dead had heeded the advice of local authorities to stay in basement shelters, where they were asphyxiated by carbon monoxide or crushed by collapsing buildings. However, taking to the streets was no guarantee of safety. Those who fled the shelters sometimes met even more horrible deaths, sucked into fires by high winds or caught in molten asphalt.

German armaments minister Albert Speer feared that if the Allies could quickly follow up with six similar devastating firestorms, the German economy might collapse. However, although RAF Bomber Command tried, it could not achieve the same result until its February 1945 assault on Dresden. Hamburg itself recovered surprisingly quickly, and the Luftwaffe changed its defensive tactics to counter the RAF night-bombing campaign. Scholarship conducted 50 years after the bombing of Dresden has considerably lowered the casualty figures from that bombing; it appears that the July 27 attack on Hamburg, not the Dresden bombing, was the deadliest air raid in the European Theater. The raids on Hamburg set a standard that RAF Bomber Command found difficult to duplicate and still provide a vivid symbol of the horrors of the bombing of cities and of total war.

CONRAD C. CRANE

See also: Dresden Bombing; Hiroshima, Bombing of; Tokyo Bombing

Further Reading

Middlebrook, Martin. *The Battle of Hamburg.* New York: Charles Scribner's Sons, 1981.

Webster, Charles, and Noble Frankland. *The Strategic Air Offensive against Germany.* 4 vols. London: Her Majesty's Stationery Office, 1961.

Haruki Isayama Trial

In July 1946, Lieutenant General Haruki Isayama was tried for war crimes along with seven other Japanese officers before the U.S. Military Commission in Shanghai, China. Isayama was the head of staff for the Japanese 15th Army in Burma from 1942 to 1943, and then served as chief of staff during the Japanese occupation of Formosa (Taiwan) until the end of the war. His co-accused were junior officers under Isayama's command in Taiwan. They included Colonel Seiichi Furukawa, Lieutenant Colonel Naritaka Sugiura, Captain Yoshio Nakano, Captain Tadao Ito, Captain Masaharu Matsui, First Lieutenant Jitsuo Date, and First Lieutenant Ken Fujikawa.

The specific charges against Isayama stemmed from the trial and execution of American prisoners of war that took place at Taihoku, Taiwan, between April 14 and June 19, 1945. The general was accused of authorizing "an illegal, unfair, unwarranted and false trial" of Americans before a Japanese military tribunal, and of forcing the tribunal to sentence the prisoners to death. The others accused along with Isayama were charged with presenting false evidence, presiding over an illegal tribunal, and carrying out the executions.

The American prisoners were airmen who had been shot down and captured by the Japanese Formosan Army between October 1944 and February 1945. Most were photographers and radiomen who had been on surveillance missions in the area. The senior commanders were sent to Tokyo for interrogation, leaving 14 of the airmen in Taiwan. They were tried under Japanese occupation law, which outlawed bombing and strafing of civilians and their property. The law also placed the accused under the jurisdiction of the 10th Area Army, commanded by Isayama. More importantly, Isayama had been given authority over any punishment, which was prescribed as death, with an allowance for life imprisonment for not less than ten years. The Japanese military tribunal presiding was made up of 10th Area Army officers, also appointed by Isayama.

The chief prosecutor was Colonel Furukawa, who, according to the evidence presented in Shanghai, flew to Tokyo for directions on how to proceed with the American airmen. Having been ordered by the Japanese government to treat them harshly, the colonel ordered his subordinates to falsify records pertaining to the airmen's interrogations. The U.S. Military Commission also heard evidence from the Japanese interpreter present for the interrogations in Taiwan, who testified that the Americans never confessed to bombing or strafing civilians as Furukawa contended. Moreover, evidence presented at Shanghai showed that Isayama was made aware of the deception, and in fact authorized the trial against the Americans based on their false confessions.

The 14 Americans were tried in six cases, all brought before the Japanese military court on May 21, 1945. None of the defendants was allowed legal counsel, or access to evidence and eyewitnesses. The proceedings of the trial were not even fully interpreted for the accused. In just one day, all 14 men were found guilty and sentenced to death. After waiting for the government in Tokyo to confirm the sentence, on June 19 the American airmen were shot and buried together in a ditch outside Taihoku.

The primary defense for the Japanese officers accused in Shanghai was that they were simply following orders given by the government in Tokyo, and in particular General Rikichi Ando, who served simultaneously as commander of the Japanese Formosan Army and as governor-general of Taiwan. Ando committed suicide before the Shanghai trial began, leaving Isayama as the most senior officer in the direct chain of command.

The prosecution against Isayama argued that he was in a position on all matters to advise General Ando, that he knew of the orders given to execute the Americans, and that he was well aware of Furukawa's actions in falsifying their confessions. Isayama's defense team, appointed by the U.S. Military Commission, argued that the airmen were denied access to the scene of their alleged bombing because of a lack of facilities and Japanese personnel. His lawyers also contended that despite their lack of representation, the airmen were allowed to make statements before the Japanese court. Lastly, in an attempt to discredit evidence against their client, Isayama's counsel pointed out that the Japanese records of the trials turned over to American officials in September 1945 were written by Furukawa, also accused of war crimes, and that they were not completed until after Japan's surrender.

On July 25, 1946, all seven defendants were found guilty. Captain Ito was sentenced to 20 years in prison. Lieutenants Date and Fujikawa were given 30 years each, while Captain Matsui received 40 years. Colonel Furukawa and Lieutenant Colonel Suguira were both sentenced to death. The Commission's Review Authority later overturned the findings against Date and Fujikawa, and commuted the death sentences against Furukawa and Suguira to life in prison. As for Isayama, he and Captain Nakano were given life imprisonment for their roles in the events at Taihoku.

ARNE KISLENKO

See also: Japan; Yamashita Trial; Yokohama Trials

Further Reading

Minnear, Richard H. *Victors' Justice: The Tokyo War Crimes Trial.* Princeton, NJ: Princeton University Press, 1971.

Piccigallo, P. R. *The Japanese on Trial: Allied War Crimes Operations in the Far East, 1945–1951.* Austin: University of Texas Press, 1979.

Hernández Martínez, Maximiliano

Maximiliano Hernández Martínez, ruler of El Salvador from 1931 to 1944, was best known for masterminding the massacre of tens of thousands of Indians after crushing an uprising in 1932.

Maximiliano Hernández Martínez was born in San Salvador on October 29, 1882, the son of lower middle class parents of predominantly Indian heritage. He acquired most of his formal education at the Military Polytechnical School of Guatemala. He joined the Salvadoran Army in 1899, seeing it as an opportunity for social advancement. He rose rapidly through the ranks of the military during a war with Guatemala in 1907. In 1930, Hernández Martínez entered the Salvadoran presidential race. He was running third in public opinion, so he offered to join the ticket of Arturo Araujo, one of the two front-runners, as vice president. Araujo lacked the military support that the other candidate (who had been a minister of war) received and needed the support that Hernández Martínez would bring. Although Hernández Martínez was not the top army officer in El Salvador, he was widely respected in military ranks.

In 1931, new President Araujo announced that the Communist Party would be allowed to participate in the upcoming elections. This announcement did not go over well in military circles, and on December 2, a group of young officers overthrew the government. Hernández Martínez was supposedly captured during the action, but a few days later, he emerged from seclusion as the officers' spokesperson. It is not clear whether he was involved in the plot or if he convinced the rebels that he was the ideal person to legitimize the coup. Araujo always believed that Hernández Martínez masterminded the operation.

In 1932, the effects of the Great Depression had caused great hardship throughout El Salvador, and working people were attracted to the Communist Party led by Farabundo Martí. Hernández Martínez confronted the possibility of a revolutionary uprising among urban workers and the indigenous population by capturing the leaders of the Communist Party and executing them. Despite efforts by the remaining Communists to call off the uprising, the indigenous peasant communities went ahead anyway, capturing much of western El Salvador.

The military responded quickly and drove back the Indians, who were mostly armed with machetes, slaughtering them along the way. The rebellious Indians engaged in some atrocities and may have been responsible for 100 deaths. In reprisal, the forces of Hernández Martínez killed not only insurgents, but any person dressed in the customary clothing of the Salvadoran peasant. Estimates range from 10,000 to 50,000 Indians killed in 1932. Just having a machete was considered proof of an Indian's guilt, despite the fact that the machete was a common farming implement, and nearly every Indian family owned at least one.

Off to a dramatic start, Hernández Martínez ruthlessly suppressed the press and eventually ensured his own reelection against constitutional principles. He fought for recognition from the United States and other Central American countries, vying with Gen. Jorge Ubico of Guatemala for power within the region. After this consolidation of power, which was to survive nonrecognition from the United States until 1934, Hernández Martínez set about ruling the country. He was known for his impeccable personal honesty, which carried through to his government. His administration stabilized the Salvadoran currency, paid off its foreign debts, and started improvements on the infrastructure of El Salvador. Extensive roads and numerous government buildings were constructed during his administration.

In 1938, Hernández Martínez lost many of his better administrators because they believed he should not run for a third term in office. As he began ignoring the advice of others and taking personal responsibility for actions he had previously delegated, his support further diminished. As the Allies began to gain the upper hand during World War II, the rhetoric of democracy and freedom flooded the world, further undermining the Hernández Martínez regime. Nevertheless, in 1944, Hernández Martínez began his fourth term in office. Housing shortages were causing unrest, labor organizations were forming, child welfare was on the agenda, and the press was protesting censorship. Hernández Martínez tried to respond with reforms of his own, but they were sorely inadequate.

The first week of May 1944, the workers in San Salvador carried out a general strike. With a huge base of support, the city shut down. Professional workers, businesspeople, and the lowest-paid manual laborers all refused to work in protest of the Hernández Martínez presidency. On May 9, Hernández Martínez stepped down and retired to exile in Honduras. Although this nonviolent revolution was short-lived, and the military soon regained control of the country, Hernández Martínez remained in exile.

Hernández Martínez was commonly nicknamed El Brujo (the witch doctor) because of his occult practices. He sold poultices for everything from toothaches to earthquakes, and seances were common in his household. He clearly held some rather unusual beliefs. He reportedly stated in a radio address to the Salvadoran people, "It is a greater crime to kill an ant than a man, because a man who dies is reincarnated while an ant dies forever."

Having never returned to El Salvador from his exile in Honduras, Hernández Martínez died on April 11, 1966.

JIM MELLEN

See also: El Salvador; United States

Further Reading

Anderson, Thomas. *Matanza: El Salvador's Communist Revolt of 1932.* Lincoln: University of Nebraska Press, 1971.

Buckley, Tom. *Violent Neighbors: El Salvador, Central America and the United States.* New York: Times Books, 1984.

Hiroshima, Bombing of

The U.S. bombing of the Japanese city of Hiroshima was the first use of the atomic bomb in combat. On July 25, 1945, commander of U.S. Strategic Air Forces General Carl Spaatz received orders to use the 509th Composite Group, Twentieth Air Force, to deliver a "special bomb" attack on selected target cities in Japan, specifically Hiroshima, Kokura, Niigata, or Nagasaki. Following rejection of conditions promulgated by the Potsdam Proclamation on July 26, a declaration threatening Japan with total destruction if unconditional surrender was not accepted, President Harry S. Truman authorized use of the special bomb.

Assembled in secrecy and loaded on the Boeing B-29 Superfortress *Enola Gay*, the bomb consisted of a core of uranium isotope 235 shielded by several hundred pounds of lead, encased in explosives designed to condense the uranium and initiate a fission reaction. Nicknamed "Little Boy," the bomb possessed a force equivalent to 12,500 tons of TNT (12.5 kilotons).

The *Enola Gay*, commanded by Colonel Paul Tibbets, departed Tinian at 2:45 A.M. on August 6. Two B-29s assigned as scientific and photographic observers followed, and the three aircraft rendezvoused over Iwo Jima for the run over Japan. Captain William Parsons of the U.S. Navy completed the bomb's arming in the air shortly after 6:30 A.M. The flight to Japan was uneventful, and Tibbets was informed at 7:47 A.M. by weather planes over the targets that Hiroshima was clear for bombing. Japan's eighth largest city (it had about 245,000 residents in August 1945), Hiroshima was an important port on southern Honshu and headquarters of the Japanese Second Army.

The Enola Gay arrived over the city at an altitude of 31,600 feet and dropped the bomb at 8:15:17 A.M. local time. After a descent of some nearly 6 miles, the bomb detonated 43 seconds later some 1,890 feet over a clinic and about 800 feet from the aiming point, Aioi Bridge. The initial fireball expanded to 110 yards in diameter, generating heat in excess of 300,000 degrees Centigrade, with core temperatures over 50 million degrees Centigrade. At the clinic directly beneath the explosion, the temperature was several thousand degrees. The immediate concussion destroyed almost everything within 2 miles of ground zero. The resultant mushroom cloud rose to 50,000 feet and was observed by B-29s more than 360 miles away. After 15 minutes, the atmosphere dropped radioactive "black rain," adding to the death and destruction.

Four square miles of Hiroshima's heart disappeared in seconds, including 62,000 buildings. More than 71,000

Japanese died, another 20,000 were wounded, and 171,000 were left homeless. Some estimates place the number of killed at more than 200,000. About one-third of those killed instantly were soldiers. Most elements of the Japanese Second General Army were at physical training on the grounds of Hiroshima Castle when the bomb exploded. Barely 900 yards from the explosion's epicenter, the castle and its residents were vaporized. Also killed was one American prisoner of war in the exercise area. All died in less than a second. Radiation sickness began the next day and added to the death toll over several years.

Following three observation circuits over Hiroshima, the *Enola Gay* and its escorts turned for Tinian, touching down at 2:58 P.M. The bombing mission, 12 hours and 13 minutes long covering 2,960 miles, changed the nature of warfare but did not end the war. Truman released a statement on August 7 describing the weapon and calling on Japan to surrender, but his message was ignored by most Japanese leaders as propaganda. The United States dropped another atomic bomb on August 9, this time on Nagasaki. Although the bomb missed its intended aiming point by 8,500 ft, it leveled one-third of the city. Called the "Red Circle of Death," the fire and blast area within the Urakami Valley section of Nagasaki destroyed more than 18,000 homes and killed 74,000 people. Another 75,000 were injured, and many later died from wounds or complications.

Survivors of the nuclear bombings of Hiroshima and Nagasaki are known as *hibakusha*. Many of them suffer from disfiguration and radiation-related illnesses, some of which have affected and will affect future generations. In 1996, the International Court of Justice issued an advisory opinion in which it found that "the threat or use of nuclear weapons would generally be contrary to the rules of international law applicable in armed conflict, and in particular the principles and rules of humanitarian law." The Court was unable to decide, however, whether or not such threat or use would be illegal in "an extreme circumstance of self-defense, in which the very survival of a State would be at stake." Because international humanitarian law was already in place at the end of World War II and the survival of the United States was not at stake, some scholars suggest that that the bombings of Hiroshima and Nagasaki could be considered illegal acts of war that violated international humanitarian law by attacking civilian populations and causing unnecessary suffering to combatants.

MARK E. VAN RHYN AND ALEXANDER MIKABERIDZE

See also: Japan; Nagasaki, Bombing of; World War II Atrocities, Pacific Theater

Further Reading

Ishikawa, Eisei. *Hiroshima and Nagasaki: The Physical, Medical, and Social Effects of the Atomic Bombings.* Translated by David L. Swain. New York: Basic Books, 1981.

Nobile, Philip. *Judgment at the Smithsonian: The Bombing of Hiroshima and Nagasaki.* New York: Marlowe and Company, 1995.

Homma, Masahura

Japanese lieutenant general Masahura Homma directed the invasion of the Philippines in 1941–1942. After a siege of six months, the island fell, and Allied prisoners of war were subjected to numerous atrocities, including the infamous Bataan Death March. Homma, disgraced for the slowness of the invasion, spent the remainder of the war in Japan. After the surrender, he was tried for war crimes, found guilty, and executed in 1946.

Born on November 27, 1887, to an aristocratic family on Sado Island off the northwest coast of Honshu, Homma was one of only a few highly cultured, brilliant, westernized Japanese generals. After graduating first in his class from the Japanese military academy in 1906, Homma was assigned to an infantry regiment as a second lieutenant; he next served as an attaché to Prince Chichibu, the youngest brother of the emperor. After attending the Army Staff College, Homma served in Europe as an observer with the British Expeditionary Force, subsequently spending a tour with the British Army's East Lancashire Brigade and then with the general staff of the British East India Army in India.

In 1925, then-Major Homma joined the staff of the Imperial Army Headquarters in Japan. Raised to the rank of colonel, he attended the League of Nation's arms conference in London. In 1933, he was given command of the 1st Infantry in Tokyo and two years later, with the rank of major general, became head of the Army Propaganda Department. After investigating charges of wanton killing and rape during the occupation of Nanking, Homma was promoted to lieutenant general in 1938 and commanded the 27th Division in China.

In December 1940, Homma took control of the army on Formosa, a position he relinquished when appointed to command the 14th Army for the invasion of the Philippines in December 1941. He was expected to complete the conquest in 50 days, but the assault turned into a siege of nearly six months. Homma neither received nor expected congratulations from his government; blamed for the slowness of the campaign, he was removed from command in June 1942. He returned to Japan in disgrace and remained essentially behind the scenes until the Japanese surrender.

Arrested after the war's end in 1945 and tried for war crimes committed during and after the Philippines campaign, Homma was arraigned before a military tribunal appointed by U.S. General Douglas MacArthur. He was prosecuted and defended by officers selected by MacArthur's command. Homma was charged with 47 counts involving atrocities committed during the Bataan Death March, against prisoners of war in the camps, against Filipino soldiers in the field, and for violating the "open city" status of Manila during the fighting. The "open city" charge could be easily refuted by the fact that Manila was never truly an "open city" because American forces remained there after MacArthur's declaration, but the allegations concerning maltreatment of prisoners in camps and soldiers in the field were certainly valid. The defense argued that as a busy commanding general, Homma had neither ordered any atrocity, nor was aware of their happening. The best the prosecution could do was prove that at least on one occasion Homma was near where maltreatment of POWs had taken place during the death march. His conviction on February 11, 1946, rested primarily on the premise that even if he did not know of or condone the atrocities as commanding officer, he bore the moral responsibility to stop them, and he had not.

The U.S. Supreme Court, having ruled in the case of *In re Yamashita*, 327 U.S. 1 (1946) that the MacArthur-established court could legally try war criminals, denied Homma's appeal. His only recourse was to ask MacArthur to have the sentence set aside, an effort that was futile, although MacArthur did change the sentence from death by hanging to death by firing squad. On April 3, 1946, Homma was executed at Los Baños in the Philippine Islands.

ROBERT S. LA FORTE

See also: Bataan Death March; Japan; United States

Further Reading

Swinson, Arthur. *Four Samurai: A Quartet of Japanese Army Commanders in the Second World War.* London: Hutchinson, 1968.

Taylor, Lawrence. *A Trial of Generals: Homma, Yamashita, MacArthur.* South Bend, IN: Icarus Press, 1981.

Houla Massacre

In 2011, the wider Arab World was shaken by a wave of popular upheaval that became known as the Arab Spring. Public demonstrations demanding greater democracy and freedoms occurred from Algeria and Tunis to Egypt and Syria. The unrest unfolded in Syria starting on January 26, 2011, and soon developed into a nationwide uprising against the regiment of Bashar al-Assad and nearly five decades of Baath Party rule. Following his father Hafez Assad's earlier example, al-Assad responded with a brutal crackdown that quickly escalated the level of violence and once again revealed deep sectarian fissures in Syrian society as the majority Sunni population remains highly discontent with the dominance of the minority Alawites.

The violence continued unabated throughout 2011 and early 2012, resulting in over 13,000 deaths, most of them civilians who perished in the government's bombardment of cities and security operations. Thus, the city of Hama was surrounded by the government forces and bombarded with heavy artillery for days at end, resulting in the deaths of hundreds of civilians, including women and children. The worst of these attacks, however, occurred in the village of Taldou, near the town of Houla on May 25, 2012. Just after midday Friday prayers, government forces fired on a protest in Taldou to disperse the crowds and, according to some reports, came under fire from opposition fighters. In response, the Syrian army shelled the town, first with tank fire, then with heavy mortars, before sending the Alawite-controlled progovernment militia, the shabiha, to conduct house-by-house searches in the ruined village. United Nations observers later confirmed that at least 108 people were killed, including 49 children and 34 women. Some were killed by shell fire, but the majority was shot or stabbed at close range.

The news of the massacres drew condemnations from around the world, even from Syria's steadfast allies like Russia. The UN Security Council issued a statement saying that "such outrageous use of force against civilian population constitutes a violation of applicable international law." However, it still remains unclear how the massacre will affect the country's 14-month-long uprising. The Syrian regime admits that a massacre did occur but claims it was the work of armed rebels who carried out the killings in order to provoke international intervention.

ALEXANDER MIKABERIDZE

See also: Syria; Syrian Civil War

Further Reading

"Houla: How A Massacre Unfolded," *BBC NEWS*, May 29, 2012, http://www.bbc.co.uk/news/world-middle-east-18233934 (accessed on 29 May 2012).

"Syria Houla Massacre: Survivors recount Horror," *BBC NEWS*, May 28, 2012, http://www.bbc.co.uk/news/world-middle-east-18245225 (accessed on 29 May 2012).

Hue Massacre

Mass killing of civilians and soldiers in the South Vietnamese city of Hue by North Vietnamese and Viet Cong forces in February 1968. More than four decades after its occurrence, the massacre of civilians and military personnel in Hue during the Communist occupation of the city during the January–February 1968 Tet Offensive remains a murky episode. Conflicting interpretations of this incident reflect the political debates regarding the Vietnam War.

In late January 1968, People's Army of Vietnam (PAVN, North Vietnamese Army) forces, assisted by the Viet Cong (VC), seized the former imperial capital of Hue. This operation was part of a Communist offensive throughout the Republic of Vietnam (RVN, South Vietnam) that took place during the Vietnamese lunar New Year holiday, known as Tet. Hue was only one of many cities and towns struck, but it and the South Vietnamese capital of Saigon were two of the principal targets. Hue saw some of the most bitter fighting of the entire offensive. Nearly a month passed before U.S. marines and Army of the Republic of Vietnam (ARVN, South Vietnamese Army) troops recaptured what remained of the largely destroyed city.

Once Hue had been secured on February 25, 1968, reports of the disappearance and execution of South Vietnamese civilians proliferated. Indeed, on February 26 allied forces uncovered the first of a number of mass graves. Eventually searchers unearthed 2,810 bodies, but many more of the missing were never found. Estimates of the dead range as high as 7,000.

One possible explanation for the bloodbath is that it was a desperate attempt to eliminate witnesses once the VC faced a return to clandestine operations. But clearly the VC had long possessed lists of assassination targets, including bureaucrats, teachers, intellectuals, ARVN soldiers, and foreigners, all of whom were presumed to oppose Communist rule.

Journalist Don Oberdorfer, who conducted an extensive investigation of the massacre in 1969, maintains that there were two classifications for those murdered in Hue. Among the first were politicians, civil servants and their families, and collaborators with U.S. forces. Among the second were civilians who tried to flee or refused to submit to questioning, those who spoke against the occupation, and those who spoke ill of or displayed a poor attitude toward the occupiers. In the Catholic section of Hue, the Communists killed virtually every able-bodied male over the age of 15, many of whom had taken refuge in the cathedral there.

After some of the details of the massacre became public, the Saigon government suggested that a similar fate lay in store for other communities should the Communists win. American officials subsequently echoed this in later public statements. Fears of a bloodbath became a justification for the continued U.S. presence.

Some compared the massacre at Hue with the slaughter of civilians by U.S. Army forces at My Lai in March 1968. Although the atrocity at My Lai was on a much smaller scale, the media proved more eager to investigate the My Lai Massacre. The killings at Hue elicited much less media coverage, in part because of the widespread nature of debate over the Tet Offensive and its consequences, and they brought only a tepid response from the U.S. public. A precise accounting of the cost of the massacre at Hue was impossible because of the great destruction in the city and the large number of civilian casualties that occurred as a consequence of the actual fighting. Not surprisingly, Hanoi denied any complicity, arguing that some Hue residents must have risen up against their oppressors in an opportunity for justice. If the executions had been conducted spontaneously rather than having been the result of meticulous planning, it would have strengthened the case that the conflict in Vietnam amounted to more of a civil war than a conventional conflict. It does appear that the massacre was solely the work of the VC rather than PAVN regular forces.

Jeffrey D. Bass

See also: My Lai Massacre; United States; Vietnam War Atrocities

Further Reading

Braestrup, Peter. *Big Story: How the American Press and Television Reported and Interpreted the Crisis of Tet 1968 in Vietnam and Washington.* Novato, CA: Presidio, 1994.

Oberdorfer, Don. *TET! The Turning Point in the Vietnam War.* Baltimore: Johns Hopkins University Press, 2001.

I

India

India is a large nation located in southern Asia with approximately 1.2 billion people; it ranks second only to China in terms of population. Since India's independence in 1947, the country has faced an enormous amount of internal turmoil and upheaval, not to mention several wars with neighboring Pakistan and China. From a domestic perspective, a good deal of the violence has stemmed from religious conflicts—chiefly Hindu versus Muslim and Hindu versus Sikh. Regional separatist insurgencies, especially in northeastern India (Jammu and Kashmir), have also wrought much violence within India. In addition, various extremist groups have periodically subjected India to terrorist-like atrocities. Finally, social conflicts that originated in India's now-abolished caste system have often brought violence to the "Dalits," members of India's lower socioeconomic class.

After the Empire of India was divided into an independent Pakistan and India in August 1947, a bloody war ensued as millions of Muslims and Hindus sought to take up residence in their respective territories (India was largely Hindu and Pakistan was overwhelmingly Muslim). In the two years of fighting, at least 200,000 Hindus and 800,000 Muslims perished; the vast majority of the dead were civilians. Meanwhile, on January 20, 1948, Hindu radicals assassinated Indian independence leader Mohandas Gandhi, which set off violent protests throughout India; hundreds were killed or wounded.

From 1947 until 1964, India was governed by Prime Minister Jawaharlal Nehru. His government generally attempted to keep domestic violence to a minimum, but his decision not to allow Kashmir residents autonomy resulted in a long-running conflict that continues to bedevil the Indian government and stymie Indo-Pakistani relations. In 1962, border tensions with the Chinese resulted in the October-November 1962 Sino-Indian War, which resulted in 3,079 Indians dead, some 4,000 captured, and another 1,000 wounded. Three years later, the second war with Pakistan began. That conflict witnessed some 3,000 Indian deaths, including a number of civilians. In 1967, the so-called Naxalite-Maoist rebellion began in West Bengal. It has since spread to the rural regions of eastern and central India and is ongoing. It is estimated that since 1967, some 10,000 people have died in the conflict, with 4,000 of those deaths occurring since 2002. The Naxalites, composed of extreme leftist groups and radical communists who revere the late Chinese leader Mao Zedong, have been fighting the Indian government for years in their attempt to form their own autonomous government. Their favored tactic is the use of terrorism against civilian populations.

Massive rioting in Gujarat broke out during September–October 1969 between Hindus and Muslims. Looting and arson were also perpetrated on a large scale. Anywhere from 660 to as many as 2,000 deaths resulted, and another 1,075 people were injured. As well, more than 48,000 people lost their homes or other property in the mayhem. In December

1971, the third Indo-Pakistani War occurred, which resulted in the deaths of 3,843 Indians; another 9,851 were wounded.

Concerned about internal threats and internal revolt, Prime Minister Indira Gandhi (Nehru's daughter) invoked a state of emergency in 1975. Civil liberties were sharply curtailed and approximately 1,000 opposition leaders were rounded up and jailed, some for years. India was relatively stable for several years thereafter, but on February 18, 1983, a major massacre occurred in Nellie, Assam when members of the Lalung tribe attacked mostly Muslim workers from Bangladesh in 14 different villages in the region. When the dust settled, 2,191 unarmed civilians lay dead (some sources claim that as many as 5,000 were killed).

In 1984, Indira Gandhi's government decided to move against a group of fundamentalist Sikh separatists who had been occupying the Golden Temple in Amritsar. The occupation was a major embarrassment to the government, and the Gandhi regime suspected the Sikhs of hoarding weapons there. During June 4–8, Indian army troops, accompanied by artillery, tanks, and armored vehicles moved into Amritsar. When the operation was over, 83 army personnel lay dead, along with some 400 civilians. The heavy-handed move outraged the Sikh community, prompting major demonstrations. Sikh Indian army officers staged a mutiny, and many Sikh government personnel resigned en masse. Just four months later, two Sikh bodyguards assigned to Gandhi's security detail assassinated her on October 31. That prompted huge anti-Sikh riots throughout India, resulting in more than 3,000 Sikh deaths.

Not long after Gandhi's assassination, one of the worst industrial accidents in history occurred at the Union Carbide India Limited pesticide plant in Bhopal. The company was a subsidiary of the American-owned Union Carbide. A massive gas leak of toxic chemicals was inadvertently released from the facility during the night of December 2–3, 1984, an event that was entirely preventable. The plant was surrounded by densely populated shanty towns. The accident claimed 2,259 victims, many of them desperately poor. The accident was attributed to lax government oversight, poor maintenance and negligence by the company, and bad working conditions. Many more victims died or became ill in the years after the disaster.

In October 1989, rioting between Hindus and Muslims in Bhagalpur killed 1,000 people (900 of them Muslims); thousands of others were displaced from their homes. Rioting involving Hindus and Muslims in Mumbai during December 1992-January 1993 resulted in some 900 deaths.

On March 12, 1993, a retaliatory strike involving the use of 13 separate bombs in Mumbai killed at least 250 and wounded 700 others. Hindu-Muslim conflict also resulted in mass violence in Gujarat in February 2002; the catalyst had been a Muslim attack on a passenger train. In that raid, 58 Hindus returning from a pilgrimage died.

In late November 2008, members of a militant Islamist group from Pakistan perpetrated a series of 12 well-coordinated bombings and shootings in Mumbai. The terrorist attacks resulted in 164 deaths; another 308 were injured. Meanwhile, the ongoing insurgency in Jammu and Kashmir grew more intense beginning in the late 1980s, with the Indian government alleging that the Pakistani government was arming and training the separatist rebels there. Between 1987 and 2009, official sources claim that the insurgency has claimed the lives of at least 47,000 people; some 3,400 others have simply disappeared. Since 2009, however, the number of insurgency-related deaths has fallen dramatically amid the ongoing Indian-Pakistani peace process. Finally, persecution and violence against India's Dalits continues to occur, with the latest figures indicating that 13,000–15,000 of them become victims of abuse or violence each year.

PAUL G. PIERPAOLI JR.

See also: Bangladesh; Pakistan; Sri Lanka

Further Reading

Bose, Sugata, and Ayesha Jalal. *Modern South Asia: History, Culture, and Political Economy.* London: Routledge, 1998.

Wolpert, Stanley. *A New History of India.* Oxford: Oxford University Press, 2004.

Indian Removal Act

Congressional legislation signed into law by President Andrew Jackson on May 26, 1830, that provided legal justification for the wholesale and forcible removal of Native Americans from the east to the west, principally Indian Territory (modern-day Oklahoma and parts of Kansas). The Indian Removal Act of 1830 was the culmination of a decades-long struggle between whites and Native Americans over who would control vast tracts of territory that had been Native American ancestral lands for several centuries, in many cases. The Indian Removal Act rendered most prior agreements and treaties between the U.S. government and Native American nations null and void, and set the stage for the government to negotiate new treaties with various tribes that would effect their removal to Indian Territory. Jackson believed that prior Indian treaties were an "absurdity" and that Native Americans were "subjects" of the United States who could not claim any rights to sovereignty, as a foreign nation could.

The Indian Removal Act was immediately aimed at the so-called five civilized tribes (Choctaw, Cherokee, Chickasaw, Creek, and Seminole), who had inhabited lands in the Southeast, ranging from parts of Alabama, Mississippi, Tennessee, Georgia, and Florida. Many southerners, principally wealthy planters, coveted the lands these tribes inhabited because they knew that they were prime agricultural lands, which could be planted with crops such as cotton, an extremely lucrative commodity in the early 19th century. Of course, the land would be worked with slave labor, making large-scale agricultural enterprises even more lucrative.

During the election campaign of 1828, Jackson and the Democratic Party made Indian removal a major issue, and Jackson saw the Indian Removal Act, which proved quite controversial, as a campaign pledge fulfilled. While Jackson was intent on placing relations with Native Americans within the complete purview of the federal government, some states, like Georgia, for example, sought to control Native American tribes themselves. In 1830, that state enacted a law that made it illegal for whites to live on Native American lands without explicit authorization and that placed tribal lands under state jurisdiction. This was aimed at white missionaries, who in some cases were helping Native Americans resist removal to the west. When this was challenged in the courts, in 1831 the U.S. Supreme Court under Chief Justice John Marshall (*Cherokee Nation v. Georgia*) ruled that Native American tribes were indeed sovereign nations, meaning that state laws (and by extension federal laws) could not apply to them. Jackson derisively spurned the court decision and essentially ignored it, as did his successors.

Within a decade or so of the 1830 Indian Removal Act, treaties had been signed with the five civilized nations that allowed for their removal. While nothing in the act suggested forcible removal per se, that is in fact what occurred. While some resisted fiercely, most saw little choice but to acquiesce, with disastrous results in many instances. Many left their ancestral homelands under the watch of well-armed U.S. Army soldiers.

The first removal treaty was with the Choctaw (chiefly in Mississippi) and saw the movement of some 14,000

Choctaw to the Red River Valley. About 7,000, however, refused to leave and stayed behind. In the ensuing years, they came under greater and greater pressure from white encroachment. During 1838–1839, the U.S. Army used force to remove thousands of Cherokee to Indian Territory, precipitating the so-called Trail of Tears, during which many died of exposure, starvation, and disease. Only a few hundred remained behind, having fled into mountainous areas. There were in fact numerous trails of tears, as most of the affected tribes suffered similar fates. When the Seminole refused forcible removal, the Second Seminole War began in 1835. The Seminole fought intrepidly, and were not ultimately subdued until the end of the Third Seminole War in 1858. The Indian Removal Act also affected tribes further north and west, including the Shawnee, Potawatomi, Sauk, and Fox, who were eventually removed to Indian Territory. The Black Hawk War of 1832 was largely a result of attempts to relocate Sauk and Fox as well as the Kickapoo.

The Indian Removal Act was certainly not without controversy, and many Americans did not support it, and for varying reasons. Numerous Christian missionaries, who had been living among the Native Americans for years, were opposed to the act, realizing that relocation would have to be de facto a forcible relocation, meaning that lives would likely be lost in the process. Some northerners were against the legislation because they knew it would mean the empowerment of southern planters who would expand slavery-based agriculture into newly acquired lands. Still others abhorred the act because it seemed to subordinate states' rights to the federal government.

The Indian Removal Act was bitterly debated in Congress before its passage, and it was not universally supported. In most cases, individual removal treaties negotiated with the Native Americans provided for an exchange of land, that is, the cession of land in the east in exchange for land in the west. The exchange was almost never one-for-one, however, meaning that tribes gave up far more land than they gained in Indian Territory. Most treaties also continued earlier annuity payments by the federal government and had provisions for additional annuities after relocation was complete.

By 1883, 25 reservations had been established in Indian Territory occupied by 37 Native American tribes. It is estimated that as many as 100,000 Native Americans were forced to move between 1830 and 1869. This mass relocation caused untold suffering. Perhaps as many as one-third of those forcibly removed died on the marches west, or died shortly after, because of disease, starvation, dehydration, or exposure. The removal permanently altered tribes' cultures, social constructs, and familial institutions. Some, like the Seneca, Navajo, Seminole, and Cherokee, were successful in resisting removal, partly or wholly. Some of these people remain today on part of their ancestral homelands. Other tribes who were removed to the west became the beneficiaries of new lands that had rich natural resources, such as minerals and oil. Those people and tribes who did relocate quickly established their own communities and began farming with considerable success. However, by the end of the 19th century, many were once more under pressure to cede land to whites in Indian Territory (Oklahoma), where oil attracted white speculators in droves.

PAUL G. PIERPAOLI JR.

See also: Native American Genocide; Trail of Tears

Further Reading

Cave, Alfred A. "Abuse of Power: Andrew Jackson and the Indian removal Act of 1830." *Historian* Vol. 65 (Winter 2003): 1130–1153.

Johansen, Bruce E. *Shapers of the Great Debate on Native Americans: Land, Spirit, Power.* Westport, CT: Greenwood Press, 2000.

Wallace, Anthony C. *The Long, Bitter Trail: Andrew Jackson and the Indians.* New York: Hill and Wang, 1993.

Indigenous Populations

The world's indigenous peoples, those also known as tribal peoples, native peoples, aboriginal peoples, Fourth World peoples, and First Nations, have been subjected to major human rights violations, massacres, and genocides in virtually every state in which they reside. Numbering some 350,000,000 to 400,000,000 in over 70 of the world's countries, indigenous peoples have experienced mass killings, arbitrary executions, torture, mental and physical mistreatment, arrests and detentions without trial, forced sterilization, involuntary relocation, destruction of their subsistence base, and the taking of children from their families. While the rate of destruction of indigenous groups may have been reduced in scale over the past 500 years, members of indigenous groups continue to be killed and mistreated in spite of efforts to protect indigenous rights and to predict potentially genocidal conditions.

As noted in the United Nations Convention on the Prevention and Punishment of the Crime of Genocide, genocide is defined as acts committed with intent to destroy, in whole or in part, a national, ethnical, racial, or religious group. Indigenous groups and their supporters sometimes draw a distinction between physical genocide, the destruction of indigenous peoples themselves, and ethnocide, or cultural genocide, the purposeful destruction of a group's culture. Examples of the physical genocide include the massacres of aboriginal peoples in Tasmania and Australia in the 19th century, the hunting down and killing of Aché (Guayaki) Indian adults and the kidnapping of their children in Paraguay in the 1960s and 1970s, and the murder and dispossession of tribal peoples in the Chittagong Hills Tracts of Bangladesh since 1971. Tens of thousands of members of indigenous groups have been killed in the late 20th century. Examples of ethnocide or cultural genocide include the efforts of the Canadian, Australian, and U.S. governments to require aboriginal children to go to boarding schools where they were required to learn and speak English, adopt European cultural pattern, and take courses on Western Civilization. The destruction of cultural identity has also occurred in places like Iran and Syria, where nomadic populations have been required to settle down, and where indigenous children were taken from their families and given to nonindigenous families to raise, as was the case in Australia.

The destruction of indigenous peoples and their cultures has been a policy of many of the world's governments, although most government spokespersons argue that the disappearance or disruption of indigenous societies was not purposeful but rather occurred inadvertently. In Brazil, for example, more than 80 Indian groups that were contacted between 1900 and 1957 were destroyed by disease and deculturation, as well as by physical destruction. The situation was especially devastating for those groups whose resource-extractive activities such as rubber and nut collection were curtailed. Overall, the numbers of indigenous peoples in Brazil declined from over 1,000,000 to 200,000, a drop of 80 percent.

Genocide is neither accidental nor an unintended result of the actions of states, armies, private companies, or development agencies. In virtually every case, genocide is a calculated and generally premeditated set of actions designed to achieve certain goals such as the removal of competitors or the silencing of opponents. Military repression of indigenous peoples that resist state-building efforts is one context in which genocide occurs. Over the past 30 years, tens of thousands of Quiche Maya and other Guatemalan Indians were killed, their villages destroyed, and their crops burned by the Guatemalan military. Many of those who were not killed sought refuge in neighboring countries, but even there they were not completely safe.

A recent example of genocidal actions against indigenous people can be seen in the case of the Lacandon Maya and other indigenous groups who support the efforts of the Zapatista National Liberation Army (EZLN) in Chiapas, Mexico. The Zapatista leadership maintain that their uprising on January 1, 1994, was linked directly to the passage of the North American Free Trade Agreement (NAFTA) and to the poor treatment of the indigenous peoples of southern Mexico by the government, companies, and non-indigenous landowners. Amnesty International and other human rights organizations reported on human rights violations by the Mexican army in its efforts to quell the Zapatista uprising; not only were members of the Zapatistas killed, but so too were Indian women and children.

States have conscripted members of indigenous groups into their armed forces, sometimes by force. The United States drew upon the services of the Montagnards of Vietnam, while the South African Defense Force (SADF) drafted members of Kung, Khwe, and Vasakela San (Bushmen) groups in the war against the South West Africa People's Organization (SWAPO) in Angola and Namibia in the 1970s and 1980s. Indeed, the San of southern Africa have been described as the most militarized ethnic group in the world.

Indigenous peoples have been persecuted mainly on the basis of who they are. They have been described by governments and the media as "vermin," people who should be removed "for the good of the country." Indigenous peoples are often seen by states as outside the universe of obligation (the other"), or as competitors for valued resources. They are sometimes said not to be utilizing land productively or are argued to be responsible for its degradation as seen, for example, in the case of rainforest depletion because of shifting cultivation by Indian communities in Latin America and tribal peoples in the Philippines and other parts of Southeast Asia. African indigenous groups like the Pygmies (Batwa) of Central Africa, the Okiek (Dorobo) of Kenya, the Hadza of Tanzania, and the San of southern Africa are criticized by governments and nongovernment environmental organizations for their hunting activities, and members of indigenous groups are arrested, held in detention, and sometimes are mistreated physically in jail. There have also been charges by indigenous groups in Africa that some governments have instituted "shoot-to-kill" policies aimed at discouraging poaching, something that indigenous groups have termed coercive conservation.

Sometimes considered "wards of the state," indigenous peoples often were not granted land and resource rights or a voice in public affairs. Efforts to remove indigenous groups from their land by governments, companies, and individuals continue to occur in the Amazon Basin, Africa, Malaysia, Indonesia, the Philippines, India, Bangladesh, and Siberia, often in the context of oil, timber, or mineral resource exploitation. Multinational corporations and multilateral development banks are sometimes complicit in these actions.

Genocide has occurred through indirect means as can be seen, for example, in the cases in North and South America, where Indians were given blankets infected by smallpox and other diseases. There is what Helen Fein has termed genocide by attrition, the process whereby indigenous and other groups, including refugees, are denied access to food and medicine by governments or other agencies. This kind of genocidal behavior has occurred over the past decade in Sudan, where thousands of Dinka, Nuer, and Nuba have died. In Somalia, sizable numbers of Eyle, a hunter-gatherer group in the Bay Region, died because of raids on humanitarian convoys by militia groups in the early 1990s.

Another context in which genocides and massive human rights violations against indigenous peoples occurs involves efforts to promote social and economic development, often characterized as being "in the national interest." Sometimes termed developmental genocides, these kinds of actions take place when states, agencies, companies, or transnational corporations oppress local peoples during the course of implementing various kinds of development projects. This can be seen, for example, in the case of the mining company Freeport Indonesia Inc. (FII), a subsidiary of the New Orleans-based multinational corporation Freeport McMoRan, in Irian Jaya (West Papua). Freeport Indonesia is said to be guilty of complicity with the Indonesian government in a whole series of human rights crimes, including assassinations, disappearances, raids on and burning of villages, detentions without trial, torture, purposeful dumping of toxic substances, and intimidation of opponents. Justifications by company executives for their actions range from protecting their assets and the security of employees to making profits for the government of Indonesia.

Numerous indigenous peoples have been forced out of development project areas, often with little or no compensation. The problem has become so widespread, in fact, that a new category of displaced persons has been proposed: "development refugees." Violence is sometimes an outgrowth of the establishment of large-scale projects, river basin development being one of the classic examples. Dam projects such as those along the Narmada River in India and the Senegal River in West Africa have seen repressive tactics employed by the companies or agencies involved in them, including the murder of political activists, disappearances, and torture of detainees. Involuntary resettlement and loss of land and resource access as a result of decisions by the state has had the effect of increasing internal social tensions, some of which are exhibited in higher rates of suicide and social stress among indigenous peoples, for example, as seen among the Guarani of Brazil.

Ecocide, the systematic destruction of ecosystems by states, agencies, or corporate entities is a problem that indigenous peoples in many parts of the world have had to face. This can be seen in the case of the Ogoni of southern Nigeria, for example, whose lands have been fouled by pollution from pipeline spills and the purposeful dumping of oil residues and other toxic substances by Shell Oil. The Ogoni and their supporters have been attacked by the Nigerian military, their homes destroyed, and sizable numbers of people arrested and jailed. The Nigerian government even went so far as to put to death a world-renowned environmental activist, Ken Saro-Wiwa, and several of his colleagues in the Movement for the Support of the Ogoni People (MOSOP) in November 1995, an action that brought widespread attention to environmental and social justice issues.

States sometimes engage in actions aimed at destroying the resource base in order to influence populations engaged in actions that they disagree with. This can be seen, for instance, in cases where herbicides such as Agent Orange were used to clear forests so that multinational development efforts or counterinsurgency actions can proceed, as was the case in Vietnam, the Amazon Basin, and Zimbabwe. The so-called drug war, orchestrated in part by the U.S. Drug Enforcement Agency (DEA) in countries such as Bolivia, Colombia, Mexico, and Peru, has had more than its share of human rights violations, some of them arising from raids on local communities and the use of toxic materials to destroy coca and marijuana crops.

Cases claiming genocide against indigenous peoples have been brought before the United Nations, but generally they have had little success, in part, as Leo Kuper pointed out, because government representatives claimed that there had been no intent to destroy indigenous peoples as such and that the groups were never eliminated "as

an ethnic or cultural group." Indigenous groups in numerous countries, including Bangladesh, Burma, and Burundi, have stressed that violations of the right to life have had a distinctly ethnic or culturally targeted character, no matter what government officials claim. Some groups have chosen to seek assistance from the Human Rights Commission of the United Nations, as the San of Botswana did in March 1996 after efforts were made by the government of Botswana to remove indigenous peoples from their ancestral territories in the Central Kalahari Game Reserve. Still others have opted to resist the actions of states to dispossess and harm them, as can be seen in the cases of the Zapatistas of Chiapas, Mexico and the Shining Path (Sendero Luminoso) and Tupac Amaru Revolutionary Movement (MRTA) in the Peruvian Andes.

Indigenous groups have begun to collaborate with a variety of support organizations in an effort to oppose genocidal practices and to promote the interests of indigenous peoples. They have also formed their own regional indigenous organizations, including COICA, the Coordinating Body for Indigenous Organizations of the Amazon Basin, and WIMSA, the Working Group of Indigenous Minorities in Southern Africa. Some indigenous groups, such as those in Guatemala, have worked with teams of forensic scientists and archaeologists who are exhuming mass graves in places as diverse as Argentina, Chile, Guatemala, Ethiopia, Rwanda, and the Former Yugoslavia. The evidence recovered in these investigations has been used in genocide and criminal trials, as was the case, for example, with the International Criminal Tribunal for Rwanda (ICTR), following the Rwandan genocide of 1994.

How successful these efforts will be very much depends on whether or not states, private companies, intergovernmental organizations, and advocacy groups are willing to collaborate in order to (1) establish strict internationally recognized indigenous rights standards; (2) enforce those standards carefully; (3) monitor and evaluate development projects and policies from the standpoint of their effects on indigenous peoples; (4) initiate changes in those projects and policies if they are found to be having a deleterious effect on the welfare of indigenous peoples and others; and (5) seek justice against those who have perpetrated genocide and human rights crimes. Governments and companies must live up to their obligation to protect indigenous peoples and their neighbors and not compromise their rights under the weight of so-called progress, economic growth, free trade, or counterinsurgency. All institutions and individuals need to work together to stop genocide and to promote the rights not just of indigenous peoples, but of all human beings.

ROBERT K. HITCHCOCK

See also: Australian Aborigines; Black War; Native American Genocide

Further Reading

Churchill, Ward. *A Little Matter of Genocide: Holocaust and Denial in the Americas, 1492 to the Present.* San Francisco, CA: City Lights Books, 1997.

Gurr, Ted Robert. *Minorities at Risk: A Global View of Ethnopolitical Conflicts.* Washington, D.C: U.S. Institute of Peace Press, 1993.

Miller, Marc S., ed. *State of the Peoples: A Global Human Rights Report on Societies in Danger.* Boston, MA: Beacon Press, 1993.

Totten, Samuel, William S. Parsons, and Israel W. Charny, eds. *Century of Genocide: Eyewitness Accounts and Critical Views.* New York: Garland Publishing, 1997.

Indonesia

Indonesia is a multiethnic, multicultural island nation located mainly in Southeast Asia. Predominantly Muslim, Indonesia is composed of more than 17,500 islands (many of which are uninhabited). Since it gained its independence from The Netherlands in 1949, Indonesia has often struggled under authoritarian regimes that committed frequent human rights abuses. Under its first president, Sukarno, Indonesians briefly enjoyed a multiparty, quasidemocratic government, but by 1957, Sukarno had declared martial law. Two years later, he dissolved the Constituent Assembly and essentially created a one-man dictatorship.

Sukarno's regime was tested in late September 1965, when a cabal of young, leftist army officers attempted a coup d'état by assassinating six rightist army generals. Sukarno ordered a massive crackdown against leftist groups, most notably the powerful Communist Party of Indonesia (PKI). What resulted over the succeeding months, and well into 1966, was a frenzy of government-sponsored violence that sought to eradicate all vestiges of communism and leftists in general. When the killing finally stopped, as many as 500,000 Indonesian communists and communist sympathizers were dead. As many as 1 million others were jailed. General Suharto, who was head of the Indonesian military and who supervised the anticommunist purges, used the tragedy to engineer Sukarno's ouster. In March 1967, Suharto deposed Sukarno and declared himself acting president. Through a series of fraudulent and rigged elections, he remained president of Indonesia until 1998. Suharto imposed his own authoritarian regime on his countrymen by severely limiting the political process, placing tight controls on the media, and relying heavily on the military to impose his will.

In December 1975, Indonesian military forces launched a full-scale invasion of East Timor, beginning a brutal occupation that would not end until 1999. The catalyst for the attack was East Timor's bid to gain independence, which the Suharto regime viewed as a significant threat. Over the course of some 24 years, which witnessed routine violence aimed at the East Timorese and a famine caused largely by occupation policies, at least 90,000 people died in East Timor (some estimates claim as many as 200,000 dead). On November 12, 1999, during peaceful proindependence demonstrations in the East Timor capital of Dili, 271 people died after being attacked by Indonesian government forces; 382 others were injured, and at least 250 were reported missing and presumed dead. In the meantime, Suharto ordered brutal crackdowns against separatists in the oil-rich region of Aceh and in West Papua, which killed tens of thousands of people.

Suharto was finally ousted from power in March 1998 after Indonesians were promised a new start engineered by a democratic government free from corruption. Suharto's successors, however, have largely paid lip service to those promises, and Indonesia remains a nation mired in cronyism and ineffective government. In more recent years, there has been a major uptick in terrorism in Indonesia, most of it perpetrated by radical, fundamentalist Islamic groups. These groups decry the secularism of the Indonesian government, not to mention its close ties to the West. In October 2002, the radical group Jemaah Islamiyah, which has ties to the Al-Qaeda terrorist organization, bombed a tourist area in Bali, killing 202 (virtually all were tourists) and injuring 240. Terrorists again struck Bali with bombs in October 2005; 20 died and more than 100 were wounded in the attacks.

Islamic terrorists struck the Indonesian capital of Jakarta in 2003, 2004, and 2009. In August 2003, a Marriott hotel was bombed, resulting in 12 deaths; an additional 150 were wounded. The Australian embassy in Jakarta was bombed in September 2004, killing nine and wounding at least 125 people. In July 2009, two exclusive tourist hotels in Jakarta were bombed. Seven people died in those attacks, and 53 more were wounded. Islamic extremist terrorism will likely remain a problem for the Indonesian government for some time to come, although the Indonesians have begun devoting more money and manpower to antiterrorist operations.

PAUL G. PIERPAOLI JR.

See also: Indonesian Killings (1965)

Further Reading

Cribb, Robert, and Colin Brown. *Modern Indonesia: A History since 1945.* London: Longman, 1995.

Ricklefs, Merle Calvin. *A History of Modern Indonesia since c. 1200.* Stanford, CA: Stanford University Press, 2001.

Indonesian Killings (1965)

From October 1965 to March 1966, conservative forces in Indonesia, including the army and Muslim militias, killed at least 100,000 Indonesians (some estimates claim as many as 500,000 deaths) as part of a sustained campaign against left-wing forces. Most of the victims were members or associates of the Indonesian Communist Party (PKI); they were killed in hundreds of local massacres.

In the early 20th century, Marxist ideas had first been introduced in Indonesia, then known as the Dutch East Indies, which influenced a wide range of thinkers in the nationalist movement. By the early 1920s, however, increasingly sharp divisions had begun to emerge between various nationalist movements, including communism, Islam, and developmental modernization. Hostility to the communists was based on both religion and class. Many Muslims and Christians objected to communism's atheism and to its opposition to state support for religion. The communists' base among plantation and factory workers, and later among peasants, also pitted them against the small middle class and the powerful landlords. A 1948 PKI uprising against the newly independent Indonesian Republic, then still engaged in a war of independence with the Dutch, helped turn many army leaders against communism.

The party regrouped in 1951 under D.N. Aidit (1923–1965), adopting a strategy of participation in democratic institutions. It emerged as the fourth largest party in Indonesia's 1955 elections. Fears that the party might soon be strong enough to demand a place in government contributed to the dismantling of the parliamentary system and the introduction of President Sukarno's "Guided

Democracy" in 1957–1959. Although Guided Democracy seemed likely at first to freeze PKI influence at 1957 levels, the party soon made itself indispensable to Sukarno as a political counterbalance to the growing influence of the army. The party developed an extensive power base amongst peasants, especially in Java and Bali, and recruited many supporters within the bureaucracy and the armed forces. Marxism, meanwhile, became a central part of the official state ideology, known as NASAKOM (taken from the Indonesian words for nationalism, religion, and communism). Many observers believed that the PKI was well placed to come to power after Sukarno's departure.

On October 1, 1965, however, an unsuccessful coup took place in the capital, Jakarta, against the conservative, anticommunist army high command. Several senior generals were killed, but the coup was suppressed by a surviving general, Suharto, who over the next five months forced Sukarno from power and destroyed the PKI, whose involvement in planning the coup was widely assumed but has never been proven. The result of Suharto's campaign was the virtual massacre of as many as 500,000 Indonesians.

The communist party was not formally banned until March 1966, but massacres of PKI members and associates began within days of the coup. The killings were sometimes carried out by military units, but were more often the work of vigilantes, generally armed and encouraged by anticommunist army units. They were most intense in Central and East Java, Bali, and North Sumatra, where the PKI had campaigned especially vigorously on behalf of landless peasants and plantation workers and where the party had become associated with social and religious tensions dating back to the early decades of the century. Many people who had made compromises with the left under Guided Democracy also were driven to take part in the killings to prove their anticommunist credentials.

ROBERT CRIBB

See also: Indonesia

Further Reading

Cribb, Robert, ed. *The Indonesian Killings of 1965–1966: Studies from Java and Bali.* Clayton, Victoria, Australia: Monash University, Centre of Southeast Asian Studies, Monash Papers on Southeast Asia, No. 21, 1990.

Robinson, Geoffrey. *The Dark Side of Paradise: Political Violence in Bali.* Ithaca, NY: Cornell University Press, 1995.

International Military Tribunal, Far East

The International Military Trials in the Far East were trials of senior Japanese leaders after World War II. General of the U.S. Army Douglas MacArthur, heading the military occupation of Japan, established the International Military Tribunal for the Far East, popularly known as the Tokyo War Crimes Trials. The body held sessions in Tokyo from May 3, 1946, to November 12, 1948. Trials conducted by the tribunal were similar to those held at Nuremberg, Germany. The defendants were 28 senior Japanese military and civilian leaders, chosen from among 250 Japanese officials originally accused of war crimes. General Tojo Hideki, who held various posts including prime minister and chief of the General Staff, was the best-known defendant among the 18 military officers and 10 civilians charged. General MacArthur, with President Harry S. Truman's support, exempted Emperor Hirohito from trial because of concerns over potential Japanese resistance to military occupation. More than 2,200 similar trials, including some held in Tokyo that preceded the tribunal, were conducted in areas formerly occupied by Japan, ranging from China to Pacific islands including Guam. The trials generated strong reactions, and they remain controversial to this day.

The Tokyo tribunal consisted of 11 judges, 1 each from Australia, Canada, China, Great Britain, the Netherlands, New Zealand, the Soviet Union, the United States, France, India, and the Philippines. The Philippine justice was a survivor of the Bataan Death March. The tribunal's chief prosecutor, Joseph B. Keenan, was appointed by President Truman. Keenan's credentials included service as a former director of the U.S. Justice Department's Criminal Division as well as assistant to the U.S. attorney general. His staff included 25 lawyers. The tribunal was not bound by technical rules of evidence normally observed in a democracy and could admit any evidence that it chose, including purported admissions or statements of the accused.

The tribunal sought to establish clearly the principle that aggressive war was a crime and to prevent or deter future crimes against peace. Those who planned and initiated aggressive war in contravention of treaties, assurances, and international agreements were to be considered common felons. The tribunal also claimed jurisdiction over conventional war crimes and crimes against humanity, such as murder, mass murder, enslavement, deportation of civilian populations, and persecutions based on political or racial grounds in connection with other crimes under tribunal jurisdiction.

Some defendants were accused of being responsible for the actions of personnel under their command who had committed crimes against prisoners of war and civilian internees. These offenses included murder, beatings, torture, ill-treatment, including inadequate provision of food and clothing and poor sanitation, rape of female nurses and other women, and the imposition of excessive and dangerous labor. Charges of murder were also leveled in cases involving the killing of military personnel who had surrendered, laid down arms, or no longer had means of defense, including survivors of ships sunk by naval action and crews of captured ships.

Seeking to conduct a fair trial, the tribunal gave each of those accused a copy of his or her indictment in Japanese, and trial proceedings were conducted in both English and Japanese. Defendants had a right to counsel, and the defense could question witnesses. Subject to court approval, the defense could also request the appearance of witnesses and the provision of documents. The mental and physical capacity of the accused to stand trial was also considered. After a conviction, the tribunal had the power to impose a death sentence or other punishment on a defendant.

Of the 28 original defendants, 25 were convicted. Seven (including Tojo) were sentenced to death by hanging, 16 to life imprisonment, one to 20 years of incarceration, and another to 7 years in prison. The remaining 3 were not convicted, one being declared mentally unstable and two dying before their trials ended.

As with the Nuremberg trials, the tribunal has been accused of promulgating "victors' justice," and some have called the proceedings racist. But fueled by horror at continuing military atrocities in places such as Bosnia and Cambodia, a legacy of the Tokyo and Nuremberg trials has been the widespread international support for a permanent war crimes tribunal. The U.S. government, however, has resisted the formation of such a body, fearing that it could be politically influenced to harass American military forces operating overseas.

GLENN E. HELM

See also: Japan; Japanese Bacteriological Weapons Trial; Tojo, Hideki; Yamashita Trial; Yokohama Trials

Further Reading

Kei, Ushimura. *Beyond the "Judgment of Civilization": The Intellectual Legacy of the Japanese War Crimes Trials, 1946–1949.* Translated by Steven J. Ericson. Tokyo: International House of Japan, 2003.

Maga, Timothy. *Judgement at Tokyo.* Lexington: University Press of Kentucky, 2001.

Iran

The modern state of Iran was born during the Pahlavi Dynasty, which fully emerged in 1925. Iran was governed by Reza Shah Pahlavi for the next 16 years. Reza Shah's rule witnessed a broad flowering of social, economic, and political reforms designed to modernize the nation and keep foreign meddling at bay. Many modern amenities first emerged in Iran during this period, including modern transportation, widely distributed electrical service, radio service, and movie theaters. Reza Shah's rule was strictly secular, however, which rankled the more conservative Islamic elements in the country. Reza Shah's government was also autocratic, stressing anticommunism, nationalism, and militarism. The regime routinely engaged in progovernment propaganda campaigns and stringently censored the press. In 1935, a revolt at the Imam Reza Shrine in Mashhad prompted by the Iranian government's permissive rules regarding Western-style clothing and liberal social interactions precipitated as many as 50 deaths and injured several hundred others. Government troops were sent in to quash the rebellion.

Because of Reza Shah's perceived tilt toward the Axis powers in World War II, British and Soviet troops occupied Iran in 1941 and Reza Shah was replaced by his son, Mohammad Reza Pahlavi, that same year. Reza Pahlavi was solidly pro-British. The new Shah governed in much the same way as his father—political freedom was only illusory, and secularism was emphasized over Islamic law. In the immediate aftermath of World War II, there was a nationalist movement among many Kurds located in Iranian Kurdistan; that development was quickly subdued by Reza Pahlavi's government. Hundreds of Kurds died or were wounded in the attempt to quash the separatists, which all but ended in 1946.

By the late 1940s, however, Reza Pahlavi's power in Iran became more tenuous, and Parliament became increasingly dysfunctional; indeed, between 1947 and 1951, Iran had six different prime ministers. At the same time, new political parties emerged that were a threat to the Shah's rule. One was the communist Thul Party, supported by the Soviets; the other was the National Front Party (NFP), a nationalist-democratic group led by Mohammed Mossadegh.

In 1951, when Mossadegh was elected prime minister, he moved to nationalize Iran's massive oil interests, which were owned by Great Britain. This prompted a full-blown diplomatic and political crisis, which resulted in Mossadegh's resignation in 1952. Within hours of the resignation, many Iranians took to the streets, shouting and chanting.

They generally voiced their support for the ex-prime minister and denounced Reza Pahlavi. Dozens of people were killed or injured in the protests, and hundreds were arrested and held without charges. Nevertheless, the Shah soon reinstated Mossadegh, who proceeded with land reform and nationalization, which deeply troubled the West. In the summer of 1953, the U.S. Central Intelligence Agency (CIA) engineered a coup against Mossadegh, with the Shah's complicity. In August, when Reza Pahlavi demanded Mossadegh's resignation, and the prime minister refused, the Shah fled the country. This prompted huge riots throughout much of Iran, killing dozens and injuring several thousand others. Eventually, the CIA and British intelligence operatives ensured that the Iranian Army, loyal to the Shah, took control in Tehran. Mossadegh was soon arrested and tried for treason while the Shah returned to Iran.

Major unrest returned to Iran in June 1963. Disillusioned with the Shah's pro-Western and secular focus, not to mention his tepid economic policies and political oppression, Islamic conservatives, who supported the cleric Ayatollah Ruhollah Khomeini's public condemnations of the Shah's regime, began rioting after Khomeini's arrest. Several days of violence brought a brutal government crackdown, with 30 leading Islamic clerics and several hundred other intellectuals and conservative Muslims arrested. At least 380 people were killed and wounded during the violence, many by government police. Khomeini went into exile and would return to lead a revolt that overthrew the Shah in 1979.

Life in the Reza Pahlavi's Iran could be dangerous, particularly for those on the extreme right or left of the political spectrum. Indeed, the Shah's dreaded secret police arrested tens of thousands of Iranians during his reign, and perhaps as many as a thousand simply disappeared. By the summer of 1978, a sizable number of Iranians had become fed up with the Shah's reign. They quickly took to the streets, and on September 8 (Black Friday), government troops and police shot and killed as many as 3,000 people in Tehran's Zhaleh Square. This was the beginning of the end for the Shah. The massacre boosted the conservative Islamists within Iran and shocked the rest of the world. By early winter of 1979, the Pahlavi Dynasty had toppled and conservative Islamists had taken over the Iranian government; Ayatollah Khomeini returned from exile in February to lead the Iranian revolutionary government.

The Khomeini regime was equally—if not more oppressive—than the one it had replaced. Insisting on the imposition of Islamic law over vast portions of government and everyday life, the new government arrested or executed dissidents, and frequently permitted ghastly punishments for those who did not observe the law, including lashings, beatings, amputations, and public executions. As Khomeini consolidated his power in the early 1980s, several separatist groups or opposition parties, including the communists and the Kurds, waged a low-level war with government forces. The Khomeini government brutally suppressed the Kurds by 1983, in the process causing some 10,000 casualties and burning dozens of villages to the ground. Thousands of others died during this period of political consolidation, although precise figures are impossible to determine.

Meanwhile, the Iran-Iraq War that began in September 1980 and that lasted until August 1988 also killed many Iranians. It is estimated that as many as 500,000 died in the bloody conflict, with another 500,000 or more wounded. Iraq's use of chemical weapons killed at least 100,000 Iranians, most of them soldiers, but many civilians died as well. In July 1988, as the war was about to end, the Iranian government murdered thousands of political prisoners throughout the country. Most were leftists or members of the People's Mujahidin Organization of Iran. The number of people killed varies from as low as 1,400 to as high as 30,000.

More recently, in the aftermath of the 2009 elections, which some have claimed were rigged in favor of the incumbent, Mahmoud Ahmadinejad, mass protests resulted in another brutal government crackdown. Anywhere from 36 to 72 protesters died in the violence, and another 4,000 were arrested. The Iranian government continues to oppress its own people and routinely resorts to strict censorship and propaganda to hide its actions from its own citizens and the international community.

PAUL G. PIERPAOLI JR.

See also: Democide; Torture

Further Reading

Ansari, Ali. *A History of Modern Iran since 1921: The Pahlavis and After*. Boston: Longman, 2003.

Schaffer, David. *The Iran-Iraq War*. San Diego, CA: Lucent Books, 2003.

Iraq

Iraq, a nation located in the Middle East with a population of about 32 million, has been badly divided and damaged by war and internal strife since the 1970s. It is somewhat ironic that it was in this ancient, blood-soaked land that a ruler gave the first recorded statement of human rights. In October, 539 BCE, the Persian ruler Cyrus II occupied ancient Babylon without bloodshed as an unopposed conqueror. He promptly issued what we know today as the "Cyrus Cylinder." That declaration is widely, if not quite accurately, perceived as the first statement of human rights.

The corresponding tragic occurrences in the land between the Euphrates and Tigris Rivers extends, literally, hundreds upon hundreds of years before the international conventions and treaties that would have delineated some of those acts as "war crimes." Hulagu Khan's February 1258 CE sacking of the Abbasid capital of Baghdad saw anywhere between 90,000 and 500,000 civilians slaughtered in a single week. Tamerlane's 1401 invasion of the region was even bloodier. At the city of Tikrit, Tamerlane ordered the decapitation of 70,000 civilians. He then moved on to Baghdad and beheaded another 20,000–90,000 people. Sadly, the justification presented by both Hulagu and Tamerlane was one of religious (Islamic) conversion and purity.

The modern interpretation of a war crime requires international laws that prohibit some behaviors. Therefore, even the deliberate and wanton slaughter of Iraqis, both Arabic and Kurdish, by the British Royal Air Force (RAF) during the Iraqi rebellion of 1920 cannot, technically, be regarded as a war crime. This is because they occurred before any treaty applying to the use of air power had been written or adopted.

After first crushing the 1920 revolt in the Euphrates River valley with both air and ground forces, the RAF was deployed against civilian villages in the Kurdish regions repeatedly throughout the rest of the decade (Iraq did not become an actual nation in even a nominal sense until 1921 and was not granted independence until 1932). One infamous British officer, Arthur Harris (later an air marshall in World War II nicknamed "Butcher" Harris), even seemed proud of these events, remarking "where the Arab and Kurd had begun to realize that if they could stand a little noise, they could stand bombing, and still argue, they now know what real bombing means, in casualties and damage; they now know that within 45 minutes a full-sized village can be practically wiped out and a third of its inhabitants killed or injured by four or five machines which offer them no real target, no opportunity for glory as warriors, no effective means of escape."

Similar dilemmas presented themselves during one of the most notorious uses of chemical weapons in history. In March 1988, Iraqi army forces under the control of Iraqi dictator Saddam Hussein attacked the village of Halabja, located in Iraqi Kurdistan. Iranian armed forces and rebellious Iraqi Kurdish fighters were, at the time, occupying the village. Because Iraq was not a signatory of the Chemical Weapons Convention, it was not technically illegal for Iraq to employ chemical weapons on the battlefield during its 1980–1988 war with Iran. The attack against the village killed an estimated 5,000 people, mostly unarmed civilians. Although not a part of Hussein's genocidal Anfal Campaign against the Kurds, which occurred on territory his troops did control and which Human Rights Watch estimated killed between 50,000 and 100,000 people, the gas and nerve agent onslaught against Halabja is more infamous.

In March 2003, the United States led a small coalition of allied nations in an attack against Iraq. Seeking regime change, ostensibly because of Hussein's apparent though not actual retention of weapons of mass destruction, the initial assault quickly toppled Hussein's Ba'athist government. During the initial fighting (March 19–April 30, 2003), it is estimated that roughly 10,000 Iraqi combatants died and approximately 4,000–7,000 noncombatants were killed. Thereafter, the situation deteriorated. Over the next three years, a small scale insurgency grew into a large-scale sectarian insurgency which, by 2006, threatened to become a full-scale quasireligious civil war. By 2007, the number of factions fighting within Iraq almost defied description. The list includes but is not limited to: American forces, the government of Iraq (which was mostly on the side of the American-led coalition), the armed forces of the various members of the coalition, the Mahdi Militia forces of radical Shiite leader Moqtada Sadr, the militia forces of various other Shiite political groups, the armed members of the various Sunni tribes, Al Qaeda in Iraq, and similar Sunni terrorist/insurgency/criminal groups such as Ansar Al Sunna.

American forces abused Iraqi prisoners, most infamously at the Abu Ghraib prison just to the west of Baghdad in late 2003. They also committed incidents of wanton rape and murder, such as the case of Mahmoudiya in March 2006, in which a squad of American soldiers killed three members of a family and raped the teenage daughter before finally murdering her. American forces also murdered unarmed civilians in retaliation for the death of a peer. An example of that occurred with U.S. Marines in the town of Haditha in 2006. The perpetrators these crimes were arrested, tried in courts, and most of them imprisoned for various terms.

In January 2007, under heavy criticism at home and abroad for its mishandling of the Iraq War, the George W. Bush administration announced a troop surge—amounting to some 20,000 additional troops—that would be deployed to Iraq and stationed in the most war-torn areas and provinces. It was hoped that the surge strategy would stem the tide of sectarian violence, relieve pressure on over-burdened U.S. troops already in Iraq, and permit the fledgling post Hussein government to take more responsibility for its own internal security. In the short term, however, the situation in Iraq worsened.

Iraqis (both Shiite and Sunni) unleashed war crimes against each other as members of organized militias, as part of rogue (and sometimes authorized) military and paramilitary units, and on behalf of the Sunni terrorist group Answer Al Sunni, as well as the small and largely non-Iraqi group Al Qaeda in Iraq. Iraqi on Iraqi violence and lawful combat had claimed the lives of at least 70,000–77,000 Iraqi civilians as of late August 2007. The overwhelming majority of these deaths came in the form of suicide bombings against Shiites, a favored Sunni tactic, and retributive murder by organized CIA militias and Shia-controlled elements of the Ministry of Interior. The most lethal attack of this kind was the August 2007 coordinated suicide bombings in the Kurdish villages of Qahtaniya and Jazeera, which killed 572 people. Considerable tensions remained between various political and sectarian factions in Iraq, and violence against civilian population remained problematic until late 2007 and early 2008, when some of the violence began to ebb and attacks on American and coalition forces dropped noticeably.

By mid-2008, at least from the Americans' perspective, the troop surge was having the desired effect. Attacks against coalition forces had been greatly reduced, sectarian violence had diminished, and the Iraqi government seemed to be on the road toward stability. The Barack Obama administration began drawing down troops in February 2009—one of the new president's campaign promises had been to end the Iraq War—and on August 31, 2010, U.S. combat operations in Iraq were declared over. The last of the American troops in Iraq were withdrawn on December 15, 2011.

ROBERT L. BATEMAN

See also: Chemical Weapons and Warfare

Further Reading
Shadid, Anthony. *Night Draws Near: Iraq's People in the Shadow of America's War*. New York: Henry Holt and Company, 2005.
Simon, Reeva Spector, and Eleanor H. Tejirian, eds. *The Creation of Iraq, 1914–1921*. New York: Columbia University Press, 2004.
Tripp, Charles. *A History of Iraq*. Cambridge, UK: Cambridge University Press, 2000.

Irish Potato Famine

As Ireland approached the 1840s, conditions were ripe for disaster. Over a fourth of its population—2 million out of 8 million—were without regular employment. Some had found shelter in workhouses built at the expense of local taxpayers as mandated by the Irish Poor Law of 1838. Many more roamed the countryside begging and sleeping in ditches. Nearly half of the country's rural families lived in windowless, mud cabins of one room and survived on the potatoes that they could grow on the half an acre or so of land for which they often paid a very high rent. Only the wealthy landowners—many of them absentee landlords living in England—had any security at all.

Potato Blight

The peasants were forced to rent the land they lived and worked on from wealthy landowners in England. The crop they depended on primarily for food and for a portion of their rent was potatoes. Since its introduction to Ireland in 1790, the potato had provided a cheap and plentiful source of food for Ireland's peasants. The potato could grow in the poorest conditions, with very little labor. That fact was important because the peasants had to spend most of their waking hours working for their landlords and had precious little time to tend their own crops.

Yet the hardy crop was no match for *Phytophthora infestans,* the potato blight that struck with a vengeance in 1845. That airborne fungus attacked the potato plants; it produced black spots and a white mold on the leaves and soon rotted the potato to a pulp. As much as 90 percent of that year's potato crop was destroyed or unfit for consumption.

Laissez-Faire Government

The government of Great Britain had long practiced an economic theory known as laissez-faire, which held that it was not a government's job to provide aid for its citizens or to interfere with the free market of goods or trade. As a result, the British government provided minimal relief to the starving peasants.

Prime Minister Sir Robert Peel did, however, push to repeal the Corn Laws, laws that had been in place since the late 1400s and that protected the investments of wealthy British landowners by subjecting any foreign crops brought into Britain to high taxes. Those laws had pretty much limited the grain supply to what was raised in Britain and guaranteed a high price for it. By repealing the laws, Parliament cleared the way for less expensive grains to be brought into Ireland to relieve the famine, but even then, the peasants had no money with which to buy bread.

Although Peel was successful in securing the repeal, the resulting protest split the British Conservative Party, and he was forced to resign. His successor, Lord John Russell, was a rigid supporter of laissez-faire and was of very little assistance to the Irish.

Evictions

The blight continued to affect crops for the next few years. Three more crop failures occurred in 1846, 1848, and 1851. Having eaten any of the potatoes spared by the blight and spent what few coins they had for food, tens of thousands of peasants were unable to pay their rents and were evicted from their homes. They had no place to go. The workhouses were already overcrowded, and there were no opportunities for employment anywhere. Matters worsened when in December 1848, cholera and typhus began to spread through the workhouses, pauper hospitals, and cramped jails in Ireland.

Emigration

It seemed that the only viable option was to leave. The Poor Law Extension Act held landowners responsible for providing for their own poor. So, many landowners evicted tenants, paid their passage to America or Australia, and ended up with the opportunity to commercialize their agricultural efforts or change from cultivation to beef and dairy farming. Between 1845 and 1855, nearly 2 million people emigrated from Ireland to America and Australia, and another 750,000 went to England.

For the emigrants, matters worsened once again. Thousands of people died while crossing the Atlantic. Unregulated shipowners often crowded hundreds of desperate emigrants onto rickety, undersupplied vessels that earned the label "coffin ships." In many cases, those ships reached port only after losing a third of their passengers to disease, hunger, and other causes.

The August 4, 1847, edition of the Toronto Globe carried this report on the arrival of an emigrant ship:

The Virginius from Liverypool, with 496 passengers, had lost 158 by death, nearly one-third of the whole, and she had 180 sick; above one half of the whole will never see their home in the New World. A medical officer at the quarantine station on Grosse Ile off Quebec reported that "the few who were able to come on deck were ghastly, yellow-looking spectres, unshaven and hollow-cheeked . . . not more than six or eight were really healthy and able to exert themselves."

Starvation in the Midst of Plenty

Authenticated research reveals that the Irish peasants starved in the midst of plenty. Wheat, oats, barley, butter, eggs, beef, and pork were exported from Ireland in large quantities during the so-called famine. All those products were the property of the wealthy, mostly absentee landowners who felt no obligation to forego profits in order to feed the masses. In fact, those goods were brought through the worst famine-stricken areas guarded by British regiments and shipped from guarded ports to England.

In 1861, author John Mitchel charged, "The Almighty indeed sent the potato blight but the English created the famine . . . a million and half men, women, and children were carefully, prudently, and peacefully slain by the English government. They died of hunger in the midst of abundance which their own hands created."

The Irish potato famine took more than a million lives and forever changed Ireland in a profound way. It also changed centuries-old agricultural practices by hastening the end of subsistence farming and ushering in the era of commercial farming. The famine also spurred new waves of emigration and thus shaped the histories of the United States, Australia, and England as well. Today, more than 13 million Americans have Irish roots.

Continuing Controversy

The Irish Potato Famine has continued to arouse controversy, with some historians arguing that it was a genocide. Recent literature, such as John Kelly's *The Graves are Walking: The Great Famine and the Saga of the Irish People* (2012) and Tim Pat Coogan's *The Famine Plot: England's Role in Ireland's Greatest Tragedy* (2012), consider British

negligence and policy and how these might be construed as genocide in the Irish context.

PAUL R. BARTROP

See also: Ukrainian Starvation (Holodomor)

Further Reading

Kinealy, Christine. *A Death-Dealing Famine: The Great Hunger in Ireland.* Chicago: Pluto Press, 1997.

O Grada, Cormac. *The Great Irish Famine.* New York: Cambridge University Press, 1995.

Schrier, Arnold. *Ireland and the American Emigration, 1850–1900.* Chester Springs, PA: Dufour Editions, 1997.

Woodham Smith, Cecil Blanche Fitz Gerald. *The Great Hunger: Ireland, 1845–1849.* London: Penguin, 1991.

Israel/Palestine

Any discussion of war crimes in Israel/Palestine is complicated by contested claims over the applicability of the Fourth Geneva Convention to the Palestinian Territories (the West Bank and Gaza Strip), which were occupied by Israel in 1967. Israel denies the applicability of the Geneva Conventions, citing its own historic claim to the territories and their lack of any full legal status prior to Israeli occupation. The issue is further complicated because according to international law, Palestinians have the legally protected right to resist occupation in their quest for self-determination. While some means of resistance fall subject to international humanitarian law (such as the proscription against targeting civilians and thereby the illegality of suicide bombings), the Palestinian right to self-determination has been affirmed by numerous United Nations (UN) resolutions, including Resolution 181 (1947), which approved the partitioning of the British Mandate of Palestine into two states, one Jewish and one Arab (Palestinian).

Sensitivities surrounding the topic of war crimes in Israel/Palestine are heightened by the fact that much of the relevant international law emerged as a result of the atrocities committed during World War II, most notably the Holocaust. Between 1940 and 1945, the Nazi regime systematically murdered some 9 million civilians, including at least 6 million European Jews. After the war, the Nuremburg Trials set the legal standards for judging war crimes. Later trials of Nazi war criminals, most notably that of Adolf Eichmann, had a significant impact on Israel's self-proclaimed identity as a place of refuge for world

Jewry. Despite the role of numerous Jews in establishing the international legal framework for upholding human rights and protecting against acts of genocide, many supporters of Israel have become disillusioned with international law, perceiving an anti-Israel bias on the part of the UN in applying international law. The example most frequently cited to support this claim is the UN resolution equating Zionism with racism.

Allegations of war crimes in Israel/Palestine commonly cite either Israel's West Bank settlement policy as a violation of the Fourth Geneva Convention prohibition against transferring civilian populations into occupied territories, or acts of terrorism committed by Palestinian groups as a violation of the Fourth Geneva Convention prohibition against intentional targeting of civilians. Although Israel rejects the applicability of Geneva IV to its settlement activity, most (with the notable exception of the United States) in the international community see Israel in repeated violation of the Convention. In support of this claim, they point to UN Security Council Resolutions 242 and 338, which call for Israel's withdrawal from territories occupied in the 1967 war and recognition of Israel within secure and recognized boundaries. Settlement growth rates have been consistently higher than the growth rate within the 1948 borders of Israel, and during the early years of the Oslo Peace Process, the number of settlers in the West Bank more than doubled. At present, over 400,000 Israeli Jewish settlers live in the West Bank.

Beyond the issue of resettlement, many of Israel's policies and actions associated with the occupation of the West Bank and Gaza, especially since September 2000, have been designated as "war crimes" or "grave breaches" by human rights groups in Israel, the Palestinian Territories, and abroad. Such policies include deliberate targeting of unarmed children, willful killing, use of torture, attacks on medical personnel, and the use of human shields. Israel has claimed that its actions have been militarily justifiable, and failed to cooperate with a UN fact-finding mission charged with investigating charges of an alleged massacre in the Jenin Refugee Camp in 2002. However, international human rights scholars like Richard Falk have argued that the persistence, frequency, and severity of Israeli violations of the Geneva Conventions may in fact amount to the commission of crimes against humanity.

In recent years several high-level Israeli military officers, including Major General Doron Almog, and former Israeli Defense Force Chief of Staff Dan Halutz, have been threatened with arrest on war crimes charges by European courts claiming universal jurisdiction. Yesh Gvul, an Israeli organization, filed a war crimes claim in Britain after several years of no progress on the complaint they filed in the Israeli court system for the men's alleged involvement in the dropping of a one-ton bomb on an apartment building in a densely populated Gaza neighborhood to assassinate Salah Shehadeh, a Hamas military commander. The bombing took the lives of 14 Palestinians in addition to Shehadeh, including 8 children, and injured 150. In June 2007 the Israeli High Court issued a ruling calling for an official Israeli investigation into the incident. In 2001, a Belgian court brought charges against (then) Prime Minister Ariel Sharon for war crimes committed in the Sabra and Shatila refugee camps in 1982. Although the case was dismissed before it ever went to trial, the case caused a diplomatic uproar. In 2004, the International Court of Justice issued an advisory opinion stating that the route of Israel's separation barrier (wall) and its attendant regime constitute a breach by Israel of its obligations under applicable international humanitarian law and human rights prescriptions, but did not charge Israel with war crimes.

The 2006 Israeli military campaigns in Lebanon and Gaza (Operation SUMMER RAINS) were widely criticized for their tactics, which directly targeted power plants, civilian neighborhoods, and bridges, and involved the use of cluster bombs. In the 34-day conflict between Israel and Hezbollah, large numbers of Israeli and Lebanese civilians were killed and even more displaced; in Lebanon 30 percent of the more than 1,000 civilians deaths were children under the age of 12. In the Gaza Strip, the June 2006 bombing of its only power station left 750,000 Palestinians without electricity for months. Human rights organizations have also condemned Palestinian factions for deliberately targeting civilians and medical facilities in inter-factional violence in Gaza during June 2007.

Several Israeli and Palestinian nongovernment organizations regularly document human rights abuses and disseminate calls for investigations of war crimes or other violations of international humanitarian law. B'Tselem, Al-Haq, Adalah, and others have raised awareness about and condemn the routine use of torture by Israel's General Security Services, the policy of administrative detention in which prisoners can be held indefinitely without formal charges being brought against them, and the policy of targeted assassinations (extrajudicial killings).

MAIA CARTER HALLWARD

See also: Iraq; Iran; Egypt; Lebanon; Syria

Further Reading

Cavanaugh, Kathleen, and Jamil Dakwar. "Grave Breaches: A View from Jenin and Nablus." *Middle East Report* Vol. 223 (2002): 30–33.

Galchinsky, Michael. "The Jewish Settlements in the West Bank: International Law and Israeli Jurisprudence." *Israel Studies* Vol. 9, no. 3 (2005): 115–36.

Lein, Yehezkel. "Absolute Prohibition: The Torture and Ill-Treatment of Palestinian Detainees." Jerusalem: B'Tselem & Hamoked-Center for the Defense of the Individual, 2007.

Moore, Wesley. "A War-Crimes Commission for the Hizbollah-Israel War?" *Middle East Policy* Vol. 13, no. 4 (2006): 61.

Itagaki Seishiro

Japanese general and war minister who played major roles in the war in China, against the Soviet Union, and in Southeast Asia, and who was found guilty of war crimes in 1948. Born on January 23, 1885, to a Samurai family in the Iwate Prefecture in northeastern Honshu, Itagaki Seishiro graduated from the Central Military Preparatory School and enlisted in the Fourth Infantry Regiment. He entered the Japanese military academy in 1903, and upon graduation returned to his regiment as a sub-lieutenant, attached to the recruited battalion. After fighting with the regiment in the Russo-Japanese War, Itagaki returned to the academy and was attached to the students' company. In 1913 he was promoted to captain and sent to the army staff college; his graduation was delayed until 1916 by combat duty in World War I.

Itagaki spent much of the next two decades in China, on the general staff and as an instructor at the staff college; he also rose rapidly in rank and was promoted to colonel in 1928 and major general in 1932. As a staff officer of the Kwantung Army, he played an important role in the conspiracy that precipitated the Mukden Incident on September 18, 1931, and which led to the occupation of northeast China and the creation of the Manchukuo puppet state. At the height of his influence in China in 1937, Itagaki was raised to lieutenant general and made commander of the army's Fifth Division. Following participation in the opening thrusts of the Sino-Japanese War of 1937, he was assigned to the Army General Staff and on June 3, 1938, became minister of war, serving in this position until August 30, 1939. A much decorated soldier and member of the "control faction" or Toseiha, which dominated Japan's military and government, Itagaki was promoted to full general in

1941 and placed in charge of the army in Korea, where he stayed until late in the war. In April 1945, Itagaki became commander of the Seventh Military District in Southeast Asia. Acting on behalf of Field Marshall Count Terauchi Hisaichi, Itagaki surrendered Japan's Southern Expeditionary Army to British Admiral Lord Louis Mountbatten, supreme commander of Southeast Asia Command, at Singapore on September 12, 1945.

In May 1946, Itagaki was formally charged with 42 of the original 55 counts brought against 28 Japanese leaders in Tokyo by the International Military Tribunal, Far East (IMTFE). During the proceedings, the tribunal dismissed 32 of the charges and tried him on the remaining 10. The prosecution's case was among the strongest mounted against Japan's wartime leaders. As a colonel on the Kwantung Army staff, Itagaki helped perpetrate the Mukden Incident, deflected attempts by moderates to keep peace with China, and later was a major force in establishing puppet regimes in Manchukuo, Inner Mongolia, and North China. As minister of war, he was responsible for setting up the government of Wang Ching-wei in central China; also, as minister of war, he advocated the Tripartite Pact, which established the Rome-Tokyo-Berlin axis. He was held responsible for attacks in 1938 and 1939 on the Soviet Union at Lake Khassan, near Vladivostok, and at Nomonhan on the Halha River in eastern Outer Mongolia. During his time in Southeast Asia, prisoners of war under Itagaki's command routinely died from starvation, malnutrition, disease, and physical mistreatment; he was held culpable for the continuation of these conditions and found guilty under count 54 of the IMTFE indictment. Likewise, he was found guilty of waging aggressive war against the Allies in East Asia and the Indian and Pacific Oceans; he was exonerated only on the aggressive war charge as applied to France.

In addition to testifying on his own behalf, Itagaki's defense counsel presented documents and witnesses to corroborate that he had no wrongful part in waging aggressive war. He alleged that the purpose of the Tripartite arrangement he supported was to stop the spread of communism in China, and that he tried to make peace in central China but was thwarted by the actions of Jiang Jieshi (Chiang Kai-shek). He claimed that he never "caused, counseled, ordered, permitted, or condoned any mistreatment of any prisoners of war at any place," and that on the contrary, he used limited supplies to keep prisoners "well-fed, housed, and clothed," claiming that although Allied sinking of Japanese cargo vessels had caused supplies to be cut, prisoners still received the same amount of food as Japanese soldiers.

Much of Itagaki's defense was contrary to what was well known. Having been found guilty, he was hanged on December 23, 1948, at Sugamo Prison in Tokyo.

ROBERT S. LA FORTE

See also: International Military Tribunal, Far East; Japan; World War II Atrocities, Pacific Theater

Further Reading

Brackman, Arnold C. *The Other Nuremberg: The Untold Story of the Tokyo War Crimes Trials.* New York: Morrow, 1987.

Yoshihashi, Takehiko. *Conspiracy at Mukden: The Rise of the Japanese Military.* New Haven, CT: Yale University Press, 1963.

Ivory Coast (Côte d'Ivoire)

Since the death of President Félix Houphouët-Boigny in 1993, the Ivory Coast has experienced almost continual civil unrest and violence. These events have largely been the result of the transition from one-man rule to a democratic form of government. The civil war that broke out in 2002 divided the country into a predominantly Muslim north and a mostly Christian south. Although positive steps have been taken to reunite the country under a shared leadership, war crimes have been committed by the different parties; even some peacekeeping forces have been accused of war crimes.

In 1960, the Ivory Coast, also known as Côte d'Ivoire, gained its independence from France. The transition to self-government was peaceful, and the new nation was relatively prosperous. It was a leading producer of coffee, cocoa, pineapples, and palm oil. French advisers were generally welcomed, and they helped to build an economy that consistently grew at an annual rate of 10 percent or more. The economic growth of the Ivory Coast attracted immigrants from neighboring countries, especially from Burkina Faso.

By 1990, however, conditions in the Ivory Coast had changed; the economy faltered chiefly because of falling falling prices for agricultural products. President Houphouët-Boigny had ruled since 1960 with an increasingly authoritarian one-party regime and spent millions to develop his home village of Yamoussoukro into a new capital. Strikes by civil servants and demonstrations by students in 1990 forced Houphouët-Boigny to promise multiparty elections. When he died in 1993, Houphouët-Boigny was succeeded by Henri Konan Bédié, who actively suppressed his political opponents and stressed the concept of "Ivority." This nationalistic idea came to represent those people who lived in the southern part of the country and whose ancestors were originally from the Ivory Coast.

Recent immigrants and those whose parents were not natives of the Ivory Coast were gradually excluded from full citizenship. Rising tensions led to racial riots in 1995 in which a number of immigrant workers were killed.

Bédié was overthrown in late 1999 by a group of army officers. General Robert Guéï assumed power but later held a presidential election in October 2000. A new law excluded anyone who did not have two parents who were Ivory Coast natives from running. The law was aimed at Alassane Ouattara, a northern politician who was popular among Muslims, immigrants, and the poor, but Guéï's attempts to fix the election failed. A popular uprising ensued, with nearly 200 civilians killed by military police under the general's command. Laurent Gbagbo subsequently assumed power. Meanwhile, eight policemen were eventually tried for some of the killings. The military court that heard the case acquitted the men on August 3, 2001, however. At the same time, an investigation into rapes committed by members of the military failed to indict anyone, despite strong evidence of wrongdoing.

Most of this violence had been directed at Muslims and immigrants. Gbagbo failed to take strong action against military leaders, leading to increasing tensions. On September 19, 2002, soldiers from the northern part of the Ivory Coast mutinied and Guéï was killed in the fighting. Although loyal troops secured the southern portion, rebels controlled the northern part. A coalition of organizations governed the rebel territory, including the Movement for Justice and Peace (MJP), the Patriotic Movement of Côte d'Ivoire (MPCI), and the West Ivorian Popular Movement (MPIGO). Each group had its own soldiers who joined together to form the New Forces. Leadership of the rebel forces eventually fell to Guillaume Soro. Loyal government soldiers were joined by the Young Patriots, nationalist paramilitaries who supported Gbagbo. Gbagbo was also accused of recruiting mercenaries for technical duties.

Fighting continued sporadically between the two sides while outside governments sought to separate them. The French sent over 7,000 soldiers to the Ivory Coast in 2003 and 2004. African peace keepers also assumed positions between the two sides under authority of the Communauté Économique des États de l'Afrique de l'Ouest, or CEDEAO (Economic Community of West African States). As the intensity of the fighting was gradually reduced, atrocities were committed against civilians by both sides. In early October 2002, the rebels massacred over 130 government gendarmes and their families at Bouaké while 50 civilians were executed by government antiriot police in Daloa later that month. Soon afterward, 50 policemen were executed by MPCI forces in retaliation. Also in November, government soldiers killed 100 West African immigrants in Monoko Zohi. In March 2003, MPIGO soldiers killed 40 civilians in Dah. That same month, 60 civilians were killed by a Liberian exile group allied with the Ivorian government. Thousands died in the fighting, and it was estimated that over 1 million people were forced from their homes.

Attempts to negotiate a lasting peace failed. A preliminary ceasefire on October 17, 2002, quickly broke down, and a deal to bring the rebels into Gbagbo's government in January 2003 was also unsuccessful; another deal was announced on July 4. French forces tried to suppress lawless elements, but relations between Gbagbo and the rebels deteriorated. In March 2004, government troops massacred 120 people at a rally organized by the opposition. A United Nations (UN) report blamed Ivorian government leaders for planning the killings. The resulting surge in violence caused French forces to evacuate most foreign nationals from the Ivory Coast. In November 2004, Gbagbo ordered his air force to strike at rebel camps in the north. In the process, an errant bomb killed nine French peace keepers, leading the French to destroy most of the air force's planes in retaliation. Anti-French riots broke out in southern Ivory Coast, forcing the remaining foreigners to flee the country.

In April 2005, South African president Thabo Mbeki facilitated a meeting between the two sides. A power-sharing deal was arranged with rebels joining the government, the army, and the police. Despite some tensions, the Pretoria agreement seems to be holding. Gbagbo's term as president was extended by the United Nations to October 2007. Additional details were agreed upon in March 2007 and Soro took office as prime minister in April 2007. On April 16, the buffer zone manned by French forces began to be dismantled, and the various pro- and antigovernment militias started surrendering their weapons in May. Gbagbo visited the northern part of the Ivory Coast in July, to mark the peace. An open presidential election that should have been organized in 2005 was postponed until November 2010. The preliminary results announced by the Electoral Commission, however, showed a loss for Gbagbo in favor of his rival, former prime minister Alassane Ouattara. Gbagbo's supporters contested the results, claiming massive voting fraud in the northern departments controlled by the rebels of the Forces Nouvelles de Côte d'Ivoire (FNCI). The Constitutional Council, which was staffed with Gbagbo supporters, declared the results of seven northern departments unlawful and granted Gbagbo a victory in the elections. Both Gbagbo and Ouattara, who was recognized as the winner by most countries and the United Nations, organized alternative inaugurations. With neither side willing to compromise, tensions quickly mounted, leading to violence. After months of unsuccessful negotiations and violence, Ouattara's forces launched an offensive, seizing control of the country and capturing Gbagbo in April 2011.

Various international groups have called for trials for those accused of war crimes in Ivory Coast. Human Rights Watch issued a report in August 2007 outlining how both the government and rebels encouraged policies of rape and violence against women as part of their war effort. Over 150 cases were documented, while many more were probably never reported by terrified women. However, an amnesty for war crimes was issued in April 2007 as part of the peace settlement, and it appears unlikely that anyone will be punished for their actions between September 2002 and April 2007. Yet, the 2010–2011 crisis produced hundreds of new victims as international organizations reported numerous instances of human rights violations by both sides. In the city of Duékoué, over 1,000 people were massacred, with the UN accusing forces of both Ouattara and Gbagbo of involvement in the killings. Gbagbo is currently being held by the International Criminal Court in The Hague, awaiting trial on charges of crimes against humanity during the dispute after 2010 elections. In the spring of 2012, the International Criminal Court announced its decision to extend its investigation into human rights abuses in Ivory Coast dating back to 2002. Meanwhile, Gbagbo's trial has been postponed indefinitely because of his poor health.

Tim J. Watts

See also: Rape

Further Reading

Calderisi, Robert. *The Trouble with Africa: Why Foreign Aid Isn't Working.* New York: Palgrave Macmillan, 2006.

Newell, Sasha. *The Modernity Bluff: Crime, Consumption, and Citizenship in Côte d'Ivoire.* Chicago: The University of Chicago Press, 2012.

Schwab, Peter. *Designing West Africa: Prelude to 21st-Century Calamity.* New York: Palgrave, 2004.

J

Japan

Only once, immediately after the end of World War II, has Japan been accused in an international military court of war crimes. In July 1945, the Americans, the Chinese, and the British issued a statement, known as the Potsdam Declaration, calling for the Japanese government to surrender. The 10th clause of the Declaration made clear that stern justice would be meted out to all Japanese war criminals, including those who mistreated allied prisoners of war (POWs).

The International Military Tribunal for the Far East (IMTFE, commonly known as the Tokyo Trial) was established by General Headquarters (GHQ) in January 1946. Trials commenced in May with the prosecution of the 28 high-priority Class-A war criminals, namely Japan's wartime leadership. Those war indictments included crimes against the peace, specifically the planning, preparation, initiation, or waging of a declared or undeclared war of aggression, or a war in violation of international law, treaties, agreements, or assurances, or participation in a common plan or conspiracy for the accomplishment of any of the foregoing. They also included conventional war crimes or violations of the laws or customs of war; crimes against humanity, including murder, extermination, enslavement, deportation, and other inhumane acts committed against any civilian population, before or during the war, or persecutions on political or racial grounds in execution of or in connection with any crime within the jurisdiction of the Tribunal. Leaders, organizers, instigators, and accomplices participating in the formulation or execution of a common plan or conspiracy to commit any of the foregoing crimes were responsible for all acts performed by any person in execution of such a plan.

However, unlike the Nuremberg Trials of Nazi war criminals, the IMTFE's written indictments did not distinguish between "conventional war crimes" and "crimes against humanity." Of the 28 accused at the Tokyo Trials, two died of natural causes during the course of the trial; one was acquitted on grounds of mental illness; and the remaining 25 were all found guilty as charged. Of this latter group, seven were sentenced to death by hanging, and 16 were sentenced to life imprisonment. Two others were given fixed sentences of 20 and seven years, respectively. The death penalty was carried out for the former prime minister, Tojo Hideki, and six others on December 23, 1947.

In addition to the above, there were also B- and C-class war criminals accused of "conventional war crimes" against allied POWs and civilians. The United States, Great Britain, Australia, the Philippines, France, the Netherlands and China each respectively tried and punished Japanese war criminals based upon their respective legal systems and territorial jurisdictions. The first trial of these two criminal classes was that of Yamashita Tomoyuki in Manila in October 1945. These hearings were concluded in May 1951 on the then-Australian territory of Manus Island. In all, 2,244 charges were levied against B- and C-class war criminals for which prosecutions were pursued against 5,700 individuals. As a result, 984 were issued the death penalty, 475 were imprisoned for an infinite period, and 2,944 imprisoned for finite periods; 1,018 were found not guilty, and 279 had their prosecutions withdrawn. There were various problems with these B- and C-Class prosecutions, however, including inadequacies in trial processes, cases of mistaken identity at both the time of trial and of arrest, and inconsistencies in the lengths of sentences handed down across jurisdictions.

The IMTFE did not pursue any prosecution against Emperor Showa who, by the Japanese constitution held the supreme position of leadership, on the grounds that it might work contrary to GHQ's control and smooth management of the occupation of Japan. Moreover, prosecutions were not aimed against the Imperial Army for its strategic bombing of Chungking. Furthermore, the chemical or germ warfare experimentation and development programs led by Unit 731 were not scrutinized during the Tokyo Trial. The activities of Unit 731 were first investigated in a Russian military court of law at Khabarovsk, in far eastern Russia, in December 1949, after the hearings of the IMTFE had come to an end. To this date, the Japanese government is still conducting clean-up operations of the Japanese Army's discarded chemical weaponry. With regards to Comfort Women, the sexual assaults inflicted upon Dutch nationals were the target of investigation, but assaults upon Asian women were not. As well, the actual control of colonial territory was not, at the time of the IMTFE, regarded as constituting an international war crime. This and other crimes, which were not included under any war crimes judgments, continue to be political and psychological points of friction between Japan and those nations concerned. To this day, the treatment of POWs by the Japanese casts a shadow over Japan's international relations.

FUMITAKA KUROSAWA

See also: Bataan Death March; Comfort Women; Harukei Isayama Trial; International Military Tribunal, Far East; Nagasaki, Bombing of; Unit 731; Yokohama Trials

Further Reading

Pritchard, R. John, and Sonia M. Zaide, eds. *The Tokyo War Crimes Trial: The Complete Transcripts of the Proceedings of the International Military Tribunal for the Far East in Twenty Two Volumes.* New York: Garland, 1981.

Yuma Totani. *The Tokyo War Crimes Trial: The Pursuit of Justice in the Wake of World War II.* Cambridge, MA: Harvard University Asia Center, 2009.

Japanese Bacteriological Weapons Trial

On December 31, 1949, a Soviet tribunal in Khabarovsk convicted 12 Japanese servicemen for their involvement in the creation, testing, production, and use of bacteriological weapons during World War II. The trial, one of few involving the Japanese germ warfare program carried out mostly by the notorious Unit 731 as well as Unit 100, was the first to punish the development, production, and use of bacteriological weapons. Most of the defendants were charged with participating in human experiments involving bacteriological agents and weapons. The experiments killed thousands, mostly Soviet and Chinese citizens suspected of anti-Japanese activity. In addition, some defendants had been engaged in the development, production, and use of bacteriological weapons in China and the Soviet Union. All of those who were eventually sentenced served their terms in a labor camp.

Yamada Otozoo, commander-in-chief of the Japanese Kwantung Army 1944, was sentenced to 25 years for supervising the preparation of bacteriological weapons, encouraging the murder of subjects of human experiments, and keeping units prepared for bacteriological warfare. Kawashima Kiyoshi was sentenced to 25 years for his role as chief of the Production Division of Units 731 and 100, and was sentenced to an additional 25 years for participating in the preparation for bacteriological warfare, directing production of enough germs to supply weapons to the Japanese Army, organizing the use of such weapons in central China, and taking part in human experiments. Karaswa Tomio, chief of a section of the Production Division of Unit 731, was sentenced to 25 years for organizing the creation of bacteriological weapons, participating in preparations for bacteriological warfare, and taking part in human experiments. Kajitsuka Ryuji, chief of the Medical Administration of the Kwantung Army, was sentenced to 25 years for supporting the use of bacteriological weapons, approving and directly supervising the work of Unit 731, and supplying resources to produce bacteriological weapons.

Nishi Toshihide, chief of Branch 673 of Detachment 731, was sentenced to 18 years for taking part in human experiments, preparing bacteriological weapons, training personnel in bacteriological warfare, and ordering the burning of buildings, equipment, and documents to conceal his branch's activities. Onoue Masao, Chief of Branch 643, was sentenced to 12 years for performing research, supervising the training of personnel in bacteriological warfare, and destroying buildings, equipment, and documents to conceal his branch's activities. Sato Shunji, chief of the bacteriological units in Canton and Nanking, was sentenced to 20 years for creating bacteriological weapons, preparing for bacteriological warfare, and later as chief of Branch 643 of Unit 731, supervising that branch while "aware of the criminal nature of the work of the detachment" and helping it produce bacteriological weapons.

Takahashi Takaatsu, chief of the Veterinary Service of the Kwantung Army, was sentenced to 25 years for organizing the production of bacteriological weapons and supervising Unit 100; Hirazakura Zensaku, member of Unit 100, was sentenced to 10 years for conducting research in the development and deployment of bacteriological weapons, and contaminating water supplies along the Soviet border with China, particularly the Tryokhrechye area. Mitomo Kazuo, member of Unit 100, was sentenced to 15 years for producing bacteriological weapons, conducting human experiments, and participating in "bacteriological sabotage" in the Tryokhrechye area; Kikuchi Norimitsu, an orderly in Branch 643 of Unit 731, was sentenced to two years for developing bacteriological weapons, growing dysentery and typhoid bacteria, and training in bacteriological warfare. Kurushima Yuji, laboratory assistant in a branch of Unit 731, was sentenced to three years for taking part in growing typhus, cholera, and other bacteria, and of testing germ warfare shells.

The defendants appeared before the Military Tribunal of the Primorye Military Area under authority of Article 1 of the Decree of the Presidium of the Supreme Soviet of the Union of Soviet Socialist Republics, issued on April 19, 1943, which was aimed as "German-Fascist Villains." The tribunal did not elaborate how a law to prosecute German nationals could apply to Japanese nationals, yet the verdicts noted that Japan had set "the objective of establishing world domination jointly with Hitler's Germany" and that the plan included use of bacteriological weapons for the "mass extermination of troops and the civilian population." Thus, the Japanese defendants were treated as accomplices to Nazi crimes.

Substantively, international law supported the verdicts. At the time of the trial, the law of war forbade inhumane treatment of detainees (including experimentation) as well as attacks on civilian populations. Additionally, the 1925 Geneva Gas Protocol, which Japan had signed, prohibited the use of bacteriological weapons. This trial served as a precedent for punishing the use of bacteriological

weapons and stands with the Medical and Milch Cases as a precedent for the criminality of employing certain medical experiments, although the Soviet military tribunal did not specify in what way the experiments at issue were unlawful. Moreover, the verdicts provide precedent for punishing complicity in war crimes, notably through preparing for and concealing war crimes.

Sato Shunji's case may have provided a precedent for convicting an individual because of his state of mind. Sato was "aware of the criminal nature of the work of the detachment" and was convicted accordingly. It should be noted, however, that international criminal law does not require that the perpetrator realize his acts are illegal. A review of the verdict and the closing speeches of defense counsel seem to support the rule that the superior orders defense may be used in mitigation of punishment. "Following orders" was explicitly offered as a mitigating factor for some defendants. In addition, defense counsel also argued that their clients' minds had succumbed to the culture of obedience and hatred of other peoples, both allegedly nurtured in Japanese society and military training. Significantly, none of the 12 defendants was sentenced to death.

Ewen Allison

See also: Japan; Unit 731; Yokohama Trials

Further Reading

Gold, Hal. *Unit 731 Testimony: Japan's Wartime Human Experimentation Program*. Boston, Charles Tuttle, 1996.

Harris, Sheldon H. *Factories of Death: Japanese Biological Warfare 1932–1945 and the American Cover Up*. New York: Routledge, 1994.

Williams, Peter, and David Wallace. *Unit 731: Japan's Secret Biological Warfare in World War II*. New York: Free Press, 1989.

Jones, Gareth

Gareth Jones was a Welsh journalist and publicist who is credited with being the first western journalist to bring attention to the famine among Soviet Ukrainians (known as the Holodomor) during 1932–1933.

Gareth Richard Vaughan Jones was born in Barry, Vale of Glamorgan, Wales (England) on August 13, 1905. He received undergraduate degrees from the University of Wales, Aberystwyth (1926) and Trinity College, Cambridge University (1929), both in modern languages. In early 1930, former British prime minister David Lloyd George hired

Jones as a foreign policy adviser, and that summer Jones made his first trip to the Soviet Union. The next year, the young journalist went to New York City, where he became involved in a project that was to result in a modern history of the Soviet Union. Jones accompanied H. J. Heinz II, the director of Heinz food products, to the Soviet Union in the summer of 1931 on a research and fact-finding mission. Jones then ghost-wrote a diary published in 1931 under Heinz's name in which the term "starvation" was first used to describe the condition of many Soviets as a result of Soviet collectivization policies.

Jones returned to London in 1932 to help Lloyd George finish his memoirs before embarking on a trip to Germany in January 1933, a trip timed to coincide with Adolf Hitler's ascension to power. In early March, he made another trip to the Soviet Union, this time to Ukraine, where he was able to witness the Holodomor first hand. Jones also traveled to Moscow, where he interviewed a number of high-ranking Soviet officials, including Foreign Minister Maxim Litvinov.

Jones returned to Germany on March 29, where he wrote his now-famous reports of the starvation occurring in Ukraine. His articles appeared widely in English-language newspapers, including the *Manchester Guardian* and *New York Evening Post*. He wrote of the people he saw in the countryside, who spoke of having no bread; many told him that "we are dying." He also reported on the Soviet government's efforts to keep foreigners and outsiders from touring the blighted areas, out of fear that the Holodomor would become known in the outside world.

Jones's articles were not well-received in some quarters. On March 21, the *New York Times* insisted that Jones had hyped his story, running an article under the headline "Russians Hungry, but not Starving." Soviet officials also denounced the Jones article as hyperbole and propaganda. In May, Jones wrote a rebuttal of the *New York Times* story, arguing that he had personally witnessed the conditions in Ukraine, and that the Soviets were engaged in an elaborate scheme to cover them up. At the time, many journalists, academics, and other intellectuals were sympathetic to the Soviet regime and thus did not wish to read or hear negative things about it. By late 1933, Soviet authorities officially banned Jones from ever traveling to their nation again.

In the closing months of 1934, Jones decided to travel to Asia, where he hoped to gather information for reports detailing the growing tensions between Japan and China. After spending some six weeks in Japan, where he interviewed a number of high-ranking military and civilian officials, he went to Beijing, China. After spending several months there, he traveled to Japanese-occupied Manchukuo (Manchuria) with a German journalist to report on conditions there. During their travels, the two men were taken prisoner by alleged bandits. The German man was released quickly, but Jones was shot and killed on August 12, 1935. Many at the time and well after the murder claim that Soviet operatives killed Jones in retaliation for his reports on the Holodomor.

PAUL G. PIERPAOLI JR.

See also: Duranty, Walter; Ukrainian Starvation (Holodomor)

Further Reading:

Conquest, Robert. *The Harvest of Sorrow: Soviet Collectivization and the Terror-Famine*. New York: Oxford University Press, 1987.

Reid, Anna. *Borderland: A Journey through the History of Ukraine*. New York: Basic Books, 2000.

K

Katyn Forest Massacre

World War II Soviet atrocity in Poland. On April 13, 1990, the Soviet news agency Tass announced that a joint commission of Polish and Soviet historians had found documents proving the involvement of personnel from the Narodnyy Kommissariat Vnutrenniakh Del (NKVD, or People's Commissariat for Internal Affairs) in the deaths of some 15,000 Polish officers in the Katyn Forest of eastern Poland in 1940; however, the total number of the executed at Katyń amounted to almost 22,000. The general secretary of the Communist Party of the Soviet Union and president of the USSR, Mikhail Gorbachev, handed over a list of the victims to Polish President Wojciech Jaruzelski. In October 1992, Russian President Boris Yeltsin produced more archival documents, helping to determine the burial sites of missing officers not found near Katyń. Even in the light of Gorbachev's glasnost and perestroika policies, this admission of Soviet responsibility for the massacre was still a bombshell.

The USSR had consistently denied murdering captured Polish army officers after its occupation of eastern Poland ever since Radio Berlin announced, on April 13, 1943, that German troops, tipped off by local inhabitants, had discovered mass graves near Smolensk. That June, the German Field Police reported that 4,143 bodies had been found in the Katyń Forest, all fully dressed in Polish army uniforms. Some 2,815 corpses were later identified by personal documents in their pockets. Without exception, all the officers, ranking from general to noncommissioned officer, had been killed by shots in the back of the head. Medical examination later showed that a few bodies had jaws smashed by blows or bayonet wounds in their backs or stomachs, probably sustained when the individuals tried to resist execution.

The Germans predictably tried to exploit the Katyn Forest murders for propaganda purposes, pointing out to their wartime enemies that any alliance with the "Bolshevik" perpetrators of this atrocity was too dangerous to continue. By then, General Władysław Sikorski's London-based Polish government-in-exile and General Władysław Anders, then commander of the Polish forces in the USSR and the Middle East, had been concerned for a considerable time over the fate of the missing Polish officers. Following the Soviet-Polish agreement in the summer of 1941, a small but steady trickle of Poles arrived at the re-opened Polish Embassy in Kuibyshev. These individuals, from prison camps scattered over the western parts of the USSR, agreed that their fellow servicemen had been transferred to unknown destinations when the NKVD liquidated these camps in April 1940. The arrivals at Kuibyshev turned out to be the few survivors of the Katyn Forest Massacre. The massacre was apparently a Soviet effort to deprive the Poles of their natural leaders, who would have undoubtedly protested a Soviet takeover.

After numerous fruitless discussions on the subject with Soviet authorities, including dictator Joseph Stalin himself, the Polish government-in-exile came to believe the German announcement of April 1943 and demanded an independent investigation by the International Committee of the Red Cross (ICRC). This move caused the Kremlin to accuse the Polish government-in-exile of siding with the "fascist aggressors" and to break off diplomatic relations. The ICRC, pursuing its policy of neutrality, could take no action without Soviet consent. London, although embarrassed by this development, made it plain that it was unwilling to risk the breakup of the alliance with the Soviet Union against Nazi Germany over such an investigation. The United States took a similar stance.

When the Red Army finally drove the German armies westward, Moscow determined it needed to present its own investigation results in 1944. A Soviet "special commission," pointing out that the bullets found on the crime scene were manufactured in Germany, concluded that the Germans had killed the Polish officers in 1941. British and American protests notwithstanding, the Soviet prosecution raised the Katyn affair at the International Military Tribunal in Nuremberg, but because the Soviets were unable to prove the Germans guilty, the tribunal simply dropped the case. Throughout the Cold War, the issue of the Katyn Forest Massacre resurfaced time and again, partly because of the efforts of the Polish émigré community. However, it remained unresolved until the demise of the USSR in 1991.

PASCAL TREES

See also: Poland; Soviet Union; Stalin, Joseph; World War II Atrocities, European Theater

Further Reading

Paul, Allen. *Katyń: The Untold Story of Stalin's Massacre.* New York: Scribner's, 1991.

Zawodny, Janusz. *Death in the Forest: The Story of the Katyn Forest Massacre.* 4th ed. Notre Dame, IN: University of Notre Dame Press, 1980.

Kesselring Trial

The trial of German Field Marshal Albert Kesselring took place in Venice, Italy, before a British Military Court from February 17 to May 6, 1947. Kesselring was charged with war crimes committed while he was commander-in-chief of the German Wehrmacht in Italy. The Kesselring trial was the longest British war crime trial ever held. Prosecutors alleged that Kesselring had been involved in the killing of 335 Italians in the Ardeatine Caves near Rome in reprisal for a March 1944 attack on German police in Rome. He

was also accused of inciting and ordering the forces under his command to kill Italian civilians as part of other reprisals between June and August 1944. While the prosecutors successfully allocated political responsibility to a military commander as the precondition for conviction, the trial did not clarify the issue of killing hostages and committing reprisals in international warfare in general.

The first charge Kesselring faced involved the aftermath of a bomb attack by Italian partisans on a German police company at Rasella Street in Rome on March 23, 1944. Numerous Germans were killed in the attack. The evidence of the first charge was the same as that presented in the Mackensen Trial in 1945; the prosecution charged that "the accused had ordered reprisals at the rate of ten to one, which was excessive, and that as he had passed the orders to subordinate army formations, he was responsible for the way in which they were carried out." In testimony that contradicted what they had said at the Mackensen trial, several of Kesselring's staff officers now claimed that early on the night of March 24, a fresh order from Adolf Hitler's headquarters had come through, commanding that the reprisals were to be carried out by the Sicherheitsdienst (SD) and not the Wehrmacht; while this testimony was not confirmed by any written record, the defense relied strongly on this second "Führer" order, which would have relieved the accused from any responsibility for the cruel manner in which the executions were carried out. In his summation, the judge advocate advised the court that should it believe "that it is right on the evidence as a whole that the shooting was clearly the responsibility of the Security Service and that all responsibility had passed from the Wehrmacht," then the court should acquit the defendant. However, the court apparently suspected perjury by the staff officers and found that Kesselring bore the primary responsibility for the shootings.

Much of the case for the second charge, that of inciting and ordering the forces under his command to kill Italian civilians as part of other reprisals between June and August 1944, focused on a series of orders Kesselring issued at that time. As partisans became an increasingly serious threat to German forces in Italy, Kesselring, as commander-in-chief of all German forces in Italy, was given overall command in antipartisan operations by Hitler on May 1, 1944; this meant that all Schutzstaffel (SS) and police forces in Italy were under his command for that purpose. On June 17, 1944, Kesselring issued an order that contained the following passage: "The fight against the partisans must be carried out with all means at our disposal and with the utmost severity. I will protect any commander who exceeds our usual restraint in the choice and severity of the means he adopts whilst fighting partisans." On July 1, 1944, Kesselring issued a second order to his troops in which he said, "all counter measures must be hard but just. The dignity of the German soldier demands it." In the course of many punitive actions during the months of July and August 1944, more than 9,000 civilians, including women and children, were killed. On August 21, 1944, Kesselring acknowledged in an order to his troops that "instances have occurred within the last few weeks which caused the greatest harm to the dignity and discipline of the German armed forces, and which had nothing to do with punitive measures." On September 24, 1944, Kesselring ordered the cessation of punitive actions.

According to the prosecution, these orders on the one hand and the atrocities on the other were cause and effect, so Kesselring was responsible for the actions of the troops under his command. The judge advocate pointed out in his summation that "the charge is a much more serious and grave one and that is that the Field Marshal deliberately and knowingly when he produced the relevant orders, was having them produced in such form that he knew what the results would be and that he intended by bringing these orders into existence, to bring about these results." The defense claimed that the orders of June 17 and July 1 were not illegal and that they meant the opposite, saying to the German forces in effect, "You must be hard, but you must keep within the law."

The accused was found guilty on both charges and sentenced to death by firing squad, but the sentence was commuted to life imprisonment at the British Military Prison at Werl, West Germany. Kesselring was released on medical grounds in October 1952 and died on July 15, 1960.

KERSTIN VON LINGEN

See also: World War II Atrocities, European Theater

Further Reading

Macksey, Kenneth. *Kesselring: German Master Strategist of the Second World War.* London: Greenhill Books, 1996.

Searle, Alaric. *Wehrmacht Generals, West German Society, and the Debate on Rearmament, 1949–1959.* Westport CT: Praeger, 2003.

Kharkov Trial

The Soviet Union held a war crimes trial between December 15 and 18, 1943, in the Ukrainian city of Kharkov. The military tribunal of the Fourth Ukrainian Front charged three Germans and a native collaborator with war crimes perpetrated during the Nazi German occupation of the region. All the defendants were indicted, sentenced to death, and executed.

The German army occupied the Kharkov region between October 1941 and February 1943 and again between March and August 1943. During these periods, German security and punitive units organized and carried out mass executions of thousands of Jews, the mentally ill, Soviet prisoners of war (POWs), and suspected communist sympathizers. A number of local residents served in German-sponsored police units and had assisted the Germans in these criminal activities.

The proceeding in Kharkov was the first public trial of Germans charged with war crimes. The accused were specifically selected to represent various German military and police branches: Corporal Reinhard Retzlaff of the Secret Field Police (GFP); Captain Wilhelm Langheld of the Military Intelligence (Abwehr); and Schutzstaffel (SS) Lieutenant Hans Ritz; the native defendant, Mikhail Bulanov, had been a chauffeur for the Kharkov security police. The defendants were charged with atrocities against the Soviet people in accordance with the government decree of April 19, 1943, and Articles 296–297 of the Criminal Procedural Code of the Ukrainian SSR, which provided that evidence presented by the prosecution would suffice for rendering a verdict.

According to Soviet legal practice, the core of the indictment rested on the confessions of the defendants, eyewitness testimonies, and the depositions of medical and legal experts. The defense was not allowed to cross examine witnesses, and its role was limited to pleading for leniency. Although a number of witnesses, including German POWs, testified about Nazi atrocities in the region, they provided no direct incriminating evidence against the defendants. The individual guilt of the defendants was established by linking them to the crimes committed by various German units. Subjected to rigorous interrogations, the defendants were pressured by the prosecution into admitting their participation in the alleged crimes and implicating their German superiors in organizing and participating in the atrocities. The trial revealed the details of mass executions of Soviet citizens and the destruction wrought upon the Kharkov region by German troops.

The carefully staged trial received widespread publicity. Set against the Moscow Declaration of November 1943, in which the Allies had pledged to hunt down and prosecute individuals guilty of war crimes, the trial demonstrated to the world that the Soviet Union was determined to implement immediately the provisions of the Declaration. The German defendants appeared in court in full uniform, and Soviet newspapers provided full coverage of the proceeding. The tribunal accentuated the premeditated and organized character of the Nazis' murder of unarmed civilians and Soviet POWs; the prosecution accused Germany of violating international conventions and specifically charged the German government, the army, civil administration, and local commanders with organizing and committing atrocities. Similarly, the defense argued that the main guilt rested with Germany's leadership, which had ordered the crimes.

In his closing statement, state prosecutor Colonel N.K. Dunayev evoked the stipulations of the post-World War I Leipzig tribunal, the Washington Treaty of 1922, and the Moscow Declaration to stress that superior order should not grant immunity from prosecution. On December 18, 1943, all four defendants were found guilty and sentenced to death by hanging. On December 19, 1943, the four were executed in public in a main city square; thousands of spectators attended.

The Kharkov trial set an important legal and political precedent for future Soviet war crime trials. By rejecting the validity of the plea of superior order, the trial implicated the entire German army as a criminal organization, whose members regardless of rank and position were equally guilty of the crimes. The trial was intended to show the inevitability of retribution for Nazi crimes as well as the impartiality of Soviet justice.

Despite the professions of the prosecution that the judgment at Kharkov was but a prologue to similar proceedings, the trial turned out to be the last highly publicized war crimes trial conducted during the war. Receptive to the pleas of the British and American governments, which were fearful of German reprisals against Allied POWs, the Soviet government suspended other open proceedings until the end of the war.

ALEXANDER V. PRUSIN

See also: Krasnodar Trial; Soviet National Trials; World War II Atrocities, European Theater

Further Reading

Dawson, Greg. *Judgment before Nuremberg: The Holocaust in the Ukraine and the First Nazi War Crimes Trial.* New York: Pegasus, 2012.

Kladov, Ignatik Fedorovich. *The People's Verdict: A Full Report of the Proceedings at the Krasnodar and Kharkov German Atrocity Trials.* London: Hutchinson & Co., 1944.

Kochang Incident

Infamous incident in which Republic of Korea Army (ROKA, South Korean Army) soldiers massacred civilians at Sinwon-myon, Kochang-kun, in South Kyongsang Province during the Korean War. Some 719 people, 75 percent of them children and the elderly, were slaughtered between February 10 and 11, 1951, by Major Han Tong Sok's 3rd Battalion, of Colonel O Ik Gyong's 9th Regiment, of Brigadier General Choe Tok Sin's 11th Division.

The 11th Division, of some 10,000 men, was created on October 2, 1950, to wipe out Korean People's Army (KPA, North Korean Army) stragglers and communist Chiri-san (Mt. Chiri) guerrillas. The Chiri-san force, estimated at about 40,000 men, had been quite active.

Suppression of the guerrillas was not easy. A succession of battles occurred between ROKA forces and the guerrillas, and there were areas where ROKA forces dominated in the daytime and the guerrillas controlled the night. Sinwon-myon township was one such area. In early December 1950, a force of some 400–500 guerrillas attacked the town and killed many policemen. The 9th Regiment was assigned the task of sweeping up the guerrillas in the southern part of the Chiri-san area.

When the 3rd Battalion of the regiment advanced on Sinwon-myon on February 7, 1951, the guerrillas had already fled. When the army left, the guerrillas returned and joined battle with the police. The 3rd Battalion, which advanced on Sinwon-myon again, first assembled about 1,000 inhabitants at Sinwon Elementary School, where they singled out and released family members of the army, police, and government officials, as well as other influential citizens. The remaining people were then accused of having betrayed the country to the communists. They were given death sentences at a summary trial of a military tribunal, with Major Han as presiding judge. These civilians were taken to a mountain valley and executed, and their bodies were burned to destroy the evidence.

Sin Chung Mok, a National Assemblyman from Kochang-kun County in the Republic of Korea (ROK, South Korea), first made public the atrocity on March 29, 1951. Because reports of the incident by the ministers of defense, home affairs, and justice conflicted, the National Assembly dispatched an investigation committee. But this team failed to reach the scene because Deputy Provost Marshal Kim Chong Won disguised a platoon of ROKA soldiers as communist guerrillas and ordered them to attack the investigators on April 7.

Subsequently, the National Assembly adopted a resolution censuring the government on this matter. As a result, the three ministers resigned, and the investigation resumed in early June 1951 on the special instruction of South Korean president Syng-man Rhee. The provost marshal headquarters then arrested O Ik Gyong, Han Tong Sok, Kim Chong Won, and Second Lieutenant Yi Chong Dae, an intelligence officer in the 3rd Battalion. These four were ordered to stand trial by court-martial. Yi Chong Dae was found not guilty; the others were convicted. O Ik Gyong received life imprisonment; Han Tong Sok was given 10 years in prison; and Kim Chong Won was sentenced to a three-year prison term. Before long, however, the three officers were released on a special amnesty from President Rhee. Even today, the real truth of the tragedy has not been fully disclosed.

JINWUNG KIM

See also: Korean War Atrocities; Nogun-ri Railroad Bridge Incident

Further Reading

Matray, James I., ed. *Historical Dictionary of the Korean War.* Westport, CT: Greenwood, 1991.

Millett, Allan R. *Their War in Korea: American, Asian, and European Combatants and Civilians, 1945–1953.* Princeton, NJ: Princeton University Press, 2002.

Kolkhoz

A kolkhoz (plural kolkhozy) was a type of collective farm that began to appear in the Soviet Union after the Bolshevik Revolution of 1917. As time went on, the number of kolkhozy increased rather dramatically, although their growth slowed after Soviet general secretary Joseph Stalin began the mass collectivization of agriculture during the early 1930s. There was a second type of collective farm in the Soviet Union at this time; they were known as sovkhozy. In most kolkhozy, farmers did not own the communally shared land, but they did collectively own nonland assets, including work animals, farm equipment, and machinery. Individuals who lived and work in them were paid strictly according to their labor (usually based on the number of days worked), and not based on revenue. In the sovkhozy, which were true state-owned enterprises, land and all nonland assets were owned and controlled by the government. Workers were paid set salaries, regardless of how much they worked.

During the 1920s, the number of kolkhozy increased dramatically; some Russians viewed them as a slightly different form of Russian farm communes, which had existed for many years. In Ukraine, which had a rich agricultural tradition, the kolkhozy and sovkhozy were viewed with more skepticism, especially among the landed kulaks, who were reluctant to dissolve their farms and turn over their operations (and profits) to faceless Soviet bureaucrats in Moscow. Farm policies were set by Soviet officials, which were then passed on to regional and provincial authorities, who were expected to carry them out. These policies dictated what crops would be planted, how much acreage would be cultivated, and which livestock would be raised. The kolkhozy had to sell their products directly to the government; they were not permitted to sell to individuals (although many did). The central governing authorities fixed prices for all agricultural products; virtually all prices were set very low. The government then sold the same products to consumers at a much higher price, yielding a tidy profit for the Soviet regime.

After the massive drive toward collectivization and "dekulakization" in the late 1920s and early 1930s, Soviet authorities used the collective farms in the Ukraine as a tool to control the Ukrainian people. The government would often force these collective farms to produce goods that were not immediately needed, or to mandate that they not plant all their acreage. This exacerbated growing food shortages in the region, which soon became a widespread famine, known by the Ukrainians as the Holodomor of 1932–1933. Some kolkhozy tried to circumvent policies forbidding sales to individuals in an attempt to ease the famine, but doing so invited retaliation—and even imprisonment—by government authorities. In the end, the efforts of some kolkhozy could not overcome mass starvation that had been largely manufactured by the Soviet central government. Kolkhozy and sovkhozy continued to function in the Soviet Union until that state collapsed in 1991. There are vestiges of them still operating today.

PAUL G. PIERPAOLI JR.

See also: First Five Year Plan; Kulaks; Soviet Collectivization; Soviet Union; Stalin, Joseph; Ukrainian Starvation (Holodomor)

Further Reading

Conquest, Robert. *The Harvest of Sorrow: Soviet Collectivization and the Terror-Famine.* New York: Oxford University Press, 1987.

Davies, R. W. *The Soviet Collective Farm, 1929–1930.* Cambridge, MA: Harvard University Press, 1980.

Kony, Joseph

Ugandan founder and leader of the Lord's Resistance Army (LRA), one of the most brutal guerrilla groups in Africa. Joseph Kony and his army have advocated a rather idiosyncratic and militant form of Christianity and have been responsible for numerous acts of violence. His troops have been responsible for massacring thousands of people and enslaving tens of thousands of children who were turned into sex slaves, forced laborers, and soldiers.

Little is known about Kony's early life. He was born sometime in 1961 into the Acholi tribe and was raised in the traditional village of Odek in northern Uganda. As a young man he came the under influence of Alice Lakwena, a spiritual medium who organized a rebel group, the Holy Spirit Movement, against the government of Yoweri Museveni in 1986. After Lakwena's revolt was suppressed, Kony became involved with other factions until proclaiming himself a prophet for the Acholi people and spreading his religious messages and prophesies. Kony has been described as a devoutly religious man whose prayer sessions combine elements of Catholic, Protestant, and even Islamic liturgy.

Kony gradually took over the Holy Spirit Movement and reorganized it into the Lord's Resistance Army, forcibly recruiting thousands of children to serve as his foot soldiers. The LRA initially received support from Sudan, which had been embroiled in an ongoing conflict with Uganda, and exploited the resentment of the Acholi people against the Ugandan government. However, as popular support for the LRA subsided, the group directed most of its attacks against the Acholi people throughout the 1990s. It is estimated that LRA violence claimed more than 10,000 lives and led to the enslavement of over 60,000 children; meanwhile, some 2 million people have been internally displaced by the violence since 1986. One of the worst atrocities committed by the LRA took place on Christmas Day 2008, when Kony's troops beat to death more than 800 people in northeastern Congo and South Sudan, and abducted hundreds others.

In 2005, the International Criminal Court (ICC) issued a warrant for Kony's arrest, accusing him of gross violations of human rights. International scrutiny forced the Sudanese government to withdraw its support for Kony, who found himself under increasing attack by Ugandan forces. This forced him to relocate to the neighboring countries of Congo and Sudan, where the LRA continued to perpetrate violence. However, increased pressures also resulted in the LRA losing membership and an attendant decline in influence. In 2006, Kony offered to negotiate, and after two years of negotiations, a peace agreement was finalized in 2008. However, Kony refused to attend the signing ceremony, demanding the suspension of the ICC's arrest warrant. In response, the governments of Uganda, Congo, and Sudan launched Operation LIGHTNING THUNDER, which targeted the LRA, inflicting considerable losses on its forces but failing to capture Kony. Military setbacks forced the elusive leader to move his movement deeper into the jungles of Congo and Central African Republic, where he launched attacks on civilians in those countries.

In its struggle against Kony, the Ugandan government received support from the United States. President George W. Bush promised financial and logistical support to Uganda in 2008, while President Barack Obama signed the Lord's Resistance Army Disarmament and Northern Uganda Recovery Act (2010), which is aimed at destroying the LRA and arresting Kony. In October 2011, the United States announced the deployment of 100 U.S. troops to central Africa to train local government forces. In 2012, Kony found himself at the center of a viral social-media campaign that revolved around a short documentary film, *Kony 2012* (produced by the U.S. company Invisible Children), which described the LRA's atrocities and called for increased efforts to bring Kony to justice. The video, seen by more than 90 million people, was instrumental in bringing worldwide attention to atrocities committed by the LRA under Kony's leadership.

Alexander Mikaberidze

See also: Obote, Milton; Uganda

Further Reading

Allen, Tim. *Trial Justice: The International Criminal Court and the Lord's Resistance Army.* New York: Palgrave Macmillan, 2006.

Allen, Tim, and Koen Vlassenroot. *The Lord's Resistance Army: Myth and Reality.* New York: Palgrave Macmillan, 2010.

Korean War Atrocities

During the 20th century, ideological wars have produced countless examples of brutality and crimes against humanity. The Korean War was no exception. From 1950 to 1953 the armies and governments of both the Democratic People's Republic of Korea (DPRK, North Korea) and the Republic of Korea (ROK, South Korea) committed or encouraged the killing of civilians and prisoners of war (POWs). Ever since, there has been historical debate over the degrees of responsibility on both sides.

U.S. and British troops were appalled by the casual brutality that they observed routinely inflicted on South Koreans by their own government. One British soldier, a Private Duncan, described a typical scene: "40 emaciated and subdued Koreans were . . . shot while their hands were tied, and also beaten unnecessarily by rifles. The executioners were South Korean military police." Such incidents created great confusion and ill-feeling toward the ROK among Western troops. "We are led to believe that we are fighting against such actions," Duncan wrote, "and I sincerely believe that our troops are wondering which side in Korea is right or wrong."

ROK treatment of Communist prisoners was particularly harsh in the days after the savage and sudden Korean People's Army (KPA, North Korean) occupation of the South. "At least many hundreds [of alleged Communists] have been shot," reported Australian delegate to the United Nations (UN) Commission for Korea John Plimsoll. He related how prisoners had been forced to dig their own graves, then "rather clumsily and inexpertly shot before the eyes of others waiting their own turn." Feelings of bitterness and the desire for revenge after the atrocities committed during the Communist occupation drove South Korean government officials to such retaliatory measures.

But the KPA occupation of much of the South conditioned this. Indeed, the widespread cruelty of the Communist occupation of South Korea during the opening months of the conflict set the moral tone for the rest of the war. It also led South Koreans who were lukewarm or opposed to the government of Syngman Rhee to rally to it as far preferable to that of the Communists.

From June to September 1950, some 26,000 South Korean civilians were murdered by the Communists. At one site near Taejon alone, 5,000 bodies were discovered after the North Korean retreat. Members of the South Korean government, police, and intelligentsia were systematically rounded up and executed. Sometimes this included entire families. During the liberation of Seoul, one group of U.S. Marines came upon a trench filled with hundreds of dead South Korean men, women, and children. "It was a ghastly sight," Marine Ed Simmons recalled, "The stench was unbearable. For days civilians were coming out from the center of Seoul in the hope of identifying them." The 5th Cavalry Regiment encountered a similar scene where 200 civilians had been executed. "Many of the murdered," Private First Class Victor Fox remembered, "were professional and business people, educators, artists, politicians,

[and] civil servants. The dead appeared to include entire families, from children to the very aged."

Even more shocking to Americans were discoveries of the corpses of American POWs who had been executed by their North Korean captors. Bodies were typically found in roadside ditches or gullies, hands tied behind the backs with barbed wire, and a single bullet wound to the back of the head. One group of 100 executed American prisoners was found in a railway tunnel during the UN advance into North Korea. Such sights enraged U.S. troops and inspired random acts of revenge killing of North Korean prisoners. One such incident occurred when the 21st Infantry Regiment took a hill along the Naktong River after a brief fire-fight. The retreating North Koreans had left a wounded officer behind. "Our officers asked for volunteers to carry him off the hill." Sergeant Warren Avery recalled. "Of course, no one volunteered; we had all heard about atrocities the North Koreans had participated in. After a little bit of argument about what we should do with this wounded officer the platoon leader went over to him and shot him between the eyes with his .45."

The Chinese, unlike their North Korean allies, were eager to take prisoners alive for propaganda purposes. For American prisoners fortunate enough to survive capture, a long, terrible march into captivity awaited them. This was particularly true during the winter of 1950–1951, when hundreds of Americans died of disease and hypothermia or were simply murdered by their guards. The survival rate for wounded soldiers during these marches was particularly dismal, although in fairness to the Chinese, with their primitive medical facilities, their own wounded were not likely to fare much better. "The signal for death was the oxcart following the column," remembered Captain James Majury. "If you had to be placed upon that, you would freeze to death."

Arrival at POW camps rarely provided any solace for American prisoners. North Korean-administered camps were the worst. The guards made little attempt to keep their prisoners alive. Starvation, disease, beatings, and months of solitary confinement were the lot of many captives. Conditions improved slightly when the Chinese assumed control of the prison camps in the spring of 1951. That summer, conditions improved further when the Chinese determined that live prisoners made better bargaining chips. Thereafter, prisoner deaths declined rapidly. But the final figures tell a stark tale: of 7,190 Americans captured by the Communists, 2,730 died in captivity. Nearly 99 percent of these died in the bitter first year of the war.

After the truce ending the Korean War on July 27, 1953, there were no trials to prosecute war criminals as had been the case at the Nuremberg Trials after World War II. However there had been discussion, early in the war, over prosecution of war criminals. During the Wake Island conference between U.S. President Harry Truman and his advisers and General Douglas MacArthur in October 1950, MacArthur had outlined a plan whereby those North Koreans who had committed atrocities would be tried by military tribunals. But the Chinese intervention in late November and the resulting stalemate precluded any formal UN attempt to bring war criminals to justice.

DUANE L. WESOLICK

See also: Kochang Incident; Nogun-ri Railroad Bridge Incident

Further Reading

Blair, Clay. *The Forgotten War: America in Korea 1950–1953.* New York: Times Books, 1987.

Halliday, Jon, and Bruce Cumings. *Korea: The Unknown War.* New York: Pantheon, 1988.

Hastings, Max. *The Korean War.* New York: Simon & Schuster, 1987.

Krasnodar Trial

A highly publicized Soviet war crimes trial, the Krasnodar Trial was held between July 14 and 17, 1943, in the city of Krasnodar in southern Russia. The military tribunal of the North-Caucasian front charged 11 native members of the Einsatzkommando 10-A with high treason and war crimes perpetrated during the German occupation of the region. Eight of the defendants received the death penalty, and three were sentenced to lengthy prison terms.

The German army occupied the Krasnodar region between August 1942 and February 1943. The Einsatzkommando 10-A and other German units organized and carried out mass executions of Jews, the mentally ill, Soviet prisoners of war (POWs), and suspected communist sympathizers. A number of local residents served with the Einsatzkommando 10-A in various capacities and assisted the Germans in these criminal activities. The defendants were charged with high treason under Articles 58–1a and 58–1b of the RSFSR Criminal Code and crimes against the Soviet people as stipulated by a special government decree of April 19, 1943. In addition, the tribunal applied Articles 319–320 of the RSFSR Criminal Procedural Code, which provided that the evidence presented by the prosecution and the "inner conviction of judges" sufficed for rendering a verdict. According to Soviet legal practice, the core of the indictment was based on the confessions of the defendants, eyewitness testimonies, and the depositions of medical and legal experts. Defense counselors were not allowed to cross examine witnesses.

Although a number of witnesses testified about German atrocities in the region, they provided no direct incriminating evidence against the defendants. The individual guilt of the defendants was established by linking them to the crimes committed by the Einsatzkommando 10-A. Subjected to a rigorous interrogation, the defendants, V. Tishchenko, N. Pushkarev, I. Rechkalov, G. Misan, M. Lastovina, G. Tuchkov, Iu. Naptsok, I. Kotomtsev, V. Pavlov, I. Paramonov, and I. Kladov admitted having participated in the alleged crimes. They revealed the details of mass executions of Soviet citizens, the brutality of the German security services, and the murderous activities of the gas vans, which killed more than 7,000 men, women, and children. In an attempt to mitigate their guilt and pressed by the prosecution, the defendants implicated their German superiors in organizing and participating in the atrocities.

The trial evolved into a highly publicized propaganda campaign. It was broadcasted around the Soviet Union and reported in the Allied press. Although the tribunal acknowledged the systematic murder of Soviet Jews, it repeatedly stressed the premeditated German plan of the total annihilation of all the Soviet people. In this venue, the prosecution and the defense counselors insisted that the ultimate responsibility for the committed crimes rested with the German government, the high command, and military and civil authorities in the occupied region.

On July 17, 1943, in accordance with the decree of April 19, 1943, and Articles 319–320 of the Criminal Procedural Code, all the defendants were found guilty under Article 58–1b. V. Tishchenko, N. Pushkarev, I. Rechkalov, G. Misan, M. Lastovina, Iu. Naptsok, I. Kotomtsev, and I. Kladov were sentenced to death by hanging, and G. Tuchkov, V. Pavlov, and I. Paramonov received 20 years at hard labor. In his closing statement, the state prosecutor, Major-General L.I. Yachenin, emphasized that Nazi crimes in the Krasnodar region were an integral part of the German war of annihilation against the Soviet Union and warned the German government of the inevitable retribution for these crimes. On July 18, 1943, the death penalty was carried out in a main city square in front of thousands of spectators.

The publicity accorded to the Krasnodar trial signified that it served several important purposes. It vividly demonstrated to the world the immeasurable suffering of the Soviet people at the hands of Nazi Germany. The sentences sent an unequivocal message both to the Germans and the Allies that the Soviet Union was committed to implementing its earlier declarations to prosecute war crimes. The tribunal implicated the entire German state in war crimes and made provisions for future proceedings against highly placed German leaders. At the same time, the trial aimed to incite the Soviet people to intensify the struggle against Nazi Germany and to deter potential collaborators in German-occupied territories. The trial also set a pattern for future war crimes trials during and after World War II.

ALEXANDER V. PRUSIN

See also: Kharkov Trial; Soviet Union; Soviet National Trials; World War II Atrocities, European Theater

Further Reading

The Trial in the Case of the Atrocities Committed by the German Fascist Invaders and Their Accomplices in Krasnodar and Krasnodar Territory Heard, July 14 to 17, 1943. Moscow: Foreign Languages Publishing House, 1943.

Kulaks

Kulak was a term used to describe and classify relatively affluent farmers in the late Russian Empire and the early years of the Soviet Union. There were many kulaks in Ukraine preceding the Holodomor (mass starvation) that occurred during 1932–1933.

After the Soviets came to power in Russia in the early 1920s, they classified peasants into three large categories: *bednyaks* (poor farmers); *serednyaks* (middle-income farmers); and *kulaks* (high-income farmers). The early Soviets believed that only the bednyaks were capable of joining the proletariat (industrial working class) in a Leninist-inspired revolution; the kulaks, on the other hand, were viewed as "class enemies" because they owned their own land and had relatively high incomes. During the Russian Revolution that began in November 1917, peasants who had refused to provide the Red Army with grain and other supplies were labeled "kulaks," and were often subjected to violence and intimidation. That general view of this group carried over into the early Soviet period. After the Soviets took control in the early 1920s, any peasant selling goods on the black market was liable to be classified as a kulak.

In 1929, Soviet general secretary Joseph Stalin ordered the complete collectivization of Soviet agriculture, meaning that farmers would no longer own their own land or livestock and that agricultural policy would be established by the central government and be carried out on collective farms. Initially, the government did not single out the kulaks for ill treatment, although Stalin soon changed that

and made them the focus of rural collectivization policies. By early 1930, Soviet policy embraced the concept that kulaks were to be eliminated as a group, a concept dubbed dekulakization. Some would be sent to gulags (prisons), others would be deported to distant and isolated parts of the country, while the remainder would be deported within their home provinces where they would be forced to live and toil on collective farms. Soon, even farmers who owned some livestock (but no land) were classified as kulaks. It seems that Stalin's goal was more than collectivization—he hoped to assert Soviet control over the entirety of the countryside and eliminate any vestiges of capitalism.

Ukraine had a large number of kulaks (known as *kurkuls* in Ukrainian), and so the policies put in place in the early 1930s had a profound effect on all Ukrainians, whether they were farmers or not. Many Ukrainian kulaks resisted collectivization, choosing to plow under crops and slaughter their livestock rather than turn them over to the state. By 1934, the Soviet government estimated that 26.6 million head of cattle had been killed along with 63.4 million sheep. This widespread slaughter, combined with failed and plowed-under crops, precipitated a major famine during 1932–1933.

Perhaps well over a million Ukrainians died in a very short period of time. As many as 1.8 million people, the vast majority of them farmers, were sent to gulags during 1930 and 1931. This compounded the famine as there were not enough people to tend farms and livestock. By 1934, some 75 percent of Soviet farms had been collectivized, but that accomplishment had resulted in devastating consequences for many Soviets, especially in the Ukraine. Untold numbers of Kulaks were either murdered on their own land, or died after being deported or imprisoned. The true enormity of these policies did not come to full light until the collapse of the Soviet Union in 1991. Many scholars have now classified the Holomodor as a genocide.

PAUL G. PIERPAOLI JR.

See also: Cannibalism in the Holodomor; Class Enemies; Dekulakization; First Five Year Plan; Great Purges; Gulags; Kolkhoz; Soviet Collectivization; Soviet Union; Stalin, Joseph; Ukrainian Starvation (Holodomor)

Further Reading

Conquest, Robert. *The Harvest of Sorrow: Soviet Collectivization and the Terror-Famine.* New York: Oxford University Press, 1987.

Werth, Nicolas, Karel Bartošek, Jean-Louis Panné, Jean-Louis Margolin, Andrzej Paczkowski, and Stéphane Courtois. *The Black Book of Communism: Crimes, Terror, Repression.* Cambridge, MA: Harvard University Press, 1999.

L

Lebanon

Since its formal independence in 1943, Lebanon, a small Middle Eastern nation located on the eastern part of the Mediterranean Sea, has been plagued by sectarian violence and civil war, often made worse by Lebanon's frequent involvement in Arab-Israeli conflicts and the ongoing Israeli-Palestinian conflict. The very makeup of Lebanese society lends itself to conflict: among the population are Sunni, Shia, and Druze sects of Islam as well as five separate Christian denominations: Maronite; Greek Orthodox; Greek Catholic; Armenian Orthodox; and the Syriacs. The diverse nature of the Lebanese population meant that various—and quite different—cultures coexisted side-by-side. Until the late 1960s, when Muslims began to outnumber Christians, there were separate educational systems based on religion, and the government has remained divided along religious lines. This badly fractured Lebanese society and led to an increasingly ineffective government.

After the 1948–1949 Arab-Israeli War, some 100,000 Palestinians sought refuge in Lebanon; this virtually guaranteed that Lebanon would become involved in the Israeli-Palestinian conflict. Soon, some Palestinians living in Lebanon began staging raids into Israel. Many more Palestinians took up residence in Lebanon during the late 1960s and early 1970s, resulting in a growing Muslim presence in the country. This also increased tensions among the various religious groups in the country. The ultimate outcome of these developments was the Lebanese Civil War, which began in 1975 and endured until 1990. The conflict commenced in earnest on April 13, 1975, when an unknown gunman opened fire on a Christian church in East Beirut; four people died in the attack. Later that same day, members of the Christian Lebanese Phalanges Party, in an apparent retaliatory move, murdered 27 Palestinians on a bus in Ayn ar Rummanah. In December 1975, four Christians died in an attack in East Beirut. The violence only escalated, and during early 1976, Muslim militias and Phalangists killed at least 600 Muslim and Christian civilians at checkpoints throughout the country.

Sectarian combat in Lebanon during April 1975–November 1976 alone killed at least 40,000 and wounded 100,000 others; many of the victims were civilians. By 1976, both Israel and Syria have become involved in the civil war. Syrian troops intervened, entering Lebanon and imposing a short-lived ceasefire. On January 20, 1976, when the predominantly Christian town of Damour fell to Muslim forces, at least 300 citizens were massacred (some sources claim over 500 died). Responding to the incursion of Syrian troops, on August 12 Christian militias perpetrated a horrific massacre of at least 2,000 Palestinians at Tal al-Zaatar, the site of a huge Palestinian refugee camp outside Beirut. Other residents were raped, beaten, or tortured. By the end of 1976, Lebanon was divided militarily. The Christians controlled East Beirut and part of Mount Lebanon, while the Palestinians and allied Muslims controlled southern Lebanon and western Beirut.

In March 1978, Palestinian militants raided northern Israel and commandeered a bus, resulting in the deaths of 34 Israelis and 6 militants. Outraged, the Israelis invaded Lebanon on March 15. Some 2,000 Lebanese died during the invasion, and another 100,000 were displaced before the Israelis withdrew. Israel, however, came under increasingly frequent raids and rocket attacks by Palestinian and allied guerilla groups. In July 1981, Israeli jets bombed Palestinian positions in a suburb of West Beirut in retaliation for rocket attacks on northern Israel. Some 200 people died in the bombardment, and another 600 were wounded, most of them civilians. The Palestinians retaliated, killing 6 Israeli civilians and wounding 59 others.

In June 1982, Israel invaded southern Lebanon in a bid to destroy Palestinian bases there. Israeli forces then moved further into Lebanon, laying siege to Beirut. During this operation, 6,700 Christian civilians in East Beirut were killed, the victims not of Israeli bombs, but rather of Palestinian and Muslim bombs. One of the worst atrocities to unfold in Lebanon occurred on September 16–18, 1982, when Christian militias massacred at least 2,000 Palestinians at the Sabra and Shatila refugee camps; this massacre unfolded in clear view of Israeli troops, who did virtually nothing to stop the carnage.

Various attempts by neighboring nations as well as the international community to stop the civil war all failed, including the ill-fated U.S. military mission to Lebanon, which was suddenly ended after the October 23, 1983, truck bombing of a barracks in Beirut. That attack killed 241 U.S. marines and 58 French troops and wounded scores of others. In the so-called War of the Camps in 1985–1986, several thousand Palestinians died in refugee camps. The Taif Accords of 1989 finally set the stage for an end to the bloody civil war, and by October 1990 a fragile peace was in place.

This did not, however, end the violence in Lebanon. In 1993 and again in 1995, the Israelis attacked Palestinian strongholds in southern Lebanon, killing hundreds and displacing several hundred thousand civilians. The attacks were an attempt to stop Palestinian rocket attacks against Israeli civilians. In 2006, another war erupted after Hezbollah, a militant Shia Islamic group in Lebanon, raided a border village and captured two Israeli soldiers. The Israelis retaliated, and the month-long conflict resulted in the deaths of as many as 700 soldiers and militants in Lebanon and 1,187 Lebanese civilians. Up to 1 million Lebanese civilians were displaced. The Israelis reported 44 civilian deaths, those the result of rocket attacks by Hezbollah.

After more infighting within Lebanon after the short summer war with Israel, the country seemed ready to embrace some semblance of normalcy by mid-2008. Lebanon remains a tinder box of sectarian and political strife, and Hezbollah's refusal to disarm casts doubt that the war-torn nation will be able to secure a lasting peace.

PAUL G. PIERPAOLI JR.

See also: Israel/Palestine; Syria

Further Reading

Fisk, Robert. *Pity the Nation: Lebanon at War.* Oxford: Oxford University Press, 2001.

Hovespian, Nubar, ed. *The War on Lebanon: A Reader.* Northampton, MA: Olive Branch, 2008.

Rabil, Robert. *Embattled Neighbors: Syria, Israel, and Lebanon.* Boulder, CO: Lynne Rienner, 2003.

Libya

A predominantly Muslim nation located in North Africa, Libya received full independence in December 1951. Although it retained a strong Arab identity, the Kingdom of Libya also cultivated close ties to the West, particularly Britain and the United States. As Arab nationalism took hold in neighboring counties beginning in the 1950s, Arab nationalism began to bloom in Libya as well. Pan-Arab nationalism received a major boost after the Arab defeat in the 1967 Six-Day War, and in 1969, a cabal of junior Libyan army officers staged a coup, overthrowing the Libyan king. The leader of the group was the charismatic Colonel Muammar Qadaffi, who quickly consolidated power as head of the Revolutionary Command Council. Qadaffi governed Libya until he was overthrown during the Arab Spring of 2011.

Qadaffi imposed an oppressive dictatorship over his people, but he steered clear of rigid political dogma and ideology. He wanted to combine Arab nationalism, which was secular, with conservative Islamic social and political structures. By the mid-1970s, he had articulated his unorthodox approach in his *Green Book* (1976), in which he staked out a political philosophy that fell somewhere between capitalism and communism. It also eschewed representative government and instead embraced direct government.

To implement his unconventional governing system, Qadaffi relied heavily on Revolutionary Committees, which reported directly to him. The Committees were also used as vehicles for internal surveillance, and by the 1980s anywhere from 10 to 20 percent of all Libyans performed some type of surveillance work for these Committees. Only in North Korea and Iraq under Saddam Hussein were there more citizens working as covert informants. In 1973, the Qadaffi regime outlawed political dissent, so the Committees were vitally important to his government. With so many informants, it is not surprising that a large number of Libyans were at one time or another detained, arrested, or imprisoned, although it is virtually impossible to know how many.

Oddly, perhaps, Qadaffi's regime generally refrained from perpetrating violent repression at home, and the dictator publicly condemned torture. Those accused of torture could receive lengthy prison sentences. Qadaffi was far more willing to engineer violent acts outside Libya, however. For nearly three decades, his regime was a known sponsor of international terrorism, and that caused frequent problems with the international community. Many nations engaged in boycotts of Libyan goods, including oil. Other nations, like the United States, retaliated militarily.

Under the Ronald Reagan administration, U.S.-Libyan relations reached a low point. In April 1986, a bomb placed in a Berlin nightclub exploded, killing two American soldiers and one Turkish soldier; more than 200 more were injured, among them many Americans. The Reagan administration claimed that Libyan agents had set off the bomb, and it was determined to strike back. U.S. attack planes bombed five separate targets in Libya on April 15. The attacks killed 45 Libyan soldiers and government officials and 15 civilians. Among the dead was Qadaffi's young adopted daughter.

Libyan terrorists struck again in December 1988, when a massive explosion blew up a Pan Am 747 airliner as it flew from London to New York. The jet disintegrated in midair over Lockerbie, Scotland, and more than 270 civilians were killed. This brought more sanctions against Libya, and for years Qadaffi dodged the question of Libyan culpability. On June 29, 1996, a massive riot at Libya's Abu Salim maximum security prison, which housed many political dissidents and enemies of the state, caused the deaths of 1,270 inmates. The prisoners were protesting the dreadful living conditions at the facility. The Qadaffi regime dispatched government troops to quash the revolt, which they did using automatic weapons. To this day, the precise events of that day remain shrouded in secrecy.

After the September 11 terrorist attacks on the United States, Qadaffi did an abrupt about-face. He now offered restitution to the families of those killed on the Pan Am flight, denounced radical Islamic terror groups like Al Qaeda, renounced his nation's stockpiles of weapons of mass destruction, and agreed to comply with nuclear nonproliferation agreements.

Despite these moves, Qadaffi's regime remained unquestionably dictatorial at home. Encouraged by revolutionary events in Tunisia and Egypt, Libyan protesters began taking to the streets in early February 2011. By February 20, the mass demonstrations had spread to the capital at Tripoli. The protesters sought political liberalization and multiparty elections. Realizing that his fate was likely to go the way of Hosni Mubarak in Egypt, who was swept from power only days earlier, Qadaffi ordered his troops to disperse the crowds, using force if necessary. When dozens of Libyans were killed and several thousand wounded or arrested, the Libyan revolt concentrated on Qadaffi's removal from office, which was championed by many in the international community.

Libya quickly descended into a civil war, and atrocities abounded. In Tripoli on August 21, 17 rebel prisoners were shot to death. On August 23, in a Tripoli suburb, 47 people died when rebel forces stormed a building which they believed Qadaffi's son was using as a makeshift prison. On August 28, 29 people in a refugee camp at Bab al-Aziza were shot to death; it is not known if they were killed by rebels or government forces. Meanwhile, by August 22, rebel troops had entered Tripoli, occupying Green Square. Qadaffi was tracked down on October 20 and was killed by rebel soldiers as they tried to apprehend him. Two days later, 53 alleged Qadaffi supporters were murdered at the Hotel Mahari in Sirte.

Libya was officially liberated on October 23, 2011. It is estimated that as many as 32,000 Libyans died in the eight-month-long civil war. Since then, Libya has remained unstable, both politically and socially, and violence between revolutionaries and pro-Qadaffi individuals remains a problem. There are some who worry that the nation might fall prey to Islamic extremists. Some of these groups have already perpetrated attacks on foreign interests in Libya, most notably on September 11–12, 2012, when radicals with ties to Al Qaeda attacked the U.S. consulate at Benghazi, killing four Americans including the ambassador and wounding 10 others. That episode has proven to be a major embarrassment for the Barack Obama administration.

Paul G. Pierpaoli Jr.

See also: Egypt; Iraq; Iran; Syria

Further Reading

Simons, Geoff. *Libya and the West: From Independence to Lockerbie.* London: I. B. Tauris, 2004.

Wright, John. *Libya: A Modern History.* Baltimore: Johns Hopkins University Press, 1981.

Lidice Massacre

The Lidice Massacre was a German wartime atrocity in Czechoslovakia on June 9–10, 1942. On June 4, 1942, Schutzstaffel (SS)-Obergruppenfuehrer Reinhard Heydrich, chief of the German Sicherheitsdienst (SD, or Security Service) and Acting Reichsprotektor (administrator) of Bohemia and Moravia, died of wounds suffered when their car was attacked with grenades in Prague, Czechoslovakia, on May 27, 1942. The attack was carried out by two agents of the London-based Czech government-in-exile, Jan Kubis and Jozef Gabcik. German reprisals for the attack on Heydrich were swift and deadly. Ultimately, the Germans raided 5,000 towns and villages. In the process, some 3,180 persons were arrested, and 1,344 were sentenced to death. German dictator Adolf Hitler ordered additional severe reprisals against the Czechs, threatening to kill 30,000 of them. This threat was not carried out. But the mining village of Lidice near Kladno, 11 miles northwest of Prague, was chosen for a conspicuous reprisal, presumably because some villagers there had sheltered Heydrich's assassins and had been otherwise identified with the Czech Resistance.

The German operation against Lidice was carried out during two days, June 9 and 10, by German police and SD personnel led by SS-Hauptsturmfuehrer Max Rostock. German police and SD troops surrounded the village on the evening of June 9, and the action began the following morning. First, the police and SD men rounded up and

The ruins of Lidice, Czechoslovakia, following its destruction by the Germans. After the death of the deputy chief of the Gestapo, Reinhard Heydrich, as a result of an ambush by Czech civilian partisans, the Nazis unleashed a retaliation campaign against the Czech civilian populace. (Library of Congress)

took away the town's children and most of the women. Then, an execution squad of 3 officers and 20 men methodically killed 172 males over the age of 16. Later that day, another 11 workers from the late shift at the Lidice mine were also executed, as were 15 relatives of Czech soldiers serving in Britain who were already in custody, bringing the total number of men murdered to 198. The Germans also executed 71 women in Lidice, and another 7 were taken to Prague, where they, too, were shot. Of the 184 Lidice women transported to Ravensbruck concentration camp and the 11 already in prison, 143 eventually survived. The 98 children in the village were transported to a camp at Gneisenau. Eighty-two of the children were gassed at Chelmno, and 8 are known to have been given to SS families to raise. In any event, only 16 surviving Lidice children could be identified in 1945. The village of Lidice itself was burned to the ground. The site was then dynamited and bulldozed, and the ground was sowed with grain.

A similar reprisal was carried out on the village of Lezaky, east of Prague, where the radio transmitter used by the Czech agents was discovered. All of the village's adult inhabitants were killed, and only two Lezaky children survived the war. On the direct orders of SS-Reichsfuehrer Heinrich Himmler, 252 friends and relatives of the Lidice inhabitants were gassed at the Mauthausen concentration camp on October 24, 1942.

No link between Lidice and the Heydrich assassination was ever proven. The village was rebuilt nearby after the war and renamed Nove Lidice. SS-Hauptsturmfuehrer Max Rostock was executed in 1951 for his part in the Lidice Massacre, which came to symbolize the Nazi oppression of Czechoslovakia.

CHARLES R. SHRADER

See also: Oradour-sur-Glane Massacre

Further Reading

Bradley, J.F.N. *Lidice: Sacrificial Village.* New York: Ballantine Books, 1972.

Wittlin, Tadeuz. *Time Stopped at 6:30.* Indianapolis, IN: Bobbs-Merrill, 1965.

Louvain, Destruction of

In August 1914, Louvain was a small Belgian clerical and university town, famed for its Gothic architecture, located 16 miles east of Brussels. During August 25–30, 1914, the town was the site of an infamous series of German war crimes against civilians. The German First Army

had occupied Louvain without a fight on August 19. Sometime around 8:00 P.M. on August 25, however, sporadic rifle fire broke out in the city streets. What provoked the initial shots is still unknown. Subsequent German claims that Belgian franc-tireurs, or irregular militiamen, had opened fire on their soldiers are highly improbable, as no claims of organized guerrilla activity anywhere in 1914 Belgium have been successfully substantiated; indeed, the Belgian government was at pains to warn its citizens not to provoke German reprisals by acts of resistance. It is more likely that retreating elements of the German First Army, temporarily pushed back into town by a counterattack by the Belgian 6th Division on the evening of the 25th, were misidentified by nervous sentries, provoking a confused and escalating exchange of "friendly fire."

As the fusillades intensified, German troops began breaking down doors to civilian homes and assaulting male inhabitants, beating and in many cases shooting people where they stood. Catholic priests, presumed by some Protestant German soldiers to be ringleaders of civilian resistance, were singled out for especially brutal treatment. Troops deliberately set fire to houses and stores. Around 11:30 P.M., soldiers broke into Louvain's historic university library with its priceless collection of 300,000 medieval books and manuscripts, doused it with gasoline, and burned it to the ground. Arson, battery, and murder continued throughout the following day, and on August 27 the German garrison commander, Major von Manteuffel, ordered the entire population of 10,000 civilians expelled. Order was only partially restored on the 30th when the German commandant in Brussels, General Walther von Lüttwitz, intervened to prevent further bloodshed. In all, 248 Belgians were killed in and around Louvain and 2,000 buildings were destroyed, one-sixth of the town's total. Thousands of citizens were deported or made refugees, some languishing in ad hoc detention camps until early 1915.

The "sack" of Louvain became a celebrated case in the Allied propaganda campaign against Teutonic "frightful" behavior in Belgium, a charge that the Germans hotly denied. In May 1915, the Reich's Ministry of Foreign Affairs published its so-called White Book on the alleged atrocities of nine months before, an unapologetic and largely fictitious diatribe against Belgian partisans in which the events in Louvain featured prominently. Responding to claims that the destruction there had be premeditated, the Germans made much of the fact that they had spared the elaborate gothic town hall. This was disingenuous, for

Manteuffel was using the building as his headquarters. The tragedy of Louvain was probably more the result of panic than cool deliberation. Inexperienced German officers and soldiers, frustrated by the Belgian army's unexpected resistance, rattled by a genuine (if imaginary) "sniper-psychosis," and conditioned by military authorities to take a hard line against any suspected civilian infractions, temporarily took leave of their senses. In so doing, however, they made the name of Louvain a permanent black mark against the pretensions of *Wilhelmine Kultur*. Although there was an investigation after the war, no one was brought to trial for what had occurred at Louvain.

ALAN ALLPORT AND GILLES BOUÉ

See also: World War I Atrocities; World War I War Crimes Trials

Further Reading

Horne, John, and Alan Kramer. *German Atrocities, 1914: A History of Denial.* New Haven, CT: Yale University Press, 2001.

Zuckerman, Larry. *The Rape of Belgium: The Untold Story of World War I.* New York: New York University Press, 2004.

Lubanga, Thomas

Thomas Lubanga Dyilo was the leader of the Union of Congolese Patriots (UPC) and is convicted war criminal from the Democratic Republic of the Congo (DRC).

Lubanga was born in Djiba (Ituri Province), DRC on December 29, 1960; he is a member of the Hema-Gegere ethnic group. After receiving a degree in psychology from the University of Kisangani, he became involved in politics and several paramilitary organizations. During the 1998–2003 Second Congo War, he served as a military commander and defense minister for the pro-Ugandan Congolese Rally for Democracy-Liberation Movement. Shortly thereafter, he established the UPC, another rebel organization vying for power and influence. In the winter of 2002, Lubanga left the Congolese Rally for Democracy, and in September of that same year became president of the UPC. At the same time, he created an armed force for the UPC, known as the Patriotic Force for the Liberation of the Congo (FPLC).

Under Lubanga's watch, the UPC and FPLC—which were chiefly staffed by the Hema-Gegere—became heavily involved in the ongoing 1997–2007 Ituri Conflict, which pitted the Hemas against the Lendu, a rival ethnic group. During this struggle, Lubanga's group was implicated in a number of alleged massacres and atrocities, including rape, mutilation, murder, and ethnic cleansing. In the Mongbwalu region, the FPLC reportedly killed some 800 civilians between November 2002 and June 2003. During February and March 2003, FPLC forces were accused of having purposely destroyed 26 villages, resulting in the deaths of at least 350 civilians and the displacement of another 60,000. At the same time, Lubanga stood accused of having employed as many as 3,000 children as soldiers, some as young as eight years old. The UPC and FPLC allegedly forced local civilians to support the war effort by donating anything they had, including young children.

In February 2005, nine United Nations peacekeepers from Bangladesh were murdered in Ituri, and Lubanga's forces were suspected of having participated in the killings. On March 19, 2005, Lubanga was arrested and detained in Kinshasa. Meanwhile, a year earlier, the International Criminal Court (ICC) had received permission from the Congolese government to investigate claims that Lubanga's forces had employed children in the ongoing conflict in the Congo. In February 2006, a preliminary ICC finding substantiated the claims, and in March Lubanga was arrested by the ICC; he was the first person to be arrested by the international tribunal. ICC officials transported Lubanga to The Hague, where he awaited trial.

Lubanga's trial commenced on January 2009. After rather tortuous proceedings, on March 14, 2012, Lubanga was found guilty of having employed child soldiers and sentenced to 14 years in prison on July 10, 2012. The court gave him credit for the six years he had spent in detention and while on trial, giving him an effective post-trial sentence of eight years. The trial was not without its critics. A number of international human rights organizations complained that the indictment had not gone far enough and did not cover ethnic cleansing, mass murder, rape, etc. Nevertheless, Lubanga's trial and conviction were important firsts for the newly created ICC and will arguably set precedents for future war crime trials.

PAUL G. PIERPAOLI JR.

See also: Congo, Democratic Republic of; Congo Mass Rapes

Further Reading

Autesserre, Séverine. *The Trouble with the Congo: Local Violence and the Failure of International Peacekeeping.* Cambridge, UK: Cambridge University Press, 2010.

Edgerton, Robert. *The Troubled Heart of Africa: A History of the Congo.* New York, St. Martin's Press, 2002.

M

Maillé Massacre

Massacre of 124 civilians, including women and children, in the central French village of Maillé on August 25, 1944, perpetrated by German occupation forces. The Maillé massacre was the second deadliest one in France during World War II. The massacre at Oradour-sur-Glane (with 642 victims), which occurred on June 10, 1944, was the deadliest. German troops also burned down large parts of Maillé. The local area had seen some French resistance activity in the weeks leading up to the massacre, which culminated in an ambush of a German jeep in the vicinity of Maillé on August 24, 1944. Although no one was reported killed, the German commandant at Tours, Lieutenant Colonel Alfred Stenger, ordered reprisals against the village, but provided no further details. In any event, the units tasked with the execution of the reprisals the following morning exceeded Stenger's vague order, carrying out a horrible bloodbath instead. After an attempted encirclement, German soldiers advanced into the village, killing inhabitants indiscriminately and torching several houses. About one quarter of the village's population was murdered. In the afternoon, two antiaircraft guns shelled the village and destroyed most of the remaining buildings. Two days later, Stenger apologized to the French prefect, Fernand Musso, for the crime, claiming that the officer in charge, Second Lieutenant Gustav Schlüter, had been relieved of his post.

For unknown reasons, French police investigated the massacre in a very haphazard manner. They were unable even to identify the specific unit responsible for the slaughter, although existing evidence should have led them to a Schutzstaffel (SS) unit garrisoned in nearby Châtellerault. Based on little evidence, a French military tribunal in Bordeaux sentenced Schlüter to death in absentia in 1951, but the French did not request his extradition. Schlüter died in Hamburg in 1965, his exact role in the massacre largely unknown.

In contrast to many other German massacres in France during World War II, the one in Maillé disappeared from collective memory for decades. This changed, however, in 2005 when German justice officials re-opened the case and German police carried out an extensive investigation. Meanwhile, a German historian was able to identify the likely perpetrators. They had been a mix of a territorial Wehrmacht unit and parts of the SS Field Replacement Battalion 17 (SS-Feldersatzbataillon 17) of 17th SS Panzer Grenadier Division. The Wehrmacht soldiers seemed to have acted with reluctance; thus, SS troops murdered the vast majority of the civilians. A local French historian was also able to shed some light on the circumstances, refuting the long-held belief that the village had been peaceful prior to the massacre. The Germans were unable, in the end, to locate any surviving perpetrators, and the case was closed in 2010. Nevertheless, the massacre has attracted much attention recently, particularly when French president Nicolas Sarkozy visited Maillé and referred to it as a "martyr village" in the summer of 2008.

PETER LIEB

See also: Oradour-sur-Glane Massacre; World War II Atrocities, European Theater

Further Reading

Gildea, Robert. *Marianne in Chains: In Search of the German Occupation 1940–1945.* London: Macmillan, 2002.
Payon, André. *Maillé Martyr: Récit du Massacre du 25 Août 1944.* Tours: Arrault, 1945.

Malmédy Massacre

Notorious incident involving the murder of unarmed American soldiers during the German Ardennes Offensive (Battle of the Bulge) in December 1944. In the offensive, I Panzer Korps had the task of breaking through Allied lines in the Monschau-Losheim sector and advancing to the Meuse. The 1st Schutzstaffel (SS) Panzer Division was on the left wing of the corps, and SS-Obersturmbannführer Joachim Peiper commanded the division's spearhead, known as Kampfgruppe Peiper.

On December 17, the second day of the offensive, 1st Panzer Division broke through the Allied lines between the Belgian towns of Malmédy and Saint Vith. At the village of Baugnez, Peiper's unit encountered a small group of trucks and jeeps belonging to Battery B of the U.S. 285th Field Artillery Observation Battalion. In the ensuing fight, some 20 U.S. soldiers were killed and Peiper's force took 125 prisoners. Peiper left behind some men to guard the prisoners before moving on to his next objective. A few hours later, another 1st SS column arrived at Baugnez, adding some additional prisoners.

The Germans herded the Americans into a snowy field, where they were held under guard. Meanwhile, another group of separated Americans who had previously escaped from the Germans moved toward the crossroads, and a firefight broke out in which more Americans were killed. This engagement led the guards in the field to fire on their prisoners, perhaps believing they would try to escape. The Germans then moved among the wounded, executing them with bullets to their heads. Most of those shot were unarmed. At least 72 men were killed, although some 30 others feigned death and later escaped to American lines.

The incident was the worst atrocity against Americans in the European Theater during the war. News of the event, which became known as the Malmédy Massacre, quickly circulated among Allied troops, and the U.S. Army made the most of it for propaganda purposes, even including civilians who had died in the fighting in the total of persons killed, although many were actually victims of U.S. bombing.

In May 1946, Peiper and 73 members of the 1st Panzer Division, a number of them selected randomly, were brought to trial by a U.S. military court for the Malmédy killings and the murder of soldiers and civilians elsewhere during the offensive. Army prosecutors presented testimony from massacre survivors and civilian witnesses, captured German documents indicating that German troops had been urged to be "ruthless" with prisoners during the offensive, and confessions from some of the accused. In response, the defense argued that pre-trial investigations had not been thorough and that confessions had been extorted by mock trials and threats of summary execution. The court dismissed these complaints and convicted all of the defendants. Peiper and 43 others were sentenced to death, and the rest were given lengthy prison sentences.

Questions about the trial results were raised almost immediately, and review boards cited errors in the court's procedural rulings. Several defendants indeed claimed that their confessions had been extracted by physical force, charges that the original prosecutors angrily denied. The army reduced the death sentences to long prison terms, but ultimately, all the defendants, including Peiper, were released from prison within a few years.

TERRY SHOPTAUGH

See also: Oradour-sur-Glane Massacre; World War II Atrocities, European Theater

Further Reading

Bauserman, John M. *The Malmédy Massacre.* Shippensburg, PA: White Mane Press, 1995.
Weingartner, James J. *Crossroads of Death: The Story of the Malmédy Massacre and Trial.* Berkeley: University of California Press, 1979.

Manila Massacre

The Manila Massacre was the purposeful killing of tens of thousands of civilian noncombatants, mainly by Japanese forces, in Manila, Philippines, during February 1945.

Much of Manila itself was looted, bombed, ransacked, or burned. During World War II, Manila was one of the largest cities in Southeast Asia, with a population of over 800,000 people. As U.S. forces drove toward Luzon (the island on which Manila is located) during early 1945, Japanese General Yamashita Tomoyuki ordered all Japanese troops to evacuate the city; Rear Admiral Iawbuchi Sanji, however, refused to follow the directive and elected to keep his troops in the city, to prevent Allied troops from taking it at virtually any cost. Under his command was a contingent of about 18,000 men, chiefly from the Japanese Imperial Navy.

On February 3, 1945, U.S. troops burst their way into the northeastern portion of Manila, a move that began the February 3–March 3 Battle of Manila. Iawbuchi now directed his troops to prevent the Americans from entering the center of the city. They did so by shelling U.S. positions with artillery, which produced numerous civilian casualties. Now faced with a stiff Japanese defense and artillery fire, the Americans were compelled to return the fire, which injured or killed scores more and which wrecked whole sections of the city. General Douglas MacArthur had already decided not to use aerial bombardment, fearing even more civilian casualties.

As the battle ground on, Japanese troops murdered perhaps thousands of civilians, looted stores and homes, bombed and burned hundreds of buildings, tortured people, and raped women and children alike. They even circumvented international agreements on the conduct of warfare by torturing and killing prisoners of war. On February 10, Japanese forces forcibly entered Manila's Red Cross Hospital, shooting or bayoneting staff and patients alike, including infants and children. After the killing stopped, they looted the building of medical supplies and food.

The Japanese carefully targeted their destruction, concentrating their efforts on churches, schools, public facilities, and any building with historical significance. The Intramuros, Manila's old walled section, which dated to the late 1500s, was almost completely destroyed. Indeed, by the time the battle ended in early March, as much as 70 percent of Manila lay in ruins. No other capital city saw such a level of destruction during the war except for Warsaw, Poland. Worse still was the human cost: an estimated 100,000 civilians were killed during the massacre (some by friendly fire). Another 16,000 Japanese troops died. U.S. casualties were estimated at 6,571, including 1,010 killed.

PAUL G. PIERPAOLI JR.

See also: Japan; World War II Atrocities, Pacific Theater; Yamashita Trial

Further Reading

Lord Russell of Liverpool. *The Knights of Bushido: A History of Japanese War Crimes during World War II.* New York: Skyhorse Publishing, 2008.

Smith, Robert Ross. *The United States Army in World War II: The War in the Pacific—Triumph in the Philippines.* Washington, DC: U.S. Government Printing Office, 1963.

Mao Zedong

Mao Zedong was the leader of the People's Republic of China. A great visionary, Mao Zedong was also one of history's deadliest tyrants. A rebel from childhood, Mao helped found the Chinese Community Party in 1921, took command of the revolution 14 years later in the midst of the Red Army's epic Long March, fought another 14 years before the Communists' final victory, and then remained China's supreme ruler for more than a quarter-century until his death at age 82.

Mao was born on December 26, 1893, in a peasant home in Hunan Province. He was educated at his village primary school and subsequently entered high school in Changsha, the provincial capital. Mao was in Changsha when, on October 10, 1911, revolution broke out against the last of the Qing Dynasty emperors. Mao promptly joined the revolutionary army, but saw no fighting and returned to his studies after six months as a soldier.

After graduating from the provincial teacher-training college, Mao went to Beijing, where he worked as an assistant librarian at Beijing University and began to learn about Marxism. In July 1921, he attended the Chinese Communist Party's founding congress in Shanghai. Seeing Marxist theories through a Chinese prism, unlike many of his more orthodox comrades, Mao believed that revolution in China had to begin among peasants, rather than in an embryonic industrial working class. During the 1920s, he spent much of his time organizing peasant unions in his native Hunan Province.

At the end of the decade, with the Communists fighting for survival against Jiang Jieshi's Nationalist (Guomindang) government, Mao retreated farther into the countryside instead of joining other communist leaders in suicidal urban uprisings. By 1934, Mao's base in Jiangxi Province was under heavy pressure from Nationalist troops. That October, some 86,000 communists slipped through the Nationalist blockade and began a 6,000-mile retreat that became known as the Long March. Mao, in political eclipse when the march began, became the party's supreme leader during the trek, a role he never relinquished. At the end of the Long March, with only about 4,000 left of the original force, Mao and his comrades established a new base in Yenan in northern China.

Between 1937 and 1945, Mao and his army fought a new enemy in Japan. In the Sino-Japanese War of 1937–1945, Mao and his commanders refined the art of "people's war." Mao summed up the strategy in only 16 Chinese characters: "The enemy advances, we retreat; the enemy camps, we harass; the enemy tires, we attack; the enemy retreats, we pursue."

The Red Army became a political as well as military organization. Instead of victimizing the peasantry, as Chinese soldiers had done from time immemorial, Mao's troops sought to win over the population to their cause. Instead of looting, raping, and destroying, communist soldiers were ordered to pay for food, respect women, and help repair war damage. The ideal, and to an extent the reality, was an army that commanded public support and could, in Mao's most famous simile, swim among the people as fish swim in the sea.

Following Japan's 1945 defeat in World War II, the struggle between the communists and Nationalists resumed, but by now the tide was running strongly in Mao's favor. By the fall of 1949, the Nationalist government and what remained of its army had fled to the island of Taiwan. On October 1, Mao stood under China's new flag, red with five gold stars, and formally proclaimed the People's Republic of China.

The Communists were not gentle in establishing their regime. "A revolution is not the same thing as inviting people to dinner or writing an essay or painting a picture or embroidering a flower," Mao once wrote. "It cannot be anything so refined, so calm and gentle." In the first years of the PRC, hundreds of thousands, perhaps millions, were executed as landlords or capitalist exploiters. Millions more were imprisoned or tortured for real or imaginary crimes against the revolution, or simply for having a privileged background. Rigid ideological controls were imposed on educators, artists, and the press.

Less than a year after he came to power, the outbreak of the Korean War presented Mao with difficult choices. His priority was on consolidating his new government and rebuilding China. But a North Korean defeat would bring hostile foreign forces to China's northeastern border and, Mao feared, might encourage Jiang to send his forces back across the Taiwan Strait to reopen the civil war on the mainland. The key issue for China was whether attacking U.S.-led forces would stop at the 38th parallel in the fall of 1950, or continue their advance into North Korea. If the latter occurred, Mao decided, China had no choice but to enter the war.

On October 8, the day after the first U.S. troops moved onto North Korean territory, Mao issued the official directive: "It has been ordered that the Northeast Border Defense Army be turned into the Chinese People's Volunteers" (the name was a fig leaf, a transparent device for China to go to war with the United States without formally avowing it) "and that the Chinese People's Volunteers move immediately into the territory of Korea to assist the Korean comrades in their struggle." Mao's decision to intervene in Korea cost the life of his oldest son.

For many ordinary Chinese, life gradually improved in the years following 1949. But Mao was impatient for faster progress. Uninformed about economics and technology, and convinced that the sheer muscle power of China's huge population could accomplish any goal if it were just mobilized properly, he began dreaming of a "Great Leap Forward" that would hurl China out of poverty and backwardness and create a modern, prosperous state virtually overnight.

The Great Leap produced numerous follies, but the worst calamity occurred in agriculture. Intoxicated by his own visions and seduced by crackpot theorists, Mao decreed an overnight transition from family or small cooperative farms to vast People's Communes, while calling for absurdly high increases in grain production. The results were devastating. From 1959 to 1961, as many as 30 million Chinese died as a direct or indirect result of Great Leap policies.

In the wake of the disaster, Mao withdrew from day-to-day administrative details. But he nursed a deep grievance against those he imagined had sabotaged his plan. In 1966, Mao struck back with the Great Proletarian Cultural Revolution, an event so irrational and bizarre that recorded history shows nothing else quite like it. Proclaiming "rebellion is justified," Mao urged China's youth to rise up against the party bureaucracy and against the "four olds": old habits, old customs, old culture, and old thinking.

At Mao's call, brigades of youthful Red Guards waving the little red book of Mao's thoughts spread out to "make revolution" in schools, factories, and offices throughout China. Within months, the country was in chaos. Red Guard groups splintered into rival mobs, each determined to outdo the other in rooting out enemies and tearing down everything that symbolized incorrect thoughts or China's past. Teachers, managers, intellectuals, and anyone suspected of insufficient revolutionary purity were paraded before howling mobs and forced to confess their misdeeds. Savage beatings were common. Many victims died under torture; constant physical and mental harassment drove many others to commit suicide.

Among those persecuted were almost all of the old cadres' party workers and Red Army soldiers whose struggle and sacrifice had brought the Communists to power. Meanwhile, the glorification of Mao reached extraordinary heights. His face, with its high-domed forehead, backswept hair tufting over each ear, and the celebrated mole just to the left of the center line of the chin, gazed out from virtually every wall in China. Badges with his image became part of the national dress. Schoolchildren and office workers began every day with bows before Mao's picture.

Not even the frenzy of leader worship could stem a growing sense that something was wrong, however. In the torrent of slogans and accusations, the movement's goals grew steadily more inexplicable. "The whole nation slid into doublespeak," Jung Chang, then a teenager, recalled in her memoir, *Wild Swans.* "Words became divorced from reality, responsibility, and people's real thoughts. Lies were told with ease because words had lost their meanings and had ceased to be taken seriously by others."

China paid a heavy price for Mao's mad fantasies: the educational system was shattered for years; economic losses were ruinous; much of China's rich artistic legacy was destroyed; society was fractured; and ideals crumbled. After two years of chaos, order was gradually restored, often at gunpoint by People's Liberation Army units, but a mood of fear and uncertainty persisted through the remaining years of Mao's rule.

The Red Guards were disbanded and millions of young people were sent from towns and cities to work as farm laborers. Out loud, nearly all of them obediently vowed willingness to "serve the people" wherever they were sent. But inwardly, many were confused, disillusioned, and hurt.

On July 28, 1976, the disastrous Tangshan earthquake struck northern China. Nearly a quarter-million people were killed, and physical destruction was immense, even in Beijing, 100 miles from the epicenter. In Chinese tradition, such disasters were thought to signal the end of a dynasty. The communist regime officially scorned such superstitions, but to many Chinese the old beliefs were vindicated when, at 10 minutes past midnight on September 9, Mao died.

Believing that sheer willpower and human muscle could overcome any obstacle, Mao had turned China into a gigantic laboratory for his experiments in transforming human society. But when his grandiose dreams failed, instead of recognizing that his policies were flawed, Mao tore China apart in mad witch-hunts for the "demons and monsters" who had frustrated his efforts.

Mao's career was rich in contradictions. He proclaimed Marxism his lifelong faith, but his revolutionary ideas owed little to Marx and much more to ancient Chinese sagas of bandits and peasant rebellions. He preached simplicity and egalitarianism, but had himself glorified as a virtual god-king. He declared war against China's feudal past and its oppressive traditions, but his reign, rife with arbitrary cruelties and constant intrigues, mirrored many of the worst aspects of imperial despotism.

Less than a month after Mao's death, his widow Jiang Qing and her three closest associates, the Gang of Four who had been the chief zealots of the Cultural Revolution, were imprisoned. Deng Xiaoping, whom Mao had twice expelled from the leadership, regained power and within a few years reversed nearly all of Mao's policies. In the end, it was the pragmatic Deng rather than the visionary Mao who laid the groundwork for economic reforms that transformed China in the 1980s and 1990s.

ARNOLD R. ISAACS

See also: China; Cultural Revolution; Great Leap Forward

Further Reading

Chang, Jung. *Wild Swans: Three Daughters of China.* New York: Simon & Schuster, 1991.

Salisbury, Harrison E. *The New Emperors: China in the Era of Mao and Deng.* Boston: Little, Brown, 1993.

Spence, Jonathan. *The Search for Modern China.* New York: W.W. Norton, 1990.

Matsui Iwane

Japanese army general and commander of forces involved in the Sino-Japanese War. Born in Aichi Prefecture, Japan, on July 27, 1878, Matsui Iwane graduated from the Military Academy in 1898. He fought in the 1904–1905 Russo-Japanese War as a captain and was awarded the Military Cross. He was a resident officer in China from 1907 to 1912 and from 1915 to 1919 and in France and Indochina between 1914 and 1915. Promoted to colonel in 1918, he commanded the 29th Infantry Regiment in Japan from 1919 to 1921, and then served as a staff officer in the Siberian Expeditionary Force at Vladivostok between 1921 and 1922.

Matsui served as a staff officer in the Guandong (Kwantung) Army from 1922 to 1924 and was promoted to major general in 1923. Between 1924 and 1925, he commanded a brigade, and he was then chief of the Intelligence Division of the Army General Staff (1925–1928).

Promoted to lieutenant general in 1927, Matsui commanded the 1st Division (1929–1931) and served as a delegate to the 1931–1933 Geneva Disarmament Conference, after which he was promoted to full general in 1933. In semiretirement, he served on the Supreme War Council between 1934 and 1935. Matsui was shocked at the Aizawa Incident of August 12, 1935, when Army Minister Lieutenant General Nagata Tetsuzan was assassinated in his office by Lieutenant Colonel Aizawa Saburoagata. Matsui then retired from the army.

After he left the army, Matsui traveled widely in China and met with Jiang Jieshi (Chiang Kai-shek), head of the Nationalist Party—the Guomindong, or GMD (Kuomintang, or KMT); he hoped to reconcile Japan and China. Ordered back to duty with the Japanese army in 1937 following the start of the Sino-Japanese War, he commanded the Japanese forces sent to capture Shanghai in Jiangsu (Kiangsu). Following heavy fighting, his forces took the city. In October 1937, Matsui was appointed to command the Central China Area Army.

In November 1937, his forces began their advance on Nanjing (Nanking), in Jiangsu. On December 1, Matsui demanded that the Chinese commander, General Tang Shengzhi (T'ang Sheng-chih), surrender the city to the Japanese, but Tang refused. On December 10, Matsui ordered his forces to attack the city, which fell three days later. During this period and afterward, Japanese troops killed thousands of prisoners of war and civilians in what became widely known as the Rape of Nanjing. Estimates of the number of victims vary widely, from 10,000 to 300,000. Although Matsui did not issue an order for his troops to kill civilians, he was held responsible as the overall Japanese commander at Nanjing.

Matsui returned to Japan in 1938 and was a cabinet adviser from 1938 to 1940, when he retired for a second and final time. Following the war, he was brought before the International Military Tribunal for the Far East on war crimes charges stemming from the atrocities at Nanjing. Found guilty, Matsui was sentenced to death and hanged on December 23, 1948, in Tokyo.

KEN KOTANI

See also: International Military Tribunal, Far East; Japan; Rape of Nanjing; World War II Atrocities, Pacific Theater

Further Reading

Fogel, Joshua. *The Nanjing Massacre in History and Historiography.* Berkeley: University of California Press, 2000.

Matsui Iwane. *Matsui Iwane Taisho no Jinchu Niishi* (The War Diary of General Matsui Iwane). Tokyo: Fuyo Shobo, 1985.

Yamamoto Masahiro. *Nanking: Anatomy of an Atrocity.* Westport, CT: Praeger, 2000.

Mexico

A large Latin American nation located between the United States and Central America, Mexico has experienced periodic episodes of internal violence over the last century, most notably during the late 1920s and during the Mexican Drug War, which began in earnest in 2006. The Mexican Revolution of 1910 ended the dictatorship of Porfirio Díaz, and the Constitution of 1917 made sweeping changes to the Mexican political and social landscapes. Among other things, it greatly limited the power and privilege of the Catholic Church and placed many restrictions on Catholic clergy—indeed monastic orders were outlawed, clergy were forbidden from wearing clerical garb, and priests were not permitted to vote. Initially, these restrictions were not frequently or uniformly enforced. That changed, however, with the advent of the Plutarco Elías Calles administration beginning in 1924. He aggressively enforced clerical restrictions and sought even tougher anticlerical laws.

Calles's persecution of the Catholic Church set off a virtual civil war between government forces and pro-Catholic rebels, known as the Cristero War (1926–1929), known by many Mexicans as La Cristiada. The term literally refers to Jesus Christ, as the insurgents believed that they were waging a war in the name of Jesus Christ. What followed over the next several years was an insurgent war fought by the Cristeros. It frequently took the form of politically inspired assassinations, terrorism, murder, and kidnappings.

The conflict began in earnest on August 3, 1926, when federal troops stormed a church in Guadalajara in which several hundred Cristeros had congregated. A stand-off ensued until government troops stormed the building, killing 18 civilians and injuring 40 others. Violence sharply escalated after this event, with incidents occurring throughout much of Mexico. When the war ended in 1929, nearly 90,000 people had died—at least 30,000 Cristeros and civilians and as many as 60,000 federal troops and police. The Mexican government attempted to mask the enormity of the event by placing sharp restrictions on the press, so many of the individual occurrences of violence are either poorly documented or cloaked in obscurity. The war took a high toll on the clergy. In 1926, there were approximately 4,500 priests in Mexico; by 1934, there were only about 350 priests. In 1935, 17 Mexican states that had no priests at all. Perhaps 100 or more priests were killed, but far more fled the country, were expelled, or simply disappeared.

Stability returned to Mexico with the ascendance of the National Mexican Party (PNM), which was later renamed the Revolutionary Institutional Party (PRI). The PRI ruled Mexico for the remainder of the 20th century and for many years relied heavily upon an authoritarian executive. The party controlled the Mexican Senate until 1988, and did not lose a gubernatorial seat until 1989. It controlled the presidency until the election of Vicente Fox Quesada in 2000.

Although violence in Mexico during the PRI ascendancy was generally subdued, there were occasional outbreaks of unrest. Perhaps the most infamous example occurred on October 2, 1968, in Mexico City's Plaza de las Culturas in the Tlatelolco section of the city. The Tlatelolco Massacre unfolded just ten days before the start of the 1968 Summer Olympic Games, which were being held in the Mexican capital. The Mexican government had spent well over $100 million dollars on improvements to Mexico City in hopes of putting Mexico's best foot forward on the world stage. As the Olympics neared, protesters, chiefly university and high-school students, began congregating in the Plaza de la Culturas to protest against government policies. Fearful that the protest would disrupt the Games and sully Mexico's image, the government decided to break up the demonstration. Using overwhelming force against the largely peaceful protest of some 10,000 people, government troops massacred anywhere from 44 to more than 300 individuals (casualty figures are much disputed) and arrested 1,345 others.

A low-level conflict involving leftist revolutionary separatists in the southern state of Chiapas and the state and federal governments began in 1994. The conflict witnessed a number of limited military and paramilitary operations against the Zapatista Army of National Liberation (EZLN), which was the chief instigator of the rebellion. The unrest had religious, economic, and political overtones. The fighting commenced in January 1994, during which 45 civilians, 51 rebels, and 3 government personnel died. Since then, there have been numerable attempts to end the unrest, but violent incidents have persisted. In December 1997, paramilitary forces murdered 45 people, mostly women and children, in Acteal. In June 1998, eight civilians and two police officers were killed in fighting at San Juan de la Libertad (El Bosque). Between 1994 and 2004 alone, at least 120 people were killed or disappeared in El Mar, northern Chiapas. Sporadic violence continues to plague Chiapas, and civilians continue to die as a result.

The Mexican Drug War, which began in 2006, has proven to be among the worst internal struggles in Mexico since the 1920s. The conflict involves drug cartels, who are fighting rival cartels as well as federal forces. The Mexican government stepped in to curb drug-related crime and murders by breaking up the cartels and killing or capturing their leadership. Drugs are big business in Mexico (many of them are imported illegally into the United States), with earnings as high as $49.4 billion per year. The conflict began in earnest with Operation MICHOACAN, launched by the Mexican government. Violence accelerated greatly thereafter. Cartels have been responsible for the murders of at least 50 journalists (two photographers were killed and dismembered on a street in Saltillo in May 2013). Families of journalists have also been targeted for intimidation, kidnapping, or murder. The drug cartels are especially leery of journalists because they often expose the activities and whereabouts of the cartel members.

In January 2008, cartel members killed 13 high-school students and two adults in Ciudad Juárez, just across the border from El Paso, Texas. In July 2010, 17 civilians were killed and 18 more wounded in Torrecon. That same month, 51 bodies were found in a mass grave near Monterrey. In April 2011, at least 450 bodies were discovered in a mass grave in Durango, Tamaulipas. In August 2011, 52 civilians died when masked gunmen set fire to a crowded casino.

It is estimated that at least 86,000 people died between 2006 and 2013, with as many as 1.6 million people displaced or made homeless. The dead include some 120,000 cartel members and more than 1,000 police and prosecutors. Among the many civilian dead were at least 1,100 children. The casually rate had grown exponentially since 2006, when 62 died. In 2012, 18,061 people died. There are signs that the Mexican government may change its policies toward the drug cartels, as their power has not greatly diminished, despite the many deaths.

PAUL G. PIERPAOLI JR.

See also: El Salvador; United States

Further Reading

Grillo, Ioan. *Narco: The Bloody Rise of Mexican Drug Cartels.* 2nd ed. London: Bloomsbury Publishing, 2012.

Meyer, Michael C., William L. Sherman, and Susan M. Deeds. *The Course of Mexican History.* 7th ed. New York: Oxford University Press, 2003.

Mothers of the Plaza de Mayo

The Mothers of Plaza de Mayo (*Madres de Plaza de Mayo*) was an organization of mothers searching for their children who had been abducted by the military during the Argentine "Dirty War" of 1976–1983. The group developed into a unique women's movement of nonviolent resistance to tyranny.

The repression carried out by the Argentine military, which seized power on March 24, 1976, quickly became a state-sponsored terrorist plan targeting civilians. Men and women of all ages were abducted by security forces in clandestine operations and taken to one of 360 hidden detention centers in the country. Usually tortured, victims were often killed in extrajudicial executions and buried in collective, unmarked graves or thrown to the sea from airplanes while still alive. Almost 10,000 people have been officially reported as *desaparecidos* ("disappeared"), although human rights organizations estimate the real figure may be closer to 30,000.

Driven by anguish about the unknown fate of their children, the mothers of the disappeared, together with other relatives and human rights supporters, stood as the only civilian resistance to the military. Their denunciations contributed to the international discrediting of the regime and eventually to its downfall. The Mothers of Plaza de Mayo did not manage to find most lost children. Instead, it provided a model of resistance against authoritarian dictatorship and greatly contributed to the reconstruction of Argentine civil society.

The mothers of the disappeared met each other while trying to determine the whereabouts of their children.

As the mothers realized that abductions of their children followed similar patterns that amounted to a systematic plan of mass murder, they decided to band together, uniting their efforts and making one claim out of their many personal losses. Because government authorities refused to grant them an audience, they gathered in front of the seat of the government at the Plaza de Mayo.

When they first demonstrated on April 30, 1977, there were only 14 mothers. Ignored by passersby in central Buenos Aires and unacknowledged by the local press, they kept meeting every week, defying police intimidation. As policemen ordered them to keep moving, hoping to get them away from the square, the mothers began to walk in pairs around the pyramid in the center of the Plaza de Mayo. Thus began their tradition of circling around this monument. They also began to wear white scarves, originally their children's diapers, as a way of recognizing each other in public. Although branded by the military as terrorists or madwomen, they were generally middle-class housewives without any previous political experience. They gradually acquired a consciousness of their resources and skills and increasingly politicized their action. The enormous risk these women took is illustrated by the fact that some of the Mothers themselves disappeared. Among them was the first president of the movement, Azucena Villaflor de Devicenzi, as well as two French nuns who supported the group; they were abducted after a church meeting in December 1977. Despite this, the movement soon counted some 150 members and had grown to comprise several thousand by the end of the dictatorship in 1983.

The prohibition and persecution of political parties, social organizations, and workers' unions had left the victims and their relatives in a situation of helplessness and isolation. Fear of state terrorism on the one hand and public indifference or even mild complicity with the military by broad sectors of Argentine society on the other left the Mothers standing alone against the regime. In the early phase of the movement, their only support came from a few engaged human rights activists and foreign journalists, who helped to make their struggle known abroad. Commitment to human rights by some U.S. State Department officials in the Jimmy Carter administration, together with pressure exerted by exiled Argentines and a growing international network of humanitarian aid, helped reverse the isolation of the Mothers. In September 1979, the Inter-American

Commission on Human Rights (IACHR) reinforced the group's credibility by registering thousands of reports of serious human rights violations. The Mothers received further international recognition when the Nobel Peace Prize was awarded to Argentine pacifist Adolfo Pérez Esquivel in 1980. In his acceptance speech, he mentioned the Mothers of the Plaza de Mayo.

Even if they had evidence of their children's murders, the Mothers of Plaza de Mayo refused to consider them dead as long as the state did not account for and take responsibility for their deaths. When the military passed a law declaring all disappeared dead in 1979, they refused its benefits and insisted on calling their children *desaparecidos.* Together with other human rights organizations, the Mothers of Plaza de Mayo played a decisive role during the transition to democracy in Argentina, placing the problem of the missing persons on the agenda of the newly elected government. They were disappointed, however, that the trial of the military chiefs in 1985, ordered by Argentina's president, dealt with only the senior members of the junta and did not divulge information about what happened to their children.

Internal dissent about its role in postdictatorship Argentina led to the split of the Mothers of Plaza de Mayo into two groups in 1986. The groups differed in their willingness to cooperate with the state, in their involvement in wider social or political causes, and in the way they wished the disappeared to be commemorated or even defined. The Asociación Madres de Plaza de Mayo (Association of the Mothers of Plaza de Mayo), led by the charismatic Hebe de Bonafini, was opposed to the search for and identification of the corpses of the missing; it also rejected any cooperation with the state. Considering themselves "revolutionary mothers," members of the Asociación thought commemoration should consist of appropriating the political goals of their children and fighting for the ideals of social justice. They founded the Universidad Popular de las Madres (Popular University of the Mothers), where courses such as popular education, history, and political thought were taught.

The other group, Madres de Plaza de Mayo (Línea Fundadora, Founding Line) also stressed the singularity of the category of the *desaparecidos,* but accepted a wider range of commemorative practices, including individual memorials. The group cooperated with other human rights organizations and with official institutions in the identification of corpses and former detention centers and was active in the projected creation of a Museo del Nunca Más (the

Never Again Museum) as well as the construction of a memorial including the names of all the missing. Both groups continue to demonstrate every Thursday at 3:30 P.M. in the Plaza de Mayo.

The struggle of the Mothers of Plaza de Mayo has been recognized worldwide as a leading example of pacific resistance to dictatorship and has had a significant moral impact in Argentine society. According to scholar Diane Taylor, however, there is controversy among feminist scholars about the extent to which the Mothers of Plaza de Mayo meant to challenge patriarchal structures. Some authors think that the struggle, although worthwhile and encouraging for other oppressed women, was based on a traditional understanding of motherhood and reinforced the role of women as suffering, self-sacrificing housewives, leaving the patriarchal values of Argentine society intact. Other authors, like Marguerite Bouvard, think instead that these women called into question the very notion of motherhood, politicizing its otherwise merely biological definition. In this interpretation, the Mothers of Plaza de Mayo consider themselves born by their own children; that is, through searching for them, they were born anew into political consciousness. They decided to "socialize" their motherhood, stating that every disappeared person is the child of every mother. Such conceptualizations, according to Bouvard, go beyond all traditional definitions and revolutionize the notion of motherhood.

The original group also led to the formation of the Grandmothers of Plaza de Mayo, made up of women who had not only children but also grandchildren among the missing. They began demonstrating together with the other mothers, but soon discovered that they shared the more specific goal of finding their abducted grandchildren. The Grandmothers of Plaza de Mayo dedicated themselves to the investigation of their children's and grandchildren's whereabouts, through the use of DNA testing to find their kin, and the restitution of their identity. By 2004, 79 out of an estimated 500 kidnapped children, who were now young adults, had been identified, and most were able to recover their true history and establish contact with their biological families.

ESTELA SCHINDEL

See also: Argentine Dirty War; Videla, Jorge Rafael

Further Reading

Arditti, Rita. *Searching for Life: The Grandmothers of the Plaza de Mayo and the Disappeared Children of Argentina.* Berkeley: University of California Press, 1999.

Bouvard, Marguerite Guzmán. *Revolutionizing Motherhood: The Mothers of the Plaza de Mayo.* Wilmington, DE: Scholarly Resources, 1994.

Fisher, Jo. *Mothers of the Disappeared.* Boston: South End Press, 1989.

Mozambique

Southeast African nation covering 304,494 square miles, roughly twice the size of the U.S. state of California. The Republic of Mozambique, with a population of approximately 27.3 million, borders on Swaziland to the south; South Africa and Zimbabwe to the west; Zambia, Malawi, and Tanzania to the north; and the Indian Ocean to the east. Portuguese navigator Vasco de Gama explored Mozambique in 1489, and Portugal colonized the land in 1505.

Mozambique fell into ruinous conditions between 1500 and 1640 as Portugal's power waned. With limited Portuguese influence, Mozambique experienced an extended period of sharecropping that kept most farmers in a state of serfdom. Also, from the mid-18th to the mid-19th centuries, large numbers of Africans were shipped away as slaves, mainly to the Macarena Islands and Brazil. By 1891, political policies of the Portuguese shifted the administration of much of Mozambique to a large, private trading organization known as the Mozambique Company, under a charter granting sovereign rights for 50 years. The Mozambique Company was one of two concession companies to which Lisbon entrusted the administration of Portuguese East Africa, although it was controlled and financed mostly by the British. Because policies in Mozambique were designed to benefit white settlers and the Portuguese homeland, little attention was paid to national integration, economic infrastructure, or education.

After World War II, Portuguese dictator António de Oliveira Salazar insisted on holding on to Mozambique and the other Portuguese colonies. A drive for Mozambican independence soon developed, and in 1962 several anticolonial political groups formed the Front for the Liberation of Mozambique (FRELIMO), a leftist, anti-Portuguese guerrilla movement under the leadership of Eduardo Mondlane.

Mondlane helped initiate an armed campaign against Portuguese colonial rule in September 1964. After some 10 years of sporadic warfare and Portugal's return to democracy, FRELIMO took control of the capital city of Maputo in a coup in April 1974. Within a year, almost all Portuguese colonists had departed. Mozambique became independent on June 25, 1975.

Mondlane responded to Mozambique's lack of resources and abysmal economy by moving into alignment with Cuba and the Soviet Union, both communist nations. After Mondlane was assassinated in 1969, FRELIMO established a one-party Marxist state under President Samora Machel. Racial violence soon ensued, and many Europeans fled the country. Meanwhile, FRELIMO banned private land ownership, nationalized all industries, and put in place educational and health reforms. The new government, sporadically supported by the Soviet Union, was economically dependent on South Africa, which at the time had a hostile apartheid government. It also had to fight the Mozambique National Resistance Movement (RENAMO), an anticommunist political organization of guerrillas sponsored by the white minority government of Rhodesia (Zimbabwe) and financed by South Africa. In 1979, Rhodesia invaded Mozambique, igniting even more violence that wrought havoc and killed scores of civilians.

In 1982, RENAMO launched a series of attacks on transport routes, schools, and health clinics, and Mozambique descended into civil war. In 1984, the South African regime agreed to stop sponsoring RENAMO under the Nkomati Accord if the Mozambican government expelled exiled members of the African National Congress (ANC) residing there. The ANC was a governing party in South Africa founded to defend the rights of the black majority. However, South Africa continued funneling financial and military resources to RENAMO until a permanent peace accord, the General Peace Agreement, was reached in 1992. In the meantime, years of violence, civil war, political instability, and gross government inefficiency all but ruined the Mozambican economy. Indeed, in 1990 Mozambique was estimated to be the world's poorest nation.

In 1994, Mozambique held national elections, which were accepted by most parties as free and fair. FRELIMO won, under Joaquim Chissano, while RENAMO ran as the official opposition. By the mid-1990s FRELIMO, which had cast aside its earlier Marxist leanings, had made progress on the economic front by introducing free-market mechanisms, cutting inflation, and stabilizing the currency. Since 2001, Mozambique's growth rate has been among the top 10 in the world; nevertheless, its people have the world's shortage life expectancy, and the nation still has one the lowest Gross Domestic Products (GDP) per capita in the world.

GLEN ANTHONY HARRIS

See also: South Africa; Uganda

Further Reading

Hanlon, Joseph. *Mozambique: The Revolution under Fire.* London: Zed, 1984.

Isaacman, Allen, and Barbara Isaacman. *Mozambique: From Colonialism to Revolution, 1900–1982.* Boulder, CO: Westview, 1983.

My Lai Massacre

The My Lai Massacre of March 16, 1968, was the most notorious U.S. military atrocity of the Vietnam War. Equally infamous was the cover-up of the incident perpetrated by the brigade and division staffs.

Located in the Quang Ngai Province, My Lai was one of a cluster of South Vietnamese hamlets making up Son My village, nicknamed "Pinkville" by U.S. soldiers because of its concentration of Communist sympathizers and Viet Cong (VC) activity. In order to snare the estimated 250 VC operating in the area, U.S. soldiers were ordered to conduct a classic search-and-destroy sweep, which had to date been characterized by lightly scattered direct VC contact and a high rate of friendly losses to snipers, mines, and booby-trap incidents.

The airmobile assault into My Lai was timed to arrive shortly after the local women had departed for market. The soldiers had expected to engage elements of one of the most successful VC units in the area, but instead found only women, children, and old men. The U.S. soldiers ran wild, particularly those commanded by First Lieutenant William Calley. They indiscriminately shot people as they ran from their huts and then systematically rounded up survivors, allegedly leading them to a nearby ditch and executing them. More villagers were killed as huts and bunkers were destroyed by fire and explosives. The killing was reported to have been halted only when Hugh Thompson, an aeroscout pilot supporting the operation, landed his helicopter between the Americans and fleeing Vietnamese and confronted the U.S. soldiers.

Between 200 and 500 Vietnamese civilians were massacred in the incident. The broad range in numbers of civilian deaths is the result of varying testimony of participants and observers. Some reports include an alleged related massacre in a nearby hamlet. Because of false reporting and the subsequent cover-up, actual casualty figures are difficult to substantiate.

The incident, uncovered a year later, was investigated by the Army Criminal Investigation Division and an army board of inquiry, headed by Lieutenant General William Peers. Although the findings of the board did not ascribe causes for the massacre, many have cited the frustrations of soldiers too long faced with unanswerable losses of comrades, poor leadership from the division commander on down the ranks, and the measurement of success by the statistical yardstick of body count.

Although the Peers report produced a list of 30 persons who knew of the atrocities, only 14 were charged with crimes. All eventually had their charges dismissed or were acquitted by courts-martial except for Calley, who was found guilty of murdering 22 civilians and sentenced to life imprisonment. Calley was seen by much of the public to be a scapegoat, and his sentence was twice reduced, eventually to 10 years. After serving about one-third of his sentence, he was paroled by President Richard M. Nixon in November 1974.

On March 6, 1998, the U.S. Army belatedly recognized Thompson, his former gunner Lawrence Colburn, and his crew chief Glenn Andreatta (who was killed in April 1968) with the Soldier's Medal for gallantry.

ARTHUR T. FRAME

See also: Hue Massacre; Tiger Force Killings; United States; Vietnam War Atrocities

Further Reading

Belknap, Michael R. *The Vietnam War on Trial: The My Lai Massacre and the Court-Martial of Lieutenant Calley.* Lawrence: University Press of Kansas, 2002.

Davidson, Phillip B. *Vietnam at War: The History, 1945–1975.* Novato, CA: Presidio, 1988.

Myanmar

Since attaining its independence from Britain in 1948, Myanmar (which was known as Burma until 1989) has been plagued by civil unrest, civil wars, and myriad human rights abuses. Since 1962, Myanmar has been governed directly or indirectly by the military. Its regimes have been despotic and repressive and have often engaged in atrocities such as mass killings and rapes, torture, human trafficking, slavery, child labor, and even the employment of child soldiers. Myanmar's government has heavily censored the domestic press and has not permitted foreign journalists into areas involved in conflict, so many of the atrocities have gone unreported, and little details are known about them. Over the years, various ethnic and political groups have waged war against each other as well as the government, and at least 25 different groups have arranged for ceasefire agreements with the government. Nevertheless, conflict and civil war still plague parts of Myanmar to the present day.

Beginning in 1962, Burmese leaders nationalized most of Myanmar's economic sectors, including the media. The government sought to install a hybridized version of socialism, known as the Burmese Way to Socialism. There have been periodic outbreaks of protests and demonstrations against the government, including one on July 7, 1962, at Rangoon University in which as many as 100 protesters were killed by government forces. In 1974, antigovernment protests during the funeral of Burmese leader and diplomat U Thant resulted in a brutal crackdown, although casualty figures are not known. Student-led demonstrations during 1975–1977 also resulted in government interventions in which scores died, were wounded, or arrested.

Antigovernment riots in 1988 spawned the so-called 8888 Uprising, which targeted the government's corruption, ineffective economic policies, and political repression. The demonstrations began in Yangon (Rangoon) and soon grew to more than 1 million protesters. After government forces moved to disperse the massive crowd, at least 10,000 lay dead, and several thousand more were wounded. Tens of thousands of others fled the country, taking up residence in Thailand. A year later, more protests resulted in a government declaration of martial law, after which hundreds of civilians died, disappeared, or fled the country.

During the spring and summer of 2007, hefty increases in the price of gasoline and diesel sparked anti-government demonstrations in Yangon, which commenced in August. The government immediately moved to arrest protest leaders, and police badly beat a number of demonstrators. That brought even larger crowds and more unrest. Soon, the so-called Saffron Revolution, led principally by Buddhist monks, emerged as a major threat to the regime. In late September, Myanmar's government moved to end the unrest. It imposed martial law, instituted strict curfews, and raided dozens of Buddhist monasteries. When the operation was over in October, 30–40 monks were dead, as

well as 50–70 civilians. Hundreds more were wounded, mainly in beatings administered by government forces. This protest and its aftermath received much international attention, which proved to be a great embarrassment to Myanmar's government.

In addition to these government crackdowns, Myanmar's population has been subjected to almost innumerable civil wars. This unrest has been chiefly the result of sub-national and ethnic/religious bids for autonomy or independence. It is estimated that as many as 210,000 people died in these struggles between 1948 and 2006. The decades-old struggle between the government and the Karen National Union (KNU), which has sought an independent Karen state in lower Myanmar, has resulted in tens of thousands of deaths. In 2010, reports surfaced that seemed to conclude that Myanmar troops have routinely engaged in gang rapes and mass murders while attempting to subdue that rebellion. The government is also engaged in military operations against the Lahu and Shan minority ethnic groups in the eastern part of Myanmar.

The Kachin Conflict, which has been waged on and off for years between government forces and the Kachin Independence Army, has resulted in many deaths. In June 2011, after a 17-year ceasefire, the war began anew. It is virtually impossible to tally the number of casualties that occurred up to 1994, although they surely number in the tens of thousands. During 2011–2012, at least 1,100 people died in the fighting, and more than 100,000 were displaced. This latest round of the conflict has seen the extensive use of landmines, torture, and child soldiers. Mass rapes have also occurred, largely perpetrated by government forces.

Conflict has also been raging in the Arakan State, which has become a virtual civil war involving Rohingya Muslims on the one side and government and nongovernment forces on the other. In 2012, mass rioting between the Rohingya Muslims and the Rakhine Buddhists in the northern part of Rakhine State resulted in as many as 10,000 civilian deaths and the displacement of some 90,000 people.

Paul G. Pierpaoli Jr.

See also: Indonesia; Torture

Further Reading

Fink, Christina. *Living Silence: Burma under Military Rule.* Bangkok: White Lotus, 2001.

Myint-U, Thant. *The River of Lost Footsteps—Histories of Burma.* New York: Farrar, Straus and Giroux, 2006.

N

Nagasaki, Bombing of

Second U.S. atomic bombing of a Japanese city. Following the Japanese refusal to surrender following the Hiroshima bombing on August 6, 1945, Twentieth Air Force headquarters on Guam issued Field Order 17 on August 8, directing that, on the following day, the second atomic bomb on Tinian Island be dropped on another Japanese city. Kokura was designated as the primary target, and Nagasaki, a city of some 230,000 persons, was the alternate.

At 3:49 A.M. on August 9, Boeing B-29 Superfortress bomber Bockscar (sometimes written as Bock's Car), commanded by Major Charles Sweeney, departed Tinian. It was followed by a second B-29 as scientific observer and a third as photographic observer. The Bockscar carried a plutonium nuclear-fission bomb nicknamed "Fat Man" that was 10 feet 8 inches long and 5 feet in diameter, with a payload greater than that of the Hiroshima bomb. The plutonium 238 isotope core consisted of two melon-shaped hemispheres surrounded by a ring of explosive charges designed to drive the sections together, achieving "critical mass" and a chain reaction releasing 22 kilotons of energy in one-millionth of a second.

Sweeney flew to Kokura but found it overcast and circled for 10 minutes. Despite the clouds, bombardier Kermit Beahan believed they could bomb visually. Sweeney, concerned about a faulty valve that limited fuel, decided to divert to Nagasaki, which was also partly obscured by clouds. Beahan believed he could bomb by radar, but a break in the clouds allowed him to bomb visually, using the Mitsubishi shipyards as his aiming point.

The Bockscar released the bomb from 31,000 feet at 11:02 A.M. local time. The bomb detonated 53 seconds later, approximately 1,500 feet over the city, destroying everything within a 1,000 yard radius. An intense blue-white explosion pushed up a pillar of fire 10,000 feet, followed by a mushroom cloud to 60,000 feet.

Although the bomb missed its intended aiming point by 8,500 feet, it leveled one-third of the city. Called the "Red Circle of Death," the fire and blast area within the Urakami Valley section destroyed more than 18,000 homes and killed 74,000 people. Another 75,000 were injured, and many later died from wounds or complications. Blast forces traveling in excess of 9,000 miles per hour damaged buildings 3 miles away, and the concussion was felt 40 miles from the epicenter. "Ashes of Death" from the mushroom cloud spread radiation poisoning, killing all who were not killed outright within 1,000 yards of the epicenter. The bomb might have killed thousands more, but it detonated away from the city center in a heavy industrial area, vaporizing three of Nagasaki's largest war factories but "minimizing" deaths.

Sweeney made one complete circle of the city to determine damage and then left after fuel concerns and heavy smoke made other circuits futile. Critically low on fuel, he flew to Okinawa, landing at Yontan Field about 12:30 P.M., his gas tanks virtually empty. After refueling, Bockscar flew to Tinian, arriving there at 10:30 P.M. local time after a 20-hour flight.

Included in the instrument bundle dropped from the observation plane was a letter addressed to Japanese physicist Professor F. Sagane that urged immediate surrender and threatened continued atomic destruction of Japanese cities. Written by three American physicists, the letter was a bluff, as no other atomic bombs were then ready. Nonetheless, the second atomic attack, coupled with the August 8, declaration of war by the Soviet Union, provided Japanese Emperor Hirohito with the excuse to end the war.

MARK E. VAN RHYN

See also: Hiroshima, Bombing of; Japan; United States

Further Reading

Chinnock, Frank W. *Nagasaki: The Forgotten Bomb.* New York: World Publishing, 1969.

Ishikawa, Eisei. *Hiroshima and Nagasaki: The Physical, Medical, and Social Effects of the Atomic Bombings.* Translated by David L. Swain. New York: Basic Books, 1981.

Nobile, Philip. *Judgment at the Smithsonian: The Bombing of Hiroshima and Nagasaki.* New York: Marlowe, 1995.

Toland, John. *The Rising Sun: The Decline and Fall of the Japanese Empire, 1936–1945.* New York: Random House, 1970.

Native American Genocide

The native nations of North America have endured relentless campaigns intent on destroying them and all aspects of their cultures for more than 500 years. Indeed, with varying intensity, government policies, corporate enterprises, and religious missions directed against American Indians can be best described as implements of genocide.

Definition

Although states have long sought to eradicate identifiably different groups, tribes, and peoples for thousands of years, the notion of genocide has a relatively recent origin, combining ancient root words, *genos* (people) and *cide* (killing). The term, coined by Raphael Lemkin, came into common usage only after World War II, largely in response to the systematic destruction of Jews, gypsies, homosexuals, and others deemed subhuman by the Nazi regime. In 1946, the United Nations codified the concept in the Convention on the Prevention and Punishment of Genocide. Article II defined it as acts "intent to destroy, in whole or in part, a national, ethnical, racial or religious group," including inflicting physical and/or psychological harm, fostering living conditions likely to lead to death and destruction, killing, the removal of children, and curtailing reproduction. Although not drafted to include the American Indian experience, activists and advocates began to reference genocide following the rise of Red Power amid the Vietnam War. More recently, the Columbian Quincentenary in 1992 sparked a wave of analytic inquiries and political applications of genocide to Native American history.

Distinctiveness

In contrast to many genocides, which have been characterized by a single, systematic, state-sponsored program directed at annihilation during a specific period of time, the native nations of North America have endured a more diffuse, extended, plural, and unrelenting onslaught. The number of tribes and nations, their geographic locations, and their unique histories of interaction with European Americans make the discussion of genocide much more complicated, as does the range of colonial powers (principally Spain, France, and Great Britain), newly established states (specifically the United States and Canada), and nongovernmental actors (especially corporate entities and Christian missionaries). As a consequence, one might be tempted to speak of multiple genocides or overlapping genocidal impulses, rather than a single destructive policy or event. Particularity and diversity, however, should not distract from the shared experience of destruction and dispossession.

Depopulation and Devastation

American Indian tribes experienced massive depopulation following (and in some cases in advance of) their exchanges with Europeans and European Americans. Indigenous communities routinely lost at least 90 percent of their members, resulting in an overall drop from more (and perhaps much more) than 5 million in the present-day United States to a low of 250,000 in 1890. To be sure, many (arguably most) of these deaths resulted from epidemic diseases; however, many others were caused by state violence, policies directed at removal, and efforts to assimilate Native Americans. In fact, guided by explicitly racist ideologies that rendered them as primitives, animals, hostiles, predators, and impediments to progress, the genocidal projects directed at American Indians exhibit two equally destructive features (biological and cultural) at once. On one hand, an array of policies and programs sought to eradicate individuals and their cultural, spiritual, and traditional beliefs and behaviors. On the other hand, more "enlightened" policies and programs intended to create new, non-Indian people through the replacement of native languages, institutions, and practice with the supposedly superior elements of Western civilization.

Destruction

Ever since the arrival of Christopher Columbus, American Indians have endured the effects of ideologies and actions aimed at their destruction. Importantly, these effects meet the United Nations definition of genocide.

Organized violence is perhaps the clearest expression of efforts to exterminate American Indians. For more than five centuries, military campaigns and vigilante actions proved pivotal to strategies to address the "Indian problem." George Washington compared indigenous peoples with wolves, deserving the same treatment, and Colonel John M. Chivington declared in 1864, "Kill them all boys, nits make lice" (Stannard 1993, 131). The governor of California officially urged the extermination of all American Indians in his state during 1851; General William Sheridan affirmed nearly two decades later, "The only good Indians I ever saw were dead" (Drinnon 1990, 539). The press also sometimes endorsed murderous actions, offering news coverage and editorials inciting settlers to take up arms against native communities. Killing, often on a massive scale, followed from these provocations.

The soldiers with Columbus delighted in the torture and mutilation of men, women, and children. Author Barry Lopez, summarizing a report by the Spanish priest Bartolomé de las Casas, wrote: "'Such inhumanities and barbarisms were committed in my sight,' he says, 'as no age can parallel. . . .' The Spanish cut off the legs of children who ran from them. They poured people full of boiling soap. They made bets as to who, with one sweep of his sword, could cut a person in half. They loosed dogs that 'devoured an Indian like a hog, at first sight, in less than a moment.' They used nursing infants for dog food" (Mass Crimes 2003). Lopez writes, "One day, in front of Las Casas, the Spanish dismembered, beheaded or raped three thousand people." Las Casas referred to the Spanish incursion as "a continuous recreational slaughter" (Lopez 1990, 6–7).

Similarly, British colonists engaged in scorched-earth campaigns against indigenous peoples, burning villages and slaughtering their occupants, perhaps most notably during the Pequot War and King Philip's War. American forces waged an unrelenting series of wars in the 19th century, each punctuated by massacres such as those at Sand Creek in 1864 and Wounded Knee in 1890. Moreover, during much of the 18th and 19th centuries, bounties were awarded for American Indian scalps.

Organized violence was expressed in another form of destruction as well, namely removal, which resulted in many deaths and the loss of indigenous traditions. Eager to claim natural resources, secure labor, and seize land, the dispossession and displacement marked British colonial efforts in the 17th and 18th centuries as well as federal and state government programs in the 19th century. The Trail of Tears clearly illustrates these undertakings and their implications. The Cherokees, Chickasaws, Choctaws, Creeks, and Seminoles all faced involuntary removal, the usurpation of national sovereignty, internment in concentration camps, forced marches from areas in the southeastern United States to what is now Oklahoma, violence, and intimidation. Combined, these traumas resulted in mortality rates ranging between 25 and 50 precent. The Cherokee Nation, for instance, lost between 4,000 and 8,000 citizens during its trek westward. This pattern of ethnic cleansing would repeat itself for the next half century, as tribal groups were pushed out of their homelands and onto reservations.

Internment of formerly free indigenous peoples on reservations dramatically altered their lives and living conditions. Conventional means of dwelling and subsistence were irrevocably altered following relocation, and, with such alterations, entire ways of knowing, being, and relating to the world suffered relentless assault. Corruption and government assistance programs brought with them malnourishment, worsening public health, and diminished life expectancy. At the same time, the traditional sources of physical and spiritual power were systematically eradicated. On one hand, white entrepreneurs and policy makers targeted the buffalo, for instance, hunting it to near extinction and with it the horse cultures of the plains dependent on it. On the other hand, lawmakers and missionaries undermined and in many cases outlawed indigenous cultural practices and traditions. Spiritual traditions, including the Sun Dance and the Potlatch, became criminal offenses.

Seemingly more benevolent programs like boarding schools, which were designed to educate and uplift

Native Americans, often had equally disastrous intentions and consequences. In reality, such undertakings sought to transform American Indians, erasing them as they made them more "American." The boarding school system stressed assimilation. American Indian children were removed from their home communities, often taken against their parents' wishes, if not by outright force, and taken to distant residential schools. Here, their hair was cut, and they were made to dress in alien and awkward attire. Living a life of structure and discipline, they were forced to speak English exclusively and taught European American history, customs, and rituals. Stripped of their cultures and isolated, children often experienced homesickness. They became vulnerable as well to physical and mental abuse and disease—which sometimes resulted in death. Boarding schools aimed, in the words of Colonel Richard Henry Pratt, founder of Carlisle Industrial School, to "[k]ill the Indian and save the man," contributing in a very real way mightily to the genocide of Native Americans.

More recently, American Indian communities have suffered from a more subtle form of genocide: population control. For many decades, until at least the late 1970s, the Indian Health Service subjected Native American women to involuntary sterilization, medical interventions with no other intent than to reduce reproduction. Some estimates suggest that upward of one-third of American Indian women of childbearing age underwent the procedure during the short period of its execution.

Past genocidal policies and practices continue to reverberate in Indian Country today, manifesting themselves in a range of social problems, including alcoholism and drug abuse, suicide and interpersonal violence, and the high number of high-school dropouts. Significantly, as they have done for more than five centuries, American Indians survive against the odds, fighting efforts to destroy native cultures and communities, while struggling to defend the validity and vitality of indigenous traditions, languages, and rights.

C. Richard King

See also: Columbian Exchange and Disease; Indian Removal Act; Trail of Tears; Wounded Knee Massacre

Further Reading

Drinnon, Richard. *Facing West: The Metaphysics of Indian Hating and Empire Building.* New York: Schoken Books, 1990.

Lopez, Barry. *The Rediscovery of North America.* Lexington: University Press of Kentucky, 1990.

"Mass Crimes against Humanity and Genocides: Past Genocide of Natives in North America." 2003. Religious Tolerance.org citing Barry Lopez. Available at: http://www.religioustolerance.org/genocide5.htm. Accessed May 30, 2006.

Niezen, Ronald. *Spirit Wars: Native North American Religions in the Age of Nation Building.* Berkeley: University of California Press, 2000.

Stannard, David E. *American Holocaust: The Conquest of the New World.* New York: Oxford University Press, 1993.

Nigeria

Since gaining its independence in 1960, Nigeria has witnessed a number of government coups, dictatorial rule, military-run regimes, a bloody civil war, and various regional and inter-ethnic conflicts. In the early years of the newly independent Nigeria, the federal-style government was democratically elected and presided over three regions. However, over time, the complex ethnic makeup of the country resulted in the creation of a number of different provinces and states, so that Nigeria is now home to 37 different states. A coup in 1966 eradicated the First Republic, and just six months later, military leaders seized control of the government through a series of coups and counter coups.

In May 1967, the Igbo ethnic group, in Nigeria's Eastern Region, voted to secede from Nigeria and form the Republic of Biafra. This triggered a nearly three-year-long civil war, known as the Biafra War, in which the Nigeria government, representing the Western and Northern Regions, fought the Biafran separatists. The conflict began on July 6, 1967, when Nigerian forces attacked Garkem in the southeastern part of the country. One of the chief catalysts of the war had been the Nigerian government's genocidal ethnic cleansing of Igbo settlers in northern Nigeria in the spring and summer of 1966, in which an estimated 50,000 people perished. The Biafra War lasted for 30 months, until Biafra's forces collapsed in January 1970.

During the conflict, anywhere from 1.5 to 3 million people died, many of them civilians. Some 200,000–300,000 died fighting for the Nigerian government; the remaining deaths occurred in Biafra. In order to quash the rebellion, the Nigerian government deliberately blockaded Biafra, not allowing any food or other supplies to enter the breakaway republic from air, sea, or land. This precipitated a full-blown humanitarian crisis as hundreds of thousands of civilians starved to death. The Nigerian government also impeded international shipments of food and other supplies to the besieged area. Thus, the majority of civilian deaths in the war resulting from malnutrition and disease were preventable.

Because Nigeria is host to some 500 different ethnic and religious groups, conflict remained endemic, although on a much smaller scale, in the aftermath of the Biafra War. Another major struggle developed in the Niger Delta region beginning in the early 1990s. This area is rich with oil deposits and is home to huge petroleum complexes. Many of the region's minority ethnic groups, who provide labor for these facilities, began to protest against foreign-owned oil companies, charging them with exploitation and environmental carelessness. This resulted in a number of small-scale protests and raids that were promptly put down by the government.

Ethnic and inter-ethnic unrest in the Niger Delta area intensified after 2000, as the competition for oil revenues and labor contracts gave rise to a host of competing ethnic militias, who fought each other and, sometimes, foreign oil companies. In May 2009, the Nigerian government launched a major military incursion into the Delta after militants had kidnapped a number of soldiers and foreign sailors. As a result, thousands of Nigerian villagers were forced to flee and hundreds—perhaps several thousand—died. One estimate claims that some 2,500 people died during the fighting in the Niger Delta between 2004 and 2009, but that is likely a very low count. The violence has continued in the area, and periodic attempts by militants to seize or sabotage the oil facilities have affected the international price of crude oil.

Since 2009, Nigeria has also been rocked by a religious-based conflict brought about by the militant Islamic group known as Boko Haram (BH), which seeks to destroy Nigeria's secular government and replace it with an Islamic government based upon sharia laws. The group, founded in 2002, has carried out almost innumerable terrorist attacks, assassinations, mass killings, and kidnappings to achieve its goal. At least 2,000 people have died in these attacks over the past four years. The violence has also displaced several thousand people, who have fled from BH strongholds. Boko Haram usually targets government buildings, Christian churches, and, more recently, schools (it has burned at least 10 schools, resulting in numerous deaths).

Among the worst atrocities committed by BH include a January 2012 attack on a church in Yola in which 17 Christian mourners were gunned down during a funeral; a bombing of a Catholic Church in Madalla in December 2011 that killed 42 churchgoers; a November 2011 multibomb attack on police headquarters in Yobe State that killed at least 150; a suicide bombing of the United Nations compound in Abuja that killed 23 in August 2011; a June 2011 bombing of a Maiduguri beer garden that killed at least 25; and bombing attacks in Jos and Maiduguri during December 24–27 that killed 86. On July 26, 2009, after BH launched a major offensive in the north, a Nigerian military counter-terrorism operation killed over 800 people, mostly BH members, including its founder, Mohammed Yusuf. A mosque in Maiduguri was also destroyed by government forces. The conflict with Islamic extremists is ongoing, although the Nigerian government has launched several bids to negotiate an end to the fighting.

Paul G. Pierpaoli Jr.

See also: Baga Massacre; Biafra

Further Reading

Falola, Toyin. *The History of Nigeria.* Westport, CT: Greenwood, 1999.

Soyinka, Wole. *The Open Sore of a Continent: A Personal Narrative of the Nigerian Crisis.* New York: Oxford University Press, 1996.

Nogun-ri Railroad Bridge Incident

Site of alleged massacre of South Korean civilians by U.S. soldiers of H Company of the 2nd Battalion, 7th Cavalry Regiment of the 1st Cavalry Division in July 1950. The railroad bridge at Nogun-ri is located near that town a few miles southwest of Hwanggan, North Chungchong Province, central Republic of Korea (ROK, South Korea). A few days after their deployment to Korea, soldiers of the U.S. 1st Cavalry Division allegedly fired on civilians at the Nogun-ri railroad bridge, killing up to 300 people.

In 1997, some 30 Korean survivors of the Nogun-ri incident filed for compensation with the South Korean government. A low-level South Korean commission found that civilians had been killed at Nogun-ri but that there was no proof of U.S. involvement. In 1998 a national panel rejected the claim on the basis that the statute of limitations had expired. The incident surfaced again when it received major press coverage in the United States in September 1999, and U.S. Secretary of Defense William S. Cohen ordered a new review of the historical evidence with a report to be issued upon its conclusion.

Allegedly, on July 26, 1950, U.S. troops instructed some 500 residents of Nogun-ri and nearby villages to gather near railroad tracks at Nogun-ri. U.S. veterans recall the subsequent events differently, although they are in agreement on a preponderance of women and children among the refugees at the bridge. Reports had circulated among U.S. troops that Korean People's Army (KPA, North Korean Army) infiltrators might attempt to use refugees to penetrate the battalion's defenses.

On July 26, the civilian refugees were resting near the railroad tracks when they suddenly came under a strafing attack by U.S. aircraft; reportedly upward of 100 refugees were killed and those who remained sought cover under the railroad bridge. Over the next several days U.S. soldiers kept the refugees pinned down under the bridge and fired on them. Some veterans recall receiving fire from the civilians at the bridge and say that they found disguised KPA soldiers among the dead. Others do not recall being fired upon and say they saw only civilians there. The Korean claimants recall only three days of carnage. On July 29 the 7th Cavalry pulled back and the KPA moved into the area. A North Korean newspaper reported several weeks later that KPA troops had found about 400 bodies in the area.

A 2001 report by the U.S. Army inspector general concluded that the Nogun-ri incident was not a deliberate or premeditated massacre of civilians but rather a tragic result of a savage war and ill-trained U.S. and South Korean troops. The Pentagon insisted that no soldiers were ordered to shoot civilians in the vicinity of the bridge. The U.S. government thus admitted that civilians had been fired upon, but the precise number of those killed varies widely; the U.S. military has estimated 50 to 100; the South Koreans claim as many as 250. The Democratic People's Republic of Korea (DPRK, North Korea) continues to claim 400 or more. Before leaving office, President Bill Clinton issued a formal statement of deep regret over the incident. There are still many people, both in the United States and South Korea, however, who believe that what happened at the railroad bridge was more nefarious than an unfortunate accident of war.

The events at Nogun-ri must be viewed against the background of the initial deployment of U.S. troops from Japan, the vast majority of whom were poorly trained and without combat experience, and their injection into the desperate fighting that marked the retreat of United Nations (UN) forces to the Pusan Perimeter. UN troops had regularly come under fire from North Korean infiltrators utilizing civilian refugees as human shields. As a consequence, U.S. commanders had indeed issued orders authorizing troops to fire on civilians as a defense against disguised KPA soldiers.

SPENCER C. TUCKER

See also: Kochang Incident; Korean War Atrocities

Further Reading

Bateman, Robert L., III. *No Gun Ri: A Military History of the Korean War Incident.* Mechanicsburg, PA: Stackpole Books, 2002.

Hanley, Charles J., Sang-hun Chol, and Martha Mendoza. *The Bridge at No Gun Ri: A Hidden Nightmare from the Korean War.* New York: Henry Holt, 2001.

O

Obote, Milton

Milton Obote was Ugandan prime minister (1962–1966) and president (1966–1971, 1980–1985).

Born on December 28, 1924, in Akokoro, northern Uganda, Obote studied at Busoga College from 1945 to 1947 and at Makerere University College beginning in 1948. Makerere officials expelled him in 1950 for political activity, and he subsequently went to Kenya to work a number of menial jobs.

On his return to Uganda in 1957, Obote organized the Lango branch of the Uganda National Congress (UNC). He was elected to membership in the Uganda Legislative Council, and in 1958 he was elected to represent the Lango district in the country's first popular election. When the UNC split in 1959, he formed the Uganda People's Congress (UPC). Obote formed a coalition with the Bagunda and three other kingdoms, and when national elections were held on April 27, 1962, the UPC majority made him prime minister. On October 9, 1962, Uganda ended 68 years as a British protectorate and gained its independence. Obote sought national unity, economic reform, and better relations with Western nations. In 1966, however, he was implicated in a gold-smuggling plot along with his protégé Idi Amin, the deputy commander of the Ugandan armed forces. In retaliation, Obote suspended the constitution, staged a coup, and declared Uganda a republic, naming himself as president on March 2, 1966.

Obote's lack of charisma, his authoritarian manner, and his widespread unpopularity doomed his first presidency. Many of his political opponents were jailed without trial and others harassed and tortured. His secret police, the General Service Unit, was responsible for many cruelties toward the civilian population. His attempts to move his country toward socialism, in what became known as the Move to the Left policy, coupled with several economic crises and scandals, further hamstrung his rule. On January 25, 1971, while the president was on a state trip to Singapore, Amin deposed Obote and immediately set up a military regime.

Obote spent nine years in exile in the Sudan and Tanzania. With the help of Tanzanian President Julius Nyerere, Obote defeated Amin in April 1979 and regained the presidency. Amin fled to Libya. The election results that followed in 1980 were not accepted by a large portion of the electorate, and Obote's opponents, including National Resistance Army, turned to armed violence in order to oust him from power. Obote responded with a brutal crackdown that resulted in the death of an estimated quarter of a million people; the worst of the atrocities took place in the so-called Luwero Triangle, an area north of the Ugandan capital of Kampala. After five years of civil strife, the army, which Obote had always used to his benefit, now turned against him. He was deposed in 1985 by General Bazilio Okello. Obote fled to Zambia and died in Johannesburg, South Africa, on October 10, 2005.

GARY KERLEY

See also: Amin, Idi; Kony, Joseph; Uganda

Further Reading

Gupta, Vijay. *Obote: Second Liberation.* New Delhi: Vikus, 1983.
Ingham, Kenneth. *Obote: A Political Biography.* New York: Routledge, 1994.

Oradour-sur-Glane Massacre

The Oradour-sur-Glane Massacre was a German atrocity against French civilians on June 10, 1944. During World War II, German armed forces committed an untold number of atrocities. Although the vast majority occurred in eastern Europe and the Soviet Union, western Europe witnessed several notorious German war crimes, including the massacre of innocent men, women, and children at Oradour-sur-Glane, France.

Located 15 miles northwest of Limoges in central France, the small village of Oradour, although it lay within the German zone of occupation since June 1940, managed to escape the horrors of World War II for the better part of four years. This all changed, however, on June 10, 1944, when Sturmbannfuehrer Otto Dickmann and troops from the 1st Battalion of the 2nd Schutzstaffel (SS) Panzer Division (Das Reich) entered the village, slaughtered its inhabitants, and looted and burned its houses and buildings.

Commanded by Obersturmbannfuehrer Heinz Lammerding, Das Reich, one of the original Waffen-SS divisions, had been transferred from the Eastern Front to Montauban in southern France in early 1944. In the immediate aftermath of the Allied Normandy Invasion of June 6, Das Reich received orders to redeploy to the Normandy Front. As it made its way north, the division came under attack from French Resistance forces and engaged in several firefights. On June 9, 1944, the Resistance captured one of the division's officers, the popular Sturmbannfuhrer Helmut Kampfe. Possibly, the massacre at Oradour was in reprisal for this act.

On entering the village, the panzergrenadiers who made up Das Reich's 1st Battalion forced the startled residents to assemble in the central square. Separating the men from the women and children, the Germans herded the former into barns and the latter into the village church. They then burned both the barns and the church, tossing in grenades for good measure and gunning down those who tried to flee. After plundering and setting fire to other buildings, the 1st Battalion withdrew. A total of 642 victims, including 207 children, lay dead. Only 7 villagers (5 men, 1 woman, and a child) managed to escape. Das Reich proceeded to the Normandy Front without encountering further Resistance activity.

At war's end, French authorities decided to maintain Oradour-sur-Glane as it had been left by the Das Reich Division, transforming the remnants of the village into a national monument. As for the perpetrators, 7 Germans and 14 Alsatians were tried by a French military court at Bordeaux in 1953. The court found 20 of the defendants guilty and sentenced 2 to death and 18 to imprisonment at hard labor camps for terms ranging from 5 to 20 years. Amnesties and pardons, however, led to all 20 being freed within 5 years.

BRUCE J. DEHART

See also: Lidice Massacre; World War II Atrocities, European Theater

Further Reading

Farmer, Sarah B. *Martyred Village: Commemorating the 1944 Massacre at Oradour-sur-Glane.* Berkeley: University of California Press, 1999.
Hastings, Max. *Das Reich: Resistance and the March of the 2nd S.S. Panzer Division through France, June 1944.* New York: Holt, Rinehart, and Winston, 1981.

P

Pakistan

Pakistan is a predominantly Muslim nation (80 percent Sunni and 20 percent Shia) strategically located in the Middle East and on the West Asian subcontinent. Since its independence in 1947, which resulted in a bloody war with its long-time adversary India, Pakistan has been plagued by autocratic, dictatorial rule, political instability, several subsequent wars with India, periodic sectarian violence, and religious-based terrorism. In the two years of fighting with India (1947–1949) that followed independence, at least 800,000 Muslims died, the vast majority of whom were unarmed civilians.

Pakistan's first democratic elections since independence occurred in 1970; those elections, however, led directly to a genocidal war with Bengali separatists and another war with India in 1971. When the East Pakistani (Bangladeshi) Awawi League won seats in the new national government, the established elite in West Pakistan would not allow its members to be seated in the national assembly. This provoked massive rioting and uprisings in East Pakistan and a brutal campaign to repress them by the Pakistani Army, code-named Operation SEARCH LIGHT, which began on March 25, 1971.

The operation was initially aimed at Hindus (the perennial enemy of Pakistan) as well as political dissidents and Bengali intelligentsia; later, the scope of the offensive would be widened to include many innocent civilians in urban as well as rural areas. The Pakistani army first instructed allied militia forces to attack Dhaka University, Bangladesh's largest and most prestigious university. On the evening of March 25, and continuing over the next several days, the militias began killing or capturing hundreds of unarmed students (most of them Hindu and other minorities), faculty, and staff members. More than 100 died, while 563 young Bengali women were seized and imprisoned in various places throughout Dhaka. They were repeatedly raped by militia men and Pakistani soldiers. Thereafter, death squads roamed the streets of Dhaka, resulting in the deaths of as many as 30,000 people in little more than a week's time. Meanwhile, half the city's population fled. Some 6,000 Pakistani soldiers also died during the offensive. On March 26, Bengali nationalists declared their independence from Pakistan.

What followed was a flurry of violence. It is estimated that during the short, nine-month conflict Pakistani and allied forces murdered 990 teachers, 49 physicians, 42 attorneys, 16 writers and artists, and 13 journalists. Some estimates suggest that as many as 200,000 women were raped. Hindus were targeted the most. On April 23 at Jathibhanga, anywhere from 3,000–5,000 Hindus were murdered in their village or while attempting to escape, but the worst atrocity of the entire war occurred on May 20, during the Chuknagar Massacre, in which some 8,000–10,000 Hindus were murdered en masse. The dead included men, women, children, and the elderly. Although it is impossible to pinpoint how many Hindus died during the entirety of the war, their fatality rate was certainly much higher than any other group.

After India entered the war in early December 1971, the conflict drew to a rapid conclusion. On December 16, Pakistani military forces surrendered, making Bangladesh's independence drive a fait accompli. During this second and brief war with India, Pakistan suffered 9,000 military deaths, 4,350 wounded, and 97,368 taken prisoner. Just three days after the surrender, however, another massacre occurred—this time in front of foreign journalists—when a group of prisoners of war were shot to death by Bengali-allied guerillas at a repatriation ceremony. The total number of those killed during the conflict varies by source. The Bangladeshi government has claimed as many as 3 million dead. Other sources, however, claim 300,000–500,000 dead. Another 8 to 10 million (mostly Hindus) were forced to flee to India as refugees. Much of the international community has since labeled the conflict a genocide.

In 1999, another war broke out between India and Pakistan. Known as the Kargil War, the conflict took place from May to July in the Kargil region of Kashmir, a long-disputed area between the Indians and Pakistanis. The war began when Kashmiri militants and Pakistani forces occupied the Indian side of the Line of Control, which serves as the de facto boundary between the two nations. Although the Pakistani government blamed the incursion solely on Kashmiri militants, it later became clear that Pakistani government forces had also been involved. The brief conflict resulted in as many as 4,000 dead and 665 wounded on the Pakistani side. This clash proved especially nerve-wracking, because by then both India and Pakistan possessed nuclear weapons.

When the War on Terror began after the attacks on the United States in September 2001, Pakistan became one of the epicenters of this difficult and diffuse struggle. Pakistan shares a long and porous border with Afghanistan to the west and north, so a number of Islamic extremists, including Taliban members, made their way into the western portions of Pakistan, where they could find refuge and regroup. The Pakistani government vowed to root them out, but these efforts were sometimes half-hearted and not well executed. Nevertheless, between 2001 and 2011, Pakistan claims that it spent $67.93 million on the War on Terror (some of that U.S. money). It has also suffered thousands of casualties, many of them civilian, and the country has had to make living arrangements for as many as 3 million civilians who have become refugees.

Sectarian and religious-based atrocities have also increased since 9/11. On March 2, 2004, 42 people died and over 100 were injured during the Quetta Ashura Massacre in the city of Quetta (in southwestern Pakistan). Most of the victims had been from the Hazara ethnic group. In the May 28, 2010, Lahore Massacre, 94 people were killed and another 120 were wounded in two simultaneous attacks on mosques in Lahore, Punjab, Pakistan. The mosques belonged to the Ahmadiyya minority group. The Kohistan Massacre near Kohistan, Pakistan, witnessed the murders of 18 Shia Muslims who were traveling on a bus. Among the dead were three children. The victims were clearly singled out because of their religious identities; other passengers on the bus remained unharmed.

Paul G. Pierpaoli Jr.

See also: Bangladesh; Bangladesh Massacres (1971); Bangladesh War Crimes Tribunal; India

Further Reading

Jones, Owen Bennett. *Pakistan: Eye of the Storm.* New Haven, CT: Yale University Press, 2002.

Zaheer, Hasan. *The Separation of East Pakistan: The Rise and Realization of Bengali Muslim Nationalism.* Oxford, UK: Oxford University Press, 1994.

People's Commissariat for Internal Affairs (NKVD)

The People's Commissariat for Internal Affairs (abbreviated as NKVD) was the chief internal law enforcement authority in the Soviet Union. Over the decades, its role and scope expanded and contracted according to the needs of the government. For much of its existence, the NKVD was far more than an internal police force, however. It oftentimes functioned as a secret internal police organization, charged with political repression, deportations, and ethnic cleansing. Sometimes, the NKVD's reach extended beyond the USSR, as it was involved in numerous assassinations of Soviet "enemies" abroad, enforcing Soviet policies in other communist nations, and infiltrating and influencing the governments of foreign countries. The NKVD also secured Soviet borders, was frequently involved in espionage, and, most notoriously perhaps, operated the vast system of gulags, or forced-labor prisons where hundreds of thousands of "class enemies," political dissidents, and other enemies of the state were interned.

The NKVD evolved shortly after the start of the November 1917 Bolshevik Revolution, when the new agency assumed the responsibilities of the old Ministry of Internal Affairs. After Joseph Stalin had consolidated his power in the USSR by the late 1920s, he used the NKVD to implement his policies and as an enforcement agency to punish those who refused to abide by his government's mandates or who disagreed with the Communist Party of the Soviet Union (CPSU). Soon, Stalin was employing the NKVD to stifle political dissent and to remake the Soviet constituent republics into an image that was acceptable to the CPSU. In Ukraine, this included the elimination of the kulaks (landed peasantry), which became an official—if unspoken—policy that began in earnest in 1929.

When collectivization of Soviet agriculture commenced in 1929, kulaks in Ukraine were expected to turn over their land to the state, which would convert it into communal farm usage. When the kulaks rebelled against this policy, NKVD personnel, along with Soviet army troops, were sent into Ukraine to enforce the collectivization policy. Those who resisted were shot, deported to a gulag, or relocated to a forced labor facility within Ukraine. The mass disappearance of so many kulaks in a short span of time crippled Ukrainian agriculture, as the region's most-experienced farmers were no longer available to tend the land.

Stalin also used the NKVD to quash what he viewed as unacceptable Ukrainian nationalism and to enforce Soviet grain requisition policies. By 1931, Ukrainian agriculture was in great disarray because of Soviet policies. Compounding that was the fact that many kulaks—in an act of desperate rebellion—had slaughtered millions of head of cattle and other livestock. This meant less food available for all Ukrainians. In 1932, in a move that many scholars claim was a deliberate act designed to induce famine, the Soviet government significantly increased its grain requisition quota in Ukraine. The NKVD enforced this policy, guarding government-owned grain silos, and forbidding hungry peasants from using the grain for their own consumption. This precipitated a full-blown mass famine, known by Ukrainians as the Holodomor. NKVD officials routinely raided peasant homes to ensure that they were not stealing or hiding grain. Those found guilty of these crimes were either murdered or disappeared within the gulag system. Thus, while hundreds of thousands of Ukrainian peasants were dying of malnutrition, government grain reserves remained plentiful—the government simply refused them access to it.

There is also considerable evidence to suggest that the NKVD prevented starving Ukrainians from traveling to other areas where food might have been more plentiful. And as the agency solely responsible for securing both internal and external borders, the NKVD more than likely prevented Ukrainians from migrating to other Soviet republics. Thus, while disastrous Soviet agricultural policies of the late 1920s and early 1930s set the stage for the Holodomor, it was the NKVD that made certain those policies had the maximum impact on the Ukrainian citizenry.

Paul G. Pierpaoli Jr.

See also: Class Enemies; Dekulakization; First Five Year Plan; Great Purges; Gulags; Kulaks; Soviet Collectivization; Soviet Grain Requisition Policies; Soviet Union; Stalin, Joseph; Ukrainian Starvation (Holodomor)

Further Reading

Conquest, Robert. *The Harvest of Sorrow: Soviet Collectivization and the Terror-Famine.* New York: Oxford University Press, 1987.

Fitzpatrick, Sheila. *The Russian Revolution. 2nd ed.* New York: Oxford University Press, 1994.

Peru

Over the last 75 years or so, the South American nation of Peru has seen its share of violence, especially between 1980 and 2000. Peru has witnessed numerous coups, military-dominated regimes, and various human rights abuses, a good number of which were perpetrated by the government or military. The last sustained period of military government occurred from 1968 until 1980. During the 1930s, a decade that ushered in a prolonged period of coups and counter-coups and alternating periods of military and democratic rule, the Peruvian government brutally repressed the American Popular Revolutionary Alliance (APRA), resulting in the deaths of hundreds and the imprisonment or repression of thousands more. Beginning in the early 1960s, leftists inspired by Cuban leader Fidel Castro's revolution went to war against the Peruvian government. The Revolutionary Left Movement spearheaded this rebellion, which was stamped out by the Peruvian army by the mid-1960s. Hundreds of communist insurgents died, and the Peruvian government resorted to wholesale civil rights restrictions to end the revolt.

The worst internal strife in Peru's history occurred between 1980 and 2000, when the country was nearly torn apart by two significant insurgencies and a series of governments that often resorted to violence in order to end violence. This period witnessed a number of massacres, terrorist attacks, forced disappearances, violence against women, and even the use of children as soldiers. It is believed that as many as 70,000 people died during this time, most of them innocent civilians. The problems began in 1980, with the coalescence of a rural-based, radical leftist group known as Shining Path, whose leaders sought to emulate Chinese leader Mao Zedong's Cultural Revolution, among other things. The Shining Path waged war against the government and against individuals and groups deemed enemies to their cause. Shining Path members exhorted the poor and rural peasants to overthrow the government; they also warred against rival groups, oftentimes killing civilians in the process. The Shining Path frequently recruited children as soldiers. In 1982, another leftist group, the Túpac Amaru Revolutionary Movement (MRTA), which was loosely allied with pro-Castro groups in Latin America, commenced a guerrilla-style war against Peru's government. The MRTA and Shining Path also fought one another.

There were a series of atrocities and massacres that unfolded as a result of this internal unrest, some of which were perpetrated by the Peruvian army or groups associated with it. In March 1983, members of a peasant-based anti-Shining Path militia assassinated a Shining Path leader in Lucanamarca; that incident resulted in a Shining Path reprisal attack in April 1983 that killed 69 people—many of them children—in the Province of Huancasancos. As many as 74 civilians—including women and children—were massacred at Accomarca in August 1985 by the Peruvian military. Many of the victims were killed by machete blows. In November 1991, a military death squad composed of soldiers from the Peruvian army massacred 15 people in the Barios Altos section of Lima. The innocent civilians were mistaken for Shining Path insurgents.

In May 1992, nine rural peasants were murdered by a military death squad in the Province of Santa. The July 1992 La Cantuta Massacre witnessed the abduction of nine students and a professor at Lima's La Cantuta University by military death squads. The disappearances occurred in the immediate aftermath of a Shining Path bombing in Tarata (Lima Province) that had left 40 people dead. The violence in Peru lessened considerably beginning in 2000, when the controversial government of Alberto Fujimori came to an end. In 2001, the Peruvian government convened the Truth and Reconciliation Commission (TRC) in order to investigate the atrocities committed during the prior two

decades. The TRC determined that the MRTA was culpable for about 1.5 percent of the 70,000 deaths; the remaining deaths were the work of Shining Path and the Peruvian government. In 2009, Fujimori was convicted of human-rights abuses during his tenure in office and was sentenced by a Peruvian court to 25 years in prison.

Although Peru's great internal struggle ended in 2000, the country has nevertheless witnessed acts of violence since then. In May 2007, a bomb hidden in a backpack in the city of Juliaca killed six people and wounded another 48. Because it occurred on the 27th anniversary of Shining Path's first attack against the Peruvian government, that organization has been blamed, although this has never been confirmed. In 2009, a crisis involving indigenous peoples in the Peruvian Amazon region, who oppose the government's oil-exploration efforts, set off more than two months of street demonstrations. In June, the Peruvian government dispatched military units to the Amazon, declared martial law there, and precipitated a two-day struggle with the protesters that resulted in the deaths of 21 soldiers and at least 30 deaths among the indigenous protesters (including three young children).

PAUL G. PIERPAOLI JR.

See also: Chile; Shining Path

Further Reading

Masterson, Daniel. *The History of Peru.* Santa Barbara, CA: Greenwood, 2009.

Palmer, David Scott, ed. *Shining Path of Peru.* 2nd ed. New York: St. Martin's, 1994.

Philippine-American War, War Crime Trials in

Little known today, the courts martial of several American army officers, in particular Brigadier Jacob H. Smith, Marine Major Littleton Waller, and Captain Edwin Glenn, during the 1899–1902 Philippine-American War, established several important legal principles that presaged those laid down in the 1945 Nuremberg Trials. The trials arose out of atrocity allegations during the Samar Campaigns of 1900–1902.

The United States had acquired sovereignty over the Philippines under the Paris Treaty of 1898, which ended the Spanish-American War. However, Filipino revolutionaries, who had been fighting for independence since 1896, and who collaborated with American naval forces under Commodore George Dewey, asserted control over the some of the islands, established a government, and declared independence. Spanish Manila surrendered to Commodore Dewey on August 13, 1898. The U.S. government declined to recognize Philippine independence or to guarantee independence at a future date. After a period of rising tensions between Filipinos and U.S. military forces, war broke out on February 4, 1899. In early 1901, Filipino revolutionary Emilio Aguinaldo was captured, and several key Filipino generals surrendered to U.S. authorities. Two provinces, however, proved particularly difficult to control, Batangas in Luzon and Samar Island.

American forces on Samar were under the command of Colonel Robert P. Hughes, who began a vigorous pacification campaign in March 1902. Giving testimony before a U.S. Senate committee in 1902, Hughes admitted that "uncivilized warfare" was being conducted in Samar by U.S. forces. A successful attack on an American garrison by the people of Balangiga, on the southern coast of Samar in September 1901, had led to the appointment of Brigadier General Jacob H. Smith to command the Sixth Separate Brigade to pacify the island. In addition to some 3,000 infantry troops and Filipino auxiliaries, a contingent of 300 U.S. Marines under the command of Major Littleton Waller were assigned to Smith.

Smith gave orders to turn the interior of Samar into a "howling wilderness," take no prisoners, and to kill all those capable of bearing arms against the United States. A public outcry erupted when these instructions were exposed in the press, however, and he was brought to trial.

Major Waller countermanded Smith's orders: "I've had instructions to kill everyone over ten years old. But we are not making war on women and children; we are making war on men capable of bearing arms." Between October 24 and November 12, 1901, Waller's forces destroyed 255 homes. In the campaign that followed, hundreds more houses and other villages were burned. More than half of the island's 44 municipalities were destroyed, together with the agricultural infrastructure necessary for its economy. Food was so scarce that some had to sell their children for a sack of rice. No accurate death toll has ever been determined, although it is now known that an oft-quoted figure of 50,000 was based on typographical errors and misreading of documents.

In December, during the rainy season, Waller set out with a contingent of 55 men and 36 Filipino bearers to open a trail across Samar. The expedition was a disaster and ten marines died of starvation and exposure. Waller,

severely sick, was persuaded by his subordinate, Lieutenant John H. Day, to order the execution of a dozen Filipino bearers for treachery, although they had, in fact, helped the marines. It was this incident that led to the court martial of Waller and Day.

All courts-martial findings under U.S. jurisdiction are reviewed, and in theory, a reviewing authority can order a retrial if fault is found, although this rarely happens. More importantly, the review can establish precedents for other similar trials even if it conflicts with the finding of the court martial.

In March 1902, Major Waller was brought to trial for violating the 58th article of war in ordering the execution of the Filipino bearers. The charge was that he "willfully and feloniously and with malice aforethought did murder and kill 11 men, names unknown, native of the Philippine Islands," by ordering his subordinate, Lieutenant John Day, to shoot them. Waller accepted responsibility for the death of the men, but pleaded not guilty to murder. His defense was that the executions were demanded by imperative necessity at the time and conformed to the laws of war. During his trial, in his defense, he cited Smith's now-infamous orders. The court found the facts correct but acquitted Waller of the murder charge. General Adna Chaffee, commander of U.S. forces, reviewed the case and found Waller's actions to be "more of unlawful retaliation than a justifiable act of war" and that they should not be used as a precedent in future cases. There was no imperative need to execute the men, and Waller could have referred the case to his superiors by telegraph.

Lieutenant Day's acquittal on charges of ordering and carrying out the executions led to an important legal precedent. In his defense, Day said that he had been obeying the orders of Major Waller. The reviewing authority decided that Day could not be acquitted for obeying Waller's order because they were of questionable legality and he should have questioned them. Had he done so, said the review, he would have prevented "one of the most regrettable incidents in the annals of the military service of the United States." Both men were returned to active duty. Waller, however, became known as the "Butcher of Samar," and the case haunted him to the end of his career, blocking his promotion to commandant of the Marines Corp.

General Jacob Smith was put on trial between late April until May 1902 on a charge of "conduct to the prejudice of good order and military discipline." The allegations against Smith were, among others, that he had ordered Waller "to take no prisoners" (meaning thereby that giving of quarter was not desired or required), and defined those to be killed as those over ten years old and capable of bearing arms. The court removed the reference to the giving of quarter, adding "and in actual hostilities against the United States" after "capable of bearing arms" and found him guilty, with a sentence recommendation that he only be admonished, believing that Smith did not mean what he said and that his orders in any event were not followed.

Secretary of War Elihu Root, who reviewed the case, disagreed strongly with the court's findings and wrote to President Theodore Roosevelt that it was the responsibility of officers like Smith not to incite subordinates to "acts of lawless violence." It was, in his view, only the good sense of his subordinates that had prevented the orders from being carried out to the letter. Despite this, Root believed that admonishment was severe for a man of Smith's age, experience, and stature. He recommended instead that Smith be retired. In notes accompanying Root's letter to Roosevelt, the Army's judge advocate general pointed out that the rules governing the behavior of American forces were not Smith's orders, but rather the laws of war, and that Smith's order was both unnecessary and illegal. The Smith trial was one of the earliest examples that upheld the principle that an officer may be prosecuted for the issuance of an illegal order even if that order is not obeyed. Roosevelt believed that the Waller and Smith cases "sullied the American name." He disapproved of the court's findings and ordered that Smith be retired immediately.

Major Edwin F. Glenn of the 5th U.S. Infantry had headed an intelligence gathering operation that included the interrogation of known or suspected members of the Filipino forces and their sympathizers as well as those favoring U.S. forces. Concerns were raised regarding the use of the "water cure," or water torture, of suspected insurgents. This involved holding the subject down and pouring or pumping water into his or her stomach, then forcing out the water and interrogating the subject. The sensation is much like drowning.

It is unknown how widely the water torture was used, but Glenn, who applied it during interrogations, regarded it as a common and acceptable technique. At the time there was considerable discussion, for instance in hearings before the congressional Committee on Affairs in the Philippine Islands, as to whether it could be properly regarded as torture if there were no lasting physical effects, deaths were few, and the subject could end his discomfort at any time by providing the information required. Nevertheless, after another public outcry, Glenn was brought to trial.

Major Glenn and his subordinates had gained a widespread reputation for their use of water torture, but he was indicted only in one case and only on the same charge as Smith, for giving orders to the prejudice of good order and military discipline. Glenn pleaded not guilty but admitted responsibility for ordering and permitting the torture for the purposes of punishment and gaining information about the insurgents. Glenn claimed that the torture was lawful because of military necessity and because it was a common method of obtaining information. The defense produced many examples of atrocities carried out by the insurgents. As a result, Glenn was found guilty but punished with a three-month suspension and $50 per month pay cut for the same period.

In a report to President Roosevelt, the judge advocate general took issue with the court's findings, stating that whatever activities the insurgents might have indulged in did not legitimize the use of torture to gain information, which was forbidden under General Order 100. While admitting that there may be exceptional circumstances that might justify the use of such cruelty, these did not apply in Glenn's case, nor, in the judge advocate general's view, was Glenn's use of torture legitimized because he claimed it as a common method.

Roosevelt concurred with the report that Glenn's punishment was inadequate but, because civil rule had by then had been instituted in the region, there was little to be gained in taking further action. Glenn later became a brigadier general. The legal principle of "obedience to orders does not constitute a defense" would be used at the Nuremberg Tribunal after World War II to limit defendants' attempts to justify their actions. The issuance of an illegal order would be used at the same tribunal by the prosecution.

Bob Couttie

See also: Spanish-American War, War Crimes; United States

Further Reading

Gates, John M. *Schoolbooks and Krags.* Westport, CT: Greenwood Press, 1973.
Linn, Brian M. *The Philippine War.* Lawrence: University Press of Kansas, 2002.

Pinochet, Augusto

Chilean general and dictator (1973 to 1990). Born in Valparaiso on November 15, 1915, Augusto Pinochet graduated in 1937 from the Chilean Escuela Militar (Military

School) and was commissioned a second lieutenant in the infantry. He spent his entire adult life in military service, during which time he served as a military attaché in Washington and as a faculty member at the Military School and the Chilean War College. In 1968 he attained the rank of brigadier general and in 1971 assumed the rank of division general. In 1972 he became chief of staff of the army. Then in August 1973, amid growing civil unrest, President Salvador Allende Gossens named Pinochet army commander in chief.

Along with most of Chile's high command, Pinochet was known for his conservative, anticommunist views. On September 11, 1973, he led the coup that brought down Allende's socialist government. Allende was killed during the struggle. In the wake of the coup, Pinochet directed a merciless military-style campaign against enemies of the new regime. Security and military officials arrested, detained, tortured, and executed thousands of Chileans.

The coup represented the final step in a carefully planned campaign that had received significant support from the U.S. government against the Allende government. Intelligence and monetary support funneled through the U.S. embassy, the Central Intelligence Agency (CIA), military contacts, and cooperative private organizations had helped Chilean opposition groups challenge the Allende government during 1970–1973.

Under Pinochet's authoritarian rule, the Chilean government promptly reversed its social and economic policies and promoted neoliberal, export-oriented reforms aimed at modernizing the country. Mixed results and mounting social problems generated a strong but cautious opposition movement in Chile during the 1980s. Despite public revelations of gross human rights violations during the 1970s that culminated in international trials against various officers who had served the dictatorship, Pinochet clung to power.

Confident that he would prevail, Pinochet held a plebiscite in 1988 in which Chileans were given a choice between a return to civilian rule or the continuation of the Pinochet presidency until 1997. Chileans voted against the dictator, and he was ultimately forced to relinquish the presidency on March 11, 1990, although he retained his position as army commander in chief until 1998.

Pinochet was arrested in London in October 1998 via an international warrant issued by a Spanish judge. International courts hounded Pinochet, intent on bringing him to trial for his various and sundry crimes as Chile's dictator. He avoided trial in Spain because of alleged ill health, was forced to return to Chile in March 2000, and was tried and convicted there. His convictions were overturned in late 2000 because his mental state was in question during the trial. In 2004, investigators discovered efforts by Pinochet to transfer financial assets out of the country illegally. This move undermined his credibility, and the government stripped him of legal immunity. In November 2005, he was charged with tax evasion for having concealed some $27 million in secret bank accounts and was ordered placed under house arrest. Never forced to stand trial and unrepentant to the end, Pinochet died in Santiago on December 10, 2006. He was accorded a military but not a state funeral. Many Chileans chose to remember him not for the abuses and atrocities of his regime but as a staunch anticommunist whose free-market policies made rapid Chilean economic growth possible.

DANIEL LEWIS

See also: Chile; United States

Further Reading

Drake, Paul, and Iván Jaksic, eds. *The Struggle for Democracy in Chile, 1982–1990.* Lincoln: University of Nebraska Press, 1991.

Pinochet Ugarte, Augusto. *The Crucial Day.* Santiago de Chile: Editorial Renaciamiento, 1982.

Spooner, Mary Helen. *Soldiers in a Narrow Land: The Pinochet Regime in Chile.* Berkeley: University of California Press, 1994.

R

Rape

Rape as a part of war has bedeviled every country that has experienced conflict. It is an age-old problem, but one that long remained hidden because of the stigma surrounding rape. Women, often seen as property owned by men, were "taken" by other men just as cattle or horses were claimed by the victor. In the 20th century, changes in attitudes toward women contributed to greater publicity about rapes during wartime. Women began to be seen as victims of war and rape became identified as a war crime.

Rape may have been used for the first time as an instrument of mass terror during World War I, although there is some evidence that Mexican revolutionaries routinely raped opposition women in the early years of the 20th century. German troops in Belgium and France raped women to such an extent during the Great War that German officers were accused of using mass rape as a weapon of war. An international war crimes tribunal that was established in 1919 reported on wartime rape and forced prostitution, but squabbling among the Allied nation meant that only a few Germans were convicted, and none served their prison terms.

During World War II, German soldiers again raped women in virtually every place that they conquered, especially in Poland and the Soviet Union. The widespread nature of the attacks indicated an organized and systemic plan to intimidate and brutalize the women of these regions. Meanwhile, in Asia, Japanese forces may have raped as many as 80,000 Chinese women during the 1937 Rape of Nanking. Japanese military authorities also forced thousands of women in conquered regions, such as Korea and the Philippines, to become sex slaves to soldiers as "comfort women." Allied troops also engaged in sexual assaults, with Soviet forces victimizing German women because of their nationality and gender.

The post-World War II International Military Tribunal at Nuremberg admitted evidence of rapes and other sexual abuse introduced by French and Russian Allied prosecutors, and witnesses testified about rapes committed by German soldiers in occupied France and on the Eastern front; testimony also informed the judges about sexual abuse, male and female, including sterilization experiments, in Nazi concentration camps. Yet, after the war crimes against women were essentially ignored, perhaps because they were viewed as less important. In its final judgments, however, the Nuremberg Tribunal did not refer even once to the crime of rape or other sexual violence, explaining that, in the section of the judgments that dealt with war crimes and crimes against humanity, "the evidence was overwhelming in its volume and detail." Unfortunately, in 1950, when the International Law Commission completed the Nuremberg Principles, it did not include rape in the list of crimes against humanity, effectively ignoring rape as a war crime during World War II.

In postwar Tokyo, the situation proved different as the International Military Tribunal for the Far East (IMTFE) charged 28 defendants, half of whom were generals, with rape as a war crime. Specifically, the defendants were indicted for "inhuman treatment," "ill treatment" and "failure to respect family honor and rights" by promoting the sexual assaults of thousands of women in Nanking. All of the defendants were convicted. Japanese General Tomoyuki Yamashita, in a trial held separately from the IMTFE because he was not waging a war of aggression but had committed traditional war crimes, received a sentence of death for permitting his troops to commit mass murder and mass rape in the Philippines. Yamashita's conviction became the first instance of a commanding officer being held criminally liable for acts committed by his troops.

In the wake of the tribunals at Nuremberg and Tokyo, the Allies also set up military courts to try minor Axis war criminals in their respective occupations zones. Within the American zone, these proceedings were established and governed by Control Council Law No. 10, which expressly named rape as one of the types of wartime atrocities. However, considering the nature of court proceedings, this provision remained only national military law and not international law. Although subsequent trials held under Control Council No. 10 have included only a few cases of rape, the true significance of the law lay in the recognition that acts of rape could be considered a crime against humanity.

In subsequent decades, other military forces would use rape as a weapon. In 1971, East and West Pakistan fought a bloody war of secession, during which tens of thousands of women were reportedly raped. Rape as a form of torture has commonly been used against Latin American political prisoners, especially during the era of dictators in Argentina, Chile, and Uruguay. During a period of intense repression in 1979, rape or the threat of rape was also used on political detainees in Colombia. In Africa, rape is still often used as a tool of war to break resistance and instill fear in the civilian population. During the 1994 Rwanda genocide, human rights groups estimate that 200,000 to 500,000 Tutsi women were raped in a 100-day period. However, most of the women were murdered afterward, making exact figures impossible to obtain. When the United Nations (UN) drafted the Statute of the Rwanda Tribunal, it included a clear provision for rape as a crime against humanity.

Bosnia is as notorious as the Congo as a place in which mass rapes occurred during political conflict. In 1991, the rapid disintegration of Yugoslavia devolved in to a brutal armed conflict during which thousands of acts of sexual violence were committed, most notably the rape of detained Bosnian Muslim and Bosnian Serb women. Systematic rape forced civilians to flee their homes and persuaded them to never return. Rape was also used as a form of ethnic cleansing, with women raped in camps until they died. Only about 20 percent of captured women survived these rape camps. Most rapes were gang rapes that were made into public spectacle, with family members, neighbors, and other women forced to watch.

Worldwide media attention and the demands of women's rights groups and other human rights organizations compelled the UN to issue Resolution 820, condemning "the massive, organized and systematic detention and rape of women and reaffirmed that those who commit . . . or order . . . the commission of such acts will be held individually responsible." In 1993, the UN Security Council established the ad hoc International Criminal Tribunal for the Former Yugoslavia to investigate, prosecute, and judge criminals from all sides of the conflict. The Tribunal's authority extended to crimes involving rape, and Article 5 of the Yugoslav Statute explicitly listed rape as a crime against humanity.

The inclusion of rape in the statutes of the Rwanda and Yugoslav tribunals marked an important development: until then, the concept of crimes against humanity had never been grounded in an international law and was in fact derived from provisions in national laws. With the inclusion of rape in the Rwanda and Yugoslav statutes, the international community underscored its acceptance that prohibitions against rape formed a part of the customary law that binds all states, even though (and unlike the crimes of apartheid, torture, or genocide), no formal international treaties dealt with this crime.

In the late 1990s, the international community also took a step forward toward developing a legal concept of crimes against humanity. The Rome Statute, signed in 1998 and ratified in 2003, outlined the jurisdiction of the International Criminal Court (ICC) whose task it is to prosecute international crimes. The Statute's Article 7(g) lists a number of violent sexual offenses under the heading of crimes against humanity, including "rape, sexual slavery, enforced prostitution, forced pregnancy, enforced sterilization, or any other form of sexual violence of comparable gravity." As of April 2012, 121 states became parties to the Statute, including all of South America, nearly all of Europe, and roughly half of the African states; another 32 countries have signed but not ratified the statute. Three states (Israel, Sudan, and the United States), however, withdrew their signatures, refusing any legal obligations arising from the Statute. In the early 21st century, the ICC was joined by several other tribunals (i.e., the Special Court for Sierra Leone, the Panels of East Timor, and the Extraordinary Chambers in the Courts of Cambodia) designed to deal with sexual assaults as crimes against humanity.

CARYN E. NEUMANN

See also: Comfort Women; Congo Mass Rapes; Rape; Rape of Nanjing

Further Reading

Frederick, Sharon. *Rape: Weapon of Terror.* River Edge, NJ: Global, 2001.

Stiglmayer, Alexandra, ed. *Mass Rape: The War against Women in Bosnia-Herzegovina.* Lincoln: University of Nebraska Press, 1994.

Rape of Nanjing

Six-week period of atrocities and terrorism, occurring from December 13, 1937, to January 22, 1938, after Japanese troops captured the Chinese capital of Nanjing (Nanking) in Jiangsu (Kiangsu) Province. In July 1937, outright war began between Japan and China after the Marco Polo Bridge/Lugouqiao (Lukouch'iao) Incident. Chinese Nationalist forces under Guomindang (GMD, [Kuomintang, KMT] Nationalist) President Jiang Jieshi (Chiang Kai-shek) initially offered strong resistance to the Japanese invasion. At the time, they were holding out at Shanghai, the country's greatest port city and the site of a major international settlement, from August 13 to November 9, 1937.

The Nationalist troops then fell back, moving inland in a near rout on the Nationalist capital of Nanjing, a symbolic location home to more than 1 million Chinese. Jiang was not prepared to abandon it without a fight, but no defense or evacuation plans had been made. Another of Jiang's objectives in defending both Shanghai and Nanjing, home to numerous foreign embassies, was to attract worldwide attention and win foreign support for China's anti-Japanese war.

In early December, Japanese troops converged on Nanjing. After Chinese troops rejected Japanese demands to surrender, on December 9 the Japanese opened a massive assault. Three days later, the Chinese defenders fell back across the Changjiang (Yangtze) River, and the following day the 6th, 9th, and 116th Divisions of the Japanese army

entered the city as two Japanese navy flotillas arrived up the Changjiang River. During the ensuing six weeks, the Japanese occupiers deliberately instituted a reign of terror, apparently designed to cow China's population into ready submission to Japanese occupation. Frustration over Jiang's refusal to surrender, which Japanese leaders had expected him to do before the end of 1937, might have been another factor contributing to the reign of terror.

Entering the city on December 13, Japanese forces fired on streets crowded with refugees, wounded soldiers, and civilians. They also fired on many thousands of refugees who were attempting to escape by swimming across the river. The occupying forces used machine guns, swords, bayonets, fire, live burial, and poison gas to massacre captured Chinese soldiers and any young men suspected of being such. Scattered atrocities and murders, often marked by great brutality, continued throughout the city for six weeks, as did heavy looting. Counts of how many soldiers and civilians died in the Nanjing Massacre vary widely, ranging from 42,000 to 300,000. During this period, Japanese soldiers raped an estimated 20,000 women, most of whom were then killed.

The Nanjing Massacre shocked the west and generated extensive international sympathy for China, although this did not necessarily translate into tangible support and assistance. It was an early example of the use of organized brutality to cow and terrorize civilian populations characteristic of many World War II military occupations. As the 21st century began, memories of the Nanjing Massacre remained bitter in China; a major museum commemorating the event exists in Nanjing. In contrast, Japanese officials sought for many decades to deny that the episode ever took place, or at least to minimize its scale, and it was omitted from official Japanese accounts of the war. In the late 1990s, however, several Japanese journalists and academics who investigated the subject mounted dedicated efforts to bring the event to the attention of the Japanese people.

PRISCILLA ROBERTS

See also: China; Japan; Matsui Iwane; Rape; World War II Atrocities, Pacific Theater

Further Reading

Honda, Katsuichi. *The Nanjing Massacre: A Japanese Journalist Confronts Japan's National Shame.* Edited by Frank Gibney. Armonk, NY: M. E. Sharpe, 1999.

Li, Fei Fei, Robert Sabella, and David Liu, eds. *Nanking: Memory and Healing.* Armonk, NY: M. E. Sharpe, 2002.

Yamamoto Masahiro. *Nanking: Anatomy of an Atrocity.* Westport, CT: Praeger, 2000.

Russia

In the post–Cold War era, Russia has seen more than its share of violence. The violence has been spawned by two separate wars with Chechnya, a constitutional crisis in 1993, a brief conflict with the Republic of Georgia over the future of South Ossetia in 2008, and ongoing terrorism and suicide bombings perpetrated by militant Islamic rebels in the North Caucasus region, particularly from Chechnya and Dagestan.

In 1993, deteriorating relations between Russian President Boris Yeltsin and Russia's Parliament led to a political stalemate by September. The crisis was sparked chiefly by Yeltsin's economic policies, which threatened to plunge the nation into a depression as it converted from a Soviet/communist system to a free-market system. A large parliamentary faction decried Yeltsin's policies and asserted that he did not have the power to institute such changes without legislative oversight. On September 21, 1993, Yeltsin unilaterally dissolved Parliament, even though he was not constitutionally authorized to do so. The move precipitated a ten-day conflict that witnessed the worst street fighting in Moscow since the Russian Revolution of 1917. Yeltsin ordered troops in to staunch the fighting, and in the process the Russian White House, home to Parliament, was badly damaged by artillery fire. When the crisis ended, more or less on Yeltsin's terms, 187 people lay dead (some sources claim the death toll was closer to 2,000), and another 437 were wounded.

A little more than a year later, in December 1994, the Russian government went to war with Chechen separatists who sought independence from Moscow. Beginning in early January 1995, Russian troops launched a brutal attack on the Chechen capital of Grozny. After surrounding the city, Russian artillery and fighter jets pounded the city, resulting in some 25,000 civilian deaths by the end of the month. In retaliation, Chechen rebels took several thousand Russians hostage, many of whom died. Russian forces also suffered high casualties in the fighting. After more fighting and many more civilian casualties, Moscow agreed to a truce in August 1996 and signed a tenuous peace treaty in May 1997. All told, 50,000–100,000 Chechen civilians died in the war. An additional 17,300 Chechen soldiers were killed, while Russia reported about 5,700 deaths among its soldiers.

A second Chechen conflict began in August 1999, a result of the Islamic International Peacekeeping Brigade's invasion of Dagestan. The Brigade was an Islamic Chechen militia that sought to help Dagestan's separatists. Russian intervened in the crisis by dispatching troops to Chechnya. The conflict ended in May 2000, with 25,000–50,000 Chechen civilians dead or missing and as many as 11,000 Russian army casualties. Although the battle phase of the conflict was terminated in 2000, Chechen rebels and Islamic extremists fought a terroristic guerilla war against Russia that did not substantially subside until 2009.

There were many atrocities and acts of terror perpetrated against the Russians between 2000 and 2009. In October 2002, militant Islamic Chechens seized a theater in Moscow and took 850 hostages. After police moved in, 130 hostages and 40 rebels lay dead; another 700 were wounded. In December 2003, the bombing of a train at Stavropol killed 46 civilians. Militants bombed a Moscow subway in February 2004, killing 40 people, and in August 2004, bombings of two Russian commercial airliners killed 89 people. In one of the worst acts of terrorism in modern Russia, Chechen and Dagestani militants stormed a school in Beslan, taking 777 children and some 320 adults hostage. The stand-off endured for three days, until police and army troops moved against the school. When the crisis ended, 380 people (many of them children) lay dead, and nearly 700 were injured.

After 2005 or so, the militants began to change their tactics, increasingly employing suicide bombers to instill terror among the Russian public. In March 2010, two female suicide bombers attacked a Moscow subway during rush hour, killing 40 and injuring 75. In January 2011, a suicide bomber blew himself up at Moscow's Domodedovo Airport, killing 36 and wounding an additional 180 people.

Russia also waged a short, five-day war against Georgia over the disputed region of South Ossetia in August 2008. The conflict ensued when Georgian forces launched a large military incursion into South Ossetia, claiming that its peacekeeping forces along the border had been fired upon. Moscow authorized an incursion into the disputed region, in the process killing 365 civilians, destroying the town of Tskhinvali and badly damaging several Georgian towns. The Russians suffered 162 deaths in the fighting, while Georgia reported 224 civilians dead, 15 missing, and 542 wounded. As long as Moscow is faced with separatist movements, terroristic violence and larger military struggles are likely to continue.

Paul G. Pierpaoli Jr.

See also: Soviet Union

Further Reading

Politkovskaya, Anna. *Putin's Russia: Life in a Failed Democracy.* New York: Holt, 2009.

Service, Robert. *A History of Modern Russia.* 3rd ed. Cambridge, MA: Harvard University Press, 2009.

S

Saudi Arabia

The Kingdom of Saudi Arabia was formally established in 1932 by King Abd al-Aziz al-Saud, who ruled the nation until his death in 1953. Since then, the House of Saud has ruled Saudi Arabia continuously, imposing its Wahhabism (a distinct branch of Sunni Islam) on its inhabitants. The country's legal system is predicated on the Hanbali school of Islamic law, with the Koran serving as the basic governing and legal blueprint for all Saudis. Since its founding, the Kingdom has seen sporadic outbreaks of violence, some precipitated by the strong Shia/Sunni Islam divide in the country, but some also the result of internal and external terrorism, particularly since the 1990s.

The Saudi government has consistently imposed a system of apartheid against its Shia Muslim minority (about 15 percent of the total population, most of who live in the Eastern Province). The Shias have been subjected to both political and economic marginalization, as well as government-sponsored and government-sanctioned violence. As late as 2002, two of Saudi Arabia's leading Wahhabi clerics referred to all Shias as apostates, and one sanctioned the murder of the members of the religious minority. Shias have been shut out of the higher echelons of government, including the military and security forces, and a number of them have been imprisoned because of their religious and political beliefs. Shias were blamed for a series of oil pipeline bombings in 1988, with no evidence to substantiate such a conclusion, and a number were arrested and executed.

From November 20 to December 4, 1979, the Saudi government faced one of its biggest domestic crises when a group of militant Islamists, who opposed the House of Saud's pro-Western foreign policy, stormed the Grand Mosque at Mecca (Islam's holiest site) and held its congregation hostage. After days of tension, Saudi security forces, with help from foreign commandos, retook the mosque, but with many casualties. At least 255 people died in the attack and counterattack (some estimates are much higher). As many as 67 of the surviving militants were arrested and summarily executed.

On July 31, 1987, violence flared between protesters and Shia pilgrims in Mecca. When Shia pilgrims from Iran confronted Saudi police, a fight ensued followed by a stampede. When the dust settled, some 400 people lay dead, including 275 Iranians, 85 Saudi police officers, and 42 pilgrims of varying nationalities.

International terrorism, likely perpetrated by Al Qaeda, resulted in the bombing of the Khobar Towers building in Khobar on June 25, 1996. The massive truck bomb killed 19 U.S. airmen stationed there and injured 372 others. A suicide bombing attack on the Vinnell Compound in Riyadh on May 12, 2002, resulted in 35 deaths and more than 200 injuries. Home-grown or foreign terrorists were the likely perpetrator. On May 24, 2004, 17 terrorists associated with Al Qaeda in the Arabia Peninsula attacked personnel employed at two major petroleum installations in Khobar, resulting in the deaths of 19 nationals and three locals. Shia unrest in Quatif, a heavily Sunni city, in March

2011 prompted Saudi security forces to open fire on a large crowd, killing several and wounding scores of others.

Major protests that began with the Arab Spring in early 2011, some of which are ongoing, have resulted in more government repression, arrests, and several deaths. Many of the protesters have been Shia, dissatisfied with their disenfranchisement and economic marginalization. Other Saudis have protested over labor rights in the region and the continued detention without trial of political dissidents. Some Saudi women have also used the Arab Spring to air their grievances, particularly their inability to drive automobiles and vote. Initially, the protests were most pronounced in the east, where most of the Shias live, but they later spread to other areas, including the capital at Riyadh. Many Shias have called for semiautonomy and an independent legislature, but the House of Saud is not likely to heed these demands. Since January 2011, 14 protesters have died, and another 150 have been arrested. The Saudi government has recently shown some willingness to meet the demands of the protesters. However, given past events, it is likely that it will fall well short of the protesters' desires.

PAUL G. PIERPAOLI JR.

See also: United States; Yemen

Further Reading

Wynbrandt, James. *A Brief History of Saudi Arabia.* New York: Checkman, 2004.

Zuhur, Sherifa. *Saudi Arabia: Islamic Threat, Political Reform and the Global War on Terror.* Carlisle Barracks, PA: Strategic Studies Institute, 2005.

Shining Path

Rural-based guerrilla organization founded in Peru and operational since 1980. Conceptually, Sendero Luminoso (Shining Path) developed in Peru during the 1960s. First established at a Peruvian regional university, the group was the result of frustration with a corrupt and unresponsive political system and the ambition of intellectuals to put theory into practice. Shining Path's key leader was Abimael Guzmán Reynoso, who headed the School of Education at the University of San Cristobal de Huamanga. During the 1960s, Guzmán, also known as "Chairman Gonzalo," recruited a core group of like-minded activists. They distinguished themselves from other Marxist groups by promoting a Maoist line of thought and action that reflected the split in the Cominform between the Soviet Union and China.

The adoption of a Maoist line, which Guzmán labeled "Marxist-Leninist–Maoist-Gonzalo Thought," fit Peru well, for its peasant population remained sizable and isolated from political affairs. As Shining Path developed, its leaders developed a strategy of action that involved the mobilization of the peasantry in a revolutionary struggle against international and domestic "oppressors of the people."

The organization used its strength among the student population to dominate university administrations into the 1970s. Graduates of the School of Education sought positions in rural schools, where they used their classrooms to develop community connections for Shining Path. Guzmán and other leaders deepened their connections with China and soon expanded their field operations beyond the university. The failure of government reforms, in particular land redistribution and rural economic development programs, convinced the Shining Path hierarchy that the revolutionary potential of the peasantry was as yet underdeveloped.

Believing that they could serve as a catalyst for a rural revolution that would expand and strangle the urban centers of capitalist exploitation, Shining Path's leaders launched its first military operation in 1980, working to create centers of revolutionary activity throughout the Andean highland region. Shining Path reorganized peasant communities and extracted cash and material goods from "liberated" and other communities by force.

Peru's civilian governments initially proved incapable of meeting Shining Path's challenge. The election of President Alberto Fujimori in 1990, however, changed that. Fujimori suspended constitutional government and launched an ambitious campaign against Shining Path and other guerrilla organizations then in operation in other parts of Peru. His government also requested help and received aid from the United States to train the military and police forces in antiguerrilla tactics. The United States provided additional support for campaigns against cocoa production, which increased the presence of security forces in rural areas. In addition, the Peruvian government trained and equipped peasant forces to separate Shining Path from its popular peasant base.

The Fujimori administration's war against Shining Path achieved success rather quickly. Peruvian forces captured Guzmán in 1992, and a series of subsequent antiguerrilla campaigns destroyed Shining Path's military capabilities. While still nominally active, Shining Path no longer represents a significant challenge to the Peruvian government.

DANIEL LEWIS

See also: Chile; Peru

Further Reading

Masterson, Daniel. *Militarism and Politics in Latin America: Peru from Sanchez Cerro to "Sendero Luminoso."* Westport, CT: Greenwood, 1991.

Palmer, David Scott, ed. *Shining Path of Peru.* 2nd ed. New York: St. Martin's, 1994.

Sierra Leone

Sierra Leone is a multiethnic, sub-Saharan nation located on the west coast of Africa. Since gaining its independence in 1961, the country had experienced numerous coups, military and one-party rule, as well as a bloody civil war that raged from 1991 until 2002. While some of the struggles have involved inter-ethnic clashes, most have involved political and economic issues. Much of the fighting during the 1991–2002 civil war, which also involved forces from nearby Liberia, was centered in the eastern part of Sierra Leone, where there are many diamond mines. Control of those mines and their revenue were a major factor in the conflict.

Between 1961 and 1967, Sierra Leone was governed by the Sierra Leone People's Party (SLLP). The 1967 nationwide elections resulted in a narrow victory for the All People's Congress (APC), and Siaka Stevens became prime minister on March 21; within hours, however, he was overthrown in a bloodless coup engineered by a disaffected army general. On March 23, another army-led coup brought another government, which constituted itself as the National Reformation Council (NRC). Yet another coup, which took place on April 18, 1968, overthrew the NRC, which was replaced by the Anti-Corruption Revolutionary Movement (ACRM). The ACRM reinstated Stevens as prime minister, who set the stage for several decades of one-party (APC) rule. Many NRC members were arrested and imprisoned, but the period of great political instability was over.

The APC governed by controlling key industries, the press, and media, although it stopped short of outright dictatorial rule. Nevertheless, corruption and nepotism were rampant during the APC-dominated years. In March 1991, antigovernment forces known as the Revolutionary United Front (RUF), with help from Charles Taylor's National Patriotic Front of Liberia (NPFL), attempted to overthrow the APC government led by President Joseph Momoh. At the time, Liberia was embroiled in its own civil war. Civil war quickly ensued in Sierra Leone. That September, Momoh, in an attempt to quash the rebellion, produced a new constitution that would allow multiparty elections in Sierra Leone. His efforts to produce more democracy were too late, however, and he was overthrown in a coup in April 1992. The new ruling junta, known as the National Provisional Ruling Council (NPRC), abandoned Momoh's constitution, strictly limited civil liberties, and invoked military rule over the country.

The NPRC attempted to formulate a peace settlement with the RUF and NPRF, which continued its operations against government forces. However, this effort did not bear fruit, and the civil war began to involve more and more civilians. Indeed, both sides in the struggle were involved in atrocities against civilians throughout Sierra Leone. There were reports of the mass murders and rapes of women, children, and the elderly. The RUF particularly engaged in forced labor and enslavement as well as abductions, torture, mutilations and amputations. The RUF and AFRC routinely abducted children and forced them to become soldiers; there were reportedly thousands of children soldiers during the civil war, and in the Kailahun District alone, some 3,000 child soldiers were carrying out military missions for the RUF and AFRC. Human rights abuses were not perpetrated solely by the RUF and AFRC; government troops also engaged in various atrocities.

In May 1997, a group of Sierra Leone's senior army officers formed a new government, known as the Armed Forces Revolutionary Council (AFRC), which announced a unilateral end to the war. This, however, only made the conflict worse, as enemy forces moved on the capital of Freetown. The number of atrocities against civilians dramatically escalated. In May 1998, a civilian woman from Koidu lost both of her children during an RUF/AFCR attack. Later that month, she witnessed the mass killing of some 50 people in Tumbodu. She was then detained by RUF/AFCR troops, who cut off her hand. In April 1999, 125 unarmed civilians were slaughtered in the town of Slongo. In January 1999, RUF troops entered Freeport and engaged in wide-spread destruction and massacres. Hundreds were killed in the violence.

The civil war ended in 2002, but only after a United Nations-led peacekeeping force and an intervention force from Britain brought an end to the hostilities. It is estimated that at least 50,000 civilians died between 1991 and

2002. Some estimates claim as many as 200,000 deaths. Perhaps a million or more others were displaced from their homes, with many thousands fleeing to neighboring Guinea. One of the worst features of this bloody conflict was the widespread use of child soldiers, which brought much international attention and indignation.

In 2002, the new government of Sierra Leone established a Truth and Reconciliation Commission to foster healing and conciliation among the perpetrators and victims of the violence. That same year, with the backing of the United Nations, the Special Court for Sierra Leone was convened to bring to justice to those who were connected with atrocities and human rights abuses in Sierra Leone. Numerous high-level individuals (from both sides of the fighting) have since been indicted, tried, and convicted. Most notably, in 2012, Liberia's Charles Taylor was convicted of atrocities for his role in the struggle.

PAUL G. PIERPAOLI JR.

See also: Special Court for Sierra Leone; Taylor, Charles

Further Reading

Kargbo, Michael. *British Foreign Policy Conflict in Sierra Leone, 1991–2001*. New York: Peter Lang, 2006.

Kulah, Arthur F. *Liberia Will Rise Again: Reflections on the Liberian Civil Crisis*. Nashville: Abingdon Press, 1999.

Somalia

Somalia is an overwhelmingly Sunni Muslim nation located in the Horn of Africa, on the continent's eastern coast. It has often been divided among rival clans, which has brought much tension and violence, particularly over the past 25 years or so. The principal clans include the Darod, Dir, Hawiye, Isaaq, and Rahanweyn. In July 1960, the United Nations trusteeship of Italian Somaliland and the old British colony of Somaliland were joined to form the modern-day nation of Somalia. Almost immediately, clan rivalry helped form a fragmented political landscape in which clan-based parties jockeyed for power and influence. Despite these rivalries, Somalia had a fairly stable government from 1960 until 1969. This changed markedly when General Mohamed Siad Barre seized power in October 1969. His regime inaugurated a period of violence and repression that continues to the present day. Indeed, by the 1990s, Somalia had descended into anarchy and almost unending violence. The government functioned as such in name only, and a grave humanitarian disaster loomed when the Somali Civil War began in 1991.

Siad ruled as a military dictator, and his regime presided over an extended period of human rights abuses, many involving innocent civilians, which wrecked Somali society and only spawned more violence. In 1977, with the initial support of the Soviet Union, Siad sent troops into the disputed region of Ogaden in Ethiopia, sparking the 1977–1978 Ogaden War. In October 1977, the Soviets ended their support for Somalia, and in March 1978 the war concluded, with nothing gained for the Somalis. The conflict did, however, result in 6,453 Somalis killed, and another 2,409 wounded. Worse still, both the Somalis and Ethiopians were guilty of wholesale atrocities aimed at civilian populations. These included mass rapes, the purposeful destruction of homes and villages, and the mass murder of civilians. Civilian casualties during the war were reportedly at least several thousand.

By August 1980, the United States had allied itself with Siad's regime, part of a broader Cold War diplomatic realignment. However, wholesale human rights violations by the Siad government compelled the U.S. government to cut off military assistance to Somalia in 1989. Meanwhile, Siad's government, which favored the Darod clan at the expense of others, sowed the seeds for a bloody civil war. By the end of the 1980s, Siad had begun losing the support of allied clans. When the United Somali Congress (USC) tried to wrest control of Mogadishu from forces loyal to Siad during 1989–1990, vicious fighting in the Somali capital virtually flattened the city. Thousands of civilians were killed, wounded, or rendered homeless. In January 1991, Siad fled Mogadishu, turning control of the capital to the USC. With Siad out of the picture, inter-clan rivalry and violence skyrocketed, setting the stage for a civil war that continues to be waged today.

During a genocidal campaign carried out by clan militias against the Bantu and Jubba Valley people in 1991, hundreds of innocent victims, including women, children, and the elderly were massacred. By then, Somalia's government existed in name only, and so there was no effective way to control these rogue militias. There were also increasing reports of the use of children as soldiers. In 1992, with hundreds of thousands of Somali refugees facing starvation and near-constant violence, the United Nations (UN) authorized a humanitarian mission to Somalia, which was almost immediately threatened by forces loyal to General Mohammed Farrah Aidid, a vicious war lord and head of the of the USC/Somali National Alliance. The United States sent a large contingent of troops to Somalia, and by the spring of 1993, conditions for the war-torn Somalis had improved appreciably.

At the same time, the UN authorized a further Somali mission, this time to disarm the warring clans and militias and to broker a peace deal. This mission soon ran into serious problems, however, as UN and U.S. troops found themselves fighting against the warring parties in Somalia, as well as troops loyal to Aidid. Reports began to surface of atrocities being committed by UN forces, involving attacks on unarmed civilians; in one instance, a hospital was attacked, killing nine patients. These incidents turned many Somalis against the UN mission, which meant more support for Aidid.

The UN mission was doomed after the October 3–4, 1993, Battle of Mogadishu, in which forces loyal to Aidid launched a major offensive, killing 18 American troops and killing or wounding scores of others, including civilians. In less than six months, U.S. troops would depart Somalia. The UN remained in the country until 1995, but fighting continued in Somalia, resulting in mounting casualties. Aidid died in August 1996, but sadly this did little to mitigate the Somali conflict. Growing Islamic radicalism began to take root in Somalia, sponsored in part by Al Qaeda, which commenced operations with local militia groups. To combat this growing threat, the United States helped create a joint task force in 2002, using some 2,000 forces from the Horn of Africa, to prevent radical Islamists from taking root in the war-torn nation. In 2004, the UN aided in the formation of the Transitional Federal Government (TFG), which struggled to rein in the violence in Somalia.

Beginning in the spring of 2006, the Union of Islamic Courts (UIC) took control over south-central Somalia, which largely defeated the warring clan-based militias. It also instituted draconian sharia laws in the areas it controlled, including Mogadishu. Some 6,000 civilians were killed in Mogadishu that year, and more than 600,000 were displaced from their homes. In late 2006 and early 2007, the TFG, along with troops from Ethiopia and African Union peacekeeping forces, defeated the UIC, but in the process another 300,000 civilians in Mogadishu were displaced. In January 2007, U.S. air strikes aimed at Al Qaeda operatives in Somalia resulted in several dozen civilian deaths. In 2008, as the TFG reached a truce with the more moderate Islamist groups, reports surfaced of atrocities against civilians committed by Ethiopian forces, which included gang-rapes of women, mutilations, and murder. On April 20, 2008, Ethiopian troops killed 21 civilians at the Al-Hidaya Mosque in Mogadishu. That same year, Ethiopian troops withdrew from Somalia as UN peacekeeping troops moved in to replace them.

The UN presence did little to stop the violence, however. In 2009, the Islamist groups reasserted themselves as the TFG's control over the conflict rapidly diminished. Somali civilians continued to be brutalized, with 150,000 more people becoming refugees. Others fell victim to rapes and artillery shelling. In June 2009, the TFG formed an alliance with two Islamic groups and agreed that sharia law would be invoked in the areas it controlled. Still, however, the fighting went on in the southern and central regions of Somalia. In late 2011, a joint operation between the TFG's army and the Kenyan military commenced against the Al-Shabaab Islamist group in southern Somalia. The move was marginally successful, and in June 2012, Kenyan troops became part of the African Union Mission to Somalia. Fighting nevertheless continues in Somalia, and it is now estimated that as many as 500,000 Somalis have died in the civil war that commenced in 1991.

Paul G. Pierpaoli Jr.

See also: Somalia Factor; United States

Further Reading

Fergusson, James. *The World's Most Dangerous Place: Inside the Outlaw State of Somalia.* New York: Da Capo Press, 2013.

Menkhaus, Kenneth. *Somalia: State Collapse and the Threat of Terrorism.* Oxford, UK: Oxford University Press, 2004.

Sook Ching Massacre

Sook Ching refers to the systematic elimination by the Japanese military of the alleged "hostile" and "uncooperative" population of Singapore following the British defeat there in February 1942. The primary target of the Japanese massacre was the Chinese population and those associated with the British colonial government. Upon the British surrender of Singapore on February 18, 1942, the Japanese military faced an unexpected problem. Because of the growing need for Japanese troops in Burma and the Philippines, the Japanese 25th Army, under the command of General Tomoyuki Yamashita, was ordered to promptly restore order in Singapore and prepare for redeployment. Control of the city had been delegated to the Japanese military police, the Kempei-tai, but it was feared that resistance to Japanese occupation might become a problem.

Yamashita had already issued orders on February 16, 1942, to eliminate members of the British-trained Chinese irregulars (Dalforce) and any Chinese who resisted the Japanese occupation. The details and conduct of the operation, however, was left up to the High Command's chief of planning and operations, Lieutenant Colonel Masanobu Tsuji. Tsuji promptly expanded the scope of Yamashita's original orders. Rather than the elimination of all armed resistance, Tsuji ordered the pacification to include all Chinese who had worked as civil servants for the British, who had joined anti-Japanese organizations, who were donors to the Chinese Relief Fund, and any Chinese male old enough to bear arms. Individuals with tattoos were believed to be connected to criminal organizations and were also to be dealt with accordingly.

Operation Sook Ching was carried out by the No. 2 Field Kempei-tai Group under the command of Lieutenant Colonel Masayuki Oishi. On February 17, 1942, the entire Chinese population of Singapore was ordered to gather at five designated assembly points throughout the city. As thousands of Chinese families turned out, organization at the assembly points broke down. Japanese officers, supplied with vague lists of names and suspects, interrogated each in search of hostile individuals. Those who were deemed nonthreatening were presented with a piece of paper stamped with "Examined" in Chinese. At some places, individuals were stamped directly on their hands.

Those Chinese detained were next loaded onto military trucks and transported to various site locations outside of the city, including the Blakang Mati and Changi beaches. The Japanese then systematically executed their victims. The Sook Ching Operation was originally intended to last for three days, but Oishi extended the massacre for two weeks. The Japanese admitted to the killing of some 6,000 during the operation. Chinese sources, however, claim that more than 50,000 were killed.

In 1947, seven Japanese officers were tried by a British military court for their role in the Sook Ching Massacre. Two, including Oishi, were sentenced to death while the remaining five received life sentences.

ROBERT W. MALICK

See also: Japan; World War II Atrocities, Pacific Theater; Yamashita Trial

Further Reading

Bayly, Christopher, and Tim Harper. *Forgotten Armies: The Fall of British Asia, 1941–1945*. Cambridge, MA: Belknap Press of Harvard University Press, 2005.

Farrell, Brian P. *The Defence and Fall of Singapore, 1940–1942*. Stroud, Gloucestershire: Tempus Publishing, 2005.

Thompson, Peter. *The Battle for Singapore*. London: Portrait Books, 2005.

South Africa

South Africa is located in far southern Africa. It is a multiethnic nation with 11 official languages, including English, Afrikaans, and nine Bantu languages. Approximately 80 percent of the country's population is of black African ancestry. The Dutch first colonized the region beginning in the late 17th century, but by the early 19th century, the British had supplanted the Dutch. Both colonial powers had introduced race-based segregation and discrimination into the region, which was not completely eradicated until the 1990s. In 1931, Britain granted the Union of South Africa independence, but the modern history of South Africa actually began in 1948, when the National Party (NP) took power. The NP dominated South African politics until the 1990s.

The NP immediately moved to formalize and codify the racial segregation that had been instituted by the former colonial powers. It classified the population into four categories—black, white, "Colored" (meaning people of mixed race), and Indian. It thereafter prescribed the rights of each group, making sure that whites received the most generous privileges and ensuring that the races did not mix. This systematic segregation came to be known as apartheid, and in it blacks were subjected to third-rate status. Millions were thus cast into institutional poverty. Blacks' movements were restricted, and they were forbidden from using facilities intended for white use or to pursue certain careers reserved for whites.

Beginning in the 1950s, and lasting until the early 1980s, the government engaged in a mass resettlement policy, designed to keep the races and varying ethnicities from comingling. After setting aside certain areas of the country based on race or ethnicity, several million people—whites included—were forced to leave their homes and resettle elsewhere. In Johannesburg in the 1950s, at least 60,000 blacks were forcibly relocated to the new black-only township of Soweto. Some 40,000 whites were similarly relocated from areas designated for blacks to white-only areas.

The South African government repressed protest and resistance movements, which forced some antigovernment groups to resort to sporadic terrorism and sabotage. Punishments for political dissidents were often summary and brutal. Under apartheid, some 40,000 people per year were arrested and subjected to whipping because of their political views or activity. The government also executed by hanging hundreds of citizens suspected of treason. The vast majority of these actions involved blacks.

The first major racially motivated uprising occurred on March 21, 1960, in the black township of Sharpeville. There, a group of about 20,000 high-school-aged students had gathered to protest against the use of pass books, which were akin to domestic passports that blacks had to carry with them at all times. They had to be able to produce the books on demand by any white person or government official or risk arrest. The books were designed to limit blacks' movement. The government responded with utter brutality, massacring 69 protesters and wounding 126 more. Thousands of others were arrested. The Sharpeville Massacre forced the government to ban protest groups like the African National Congress (ANC) and the Pan Africanist Congress (PAC). This forced many dissidents underground. In 1962, the NP arrested Nelson Mandela of the ANC—he remained a political prisoner until 1990. In 1963, the government arrested a host of other dissident leaders.

The Soweto Uprising of June 16, 1976, commenced when students began protesting the government mandate that they be taught exclusively in Afrikaans rather than their own language. The crowd grew to nearly 20,000 before government forces moved in to break up the demonstration. In the process, at least 176 people were killed (some estimates claim as many as 700 died). That massacre also sparked a week-long revolt that resulted in at least 1,000 more deaths. The Soweto debacle forced the NP to become even more repressive.

Large demonstrations after Soweto were discouraged by the government, which acted proactively to stop them before they began. More arrests of alleged "troublemakers" and political dissidents also helped to combat widespread violence. After P. W. Botha came to power in 1978, he promised to reform South Africa socially and economically. But it soon became clear that he had no intention of casting apartheid aside. In 1983, a new constitution he championed extended the vote to Indians and "Coloreds," but did nothing for the large black majority. This sparked outrage among many blacks and brought demonstrations that were quickly dispersed. Disturbances during 1984–1986, some now involving white labor unions, seemed to suggest that the NP was beginning to lose its grip on South Africa. By then, even many whites had begun to question the government amid economic stagnation made worse by increasing sanctions against South Africa by foreign nations that decried the apartheid regime.

In an attempt to deal with the deteriorating situation, in August 1985 Botha announced a series of new, incremental reforms, but without dismantling apartheid. The announcement placated virtually nobody and actually increased foreign criticism of the NP government. Botha resigned in 1989 because of failing health, and the advent of F. W. de Klerk eventually paved the way for sweeping reforms and the end of apartheid, which was aided by the simultaneous end of the Cold War. In early 1990, the NP government ended the bans on opposition groups, including the ANC, and it released Mandela from prison in February 1990. Within four years, apartheid was gone, and Mandela had been elected South Africa's first black president.

The transition to freedom and democracy was not an entirely smooth one, however. Some 40 people were killed in the Boipatong Massacre on June 17, 1992, when supporters of the Inkatha Freedom Party (IFP) opened fire on local workers. The Bisho Massacre of September 7, 1992, witnessed the killing of 28 ANC supporters and one soldier by a homeland defense force in Ciskei. On July 25, 1993, 11 churchgoers died and 58 more were injured when an armed wing of the PAC opened fire in Kenilworth, Cape Town. On March 28, 1994, thousands of Inkatha Freedom Party (IFP) protested against the 1994 elections at the ANC headquarters in Johannesburg; ANC security forces panicked, and 19 protesters were gunned down.

In 1995, the new South African government established the Truth and Reconciliation Commission (TRC). The purpose of this quasilegal entity was to identify victims of human-rights abuses and solicit their testimony. Perpetrators were also encouraged to participate, with the understanding that they would be immune from any civil or criminal charges related to these abuses. The TRC has since been disbanded, but it was viewed by many South Africans as an absolute prerequisite to the inauguration of true, multiracial democracy.

Since the 1990s, violence in South Africa has decreased. Today, conflicts involving economics, rather than race alone, are most prevalent. The global economic recession that hit in late 2007 affected South Africa's economy quite profoundly, as was seen on August 16, 2012, when large-scale labor strikes in Marikana resulted in the deaths of 44 strikers and the wounding of 78 others.

PAUL G. PIERPAOLI JR.

See also: Indigenous Populations; Truth Commissions

Further Reading

Marx, Anthony W. *Lessons of Struggle: South African Internal Opposition, 1960–1990.* New York: Oxford University Press, 1992.

Ross, Robert. *A Concise History of South Africa.* 2nd ed. Cambridge, UK: Cambridge University Press, 2009.

Thompson, Leonard Monteath. *A History of South Africa.* New Haven, CT: Yale University Press, 1990.

Soviet Collectivization

Soviet collectivization refers to the Soviet government's efforts to eradicate all privately owned and operated farms in the USSR, which were to be replaced by state-owned farms (known as sovkhozy) or state-supervised communal farms (known as kolkhozy). Mass collectivization occurred roughly between 1929 and 1940 and was directly connected to the Soviets' mass industrialization drive, which began in earnest with the First Five Year Plan of 1928–1932. Soviet collectivization played a major role in the Holodomor (mass starvation) in Ukraine during 1932–1933.

Since the beginning of the Russian Revolution of November 1917, Soviet leaders had hoped to rid Russia of private property in terms of the agricultural sector. Early on, Vladimir Lenin saw it as antithetical to the communist revolution because it bred capitalism and a bourgeoisie. The Kremlin under Soviet general secretary Joseph Stalin believed that collectivization was necessary to accomplish several important goals. First, Soviet officials hoped and expected that state-run agriculture would alleviate food shortages and alleviate food distribution problems. Second, they believed that collectivization was necessary to carry out Stalin's ambitious industrialization drive by providing larger crop surpluses that could be used to feed the swelling industrial workforce in Soviet cities. Third, Soviet leaders believed that collectivization would result in enough agricultural surpluses so that the USSR could export food products, enabling it to purchase more machinery. Finally, Stalin and his henchmen had a rather more sinister purpose for instituting a crash course in collectivization: doing so would allow the regime to imprison or otherwise eradicate class enemies, especially the landed peasantry, known as kulaks.

There were many kulaks in Ukraine, which was one of the USSR's most fertile and productive agricultural regions. Not surprisingly, many of them passively or actively resisted Soviet collectivization, which had disastrous long-term consequences for Ukraine. Many kulaks simply refused to turn over their land to the state or to work in the kolkhozy. Untold thousands were killed, imprisoned, or deported, which meant that there were far fewer farmers to tend the land. Many kulaks also plowed under or burned crops, refused to plant crops, and slaughtered millions of head of livestock in protest. The results were growing food shortages.

At the same time, the Soviet government insisted on imposing unrealistic grain requisition quotas on Ukrainian farmers, which further exacerbated the problems. Meanwhile, during 1930, Soviet bureaucrats accelerated collectivization, and during January and February of that year alone, some 11 million households joined collective farms. Such massive change, which occurred in a very short time span, understandably created chaos in the agricultural sector and worked against higher crop yields. At the same time, the USSR insisted on exporting grain (5.832 tons during 1930–1931 alone), while many of its own people went hungry.

Thus, the Holodomor in Ukraine was largely created by the Soviet regime and its insistence on rapid farm collectivization at all costs. While collectivization accomplished almost none of its goals in the short term, it did permit Stalin to move forward with the eradication of the kulaks (a process known as dekulakization). It also allowed him to purge many Ukrainian leaders, whom he suspected of disloyalty, and Ukrainian intellectuals, whom he did not trust at all. Indeed, in Stalin's mind, the problems in Ukraine had been caused chiefly by the kulaks and local Ukrainian leadership. The Ukrainian crop failures of 1932, combined with increased government grain requisitions that same year, created a perfect storm of misery that precipitated the Holodomor of 1932–1933. Stalin compounded the catastrophe by suppressing news of the famine in the USSR and around the world and by closing off the Ukrainian borders so starving Ukrainians could not escape.

PAUL G. PIERPAOLI JR.

See also: Cannibalism in the Holodomor; Class Enemies; First Five Year Plan; Great Purges; Kolkhoz; Kulaks; People's Commissariat for Internal Affairs (NKVD); Soviet Grain Requisition Policies; Soviet Union; Stalin, Joseph; Ukrainian Starvation (Holodomor)

Further Reading

Conquest, Robert. *The Harvest of Sorrow: Soviet Collectivization and the Terror-Famine.* New York: Oxford University Press, 1987.

Davies, R. W. *The Soviet Collective Farm, 1929–1930.* Cambridge, MA: Harvard University Press, 1980.

Soviet Grain Requisition Policies

During the First Five Year Plan, in which the Soviet government under Joseph Stalin sought to transform the USSR into an industrialized nation and collectivize agriculture, unrealistic grain requisition policies set for Ukraine played a sizable role in the Holodomor (mass starvation) of 1932–1933. Ukrainian agriculture had already been badly disrupted by mass collectivization that had begun in 1929, and the refusal of many kulaks to turn over their farms to state control only compounded the problems. By the early 1930s, Soviet bureaucrats had begun setting quotas for most agricultural products, including grain. Grain was a major crop cultivated in Ukraine and was perhaps one of the most critical of all agricultural staples. In 1932, the Soviet government significantly increased the grain quota for Ukrainian farms. This decision was based on the abundant crop of 1931, which bureaucrats assumed would be sustained for 1932. But Ukrainian grain output plummeted during 1932, chiefly because of adverse weather and the chaos caused by collectivization.

When Soviet officials realized that Ukraine would not meet its grain requisition quota, in the late fall of 1932 they instituted a disastrous set of requisition policies designed to punish recalcitrant Ukrainians and shift the blame for the crop failure to the Ukrainians themselves. It was clear that these polices, which played a key role in the Holodomor, had more to do with politics than agricultural output. The Kremlin was already angered by resistance from the kulaks and the mass slaughter of livestock in protest of collectivization. So, the new and draconian requisition offensive was in part retribution for these developments. But it went beyond that. Many Kremlin officials, including Stalin himself, feared Ukrainian nationalism, so the new grain requisition policies were also an attempt to quash nationalism and repopulate Ukrainian leadership with loyal Stalinists.

To force Ukrainians to turn over as much grain as possible, the Soviets sent troops to the Ukrainian countryside to compel peasants and others to turn over all grain stores to the government. Often, they were forced to turn over grain to be used for their own use, and they were frequently compelled to turn over other foodstuffs as well. Resistors were either imprisoned, or more often, shot. At the same time, the Ukrainian borders were sealed off, preventing starving peasants from escaping the growing famine. Strict new laws were also instituted, designed to deter grain theft. Thieves were subjected to imprisonment or execution without a trial. Many kulaks were killed as a result of this; they also received the lion's share of the blame for the crop failure. By January 1933, at least 14,000 Ukrainians had been sentenced to prison for alleged infractions of the grain laws. After a full-blown famine had set in during 1933, Kremlin officials revised the grain quotas, but that came too late to save hundreds of thousands of Ukrainians from starvation and death.

Paul G. Pierpaoli Jr.

See also: Cannibalism in the Holodomor; Dekulakization; First Five Year Plan; People's Commissariat for Internal Affairs (NKVD); Soviet Collectivization; Soviet Union; Stalin, Joseph; Ukrainian Starvation (Holodomor)

Further Reading

Conquest, Robert. *The Harvest of Sorrow: Soviet Collectivization and the Terror-Famine.* New York: Oxford University Press, 1987.

Fitzpatrick, Sheila. *The Russian Revolution. 2nd ed.* New York: Oxford University Press, 1994.

Soviet National Trials

Trials related to war crimes committed by the Axis powers and their indigenous accomplices in the Soviet Union (USSR) during World War II were held in the Soviet Union both during and after the war. In most cases, the trials were convened by military tribunals, which were authorized to prosecute such offenses under government decrees of June 22 and 24, 1941, and, more specifically, under a decree of April 19, 1943.

During the inter-war period, Soviet criminal laws did not specifically address war crimes. Instead, military crimes (crimes committed by the personnel of the Red Army) were listed among the most dangerous state offenses. A "Statute on Military Crimes" of 1927 had provided military tribunals with the authority to dispense justice in the territories under martial law. At the beginning of the Soviet-German war in June 1941, the jurisdiction of military tribunals was further extended, as they were now empowered to prosecute foreign culprits under the articles of the Republics' criminal codes related to banditry, arson, and terrorism. The tribunals were authorized to apply Articles 318–320 of the Criminal Procedural Code of the RSSFR and similar articles of the Republics' criminal procedural codes, which stipulated that the "inner conviction of the judges" and the evidence presented by the prosecution sufficed for indictment and sentencing. In addition, Soviet citizens could be charged with high treason under Article 58 of the criminal codes of the various Soviet republics.

In the international arena, in 1925 and 1931 the USSR joined the Geneva Conventions of 1906 and 1929 regarding, respectively, the prohibition of the use of chemical and biological agents and the humane treatment of the sick, the wounded, and prisoners of war (POWs) in a war theater; it did not, however, sign the Hague Convention of 1907 regarding the rules of land warfare. In July 1941, the Soviet government passed several resolutions that guaranteed all foreign POWs life and safety according to the existing international conventions. The USSR announced that contingent on Germany's reciprocity, it would also abide by the 1907 Hague Convention. Throughout the war, the USSR unilaterally and jointly with the Allies issued several declarations denouncing Nazi atrocities in German-occupied territories and accusing Germany of brazen violations of international laws. In November 1942, the Soviet government announced the creation of the Extraordinary State Commission, whose primary task was to collect evidence of Nazi war crimes.

On April 19, 1943, the Soviet government signed (but never published) a special decree, which delegated the prosecution of foreign and domestic war criminals to drumhead courts martial, and stipulated two measures of punishment: public execution by hanging or forced labor terms from 15 to 20 years. The April decree became the binding legal tool and the main basis for indictment in subsequent war crimes trials, both during and after the war; the decree was also intended to serve as a deterrent against potential collaborators. Until the end of the war, the military tribunals and courts martial applied the April decree in thousands of cases. The decree was especially highlighted as the "punishing sword of Soviet justice" in the Krasnodar and Kharkov trials in 1943. In 1943–1944, public war crimes trials also took place in Krasnodon, Mariupol, Nikolayev, and Kiev. In accordance with normative Soviet legal practice, the indictments in all trials were based on the confessions of the defendants, eyewitness testimonies, and the evidence presented by the Extraordinary State Commission.

In 1945–1946, open trials were staged in Smolensk, Riga, Leningrad, Kiev, Velikie Luki, Minsk, and other cities; a total of 86 German military personnel were indicted during these trials under the April decree, Articles 318–320, and the corresponding articles of the criminal procedural codes of the Soviet republics. The defendants represented all branches of the German army, administration, security, and police forces, including the former chief of the Schutzstaffel (SS) and police in south Russia and the Baltic region and SS General Friedrich von Jeckeln. Held concurrently with the Nuremberg International Tribunal, the trials were publicized as a part of the unified international campaign to punish war criminals. Sixty-seven defendants, including 18 generals, were sentenced to death and hanged in public.

In October 1947, the second wave of public trials began in the Soviet sector of Berlin, Stalino (Donetsk), Bobruisk, Sevastopol, Chernigov, Poltava, and Kishinev. The defendants were German, Hungarian, and Romanian military, police, and concentration camp personnel. Because the death penalty had been abolished in May 1947, the majority of the defendants received a long sentence of hard labor.

During 1949–1952, in closed proceedings, Soviet military tribunals indicted hundreds of Axis military personnel, including the German Field Marshals Ewald von Kleist and Ferdinand Schoerner, Colonel General Erwin Jaenecke, and the former commander of the Japanese Kwantoong Army, General Yamada Otosoo. Similar to the Nuremberg and Tokyo International Tribunals, in all Soviet post-World War II trials the prosecution dismissed the defense plea of superior order and insisted that all the defendants were responsible for the committed crimes. By the mid-1950s, the Axis personnel who had survived Soviet prisons and camps were released and repatriated to their countries of residence.

Until 1958, all defendants in war crimes trials were indicted under the April decree of 1943 and Article 58. A new statute of state crimes and new criminal codes were introduced on December 25, 1958. The statute and the codes stipulated the death penalty by shooting and long prison terms for high treason, terror, membership in anti-state organizations, and brutal treatment of civil population in wartime.

Between the end of World War II and mid-1980s, Soviet military tribunals also indicted more than 50,000 Soviet citizens accused of war crimes and collaboration with Germany. Public and closed trials took place in Krasnodar, Tallin, Lviv, Vitebsk, Minsk, Tarnopol, Elista, Mirhorod, Kiev, Moscow, and many other cities of the Soviet Union. The defendants were either individuals or entire groups, representing various German-sponsored military, police, and security units. In August 1946, the Military Board of the Soviet Supreme Court sentenced to death General Andrei

Vlasov and his associates, who had organized the so-called Russian Liberation Army that fought on the side of Germany. In October 1963, the military tribunal of the North-Caucasian Military Region indicted nine former members of the Einsatzkommando 10-A in the "second" Krasnodar trial.

Soviet war crimes trials conveniently fulfilled two political purposes: they demonstrated a fair and "long-reaching hand" of Soviet justice and aimed to educate the younger generation in Soviet ideals. In March 1965, the Soviet government announced that the statute of limitations would not be extended to war crimes, and repeatedly requested the extradition of alleged war criminals from the United States, Canada, Australia, West Germany, and other countries. In only a few cases, however, were the extradition requests granted. Thereafter, the Soviet government consistently used war crime trials as a propaganda tool in order to accuse the West of harboring war criminals.

ALEXANDER V. PRUSIN

See also: Kharkov Trial; Krasnodar Trial; Soviet Union

Further Reading

Brand, Emanuel. "Nazi Criminals on Trial in the Soviet Union." *Yad Vashem Bulletin* Vol. 19 (1966): 36–44.

Dawson, Greg. *Judgment before Nuremberg: The Holocaust in the Ukraine and the First Nazi War Crimes Trial.* New York: Pegasus, 2012.

Ginzburgs, George. "Laws of War and War Crimes on the Russian Front during World War II: The Soviet View." *Soviet Studies* Vol. XI, no. 3 (1960): 253–285.

Soviet Union

The Soviet Union was a large Eurasian country encompassing many different ethnicities and religions. It was founded in 1922, a result of the November 1917 Russian Revolution, and existed until its dissolution into various constituent republics in 1991. The government of the Soviet Union (USSR) imposed on its far-flung population a Marxist economic system that was maintained by a powerful, oftentimes dictatorial, centralized regime in Moscow. The Soviets had an abysmal record of human rights abuses, particularly during the long reign of Soviet dictator Joseph Stalin, who was the key leader of the USSR from the 1920s until his death in 1953. For the purposes of this essay, human rights abuses committed by foreign powers within the USSR (like Germany during World War II) and human rights abuses perpetrated by Soviet forces outside the Soviet Union will not be examined. Only atrocities committed by the Soviets within the USSR will be examined.

One of the great vehicles of state-sponsored violence in the Soviet Union was the People's Commissariat for Internal Affairs (NKVD). The NKVD combined the attributes of an internal spy organization, a secret police force, and a willing executioner. From the late 1920s until the early 1950s, the NKVD was directly responsible for the murder of millions of Soviet citizens and the jailing of millions of others. Indeed, during this period the NKVD sent perhaps as many as 75–85 million people to Gulags (forced labor camps usually located in desolate places, like Siberia). People from virtually every walk of life were sent to the Gulags—from peasants to intellectuals to disaffected military officers. Any individual whom the state believed to be "subversive" or dangerous to the regime was liable to be arrested and deported to a Gulag. The conditions in these prison camps were often inhumane, and it is estimated that as many as 50 million Soviets died in these facilities between 1930 and 1950 alone. A former village known as Bykivnia in Ukraine was the site of one mass grave filled with the bodies of those killed by the NKVD. After the collapse of the USSR, some 200,000 human remains were found there.

The forced Soviet collectivization of agriculture, which commenced in earnest in the late 1920s, resulted in a massive humanitarian catastrophe throughout the Soviet Union, resulting in millions of deaths, mainly due to starvation. Nowhere was this policy more tragic than in Ukraine. During the 1932–1933 Holomodor (Great Starvation) there, 3–3.5 million people died and another 1.8 million were sent to Gulags (where most perished). Scholars have since termed this a genocide.

Equally appalling were the Great Purges of Soviet society spurred on by Stalin's rampant paranoia and insatiable need for complete control. The 1930s became infamous for these purges, which affected artists, writers, intellectuals, army commanders/officers, political rivals, "enemies of the state," ex-kulaks, etc. During 1937–1938 alone, it is estimated that some 700,000 Soviets were murdered by state authorities (chiefly the NKVD), or nearly 1,000 people every week for two years. The Vinnytsia Massacres in Ukraine during 1937–1938 witnessed the mass murder of several thousand ethnic Ukrainians by NKVD personnel. Although the worst of the bloodshed associated with the Great Purges tapered off after 1937, Soviet authorities continued to kill or imprison thousands of people every year. At Sandarmokh (Karelia, Russia) in late 1937, some 9,000 people were executed, many of them inmates from the nearby Solovki Prison.

In the spring of 1940, during World War II, NKVD operatives and Soviet secret police executed 4,143 Polish army officers who had been taken prisoner by the Soviets. The massacre occurred in the Katyn Forest. Several thousand other Polish nationals were also killed. Sometime during 1941, the NKVD murdered at least 524 civilians (150 or whom were women and children) at Dem'ianiv Laz, Ukraine. On April 1, 1941, at least 200 civilians were killed by Soviet troops as they attempted to cross the border from the USSR into Romania. That massacre occurred at Fantana Alba, Northern Bukovina. The Medvedev Forest Massacre of September 11, 1941, involved the mass execution of political prisoners at the Oryol Prison; at least 157 were murdered there. In February 1944, NKVD forces murdered some 700 villagers at Khaibakh, Chechnya. Many were children and women who were locked in a barn and then burned to death.

Stalin's anti-Semitism fueled more purges in the early 1950s. During the August 12–13, 1952, "Night of the Murdered Poets," 13 prominent Jewish writers were summarily executed. Their only transgression was their religion. Increasingly obsessed with a Jewish "conspiracy" against Soviet authority, Stalin and his handlers discovered the "Doctor's Plot" in January 1953, in which an alleged cabal of Jewish physicians was plotting to decapitate the Kremlin leadership by poisoning or by bogus medical procedures. The doctors were promptly arrested. Stalin's death in March 1953 ended the absurd preoccupation with Jewish conspiracies, but post-Stalinist Russia was no less capable of perpetrating human rights abuses.

During May-June 1954, an uprising at Kengir, a Soviet Gulag, resulted in the deaths of as many as 100 inmates and 40 Soviet soldiers; another 100 people were injured. Riots in Tbilisi, Georgia, spurred on by Soviet leader Nikita Khrushchev's de-Stalinization policies, resulted in the deaths of as many as 800 demonstrators and the wounding of hundreds of others on March 9, 1956. The massacre was perpetrated by Soviet troops. Several hundred Georgians were also imprisoned. On June 1–2, 1962, mass rioting associated with a labor strike in Novocherkassk resulted in Soviet troops opening fire. Twenty-six rioters died and 87 others were injured. Increased internal stability and improving relations with the West beginning in the mid-1960s helped curb the worst human rights violations in the USSR, but they by no means disappeared. The

Gulag system, while relatively small compared to Stalin-era standards, continued to hold thousands of political dissidents and "enemies of the state." Although the April 1986 Chernobyl Nuclear Disaster in the Ukraine was termed an accident, Soviet policies before, during, and after the event clearly played a role in the casualties there. The USSR attributed 31 direct deaths to the meltdown, with an additional 64 later deaths due to radiation sickness and associated cancers. The death toll might reach as high as 4,000 as more people become sick. Hundreds of thousands of others were exposed to radioactive fallout, many of whom had to abandon their homes. The Soviet government was slow to alert the citizenry of the accident, which undoubtedly contributed to the deaths.

More recently, on April 9, 1989, anti-Soviet demonstrations in Tbilisi were brutally suppressed by Soviet troops. By day's end, 20 protesters lay dead and hundreds lay injured. On January 20–21, 1991, less than a year before the collapse of the USSR, Soviet army troops invaded Baku, Azerbaijan, to stem the independence movement there. At least 135 civilians were killed in the fighting, and 800 more were wounded.

PAUL G. PIERPAOLI JR.

See also: Dekulakization; Great Purges; Gulags; Katyn Forest Massacre; Kulaks; People's Commissariat for Internal Affairs (NKVD); Russia; Soviet Collectivization; Soviet Grain Requisition Policies; Stalin, Joseph; Ukrainian Starvation (Holodomor)

Further Reading

Barber, John, and Mark Harrison. *The Soviet Home Front, 1941–1945: A Social and Economic History of the USSR in World War II.* London: Longman, 1991.

Conquest, Robert. *The Harvest of Sorrow: Soviet Collectivization and the Terror-Famine.* New York: Oxford University Press, 1987.

Lowe, Norman. *Mastering Twentieth-Century Russian History.* Houndsmill, UK: Palgrave, 2002.

Spain

During the July 1936–April 1939 Spanish Civil War, countless atrocities, massacres, and human rights abuses occurred throughout Spain. They were committed by both the so-called Nationalists, led by General Francisco Franco, and the Republicans, who represented antimonarchists and various centrist and leftist groups who favored a republican-style government. During the course of the conflict, some 600,000 Spaniards died, and perhaps a million or more were injured. A good number of the casualties were civilians. An additional 450,000–500,000 people were displaced during the fighting, and after the Nationalist victory, Franco's regime executed some 100,000 enemies, including anarcho-syndicalists, communists, socialists, antimonarchists, and Republican army commanders and soldiers. What made the civil war in Spain so deadly was the intervention of both Germany and Italy in the conflict early on; the Soviet Union decided to aid the Republicans late in the war, while some 40,000 men from 54 nations (many of them communists) fought alongside the Republicans.

On August 7, 1936, Nationalist troops under Franco attempted to root out Republican forces in the village of Almendralejo, in the process killing at least 1,000 civilians. The Badajoz Massacre of August 14, 1936, witnessed the killing of as many as 1,340 alleged Republican supporters by Nationalist troops. On November 8 and 9, 1936, Republican militiamen killed anywhere from 1,000–4,000 civilians (estimates vary widely) in Paracuellos del Jarama, during the nearby Battle of Madrid.

On February 7, 1937, a major atrocity occurred on the Málaga-Almería Road after more than 100,000 civilians were forced to flee their homes. Nationalist aircraft bombed and strafed the refuges while artillery guns shelled them. Several thousand died in the attacks, although the precise figure is still not known. On March 31, 1937, Italian and German war planes bombed the Republican stronghold of Durango, killing 250 civilians including a Catholic priest and 14 nuns. On April 1, Nationalist-allied aircraft attacked Jaén in retaliation for a Republican air raid on Córdoba; at least 159 died in the attack. Perhaps the worst atrocity of the war occurred on April 26, 1937, when German and Italian aircraft carpet-bombed the town of Guernica, resulting in 7,000 civilian casualties. Guernica received international media coverage and outraged the international community. On May 31, 1937, the German pocket battleship *Admiral Scheer,* along with four destroyers, opened fire on the coastal town of Almería in retaliation for a Republican air attack on a German naval cruiser. The bombardment wrecked 35 buildings, killed 20 civilians, and wounded 50 more.

The Italian bombing of Alicante on May 25, 1938, resulted in as many as 400 civilian deaths. On November 7, 1938, the Republican air raid on Cabra (Andalusia) killed 107 civilians and wounded 200 others. National air attacks on La Garriga during January 28–29, 1938, resulted in at least 13 deaths.

The war ended in a clear Nationalist victory in 1939. Franco moved quickly to consolidate his power, in the process bringing forth a one-party dictatorship managed by the Falange Party. The Falangists focused on Spanish nationalism, traditionalism, rabid anticommunism, and conservative Catholicism. The national assembly was a rubber-stamp body that was bound to uphold the Falange Party. Although Franco and his Falangists were often referred to as fascists, especially during and immediately after the Civil War, this label is highly misleading. Unlike Italian dictator Benito Mussolini, who had pioneered fascism in the 1920s, or German dictator Adolf Hitler, Franco did not hold any strong ideological beliefs. Instead, he focused on consolidating and maintaining his power and keeping Spain aloof from foreign conflicts, including World War II.

Compared to Mussolini, and certainly Hitler, Franco was almost a benevolent despot. He enjoyed the trappings of solitary rule and cultivated some semblance of a cult of personality, but his regime did not generally engage in wholesale persecutions of minorities or political enemies. That being said, Franco's government certainly engaged in political repression, especially toward the left, and tolerated no measure of influence by communists. The Catholic Church was given special privileges, both economic and social, which helped keep most Spaniards in line. After Franco's death in 1975, Spain witnessed sporadic unrest as it transitioned from one-party rule to democratic republicanism under King Juan Carlos I. On January 24, 1977, a Falange/neo-fascist attack on a building in central Madrid resulted in five civilian deaths and the wounding of four others.

PAUL G. PIERPAOLI JR.

See also: Spanish-American War, War Crimes; Total War

Further Reading

Graham, Helen. *The Spanish Republic at War, 1936–1939.* New York: Cambridge University Press, 2002.

Preston, Paul. *Franco: A Biography.* New York: Basic Books, 2004.

Yglesias, Jose. *The Franco Years.* Indianapolis: Bobbs-Merrill, 1977.

Spanish-American War, War Crimes

Atrocities were known to have taken place in Cuba well prior to the outbreak of the Spanish-American War in April 1898. Most had been perpetrated by Spanish colonial officials who had governed Spain for many years. No side was immune from committing such acts, however, and they involved the Spanish, American forces, and the Cuban rebels. Atrocities in this period are somewhat harder to study for two primary reasons: alleged incidents were often sensationalized by the salacious yellow press in the United States, and actions that would today be perceived as atrocities were not always perceived as such at the time they were committed.

During Cuban efforts to throw off Spanish colonial rule during the Cuban War of Independence (1895–1898), both sides engaged in atrocities. Although perceived Spanish brutality in Cuba was a key factor in the U.S. decision to declare war on Spain, the perception that the Spanish deliberately and routinely committed atrocities was primarily the creation of the yellow press, which ran stories reported by Cuban revolutionaries without scrutiny or investigation. Spanish governor-general Valeriano Weyler y Nicolau attempted through his *reconcentrado* (reconcentration) policy of 1896 to weaken the insurgency in the countryside. Weyler initially ordered civilians in one province to detention camps near garrisoned military headquarters. He also gave military commanders broad powers to execute people who evaded the requirement to register with the government, and he subjected those who aided the rebels to military rather than civilian law. Later, the reconcentration camps were greatly expanded. The camps were overcrowded, and shelter consisted mostly of dilapidated warehouses without plumbing. The government also failed to provide adequate food or arable land for the internees. As a result, between 200,000 and 400,000 civilians in the camps died from diseases such as yellow fever and smallpox or starvation during the two years that the policy remained in effect.

The Cuban rebels also committed atrocities as part of their military strategy, but few of these are well documented. One major exception is José Maceo Grajales's march of some 6,000 men through Havana Province in the spring of 1897. In an effort to put economic pressure on Spain to end its rule of the island, the rebels raided fellow Cubans' shops and killed civilians working on railways and in sugarcane fields.

Atrocities were relatively few during the brief Spanish-American War of 1898. One grisly incident occurred when Americans in the Cuban village of El Caney placed some prisoners of war captured during the Battle of San Juan Hill under the control of Cuban rebels, who murdered 40 of the prisoners by decapitation. Some historians have argued that the U.S. Navy's bombardment of the city of Santiago de Cuba for two days prior to the August 12, 1898, truce may also be considered an atrocity.

While atrocities have been a part of warfare since the beginning of history, the modern press's reporting of such acts and increased government scrutiny of them before, during, and after the Spanish-American War led to a general heightened awareness of such acts. Indeed, a number of atrocities and massacres occurred during the American pacification of the Philippines, which began in 1899 and lasted until 1902. As a result of the Spanish-American War, the United States had annexed the Philippines, a former Spanish colony where an independence movement had also been underway before that conflict began.

Matthew J. Krogman

See also: Philippine-American War, War Crime Trials in; Spain

Further Reading

Boot, Max. *The Savage Wars of Peace: Small Wars and the Rise of American Power.* New York: Perseus, 2002.

Trask, David F. *The War with Spain in 1898.* Lincoln: University of Nebraska Press, 1996.

Special Court for Sierra Leone

Often referred to simply as the Special Court, the Special Court for Sierra Leone (SCSL) is a judicial body established by the United Nations (UN) and the government of Sierra Leone in 2002 to investigate crimes committed during that country's brutal civil wars. Unlike the International Criminal Tribunal for the former Yugoslavia (ICTY) and the International Criminal Tribunal for Rwanda (ICTR), the SCSL was established under the joint authority of the Sierra Leonese government and the United Nations to prosecute violations of international humanitarian law. As such, it features both international and national elements and is often described as a hybrid court.

The court consists of two trial chambers and an appeals chamber. Each trial chamber consists of three judges, two selected by the UN secretary-general and one by the government of Sierra Leone. The appeals chamber consists of five judges, two nominated by the government of Sierra Leone and three by the UN secretary-general. All judges serve three-year terms. While both the ICTR and the ICTY Statutes include genocide as a listed crime, the SCSL Statute does not. In the case of the SCSL, the secretary-general explicitly noted that genocide had been excluded from the draft presented to the Security Council because no evidence existed to show that the killings, while widespread and systematic, were directed against any of the protected groups in the Convention 103.

The prosecutor issued 13 indictments in 2003, but later withdrew two of them because the accused had died. The trials of three former leaders of the Armed Forces Revolutionary Council (AFRC), three former Revolutionary United Front (RUF) leaders, and two members of the Civil Defense Forces have been completed. Alex Brima and Brima Bazzy Kamara, former military commanders in the AFRC, were sentenced to 50 and 45 years of imprisonment respectively. Morris Kallon, who commanded troops in the RUF, was found guilty of 16 of the 18 charges of crimes against humanity and war crimes and sentenced to 40 years imprisonment. Similarly, Issa Hassen Sesay was sentenced to a 52-year imprisonment for war crimes that included terrorizing civilians, unlawful killings, sexual violence, use of child soldiers, abductions and forced labor, looting, and burning. The court's most famous case involved former Liberian President Charles Taylor, who was accused of providing support to Sierra Leonese forces. On April 26, 2012, he became the first African head of state to be convicted for his part in war crimes. The following month, he was given a 50-year prison sentence.

ALEXANDER MIKABERIDZE

See also: Sierra Leone; Taylor, Charles

Further Reading

Huband, Mark. *The Liberian Civil War.* London: Frank Cass, 1998.
Special Court for Sierra Leone, official Web site, http://www.sc-sl.org/.

Sri Lanka

Known as Ceylon until 1972, Sri Lanka is an island nation situated some 20 miles off the southern tip of India, between the Arabian Sea and the Bay of Bengal. The British ruled the country until it attained independence in 1947; in 1948 it became part of the British Commonwealth, but was governed independently. It later opted out of the Commonwealth. During the government of Solomon Bandaranaike, most of Sri Lanka's principal industries were nationalized. He stoked considerable ethnic and religious unrest after declaring that only Sinhalese would be used by government officials and in schools; this angered the minority Tamils. The Sinhalese are Buddhists while the Tamils are Hindus. Thereafter, the Tamils engaged in a growing insurgency against the government that morphed into a bloody civil war that endured for more than 26 years. After Bandaranaike's 1950 assassination, his widow, Sirimavo, became head of state. She further antagonized the Tamils by declaring Buddhism as the official state religion.

In April 1971, the Sri Lankan government faced another threat, this time from the Marxist political group known as the Maoist People's Liberation Front (MPFL), which commenced a full blown rebellion that was largely quashed by June 1971, although the MPLF would wage a guerilla-style conflict for years thereafter. Between 1971 and 1977, the government of Sri Lanka ruled using emergency powers to deal with the MPLF and Tamil separatists. During the 1971 revolt, as many as 5,000 people were killed, many of them civilians in rural areas. Meanwhile, by the 1970s the Tamils, who sought an independent nation separate from Sri Lanka, had organized the Liberation Tigers of Tamil Eelam (LTTE), which waged a low-level guerilla war against the Sri Lankan government. That became a full-fledged civil war beginning in 1983.

In May 1983, LTTE militants killed 13 Sri Lankan soldiers. This prompted bloody reprisals from the Sinhalese, who rioted against the Tamils beginning in June. Many Tamil civilians died in the unrest, with the total death toll perhaps as high as 3,000. This marked the beginning of the long-running war between the LTTE and the Sri Lankan government. Early on, the LTTE was clandestinely aided by the southern Indian state of Tamil Nadu, which made the LTTE's insurgency all the more potent. An accord between the Indian and Sri Lankan governments in 1987 largely cut off this aid, and India sent peacekeeping troops to the Tamil-dominated portions of Sri Lanka, although in 1990 the Tamils turned against the Muslim minority, which they claimed was supporting the Sinhalese. This escalated the conflict. The MPLF launched another major offensive against the Sri Lankan government in 1987, necessitating more Indian peacekeepers.

Although the LTTE and MPLF were fighting for fundamentally different reasons, both groups played off the other, taking advantage of a government that seemed ill-equipped to deal with a prolonged civil war. Indeed, sometimes they coordinated their attacks in order to multiply their shock value. There were many atrocities committed by the LTTE, MPLF, and Sri Lankan forces during the civil war. The December 4, 1984, attack against Tamil civilians by Sri Lankan military forces at Mannar resulted in as many as 150 deaths. The LTTE carried out a massacre of Sinhalese civilians at Anuradhapura on May 14, 1985, that killed 145 people. On August 18, 1987, an MPLF guerilla threw grenades into the Sri Lankan Parliament, killing an assembly member and a cabinet secretary. On October 21–22, 1987, Indian peacekeeping troops raided a hospital in Jaffna, killing 60–70 patients and staff members. On February 8, 1989, an attack by the MPLF on a Buddhist shrine that houses the relic of the tooth killed 17 and wounded 25 more.

The killings continued unabated through the 1990s. On June 11, 1990, LTTE fighters reportedly murdered some 600 Sri Lankan police officers in the Eastern Province. On July 9, 1995, the Sri Lankan air force mistakenly killed at least 125 civilians (some estimates claim as many as 750) in Navaly (Navali) as they took shelter in a local church. The unarmed civilians had previously been told by Sri Lankan forces to seek refuge in the church. A truck bomb planted by the LTTE killed 15 and injured 150 more at the Colombo World Trade Center on October 15, 1997. Meanwhile, the LTTE and the Sri Lankan government engaged in several fruitless ceasefires and peace negotiations between 1985 and 2006, when the fighting intensified exponentially. Meanwhile, both the MPLF and LTTE committed numerous political assassinations of both Sri Lankan and Indian leaders.

When the Sri Lankan-LTTE fighting was renewed and reinvigorated in 2006, more massacres ensued, and on a scale not seen before. At Kebithigollewa, an LTTE attack on a bus on June 15, 2006, killed 60 civilians. The rising violence was made much worse by the massive tsunami that struck Sri Lanka's coast in December 2004, killing at least 35,000 people. Tamil guerillas carried out a suicide truck bombing on October 16, 2006, against a military convoy between Dambulla and Habarana, killing at least 200 and perhaps as many as 350, and wounding 150 others. A large number of civilians also died in the attacks.

The final months of the war between the LTTE and the Sri Lankan military, in 2009, were among the bloodiest of the entire conflict. There were wholesale massacres of civilians by both sides, hundreds of disappearances, and food, water, and medicine shortages among the many civilians displaced by the fighting. There were also reports that the LTTE used child soldiers toward the end of the war. Between January and April 2009 alone, some 6,500 civilians died, and another 14,000 were injured. Thousands more became homeless. By mid-April, some 1,000 civilians per day were being killed. The following month, the Sri Lankan

government declared victory, and the majority of the fighting ceased. The 1983–2009 civil war resulted in 22,327 Sri Lankans killed and 60,000 more wounded. The Tamils and the LTTE suffered 27,000 deaths, while Indian peacekeeping forces suffered 1,200 deaths. During the last six months of the war alone, 294,000 civilians became refugees.

There remains an uneasy truce in Sri Lanka today, although sporadic violence and terrorism perpetrated by extremists continues to haunt its citizenry. The MPFL, meanwhile, purged itself of militant extremists in the 1990s, and is now a viable political party with considerable clout in the Parliament and government.

PAUL G. PIERPAOLI JR.

See also: India; Myanmar

Further Reading

De Silva, Chandra Richard. *Sri Lanka: A History.* 2nd ed. New Delhi: Vikas, 1997.

Nubin, Walter. *Sri Lanka: Current Issues and Historical Background.* Bloomington: Indiana University Press, 2004.

Stalin, Joseph

Joseph Stalin was general secretary of the Central Committee of the Communist Party, supreme commander of the Soviet armed forces, marshal of the Soviet Union, and Soviet dictator. He was indisputably one of the most powerful rulers in history, as well as one of the greatest murderers.

Born Iosif Vissarionovich Dzhugashvili in the Georgian town of Gori on December 21, 1879, Stalin was the only child of his parents to survive infancy. His parents were semiliterate peasants, the descendants of serfs; his father worked as cobbler and his mother as a washerwoman and domestic. Soso, the common Georgian nickname for Iosef, was admitted to the four-year elementary ecclesiastical school in Gori in September 1888 and graduated in July 1894. His mother wished a career in the priesthood for him, so in September 1894, he entered the Tiflis theological seminary on a free scholarship.

Stalin's "official" biographies obscure more than they reveal, and they differ for the most part on the cause of Soso's exit from the seminary in 1899. Some say he was expelled for revolutionary activity, and others claim that he quit, but it was at seminary that Dzhugashvili was introduced to Russian socialism and Marxism. His career as a low-level party functionary began in 1901 and included "expropriations" (robbery) and counterfeiting in support of the Russian Social Democratic Labor Party (RSDLP). Arrested, he was tried, convicted, and exiled to Siberia in 1903 under the pseudonym Koba.

Koba escaped from exile in 1904, and the next year he joined the Bolshevik faction of the RSDLP (Georgia being a stronghold of the Menshevik faction), which was led by Vladimir Lenin. By 1907, he was recognized as an outstanding Bolshevik propagandist. By 1912, he was sponsored by Lenin to membership in the Bolshevik-controlled RSDLP Central Committee at the Prague conference where the final split between the Bolsheviks and Mensheviks took place. Stalin (steel), as he was then known, was freed from Siberian exile by the Russian Revolution of March 1917. He returned to Petrograd and became editor of the party newspaper *Pravda*. His seniority on the Central Committee allowed him to assume leadership of the Bolsheviks until Lenin's return to Petrograd from Switzerland in April 1917. Stalin seems to have played little role in the Bolshevik seizure of power in October 1917.

Stalin's alleged expertise on the nationalities question led to his appointment as commissar of nationalities in the new Bolshevik government. Through the Russian Civil War period, the real government of Russia was the Bolshevik Politburo of five men: Lenin, Leon Trotsky, Lev Kamenev, Nikolai Bukharin, and Stalin. To Stalin fell the day-to-day management of the party, which gave him considerable power. In 1922, his power base was expanded when he was appointed general secretary of the Central Committee, whereby de facto control of the Politburo accrued to him.

Following Lenin's incapacitation by stroke in 1923 and his death on January 21, 1924, over time Stalin was able to parlay his base of power into control of the organs of Soviet governance. By 1929, his accumulation of power was complete and unchallenged. In the 1930s, he began to purge "old Bolsheviks," who were his former adversaries, in his quest to maintain and strengthen his hold on power.

Periodic purges were not unprecedented after the Bolshevik seizure of power. Most were directed at subordinate officials and low-ranking party members, who bore the brunt of policy failures. The Great Purges, conducted on Stalin's orders, were characterized by their focus on party and state elites, the use of mass terror, and dramatic public "show trials" and "confessions" by the accused.

Beginning in 1936, in a series of show trials held in Moscow, numerous leading Communists and old Bolsheviks were tried; they confessed and were executed or sentenced to hard labor. At the same time, millions of ordinary Soviet citizens simply disappeared in what became known as the "deep comb-out." Eventually some 8 million people were arrested, 1 million of whom were executed; the remainder were sent to the gulags. In 1937, after the destruction of his former adversaries, Stalin began to eliminate potential threats to his power with the purge of Red Army leaders. Eventually, 40 to 50 percent of the senior officer corps disappeared. Not all were executed or died in the gulags; many survived and were rehabilitated in World War II. Others left in the army found the previously closed path to military prominence open.

Simultaneously, Stalin reversed Lenin's New Economic Policy (NEP), which had introduced a degree of capitalism in order to revive the economy, purged the middle-class peasants who had emerged under that policy (the kulaks), and carried out the collectivization of agriculture. Reliable casualty figures for the collectivization drive are unavailable, but if one includes the famine fatalities, the number of those who died may have exceeded 10 million people. Russian writer Nikolai Tolstoi put the number who died in the gulags under Stalin at 12 million people. These numbers compare with a total of 15,000 executions in the last 50 years of the tsars. In terms of the sheer number of victims, the Soviet Union under Stalin unquestionably outdistanced Hitler's Germany.

In addition to pushing the collectivization of agriculture, Stalin also implemented a series of five-year plans that set quotas for growth in all areas of the economy. Much of this effort was devoted to the exploitation of Soviet natural resources and development of heavy industry. The last of these plans prior to World War II also emphasized armaments production. Although growth was uneven, considerable progress was registered, much of which came at the expense of the living standards of the Soviet people.

In the 1930s, German ambitions alarmed Stalin, who grew interested in collective security. He instructed People's Commissar for Foreign Affairs Maksim Litvinov to pursue an internationalist course. In 1934, the USSR joined the League of Nations. Stalin also secured defensive pacts with other nations, including France. In the late 1930s, many western leaders still distrusted the Soviet Union; thus, even though the Kremlin was willing to enter into arrangements with the West against Germany and Japan, no effective coalition was forged, and events during the decade took a course that largely ignored the Soviet Union. Unsentimental in such matters, in August 1939 Stalin arranged a nonaggression pact with Germany that allowed

Adolf Hitler to invade Poland without fear of war with the Soviets. Stalin hoped, thereby, to gain time to strengthen his own military. He also gained territory in eastern Poland and the Baltic states. When Finnish leaders rejected his demands, in November 1939 Stalin ordered Soviet forces to invade Finland in order to secure territory and bases against a potential German attack.

Stalin rejected numerous western warnings in the winter and spring of 1941 that Germany was preparing to attack the Soviet Union, viewing these as efforts by the Allied powers and the United States to trick the Soviet Union into war with Germany. In consequence, Soviet forces were largely unprepared for Operation BARBAROSSA, the German invasion of the Soviet Union on June 22, 1941. Soviet military units were not even immediately authorized to return fire.

For nearly two weeks after the German attack, Stalin remained incommunicado, but he finally reappeared to proclaim the "Great Patriotic War" and rally his people and the Red Army to the defense of the "motherland." During the course of the fighting on the Eastern Front, Stalin grew dramatically as a military commander. All important strategic and operational decisions required his personal approval as supreme commander. He also absorbed specialist military knowledge, although he held no strategic dogmas or pet operational blueprints. For the most part, Stalin allowed his generals to formulate their own views and develop their own plans following his general ideas, based on well-founded knowledge of the situation. If Stalin bears great responsibility for the early defeats suffered by the Soviet Union in the first two years of the war, he must also be credited for Soviet successes in its last two years.

Besides rallying the Soviet people and armed forces with speeches and rhetoric, Stalin demonstrated his own readiness to stand firm against the German onslaught. On October 15, 1941, the Germans having driven to within 50 miles of Moscow, the Soviet government and diplomatic community were evacuated to Kuibyshev on the Volga. This caused a panic among the Muscovites, who believed they had been abandoned. The announcement on October 17 that Stalin was in the Kremlin restored relative calm to the city. Stalin remained in the Kremlin, directing strategic operations throughout the siege of Moscow and, with rare exceptions, for the remainder of the war.

During the war, Stalin had a clear picture of his postwar objectives. As the western powers had used the new eastern European states after World War I to isolate Communist Russia and contain Bolshevism, so Stalin planned to use the same states, under Soviet control as satellites, to exclude western influences from his own empire. At no time in the war after June 1941 was less than three-quarters of the German army committed on the Eastern Front. Stalin used this fact, delays by the western Allies in opening a true second front, and the great suffering of the Soviet Union (up to 27 million dead in the war) to secure massive amounts of Lend-Lease aid. He also used the actual occupation of eastern and much of central Europe by the Red Army to secure major concessions from the west at conferences at Tehran, Yalta, and Potsdam, thereby ushering in the Soviet empire.

Stalin continued to rule the Soviet Union with an iron fist almost until the day of his death. He died on March 5, 1953, a month after suffering a stroke, at Kuntsevo near Moscow.

ARTHUR T. FRAME AND SPENCER C. TUCKER

See also: Beria, Lavrenty; Class Enemies; First Five Year Plan; Great Purges; Kolkhoz; Kulaks; People's Commissariat for Internal Affairs (NKVD); Soviet Collectivization; Soviet Union; Ukrainian Starvation (Holodomor)

Further Reading

Conquest, Robert. *Stalin: Breaker of Nations*. New York: Penguin, 1991.

McNeal, Robert H. *Stalin: Man and Ruler*. New York: New York University Press, 1988.

Tucker, Robert C. *Stalin as Revolutionary 1879–1929*. New York: W. W. Norton, 1973.

Tucker, Robert C. *Stalin in Power: The Revolution from Above, 1928–1941*. New York: Norton, 1990.

Stolen Generations

Term that refers to children of Aboriginal descent who were removed permanently from their parents' homes and placed with non-Aboriginal families with the intention of imposing Western culture, mores, and languages on them. The policy that created the Stolen Generations was maintained by Australia's state and federal governments between from the 1930s to 1970s, profoundly impacting several generations of Aborigines. Children were taken away as early as at birth, shattering families and leaving deep psychological scars. Many children suffered physical and/or sexual abuse with their foster families. A 1997 Human Rights and Equal Opportunity Commission in Sydney released a report, *Bringing Them Home*, which indicated that between one in three and one in ten

Aboriginal children had been taken away from their families, resulting in the removal of tens of thousands of children. The report condemned the practice and suggested that it fell under the provisions of Article 2 (e) of the 1948 UN Genocide Convention.

In the 2000s, some Aborigines resorted to judicial proceedings to seek compensation for the ills they had suffered. In a landmark case in 2008, the South Australian Supreme Court awarded Bruce Trevorrow, who was unlawfully taken from his family by the state Aboriginal Protection Board, more than $500,000 in compensation. Trevorrow became the first member of the Stolen Generations to successfully sue an Australian government for compensation, opening the way for other Aborigines. In 2008, the Australian government issued a formal apology for the past wrongs perpetrated against the indigenous Aboriginal population.

Alexander Mikaberidze

See also: Australia; Australian Aborigines

Further Reading

Australian Government. *Bringing Them Home: Report of the National Inquiry into the Separation of Aboriginal and Torres Strait Islander Children from Their Families.* Sydney: Human Rights and Equal Opportunity Commission, 1997.

Manne, Robert. "The Stolen Generation." *Quadrant* (January–February 1998): 53–63.

Syria

An organized political system existed in the region now known as Syria as long ago as 3000 BC. For much of its history the region was subject to invasion and occupation because it lay along the key invasion and trade routes between the Mediterranean, North Africa, and Mesopotamia. Among its conquerors were Egypt, the Hittites, the Assyrians, the Persians, and the Greeks. Syria became a part of the Roman Empire in 64 BC and following the collapse of the Western Roman Empire it became a part of the Byzantine Empire.

The most significant conquest of Syria came in the seventh century AD when the Muslim Amayyad Empire took over. Christianity had been prevalent in Syria since soon after the birth of the faith but most Syrians converted to Islam after the Amayyad conquest. The country was soon in the hands of another ruler, the Abbasid, who were followed by the Seljuk Turks, the Crusaders, the Mamelukes, and the Mongols before the Ottoman Empire began its

400-year dominance in the region. There was a brief period of Egyptian control in the 19th century but European powers "persuaded" Cairo to return control to the Ottomans.

During World War I Syrian nationalists were persuaded to fight with the Allies in exchange for a promise of independence after the war ended. The promise was broken as the new League of Nations divided what are now Syria, Lebanon, Israel, and Jordan between the French and the British, with France gaining control of the first two. Not surprisingly, Arab nationalists did not take well to the arrangement, and some serious unrest in 1925 prompted France to begin yielding ground. Lebanon became a separate state in 1926 and after long-winded talks France began granting Syria autonomy in 1936. The Arab struggle continued after the fall of France to Germany at the start of World War II. The Vichy government retained control of Syria and even before the fall to the Germans the government had suspended Syria's constitution. After Allied forces discovered that Syrian airfields were being used by German forces, the United Kingdom and the Free French forces invaded Syria in 1941. The Free French then granted Syria and Lebanon independence, with the Syrian change being completed in 1946. Shukri al-Kuwatli, the nationalist leader who led the drive for independence.

The early life of independent Syria was stormy. From 1949 to 1963 the country was beset by numerous coups and changes of government. It was undermined by the ideological and regional differences within the country as well as the distractions caused by the Cold War and Syria's resistance to the creation of the state of Israel. During this period the socialist and Arab nationalist Baath Party became the nation's most important political grouping, and the nation joined with Egypt to establish military and economic agreements with the Soviet Union in an effort to counteract the growing influence of the West within the Middle East. However, political leaders were concerned that the Soviet influence would also grow too great, so to reduce Soviet influence and put off the possibility of a communist takeover, Syria agreed in February 1958 to join with Egypt in forming the United Arab Republic (UAR). The UAR did not last long because conservative elements in Syria were opposed to the growing dominance of Egypt within the republic and to the nationalization of the economy. On Sep 28, 1961, military officers launched a coup, withdrew Syria from the UAR, and founded the Syrian Arab Republic.

The new regime was dominated by the Baath Party, which started redistributing wealth by a process of nationalization and land reform, thereby reducing the power of the traditional, land-based ruling class. The party was factionalized and in 1966 a more radical branch of the party took control of the country. This lasted until 1970, when the present leader, moderate Hafez al-Assad gained power through a bloodless coup. Assad's main goals were to challenge the existence of Israel and to reduce Syrian dependence on the Soviet Union. In the 1970s Syria grew rich from the Arab oil boom, and support for Assad increased after he attacked Israel in the Golan Heights in the October 1973 Yom Kippur War. Israel drove the Syrian forces to within 20 miles of Damascus, the capital, but the two sides signed a disengagement agreement the following year that returned part of the Golan Heights to Syria as well as providing for prisoner exchanges and patrols by United Nations (UN) forces.

Assad's problems increased in the 1970s, in large part because of his intervention in the civil war in Lebanon. He ultimately sent in as many as 50,000 troops. Israel became concerned at the growing Syrian involvement and invaded Lebanon in 1982, provoking clashes with Syrian forces. By the time the civil war ended, Lebanon had effectively become a client state of Syria with the political scene heavily controlled by Damascus. The heavy military involvement took a significant toll on Syria's economy. The situation was worsened by the growing resentment Sunni Muslims were feeling toward the Alawite Muslims who had dominated the political scene since Assad had taken power. In 1976 fundamentalists began killing and launching bomb attacks against prominent Alawites, worsening the division of the nation. The government stepped up its repression but rebellions continued in 1980 and 1982. Assad has remained a powerful figure by combining necessary force and diplomatic skill, although the Arab world distanced itself from him during the 1980s because of his support for non-Arab Iran in the 1980–88 Iran-Iraq War and his involvement in efforts to oust Yasir Arafat from the leadership of the Palestine Liberation Organization (PLO). Despite his skills, Assad was also isolated from the West during the 1980s, when some nations imposed sanctions because of the belief that Syria was a major supporter of international terrorism.

In the 1990s Syria took steps to improve its image, partly by acting to help bring about the release of Westerners being held hostage in Lebanon and by siding with Kuwait and its Western allies in the Persian Gulf War. Although Syria supports the principle that Israel exchange occupied Arab territory for peace, Damascus has generally opposed the self-rule agreements established between Israel and the PLO. In 1994, Syria held negotiations with Israel regarding the possible return to Syria of the Golan Heights, which Israel had annexed in 1982, but the talks did not bear fruit. Syria remains influential in Lebanon: it indirectly supported Hezbollah attacks against northern Israel during the 1990s.

With the death of Hafez al-Assad and the ascension of his son, Bashar al-Assad, to the presidency in 2000, Syrians and the world community began to tire of the hardline Assad political dynasty. Then, with the explosion of successful antigovernment protests in Tunisia and Egypt during the Arab Spring of 2011, many Middle Eastern dictatorships came under threat from their own people, and Syria was no exception. But unlike the former leaders of Tunisia and Egypt, the younger Assad would not go quietly. Adopting the violent tactics of Libya's Muammar Qaddafi, Assad's forces began to fire on unarmed protesters and medical aid personnel, killing thousands, and arrested hundreds of citizens. As the violence intensified through 2011, Assad was vilified by foreign governments, the UN, and human rights groups, all demanding that he step down. As a result, protesters took up arms and fought back, as Syria moved toward civil war.

Paul R. Bartrop

See also: Assad, Bashar al-; Houla Massacre; Syrian Civil War

Further Reading

Dam, Nikolaos van. *The Struggle for Power in Syria: Politics and Society under Asad and the Ba'ath Party,* London: I.B. Tauris, 1996.

Dawisha, Adeel I. *Syria and the Lebanese Crisis,* London: Palgrave Macmillan, 1980.

Devlin, John F. *Syria: Modern State in an Ancient Land,* London: Croom Helm, 1983.

Tibawi, A.L. *A Modern History of Syria Including Lebanon and Palestine,* London: Macmillan, 1969.

Syrian Civil War

The Syrian Civil War is a popular and ongoing rebellion against Syrian President Bashar al-Assad's government and the Baath Party that began in January 2011. Since then, events within Syria have sharply escalated as Syrian armed forces have attempted to quell the rebellion using violent means. Anti-government protesters, meanwhile, have become better organized and equipped, leading to an escalatory spiral of attacks and counterattacks that have frequently claimed the lives of innocent civilians. The Syrian government has been roundly condemned in the international community, but outside attempts to mediate a peaceful resolution to the conflict unraveled during the summer of 2012. As of September 1, 2012, it is estimated that as many as 38,000 Syrians have died in the struggle, half of whom were civilians. Some 1.5 million others have been driven from their homes, and at least 250,000 fled to neighboring nations.

Although the immediate catalyst of the Syrian Civil War seemed to have emerged from the wider Arab Spring, which saw protests sweep other Arab nations, including Tunisia, Yemen, Libya, and Egypt, the violence in Syria is actually rooted in its immediate past. Since al-Assad's father, Hafez, began ruling the nation with an iron hand in the early 1970s, Syrians have been routinely subjected to severe political repression, human right abuses, and periodic crack downs against alleged government dissidents that resulted in perhaps thousands of deaths. The government also employs torture and incarceration without due process. Some Syrians had hoped that Bashar al-Assad would liberalize their country when he took power in 2000. However, despite some early rhetoric, al-Assad apparently had no intention of engaging his nation in meaningful political reform. To make matters worse, al-Assad and much of the leadership in his government are Alawite, a sub-group of Shiite Islam that represents only 12 percent of the Syrian population; Sunni Muslims comprise nearly 75 percent of the population.

In addition to the obvious problems caused by minority rule, Syrians began to chafe under their government's restrictive laws that limited or eliminated freedom of expression, assembly, or association. The al-Assad regime strictly censors the press, and until 2011 many popular Web site were blocked. Women and ethnic minorities—especially the Kurds—have also been subjected to discrimination and even violence. At the same time, the economic situation in Syria began to badly deteriorate, particularly after the global financial crisis and recession that began in 2007. Unemployment rates soared, government aid to the poor declined, and government subsidies for basic food crops resulted in climbing prices.

By 2011, Syria seemed ripe for popular unrest, and by then many Syrians had taken notice of rebellions occurring in other Arab nations. Protests in Syria commenced on January 26, 2011, when antigovernment activist Hasan Ali Akleh immolated himself in a public square. Sporadic protests occurred throughout Syria thereafter, but not until mid-March did the protests begin to escalate. The al-Assad government moved swiftly, and with an iron fist, to quash the rebellions. Thousands were arrested and detained for indefinite periods of time. Many of those arrested were tortured or treated abhorrently. By April, the government had sent troops and tanks into towns and cities across Syria; troops frequently opened fire, killing or wounding scores of civilians. Although al-Assad imposed an absolute blackout of all media and news coverage, the outside world nevertheless learned of the atrocities and was deeply disturbed by them. Foreign journalists caught in Syria were subject to arrest, and several were killed.

By the summer of 2011, a sizable number of Syrian soldiers and officers began to defect, claiming that they could not support a government that wages war on its own people. By the end of July, many of these defectors formed the Free Syrian Army (FSA), which would soon become the chief adversary of the regular Syrian Army. Throughout the autumn of 2011, government troops continued to quash protests by force, but on November 3, al-Assad's government agreed in principle to a plan put forth by the Arab League to end the violence. That overture, however, was virtually stillborn, as government forces continued to fire on civilians. In February 2012, the United Nations (UN) appointed Kofi Annan, former UN general-secretary, as UN-Arab League envoy to Syria. A ceasefire was agreed to on April 12, but Syrian armed forces, including the pro-government Shabiha (militia), and rebel forces routinely violated it. By June, the UN-Arab League effort had collapsed, and Annan resigned and left Syria in August 2012.

Meanwhile, reports of atrocities in Syria proliferated. On May 25, 2005, at least 108 civilians (49 children and 34 women) were killed in the Houla Massacre after Syrian forces shelled the village of Taldou. On June 6, some 78 civilians died in the al-Qubair Massacre, when government forces shelled a civilian area. The al-Assad government has indiscriminately shelled many other areas, including large towns and cities, and even unleashed Syrian military jets on areas that were inhabited by innocent civilians.

Meanwhile, the UN has issued several statements condemning the civilian killings, but China and Russia have been unwilling to take stronger action against Syria for both political and economic reasons. Unless their intransigence changes, the UN is unlikely to take any more substantive steps to quell the uprising. Syria has a strong backer in Iran, which has been a long-time strategic ally and has sent supplies and troops to Syria, but the Arab League has sharply condemned al-Assad's actions. Unless an outside entity provides substantial aid to the rebels, or intervenes in the struggle itself, which is unlikely, the Syrian Civil War may well endure for some time. As of this writing, neither the rebels nor Syrian government forces seem to possess adequate force to completely subdue the other. And the international community appears incapable of presenting a united front against al-Assad. This spells tragedy for the Syrian people, who will continue to endure random violence, organized government killing, arrests, and torture. In a wider context, the unrest in Syria will further destabilize an already volatile Middle East and make it much more difficult to achieve lasting peace and stability in the region.

PAUL G. PIERPAOLI JR.

See also: Assad, Bashar al-; Houla Massacre; Syria

Further Reading

Dam, Nikolaos van. *The Struggle for Power in Syria: Politics and Society under Asad and the Ba'ath Party.* New York: I.B. Tauris, 1996.

Hinnesbusch, Raymond. "Syria: From 'Authoritarian Upgrading' to Revolution?" *International Affairs* Vol. 88, no.1 (2012): 95–113.

"Syria: A Divided Nation," *BBC News,* September 6, 2012, http://www.bbc.co.uk/news/world-middle-east-17258397 (accessed September 13, 2010).

T

Taylor, Charles

Civil war marked both the beginning and end of Charles Taylor's tenure as president of Liberia, which lasted from July 1997, when he won democratic elections following a long career as a guerrilla soldier, until August 2003, when he was forced into exile in Nigeria by a new group of rebels. Before winning the presidency, Charles Taylor was head of the National Patriotic Front of Liberia (NPFL) guerrilla army, whose forces launched a bloody civil war against rival groups in 1990. The NPFL was accused of wanton disregard for human rights during the conflict, which finally ended in August 1996. Taylor was later indicted, in June 2003, on charges of crimes against humanity and war atrocities by a United Nations (UN) court for his role in the civil war in neighboring Sierra Leone. He stepped down from the presidency in 2003, and in 2006 was flown to The Hague, Netherlands to face trial. The trial began in 2008, and Taylor was convicted in April 2012, becoming the first former head of state in Africa to be convicted by an international court. The following month he received a 50-year prison sentence.

Charles Ghankay Taylor was born to Americo-Liberian parents on January 27, 1948, in Artiton, a wealthy district of Monrovia, the Liberian capital. He received an economics degree at Bentley College in Waltham, Massachusetts in 1977 and went to work in Boston as an automobile mechanic. He returned to Liberia to work for the Samuel Doe government after a coup overthrew William Tolbert in 1980. Taylor became one of Doe's top advisers, but he fled the country in 1983 when he was accused of defrauding the government of $900,000. He returned to the United States only to face extradition back to Liberia. However, he escaped again and spent the next several years roaming northwestern Africa and plotting to overthrow Doe's government.

Taylor announced the formation of the NPFL at the start of 1989, with financial support from the governments of Libya and Burkina Faso. As dissatisfaction with the repressive Doe regime mounted, he launched an armed resistance in December 1989. The NPFL soon overran most of the countryside and Doe holed himself up in the capital, Monrovia. Taylor won support among the Gio and Manos peoples and began to rely heavily on mercenaries from other West African countries. Neighboring governments began to worry that Taylor's movement might destabilize the region. Before Doe was overthrown in September 1990, a West African peacekeeping force known as the Economic Community of West African States Monitoring Group (ECOMOG), had occupied Monrovia.

ECOMOG set up an interim government in Monrovia under Amos Sawyer in October 1990, while Taylor proclaimed himself president a month later, setting up a separate capital in Gbarnga. Taylor was accused of countless abuses of human rights throughout the early 1990s as the civil war raged on. Peace accords were signed between the warring factions in July 1993 and September 1994. During the second half of 1994, however, Taylor faced increasing opposition from within the NPFL and lost control of Gbarnga to dissident forces. A December 1994 accord also faltered and was succeeded by a new peace pact, signed in August 1995. Taylor subsequently became a member of a new ruling Council of State that was inaugurated in September 1995. In April 1996, Taylor's attempts to arrest Roosevelt Johnson, a rival militia leader, set off a new round of violence that derailed the nation's fragile peace process and left the capital, Monrovia, in ruins.

Following the signing of a new peace accord in August 1996, Taylor declared his candidacy for the national presidency. He and his National Patriotic Party (formerly the political wing of the NPFL) captured close to 75 percent of the vote in July 1997 elections. Some political analysts suggested that voters decided it would be better to elect Taylor than to risk his returning to warfare if he did not win.

Taylor has been accused of providing arms and training to rebels of the Revolutionary United Front (RUF) in neighboring Sierra Leone. The RUF, whose brutality has been likened to that of Taylor's NPFL, funded their insurgency through the illegal mining and exporting of Sierra Leone's diamonds. In July 2000 the UN imposed a worldwide ban on the trade of rough Sierra Leone diamonds after it accused Taylor of enriching himself through arms-for-diamonds trading with the RUF. The UN also imposed travel sanctions on Taylor and banned the trade of weapons and diamonds with Liberia. The international body extended the sanctions in May 2003, citing the government's "active support" of various rebel groups destabilizing West Africa, and added a ban on timber sales, as tropical hardwoods were another main source of Liberia's income. The following month, the UN Sierra Leone Special Court indicted Taylor for his role in the Sierra Leone conflict, a move applauded by many but condemned by others who feared that the indictment could increase factional fighting in Liberia.

As he lost support on the international scene, Taylor also came under increasing pressure from the rebel Liberians United for Reconciliation and Democracy (LURD), which along with the Movement for Democracy in Liberia had taken over two-thirds of the country by early 2003. Taylor's government battled LURD for four years, causing destruction that left tens of thousands of refugees and little remaining infrastructure in the war-torn nation. In July and August 2003, LURD rebels advanced on the capital, Monrovia, taking control of the main port and saying they would not lay down their arms until Taylor resigned. The

siege lasted for three weeks, with Taylor repeatedly promising to step down and then reneging on his pledge. With the arrival of West African peacekeepers, he finally agreed to leave the country. On August 11, 2003, Taylor handed over power to his vice president, Moses Blah, who had fought alongside him in the previous civil war, and LURD rebels agreed to end their assault. Blah relinquished power to a transitional government in October 2003.

Taylor lived in exile in Nigeria from 2003 to 2006, all the while saying he hoped to return to his home country. One month after he left for Nigeria, a UN investigation charged Taylor with stealing or illegally diverting at least $100 million during his years in office. In March 2006, Taylor was arrested as he tried to escape Nigeria. He was flown to Sierra Leone, where the UN-backed Special Court for Sierra Leone charged him with 11 counts of crimes against humanity and war atrocities, including leading and financing a rebel army that murdered, mutilated, raped, and abused tens of thousands of civilians. He pleaded not guilty to all 11 charges and said he could not afford defense attorneys. In June 2006, Taylor was extradited to The Hague, Netherlands for trial, as officials feared tension over the case in Sierra Leone would lead to renewed violence. After several delays, the trial began in January 2008 as Taylor became the first former African ruler to stand trial for war crimes. He was convicted on April 26, 2012, on all 11 counts, but of "aiding and abetting," rather than leading, rebel militia groups in the specified atrocities and crimes against humanity.

PAUL R. BARTROP

See also: Sierra Leone; Special Court for Sierra Leone

Further Reading

Huband, Mark. *The Liberian Civil War.* London: Frank Cass, 1998.

Kulah, Arthur F. *Liberia Will Rise Again: Reflections on the Liberian Civil Crisis.* Nashville: Abingdon Press, 1999.

Tiananmen Square Incident

A large public plaza in Beijing, capital of the People's Republic of China (PRC), Tiananmen Square, literally meaning "Gate of Heavenly Peace," has been the site of student movements since the 1919 May Fourth Movement. The Tiananmen Square protests of 1989 (April 15–June 4) were of the utmost importance in both their domestic and international contexts. The protests began on April 15 when

Beijing's students gathered in the square, mourning the death of Hu Yaobang, former secretary-general of the Chinese Communist Party (CCP) (1980–1987). That Hu was ousted from office in January 1987 because of his sympathetic stance toward the prodemocracy student movement of 1986 helped transform mourning activities into a series of nation-wide student demonstrations. Students renewed their calls for immediate democratization and demanded direct dialogues with senior leaders. The movement employed mass sit-ins, boycotts of classes, public forums, bicycle demonstrations, and hunger strikes.

On May 4, 1989, organized prodemocracy demonstrations occurred in 51 Chinese cities. Other sectors also expressed their discontent with the CCP. Coincident with the visit of Soviet leader Mikhail Gorbachev in mid-May, the protests received global media coverage.

The world-wide attention and escalation of the student movement irritated PRC leaders. The handling of students' demands renewed the factional struggles between the liberal reformers and the conservatives, whose origins dated to 1979 when the paramount leader Deng Xiaoping introduced a market economy and open-door policy to modernize China. This time, the struggle was personalized by the liberal reformist CCP secretary-general Zhao Ziyang and the conservative hard-liner Premier Li Peng. Zhao preferred a conciliatory stance, arguing that the protest was of a patriotic nature and political reform should be accelerated to facilitate economic modernization. Li, by contrast, insisted on clear-cut coercive measures to disperse the demonstrators and restore stability.

Although away from the front line since the early 1980s, Deng remained highly influential as the chairman of the Central Military Commission. Fearing that his economic program would be jeopardized, Deng supported Zhao's soft-line and accommodating posture. The government's dialogues with students, however, proved fruitless. With no sign that the protests would soon end, Deng's patience was exhausted and he decided to adopt Li's hard-line approach.

On May 20, 1989, Li declared martial law in Beijing, ordering the People's Liberation Army (PLA) to clear Tiananmen Square, on conditions that no bloodshed occur. Owing to the students' blockade, the army stopped on the outskirts of Beijing city, resulting in a stalemate for the rest of the month. Meanwhile, the government was preoccupied with two issues: preparing a change in leadership to end the factional struggles; and regaining Tiananmen Square to end the protests. On May 28, Zhao was placed under house arrest, and was replaced by Jiang Zemin, the party secretary of the Shanghai Municipal Committee, whose decisive action in closing down a newspaper for reporting the Tiananmen Square protests drew the conservatives' attention.

After consulting retired elder statesmen like Li Xiannin and Bo Yibo and PRC President Yang Shangkun, Deng finally agreed on more forceful means to end the standoff, implying the clearance of the square at all cost. On June 2, Yang ordered a military crackdown on the student-demonstrators and the clearance of Tiananmen Square on the grounds that a "counter-revolutionary riot" was fermenting and continued instability would retard economic reform. On June 4 at midnight, the PLA marched into the Square and by dawn had successfully fulfilled its orders, thereby ending the seven-week long protests. Because of a press blackout, the estimated deaths and injuries on that night vary from 240 to 10,000.

To prevent a reoccurrence, on June 9 the government ordered the arrest of all student leaders and activists. Some leaders, such as Wang Dan, were arrested and sentenced to long prison terms, while others like Chai Ling and Wuer Kaixi fled abroad. On June 10, the PRC claimed that a total of 468 "trouble-makers" had been arrested and that calm had been restored in Beijing.

The PRC's use of the PLA to suppress the student demonstrations stunned the world. Some contemporaries labeled the incident the "Tiananmen Massacre." Foreign condemnations, including those from the Soviet bloc, flooded in, followed by a number of punitive sanctions, like the suspension of arms sale to China, the linking of human rights issues to the PRC's entry into the World Trade Organization, and economic embargoes. From a broader perspective, the legacy of the Tiananmen Square Protests was two-fold. In the PRC, the protests enabled the conservatives to gain the upper hand. In November 1989, Deng relinquished his remaining post to Jiang, passing the ruling power to the "third generation," and his economic modernization was slowed down. In the Cold War context, there is a consensus that the Tiananmen Square Protests had in some ways inspired the liberation of Eastern Europe from Soviet control, precipitating the Cold War's end.

Debbie Law Yuk-fun

See also: China; Cultural Revolution; Great Leap Forward; Tibet Annexation

Further Reading

Blecher, Marc J. *China against the Tides: Restructuring through Revolution, Radicalism and Reform*. London: Continuum, 2003.

Evans, Richard. *Deng Xiaoping and the Making of Modern China.* Rev. ed. London: Penguin Books, 1997.

Nathan, Andrew J., and Perry Link, eds. *The Tiananmen Papers: The Chinese Leadership's Decision to Use Force against Their Own People—In Their Own Words.* New York: Public Affairs, 2001.

Tibet Annexation

In 1949, the People's Republic of China (PRC) launched a campaign to "liberate" Tibet from imperialism. However, for Tibet, the campaign resulted in death and destruction, as well as the exile of the Dalai Lama. Tibet is still fighting for freedom from China.

In September 1949, the People's Liberation Army (PLA) entered rural Tibet in the areas of Gansu and Qinghai. That incursion, however, was met with little resistance. In October 1949, during the Chinese Communist Revolution, the Chinese Nationalist Party (Kuomintang) retreated to Taiwan; subsequently, on October 1, 1949, the revolution ended, and Mao Zedong proclaimed the PRC. Soon after, the communists focused on liberating Tibet from supposed imperialism. However, no imperial powers had taken an interest in Tibet since Great Britain, which granted India independence and had been out of the region since 1947. The strategic position of Tibet, located in the Himalayas between China and India, is a more plausible explanation for China's interest.

On November 2, 1949, Tibet's foreign office proposed negotiations to Mao to settle territorial disputes. Great Britain, India, and the United States supported that proposal over other alternatives. Despite the West's containment policy against communism, those countries wanted to eliminate any chance of a military conflict with China. The PLA invaded Qamdo, the provincial capital of eastern Tibet, on October 7, 1950, the same day that China entered the Korean War. The 40,000-troop PLA force destroyed an ill-equipped 8,000-troop Tibetan force in only two days. The PLA captured the Tibetan regional governor and killed more than 4,000 Tibetan troops. In response to the invasion of Lhasa, the Tibetan National Assembly granted Tenzin Gyatso, the 15-year-old 14th Dalai Lama, full powers as the head of state. The assembly also asked the Dalai Lama to leave Lhasa for Dromo, which is near the Indian border.

On November 7, 1950, the Tibetan government appealed to the United Nations (UN) for intervention, and 10 days later, El Salvador appealed to the UN for assistance to Tibet, which was not a UN member nation. Great Britain maintained that Tibet was an independent state and looked to India for leadership in the region. Fearing tension with China, India lobbied against any UN action against the invasion. India, Great Britain, and the United States believed a peaceful solution was still possible, and on November 24, the UN General Committee unanimously voted to postpone talks over the Tibetan issue. The PLA defeated Tibetan resistance, and in December 1950, the Dalai Lama fled Lhasa.

Although India condemned the invasion, with an overwhelming lack of international support, Tibet sent a delegation to Beijing to negotiate with the Chinese government. The delegation was threatened with violence, and some members were held prisoner. The Chinese government told the delegation to sign the agreement or face military action against Lhasa. On May 23, 1951, the Tibetan delegation and the Chinese government signed the 17-point Agreement on Measures for the Peaceful Liberation of Tibet. The agreement was said to provide national defense to Tibet, to eliminate the "aggressive imperialist forces," to unify the territory of the PRC, and to return Tibet to the "big family" of the PRC. The agreement offered Tibet equality and regional autonomy, and initially, Tibetans believed that their monastic and religious life would not be affected.

On May 27, 1951, Radio Beijing broadcast the full text of the agreement, the first time that the Dalai Lama and the Tibetan government became aware of the agreement. The Dalai Lama returned to Lhasa on August 17 to renegotiate the treaty. On September 9, 1951, 3,000 PLA troops entered Lhasa. Soon after, they occupied the cities of Ruthok, Gartok, Gyangtse, and Shigatse. The Dalai Lama was not allowed to negotiate the treaty, and the Tibetans maintained that the agreement had never been accepted. The agreement was reportedly ratified by Tibet on September 28, 1951. However, Tibet signed the agreement to avoid further aggression, and the Chinese government has been accused of using a forged Dalai Lama seal to ratify the agreement. The Chinese government held a public signing ceremony and announced to the international community that an agreement had been reached, and the "peaceful liberation of Tibet" had been concluded.

During its first stages, the occupation was not violent. By 1954, famine-like conditions and hyperinflation were the result of the strain on the country's agriculture by the 222,000 PLA troops in Tibet. In response, tension grew between Tibetans and the PLA. In February 1956, a revolt began in eastern Tibet. Tibetan guerrillas inflicted heavy casualties on the Chinese, and the Chinese began a bombing campaign against the villagers as well as the public execution and torture of the rebels. By the end of 1958, more than 20,000 guerrilla fighters were fighting the PLA, and China threatened to bomb Lhasa as well as the Dalai Lama's Norbulingka palace.

On March 1, 1959, the Chinese government invited the Dalai Lama to the military base at Lhasa to see a performance of a Chinese dance group. The Dalai Lama was expected to attend in secret, without his customary group of 25 bodyguards. The Dalai Lama agreed to attend, but a rumor that it was a Chinese plot to kidnap the Dalai Lama spread throughout Lhasa. Swearing to protect the Dalai Lama, a large crowd assembled at the Dalai Lama's Norbulingka palace on March 10. In response, the Dalai Lama canceled his appointment, but the uprising continued. Tibetan soldiers in the PLA defected from the army and began to pass out weapons to the civilians. Tibetan government officials renounced China's authority and stated that the agreement was null and void. On March 12, 5,000 Tibetan women marched through Lhasa shouting "From today Tibet is Independent" and holding banners that read "Tibet for Tibetans." In the afternoon of March 17, 1959, the PLA fired two mortar shells at the Norbulingka palace. Later that night, the Dalai Lama, disguised as a soldier, escaped from the Norbulingka summer palace and began the treacherous 14-day journey to India. After three days of fighting, the PLA killed an estimated 10,000 to 15,000 Tibetans, and on March 20, the troops discovered that the Dalai Lama had escaped. In response, the Chinese seized control of all the high passes between Tibet and India. Over the next few days, the PLA defeated the outnumbered Tibetan resistance.

On March 31, the Dalai Lama and his party crossed the Indian border at Khenzimane Pass, and on April 3, Indian prime minister Jawaharlal Nehru announced that the Indian government had granted asylum to the Dalai Lama. On April 18, the Dalai Lama left for Tezpur, where he made the Tezpur Statement, disavowing the 17-point agreement by stating that it was "thrust on the Tibetan Government and people by the threat of arms." The Dalai Lama eventually settled in Dharamsala, the seat of Tibetan government in exile, where he still resides.

The Chinese government abolished the Tibetan government and implemented a Marxist government that controlled Tibetan religious life and agriculture. Among many changes, Chinese government stopped many farmers from producing barley and made them grow wheat and rice; wheat and rice do not grow well in the high altitude, and a famine ensued. An estimated 70,000 Tibetans died of starvation by 1961. In 1959, 1961, and 1965, after appeals from the Dalai Lama, the UN passed resolutions that demanded respect for human rights in Tibet. In response to the UN demands, the Chinese government began a campaign to harass monks and destroy monasteries. The campaign eventually resulted in the destruction of almost every historical structure in Tibet.

Continuous rebellion in Tibet eventually caused financial strain to the Chinese government. China granted limited religious freedom during the early 1980s. In 1984, Tibet was reopened to foreign tourism, which brought outside attention to the Tibetan situation. In September 1987, during the 37th anniversary of the Tibetan Annexation, 30 Buddhist monks began marching around the Jokhang Temple, Tibetan Buddhism's most sacred temple, and calling for independence for Tibet. The monks, along with many bystanders, were beaten and arrested. Four days later, a similar protest, with similar results, was witnessed by Western tourists. Soon after, Western media was reporting on the violence in Tibet. In response, the Chinese government closed the entire country to foreign tourism until 1992.

In March 2008, large-scale protests erupted in Tibet as international attention was drawn to China during preparations for the Summer Olympics set to take place in Beijing later in the year. The protests were organized by Tibetan monks to commemorate the anniversary of the failed 1959 uprising and began peacefully with hunger strikes and demonstrations. The situation soon became violent, however, as Chinese troops cracked down on the dissidents. Though many Tibetans were killed, the protests continued as the Dalai Lama declared that China was engaged in "cultural genocide" against Tibet.

Throughout the years, the Dalai Lama has preached civil disobedience and has demanded that China withdraw from Tibet, though he has stated that he may accept Chinese authority provided that China allow for total religious, cultural, and environmental autonomy in the region. On September 21, 1987, he addressed the U.S. Congress and outlined a five-point peace process that stressed nonviolence. In 1989, he was awarded the Nobel Peace Prize for those efforts. A visit by U.S. president Bill Clinton in 1998 brought more attention to the Tibetan situation, and the U.S. government bestowed the Congressional Gold Medal upon the Dalai Lama in 2007 for his tireless efforts to promote peace and publicize the Tibetan situation.

Yet, Chinese control over Tibet's economy, as well as Chinese settlements in Tibet, continue to make the prospect of independence difficult. Under Chinese occupation, more than 1 million Tibetans have been killed or exiled. In 2005, the Chinese government offered to meet with the Tibetan government-in-exile, and the Dalai Lama seemed opened to the possibility; however, no such meeting has yet occurred.

PHILIP J. MACFARLANE

See also: China; Cultural Revolution; Great Leap Forward

Further Reading

Dalai Lama XIV. *Freedom in Exile: The Autobiography of the Dalai Lama.* New York: HarperCollins, 1990.

Dalai Lama XIV. *My Land and My People.* New York: Potala, 1977.

Tiger Force Killings

Tiger Force was one of the elite long-range reconnaissance platoons (LRRPs) established by U.S. forces during the Vietnam War. Formed within the 1st Battalion, 327th Infantry Regiment of the 101st Airborne Division in South Vietnam in 1967, its field commanders were First Lieutenant Jim Gardner (killed in action, February 1967) and his replacement First Lieutenant James Hawkins. Overall commander and founder of the unit was Colonel David Hackworth. Hackworth had conceived the unit in 1966 and asked for volunteers, who he said had to be "hard-charging men" who would carry the guerrilla fight to the enemy. This would be accomplished through deep penetration missions into territory held by Viet Cong (VC) and People's Army of Vietnam (North Vietnamese) forces. Tiger Force was stationed in Quang Ngai Province in the Central Highlands. As a secret LRRP unit, Tiger Force was permitted considerable leeway in command, equipment, and operational policies.

At age 40 in 1971, Hackworth was the youngest colonel to serve in Vietnam. He was a career military officer who became second in command of the 1st Battalion in 1967. When he arrived in Vietnam in 1966, Hackworth, then a major, established Tiger Force. His concept of an elite commando unit and unorthodox tactics won command approval on February 7, 1966. Hackworth and Tiger Force were tasked with rescuing a unit cut off by a large communist guerrilla force in the village of My Canh. Hackworth ordered a bayonet charge to break through the enemy forces, but this went awry as hidden guerillas opened fire, killing unit commander Lieutenant Gardner and killing or wounding every man in the unit.

Gardner was posthumously awarded the Medal of Honor, and Hackworth received the Distinguished Service Cross for this battle. Although a tactical failure, My Canh "blooded" Tiger Force and gave it a reputation that was to remain unsullied until an investigation by the Toledo Blade newspaper 36 years later. According to subsequent interviews, many of the men in the unit were bitter after My Canh, believing that Hackworth and Gardner received all the glory while the men who had done the bulk of the fighting had gone unrecognized.

Tiger Force was reconstituted following the Battle of My Canh and between May and November 1967 it is alleged to have carried out the single longest sustained series of war crimes and atrocities in modern U.S. military history. Tiger Force created a ferocious reputation for itself and created a wave of destruction, murder, and mayhem in its operational area.

Among atrocities charged to the unit (many of which have been verified by remorseful veterans, and only exposed due to the investigative work of *Toledo Blade* journalists Michael D. Salaam, Joe Mar, and Match Weirs) include the burning of Vietnamese villages without any proof of the involvement of their inhabitants with the National Liberation Front (Viet Cong), and the murder of hundreds of Vietnamese civilians, including a large number of elderly men, women, and children.

Indeed it was the report of a Tiger Force sergeant about a unit member decapitating an infant that turned a secret inquiry into an official army investigation into Tiger Force activities in 1971. Tiger Force is also to have been charged with running an illegal brothel staffed by young women and girls impressed from the local villages; wholesale rape; the mutilation of corpses, including collecting human ears and stringing them on necklaces as souvenirs; scalping the dead and decorating rifles with the scalps; kidnappings; shooting of prisoners; black market dealings including the sale of military scrip that netted substantial profits to those involved; and the torture of prisoners and civilians.

Ironically, as Tiger Force was rampaging through Quang Ngai, less than 25 miles away also in Quang Ngai, a task force of the 11th Infantry Brigade under First Lieutenant William Calley burned the village of My Lai and killed its inhabitants. This atrocity was subsequently reported and

Calley was court-martialed (although hardly punished), while Tiger Force continued its activities unchecked.

Sergeant Dennis Stout, a military journalist, witnessed and reported Tiger Force atrocities in 1967. Stout was ordered by military superiors to "forget" the atrocities, and even an army chaplain he approached counseled him not to pursue the matter. The army, however, opened a secret two and a half year investigation over the "Stout allegation." The army investigators found considerable evidence supporting the allegations, yet no charges were filed. Colonel Hackworth (by that time back in the United States) was not questioned, and although the army had planned to court martial him in 1971 for anti war activities, he was later allowed to resign with honor, even in light of the large number of atrocity counts for which he could have been held accountable.

In 1971, however, the army opened a formal investigation. Criminal investigative interviews included one with Sergeant Gary Coy, who recounted the story of the decapitation of the infant. Ironically, in light of his statements Coy found himself along with 18 other men implicated and facing possible charges unless they remained silent. Even though the army substantiated at least 20 incidents of war crimes (sufficient to proceed with courts martial) no member of Tiger Force was ever charged. The Pentagon kept the matter quiet until the *Toledo Blade* journalists got on the case.

Although Hackworth denied any knowledge of atrocities, former members of the unit, bothered by conscience, spoke to the *Toledo Blade* and verified many of the stories. The army reopened the case in 2002, but no charges or additional information have been forthcoming. Army spokesmen have stated, however, that murder charges could still legally be prosecuted. Sallah, Mahr, and Weiss received the 2004 Pulitzer Prize for their articles on the Tiger Force killings.

RODERICK S. VOSBURGH

See also: My Lai Massacre; United States; Vietnam War Atrocities

Further Reading

Belknap, Michael R. *The Vietnam War on Trial: The My Lai Massacre and the Court-Martial of Lieutenant Calley.* Lawrence: University Press of Kansas, 2002.

Congressional Medal of Honor Society. "Bazaar, Philip." http://www.cmohs.org/recipient-detail/73/bazaar-philip.php.

Hackworth, David H. *About Face: The Odyssey of an American Warrior.* New York: Touchstone Press. 1990.

Shay, Jonathan. *Achilles in Vietnam: Combat Trauma and the Undoing of Character.* New York: Scribner. 1995.

Tojo, Hideki

Japanese military and political leader during World War II, who served as minister of the army from 1940 to 1944 and as prime minister from 1941 to 1944. Tojo Hideki was born on December 30, 1884, in Tokyo. A career soldier, his first posting after officer training was as an army attaché in Germany between 1919 and 1922. He returned to Japan in 1922 to teach at a military academy and then transferred to the Ministry of the Army's administrative staff in 1926. After a brief field command, he joined the Army General Staff in 1931.

During the mid-1930s, the Japanese military underwent profound political changes; several factions emerged, some of which favored a more nationalistic and militaristic foreign policy. Tojo became prominent in the conservative *toseiha* or "control faction," which demanded military action in China and an increased role for the army in the government. Nicknamed *kamisori* ("Razor") for his strictness, Tojo in 1935 became commander of the military police for the Kwantung Army, which had invaded and occupied Chinese Manchuria; in 1937 he joined the Kwantung's General Staff and was instrumental in the decision to invade the remainder of China that same year.

The successful campaign in China enhanced Tojo's military and political career, and by 1938 he was one of the top military leaders in Japan. He and other conservatives swept aside those who opposed the war in China. Appointed minister of the army in 1940, Tojo insisted on continuing the war in China, and his anti-Western views also shaped Japan's foreign policy toward the U.S. and European powers. The success of Adolf Hitler's military campaigns beginning in 1938 led Tojo to favor the alignment of Japan with Germany and Italy in the Tripartite Pact, the signing of which in September 1940 effectively committed Japan to war against the Allies. The Tripartite Pact, in addition to the German victory over France in the summer of 1940, gave Japan the opportunity to extend its Far Eastern empire by seizing French Indochina, although Japanese occupation of the region in July 1941 resulted in a crippling economic embargo by the United States against Japan. Tojo warned darkly that unless the embargo was lifted, especially the restrictions on oil, war with the Allies was inevitable.

With the resignation of Prime Minister Fumimaro Konoe in October 1941, Tojo formed a new military government in which he served as prime minister, and he quickly dismantled all political parties. In November 1941, Tojo refused a U.S. demand that Japan withdraw from

China. Under his leadership, Japan in fact extended its military operations in Southeast Asia and cemented its hold on China. Moreover, Tojo purposely steered Japan on a collision course with the Americans, ordering preparations for the attack on Pearl Harbor in December 1941.

As prime minister, Tojo put in place strict economic and political controls and suppressed opposition to his government; however, unlike Hitler or Benito Mussolini, he was not ideological and was not wedded to a particular governing philosophy. He was certainly militaristic and ultra-nationalist, but he did not identify with European fascism. Indeed, Tojo's rise to power was in accordance with Japanese constitutional and political traditions, and most importantly, his rule was not absolute. He frequently battled ambitious bureaucracies, rival factions, and uncooperative government officials; in fact, opposition to Tojo from within the military eventually forced his removal as prime minister in July 1944 after mounting Japanese defeats throughout Asia and the Pacific.

Tojo spent the rest of the war as a civilian. After Japan surrendered in August 1945, he attempted suicide, but was arrested by American officials. He was prosecuted as a war criminal during the Tokyo trials of the International Military Tribunal for the Far East. The trials lasted from May 1946 until November 1948, and Tojo was the most important defendant, especially for the Americans, who viewed him as a "Japanese Hitler" and who invoked his name as a pejorative reference to all Japanese during the war. The Japanese public also scorned him for his harsh rule and military failures. Accused of waging aggressive war, conspiracy, and authorizing atrocities, the former prime minister maintained his innocence throughout the trials. He was, nevertheless, convicted and hanged in Tokyo on December 22, 1948.

Today, Tojo remains a controversial figure. Some sympathetic Japanese have tried to rehabilitate him, believing that he was a scapegoat who accepted responsibility for the war to spare Emperor Hirohito. To his defenders, Tojo is a national hero; he has even been commemorated at the Yasukuni shrine, Japan's most important military memorial. Tojo has also been honored in books and movies. Despite official government opposition to such acknowledgments, however, Tojo remains a powerful figure in Japanese history.

ARNE KISLENKO

See also: International Military Tribunal, Far East; Japan; World War II Atrocities, Pacific Theater

Further Reading

Hayner, Priscilla B. *Unspeakable Truths: Confronting State Terror and Atrocity.* New York. Routledge, 2000.

Maga, Timothy. *Judgement at Tokyo.* Lexington: University Press of Kentucky, 2001.

Shillony, Ben-Ami. *Politics and Culture in War-Time Japan.* Oxford, UK: Clarendon, 1981.

Tokyo Bombing

The B-29 incendiary raid on Tokyo on the night of March 9–10, 1945, was the deadliest air attack of World War II. Conducted as a test of new tactics after disappointing results with precision methods, the raid set the pattern for a new firebombing campaign that devastated Japanese cities over the next five months.

By February 1945, the U.S. Twentieth Air Force's strategic bombing campaign against Japan was in trouble. The new commander of its combat operations from the Marianas, Major General Curtis LeMay, knew he had been given the assignment in January to get results. He had reorganized the staff, instituted new training, and designed new maintenance programs, but the achievements of his high-altitude precision-bombing attacks remained disappointing. Besides technological problems with the hastily fielded B-29 Superfortress, the biggest difficulty he faced was the weather. Overcast skies and jet stream winds at normal bombing altitudes obscured targets and negated flight patterns.

Other theater commanders were trying to gain control of the expensive B-29s, and LeMay knew he could be relieved just as his predecessor had been if he did not produce significant success. He had had some experience with fire raids in China and had conducted some experiments over Japan. Although unsure how higher headquarters would react to a departure from precision bombing, he and his staff decided to destroy key targets by burning down the cities around them. This result would be achieved with low-level, mass night raids. These tactics would avoid high winds, reduce the strain on the B-29s' problematic engines, allow aircraft to carry more bombs, and exploit weaknesses in the Japanese air defenses.

The first raid employing these new tactics, Operation MEETINGHOUSE, was conducted against Tokyo beginning on the night of March 9. The selected zone of attack covered six important industrial targets and numerous smaller factories, railroad yards, home industries, and cable plants, but it also included one of the most densely populated areas of the world, Asakusa Ku, with a population of more than 135,000 people per square mile. For the first time, XXI Bomber Command had more than 300 bombers on a mission (325 to be exact) and they put more than 1,600 tons of incendiary bombs on the target.

Before the firestorm ignited by Operation MEET-INGHOUSE had burned itself out, between 90,000 and 100,000 people had been killed. Another million were rendered homeless. Sixteen square miles were incinerated, and the glow of the flames was visible 150 miles away. Victims died horribly as intense fires consumed the oxygen, boiled water in canals, and sent liquid glass rolling down streets. The B-29 crews fought superheated updrafts that destroyed at least 10 aircraft. They also wore oxygen masks to avoid vomiting from the stench of burning flesh. A total of 14 Superfortresses were lost on the mission.

The attack on Tokyo was judged a great success. It resuscitated the flagging strategic bombing campaign against Japan and restored the hopes of Army Air Forces leaders that the B-29s could prove the worth of independent airpower by defeating an enemy nation without the need for an invasion. MEETINGHOUSE set the standard for the incendiary raids that dominated Twentieth Air Force operations for the remainder of the war.

Conrad C. Crane

See also: Dresden Bombing; Hiroshima, Bombing of; Japan; World War II Atrocities, Pacific Theater

Further Reading

Edoin, Hoito. *The Night Tokyo Burned.* New York: St. Martin's Press, 1987.

Werrell, Kenneth P. *Blankets of Fire: U.S. Bombers over Japan during World War II.* Washington, DC: Smithsonian Institution Press, 1996.

Torture

The United Nations Convention against Torture and Other Cruel, Inhuman or Degrading Treatment or Punishment is the most widely ratified international treaty aimed to prevent torture. The UN Convention against Torture defines torture as "any act by which severe pain or suffering, whether physical or mental, is intentionally inflicted on a person for such purposes as obtaining from him or a third person information or a confession, punishing him for an act he or a third person has committed or is suspected of having committed, or intimidating or coercing him or a third person, or for any reason based on discrimination of any kind, when such pain or suffering is inflicted by or at the instigation of or with the consent or acquiescence of a public official or other person acting in an official capacity. It does not include pain or suffering arising only from, inherent in or incidental to lawful sanctions (Article 1)." Established in 1984, and presently ratified by 147 countries, the UN Convention against Torture represents an international human rights response to the widespread proliferation of both psychical and psychological torture that has occurred in the second half of the 20th-century.

Following the brutality and atrocities of World War II, the international community moved to establish a legal framework that would ban the practice of torture in times of both war and peace. What resulted were the first international treaties against torture. Article 5 of the Universal Declaration of Human Rights (1948) asserts that "No one shall be subjected to torture or to cruel, inhuman or degrading treatment or punishment." Article 17 of the Third Geneva Convention (1949) explicitly bans the use of "physical or mental torture" or "other form of coercion" for the purpose of obtaining information. The United Nations Standard Minimum Rules for the Treatment of Prisoners (1955) similarly stipulates that "corporal punishment, punishment by placing in a dark cell, and all cruel, inhuman or degrading punishments shall be completely prohibited as punishments for disciplinary offences."

The Inter-American and European communities also took steps to prevent torture. Established in 1950, the Council of Europe Convention for the Protection of Human Rights and Fundamental Freedoms prohibits torture in Article 3: "No one shall be subjected to torture or to inhuman or degrading treatment or punishment." Although in the Western Hemisphere, the Organization of American States (OAS), Inter-American Convention to Prevent and Punish Torture (IACPPT) was not put into force until 1987, it provides perhaps the most comprehensive definition of torture to date. Going beyond the UN Convention Against Torture, the IACPPT definition of torture includes "the use of methods upon a person intended to obliterate the personality of the victim or to diminish his physical or mental capacities, even if they do not cause physical pain or mental anguish." Part of the broader American Convention on Human Rights, the IACPPT is currently ratified by 18 states.

Despite such a concerted, transnational commitment to the prevention of torture, the use of torture increased at an alarming rate during the Cold War, and its practice became synonymous with the modern authoritarian age. A bipolar ideological struggle between divergent political, economic, and social systems, the Cold War was largely fought in the so-called Third World as both Washington and Moscow struggled to extend their respective spheres of influence. While torture was routine in Josef Stalin's re-education camps as well as Pol Pot's prisons, it was most often the rabidly anticommunist, right-wing, nationalist dictators of the postcolonial nation-states of Africa, Asia, Latin America, and the Middle East who deployed torture as part of more elaborate systems of state terror intended to eviscerate opposition and consolidate their often illegitimate regimes. It is important to note, however, that European governments also widely employed torture in various struggles to maintain their colonial holdings in Africa and Asia during the 1950s and 1960s, the most notorious case being the French in Algeria.

The use of torture generally arises from the need for information and is often driven by the nature of the enemy. In subversion and insurgency movements—whether communist or nationalist—local security forces often confront clandestine cells of ideologically motivated militants that, operating under furtive command structures, rely on propaganda and terrorism to realize their objectives. Internal security forces frequently rely on torture to identify, infiltrate, and ultimately defeat this often invisible adversary.

Contested processes of democratization during the 1980s and 1990s revealed the extent to which state security forces of several nations relied on torture for the duration of the Cold War. In Chile, Augusto Pinochet's regime produced 30,000 torture victims in its internal anticommunist crusade between 1973 and 1991. Argentina's internal war against communism between 1976 and 1983, called the Proceso de Reorginización Nacional (National Reorganization Process) by the military government, or the "Dirty War" by most observers, left upward of 30,000 torture victims, most of which were "disappeared" after their interrogation. Over twenty years of right-wing dictatorship in Brazil (1964–1986) left thousands of torture victims. Ferdinand Marcos's Philippines left an estimated 35,000 torture victims. Before Iran's 1979 Islamic Revolution, Amnesty International reported that SAVAK, the dreaded state intelligence services, had brutally tortured thousands of political dissidents and prisoners. U.S. military and intelligence forces, in tandem with South Vietnamese

security forces, were also culpable in the widespread practice of torture during the Vietnam War specifically through the Phoenix Program, a CIA-led counter-terror and assassination program targeting the command structure of the National Liberation Front (NLF) operational from 1967 to 1972.

The declassification of documentation through the United States Freedom of Information Act (FOIA) has begun to reveal the extent to which the U.S. Central Intelligence Agency (CIA) was culpable in not only the development of a new psychological torture paradigm during the 1960s, but also the propagation of that paradigm to police and internal security forces throughout the Third World. A FOIA request filed by the *Baltimore Sun* in 1996 revealed two CIA interrogation manuals, *KUBARK Counterintelligence Interrogation* (1963) and the *Human Resources Exploitation Handbook* (1983). These "torture manuals" present a novel approach to torture that eschewed physical duress and instead targeted human psychology. Isolation, degradation, threats, sleep deprivation, temporal disorientation, sensory manipulation, and narcosis were all part of a new psychological torture paradigm that the CIA deployed as a secret weapon in a broader U.S. Cold War foreign policy strategy aiming to suppress "communist subversion" throughout the Third World.

For 25 years (1963–1987), the CIA disseminated its psychological torture model to foreign police and internal security forces. After developing *KUBARK* in 1963, the CIA began working through a U.S. foreign police training program called the Office of Public Safety (OPS). Yet, in 1975, when Congress shut down all U.S. foreign police training programs in response to widespread allegations of OPS torture training, the Agency was forced to seek a new intermediary. It soon found one in the U.S. Army Green Berets and, from 1982 to 1987, the CIA collaborated with Mobile Training Teams in Central America to instruct local security forces in psychological torture. The extent to which the CIA was culpable in the proliferation of particular methods of psychological torture in the Third World during the 1960s, 1970s, and 1980s awaits further historical research and the declassification of documents in several nations.

Indeed, it is these very methods of psychological torture created and refined in the crucible of Cold War containment that the CIA has once again deployed as a crucial weapon in Washington's War on Terror. In the wake of the attacks of September 11, the CIA redeployed psychological torture to confront the new and perhaps more potent enemy of the "non-state actor" manifest in fundamentalist

Islamic terrorism. Abandoning national allegiance for ideology, these militants operate in clandestine networks that extend from metropolitan Europe to the remote jungles of the Philippine archipelago and rely on propaganda and terrorism to realize their objectives. Lacking the human intelligence capacities to identify, infiltrate, and ultimately suppress this often invisible enemy, both the CIA and the U.S. Military have fallen back on psychological torture to obtain this intelligence at Abu Ghraib, Guantánamo Bay, various "black sites" scattered about the globe and through "extraordinary renditions" (also known as "torture by proxy").

As lawyers, politicians, and pundits increasingly debate the ethics of torture, continuing legal discussion over what actually constitutes torture, particularly in its psychological manifestation, have not only caused further complication of the issue, but also created legal loopholes that enable governments to continue its practice. However, with the increase of terrorism committed by non-state actors, torture continues. What is needed in the world environment today is not only a clearer, internationally recognized legal definition of torture (particularly, psychological torture), but also stricter international mechanisms to both its use and to prosecute its perpetrators. The successful global prevention of torture is ultimately predicated upon the respect of international law.

R. MATTHEW GILDNER

See also: Argentine Dirty War; Great Purges; Pinochet, Augusto; United States

Further Reading

Greenberg, Karen J. and Dratel, Joshua L. *The Torture Papers. The Road to Abu Ghraib.* Cambridge, Cambridge University Press. 2005.

Margulies, Joseph. *Guantánamo and the Abuse of Presidential Power.* New York, Simon and Shuster, 2006.

McCoy, Alfred W. *A Question of Torture: CIA Interrogation, From the Cold War to the War on Terror.* New York: Metropolitan Books/Henry Holt and Co. 2006.

Schulz, William F, ed. *The Phenomenon of Torture: Readings and Commentary.* Philadelphia: University of Pennsylvania Press, 2007.

Total War

The term "total war" denotes a concept that has come into increasing use in the modern age. It describes the transformation of modern war over the last two centuries from a limited activity, carried out by professional armies on clearly defined battlefields, to the all-encompassing efforts of entire nations to destroy their enemies completely. The development of total war began in Europe at the end of the 18th century and has extended into the age of nuclear weapons.

War in the 18th century was relatively limited, and it could even be conducted without disturbing large parts of the belligerent nations' territories or populations. To be sure, war was terrible, and had been since human beings first began to commit organized violence against one another, but the French Revolution at the end of the 18th century inaugurated a style of warfare that would change the face of armed conflict.

As the new revolutionary government struggled to gain control over France in the spring and summer of 1793, the allied armies of the European monarchies marched into French territory intent on ending the uprising and restoring the French royal family to the throne. The revolutionaries were ill-equipped to deal with such an invasion force and so called on the entire French people to aid in hurling the invaders back. On August 23, 1793, the French government decreed the *levée en masse* (a mass rising of the French people):

Henceforth, until the enemies have been driven from the territory of the Republic, the French people are in permanent requisition for army service. The young men shall go to battle; the married men shall forge arms and transport provisions; the women shall make tents and clothes, and shall serve in the hospitals; the children shall turn old linen into lint [for musket cartridges]; the old men should repair to the public places, to stimulate the courage of the warriors and preach the unity of the Republic and hatred of kings.

The rest of the decree outlined the use of everything from horses to arms to buildings, all to be in service of the war effort. The French were thus able to field an enormous army of 800,000 men, and though disputes among the allied invaders also contributed to the eventual French victory, the *levée en masse* clearly helped mobilize the entire nation behind the war effort. The Napoleonic Wars following the French Revolution were massive affairs, but Napoleon I was suspicious of the popular ferment implied by the *levée en masse*. Thus, total war would have to wait for the 20th century to come to complete fruition.

In the meantime, however, events in the United States foreshadowed the nature of future wars. The American Civil War demonstrated many of the characteristics of total war. More accurate weapons increased the numbers of casualties in a horrifying manner, as the minié ball, a new rifle bullet, could kill at half a mile and was accurate at 250 yards. Though commanders still insisted on frontal assaults with bayonets fixed, such tactics were obsolete in the face of the murderous firepower.

As the war dragged on for four years, new and terrible weapons that increased the lethality and destruction of battle came into use, most notably ironclad battleships, railroad artillery, land mines, hand grenades, and telescopic sights. Scale and logistics were also transformed, as railroads served to move men and supplies around the country, telegraphs increased the speed and length of communications, and hot air balloons even allowed generals to obtain reconnaissance from farther behind the front. Field fortifications underwent important transformations as well, and trench warfare even appeared in some locations, foreshadowing the kind of defensive stalemate that would characterize World War I. The production of armaments and supplies were industrialized, and prolonged combat required the mobilization of the entire economy and society.

Most important, the theater of operations expanded during the Civil War to include civilians and their property, both of which were essential to sustaining the war effort—a logical extension of the process that had begun during the French Revolution. If an entire society and economy was mobilized to support military activity, then belligerents must attack that economy and society to secure victory.

Perhaps no one grasped this truth more readily that Union general William T. Sherman. In the summer of 1864, Sherman laid siege to Atlanta: he bombed and destroyed much of the important Confederate rail and industrial center. When he finally conquered the city, he began a march through Georgia and South Carolina that would demonstrate his full understanding of the necessity to destroy both the will and the means of the South to continue fighting. During Sherman's infamous March to the Sea, he and his men destroyed everything they could lay their hands on, including railroads (by twisting rails into irreparable shapes known as "Sherman's neckties"), crops, livestock, homes, and what little industry the South possessed.

The campaign was different from previous ones, which had been designed to chase enemy armies and defeat them in battle. At one point in his march, Sherman remarked, "We cannot change the hearts of these people of the South, but we can make war so terrible . . . and make them so sick of war that generations pass away before they again appeal

to it." Sherman and the Union Army's strategy of denying the Confederate Army the essential labor and moral and material support of civilian society marked an important stage in the transformation of modern war into total war.

The Franco-Prussian War of 1870–1871 was another conflict that gave many indications that war was becoming total, but it was World War I that fully displayed the increasing scale and destruction of armed conflict in the modern age. Nations went to war in 1914 largely ignorant of the effects that modern weapons would have. Though there were many theaters of operations around the globe, the decisive front was in France, where the German Army faced French and British forces in a stalemate of trenches and barbed wire.

As the war dragged on and months faded into years, each belligerent mobilized more and more of its national resources. Gigantic artillery pieces, machine guns, submarines, flame throwers, poison gas, airplanes, and other new weapons made the battlefield a nightmare landscape of death and suffering, while the need to produce those weapons oriented entire national economies toward production for the war effort.

Women entered the workforce in large numbers for the first time in many countries, and rationing and shortages on the home front became common as the armies' insatiable need for supplies emerged as the primary concern of governments. Nations took control of key industries and generally directed the war effort in a more intrusive fashion than would have been tolerated in peacetime. Each country put every able-bodied man it could into the army; in France alone, 8 million men served, which represented 20 percent of its entire population and 40 percent of all males.

The United States did not become involved in the war until 1917 and did not mobilize its resources or population in nearly the same way as the European powers. However, Americans did take important steps toward such mobilization with the institution of conscription, the use of state-sponsored propaganda to mobilize public opinion in support of the war effort, the build-up of industry, and the appearance of government direction of and cooperation with big business to ensure efficient war production.

If U.S. involvement in World War I was too brief to allow the nation to enter fully into total war, the same was not true of World War II. This global conflict was the apotheosis of modern conventional warfare and saw the realization of the true potential of the dual nature of total war: the complete mobilization of entire nations' populations and economies to field large armies with weapons of enormous destructive power, and the targeting of those populations and resources by enemy militaries so as to deny the armies the sustenance they needed. Such developments transformed the world into a battlefield, and the distinction between the front lines and the home front nearly disappeared. Everything became a military target, from soldiers, tanks, and battleships to civilian workers, factories, and homes.

During World War I, the British blockade of Germany, which denied the Germans important natural resources and food, and German submarine warfare had demonstrated the trend toward this kind of total war, but World War II took those practices to extremes. Planes bombed cities to destroy both industry and the will of the enemy to fight. Surface naval and submarine warfare once again sought to deny essential resources to the enemy in an even more intensive fashion than in the previous conflict.

German leader Adolf Hitler even made war against entire peoples, as he sought to exterminate Jews, Slavs, Russians, and any others he thought undermined or stood in the way of Germany's victorious destiny. At least 50 million people died during the war. Added to that appallingly high cost of lives was the trillions of dollars' worth of wealth consumed. Sherman's observations about war's cruelty were even more applicable 80 years after his march through the South.

World War II also produced a weapon that would propel modern war into an entirely new dimension of destruction and help define the 20th century as the "century of total war," as one scholar has called it. On August 6, 1945, the United States dropped the first atomic bomb on the Japanese city of Hiroshima, and three days later, it dropped another one on Nagasaki. The scale of destruction was enormous and brought warfare into the nuclear age.

Though nuclear weapons have not been used since, many nations around the world have developed ever more powerful warheads and ever more accurate and rapid delivery systems, including missiles that can cross oceans and continents. Many believe that nuclear weapons have transformed warfare into complete total war. A nuclear conflict would likely destroy the entire planet, or large parts of it, including all plant and animal life, for eons to come. With missiles equipped with nuclear warheads still targeting major population centers, nothing is safe from total destruction now.

The nuclear threat is belied somewhat by the fact that none of the wars since 1945 have been total wars in the same way that World War II was. The Korean War, the Vietnam War, the Persian Gulf War, and the Yugoslavian Civil War did not disrupt the societies and economies of the major Western powers nearly as dramatically as World War II did. However, post-World War II conflicts were indeed total wars for the societies that hosted them. Civilians and production centers were major targets in Vietnam and elsewhere.

Nevertheless, the trend in the present day may be toward an increasingly technological and precise form of warfare between smaller professional armies. Weapons are still hugely destructive, but their use is less indiscriminate. Many feel that a vast conflict like World War II is no longer likely or even possible. Still, weapons like nuclear missiles and chemical and biological agents exist, and many argue that there is a distinct possibility that they will be used—giving new and unprecedented meaning to the term total war.

PAUL R. BARTROP

See also: World War I Atrocities; World War II Atrocities, European Theater

Further Reading

Aron, Raymond, *The Century of Total War.* Garden City, NY: Doubleday, 1954.

Boemeke, Manfred F., Roger Chickering, and Stig Förster, eds., *Anticipating Total War: The German and American Experiences, 1871–1914.* New York: Cambridge University Press, 1999.

Chickering, Roger, and Stig Förster, eds., *Great War, Total War: Combat and Mobilization on the Western Front, 1914–1918.* New York: Cambridge University Press, 2000.

Förster, Stig, and Jörg Nagler, eds., *On the Road to Total War: The American Civil War and the German Wars of Unification, 1861–1871.* New York: Cambridge University Press, 1997.

Wright, Gordon, *The Ordeal of Total War, 1939–1945.* New York: Harper & Row, 1968.

Trail of Tears

Trail of Tears is the name given to the forced relocation of the Cherokee tribe from Georgia to the western United States by the U.S. Army. This movement, which consisted of a series of brutal forced marches, began on May 26, 1838, and was part of the U.S. government's Indian Removal Policy. Some 17,000 Cherokees were gathered together, mostly in Georgia and Tennessee, and were then forced to travel nearly 1,200 miles to Arkansas and Oklahoma. In the Cherokee language, the removal was referred to as "the trail where we cried," a name that has described the grim event ever since.

Tensions between the Cherokee Nation and white settlers had reached new heights in 1829, when gold was discovered in Dahlonega in northwestern Georgia. The Cherokees considered this area their tribal land and insisted on exercising sole sovereignty over it. In 1830, the State of Georgia sought legal clarification of the land dispute in a case that ultimately went to the U.S. Supreme Court, which refused to hear it because it did not consider the Cherokee Nation a sovereign state. However, in another U.S. Supreme Court case in 1832, the Court ruled that state governments could not invoke sovereignty over the Cherokees, arguing that this was the prerogative of the federal government. After his landslide 1832 reelection to the presidency, Andrew Jackson was more determined than ever to pursue with vigor the removal of the Cherokees, which had been made easier by the 1830 Indian Removal Act.

Soon thereafter, a splinter faction of the Cherokees called the Ridge Party or Treaty Party formed, led by Cherokees Major Ridge and Stand Watie. They began negotiations with the Jackson administration to secure equitable treatment, believing that removal was inevitable. However, Ridge and others acted without the support of the Cherokee elected council, headed by Chief John Ross, who was firmly opposed to any kind of removal and thus unwilling to negotiate such terms. This created a split among the Cherokees, with the Ridge contingent forming its own ruling council and becoming known as the Western Cherokees. Those loyal to Ross were then known as the Eastern Cherokees.

In 1835, President Jackson appointed Rev. John Schermerhorn as a treaty commissioner to enter into detailed negotiation with the Cherokees. That same year, the U.S. government proposed to pay $4.5 million to the Cherokees as compensation for their land. In return, they were to vacate the area voluntarily. Schermerhorn then organized a meeting with a small number of Cherokee council members who were prepared to accept removal. Not more than 500 Cherokees (out of many thousands) parlayed with the commissioner, but nevertheless 20 Cherokees, including Ridge, signed the Treaty of New Echota on December 30, 1835. It was also signed later by Ridge's son John and by Watie. No members of the main Cherokee Council signed the document, however.

This treaty ceded all Cherokee lands east of the Mississippi River. Naturally, Ross rejected the treaty out of hand. The U.S. Senate nevertheless barely ratified it on May 23, 1836, and set the date of May 23, 1838, as the deadline for the removal of the Cherokees. Although Ross presented a 15,000-signature petition to Congress in support of the Cherokees and against the treaty, this appeal fell on deaf ears. Meanwhile, Cherokees who had supported the removal policy began to migrate from Georgia to Oklahoma and Arkansas. By the end of 1836, it is estimated that at least 6,000 Cherokees had voluntarily left their ancestral lands. But some 17,000 Cherokees remained.

In May 1838, with the removal deadline looming, President Martin van Buren appointed Brigadier General Winfield Scott to oversee the forcible removal of the recalcitrant Cherokees. By May 17, Scott had reached New Echota, Georgia, the heart of Cherokee country, with 7,000 troops. They began to round up the Cherokees in Georgia beginning on May 26. Operations in Tennessee, North Carolina, and Alabama began on June 5. Systematically, the Cherokees were forced from their homes at gunpoint and marched to a series of camps. They were allowed to take no belongings with them, and they offered little resistance.

Thirty-one forts, which were basically makeshift detention camps, had been built to aid in the removal. Thirteen of them were in Georgia. The Cherokees were then moved from these temporary encampments to 11 fortified camps, of which all but one was in Tennessee. By late July 1838, some 17,000 Cherokees and an additional 2,000 black slaves owned by wealthy Cherokees were in the camps.

Conditions in the camps were appalling, and diseases including dysentery were rife. As a result, there was a very high mortality rate in the camps. The Cherokees were then gradually removed to three transfer points: Ross's Landing (Chattanooga, Tennessee), Gunter's Landing (Guntersville, Alabama), and the Cherokee Agency (Calhoun, Tennessee).

Three groups of Cherokees, totaling 2,800 people, were moved from Ross's Landing by steamboat along the Tennessee, Ohio, Mississippi, and Arkansas rivers to Sallisaw Creek in Indian Territory by June 19. However, the majority of the Cherokees were moved in groups of 700 to 1,500 people, along with guides appointed by Ross, on overland routes. Ross had received the contract to oversee the relocation under Cherokee supervision despite resistance from within his own nation and from members of Congress who resented the extra cost. In the end, the army was to be used only to oversee the removal and to prevent outbreaks of violence. The one exception to this mass removal was the small group of Cherokees who had signed the New Echota Treaty. They were escorted by Lieutenant Edward Deas of the army mainly for their own protection.

The movement of detachments began on August 28, 1838. For most, the journey was about 1,200 miles. Although there were three distinct overland routes, the majority took the northern one through central Tennessee, southwest Kentucky, and southern Illinois. These groups crossed the Mississippi at Cape Girardeau, Missouri, and trekked across Missouri to northern Arkansas. They then entered Oklahoma near Westville, having met troops from Fort Gibson.

The conditions on the march varied. The first groups to undertake the journey experienced high temperatures, and many suffered from heat exhaustion. In the winter, many Cherokees suffered from frostbite and hypothermia while waiting to cross frozen rivers. Most Cherokees marched on foot, but some were loaded into overcrowded wagons. It was customary for the detachments to be accompanied by a physician and a clergyman. Many Cherokees died on the way. The official government total was 424, but the most widely cited number is 4,000, half of them in the camps and half on the march. A recent scholarly study, however, has come up with a much higher figure of 8,000 dead.

Many of the Cherokees settled around Tahlequah, Oklahoma, which became the center for the tribal government. Local districts were established that elected officials to serve on the new National Council. Bilingual schools were created, and missionaries from the American Board of Commissioners for Foreign Missions built churches on the reservations. There was great resentment on the part of many Cherokees against Ridge, Watie, and the signatories of the New Echota Treaty. Ridge and his son John were killed on June 22, 1839, in separate incidents. The Trail of Tears is generally considered to be one of the most deplorable eras in American history.

RALPH MARTIN BAKER AND PAUL G. PIERPAOLI JR.

See also: Indian Removal Act; Native American Genocide

Further Reading

Ehle, John. *Trail of Tears: The Rise and Fall of the Cherokee.* New York: Anchor, 1988.

Remini, Robert V. *Andrew Jackson and His Indian Wars.* New York: Viking, 2001.

Truth Commissions

The international community has principally used two methods to establish and evaluate the record of grave human rights crimes following an international conflict or civil war. The first method is international prosecutions, such as those conducted at Nuremberg and Tokyo following World War II, and, more recently, at The Hague, Netherlands, and in Arusha, Tanzania, following the conflict in the former Yugoslavia and Rwanda. The second method is the establishment of commissions of inquiry, now commonly referred to as "truth commissions," which investigate incidents and submit reports on their findings.

The first international truth commission was established by the Carnegie Endowment for International Peace to investigate alleged atrocities committed against civilians and prisoners of war during the Balkan Wars of 1912–1913. In 1919, after World War I, the allies created the Commission on the Responsibility of the Authors of the War, and on Enforcement of Penalties, which investigated German and Turkish atrocities committed during the war. After World War II, the Allies established the United Nations War Crime Commission to investigate German war crimes, and the Far Eastern Commission to investigate Japanese war crimes. In 1978, the parties to Additional Protocol I to the Geneva Conventions of 1949 set up an International Fact-Finding Commission to investigate serious violations of the Geneva Conventions. During the 1990s, the international community, via the United Nations, established truth commissions in several countries, including El Salvador, Guatemala, Somalia, the former Yugoslavia, and Rwanda. Moreover, in the past decade over a dozen states have set up their own domestic truth commissions to document atrocities within their borders and to facilitate national reconciliation.

Truth commissions are, in most cases, officially sanctioned, authorized, or empowered by the state. They focus on the recent past and investigate politically motivated repression and patterns of widespread abuse rather than a single event. Truth commissions are unavoidably affected by their internal makeup and resources, as well as by outside factors such as the continued power of perpetrators, the strength of civil society, the attention of the international community, and the wider political and social culture within which they operate. Among the more critical mandates of truth commissions are: reaching out to victims; documenting and corroborating cases for a reparations program; arriving at firm and irrefutable conclusions on controversial cases and patterns of abuse; engaging the country in a process of national healing; contributing to justice; producing an accessible public report; outlining possible reforms; and giving victims a voice.

The work of truth commissions has implications for justice, reconciliation, historical understanding, political transformation, institutional reform, accountability, and even personal healing. Truth commissions address both conceptual issues, that is, how the pursuit of truth affects the pursuit of justice, and practical matters, that is, precisely how data should be collected, organized, and evaluated. Key questions in establishing a commission include: What level of funding is adequate? What type of training might staff members need? Should testimony be public? Should perpetrators be named?

Truth commissions are not courts, and they are not a replacement for criminal prosecutions. While truth commissions have fewer powers than courts, cannot compel testimony, put anyone in jail, or enforce recommendations, truth commissions are free of some of the narrower rules of evidence and restricted focus on individual responsibility that often characterize court systems. The purpose of criminal trials is not to expose the truth, but to find whether the criminal standards of proof have been satisfied on specific charges. A measure of truth may emerge in this process, but criminal trials are limited in the truth they are able to tell as they must comply with rules of evidence, which often exclude important information.

The mandates of truth commissions are much broader, examining larger patterns, discerning the responsibility of the state, and helping to establish accountability and a shared understanding of history. Truth commissions explore not only the facts and figures, but also the underlying causes of past repression. If properly constructed (e.g., in El Salvador) truth commissions may be strong even where judiciaries are quite weak, corrupt, or compromised.

While truth commissions are not courts and should not be a replacement for criminal prosecutions, the difficult decision is whether or not to grant amnesty. Truth Commissions granting amnesty are often viewed as an alternative to prosecutions. For example, the same day the Haitian parliament established a seven-member truth commission to investigate and document human rights crimes committed in Haiti during President Jean-Bertrand Aristide's exile, it enacted an amnesty for members of the military regime responsible for those abuses. Following the publication of the El Salvador truth commission's report, El Salvador's government enacted an amnesty preventing the prosecution of those named in the report. Similarly, the South African truth commission itself was empowered to grant amnesty as an inducement for the giving of testimony before the commission.

Viewing truth commissions as a substitute for prosecutions exposes two problems. First, in some situations, the granting of amnesty may be in violation of international legal instruments, such as 1949 Geneva Convention, the Genocide Convention, the Torture Convention, and, in the case of South Africa, the Apartheid Convention, which contain an absolute obligation to prosecute the crimes enumerated therein. Additionally, a blanket amnesty may violate general human rights conventions such as the International Covenant on Civil and Political Rights, the European Convention on Human Rights, and the American Convention on Human Rights, which obligate states to "ensure" or "secure" the rights enumerated therein. As Article 27 of the Vienna Convention on the Law of the Treaties provides, "a party may not invoke the provisions of its internal law as justification for failure to perform a treaty." Second, even when amnesties do not run afoul of these treaties, the creation of impunity through an amnesty can have the effect of encouraging future violations of the law. The granting of amnesty may erode the rule of law by blurring the norms of right and wrong while encouraging victims to resort to vigilante justice; and, most worrisome of all, an amnesty that has the imprimatur of the international community encourages a repetition of similar abuses by perpetrators throughout the world. The issue of amnesty can best be resolved by including a statement in the originally document emphasizing that the truth commission is intended to be complementary to national and international prosecutions, not a substitute for them.

This is not to suggest that a country should rush ahead with prosecution at the cost of political instability and social upheaval or that every single perpetrator must be brought to justice. By documenting abuses and preserving evidence, a truth commission can enable a country to delay prosecutions until the international community has acted, or a new government is secure enough to take such action against members of the former regime, paramilitary, or guerrilla movements. International law recognizes the legitimacy of prosecutorial discretion, both in terms of the selection of defendants and the timing of prosecutions, as long as the criteria are not arbitrary.

A long-term goal of truth commissions is to facilitate reconciliation. Many elements contribute to reconciliation: an end to violence or threat of violence; reestablishment of respectful relations; acknowledgments of and reparations for wrongdoing; projects that bring former opponents together; correction of structural inequalities; meeting of material needs; and the passage of time. However, the role truth commissions play in reconciliation is fundamental to the previously mentioned elements. Truth commissions have the task of forging a single shared account of the past, making the varied and often contradictory stories compatible, consistent, and accepted. While there is rarely, if ever, one truth, there are facts that are fundamental enough that broad acceptance of the truth is necessary before reconciliation can take place. This is a fundamental responsibility of truth commissions.

Creating a single shared account of the past may lead to long-term reconciliation, but generate further trauma in the short term. Truth commissions give victims an opportunity to recount their stories, helping them to deal with their trauma. Short- and long-term studies on the psychological impact of truth commissions on survivors have not yet been conducted. Truth commissions do not offer long-term therapy or any psychological support services. The entire process of truth finding can also generate further trauma. For example, discovering the identity of individual perpetrators can reawaken enormous pain and anger. The issue of how to handle the potential for retraumatization has not been addressed by truth commissions. Priscilla Hayner writes, "perhaps more important than the lack of personnel or resources is the point that Western psychology may not be appropriate means of response in some cultures. The impact of culture on how people respond to and recover from extreme trauma is not yet well understood." It is possible that local community organizations, civic groups, traditional healers, churches, or extended families might contribute more to the complex process of healing trauma than truth commissions can, depending on the character of the society.

Acknowledging the problems facing truth commissions is a positive step toward a full and inclusive national memory. Allowing the voices of the victims and survivors to be heard is a crucial step in transitional processes. The overall record of past truth commissions has been positive. Despite political constraints and pressures, most have documented the testimonies of thousands of victims and witnesses, producing strongly worded and politically unbiased reports.

LARRY HUFFORD

See also: International Military Tribunal, Far East

Further Reading

Freeman, Mark. *Truth Commissions and Procedural Fairness.* Cambridge, UK: Cambridge University Press, 2006.

Hayner, Priscilla B. *Unspeakable Truths: Confronting State Terror and Atrocity.* New York: Routledge, 2000.

Rotberg, Robert, and Dennis Thompson. *Truth v. Justice: The Morality of Truth Commissions.* Princeton, NJ: Princeton University Press, 2000.

Turkey

Since its modern foundation in the 1920s, Turkey has witnessed a great deal of periodic violence, the result of ethnic-, religious- and politically based unrest and conflict.

During the Turkish War of Independence (1919–1922), during which the Turks fought Greece, thousands of civilians were killed in the fighting. The 1919 Battle of Aydin resulted in the leveling of the city and the deaths of 2,000–3,000 civilians, most of them Greek. Greek troops and Greek locals perpetrated a massacre of Turkish civilians during 1920–1921 on the Gemlik-Yalova Peninsula, resulting in mass rapes and the deaths of as many as 6,500 people. In 1922 at Akhisar, Turkish troops murdered en masse virtually all Greeks living in the city, resulting in some 7,000 deaths. During September 13–22 1922, a massive conflagration in Izmir (Symrna) and a retaliatory campaign by Turkish troops resulted in the deaths of as many as 100,000 Armenians and Greeks. In the final stage of the war, Greek troops implemented a scorched-earth policy that leveled Manisa and killed as many as 30,000 Turks.

By 1923, when the Republic of Turkey was formally founded, Turkish forces and officials were responsible for the deaths of 3.5 to 4.3 million Greeks, Armenians, and various other Christian groups. Estimates claim that between 1919 and 1922 alone, 440,000 Armenian civilians and 264,000 Greek civilians died. The Turks suffered as many as 100,000 dead, including at least 15,000 civilians.

In July 1930, Turkish forces killed between 5,000 and 45,000 (estimates vary widely) Sunni Kurds at Zilan. The Dersim Massacre of 1937–1938 witnessed the mass killing of as many as 70,000 Alevi Zazas people (a minority in East Anatolia that self identifies as Kurds) by Turkish forces. A pogrom in Istanbul in September 1955 against Jews and Greek and Armenian Christians resulted in the deaths of some 30 people and forced most of the Greek minorities in the city to flee the country. Meanwhile, during 1955–1963, sporadic violence between Turkish and

Greeks in Cyprus resulted in the deaths of 365 Turks and 175 Greeks. Between December 21 and 31, 1963, alone as many as 133 Turkish Cypriots died in the violence.

On July 1974, Turkey invaded the disputed territory of Cyprus to reverse a Greek-supported coup on the island. During the resulting fighting there, Turkish troops engaged in mass rapes against Greek women. The Turks suffered 568 killed and 3,500 more wounded, including civilians. The Greeks reported as many as 6,000 killed or wounded and some 3,000 missing. Among the casualties were many civilians.

Beginning in 1977, Turkey was also rocked by serious political upheaval and violence, much of which pitted rightist groups against leftist groups and the Turkish government. At least 5,000 civilians died in this unrest between 1977 and 1980. The Taksim Square Massacre of May 1, 1977, saw the deaths of some 40 leftist protesters at the hands of Turkish police. The Maras Massacre (December 19–26, 1978), which ensued from a confrontation between Alevi Kurds and the Grey Wolves, a neo-fascist, ultra-nationalist group, witnessed the deaths of 109 people. During May-June 1980, fighting in Corum between the Grey Wolves and Alevi Kurds resulted in 57 deaths. In the meantime, the ongoing 1979–2013 fighting between the Turkish government and various Kurdish insurgents seeking Kurdish independence, has resulted in at least 45,000 verifiable deaths (although the Kurds claim larger losses). This conflict has been dominated on the Kurdish side by the armed branch of the Kurdistan Workers' Party (PKK), which was founded in 1978. The Turks have reported nearly 7,000 killed and over 13,000 wounded; the Kurds have suffered well over 30,000 deaths, and at least 14,000 wounded or captured. Moreover, some 3 million Kurds have been displaced.

In July 1993, 37 people died in communal violence between Alevi intellectuals and rightist Islamists in Sivas, Turkey. The so-called Gazi Quarter Massacre in Istanbul, which pitted Alevi Kurds against Turkish government troops, resulted in 23 deaths and more than 400 injured. In May 2009, an inter-clan feud among Kurdish civilians in Bilge, Mardin during an engagement ceremony resulted in 44 deaths. The massacre was termed one of Turkey's worst civilian-based atrocities in the country's modern history.

More recently, in the spring and early summer of 2013, the government of Prime Minister Recep Tayyip Erdogan has faced off against a potent resistance movement, which has resulted in several hundred thousand protesters flooding and occupying Ankara's and Istanbul's squares and public parks. As of this writing, at least a dozen people have been killed in the unrest, with more than 5,000 injured. Unlike most previous antigovernment movements, the current impasse involves large numbers of middle-class Turks. Erdogan's police forces and security personnel have often employed brute violence to disperse the crowds of mainly unarmed civilians, a move that has outraged and unnerved the international community, especially North Atlantic Treaty Organization (NATO) states (Turkey is a member of NATO). Some observers have begun to speculate that the Arab Spring movement that swept parts of the Middle East beginning in late 2010 may be taking shape in Turkey as well.

PAUL G. PIERPAOLI JR.

See also: Class enemies; Torture

Further Reading

Mango, Andrew. *The Turks Today: Turkey after Ataturk.* London: John Murray, 2005.

Zürcher, Erik J. *Turkey: A Modern History.* London and New York: I. B. Tauris, 1993.

U

Uganda

Uganda, a land-locked nation in east-central Africa, has been plagued by human rights abuses, corruption, and war crimes since its independence from European rule. Beginning in 1986, a shadowy rebel group calling itself the Lord's Resistance Army (LRA) began committing atrocities in northern Uganda. The LRA's war crimes include the kidnapping and forced recruitment of children as soldiers and sexual slaves. In fighting the LRA, Ugandan government forces have also committed war crimes. The issue of war crimes in Uganda became the first case referred by a government to the International Criminal Court (ICC).

Uganda's future held promise in 1962, when the British colonial government turned power over to Milton Obote and a parliamentary government. Obote was a corrupt ruler, however, who relied upon the army to remain in power. In 1966, he used the army to dissolve Parliament and forced through a new constitution granting him dictatorial powers. Obote's protégé, Idi Amin, overthrew Obote in 1971. Amin was overthrown in turn by Ugandan exiles in 1979, who returned Obote to power. Obote, however, resumed his misrule, killing as many as a half million Ugandans between 1979 and 1985.

In July 1985, Ugandan army units overthrew Obote. After a year of uncertainty, Yoweri Museveni took power. He was a former government official who headed the National Resistance Party (NRP). Although not elected, Museveni introduced democratic reforms to Uganda. In 1996,

he won the first direct presidential election in Uganda's history. Five years later, he was reelected. Although critics have criticized Museveni for organizing single-party rule, individual candidates were allowed to run for office as long as they did not organize a competing party. Museveni also received praise from the international community by sponsoring aggressive measures to reduce AIDS cases in Uganda. By 2007, Museveni's leadership had brought a measure of stability and prosperity to Uganda.

Nevertheless, Museveni's regime has a history of human rights violations. Ugandan forces intervened in the Congo in the late 1990s, during which they were accused of war crimes including killings, torture, and illegal detention. Museveni also supported rebels in southern Sudan. In reprisal, the Sudanese government supported the Lord's Resistance Army (LRA), founded in 1986 in northern Uganda, in opposition to Museveni. Its leader is Joseph Kony, a member of the Acholi people. The fundamentalist Christian group's goal is to establish a government based on the Ten Commandments. Most Ugandan Christians, however, have denounced the LRA's activities. The U.S. State Department has labeled the LRA a terrorist group. Even so, the LRA is well supplied with automatic weapons, mortars, and shoulder-launched rockets. Its firepower is the equal of many African armies. Most LRA atrocities have taken place among the Acholi people of northern Uganda. Only a small portion of the LRA is made up of adults. An estimated 85 percent are children, forced to serve. LRA soldiers attack isolated settlements and take children between 11 and 15 years old as captives. The children are forced to choose between death and fighting for the LRA. Some have been forced to kill their parents or commit other atrocities. While the boys serve as soldiers, the girls are forced into a variety of roles. Some also fight, while others serve as porters or laborers. Many are also forced to serve as sexual slaves for LRA leaders, including Kony. Boys and girls are sometimes released from the LRA when their usefulness is over. Programs have been set up to reintegrate these children back into society.

LRA war crimes include mutilations, murders, and looting. Individuals suspected of supporting the government are killed or have had hands, ears, and lips cut off. In 2003, a report prepared by non governmental organizations in Uganda estimated that at least 1,946 houses and 1,600 storage granaries had been burned by the LRA. Another 1,327 houses, 116 villages, and 307 shops had been looted of all valuables by the LRA. A majority of the population in the districts of Gulu and Kigum/Pader in northern Uganda have fled to refugee camps for safety. By 2003, 1.6 million people resided in the camps. Those families that remained in their villages adopted a practice of sending their children to places of safety during the night. Churches and factories in cities served as nightly shelters for children, who return to their homes during the day. Even so, by 2007, the LRA had abducted 38,000 children and 37,000 adults since 1996.

The Ugandan People's Defense Forces (UPDF) responded to these developments with escalating violence. In March 2002, the government launched Operation IRON FIST, sending 10,000 soldiers into northern Uganda. The offensive met unexpectedly stiff resistance. In response, the LRA attacked refugee camps and targeted international aid workers. Within weeks, LRA soldiers had attacked a refugee camp with automatic weapons and mortars, killing 50 refugees. Other attacks followed, including one in February 2004, which left over 200 dead. Many aid organizations reduced their operations. LRA refuges in Sudan prevented a decisive government victory. The frustrated UPDF was soon accused of having committed war crimes, and suspected guerillas or sympathizers were subject to summary execution or imprisonment. Crops, animals, and other resources that could be used by LRA were also destroyed.

Stymied militarily, the Museveni government turned to diplomatic solutions. In 2000, the government passed the Amnesty Act. Rebels who turned in their weapons were pardoned and allowed to live in peace. By 2005, 10,000 LRA soldiers had turned themselves in. On December 16, 2003, the government referred the prosecution of LRA leaders to the International Criminal Court. After an investigation, on May 6, 2005, the prosecutor for the Court requested arrest warrants for five LRA leaders, including Kony, Vincent Otti, Okot Odhiambo, Raska Lukwiya, and Dominic Ongwen. Their crimes included systematic murder, sexual enslavement, and forcing children to serve as soldiers. Some feared the prosecutions would prevent peace, because the LRA leaders had no chance for amnesty. The Museveni government also reached an agreement with Sudan in 2003 to allow pursuit of LRA soldiers across the border

During the summer of 2007, reports surfaced that some of the LRA leaders had been killed. Although these reports were not confirmed, many Ugandan leaders were anticipating peace. Acholi members of the Ugandan Parliament were compiling a list of war crimes committed by both the LRA and the UPDF, with accompanying evidence. They, and others, called for a public truth commission to examine all crimes, no matter which side committed them. Whether the Museveni government would allow its soldiers to stand trial for war crimes remains unknown.

Tim J. Watts

See also: Amin, Idi; Kony, Joseph

Further Reading

Allen, Tim. *Trial Justice: The International Criminal Court and the Lord's Resistance Army.* New York: Palgrave Macmillan, 2006.

Boas, Morten, and Kevin C. Dunn. *African Guerrillas: Raging against the Machine.* Boulder, CO: Lynne Rienner, 2007.

Ukrainian Starvation (Holodomor)

Referred to as Holodomor ("killing by hunger" in Ukrainian), the Ukrainian starvation was a man-made famine in the Ukrainian Soviet Socialist Republic between 1932 and 1933. During the famine, which is also known as the "terror-famine in Ukraine" and "famine-genocide in Ukraine," between five and 7 million peasants—most of them Ukrainians living in Ukraine and the traditional Cossack territories of the North Caucasus (now the Krasnodar, Stavropol, and Rostov on the Don regions of the Russian Federation)—starved to death because the government of the Soviet Union seized the 1932 crop and foodstuffs from the population.

The question of genocide in the USSR is inevitably connected with the policies of social engineering carried out under the leadership of Joseph Stalin from the late 1920s until his death in 1953. The main transformations of this period include the forced collectivization of agriculture on the basis of the liquidation of the kulaks as a class, rapid industrialization made possible by the lowering of real labor costs through the drastic reduction in the living standards of free workers and the extensive use of forced labor, the absolute standardization of all spheres of intellectual activity and their strict subordination to state priorities, and the integration of a large and varied collection of national and religious groups into a Russocentric political structure. Moreover, a massive blood purge of real and imagined "enemies of the people" took place.

The famine of 1932–1933 poses particular problems from the standpoint of internationally accepted definitions of genocide, since its focus was geographic rather than discriminatory against specific groups within a given area, and it was clearly not an attempt to destroy all members of a given group. Rather, its national and ethnic target (i.e., genocidal nature) must be inferred from the clarity in which it was geographically focused against areas containing target populations and from the particularly harsh policies of the Soviet authorities in the national sphere as applied to the main victimized group, the Ukrainians.

With the famine and other policies that have been argued to have been genocidal, the issue of intent is particularly difficult because the Soviet state, including Stalin, decreed a massive denial of everyday reality from the very pinnacle of authority to the lowest level of execution and victimization.

After over half a century of denial, in January 1990 the Communist Party of Ukraine adopted a special resolution admitting that the Ukrainian Famine had indeed occurred, cost millions of lives, had been brought about by official actions, and that Stalin and his associates bore criminal responsibility for those actions.

In 1986, the U.S. government created a Commission on the Ukraine Famine, under the leadership of James Mace, formerly of Harvard University. The commission held hearings throughout the nation and heard testimony from 57 eyewitnesses to the famine. The Commission's Report to Congress with appendices and supporting materials was prepared for publication by the Government Printing Office. The commission also transcribed for publication a supplement of over 200 in-depth interviews with eyewitnesses.

In its concluding report, the commission stated that Stalin and those around him committed genocide against the Ukrainians in 1932–1933. The commission adopted the following findings:

- There is no doubt that large numbers of inhabitants of the Ukrainian SSR and the North Caucasus Territory starved to death in a man-made famine in 1932–1933, caused by the seizure of the 1932 crop by the authorities.
- Victims of the famine numbered in the millions.
- Official Soviet allegations of "kulak sabotage," upon which all "difficulties" were blamed during the famine, are false.
- The famine was not, as is often alleged, related to drought.
- In 1931–1932, the official Soviet response to a drought-induced grain shortage outside Ukraine was to send aid to the areas affected and to make a series of concessions to the peasantry.
- In 1932, following complaints by officials that excessive grain procurements had led to localized outbreaks of famine, Moscow reversed course and took an increasingly hard line.
- The inability of Soviet authorities in Ukraine to meet the grain quota forced them to introduce increasingly severe measures to extract the maximum quantity from the peasants.
- In the fall of 1932, Stalin used the "procurements crisis" in Ukraine as an excuse to tighten his control and to further intensify grain seizures.
- The Ukrainian famine of 1932–1933 was caused by the maximum extraction of agricultural produce.
- Officials in charge of grain seizures also lived in fear of punishment.
- Stalin knew that people were starving to death in Ukraine by late 1932.
- In January 1933, Stalin used the alleged laxity of the Ukrainian authorities in seizing grain to further strengthen his control over the Communist Party of Ukraine and mandated actions which maximized loss of life.
- Officials had a dual mandate from Moscow: to intensify grain seizures in Ukraine and to eliminate such national self-assertion as Ukrainians had been allowed.
- While famine also took place during the 1932–1933 agricultural year in the Volga Basin and the North Caucasus Territory, Stalin's interventions in

the Ukraine are paralleled only in the ethnically Ukrainian Kuban region of the North Caucasus.

- Attempts were made to prevent the starving from traveling to areas where food was more available.
- Joseph Stalin and those around him committed genocide against Ukrainians in 1932–1933.
- The American government had ample information about the famine but failed to take any steps which might have ameliorated the situation. Instead, the administration extended diplomatic recognition to the Soviet government in November 1933, immediately after the famine.
- During the famine certain members of the American press cooperated with the Soviet government to deny the existence of the Ukrainian famine.

In recent years, scholarship in both the West and, to a lesser extent, Russia has made substantial progress in dealing with the famine—although official Russian historians and spokespersons have never given a fully accurate account.

James E. Mace

See also: Cannibalism in the Holodomor; Class Enemies; Dekulakization; Duranty, Walter; Famine; First Five Year Plan; Great Purges; Gulags; Jones, Gareth; Kolkhoz; Kulaks; People's Commissariat for Internal Affairs (NKVD); Soviet Collectivization; Soviet Grain Requisition Policies; Soviet Union; Stalin, Joseph

Further Reading

Mace, James E. "Genocide in the USSR." In *Genocide: A Critical Bibliographic Review*. Edited by Israel W. Charny, 116–136. London: Mansell Publishing, 1988.

Mace, James E. "Soviet Man-Made Famine in Ukraine." In *Century of Genocide: Eyewitness Accounts and Critical Views*. Edited by Samuel Totten, William S. Parsons, and Israel W. Charny, 78–112.

United States Commission on the Ukraine Famine. Report to Congress. Washington, DC: U.S. Government Printing Office, 1988.

Unit 731

Unit 731 was the Japanese Army's secret biological warfare unit. Established under the command of Lieutenant Colonel Ishii Shiro in Haerbin (Harbin), Manchuria, in August 1936, Unit 731 was officially known as the Epidemic Prevention and Water Purification Bureau. Some 3,000 personnel worked to produce bacteria for anthrax, bubonic plague, cholera, dysentery, tetanus, typhoid, typhus, and other infectious diseases. To develop methods to disperse biological agents and enhance their effectiveness, Unit 731 infected prisoners of war. At least 3,000 of them died in these experiments. Unit personnel referred to the prisoners, who were mostly Chinese, Koreans, and Soviets, as *maruta* (logs) because the Japanese informed the local Chinese that the Unit 731 facility was a lumber mill. American, British, and Australian prisoners were also used as human guinea pigs.

Unit 731's activities amounted to outrageous crimes against humanity. After infecting a prisoner with a virus or bacteria, researchers might then cut open his body, sometimes while he was still alive, to determine the effects of the disease. No anesthetics were employed, as these might have affected the results of the experiment. Medical researchers also confined infected prisoners with healthy ones to determine how rapidly diseases spread. In addition, Unit 731's doctors conducted experiments on compression and decompression and the effects of extreme cold on the body, subjecting limbs to ice water and then amputating them to determine the effects. The Japanese army also repeatedly conducted field tests using biological warfare against Chinese villages.

Japanese aircraft also spread plague-infected fleas over Ningbo (Ningpo) in Zhejiang (Chekiang) Province in eastern China in October 1940, causing 99 deaths. The Chinese government correctly concluded that an epidemic of plague in these areas had been caused by Japanese biological weapons, and it publicized its findings. Japanese troops also dropped cholera and typhoid cultures into wells and ponds. In 1942, germ-warfare units deployed dysentery, cholera, and typhoid in Zhejiang Province.

At the end of the Pacific war, Ishii and other researchers escaped to Japan. They left behind their laboratory equipment, as well as plague-infected mice that produced outbreaks of the disease in the Haerbin area between 1946 and 1948. The U.S. government feared that the Japanese might employ biological warfare against North America via balloon bombs from Japan, but such a plan was never carried out.

After the Japanese surrender, the United States did not bring Ishii and his colleagues before the International Military Tribunal for the Far East (the Tokyo War Crimes Trials) for their crimes. Instead, they were granted immunity in exchange for providing information on the experiments to U.S. authorities, which Washington considered invaluable to its own biological warfare program. The Soviet government did prosecute 12 members of the unit at

Khabarovsk in December 1949, all of whom admitted to their crimes. They were convicted and received sentences from 2 to 25 years in a labor camp.

KEN KOTANI

See also: Japan; Japanese Bacteriological Weapons Trial; Yokohama Trials

Further Reading

Harris, Sheldon H. *Factories of Death: Japanese Biological Warfare 1932–1945 and the American Cover Up.* New York: Routledge, 1994.

Williams, Peter, and David Wallace. *Unit 731: Japan's Secret Biological Warfare in World War II.* New York: Free Press, 1989.

United States

For more than a century, the United States has been prominent among Western nations in its unequivocal condemnation of both individuals and states who commit wartime atrocities, particularly when such outrages are perpetrated against innocent noncombatants. This extensive record of human rights activism notwithstanding, the United States has also been called to account for instances during the same period when it, too, was accused of engaging in behaviors and activities broadly categorized by the international community as war crimes. Not surprisingly, allegations of this kind, whether verified or not, have collectively operated to challenge the mantel of moral authority the United States routinely evinces in its relations with the rest of the world.

At the outset of the 20th century, the Americans' heavy-handed prosecution of the Philippine-American War (1899–1902), occasioned the nation's own war correspondents to regularly accuse the American military of implementing a nefarious program of misconduct and brutality against the Philippine populace. Ranging from reported incidents of robbery and physical abuse to torture and murder, these allegations were typically made in connection with American soldiers' treatment of both surrendering and already captured enemy regulars and insurgents. That said, claims of unwarranted violence against Filipino civilians were hardly uncommon, the most notorious of which included the purported American massacre of approximately 1,000 men, women, and children in the village of Titatia during the spring of 1899.

In mid-1902, a pair of high-profile court-martial proceedings involving several American officers accused of having directed troops under their respective commands to commit outrages on the island of Samar confirmed the veracity of at least some of these claims. Charged with murder for ordering the execution of 11 Filipino citizens without benefit of due process, Major Littleton W.T. Waller, U.S. Marine Corps, was the first of the two officers to be tried. Shockingly, Waller was acquitted by the members of the court-martial board just weeks after the trial began on March 17, 1902, when he presented to them copies of orders written by his immediate superior, Brigadier General Jacob H. Smith, U.S. Army, that plainly instructed him to take no prisoners and to eradicate all Filipino males over ten years of age. This incriminating testimony not only concluded the Waller case, but it also led directly to the commencement of General Smith's own court-martial that May. Within a month, the court had convicted Smith, having found him guilty of "conduct to the prejudice of good order and military discipline." He was subsequently sentenced "to be admonished by the reviewing authority" and forced to retire from the U.S. Army. Although neither Waller's nor Smith's courts-martial specifically defined the officers' offenses as war crimes, both trials illuminated the likelihood that American troops had committed atrocities on Samar and possibly elsewhere during the course of the conflict.

Some 60 years later, perhaps the most infamous act of unlawful aggression perpetrated by American troops against enemy civilians unfolded amid the American involvement in the Vietnam War. On the morning of March 16, 1968, the men and officers of Charlie Company, 1st Battalion, 20th U.S. Infantry, 11th Infantry Brigade (Light) of the 23rd Infantry (Americal) Division rushed into the sleepy South Vietnamese hamlet of My Lai fully expecting to confront and engage elements of the 48th Vietcong Local Force Battalion that reportedly controlled the area. Upon entering the village, what the soldiers actually encountered were hundreds of startled civilians, most of whom were elderly men, women, and children. Controversy still abounds over what Charlie Company's commanding officer, Captain Ernest Medina, had truly directed the men of his unit to accomplish the next day in My Lai in a briefing conducted the night before. Although Medina later insisted in sworn testimony that he had not ordered his soldiers to kill noncombatants, many of them contradicted this statement, recalling that his instructions had been chillingly emphatic: destroy everything and everyone in My Lai. In any event, almost immediately after arriving on the outskirts of the village, the members of Medina's company proceeded to indiscriminately fire in all directions. For the better part of the next four hours, the American GIs methodically swept through My Lai, slaughtering innocent villagers of all ages. The 1st Platoon, commanded by Lieutenant William L. Calley Jr., allegedly killed as many as 200 people alone. In addition to the massacre of some 500 Vietnamese civilians altogether, Charlie Company also devastated the town itself by destroying most of it dwellings, livestock, and crops. Thus, at the operation's end, where My Lai had stood just hours before, only gruesome stacks of bodies and smoking ruins remained.

During the weeks and months that followed the massacre at My Lai, army officials either willfully ignored or, in some instances, actively concealed evidence of what had occurred there. Indeed, despite the desire of a few soldiers who had witnessed, but not participated, in the mass executions to initiate criminal investigations of the operation, the army quickly stifled all such efforts before they could progress. Still, however much the army attempted to suppress them, lingering reports of the atrocities committed at My Lai continued to circulate. Ultimately, between April 1969 and July 1970, the persistence of these rumors prompted the Office of the Inspector General, of the army's Criminal Investigation Division, and the Investigative Subcommittee of the U.S. House Armed Services Committee, to open formal investigations into the massacre. The combined results of these inquiries directly led to the prosecution of several dozen enlisted men and officers for criminal offenses ranging from dereliction of duty to premeditated murder.

Of these individuals, Calley became the public face of Charlie Company's rampage through My Lai. Convicted on March 29, 1971, of the premeditated killing of at least 22 Vietnamese civilians, Calley was sentenced to life in prison by the court-martial board that heard his case. Utterly disenchanted with their government's handling of the Vietnam conflict, most Americans elected to view Calley as a victim of a war gone bad and were consequently incensed by the outcome of his lengthy court-martial trial. To be sure, public support for Calley was so intense that President Richard M. Nixon intervened on his behalf, ordering that the officer remain under house arrest in his Fort Benning quarters while awaiting an appeal of the court's verdict. Calley subsequently served just three and a half years of his initial sentence, after which the army paroled him on November 8, 1974, in response to an order issued by the Fifth Circuit Court of Appeals that released the former lieutenant on bail.

More recently, U.S. military involvement in Afghanistan and Iraq, the two principal fronts of the nebulous Global War on Terror, has not only provoked sharp international scrutiny of the nation's foreign policy endeavors, but also numerous allegations of unlawful conduct on the part of American armed forces and intelligence services. Many of these claims are either currently unverifiable or have yet to be fully investigated, including possible atrocities committed at Haditha, Iraq, and the alleged maltreatment of terror suspects housed at the Guantanamo Bay detainment facility in Cuba. At least one instance of American wrongdoing, however, has been thoroughly substantiated. Initially made public in April 2004, the revelation of systematic abuse and torture of detainees confined in Iraq's Abu Ghraib prison by certain members of the U.S. Army's 372nd Military Police Company proved to be a bombshell to the U.S. public. As indicated by the official investigations of the matter, the mistreatment of prisoners at Abu Ghraib had been routinely undertaken, ostensibly for intelligence purposes, since Iraq's liberation from Saddam Hussein's tyrannical rule by American forces the previous spring. Compelling eyewitness accounts alleged that American soldiers and intelligence officers subjected prisoners to an astonishing array of physical, psychological, and sexual abuse during that one-year period. Moreover, widely circulated photographs depicting the abuse of detainees at Abu Ghraib graphically documented some of the techniques employed as well as two of the scandal's key participants: Specialists Charles Graner and Lynndie England.

In light of this evidence, the U.S. Department of Defense moved to identify and punish those responsible for the dreadful excesses at the prison. Brigadier General Janis Karpinski, commanding officer at Abu Ghraib, was relieved of command of the 800th Military Police Brigade on April 8, 2005, with a subsequent reduction in rank to colonel. In early May 2005, the commander of the 205th Military Intelligence Brigade, Colonel Thomas Pappas, was also removed from command after receiving nonjudicial punishment for dereliction of duty. Eleven enlisted personnel were likewise penalized for their involvement, seven of whom faced court-martial proceedings. Of these, Specialists Graner and England endured the most heavily publicized trials because of their extensive and consistently lewd participation in the photographic portrayals of misconduct at Abu Ghraib. Convicted of multiple offenses, including assault and obstruction of justice, Graner was sentenced on January 15, 2005, to serve

10 years in military prison. England, on the other hand, was similarly found guilty of various charges on September 26, 2005, but received a far lighter sentence of three years confinement.

PHILLIP M. SOZANSKY

See also: Balangiga Massacre; My Lai Massacre; Philippine-American War, War Crime Trials in; Vietnam War Atrocities

Further Reading

Belknap, Michael R. *The Vietnam War on Trial: The My Lai Massacre and the Court-Martial of Lieutenant Calley.* Lawrence: University Press of Kansas, 2002.

Danner, Mark. *Torture and Truth: America, Abu Ghraib, and the War on Terror.* New York: New York Review of Books, 2004.

Miller, Stuart Creighton. *"Benevolent Assimilation": The American Conquest of the Philippines, 1899–1903.* New Haven CT: Yale University Press, 1982.

V

Videla, Jorge Rafael

Gen. Jorge Rafael Videla led the military junta that ruled Argentina after the overthrow of Isabel Perón, serving as president from 1976 to 1981. During this time, he purged Perónistas from office and led what became known as the Argentine Dirty War against suspected leftists, a campaign that resulted in the illegal imprisonment, torture, death, or disappearance of thousands of innocent Argentineans.

Videla was born on August 2, 1925, in Mercedes, Argentina, in the province of Buenos Aires. He entered the Colegio Militar, Argentina's military academy, in 1942 and began his military career as an infantry second lieutenant in 1944. After serving a term as an instructor at the Colegio Militar and attending the Escuela Superior de Guerra, in 1956 he went to Washington, D.C., as an aide to the chief of Argentina's mission to the Inter-American Defense Council. He returned home in 1959. For the next two years, he taught military intelligence courses, and then in 1961, Videla became superintendent of cadets at the Colegio Militar. In 1962, he took an administrative position in the Defense Ministry, leaving in 1964 to study counterinsurgency at the U.S. School of the Americas in the Panama Canal Zone. He was promoted to the rank of colonel in 1965 and was made general in 1971. Appointed chief of the Army General Staff in 1973, in August 1975, he became commander in chief of the army and in November of that same year he was promoted to lieutenant general. In these positions, he removed Perónistas from active duty and masterminded the army's bitter campaign against Marxist and Perónista guerrillas in the provinces.

Since the 1950s, the once prosperous Argentina had undergone a seemingly permanent economic cycle of boom and bust, and its political developments had added to the turmoil, alternating between military and civilian regimes. In 1973, military leaders demonstrated their exasperation and inability to right the country's political and economic woes by agreeing to allow the election of a Perónista president and then allowing Juan Perón himself to return from exile after nearly 20 years. For two decades, the military had been working to stamp out Perónista influence; the return of the old caudillo indicated their desperation.

Perón managed to achieve a tentative national reconciliation, but he died in 1974. The presidency went to his vice president and widow Isabel Perón, who was ill prepared to lead a country. Immediately, all the cleavages in Argentine society reassumed their former bitterness, and political struggles took more violent forms.

On March 24, 1976, Videla and other high-ranking officers removed Perón from power during the Argentine Revolution of 1976 with little resistance. Aware of her obvious incompetence and the chaos that had characterized Argentina's political life, Videla and his fellow officers came into power with more freedom to act than any previous military administration. With Juan Perón dead, his movement partially discredited, the economy suffering dramatic inflation, labor unrest, and even the Marxist and Perónista guerrillas on the run, the country was open to strong measures to restore stability and prosperity. The program put forward by the armed forces was known as the Process of National Reorganization, or simply the *Proceso*.

Videla led the military in the repression of Perónistas and leftists. An extremely well-organized secret police force coordinated the work of the armed forces and crushed all major guerrilla bands by 1978. Having won the war against armed resistance, Videla had no plan for what came next. He personally favored a restricted democracy, one that would exclude Marxists and avowed Perónistas, as military governments in the late 1950s had attempted. Videla was nonetheless directly involved in the war against "subversion" and the human rights abuses that accompanied it. He justified the actions of the military regime by claiming that subversives had abused their freedoms, and that in order to defend Western civilization, the armed forces had to temporarily suspend liberties and constitutional protections in the interests of the nation. Videla himself said that one of the main goals of the *Proceso* was to restore "a republican, representative, and federal democracy."

The *Proceso* went well beyond the repression of subversives, however, by implementing a policy of state terror that arbitrarily targeted Argentineans from all walks of life. Although young people involved in social work were the majority of the disappeared, the fact that anyone could simply be taken out of his or her home or off the street at any time instilled tremendous fear in the Argentine population, effectively silencing any opposition to the other programs enacted by the military regime.

For the majority of Argentineans, the most painful of these measures was the neo-liberal economic program implemented to lower inflation and improve Argentina's balance of payments with other countries. The idea was to correct the mistakes made during years of state-run economies by cutting government employment, ending subsidies to inefficient industries, and freezing wages. All other economic indicators floated freely, although labor unions were banned and strikes became illegal. This program generally succeeded at limiting inflation; it also slashed the living standards of the urban working classes and greatly reduced the industrial sector of the economy. By late 1979, however, even Videla and his allies in the government became concerned that perhaps their economic austerity program had gone too far and drew the line at privatization, cuts in subsidies to public corporations, or increases in unemployment. Too late to help many workers, these measures led to renewed inflation and other economic

difficulties. By 1981, foreign debt had mushroomed to more than $25 billion, or 42 percent of the gross domestic product.

Videla retired as a lieutenant general in August 1978, turning over command of the army to Gen. Roberto Viola. He continued as the civilian president of Argentina until 1981. Of the non elected Argentine military dictators of this century, he was the only one to serve out his term as initially stipulated by the armed forces and left office in 1981 as previously agreed by the generals. The regime itself lasted only until 1983, when the debacle of the Falkland Islands War and continuing economic difficulties forced the military regime to surrender power and hold elections for a civilian government. The new civilian president, Raúl Alfonsín, promised to hold those who had tortured and killed Argentine citizens responsible for their actions. Although military courts refused to try Videla and others during 1983–1984, Argentina became the only Latin American nation to bring the perpetrators of such massive human rights abuse to trial in civilian courts.

The trial of the former junta leaders began on April 22, 1985, and lasted five months. Videla did not recognize the legitimacy of the civilian court that tried him, boycotted the process by remaining in his cell, and refused to select a counsel to argue in his defense. Despite this protest, on December 9, Videla received a life sentence for his crimes and went to prison. Five years later, on December 28, 1990, he and the other convicted officers were pardoned during a general amnesty.

Although the amnesty reduced the possibility of further military revolt, many Argentineans (especially those who had lost friends and family to the horrors of the *Proceso*) were dissatisfied with the release of the generals from prison. In the summer of 1998, new evidence was brought forward, and Videla was arrested and indicted again, this time for his part in authorizing the abduction and illegal adoption of the children of those killed by the military regime. Videla remained under house arrest. An Argentinean court later ruled Videla's prior amnesty invalid, and he was again placed on trial. On July 5, 2012, Videla was found guilty of having orchestrated the mass removal of babies from their parents' homes. He received a 50-year prison sentence.

On May 17, 2013, Videla died at Marcos Paz prison while serving a life sentence for crimes against humanity.

WAYNE BOWEN

See also: Argentine Dirty War; Mothers of the Plaza de Mayo

Further Reading

Hodges, Donald Clark. *Argentina's "Dirty War": An Intellectual Biography.* Austin: University of Texas Press, 1991.

Wynia, Gary W. *Argentina: Illusions and Realities.* 2nd ed. New York: Holmes & Meier, 1992.

Vietnam War Atrocities

The Communist insurgents in Vietnam, the Viet Cong (VC), outmatched by the Army of the Republic of Vietnam (ARVN) and the United States in a material sense, carried out guerrilla warfare. Evasion of decisive, "set-piece" battles, surprise attacks, and civilian cover served to counterbalance limited resources. The practice of seeking refuge in the guise of civilians frustrated and infuriated American troops and led to misdirected reprisals. Likewise, the VC perpetrated a number of massacres to achieve political ends. Writers on both sides of the conflict have also employed the term "atrocity" to describe every action from bombing raids to American involvement in the war. To avoid such philosophical questions, the present discussion describes only those situations in which an unarmed, nonresisting noncombatant or prisoner died as the result of small-arms fire, beating, or other corporal assault.

Most U.S. atrocities occurred because of the nature of the American response to guerrilla tactics. Search-and-destroy missions, designed to deprive the VC of civilian cover and supplies, replaced conventional large-unit tactics early in the war. A search might reveal hidden weapons caches, rice stores, or a variety of booby traps. Small units patrolled the countryside in pursuit of the VC, who left mines or punji pits in their wake. Viciously efficient, these booby traps killed or maimed many GIs, and left their frightened and angry comrades with no means for revenge. Veterans regaled new soldiers arriving in country with tales of buddies who had been blown up while buying soft drinks or cigarettes from children. Although in truth only a small minority of American soldiers in Vietnam experienced an ambush or encountered mines or booby traps, the stories created an atmosphere of distrust toward all Vietnamese civilians.

Retribution, or "payback" as it was known to GIs, took several forms. Mutilation was by far the most prevalent. Taking an ear or finger from a dead enemy, or emptying a clip of ammunition into an incapacitated foe proved adequate vindication for some. Others were not so easily satisfied. One of the most horrific examples of a U.S. atrocity occurred in 1966 when members of an off-duty battery support unit stopped a passing flatbed truck, claiming that they were out of gas. When the driver consented, the soldiers siphoned fuel from the tank and carried it to the middle of a field where a young Vietnamese girl had been staked to the ground. Soaking her with the gasoline, they set fire to her. Some GIs sought recreation in taking target practice on farmers or their stock. Less random was the torture of captured VC suspects, which ranged from bare-knuckle beatings to forcible ejection from airborne helicopters. Members of the Republic of Vietnam (RVN) police accompanied American units in the field, serving as interpreters and, on occasion, as executioners.

American forces also committed atrocities in a more organized fashion. The Central Intelligence Agency (CIA) designed and implemented the Phoenix Program in 1967 to weaken the VC infrastructure and cripple its capacity for espionage and terrorism. Myra MacPherson notes in Long Time Passing that by 1969, Phoenix teams became known as "heads and ears guys" for the decapitations that were their trademark.

Some operations that seemed routine at the outset degenerated into massacres. Early in 1967, two marine companies advanced on Thuy Bo expecting only token resistance. The engagement lasted for three days, however, resulting in heavy casualties for the Americans. Upon withdrawal of the VC, the Marines entered the village and, by their own account, began shooting anything that moved. In 1968, three companies of the Americal Division committed what were probably the best-known atrocities of the war at My Lai. Unlike Thuy Bo, American forces expected heavy resistance, but met with little or none. Estimates of Vietnamese civilian dead, however, ranged from 100 to 400 women, children, and elderly men.

The unpredictable nature of the war dictated tactical adjustments. The method of drawing the enemy out and annihilating him, so effective in two world wars and in the Korean War, no longer sufficed. The Military Assistance Command, Vietnam (MACV) thus resorted to a policy of attrition. "Body counts" replaced "area secured" as a measure of progress. As support for the war waned, and pressure for some indication of success mounted, the counts became increasingly inflated. Commanders padded mission reports at every level; some offered extra leave to units with the highest counts. Many GIs, already disillusioned about their role in the conflict, interpreted the incentive as tacit approval for indiscriminate killings. Attrition policy thus gave rise to the philosophy "if it's dead and Vietnamese, it's VC." In this context, such horrendous practices as counting the pregnant dead as two kills became a sort of morbid "bargain."

The VC engaged in atrocities as well, but in different situations and for different reasons. Emotional outbursts triggered American atrocities, and, excluding some Phoenix operations, few were planned as such. In contrast, the Vietnamese Communists killed systematically, most often with a political end in mind. The VC assassinated village leaders, disemboweling and decapitating them in full view of the rest of the village to demonstrate their primacy in a given area. They also used terror tactics during the 1968 Tet Offensive, most notably in the ancient imperial capital of Hue, where they killed thousands of people judged to be hostile to their side in the war.

Communist operatives abducted "enemies" and either clubbed, shot, or buried them alive. In battle, VC units skinned or eviscerated captured GIs. Hung in the paths of American patrols, the defiled corpses elicited rage in some and fear in others, robbing commanders of control and the entire unit of its focus.

Little evidence exists to suggest that the VC ever committed rape as a matter of course. Unfortunately, the same cannot be said of American soldiers. As early as 1966, a reconnaissance patrol in the Central Highlands embarked on a mission with explicit orders to kidnap a Vietnamese girl. The team commander gave the men instructions to carry the girl along for some "boom-boom," and then kill her when the operation was completed. In 1968, a company commander in the American division reportedly stood 60 feet away from a group of soldiers who raped and sodomized two Vietnamese nurses. Seven Marines stationed at a hospital in Da Nang murdered a South Vietnamese nurse after raping her repeatedly. Nor did the sexual abuse end there. Women suspected of collaborating with the VC had their vaginas sewn shut or their breasts branded with heated bayonets.

Allied Republic of Korea (ROK) units also contributed to the gruesome litany of human suffering. Like many U.S. atrocities, a surprise mine detonation triggered the Korean action at Phong Nghi, Quang Nam Province, in 1968. After the explosion had destroyed one of their armored personnel carriers, the 2nd ROK Marine Brigade turned on the hamlet. The Koreans leveled the village, and the evidence suggested that they had shot women and children at point-blank range.

Although it is unclear whether the Korean troops involved in the Phong Nghi massacre received disciplinary action, at least some war crimes did not go unpunished. The records of the U.S. judge-advocate general show that between 1965 and 1971 courts martial convicted 201 Army personnel and 77 Marines of murder, rape, and assault. Interestingly, over three-quarters of this number received sentences after public revelation of the My Lai massacre in September 1969. More enlisted men served time than did officers, and few of either group served the entire length of their sentences.

Atrocities in war are axiomatic, perhaps even inevitable. The conflict in Vietnam, however, bears the dubious distinction of having been especially "dirty" and loathsome. Advances in communications technology allowed almost instantaneous dissemination of reports of search-and-destroy missions, torture of prisoners, and other alleged misdeeds. For the first time, national and local news services broadcast a war, concentrated to fit the demands of scheduling, to an already antagonized and confused public.

The U.S. Army may have conducted ground operations with less concern for the civilian population in Vietnam than in the two world wars or Korea. The perception of the Vietnam War as "atrocity-ridden," however, owes as much to the various sociopolitical contexts of American wars in this century as to any illegal military action.

Benjamin C. Dubberly

See also: Hue Massacre; Tiger Force Killings; United States

Further Reading

Karnow, Stanley. *Vietnam: A History.* Rev. ed. New York: Penguin Books, 1991.
MacPherson, Myra. *Long Time Passing.* New York: Doubleday, 1984.

Volhynian Poles Massacres

The region of Volhynia, currently Volyn in Western Ukraine, is the site of the 1943 massacre of tens of thousands of Volhynian Poles by Ukrainians. This is best explained in the context of the interwar period, even though Poles and Ukrainians fought over Volhynia for centuries. After World War I and the establishment of the Second Polish Republic, regional disputes led to the 1923 granting of Volhynia and Eastern Galicia to Poland and the Soviet annexation of Ukraine. President Józef Pilsudski initiated policies of religious and cultural freedom for Jews and Ukrainians living in Poland. With his death in 1935, the Polish state forced the conversion of Orthodox

Christians to Catholicism and limited Ukrainian freedoms. This led to Ukrainian terrorist activities and the strengthening of the extremist faction of the Organization of the Ukrainian Nationalists (OUN), led by Stepan Bandera and referred to as OUN-B. Polish repression of the Ukrainians in Poland left nonterrorists dead and exacerbated tensions.

The 1939 German and Soviet invasion into Poland left Volhynia under Soviet control. Soviets deported hundreds of thousands of Poles to Siberia, including Polish Jews. Ukrainian political parties were banned, which forced the extremist OUN-B underground. In 1941, the Germans invaded Volhynia, pushing the Soviets eastward. To avoid slave labor in the German Reich, many Ukrainians enlisted as police or in positions in the German civilian administration, the Reichskommissariat Ukraine. Between 1941 and 1942, thousands of Ukrainian police assisted the Germans in killing approximately 200,000 Volhynian Jews, thereby learning Nazi methods of well-planned, widescale murder.

In 1942, the OUN-B formed paramilitary groups, secured its command in Volhynia, and instituted extensive propaganda against Poles. Germans and Poles terrorized Ukrainians who joined the nationalists, but the nationalists, well-armed and well-trained police or administrators, prevailed. With the German defeat at Stalingrad, the situation escalated in March 1943 when the OUN-B formed the Ukrainian Insurgent Army (UPA), and called for a full-scale liquidation of the Poles to ensure a Pole-free Ukrainian Volhynia. Ukrainians surrounded villages across the region, murdered unsuspecting civilians, then destroyed their villages. The UPA gave Ukrainian civilians the choice to join their efforts or risk arrest or death. Nevertheless, some Ukrainians sheltered Poles. Mixed families often lost both Poles and Ukrainians. The Poles counterattacked, murdering thousands of Ukrainians, many of whom were innocent of bloodshed.

The UPA killed some 7,000 unarmed civilians in late March and early April 1943. In July 1943 alone, the UPA attacked 167 towns and villages, slaying an estimated 10,000 Poles. Evidence of wide-scale torture, rape, disembowelment, and murder of the Polish minority population originate from eyewitness accounts, German and Soviet documents, and more recently, from mass grave excavations. The final attack in Volhynia occurred on Christmas of 1943 when hundreds of Poles were burned alive in their churches. The ethnic cleansing then spread south to Eastern Galicia, where it continued into 1945.

Estimates of the numbers of Volhynian Poles the UPA murdered range from 35,000 to 60,000, with several thousand Ukrainians also slaughtered by either Poles or the UPA. Historians and activists debate the numbers. Although the Polish government issued a statement concerning the guilt of individuals rather than of the Ukrainian nation, the Ukrainian government has not apologized.

WENDY JO GERTJEJANSSEN

See also: Soviet Union; Ukrainian Starvation (Holodomor)

Further Reading

Berkhoff, Karel C. *Harvest of Despair: Life and Death in Ukraine under Nazi Rule.* Cambridge, MA: Belknap Press of Harvard University Press, 2004.

Gross, Jan Tomasz, *Revolution from Abroad: The Soviet Conquest of Poland's Western Ukraine and Western Belorussia.* Princeton: Princeton University Press, 1988.

Kamanetsky, Ihor. *Hitler's Occupation of Ukraine, 1941–1944: A Study of Totalitarian Imperialism.* Milwaukee: Marquette University Press, 1956.

Lotnik, Waldemar. *Nine Lives: Ethnic Conflict in the Polish-Ukrainian Borderlands.* London: Serif, 1999.

Motyl, Alexander J. *The Turn to the Right: The Ideological Origins and Development of Ukrainian Nationalism, 1919–1929.* Boulder: East European Monographs, 1980.

W

World War I Atrocities

Atrocities are omnipresent in war, and World War I was no exception. Although nowhere as extensive as in World War II, random killing of civilians occurred between 1914 and 1918. At the same time there were instances of officially sanctioned extermination policies. Many incidents were exaggerated for propaganda purposes. Other so-called atrocities lacked documentary evidence and witness corroboration. Many were simply ignored, in part because of the realization that all armies sometimes commit horrible acts. Nonetheless atrocities did occur, echoing on the home front the savagery seen on the war's battlefields.

Allied propaganda portrayed the German invasion of Belgium in August 1914 not as a military campaign but as an attack on civilization. Belgium was a neutral state, protected by an internationally recognized treaty of which Prussia was a signatory in 1839. The Germans invaded Belgium because "necessity knows no law." German army leaders believed that a rapid invasion of northeastern France through Belgium offered the best chance at victory in the war. Rumors of German brutality against civilians in Belgium added grist to the Allied propaganda mill. Within a few days of the German invasion, stories appeared of Belgian homes being looted and burned, priests being strung up and used as church bell clappers, nuns being raped, and prisoners of war being crucified.

While such stories were purposely exaggerated by the Allied government to enrage their soldiers and recruit volunteers for the front, there was also some truth to them. On August 23, 1914, German soldiers torched the Belgian town of Visé, killing several hundred innocent civilians. More than 700 other residents were forcibly deported to Germany to work as slave labor, while 4,000 fled as refugees to France and Holland. In the town of Dinant, 600 people, including a number of women and children, were lined up in the town square and shot. The Germans also destroyed a number of important medieval buildings in Louvain, including the university library with its priceless collection of manuscripts. More than 200 people were killed and some 600 more deported east.

Similar atrocities occurred in France as the Germans advanced. Random attacks on civilians there revealed the indiscriminate nature of German killing, often in bizarre contexts. Sixteen birders in northern France were summarily executed when German soldiers thought the raptors they kept were pigeons being used to send messages to the French Army.

Excused by some as the infrequent actions of soldiers gripped by war, the reality turned out to be something quite different. In Visé and Dinant, atrocities were committed by German soldiers belonging to primarily rear echelon units that had yet to see any fighting. Moreover, these were deliberate acts, orchestrated or legitimized by the German high command. German military leaders such as Chief of the German General Staff General Helmuth von Moltke adhered to the belief that if a civilian population fully experienced the ravages of war, this would lead to a more rapid enemy capitulation. The diaries and letters of German soldiers confirmed this brutal truth.

Estimates place the number of Belgian civilians wantonly slain by the German army in August 1914 at some 5,500 people. Another 500 died in France. Many of the dead were women and children. Some had been used as human shields, and others had been raped. One account told of an 18-year-old Belgian woman who was bayoneted for resisting the sexual advances of a German soldier. Another detailed the stabbing of babies, still clutched in the arms of their dead mothers.

The German government denied the atrocities. Officials conceded that some people were killed under the German occupation but described the actions of their soldiers as motivated only by self-defense. They labeled all those killed as *francs-tireurs,* after the irregular French forces who had fought against the Germans during the Franco-Prussian War of 1870–1871. After all, the 1899 Hague Convention permitted the execution of resistance fighters and saboteurs. Stories coming out of Belgium were powerful propaganda, particularly in the neutral United States, and they significantly influenced world opinion in favor of the Allies.

Another powerful propaganda piece was the May 7, 1915, sinking by the German U-20 submarine of the British passenger liner *Lusitania.* A total of 1,198 died, including 128 Americans. Allied propaganda made much of this action, pointing out that submarine attacks against civilian vessels were unique to the Central Powers. They stressed that the British navy never preyed upon neutral shipping. Again, there was some truth to this claim, certainly in the loss of civilian life. Innocent civilians died on other fronts. By February 1915, Austro-Hungarian soldiers had killed more than 1,000 Serb civilians, whereas Russian soldiers in Galicia had executed only 22 noncombatants in the same time period.

Seeking to capitalize on the far more numerous atrocities committed by the Central Powers, in May 1915 the British government established the Bryce Commission. Its report, printed in 30 languages, detailed the extent of atrocities committed by the Central Powers. The Germans countered the Bryce Commission Report with their own detailed exposé alleging Belgian and French atrocities against German soldiers. The damage, however, had been done, and the Allies had won the first round in the propaganda war. In the eyes of many people, Germany was alone guilty of horrific crimes. This weighed heavily in the U.S. decision to declare war on Germany in April 1917.

Other actions were also labeled atrocities. German bombing raids against Britain and the shelling of civilian centers in France were considered beyond the course of normal warfare. So too was the use of certain weapons in the field, such as poison gas and bullets that expanded on impact. The writer Robert Graves, who fought in the war, said that both sides were guilty of atrocities. He noted the savagery of Canadian soldiers toward prisoners after rumors that the Germans had crucified one of their men. Whose behavior was worse was, Graves observed, was a matter of opinion. The Allies labeled Bulgarian actions aimed at crushing rebellions in Serbia, Macedonia, and Moravia as major war crimes, while British operations to suppress the Easter Rising rebellion in Ireland were not so characterized.

In 1915, the Ottoman Empire began a systematic campaign of genocide against the Armenians who, along with others in the Caucasus region, struggled for independence during the war. Between 600,000 and 1.5 million Armenians died as a result of Turkish government policies. Many were killed, while many more died of disease and malnutrition in the forced relocation of the Armenian population. The extent of the Turkish action prompted the British government to accuse Turkey of "crimes against humanity," the first time that term was ever officially used by the government of a major state. Russia hoped to profit from the atrocity, believing that, as a result, its own Armenian population would fight the Turks more tenaciously. Even after the war, when Britain successfully forced the defeated Turks to hold war crimes trials to account for the massacre, politics prevailed. Against the backdrop of the nationalist revolution in Turkey and war against Greece led by Mustafa Kemal (Ataturk), the Armenian genocide went largely unpunished. Only two of the nine top Ottoman officials implicated in the genocide were convicted. Although the Treaty of Sèvres, imposed by the Allies on Turkey in August 1920, contained five provisions for dealing with war crimes and that advocated the establishment an independent Armenia, most Turks responsible for the atrocities were never brought to justice.

As with Turkey, the other defeated Central Powers were supposed to be held accountable for wartime atrocities. In the Treaty of Versailles, the Germans were accused of crimes against Belgian and French citizens and Allied prisoners of war. They were also held responsible for specific events, such as the sinking of the *Lusitania.* Even individual deaths, such as the execution of British nurse Edith Cavell in Belgium by the Germans, were labeled atrocities.

However, subsequent war crimes trials held at Leipzig proved to be a fiasco in which few Germans were ever convicted. Almost all atrocities committed in Belgium and France went unpunished.

Not surprisingly, after the war little attention was paid to atrocities committed by Allied soldiers against the Central Powers. These paled in comparison to the offenses committed by the Central Powers, but it is also true that history is written by the victors, and in this respect the extent of Allied crimes was never fully gauged. It is also important to note that identifying all atrocities committed during the war is an impossible task, just as proved to be the case in World War II. One need only consider events in Russia to understand the problem. The Russian Civil War claimed the lives of millions of innocent civilians, many the result of atrocities committed by both the Red (Bolshevik) and White (counterrevolutionary) forces.

ARNE KISLENKO

See also: Louvain, Destruction of; World War I War Crime Trials

Further Reading

Ferguson, Niall. *The Pity of War: Explaining World War I.* New York: Basic Books, 1999.

Graber, G.S. *Caravans to Oblivion: The Armenian Genocide, 1915.* New York: Wiley, 1996.

Horne, John, and Alan Kramer. *German Atrocities, 1914: A History of Denial.* New Haven, CT: Yale University Press, 2001.

World War I War Crimes Trials

The unprecedented but unsuccessful effort by the victorious Entente powers to conduct postwar trials. Each of the five treaties ending World War I had clauses providing for the trial of defeated leaders and soldiers. Although trials of Germans, Bulgarians, and Turks did take place, these differed from the procedures provided in these treaties.

Throughout the war, a chorus of voices in Allied nations, especially in Britain, called for prosecution of alleged war criminals. Statements from opinion leaders waxed and waned as prospects for victory changed, but they reached a crescendo at dramatic incidents: the German invasions of Belgium and France, with accompanying executions of civilian hostages; U-boat attacks and the sinking of the *Lusitania;* Young Turk massacres of Armenians; zeppelin raids on London; the executions of Edith Cavell and Charles Fryatt; mistreatment of prisoners; and the deportation and forced labor of Belgian and French civilians. Calls for trials arose partly from vengeful hatreds fueled by atrocity propaganda and partly from idealistic intentions to vindicate the laws of war so recently codified at the 1899 and 1907 Hague Conferences in order to advance international law.

In 1914 French courts-martial sentenced captured German soldiers, and in March 1915 First Lord of the Admiralty Winston Churchill ordered special detention for future trials of captured U-boat crews. But the Germans made hostages of Allied prisoners of war, forcing an end to such measures. Threats of trials, however, continued. A joint Allied statement on May 24, 1915, declared that leaders and subordinates would be held personally responsible for the "crimes of Turkey against humanity and civilization." British prime minister Herbert Asquith on July 31, 1916, denounced German "terrorism" and said that the British were "resolved that such crimes shall not, if they can help it, go unpunished. When the time arrives they are determined to bring to justice the criminals, whoever they may be and whatever their station." At the same time, the British unsuccessfully sought French and Russian support for a joint declaration on war crimes trials. Separately, the French Ministry of Justice drafted a plan in 1917 to bring Germans before an inter-Allied criminal court at war's end. The British and French issued new threats in October 1918. As the war ended, British attorney general F. E. Smith announced on November 7, 1918, the appointment of a Committee of Enquiry into Breaches of the Laws of War. It began drafting legal opinions and drawing up lists of possible prosecutions. Throughout 1919–1920, the French and British arrested accused individuals.

The most wanted man was German kaiser Wilhelm II, who had fled revolution in his homeland to seek refuge in the Netherlands. "Hang the Kaiser" became the most popular slogan of the December 1918 British election. Prime Minister David Lloyd George, wrongly blamed for this demagoguery, wished to bring the kaiser before an international tribunal for having started the war, thus establishing a new precedent and crime in international law. He insistently pressed reluctant cabinet ministers to acquiesce and secured support from French and Italian leaders at a London conference held during the election.

In 1919 the Paris Peace Conference quickly addressed the war crimes issue. Its first major action was the appointment of a Commission on the Responsibilities of the Authors of the War and the Enforcement of Penalties. This commission, however, proved an obstacle to British and French plans. Opposition from its chairman, U.S. secretary of state Robert Lansing, who objected primarily to the unprecedented, ex post facto character of the plans, undermined the whole project. When Allied leaders resolved the dispute, President Woodrow Wilson backed Lansing, despite strong support for an international tribunal among American lawyers and the general public.

The result was Articles 227–230, the war crimes clauses of the Treaty of Versailles, more limited in design than the French and British had proposed. There would be no grand international criminal tribunal to judge individuals accused of violating the laws of war. The kaiser would not be arraigned for violating international law in starting a war of aggression or invading neutral Belgium, or even for ordering or failing to halt violations of the ordinary laws of war. Rather, trials of accused German soldiers and sailors would occur before national military tribunals or if necessary before ad hoc, mixed tribunals of several nations to prosecute an individual whose alleged war crime affected citizens of more than one nation. The kaiser's trial would be a political rather than a legal proceeding, for the charge leveled against him in Article 227 was "a supreme offense against international morality and the sanctity of treaties." The famed war-guilt clause, Article 231, blaming Germany for causing the war was not drafted by those who created the war crimes articles but was prepared separately by experts working on reparations in order to justify saddling Germany with the costs of the war. The Germans and other opponents of the treaty, however, often linked Article 231 to Articles 227–230.

The long delay in asking the Dutch to hand over the kaiser and Allied disagreements about bringing him to trial enabled the Dutch to refuse an "extradition" demand in early 1920. The Dutch stood firm on their tradition as a country of political asylum. Opposition by King George V prompted other British leaders and diplomats to secretly undercut Lloyd George, as did messages to the Dutch from prominent figures in France and Italy. Almost alone, Lloyd George remained committed to a trial but in the end was forced to give way. The kaiser remained in the Netherlands. No trial was ever held.

Nor were there Allied trials of Germans as provided for in the Treaty of Versailles. Opposition from conservatives, nationalists, and the military made it virtually impossible for any German government to cooperate with the Allies who came to fear chaos and bolshevism if they strongly pressed fulfillment of war crimes clauses. After an official demand in early 1920 for the surrender of 854 accused persons, including the highest-ranking admirals and generals,

the Allies quickly agreed to a compromise that permitted a selected number of cases to be tried before the German Supreme Court at Leipzig.

The Allies requested the trial of 45 individuals, none very prominent. In 1921 the Germans tried 12 persons, finding most of them innocent and secretly paying for the defense of all of the accused. Convicted war criminals received notably light sentences. French and Belgian officials and witnesses who went to Leipzig were met by hostile crowds and left to protest innocent verdicts even before all trials were concluded. The British found the trials more satisfactory, reflecting a more conciliatory attitude and policy toward Germany.

For the development of international law, the most significant verdict at Leipzig came in the *Llandovery Castle* case. Two U-boat lieutenants were found guilty of firing on survivors of the torpedoed hospital ship, and the court rejected their defense of superior orders.

Repudiating the Leipzig trials, the French and Belgians began to try in absentia all accused Germans. The original French list of alleged criminals, before its reduction in 1920, contained the names of more than 2,000 individuals. They were now prosecuted, case by case, over the next several years. These proceedings came to an end only after the Locarno Pacts of 1925. The French denied visas to convicted Germans until 1929. For years, the Germans also continued proceedings in order to establish the innocence of accused soldiers and sailors and to defend the military and the nation's honor. Germany's Supreme Court processed cases until almost all of the 854 individuals whose surrender the Allies had demanded were pronounced innocent. Secretly, the court also reversed the verdict of the *Llandovery Castle* case.

The greatest failure of this first major effort to hold postwar international war crimes trials was not holding the Young Turks responsible for the deaths of hundreds of thousands of Armenians. Allied focus was largely on Germany. Little heed was given to accusations against Austrians, Hungarians, and Bulgarians; although the peace treaties provided for trials, none were held in Austria or Hungary. There were a small number of war crimes prosecutions in Bulgaria, although most trials initiated by the Bulgarians were political trials of former leaders. There were trials, too, by Turkish authorities in Constantinople in 1919–1920. A few persons were convicted and executed before a nationalist backlash halted these proceedings. To prevent the release or escape of other accused Turks, the British removed them to detention on Malta, where eventually more than a hundred were held. The British undermined the legitimacy of this action by mixing political detainees troublesome to occupation authorities in Turkey with individuals thought truly responsible for the massacres. Article 230 of the Treaty of Sèvres in 1920 provided for a tribunal, possibly to be created by the League of Nations, to deal with persons accused of massacres. No such tribunal was established. Eventually, the British exchanged all individuals held on Malta in 1921 for hostages taken by Kemal Ataturk's Nationalist movement. After the new Treaty of Lausanne, the last alleged Turkish war criminal was released in 1923 from an Indian prison.

The effort to try individuals for war crimes during World War I, which would have represented a veritable revolution in international law and relations, thus ended largely in failure. Nonetheless, the experience helped pave the way for the International War Crimes Tribunals of World War II.

JAMES F. WILLIS

See also: World War I Atrocities

Further Reading

Bass, Gary Jonathan. *Stay the Hand of Vengeance: The Politics of War Crimes Tribunals.* Princeton, NJ: Princeton University Press, 2001.

Dadrian, Vahakn N. *The History of the Armenian Genocide: Ethnic Conflict from the Balkans to Anatolia to the Caucasus.* Oxford: Berghahn Books, 1995.

Horne, John, and Alan Kramer. *German Atrocities, 1914: A History of Denial.* New Haven, CT: Yale University Press, 2001.

Willis, James F. *Prologue to Nuremberg: The Politics and Diplomacy of Punishing War Criminals of the First World War.* Westport, CT: Greenwood, 1982.

World War II Atrocities, European Theater

World War II, officially waged between 1939 and 1945, was the most expansive, destructive, and deadly war in human history. It was a total war, which blurred completely the lines between civilians and combatants, and featured military technology that greatly increased casualties among both civilians and military personnel. It is believed that as many as 60 million people died in the conflict, and for the first time in the history of warfare, there were more civilian deaths (some 35–40 million) than military deaths (some 20 million). The number of atrocities that occurred among the belligerents in Europe was truly staggering, and it is not possible to list them all here or discuss them with any great detail. To further complicate matters, there were at least 20 civil wars going on simultaneously throughout the world, including one in Yugoslavia and one that pitted the Croats and Slovenes against the Serbian Chetnik ultranationalists. This essay will not discuss the Holocaust, which unfolded in Europe and was perpetrated by the Nazis and their collaborators. That cataclysm claimed the lives of 6 million Jews, 200,000 Romani, 200,000–250,000 disabled persons, 5,000–15,000 homosexuals, and 2,500–5,000 Jehovah Witnesses, among others.

What made World War II so genocidal in nature were several developments, which taken together formed a perfect storm of unprecedented carnage. Massive aerial bombardment of civilian areas occurred on a scale never before seen. Civilians were now seen as legitimate targets because many worked in arms factories and were no longer "innocent" bystanders. This upended longstanding understandings and international conventions guiding the terms and conduct of warfare. Also contributing to the peculiarly virulent nature of World War II were stark and competing socio-political ideologies. Although many wars have had their political components, the clash between the right-wing extremism and collectivism of Nazism and Fascism and the left-wing extremism and collectivism of Communism ensured that the conflict would have apocalyptic overtones. Neither ideology believed that it could survive alongside the other, so both sides fought to literally exterminate the other. Finally, World War II had significant ethnic, racial, and religious overtones that set the stage for unimaginable mass murder. Germany especially combined extreme nationalism, racism, and a secular holy war against Jews to form a toxic stew so poisonous that few who fell under its grip were safe.

Among the belligerents in Europe, Germany was, by far, the most genocidal. In addition to killing 6 million civilian Jews, the Germans were also responsible for the deaths of 12–15 million Slavs, Poles, Russians, and other civilians, and at least 1 million prisoners of war (POWs), hostages, partisans, and forced laborers. On the other end of the spectrum, Poland was by far the biggest victim of World War II. Out of a prewar population of 34 million, 6 million Poles died between 1939 and 1945; all but 100,000 or so of that 6 million were civilians. The Poles were killed not only by the Germans, but also by the Soviets. Germany itself lost 5 million (military and civilians) people, out of a population of 78 million.

Soviet troops committed a major atrocity in Poland's Katyn Forest in the spring of 1940, when some 22,000 Poles were summarily shot to death and buried in mass graves. Most of the victims were Polish army officers who had been captured as POWs. The graves were discovered by the Germans in April 1943, who used this evidence of a Soviet massacre as potent wartime propaganda. The Soviets at first denied involvement in the killings and then later blamed the Germans for the atrocity. Not until the end of the Cold War in the 1990s did the Russians make clear the extent of Soviet involvement.

The September 1941 Babi Yar Massacre, which occurred near Kiev, Ukraine, was a very significant war atrocity. In that tragedy, German troops shot en masse 33,771 innocent Jewish civilians, including women and children. Later, the Nazis tried to cover up the killings, but vestiges of them remained and were uncovered by Soviet troops in November 1943.

In Czechoslovakia, during the June 1942 Lidice Massacre in Czechoslovakia, the Germans summarily executed or deported a number of civilians in retaliation for the assassination of two high-ranking Nazi officials in Prague on May 27. In the end, German soldiers killed 172 males and 71 women at Lidice. Seven other women were taken to Prague, where they were shot to death, and another 184 women were deported to the Ravensbruck concentration camp. Eighty-two children from Lidice were eventually gassed to death while the town itself was completely destroyed. None of the victims had anything to do with the assassinations.

The April–May 1943 Warsaw Ghetto Uprising, involving Warsaw's interned Jewish community, resulted in the deaths or deportation of at least 300,000 people. That tragedy unfolded after a group of armed Jews, the Jewish Fighting Organization (ZOB), decided to fight the Germans and resist deportation. The German responded with a brutal crackdown. Thousands of Jews were shot and killed while many thousand more were deported to death camps. Of the deportees, very few survived the war.

In September and October 1943, right after Italian dictator Benito Mussolini was deposed and the Italians switched sides in the war to join the Allies, the Germans perpetrated a terrible massacre against Italian POWS on the Greek island of Cephalonia. About 4,750 soldiers were summarily shot in the first phase of the Acqui Division Massacre in September; another 4,000 Italian POWs were either drowned at sea or shot and killed in October. In all,

nearly 9,000 Italian POWs perished during one of the war's greatest atrocities against POWs.

In the March 1944 Ardeatine Massacre, outside Rome, German occupation forces murdered 335 Italian civilians—75 of whom were Jews—in reprisal for a partisan bombing against German police. None of those who were executed had any role in the bombing.

On June 10, 1944, German Waffen-SS forces murdered 218 men, women, and children in the Greek village of Distomo. The atrocity was committed allegedly to avenge a deadly Greek partisan attack against the Germans. German troops went door to door, flushing out residents and shooting them in their homes or when they attempted to escape.

That very same day, German forces committed another atrocity in the French town of Oradour-sur-Glane. Occurring only days after the Allied landings at Normandy, France, German troops entered the sleepy village, separated the men from the women and children, and herded them into a barn and a church. The Germans then tossed grenades into the buildings, burning the French civilians alive. The death toll included 642 victims (only seven villagers escaped death); among the dead were 207 children.

The December 1944 Malmédy Massacre in Belgium witnessed the mass murder of 72 U.S. POWs. The incident, perpetrated by the Germans, occurred during the Battle of the Bulge (December 16, 1944–January 16, 1945). The killings at Melmédy represented the worst atrocity against Americans in the European Theater of war.

Finally, no treatment of World War II atrocities would be complete without mention of the devastating Allied air attacks against Dresden, Germany, in February 1945. During the first two waves of bombings, 2,600 tons of ordnance was dropped over the city; the following day, an additional 700 tons of bombs were dropped on Dresden. The bombings created a raging firestorm that consumed vast portions of the city. The fires became so intense that many people died of oxygen deprivation rather than from burns or smoke inhalation. It is estimated that 45,000 Germans were killed in the bombings.

Clearly, World War II was a conflict without parallel in terms of scope, destruction, and loss of life. Earlier attempts to shield civilians from combat or harm's way were no longer operable in this total war. Indeed, civilians seemed often to be specifically targeted to produce terror and demoralization among enemy populations. And if they were not consciously targeted, little thought went into protecting them from the depredations of war. Modern technology, meanwhile, made killing on a vast scale an easy and largely impersonal task. Aerial bombardment especially made every civilian in the theater of war a potential casualty. In a very significant sense, the entirety of World War II was one long, nightmarish atrocity.

PAUL G. PIERPAOLI JR.

See also: World War II Atrocities, Pacific Theater

Further Reading

Crane, Conrad C. *Bombs, Cities, and Civilians: American Airpower Strategy in World War II.* Lawrence: University Press of Kansas, 1993.

Dziewanowski, M.K. *War at Any Price: World War II in Europe, 1939–1945.* New York: Prentice Hall, 1991.

Hastings, Max. *Das Reich: Resistance and the March of the 2nd S.S. Panzer Division through France, June 1944.* New York: Holt, Rinehart, and Winston, 1981.

Weinberg, Gerhard L. *A World at Arms: Global History of World War II.* New York: Cambridge University Press, 1994.

World War II Atrocities, Pacific Theater

World War II was not unlike other wars in terms of atrocities and human-rights abuses. In the fog of war, atrocities are often a tragic byproduct of human conflict; some are intentional, while others are not. But what makes World War II stand out from any other war in human history was its scale and scope. It involved more nations and more people than any other recorded war. It was also history's most expensive, destructive, and deadly conflict. It is believed that as many as 60 million people died in the conflict, and for the first time in the history of warfare, there were more civilian deaths (some 35–40 million) than there were military deaths (some 20 million). Although the majority of those deaths occurred in the European Theater, the Pacific War nevertheless produced horrendous casualties, many of them among civilian populations.

As in Europe, the war in the Pacific often involved civilians on an unprecedented scale. Chinese civilian deaths, dating back to the beginning of the Sino-Japanese War in 1937, were staggering. The Philippines also suffered high civilian casualties at the hands of the Japanese. It is estimated that China and the Philippines alone may have suffered 8–9 million total deaths between 1937 and 1945. The Japanese militarists in fact showed little mercy in their quest to dominate Asia, which besides China and the Philippines also included Indochina and Malaysia. The Soviets, too, were involved in atrocities involving Japanese and Korean prisoners of war (POWs), and many would argue that the U.S. atomic bombings of Hiroshima and Nagasaki, Japan in August 1945, no matter how militarily necessary they may have been, resulted in a massive atrocity against unarmed civilians.

The Japanese frequently mistreated, abused, tortured, and murdered prisoners of war from all the nations it fought, including the United States. The Japanese refused to abide by international conventions stipulating the humane treatment of POWs, and therefore contributed to untold numbers of deaths among prisoners under their care. Indeed, the war in the Pacific exhibited a virulent racism to it that was perhaps as stark as that of the European war. The Japanese hatred and disdain toward Europeans is grimly illustrated by the low percentage of European POWs who survived captivity: Of the approximately 80,000 European prisoners taken by the Japanese between 1939 and 1945, only 65 percent of them survived. The Japanese themselves lost some 2 million servicemen during the war, while about 500,000 Japanese civilians died, of all causes.

Although the official start of World War II came on September 1, 1939, in Asia the war actually began in 1937, when the Japanese launched an all-out offensive to capture and control as much of China as they could. Thus, the first great atrocity of the war in the east was the Nanjing Massacre of December 1937–January 1938. When Chinese troops refused to surrender the city, Japanese forces unleashed a hellish series of events designed to intimidate and destroy the Chinese. In just six weeks' time, perhaps as many as 300,000 Chinese soldiers and civilians were killed. The Japanese also subjected some 20,000 Nanjing women to mass rapes. The majority of those victims were later killed.

In January 1942, in Johor, Malaysia, Japan's Imperial Guards Division perpetrated a massacre against Indian and Australian troops. Following the bloody Battle of Muar, which involved the Australian 8th Division and the Indian 45th Brigade, a number of troops from those units had to be left behind because of injuries. Taken prisoner by the Japanese, some soldiers were shot while others were burned alive. Their bodies were then repeatedly run over by trucks. At least 150 Indian and Australian troops died.

After Singapore, a British colony, surrendered to the Japanese in February 1942, Japanese troops perpetrated another massacre, this one at Sook Ching. That atrocity was aimed at the Chinese population in the area and lasted from mid-February until early March 1942. The operation, which was pre planned, was designed to get rid of all Chinese opposition. Although the casualty figures are still being debated today, it is estimated that the Japanese killed at least 50,000 civilians, the vast majority of whom were ethnic Chinese.

Meanwhile, the collapse of the U.S.-controlled Philippines and the Japanese seizure of the Bataan Peninsula in April 1942 precipitated the infamous Bataan Death March. Japanese troops forced-marched 12,000 American soldiers and 64,000 Filipino soldiers, who were now POWS, some 52 miles through tropical heat virtually without water or food. Along the way, the Japanese kicked and beat stragglers; those who collapsed were shot and killed. The death toll from this notorious incident was estimated at 7,000 to 10,000. Another 1,600 Americans and 16,000 more Filipinos died in the first two months of captivity.

In the Palawan (Philippines) Massacre of December 1944, Japanese troops burned to death some 150 American POWs at a Japanese prison camp to prevent the Allies from reaching the facility and freeing the prisoners. Only 11 men survived the ordeal.

In February 1945, Japanese occupation troops in Manila (the Philippines) perpetrated a ghastly atrocity against that city's civilian population as Allied troops closed in. In the span of less than a month, it is estimated that the Japanese systematically murdered as many as 100,000 Filipinos. Women were raped, children tortured, and the city itself lay in ruins by the time it was liberated.

On March 9–10, 1945, American B-29 bombers unleashed a fire storm over Tokyo, using massive amounts of conventional incendiary bombs. The air raid involved 325 bombers and 1,600 tons of bombs. Tokyo's crowded conditions and wooden buildings greatly magnified the destruction. The glow of the firestorm was visible 150 miles away as water literally boiled in canals and glass melted into liquid and ran down the streets. Some 90,000–100,000 people died in the Tokyo Bombing, making it the war's deadliest air attack, even more deadly than the atomic bomb attacks on Hiroshima and Nagasaki later that same year.

The U.S. atomic bombings of Hiroshima (August 6, 1945) and Nagasaki (August 9), while viewed as military necessities designed to end the Pacific War quickly and thus save lives, nevertheless involved the deaths of tens of thousands of Japanese civilians. The nuclear weapon dropped on Hiroshima resulted in a mushroom cloud more than 50,000 feet high visible to aircraft more than 350 miles away. Confirmed deaths were 71,000, many of whom were simply vaporized by the bomb; another 20,000 were wounded while 170,000 more were left homeless. Radiation sickness and related diseases killed scores more in the weeks, months, and years following the bombing.

The atomic bombing of Nagasaki, which is more controversial than that of Hiroshima, killed 74,000 people and injured 75,000 more. The mushroom cloud from that detonation rose to 60,000 feet and was visible by aircraft some 400 miles away. One-third of the city was completely leveled, and some 18,000 homes were destroyed. Some historians have argued that this second atomic bombing was unnecessary and that the Allies had not allowed sufficient time for the Japanese to respond to the Hiroshima bombing.

What made World War II so deadly and destructive was not only the scale and scope of the conflict, but also the inclusion of civilians on a large scale. Ever-more deadly weaponry also magnified the casualties. Indeed, modern technology made killing on a vast scale an easy and largely impersonal task. Aerial bombardment especially made every civilian in the theater of war a potential casualty. Long-held cultural biases and ethnic and racial hatred also virtually ensured that the Pacific War would take on apocalyptic overtones that often manifested themselves in war-time atrocities.

PAUL G. PIERPAOLI JR.

See also: World War II Atrocities, European Theater

Further Reading

Crane, Conrad C. *Bombs, Cities, and Civilians: American Airpower Strategy in World War II.* Lawrence: University Press of Kansas, 1993.

Dower, John W. War *Without Mercy: Race and Power in the Pacific War.* New York: Pantheon, 1987.

Lord Russell of Liverpool. *The Knights of Bushido: A History of Japanese War Crimes during World War II.* New York: Skyhorse Publishing, 2008.

Thompson, Peter. *The Battle for Singapore.* London: Portrait Books, 2005.

Weinberg, Gerhard L. *A World at Arms: Global History of World War II.* New York: Cambridge University Press, 1994.

Wounded Knee Massacre

For all intents and purposes, the Wounded Knee Massacre of 1890 marked the end of organized American Indian resistance to the white culture that had arrived in the New World four centuries earlier.

Aftermath of the Wounded Knee Massacre at the Pine Ridge Agency in South Dakota in 1890. (Library of Congress)

The Ghost Dance, a nonmilitant, quasireligious movement among many Indian tribes during the late 19th century, had a reverse effect on the Lakota Sioux. Militant leaders among the Sioux, angered by the plight of their people who were suffering from hunger and sickness, capitalized on the Ghost Dance fervor by preaching the overthrow of the white man and his rule. They promised that the sacred ghost shirt would protect them from soldiers' bullets.

Government officials watched with growing concern. At the Pine Ridge Agency and the Rosebud Agency, emotions ran high, and nearby settlements feared an uprising. In response to settlers' cries for military protection, President Benjamin Harrison ordered the War Department to take control of a rapidly deteriorating situation. Accordingly, in mid-November 1890, army troops occupied both agencies.

Within the Sioux tribe, two factions had emerged: friendlies (those not wanting trouble) and hostiles (the militants). In December, the hostile ghost dancers, numbering perhaps 500 or 600, had come together in the northwest corner of the Pine Ridge Reservation. Elsewhere, other Sioux bands, notably that of Sitting Bull, also appeared threatening. One in particular, that of Big Foot, steadfastly refused the army's efforts at pacification.

Meanwhile, General Nelson A. Miles, having recently assumed command of the Military Division of the Missouri, ordered the arrest of Big Foot and Sitting Bull. Much to Miles's chagrin, however, the death of Sitting Bull, killed by Indian policemen attempting to arrest him, further provoked a charged situation, which was beginning to receive considerable media attention. Most of Sitting Bull's Hunkpapa band agreed to be relocated, but a few hard-liners joined Big Foot's band. Lieutenant Colonel Edwin Sumner,

with orders to arrest Big Foot, deemed it more prudent to hold off temporarily on the execution of his orders to avoid trouble. His delay led to trouble nevertheless.

Although militant, Big Foot had a reputation as a peacemaker and had been asked by some of the Oglalas to come down from his Cheyenne River camp to Pine Ridge to help ease tensions. When Sumner finally decided to carry out his orders, he found that Big Foot and his band had quietly slipped away under cover of night for Pine Ridge. On December 17, an angry Miles took personal charge of a situation that he felt had been bungled. His troops were still trying to persuade the militants to come in from the remote corner of Pine Ridge where they had been holding out, and Miles now sought to keep Big Foot from joining them. Accordingly, elements of the 6th and 9th Cavalry were directed to prevent such a union.

Big Foot, however, managed to elude the cavalry patrols and made his way toward Pine Ridge by way of the Badlands. Along the way, the Oglala leader was stricken with pneumonia. Meanwhile, a frustrated Miles ordered George Armstrong Custer's old regiment, the 7th Cavalry, now commanded by Colonel James W. Forsyth, to intercept the elusive Oglalas. Forsyth succeeded where the others had failed. On the night of December 28, 1890, his advance units located and surrounded Big Foot's camp along Wounded Knee Creek.

Surrounded by 500 soldiers and four field pieces, the Sioux, numbering about 100 men and perhaps 200 women and children, readily agreed to be escorted to the railhead for transfer to Omaha. However, when Forsyth demanded surrender of all weapons, the Sioux grew angry and refused to comply. Soldiers, understandably nervous, were sent in among the throng of murmuring Indians to search for concealed weapons. It was a volatile situation. In a disagreement between one of the soldiers and a Sioux, a rifle was discharged. Suddenly both sides were firing at each other. Brutal, close-in fighting ensued, with shooting and stabbing.

As the fighting broke off and the two sides gradually separated, Forsyth's Hotchkiss guns began firing into the camp with deadly effect, scattering the Indians. When the shooting finally ended, some 150 Sioux including Big Foot lay dead, and another 50 were wounded. Army losses amounted to 25 killed and 40 wounded.

Miles was furious. He considered the massacre totally unnecessary, a blunder, and relieved Forsyth of command (that decision was later overturned). Wounded Knee was a genuine tragedy, but it was not a massacre in the sense that Sand Creek was a massacre, as it was neither deliberate nor indiscriminate. Further violence was averted, due mainly to Miles's avoidance of dangerous situations. The power and attraction of the Ghost Dance waned after that.

JERRY KEENAN

See also: Native American Genocide; Trail of Tears

Further Reading

Brown, D. Alexander. *Bury My Heart at Wounded Knee: An Indian History of the American West.* New York: Holt, Rinehart & Winston, 1973.

Utley, Robert M. *The Last Days of the Sioux Nation.* New Haven, CT: Yale University Press, 1963.

Y

Yamashita Trial

Japanese general Tomoyuki Yamashita petitioned the U.S. Supreme Court to review his case after being sentenced to death for war crimes by a military tribunal. The Court refused to hear Yamashita's petition, and its majority opinion found that military tribunals comply with the Constitution and that command responsibility may be judged by a strict standard.

Yamashita's reputation was built on military successes in Malaya and Singapore, and in 1944 he became Commanding General of the Imperial Japanese Army's Fourteenth Army Group in the Philippines. Forces under Yamashita's command committed atrocities including killing, rape, torture and other forms of brutality. These events were the basis for 123 war crimes charges against Yamashita. After a military tribunal found him responsible, Yamashita unsuccessfully petitioned the U.S. Supreme Court to review the proceedings. By a 6 to 2 margin, the Court refused to do so, and Yamashita was hung in the Philippines on February 23, 1946.

Yamashita was not charged with intentional war crimes or even with acting recklessly; rather, the charge was that he should have known of the crimes. If the standard of intent imposed wasn't strict liability, then it was at most a negligence test, stating that a commander acting "reasonably" would ensure that troops under his command wouldn't commit such crimes.

A five-member military commission composed of U.S. generals without legal training sentenced Yamashita to death in December 1945. In his trial, procedural guarantees of civilian U.S. courts such as the right to a jury trial and standards of evidence were weaker or absent. The tribunal denied a motion for continuance for preparation of the defense case, as well as a motion to allow Yamashita to represent himself. Through his lead defense lawyer A. Frank Reel, Yamashita contended that he had no knowledge of the atrocities, that he would not have approved of them, and that he should not be held accountable. Reel claimed that the result of the military trial was foreordained by General Douglas MacArthur.

At issue, also, was whether President Franklin D. Roosevelt had the authority to set up military courts. The Supreme Court held that he did, at least during wartime. Chief Justice Harlan Fiske Stone's majority opinion (in which he was joined by Justices Hugo Black, Stanley F. Reed, Felix Frankfurter, William O. Douglas, and Harold H. Burton) found the military war crimes commission legitimately created. Justices Frank Murphy and Wiley B. Rutledge, Jr. sided with Yamashita; both dissents went beyond challenging the propriety of military tribunals to challenge the conception of "command responsibility" under which Yamashita was convicted. Rutledge opined that the decision was the worst in U.S. Constitutional history, even worse than Dred Scott. The majority's view, however, set a precedent.

Arthur W. Blaser

See also: Harukei Isayama Trial; International Military Tribunal, Far East; Japan; Manila Massacre

Further Reading

Lael, Richard L. *The Yamashita Precedent: War Crimes and Command Responsibility.* Wilmington, DE: Scholarly Resources Inc., 1982.

Reel, A. Frank. *The Case of General Yamashita.* New York: Octagon Books, 1971.

Taylor, Lawrence. *A Trial of Generals: Homma, Yamashita, MacArthur.* South Bend, IN: Icarus Press, 1981.

Yemen

Yemen, a Muslim nation located in the southern Arabian Peninsula, has had a long history of civil and political violence. Since the late 1990s, it has also become caught up in the Global War on Terror, and has been rocked by domestic terrorism and insurgencies against the government, perpetrated chiefly by militant fundamentalist Islamic groups.

In 1918, northern Yemen gained independence under Imam Yahya, of the Hamiddadin family. That family ruled North Yemen until 1962, when a royal succession crisis sparked an army-supported coup d'état.

The coup in turn precipitated a bloody, eight-year-long civil war (1962–1970), which soon involved outside powers. The royalists were backed by Saudi Arabia, Jordan, and Britain, while the republicans were supported by Egypt and the Soviet Union. During the fighting, as many as 200,000 North Yemenis were killed. Egypt lost some 26,000 soldiers, while the Saudis suffered about 1,000 killed.

At the same time, beginning in 1963, the British, who had controlled Aden and Southern Yemen since the late 1830s, faced their own insurgency, known as the Aden Emergency (1963–1967). That crisis began on December 10, 1963, when an unknown assailant threw a grenade at British officials at the Aden airport. The British thereafter declared a state of emergency, but were unable to quell the growing unrest. The insurrection intensified in 1967, aided by Egyptian forces and insurgents in North Yemen, and the British were compelled to withdraw from the south in late November 1967. The People's Republic of South Yemen was subsequently declared, but not before at least 2,100 people had died during the Aden Emergency.

Thereafter, there was sporadic but generally limited conflict between North and South Yemen, which nevertheless escalated beginning in 1979. Meanwhile, in South Yemen, a civil war erupted during January and February 1986, a result of conflicting factions in the Yemeni Socialist Party. The war became a bloody affair, and even though it lasted for barely a month, it claimed as many as 10,000 lives. The nearly constant fighting in both the North and South hamstrung Yemen's economy, making them among the poorest nations in the Arab world.

After years of squabbling and fighting, both Yemeni nations agreed on a unification plan, and Yemen became one nation on May 22, 1990. Shortly thereafter, the Persian Gulf War began, and Yemen's government refused to support the Western coalition against Saddam Hussein's Iraq. This further hobbled the country's weak economy and compelled hundreds of thousands of Yemenis to leave the country to seek employment in other Arab states. After the war ended in early 1991, a flood of expatriate Yemenis returned to Yemen, which caused nearly insurmountable unemployment and economic chaos. Yemen now found itself at the epicenter of the growing terrorist threat encouraged by radical Islamic groups like Al Qaeda. Indeed, Al Qaeda's first attack was carried out in Aden, Yemen, on December 29, 1992, when bomb attacks on a hotel killed two Australian visitors and wounded scores more.

Another brief civil war that occurred between May and July 1994 involved supporters of the former North and South Yemen, including members of the Yemeni Socialist Party, and the Yemeni government. The South Yemeni forces were defeated, but 7,000–10,000 people lost their lives in the brief secessionist crisis. In October 2000, Yemen was the site of a terrorist bombing (most likely by Al Qaeda) of the U.S. warship *Cole*. Seventeen U.S. sailors were killed, and many others injured. The attack not only strained Yemeni-American relations, but also seemed to indicate that radical Islamic extremism was taking firmer hold in Yemen.

In the summer of 2004, a rebellion led by dissident fundamentalist cleric Hussein Badreddin al-Houthi commenced in Yemen. Al-Houthi and his followers sought the overthrow of the Yemeni government and the installation of a new regime based strictly on sharia law. This rebellion is ongoing, and some reports claim as many as 25,000 people have died in the fighting; 9,000 more have been wounded, and the government has arrested at least 3,000 dissidents and rebels. Meanwhile, Yemen has experienced U.S. cruise missile and drone strikes on its territory as American policymakers have tried to zero in on and eliminate terrorists connected to Al Qaeda in the Arabian Peninsula, an off-shoot of Osama bin Laden's Al Qaeda organization. On December 17, 2009, an American cruise missile attack on suspected Al Qaeda leaders in al-Majala, in southern Yemen, reportedly killed scores of civilians, including, by some reports, 22 children and 5 women. The U.S. government has steadfastly refused to either confirm or deny the casualty reports, but it is believed that others have died in similar U.S. attacks elsewhere in Yemen. Al Qaeda and affiliated groups have also been active in the al-Houthi uprising, and they have perpetrated some grisly human rights abuses. In southern Yemen, where the rebels are strongest, there have been reports of beheadings, crucifixions, and amputations committed against civilians who have allegedly violated sharia law.

As the so-called Arab Spring swept across much of the Middle East beginning in early 2011, demonstrators in the Yemeni capital of Sanaa took to the streets to protest against the government. By February 3, at least 20,000 people jammed the streets and squares of the capital, overwhelming the police force. Initially, the demonstrators were rallying against high unemployment, a bad economy, and government corruption. Soon, however, they began demanding the ouster of President Ali Abdullah Saleh. This prompted large defections from the Yemeni military and police forces and, ultimately, Saleh's exit in February 2012. On Friday March 18, 2011, Yemeni forces killed 45 people and wounded at least 200 others in a massacre in Sanaa; this was the worst single act of violence during the entire uprising. The uproar became more subdued after Saleh's departure, but Yemen remains a violent and dangerous place. It is estimated that 2,000 or more people died in the Arab Spring unrest, with as many as 20,000 injured.

Al Qaeda and other extremist groups continue to perpetrate suicide bombings and other acts of terror in which Yemeni civilians have been injured or killed. In early March 2012, the Yemeni government reported the massacre of some 60 Yemeni soldiers in the southern province of Abyan by members of Al Qaeda in the Arabian Peninsula. In May, a suicide bomber struck a military parade in Sanaa, killing 96 soldiers and injuring more than 100 others. The violence in Yemen is not likely to diminish so long as the country remains a haven for Islamic extremists who are able to defy the weak and chaotic government there.

PAUL G. PIERPAOLI JR.

See also: Egypt; Saudi Arabia

Further Reading

Dresch, Paul. *A History of Modern Yemen.* Cambridge, UK: Cambridge University Press, 2008.

Mackintosh-Smith, Martin. *Yemen: The Unknown Arabia.* Woodstock, NY: Overlook, 2001.

Yokohama Trials

At the end of World War II, the Allied powers conducted war crimes trials involving Japanese defendants primarily through the International Military Tribunal for the Far East (IMTFE) as 'class A' defendants. Other Japanese officials—5700 in total—were tried as "class B and C" defendants for war-time offenses before Allied military courts throughout Asia-Pacific. There were more than 2,000 regional trials, held before 50 tribunals. One ran between 1946 and 1951 in Yokohama, Japan, before commissions of the U.S. Eighth Army.

One of Japan's largest cities, a major port, and just 30 miles from Tokyo, Yokohama saw much of the war. It was a target of the famous Doolittle raids in April 1942. In May 1945, nearly half the city was destroyed in incendiary bombing. That August, the Supreme Commander of Allied forces in the Pacific, U.S. general Douglas MacArthur, set up his command headquarters there. Yet in some respects, Yokohama saw even more of the war with the parade of Japanese officials tried before it. Among the accused were military men from all services and ranks, but also medical personnel and bureaucrats. Most crimes involved the abuse of prisoners of war, who endured severe malnutrition, torture, and even summary execution. Whereas only 4 percent of American, British, or Commonwealth prisoners held by the Germans and Italians died in captivity, 27 percent died in Japanese camps. With this in mind it is not surprising that many class B defendants at Yokohama were prison guards. Class C defendants were predominantly senior military officers who ordered or failed to prevent such crimes.

Also in class B at Yokohama were members of Japan's notorious Kempei-tai, or secret police. Over 1,500 men in this service were tried at regional trials; representing about one-quarter of all Japanese war criminals. Yokohama trials also saw doctors, scientists, and technicians who took part in barbaric experiments on Allied personnel. Many of the accused worked for the Japanese Imperial Army's Unit 731, which developed biological and chemical weapons. In March 1948, thirty members of Unit 731 were tried at Yokohama for unlawful vivisection and the removal of body parts. Charges of cannibalism against some defendants were also laid. Twenty-three were convicted. Five were sentenced to death. Four received life sentences. Fourteen were given prison terms. However, in September 1950, with the Korean War underway, General MacArthur commuted most of the sentences. By 1958, all were released. Facing increasing Cold War tensions, some believe that senior U.S. officials quietly intervened to free the accused: anxious to use the Unit's research for similar American programs.

Also tried at Yokohama were Japanese sailors charged in the deaths of more than 1,300 men aboard the ill-fated Oryoku Maru. One of the infamous "hell-ships"—unmarked freighters used to transport prisoners—Oryoku Maru was packed with 1,619 men in abysmal conditions. En route from Manila to Japan in December 1944, the ship was attacked by American planes, unaware of the captives on-board. In the ensuing chaos, Japanese guards killed 286 prisoners. The survivors were re-boarded on the Enoura Maru, which was also hit by an American attack with the loss of several hundred more. Only 490 reached Japan in late-January 1945. One hundred sixty-one more died shortly thereafter of disease and malnutrition. In total, only 271 men survived the affair. At Yokohama, the captain of the guards and an interpreter on Oryoku Maru were sentenced to death, while four others drew prison sentences.

Arraigned as class B criminals, employees of prominent Japanese businesses were also tried at Yokohama. Best known was Kajima Corporation—today one of the largest construction companies in the world—which during the war used thousands of Chinese slave-laborers. In June 1945, at its copper mine facility in Hanaoka, Japan, about 1,000 starving Chinese revolted. Nearly all were savagely hunted down, tortured, and killed. Only three Kajima executives were implicated: they were found guilty and sentenced to death. However, in 1956, all three were released. The Japanese government even compensated the corporation for the loss of its slaves.

As was the case with most regional trials, at Yokohama many of the accused were tried co-jointly on charges stemming from specific incidents. The hearings at Yokohama were also noted for large amounts of documentary evidence submitted by the prosecution; chiefly eye-witness affidavits. The trials, however, may be best remembered for the relatively lenient treatment of many accused. Anxious to re-build Japan and count it as an ally in the Cold War, American officials were evidently willing to forget some of the worst war-crimes in history, just as occurred in Germany.

ARNE KISLENKO

See also: Harukei Isayama Trial; International Military Tribunal, Far East; Japan; Japanese Bacteriological Weapons Trial; Unit 731

Further Reading

Buruma, Ian. *Wages of Guilt: Memories of War in Germany and Japan.* New York: Farrar, Straus, and Giroux, 1994.

Dower, John W. *Embracing Defeat: Japan in the Wake of World War II.* New York: W.W. Norton, 1999.

Hosoya, Chihiro, ed. *The Tokyo War Crimes Trials: An International Symposium.* Tokyo: Kodansha, 1986.

Minnear, Richard. *Victor's Justice: The Tokyo War Crimes Trial.* Princeton, NJ: Princeton University Press, 1971.

Piccigallo, P.R. *The Japanese on Trial: Allied War Crimes Operations in the Far East 1945–1951.* Austin: University of Texas Press, 1979.

Historical Dilemmas

The Historical Dilemma section introduces students and researchers to debates and controversies in the study of certain genocides and atrocities. It presents a historical question with different perspectives on the issue, showing users not only how scholars utilize evidence to present their respective arguments, but how certain topics in genocide studies continue to be debated.

Was the Ukrainian Famine (The Holodomor of the Early 1930s) a Genocide?

Introduction

The Holodomor, a major 1932–1933 famine created by Soviet policies in Ukraine, led to an estimated death toll ranging from 3 to 7 million people. The Soviet Union, then under the rule of Joseph Stalin, implemented an array of social, economic, and political reforms across the country. This included the collectivization of agriculture, which meant the removal of the kulaks (small farmers) from Soviet society in an effort to create large state-owned farms. As part of these agricultural reforms, Soviet grain quotas, with much of the crop marked for export, were unusually high. As a result, after poor weather led to a subpar harvest in 1932, Soviet requisitions of Ukrainian grain stocks contributed to a massive food shortage. As part of an ideological drive to expand the Soviet economy and remove "class

enemies" from society, collectivization policies also overlooked the realities of Ukrainian food supplies, directly contributing to the famine.

The Holodomor continues to be an issue of historical controversy because there is no consensus within the international community on whether it is an instance of genocide as defined by the 1948 United Nations Convention on the Prevention and Punishment of the Crime of Genocide (UNCG). Much of this debate is around the issue of whether the Soviet regime implemented these policies with the intention of causing the deaths of Ukrainians through famine or whether it was merely consequential. Thus, this raises the question: Was the Ukrainian famine (the Holodomor of the early 1930s) a genocide?

In his Perspective Essay, Joshua Rubenstein states that the Soviet regime's collectivization policy and reluctance to assist the victims of famine in Ukraine was illustrative of its intent to murder the population. Rubenstein further argues that ideological considerations on the part of Joseph Stalin and Soviet officials shaped the policies that resulted in the Holodomor. Moreover, inaction, in and of itself, showed that the Soviet regime intended for the deliberate murder of Ukrainians in the famine. In his Perspective Essay, Bohdan Klid argues that the Holodomor fits the criteria of the UNCG. Klid states that one must consider that the wording of in Article 2 (c), "Deliberately inflicting on the group conditions of life calculated to bring about its physical destruction in whole or in part," fits the characteristics of the Holodomor. Lastly, in his Perspective Essay, Alexander Mikaberidze argues that despite the catastrophic famine in Ukraine, the Holodomor does not constitute an act of genocide given that it does not meet the UNCG legal definition of genocide.

Perspective 1: Deliberate Inaction

The numbers of the dead only begin to suggest the full scale of the horror that the Ukrainian people suffered during the killer famine of the early 1930s. Based on documentation that has become available since the collapse of the Soviet Union, it is now believed that in 1932 and 1933, between 3 to 5 million people died of starvation and diseases associated with the famine in Ukraine and in the northern Kuban, an area of southern Russia with a significant Ukrainian population. The famine was not a natural disaster. It was not the result of a severe drought, which can devastate an otherwise productive agricultural region. The famine that engulfed Ukraine was part of a broader disaster that affected the whole country and resulted in the total deaths of between 6 to 8 million people.

The regime's policies created this catastrophe. When the Bolsheviks took control of the Russian Empire in 1917, the population was still made up primarily of peasants who worked small plots of land. In order to overcome the country's economic backwardness, Soviet dictator Joseph Stalin decided to carry out a program of forced industrialization that would require the consolidation of peasant holdings into collective farms, thereby "encouraging" millions of peasants to move to the cities where they would become the workers and builders of a new Soviet industrial landscape. At the same time, the regime targeted richer peasants, the so-called kulaks, who were accused of owning more land and livestock than other peasant households; they were accused of resisting collectivization. With the beginning of the first Five-Year Plan and forced collectivization in 1928 and 1929, agricultural productivity and grain deliveries were already being disrupted, a process that accelerated as the regime collected a greater and greater portion of the harvest, as well as the seed grain that peasants needed to plant for the following year. As the peasants were left with inadequate wheat for themselves, they began to slaughter their livestock, in part for food for themselves but also because with less grain on hand, there was considerably less food for the animals.

Stalin particularly mistrusted Ukraine and the Ukrainian communities in northern Kuban. The Bolsheviks regarded the peasants as their natural opponents. They were culturally and economically backward, resistant to modernization, "counterrevolutionary." But Ukrainians were deeply attached to their own language and national culture, and it was the peasants who were seen as primarily responsible for celebrating and preserving Ukrainian national traditions.

This made Stalin all the more determined to impose collectivization on Ukraine, both to consolidate its small land holdings, but also to break the political and cultural dominance of the Ukrainian peasants in particular. As the growing lack of grain and food in general spread throughout the republic, starvation took hold. Local officials who were witnessing the spread of famine and starvation appealed to the Kremlin to relax its policies. But Stalin would not relent. On June 21, 1932, Stalin and Vyacheslav Molotov, the chairman of the Council of People's Commissars, made clear to officials in Ukraine that there was no turning back. "No manner of deviation—regarding either amounts or deadlines set for grain deliveries—can be permitted from the plan established for your region for collecting grain from collective and private farms or for delivering grain to state farms," they wrote. Any peasant who resisted was subject to arrest.

As the famine took hold and brought misery and mass death throughout Ukraine and the northern Kuban, tens of thousands of peasants left the region in search of food, crossing into Russia and other republics. Their presence provoked Stalin who complained that they were "demoralizing our collective farms with their complaints and whimpering." He ordered the sealing of the borders between Ukraine and Russia, not only to prevent Ukrainian peasants from seeking food supplies elsewhere in the country but also to prevent the rest of the country and the outside world from knowing the full details of the catastrophe. The regime employed draconian measures to enforce the isolation of Ukraine and control victims of the famine who were still alive from seeking assistance. In one typical month, February 1933, large units of secret police troops intercepted and arrested 220,000 Ukrainian peasants who were attempting to escape from their villages. An overwhelming proportion—190,000—were sent back home, essentially condemned to death. The remaining 30,000 were dispatched to the Gulag where the mortality rate was higher than usual during the famine years.

Still, there was the occasional witness. The writer Arthur Koestler had recently joined the communist party and came to the Soviet Union out of ideological commitment.

In his 1945 book, *The Yogi and the Commissar,* Koestler described how he spent the winter of 1932–1933 in Kharkov, which was the capital of Ukraine at the time. "The peasants had killed their cattle, burned or hidden their crops and were dying of starvation and typhoid. . . . the [train] stations were lined with begging peasants with swollen hands and feet, the women holding up to the carriage windows horrible infants with enormous wobbling heads, stick-like limbs, and swollen, pointed bellies." For Koestler, these famished children "looked like embryos out of alcohol bottles."

Part of the tragedy was the silence on the part of such witnesses. Koestler and others regarded the famine and other crimes as part of the necessary historical process of building socialism. It took several years before he would write honestly about what he had seen. He first had to quit the Communist Party and acknowledge to himself how and he his former comrades each carried "a skeleton in the cupboard of his conscience."

The scale of the famine was matched by the regime's merciless determination to do nothing to ameliorate conditions or to welcome support from outside the country. Even within Ukraine, the regime set up roadblocks to keep peasants away from the cities where there were at least some food reserves. Doctors and nurses were not allowed to treat or feed the starving who reached their clinics. And when famished peasants reached urban areas, they were often so weak that many collapsed and died on the streets. Officials quickly disposed of the bodies in order to insure that concrete evidence of the famine was neither documented nor acknowledged. There were even orders to round up hungry children and keep them out of sight.

Stalin and his colleagues on the Politburo were well aware of the scale of the suffering. In April 1933, when the Soviet writer Mikhail Sholokhov wrote to Stalin directly, urging him to intervene, Stalin dismissed his concerns out of hand. "The fact that this sabotage was silent and appeared to be quite peaceful (there was no bloodshed) changes nothing—these people deliberately tried to undermine the Soviet state. It is a fight to the death Comrade Sholokhov!" In Stalin's eyes, his victims were always at fault for their own suffering. The regime refused to suspend the export of grain or to release grain reserves, measures that could have limited the number of victims.

The regime's utter refusal to help the victims even as millions were succumbing to starvation reinforces the charge that the famine was an act of genocide. A dispute among scholars persists, however, on whether or not the Holodomor should be considered an act of genocide within the definition framed by the 1948 United Nations Genocide Convention. But Article 2 of the convention, which refers to the acts "committed with intent to destroy, in whole or in part, a national, ethnical, racial or religious group," includes a clause which forbids "deliberately inflicting on the group conditions of life calculated to bring about its physical destruction in whole or in part." The famine was the result of government policies and the same government could have taken measures to prevent or at least ameliorate the underlying reasons for such widespread and tragic starvation. Stalin's regime chose not to do so.

JOSHUA RUBENSTEIN

Perspective 2: Holodomor and UN Genocide Convention Criteria

The famine of 1932–1933 in Ukraine, called the Holodomor (a word coined in the late 1980s, meaning a famine deliberately initiated to cause suffering and death) can be considered genocide according to the 1948 United Nations Convention on the Prevention and Punishment of the Crime of Genocide (UNCG) in light of Article 2 (c). This clause identifies as genocide deliberate actions that create conditions of life leading to the physical destruction in whole or in part of a national, ethnic, religious or racial group.

The famine in Ukraine began in late 1931 during the Soviet Union's first Five-Year plan, which called for rapid industrialization and the forced collectivization of agriculture. During the collectivization drive that began in 1929, private farms were abolished, and in their place state-owned and collective farms were established. Ostensibly run by the collective farmers themselves, the collective farms were actually controlled and monitored by Soviet or Communist Party officials. At the same time, successful, well off-farmers, labeled kulaks (according to the Soviet regime, these were exploiters of poorer peasants), were persecuted, stripped of their possessions, arrested and deported. Many were sent to far-off lands, and some were even executed. In practice, any farmer opposed to collectivization, even if not well off, was often labeled a kulak or kulak supporter.

Most peasants (subsistence and small-scale farmers) in the Soviet Union were reluctant to give up private farming to join the new collectives. In Ukraine, which had a strong tradition of private farming, resistance was particularly strong. In some cases, Ukrainian peasants and urban dwellers resented collectivization and other policies that emanated from Moscow. Reaction to these policies reinforced sentiment for more autonomy or even independence for Ukraine. Ukrainians had established an independent state in 1918, but this attempt at achieving full-fledged statehood failed by 1920 owing mainly to military intervention from Communist Russia. In 1922, Ukraine became incorporated into the Soviet Union as a republic, retaining nominal forms of statehood and autonomy.

The establishment of state and collective farms in the Soviet Union was justified by its leaders as an essential part of building socialism. Soviet officials also considered them more reliable than individual farms as sources of surplus grain production, which was to fulfill compulsory state grain collection quotas. Grain collected by the state was used to feed the rapidly growing urban population, and for exports to finance purchases of machinery abroad to support the industrialization drive. However, the collectivization of agriculture led to chaos and a drop in farm production in Ukraine, which was a key grain-producing area in the Soviet Union. Despite this, the Soviet leadership maintained high quotas for Ukraine's farmers to deliver grain to the state.

When famine broke out in Ukraine—triggered by confiscatory measures taken by Soviet officials to fulfill unrealistically high grain collection targets in the wake of the substantial drop in agricultural production—top Soviet Ukrainian government leaders informed the Kremlin of starvation, requesting aid and a reduction in the grain quota for the country. The Soviet leader, Joseph Stalin, called instead for an intensification of grain collection efforts. He also voiced his distrust of Ukrainian officials, suspecting many of them as nationalists, and expressed fear that opposition to his policies in Ukraine could intensify, possibly leading to Ukraine's secession from the Soviet Union.

Stalin's response was catastrophic for Ukraine. Under his urging, the Soviet leadership passed draconian laws and adopted punitive and repressive policies, ostensibly to help meet the grain quota. Special teams were sent to the countryside, headed by Stalin's top lieutenants, to collect more grain, even though farmers had little stored for the winter and spring months ahead. Even seed grain was taken, and fines in meat and potatoes were instituted for those who had not fulfilled the grain collection plan. Other foodstuffs were also confiscated by search squads.

Unsurprisingly, the situation in the Ukrainian countryside became desperate by winter. But the regime did not relent from its policies of confiscation, punishment and repression. On January 22, 1933, in response to large numbers of hungry Ukrainian farmers leaving their villages in search of food, primarily to Russia, the Soviet leadership issued an order prohibiting their departure from the republic. Around the same time, Stalin began replacing some of Ukraine's leaders and changed state policy that had supported the development and use of the Ukrainian language. A campaign of persecution and destruction of many Ukrainian intellectuals and officials who were accused of being Ukrainian nationalists also began.

The famine in Ukraine subsided in summer 1933 as that year's harvest was gathered. By that time, resistance in the countryside had been broken. Demographers estimate that close to 4 million residents of Ukraine, mostly Ukrainian peasants, perished as a direct result of starvation.

Any discussion of the famine as genocide should begin with a review of the ideas of Raphael Lemkin, a legal scholar who was the "father" of the UN's genocide convention. In a speech delivered in 1953, he called the USSR's policies toward Ukraine under Stalin "the classic example of Soviet genocide." He viewed the famine in Ukraine as a key component of what he called the "Ukrainian genocide," which he understood as a series of actions that also included the destruction and subjugation of Ukraine's intellectuals and political elite, the liquidation of the independent Ukrainian Orthodox Church, and the government-directed settlement of Ukraine's farmlands by non-Ukrainians, which took place in the wake of the famine of 1932–1933.

In assessing the charge of genocide, one should recognize that it carries legal and political implications, and thus could be controversial. Political figures and entities have sometimes made statements or offered opinions on specific cases where the question of genocide has been raised. This is true of the famine in Ukraine. In 1988, a special commission of the U.S. Congress established to investigate the Ukrainian famine concluded that "Joseph Stalin and those around him committed genocide against Ukrainians in 1932–33." In 2006, Ukraine's legislature, the Verkhovna Rada, adopted a law that called the Holodomor genocide. Some countries, like Canada, have adopted resolutions or statements recognizing the Holodomor as genocide. However, Russia's national legislature, the Duma, stressed in a declaration that famine in these years was a pan-Soviet tragedy and denied that the Ukrainian situation was specific.

Controversy can also occur because of a lack of consensus among scholars. There is general agreement among scholars that the Holodomor resulted from the actions of Soviet authorities and was thus man-made and avoidable. However, some scholars as well as political figures have argued that the charge of genocide in Ukraine cannot be substantiated because famine occurred at the same time in other republics of the Soviet Union, including Russia. It has also been argued that the famine was used as a weapon aimed against peasants as a social group, and not against Ukrainians as an ethnic group. Two scholars of the Soviet Union, Robert E. Davies and Stephen G. Wheatcroft, have argued that the Soviet leadership caused the famine partly through "wrongheaded policies," but that it was "unexpected and undesirable." The famine, they argue, was "a consequence of the decision to industrialize this peasant country [the Soviet Union] at breakneck speed."

The Italian scholar Andrea Graziosi, in support of the genocide interpretation, has argued that in assessing the issue one must take into account the extremely high mortality rate in Ukraine—triple the mortality rate in Russia. This was caused by the additional measures taken by Soviet authorities that intensified the famine in Ukraine. Graziosi also stresses Stalin's understanding of the peasant and national questions as closely linked in largely peasant-based countries like Ukraine. He thus concludes that the Ukrainian villages were "indeed targeted to break the peasants, but with the full awareness that the village represented the nation's spine."

There are other arguments to be made in favor of the genocide interpretation. Grain exports continued during the worst months of the famine, and Soviet government reserves contained enough grain to feed the starving. When aid was first authorized in February 1933, it was selective, and not nearly enough grain was released to save millions from starvation. The mobility of Ukraine's peasants was blocked through the January 22, 1933, decree depriving them of possible access to food in other regions of the Soviet Union. It is also clear that Stalin in 1932 was worried about losing Ukraine, tied the shortfall in grain collections in Ukraine to perceived failures of the republic's leadership, and referred to this to justify removing some of Ukraine's leaders when he replaced them with loyal followers. He also saw resistance in the Ukrainian countryside to grain collection as motivated by both class antagonisms and nationalism. If one considers the anti-Ukrainian measures he promoted, including authorizing persecutions of Ukrainian intellectuals and of the more nationally oriented political leadership, the overall antinational thrust of Stalin's decisions in 1932–1933 becomes more evident.

Finally, news of the famine was suppressed in the Soviet Union, offers of outside aid were refused, and until the late 1980s the Soviet government denied that a famine had even taken place.

BOHDAN KLID

Perspective 3: Intentionality and the Holodomor

The Holodomor was not a genocide. The famine was clearly man-made in the sense that it would not have occurred without unattainable grain procurement quotas that the Soviet authorities established and enforced. However, it does not meet strict legal definition of genocide under the 1948 United Nation's Convention on the Prevention and Punishment of the Crime of Genocide.

The Holodomor, a large scale famine created by the Soviet government in the Ukrainian Soviet Socialist Republic and other parts of the Soviet Union, is estimated to have claimed at least 4 million lives in Ukraine alone. While general outline of events of the Holodomor has been widely acknowledged, interpretation of facts continues to elicit contrasting responses and sustains a bitter divide between Ukraine and Russia. In November 2006 the Ukrainian parliament approved the "Law on the Holodomor in Ukraine in 1932–1933" that declared Holodomor as an "act of genocide against the Ukrainian people." The Russian Federation condemned this law and issued its statement acknowledging historical facts of mass deaths in Ukraine and other parts of the Soviet Union but rejecting their characterization as a genocide.

So was the Holodomor a genocide? To answer this question, we must first turn to legal definition of a genocide. In 1948, the UN approved the Convention on the Prevention and Punishment of the Crime of Genocide (UNCG). The convention's Article 2 defined defines genocide as "any of the following acts committed with intent to destroy, in whole or in part, a national, ethnical, racial or religious group, such as killing members of the group; causing serious bodily or mental harm to members of the group; deliberately inflicting on the group conditions of life, calculated to bring about its physical destruction in whole or in part; imposing measures intended to prevent births within the group; forcibly transferring children of the group to another group."

This article sits at the heart of legal definition of genocide. Listing just five punishable acts, it offers a rather narrow classification of genocide and leaves out many atrocities that due to the nature of their crimes can be easily considered as genocidal. It is, thus, very important to keep in mind these preconditions and limitations because, legally speaking, not all events involving mass slaughter and atrocities can be considered genocides. Everything depends on how strict or relaxed legal interpretation of crime of genocide is.

If we examine the famine through the prism of strict legal definition, we will find that while the constituent elements of genocide—"killing," "inflicting serious bodily or mental harm," "deliberately inflicting on the group conditions of life"—are present in the Holodomor, the event as a whole does not constitute a genocide. In this respect two issues are fundamental to the legal crime of genocide: criminal intent and extent. During the Holodomor, the Soviet government had no "intent to destroy" Ukrainian ethnicity-nationality but rather pursued a series of broad policies that aimed at collectivization, dekulakization, and suppression of nationalist tendencies that could threaten the unity of the Soviet Union. When they initiated the collectivization policy, Joseph Stalin and his colleagues in the Soviet government did not intend to massacre millions of Ukrainian peasants because they were Ukrainian. Instead, Soviet leaders' ignorance of agricultural reality and peasants' abilities, not to mention overly optimistic assessment of their own policies, played decisive role in the making of this catastrophe. When discussing the Holodomor, it is important to bear in mind that Stalin and his colleagues had been deeply entrenched in Marxism and subscribed to the class-historical approach. They regarded peasants as "second-class citizens" and genuinely believed in the "class war" waged by "enemy classes" that transcended national, ethnical, racial or religious boundaries.

The UN Convention on Genocide specifies that the crime of genocide involves "intent to destroy, in whole or in part, a national, ethnical, racial or religious group." Yet, the victims of the Holodomor were not limited to just one national, ethnical, racial, or religious group. The Soviet policy of collectivization and dekulakization provoked fierce resistance among many ethnic groups Ukrainians, who had a long tradition of individuality and personal independence. It is certain that the Soviet authorities used these policies to undermine nationalist tendencies (affluent peasants traditionally fostered strong national feelings), but this was not applied exclusively to Ukraine, and other Soviet republics had been subjected to them as well. Although the term Holodomor is associated with in Ukraine, the famine did not spare non-Ukrainians either.

Within Ukraine, Moldavian, Russian, Polish, German, and Bulgarian populations suffered in the same proportion as the rural Ukrainian population. Furthermore, the famine was not limited to Ukraine itself but rather extended to the Don and Kuban areas of North Caucasus, the Volga basin, parts of Kazakhstan and Western Siberia; in fact, chronologically Kazakhstan was first to be affected by famine, which caused even greater suffering among the local nomadic herders than among sedentary Ukrainian peasants, though the loss of life in absolute numbers was not as high as in Ukraine.

In the Volga basin, the Soviet policies had a devastating impact on the population of mixed ethnic origins, with the Volga Germans (who had been settled here in the 18th century) being among the most affected. It is estimated that at least 1 million people had perished during the Holodomor in Kazakhstan and North Caucasus. Some of these regions were still recovering from the devastating Povolzhye famine of 1921, which was also largely caused by the Soviet government's "Prodrazvyorstka" campaign of confiscation of grain and other agricultural produce, and claimed at least 1.5–2 million lives. In rejecting the Holodomor's characterization as genocide, the Russian government has repeatedly pointed out that among the affected by the famine were non-Ukrainians, including tens of thousands of ethnic Russians. Thus the question is how one should treat these non-Ukrainian victims of the famine since current legal definition of genocide revolves around "national, ethnical, racial or religious" identity of the victim group. This issue becomes particularly important when discussion touches upon the issue of intent. Genocide requires establishing the highest level of specific intent of destroying a particular group. Yet, evidence for such an intent is not solid. For example, the Soviet government did impose a special migration ban on areas largely inhabited by the Ukrainians but the Soviet secret police did not differentiate between Ukrainians and non-Ukrainians, preventing all of them from leaving the famine-stricken areas.

The next question we must consider is whether one can speak of genocide when most of the victim group survives. The UN Convention specifically refers to the destruction of a group "in whole or in part." The Holodomor claimed at least 4 million lives in Ukraine but, tragic as this number is, it represents a relatively small proportion (roughly a tenth) of the total Ukrainian population. Yet contemporary case law and jurisprudence remain divided on the meaning of "in part" element of the legal definition. In 2001, the International Criminal Tribunal for the Former Yugoslavia considered the issue of whether the destruction 'in part' of the group constitutes a genocide. It ruled that:

"the intent to destroy a group, even if only in part, means seeking to destroy a distinct part of the group as opposed to an accumulation of isolated individuals within it. Although the perpetrators of genocide need not seek to destroy the entire group protected by the Convention, they must view the part of the group they wish to destroy as a distinct entity which must be eliminated as such. A campaign resulting in the killings, in different places spread over a broad geographical area, of a finite number of members of the protected group might not thus qualify as genocide, despite the high total number of casualties, because it would not show an intent by the perpetrators to target the very existence of the group as such."

This case law thus rules out characterization of the Ukrainian Starvation as a genocide: although the famine involved "a broad geographical area," it was not an attempt to "target the very existence" of the Ukrainians "as such" and the overwhelming majority of Ukrainians had survived it.

In final analysis, whether the Holodomor was a genocide depends on how "genocide" is defined. Based on a strict legal interpretation of the UN Genocide Convention, this mass atrocity does not meet legal preconditions of a genocide but does clearly constitute a series of crimes against humanity. Current legal definition of genocide is too narrow and most probably it was intentionally designed so. In his recent history of Eastern Europe, Timothy Snyder of Yale University argued that the Soviet government "made sure that the term genocide, contrary to Lemkin's intentions, excluded political and economic groups." Thus the Ukrainian famine can be presented as "somehow less genocidal because it targeted a class, kulaks."

This technicality, however, should not obscure the fact that millions of people had lost their lives as the result of Soviet government's actions. Genocide or not, the Holodomor represents a human tragedy of enormous scale.

ALEXANDER MIKABERIDZE

Did the Indian Wars Constitute Genocide?

Introduction

On December 29, 1890, a confrontation erupted between soldiers of the U.S. 7th Cavalry, led by Colonel James Forsyth, and a group of Lakota Sioux under Spotted Elk who had been moved to Wounded Knee Creek, South Dakota,

and disarmed. When it was all over, more than 150 Indians had been killed, many of them women and children. This image depicts a mass burial of the victims on January 1, 1891.

The Wounded Knee Massacre is generally considered to be the culminating event of the Indian Wars. This protracted conflict, which began in colonial times, saw a precipitous decline in the Native American population, perhaps by as much as 98 percent. Although it is clear that American Indians suffered in the face of first white colonialism and, later, U.S. expansionism, scholars continue to disagree on the question of whether or not the Indian Wars constituted genocide as we understand the term today.

In his essay, Dr. Jim Piecuch asserts that the Indian Wars did indeed constitute genocide. Beginning in colonial times, he highlights a number of important events, including the Pequot War, King Philip's War, the Trail of Tears, the Sand Creek Massacre, and the Battle of Wounded Knee. Taking a slightly different approach, Dr. Justin Murphy uses Raphael Lemkin's broader definition to argue that the Indian Wars represent cultural genocide. He examines the ways in which Indians were deprived of land and economic resources and forced to adopt white cultural practices. By contrast, Dr. Jerry Morelock argues that the Indian Wars were not genocide, but rather a clash of two entrenched, incompatible cultures. He believes that to call them genocide is a gross oversimplification and demonstrates a seriously flawed understanding of what was a complex interaction of multiple cultures.

Perspective 1: Three Centuries of Genocide

Between 1607 and 1890, one of the greatest acts of genocide in human history occurred as European colonists and their descendants nearly exterminated the native population in the territory of the future United States. In 1492, an estimated 4.4 million Native Americans inhabited the portion of the Americas north of Mexico, with the vast majority living in the area south of present-day Canada. By 1890, the Native population of the United States had been reduced to about 250,000. The attitudes and policies that resulted in the annihilation of millions of the original North American inhabitants, and millions more born during the four centuries since Europeans began colonizing the Americas, was established in the early years of the colonial period and continued virtually without interruption until the last Native resistance was crushed in 1890.

When English colonists established their country's first permanent settlement in North America at Jamestown, Virginia, in 1607, the natives had already suffered serious population losses. Spanish expeditions into the southeastern United States and Spain's subsequent colonization of Florida had introduced diseases such as smallpox, to which the natives had no natural immunity, sparking waves of epidemics across the continent. Violent assaults on the natives and slave raids to supply labor for Spain's Caribbean colonies took a further toll.

Thirteen years later, English settlers at Plymouth encountered a similarly decimated native population. Colonist Robert Cushman estimated that only 1 native out of 20 remained alive in the area. Although the colonists cannot be directly blamed for the epidemics that ravaged the native population, they were able to take advantage of the social and political chaos that such high mortality rates produced in native society.

As they embarked on the colonization of North America, the English had at hand a well-known lesson of how not to treat the natives. Bartoleme de las Casas, the Spanish priest who in the 16th century had fought a long and largely futile battle to defend the natives of Spanish America, had chronicled in gory detail the ruthless violence with which the Spaniards treated the natives. One of Las Casas's accounts was translated into English with the title *Tears of the Indians.* English advocates of colonization attempted "to define their colonial ventures in opposition to [the Spanish] model" and urged a policy of kindness toward the natives.

These ideals conflicted with the colonists' other goals. Although the Virginia settlers had been ordered "not to Offend the naturals," they were also supposed to establish England's title to the land and find ways to make a profit. The colonists therefore showed little respect for the Powhatans' land ownership, considering native rights to the territory no more than "temporary . . . impediments to the superior 'civil' claims" of the English.

Violence against the Native Americans and seizure of their lands were justified in English eyes by the natives' inferiority. John Smith, one of the leaders of the Virginia Colony, described the Powhatan Confederacy that inhabited the shores of Chesapeake Bay and its tributaries as "inconstant in everything but what fear constraineth them to keep. Crafty, timorous, quick of apprehension, and very ingenuous. Some are of disposition fearful, some bold some cautelous [deceitful], all savage . . . They are soon moved to anger, and so malicious that they seldom forget an injury."

As Smith made clear, the natives' very inferiority—their savagery and cunning—made them dangerous to the English.

The English colonists' sense of inherent superiority led them to demonstrate a callous disregard for native lives. When their own provisions ran out as a result of laziness and neglecting agriculture in favor of seeking nonexistent gold, the Virginians resorted to force to obtain food from the native Powhatans. Armed parties burned native towns, tortured and killed natives, and carried off what they wanted.

Such practices, along with the seizure of native lands, prompted Powhatan retaliation and resulted in three Anglo-Powhatan wars that ended in 1646 with the complete defeat of the natives. The brutalities committed by the English included throwing native children into the James River and shooting them in the head as they struggled to stay afloat; killing 200 Powhatans during peace negotiations by giving them poisoned wine, and massacring the 50 survivors on May 18, 1623; and repeatedly employing what became customary English practice: devastating the natives' dwellings and food supplies. Less than 40 years after the English landed at Jamestown, the Powhatans, who had numbered some 14,000 in 1607, were decimated. The English confined the few survivors to small reservations.

A similar attitude of superiority toward the natives prevailed in New England, where

Puritan settlers in the Connecticut River Valley came into conflict with the Pequot Nation of some 3,000 natives. War broke out in 1636, and the next year a New England expedition brutally destroyed a Pequot village. Captain John Mason, leader of the New England troops, noted that "we had formerly concluded to destroy them by the sword," and he achieved his goal. After setting the village afire, the colonists slaughtered the Pequots as they fled, killing between 400 and 700, including women and children.

The colonists killed more Pequots "in massacres or mass executions," until the survivors signed the Treaty of Hartford in 1638. The treaty dissolved the Pequot Nation and achieved Mason's goal "to cut off remembrance of them from the earth." The destruction of as many as 2,000 Pequots and the dissolution of their nation by the English have been characterized as genocide by many scholars.

Less than 40 years later, the remaining New England tribes were nearly annihilated in King Philip's War. As the colonies expanded onto native territory and forced the natives to accept English authority, Wampanoag leader Metacom, called King Philip by the English, attempted to defend what remained of his people's land and autonomy. The war began in June 1675. Despite some success, the natives quickly found themselves facing an English counteroffensive that resulted in several massacres. The largest of these occurred in Rhode Island, where the English surrounded an estimated 3,000 to 4,000 Narragansetts, mostly women and children, and slaughtered as many as 2,000. Fighting subsided with Metacom's death in August 1676. Hundreds of captured natives were sold into slavery in the West Indies. Many of those who avoided death or capture fled north or west to escape the English. Meanwhile, the English justified the carnage as simple self-defense against a savage enemy.

The destruction of the natives of Virginia and New England in the 17th century, without regard for age or gender, established a pattern that was repeated over the next two centuries. Native nations that responded to English abuse and encroachments with force, such as the Tuscaroras in North Carolina in 1711 and the Yamasees in South Carolina four years later, were ruthlessly crushed. Other conflicts between the English and Native Americans were absorbed into the larger struggle between England and France that began in 1689. Many natives allied with the French, while some believed that the best chance for survival lay in aiding the English. Native involvement in the imperial wars cost thousands of lives, and when France was defeated and ousted from North America in 1763, Native Americans could no longer rely on that nation's assistance to stem the westward expansion of the British colonies.

In a desperate effort to reverse the British ascendancy, Pontiac of the Ottawa Nation led a coordinated native offensive against British posts in the Great Lakes region in 1763. The natives failed to secure a decisive victory; however, Pontiac's Rebellion convinced British officials to change their policy toward the natives. The Royal Proclamation of 1763 forbade colonial settlement west of the Appalachians and gave British Indian agents more authority to halt trade abuses. The new British policy earned the goodwill of the natives but incurred the wrath of the colonists whose desire for native land appeared limitless. Britain's conciliatory efforts resulted in most native nations supporting the British during the American Revolution. Once again, the natives suffered heavy losses in lives and land only to find themselves on the losing side. Yet even those native nations that supported the Americans benefited little. The Oneidas, one of the six nations that composed the Iroquois Confederacy, allied with the revolutionaries only to have most of their land taken by the state of New York without their consent.

Freed from the constraints of British imperial policy, the independent United States resumed westward expansion at the natives' expense. After two humiliating defeats in 1790 and 1791, American forces triumphed over a coalition of Native American nations in 1794. In the wake of this disaster, Tecumseh of the Shawnees arose as a new native leader. His knowledge of the Americans' treachery, including the slaughter of 90 Christian natives of the Delaware Nation at Gnadenhutten, Pennsylvania, in 1782, convinced Tecumseh that the natives' survival depended on uniting to resist the Americans.

Tecumseh succeeded in uniting several native nations and assisted the British in the War of 1812. He was killed at the Battle of the Thames in 1813, and with him died Native American hopes of continuing resistance to the United States in the north. In 1814, Andrew Jackson ended native opposition in the south when he killed some 800 Creeks at Horseshoe Bend, Alabama. Jackson had the assistance of several hundred natives, but this effort to avoid destruction by allying with the Americans proved futile. Jackson imposed a punitive treaty upon the Creeks in 1814, forcing them to cede 23 million acres of land to the United States. He ignored the protests of those Creeks who had aided him in his campaign. When Jackson became president in 1829 he convinced Congress to approve his "Indian removal" policy. Tens of thousands of Creeks, Choctaws, Chickasaws, Seminoles, and Cherokees were relocated to Indian Territory (present-day Oklahoma). The Cherokees, who had labored the hardest to adopt American culture, suffered the most. Some 4,000 Cherokees, perhaps one-fourth of the nation's population, died while being forcibly rounded up and marched westward along the "Trail of Tears."

Having killed or removed all but a few scattered remnants of Native Americans east of the Mississippi River, Americans turned their eyes farther westward. As settlers, traders, and prospectors began occupying native lands, conflicts resulted. From 1849 to 1881, the U.S. Army fought 1,073 battles against the natives to suppress resistance and force land cessions. Additional battles were fought between natives and settlers and between the army and natives from 1881 to 1890.

Many of these battles were fought without regard for accepted rules of warfare. Little effort was made to distinguish between peaceful and warring Native American nations, or to spare noncombatants or prisoners. Army commanders set the tone for the behavior of their troops. Lieutenant General William T. Sherman, commander of the U.S. Army, declared that his soldiers should "get them [natives] out as soon as possible, and it makes little difference whether they be coaxed out . . . or killed."

Encouraged by such attitudes, soldiers and civilians slaughtered large numbers of natives. In 1864, troops under Colonel John Chivington attacked a peaceful band of some 650 Cheyennes and Arapahos at Sand Creek, Colorado. The natives, who were ostensibly under the protection of the U.S. government, lost 28 men killed and 105 women and children. Most of the native dead were scalped and many of the bodies mutilated, the soldiers displaying body parts as trophies.

Other Native American nations suffered similar attacks. Learning that some 200 Apaches had surrendered, been disarmed, and were at Camp Grant in present-day Arizona, Tucson residents mounted an attack in 1871 that killed 144 natives, the majority of them women and children. Twenty-eight captured children were sold into slavery in Mexico. Such events continued until the final battle of the Indian Wars at Wounded Knee, South Dakota. There, on December 29, 1890, a Lakota band of some 350 people attempting to surrender were fired on by soldiers after a scuffle broke out while the natives were being disarmed. As many as 300 natives were killed.

Natives who remained peaceful or surrendered found themselves little better off than those who died resisting the Americans. Leaders such as Mangas Coloradas of the Apaches and Crazy Horse and Sitting Bull of the Lakotas were murdered in captivity or on the reservations. Apache leader Geronimo and many of his warriors were imprisoned in Florida, where over 100 died. Thousands of Nez Perce, Cheyennes, Poncas, and others were forcibly relocated to Oklahoma, where large numbers perished. Eventually some native nations were allotted reservations on small portions of their original lands.

When the Wounded Knee Massacre brought the fighting between Native Americans and the United States to a close, the native population had reached its nadir. From an estimated 600,000 in 1800, it had been reduced in the span of 90 years to about 250,000. Of the roughly 4 million people who had inhabited the region that became the United States in 1492, and their descendants born over the next four centuries, only a fraction remained. Much of the destruction of the native population can be attributed to the introduction of Old World diseases. However, any chance at population recovery was eliminated by the English colonists and their heirs in the independent United States, whose policies accelerated the decline. Having

characterized the natives as inferior and impediments to their own vision of progress, the newcomers produced a "holocaust of North American Indians" resulting in "millions of deaths." The destruction of so many native people, carried out over nearly three centuries, constitutes nothing less than genocide. The fact that several thousand natives survived, as did many intended Jewish victims of Nazi genocide in the 1940s, does not mitigate the crime.

JIM PIECUCH

Perspective 2: Cultural Genocide of Native American Peoples

Determining whether the Indian Wars constituted genocide is complicated by the tendency to use the Holocaust as a basis for comparison. It is important, therefore, to begin by examining the definition of genocide as first developed by Raphael Lemkin, a Polish Jewish lawyer who had fled to the United States in 1939 and in 1944 published *Axis Rule in Occupied Europe: Laws of Occupation, Analysis of Government, Proposals for Redress.* Lemkin coined the term "genocide" from the Greek word *genos,* which means "tribe or race," and the Latin word *cide,* which means "killing," to denote the mass extermination of Jews in the Holocaust. Lemkin did not restrict the definition of genocide to the mass extermination of a race, but instead provided a much broader definition:

Generally speaking, genocide does not necessarily mean the immediate destruction of a nation, except when accomplished by mass killings of all members of a nation. It is intended rather to signify a coordinated plan of different actions aiming at the destruction of essential foundations of the life of national groups, with the aim of annihilating the groups themselves. The objectives of such a plan would be disintegration of the political and social institutions, of culture, language, national feelings, religion, and the economic existence of national groups, and the destruction of the personal security, liberty, health, dignity, and even the lives of the individuals belonging to such groups. Genocide is directed against the national group as an entity, and the actions involved are directed against individuals, not in their individual capacity, but as members of the national group.

By applying Lemkin's broader definition of genocide and considering the broader policies toward Native Americans, this essay will argue that the Indian Wars constituted cultural genocide.

The policies the United States pursued toward Native Americans followed a pattern similar to that established when the first English colonists arrived in North America. At first Native Americans welcomed colonists for the trade goods they provided, while colonists depended on Native Americans for food. In addition, some tribes saw the English as allies against enemy tribes. For example, when the Puritans began arriving in the Massachusetts Bay Colony in 1629, the Narragansetts and other smaller tribes sought an alliance with the Puritans against the Pequots, a powerful tribe that had recently entered the region and encroached upon Narragansett hunting lands. When the Pequot War broke out in 1636, the Puritans saw the Pequots as enemies of God and descended upon them with a fury that shocked their Indian allies. After surrounding the chief Pequot village on the Mystic River on May 26, 1637, the Puritans and their native allies set fire to the village and killed some 400–700 men, women, and children. The Puritans emerged from the Pequot War as the leading power in New England and, 40 years later in King Philip's War (1676–1677), effectively destroyed the Narragansetts as an independent tribe. To the extent that the policies of the Puritans toward the Pequots and Narragansetts resulted in their virtual annihilation, they meet the standards of Lemkin's definition of genocide.

The most important factor that created conflict between English colonists and Native Americans was the seizure of Indian lands as the colonial population expanded westward. Although a few colonial leaders advocated purchasing Indian lands, the overall English practice was simply to take them without compensation. This pattern of land seizure also demonstrates that the English, unlike the French and Spanish, made little effort to incorporate Native Americans into colonial society. Although Puritan missionary John Eliot was an exception in attempting to convert Native Americans to Christianity, it is important to note that native converts were segregated into "praying towns" and forced to adopt English cultural customs. By depriving Native Americans of their ancestral hunting lands, upon which their economic existence and culture depended, or forcing them to convert and adopt white culture in order to remain on their lands, these policies amount to cultural genocide by Lemkin's standards.

Great Britain's defeat of the French in the French and Indian War marked a major turning point in the relationship between Native Americans and colonists. With the French forced to cede Canada and all their lands east of the Mississippi to Great Britain and the Louisiana Territory to Spain, all the tribes east of the Mississippi were in a far weaker position. Although the British issued the Proclamation of 1763, forbidding white expansion beyond the Appalachian Mountains in an effort to prevent Indian unrest, enforcing the proclamation was a different matter. White encroachments on Indian land in Kentucky and the Ohio Valley resulted in Lord Dunmore's War against the Shawnees and their allies in 1774. Although the American Revolution brought a temporary respite for Native Americans, Lord Dunmore's War clearly demonstrated what would become a recurring pattern over the next century—the inability of governing authorities to prevent white settlers on the frontier from encroaching on Indian lands.

The success of the United States in achieving its independence placed Native Americans in a far more precarious position because, through the Treaty of Paris of 1783, the United States gained sovereignty over the land south of the Great Lakes and east of the Mississippi River (excluding Florida, which went to Spain). Tribes soon discovered that the federal structure of the U.S. Constitution meant that they had to contend not only with the federal government but also with state governments. In addition, the federal government was ineffective in forcing white settlers to abide by treaties negotiated with tribes. States often pursued their own policies against Native Americans, especially in regard to Indian lands, often in contradiction to the federal government.

Perhaps nothing better symbolizes the relationship between the United States and Native Americans than the decision of the first Congress in 1789 to place relations with Indian tribes under the jurisdiction of the War Department rather than the State Department. It clearly revealed that the United States regarded tribes to be in a subordinate position whereby the United States reserved the right to impose terms by military force. With the exception of three military campaigns in the Old Northwest during the early 1790s, however, the War Department generally succeeded in avoiding armed conflict with Native Americans during the first two decades by negotiating treaties that secured title to Indian lands. At the same time, the War Department controlled trade with Native Americans through the so-called factory system, whereby it licensed traders to trade with specific tribes. One of President George Washington's goals in promoting the factory system was to introduce white culture to tribes and encourage them to turn from hunting to agriculture. Assimilation was therefore a stated objective of federal policy and it involved compelling Native Americans to change their culture so they could coexist with whites.

After President Thomas Jefferson's administration successfully negotiated the Louisiana Purchase, the prospect of removing Eastern tribes to west of the Mississippi gradually emerged as a new aspect of federal policy. In an 1803 letter to William Henry Harrison, governor of the Indiana Territory, Jefferson expressed the goal of Indian policy to be promoting trade with Native Americans so that their indebtedness would force them to cede lands to the point that they were so surrounded by whites that they would have to choose between becoming citizens or removing west of the Mississippi. At the same time, Jefferson prevailed upon Congress to provide funds whereby Native Americans could be assimilated by inducing them to abandon hunting and adopt agriculture.

In 1819, Congress established the Civilization Fund for Indian education, dispensing funds through missionary organizations such as the American Board of Commissioners for Foreign Missions, which established missions and schools among Native Americans. While many of the tribes of the Old Northwest would resist under the leadership of Shawnee war chief Tecumseh in an attempt to preserve their way of life, the five leading Southern tribes—the Cherokees, Choctaws, Chickasaws, Creeks, and Seminoles—actively adopted aspects of white culture, including plantation agriculture, black slavery, schools, churches, newspapers, and written laws and constitutions. These "Five Civilized Tribes," however, were sharply divided as factions sought to retain their traditional hunting lifestyle. This resulted in conflicts with white settlers, leading to the Creek War during 1813–1814 and a series of Seminole Wars, but also produced what amounted to a civil war within the tribes themselves.

President Andrew Jackson's election in 1828 made the shift to removal as the preferred policy official with the passage of the controversial Indian Removal Act in 1830. The Cherokees resisted the Indian Removal Act and Georgia's extension of state jurisdiction over Cherokee lands by filing suit in the U.S. Supreme Court. In *The Cherokee Nation v. Georgia* (1831), Chief Justice John Marshall ruled that Native American tribes were "domestic dependent nations" that were not sovereign entities but were subject to the jurisdiction of the United States with tribal members being in the position of federal wards.

Although Jackson has been vilified for the tragic "Trail of Tears," in which approximately 25 percent of Cherokees, Choctaws, Chickasaws, Creeks, and Seminoles died of exposure and starvation during their forced removal to Indian Territory, these deaths were the result of the policy's flawed implementation rather than a stated objective of the policy per se. In addition, F. P. Prucha forcefully argues in "Andrew Jackson's Indian Policy: A Reassessment" that Jackson's policy was not based on hatred of Indians, but was more a practical matter of denying dual sovereignty. Those Indians who were ready to enter white society could remain behind and become citizens, while those who wished to retain their tribal identity could do so by removing to Indian Territory, where they would gain the time to evolve further on the path to civilization, which in Jackson's view was essential to prevent their extinction. The "Trail of Tears" does not quite meet Lemkin's standard of genocide, and the extent to which tribes were allowed to retain their identity, albeit by removal, does not quite meet Lemkin's standard of cultural genocide.

The annexation of Texas in 1845, the acquisition of the Oregon Territory in 1846, and the Mexican Cession following the Mexican-American War marked the beginning of the Indian Wars that ended with the Battle of Wounded Knee in 1890. There were numerous individual actions that in themselves can be considered genocide. By far the most infamous was the Sand Creek Massacre on November 29, 1864, when Colorado militiamen under Colonel John M. Chivington attached Cheyenne chief Black Kettle's peaceful village of 500 Indians. Even though Black Kettle vainly waved an American flag and white flag from his lodge, Chivington's troops ruthlessly slaughtered at least 300 individuals.

Although the Indian Wars against the Plains Indians and the Apaches and Navajos in the Southwest do not necessarily meet Lemkin's standard of genocide in that there was not a systematic attempt of mass extermination, there are many aspects of federal Indian policy that do meet Lemkin's broader definition in that there was a systematic attempt to destroy Native American culture. Ironically, many of those who promoted this effort were well-intentioned reformers, such as Senator Henry L. Dawes of Massachusetts, Editor Lyman Abbot of the *Christian Union,* and Reverend F. F. Ellinwood of the Presbyterian Board of Foreign Missions. Along with other reformers, they met numerous times beginning in the 1880s. Committing themselves to save Native Americans from extinction, they launched a "reform" movement designed "to destroy traditional Indian life by dissolving all tribal bonds, ending the practice of communal land ownership, overthrowing native religions, and eradicating traditional social customs." Their efforts resulted in Dawes's General Allotment Act of 1887, which divided reservations into individual homesteads with the extension of citizenship to Native Americans.

The Dawes Act resulted in the opening of 90 million acres of excess land left over from individual allotments to white settlers. Succeeding generations of Native Americans saw their land holdings grow smaller because original allotments were divided equally among children and grandchildren, making it impossible for them to be economically viable. Education policy was designed to forcibly eradicate native culture by moving children to off-reservation boarding schools, where they were often punished for speaking their native language, were given Anglo names, and were often placed into white families in an effort to force them to adopt white culture. Meanwhile, clergymen serving as Indian agents made a concerted effort to eradicate native religion. The Curtis Act of 1898, in blatant disregard of treaties with the tribes within Indian Territory, abolished tribal government. In short, reformers sought to save Native Americans from physical extinction by trying to destroy the very characteristics that made them Native Americans. In this regard, these policies meet Lemkin's broader definition of genocide.

Nevertheless, Native Americans, despite overwhelming odds, resisted efforts to eradicate their culture. During the 20th century, several Native American leaders emerged to champion Indian rights. The Civil Rights Movement of the 1960s led to the Indian Civil Rights Act of 1968, which accepted tribal laws based on tribal culture. More importantly, the Indian Self-Determination and Education Assistance Act of 1975 empowered tribal governments by allowing them to administer federal assistance programs. As a result of their perseverance, Native Americans have managed to survive and retain their cultural heritage, even though the extreme poverty and appalling health conditions on reservations clearly demonstrate that Native Americans continue to suffer the long-term effects of the cultural genocide inflicted upon them.

JUSTIN D. MURPHY

Perspective 3: Clash of Incompatible Cultures

The Indian Wars did not constitute genocide as we understand that term today. Genocide is a conscious, deliberately chosen policy of extermination of a targeted population through organized, state-sanctioned mass murder. What we refer to as the "Indian Wars" was a tragic clash of two entrenched, incompatible cultures in which neither side was willing to accept compromise on the other's terms. Although Indians adopted some items and elements of European American culture that made their daily lives easier, they were determined to preserve and pursue their way of life. To European Americans, Indians were simply "in the way" of westward expansion—Indian assimilation or removal, not genocidal extermination, was U.S. government Indian policy.

Neither side showed much willingness to understand the other's culture or to pursue interaction within their opposite number's very different cultural framework and worldview. One telling indication of this cultural bias is the European Americans' naive and unrealistic insistence on dealing with the many individual Indian tribes as "nations," in which tribal chiefs not only spoke for the entire tribe (typically made up of various smaller bands who might have only infrequent contact with each other), but were also expected to *force* tribal members to abide by treaty provisions. Native Americans violated the treaties more often than European Americans; yet this is understandable and predictable given the individualistic nature of Indian culture and the typically one-sided treaties. European Americans either did not understand the nature of Indian culture or were unwilling to try to understand it and work within the Indians' frame of reference since it made dealing with the numerous tribes very complicated. Both sides' cultural blindness was also evident in the way Indians and European Americans retaliated for wrongs against them committed by the other: Indians attacked European Americans who had nothing to do with the act being retaliated for, and European Americans murdered Indians who may not have even been members of the same tribe responsible for the incident that had set the European Americans on a quest for revenge. Both sides could—and did—kill the other's women and children, mutilate their opponents' corpses, and perpetrate massacres in brutal "no-quarter" combat.

Applying the term genocide to what transpired in the West during the 19th century is not only an inappropriate use of the term, it also reveals at best a gross oversimplification and at worst a seriously flawed understanding of what was a complex interaction of *multiple* cultures. Even the term "Indian" is misleading and imprecise, since it implies a monolithic entity with shared values and a single common culture. In fact, "Indian" encompassed numerous different tribes and cultural groupings with often quite different customs, attitudes, and behavior. Many tribes had traditionally warred against other tribes for ages be-fore European Americans arrived on the scene. Indeed, some Indian tribes could be as "imperialistic" as European Americans. For example, the Lakota people erupted from their original Minnesota homeland in the late 18th and early 19th centuries to conquer huge tracts of territory in present-day Montana, Wyoming, and the Dakotas, includ-ing the sacred Black Hills, forcibly displacing the Crows and other less powerful tribes that had traditionally oc-cupied that region. The various Western Indian tribes re-acted to the aggressive European American encroachment in different ways. Some (e.g., Lakotas, Cheyennes, Co-manches, Apaches) fiercely resisted; others (e.g., Crows, Tonkawas, Pawnees) allied themselves with European Americans in wars against other tribes for various reasons. The Western "Indian Wars" was not a single, genocide-motivated war of extermination waged by European Americans against all "Indians"; in fact, it played out as a series of widely scattered, separate campaigns waged against individual tribes in which Indians were allies as well as opponents.

Genocide implies essentially defenseless victims pow-erless to prevent their mass murder by the irresistible force of those bent on their extermination. This is another rea-son why "genocide" fails to accurately describe the West-ern Indian Wars. Those who hold such a view rob Indians of what social scientists and anthropologists refer to as "agency"—the power and ability to influence the events that have an impact on one's life—by treating them merely as helpless victims of European American aggression and as if nothing any Indians did had any influence on what transpired or on their ultimate fate. This seems an unnec-essarily condescending attitude and is simply wrong.

To find only one notable example among many illustrat-ing how Indians were actors in this American tragedy and not merely helpless victims, one need only examine the Comanche people of the Southern Plains region. Number-ing perhaps as few as 30,000 individuals with only about one-sixth of this number warriors, the various bands that made up the people known as "Comanche" dominated a huge area ("Comancheria") stretching from Colorado to Mexico and from central Texas to eastern New Mexico. These "Lords of the Southern Plains" reigned as the region's true power brokers for over a century—overwhelming and displacing less powerful tribes (Apaches, Tonkawas, etc.); stopping the Spanish colonization of the Plains in its tracks; preventing the French from advancing into the Southwest; and effectively blocking European American

settlement of western Texas for a half-century. Coman-che power finally ended when their European American enemy, desperate to devise an effective military strategy, ruthlessly targeted and eliminated the key elements of the Comanches' way of life: the horse and the buffalo. The Eu-ropean Americans' wholesale slaughter of the immense buffalo herds that provided Comanches and other Plains tribes with sustenance, and the mass killings of Comanche pony herds captured during winter campaigns that robbed the tribe of its mobility, seem today to represent brutal and unnecessarily harsh acts; yet, the draconian strategy's aim was Indian removal—forcing the tribes onto government-run reservations—not genocidal extermination.

Indeed, the culminating action of the 1874 Red River War, the final campaign that forced the Comanches onto a reservation at Fort Sill, was the September 28, 1874, sur-prise attack by Colonel Ranald Mackenzie and the 4th U.S. Cavalry Regiment on the tribe's Palo Duro Canyon sanctu-ary during which only one soldier and three Indians were killed. Instead of committing a wholesale slaughter of sleeping Indians (Mackenzie had achieved complete sur-prise), he targeted and destroyed the Indians' pony herd and winter supplies, which gave the Comanches no choice but to seek shelter and food at the Fort Sill reservation. The fact that European Americans had to resort to such an ex-treme strategy, born out of frustration and desperation, of eliminating Comanche mobility and sustenance starkly emphasizes the real power the Comanches wielded for over a century. Indians were actors in the American trag-edy that was the Western Indian Wars, not helpless victims.

Although today often portrayed as the willing perpetra-tors of Indian genocide, the U.S. Frontier Army was often caught in the middle in this clash of incompatible cultures. Never numbering more than about 25,000 cavalrymen and infantrymen, the U.S. regular army was scattered in small detachments over an area of about 2 million square miles. Led by a small, mainly West Point–trained officer corps, the U.S. Frontier Army was manned mostly by sol-diers recruited from the bottom tier of American society, and drunkenness, desertion, and psychologically numb-ing isolation were constant plagues that vexed command-ers even more than their infrequent armed clashes with Indians. Frontier army service was typically an onerous *duty* that the army was compelled to perform, carrying out frequently misguided policies originating in Washington, formed by politicians and government officials who usu-ally had no idea of the actual situation on the ground in the West.

One of the most notorious Indian Wars incidents used to justify claims that the U.S. Army pursued genocide is the infamous 1864 Sand Creek Massacre; yet, the wholesale killing of 70–160 Cheyenne men, women, and children at Sand Creek was neither perpetrated by nor condoned by the U.S. Army. Poorly trained, ill-disciplined Colorado territorial militia (many reportedly drunk at the time) under the command of a racist bigot, Colonel John M. Chivington, committed this crime that was later repudiated by the U.S. Congress Joint Committee on the Prosecution of the [Civil] War. Indeed, some U.S. Frontier Army regular officers later became public champions of Indian rights. Probably the most notable of these is Brigadier General George Crook, who was one of the army's most successful "Indian fighters," but who spent the last decades of his life fighting for Indian rights and justice for the tribes.

Claims that this clash of incompatible cultures constituted genocide typically focus on only a select few of the more than 1,500 armed clashes—from minor skirmishes to pitched battles to undeniable massacres committed by both sides—between Indians and European Americans in the West from 1850 to 1890. Gregory Michno in *The Encyclopedia of Indian Wars* calculates that there were about 21,000 total casualties in these armed clashes, with European Americans (soldiers and civilians) accounting for about 6,600 (31 percent) and Indians suffering about 15,000 (69 percent). Although these casualty figures do not include Indian deaths from disease, sickness, or displacement-induced starvation, they are hardly lopsided enough to support claims of genocide. In addition to Sand Creek (committed by civilian volunteers), the other most-often cited example used to support genocide claims does involve the U.S. regular army: the 1890 tragedy at Wounded Knee.

The tragedy that took place December 29, 1890, at Wounded Knee Creek, South Dakota—the final armed encounter that marked the end of the Western Indian Wars—is a compelling illustration of how the clash of Indian and European American cultures could produce a horrific and bloody outcome that neither side intentionally sought. What we today call the Wounded Knee Massacre was set in motion by desperation and fear, not by some desire for "revenge" by the 7th Cavalry Regiment for its losses at the 1876 Battle of the Little Bighorn (a motivation attributed to the troopers after the fact, created by sensationalist Eastern newspaper accounts). The Lakotas, by 1890 confined to a bleak existence on South Dakota reservations and desperate at the loss of their way of life, turned for solace to the Ghost Dance religion. Misunderstanding this new Indian religious movement, reservation agents and the area's European American settlers feared it was a precursor to a Lakota "uprising" and sent panicked pleas to Washington to send troops. In turn, the arrival of U.S. Army soldiers spread corresponding fear among the Lakotas, and some bands, including one of about 350 men, women, and children led by Big Foot (Spotted Elk) fled the reservation.

Intercepted by 7th Cavalry troopers, Big Foot's band was being escorted back to the reservation when, at a campsite on Wounded Knee Creek, the soldiers' attempt to disarm the Lakotas went horribly wrong. Surrounded by armed troopers but refusing to reveal and surrender the numerous repeating rifles they had been seen carrying when they surrendered the day before, about 100 Lakota warriors were being harangued by a medicine man, Yellow Bird, to resist: "Do not be afraid . . . their bullets will not penetrate you!" As the soldiers grabbed the rifle of an unstable Indian named Black Coyote, the weapon discharged; simultaneously, Yellow Bird threw a handful of dust into the air. At this signal, several Lakota warriors threw back their blankets, raised their Winchester rifles, and fired a volley into the troopers' ranks, killing and wounding several soldiers and possibly hitting women and children in the Lakota camp beyond. The troopers fired back and, supported by four rapid-firing Hotchkiss Guns, delivered an overpowering fusillade that struck down Lakota warriors, women, and children. Once the shooting started, it was difficult to stop; the end result was tragically inevitable: 84 Lakota warriors, 44 women, and 18 children were killed. Yet, soldier casualties were also heavy, totaling 64 (25 killed and 39 wounded).

Some accounts claim that the high soldier casualties were mainly due to "friendly fire," but the evidence to support this claim is sketchy and inconclusive. In the wake of the shooting, 7th Cavalry troopers loaded surviving Lakotas (51 were found in the area) into wagons and transported them to shelter and to receive medical treatment at the reservation hospital—hardly the actions of soldiers who were intent on killing all the Indians.

Claims that the Western Indian Wars constituted genocide grossly misread and incorrectly label a complex clash of incompatible cultures. Calling the American tragedy that was the Indian Wars "genocide" not only condescendingly idealizes and oversimplifies Indian culture while unfairly demonizing European American culture, it demeans the experience of the victims of actual genocide in the 20th century.

JERRY D. MORELOCK

Appendix II: International Law and Organizations

As the scale of human rights violations and incidents of mass murder increased in the 19th and 20th centuries, so did the attempts of the international community to address them. Through various international legal conventions and organizations, international law evolved in an attempt to define genocide, war crimes, and crimes against humanity. Key international organizations, notably the United Nations (UN), and international legal conventions, such as the 1948 UN Convention on the Prevention and Punishment of the Crime of Genocide, were crucial in the development of the prevention and prosecution of war crimes, crimes against humanity, and genocide. Nongovernmental organizations (NGOs), such as Amnesty International, and international figures, such as UN ambassador Samantha Power, have also worked to draw international attention to episodes of violence that have the potential to escalate into genocide in an effort to prevent future occurrences. This section includes individuals, organizations, conventions, and concepts important in understanding the relationship between international law and genocide.

Topical List of Entries

INDIVIDUALS
Annan, Kofi
Bassiouni, M. Cherif
Boutros-Ghali, Boutros
Brauman, Rony
Egeland, Jan
Kuper, Leo
Pilger, John
Power, Samantha
Proxmire, William

IDEAS
Upstander

INSTITUTIONS
International Court of Justice
International Criminal Court
League of Nations
United Nations
United Nations Commission of Experts
United Nations Commission on Human Rights
United Nations War Crimes Commission

ORGANIZATIONS
Amnesty International
Coalition for International Justice
Human Rights Watch
Prevent Genocide International
Truth Commissions
War Crimes Tribunals

LAWS AND CONVENTIONS
European Convention on the Non-Applicability of Statutory Limitations to Crimes
Geneva Convention, Protocol I
Geneva Convention Protocol II (1977)
Responsibility to Protect (R2P)
United Nations Convention on the Prevention and Punishment of the Crime of Genocide (UNCG)
Universal Declaration of Human Rights
Whitaker Report

A

Amnesty International

Amnesty International is a worldwide movement that works to free prisoners of conscience, assist political prisoners, abolish the death penalty, and end extrajudicial executions and disappearances through education, grassroots efforts, and letter-writing campaigns.

The organization was founded in May 1961, when Peter Benenson, a lawyer in London, England, read in the London Observer about a group of students in Portugal who had been jailed for proposing a toast to "freedom" in a public restaurant. Benenson launched a campaign called "Appeal for Amnesty 1961," which kept the issue in the columns of the Observer for a year and encouraged people to write letters to officials in all countries where people were imprisoned for their political beliefs. The campaign was a great success, even spreading to other countries. By the end of 1961, Amnesty International was formed to organize these efforts.

Amnesty International based its principles on the United Nations' Universal Declaration of Human Rights, which had been adopted by the United Nations General Assembly in 1948. Defining "prisoners of conscience" as people unjustly imprisoned solely because of their beliefs, race, gender, or ethnic origin, the agency began by investigating the cases of individual prisoners. Those who were indeed prisoners of conscience would be adopted by the agency, and a letter-writing campaign would commence.

When it was deemed safe, the families of such prisoners were also contacted and assistance offered. The early emphasis was on freeing individuals, not on changing political systems.

By the late 1960s, Amnesty International had expanded some of its efforts into education, grassroots fund-raising, and reaching out to churches, schools, businesses, and labor unions to spread awareness of its campaigns. After some trial and error, the agency adopted the rule that organization members could only work on cases outside their own country. This helped to preserve impartiality in the investigations of human rights abuses and thereby maintained the reputation of the organization. Despite growing international opposition by human rights abusers, Amnesty International was awarded the Nobel Peace Prize in 1977.

Many of the first members of Amnesty International were professors, but during the 1980s the number of students grew rapidly. The student membership did not adopt prisoners but instead organized publicity about unjust political systems and helped to write letters for prisoners adopted by other groups. The tendency to call attention to particular injustices became even more pronounced as prominent musicians and artists adopted Amnesty International as a special cause. Concerts and other events not only provided a major boost to the organization's budget, they expanded the reach of educational campaigns.

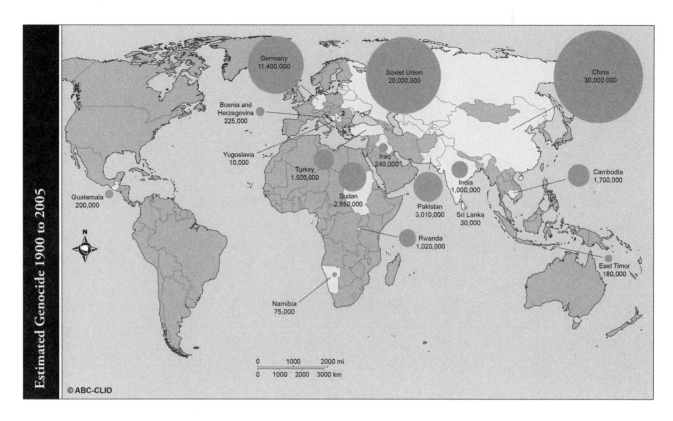

Estimated Genocide 1900 to 2005

The organization remains independent of any government, political party, religious faction, or economic interest. Its emphasis on accuracy and impartiality has established its reputation as a credible source of information. A good part of the budget of the International Secretariat, in the central headquarters based in London, goes toward careful research into the situations of political prisoners.

Amnesty International has more than a million members, supporters and subscribers in more than 150 countries and territories, and it has offices in more than 70 countries. The organization is headed by an International Council that meets every two years and has representatives from each section (a section is a group of members in a given country). The International Executive Committee meets at least twice a year and includes the treasurer, a representative from the International Secretariat staff, and seven regular members. The International Executive Committee appoints the organization's secretary-general. The organization is funded by its membership, as well as by donations and fund-raising.

The group's Urgent Action Network conducts letter-writing campaigns on behalf of people who are in grave danger. The group issues an annual newsletter as well as reports and studies, annuals, and audiovisual resources. Amnesty International has been successful in getting 50 percent of designated "prisoners of conscience" released within a short time.

PAUL R. BARTROP

See also: Egeland, Jan; Save Darfur Coalition; United Nations Convention on the Prevention and Punishment of Genocide

Further Reading

Clark, Ann Marie. *Diplomacy of Conscience: Amnesty International and Changing Human Rights Norms.* Princeton: Princeton University Press, 2001.

Desmond, Cosmas. *Persecution East and West: Human Rights, Political Prisoners, and Amnesty.* New York: Penguin Books, 1983.

Power, Jonathan. *Amnesty International, the Human Rights Story.* New York: Pergamon Press, 1981.

Annan, Kofi

Kofi Annan was the 7th secretary-general of the United Nations (UN), serving between 1997 and 2006. He was born in Kumasi, in what was then the British Gold Coast colony (now Ghana), on April 8, 1938. He came from an upper-class merchant family that had descended from tribal chiefs.

As a teenager, Annan attended a local boarding school and in 1958 entered the Kumasi College of Science and Technology (now Kwame Nkrumah University), where he studied economics. Whilst there, he received a grant to complete his studies at Macalester College, St. Paul, Minnesota. Between 1961 and 1962, he undertook a degree in international relations at the Graduate Institute of International and Development Studies in Geneva, Switzerland, and also studied at the Massachusetts Institute of Technology's Sloan School of Management, where he earned an MSc degree in management in 1972.

In 1962, Annan joined the World Health Organization (WHO) before returning to Ghana, where he worked as the country's director of tourism between 1974 and 1976. By 1987, he had become a key bureaucrat with the UN in New York, serving successively in senior positions in a diverse range of departments, including Human Resources Management (1987–1990), Budget and Finance (1990–1992), and Peacekeeping (March 1992–December 1996). One of his special assignments saw him given the task in 1990 of facilitating the repatriation of international staff and citizens of Western countries from Iraq after that country, led by Saddam Hussein, invaded Kuwait.

As head of the Department of Peacekeeping Operations (DPKO), Annan presided over an undertaking that at one time saw nearly 70,000 military and civilian personnel deployed in UN operations around the world. While many of these operations were successful, everything else during his tenure paled when measured against the UN's unproductive handling of the crisis in Rwanda prior to, during, and after the genocide that took place there in 1994.

The UN's efforts in halting the tragedy were thoroughly inadequate, a point subsequently acknowledged by Annan on a number of occasions. He in fact later apologized for the UN's role during the genocide, expressing "deep remorse" that more was not done to stop it. Annan was criticized by many, both at the time and later, for adopting a passive approach to pleas for help from the commander of the United Nations Assistance Mission for Rwanda, Lieutenant General Roméo Dallaire, who argued that Annan wavered over whether or not to reinforce the mission or try to arrange a new mandate that would allow for more effective action. Dallaire also claimed that Annan refused to respond to his repeated calls for authority to take action on the ground. In this, some have asserted, Annan was restricted by the lines of demarcation within the UN bureaucracy and was overruled by his immediate superior, Iqbal Riza, and, further up the chain, the then-secretary-general, Boutros Boutros-Ghali.

In 2004, Annan said he could and should have done more to stop the genocide in Rwanda and acknowledged that he did not push hard enough for action to be taken by UN member states or the Secretariat. The painful memory of this inaction was profound, and he became determined from this point on never to allow a repetition of what had happened to again occur on his watch. Rwanda thus influenced many of Annan's later decisions once he became secretary-general.

After Rwanda, Annan served as UN under-secretary-general between March 1994 and October 1995, prior to an appointment as special representative of the secretary-general (SRSG) for the former Yugoslavia from November 1995 to March 1996. He resumed his position as under-secretary-general in April 1996. On December 13, 1996, Annan was recommended by the UN Security Council to be the next secretary-general. Succeeding Boutros-Ghali, he would be the second successive African to serve in the post, and the first from sub-Saharan Africa. He was also the first secretary-general to be elected from the ranks of the UN bureaucracy. His five-year term began on January 1, 1997; this was renewed after Annan was reappointed in June 2001 for a second term that began on January 1, 2002.

As secretary-general, Annan negotiated or presided over a number of highly delicate situations, including an attempt in 1998 to gain Iraq's compliance with Security Council resolutions and a mission that same year to promote the transition to civilian rule in Nigeria. In 1999, he helped to resolve a stalemate between Libya and the Security Council and to forge an international response to preindependence violence in East Timor.

Much of his work in the international arena focused on issues related to global health, in particular HIV/AIDS, and he took a leading role in mobilizing the global community in the battle against the AIDS pandemic. In April 2001, he proposed a Global AIDS and Health Fund to help developing countries confront the crisis, and for this both he and the UN were awarded the 2001 Nobel Peace Prize.

Annan was secretary-general during the first four years (2003–2006) of the genocidal crisis in Darfur, Sudan, during which the UN did little that was effective in stopping the killing. Annan supported the sending of a UN peacekeeping

Kofi Annan, then secretary-general of the United Nations, and spouse Nane Annan, are shown the burial site of genocide victims in Kigali, Rwanda, 1998. (UN Photo/Milton Grant)

mission and worked with the government of Sudan (GOS) to accept a transfer of power from an African Union monitoring force to one under the authority of the UN.

On April 7, 2004, in a speech in Geneva commemorating the 10th anniversary of the genocide in Rwanda, Annan launched a five-point Action Plan to Prevent Genocide. This included: (1) preventing armed conflict, which usually provides the context for genocide; (2) protection of civilians in armed conflict, including a mandate for UN peacekeepers to protect civilians; (3) ending impunity through judicial action in both national and international courts; (4) information gathering and early warning through a UN special adviser for genocide prevention making recommendations to the UN Security Council on actions to prevent or halt genocide; and (5) swift and decisive action along a continuum of steps, including military action.

The fourth point, the future appointment of a special adviser on genocide prevention, was a pledge to designate an official who would collect data and monitor any serious violations of human rights or international law that have

racial or ethnic dimensions that could lead to genocide. By July 14, 2004, the appointment was made. Juan E. Méndez, an Argentinean lawyer, took up the position, charged with the task of acting in an early-warning capacity that would advise the secretary-general and the Security Council about potential genocidal situations. Once this determination was made, he would then make recommendations to the Security Council about how the UN could prevent these events.

As secretary-general, Annan gave priority to strengthening and revitalizing the UN's work and to improve its image through a comprehensive program of reform. This included strengthening the UN's traditional work in the areas of development and the maintenance of international peace and security; advocating human rights, the rule of law, and the universal values of equality, tolerance, and human dignity; and restoring public confidence in the UN by reaching out to new partners.

To help achieve this, in April 2000 he issued a report that considered what the UN's role should be in the 21st century. The so-called Millennium Declarations that followed were adopted by many of the world's leaders attending the UN Millennium Summit that September. These "Millennium Development Goals" set specific targets to end poverty and inequality, improve education, protect vulnerable groups from violence, combat HIV/AIDS, and protect the environment.

On December 31, 2006, Annan retired as secretary-general, to be succeeded by South Korean statesman Ban Ki Moon. He returned to Ghana but has maintained an active role as one of Africa's senior statesmen through to the present day.

PAUL R. BARTROP

See also: Boutros-Ghali, Boutros; United Nations

Further Reading

Meisler, Stanley. *Kofi Annan: A Man of Peace in a World of War*. New York: Wiley, 2008.

United Nations. *Atrocities and International Accountability: Beyond Transitional Justice*. New York: United Nations, 2008.

B

Bassiouni, M. Cherif

Mahmoud Cherif Bassiouni is a distinguished research professor of law emeritus at DePaul University College of Law in Chicago, Illinois (where he has taught since 1964). He has also been president emeritus of DePaul's International Human Rights Law Institute on two occasions (1990–2006 and 2007–2009). In addition, since 1988 he has been president of the Istituto Superiore Internazionale di Scienze Criminali (International Institute of Higher Studies in Criminal Sciences, or ISISC), in Siracusa, Italy, and honorary president of the International Association of Penal Law in Paris (1989–2004).

A visionary in the field of international law, Bassiouni, through his writings and speeches, was an early and strong advocate of the establishment of an international criminal tribunal to try major crimes against the human person. Ultimately, he played a major role in the establishment of both the International Criminal Tribunal for the Former Yugoslavia (ICTY) and the International Criminal Court (ICC).

Born in Cairo in 1937, Bassiouni was educated in Egypt (University of Cairo), France (University of Burgundy), Switzerland (University of Geneva), and the United States (Indiana University, John Marshall Law School, and George Washington University). He was a Fulbright-Hays professor of international criminal law at the University of Freiburg, Germany, in 1970, and then a visiting professor of law at New York University Law School in 1971. In 1972 he was a guest scholar at the Woodrow Wilson International Center for Scholars in Washington, D.C. He served as a consultant to the U.S. Departments of State and Justice on projects relating to international drug trafficking (1973) and international control of terrorism (1975 and 1978–1979). Bassiouni also acted as a consultant to the U.S. Department of State regarding the U.S. hostages in Iran between 1979 and 1980.

Between 1975 and 2005, Bassiouni served in a number of important United Nations positions. These saw him act as honorary vice-president of the Fifth United Nations Congress on Crime Prevention (1975); co-chairman of the Independent Committee of Experts on Drafting the Convention on the Prevention and Suppression of Torture (1978); consultant to the Southern African Commission on Human Rights from 1980–1981 (in this capacity he prepared a draft statute for the creation of an international criminal court to prosecute apartheid); consultant to the Sixth and Seventh United Nations Congresses on Crime Prevention (1980 and 1985); chairman of the United Nations Commission of Experts Established Pursuant to Security Council 780 (1992) to Investigate Violations of International Humanitarian Law in the Former Yugoslavia (1993–1994), and the Commission's Special Rapporteur on Gathering and Analysis of the Facts (1992–1993); vice-chairman of the General Assembly's Ad Hoc Committee on the Establishment of an International Criminal Court (1995); vice-chairman of the General Assembly's Preparatory Committee on the Establishment of an International Criminal Court (1996–1998); chairman of the Drafting Committee, United Nations Diplomatic Conference on the Establishment of an International Criminal Court (1998); independent expert on the Rights to Restitution, Compensation and Rehabilitation for Victims of Grave Violations of Human Rights and Fundamental Freedoms (1998–2000); and independent expert on the Commission on Human Rights in Afghanistan (2004–2005).

As chairman of the United Nations Commission of Experts investigating the Former Yugoslavia, and the Commission's Special Rapporteur on Gathering and Analysis of the Facts (1992–1993), Bassiouni's team compiled 65,000 pages of evidence. The Commission's report, issued in June 1994, concluded that 80 percent of the victims of the war crimes investigated were Bosniaks, and 80 percent of the perpetrators were Serbs; that mass rapes perpetrated by Serbs took place as a matter of policy; and that Serb-directed ethnic cleansing amounted to "crimes against humanity" which the United Nations is committed to punish.

Earlier, it had been suggested in some quarters that Bassiouni had established strong qualifications to become the first prosecutor of the ICTY, a position that was assumed by South African judge Richard Goldstone. When the vote was taken in the UN Security Council, the first ballot saw Bassiouni's candidature supported by seven member states, with seven opposing him and one abstention. His failure was believed to be due to political pressure from the United Kingdom, which was concerned that Bassiouni would not be impartial, and inclined to charge Serbs ahead of other actors in the former Yugoslavia such as Croats and Bosniaks.

While this setback was of course noticed in international circles, the high esteem in which Bassiouni was held saw him nominated for the 1999 Nobel Peace Prize for his work in the field of international criminal justice and for his contribution to the creation of the International Criminal Court.

One of the most eminent and well-credentialed of United Nations war crimes experts, Bassiouni's written works run to well over 200 legal articles and nearly 80 books as author and editor, published in Arabic, Chinese, English, Farsi, French, Georgian, German, Hungarian, Italian, Russian, and Spanish. He has written seminal works in the field of international law, particularly as they apply to the issues of human rights, crimes against humanity, and genocide. His published works have been cited by the International Court of Justice, the International Criminal Tribunal for the Former Yugoslavia, and the International Criminal Tribunal for Rwanda.

In 2007, he was awarded the Hague Prize for International Law, a prize awarded every two years to individuals and/or organizations who have made, through publications or achievements in the practice of law, a special contribution to the development of public international law, private international law, or to the advancement of the rule of law in the world. Considered to be "without peer when it comes to the advocacy of international criminal justice," especially through his promotion of the establishment of an International Criminal Court, the Hague Prize jury assessed him as one of the world's most authoritative experts in the field of international law.

Paul R. Bartrop

See also: International Court of Justice

Further Reading

Hagan, John. *Justice in the Balkans: Prosecuting War Crimes in the Hague Tribunal.* Chicago, IL: University of Chicago Press, 2003.

Sriram, Chandra Lekha, Olga Martin-Ortega, and Johanna Herman. *War, Conflict and Human Rights: Theory and Practice.* New York: Routledge, 2010.

Boutros-Ghali, Boutros

Boutros Boutros-Ghali is a former Egyptian statesman who served as United Nations secretary-general during one of its most challenging periods, between January 1, 1992, and December 31, 1997. He was born in Cairo to an elite Coptic Christian family on November 14, 1922. His grandfather, Boutros Ghali, had been prime minister of Egypt from 1908 until his assassination in 1910. His uncle, Wassif Ghali Pasha, served as Egypt's foreign minister.

Boutros Boutros-Ghali graduated from Cairo University in 1946, and obtained a PhD in international law from the University of Paris in 1949 with a thesis on the study of regional organizations. Much of his early career was in academic scholarship. He was a Fulbright Research Scholar at Columbia University (1954–1955), director of the Centre of Research of The Hague Academy of International Law (1963–1964), and a visiting professor in the faculty of law at the University of Paris (1967–1968). In 1979, he was appointed professor of international law and international relations at Cairo University, a position he held until 1999.

Between 1974 and 1977 he was a member of the central committee of the Arab Socialist Union, and in the latter year was appointed by Egyptian president Anwar Sadat to the position of Minister of Foreign Affairs, a position he held until 1991. In September 1978 he attended the Camp David Peace Conference and had a role in negotiating the subsequent Camp David Accords between Egypt and Israel, signed between Sadat and Israeli prime minister Menachem Begin on March 26, 1979. He led many Egyptian delegations to meetings of the Organization of African Unity (OAU) and the Movement of Non-Aligned Countries, as well as to the summit conference of French and African heads of state. He also headed Egypt's delegation to the General Assembly sessions in 1979, 1982, and 1990. He became a member of the Egyptian parliament in 1987, and a member of the National Democratic Party secretariat from 1980. Until assuming the office of secretary-general of the United Nations, he was also vice president of the Socialist International.

On December 3, 1991, Boutros-Ghali was appointed by the UN General Assembly to become its sixth secretary-general, his five-year term to commence on January 1, 1992. That year, he was the architect and author of the UN's *Agenda for Peace,* which, at the time, was considered to be one of the most comprehensive statements vis-à-vis the role of the United Nations relative to violent conflict in the post–Cold War period. By his own admission, expressed later, he was under the illusion that the UN's role in the future would be to find a solution that would manage the post–Cold War situation. In doing so, however, the UN became involved in a number of peacekeeping fiascos during the early 1990s which cast doubt over its effectiveness as the world's preeminent decision-making body. Looked at in this light, the *Agenda for Peace* was a solid piece of academic scholarship, though not sound practically.

It was Boutros-Ghali's misfortune that he oversaw the UN at a time when two major genocidal crises, in the former Yugoslavia (1991–1995) and Rwanda (1994), threatened the very bases upon which the UN rested—nonintervention, realpolitik, and the authenticity of the contemporary states system. His term also included a disastrous peacekeeping mission in Somalia in 1993, when 24 UN peacekeepers from Pakistan were killed in a firefight with members of warlord Mohammed Farrah Aideed's militia. Sent to help keep the peace and distribute aid in Somalia, these troops were followed on October 3, 1993,

by U.S. Army Rangers and Delta Special Forces, who were ambushed by this same militia. Eighteen U.S. soldiers were killed, 73 wounded, and a Black Hawk helicopter crashed, the pilot kidnapped. Newscasts around the world showed the members of the militia dragging the naked, dead body of a U.S. Ranger through the streets of the capital, Mogadishu. Both the attack and the brutal aftermath caused such great consternation amongst U.S. citizens that it impacted future U.S. foreign policy decisions. More specifically, U.S. foreign policy makers became extremely tentative about deploying any U.S. troops in violent conflicts far from home in which the United States ostensibly had little to no direct strategic interests. Ultimately, due in large part to this "Somalia Factor," U.S. president Bill Clinton decided not to attempt to prevent, or even halt, the 1994 Rwandan Genocide a few months later.

In a 2004 interview for the U.S. documentary *Ghosts of Rwanda* (dir. Greg Barker, 2004), aired on the program *Frontline,* Boutros-Ghali reflected on his term as secretary-general during the period of Bosnia and Rwanda, and concluded, in relation to the latter, that it was one of his greatest failures in view of the fact that he was unaware of the degree of the disaster. (He also said as much in public interviews reported in U.S. news magazines at the time.) Further, he argued, it was an added failure that he was not able to convince the members of the UN Security Council to intervene. That acknowledgement made, he was criticized for the UN's failure to act during the genocide, as well as for his inability to generate sufficient support for other UN peacekeeping activities from among member states. In his defense, he argued later—quite accurately—that the United Nations, being comprised of individual sovereign states, runs in accordance with the principle of national interests. Given that, states can choose whether or not to intervene in a situation, and cannot be compelled to do so even for the sake of the greater good.

However, Boutros-Ghali identified a larger issue that was holding back effective UN intervention in genocidal situations, an institutionalized racism particularly regarding Africa and other Third World regions. In his view, genocide in Africa does not receive the same priority in world capitals that genocide in Europe or elsewhere does. In his view, this certainly hampered endeavors for effective intervention in Rwanda and other African crises during his term as secretary-general. What he referred to as a "marginalization of Africa" led to what he saw as a hierarchy of assistance that siphoned off much larger amounts of assistance money to Bosnia than to Africa—whether to Sierra Leone, Rwanda, Burundi, Angola, Liberia, or elsewhere. He also bemoaned the fact that international peacekeeping appeared to be dominated by U.S. interests and priorities, rather than being even-handed and impartial.

As Boutros-Ghali's administration was forced to confront war in Bosnia and genocide in Rwanda, this inevitably had an impact on how his tenure played out. While a tradition was developing within the UN that a secretary-general would have the opportunity of serving two terms, an active lobby developed that Boutros-Ghali should not serve more than one. In 1996, 10 member states in the Security Council sponsored a resolution supporting him for a second term as secretary-general, but this was vetoed by the United States supported by a number of other influential states. Boutros-Ghali turned out to be the only secretary-general not to be elected to a second term in office, and on January 1, 1997, he was succeeded at the UN by Kofi Annan.

After his term at the United Nations, Boutros-Ghali served as secretary-general of the French equivalent to the British Commonwealth, *La Francophonie* (1997–2002), and in 2003 he was appointed as director of the Egyptian National Council of Human Rights.

PAUL R. BARTROP

See also: Annan, Kofi; United Nations

Further Reading

Boutros-Ghali, Boutros. *An Agenda for Peace: Preventive Diplomacy, Peacemaking and Peace-Keeping.* New York: United Nations, 1992.

United Nations. *Atrocities and International Accountability: Beyond Transitional Justice.* New York: United Nations, 2008.

Brauman, Rony

Rony Brauman was the president of Médecins Sans Frontières (Doctors without Borders, or MSF) from 1982 to 1994. Born of French nationality in Jerusalem on June 19, 1950, he was educated at Lakanal de Sceaux secondary school and the medical faculty of Cochin-Port-Royal de Paris, where he qualified as a doctor in tropical medicine, public health, and epidemiology.

Between 1975 and 1978, he was shipboard doctor on a vessel laying underwater cables along the African coast. Joining MSF as a medical officer in 1978, he became a physician, and from then until 1982 oversaw a number of field missions, both in the direct line of fire in conflict situations and in refugee camps in Asia, Africa, and Central America. In 1982 he became president of MSF.

As president from then until 1994, Brauman's experience unfolded primarily in medical relief in crisis situations, particularly civil strife, war, famine, and refugee issues. His term coincided with the collapse of communism and the end of the Cold War, and saw the greatest spread of intensive MSF work in wartorn Bosnia-Herzegovina and Rwanda. His effectiveness as an administrator, despite the challenges facing MSF at this time, saw the organization both increase its activity and expand its budget tenfold in the space of 12 years.

Brauman elaborated a doctrine of humanitarian action that outlined both the promise and limits of humanitarianism, and unraveled its inherent dilemmas. This saw the introduction of the term "humanitarian space" (espace humanitaire) as a way of describing "a space of freedom in which we are free to evaluate needs, free to monitor the distribution and use of relief goods, and free to have a dialogue with the people." In effect, this is an operating environment in which humanitarian agencies and organizations can establish and maintain a regime conducive to the humanitarian operating environment in which they are deployed when they go out into the field. The preservation of humanitarian space has since become an issue of concern to the United Nations (UN), particularly the department of peacekeeping operations. There is a fear that this space is shrinking, particularly in integrated UN peacekeeping missions.

One of the major areas in which international aid organizations have addressed themselves to issues relating to humanitarian space has been the question of impartiality, as most civilian or military actors, whether working for state or non state agencies, seek to comply with the principles dictated by the need to remain neutral in order to act as an intermediary between conflicting parties, be accepted by all parties, and recognized as having a specific role without identifiable political or military ambitions. The irony of this for Brauman is that this is specifically expected of the International Committee of the Red Cross (ICRC), though not of MSF—which was one of the key elements leading to Bernard Kouchner and other French doctors breaking away from the ICRC during the Nigeria-Biafra War (1967–1970) and then forming MSF in December 1971.

From 1984 to 1988 Brauman served as cofounder and director of a new organization, Liberté sans Frontières (Freedom without Borders), working on issues concerning underdevelopment and helping to shed light on many of the connections between autonomy and civil society, the democratization movement, and economic development.

In 1994, Brauman left MSF and became a professor at the Institut d'études politiques in Paris, where he remained until 1997. While there, he also worked as research director at the Doctors without Borders Foundation, helping to raise funds to continue the work for the organization to which he had already devoted so much of his time and energy. In 1997, he received the highly prestigious Prix Henry Dunant, awarded to individuals or organizations that have made significant contributions to the study, spread, and renewal of the ideas and achievements of Henry Dunant, the founder of the ICRC in 1863. It was recognized that Brauman overcame numerous obstacles on the road to transforming MSF into the organization it became under his leadership, and that he had in addition established Freedom without Borders to work for the cause of human dignity.

In 1999, MSF created the Centre de réflexion sur l'action et les savoirs humanitaires, or CRASH. Its objective is to encourage debate and critical reflection on MSF's humanitarian practices so as to improve the organization's effectiveness. CRASH carries out in-depth studies and analyses of MSF's activities. The aim of its work is to contribute to ongoing discussions concerning the challenges, constraints, and limits of humanitarian action. Brauman is the current research director of CRASH, helping to direct its training and evaluation processes.

Brauman's concern regarding the provision of government assistance in crisis situations has seen him call on states to make use of the instruments of international humanitarian law they have ratified. He is concerned that too much is left to the efforts of humanitarian organizations when governments can themselves be doing a great deal to help affected populations. Thus, in 2010, Brauman protested against the fate of the Foundation of France (Fondation de France), a private, independent organization founded in 1969 that helps to implement philanthropic, educational, scientific, social, and cultural projects and provides assistance to people in need. Brauman saw that the government was hiding behind the foundation's work as a mask for its own inaction, and that funds management and the use of mass media was part of a "propaganda" campaign to mobilize donors in the face of humanitarian disasters.

A member of the National Consultative Commission of Human Rights, Brauman has also turned his attention to movies. In 1999, he and Israeli director Eyal Sivan codirected *The Specialist,* a documentary on the 1961 trial of Adolf Eichmann.

PAUL R. BARTROP

See also: Human Rights Watch; Universal Declaration of Human Rights

Further Reading

Bortolotti, Dan. *Hope in Hell: Inside the World of Doctors Without Borders.* New York: Firefly Books, 2010.

Morley, David. *Healing Our World: Inside Doctors Without Borders.* Markham, Canada: Fitzhenry and Whiteside, 2008.

C

Coalition for International Justice

The Coalition for International Justice (CIJ) was an international, not-for-profit organization formed in 1995 and initially designed to support war-crimes trials for the Rwandan Genocide and the atrocities committed in the former Yugoslavia. The CIJ later supported criminal-justice initiatives in East Timor, Sudan, Sierra Leone, and Cambodia. The CIJ was headquartered at The Hague in the Netherlands and maintained an office in Washington, D.C. Among other things, the CIJ provided legal and technical assistance to international tribunals as well as individual governments, conducted outreach and public-education programs related to war crimes and atrocities, and compiled analyses and critiques of cases being assembled by tribunals in order to maximize the effectiveness of prosecutorial teams.

The CIJ also worked to educate and reach out to world leaders and decision-makers and maintained an archive of all reports from various war-crime trials held between 1995 and 2006. In 2000, the organization branched out and began covering war-crime happenings in Africa and Cambodia. During 2004–2005, the CIJ sponsored a team of historians and other experts who conducted some 1,200 interviews with refugees in Chad who had sought a safe haven from the violence in Darfur, Sudan. The organization was also involved in gathering information on atrocities in Sierra Leone, East Timor, and Cambodia. The CIJ ceased its operations on March 31, 2006. Its board issued a statement at that time stating that the organization was not designed to be a permanent group.

Paul G. Pierpaoli Jr.

See also: Human Rights Watch; Amnesty International; United Nations Commission on Human Rights

Further Reading

Web site of the Coalition for International Justice: www.hague justiceportal.net/index.php?id=3663.

E

Egeland, Jan

Jan Egeland is a former United Nations (UN) undersecretary-general for Humanitarian Affairs and emergency relief coordinator, having served in this role between June 2003 and December 2006. He was born on September 12, 1957, in the small Norwegian city of Stavanger and educated at the University of Oslo. He has been a Fulbright Scholar at the University of California, Berkeley, and a fellow at both the International Peace Research Institute, Oslo, and the Truman Institute for the Advancement of Peace, Jerusalem.

In 1980, Egeland became chairman of Amnesty International in Norway. During his tenure in that office, he was elected as vice-chairman of the International Executive Committee of Amnesty International. He remained in both positions until 1986. Then, between 1990 and 1997, Egeland was state secretary in the Norwegian Ministry of Foreign Affairs, engaged in humanitarian relief work. He joined the UN as the secretary-general's special adviser on Colombia from 1999 to 2002. In August 2003, he was appointed by Secretary-General Kofi Annan as undersecretary-general for Humanitarian Affairs and emergency relief coordinator, making him also head of the UN Office for the Coordination of Humanitarian Affairs (OCHA). He served in that post until December 2006, after which, in September 2008, he became Secretary-General Ban Ki-moon's special adviser for conflict prevention and resolution. During the period 2001–2003 he also served as secretary-general of the Norwegian Red Cross.

As a young diplomat in 1992, Egeland helped establish the back-channel diplomacy that started negotiations between representatives of Israel and the Palestine Liberation Organization (PLO). These initiatives would lead eventually to the Oslo Agreement between Israel and the PLO (the so-called Declaration of Principles) in September 1993. Later, in 1996, he helped facilitate the UN-led peace talks leading up to a cease-fire agreement between the government of Guatemala and the Unidad Revolucionaria Nacional Guatemalteca (Guatemalan National Revolutionary Unity, or URNG) guerrillas—an agreement signed at Oslo City Hall. A further success saw the Ottawa Treaty to ban landmines negotiated and adopted in Oslo in 1997, with Egeland as the Norwegian delegation leader.

In December 2003, soon after becoming UN undersecretary-general for Humanitarian Affairs, Egeland was forced to address the new humanitarian crisis in Darfur, Sudan. He relentlessly tried to bring the situation in Darfur to the world's attention, just as Mukesh Kapila, in Khartoum, was attempting closer to the scene. In 2004, Egeland went to Darfur, where already there were a million people in need. Within three years, this had risen to 4 million. In short time, Egeland was warning of a possible collapse of humanitarian assistance programs in Darfur and neighboring areas, due to what he referred to as a "meltdown in security." He was desperate for urgent action to be taken, although he was all too aware that the response of the international community was haphazard, uneven, and, all too often, feeble.

By 2006, Egeland's criticisms of the regime in Khartoum and the international community's response had led to an unlikely outcome: the most senior humanitarian officer of the UN, appointed directly by the secretary-general, was forbidden entry by the Sudanese government. His accusations against Sudan of deliberately hindering relief aid in Darfur, attacking villages, and arming the Janjaweed militias were made at a terrible cost to the local population in Darfur, as the killing continued and there was still little in the way of effective action forthcoming from the international community.

As well as addressing the crisis in Darfur, Egeland also coordinated relief efforts in what would have been otherwise neglected emergency situations, such as in northern Uganda (where the Lord's Resistance Army, under Joseph Kony, had been murdering tens of thousands for decades), in Somalia, and in the Democratic Republic of the Congo. He traveled to the frontlines of conflicts, meeting with Kony and his deputy, Vincent Otti, in November 2006, as well as other sites of human catastrophe such as Colombia, Lebanon, and the Palestinian Territories. And while he sought to draw international attention at all times to the need to alleviate distress, he was often just as critical of local conditions and leaders and their part in the crisis situations he was attempting to ease.

Apart from manmade disasters such as these, during his period with OCHA Egeland was also confronted by natural calamities and the need to provide desperately needed relief in these situations. These included earthquakes, droughts, the 2004 Indian Ocean tsunami, and the 2005 Atlantic hurricane that devastated large parts of the southern United States and the Caribbean, Hurricane Katrina.

In July 2006, Egeland launched a huge U.S. appeal to aid the reconstruction of Lebanon following the destruction of parts of the country by Israeli forces and the displacement of many thousands of refugees. Although critical of Israel, referring to its invasion of Lebanon as a violation of humanitarian law, he drew the intense ire of Hezbollah, lashing out at the movement for its use of women and children as human shields, and effectively blaming it for much of the loss of life through this tactic.

During Egeland's tenure at the UN, he oversaw the creation of the Central Emergency Response Fund (CERF), a humanitarian funding mechanism established to enable more timely and reliable assistance to victims of natural disasters and armed conflicts. It was approved by the General Assembly on December 15, 2005, when the former Central Emergency Revolving Fund (a loan facility of $50 million established by the General Assembly in 1991) was upgraded by adding a grant element for the disbursement of further emergency assistance. The CERF, which allocates one-third of its resources to core, life-saving activities in chronically underfunded crises, was launched in March 2006.

On September 1, 2007, Egeland returned to Norway to take up the position of director of the Norwegian Institute of International Affairs. He also became a professor at the University of Stavanger, established in 2005, while remaining an adviser to the UN secretary-general. In 2008, Egeland published a memoir, *A Billion Lives: An Eyewitness Report from the Frontlines of Humanity,* dealing with his time at the UN between 2003 and 2006.

PAUL R. BARTROP

See also: Amnesty International

Further Reading

Anderson, Scott. "How Did Darfur Happen?" *The New York Times,* October 17, 2004.

Scherrer, P. Christian. *Genocide and Crisis in Central Africa: Conflict Roots, Mass Violence, and Regional War.* Westport, CT: Praeger, 2002.

European Convention on the Non-Applicability of Statutory Limitations to Crimes

Similar to the United Nations (UN) convention of the same name introduced in 1968 and ratified two years later, the European convention, concluded on January 25, 1974, draws its legality from the post–World War II Nuremberg Trials, the 1948 UN Convention on Genocide, and the 1949 Geneva Conventions. It declared that war crimes and crimes against humanity have no statutory limitations. A key difference between the European and UN conventions is that the former specifically mentions apartheid as a crime against humanity while the UN convention does not. None of the member nations of the European Council at that time ratified the UN convention because European nations were uncomfortable with classifying apartheid as a crime against humanity, fearing that their former colonies might use it to prosecute former imperial officials.

Although thinkers such as Cesare Beccaria and John Locke had argued for a legal definition of crimes against humanity as early as the 17th century, the atrocities of the Holocaust and World War II brought renewed interest to the topic. At the end of World War II, Allied powers prosecuted major German and Japanese war criminals at the Nuremberg and Tokyo trials. While there was consensus in Europe to punish former German officials, there was a great deal of ambivalence concerning the prosecution of their own domestic war criminals. European nations that had been occupied by Germany during the war had little interest in opening the wounds of the past by prosecuting citizens for collaboration with Nazi officials, specifically for aiding and abetting the transportation of individuals to certain death in concentration camps. The issue was complicated by Cold War politics and a fear of giving the Soviet Union any propaganda victories.

France provides an excellent example of this ambivalence. After the war, the French government granted amnesty to officials of the German-allied Vichy government. In 1964, France added a domestic law that made war crimes and crimes against humanity a criminal act. This seeming reversal was more than offset by the reluctance of the French government to use the law as a basis of prosecution. In the 1980s, Klaus Barbie was brought to trial for participation in the Holocaust. Many charges against him were dismissed under the pre-1964 statutes, although he was ultimately convicted of war crimes. The trial of Maurice Papon, which lasted from 1981 until 1998, likewise demonstrated the ambiguity of prosecuting war crimes in France. Like Barbie, Papon was found guilty, but only served three years of his sentence.

In 1965 the parliamentary assembly of the European Council recommended that a convention be drawn up to bring consistency and order to the subject of war crimes and crimes against humanity. In the meantime, the UN began work on a similar convention. Nine years later, on January 25, 1974, the European convention declaration that there were no statutory limitations to war crimes and crimes against humanity was concluded in Strasbourg, France.

The convention required the ratification of three nations before it would enter into force. Despite this fairly low threshold, it would be 29 years before it was ratified. France signed the treaty in 1974, but never ratified it. The Netherlands was the first country to ratify the convention in 1981. The collapse of the Iron Curtain in 1989 breathed new life into the convention, however. Nineteen years after the Netherlands, Romania became the second nation to ratify the convention. In 2003, Belgium ratified the treaty, enabling it to finally enter into force. Since then, the convention has been ratified by Ukraine (2008), Bosnia and Herzegovina (2009), Serbia (2011), and Montenegro (2011).

Other European nations objected to the convention for several reasons. Some claimed that existing agreements already rendered the convention irrelevant. This position was clearly stated in 1983 by the French Supreme Court when it ruled that the nonstatutory limitation to crimes against humanity and war crimes was an accepted international legal standard that required no further legislation. Some legal scholars questioned the retroactive nature of domestic laws and international conventions related to the nonapplicability of statutory limitations to war crimes and crimes against humanity.

The Strasbourg Convention has been superseded by Article 29 of the Rome Agreement of 2002, which explicitly states that there are no statutory limitations to war crimes and crimes against humanity. The Rome Agreement also created an International Criminal Court (ICC) to adjudicate cases under this law. Unlike the Strasbourg Convention, which evoked little interest, most European countries have signed the Rome Agreement.

Gregory J. Dehler

See also: Hague Conventions; United Nations; United Nations Convention on the Prevention and Punishment of Genocide

Further Reading

Bassiouni, M. Cherif. *Crimes against Humanity in International Criminal Law.* 2nd Rev. ed. Boston: Kluwer Law International, 1999.

Cryer, Robert, Hakan Friman, Darryl Robinson, and Elizabeth Wilmhurst. *An Introduction to International Criminal Law and Procedure.* Cambridge, UK: Cambridge University Press, 2007.

G

Geneva Convention, Protocol I

The additional Protocol I to the Geneva Conventions of 1949, which applies to international armed conflicts and the protection of war victims, was adopted in 1977 following a four-year negotiating process. As of May 11, 2011, 170 states were party to Protocol I; this group does not include the United States or Israel.

Protocol I was negotiated during and in the immediate aftermath of the Vietnam Conflict and constituted an attempt to update both the Geneva Convention of 1949 concerning the protection of victims and the 1907 Hague Convention concerning methods and means of war. The 102 articles are divided into six parts: part 1 (Articles 1–7) general provisions; part 2 (Articles 8–34) wounded sick and shipwrecked; part 3 (Articles 35–47) methods and means of warfare and combatant and prisoner of war status; part 4 (Articles 48–79) civilian population; part 5 (Articles 80–91) execution of the conventions; and, the protocol, part 6 (Articles 92–102) final provisions.

One particularly contentious issue during the negotiating process was the scope of application of the protocol, in particular whether it should apply exclusively to traditional interstate armed conflicts or also to some or all conflicts involving liberation movements of various types. Indeed, some delegations favored the development of a uniform body of law applicable to all conflicts. In the end, the conference adopted Article 1 (4) whereby Protocol I was regarded as applicable to traditional interstate armed conflicts and also to "armed conflicts in which peoples are fighting against colonial domination and alien occupation and against racist regimes in the exercise of their right of self-determination." The adoption of this provision probably ensured that some countries would not immediately ratify the protocol, but it does not appear to have had a substantial long-term effect.

Combatant and prisoner of war status was another contentious issue during the negotiation process, and the issue continues to be regarded as contentious in some circles. Under the older law, as embodied in Article 4 of the 1949 Geneva Prisoner of War Convention, members of organized resistance movements had to meet several criteria, including requirements to wear some kind of uniform and to carry their arms openly, in order to be regarded as prisoners of war upon capture; members of resistance movements, however, found it difficult both to meet these criteria and remain effective. Article 44 of Protocol I eliminates the requirement that resistance fighters wear some kind of uniform; it also modifies the arms obligation, so that arms now are required to be carried openly only during each military engagement and while the fighter is visible to an adversary when engaged in a military deployment prior to an attack.

Parts 3 and 4 of the protocol substantially update the old body of law concerning the conduct of hostilities; many of the provisions in these parts are regarding as stating current customary law. In brief, the protocol defines the expression "military objective" and then states that military commanders are required not only to direct their operations against military objectives, but also to ensure that losses to the civilian population and damage to civilian property are not disproportionate to the concrete and direct military advantage anticipated. Attacks that are not directed against military objectives, particularly attacks directed against the civilian population, and attacks that cause disproportionate civilian casualties or civilian property damage may constitute the offense of unlawful attack. In determining whether or not such an offense has been committed, the following duties of commanders must be considered. Military commanders must: a) do everything practicable to verify that the objectives to be attacked are military objectives; b) take all practicable precautions in the choice of methods and means of warfare in order to avoid or minimize incidental civilian casualties or civilian property damage; and c) refrain from launching attacks that may be expected to cause disproportionate civilian casualties or civilian property damage.

The protocol imposes obligations on defenders as well as attackers. In particular, defenders are obligated to take precautions to protect civilians under their control against dangers resulting from military operations and, to the extent practicable, to avoid undertaking military operations where civilians and civilian property are present.

WILLIAM J. FENRICK

See also: Geneva Convention Protocol II (1977); Hague Conventions

Further Reading

Bothe, M., K. J. Partsch, and W. A. Solf. *New Rules for Victims of Armed Conflicts.* The Hague: Martinus Nijhoff Publishers, 1982.

Sandoz, Y., C. Swinarski, and B. Zimmerman, eds. *Commentary on the Additional Protocols of 8 June 1977 to the Geneva Conventions of 12 August 1949, International Committee of the Red Cross.* The Hague: Martinus Nijhoff Publishers, 1987.

Geneva Convention Protocol II (1977)

Protocols I and II Additional to the Geneva Conventions of 1949 were negotiated at a diplomatic conference held in Geneva between 1973 and 1977; both were adopted in 1977. Protocol II applies to noninternational armed conflicts and, as of May 2011, 165 states were party to it. The United States is a nonparty. Protocol II consists of 28 Articles in five parts: part 1 (Articles 1–3) scope of application; part 2 (Articles 4–6) humane treatment; part 3 (Articles 7–12) wounded, sick, and shipwrecked; part 4 (Articles 13–18) civilian population; and part 5 (articles 19–28) final provisions.

Protocol II is a truncated document because of its negotiating history. As indicated above, both additional protocols were negotiated at the same diplomatic conference; one of the main issues at the conference, which occurred during and in the aftermath of both the Vietnam War and the decolonization process, was the treatment of national liberation movements. A variety of options were explored and kept open until late in the negotiation process, including: a) producing a single protocol for all conflicts; b) classifying national liberation conflicts as international conflicts; and c) classifying national liberation conflicts as internal conflicts. As long as option (c) above remained open, the draft Protocol II remained a substantial document. Once it became apparent that conflicts involving national liberation movements would be classified as international conflicts because of the adoption of Article 1(4) of Additional Protocol I, many delegations, particularly those from developing countries, attempted to jettison some or all of Additional Protocol II. The present Additional Protocol II is the result of a partially successful salvage operation conducted in the final phase of negotiations. As a result, it contains an oddly assorted grab bag of provisions.

Protocol II is the first treaty instrument devoted exclusively to noninternational armed conflicts. Its content and scope of application must be considered in relation to Common Article 3 of the Geneva Conventions of 1949, the only provision of the Conventions that applies to noninternational armed conflicts. This article does not define noninternational armed conflict, but it is generally regarded as having a low threshold of application. It is also regarded as restating the core of the Geneva Conventions, a set of minimum standards applicable to all armed conflicts.

Protocol II has a narrower scope of application than Common Article 3 and applies to armed conflicts between government armed forces and dissident armed forces or organized armed groups, which meet certain criteria. It does not apply to situations of internal disturbances and tensions, such as riots or isolated and sporadic acts of violence, not does it apply to armed conflicts between organized armed groups or dissident armed forces. The involvement of government armed forces in the conflict is an essential element.

In addition to restating, updating, and amplifying the provisions of Common Article 3 related to the protection of victims of war, Protocol II briefly addresses conduct of hostilities issues. The provisions related to these issues, Articles 13–18, are similar to almost randomly selected provisions in Protocol I. For example, Article 13(2) of Protocol II states: "The civilian population as such, as well as individual civilians, shall not be the object of attack. Acts of, or a threat of, violence the primary purpose of which is to spread terror among the civilian population, is prohibited." This is identical to Article 51(2) of Protocol I, but Protocol I also contains several other provisions that are related to or amplify this statement.

WILLIAM J. FENRICK

See also: Hague Conventions; Geneva Convention, Protocol I

Further Reading

Bothe, M., K.J. Partsch, and W.A. Solf. *New Rules for Victims of Armed Conflicts.* The Hague: Martinus Nijhoff Publishers, 1982.

Levie, Howard. *The Law of Non-International Armed Conflict: Protocol II to the 1949 Geneva Convention.* The Hague: Martinus Nijhoff Publishers, 1987.

Sandoz, Y., C. Swinarski, and B. Zimmerman, eds. *Commentary on the Additional Protocols of 8 June 1977 to the Geneva Conventions of 12 August 1949, International Committee of the Red Cross.* The Hague: Martinus Nijhoff Publishers, 1987.

Hague Conventions

The Hague Peace Conferences originated from the desire to codify certain principles of justice that existed in the public conscience and that were often manifested by general customs in the international community. There are multiple parallels between The Hague Convention of 1899 and the Brussels Declaration of 1874; therefore, many scholars believe that Brussels was the inspiration for 52 of the 60 Hague Convention articles (1899). The Oxford Manual of 1880 is also mentioned as a possible influence, but Brussels is considered the most significant predecessor to the Hague Convention of 1899. Another Hague Convention was held in 1907, which dealt primarily with establishing international norms for warfare, including crimes against humanity.

The conference that directly preceded the Hague Conventions was convened on the initiative of Czar Nicholas II of Russia and was meant to include all the nations of Europe and the United States. All of the formal invitations were accepted, and 26 nations sent 100 delegates to the peace conference. Although the majority of Europe, the United States, Russia, Mexico, Turkey, Siam, and Bulgaria were all in attendance, there were numerous omissions (such as the whole of South America and Korea), which caused some resentment. The Netherlands was chosen as the seat of the Conference because it was seen at the time as a neutral country, had hosted international conferences in the past, and Queen Wilhelmina was free

from international scandal because of her short time on the throne. The conference opened at The Hague on May 18, 1899, and continued for more than two months, until the final plenary session on July 29, 1899.

The total number plenary sessions held was ten, but nearly all of the vital work of the Hague Conference occurred within its committees or commissions. The first commission addressed the limitation of armaments and the "humanizing" of war; it was deemed to be the most relevant and crucial of all commissions at the time. The second commission dealt with maritime warfare and the laws and customs of war. It was the third commission that addressed the subjects of mediation and arbitration, which would leave a lasting legacy for international jurisprudence. The fourth commission, generally designated as a subcommittee of the third commission, was developed to promote good relations within the commissions themselves.

The primary objective of the conference was to seek "the most effectual means of insuring to all peoples the benefits of a real and durable peace." A general theme was the peaceful settlement of disputes between sovereign and equal states, which would be achieved through the creation of mechanisms for the judicial settlement of disputes. The third commission handled this undertaking with the establishment of the Permanent Court of Arbitration. This tribunal was designed to utilize methods of conciliation, mediation, arbitration, and judicial settlement in order to avoid armed conflict between and among nations. The Permanent Court of Arbitration gave rise to the most contentious debate during the Hague Conference, with Germany and the United States pitted against the rest of the nations. The German kaiser was strongly opposed to the Court, and relented to its creation only after much pressure from his inner circle of advisers forced his hand. The United States reneged at the last minute, fearing that the Court might precipitate a war between Europe and the United States sometime in the future. Eventually, the Americans did comply with the establishment of the Court, however.

Another aspiration of the 1899 Hague Peace Conference was the global reduction in armaments, or military charges, as it was termed at the time. The first commission handled this subject and termed armaments to be a serious economic burden on the international community. In the final act of 1899, the first commission promoted the restriction of military charges as extremely desirable in order to increase the material and moral welfare of mankind. The commission explored the desirability of limited war budgets and quotas for land and sea troops in an effort to limit the global economic burden of war and war preparations. The goal to reduce armaments was also grounded in the belief that the cruelty of war could be minimized through arms control and prohibitions on specific categories of weapons.

The third major goal of the Hague Peace Conference of 1899 was rooted in humanitarian purposes and focused on the restriction of the means and methods of warfare. The second commission determined that the primary purpose of war was to gain territory and not to inflict pain and suffering on the general populace; therefore, any acts that did specifically target civilian populations could not be justified and had to be avoided on humanitarian grounds. This reasoning was justified only if civilians did not take up arms, in which case the restriction of military action against those civilians would be null and void. The second commission also determined that warfare did not require the unnecessary maiming of the enemy, only enough injury to disable the soldier so he could no longer participate in an armed contest. This idea was derived from the formulations of the St. Petersburg declaration of 1868, which had espoused that the only legitimate object of the state at war was to weaken the military forces of the enemy by disabling as many combatants as possible.

The Hague Peace Conference focused on the reduction of the horrors of war and emphasized that combatants do not have limitless means available to them in order to neutralize the enemy. Consequently, the second commission solidified the restriction of some weapons and established the complete prohibition of other weapons, thereby establishing precedence for modern just rules of warfare. The launch of projectiles and explosives from balloons and any other similar methods was banned because the risk to the unarmed civilian population was deemed unnecessary. The Hague Peace Conference of 1899 also banned the "dum-dum bullet," which would expand or flatten easily in the human body. Finally, the Conference of 1899 banned the use of projectiles that could diffuse asphyxiating or deleterious gases, because they were deemed to be unnecessary and cruel in nature.

The 1899 Hague Peace Conference was the first such meeting that was not assembled after a major global conflict. The Conference also represented the start of an international era in which a diverse array of global players was invited to the meeting table, not just the European powers. Moreover, the Conference established the first global tribunal and took the first step toward establishing permanent institutions for promoting international peace. Although the Permanent Court of Arbitration was not a permanent judicial body, this tribunal provided a precedent for the Permanent Court of International Justice founded by the League of Nations in 1920. The United Nations later revised the statute of the World Court in 1945 and changed the official name of the Permanent Court of International Justice to the International Court of Justice. Although modern international judicial developments can be traced to the First Hague Peace Conference of 1899, the avowed purpose of the Conference was to promote peace, and so many scholars therefore consider it a failure. Indeed, the armaments race was not checked, and the arbitration agreements established in 1899 did not prevent World War I.

Another global peace conference would not convene at The Hague until Russia proposed an international meeting following the conclusion of the 1904–1905 Russo-Japanese War. In 1907, delegates from 46 countries gathered at The Hague with the primary goal of establishing a world court. This new court would function in an entirely different capacity than the Permanent Court established during The Hague Peace Conference of 1899, which largely dealt with arbitration issues. The world court would function as a supreme international tribunal and would issue decisions based on international law and precedent. However, a world court did not emerge from the Hague Conference of 1907 because of an impasse over the selection of judges for the court. The meeting was successful in defining some rules of conduct in modern warfare, but many nations failed to ratify the resolutions, so they became largely moot. Moreover, the delegates agreed to the wording of a model arbitration treaty that did not consider sovereignty, vital interests, or national honor. Perhaps the most lasting and relevant portion of the Hague Convention of 1907 was the development of the concept of "crimes against humanity," taken from the Martens Clause. This clause stated in cases not otherwise covered by the convention that "the inhabitants and the belligerents remain under the protection and the rule of the principles of the law of nations, as they result from the usages established among civilized people, from the laws of humanity, and the dictates of public conscience." Ultimately, the legacies of The Hague Conventions did promote the growth of international humanitarian law, which have become a vital part of modern international jurisprudence.

MARGARET DETRAZ

See also: Coalition for International Justice; International Court of Justice; International Criminal Court

Further Reading

Kalshoven, Frits, ed. *The Centennial of the First International Peace Conference: Reports and Conclusions.* Boston, MA: Kluwer Law International, 2000.

Schucking, Walther. *The International Union of the Hague Conferences.* Oxford, UK: Clarendon Press, 1918.

Human Rights Watch

Human Rights Watch (HRW) is a human rights organization based out of New York, New York, with a staff of 150 workers. It investigates human rights problems around the world and leads campaigns against particular abuses.

HRW was founded as Helsinki Watch in 1978. Its original mission was to make sure the Soviet Union adhered to the human rights provisions of the Helsinki Accords, signed in 1975. Various other "Watch" committees formed over the next few years, including Americas Watch in 1981, Asia Watch in 1985, the Prison Project in 1987, and Africa Watch in 1988. That year the groups assembled into one organization called Human Rights Watch.

One of HRW's main missions is fact gathering. Every year HRW sends researchers to investigate human rights abuses. It compiles facts and publishes reports in the news media and in books. Part of its goal in making media reports is to embarrass governments that abuse citizens. During crises, HRW makes multiple daily reports on dangerous situations. Members of HRW also meet with government representatives to discuss human rights abuses and suggest changes. The organization uses its reports to persuade governments and international organizations to take action against abuses, and recommends appropriate responses.

HRW currently follows human rights events in 70 countries, including issues of women's rights, child abuse and exploitation, the sale of arms to abusive armies, international justice, prisons, drugs, refugees, and academic freedom. It has called international attention to genocide and ethnic violence in Rwanda, Serbia and Croatia, Kosovo, Israel and Palestine, Indonesia, and Sudan. It has also identified human rights abuses within the United States. HRW has led efforts to formalize an international treaty against the use of child soldiers. It campaigned for an international ban on landmines. It has provided evidence for tribunals in the former Yugoslavia, Rwanda, and Chile.

About 150 people work for HRW. They include journalists, scholars, lawyers, and cultural experts. Numerous volunteers help the organization with its projects. HRW is based in New York and maintains offices in Washington, D.C., San Francisco, Los Angeles, Toronto, London, Brussels, Moscow, Tashkent, and Hong Kong. To maintain its fairness in reporting, HRW does not accept money from any government or government-funded agency. It is funded entirely by donations from individuals and private groups.

AMY HACKNEY BLACKWELL

See also: Amnesty International; Human Rights Watch; Prevent Genocide International

Further Reading

Mann, Michael. *The Dark Side of Democracy: Explaining Ethnic Cleansing.* Cambridge, UK: Cambridge University Press, 2004.

Power, Samantha. *"A Problem from Hell": America and the Age of Genocide.* New York: Harper Perennial, 2007.

I

International Court of Justice

Also known as the World Court, the International Court of Justice (ICJ) sits at The Hague in the Netherlands. As the principal judicial organ of the United Nations, the ICJ adjudicates disputes between states that have recognized its competence.

Created in the wake of World War II, the ICJ provides a mechanism for states to resolve their differences peacefully, without resort to war or violence. The ICJ endeavors to fulfill the primary goal stated in the United Nations (UN) Charter: "to bring about by peaceful means, and in conformity with the principles of justice and international law, adjustment or settlement of international disputes or situations that might lead to a breach of the peace." The ICJ also provides advisory opinions on legal questions referred to it by the organs and agencies of the UN.

Although the ICJ itself was founded as part of the United Nations system in 1945, its history extends back to 1919, when the Permanent Court of International Justice (PCIJ) was created. The PCIJ was the first body of its kind to offer states a permanent body for dispute resolution that also allowed for consistent interpretation and development of international law. Active between 1919 and 1940, the PCIJ rendered 29 decisions in contentious cases and 27 advisory opinions. With the onset of World War II, however, the PCIJ fell into disuse. As World War II drew to a close and steps were taken to establish the United Nations, the future of the PCIJ was questioned. The PCIJ had been affiliated with the now-defunct League of Nations. The founders of the UN wanted to maintain an international court, but believed it necessary to distance themselves symbolically from the PCIJ. The ICJ, based largely on the statute of the PCIJ, provided a judicial forum for dispute resolution within the United Nations.

There have been few formal changes in the structure of the ICJ since its creation in 1945. Informal changes include increased membership and caseload, greater diversity of subject matter, modification of the rules of the court regarding the creation and composition of chambers, and new patterns of mobilization.

Not only has the ICJ increased in membership as more states have joined the United Nations, but since the end of the Cold War in 1991 many countries have withdrawn their reservations to the arbitration clauses of various treaties requiring the submission of disputes to the ICJ. This change makes it much easier to bring disputes arising under these treaties before the ICJ. It also encourages greater use of such clauses in future treaties. With more members and more functioning treaties, the ICJ has seen a steady increase in its caseload since 1986. Since 1993 the ICJ has gained or solidified authority over various policy areas, most notably human rights and the law of the sea. Early ICJ cases focused on land frontiers and maritime boundaries; more recently, the court has also reviewed cases relating to nuclear testing and nuclear weapons, self-determination, and genocide.

The ICJ revised its rules in 1978 to give litigants the option of bringing cases before chambers of the ICJ. The use of chambers allows disputing parties to indicate which judges they prefer to hear their case. The parties, in consultation with the ICJ, can determine the composition of the chamber, as well as the chamber's procedural rules. Proponents of chambers argue for their political and practical value; states that would otherwise avoid the ICJ make use of chambers and thereby increase the ICJ's overall workload. Chambers encourage states to bring controversial or sensitive cases to the ICJ, but, critics argue, they also tend to lower trust in the ICJ as a whole. These critics are encouraged by the renewed use of the full body of the ICJ, which they believe increases the legitimacy of the body and returns the rule of law to the proceedings.

The mechanisms of the ICJ have been increasingly mobilized in new and creative ways. Historically, states have turned to the ICJ as a last resort. Now the court is a natural step in the process of resolving international disputes. Many more cases are being settled before reaching the end of the dispute settlement process. States parties are turning to the ICJ earlier, using it as a resource for advice and a mechanism for leverage. Disputing states refer specific legal questions to the ICJ even as they engage in political negotiations to resolve the dispute on their own.

The ICJ decides cases in accordance with international law. Article 38, paragraph 1 of the statute of the court states that international law may be derived from the following sources: international conventions; international customs; general principles of law; and, as a secondary source, "judicial decisions and the teachings of the most highly qualified publicists of the various nations." It is clear from the ICJ's decisions that this is not an exhaustive list. Nevertheless, the ICJ relies heavily on treaties, conventions, and established state behavior to decide cases that come before it.

Only states parties to the statute of the court may submit contentious cases. Member states of the UN are automatically parties to the statute of the court. Switzerland is also a party to the statute of the court. However, the ICJ does not have compulsory jurisdiction over these parties. It obtains jurisdiction over a state in one of three ways: two or more states agree to submit a dispute to the ICJ; states are party to a treaty that refers disputes to the ICJ; or disputing parties have made prior declarations recognizing as compulsory the jurisdiction of the ICJ. In the last case, states are bound only insofar as their declarations coincide. Organs and agencies of the United Nations may also submit legal questions to the ICJ for advisory opinions.

Requests must fall within the scope of the activities of the requesting agency. Advisory opinions are nonbinding in nature.

A case may be lodged with the ICJ either by a single state or by states parties to a dispute. Once a case has been brought before the ICJ, it is registered by the registry of the court, communicated to the respondent party and to the press, and placed on the ICJ's docket. The ICJ then works with the parties to establish guidelines and time limits for written pleadings and considers any preliminary objections challenging the ICJ's jurisdiction in the case.

Once it has been established that the ICJ has jurisdiction, the case continues through the written phase of the proceedings. The parties to the case submit extensive written arguments to the ICJ. These pleadings are confidential, pending the outcome of the case. Oral hearings make up the next phase of the case. Each party to a case presents oral arguments at a public hearing of the ICJ, which then has an opportunity to ask questions and request further information from the parties, if necessary. The judges meet privately to discuss the case and then render the written judgment of the ICJ. Judges may also submit concurring and dissenting opinions. The decision of the court is binding.

The ICJ consists of 15 judges who are elected by the United Nations General Assembly and Security Council to nine-year terms. All states parties to the statute of the court may propose candidates to the ICJ. Judges are eligible for reelection. According to the statute of the court, judges must be persons of "high moral character, who possess the qualifications required in their respective countries for appointment to the highest judicial office or are jurisconsults of recognized competence in international law." No two judges may be from the same country, and the body as a whole must represent "the main forms of civilizations and the principal legal systems of the world."

Members of the ICJ act in their individual capacity to uphold the law. When a case comes before the ICJ in which nationals of one or both of the states parties to the dispute do not sit on the court, the party may choose a person to sit independently as an ad hoc judge in the case. This is done to guarantee fairness and to assure that the complexities of the state's domestic law are fully understood.

The registry of the court supports the judges in their work. Members of the registry are chosen for their administrative, legal, or linguistic skills. Registry officials must be proficient in both English and French, the ICJ's two official languages.

Since 1984, the ICJ has experienced an increased caseload and a notable shift in the issues brought before it. Patterns of mobilization vary for all courts over time. During the late 1970s and early 1980s, the ICJ experienced diminished use, but has since experienced a steady increase in its workload. The current level of use exceeds the ICJ's previous period of increased mobilization (1971–1975) and represents a greater diversity of litigants.

Beginning in 1978, the ICJ revised its rules to allow parties to bring questions before a chamber of the court. The ICJ works with the parties to establish the composition of the chamber and determine the rules governing the proceedings. This practice increased the ICJ's workload at a critical juncture, but no chamber has been convened since 1992.

The ICJ lacks any enforcement powers and is dependent on the will of the parties to a case for implementation. The statute of the court provides for enforcement of court decisions by the United Nations Security Council; but the viability of such an enforcement mechanism is questionable because of the veto powers of Britain, China, France, Russia, and the United States. Enforcement was not possible during the Cold War, and this possibility has not since been pursued. Nevertheless, the parties to a case have implemented the vast majority of the ICJ's decisions without recourse to the Security Council.

Controversy surrounds the question of the ICJ's efficacy. Critics of the ICJ argue that the court's relatively light caseload is an indication that the ICJ is not effective. They also contend that the ICJ is too steeped in a Western legal tradition, that it is too accommodating of the parties, that it has no enforcement powers, and that the process takes too long. Proponents counter that the ICJ is only one of several options states might legitimately pursue in their efforts to attain a peaceful settlement to a dispute; as long as the ICJ assists states in the peaceful resolution of disputes, then it is successful, regardless of the number of cases it hears. Stephen Schwebel, a member of the court from 1981 to 2000, provides the example of a border dispute between Botswana and Namibia. He contrasts the peaceful settlement of this dispute with a similar dispute between Ethiopia and Eritrea that has led to a great deal of violence and unnecessary bloodshed. Proponents further argue that the increased use of the ICJ by non-Western states indicates that the criticism of a Western bias is no longer appropriate. They also note that little is gained if the ICJ extends a ruling that the parties will not follow and that a high measure of implementation belies the need for enforcement powers. Finally, a lengthy process is necessary not only

to resolve the complex issues that come before the court but also to accommodate differences in legal traditions that emphasize either extensive written pleadings or oral pleadings. It should also be noted that the average length of the court's proceedings is not significantly longer than comparable institutions dealing with dispute resolution, such as arbitration.

The ICJ serves the interests of the international community. In many ways, the tribunal exemplifies the community's commitment to consistency, predictability, and the development of a coherent body of international law. The ICJ has not always been a huge success, but it has served to elaborate upon the ever-burgeoning field of international law and is growing into the role of a "supreme court" similar to those found in the UN's member states. And, like every "supreme court," the ICJ experiences periods of growth, stagnation, and even decline. Through it all, the ICJ reflects the international community's need for a legitimate, trustworthy, independent tribunal. The current change in the ICJ's agenda, that is, its enhanced jurisdiction and use, is itself a reflection of an expanded global agenda.

Sonya Brown

See also: International Criminal Court; United Nations

Further Reading

Lowe, Vaughan, and Malgosia Fitzmaurice, eds. *Fifty Years of the International Court of Justice: Essays in Honor of Sir Robert Jennings.* New York: Cambridge University Press, 1996.

Rosenne, Shabtai. *The World Court: What It Is and How It Works.* 5th ed. Dordrecht, The Netherlands: Martinus Nijhoff Publishers, 1995.

International Criminal Court

The first permanent international institution to address the most heinous international crimes. Critics of the International Criminal Court (ICC) maintain that such an institution threatens state sovereignty and advocate further limitations of the Court's jurisdiction. Proponents of the institution view the Court as a potential deterrent and as a tool to empower and provide legal proceedings to victims of the gravest breaches of international law.

On July 1, 2002, the ICC became a reality with more than one 120 nations attending the final convention of the Rome Statute. The Rome Statute required 60 states to become signatories by December 31, 2000 (Article 126), for the statute to enter force. That goal was far exceeded with 139 state signatories at the closing date. The endorsement of the Rome Statute requires states to be signatories and ratified members. The ratification of a state's signature varies with each state's domestic legal system. For example, the United States would need the approval of the Senate for the international signature to be ratified. Support of the ICC stands to become stronger as the 139 states that have endorsed the Rome Statue with their signature become ratified members; as of March 2006, 100 states had become ratified members in accordance with their domestic legal systems. A few states have failed to become signatories because of domestic strife, but are willing to participate in the ICC, such as Kazakhstan, Indonesia, and Malaysia. Other states are adamantly opposed to the ICC, such as the Libyan Arab Jamchiriya, India, Pakistan, Saudi Arabia, Turkey, Iraq, and Myanmar.

The idea of an international court to adjudicate disputes over international law is not a new idea. Throughout the late 19th and 20th centuries, the idea had been pursued and explored within the international arena. One of the founders and acting president of the International Committee of the Red Cross, Gustave Moynier, was the first to formally propose an international criminal court in 1872. The Franco-Prussian War was plagued by mass atrocities committed by both sides, despite obligations under the First Geneva Convention of 1864. Moynier, distraught at the violations of international treaties, proposed an international criminal court to try persons accused of war crimes. The proposed international court never received support from international lawyers or state parties. The concept of an international criminal court was not revisited again until after World War I; the framers of the 1919 Treaty of Versailles revived the vision of an international criminal court to try the Kaiser Wilhelm and German war criminals. The call for an international criminal court was compromised, however; punishment for war crimes was to be handled by existing national military tribunals. The failure of the proposed court resulted in trials held in Leipzig, where 888 of the 901 persons accused of war crimes were acquitted, released, or not tried.

In 1937, the League of Nations attempted to establish an international criminal court. Two international conventions were concluded in Geneva, Switzerland, on November 16 of that year: the Prevention and Repression of Terrorism and the Creation of an International Criminal Court. The charter for the creation of an international criminal court required the ratification of the Prevention and Repression of Terrorism Treaty. Neither convention, however, obtained sufficient support for ratification.

World War II postponed any collective interest in an international criminal court. As the war was coming to an end, however, the Allied powers directed their attention to the creation of an international institution to try individuals for the most heinous crimes of war. The need for and call to international justice resonated throughout the world. Some had hopes that with the end of the League of Nations and the development of the United Nations (UN), the world was a step closer to instituting a permanent criminal court. The outcome was not an international criminal court, however, but international military tribunals instituted to address crimes against humanity. Nonetheless, this collective drive produced the Nuremberg Principles, which would sit as the foundation of future international law directed at war crime and crimes against humanity. But the hope of a permanent international criminal court was again discouraged.

Although efforts to establish an international criminal court continued over the next several decades by institutional reformers and civil society actors, it was not until 1989 that the international society began to seriously reconsider the establishment of an international criminal court. In 1989, Trinidad and Tobago approached the UN with a proposal for an international criminal court as a device to address drug trafficking and terrorism. Contemporaneously, the International Institute of Higher Studies in Criminal Sciences, in conjunction with the UN, prepared a draft statute that proposed an international criminal court with jurisdiction over all international crimes. This draft was submitted to the Eighth United Nations Congress on Crime Prevention and Treatment of Offenders in 1990, recommending that the International Law Commission (ILC) consider the draft. The ILC completed its report, which the UN General Assembly had assigned it in 1989, and submitted it to the 45th session of the General Assembly. The report did not limit the concept of a court to drug trafficking but was expanded to include a more universal criminal court that would cover other forms of international crimes. Although there were states that would strongly resist this court, an overwhelming number of nation-states appeared ready for the concept and reality of an international criminal court.

The following nine years proved to be challenging as the UN General Assembly, preparatory committees, and nongovernmental agencies worked on a proposal for an international criminal court: the Rome Statute. During this time, state representatives, international lawyers, and nongovernmental organizations prepared many drafts stating their preferences for what role the court should play and what crimes would fall within the court's jurisdiction. Ultimately, many compromises had to be made. On July 18, 1998, a final vote on the Final Act of the Diplomatic Conference was taken: 120 delegations voted in favor of the Rome Statute, 7 voted against, and 21 abstained. The final vote represented the end of years of efforts to establish a statute for an international criminal court. As a result, the Rome Statute was officially opened for state signatures on July 18, 1998.

During the process of negotiations, significant conflicts occurred over issues of the Court's jurisdiction and its ability to exercise that jurisdiction. States held incompatible views regarding the role of the Court. Many states supported universal jurisdiction of the Court, ensuring universal justice, whereas other states (mainly the United States) insisted that the acceptance of the ICC's jurisdiction by states was a necessary precondition to jurisdiction. These two positions were heavily debated and resulted in a compromise that was not fully satisfactory to either of the conflicting forces: the like-minded states (LMS), which wanted universal jurisdiction, and the United States (the main challenger), which wanted a system based on compliance at will.

Although there was a general consensus that crimes of genocide, war crimes, and crimes against humanity should be covered by the court's jurisdiction, there were conflicts over the scope of crimes covered under war crimes, crimes against humanity, and the definition for crimes of aggression. Despite the fact that precedence had been set for the definition of aggressive crimes during the International Military Tribunal of the Nuremberg defendants after World War II and in the General Assembly Resolution 3314 of December 1974 (passed with a consensus for the definition of aggression), it remained an irresolvable issue for the committee meeting members.

Crimes of aggression were not the only controversial crime debated during the conference. For example, U.S. delegates insisted that the Court's jurisdiction should only occur if a state was a signatory when war crimes were committed on a large scale. This would mean that war crimes would essentially also have to be crimes against humanity before the Court could interject its jurisdiction. The United States was triumphant in this debate, and the condition of jurisdiction over war crimes was included in Article 8 (1) as a part of Part 2 Jurisdiction, Admissibility and Applicable Law. Article 8 (1) states, "the Court shall have jurisdiction in respect of war crimes in particular when committed as part of a plan or policy or as part of a large-scale commission of such crimes."

In summary, during the process of negotiations of the plenipotentiaries meeting, no one state (including the United States) was a monolithic obstacle. The proceedings were divided rather conspicuously between those like-minded states—more than 60 states, led by Canada, Australia, and the United Kingdom—that wanted universal jurisdiction, expanded definition of war crimes, an empowered prosecutor, and the exclusion of the Security Council in the court's decision, versus the non-like-minded states, such as the United States, Iraq, Qatar, and China. One of the major concessions made upon the insistence of the United States was the inclusion of a complementary court. This ensured that the concept of universality would be diminished by the recognition of the primacy of domestic courts. Another major compromise made at the insistence of the United States was the need for a state to be a signatory. This ensured state willingness to participate in the court versus a court empowered under a universal system of international law governing all of international society.

The ICC consists of over 120 states (as of 2012) forming the Assembly of States Parties (ASP) to the Rome Statue. The Assembly of States Parties is the management oversight and legislative body of the ICC. It is composed of representatives of the states that have ratified and acceded to the Rome Statute. The ASP has a main bureau, consisting of a president, 2 vice presidents, and 18 elected members for a three-year term. The ASP's role is to decide on issues including the adoption of normative texts, the budget, and the election of the judges, the prosecutor, and the deputy prosecutor(s). According to Article 112:7 of the Rome Statute, each state party has one vote, although every effort has to be made to reach decisions by consensus both in the ASP and the bureau. If consensus cannot be reached, decisions are taken by vote.

The Court consists of four chambers: (1) the Presidency; (2) Registry; (3) Judicial Court (made up of the Appeals Chamber, Trial Chamber, and a Pre-Trial Chamber); and (4) Office of the Prosecutor. Each of these plays a significant role in the Court's processes. The Presidency is an elected office with a term of three years, and it holds responsibility for the administrative duties of the Court, excluding the Office of the Prosecutor. The Presidency coordinates and seeks the concurrence of the Office of the Prosecutor on all matters of mutual concern. The president serves a six-year term on the Appeals Court. The first and second vice presidents serve nine-year terms in the Trial Division. The judges composing the Presidency also serve on a full-time basis. The president and first and second vice presidents are to elected by an absolute majority of the 18 judges of the Court.

The Registry is solely responsible for the administrative and nonjudicial aspects of the Court and for creating a Victims and Witness Unit that provides protective and security measures for witnesses, victims, or others at risk due to testimony given to the court. More specifically, the registrar is responsible for the administration of legal aid matters, court management, victims and witness matters, defense counsel, detention unit, finances, translation, and personnel. In relation to victims, the registrar is responsible for providing notice of the case to victims, assisting them in obtaining legal advice and representation, and, if necessary, providing agreements for relocation and support services (Rule 16 of the Rules of Procedure). The registrar is also responsible for receiving, obtaining, and providing information with states and as the main channel of communication between the Court, states, intergovernmental organizations, and nongovernmental organizations. The ASP by an absolute majority elects the registrar.

The functions of the Judicial Court are divided into chambers, which allow the judges to be on more than one chamber if it serves the functioning of the court in a more efficient manner. The Appellate Chamber is exempt from this, as an appellate judge is prohibited from serving on other chambers (Article 39). The judges constitute a forum of international experts that represents the world's principal legal systems. After the election of the judges, the Court organized itself into Appeals, Pre-Trial, and Trial Chambers.

The Office of the Prosecutor is a separate division of the Court with the responsibility for the investigation of referrals on crimes covered by the ICC. The prosecutor has full authority over the administration of the Prosecutorial Division (Article 42, Rome Statute). Cases brought to the ICC are handled independently by this office, unlike the system used by the UN Security Council, where there must be joint agreement to charges brought forth against individuals for crimes covered under international laws and treaties. A state may refer cases to the Office of the Prosecutor, or the prosecutor may initiate the investigations based on information of a crime being committed within the jurisdiction of the Court (Articles 14 and 15, Rome Statute). The prosecutor may start an investigation upon referral of situations in which there is a reasonable basis to believe that crimes covered by the Rome Statute have been or are being committed. Such referrals must be made by a state party or the UN Security Council. In accordance with the Rome Statute and the Rules of Procedure and Evidence,

the chief prosecutor must evaluate the material submitted to him before making the decision to proceed. In addition to state party and Security Council referrals, the chief prosecutor may also receive information on crimes within the jurisdiction of the Court provided by other sources, such as individuals or nongovernmental organizations.

The prosecutor then conducts a preliminary examination of the information in every case. If the prosecutor decides not to pursue a case due to lack of credible information or facts, he or she must provide prompt notice informing the state or states that referred the situation under Article 14 or the Security Council under Article 13 (b). If the chief prosecutor decides that there is a reasonable basis to proceed with an investigation, he or she will request the Pre-Trial Chamber to authorize such. The prosecutor evaluates the information and investigates to determine whether there is sufficient basis to prosecute. The prosecutor is solely responsible for the retention, storage, and security of all information and physical evidence obtained during the course of investigation (Rule 10, Rules of Procedure and Evidence). If the prosecutor decides to proceed with the investigation, he or she must first obtain authorization from the Pre-Trial Chamber. Formal prosecution then begins once a Pre-Trial Chamber judge issues an arrest warrant or summons for the accused individual to appear before the Court based on the charges filed by the prosecutor.

Once the accused appears, a hearing is held to determine whether sufficient evidence exists to proceed to the trial stage. It is at this point that the domestic states of those individuals may appear at the Court to challenge its jurisdiction or the admissibility of the case based on state primacy to prosecute.

GREGG BARAK

See also: International Court of Justice; Prevent Genocide International

Further Reading

Harrington, Joanna, ed. *Bringing Power to Justice?: The Prospects of the International Criminal Court.* Montreal, Canada: McGill-Queen University Press, 2006.

Roach, Steven. *Politicizing the International Criminal Court: The Convergence of Politics, Ethics, and Law.* Lanham, MD: Rowman and Littlefield Publishers, Inc., 2006.

Schabas, William A. *An Introduction to the International Criminal Court.* 2nd ed. Cambridge: Cambridge University Press, 2004.

Sewall, Saray, and Carl Kaysen. *The United States and the International Criminal Court.* Lanham, MD: Rowman and Littlefield Publishers, Inc., 2000.

K

Kuper, Leo

Leo Kuper was a South African lawyer, sociologist, teacher, and eminent genocide scholar.

Kuper was born in Johannesburg, South Africa on November 28, 1908, and was of Lithuanian-Jewish ancestry. After studying law, he commenced legal practice in South Africa, joining the British Army at the beginning of World War II. He eventually worked as a British intelligence officer. After the war, he settled in Britain and took a position teaching sociology at the University of Birmingham. He later held a faculty position at South Africa's University of Natal, where he published work that was critical of South Africa's apartheid government. His books *Passive Resistance in South Africa* and *An African Bourgeoisie,* published in the early 1960s, were both outlawed by South African officials. Kuper took a faculty position at the University of California-Los Angeles (UCLA) in 1961, and remained there for much of the remainder of his career. He also headed UCLA's African Studies Center for a number of years.

At UCLA, he continued researching and writing about South Africa, garnering numerous awards and accolades for his work. His most influential books in this field include *Race, Class, and Power, The Pity of it All: Polarisation of Racial and Ethnic Relations* (edited with M.G. Smith), and *Durban: A Study in Racial Ecology.* Kuper's satirical novel *The College Brew,* set in a fictitious tribal university in South Africa, was also well-received. One of Kuper's most outstanding contributions to the field of modern South African studies occurred when he identified ways in which marginalized or subjugated groups could reorder their relationships with elites and ruling groups short of violence or war.

Beginning in the 1970s, Kuper's intellectual curiosity and knack for synthesizing complex sociological ideas led him to the study of genocide. In 1981, Kuper published his first major work on the subject, the path breaking *Genocide: Its Political Use in the Twentieth Century.* In it, he brought to light the commonality of genocide throughout disparate cultures and devised a classification system of genocide that helped explain the subject as a whole. The book was heralded for its research and insight both by academics and generalists. In 1985, Kuper published *The Prevention of Genocide,* which was similarly praised. In it, he articulated the international community's chief impediments to preventing genocide, with a particular focus on the United Nations, and offered ways in which to circumvent those obstacles.

Kuper was a co-founder of the Institute on the Holocaust and Genocide and frequently published in its journals and proceedings. He also played a vital role in the establishment of International Alert, a supranational organization headquartered in London that monitors situations that may devolve into genocide. Kuper remained active in the organization until his death.

Upon his death in Los Angeles on May 23, 1994, Kuper was considered one of the best and most influential genocide scholars of the late 20th century.

PAUL G. PIERPAOLI JR.

See also: United Nations

Further Reading

Kuper, Leo. *Genocide: Its Political Use in the Twentieth Century.* New Haven, CT: Yale University Press, 1983.

Kuper, Leo. *The Prevention of Genocide.* New Haven, CT: Yale University Press, 1985.

L

League of Nations

In 1919, the victorious nations in World War I called for the establishment of an international organization in which countries could meet to discuss their differences and resolve their problems without resorting to war. The resulting League of Nations, whose greatest champion was U.S. president Woodrow Wilson, would also establish a tribunal to try individuals responsible for war crimes in the event a war did occur. The League was based in Geneva, Switzerland. The articles of the covenant forming the organization's charter and laying out its mandate were incorporated into every peace treaty that ended World War I. Because of political wrangling and President Wilson's refusal to accept any compromises concerning the League, however, the United States never joined the organization. The first meeting of the League Council was held in Paris on January 16, 1920, and the first Assembly was held on November 15, 1920, in Geneva.

The League was formed principally to promote international cooperation, allow for open relations among nations thereby avoiding the secret alliances that had contributed to the outbreak of World War I, establish a basis of international law as it governed conduct among governments, and maintain respect for all treaty obligations. The League had little success in any area, however. When a nation submitted a dispute to the League, the process of adjudicating it tended to be long and drawn out. The League could settle disputes only among member nations, and Germany did not become a member until 1927. Most of the major interwar disputes in fact involved German reparations, borders, etc., so there was little the League could do. Most often, the great powers of Great Britain, France, Italy, and Germany proceeded as they always did, settling issues among themselves. Furthermore, The important treaties of the era, Locarno, Rapallo and Kellogg-Briand, were all settled outside of the League's purview. The main function of the League seemed to be to serve as a central repository for treaties, and enforcement of them was left up to the individual nations involved.

The League did not become more effective in the 1930s, when faced with significant international crises. For example, when Italy's invasion of Ethiopia in 1935 resulted in a vote of sanctions against Italy by the League, Italy simply withdrew from the League, releasing it from its obligations to follow the League's mandates. Meanwhile, Germany remilitarized the Rhineland and denounced the Treaty of Versailles in 1936. Again, the League protested, but did nothing of substance to reverse these provocative actions. Germany quit the League that same year. With Germany rearming, the League became increasingly ineffective; meanwhile, the great powers continued to act as the arbitrators of international action, very imperfect ones at that.

In September 1939, Germany invaded Poland, sparking World War II. The League of Nations was now effectively neutralized. Although technically continuing in existence throughout the war, the Allies fought without a League mandate or even a reference to it. After the war began, U.S. president Franklin D. Roosevelt called for a stronger organization, and the United Nations (UN) became a reality in October 1945. One of its first acts was to terminate the League and turn over all its functions to the newly created UN. The League failed in its purpose principally because of a lack of will and enforcement powers.

ELIZABETH PUGLIESE

See also: United Nations

Further Reading

Albrecht-Carrie, Rene. *A Diplomatic History of Europe since the Congress of Vienna.* New York: Harper & Brothers, 1958.

Carr, Edward Hallett. *The Twenty Years Crisis, 1919–1939.* London: Macmillan and Company, Limited, 1962.

P

Pilger, John

John Pilger is an Australian-born journalist and documentary filmmaker who has examined the genocides in Cambodia and East Timor.

John Pilger was born outside Sydney, Australia, on October 9, 1939. Interested in journalism from an early age, he participated in a four-year training program for journalists with an Australian newspaper before taking a position with the *Daily Telegraph* in Sydney. In 1962, he moved to the United Kingdom, where he eventually joined the staff of the *Daily Mirror,* with which he has been long associated. A consistent critic of American and British foreign policies, he produced several television documentaries on the Vietnam War beginning in 1970. He also hosted a number of shows on the BBC covering foreign events.

Immediately following the Cambodian Genocide of 1975–1979, Pilger went to Cambodia with a photographer and documentary film producer. Pilger was among the first Western journalists to document the horrors of the genocide, and went on to co-produce a well-received television documentary on it (*Year Zero: The Silent Death of Cambodia*). Pilger has also been a long-term critic of Australian government policies toward its indigenous population, and he has made several documentaries on that issue as well.

In 1993, Pilger and a skeletal film crew clandestinely visited East Timor, where he shot *Death of a Nation: The Timor Conspiracy.* The documentary was credited for having turned the world's attention to the ongoing tragedy there. Pilger has also done television exposés on the Palestinian situation as well as the British government's policies toward the inhabitants of Diego Garcia in the Indian Ocean.

More recently, Pilger was a strong critic of U.S. president George W. Bush and British prime minister Tony Blair, whom he once characterized as a war criminal. Pilger has supported the actions of international whistle-blower Julian Assange, even helping him raise bail in late 2010. The journalist has long criticized the mainstream media for its failure to probe thorny issues and for virtually backing wrong-headed policies, including the Iraq War. His uncompromising positions and harsh rhetoric aimed largely at the United States has won him as many critics as supporters, but it is undeniable that Pilger has delved into issues that most journalists dare not take on.

PAUL G. PIERPAOLI JR.

See also: Power, Samantha; Upstander

Further Reading

Greenslade, Roy. *Press Gang: How Newspapers Make Profits From Propaganda.* London and Basingstoke, UK: Macmillan, 2003.

Hayward, Anthony. *In the Name of Justice: The Television Reporting of John Pilger.* London: Bloomsbury, 2002.

Power, Samantha

Samantha Power is a special assistant to U.S. president Barack Obama, administering the Office of Multilateral

Affairs and Human Rights as senior director of multilateral affairs on the staff of the National Security Council (NSC). She is also the Anna Lindh Professor of Global Leadership and Public Policy at Harvard University and the founding director of Harvard's Carr Center for Human Rights Policy.

An award-winning journalist and writer, Power was born on September 21, 1970, in Dungarvan, Waterford, Ireland. She migrated to the United States in 1979 and grew up in Pittsburgh, Pennsylvania, and Atlanta, Georgia. Although originally aspiring to become a newspaper sports reporter, upon graduation from Yale University her journalistic career took her down a different path. She began covering genocidal conflicts and gross human rights violations in a number of the world's hot-spots, including Bosnia, Burundi, Darfur, East Timor, Kosovo, Rwanda, and Zimbabwe. Seeing first-hand the all-too-often impotence of international efforts to combat genocide, particularly those of the United States, led in 2002 to her Pulitzer Prize–winning book *"A Problem from Hell": America and the Age of Genocide,* for which she also received the 2003 National Book Critics Circle Award for general nonfiction and the 2003 Council on Foreign Relations Arthur Ross Prize for the best book on U.S. foreign policy. She followed this up with an article in the *New Yorker* in August 2004 titled "Dying in Darfur: Can the Ethnic Cleansing in Sudan be Stopped?," which won the 2005 National Magazine award for best reporting.

As a working journalist as well as a scholar and government official, Power continues to write on foreign policy issues and matters for a number of major periodicals syndicated throughout the world. In 2000, she coedited, with Graham Wilson, *Realizing Human Rights: Moving from Inspiration to Impact.* Her most recent major project was a biography of Sergio Vieira de Mello, the United Nations (UN) envoy killed by a suicide bomber in Iraq along with 14 others in 2003. Entitled *Chasing the Flame: Sergio Vieira de Mello and the Fight to Save the World,* this study appeared in early 2008.

Prior to the release of *A Problem from Hell,* Power wrote "Bystanders to Genocide" in *Atlantic Monthly,* which in many ways summarized the arguments that would follow in the larger work. In this lengthy article—the result of a three-year investigation—she criticized the administration of President Bill Clinton for its ongoing failures to do anything substantive to halt the genocide in Rwanda in 1994. Power asked a range of questions that would frame her investigation regarding the lack of past U.S. involvements in

previous cases of genocide. These included: Why did the United States not do more for the Rwandans at the time of the killings? Did the president really not know about the genocide, as marginal comments in his memoranda suggested? Who were the people in Clinton's administration who made the life-and-death decisions that dictated U.S. policy? How did they arrive at their decisions? Were any voices inside or outside the U.S. government demanding that the United States do more? If so, why were they not heeded? And, most crucially, what could the United States have done to save lives? In response to such concerns, Power would later admit that her own moral passion when she wrote both of her early articles, and at the time of the appearance of *A Problem from Hell,* reflected her own naiveté with regard to political realism and the affairs of states.

Rejecting claims of ignorance over what was happening in Rwanda, of a lack of compassion, or a lack of concrete action as to what could have been accomplished, Power's research conclusively showed that an absence of U.S. involvement was not a case of inactive "bystanderism," but instead the result of *active noninvolvement.* The scenario of "active noninvolvement," in fact, was consistent with what Power regarded as the "major findings" of *A Problem from Hell* relating to U.S. policy responses to genocide.

Power wrote this book, she said later, for "the screamers," those persons in positions of responsibility who choose to speak out against government policies, often at great personal and professional sacrifice (a number of whose stories are told throughout the book), as well as in the hope that the learning curve concerning what is and what is not genocide—and what can and what cannot be done in the future—will prove far less difficult to surmount than it has been in the past.

Power was an early and outspoken supporter of Obama's presidential campaign and spent 2005–2006 working in his office as a foreign policy fellow. Her support for Obama was prompted in part by his advocacy of U.S. and UN action over the ongoing genocide in Darfur. Until March 2008, Power was a senior adviser to Obama, until she resigned after a controversial swipe at Obama's main political rival (and later, his secretary of state), Hilary Clinton. After the 2008 presidential election, Power returned to work for Obama, where she became a member of the transition team and worked for the Department of State. In January 2009, President Obama appointed Power to the NSC staff.

During 2011, Power was held by many to be the most important figure within the Obama administration pushing for military intervention in Libya and in persuading the president to intervene on moral and humanitarian grounds.

Overall, it can be said that Power is an important critical voice in policies regarding genocide. She continues to bring to the table the intellect and insights of a scholar, the eye and talents of a journalist, and the moral passion of a human being truly concerned about others caught in the grip of a crime that shows few signs of abating. She has not been without her detractors, some of whom have argued that her reliance on an idealized vision of "political will" as a way to stop genocide does not take into account the actuality of a world system that is still founded on political realism. Her influence, however, has been widespread, with a broad readership in the nonspecialized general community embracing her ideas and taking her theoretical perspectives on international action to a new level of direct action when meeting with their elected representatives.

PAUL R. BARTROP

See also: Upstander

Further Reading

Power, Samantha. *Chasing the Flame: Sergio Vieira de Mello and the Fight to Save the World*. New York: Penguin, 2008.

Power, Samantha. *"A Problem from Hell": America and the Age of Genocide*. New York: Harper Perennial, 2007.

Prevent Genocide International

Prevent Genocide International is a nonprofit organization dedicated to ending genocide by educating the world's inhabitants about the crime. It was founded in 1998. Its Web site contains a vast amount of information on genocide and ethnic cleansing.

Prevent Genocide uses the Internet as its primary means of disseminating information. The group believes that the Internet is a good means of organizing a group of individuals and local, national, and international organizations, and persuading them to use their influence to help stop genocide. It hopes that by spreading information about genocide, individuals and groups will speak out in their own localities and thus mobilize the general public all over the world.

The organization's Web site contains a great deal of information on genocide all over the world. It includes various definitions of genocide and ethnic cleansing, the elements of the crime of genocide as defined by the International Criminal Court, and links to numerous articles on ethnic cleansing and what makes people mass murderers. The "Law" page of the Web site contains links to a vast amount of legal information. It includes links to the United Nations Genocide Convention and a list of the parties to it, a report on the convention's first 50 years of existence, and information on genocide laws in several different nations. The "Education" section has links to numerous resources on the nature of genocide and ethnic cleansing, accounts of 20th- and 21st-century genocides, and information on conferences and courses on the subject.

Prevent Genocide International wants to prevent genocide. It has assembled several links to documents related to this topic, including the text of the Stockholm Declaration on Genocide Prevention from 2004, United Nations Documents on Genocide Prevention, articles on preventing genocide, and a link to a global news monitor that follows cases of genocide. In order to give visitors a concrete way to fight genocide, the organization posts regular action alerts that provide visitors with letters to send to their elected officials demanding the end of particular genocides. Prevent Genocide International is a founding member of the International Campaign to End Genocide, established at The Hague in 1999; this group is a coalition of human rights organizations dedicated to ending genocide and ethnic cleansing.

AMY HACKNEY BLACKWELL

See also: International Court of Justice; International Criminal Court

Further Reading

Mann, Michael. *The Dark Side of Democracy: Explaining Ethnic Cleansing*. Cambridge, UK: Cambridge University Press, 2004.

Power, Samantha. *"A Problem from Hell": America and the Age of Genocide*. New York: Harper Perennial, 2007.

Proxmire, William

(Edward) William "Bill" Proxmire was a U.S. senator for Wisconsin from 1957 to 1989. The son of a wealthy surgeon, he was born in Lake Forest, Illinois, on November 11, 1915, and educated at Yale and Harvard universities. He served as a member of the Military Intelligence Service of

Senator William Proxmire at the CBS Television studios before a taping of *Face the Nation,* September 3, 1967. (AP Photo)

the U.S. Army during World War II, assigned to counterintelligence work. He was discharged in 1946 with the rank of first lieutenant.

After the war he moved to Wisconsin to take up a position as a reporter, viewing this as a form of access to a political career. A member of the Democratic Party, he served as a member of the Wisconsin State Assembly during 1951–1952 and attempted to become state governor in 1952, 1954, and 1956. He finally achieved high office in 1957 when he was elected to the U.S. Senate to fill the vacancy caused by the death of Senator Joseph R. McCarthy. He was reelected in 1958, 1964, 1970, 1976, and 1982, always by wide margins.

A member of the United Church of Christ, Proxmire was a strong supporter of civil rights. Soon after his election, in his first term, he clashed with the Senate majority leader (and later U.S. president), Lyndon B. Johnson, on account of what he perceived to be Johnson's blocking of civil rights legislation. Then, during the Vietnam War, Proxmire was an early critic of U.S. involvement in that conflict. He used his seat on the Senate Armed Services Committee to spotlight wasteful military spending, and frequently criticized President Johnson and his successor, Richard Nixon for their conduct of the war and foreign policy decisions.

During the period 1967 to 1986, Proxmire came to see that there was a massive anomaly in the United States holding itself up as the world's arbiter of freedom and democratic values, but at the same time not being a signatory to the United Nations Convention on the Prevention and Punishment of the Crime of Genocide (UNCG). At the urging of a Milwaukee lawyer and leading supporter of the United Nations (UN), Bruno Bitker, Proxmire began his campaign with the words that the Senate's failure to approve the treaty to that point was a "national shame." From that first day, January 11, 1967, he took a personal responsibility to bring U.S. ratification of the UNCG to fruition. Using his position as a U.S. senator to draw attention to the issue, he made repeated and frequent speeches calling for Senate ratification. These speeches became a daily occurrence across every day that the Senate was in session across the 20-year period he waged his campaign. Proxmire's dedication to the cause he championed knew few bounds. He never missed a sitting day in the Senate, as a result of which he still holds the record for the greatest consecutive roll call of votes cast. Between April 20, 1966, and October 18, 1988, he cast 10,252 consecutive votes, and delivered a total of 3,211 speeches on genocide to the floor of the Senate—an average of 168 for every year of his campaign. Each speech was unique, focusing variously on the historical context that led to the drafting of the treaty, the treaty's provisions, its negotiating history, and contemporaneous events germane to the treaty.

Treaty ratification in the U.S. Senate requires the votes of two-thirds of senators for approval. Proxmire, and his allies Jacob Javits and Claiborne Pell, were tireless in their devotion to their cause, but they were opposed by equally determined adversaries in Senators Sam Ervin and Jesse Helms. Proxmire's speeches kept the question of ratification an open sore for the Senate, but with memories of his wartime experience and his horror at news from such overseas situations as those in Biafra, Bangladesh, Uganda, and Cambodia, he remained totally committed to the issue and enthusiastic to see the issue resolved in favor of ratification.

Proxmire gave his last speech on the matter early in 1986. On February 19 of that year, the Senate ratified the UNCG by a vote of 86–11, but only after incessant wrangling and with reservations that Proxmire reluctantly agreed to accept. Implementation legislation, named the "Proxmire Act," was passed two years later and signed by President Ronald Reagan. On November 25, 1988, only weeks before the 40th anniversary of the convention's

1948 approval by the UN General Assembly, the United States deposited instruments of ratification at UN headquarters in New York. The Genocide Convention Implementation Act of 1988 would make genocide a crime punishable in the United States, with legal sanctions of life imprisonment and fines of up to $1 million.

While passage of the Genocide Convention Implementation Act was hailed as a milestone, many saw it as tainted. Certain senators insisted that a reservation be attached to the ratification, stating that *before* the United States could be called before any international tribunal the president of the United States would have to consent to that court's jurisdiction. The reservation resulted in the U.S. being the only country in the world that would decide whether or not it would appear before a court determining guilt for the crime of genocide. It is noteworthy that some 97 nations had ratified the convention ahead of the United States.

Proxmire retired from the Senate in 1988. In 1998 he announced his treatment for Alzheimer's disease, and, after struggling with the disease for several years, he died in a nursing home in Sykesville, Maryland, on December 15, 2005, aged 90.

PAUL R. BARTROP

See also: Proxmire, William; United Nations Convention on the Prevention and Punishment of Genocide

Further Reading

Proxmire, William. *Fleecing of America.* New York: Houghton Mifflin, 1980.

Proxmire, William. *Report from Wasteland: America's Military-Industrial Complex* Westport, CT: Praeger, 1970.

R

Responsibility to Protect (R2P)

The Responsibility to Protect, often abbreviated as R2P, is a relatively new set of international guidelines designed to prevent genocide and to suggest ways in which to deal with genocide once it is underway. R2P is considered an international norm, rather than an international law, although it is predicated on previously established international law. The genesis of R2P may be traced to the Canadian government, which created the International Commission on Intervention and State Sovereignty (ICISS) in September 2000. That effort brought together genocide and legal experts from around the world, and the ICISS published a far-reaching report entitled *The Responsibility to Protect* in December 2001. The Canadians' chief reason for establishing the ICISS was to prevent a repeat of the 1994 Rwanda Genocide, in which nearly 1 million Rwandans were slaughtered in just a few short months while most of the rest of the world stood idly by.

The United Nations (UN) World Summit unanimously approved the ICISS report in 2005. The R2P embraces three major premises. First, it asserts that every nation is responsible for avoiding genocide, war crimes, ethnic cleansing, and crimes against humanity within its own borders. Second, it states that the international community has an obligation to ensure that every nation adheres to the first guideline and that the international community should assist in helping any state that is facing circumstances that may bring about genocide, etc. Third, it stipulates that the international community must be prepared to act in a decisive and timely manner, in accordance with the UN Charter, to protect any population threatened by genocide and the like.

It is understood that military intervention designed to prevent or halt such activities should be used only as a last resort, after diplomacy as well as political and/or economic sanctions have been thoroughly exhausted. The UN has further stated that the use of military force must only be invoked by the UN Security Council, rather than on an ad hoc basis by individual states.

R2P has given birth to a number of international initiatives, both within and outside of the UN, to fine-tune and further the message of the ICISS. These include the Working Group on R2P, a joint task force of the U.S. Holocaust Memorial Museum, the Brookings Institution, and the U.S. Institute of Peace; the Genocide Prevention Task Force; and the International Coalition for the Responsibility to Protect (ICRtoP).

R2P has not been fully embraced by everyone, however. Some detractors fear that the obligation to intervene might invite unnecessary use of force and might embolden some nations to undertake military force in an effort to further their own goals rather than to stop genocide per se. Others have argued that any use of outside force to prevent genocide is a de facto infringement of state sovereignty. Still others claim that R2P does not go far enough. The situation in Syria has certainly tested R2P, as has the violence in the Central African Republic (CAR). In 2013, France asserted that the carnage in the CAR warranted international intervention, but to date the UN Security Council has not approved such action.

PAUL G. PIERPAOLI JR.

See also: United Nations

Further Reading

Badescu, Cristina G. *Humanitarian Intervention and the Responsibility to Protect: Security and Human Rights.* New York: Routledge, 2011

Evans, Gareth, and Mohamed Sahnoun, Co-chairs. *The Responsibility to Protect: Report of the International Commission on Intervention and State Sovereignty.* Ottawa, ON, Canada: International Development Research Centre, Minister of Foreign Affairs, 2001.

T

Truth Commissions

The international community has principally used two methods to establish and evaluate the record of grave human rights crimes following an international conflict or civil war. The first method is international prosecutions, such as those conducted at Nuremberg and Tokyo following World War II, and, more recently, at The Hague, Netherlands, and in Arusha, Tanzania, following the conflict in the former Yugoslavia and Rwanda. The second method is the establishment of commissions of inquiry, now commonly referred to as "truth commissions," which investigate incidents and submit reports on their findings.

The first international truth commission was established by the Carnegie Endowment for International Peace to investigate alleged atrocities committed against civilians and prisoners of war during the Balkan Wars of 1912–1913. In 1919, after World War I, the allies created the Commission on the Responsibility of the Authors of the War, and on Enforcement of Penalties, which investigated German and Turkish atrocities committed during the war. After World War II, the Allies established the United Nations War Crime Commission to investigate German war crimes, and the Far Eastern Commission to investigate Japanese war crimes. In 1978, the parties to Additional Protocol I to the Geneva Conventions of 1949 set up an International Fact-Finding Commission to investigate serious violations of the Geneva Conventions. During the 1990s, the international community, via the United Nations, established truth commissions in several countries, including El Salvador, Guatemala, Somalia, the former Yugoslavia, and Rwanda. Moreover, in the past decade over a dozen states have set up their own domestic truth commissions to document atrocities within their borders and to facilitate national reconciliation.

Truth commissions are, in most cases, officially sanctioned, authorized, or empowered by the state. They focus on the recent past and investigate politically motivated repression and patterns of widespread abuse rather than a single event. Truth commissions are unavoidably affected by their internal makeup and resources, as well as by outside factors such as the continued power of perpetrators, the strength of civil society, the attention of the international community, and the wider political and social culture within which they operate. Among the more critical mandates of truth commissions are: reaching out to victims; documenting and corroborating cases for a reparations program; arriving at firm and irrefutable conclusions on controversial cases and patterns of abuse; engaging the country in a process of national healing; contributing to justice; producing an accessible public report; outlining possible reforms; and giving victims a voice.

The work of truth commissions has implications for justice, reconciliation, historical understanding, political transformation, institutional reform, accountability, and even personal healing. Truth commissions address both conceptual issues, that is, how the pursuit of truth affects the pursuit of justice, and practical matters, that is, precisely how data should be collected, organized, and evaluated. Key questions in establishing a commission include: What level of funding is adequate? What type of training might staff members need? Should testimony be public? Should perpetrators be named?

Truth commissions are not courts, and they are not a replacement for criminal prosecutions. While truth commissions have fewer powers than courts, cannot compel testimony, put anyone in jail, or enforce recommendations, truth commissions are free of some of the narrower rules of evidence and restricted focus on individual responsibility that often characterize court systems. The purpose of criminal trials is not to expose the truth, but to find whether the criminal standards of proof have been satisfied on specific charges. A measure of truth may emerge in this process, but criminal trials are limited in the truth they are able to tell as they must comply with rules of evidence, which often exclude important information.

The mandates of truth commissions are much broader, examining larger patterns, discerning the responsibility of the state, and helping to establish accountability and a shared understanding of history. Truth commissions explore not only the facts and figures, but also the underlying causes of past repression. If properly constructed (e.g., in El Salvador) truth commissions may be strong even where judiciaries are quite weak, corrupt, or compromised.

While truth commissions are not courts and should not be a replacement for criminal prosecutions, the difficult decision is whether or not to grant amnesty. Truth Commissions granting amnesty are often viewed as an alternative to prosecutions. For example, the same day the Haitian parliament established a seven-member truth commission to investigate and document human rights crimes committed in Haiti during President Jean-Bertrand Aristide's exile, it enacted an amnesty for members of the military regime responsible for those abuses. Following the publication of the El Salvador truth commission's report, El Salvador's government enacted an amnesty preventing the prosecution of those named in the report. Similarly, the South African truth commission itself was empowered to grant amnesty as an inducement for the giving of testimony before the commission.

Viewing truth commissions as a substitute for prosecutions exposes two problems. First, in some situations, the granting of amnesty may be in violation of international legal instruments, such as 1949 Geneva Convention,

the Genocide Convention, the Torture Convention, and, in the case of South Africa, the Apartheid Convention, which contain an absolute obligation to prosecute the crimes enumerated therein. Additionally, a blanket amnesty may violate general human rights conventions such as the International Covenant on Civil and Political Rights, the European Convention on Human Rights, and the American Convention on Human Rights, which obligate states to "ensure" or "secure" the rights enumerated therein. As Article 27 of the Vienna Convention on the Law of the Treaties provides, "a party may not invoke the provisions of its internal law as justification for failure to perform a treaty." Second, even when amnesties do not run afoul of these treaties, the creation of impunity through an amnesty can have the effect of encouraging future violations of the law. The granting of amnesty may erode the rule of law by blurring the norms of right and wrong while encouraging victims to resort to vigilante justice; and, most worrisome of all, an amnesty that has the imprimatur of the international community encourages a repetition of similar abuses by perpetrators throughout the world. The issue of amnesty can best be resolved by including a statement in the originally document emphasizing that the truth commission is intended to be complementary to national and international prosecutions, not a substitute for them.

This is not to suggest that a country should rush ahead with prosecution at the cost of political instability and social upheaval or that every single perpetrator must be brought to justice. By documenting abuses and preserving evidence, a truth commission can enable a country to delay prosecutions until the international community has acted, or a new government is secure enough to take such action against members of the former regime, paramilitary, or guerrilla movements. International law recognizes the legitimacy of prosecutorial discretion, both in terms of the selection of defendants and the timing of prosecutions, as long as the criteria are not arbitrary.

A long-term goal of truth commissions is to facilitate reconciliation. Many elements contribute to reconciliation: an end to violence or threat of violence; reestablishment of respectful relations; acknowledgments of and reparations for wrongdoing; projects that bring former opponents together; correction of structural inequalities; meeting of material needs; and the passage of time. However, the role truth commissions play in reconciliation is fundamental to the previously mentioned elements. Truth commissions have the task of forging a single shared account of the past, making the varied and often contradictory stories compatible, consistent, and accepted. While there is rarely, if ever, one truth, there are facts that are fundamental enough that broad acceptance of the truth is necessary before reconciliation can take place. This is a fundamental responsibility of truth commissions.

Creating a single shared account of the past may lead to long-term reconciliation, but generate further trauma in the short term. Truth commissions give victims an opportunity to recount their stories, helping them to deal with their trauma. Short- and long-term studies on the psychological impact of truth commissions on survivors have not yet been conducted. Truth commissions do not offer long-term therapy or any psychological support services. The entire process of truth finding can also generate further trauma. For example, discovering the identity of individual perpetrators can reawaken enormous pain and anger. The issue of how to handle the potential for re-traumatization has not been addressed by truth commissions. Priscilla Hayner writes, "perhaps more important than the lack of personnel or resources is the point that Western psychology may not be appropriate means of response in some cultures. The impact of culture on how people respond to and recover from extreme trauma is not yet well understood." It is possible that local community organizations, civic groups, traditional healers, churches, or extended families might contribute more to the complex process of healing trauma than truth commissions can, depending on the character of the society.

Acknowledging the problems facing truth commissions is a positive step toward a full and inclusive national memory. Allowing the voices of the victims and survivors to be heard is a crucial step in transitional processes. The overall record of past truth commissions has been positive. Despite political constraints and pressures, most have documented the testimonies of thousands of victims and witnesses, producing strongly worded and politically unbiased reports.

LARRY HUFFORD

See also: South Africa

Further Reading

Freeman, Mark. *Truth Commissions and Procedural Fairness.* Cambridge, UK: Cambridge University Press, 2006.

Hayner, Priscilla B. *Unspeakable Truths: Confronting State Terror and Atrocity.* New York: Routledge, 2000.

Rotberg, Robert, and Dennis Thompson. *Truth v. Justice: The Morality of Truth Commissions.* Princeton, NJ: Princeton University Press, 2000.

U

United Nations

The United Nations' charter, finalized on June 26, 1945, makes the United Nations (UN) the only international organization with a global reach on matters of war and peace; even many nonmembers states follow UN rules (article 2 (6) UN Charter). According to article 1 of the Charter, it is the organization's principal aim to "maintain international peace and security, and to that end to take effective collective measures for the prevention and removal of threats to the peace, and for the suppression of acts of aggression or other breaches of the peace, and to bring about by peaceful means, and in conformity with the principles of justice and international law, adjustment or settlement of international disputes or situations which might lead to a breach of the peace."

Apart from activities of auxiliary UN institutions, like the Economic and Social Council, there have been three main avenues of UN action concerning the strengthening of rules and procedures of international law as they pertain to war crimes. First, the General Assembly has adopted several resolutions (GA res.) which are relevant to the prevention and prosecution of war crimes. The most important ones are GA res. 3 (I) and 170 (II) of 1946 and 1947 on the extradition and punishment of war criminals, 95 (I) of 1946 on the principles of international law according the Charter of the International Military Tribunal (IMT) of Nuremberg, 96 (I) of 1946 on genocide being a crime under international law, 2184 (XXI) and 2202 (XXI) of 1966 declaring the violation of the rights of indigenous populations and the policies of apartheid crimes against humanity, and 3074 (XXVIII) of 1973 on the principles of international co-operation in the prosecution of persons guilty of war crimes and crimes against humanity. In these resolutions, the GA has successively broadened the legal foundations of the Nuremberg Tribunal of 1945–1946, including the IMT definitions of war crimes and crimes against humanity as parts of general international law.

The second manner of UN action on war crimes has been conventions, that is, international treaties among states, created by international cooperation and negotiation, chiefly via the UN General Assembly. The three most important ones are the Convention on the Prevention and Punishment of the Crime of Genocide of 1949 (entered into force in 1951); the Convention on the Non-Applicability of Statutory Limitations to War Crimes and Crimes against Humanity of 1968; and the Rome Statute of the International Criminal Court (ICC) of 1998 (entered into force in 2002). According to the Genocide Convention, "genocide means any . . . acts committed with intent to destroy, in whole or in part, a national, ethnical, racial or religious group" (article 2). Punishable acts not only include genocide itself, but also all kinds of genocide preparations (article 3). Contrary to traditional international law, the Genocide Convention stipulates that any person guilty of genocide is to be punished by the state in which the act was committed, or by an international penal tribunal (article

6), including "constitutionally responsible rulers" (article 4). Additionally, article 1 and 3 of the Convention of 1968 assert that no statutory limitation shall apply to war crimes and crimes against humanity, including genocide, and that the states undertake all necessary domestic measures in order to make extradition of war criminals possible. Because national prosecutions and extradition have generally prevailed, however, only the recent Rome Statute of the ICC has established a permanent international court for genocide, crimes against humanity, war crimes, and aggression.

Finally, the UN Security Council has adopted several resolutions (S/RES) concerning war crimes. While GA resolutions are only proposals from a formal point of view, and conventions are in principle only legally binding for their member states, Security Council resolutions are generally binding according to article 25 of the charter of the UN. The most relevant resolutions are S/RES/688 condemning Iraqi atrocities against the Iraqi Kurdish minority (1990), S/RES/827, the International Tribunal for the Prosecution responsible for Serious Violations of International Humanitarian Law committed in the Territory of the Former Yugoslavia (ICTY) and its annex on the Statute of the Tribunal (1993), and S/RES/955 establishing the International Criminal Tribunal for Rwanda (ICTR), including the annex on its Statute (1995). Until early 2002, 118 and 62 persons were indicted at the ICTY and ICTR, respectively, with about 900 war crimes suspects recorded in prosecution files of the ICTY.

Although the UN has intensified its activities concerning legally binding and enforceable international rules against war crimes after the end of the Cold War, there are still fundamental problems concerning its role in that matter. First, there remains the core problem of exact and detailed legal definitions of war crimes and crimes against humanity, especially in the case of genocide. In September 1998, for example, the ICTR decided that the Genocide Convention definition was meant to protect all "stable" groups that "constituted in a permanent fashion and membership of which is determined by birth, with the exclusion of the more 'mobile' groups which one joins through individual voluntary commitment, such as political or economic groups." This leaves the obvious problem that changes of religion and nationality are possible, which might make individuals potential victims of atrocities. Second, there is the central role of major nations, especially the United States, which is

indispensable to the functioning of UN institutions and the promotion of UN action against war crimes, whose effectiveness depend on the participation of those states. This has been demonstrated by the restricted global relevance of the ICC because the United States, Russia, Israel, and China did not ratify the Rome Statute in 2002. Third, because the General Assembly has no legally binding power and negotiations about conventions may take years or even decades, the most efficient way to promote the international law on war crimes is through Security Council Resolutions, as demonstrated in the case of the ICTY and ICTR. The structure of the Security Council, however, again links progress in this field to the goodwill and interests of its member states, especially the permanent ones. An example of this structural problem was the Security Council's hesitation in April and May 1994 to use term the "genocide" in describing the massacre of Rwandan Tutsis. According to the UN General Secretary Boutros Boutros-Ghali, this over caution was out of fear that the Security Council would have no alternative but to intervene militarily against such a genocide, which was not in the interest of the Western powers at that time.

RALPH ROTTE

See also: Annan, Kofi; Boutros-Ghali, Boutros; United Nations Commission of Experts; United Nations Commission on Human Rights; United Nations War Crimes Commission; Universal Declaration of Human Rights

Further Reading

Fasulo, Linda. *An Insider's Guide to the UN*. New Haven, CT: Yale University Press, 2003.

Gutman, Roy, ed. *Crimes of War: What the Public Should Know*. New York: W.W. Norton & Company, 1999.

Roberts, Adam, and Richard Guelff. *Documents on the Laws of War*. Oxford: Oxford University Press, 2000.

United Nations Commission of Experts

In 1992, the United Nations (UN) Security Council requested that the secretary-general of the UN establish a Commission of Experts in connection with conflicts in Eastern Europe and Africa. By Resolution 780 of October 6, 1992, a Commission of Experts was duly established to review available information and to provide the secretary-general with evidence of violations of international humanitarian law committed in the territory of the former

Yugoslavia. By Resolution 935 of July 1, 1994, a similar Commission of Experts was established concerning Rwanda and the genocide there.

The Commission of Experts for the former Yugoslavia was, in theory, except for the chairman, a group working on a part-time basis; it filed interim reports on February 9 and October 5, 1993, and a final report on May 24, 1994, together with a wide range of subsidiary reports. Extremely productive for an entity that functioned only on a part-time basis and that depended to a large extent on trust-fund donations, the commission's work was partially responsible for the creation of the International Criminal Tribunal for the Former Yugoslavia (ICTY) by Security Council Resolution 827 on May 25, 1993. The archives of the commission, which were turned over to the Tribunal after the final report was submitted, provided useful leads for the ICTY's prosecutors in its early days.

In contrast, the Commission of Experts for Rwanda was composed of members working on a full-time basis and was given a temporally defined mandate; the secretary-general was requested to report to the Security Council on the commission's conclusions within four months of its establishment. The Rwanda Commission submitted a preliminary report on October 1, 1994, followed by a final report on December 9. The International Criminal Tribunal for Rwanda (ICTR) was established by Security Council Resolution 955 of November 8, 1994, and the work of the Rwanda Commission contributed to its creation.

The Security Council has neither directed the secretary-general to establish commissions of experts nor established new ad hoc international tribunals since 1994. The International Criminal Court, as conceptualized in the Rome Statute adopted on July 1, 1998, came into existence on July 1, 2002, and is the international criminal tribunal wave of the future, as the Security Council can refer situations directly to it.

Although commissions of experts were created before the ICTY and the ICTR were established, the commissions and their work, at most, provided some support for the establishment of the ad hoc tribunals. For example, the Security Council decided to establish the ICTY when it adopted Resolution 808 on February 22, 1993; by that time, the Yugoslav Commission of Experts had filed its first preliminary report but was over a year away from filing its final report. Further, neither the Yugoslav nor the Rwanda Commission had the resources to conduct the in-depth investigations necessary to prepare indictments or inform trials. The commissions did, however, make useful first efforts to construct model procedures to be followed by the ICTY and the ICTR.

William J. Fenrick

See also: United Nations

Further Reading

Fenrick, W. J. "In the Field with UNCOE: Investigating Atrocities in the Territory of the Former Yugoslavia." *Military Law and Law of War Review* Vol. 34 (1995): 34–66.

Weiss, Thomas G., David P. Forsythe, and Roger A. Coate. *The United Nations and Changing World Politics.* Westport, CT: Westview Press, 2004.

United Nations Commission on Human Rights

The United Nations (UN) Commission on Human Rights (UNCHR), established in 1946, became the first international body empowered to promote global human rights. The founders of the Commission assumed that improved respect for human rights would serve the primary goal of the UN, namely peacekeeping, by eliminating repressive practices that promoted war.

The UNCHR, which fell under the aegis of the Economic and Social Council of the UN, was led initially by former U.S. first lady Eleanor Roosevelt. The Commission had no permanent members. Instead, members were appointed for three-year terms. Long-time members were the Soviet Union, the United States, the United Kingdom, France, India, Chile, and Uruguay. Most nations had membership on the UNCHR at some point.

During its first 20 years, the Commission established most of the contemporary standards of human rights. It scrutinized practices that previously had been within national governments' sovereign jurisdiction. However, it had no power to take any action in regard to human rights complaints and declined to review specific complaints by individuals. Governments would receive a copy of a complaint, with the author's name concealed, and could respond to these complaints. The complainants were informed that their communications had been received and that the UNCHR had no power to act. The vast majority of the complaints received in the 1940s and 1950s focused on political persecution, with a small number devoted to genocide, freedom of assembly and association, trade union rights, and the rights of minorities. Most governments did not respond to the complaints.

The Commission's chief success in its early history was the drafting of a Universal Declaration of Human Rights in 1947.

Increased social awareness in the 1960s enabled the UNCHR to shift focus to enforcement activities. It responded to specific complaints from individuals and nongovernmental organizations and pressured more than 70 offending governments by using various measures that ranged from exhortation and mediation to sanctions designed to isolate violators. This change in focus increased the Commission's visibility and dramatically transformed its operation. At the same time, however, it exacerbated differences among UN members over whether individual or collective rights deserved priority.

National self interests and the struggle for power were issues for the Commission from its very beginning. The Soviet Union, an original member, clashed with Western powers over economic rights, with the United States and its supporters preferring to focus primarily on civil and political rights. As representatives of governments, the UNCHR's members operated to varying degrees on instructions from their own governments. As a result of such control, the Commission often became a forum for political conflict.

African and Asian representatives joined the Commission for the first time in 1967. Determined to combat racial discrimination and advance the right of self determination, they sought enforcement powers to halt egregious human rights violations. Thus, the Economic and Social Council gave the Commission investigative powers. Several African countries then challenged South Africa's apartheid policy while Arab states complained about human rights violations in the territories occupied by Israel. The Soviet Union complained about American Jewish organizations composed of dissident exiles protesting on behalf of Soviet Jewry. The Non-Aligned Movement, consisted of countries from Asia, Africa, and Latin America, constituted a majority of Commission members and made self determination, South African apartheid, and Israeli violations the exclusive concerns of the Commission.

The United States was ousted from the Commission in 2001, while countries with notorious human rights histories, including Libya, Algeria, Cuba, and Syria, remained. American diplomatic officials blamed the ouster on American willingness to focus world attention on violations of human rights and European Union unwillingness to risk offending possible trade partners with public condemnations. By that time, the UNCHR had become discredited among most human rights activists. It seemed to be used mostly for finger-pointing and criticism rather than constructive efforts to further human rights. The Commission held its final meeting in Geneva on March 27, 2006. Earlier that month, the UN had overwhelmingly voted to replace the UNCHR with the Human Rights Council, which consists of representatives from 47 countries. It also has the goal of addressing human rights violations and making recommendations about how to address them.

CARYN E. NEUMANN

See also: United Nations; Universal Declaration of Human Rights

Further Reading

Mertus, Julie. *The United Nations and Human Rights: A Guide for a New Era.* New York: Routledge, 2005.

Tolley, Howard, Jr. *The U.N. Commission on Human Rights.* Boulder, CO: Westview Press, 1987.

Weiss, Thomas G., David P. Forsythe, and Roger A. Coate. *The United Nations and Changing World Politics.* Westport, CT: Westview Press, 2004.

United Nations Convention on the Prevention and Punishment of the Crime of Genocide (UNCG)

The United Nations Convention on the Prevention and Punishment of the Crime of Genocide (UNCG) is a comprehensive, international legal convention that details the definition and meanings of genocide and that provides very general guidelines for the punishment of genocide perpetrators. The UN General Assembly officially enacted the UNCG on December 11, 1948, when 22 member states signed the declaration to proceed to ratification by their own home governments. The Convention, which remains in force, recognizes that genocide is a crime under international law.

The UNCG's definition of genocide has not been without its critics. Some have argued that it is unnecessarily expansive, as it enumerates behaviors that are not necessarily lethal. That seems to fly in the face of the very term "genocide," which literally means the killing of people. Others detractors have asserted that the Convention does not go far enough, because it does not include the killing of people on the basis of political or social affiliations in the definition of genocide. This was the result of several nations' efforts, including those of the United States and Soviet Union, to exclude politics and social affiliations from the

The president of the United Nations General Assembly, Dr. Herbert Evatt of Australia, signs the Convention on the Prevention and Punishment of the Crime of Genocide on behalf of his government. Standing by is Jehan de Noue, chief of Protocol. The Convention was held in Paris, France, on December 11, 1948. (UN Photo/MB)

definition for specific internal political reasons. Despite these concerns, however, the UNCG has remained an important component of international law and has been invoked many times since 1948.

The UNCG would probably not have been approved when it was had it not been for the herculean effort of one man: Raphael Lemkin. Lemkin, a Polish Jew, was a lawyer and historian who had fled Poland in 1939 and settled in the United States in 1941. By then, he had already spent much time contemplating mass murder and its implications for the international community. He published and lectured widely on the subject, and in 1944 he was credited with coining the term "genocide" in his *Axis Rule in Occupied Europe: Laws of Occupation, Analysis of Government, Proposals for Redress*. That book made Lemkin famous, but more importantly, it placed his quest to enact an international convention against genocide in the public spotlight. In 1945, he published an article, "Genocide—A Modern Crime," which was read widely and lent even more credence to his efforts.

In 1945–1946, Lemkin served as a legal adviser to the Nuremberg war-crime trials in Germany, and he redoubled his efforts to push for a global convention against genocide. In 1946, Lemkin was told that his idea of a genocide

President Ronald Reagan signs the United Nations Convention on Genocide in Chicago, Illinois, on November 5, 1988. (Courtesy Ronald Reagan Library)

convention would be formally considered by a UN committee. Although the proposal encountered some turbulence early on, the UN General Assembly unanimously approved a convention banning genocide on December 11, 1948. By then, however, Lemkin had seriously undermined his own health in his quest to establish a genocide convention. The convention went into effect on January 21, 1951, and until the end of his life in 1959, Lemkin worked tirelessly to secure U.S. ratification of the measure. That would not occur until November 4, 1988, however, when President Ronald Reagan signed the ratification agreement.

Today, there are still only 41 signatories to the UNCG. Nevertheless, it is regarded as the bedrock of international law dealing with war crimes, crimes against humanity, and genocide. A number of courts that have since been established to indict and prosecute such crimes—including the International Criminal Tribunal for the Former Yugoslavia and the International Criminal Tribunal for Rwanda—owe at least part of their jurisdiction to the UNCG.

PAUL G. PIERPAOLI JR.

See also: United Nations

Further Reading

LeBor, Adam. *"Complicity with Evil": The United Nations in the Age of Modern Genocide.* New Haven, CT: Yale University Press, 2008.

United Nations. *Atrocities and International Accountability: Beyond Transitional Justice.* New York: United Nations, 2008.

United Nations War Crimes Commission

The creation of United Nations War Crimes Commission (UNWCC) was announced in a joint declaration on October 7, 1942, by the British lord chancellor, Lord Simon, and U.S. president Franklin D. Roosevelt. The UNWCC was initially called the United Nations Commission for the Investigation of War Crimes. The aim of the UNWCC would be to collect and assess all available evidence with a view toward establishing the responsibility of the those individuals guilty of war crimes and to limit the number of people to be tried at the end of World War II. The constituent meeting of the commission finally took place on October 20, 1943, at the Foreign Office in London. The most important members appointed on that day were Cecil J. B. Hurst for Great Britain, Herbert Pell for the United States, André Gros for France, Vaclav Benes for Czechoslovakia, Marcel de Baer for Belgium, and Stefan Glaser for Poland. Later, Baron Robert Wright of Durley joined the commission as a member for Australia. Hurst became the first chairman of the commission and was succeeded by Baron Wright when he retired in January 1945.

The final establishment of the UNWCC was delayed because many governments were reluctant to embark on measures that might have led to a fiasco similar to the one that occurred at the end of World War I, after which virtually no war crime trials were held. The fact that the Soviet government was suspicious of Western intentions pertaining to the punishment of war crimes was also a factor. The Soviet government finally decided not to take part in the deliberations of the UNWCC, citing that its demand for representation from all the Soviet republics touched by the war had been refused. Because no precise rules for the organization and structure of the UNWCC had been laid down prior to the constituent meeting, the commission decided to establish its own organization and set up three committees concerned with the investigation of war crimes, the question of enforcement, and technical advice.

The first committee was headed by Marcel de Baer for almost the whole period of its existence and was concerned with the coordination of the efforts of national offices for the punishment of war crimes. These national offices were organs of their respective governments, but affiliated with the UNWCC. Their main aim was to collect any available information on war crimes and to set up lists of persons who should be indicted at the end of the war. The main efforts of the second committee, headed successively by Herbert Pell and Colonel J. Hodgson, were directed at the elaboration of clauses to be inserted into the expected armistice with Germany to ensure the apprehension of war criminals, the provisioning of draft conventions for the establishment of courts for the trial of war criminals that could not be judged conveniently by national courts, and the creation of war crimes offices in occupied nations for the detection and arrest of war criminals. The third committee was made up of legal experts and handled several important items, including the definition of a war crime, the issue of superior orders at trial, gaps in national legislation, and collective responsibility. On November 29, 1944, the UNWCC set up a Far Eastern and Pacific Sub-Commission, which focused on war crimes in the Far East.

The history of the commission falls into four principal phases. First was the preparatory phase while the war was still in progress, during which important questions of principle and procedure were debated. The second phase was characterized by the support given by the UNWCC to the constitution of tribunals for the punishment of war crimes and to the trials against the major war criminals at Nuremberg. In the third phase, which extend to the latter part of 1947, the commission examined and reported on numerous problems of law arising from treaties and charges in the context of the trials of war criminals by courts set up by the Allied powers. Finally, the latter part of 1947 and the spring of 1948 formed the fourth phase of UNWCC, which focused on winding up the commission's activities, transferring them to other bodies, and writing a history. The commission was dissolved in May 1948.

DANIEL MARC SEGESSER

See also: War Crimes Tribunals

Further Reading

Kochavi, Arieh. *Prelude to Nuremberg: Allied War Crimes Policy and the Question of Punishment.* Chapel Hill: University of North Carolina Press, 1998.

United Nations War Crimes Commission. *History of the United Nations War Crimes Commission.* London: His Majesty's Stationary Office, 1948.

Universal Declaration of Human Rights

The Universal Declaration of Human Rights was adopted on December 10, 1948, by the United Nations (UN) General Assembly. Although not legally binding, the declaration sought to codify and protect five categories of human rights: civil rights, political rights, economic rights, social rights, and cultural rights. Serving as the foundation of future human rights statements, over the interceding decades, this declaration has significantly affected the international political atmosphere through its emphasis on equality and the right to life, liberty, and security.

The declaration largely focuses on the category of civil rights. This first section seeks to protect individuals from discrimination, the depravation of life, liberty, and security, slavery, inhuman treatment, arbitrary arrest, and other various infringements. These protections served as foundations for later UN resolutions and programs including the International Covenant on Economic, Social, and Cultural Rights, the Declaration on the Elimination of Discrimination against Women, and the Universal Declaration on the Eradication of Hunger and Malnutrition.

Further rights that are to be protected are listed in the sections pertaining to political, economic, social, and cultural rights. Many of these rights and goals require positive action on the part of states. Stemming from a belief that poverty, exploitation, and discrimination are not only threats to human welfare, but also the welfare of the state, the enumerated rights seek to ameliorate and end these exploitations through positive governmental action. Seeking full equality, the document argues against the favoring of any group over another, in order to bring about greater prosperity and promote human welfare.

The Universal Declaration of Human Rights serves as the foundation of the United Nations' system. Its structure and emphasis on equality and human rights at all levels of life has brought about progressive legislation over the last half century, which has sought to better the lives of all humans worldwide.

ALEXANDER MIKABERIDZE

See also: United Nations; United Nations Commission on Human Rights

Further Reading

Donnelly, Jack. *Universal Human Rights in Theory and Practice.* 2nd ed. Ithaca, NY: Cornell University Press, 2002.

Morsink, Johannes. *The Universal Declaration of Human Rights: Origins, Drafting, and Intent.* Philadelphia: University of Philadelphia Press, 2000.

Upstander

An upstander is an individual, group, or institution that performs a positive action in order to aid a person or group of people who are the victims of injustice and/or are in distress. The term is most commonly associated with those who have stood up to help the victims of genocide and persecution, sometimes at great personal risk. But there are in fact different types of upstanders, including those who help the poor and disadvantaged and civil rights activists, among many others. Common tactics employed by upstanders include bringing attention to the plight of victims, advocating for government policies to help those being persecuted, and directly intervening in situations in order to protect and save lives. An example of this would be the people in German-occupied countries during World War II who let Jews hide in their homes in order to protect them from the Nazis. This is in contrast to a bystander, who knows that someone is suffering injustice but takes no action. In more recent years, the term upstander has been employed to counter bullying, mostly in primary and secondary schools. In this case, upstanders can play a wide variety of roles, from directly challenging a bully, protecting a person or group from bullying, or promoting an atmosphere in which bullying is discouraged.

The Nazi-inspired Holocaust of the late 1930s and early 1940s spawned countless upstanders who assisted Jews in one way or another or helped hide them. There were upstanders in every nation touched by the Holocaust, and many tried to help or intervene at great peril to themselves, as most countries occupied by the Germans had passed laws that made aiding or hiding Jews a very serious crime. In some cases, the death penalty could result. Some of the more famous Holocaust upstanders, whom the world Jewish community and Israel often refer to as Righteous Gentiles, or Righteous Among the Nations, include: Miep Gies, who hid Anne Frank, her family, and several other Jews in Amsterdam between 1942 and 1944; Raoul Wallenberg, who helped rescue thousands of Jews from near certain-death in Hungary; and Oskar Schindler, who shielded some 1,200 Jews from deportation or death by employing them in his manufacturing business.

Examples of upstanders who in some way intervened in other genocides include: Nicholas D. Kristof an American journalist who helped publicize the recent genocide in Darfur; Paul Rusesabagina, a hotel manager in Kigala who shielded some 1,300 mostly Tutsi refugees during the 1994 Rwandan Genocide; Rigoberta Menchú, who wrote passionately about her experiences during the Guatemalan Genocide, thus focusing world attention on it; and Dith Pran, a Cambodian journalist who revealed fully to the world the horrors of the genocide in Cambodia.

Upstanders not tied to a genocide per se are legion, and they include civil and human rights activists in the United States and abroad, women's rights activists, antiwar activists, antipoverty activists, and even environmental activists. People involved in these activities are considered upstanders because they adopt a positive stand toward a particular wrong or problem, and are acting on behalf of others or themselves.

In recent years, upstanders have been linked with antibullying efforts in U.S. primary and secondary schools. Indeed, in states like Texas, educators have gone even further, teaching about genocide within the context of bullying. Upstanders in antibullying programs can include students who positively defend themselves or others from bullies; individuals who report bullying to teachers, parents, or others in authority; or those who attempt to change social and cultural attitudes to ensure that bullying is discouraged or eliminated. There are currently a number of Web site and organizations that focus on upstanders and bullying, such as the National School Climate Center, the Holocaust Memorial Resource and Education Center of Florida, Stomp out Bullying, and the National Bullying Center.

Paul G. Pierpaoli Jr.

See also: Power, Samantha

Further Reading

Facing History and Ourselves. *Decision-Making in Times of Injustice.* Brookline, MA: Facing History and Ourselves National Foundation, 2009.

Miller, Cindy and Cynthia Lowen. *The Essential Guide to Bullying: Prevention and Intervention.* New York: Alpha Books, 2012.

W

War Crimes Tribunals

International War Crimes Tribunals have been established on an ad hoc basis in response to violations of the laws of war and other serious violations of international humanitarian law.

Following World War I, a 15-member commission appointed by the Allies recommended to the Paris Peace Conference that "violations of the laws and customs of war and the laws of humanity" be punished. The Treaty of Versailles provided for the trial of Kaiser Wilhelm II "for a supreme offense against international morality and the sanctity of treaties," and for trial of Germans accused of violating the laws and customs of war before allied tribunals. However, the Allies did not hold any trials and the Kaiser was never put on trial. Instead, a dozen defendants accused of war crimes were prosecuted before the German Supreme Court in Leipzig but were given minimal sentences.

The Nuremberg tribunals established after World War II is the most significant war crimes tribunal in history. Under the Allies' November 1943 Moscow Declaration, minor Nazi war criminals were to be judged and punished in the countries where they committed their crimes, while the major war criminals would be tried and punished by joint decision of the governments of the Allies. On August 8, 1945, the Allies signed the London Agreement by which they adopted the Charter of the International Military Tribunal (IMT), setting for the jurisdiction substantive law and procedure governing the Nuremberg Tribunal. The

International Military Tribunal for the Far East, commonly known as the Tokyo Tribunal, was created by order of Gen. Douglas MacArthur. The jurisdiction, powers, and procedures were similar to the Nuremberg Tribunal.

The IMT at Nuremberg established the principle of individual responsibility for acts committed by persons against their own nationals and foreigners during wartime. The major leaders of the Axis efforts were brought to trial and sentences including death were imposed.

The charter establishing the Nuremberg Tribunal also established the procedures to be followed. Proceedings were initiated by indictment against defendants who had been designated by the Committee of the Chief Prosecutors as major war criminals. Procedure before the Nuremberg Tribunal war was based on the Anglo American adversarial system, and defendants were granted specified rights, including the right to counsel, to testify on their own behalf, to present evidence, and to cross-examine witnesses. Trials in absentia were authorized and the death penalty could be and was imposed.

The judgment of the IMT stated that the IMT Charter establishing the Nuremberg Tribunal "was the exercise of the sovereign legislative power by the countries to which the German Reich unconditionally surrendered." The charter granted the tribunal jurisdiction over individuals who, as individuals or as members of organizations, committed crimes against peace, war crimes, or crimes against humanity. In addition, responsibility was imposed on leaders, organizers, instigators, and accomplices for all acts performed in execution of a common plan or conspiracy. The jurisdiction of the tribunal was limited to those war criminals whose crimes had no particular location and did not prejudice the jurisdiction of any of the national or occupation courts. The jurisdiction, powers, and procedures of the Tokyo Tribunal were essentially similar to the Nuremberg Tribunal.

Despite the efforts to create a fair and impartial tribunal, the Nuremberg Tribunal was criticized. It was argued that the trials violated the principle against ex post facto laws particularly with respect to the charges pertaining to crimes against the peace. Additionally, it was argued that the tribunals tried only the vanquished and that the judges, all allied nationals, were not impartial. Similar criticisms were directed to the Tokyo Tribunals.

The Nuremberg tribunal consisted of four judges, one appointed by each of the Allied powers, Britain, France, the Soviet Union, and the United States. The chief prosecutor was Justice Robert H. Jackson.

The Tokyo Tribunal consisted of 11 judges, from 11 countries, Australia, Canada, China, France, Britain, India, the Netherlands, New Zealand, the Philippines, the Soviet Union, and the United States, all appointed by Gen. MacArthur.

The Nuremberg Tribunal initially indicted 24 defendants and ultimately tried 22 of them, one in absentia. Of the 22 tried, the tribunal convicted 19 defendants. In addition, several thousand Nazi war criminals were tried before national courts or before tribunals administered by the Allies after the war.

The post–World War II tribunals were important not only because they brought to justice those accused of the most heinous crimes but also because they served an educational purpose, bringing to widespread public attention the atrocities committed by the Axis powers during World War II. In addition, several important principles called the Nuremberg Principles emerged and were adopted by the General Assembly of the United Nations on December 11, 1946. These included: the principle that an individual could be held responsible for violating international law, that reliance on domestic law does not excuse an individual of responsibility, that heads of state are not immune from prosecution, and that following superior orders is not a defense.

The United Nations has been involved with efforts to create an international criminal court almost from its inception. In 1948, the General Assembly requested the International Law Commission to examine the establishment of an international criminal court with jurisdiction over genocide and other crimes. These efforts, however, fell casualty to the Cold War, and efforts to create such a court were held in abeyance.

Following these tribunals, no international war crimes tribunals were established until the 1990s. In response to evidence of serious violations of international humanitarian law taking place in the conflict in the former Yugoslavia, the International Criminal Tribunal for the former Yugoslavia (ICTY) was established by a Security Council Resolution on May 25, 1993. The jurisdiction of the court is limited to serious violations of international humanitarian law committed in the former Yugoslavia since 1991 and includes war crimes, genocide, and other crimes against humanity.

The International Criminal Tribunal for Rwanda (ICTR) is similar to the Yugoslav War Crimes Tribunal. It was established by the Security Council of the United Nations to prosecute persons responsible for genocide and other serious violations of international humanitarian law committed in the territory of Rwanda between January 1, 1994, and December 31, 1994. It may also prosecute Rwandan citizens charged with such crimes committed in the territory of neighboring states during the same period.

The International Law Commission, as mandated by the United Nations General Assembly, issued a draft statute for an international criminal court in 1994, and a diplomatic convention was convened in Rome in 1998 to adopt a statute for the creation of an international criminal court. On July 17, 1998, the UN diplomatic conference adopted the statute for a permanent international criminal court (ICC) by a vote of 120 in favor, 7 against, and 21 abstentions. The international criminal court will come into existence when 60 states ratify the statute.

The Yugoslav and Rwanda Tribunals were created by a resolution of the Security Council acting under Chapter VII of the Charter United Nations and sets forth the substantive jurisdiction of the courts. Rules of Procedure were adopted by the judges of tribunal pursuant to the statute. Some states have voiced criticism of the courts, arguing that the creation of the courts exceeded the power of the Security Council.

The ICTY and ICTR were created by a resolution of the United Nations Security Council and bind all member states of the United Nations. Their jurisdiction extends to natural persons, and states are required to cooperate with the tribunals in the investigation and prosecution of persons accused of committing serious violation of international humanitarian law.

The ICTY is situated in the Hague and enjoys primacy over national courts. The statute prohibits double jeopardy, except that the tribunal may try a person who has been tried by a national court where the relevant act was characterized as an ordinary crime or where the national court proceedings were not impartial or independent, were designed to shield the accused from international criminal responsibility, or were not diligently prosecuted. The statute requires that trials be fair and expeditious and guarantees suspects and the accused internationally recognized rights. Thus, the accused is presumed innocent and among the rights guaranteed are the right to be informed promptly and in detail of the charges against him, to have adequate time and facilities for preparation of a defense, and to communicate with counsel of his own choosing, to have legal counsel provided if he cannot afford it, to be tried without undue delay; to cross-examine witnesses; to remain silent; and to obtain disclosure of certain evidence.

The ICTY is composed of three organs, the prosecutor, the Chambers, and the Registry. The prosecution acts independently as a separate organ of the tribunal to investigate the crimes within the tribunal's jurisdiction, prepare charges, and prosecute accused persons. She may request a state to arrest a suspect provisionally and to seize evidence. Upon sufficient evidence of reasonable grounds to believe that the suspect committed a crime, the indictment is submitted to a trial chamber judge, who, if he concurs, confirms the indictment and may issue any necessary orders, including order for the arrest, surrender, and transfer of the accused.

The defendant then enters a plea and the parties may make preliminary or other motions, including dismissal for lack of jurisdiction and exclusion of evidence.

Trials begin with optional opening statements followed by presentation of the evidence. Witnesses are examined by the parties, though judges may call witnesses and pose questions. In addition to the parties, the tribunal may invite or permit any state, organization, or person to appear before it and make submissions. After presentation of the evidence, the parties may present closing arguments.

Although a trial in absentia is not permitted, if the custody of the accused cannot be obtained, the prosecutor may nevertheless present the case to the trial chamber and if the chamber finds that there are reasonable grounds to find that the defendant committed the crime, an international arrest warrant can be issued. Penalties include imprisonment.

Upon conviction, penalties of imprisonment restriction can be imposed but the death penalty cannot be imposed. Both the defendant and the prosecution can appeal judgment.

The Rwanda War Crimes Tribunal is appended to the Yugoslavia Tribunal, and its statute is closely based on the latter's. It is situated in Arusha, Tanzania. Like the ICTY it is technically a subsidiary, though independent, organ of the Security Council. Its organization is identical to that of the Yugoslav Tribunal, with separate prosecutorial, judicial, and administrative organs. Although its trial chambers are separate from those of ICTY, the organization and procedure of the trial chambers are basically identical, and the two tribunals share a common appellate chamber, as well as a common prosecutor and some common prosecutorial staff.

The Rwanda Tribunal's jurisdiction extends to genocide, crimes against humanity, and war crimes. Jurisdiction is concurrent with national courts, although the tribunal has primacy over national courts. The statute's provisions on individual responsibility, defenses, immunities, and double jeopardy are identical to those in the ICTY statute.

In accordance with the tribunal's statute, the ICTR's judges adopted the Rules of Procedure and Evidence of the ICTY, with only minor changes. Both the ICTY rules and the ICTR rules have been revised on several occasions to enhance efficiency and reflect tribunal practice.

The Yugoslav War Crimes Tribunal is composed of 16 permanent independent judges and a maximum of nine ad litem independent judges. No two judges may be nationals of the same state. Each trial chamber is composed of three permanent judges and a maximum of six ad litem judges. The appeals chamber is composed of seven permanent judges, two of whom are appointed from the International Tribunal for Rwanda. The qualifications of the judges are set forth in Article 13 of the International Tribunal Statute and require that:

The permanent and ad litem judges shall be persons of high moral character, impartiality and integrity who possess the qualifications required in their respective countries for appointment to the highest judicial offices. In the overall composition of the Chambers and sections of the Trial Chambers, due account shall be taken of the experience of the judges in criminal law, international law, including international humanitarian law and human rights law.

Judges of the ICTY and ICTR are nominated by member states of the United Nations. The General Assembly then elects the permanent judges from a list of candidates submitted by the Security Council for a term of four years and there are no term limitations for reelection.

The permanent judges of the International Tribunal elect a president from among their number. The president is a member of the appeals chamber and assigns four others to work with the appeals chamber and nine to work with the trial chamber. The permanent judges of each trial chamber elect a presiding judge from among their number, who oversees the work of the trial chamber as a whole.

The prosecutor is appointed by Security Council on nomination by the secretary-general for a four-year term and can be reelected. The prosecutor must be "of high moral character and possess the highest level of competence and experience in the conduct of investigations and prosecutions of criminal cases."

The acceptance of the Nuremberg Principles was the first step in the development of international human rights law. These principles were elaborated on and embodied in the International Human Rights Conventions that followed. The international community affirmed that how a nation treated its own nationals is of concern to the international community and that governments would be held accountable.

Further, the principle of individual responsibility for violation of international law has been developed and strengthened by the ad hoc tribunals established in Nuremberg, the former Yugoslavia, and Rwanda.

ELIZABETH F. DEFEIS

See also: International Criminal Court; Kuper, Leo; Proxmire, William; United Nations War Crimes Commission

Further Reading

Aldrich, George. "Jurisdiction of the International Criminal Tribunal for the Former Yugoslavia." *American Journal of International Law* Vol. 64 (1996): 90.

Bassiouni, M. Cherif, and Peter Manikas. *The Law of the International Criminal Tribunal for the Former Yugoslavia.* Irvington-on-Hudson, NY: Transnational Publishers, 1996.

Bassiouni, M. Cherif. *Crimes Against Humanity in International Criminal Law.* 2nd Rev. ed. Boston: Kluwer Law International, 1999.

Bassiouni, M. Cherif, ed. *International Criminal Law.* Ardsley, NY: Transnational Publishers, 1999, 3 vols.

Ferencz, Benjamin B. *An International Criminal Court: A Step toward World Peace.* New York: Oceana Publications, 1980, 2 vols.

Taylor, Telford. *The Anatomy of the Nuremberg Trials.* New York: Alfred A. Knopf, 1992.

Whitaker Report

The Whitaker Report was a wide-ranging special report on genocide, which was formally submitted to the United Nations (UN) Sub-Commission on Prevention and Discrimination and Protection of Minorities (Commission on Human Rights of the UN Economic and Social Committee) on July 2, 1985. The report was compiled and written by now-retired British Labour Party politician Benjamin Whitaker, whom the UN had tasked with writing the comprehensive report. The Whitaker Report was formally entitled *Revised and Updated Report on the Question of the Prevention and Punishment of the Crime of Genocide.* Because of problems with a 1978 UN report on genocide, known as the Ruhashyankiko Report, in 1983 the Sub-Commission requested that the United Nations Economic and Social Council (ECOSOC) permit a new and revised report to be compiled, and Whitaker was given the title of special UN rapporteur that same year.

The Whitaker Report consisted of a Forward, Introduction, Appendix, and a four-part analysis. Part I provided an Historical Overview; Part II provided a detailed analysis of the existing United Nations Convention on the Prevention and Punishment of the Crime of Genocide (UNCG); Part III discussed the future of genocide and the prevention of it; and Part IV listed recommendations and conclusions.

In Part I, Whitaker discussed past genocides, and made specific reference to the 1915–1923 Armenian Genocide, which earlier UN reports had failed to do. This was the first written document from the UN that acknowledged those tragic events. In Part II, Whitaker took up the deficiencies of the UNCG of 1948. Here he tackled a number of issues, some of them quite controversial. They included the determination of groups that were not then protected by the UNCG, the intent to commit genocide, the definition of the acts that constitute genocide, UNCG enforcement, and the statute of limitations involving genocidal crimes. In Part III, Whitaker prescribed the need to institute mechanisms by which genocides may be predicted, prevented, or stopped once they begin. He also discussed the need for an international court of human rights, where those accused of war crimes and crimes against humanity may be tried in a supranational criminal tribunal.

Part IV of Whitaker's report was perhaps the most illuminating but also the most controversial. Among other things, he urged that the UNCG be expanded to include groups who had been previously left out of the Convention because of political or cultural considerations. Those groups included political groups as well as groups targeted because of their sexual orientation. He also suggested that ecocide (the purposeful destruction of the natural environment), and cultural genocide be studied further and, perhaps, added to the UNCG.

The Sub-Commission formally accepted Whitaker's report, although it failed to "approve" it because of political considerations. Indeed, a number of its suggestions and recommendations were virtually ignored. The establishment of the International Criminal Court (ICC) at The Hague in 2002, however, was a significant vindication of Whitaker's work, as he had specifically called for such a tribunal in Part III of his report. In 1993–1994, the Sub-Commission revisited the issue of genocide and vowed to institute some of Whitaker's other recommendations.

PAUL G. PIERPAOLI JR.

See also: United Nations

Further Reading

Kennedy, Paul. *The Parliament of Man: The Past, Present, and Future of the United Nations.* New York: Vintage, 2007.

Schabas, William A. *Genocide in International Law: The Crime of Crimes.* Cambridge, UK: Cambridge University Press, 2000.

Historical Dilemmas

The Historical Dilemma section introduces students and researchers to debates and controversies in the study of certain genocides and atrocities. It presents a historical question with different perspectives on the issue, showing users not only how scholars utilize evidence to present their respective arguments, but how certain topics in genocide studies continue to be debated.

What Are the Most Effective Ways to Prevent Future Genocides?

Introduction

In an attempt to draw attention to a conflict and garner enough international attention and action before the situation turns into an episode of mass murder, potential genocide prevention strategies are compiled by various scholars, organizations, government officials, politicians, activists, and international institutions—sometimes working in tandem or separately. Those who are familiar with the criteria necessary for a conflict to escalate to a genocide have found it essential to research, analyze, and present information to draw attention to and shape international opinion on these events as well as propose potential solutions in order to quell such scenarios prior to them becoming genocide.

Genocide prevention activism in the late 20th and early 21st centuries has been successful in creating international awareness of gross human rights violations and violent conflicts that could potentially turn into genocidal events. However, despite these successes, genocidal actions were conducted in Bosnia, Rwanda, and Darfur, as the world watched and did little in response. Nonetheless, genocide prevention models and strategies provide a valuable set of tools for forecasting potential hotspots and providing solutions to major powers and international organizations so they can take action. In light of this, it is fair to ask the question: What are the most effective ways to prevent future genocides?

In the first Perspective essay, Gregory H. Stanton argues that organizations dedicated to genocide prevention can make a significant difference in preventing genocidal incidents. Stanton uses his personal experience through his work with Genocide Watch as an example of how such activism can be successful in drawing attention to and encouraging responses from the international community. In the second Perspective essay, Henry C. Theriault argues that while genocide prevention can be successful in certain instances, more often than not, complications arise that can make it difficult for international action to be prompt in responding to instances of genocide. However, Theriault still thinks it is possible and necessary to bring attention to and educate the public about the potential for genocide. In the third Perspective essay, Colin Tatz discusses the limits of genocide prevention. Tatz argues that despite the best attempts at international intervention through sanctions or military action, prevention schemes often overlook the political and social factors which created the context for potential genocidal events.

Perspective 1: Genocide Watch

Genocide Watch has developed an early warning system using our understanding of the genocidal process to predict and recommend policies to prevent genocide. Through the International Alliance to End Genocide, the first anti-genocide coalition (founded in 1999), we maintain close relations with policy makers who can take preventive action. Rapid response by regional alliances has prevented or stopped several genocides: in East Timor, Kosovo, Ivory Coast, Ethiopia, and Sierra Leone.

We have created international tribunals to try genocidists in former Yugoslavia, Rwanda, Sierra Leone, East Timor, and Cambodia. And we finally have an International Criminal Court (the ICC). The UN Security Council has referred the situation in Darfur to the ICC. It has indicted President Omar al-Bashir, Abdul Rahim, and Ahmed Harun for crimes against humanity and genocide in Darfur. But al-Bashir has just laughed. He even appointed Harun (one of those indicted) to be Governor of South Kordofan where he is leading another genocide against the people of the Nuba Mountains.

The International Criminal Tribunal for Rwanda (ICTR) has finished 50 trials and convicted 29 persons. The Cambodian Tribunal has sentenced Comrade Duch, the commander of the Tuol Sleng Prison that tortured and killed 14,000 Cambodians, to life in prison. And the surviving leaders of the Khmer Rouge are finally on trial, 30 years after I founded the Cambodian Genocide Project while still a student at Yale Law School in 1982.

In 30 years of work against genocide, I have learned two things about genocide prevention. The first lesson is the direct result of our own human incapacity to comprehend or feel sympathy for large groups of people half way around the world. Because individuals cannot do that, we need permanent institutions established that will watch out for precursors of genocide, take action to prevent it, intervene to stop it, and arrest and prosecute those who commit it.

Institutions are necessary to overcome the fleeting nature of our concern. That is why in 2000, I proposed and the International Alliance to End Genocide lobbied, and in 2004 the UN Secretary General created the UN Special Advisor for the Prevention of Genocide. It is why we support President Barack Obama's U.S. Atrocities Prevention

Board and the creation of similar institutions in Britain, France, Germany, India, Nigeria and other nations around the world. But warning is not enough.

We must also create institutions for action. Unfortunately, President Obama has not matched his promise of "Never again" with any concrete action to stop the Sudanese government's genocide in the Nuba Mountains and Darfur. President Obama should impose a NO FLY Zone over the Nuba Mountains. Any Sudanese bomber or helicopter gunship that attacks a Nuba village should be allowed to land and then destroyed (when their crews have left at night) by cruise missiles fired from American warships in the Indian Ocean. And their runways should be destroyed. North Atlantic Treaty Organization (NATO) airstrikes in Libya took control of the skies from Muammar Gaddafi. The same should be done with Omar Hassan Ahmad al-Bashir's Sudan.

The UN has completely failed to prevent or stop genocide, largely because of paralysis by threatened vetoes by one or more of the permanent members so the Security Council, but also because of the UN's continuing unwillingness to offend member states. Regional alliances like NATO, ASEAN (Association of Southeast Asian Nations), the OAS (Organization of American States) and ECOWAS (the Economic Community of West African States, led by Nigeria), have been effective interveners. The UN Charter specifically authorizes regional intervention.

The International Criminal Court needs an Optional Protocol to create an international police force with the sole mandate to arrest leaders indicted by the ICC. This police force could be created without any action by the UN—through a treaty among the Assembly of States-Parties to the ICC.

The second lesson I have learned is that genocide prevention must start and be led by people from countries at risk. It cannot be led by an American organization in Washington D.C., led by a pacifist director, that is unwilling to advocate the use of force to stop genocide. Prevention must especially begin from the ground up in countries at risk of genocide. A true International Alliance to End Genocide can support such local efforts and create an international mass movement to end genocide. The best example is Liberia.

Leemah Gbowee, a fish seller in Monrovia, Liberia had a strange dream one night. She dreamed that the market women of Monrovia should begin each week with an hour of prayer for peace in Liberia, a country then torn apart by civil war between Charles Taylor's government and the

Revolutionary United Front (RUF). Both sides cut off arms and hands, raped women, conscripted child soldiers and turned them into killers on drugs—they committed every war crime. She told her dream to a Muslim friend who also sold fish in the market, and they began the weekly prayer meetings in the fish market. More and more women joined until 5,000 women were praying every week. Taylor's entourage drove blithely by in their Mercedes limousines.

Then Leemah Gbowee and the other women demanded a meeting with Taylor and with the leaders of the RUF. When they met them, the women demanded an immediate ceasefire and negotiations to end the war. Both sides agreed; and talks began in Accra, Ghana. But the women did not trust the men to make peace. They pooled their nickels and quarters, rented buses, and went to Accra themselves. They slept outside, sometimes in the rain, while the men slept in four-star hotels. The talks between the men, led by a former Nigerian President, went nowhere.

Finally, fed up, the women walked into the building where the talks were underway and sat down in the hallways. The Ghanaian police threatened to arrest them. One of the senior women said she would make it easy for them by removing all her clothes. (One of the most humiliating things that can happen to a man in Ghana is for a grandmother to disrobe in front of him.) The police backed off.

Finally the Nigerian ex-President told the men that if they did not come to agreement in three days, he would turn the talks over to the women. The agreement they reached included the exile of Charles Taylor to Nigeria.

Peace returned to Liberia and in the next election, with the women's crucial votes, Dr. Ellen Johnson Sirleaf become the first woman elected President of an African country. Leymah Gbowee, Ellen Johnson Sirleaf, and the Yemeni woman human rights activist, Tawakkul Karman won the Nobel Peace Prize in 2011. Charles Taylor was tried for his crimes and convicted. He will likely spend the rest of his life in prison.

GREGORY H. STANTON

Perspective 2: Studies and Recommendations for Prevention

Recently, scholars, policy makers, and human rights activists have focused on intervention against genocides. For instance, many organizations entreated the United Nations and individual countries to stop the 1994 Rwandan Genocide and the 1992–1995 Bosnia Genocide. Scholars and activists continue today to urge intervention against Sudan government's nine-year genocide in Darfur and violence against groups in the Nuba Mountains and South Kordofan since 2011. In case after case, however, little or nothing has been done to intervene. Furthermore, even in cases of intervention, it occurred only after much death and suffering. The 1999 North Atlantic Treaty Organization (NATO) bombing of Serbia to prevent escalating violence in Kosovo happened after 100,000 to 200,000 Bosnians and others had been murdered and countless raped in the Bosnia Genocide. Intervention in East Timor came only when the same government that had already killed 250,000 people a few years earlier started killing thousands more.

Because intervention happens only too late or not at all, many scholars, activists, and policy makers now emphasize prevention. Governments and organizations outside a country that might commit genocide as well as citizens and political leaders inside that country can try to stop a genocide before it even begins.

There are, unfortunately, many difficulties with prevention. First, it requires making an educated guess whether genocide is truly going to happen. Since we cannot predict the future accurately, this requires "judgement calls" by qualified experts based on "early warning signs." For instance, some scholars have said that national identification cards that record an individual's tribal, ethnic, or religious group are a genocide warning sign, because the cards help mark off potential victims from potential perpetrators. Some scholars also point to violence by a government, particularly one that is not democratic: if a government believes that it is acceptable to commit violence against its own or another society's people, it might come to think that mass murder of such people is acceptable.

Yet, even when the warning signs of genocide seem reasonably clear, that does not mean outside or inside groups will act to prevent genocide. Often, nonexperts and even some experts disagree that genocide is a threat or tell themselves that it is not even though they should know better. And, when many people agree that there is a danger of genocide, the question becomes, what can be done to prevent it? Should military forces from other countries go in and remove the potentially genocidal government from power? But, in a world where we are supposed to be innocent until proven guilty, unless we can be 100 percent sure that a government is about to commit genocide, what gives us the right to remove it from power? Also, often outside groups are not willing to risk the deaths of their own citizens to stop a genocide against some other group. What is more, if there is military action, this could lead to a big war in which many people are killed on all sides, including in the victim group that outsiders were trying to save from genocide.

Prevention is also complicated because the earlier in time we are, the harder it is to see warning signs and have some level of certainty that they are leading to genocide. For all of these reasons, genocide prevention is a very difficult issue even for the most experienced scholars and policy makers.

That does not mean, however, that we should not try to prevent genocide. Because genocide is so constant in our world—it is difficult to think of a period in the past 520 years, for instance, in which there has been no genocidal activity in the world—and destroys so many people—R. J. Rummel of the University of Hawai'i estimates that between 170 and 360 million people were killed by governments from 1900 to 1987—most people would agree we must try.

Some policy makers have made concrete proposals. The Genocide Prevention Task Force led by former U.S. secretary of state Madeleine Albright and former U.S. secretary of defense William Cohen, in 2008's *Preventing Genocide: A Blueprint for U.S. Policymakers,* discuss many prevention strategies. For instance, outside powers can use incentives such as increased trade to gain better treatment of potential victim groups, or they can use consequences, such as trade embargoes or denial of favorable trade status, to coerce a government into better treatment. Such approaches have the potential to work well when a genocide is motivated by economic or national security concerns, for instance, as is the case with the destruction of indigenous peoples in the Amazon Basin area during the past four decades.

Another method promises even better results than the Albright-Cohen piecemeal approach. This takes recognizing that the United States and other great powers are not simply bystanders to genocides that happen somewhere else, but are sometimes active participants themselves. The United States provided military and political support to Guatemala's government as it murdered approximately 200,000 members of its indigenous Mayan population in the 1970s-1990s and to the Indonesian government as it killed about 500,000 "communists" in 1965–66 and 250,000 East Timorese starting in 1975. Support has included guns, help from U.S. Navy ships, efforts in the UN to prevent discussion, etc. One very good prevention strategy is to withdraw military and political support from

governments that appear to be heading toward genocide. In this way, such governments might have fewer guns to commit genocide and will not have political support to hide from the consequences of genocidal acts.

This discussion has been about prevention in other societies, as if our own has no chance of committing genocide. But it has committed genocide, for instance, against Native Americans. How can we prevent our own society—and how can other societies prevent themselves—from committing genocide in the future? Psychologist Ervin Staub has argued that an important concern for genocide prevention is how we educate and "socialize" people in our society, particularly children. If people grow up learning that prejudice and violence are acceptable, they are more likely to participate in genocide. As Staub says, there is always an extremist leader or group in any society; genocides occur when people follow that extremist. By educating and socializing people against violence and prejudice, we can reduce the number of people willing to follow such leaders and commit genocide. If we make sure our society is truly committed to nonviolence and human rights, we can make it much less likely to commit genocide.

There is still another level of prevention. It is easy not to notice, but our current world has come about through past genocides and other mass human rights violations such as slavery, as much as by any other force. The land of the United States was depopulated of its 10 million native inhabitants largely through genocide and the bulk of the labor that build the colonies and then United States in their first 250 years was from slaves. A similar situation exists around the world, from Ireland to Australia. The awful truth is that genocide usually helps those committing it a great deal. They get land, wealth, and power. What is more, genocide has become part of the very way we do politics and fight wars. Real prevention of genocide will require us to change the way we do politics and fight wars. Perhaps the way to start this is to recognize the wrongs of the past and try to address them, so that genocide no longer is a benefit for perpetrators.

HENRY C. THERIAULT

Perspective 3: Reservations about Genocide Prevention

The concept of prevention is in the forefront of both suicide and genocide studies. I am a student of both. We do not know the precise causes of self-death or of mass death, and so the word prevention is misleading and pretentious. Neither case is like measles or smallpox, and no inoculation or prophylactic is to hand. Early detecting of symptoms, perhaps deflecting and intervening are possible—but not obviating, precluding, excluding or pre-empting the phenomena.

Genocide is never spontaneous. Always incremental, it is an accretion of ideas and actions like a set of building blocks or an engine assembly. There is always a context which allows for diagnosis and analysis, perhaps an autopsy, of what has gone before—the terrain, the antecedent events, precursory signs and actions. Two scholars—Yehuda Bauer on the Judeocide and Richard Dekmejian on the Armenian Genocide—talk of five factors that produce or occasion genocidal events: an ancient hatred or ideological imperative, a brutal dictatorship, a war setting, a compliant bureaucracy and a use of technology. Their paradigm derives from European experiences, but when we look at Rwanda, as one example, some of these elements are missing, or are different. Post-Holocaust research has also shown that democracies, like Australia, can commit genocide, even outside of a war setting.

We can try to predict a genocidal event by a focus on at-risk factors, early warning signs and symptoms, cries for help (as with suicide). But when or what precisely is "early" and what is a "warning sign"? American scholars Ted Gurr and Barbara Harff have done fine service in producing politico-sociological analyses of "at-risk" societies, assigning graduated weightings to the most likely to the less likely victim groups. With their checklist, we may get it right in some instances. Yet coming from South Africa, as I did, one could see all the outward signs, the "downstream factors"—of authoritarianism, race hatred and division, oppression, suppression, violence, censorship, exile of citizens, imprisonments without trial, politically motivated murders; assessors would have been right in defining crimes against humanity but they would have been wrong in diagnosing genocide.

The Carnegie Commission on Preventing Deadly Conflict (1994–1999) outlined two broad strategies: *operational* prevention and *structural* prevention. The former is really *intervention,* of how to respond to an immediate crisis. The latter is intended as keeping crises from occurring. In essence, that means trying to teach people about the rule of law, democratic processes, open economies and social "safety nets." Unashamedly American, these structural proposals are essentially about democracy as the antidote to all, or most, conflicts.

The topic here is prevention, that is, the quick extinguishment of the sparks that may, or are likely to, cause something to flare, or which has begun to show actual signs of escalating into that ultimate crime. What exactly can hinder, impede, frustrate or forestall what German author Christian Pross calls the use of "ideological tools for a biological solution to a social [or political] problem." That is an accurate and astute description of what genocide is, and so the question is, how do we stop *that* mindset?

Outlawing the crime of genocide has not stopped it, and punishment has been absent, or tardy and slow enough, or so bogged down in technicalities, as to be seen as an insufficient, even a poor, deterrent to potential génocidaires. The Turkish courts-martial in 1919, the Leipzig trials in Germany after World War I, the Nuremberg Trials and over 100,000 "smaller" trials that followed in the two Germanys and Austria after the International Military Tribunal, and the Rwanda and Former Yugoslavia special tribunals of more recent times have not produced a sufficient fear of public trial and punishment to prevent repetition.

Sanctions of arms, fuels, finance, goods and services, have not proven prophylactic enough, whether against murderous Italy in Abyssinia (Ethiopia) or neo-genocidal Japan in China's Nanking in the 1930s. Sanctions against Syria some 77 years later did not stop the death of some 60,000 civilians by the end of 2012, with many more dead to come.

We need a close look at "upstream" factors or signs. First, at *political geography,* a lens of great value but too rarely used. Who, for example, blocks the pathway to expanded territorial boundaries; which domains, like Kashmir, frustrate the ambitions of powerful neighbors? Where do we find valued resources, like crops or cattle or minerals, seemingly in the hands of minorities who will not share the goods? Who has grain and who does not in a climate change vortex? Where do potential victims have assets which others covet and which would be available readily if the owners were simply not there, as in many Amazonian cases? Where have populations been moved across earlier maps, where have populations disappeared from such maps? What exactly have been the factors in what look like (and often are not) voluntary migrations?

Landscape is a good a place to begin. The political maps drawn in the 19th century "scramble for Africa" produced fatal results because of the casting aside of tribal boundaries and affiliations in favor of "desirable" or neat political units. Some units in Asia (and Britain) have had to resort to partition because conflicting groups have been unable to coexist within a new political domain. Landscapes are as important as the examination of local history, politics, and sociology. It is not difficult to find evidence of both episodic and chronic violence as a means of resolving disputes, of enslavement or deportation or exile as evidence that a biological remedy has been adopted as a solution to "problems."

An "upstream" examination of the physical place and plight of Christian minorities in the Near East (circa 1880–1915), at their lack of a "homeland" shield, at the history of their vilification—politically, culturally, linguistically and religiously—would have signaled the events to come, especially after the massacre of some 200,000 Armenians in 1894 by Sultan Hamid II. "Upstream" factors were always visible in modern Europe in relation to Jews and Romani peoples, and there was no shortage of evidence that these were "undesirable" people. The homicidal texts underlying both Christian and "racial science" doctrines were not that difficult to detect. The genocidal engines that finally destroyed them did not land in a Nazi space ship in 1933: they were built, by accretion, with each engine part or building block evident "upstream" in time. That people, including the victims, did not want to see "things" is not to say that those "things" were not present. Kurds in Turkey, Iraq and Iran today are the obvious case of landscape and history leading to genocide in embryo. Extra lessons in democracy are neither curative nor preventative.

The *CIA World Factbook* offers a good starting point. It details 267 political entities, listing their physical attributes, population composition, geography, history, systems of government, economies, communications, transport systems and the like. Applying a template of past genocides and neo-genocides, it cannot be that difficult to locate "sparks" or even "embers," let alone "fires." But having found something indicative, what is missing, and will always remain missing, is the concerted political will to avert the possibly avertable. One need look no further than the attitudes of Belgium, France and the United States as the Rwandan events of 1994 began to unfold—especially against the landscape-history of what happened in Burundi in 1972. The world gets better at intervening, as with "no-fly" zones in Iraq in 1991 to *further protect* Kurds from chemical and bacterial weapons already used. But intervening and stopping are not synonyms for preventing.

Colin Tatz

Can Humanitarian Intervention in Countries Suffering from Genocidal Violence Be Justified, Even though Such Intervention Conflicts with International Law?

Introduction

The incidence of genocide in the contemporary world often raises the question of whether humanitarian intervention is a viable option to quell the situation. While the international community observes such deteriorating situations and attempts diplomatic solutions to prevent the violence from escalating, quite often, this does little to nothing in ending the slaughter of innocents. Despite the instruments of international law designed at ensuring military action to stop genocidal policies, international disagreements over intervention, the primacy of domestic politics, and military considerations over national interests, often shape the desire or reluctance to become involved in humanitarian intervention. Moreover, questions of national sovereignty and its infringement by international military actions are frequently raised by proposed humanitarian interventions. Recent genocides, most notably Rwanda and Bosnia, resulted in limited international intervention under the support of the United Nations and/or the North Atlantic Treaty Organization (NATO), which limited the damage to some extent, but were often controversial due either to inaction or questionable military strikes. Moreover, the sanctity of national sovereignty as upheld by international law conflicts with the existing international instruments of law to ensure military action to prevent and end genocidal policies. Can humanitarian intervention in countries suffering from genocidal violence be justified, even though such intervention conflicts with international law?

In his Perspective essay, Henry C. Theriault argues the international principle of national sovereignty is sacrosanct and should not be violated, lest it set a precedent for interventions that would violate the precept that protects the existence of nation-states. While international legal instruments exist to prevent genocidal excess, these are typical in conflict with international law in certain instances. Moreover, major world powers have often used genocidal violence as an excuse to engage in aggression abroad. Lastly, sometimes intervention creates more problems than it solves, unleashing greater instability in already troubled world regions. In contrast, in his Perspective essay, Henry

Carey maintains that saving human lives trumps national sovereignty and the international community has a responsibility to intervene to stop genocidal violence. Carey recognizes that much needs to be done in the realm of international law to create more concrete guidelines for intervention, but that noninvolvement is not an option when a genocide is clearly being undertaken by a regime against people under its power. Lastly, in his Perspective essay, Alexander Mikaberidze traces the complex history of international intervention in genocidal episodes and how international law has evolved over time. He concludes that these events should be stopped by the international community only when warranted and not as an excuse to begin aggression against a particular nation-state (i.e., U.S. 2003 invasion of Iraq). Only through the proper channels of international order, namely through cooperation with the United Nations (UN) should interventions be exercised. In this manner, national sovereignty is not violated, but sanctioned by the necessity of saving the civilian population of a rogue regime bent on their death.

Perspective 1: Military Intervention Not Justified

"Intervention" can mean military or nonmilitary intervention. However, in most cases, nonmilitary intervention, that is, intervention that does not use violence or other force, does not conflict with international law. For instance, under most conditions, any country is free to choose to invoke economic sanctions against another country; it is only a violation of international law if force is used without United Nations (UN) or other international legal sanction. Similarly, any country can send relief aid to another country, which can accept or refuse it as it wishes; it is only a violation of international law if force is used to impose the relief aid on the country in question.

Military intervention is use of force to protect victims and/or to prevent perpetrators from committing violence, whether by degrading their ability to commit the violence or defeating them and taking them out of power. Military intervention can be authorized by, for instance, a United Nations Security Council resolution, or it can be unauthorized, such as the unilateral 1999 North Atlantic Treaty Organization (NATO) bombing of Serbia in response to violence against Kosovo Albanians.

Is military intervention that is not authorized legally justifiable in cases of genocide? It goes without saying that, if a genocide can be prevented or stopped by nonmilitary means that do not conflict with international law, then clearly military action is not justified. What of cases in which it appears that military intervention is the best option, however? If it is the case that international law is flawed or has gaps that allow genocides that should be prevented based on international human rights law, then unauthorized intervention might be justified.

But international law does not seem to be flawed or incomplete, at least for more than a decade, with the general acceptance of the concept of the "responsibility to protect." This principle has two core elements. First, a government that enjoys sovereign rule over its population also has the responsibility to protect the human rights of that population from others and to promote rather than abuse those human rights itself. Second, when a government fails in its responsibility toward its own people, not only do other governments have the right to intervene, but they have the responsibility to intervene. The "responsibility to protect" is now generally understood as an interpretation of the implications of current international law. Thus, in cases of serious human rights abuse such as genocides, international law allows for intervention even when this will violate state sovereignty.

Even if the formal legal mechanisms for intervention despite state sovereignty exist, however, military intervention might still be justified if in practice, due to political manipulations, the "responsibility to protect" is not enforced when it should be. This seemed to happen, for instance, in the case of Rwanda. In recent years, the view that failures such as Rwanda show that there should generally be much more military intervention than there is has become prevalent. As an example, Samantha Power's *A Problem from Hell* (2003) can, in fact, be read as an extended, emotionally manipulative polemic aimed at convincing readers that the United States should be intervening militarily much more than it does. While Power certainly and rightly exposes UN inaction on genocides as a serious problem, she also appears to advocate unilateral military action as a response to UN and other failures, as in Kosovo.

But, as much as there are cases in which formal legal mechanisms are not applied to authorize legitimate humanitarian intervention, the opposite is true as well: there appear to be many cases in which humanitarian reasons have been asserted in cases in which the goal might not have been the protection of human rights but the subversion of state sovereignty by the invading power to gain its own economic, political, and/or military advantages. This, for instance, is a criticism often made of the U.S. invasion and occupation of Iraq, which has installed a pro-U.S. government in place of an anti-U.S. government. Herb Hirsch also points out that the promotion of humanitarian military intervention gives great power militaries, especially the United States', continued legitimacy in the post–Cold War era, when questions arise about why the United States and other countries are maintaining the massive military spending levels of the Cold War.

The principle of sovereignty is an important protection against external military and political intrusions of the sort that were the global rule in the age colonialism. It cannot be set aside without good reason. The imperfect application of international law to human rights issues can be seen to work in both directions, that is, to produce some cases in which intervention should have occurred and others in which it should not have but did. Once we remove the moral force of international legal protections against unilateral military actions, we are likely to increase the number of human rights-abusing interventions at least as much as those that protect human rights, while weakening the very international legal structures that are the foundation of human rights protections in the first place. If the law is not applied perfectly, this is because the tension between sovereignty and the responsibility to protect is (1) subject to political manipulation and (2) is complex and uncertain. The solution to this problem is not to do away with state sovereignty, but to stop political manipulation of international law regarding human rights crises.

There is another issue regarding unlawful intervention. Cases for morally justified unlawful military intervention assume that military intervention is effective at stopping genocidal violence and the only problem is that sometimes international law stands in the way of intervention. But, is even legal military intervention generally successful in stopping or reducing violence? According to genocide scholar Alan Kuperman, military as well as other forms of intervention, such as economic sanctions, can in fact increase the level of violence in a human rights crisis. For instance, it can provoke a backlash by a government that is committing genocide or on a path to do so. It can also embolden armed rebel groups to increase their level of violence, with the result that civilians are caught between government and rebel troops. We can add further that intervention can destabilize a society. As I have argued, in many cases of authorized intervention, intervening forces have also committed significant violations of human rights. If legally authorized military intervention is not morally justified in cases in which it has a reasonable

chance of not being effective, then certainly neither is unauthorized military intervention.

What is more, genocide scholar Daniel Feierstein has argued that the problem is not too little intervention, but too much intervention. His main example is the United States. He points out that the United States has been involved in human rights abuses in various Latin American countries, including direct involvement in the Guatemalan Genocide. The solution for him is ending military and other intervention, not increasing it. This is borne out by evidence from other areas of the world. For instance, the second phase of the East Timor Genocide was prevented when the United States, Britain, and Australia withdrew their military and political support for the Indonesian government, support that made the first phase of the genocide starting in 1975 possible.

In sum, not only does unauthorized military intervention undermine the very legal foundations of human rights themselves, but the assumption that it will stop or prevent an on-going or potential genocide is not well-supported. Unauthorized military intervention is, therefore, not justified.

HENRY C. THERIAULT

Perspective 2: Humanitarian Intervention and National Sovereignty

The debate over legalizing "humanitarian intervention" has occurred over the past century, since the Balkan Wars in the early 20th century, when a Christian empire like Britain intervened to protect Christians from attack by the Muslim Ottoman Empire. Initially, there was some acceptance by states that international law would accept armed intervention to protect fellow citizens whose lives were threatened in a foreign country. When the United Nations (UN) Charter became the basis for international law in 1945, the legal prohibition against any armed intervention not sanctioned by the UN Security Council (UNSC) was strengthened, except for unilateral state intervention for individual or collective self-defense, which as regarded by the Charter as an 'inherent' right, that is part of customary international law. States have conducted unilateral military interventions which halted or prevented genocide but violated international law. Humanitarian interventions in the 1970s, such as in Tanzania to stop Idi Amin in Uganda, India to stop Pakistan in East Pakistan (what subsequently became Bangladesh), and Vietnam in to stop mass murder by the Khmer Rouge in Cambodia in the 1970s has been limited and selective. Section 139 of the 2005 "World Summit" Resolution of the UN General Assembly authorizes armed intervention only via UNSC authorization.

In addition, the UN Charter permits armed intervention for "individual and collective self-defense." Self-defense does not legally extend to armed intervention to protect citizens of a foreign government in that foreign country, and assertions that human rights, which are a main Purpose of the UN as stated in its Charter, armed intervention to protect human rights as a legal remedy remains controversial. Even in cases of genocide, legalizing humanitarian intervention remains challenged by legal scholars.

The UN General Assembly passed a recommendation in 2005 for the Responsibility to Protect (R2P), defined as, "the responsibility (of each state) to protect its populations from genocide, war crimes, ethnic cleansing and crimes against humanity." However, that R2P doctrine, which was also controversial because the Charter seems to require a threat to international peace, which is not present in genocide, required UN Security Council authorization, whereas humanitarian intervention, such as the North Atlantic Treaty Organization's (NATO's) 1999 humanitarian intervention against Serbia to halt the incipient genocide in Kosovo, lacked the UNSC endorsement, which was provided for NATO's intervention in Libya. It is a responsibility that extends to the international community as a whole. In the event an individual state cannot or will not protect its population R2P requires that appropriate action be taken through the UNSC. While genocide, as the "crime of crimes," might naturally seem to make sense as a near-automatic exception to prohibitions against intervention, there remain questions about methods and motives. The Charter requires the exhaustion of peaceful methods of dispute resolution prior to recourse to force—though time is of the essence in halting or preventing genocide. Even where successfully preventing genocide and other crimes against humanity, as in Libya, NATO went beyond protecting the ethnic groups in the eastern part of the country to effecting regime change, thereby violating Article 2(4), by changing the government's "political independence." Even when a humanitarian intervention has UNSC authorization, it must "[bear] in mind the principles of the [UN] Charter and international law," according to the 2005 General Assembly Resolution from the "World Summit Outcome."

Australian scholar Luke Glanville and others suggest that humanitarian intervention has been asserted by proponents like Ellary Stowell, who in the early 20th century argued that sovereignty was not a legal absolute, under the "universally recognized principles of decency and humanity." As the 2005 UN World Summit indicates, the "collective responsibility to act to protect populations in instances where states fail to do so."

Perhaps most vexing about genocide is that it is an "intent crime," which can occur so long as there is a plan to perpetrate genocide. Thus, even before large number of murders of racial, religious, ethnic groups, a genocide has legally occurred. However, the early stages of genocide are the time when diplomacy to avoid war—and thus greater numbers of deaths in the short run, are a distinct possibility, especially if a humanitarian intervention is less than quickly successful. Moreover, the initial crisis may turn out to be less than what are conventionally regarded as genocides—after the murders have been perpetrated—in other words, after it is too late.

The argument in favor of humanitarian intervention is based on the human right to life, as the overriding right that permits all other human rights. Humanitarian intervention is necessary, proponents argue, because the UN Genocide Convention provides not merely for the discretion to intervene, the obligation of states parties to prevent and punish genocide. Furthermore, the four 1949 Geneva Conventions, at the heart of international humanitarian law, require states to facilitate and/or seek disaster relief, a nonviolent form of intervention, in all international armed conflict to curtail the loss of life. Most legal scholars feel these requirements also extend to internal wars, which are typical of many genocides. Strengthening international law to ensure that states meet their obligations makes both armed and aid-based humanitarian interventions, with or without UNSC authorization, as desirable under specific conditions.

Among the necessarily legal conditions for success would include: a) the need to act quickly before more people die; b) the futility of continuing diplomatic and other voluntary measures of conflict resolution; c) the high probability of success of military and aid-based interventions; d) acting through multilateral sanction through the UN or other international organizations or coalitions of willing states, where possible. Of all these requirements, the *sine qua non* is the probability that attempting to stop a genocide will succeed and not produce more deaths than it prevents, not only in the short, but also in the long run.

There always remains, given the reality that humanitarian intervention usually has a strategic or political motive, in addition to the altruistic one, that the humanitarian motive is less significant to political-military calculations of the intervening parties. Legal scholar Stuart Ford argues that, "It seems futile to rely on the state to prevent crimes that it is committing, and encouragement by the international community [as in the case of Myanmar] is unlikely to be of much use either." There could be other situations where other states might conduct forcible interventions against the wishes of host states, particularly when the host state might claim it was not responsible, such as natural disasters, like tsunamis, earthquakes, hurricanes and even deforestation where sovereign governments may not appear responsible, but they may still retain good faith desires to utilize international assistance on their own, without dictates by the international community.

It is possible that humanitarian interventions could not save lives, just as state actions may not lead to genocide or crimes against humanity. Syria, Yemen, Bahrain, and the Democratic Republic of the Congo are potential genocides, at the time of writing, where humanitarian intervention might have been used to stop mass repression and murder in recent years. They may not have led to further deaths, however, only because repressive states halted uprisings. Genocides usually or always have occurred during war when states feel most threatened and rebellions have the greatest chance of success. In such situations, calculations about humanitarian intervention are difficult and also can be ethically murky, given this uncertainty. Still, the stakes are greatest during war and failure to act, can appear to be immoral, even though humanitarian intervention may not succeed, epitomized by the current humanitarian dilemma in Syria, where both sides are backed by strong powers.

To become legal, humanitarian intervention will require a reconceptualization of the concepts of national sovereignty and human security. Legal scholar J. Benton Heath suggests that a distinction should be made between internal and external sovereignty. Internal sovereignty derives from external sovereignty and pertains to the obligations leaders owe to their citizenry. Humanitarian intervention under the aforementioned restrictions would not violate sovereignty as sovereignty is commonly understood (e.g., as external sovereignty). Moreover by signing treaties and joining international and regional organizations for example, states are placing limitations on their sovereignty. Seen in this light, humanitarian intervention is just an extension of this trend.

Henry Carey

Perspective 3: The Complex History of International Law and Humanitarian Intervention

On April 6, 1994, President Juvénal Habyarimana of Rwanda and several senior government officials were killed when their plane was shot down by a surface-to-air missile near the Kigali airport. Within hours of this event, leading members of the Hutu-dominated government, police, and military started rounding up and executing opposition Tutsi politicians. Special lists of prominent Tutsi community leaders were drafted and "every journalist, every lawyer, every professor, every teacher, every civil servant, every priest, every doctor, every clerk, every student, every civil rights activist were hunted down in a house-to-house operation." Once the Tutsi leadership was killed, the Hutu-dominated army and militia, along with numerous thugs, hunted down anyone identified as Tutsi. Over the subsequent 100 days, as the world stood by and watched, large scale massacres occurred across Rwanda: 5,500 were killed in Cyahinda, 43,000 Tutsis in Karama Gikongoro and some 100,000 in Butare. By early May, one mutilated body plunged over the Rusomo Falls on the Kagera River every minute. In just 100 days (from April 6 to mid-July) this genocidal mass slaughter claimed over 800,000 lives in Rwanda. And all the while the international community did nothing to stop this massacre. In fact, this tragedy might have continued if not for the military victory of the Rwandan Patriotic Front, a Tutsi force that rallied in the north of Rwanda and successfully counter-attacked. In the wake of this tragedy, many pondered the question of whether the international community should have intervened to stop the carnage? Did it have a legal right to do so? And what about a moral duty to intervene?

Although we tend to think of "humanitarian intervention" as a modern-day matter, the issue of protecting human rights and safeguarding human security has long beleaguered the international community. Its history did not begin in the post–Cold War era and can be traced at least two centuries back. The term itself dates from the 19th century but remains subject of continued debate. Broadly speaking, humanitarian intervention refers to involvement across state borders by a state or international community of states aimed at preventing or ending grave violations of fundamental human rights and suffering or death among inhabitants. The vague nature of the term means that, in practice, it can be difficult to differentiate between different types of involvement in another state's affairs since there are so many diverse diplomatic and economic activities that may constitute intervention. Nevertheless, in most cases, the term implies the threat or actual use of force inside a given state, an act that necessarily implies violation of international law since it requires action without the permission of the state within whose territory force is applied. So the central question is whether such interventions can be justified.

From ethical and moral considerations, humanitarian intervention can be fully justified where violations are intentional, widespread and systematic. Moral conceptions are important dimensions of human life and teach us differences between right and wrong and responsibility to do the right thing to become a better person. Ancient Greek philosophers argued that the only true harm we can suffer is the harm of doing wrong. Major religions advise believers that moral worthiness is the basis on which God would judge them in afterlife and urge them to cherish their fellow human beings. In this respect, humanitarian intervention can be styled as a product of the duty of beneficence—Leviticus 19:16, for example, contains biblical injunction that "thou shalt not stand idly by the blood of thy neighbor"—and of the responsibility to use force to protect the innocent. rights. To use an oft-cited but instructive example, it is generally accepted that the Allies were morally justified in fighting the Nazis in World War II not simply by virtue of repulsing an aggressor, but also in morally opposing and condemning radical Nazi ideology that sanctioned widespread atrocities.

Timeliness constitutes an important element in this discussion. Intervention must be directed at preventing or ending ongoing humanitarian crisis. Recent events in Iraq offer a good example of this point. American invasion of Iraq in the spring of 2003 was oftentimes justified on the basis of Iraq's past atrocities. It is true that Saddam Hussein's regime had a well-documented history of atrocities, including the famous al Anfal Campaign (1988) in which some 100,000 Kurds were slaughtered. However, by 2003, the level of the Iraqi government's human rights abuses had declined significantly, largely due to the protective no-fly zones enforced by the international community. Thus, the 2003 invasion could not be justified on the basis of Iraq's past humanitarian atrocities—it may well have been morally permissible in 1988 but a "punitive" intervention 15 years after the event fails to justify the deaths of tens of thousands of Iraqi civilians that have perished in the decade-long violence this invasion unleashed.

Legal concepts can also be used in support of intervention. If we are to discuss the justification for the existence of the modern state, it would be for the protection and enforcement of the natural rights of its citizens. Whenever the state fails in its duties to protect its citizens and their rights, it makes intervention permissible. Natural law that contends that all human beings have certain natural rights and moral duties that are universal and immutable. If persons have certain rights, one legal scholar argues, "then surely one ought not only to respect persons' rights by not violating them. One ought also to contribute to creating arrangements that will ensure that persons' rights are not violated. To put the same point somewhat differently, respect for persons requires doing something to ensure that they are treated respectfully." Natural law proponents argue that our moral obligations to others are not "limited to people with whom we are bound in community by contract, political ties, or common locale. We are obliged to help whoever we can . . . This general duty to help others is the most basic ground within this common morality for interference in the internal affairs of one nation by outsiders, including other nations and international bodies."

Indeed, one of the founding fathers of international humanitarian law, the great 16th century Dutch jurist Hugo Grotius argued that, where a tyrant "should inflict upon his subjects such treatment as no one is warranted in inflicting, "other states have the right to intervene. Grotius justified such action based on the natural law notion of universal community of humankind. The Dutch jurist argued that government has the right to prosecute not just those who commit crimes against itself or its subjects/citizens, but "also on account of injuries which do not directly affect them but excessively violate the law of nature or of nations in regard of any person whatsoever." Similarly, St. Thomas Aquinas, the 13th century Christian theologian who wrote a series of influential treatises on war and government, argued that tyranny was the worst of crimes and could be legitimately opposed, including by military action. Starting in the 19th century, proponents of Utilitarianism, which promotes actions that maximize human well being and reduce suffering, also advocate interventionism, arguing that justice of any humanitarian intervention depends entirely on its ultimate results. If it helps increase aggregate well-being, then it is just; and if its direct effect is to decrease aggregate well-being, then it is unjust. Therefore, argue modern day proponents, "allowing humanitarian intervention . . . would promote overall well-being."

The most important international document regulating the exercise of armed force in the international community is the United Nations (UN) Charter. Although Article 2 safeguards states' absolute sovereignty and territorial integrity, the Charter does contain other provisions that create legal grounds for intervention. For example, some legal scholars point to a technical loophole in Article 2 forbidding threat or use of force against states only when it affects their territorial integrity or political independence. Humanitarian intervention, one may argue, does not seek territorial conquest or political subjugation but rather strives to uphold other fundamental goals of the United Nations—the protection of human rights (Articles 1(3); 55 and 56). Indeed, Article 39 of the UN Charter specifically states that the use of force can be sanctioned in response to "any threat to the peace, breach of the peace or act of aggression." Thus, large scale massacres, like in Rwanda, Cambodia or Sudan, can be interpreted as threats to international peace, which would constitute legal grounds for violating state's sovereignty. The United Nations, in fact, had done this in the past and its interventions in Somalia (1992), Rwanda (1994), and Haiti (1994) were sanctioned under Chapter VII of the UN Charter to use military force to end massive human rights abuses.

ALEXANDER MIKABERIDZE

Should Military Personnel Be Treated Differently from Other Perpetrators in Cases of Genocide?

Introduction

During the 20th century, the role of military personnel in genocide has been a particularly complex issue in international law. While it is understood that military forces operate under a command structure that limits their individual level of decision making, they are also to be held accountable under international legal conventions. The conduct of military forces in relation to civilians, established in a variety of international legal conventions, most notably the Geneva Conventions of the late 19th and early 20 centuries, have been heavily regulated. However, the development of technology and warfare in the 20th century has blurred the lines between armed combatants and civilians. As a result, regimes, such as the Young Turks in the Ottoman Empire, and the Nazis in Germany, used the pretext of attacking civilians to deter treason. Later genocides, in Bosnia, Cambodia, Guatemala, and Rwanda also showed how

military forces, under orders from civilian authorities, perpetrated war crimes.

In the major genocides of the 20th century, military forces, despite operating under the command of their superior officers, arguably made the personal decision to commit murder. However, it is also arguable that they could be held accountable to their respective civilian and military authorities, and thus were acting under coercion. Moreover, some individuals could have been acting under loyalty to the regime or their code of honor, which many in the German Wehrmacht argued was the case in their actions against Jews and the peoples of Eastern Europe during World War II. Nonetheless, these actions raise the question: Should military personnel be treated differently from other perpetrators in cases of genocide?

In her Perspective Essay, Sarah E. Brown states that military personnel should be held accountable for acts of genocide, considering they have received special training on warfare and the rules of war. Moreover, they also enjoy a unique position in their respective societies that sets a standard. Thus, their actions can set a bad precedent for the rest of society to follow, particularly in cases of war crimes and genocide. In his Perspective Essay, Henry Carey sustains that military forces should not be treated differently from other genocide perpetrators since they are accountable to the Nuremberg Principles. The Nuremberg Principles are considered a higher legal authority by the international community that exceeds any national directive to commit acts deemed as war crimes or genocide. As such, the "following orders" defense is not applicable to military personnel. Lastly, in his Perspective Essay, Alexander Mikaberidze similarly argues that soldiers and officers are subject to the rule of international law and should be held accountable for their actions. Much like Carey, Mikaberidze argues that international standards for individual conduct and action override any command that leads to genocidal violence against civilian populations.

Perspective 1: Specialized Training and Personal Responsibility

From Rwanda to Srebrenica to the Holocaust, military personnel have played an active role in facilitating and perpetrating genocide; oftentimes, genocide would not have been possible without their participation. In the instance of genocide, military personnel should be held culpable for crimes of genocide and given no leniency. This rationale is built upon the fact that military personnel receive special training on warfare and the rules of war and enjoy a unique position of authority in society. As such, their participation in the perpetration of genocide is especially heinous.

New recruits to the military receive extensive training on warfare, weaponry, and on the Law of War, otherwise referred to as International Humanitarian Law, which is founded upon the Geneva Conventions. These treaties and laws dictate conduct during violent conflict and ensure that noncombatants, including the wounded and sick, shipwrecked, prisoners of war, and most importantly, civilians, are treated with dignity and respect. Additional protocols were added in 1977 that account for international (inter-state) and noninternational (intra-state) violent conflict and further elaborate on the protection of civilians. Unlike many civilians, military personnel, as members of a trained body responsible for violent conflict, have a heightened awareness of the rules that dictate violent conflict and their responsibility to protect and respect civilians. As such, when they target noncombatants for annihilation as part of a policy of genocide, they do so with the knowledge that they are violating international humanitarian law.

During the Rwandan Genocide, Colonel Théoneste Bagosora played a crucial role in inciting and perpetrating genocide. When he was caught, Bagosora was brought before the International Criminal Tribunal for Rwanda (ICTR) and charged with genocide, conspiracy to commit genocide, crimes against humanity, and violation of the Geneva Conventions. Bagosora was a high ranking officer who received extensive military training in Rwanda as well as in Belgium and France. There is little doubt that during the course of his extensive training, Bagosora was instructed on the Geneva Conventions, the very foundation of the laws of war. Nevertheless, he chose to violate those very laws and perpetrate genocide against Rwanda's Tutsi population.

At the same time, not knowing the details of the Geneva Conventions and the additional Protocols that comprise international humanitarian law does not exempt a perpetrator of genocide from punishment by law. Ignorance is not a defense. The attempt to eradicate a population based upon their race, religion, ethnicity, or nationality is genocide and the perpetration of such crimes, by civilians and soldiers alike, is a crime punishable by law.

Being in a position of authority with clearly identifiable uniforms, military personnel often serve as role models, examples of how an ideal citizen should behave. In addition,

due to their training in warfare and weapons, military personnel often command a certain degree of power over the civilian population. This can have a detrimental impact in instances when military personnel participate in genocide. When a soldier decides to participate in genocide, they set an example for their citizens and sanction genocidal violence due to their position of authority.

Colonel General Ratko Mladic, a military commander of the Bosnian Serb Army (VRS), directed the forces that perpetrated genocide at Srebrenica. Mladic and his rank were easily identifiable due to his military uniform and various decorations. During the violence that took place in Bosnia-Herzegovina, Mladic was renowned by fellow Serbs as a war hero and regularly featured by Serbian media outlets. Since 2013, Mladic has been on trial at the International Criminal Tribunal for the Former Yugoslavia (ICTY) for his role as commander of a force that murdered 7,000 to 8,000 Bosnian Muslim men from Srebrenica. But for many in Serbia, Mladic remains a hero, with videos, publications, and media propaganda extolling his virtues and heroism. As a highly visible military commander, not only did Mladic perpetrate genocide, he served as a role model for others who followed his example.

Worse still, as a high ranking military officer, Mladic commanded authority, even over members of the United Nations Protection Force (UNPROFOR) tasked with protecting civilians in the region. Therefore, when Mladic said, "I am in charge here. I decide what happens. I have my plans and I'm going to carry them out. It will be best for you if you cooperate," he was obeyed. Up to 8,000 Bosnian Serb men were loaded onto buses and slaughtered without interference from UNPROFOR.

Oftentimes, military personnel claim that they were "following orders" issued by their superiors who commanded them to perpetrate genocide and are therefore not responsible for their actions. This line of defense was dismissed by the International Military Tribunal at Nuremberg, the court established by the Allied Powers following World War II and the Holocaust to try suspected Nazi war criminals. Article 8 of its Constitution specifically states that following orders did not free a perpetrator from responsibility. When trying perpetrators of the Holocaust, the court decided that the agency exercised by the individual, meaning their capacity to choose one action over another, took precedence over the orders of a commanding officer. The "following orders" defense does not ease the responsibility born by a soldier who commits genocide.

Each individual, be they a soldier or a civilian, has a choice. In the instance of a trained member of the military, that decision making process is aided by knowledge of international humanitarian law which instructs them to protect noncombatants, not mass murder them. Therefore, when a soldier attempts to destroy, in whole or in part, a portion of their population, they are violating the laws of war and perpetrating genocide. As mentioned above, soldiers, easily identifiable and respected as authoritative figures in society, are often role models for citizens. Should a member of a military force participate in genocide, they are setting an example and sanctioning the perpetration of crimes that may result in the destruction of a population. This sanctioning of genocide has a detrimental impact on society, as can be seen by the example of Ratko Mladic who mass murdered nearly 8,000 individuals and is still hailed as a war hero by many Serbians. Many soldiers claim that they were "following orders" and are therefore not accountable for their genocidal crimes. This is not an accepted line of defense. Due to their training and their position of authority, military personnel should be held especially culpable and given no leniency when they choose to perpetrate genocide.

Sara E. Brown

Perspective 2: International Law and Military Personnel

Military personnel should not be treated differently from other genocide perpetrators. While all known genocides have occurred during war, that does not mean that genocide is a militarily specific crime. The 1948 United Nations Convention on the Prevention and Punishment of the Crime of Genocide (UNCG) bans genocide during either armed conflict or peacetime and is therefore not intended to have any double standards about the context for its perpetration or its perpetrators. The degree of culpability of military personnel would reflect the facts in question, not their employment status. A soldier has the obligation under the Nuremberg Principles, which are accepted as binding under customary international law, to disobey manifestly illegal orders.

It might be that civilian leaders would be more culpable and deserving of greater criminal responsibility for genocide if they were in superior positions giving orders to a subordinate military, such as the Serbian genocide in Bosnia (for which Serbian president Slobodan Milosevic

was arguably even more guilty than those military officers who were convicted of genocide by the International Criminal Tribunal for the Former Yugoslavia (ICTY), but the late President died before his trial ended). In other factual situations, such as a military dictatorship (such as the Armenian Genocide), the greater culpability might have been with the military leaders. As part of the trial of *Bosnia v. Serbia* at the International Court of Justice, two "provisional protective measures" were issued in April and September 1993. The then Federal Republic of Yugoslavia (FRY, later renamed Serbia and Montenegro) was ordered explicitly "to do everything in its power to prevent the crimes of genocide and to make sure that such crimes are not committed by military or paramilitary formations operating under its control or with its support." At that trial's conclusion, Serbia was absolved of genocide, but it was found guilty of not preventing the genocide, a violation of the Genocide Convention that fell upon FRY leaders like Milosevic. (*Bosnia and Herzegovina v. Serbia and Montenegro* ("Case concerning the application of the Convention on the Prevention and Punishment of the Crime of Genocide") In this particular case, the ICJ suggested that military officers and civilian leaders were guilty, but only missing was the requisite level of proof, much of which was denied to the ICJA because that Supreme Defense Council records of Serbia had been granted to the ICTY on the condition that they would not be revealed publicly to anyone else. While the Bosnian Serb military leadership was financed and directed by Serbia, the court did not hold either the Serbian military and civilian leaders of their country implicitly not guilty of genocide, though guilty of violating the UNCG's genocide provisions mandates when they were so clearly in the position to stop such acts, if only be halting the financing of genocide, which would have been considered genocide of greater evidence of intent were present.

Another category where soldiers might not be prosecuted for genocidal crimes because of the specific facts would include situations where the particular atrocities occurred in combat and not in detention where the "acts may speak for themselves" as genocide. In combat, the motive of soldiers might be that the enemy were killed because they were the enemy. Some ostensibly noncombatant civilians might number among the victims, but because of the combat context, there might not be independent witnesses and other evidence form which "guilt beyond a reasonable doubt" could not be achieved. In *Bosnia v. Serbia*, the ICJ accepted that acts of genocide certainly were perpetrated by Serb forces, but could not find conclusive evidence of the specific intent to destroy the ethnic Bosniaks as a group in whole or in part. In other words, the civilians killed were perceived to be as combatants because they were of "fighting age." What made the soldiers less likely to be prosecuted is that the test of the mental element of the crime of genocide is subjective, as determined by the UNCG. Instead of the presumptive objective test for the *mens rea* (guilty mind), based on what the reasonable person would have thought, this statute asserts that what matters is the subjective mind of any defendant. Thus, it would not matter that a reasonable person would have or should have known about the protective status of civilians killed in combat, so long as the defendant thought that they were enemy combatants and not members of racial, ethnic, religious, or national group being killed to destroy it in whole or in part.

Soldiers are more often involved in acts of ethnic cleansing than are civilians. While such expulsions under threats or acts of violence are certainly war crimes and crimes against humanity under most circumstances, they often do not constitute genocide (though in some factual situations, they might so constitute genocide. In the European Court of Human Rights case, *Jorgic v. Germany* on July 12, 2007, the court held that rendering an area "ethnically homogeneous," is not genocide unless the mental element of an intent "to destroy, in whole or in part" a particular group is required. The International Court of Justice (ICJ) found under the heading of "intent and 'ethnic cleansing'" § 190 Displacement or deportation of members of such a group, even if effected by force, is not necessarily equivalent to that group's destruction. Only if the ethnic cleansing met the UNCG requirement of "'deliberately inflicting on the group conditions of life calculated to bring about its physical destruction in whole or in part,'" would violate Article II, paragraph (c), of the UNCG, provided that the mental element was also present. Similarly, the International Criminal Tribunal for the Former Yugoslavia held (Krstić, IT-98–33-T, Trial Chamber Judgment, 2 August 2001, para. 562), that while "there are obvious similarities between a genocidal policy and the policy commonly known as 'ethnic cleansing,' a clear distinction must be drawn between physical destruction and mere dissolution of a group. The expulsion of a group or part of a group does not in itself suffice for genocide."

The ICJ's holding effectively concluded that Serbia was legally complicit in genocide by not preventing it, while having both the duty and the power to do so. Under this ruling, the civilian leaders of Serbia are absolved when they violate the UNCG. As a result, civilians, in practice, have not been held guilty for genocide more often than military officers have, even though the civilian leaders were more responsible for the conditions that enabled the crime of genocide to take place. The International Criminal Tribunal for Rwanda (ICTR) did convict some civilian leaders, including Rwandan prime minister Jean Kabanda, and a Mayor, Akeyesou. However, the majority of ICTR defendants convicted of genocide were paramilitary and military officials. The reason that, so far in practice, that military officers have been convicted more often is that there are more of them who can more easily be identified as having killed civilians in detention without due process, a situation where it is far easier to prove the mental element of the crime of genocide. By contrast, a civilian leader would have to be linked to a plan, based on eye witness testimony or written document that indicated what may be clear, but hard to prove beyond a reasonable doubt, that the civilian leader intended to eliminate a part of a group.

HENRY CAREY

Perspective 3: Responsibility of Military Personnel and International Law

One of the fundamental concepts in the contemporary democratic order revolves around the supremacy of the law which means that all persons—individuals, institutions, and government—must be subject to the rule of law without an exception. Contemporary international criminal law is based on this principle and speaks of duty of every state to prosecute those responsible for international crimes.

In international criminal law, the supremacy of the law manifests itself in the principle of individual responsibility whose origins can be traced to the mid-20th century. The international community was appalled by the vast and horrific nature of atrocities committed during World War II and felt the responsibility to act. The war was still underway when the Allied powers agreed to create a new legal system to prosecute perpetrators of war crimes and crimes against humanity. The Moscow Declaration of October 30, 1943, signed by the United States, Britain and the Soviet Union, called for dual responsibility of state and individuals involved in atrocities and specified that "German officers and men and members of the Nazi Party who have been responsible for or have taken part in the . . . atrocities, massacres and executions will be sent back to the countries in which their abominable deeds were done in order that they may be judged and punished according to the laws of these liberated countries and of free governments which will be erected therein."

The subsequently established International Military Tribunal (IMT) and International Military Tribunal for the Far East (IMTFE) developed clear provisions for the prosecution of individuals, including military personnel, with the IMT charter's article 6 explicitly referring to the tribunal's power to try and punish any persons who whether as individuals or as members of organizations committed crimes against peace and crimes against humanity. Both tribunals argued that these individuals' official positions, whether as heads of state, ministers or members of armed forces, should not negate their responsibility or mitigate their punishment for crimes committed. In calling for individual responsibility for war crimes and crimes against humanity, IMT and IMTFE entered new legal grounds since there was no judicial precedent for it. Nevertheless, IMT's chief prosecutor Justice Robert Jackson argued that "unless we are prepared to abandon every principle of growth for international law, we cannot deny that our own day has the right to institute customs and to conclude agreements that will themselves become sources of a newer and strengthened international law."

The IMT and IMTFE charters represented the first attempt to establish individual responsibility for war crimes and crimes against humanity. Over the last seven decades international criminal law had grown exponentially as many European states set up special courts and military tribunals to prosecute suspected perpetrators of genocides and war crimes while international community had established new mechanisms of enforcement, most notably the International Criminal Court (ICC) that serves as a permanent tribunal to prosecute perpetrators of genocide, crimes against humanity, and war crimes. The ICC embraces the notion of individual responsibility and its charter targets any person committing crimes against humanity or war crimes would be "individually responsible and liable for punishment." In fact, Article 27 of the ICC charter explicitly state that the court's authority applies "equally to all persons without any distinction based on official capacity." Thus, the ICC devotes a separate provision to the responsibility of the military personnel but

here it once again emphasizes individual responsibility of any military commander whose forces committed atrocities and war crimes whether as a result of his/her direct orders or failure to exercise proper control and supervision.

This last element is particularly noteworthy because it is directly connected to one of the most widely debated and controversial issue in international criminal law: the notion of "superior orders." Armed forces represent a unique institution that is based on distinct and strict principles, one of which emphasizes obedience. Soldiers are duty bound to accept authority of their superiors and obey orders without questioning their legality. This concept of "duty and obedience," however, makes it very difficult to determine the guilt of individuals who have been involved in an atrocity and can claim that they did not commit offenses of their own free will but were instead acting under orders of their superior. During an armed conflict, a soldier can face a crucial predicament—should he/she obey the order at the risk of being held responsible for a crime or should he/she disobey this order and risk being court-martialed? This situation is well illustrated by the case of a German officer who had been tried for atrocities in a Belgian village during World War I. When asked about his crimes, the officer replied, "Yes, I know it was contrary to the law of nations for I am a doctor of law. I did not wish to do it, but I did it in obedience to the formal order of the Governor General of Brussels." The question here is who should be held responsible for a crime—a soldier who commits it, an officer who commands it, a superior officer who initiated the order or all of them? And what share of responsibility for a crime do they bear?

The atrocities of World War I and World War II had a major impact on legal approach to "superior orders" defense, with the IMT and IMTFE embracing the principle of "absolute liability," also known as the "Nuremberg Model." This approach holds military personnel directly responsible for crimes committed while following orders because it argues that a soldier is a rational individual who is capable of appraising circumstances and orders he/she has received. In the wake of genocidal massacres in Rwanda and Yugoslavia, this approach has been embraced in the statutes of the two tribunals that the United Nations had established to prosecute the perpetrators in the affected regions. But this approach has been modified over the years and nowadays many states (e.g., Denmark, The Netherlands, Germany, Israel, Switzerland, Italy, etc.) have reverted to the conditional liability. For example, the *U.S. Department of the Army Field Manual* specifies that a soldier would not be held responsible for criminal acts he had performed on an order of a superior authority as long as he "did not know and could not reasonably have been expected to know that act ordered was unlawful." However, some states adopted a "mixed" system applying two sets of standards in cases of international crimes. Norway, for example, the doctrine of "conditional liability" is applied to war crimes committed by Norwegian citizens while "absolute liability" is employed for "enemy" nationals.

During the drafting of the statute of the ICC, a key source of contemporary international criminal law, national delegates had long argued over "conditional" and "absolute" approaches, with the German delegation calling for the latter and the U.S. delegates strongly advocating the former. A compromise was eventually reached. While Article 28 clearly speaks of responsibility of commanders and other superiors for any actions committed by their forces, Article 33 focuses on the actions of their subordinates. This provision argues that when it comes to war crimes military personnel cannot be treated differently from other perpetrators unless they satisfied three legal requirements: 1. they were under a legal obligation to obey orders; 2. They did not know that the order was unlawful; 3. The order was not manifestly unlawful. Yet, Article 33 makes an important distinction in the responsibility of military personnel for war crimes and crimes against humanity. It argues that while military personnel may claim "the superior orders" defense in some instances of war crimes, it can never be done to charges of genocide and crimes against humanity since orders to commit these crimes are always "manifestly unlawful."

The "conditional" and "absolute" approaches are not mutually exclusive. The former, as expressed in national laws and the ICC statute, is aimed at minor violations of the laws of warfare when military personnel can justify its actions by referring to superior orders and may seek mitigation of its responsibility of crimes. In effect, it seeks to ensure the ability of the military personnel to carry out combat operations without constantly interrupting them to consider potential international criminal responsibility for orders issued. Yet, when it comes to the crimes against humanity and war crimes—widespread, systematic and willful murder, extermination, enslavement, forcible deportation, rape and sexual slavery, torture, etc.—when illegality of orders is manifest and any rational being can

anticipate the ill effects of his/her actions, military personnel cannot excuse their action through the "superior orders" defense and should be held responsible under the doctrine of individual responsibility to the full extent of the law.

ALEXANDER MIKABERIDZE

Why Did It Take the United States Almost 40 Years to Ratify the 1948 UN Convention on Genocide?

Introduction

With the end of World War II, as the Nazi regime's Final Solution was revealed to the world in all its details, the effort to codify a set of international laws to prevent this from ever occurring again became a priority for the newly formed United Nations (UN). The resultant 1948 United Nations Convention on the Prevention and Punishment of the Crime of Genocide (UNCG) became the standard definition of what constituted the crime of genocide, accepted by many of the member states of that international body. However, the United States, one of the major Allied powers, did not immediately ratify the UNCG. Rather, it took 40 years of debates and deliberations before ratification.

Despite the initial support of the Harry S. Truman administration and many members of Congress at the time of its drafting, political and military considerations, many of them arising out of the Cold War, hindered the ratification of the UNCG for four decades. While the aftermath of the Holocaust was one of the myriad reasons many of the advocates of the UNCG used to press for Senate ratification, issues over national sovereignty, past U.S. actions that might be considered genocide, and/or potential redundancy with existing international laws, were argued by critics of ratification. This raises the question: Why did it take the United States almost 40 years to ratify the 1948 UN Convention on Genocide?

In his Perspective Essay, Roger W. Smith provides the broad contours for the reasons that the United States was hesitant to ratify the UNCG. Foreign policy, domestic politics, redundancy, racism, and national sovereignty were among the various factors considered by critics of ratification, factors that held for four decades. In his Perspective Essay, Henry C. Theriault states many of the same reasons brought up by Smith, and further argues that the United States was also hesitant to ratify due to past or present actions that might be used to bring up charges in accordance with the UNCG.

Perspective 1: Reluctance to Ratify

When the United Nations Convention on the Prevention and Punishment of the Crime of Genocide (UNCG) was ratified by the U.S. Senate in 1986, it had been before that body longer than any other treaty in U.S. history. Drafted by the United Nations (UN) as a response to the Holocaust, and with active support from the U.S. representatives, it was adopted by the UN General Assembly without opposition on December 9, 1948. After sufficient ratifications, it went into effect in January 1951. The Convention defined the crime of genocide, specified the acts that constitute it, provided (inadequate) means for enforcing the rule, and assigned questions of interpretation, application, and fulfillment of the Convention to the International Court of Justice.

President Harry S. Truman sent the Convention to the Senate for approval in 1949 with every expectation of ratification. The hearings in 1950, however, were acrimonious in the extreme, characterized by charges that the Convention was a "sell-out" to the Communists, an attack on civil liberties, a subversion of U.S. sovereignty, a grab for power by the president, and a threat to the powers of the states within the federal system. There was also the claim that there was no need for the Convention since genocide was murder and laws against murder were already in place, and the United States as a righteous nation would never commit genocide. These arguments set the stage for all other hearings and subsequent debates. Opponents also had the support, until 1976, of the American Bar Association (ABA), which lent respectability to arguments that, though legal in form, were the embodiment of political conservatism, not excluding racism.

For 20 years, no new hearings were held: opposition in the Senate persisted, the Convention did not receive the support of President Dwight D. Eisenhower, and Presidents John F. Kennedy and Lyndon B. Johnson did not give ratification concerted attention. President Richard Nixon, however, did offer strong support for ratification, and the Senate Foreign Relations Committee held a series of hearings beginning in 1970, but to no avail. In 1984, when President Ronald Reagan announced his support for the Convention, a crucial step since by the 1980s, most of the opposition to ratification lay within the Republican Party. Finally, after almost 40 years and seven hearings, the Convention was ratified in 1986 by a vote of 83 to 11. Ratification, however, was conditional: there were reservations and understandings that became an integral part of the treaty. Many of the provisions were defensible, but the rejection of compulsory jurisdiction of the International Court of Justice (ICJ) left no doubt that the United States had serious misgivings about the adequacy and fairness of international legal institutions.

Racism was a motive for opposition, which was aided by carelessness by the UN in drafting the Convention. Many opponents of the Convention, for example, feared that the United States could be charged with genocide for its harsh treatment of African Americans and Native Americans. They reasoned that lynching could be construed as genocide since it involved the killing of a "part" of a group for racial reasons, and that discrimination could be equated with "mental harm" to a group, an act defined under the Convention as genocide. Accordingly, two "understandings" were produced: "part of a group" now became a "substantial part," and "mental harm" was defined as "permanent impairment of mental faculties through drugs, torture, or similar techniques."

What led to the delays, acrimony, and conditional ratification of the Convention? Racism, suspicion of the Soviet Union and any role it may have had in crafting the Convention, the desire to limit both presidential and federal power, and a sense that the Convention was simply not needed. However, suspicion of international organizations, especially courts and the UN, was also crucial, buttressed by that peculiar American sense of righteousness (the City on the Hill complex).

In the end, when approval came, there was no unified vision of why the Convention should be ratified; rather, there was a range of answers. During the final debate on the treaty, proponents gave the following reasons for ratification: morality requires it, it will demonstrate the U.S. commitment to human rights and the rule of law, it will help recall the Holocaust, it will end unfair criticism of the United States on human rights, and ratification will help prevent future genocides. Others who supported the Convention thought that ratification was important as a "symbol," but that this must be followed by "action." What this action must be they did not specify, but this is surely the crucial issue: ratification of a treaty does not in itself translate into protection of rights.

ROGER W. SMITH

Perspective 2: International and Domestic Factors Hindering Ratification

The United Nations General Assembly passed the Genocide Convention on December 9, 1948, and President Harry S. Truman submitted it to the U.S. Senate in June 1949. Yet, the Senate did not consent to ratification of the Convention until February 19, 1986, with President Ronald Reagan not signing enabling legislation until November 5, 1988. The obvious question is: Why did it take the United States nearly 40 years to ratify the Genocide Convention?

There are two challenges that any attempt to answer this question faces. First, the U.S. government, and even just the Senate, are complex institutions involving many different political and social forces and agendas, all the more when considered over a 40-year period. Any comprehensive analysis of this issue would require looking in great detail at all of the people, groups, offices, institutions, and historical context involved, which would surely require hundreds if not thousands of pages just to summarize. Second, when considering the actual reasons causing individual political leaders as well as political institutions to make certain decisions, stated reasons and official documents, while useful, should never be taken at face value. A politician refusing to support ratification of the Genocide Convention for immoral reasons, for instance, could hardly state those in public, but would have to rationalize his/her refusal in acceptably moral terms. Similarly, if, say, U.S. Department of State opposition had been based on fears that ratification would interfere with U.S. support for the genocide perpetrated without our help in Guatemala in the early 1980s, its spokespeople could not come out and say this. By necessity, then, this short essay is limited to sketching out the main possible reasons for the 40-year delay and discussion of the available evidence for or against the relevance of each reason.

When we consider the question of why the United States took nearly 40 years to ratify the UN Genocide Convention, eight general reasons appear possible.

1. Arguably, U.S. leadership was indifferent to the issue of genocide. In this period, genocide was not a priority for U.S. leaders, nor was there the kind of popular concern that could have pushed leaders to action. While at the end of World War II some attention was given to the genocide of Jews and others, this was not a focal issue of the Nuremberg Trials. The Holocaust had some public prominence with the Adolf Eichmann trial of the early 1960s, but it was only from the late 1970s on that the Holocaust began gaining the significant importance in the U.S. press, education system, and political discourse that it has today. It is likely no coincidence that ratification occurred as the prominence of the Holocaust, and to a lesser extent genocide more generally (in the aftermath especially of the Cambodian Genocide), rose. It is worth noting that this indifference is evidence against any claim that the United States rejected the Convention out of fear that it would require the United States to act against genocide if it occurred, as this principle did not emerge until much later, particularly with the 2001 Responsibility to Protect (R2P) report.

2. U.S. leadership did not see support for the Convention as politically expedient. The 1950s, 1960s, and 1970s saw dramatic antiwar, anti-racism, antisexism, and other prodemocracy movements shake the United States politically and culturally. Yet, while the civil rights movement as well as the antiwar movement routinely cited human rights concerns, including the problem of mass killing and imperialism, genocide was not a major or really even a minor issue in any of these movements. The 1980s saw the United States particularly criticized for its military and political participation in anticommunist civil wars and related mass violence, including the prevalence of death squads, in Central America as well as its stalwart support for South African apartheid. In this context, political leaders, including President Reagan, might have seen ratification of the Genocide Convention as a useful public relations move. Genocide scholar Samantha Power argues that Reagan's participation in a wreath-laying ceremony for about 2,000 German soldiers, including about 50 from the Schutzstaffel (SS), on May 5, 1985, created such a public relations crisis that he began supporting the Convention in order to appease critics.

3. The United States had been dissatisfied with the specifics of the Convention, such as its definition or punishments, for altruistic reasons. The general lack of policy interest in genocide means, of course, that there was no resistance from policy

makers to the Convention. Political leaders did not support the Convention because they were largely indifferent to genocide, not because they focused a great deal of attention on the issue and had principled objections to the specific formulation of the UN Genocide Convention.

4. The U.S. government was dissatisfied with the specifics of the Convention, such as its definition or punishments, because it was perceived not to serve the global interests of the United States. The only partial exception to the foregoing point is regarding "political groups." Because of political maneuvering during the negotiation of the Convention, political groups were excluded from the list of possible targets of UN-defined genocide. This exclusion had long been strongly criticized by scholars, the press, and, in 1985, even UN Special Rapporteur Benjamin Whitaker. And, when the U.S. Senate finally did consent to ratification of the Convention, it voted 93 to 1 to direct the Reagan administration to try to get the Convention changed to include political groups. But selection of this sole issue from many points of criticism of the Convention suggests a political rather than altruistic motive. It was the Soviet bloc that successfully pushed for removal of political groups from the UN definition, which then clearly exempted the mass killings under Joseph Stalin and other Soviet leaders from coverage by the Convention. Given the Cold War, it is no surprise that, once U.S. policy makers actually did focus on genocide, the main concern regarding the Convention was that it did not include political groups and therefore was not applicable to communist regimes. Thus, while the exclusion of political groups were not the reason that the United States did not ratify the Convention for so long, it is virtually assured that, had political groups been included in the definition, U.S. policy makers even in the 1950s would have recognized the political utility of the Convention for advancing U.S. interests against the Soviet Union, and this might have been sufficient to drive ratification much earlier than 1988.

5. U.S. leaders felt that felt the Convention alone to be inadequate to impact genocide. A corollary argument to that given in 3 applies to this issue

as well, so it was unlikely a factor. Only after the 1992–1995 Bosnia Genocide and the 1994 Rwanda Genocide did the criticism of inaction against genocide despite the Convention become widespread.

6. U.S. policymakers viewed the Convention as redundant for U.S. law. There is a hint of this discussed by scholar Leo Kuper, but the argument in point 3 also applies to this issue.

7. U.S. leaders opposed subjecting the United States to international human rights law of any sort. Early on, this does seem to have been a factor. At the same time, this does not seem to have been a central factor for most of the nonratification period. It was only with the UN peacekeeping activities of the 1990s and the U.S. refusal to sign the 1998 Rome Statue creating the International Criminal Court (ICC) that U.S. rejection of subjugation of citizens, particularly in the armed forces, to international authority and to international legal structures, respectively, emerged.

8. Lastly, U.S. policymakers feared application of the Convention to past or future actions of the United States. While Power recognizes that early in the nonratification period, the fear that, if the United States ratified the Convention, it would be used to investigate U.S. treatment of Native Americans in the 19th century, she does not consider this a significant factor in the nonratification. But Ward Churchill argues that fear of application of the Convention to U.S. actions was the key factor preventing ratification. He cites the U.S. reaction to the 1951 240-page report submitted to the UN by the American Civil Rights Congress, on forced sterilization of African Americans (a form of genocide according to the UN definition) that specifically charged genocide against the United States, as one example of the U.S. attitude. Churchill also cites the major impact of the tribunal sponsored by one of the most important and respected public figures of the 20th century, philosopher Bertrand Russell, and presided over by one of the other most important and respected public figures of the 20th century, French philosopher Jean-Paul Sartre, which found the United States guilty of genocide in Southeast Asia through pursuit of the Vietnam War. One might add the U.S. participation in genocides

in Bangladesh, East Timor, and Guatemala in the 1970s and 1980s as further reasons for why the policy establishment did not want to strengthen the Convention by having the United States ratify it.

Churchill pointed out that Senate debates over the Convention did not discuss Native Americans at all, but he argues that this was because to have merely mentioned this elephant in the room in the context of discussion of genocide would have opened the Pandora's Box of not only the 20th century genocidal use of boarding schools against Native Americans but the widespread, undeniable mass extermination campaigns of the 19th century.

Given the foregoing, the explanation of why the United States did not ratify the UN Genocide Convention for nearly 40 years includes a combination of factors. Certainly the fact that genocide itself was neither a major political or popular issue was crucial in preventing the kind of public debate that might have fostered broad support for such an obvious human rights-supporting step. One reason for the lack of political interest was the fact that the specifics of the Convention were of little use in the Cold War, which was the focus of U.S. international (and much domestic) policy in the nonratification period. If these two factors produced a lack of movement toward ratification, the final factor, fears of the United States' own historical and contemporary susceptibility to charges of genocide, seems to have repelled policy makers away from ratification.

HENRY C. THERIAULT

Is the United Nations' 1948 Definition of Genocide Still Viable Given More Recent Genocidal Events?

Introduction

The 1948 United Nations Convention on the Prevention and Punishment of the Crime of Genocide (UNCG) was a major attempt by the international community to define genocide, created in the aftermath of World War II, when the Holocaust had shocked much of the world in terms of its scale and severity. The United Nations, established in 1945 to replace the impotent League of Nations, sought to create a standard of international law to which such crimes could be attributed and defined. Taking the Holocaust and the subsequent Nuremberg Trials as a template, the UNCG became the accepted piece of international legislation to define genocide.

However, critics of the UNCG definition were not content with the arguably ambivalent language in the passage, "deliberate and systematic destruction, in whole or in part, of an ethnic, racial, religious, or national group." Questions were raised about "intention" to kill "part" or the "entirety" of a group. As the call to "never again" repeat the egregious mass murder of the Holocaust became unheeded and newer cases of genocide emerged in the later 20th century, such as those in Bosnia, Cambodia, Darfur, East Timor, Iraqi Kurdistan, and Rwanda, the UN definition of genocide was further questioned. Therefore, it is fair to ask the question: Is the United Nations' 1948 definition of genocide still viable given more recent genocidal events?

In his Perspective Essay, Roger W. Smith argues that while the scope of the UN definition is unsatisfactory, it still serves an important purpose. Moreover, Smith contends that further acts of international law, such as the Rome Statute (1998), continue to add to what acts are considered genocide. In contrast, Colin Tatz argues in his essay that the language of the Convention, complicates its effectiveness in defining genocide. Lastly, Henry Theriault argues in his essay that the Convention stands as a product of its time and that current developments in world affairs illustrate the needs to update international legal standards in regards to genocide.

Perspective 1: The Concept of Genocide

What we term "genocide" has a long history and continues into the present, but the concept dates only from 1944 when introduced by the international lawyer Raphael Lemkin. The term was based on the Greek "genos" (race, group) with the Latin "cide" (killing). For Lemkin the emphasis was on the destruction of groups rather than on the individuals who formed the group. But with so many genocides, different motives, victim groups, and consequences, it has been difficult to define "genocide" in ways that everyone would accept. Nevertheless, the definition of genocide that is contained in the United Nations Convention on the Prevention and Punishment of Genocide, though widely criticized, is the one that prevails among scholars, and is the international legal standard. Yet the question arises "Is the United Nations' 1948 definition of genocide still viable, or does it need to be revised based on genocidal events that have occurred since that time?"

I would go further, was the definition in the Convention ever satisfactory? No. Can the Convention be revised extensively? No, because of the structure of the UN and the complex interests of the members of that body.

Nevertheless, in some ways the international courts have, through interpretation, clarified and expanded the Convention. A single example: it is now settled international law under the Convention that systematic rape, when committed with the intent to destroy a group in whole or in part, constitutes genocide. And do recent events, the many atrocities that have occurred since the Convention went into effect, require a revision of the concept of genocide? No, but it does require a new set of laws that have now come into being under the Rome Statute (1998) that deal with "crimes against humanity." The latter include genocide, but go well beyond it to touch on acts that are similar to genocide, and perhaps equally horrible, but about which the Genocide Convention is silent. The argument then is that we need both the Genocide Convention, despite its defects and limitations, and the Rome Statute with its potential to prosecute, and perhaps deter, other crimes against humanity.

The Convention makes genocide a crime under international law, "whether committed in time of peace or in time of war." But the heart of the Convention is found in Article II, where the crime of genocide is defined, and where many of the problems with the concept begin:

"In the present Convention, genocide means any of the following acts committed with intent to destroy, in whole or in part, a national, ethnical, racial or religious group, as such:

(a) Killing members of the group;
(b) Causing serious bodily or mental harm to members of the group;
(c) Deliberately inflicting on the group conditions of life calculated to bring about its physical destruction in whole or in part;
(d) Imposing measures intended to prevent births within the group;
(e) Forcibly transferring children of the group to another group."

Many important issues arise from this conception of genocide. First, not all groups are protected; political and social groups, such as classes, are not included. Second, the intent to destroy a group must be "specific intent," that is, the intent to destroy the group must be because of its specific characteristics (national, ethnical, racial, or religious).

Destroying such a group for economic reasons, for example, would not count as genocide. Third, the question, now more or less resolved, about destroying a group "in part," raised the issue of how large a part, and whether this was a matter of numbers or a percentage of the overall group that counts. These issues are now seen as involving a "substantial part," leaving it to courts to draw the boundary. Fourth, why there such be a focus on the destruction of the group rather than the members who constitute the group is not touched upon in the Convention nor has it been dealt with to any extent by scholars. There may be justification for the emphasis on the group, but so far no one has given a compelling argument for it as a result, a mystery lies at the heart of the Convention. Finally, of the five acts listed, any one of which constitutes genocide, only one of them actually involves killing, though all aim at the destruction of the group. The UN definition focuses on intent not results. That genocide could occur with few or no deaths, is a surprising conceptual outcome of the UN's approach and contrary to both scholarly analysis and public understanding of what is meant by genocide.

If there were space, one could deal with how other concepts bear a resemblance to "genocide," but can be differentiated from it: war, massacre, and ethnic cleansing. For example, "ethnic cleansing" is often part of a genocidal process, but in theory it means using violence, rape, terror, and forced deportation to drive out or remove a particular group from a common territory. The emphasis is on creating a homogenous society through fear and expulsion, not as in genocide on annihilating the group.

There are also legal and instructional developments that relate to the status of genocide under international law. In 1998, the Rome Statute created an International Criminal Court (ICC), with the following crimes within its jurisdiction: genocide, crimes against humanity, war crimes, and the crime of aggression. In the statute, crime against humanity is defined in terms of a number of particular acts, including murder, extermination, and forcible transfer of population, but more widely to include torture and "other inhuman acts of a similar character intentionally causing great suffering, or serious injury to body or mental or physical health." Any of these acts "when committed as part of a widespread or systematic attack directed against any civilian population" constitutes a crime against humanity. The key category here is "civilian population," not particular groups as indicated in the Genocide Convention; and the question of intent is different from that required under the Convention: here no "specific intent" is required.

Though one can differentiate "genocide" and "crimes against humanity" in important respects, the two concepts overlap in many ways. But it is much easier to prosecute actions as crimes against humanity than as genocide; the former also have a wider reach, not being restricted to crimes against particular groups named in the Convention. Some international legal scholars suggest that with the increased emphasis on crimes against humanity, the international community could dispense with the Genocide Convention. Prosecution of crimes against humanity would thus provide alternatives to the conceptual confusions and limitations of the Convention. Yet the Rome Statute seems to indicate a different perspective: it retains the definition of genocide that the UN specified in 1948.

ROGER W. SMITH

Perspective 2: The Definition Problem

Apart from the incomparable *American Webster's*, dictionaries have made a mess of defining genocide. Britain's *Shorter* and *Greater Oxford* confine the meaning to "annihilation of a race." Australia's *Macquarie Dictionary* follows in that vein: "extermination of a national or racial group as a planned move." *Webster's* comes closest to what international law has defined as genocide: "the use of deliberate systematic measures (as killing, bodily or mental injury, unlivable conditions, prevention of births) calculated to bring about the extermination of a racial, political or cultural group or to destroy the language, religion, or culture of a group." *Webster's* has added a few cultural aspects not found in the United Nations Convention on the Prevention and Punishment of the Crime of Genocide (hereafter GC), but it does convey the substance and essence of the crime as recognized internationally.

Scholars have rightly railed against the flawed GC definition, agreed to by the United Nations in 1948 and operational from January 1951. The identical wording has been adopted in the scheduled crimes in the Statute of the International Criminal Court, 2002, at Articles 6 and 25(e):

GC ARTICLE II

In the present Convention, genocide means any of the following acts committed with intent to destroy, in whole or in part, a national, ethnical, racial or religious group, as such:

(a) Killing members of the group;

(b) Causing serious bodily or mental harm to members of the group;

(c) Deliberately inflicting on the group conditions of life calculated to bring about its physical destruction in whole or in part;

(d) Imposing measures intended to prevent births within the group;

(e) Forcibly transferring children of the group to another group.

ARTICLE III

The following acts shall be punishable:
Genocide;
Conspiracy to commit genocide;
Direct and public incitement to commit genocide;
Complicity in genocide.

The flaws are many and of serious concern. First, the context of the Convention—war-torn, ravaged and homicidal Europe—leads to a legitimate assumption that "intent to destroy" is baleful, malevolent and indeed murderous. But the nature of the intent is not specified and so it is left open to argue that genocide can be committed with "good intent." There is historical evidence for this, particularly the forcible removal of Australian Aboriginal children, said to have been "in their best interests." Second, we intuitively understand what "in whole" is, but what exactly (or inexactly) constitutes "in part"? How small a number warrants examination for a probable crime?

Third, the targeted groups are listed as national, ethnical (ethnic), racial or religious. Groups defined as "political" do not appear, mainly because of Soviet Union opposition to such inclusion. Thus, the 50 million kulaks (peasants) and "enemies of the people" who died by intent between 1917 and 1939 are excluded from the purview of the new law. So, too, are the 500,000 victims of Indonesia's genocidal purge of the "Communists" in 1965–1966.

Fourth, the acts of genocide must be intended against these groups "as such"—that is, because they are those groups. Thus, in 1974 the case brought against Paraguay for the killing of Guayaki Indians came to nought because of the defense that while there were victims and perpetrators, there was no intent to kill these people because they were Guayaki. They died in the way of agricultural and other acts of "progress."

Perhaps the greatest fault lies in the co-equating of non-synonymous acts. Physical killing is understood easily enough. Causing people "serious bodily or mental harm" is ambiguous—not so much the physical aspect as the mental. How does one arrive at a universal concept of "mental harm"? Inflicting deleterious and destructive conditions of life—like slavery, or banishment to a remote gulag—is heinous, but again there is no median line to indicate any degree of severity. These first three acts are suggestive of short, sharp events, such as the fate of Armenians, Assyrians, and Pontian Greeks between 1915 and 1922, of Jews between 1939 and 1945, of Tutsi in Rwanda in 100 days in 1994. But the two remaining acts of genocide, Article II(d) on sterilization and II(e) on forcible child removal, suggest a quite different time-scale, a much longer range vision of "annihilation of a race."

The early drafting committees of the United Nations Convention, 1946 to 1948, wanted to divide genocide into three types: physical, biological, and cultural. They decided to exclude the cultural category (which *Webster's* includes by way of language) but, by the smallest of margins, included as "cultural" genocide the forcible remove of children from one group to another. The drafters may have had in mind the coercive "Turkification" of Christian minorities in the Ottoman Empire, or of East European children kidnapped by the Nazis for "Germanization." [Jewish children were destined for death, not transfer.] By any subjective or objective yardsticks, killing people, causing them harm, inflicting life-threatening actions and even resorting to sterilization is not quite the same as "transferring" children. This is not to say that forcible removal, child abuse, lifelong scarring is less than atrocious, but it is the equation of that behavior with killing that remains problematic.

Other flaws lie in Article III which equates conspiracy, incitement and complicity with the very crime itself. Most criminal justice systems differentiate between an attempt to commit a crime and its physical act of commission (or sometimes omission).

Despite some scholarly attacks on the "narrowness" of the UN definition, it is the breadth of the wording that bedevils this "crime of crimes." English-speaking scholars have railed against the GC definition since 1948 and have produced a sometimes bewildering array of new wording. Raphael Lemkin, the Polish jurist who coined the term "genocide" in 1944, was clear enough: he saw it as "the destruction of the essential foundations of the life of national groups, with the aim of annihilating the groups themselves." In 1959, Pieter Drost confined the concept to "deliberate destruction of physical life." In 1976, Irving Louis Horowitz saw the crime as the "structural and systematic

destruction of innocent people." In 1988, Henry Huttenbach talked of "any act that puts the very existence of a group in jeopardy." In 1993, Helen Fein called it "the sustained purposeful action . . . to physically destroy a collectivity directly or indirectly, through interdiction of the biological and social reproduction of group members." Others, like Frank Chalk and Kurt Jonassohn, Jennifer Balint, and Israel Charny in the 1990s were almost as one in emphasizing the physical killing of a targeted group.

Whatever their merits, chipping away by academic criticism is unlikely to change matters. The harsh reality is that we have been saddled with the UN Convention definition since 1948, and we are likely to be stuck with it for perhaps another 50 years in the ICC Statute. When a U.S. delegate to the Rome discussions on the ICC Statute tried to revisit the definition issue, it became clear soon enough that re-opening of the definition would lead several key states—including the United States, Australia and some former colonial empires—to say that they would not ratify any new broader, more encompassing and better definitions, lest, it seems, they found themselves accused of the crime.

Judicial decisions may well be an answer to some of these problems. The 1998 Akayesu case in Rwanda has helped liberate some of the constraints imposed by the GC and ICC definitions. The International Criminal Tribunal for Rwanda (ICTR) declared that it is possible to deduce a genocidal intent in a particular act from the general context of other culpable acts directed against a particular community, in short, evidence from the circumstances. Courts have now declared rape in such circumstances as an act of genocide because it contributes to the degradation and destruction of a people.

COLIN TATZ

Perspective 3: Definition of Genocide Still Viable?

To address this question, it is important to understand how the United Nations definition was first formulated. There are two key influences. First, Raphael Lemkin coined the term and offered a detailed account of its meaning in *Axis Rule in Occupied Europe* (1944). Second, as Leo Kuper details, in the post–World War II context, various powers negotiated the United Nations Convention on the Prevention and Punishment of the Crime of Genocide through a process heavily influenced by political considerations.

Lemkin's concept of genocide represents a tension between his specific, detailed, and brilliantly insightful analysis of how the Nazis were destroying Jews and others in Europe and a more general pre-Holocaust study of a range of historical cases, going back from the Armenian Genocide to ancient times. It would be a mistake to misunderstand the Holocaust element of Lemkin's concept as narrowing; quite the contrary, Lemkin's analysis at once held Poles and others to be victims of genocide under the Nazis and engaged a variety of elements and techniques of which direct killing was only one. For instance, Lemkin discussed the undermining of national cohesion by imposed moral degradation through pornography, alcohol consumption, and gambling, as well as by separation of women and men of victim populations to lower birthrates.

In the opposite direction, Lemkin's historical survey, though penetrating and foundational, was empirical and limited to three main forms of genocide, the destruction of captive or defeated populations, as in the cases of Melos and Carthage; the destruction of national patterns of social and individual life by colonizers or conquerors; and the combination of the first two forms, especially by the Nazis. If Nazi methods of genocide, including an industrial concentration camp "liquidation" system integrated into finance and manufacturing capitalism, were highly innovative, the overarching form of genocide—who it targeted and why, not simply in the sense of biological racism but also including populations that had been conquered—were much less so, even atavistic.

This is not a problem at all. Even setting aside his coining of the term, one would be hard-pressed to find a scholar or international lawyer who would dispute the claim that Lemkin remains the figure who has contributed the most to the field of genocide studies and law. But Lemkin worked in the 1920s to 1950s and had only available to him the history and conceptual tools that existed in that era. It would have required prescience more than simple extrapolation from existing cases to anticipate some of the dimensions of genocide that have emerged in the seven decades since Lemkin.

Similarly, it would be a mistake to see the compromise UN definition resulting from the highly politicized process of great and small power negotiations as simplistically limited and flawed. That definition in fact has allowed for a significant range of applicability and has been used, though with some Ptolemaic stretching, to fit cases such as Cambodia and the Ukraine famine—cases of a form that was originally meant to be excluded from applicability. The

exclusion of political groups has been a hindrance but not debilitating for the definition, especially given the influence of the 1985 Whitaker Report arguing against exclusion of political, gender, and other groups as targets and what William Schabas has claimed to be a recent history of case law that has adequately expanded the applicability of the legal definition to fit all recent cases that it should have. While Schabas's own restricted application of the term weakens this point a good deal, it is still the case that the UN definition has not so far been excessively limiting when applied in an objective manner.

This does not mean that we can answer the opening question affirmatively. In fact, the UN definition is no longer viable because it was never viable as a universal definition. Neither was Lemkin's or any other fixed definition proposed since his initial formulation. This is especially clear regarding Lemkin. As Chalk and Jonassohn point out, while Lemkin's definition could be applied to "domestic genocide," that is, a genocide launched by one segment of a society against another segment of the same society, Lemkin's focus, especially early on, was not on this form and his later work does not seem to include this as a specific type. Thus, the general concept of genocide Lemkin developed was broader than his own understanding of its potential applicability. This is good, but ultimately that broadness is limited by the grounding understanding of its applicability. The same is true of the UN definition, which is different from Lemkin's mainly in that it narrows the methods of genocide used and shifts his balanced emphasis on many elements to a focus on direct and indirect destruction of the physical lives of victim group members. Greater and greater effort is required to fit more and more recent cases of genocide into the range of applicability. One result is that application of the term requires more and more time, so that the term becomes applicable only after the bulk of the destruction has taken place, as in the Rwanda case. What is more, contemporary cases such as Bosnia and Darfur continue to be contested based on definitional concerns that cannot be reduced to simple, cynical denialism. Because of the limits of the UN definition, these cases remain open to debate. In the case of Darfur, this is a contributing factor in the continuation of the genocide as well as the ability of the al-Bashir government to engage in mass violence on a path to genocide against the peoples of South Kordofan and the Nuba Mountains today.

The UN definition is not keeping up because it cannot. The forms of genocide have evolved historically and any attempt to define the term must capture this evolution. To date, all definitions, including Lemkin's and the UN definitions, have been fixed (if flexible and open) definitions that at the very best (and most do not achieve this) combine a summary of past cases gathered under the term defined and extrapolations to future cases from past cases. Such definitions simply cannot anticipate future changes in the forms of genocide. This is especially true as sophisticated perpetrators intentionally construct their actions to just not fit the UN definition as they attempt to prevent their actions being labeled "genocide." As an example, even though a definition of genocide might anticipate new groups to be targeted, such as homosexuals, it cannot anticipate kinds of groups that do not yet exist or whose existence is not understood adequately when the definition is developed. Could the framers of the UN definition, for instance, have conceptualized the group "Queer Nation," which is a subset of homosexuals self-defined in a complex contemporary manner? On the UN definition even expanded to include homosexuals as a social group, a perpetrator could easily argue that in destroying "Queer Nation" it was not targeting people as homosexuals as a social category.

Fixed definitions also cannot keep pace with innovations in scholarship. Re-reading Lemkin's work on genocide, one is struck as much by its representation of the scholarship and political situation of a particular time as of the bold innovations carrying his work beyond those

limits. "Intent" in the UN definition, as interpreted in case law, is an individual and specific form of intent that depends on the notion that the decision to commit genocide (or continue in the case of an organic process of increasing violence that reaches the threshold of genocide) is in some way is housed in individual human consciousnesses. While this approach is appropriate to standard criminology and its concern with assessing the guilt and innocence of particular individuals, it is not especially useful for determining that a genocide is occurring or has occurred when intervention or group reparations is the concern, rather than individual prosecution. It ignores newer, more complex and subtler concepts of social causation that recognize genocide as the produce of a social process in which various actors participate but none has an overarching intent of the individual and explicit form. Thus, new intellectual insights into the elements even of past genocides require modifications of the definition.

Ultimately, some kind of evolving concept of genocide should replace the fixed definition of the UN. The challenge is to create a process for the evolution that will still allow legal action based on the definition. One solution might be regularly scheduled revisions. The problem with that, of course, is that it could lead to renewed efforts by members to manipulate the definition to protect themselves, as in the original process developing the 1948 definition.

HENRY C. THERIAULT

Documents

---

1. Raphael Lemkin Introduces the Concept of Genocide

Though somewhat ironically a small chapter in this overall volume of 674 pages, totaling only 17 pages, and not a central focus of the book, Lemkin (1900–1959) would ultimately embrace this concept as his life's mission and saw its realization in the 1948 UN Convention on the Punishment and Prevention of the Crime of Genocide. The chapter itself is subtitled "A New Term and New Conception for Destruction of Nations," and begins "New conceptions require new terms. By 'genocide,' we mean the destruction of a nation or of an ethnic group." (This would later be expanded to include racial and religious groups and though originally including political groups as well, this last reference was omitted due to the political machinations of the Soviet Union.) Often overlooked in Lemkin's chapter was his first footnote where he wrote that would be equally comfortable with the word "ethnocide" to denote the same crime. The chapter then goes on to explore the various techniques of genocide in these fields—political, social, cultural, economic, biological, physical, religious, and moral, and ends with a series of recommendations for the future, addressing genocide in both war and peace and pressing for "international control of occupation practices."

Chapter IX Genocide

I. Genocide—A New Term and New Conception for Destruction of Nations

New conceptions require new terms. By "genocide" we mean the destruction of a nation or of an ethnic group. This new word, coined by the author to denote an old practice in its modern development, is made from the ancient Greek word *genos* (race, tribe) and the Latin *cide* (killing), thus corresponding in its formation to such words as tyrannicide, homocide, infanticide, etc.[1] Generally speaking, genocide does not necessarily mean the immediate destruction of a nation, except when accomplished by mass killings of all members of a nation. It is intended rather to signify a coordinated plan of different actions aiming at the destruction of essential foundations of the life of national groups, with the aim of annihilating the groups themselves. The objectives of such a plan would be disintegration of the political and social institutions, of culture, language, national feelings, religion, and the economic existence of national groups, and the destruction of the personal security, liberty, health, dignity, and even the lives of the individuals belonging to such groups. Genocide is directed against

---

1. Another term could be used for the same idea, namely, ethnocide, consisting of the Greek word "ethnos"—nation-and the Latin word "cide."

the national group as an entity, and the actions involved are directed against individuals, not in their individual capacity, but as members of the national group.

The following illustration will suffice. The confiscation of property of nationals of an occupied area on the ground that they have left the country may be considered simply as a deprivation of their individual property rights. However, if the confiscations are ordered against individuals solely because they are Poles, Jews, or Czechs, then the same confiscations tend in effect to weaken the national entities of which those persons are members.

Genocide has two phases: one, destruction of the national pattern of the oppressed group: the other, the imposition of the national pattern of the oppressor. This imposition, in turn, may be made upon the oppressed population which is allowed to remain, or upon the territory alone, after removal of the population and the colonization of the area by the oppressor's own nationals. Denationalization was the word used in the past to describe the destruction of a national pattern.[1a] The author believes, however, that this word is inadequate because: (1) it does not connote the destruction of the biological structure; (2) in connoting the destruction of one national pattern, it does not connote the imposition of the national pattern of the oppressor; and (3) denationalization is used by some authors to mean only deprivation of citizenship.[2]

Many authors, instead of using a generic term, use currently terms connoting only some functional aspect of the main generic notion of genocide. Thus, the terms "Germanization," "Magyarization," "Italianization," for example, are used to connote the imposition by one stronger nation (Germany, Hungary, Italy) of its national pattern upon a national group controlled by it. The author believes that these terms are also inadequate because they do not convey the common elements of one generic notion and they treat mainly the cultural, economic, and social aspects of genocide, leaving out the biological aspect, such as causing the physical decline and even destruction of the population involved. If one uses the term "Germanization" of the Poles, for example, in this connotation, it means that the Poles, as human beings, are preserved and that only the national pattern of the Germans is imposed upon them. Such a term is much too restricted to apply to a process in which the population is attacked, in a physical sense, and is removed and supplanted by populations of the oppressor nations.

Genocide is the antithesis of the Rousseau-Portalis Doctrine, which may be regarded as implicit in the Hague Regulations. This doctrine holds that war is directed against sovereigns and armies, not against subjects and civilians. In its modern application in civilized society, the doctrine means that war is conducted against states and armed 'forces and not against populations. It required a long period of evolution in civilized society to mark the way from wars of extermination[3], which occurred in ancient times and in the Middle Ages, to the conception of wars as being essentially limited to activities against armies and states. In the present war, however, genocide is widely practiced by the German occupant. Germany could not accept the Rousseau-Portalis Doctrine: first, because Germany is waging a total war; and secondly, because, according to the doctrine of National Socialism, the nation, not the state, is the predominant factor.[4] In this German conception the nation provides the biological element for the state. Consequently, in enforcing the New Order, the Germans prepared, waged, and continued a war not merely against states and their armies[5] but against peoples. For the German occupying authorities war thus appears to offer the most appropriate occasion for carrying out their policy of genocide. Their reasoning seems to be the following:

The enemy nation within the control of Germany must be destroyed, disintegrated, or weakened in different degrees for decades to come. Thus the German people in the post-war period will be in a position to deal with other European peoples from the vantage point of biological superiority. Because the imposition of this policy of genocide is more destructive for a

---

1a. *See Violation of the Laws and Customs of War: Reports of Majority and Dissenting Reports of American and Japanese Members of the Commission of Responsibilities, Conference of Paris*, 1919. Carnegie Endowment for International Peace, Division of International Law, Pamphlet No. 32 (Oxford: Clarendon Press, 1919), p. 39.

2. See Garner, *op. cit.*, Vol. I, p. 77.

3. As classical examples of wars of extermination in which nations and groups of the population were completely or almost completely destroyed, the following may be cited: the destruction of Carthage in 146 B.C.; the destruction of Jerusalem by Titus in 72 A.D.; the religious wars of Islam and the Crusades; the massacres of the Albigenses and the Waldenses; and the siege of Magdeburg in the Thirty Years' War. Special wholesale massacres occurred in the wars waged by Genghis Khan and by Tamerlane.

4. "Since the State in itself is for us only a form, while what is essential is its content, the nation, the people it is clear that everything else must subordinate itself to its sovereign interests."—Adolf Hitler, *Mein Kampf* (New York: Reynold & Hitchcock, 1939), p. 842

5. See Alfred Rosenberg, *Der Mythus des 20. Jahrhunderts* (München: Hoheneichenverlag, 1935), pp. 1–2: "History and the mission of the future no longer mean the struggle of class against class, the struggle of Church dogma against dogma, but the clash between blood and blood, race and race, people and people."

people than injuries suffered in actual fighting[6], the German people will be stronger than the subjugated peoples after the war even if the German army is defeated. In this respect genocide is a new technique of occupation aimed at winning the peace even though the war itself is lost.

For this purpose the occupant has elaborated a system designed to destroy nations according to a previously prepared plan. Even before the war Hitler envisaged genocide as a means of changing the biological interrelations in Europe in favor of Germany[7]. Hitler's conception of genocide is based not upon cultural but upon biological patterns. He believes that "*Germanization* can only be carried out with the soil and never with men."[8]

When Germany occupied the various European countries, Hitler considered their administration so important that he ordered the Reich Commissioners and governors to be responsible directly to him.[9] The plan of genocide had to be adapted to political considerations in different countries. It could not be implemented in full force in all the conquered states, and hence the plan varies as to subject, modalities, and degree of intensity in each occupied country. Some groups-such as the Jews-are to be destroyed completely.[10] A distinction is made between peoples considered to be related by blood to the German people (such as Dutchmen, Norwegians, Flemings, Luxemburgers), and peoples not thus related by blood (such as the Poles, Slovenes, Serbs). The populations of the first group are deemed worthy of being Germanized. With respect to the Poles particularly, Hitler expressed the view that it is their soil alone which *can and should be profitably Germanized.*[11]

II. Techniques of Genocide in Various Fields

The techniques of genocide, which the German occupant has developed in the various occupied countries, represent a concentrated and coordinated attack upon all elements of nationhood. Accordingly, genocide is being carried out in the following fields:

Political

In the incorporated areas, such as western Poland, Eupen, Malmédy and Moresnet, Luxemburg, and Alsace-Lorraine, local institutions of self-government were destroyed and a German pattern of administration imposed. Every reminder of former national character was obliterated. Even commercial signs and inscriptions on buildings, roads, and streets, as well as names of communities and of localities, were changed to a German form.[12] Nationals of Luxemburg having foreign or non-German first names are required to assume in lieu thereof the corresponding German first names; or, if that is impossible, they must select German first names. As to their family names, if they were of German origin and their names have been changed to a non-German form, they must be changed again to the original German. Persons who have not complied with

---

6. The German genocide philosophy was conceived and put into action before the Germans received even a foretaste of the considerable dimensions of Allied aerial bombings of German territory.

7. See Hitler's statement to Rauschning, from *The Voice of Destruction*, by Hermann Rauschning (New York, 1940), p. 138, by courtesy of G. P. Putnam's Sons:

    ". . . The French complained after the war that there were twenty million Germans too many. We accept the criticism. We favor the planned control of population movements. But our friends will have to excuse us if we subtract the twenty millions elsewhere. After all these centuries of whining about the protection of the poor and lowly, it is about time we decided to protect the strong against the inferior. It will be one of the chief tasks of German statesmanship for all time to prevent by every means in our power, the further increase of the Slav races. Natural instincts bid all living beings not merely conquer their enemies, but also destroy them. In former days, it was the victor's prerogative to destroy entire tribes, entire peoples. By doing this gradually and without bloodshed, we demonstrate our humanity. We should remember, too, that we are merely doing unto other as they would have done to us."

8. *Mein Kamff*, p. 588.

9. See "Administration," above, pp. 9–10.

10. *Mein Kampf*, p. 931: ". . . the National Socialist movement has its mightiest tasks to fulfill . . . it must condemn to general wrath the evil enemy of humanity [Jews] as the true creator of all suffering."

11. *Ibid.*, p. 590, n. ". . . The Polish policy in the sense of a Germanization of the East, demanded by so many, rooted unfortunately almost always in the same wrong conclusion. Here too one believed that one could bring about a Germanization of the Polish element by a purely linguistic integration into the the German nationality. Here too the result would have been an unfortunate one: people of an alien race, expressing its alien thoughts in the German language, compromising the height and the dignity of our own natronality by its own inferiority." As to the depopulation policy in occupied Yugoslavia, see, in general, Louis Adamic, *My Native Land* (New York: Harper & Brothers, 1943).

12. For Luxemburg, see order of August 6, 1940, below, p. 440.

these requirements within the prescribed period are liable to a penalty, and in addition German names may be imposed on them.[13] Analogous provisions as to changing of names were made for Lorraine.[14]

Special Commissioners for the Strengthening of Germanism are attached to the administration, and their task consists in coordinating all actions promoting Germanism in a given area. An especially active role in this respect is played by inhabitants of German origin who were living in the occupied countries before the occupation. After having accomplished their task as members of the so-called fifth column, they formed the nucleus of Germanism. A register of Germans (*Volksliste*) [15] was established and special cards entitled them to special privileges and favors, particularly in the fields of rationing, employment, supervising enterprises of local inhabitants, and so on. In order to disrupt the national unity of the local population, it was declared that non-Germans, married to Germans, may upon their application be put on the *Volksliste.*

In order further to disrupt national unity, Nazi party organizations were established, such as the Nasjonal Samling Party in Norway and the Mussert Party in the Netherlands, and their members from the local population were given political privileges. Other political parties were dissolved.[16] These Nazi parties in occupied countries were also given special protection by courts.

In line with this policy of imposing the German national pattern, particularly in the incorporated territories, the occupant has organized a system of colonization of these areas. In western Poland, especially, this has been done on a large scale. The Polish population have been removed from their homes in order to make place for German settlers who were brought in from the Baltic States, the central and eastern districts of Poland, Bessarabia, and from the Reich itself. The properties and homes of the Poles are being allocated to German settlers; and to induce them to reside in these areas the settlers receive many privileges, especially in the way of tax exemptions. [17]

Social

The destruction of the national pattern in the social field has been accomplished in part by the abolition of local law and local courts and the imposition of German law and courts, and also by Germanization of the judicial language and of the bar.[18] The social structure of a nation being vital to its national development, the occupant also endeavors to bring about such changes as may weaken the national spiritual resources. The focal point of this attack has been the intelligentsia, because this group largely provides national leadership and organizes resistance against Nazification. This is especially true in Poland and Slovenia (Slovene part of Yugoslavia), where the intelligentsia and the clergy were in great part removed from the rest of the population and deported for forced labor in Germany. The tendency of the occupant is to retain in Poland only the laboring and peasant class, while in the western occupied countries the industrialist class is also allowed to remain, since it can aid in integrating the local industries with the German war economy.

Cultural

In the incorporated areas the local population is forbidden to use its own language in schools and in printing. According to the decree of August 6, 1940,[19] the language of instruction in all Luxemburg schools was made exclusively German. The French language was not permitted to be taught in primary schools; only in secondary schools could courses in that language continue to be given. German teachers were introduced into the schools and they were compelled to teach according to the principles of National Socialism.[20]

13. See order concerning the change of first and family names in Luxemburg, of January 31, 1941, below, p. 441.
14. Verordnungsblatt, 1940, p. 60
15. As to Poland, see order of October 29, 1941, below, p. 552.
16. As to Norway, see order of September 25,1940, below, p. 499.
17. See above, chapter on "Finance."
18. See above, chapters on "Law" and "Courts."
19. See below, p. 440.
20. "It is the task of the director to orient and conduct the school systematically according to National Socialist principles." See announcement for execution of the order concerning the elementary school system, February 14, 1941, promulgated in Lorraine by the Chief of Civil Administration, below, p. 388.

In Lorraine general compulsory education to assure the upbringing of youth in the spirit of National Socialism begins at the age of six.[21] It continues for eight years, or to the completion of the grammar school (*Volksschule*), and then for three more years, or to the completion of a vocational school. Moreover, in the Polish areas Polish youths were excluded from the benefit of liberal arts studies and were channeled predominantly into the trade schools. The occupant apparently believes that the study of the liberal arts may develop independent national Polish thinking, and therefore he tends to prepare Polish youths for the role of skilled labor, to be employed in German industries.

In order to prevent the expression of the national spirit through artistic media, a rigid control of all cultural activities has been introduced. All persons engaged in painting, drawing, sculpture, music, literature, and the theater are required to obtain a license for the continuation of their activities. Control in these fields is exercised through German authorities. In Luxemburg this control is exercised through the Public Relations Section of the Reich Propaganda Office and embraces music, painting, theater, architecture, literature, press, radio, and cinema. Every one of these activities is controlled through a special chamber and all these chambers are controlled by one chamber, which is called the Reich Chamber of Culture (*Reichskulturkammer*).[22] The local chambers of culture are presided over by the propaganda chief of the National Socialist Party in the given area. Not only have national creative activities in the cultural and artistic field been rendered impossible by regimentation, but the population has also been deprived of inspiration from the existing cultural and artistic values. Thus, especially in Poland, were national monuments destroyed and libraries, archives, museums, and galleries of art carried away.[23] In 1939 the Germans burned the great library of the Jewish Theological Seminary at Lublin, Poland. This was reported by the Germans as follows:

For us it was a matter of special pride to destroy the Talmudic Academy which was known as the greatest in Poland.... We threw out of the building the great Talmudic library, and carted it to market. There we set fire to the books. The fire lasted for twenty hours. The Jews of Lublin were assembled around and cried bitterly. Their cries almost silenced us. Then we summoned the military band and the joyful shouts of the soldiers silenced the sound of the Jewish cries.[24]

Economic

The destruction of the foundations of the economic existence of a national group necessarily brings about a crippling of its development, even a retrogression. The lowering of the standard of living creates difficulties in fulfilling cultural-spiritual requirements. Furthermore, a daily fight literally for bread and for physical survival may handicap thinking in both general and national terms.

It was the purpose of the occupant to create such conditions as these among the peoples of the occupied countries, especially those peoples embraced in the first plans of genocide elaborated by him-the Poles, the Slovenes, and the Jews.

The Jews were immediately deprived of the elemental means of existence.[25] As to the Poles in incorporated Poland, the purpose of the occupant was to shift the economic resources from the Polish national group to the German national group. Thus the Polish national group had to be impoverished and the German enriched. This was achieved primarily by confiscation of Polish property under the authority of the Reich Commissioner for the Strengthening of Germanism. But the process was likewise furthered by the policy of regimenting trade and handicrafts, since licenses for such activities were issued to Germans, and only exceptionally to Poles. In this way, the Poles were expelled from trade, and the Germans entered that field.

As the occupant took over the banks a special policy for handling bank deposits was established in order to strengthen the German element. One of the most widely patronized Polish banks, called the Post Office Savings Bank (P.K.O.), possessed, on the day of the occupation, deposits of millions of Polish citizens. The deposits, however, were repaid by the occupant only to the German depositors upon production by them of a certificate of their German origin.[26] Thus the German element in Poland was immediately made financially stronger than the Polish. In Slovenia the Germans have liquidated the

21. *Verordnungsblatt, 1941,* p. 100. See below, p. 386.
22. As to or organization of the Reich Chamber of Culture, see law of November I, 1933, *Reichsgesetzblatt,* I, *p. 979.*
23. See note of the Polish Minister of Foreign Affairs of the Polish Government-in-Exile to the Allied and neutral powers of May 3, 1941, in *Polish White Book:* Republic of Poland, Ministry of Foreign Affairs, *German Occupation of Poland-Extract of Note Addressed to the Allied and Neutral Powers* (New York: The Greystone Press [1942]), pp. 36–39
24. *Frankfurter Zeitung,* Wochen-Ausgabe, March 28, 1941.
25. See above, chapter on "Legal Status of the Jews."
26. See ordinance promulgated by the German Trustee of the Polish Savings Bank published in *Thorner Freiheit* of December 11, 1940

financial cooperatives and agricultural associations, which had for decades proved to be a most efficient instrumentality in raising the standard of living and in promoting national and social progress.

In other countries, especially in Alsace-Lorraine and Luxemburg, genocide in the economic field was carried out in a different manner. As the Luxemburgers are considered to be of related blood, opportunity is given them to recognize the Germanic elements in themselves, and to work for the strengthening of Germanism. If they do not take advantage of this "opportunity," their properties are taken from them and given to others who are eager to promote Germanism.[27]

Participation in economic life is thus made dependent upon one's being German or being devoted to the cause of Germanism. Consequently, promoting a national ideology other than German is made difficult and dangerous.

Biological

In the occupied countries of "people of non-related blood," a policy of depopulation is pursued. Foremost among the methods employed for this purpose is the adoption of measures calculated to decrease the birthrate of the national groups of non-related blood, while at the same time steps are taken to encourage the birthrate of the *Volksdeutsche* living in these countries. Thus in incorporated Poland marriages between Poles are forbidden without the special permission of the Governor (*Reichsstatthater*) of the district; and the latter, as a matter of principle, does not permit marriages between Poles.[28]

The birthrate of the undesired group is being further decreased as a result of the separation of males from females[29] by deporting them for forced labor elsewhere. Moreover, the undernourishment of the parents, because of discrimination in rationing, brings about not only a lowering of the birthrate, but a lowering of the survival capacity of children born of underfed parents.

As mentioned above, the occupant is endeavoring to encourage the birth-rate of the Germans. Different methods are adopted to that end. Special subsidies are provided in Poland for German families having at least three minor children.[30] Because the Dutch and Norwegians are considered of related blood, the bearing, by Dutch and Norwegian women, of illegitimate children begotten by German military men is encouraged by subsidy.[31] Other measures adopted are along the same lines. Thus the Reich Commissioner has vested in himself the right to act as a guardian or parent to a minor Dutch girl if she intends to marry a German.[32] The special care for legitimation of children in Luxemburg, as revealed in the order concerning changes in family law of March 22, 1941,[33] is dictated by the desire to encourage extramarital procreation with Germans.

Physical

The physical debilitation and even annihilation of national groups in occupied countries is carried out mainly in the following ways:

27. See "Property" above, p.38
28. See Report of Primate of Poznan to Pius XII, *The Black Book* of Poland (New York: G. P. Putnam's Sons, 1942), p. 383.
29. That the separation of males from females was preconceived by Hitler as an element of genocide is obvious from his statement: "*We are obliged to depopulate*," he went on emphatically, 'as part of our mission of preserving the German population. We shall have to develop a technique of depopulation. If you ask me what I mean by depopulation, I mean the removal of entire racial units. And that is what I intend to carry out—that, roughly, is my task. Nature is cruel, therefore we, too, may be cruel. If I can send the flower of the German nation into the hell of war without the smallest pity for the spilling of precious German blood, then surely I have the right to remove millions of an inferior race that breeds like vermin! And by" remove "I don't necessarily mean destroy; I shall simply take the systematic measures to dam their great natural fertility. For example, I shall keep their men and women separated for years. Do you remember the falling birthrate of the world war? Why should we not do quite consciously and through a number of years what was at that time merely the inevitable consequence of the long war? There are many ways, systematical and comparatively painless, or at any rate bloodless, of causing undesirable races to die out.'"—Rauschning, *op.cit.*, pp. 137–38, by courtesy of G.P Putnam's Sons.
30. See order concerning the granting of child subsidies to Germans in the Government, of March 10, 1942, below, p.553.
31. See order of July 28, 1942, concerning the subsidizing of children of members of the German armed forces in occupied territories, *Reichsgesetzblatt*, 1942, I, p. 488:
    "To maintain and promote a racially valuable German heritage, children begotten by members of the German armed forces in the occupied Norwegian and Dutch territories and born of Norwegian or Dutch women will upon the application of the mother be granted a special subsidy and benefit through the offices of the Reich Commissioners for the occupied Norwegian and Dutch territories."
32. See order of February 28, 1941, below, p.474
33. See below, p. 428

I. *Racial Discrimination* in *Feeding.* Rationing of food is organized according to racial principles throughout the occupied countries. "The German people come before all other peoples for food," declared Reich Minister Göring on October 4, 1942.[34] In accordance with this program, the German population is getting 93 per cent of its pre-war diet, while those in the occupied territories receive much less: in Warsaw, for example, the Poles receive 66 per cent of the pre-war rations and the Jews only 20 per cent.[35] The following shows the difference in the percentage of meat rations received by the Germans and the population of the occupied countries: Germans, 100 per cent; Czechs, 86 per cent; Dutch, 71 per cent; Poles (Incorporated Poland), 71 per cent; Lithuanians, 57 per cent; French, 51 per cent: Belgians, 40 per cent; Serbs, 36 per cent; Poles (General Government), 36 per cent; Slovenes, 29 per cent; Jews, 0 per cent.[36]

The percentage of pre-war food received under present rations (in calories per consumer unit) is the following:[37] Germans, 93 per cent; Czechs, 83 per cent; Poles (Incorporated Poland), 78 per cent; Dutch, 70 per cent; Belgians, 66 per cent; Poles (General Government), 66 per cent; Norwegians, 54 per cent; Jews, 20 per cent.

As to the composition of food, the percentages of required basic nutrients received under present rations (per consumer unit) are as follows:[38]

The result of racial feeding is a decline in health of the nations involved and an increase in the deathrate. In Warsaw, anemia rose 113 per cent among Poles and 435 among Jews.[39] The deathrate per thousand in 1941 amounted in the Netherlands to 10 per cent; in Belgium to 14.5 per cent; in Bohemia and Moravia to 13.4.[40] The Polish mortality in Warsaw in 1941 amounted in July to 1,316;[41] in August to 1,729[42] and in September to 2,160.[43]

2. *Endangering of Health.* The undesired national groups, particularly in Poland, are deprived of elemental necessities for preserving health and life. This latter method consists, for example, of requisitioning warm clothing and blankets in the winter and withholding firewood and medicine. During the winter of 1941, only a single room in a house could be heated in the Warsaw ghetto, and children had to take turns in warming themselves there. No fuel at all has been received since then by the Jews in the ghetto.[44]

Consumer Units	Carbohydrates %	Proteins %	Fats %
Germans	100	97	77
Czechs	90	92	65
Dutch	84	95	65
Belgians	79	73	29
Poles (Incorporated Poland)	76	85	49
Poles (General Government)	77	62	18
Norwegians	69	65	32
French	58	71	40
Greeks	38	38	1.14
Jews	27	20	0.32

34. See *New York Times*, October 5, 1942, p.4, col.6.
35. The figures quoted in this and the following two paragraphs have been taken, with the permission of the Institute of Jewish Affairs, from its publication entitles *Starvation over Europe* (*Made in Germany*); *A Documented Record* 1943 (New York, 1943), pp. 37, 47, 52.
36. *Ibid.*, p.37
37. *Ibid.*, p.47
38. *Ibid.*, p.52. For further details, see League of Nations, *World Economic Survey* (Geneva, 1942), pp. 90–91
39. See *Hitter's Ten-Year War on the Jews* (Institute of Jewish Affairs of the American Jewish Congress, World Jewish Congress, New York, 1943), p. 144.
40. League of Nations, *Monthly Bulletin of Statistics* (Geneva, 1942), Nos. 4, 5, 6.
41. *Nowy Kurjer Warszawski* (Warsaw), August 29, 1941.
42. *Die Nation* (Bern), August 13, 1942.
43. *Poland Fights* (New York), May 16, 1942.
44. *Hitler's Ten-Year War on the Jews*, p. 144.

Moreover, the Jews in the ghetto are crowded together under conditions of housing inimical to health, and in being denied the use of public parks they are even deprived of the right to fresh air. Such measures, especially pernicious to the health of children, have caused the development of various diseases. The transfer, in unheated cattle trucks and freight cars, of hundreds of thousands of Poles from Incorporated Poland to the Government General, which took place in the midst of a severe winter, resulted in a decimation of the expelled Poles.

3. *Mass Killings.* The technique of mass killings is employed mainly against Poles, Russians, and Jews, as well as against leading personalities from among the non-collaborationist groups in all the occupied countries. In Poland, Bohemia-Moravia, and Slovenia, the intellectuals are being "liquidated" because they have always been considered as the main bearers of national ideals and at the time of occupation they were especially suspected of being the organizers of resistance. The Jews for the most part are liquidated within the ghettos,[45] or in special trains in which they are transported to a so-called "unknown" destination. The number of Jews who have been killed by organized murder in all the occupied countries, according to the Institute of Jewish Affairs of the American Jewish Congress in New York, amounts to 1,702,500.[46]

Religious

In Luxemburg, where the population is predominantly Catholic and religion plays an important role in national life, especially in the field of education, the occupant has tried to disrupt these national and religious influences. Children over fourteen years of age were permitted by legislation to renounce their religious affiliations,[47] for the occupant was eager to enroll such children exclusively in pro-Nazi youth organizations. Moreover, in order to protect such children from public criticism, another law was issued at the same time imposing penalties ranging up to 15,000 Reichsmarks for any publication of names or any general announcement as to resignations from religious congregations.[48] Likewise in Poland, through the systematic pillage and destruction of church property and persecution of the clergy, the German occupying authorities have sought to destroy the religious leadership of the Polish nation.

Moral

In order to weaken the spiritual resistance of the national group, the occupant attempts to create an atmosphere of moral debasement within this group. According to this plan, the mental energy of the group should be concentrated upon base instincts and should be diverted from moral and national thinking. It is important for the realization of such a plan that the desire for cheap individual pleasure be substituted for the desire for collective feelings and ideals based upon a higher morality. Therefore, the occupant made an effort in Poland to impose upon the Poles pornographic publications and movies. The consumption of alcohol was encouraged, for while food prices have soared, the Germans have kept down the price of alcohol, and the peasants are compelled by the authorities to take spirits in payment for agricultural produce. The curfew law,

45. See the Joint Declaration by members of the United Nations, issued simultaneously in Washington and in London, on December 17, 1942:

"The attention of the Belgian, Czechoslovak, Greek, Jugoslav, Luxembourg, Netherlands, Norwegian, Polish, Soviet, United Kingdom and United States Governments and also of the French National Committee has been drawn to numerous reports from Europe that the German authorities, not content with denying to persons of Jewish race in all the territories over which their barbarous rule has been extended, the most elementary human rights, are now carrying into effect Hitler's oft-repeated intention to exterminate the Jewish people in Europe.

"From all the occupied countries Jews are being transported in conditions of appalling horror and brutality to Eastern Europe. In Poland, which has been made the principal Nazi slaughterhouse, the ghettos established by the German invader are being systematically emptied of all Jews except a few highly skilled workers required for war industries. None of those taken away are ever heard of again. The able-bodied are slowly worked to death in labor camps. The infirm are left to die of exposure and starvation or are deliberately massacred in mass executions. The number of victims of these bloody cruelties is reckoned in many hundreds of thousands of entirely innocent men, women and children.

"The above-mentioned governments and the French National Committee condemn in the strongest possible terms this bestial policy of cold-blooded extermination. They declare that such events can only strengthen the resolve of all freedom-loving peoples to overthrow the barbarous Hitlerite tyranny. They reaffirm their solemn resolution to insure that those responsible for these crimes shall not escape retribution, and to press on with the necessary practical measures to this end." *The United Nations Review,* Vol. III (1943), No. I, p. I.

46. *Hitler's Ten-Year War on the Jews*, p. 307.

47. See order of December 9, 1940, below, p. 438.

48. *Ibid.*

enforced very strictly against Poles, is relaxed if they can show the authorities a ticket to one of the gambling houses which the Germans have allowed to come into existence.[49]

III. Recommendations for the Future

Prohibition of Genocide in War and Peace

The above-described techniques of genocide represent an elaborate, almost scientific, system developed to an extent never before achieved by any nation.[50] Hence the significance of genocide and the need to review international law in the light of the German practices of the present war. These practices have surpassed in their unscrupulous character any procedures or methods imagined a few decades ago by the framers of the Hague Regulations. Nobody at that time could conceive that an occupant would resort to the destruction of nations by barbarous practices reminiscent of the darkest pages of history. Hence, among other items covered by the Hague Regulations, there are only technical rules dealing with some (but by no means all) of the essential rights of individuals; and these rules do not take into consideration the interrelationship of such rights with the whole problem of nations subjected to virtual imprisonment. The Hague Regulations deal also with the sovereignty of a state, but they are silent regarding the preservation of the integrity of a people. However, the evolution of international law, particularly since the date of the Hague Regulations, has brought about a considerable interest in national groups as distinguished from states and individuals. National and religious groups were put under a special protection by the Treaty of Versailles and by specific minority treaties, when it became obvious that national minorities were compelled to live within the boundaries of states ruled by governments representing a majority of the population. The constitutions which were framed after 1918 also contain special provisions for the protection of the rights of national groups. Moreover, penal codes which were promulgated at that time provide for the protection of such groups, especially of their honor and reputation.

This trend is quite natural, when we conceive that nations are essential elements of the world community. The world represents only so much culture and intellectual vigor as are created by its component national groups.[51] Essentially the idea of a nation signifies constructive cooperation and original contributions, based upon genuine traditions, genuine culture, and a well-developed national psychology. The destruction of a nation, therefore, results in the loss of its future contributions to the world. Moreover, such destruction offends our feelings of morality and justice in much the same way as does the criminal killing of a human being: the crime in the one case as in the other is murder, though on a vastly greater scale. Among the basic features which have marked progress in civilization are the respect for and appreciation of the national characteristics and qualities contributed to world culture by the different nations-characteristics and qualities which, as illustrated in the contributions made by nations weak in defense and poor in economic resources, are not to be measured in terms of national power and wealth.

As far back as 1933, the author of the present work submitted to the Fifth International Conference for the Unification of Penal Law, held in Madrid in October of that year in cooperation with the Fifth Committee of the League of Nations, a report accompanied by draft articles to the effect that actions aiming at the destruction and oppression of populations (what would amount to the actual conception of genocide) should be penalized. The author formulated two new international law crimes to be introduced into the penal legislation of the thirty-seven participating countries, namely, the crime of barbarity, conceived as oppressive and destructive actions directed against individuals as members of a national, religious, or racial group, and the crime of vandalism, conceived as malicious destruction of works of art and culture because they represent

---

49. Under Polish law, 1919–39, gambling houses were prohibited; nor did they exist on Polish soil when it was under Russian, German, and Austrian rule before 1914, See *The Black Book of Poland*, pp. 513, 514.

50. "No conqueror has ever chosen more diabolical methods for gaining the mastery of the soul and body of a people."—*Manchester Guardian*, February 28, 1941.

 "We know that there is no war in all our history where such ruthless and deliberate steps have been taken for the disintegration of civilian life and the suffering and the death of civilian populations."—Hugh R. Jackson, Special Assistant to the Director of Forein Relief and Rehabilitation Operations, U.S. Department of State, in an address before the National Conference of Social Work, New York, March 12, 1943; printed in Department of State, *Bulletin,* Vol. VIII, No. 194 (March 13, 1943) p. 219

51. The idea of a nation should not, however, be confused with the idea of nationalism. To do so would be to make the same mistake as confusing the idea of individual liberty with that of egoism.

the specific creations of the genius of such groups. Moreover, according to this draft these new crimes were to be internationalized to the extent that the offender should be punished when apprehended, either in his own country, if that was the situs of the crime, or in any other signatory country, if apprehended there.[52]

This principle of universal repression for genocide practices advocated by the author at the above-mentioned conference, had it been accepted by the conference and embodied in the form of an international convention duly signed and ratified by the countries there represented in 1933, would have made it possible, as early as that date, to indict persons who had been found guilty of such criminal acts whenever they appeared on the territory of one of the signatory countries. Moreover, such a project, had it been adopted at that time by the participating countries, would prove useful now by providing an effective instrument for the punishment of war criminals of the present world conflict. It must be emphasized again that the proposals of the author at the Madrid Conference embraced criminal actions which, according to the view of the author, would cover in great part the fields in which crimes have been committed in this war by the members of the Axis Powers. Furthermore, the adoption of the principle of universal repression as adapted to genocide by countries which belong now to the group of non-belligerents or neutrals, respectively, would likewise bind these latter countries to punish the war criminals engaged in genocide or to extradite them to the countries in which these crimes were committed. If the punishment of genocide practices had formed a part of international law in such countries since 1933, there would be no necessity now to issue admonitions to neutral countries not to give refuge to war criminals.[53]

It will be advisable in the light of these observations to consider the place of genocide in the present and future international law. Genocide is, as we have noted, a composite of different acts of persecution or destruction. Many of those acts, when they constitute an infringement upon honor and rights, when they are a transgression against life, private property and religion, or science and art, or even when they encroach unduly in the fields of taxation and personal services, are prohibited by Articles 46, 48, 52, and 56 of the Hague Regulations. Several of them, such as those which cause humiliations, debilitation by undernourishment, and danger to health, are in violation of the laws of humanity as specified in the preamble to the Hague Regulations. But other acts falling within the purview of genocide, such as, for example, subsidizing children begotten by members of the armed forces of the occupant and born of women nationals of the occupied area, as well as various ingenious measures for weakening or destroying political, social, and cultural elements in national groups, are not expressly prohibited by the Hague Regulations. The entire problem of genocide needs to be dealt with as a whole; it is too important to be left for piecemeal discussion and solution in the future. Many hope that there will be no more wars, but we dare not rely on mere hopes for protection against genocidal practices by ruthless conquerors. Therefore, without ceasing in our endeavors to make this the last war, we must see to it that the Hague Regulations are so amended as expressly to prohibit genocide in any war which may occur in the future. *De lege ferenda,* the definition of genocide in the Hague Regulations thus amended should consist of two essential parts: in the first should be included every action infringing upon the life, liberty, health, corporal integrity, economic existence, and the honor of the inhabitants when committed because they belong to a national, religious, or racial group; and in the second, every policy aiming at the destruction or the aggrandizement of one of such groups to the prejudice or detriment of another.

Moreover, we should not overlook the fact that genocide is a problem not only of war but also of peace. It is an especially important problem for Europe, where differentiation in nationhood is so marked that despite the principle of political and territorial self-determination, certain national groups may be obliged to live as minorities within the boundaries of other states. If these groups should not be adequately protected, such lack of protection would result in international disturbances, especially in the form of disorganized emigration of the persecuted, who would look for refuge elsewhere.[54] That being the case, all countries must be concerned about such a problem, not only because of humanitarian, but also because of practical, reasons affecting the interest of every country. The system of legal protection of minorities adopted in the past, which

---

52. See Raphaël Lemkin, "Terrorisme," *Acts de la Ve Conférence Internationale pour l'Unification du Droit Pénal* (Paris, 1935), pp. 48–56; see *also* Lemkin, "Akte der Barbarei und des Vandalismus als *delicti iuris gentium*," *Internationales Anwaltsblatt* (Vienna, November, 1933).

53. See statement of President Roosevelt, *White House Press Release,* July 30, 1943, Department of State, *Bulletin,* Vol. IX, No. 214 (July 31, 1943), p. 62.

54. Adequate protection of minority groups does not of course mean that protective measures should be so stringent as to prevent those who so desire from leaving such groups in order to join majority groups. In other words, minority protection should not constitute a barrier to the gradual process of assimilation and integration which may result from such voluntary transfer of individuals.

was based mainly on international treaties and the constitutions of the respective countries, proved to be in-adequate because not every European country had a sufficient judicial machinery for the enforcement of its constitution. It may be said, in fact, that the European countries had a more efficient machinery for enforcing civil and criminal law than for enforcing constitutional law. Genocide being of such great importance, its repression must be based not only on international and constitutional law but also on the criminal law of the various countries. The procedure to be adopted in the future with respect to this matter should be as follows:

An international multilateral treaty should provide for the introduction, not only in the constitution but also in the criminal code of each country, of provisions protecting minority groups from oppression because of their nationhood, religion, or race. Each criminal code should have provisions inflicting penalties for genocide practices. In order to prevent the invocation of the plea of superior orders, the liability of persons who order genocide practices, as well as of persons who execute such orders, should be provided expressly by the criminal codes of the respective countries. Because of the special implications of genocide in international relations, the principle of universal repression should be adopted for the crime of genocide. According to this principle, the culprit should be liable to trial not only in the country in which he committed the crime, but also, in the event of his escape therefrom, in any other country in which he might have taken refuge.[55] In this respect, genocide offenders should be subject to the principle of universal repression in the same way as other offenders guilty of the so-called *delicta juris gentium* (such as, for example, white slavery and trade in children, piracy, trade in narcotics and in obscene publications, and counterfeiting of money).[56] Indeed, genocide should be added to the list of *delicta juris gentium*.[57]

International Control of Occupation Practices

Genocide as described above presents one of the most complete and glaring illustrations of the violation of international law and the laws of humanity. In its several manifestations genocide also represents a violation of specific regulations of the Hague Convention such as those regarding the protection of property, life, and honor. It is therefore essential that genocide procedures be not only prohibited by law but prevented in practice during military occupation.

In another important field, that of the treatment of prisoners of war, international controls have been established in order to ascertain whether prisoners are treated in accordance with the rules of international law (see Articles 86 to 88 of the Convention concerning the Treatment of Prisoners of War, of July 27, 1929).[58] But the fate of nations in prison, of helpless women and children, has apparently not seemed to be so important as to call for supervision of the occupational authorities. Whereas concerning prisoners of war the public is able to obtain exact information, the lack of direct-witness reports on the situation of groups of population under occupation gravely hampers measures for their assistance and rescue from what may be inhumane and intolerable conditions. Information and reports which slip out from behind the frontiers of occupied countries are very often labeled as untrustworthy atrocity stories because they are so gruesome that people simply refuse to believe them. Therefore, the Regulations of the Hague Convention should be modified to include an international controlling agency vested with specific powers, such as visiting the occupied countries and making inquiries as to the manner in which the occupant treats nations in prison. In the situation as it exists at present there is no means of providing for alleviation of the treatment of populations under occupation until the actual moment of liberation. It is then too late for remedies, for after liberation such populations can at best obtain only reparation of damages but never restoration of those values which have been destroyed and which cannot be restored, such as human life, treasures of art, and historical archives.

Source: Raphael Lemkin, *Axis Rule in Occupied Europe: Laws of Occupation, Analysis of Government, Proposals for Redress.* Chapter IX, pp, 79–95 with footnotes. Washington, DC: Carnegie Endowment for International Peace, 1944. Available online at http://ess.uwe.ac.uk/genocide/Lemkina .html.

---

55. Of course such an offender could never be tried twice for the same act.
56. Research in International Law (Under the Auspices of the Faculty of Harvard Law School), "Part II. Jurisdiction with Respect to Crime," (Edwin D. Dickinson, Reporter), *American Journal of International Law, Supp., Vol. 29* (1935), pp. 573–85.
57. Since not all countries agree to the principle of universal repression (as for example, the United States of America), the future treaty on genocide might well provide a facilitative clause for the countries which do not adhere to this principle.
58. League of Nations, *Treaty Series,* Vol. 118, p. 343.

2. UN Convention on the Prevention and Punishment of the Crime of Genocide

In the aftermath of the horrors of World War II, though not specifically referencing the genocidal tragedy of the Jews of Europe between 1939 and 1945, this legally affirmed UN Convention defines what constituted genocide against which groups as punishable acts, and further details the process by which it would become international law. Though not without controversy and critique even today by both the academic and legal communities, it remains the only legal instrument possessing international standing. It should also be noted that the United States, while originally affirming its validity under President Harry Truman (1884–1972), hindered its own ratification until 1988 under the presidency of Ronald Reagan (1911–2004).

Convention on the Prevention and Punishment of the Crime of Genocide

Adopted by Resolution 260 (III) A of the United Nations General Assembly on 9 December 1948.

The Contracting Parties,

Having considered the declaration made by the General Assembly of the United Nations in its resolution 96 (I) dated 11 December 1946 that genocide is a crime under international law, contrary to the spirit and aims of the United Nations and condemned by the civilized world;

Recognizing that at all periods of history genocide has inflicted great losses on humanity; and

Being convinced that, in order to liberate mankind from such an odious scourge, international co-operation is required;

Hereby agree as hereinafter provided.

Article 1. The Contracting Parties confirm that genocide, whether committed in time of peace or in time of war, is a crime under international law which they undertake to prevent and to punish.

Art. 2. In the present Convention, genocide means any of the following acts committed with intent to destroy, in whole or in part, a national, ethnical, racial or religious group, as such:

(a) Killing members of the group;
(b) Causing serious bodily or mental harm to members of the group;
(c) Deliberately inflicting on the group conditions of life calculated to bring about its physical destruction in whole or in part;
(d) Imposing measures intended to prevent births within the group;
(e) Forcibly transferring children of the group to another group.

Art. 3. The following acts shall be punishable:

(a) Genocide;
(b) Conspiracy to commit genocide;
(c) Direct and public incitement to commit genocide;
(d) Attempt to commit genocide;
(e) Complicity in genocide.

Art. 4. Persons committing genocide or any of the other acts enumerated in Article 3 shall be punished, whether they are constitutionally responsible rulers, public officials or private individuals.

Art. 5. The Contracting Parties undertake to enact, in accordance with their respective Constitutions, the necessary legislation to give effect to the provisions of the present Convention and, in particular, to provide effective penalties for persons guilty of genocide or any of the other acts enumerated in Article 3.

Art. 6. Persons charged with genocide or any of the other acts enumerated in Article 3 shall be tried by a competent tribunal of the State in the territory of which the act was committed, or by such international penal tribunal as may have jurisdiction with respect to those Contracting Parties which shall have accepted its jurisdiction.

Art. 7. Genocide and the other acts enumerated in Article 3 shall not be considered as political crimes for the purpose of extradition.

The Contracting Parties pledge themselves in such cases to grant extradition in accordance with their laws and treaties in force.

Art. 8. Any Contracting Party may call upon the competent organs of the United Nations to take such action under the Charter of the United Nations.

Source: A/RES/260 (III). December 9, 1948. http://www.un.org/ga/search/view_doc.asp?symbol=a/res/260(III). Used by permission of the United Nations.

3. Principles of the Nuremberg Tribunal, 1950

A set of precepts emerging from the Nuremberg Trials of 1945–1946 was adopted by the United Nations International Law Commission in 1950, the essential implication being that every person is responsible for his or her own actions, and that, as a result, no one stands above international law. By these principles, the defense of "following superior orders" is nullified. The Nuremberg Principles have been incorporated into a number of multilateral treaties, most notably that which established the International Criminal Court.

Principle I

Any person who commits an act which constitutes a crime under international law is responsible therefor and liable to punishment.

Principle II

The fact that internal law does not impose a penalty for an act which constitutes a crime under international law does not relieve the person who committed the act from responsibility under international law.

Principle III

The fact that a person who committed an act which constitutes a crime under international law acted as Head of State or responsible Government official does not relieve him from responsibility under international law.

Principle IV

The fact that a person acted pursuant to order of his Government or of a superior does not relieve him from responsibility under international law, provided a moral choice was in fact possible to him.

Principle V

Any person charged with a crime under international law has the right to a fair trial on the facts and law.

Principle VI

The crimes hereinafter set out are punishable as crimes under; international law:
   Crimes against peace:

   (i) Planning, preparation, initiation or waging of a war of aggression or a war in violation of international treaties, agreements or assurances;
   (ii) Participation in a common plan or conspiracy for the accomplishment of any of the acts mentioned under (i).

   War crimes:
   Violations of the laws or customs of war which include, but are not limited to, murder, ill-treatment or deportation to slave-labor or for any other purpose of civilian population of or in occupied territory, murder or illtreatment of prisoners of

war, of persons on the seas, killing of hostages, plunder of public or private property, wanton destruction of cities, towns, or villages, or devastation not justified by military necessity.

Crimes against humanity:

Murder, extermination, enslavement, deportation and other inhuman acts done against any civilian population, or persecutions on political, racial or religious grounds, when such acts are done or such persecutions are carried on in execution of or in connection with any crime against peace or any war crime.

Principle VII

Complicity in the commission of a crime against peace, a war crime, or a crime against humanity as set forth in Principles VI is a crime under international law.

> **Source:** Report of the International. Law Commission covering its Second Session, June 5—July 29, 1950, Document A/1316. Available online at http://www.icrc.org/ihl.nsf/full/390.

4. The Rome Statute of the International Criminal Court, July 17, 1998

This legal document from 1998 is divided into the following parts: I. Establishment of the Court, II. Jurisdiction, Admissibility, and Applicable Law, III. General Principles of Criminal Law, IV. Composition and Administration of the Court, V. Investigation and Prosecution, VI. The Trial, VII. Penalties, VIII. Appeal and Revision, IX. International Cooperation and Judicial Assistance, X. Enforcement, XI. Assembly of States Parties, XII. Financing, XIII. Final Clauses. Of particular important are Articles 6 Genocide, 7 Crimes against Humanity, and 8 War Crimes, further spelling out what categories of crimes are to be addressed. It should be noted that President Bill Clinton (b. 1946) signed onto the Rome Statutes, President George Bush Jr. (b. 1961) reversed that decision, and, as of this date (2014), President Barack Obama (b. 1961) has yet to urge the United States to become a signatory.

Part 1. Establishment of the court
Article 1

The Court

An International Criminal Court ("the Court") is hereby established. It shall be a permanent institution and shall have the power to exercise its jurisdiction over persons for the most serious crimes of international concern, as referred to in this Statute, and shall be complementary to national criminal jurisdictions. The jurisdiction and functioning of the Court shall be governed by the provisions of this Statute.

Article 2

Relationship of the Court with the United Nations

The Court shall be brought into relationship with the United Nations through an agreement to be approved by the Assembly of States Parties to this Statute and thereafter concluded by the President of the Court on its behalf.

Article 3

Seat of the Court

1. The seat of the Court shall be established at The Hague in the Netherlands ("the host State").
2. The Court shall enter into a headquarters agreement with the host State, to be approved by the Assembly of States Parties and thereafter concluded by the President of the Court on its behalf.
3. The Court may sit elsewhere, whenever it considers it desirable, as provided in this Statute.

Article 4

Legal status and powers of the Court

1. The Court shall have international legal personality. It shall also have such legal capacity as may be necessary for the exercise of its functions and the fulfilment of its purposes.
2. The Court may exercise its functions and powers, as provided in this Statute, on the territory of any State Party and, by special agreement, on the territory of any other State.

Part 2. Jurisdiction, admissibility and applicable law

Article 5

Crimes within the jurisdiction of the Court

1. The jurisdiction of the Court shall be limited to the most serious crimes of concern to the international community as a whole. The Court has jurisdiction in accordance with this Statute with respect to the following crimes:

   (a) The crime of genocide;
   (b) Crimes against humanity;
   (c) War crimes;
   (d) The crime of aggression.

2. The Court shall exercise jurisdiction over the crime of aggression once a provision is adopted in accordance with articles 121 and 123 defining the crime and setting out the conditions under which the Court shall exercise jurisdiction with respect to this crime. Such a provision shall be consistent with the relevant provisions of the Charter of the United Nations.

Article 6

Genocide

For the purpose of this Statute, "genocide" means any of the following acts committed with intent to destroy, in whole or in part, a national, ethnical, racial or religious group, as such:

   (a) Killing members of the group;
   (b) Causing serious bodily or mental harm to members of the group;
   (c) Deliberately inflicting on the group conditions of life calculated to bring about its physical destruction in whole or in part;
   (d) Imposing measures intended to prevent births within the group;
   (e) Forcibly transferring children of the group to another group.

Article 7

Crimes against humanity

1. For the purpose of this Statute, "crime against humanity" means any of the following acts when committed as part of a widespread or systematic attack directed against any civilian population, with knowledge of the attack:

   (a) Murder;
   (b) Extermination;
   (c) Enslavement;

(d) Deportation or forcible transfer of population;

(e) Imprisonment or other severe deprivation of physical liberty in violation of fundamental rules of international law;

(f) Torture;

(g) Rape, sexual slavery, enforced prostitution, forced pregnancy, enforced sterilization, or any other form of sexual violence of comparable gravity;

(h) Persecution against any identifiable group or collectivity on political, racial, national, ethnic, cultural, religious, gender as defined in paragraph 3, or other grounds that are universally recognized as impermissible under international law, in connection with any act referred to in this paragraph or any crime within the jurisdiction of the Court;

(i) Enforced disappearance of persons;

(j) The crime of apartheid;

(k) Other inhumane acts of a similar character intentionally causing great suffering, or serious injury to body or to mental or physical health.

2. For the purpose of paragraph 1:

(a) "Attack directed against any civilian population" means a course of conduct involving the multiple commission of acts referred to in paragraph 1 against any civilian population, pursuant to or in furtherance of a State or organizational policy to commit such attack;

(b) "Extermination" includes the intentional infliction of conditions of life, *inter alia* the deprivation of access to food and medicine, calculated to bring about the destruction of part of a population;

(c) "Enslavement" means the exercise of any or all of the powers attaching to the right of ownership over a person and includes the exercise of such power in the course of trafficking in persons, in particular women and children;

(d) "Deportation or forcible transfer of population" means forced displacement of the persons concerned by expulsion or other coercive acts from the area in which they are lawfully present, without grounds permitted under international law;

(e) "Torture" means the intentional infliction of severe pain or suffering, whether physical or mental, upon a person in the custody or under the control of the accused; except that torture shall not include pain or suffering arising only from, inherent in or incidental to, lawful sanctions;

(f) "Forced pregnancy" means the unlawful confinement of a woman forcibly made pregnant, with the intent of affecting the ethnic composition of any population or carrying out other grave violations of international law. This definition shall not in any way be interpreted as affecting national laws relating to pregnancy;

(g) "Persecution" means the intentional and severe deprivation of fundamental rights contrary to international law by reason of the identity of the group or collectivity;

(h) "The crime of apartheid" means inhumane acts of a character similar to those referred to in paragraph 1, committed in the context of an institutionalized regime of systematic oppression and domination by one racial group over any other racial group or groups and committed with the intention of maintaining that regime;

(i) "Enforced disappearance of persons" means the arrest, detention or abduction of persons by, or with the authorization, support or acquiescence of, a State or a political organization, followed by a refusal to acknowledge that deprivation of freedom or to give information on the fate or whereabouts of those persons, with the intention of removing them from the protection of the law for a prolonged period of time.

3. For the purpose of this Statute, it is understood that the term "gender" refers to the two sexes, male and female, within the context of society. The term "gender" does not indicate any meaning different from the above.

Article 8

War crimes

1. The Court shall have jurisdiction in respect of war crimes in particular when committed as part of a plan or policy or as part of a large-scale commission of such crimes.
2. For the purpose of this Statute, "war crimes" means:

   (a) Grave breaches of the Geneva Conventions of 12 August 1949, namely, any of the following acts against persons or property protected under the provisions of the relevant Geneva Convention:

      (i) Wilful killing;
      (ii) Torture or inhuman treatment, including biological experiments;
      (iii) Wilfully causing great suffering, or serious injury to body or health;
      (iv) Extensive destruction and appropriation of property, not justified by military necessity and carried out unlawfully and wantonly;
      (v) Compelling a prisoner of war or other protected person to serve in the forces of a hostile Power;
      (vi) Wilfully depriving a prisoner of war or other protected person of the rights of fair and regular trial;
      (vii) Unlawful deportation or transfer or unlawful confinement;
      (viii) Taking of hostages.

   (b) Other serious violations of the laws and customs applicable in international armed conflict, within the established framework of international law, namely, any of the following acts:

      (i) Intentionally directing attacks against the civilian population as such or against individual civilians not taking direct part in hostilities;
      (ii) Intentionally directing attacks against civilian objects, that is, objects which are not military objectives;
      (iii) Intentionally directing attacks against personnel, installations, material, units or vehicles involved in a humanitarian assistance or peacekeeping mission in accordance with the Charter of the United Nations, as long as they are entitled to the protection given to civilians or civilian objects under the international law of armed conflict;
      (iv) Intentionally launching an attack in the knowledge that such attack will cause incidental loss of life or injury to civilians or damage to civilian objects or widespread, long-term and severe damage to the natural environment which would be clearly excessive in relation to the concrete and direct overall military advantage anticipated;
      (v) Attacking or bombarding, by whatever means, towns, villages, dwellings or buildings which are undefended and which are not military objectives;
      (vi) Killing or wounding a combatant who, having laid down his arms or having no longer means of defence, has surrendered at discretion;
      (vii) Making improper use of a flag of truce, of the flag or of the military insignia and uniform of the enemy or of the United Nations, as well as of the distinctive emblems of the Geneva Conventions, resulting in death or serious personal injury;
      (viii) The transfer, directly or indirectly, by the Occupying Power of parts of its own civilian population into the territory it occupies, or the deportation or transfer of all or parts of the population of the occupied territory within or outside this territory;
      (ix) Intentionally directing attacks against buildings dedicated to religion, education, art, science or charitable purposes, historic monuments, hospitals and places where the sick and wounded are collected, provided they are not military objectives;

(x)   Subjecting persons who are in the power of an adverse party to physical mutilation or to medical or scientific experiments of any kind which are neither justified by the medical, dental or hospital treatment of the person concerned nor carried out in his or her interest, and which cause death to or seriously endanger the health of such person or persons;

(xi)   Killing or wounding treacherously individuals belonging to the hostile nation or army;

(xii)   Declaring that no quarter will be given;

(xiii)   Destroying or seizing the enemy's property unless such destruction or seizure be imperatively demanded by the necessities of war;

(xiv)   Declaring abolished, suspended or inadmissible in a court of law the rights and actions of the nationals of the hostile party;

(xv)   Compelling the nationals of the hostile party to take part in the operations of war directed against their own country, even if they were in the belligerent's service before the commencement of the war;

(xvi)   Pillaging a town or place, even when taken by assault;

(xvii)   Employing poison or poisoned weapons;

(xviii)   Employing asphyxiating, poisonous or other gases, and all analogous liquids, materials or devices;

(xix)   Employing bullets which expand or flatten easily in the human body, such as bullets with a hard envelope which does not entirely cover the core or is pierced with incisions;

(xx)   Employing weapons, projectiles and material and methods of warfare which are of a nature to cause superfluous injury or unnecessary suffering or which are inherently indiscriminate in violation of the international law of armed conflict, provided that such weapons, projectiles and material and methods of warfare are the subject of a comprehensive prohibition and are included in an annex to this Statute, by an amendment in accordance with the relevant provisions set forth in articles 121 and 123;

(xxi)   Committing outrages upon personal dignity, in particular humiliating and degrading treatment;

(xxii)   Committing rape, sexual slavery, enforced prostitution, forced pregnancy, as defined in article 7, paragraph 2 (f), enforced sterilization, or any other form of sexual violence also constituting a grave breach of the Geneva Conventions;

(xxiii)   Utilizing the presence of a civilian or other protected person to render certain points, areas or military forces immune from military operations;

(xxiv)   Intentionally directing attacks against buildings, material, medical units and transport, and personnel using the distinctive emblems of the Geneva Conventions in conformity with international law;

(xxv)   Intentionally using starvation of civilians as a method of warfare by depriving them of objects indispensable to their survival, including wilfully impeding relief supplies as provided for under the Geneva Conventions;

(xxvi)   Conscripting or enlisting children under the age of fifteen years into the national armed forces or using them to participate actively in hostilities.

(c)   In the case of an armed conflict not of an international character, serious violations of article 3 common to the four Geneva Conventions of 12 August 1949, namely, any of the following acts committed against persons taking no active part in the hostilities, including members of armed forces who have laid down their arms and those placed *hors de combat* by sickness, wounds, detention or any other cause:

(i)   Violence to life and person, in particular murder of all kinds, mutilation, cruel treatment and torture;

(ii)   Committing outrages upon personal dignity, in particular humiliating and degrading treatment;

(iii)   Taking of hostages;

(iv)   The passing of sentences and the carrying out of executions without previous judgement pronounced by a regularly constituted court, affording all judicial guarantees which are generally recognized as indispensable.

(d) Paragraph 2 (c) applies to armed conflicts not of an international character and thus does not apply to situations of internal disturbances and tensions, such as riots, isolated and sporadic acts of violence or other acts of a similar nature.

(e) Other serious violations of the laws and customs applicable in armed conflicts not of an international character, within the established framework of international law, namely, any of the following acts:

    (i) Intentionally directing attacks against the civilian population as such or against individual civilians not taking direct part in hostilities;

    (ii) Intentionally directing attacks against buildings, material, medical units and transport, and personnel using the distinctive emblems of the Geneva Conventions in conformity with international law;

    (iii) Intentionally directing attacks against personnel, installations, material, units or vehicles involved in a humanitarian assistance or peacekeeping mission in accordance with the Charter of the United Nations, as long as they are entitled to the protection given to civilians or civilian objects under the international law of armed conflict;

    (iv) Intentionally directing attacks against buildings dedicated to religion, education, art, science or charitable purposes, historic monuments, hospitals and places where the sick and wounded are collected, provided they are not military objectives;

    (v) Pillaging a town or place, even when taken by assault;

    (vi) Committing rape, sexual slavery, enforced prostitution, forced pregnancy, as defined in article 7, paragraph 2 (f), enforced sterilization, and any other form of sexual violence also constituting a serious violation of article 3 common to the four Geneva Conventions;

    (vii) Conscripting or enlisting children under the age of fifteen years into armed forces or groups or using them to participate actively in hostilities;

    (viii) Ordering the displacement of the civilian population for reasons related to the conflict, unless the security of the civilians involved or imperative military reasons so demand;

    (ix) Killing or wounding treacherously a combatant adversary;

    (x) Declaring that no quarter will be given;

    (xi) Subjecting persons who are in the power of another party to the conflict to physical mutilation or to medical or scientific experiments of any kind which are neither justified by the medical, dental or hospital treatment of the person concerned nor carried out in his or her interest, and which cause death to or seriously endanger the health of such person or persons;

    (xii) Destroying or seizing the property of an adversary unless such destruction or seizure be imperatively demanded by the necessities of the conflict;

(f) Paragraph 2 (e) applies to armed conflicts not of an international character and thus does not apply to situations of internal disturbances and tensions, such as riots, isolated and sporadic acts of violence or other acts of a similar nature. It applies to armed conflicts that take place in the territory of a State when there is protracted armed conflict between governmental authorities and organized armed groups or between such groups.

3. Nothing in paragraph 2 (c) and (e) shall affect the responsibility of a Government to maintain or re-establish law and order in the State or to defend the unity and territorial integrity of the State, by all legitimate means.

Article 9

Elements of Crimes

1. Elements of Crimes shall assist the Court in the interpretation and application of articles 6, 7 and 8. They shall be adopted by a two-thirds majority of the members of the Assembly of States Parties.

2. Amendments to the Elements of Crimes may be proposed by:

(a) Any State Party;
(b) The judges acting by an absolute majority;
(c) The Prosecutor.

Such amendments shall be adopted by a two-thirds majority of the members of the Assembly of States Parties.

3. The Elements of Crimes and amendments thereto shall be consistent with this Statute.

Article 10

Nothing in this Part shall be interpreted as limiting or prejudicing in any way existing or developing rules of international law for purposes other than this Statute.

Article 11

Jurisdiction ratione temporis

1. The Court has jurisdiction only with respect to crimes committed after the entry into force of this Statute.
2. If a State becomes a Party to this Statute after its entry into force, the Court may exercise its jurisdiction only with respect to crimes committed after the entry into force of this Statute for that State, unless that State has made a declaration under article 12, paragraph 3.

Source: Rome Statute of the International Criminal Court (1998). Artices 1 to 11. http://www.icc-cpi.int/nr/rdonlyres/ea9aeff7–5752–4f84-be94–0a655eb30e16/0/rome_statute_english.pdf Used by permission of the United Nations.

5. The Eight Stages of Genocide

Gregory Stanton, past president of the International Association of Genocide Scholars (IAGS), lawyer and anthropologist, and creator and maintainer of the Web site www.genocidewatch.org has presented the concept and practice of genocide as a series of "stages," whose borders and boundaries are porous, as perpetrators move from one stage to the next. They are (1) classification, (2) symbolization, (3) dehumanization, (4) organization, (5) polarization, (6) preparation, (7) extermination, and (8) denial. It should be noted that these stages are applicable historically, and includes the Herero Genocide, the Armenian Genocide, the Holocaust of World War II, as well as the contemporary genocides of Cambodia/Kampuchea (where much of his scholarly work has been done), Guatemala, the Kurdish Genocide, East Timor, Bosnia, Rwanda, and Darfur.

The 8 Stages of Genocide By Gregory H. Stanton

The International Convention for the Prevention and Punishment of the Crime of Genocide defines "genocide."

"In the present Convention, genocide means any of the following acts committed with intent to destroy, in whole or in part, a national, ethnical, racial or religious group, as such:

(a) Killing members of the group;
(b) Causing serious bodily or mental harm to members of the group;
(c) Deliberately inflicting on the group conditions of life calculated to bring about its physical destruction in whole or in part;
(d) Imposing measures intended to prevent births within the group;
(e) Forcibly transferring children of the group to another group."

Acts of genocide

During the Rwandan genocide, the U.S. State Department's lawyers infamously directed U.S. diplomats to avoid use of the word genocide. Only "acts of genocide" were being committed, they said. It was a distinction without a difference.

The crime of genocide is defined by the Genocide Convention as "acts of genocide." It does not exist apart from those acts. A pattern of acts of genocide is frequently called "genocide" and evidence of such a pattern of ethnic, racial, or religious massacres is strong evidence of genocidal intent.

The Convention declares the following acts punishable:

"(a) Genocide;
 (b) Conspiracy to commit genocide;
 (c) Direct and public incitement to commit genocide;
 (d) Attempt to commit genocide;
 (e) Complicity in genocide."

The Genocide Convention is sometimes misinterpreted as requiring the intent to destroy **in whole** a national, ethnical, racial or religious group. Some genocides have fit that description, notably the Holocaust and Rwanda. But most do not. Most are intended to destroy only **part** of a group. The Genocide Convention specifically includes the intentional killing of part of a group as genocide. It reaffirms this definition when it includes as among the acts that constitute genocide "deliberately inflicting on the group conditions of life calculated to bring about its physical destruction in whole **or in part**". Those who shrink from applying the term "genocide" usually ignore the "in part".

Intent

Intent can be directly proven from statements or orders by the perpetrators. But more often, it must be deduced from the systematic pattern of their acts, a pattern that could only arise out of specific intent.

Criminal law distinguishes intent from motive. A murderer may have many motives—gaining property or eliminating a rival for power. But his intent is determined by the purpose of his act: Did he purposely kill the victim? Genocidal intent is determined by the specific purpose of the act: Did the killer purposely kill the victim as part of a plan to destroy a national, ethnic, racial, or religious group, at least in part?

The motive of the killer to take the victim's property or to politically dominate the victim's group does not remove genocidal intent if the victim is chosen because of his ethnic, national, racial, or religious group.

A plan for genocide doesn't need to be written out. An act of genocide may arise in a culture that considers members of another group less than human, where killing members of that group is not considered murder. This is the culture of impunity characteristic of genocidal societies. In Burundi, Tutsis who kill Hutus have seldom been convicted or even arrested. Massacres are ethnic, intended to destroy parts of the other ethnic group.

Leo Kuper calls such mass killings genocidal massacres. They are acts of genocide even if only a part of a group (the intellectuals, officers, leaders) is targeted.

The Genocidal Process

Prevention of genocide requires a structural understanding of the genocidal process. Genocide has eight stages or operational processes. The first stages precede later stages, but continue to operate throughout the genocidal process. Each stage reinforces the others. A strategy to prevent genocide should attack each stage, each process. The eight stages of genocide are classification, symbolization, dehumanization, organization, polarization, preparation, extermination, and denial.

Classification

All languages and cultures require classification—division of the natural and social world into categories. We distinguish and classify objects and people. All cultures have categories to distinguish between "us" and "them," between members of our group and others. We treat different categories of people differently. Racial and ethnic classifications may be defined by absurdly detailed laws—the Nazi Nuremberg laws, the "one drop" laws of segregation in America, or apartheid racial classification laws in South Africa. Racist societies often prohibit mixed categories and outlaw miscegenation. Bipolar societies are the most likely to have genocide. In Rwanda and Burundi, children are the ethnicity of their father, either Tutsi or Hutu. No one is mixed. Mixed marriages do not result in mixed children.

Symbolization

We use symbols to name and signify our classifications. We name some people Hutu and others Tutsi, or Jewish or Gypsy, or Christian or Muslim. Sometimes physical characteristics—skin color or nose shape—become symbols for classifications. Other symbols, like customary dress or facial scars, are socially imposed by groups on their own members. After the process has reached later stages (dehumanization, organization, and polarization) genocidal governments in the preparation stage often require members of a targeted group to wear an identifying symbol or distinctive clothing—e.g. the yellow star. The Khmer Rouge forced people from the Eastern Zone to wear a blue-checked scarf, marking them for forced relocation and elimination.

Dehumanization

Classification and symbolization are fundamental operations in all cultures. They become steps of genocide only when combined with dehumanization. Denial of the humanity of others is the step that permits killing with impunity. The universal human abhorrence of murder of members of one's own group is overcome by treating the victims as less than human. In incitements to genocide the target groups are called disgusting animal names—Nazi propaganda called Jews "rats" or "vermin"; Rwandan Hutu hate radio referred to Tutsis as "cockroaches." The targeted group is often likened to a "disease", "microbes", "infections" or a "cancer" in the body politic. Bodies of genocide victims are often mutilated to express this denial of humanity. Such atrocities then become the justification for revenge killings, because they are evidence that the killers must be monsters, not human beings themselves.

Organization

Genocide is always collective because it derives its impetus from group identification. It is always organized, often by states but also by militias and hate groups. Planning need not be elaborate: Hindu mobs may hunt down Sikhs or Muslims, led by local leaders. Methods of killing need not be complex: Tutsis in Rwanda died from machetes; Muslim Chams in Cambodia from hoe-blades to the back of the neck ("Bullets must not be wasted," was the rule at Cambodian extermination prisons, expressing the dehumanization of the victims.) The social organization of genocide varies by culture. It reached its most mechanized, bureaucratic form in the Nazi death camps. But it is always organized, whether by the Nazi SS or the Rwandan *Interahamwe*. Death squads may be trained for mass murder, as in Rwanda, and then force everyone to participate, spreading hysteria and overcoming individual resistance. Terrorist groups will pose one of the greatest threats of genocidal mass murder in the future as they gain access to chemical, biological, and even nuclear weapons.

Polarization

Genocide proceeds in a downward cycle of killings until, like a whirlpool, it reaches the vortex of mass murder. Killings by one group may provoke revenge killings by the other. Such massacres are aimed at polarization, the systematic elimination of moderates who would slow the cycle. The first to be killed in a genocide are moderates from the killing group who oppose the extremists: the Hutu Supreme Court Chief Justice and Prime Minister in Rwanda, the Tutsi Archbishop in Burundi. Extremists target moderate leaders and their families. The center cannot hold. The most extreme take over, polarizing the conflict until negotiated settlement is impossible.

Preparation

Preparation for genocide includes **identification.** Lists of victims are drawn up. Houses are marked. Maps are made. Individuals are forced to carry ID cards identifying their ethnic or religious group. Identification greatly speeds the slaughter. In Germany, the identification of Jews, defined by law, was performed by a methodical bureaucracy. In Rwanda, identity cards showed each person's ethnicity. In the genocide, Tutsis could then be easily pulled from cars at roadblocks and murdered. Throwing away the cards did not help, because anyone who could not prove he was Hutu, was presumed to be Tutsi. Hutu militiamen conducted crude mouth exams to test claims of Hutu identity.

Preparation also includes **expropriation** of the property of the victims. It may include **concentration:** herding of the victims into ghettos, stadiums, or churches. In its most extreme form, it even includes construction of extermination camps, as in Nazi-ruled Europe, or conversion of existing buildings—temples and schools—into extermination centers in Cambodia. **Transportation** of the victims to these killing centers is then organized and bureaucratized.

Extermination

The seventh step, the final solution, is extermination. It is considered extermination, rather than murder, because the victims are not considered human. They are vermin, rats or cockroaches. Killing is described by euphemisms of purification: "ethnic cleansing" in Bosnia, "ratonade" (rat extermination) in Algeria. Targeted members of alien groups are killed, often including children. Because they are not considered persons, their bodies are mutilated, buried in mass graves or burnt like garbage.

Denial

Every genocide is followed by denial. The mass graves are dug up and hidden. The historical records are burned, or closed to historians. Even during the genocide, those committing the crimes dismiss reports as propaganda. Afterwards such deniers are called "revisionists." Others deny through more subtle means: by characterizing the reports as "unconfirmed" or "alleged" because they do not come from officially approved sources; by minimizing the number killed; by quarreling about whether the killing fits the legal definition of genocide ("definitionalism"); by claiming that the deaths of the perpetrating group exceeded that of the victim group, or that the deaths were the result of civil war, not genocide. In fact, civil war and genocide are not mutually exclusive. Most genocides occur during wars.

Prevention

A full strategy for preventing genocide should include attack on each of genocide's operational processes.

Classification may be attacked either through devaluation of the distinctive features used to classify (e.g. amalgamation of regional dialects and accents by exposure to mass media, standardized education, and promotion of a common language) or through use of transcendent categories, such as common nationality or common humanity. Promotion of mixed categories, such as the financial incentives for inter-caste marriages in Tamil Nadu, India, may help break down group endogamy, but do not combat genocide in bipolar societies where mixed categories have no recognition. In bipolar societies, transcendent institutions like the Catholic Church should actively campaign against ethnic classifications. Special effort should be made to keep such institutions from being captured and divided by the same forces that divide the society, e.g. through hierarchical discipline from Rome for the Roman Catholic Church.

Symbolization can be attacked by legally forbidding use of hate symbols (e.g. swastikas) or ethnic classification words. "Nigger" or "kaffir" as racial expletives may be outlawed as "hate speech." Group marking like tribal scarring may be outlawed, like gang clothing. The problem is that legal limitations on hate speech will fail if unsupported by popular cultural enforcement. Though Hutu and Tutsi were forbidden words in Burundi until the 1980's, the prohibition had little effect, since other euphemisms and code-words replaced them. Prohibition may even become counter-productive, as part of an ideology of denial, which prevents people from naming, discussing and overcoming deep cultural divisions. However, without symbols for our classifications, they would become literally insignificant. Yellow stars became insignificant in parts of France and Bulgaria because many Jews refused to wear them and were not turned in by their Christian neighbors, who rejected the Nazi's classification system. In cultures that reject negative symbolization, resistance can be a powerful preventive tactic. In Denmark, the popular resistance to Nazi classification and symbolization was so strong that the Nazis did not even dare to impose the yellow star, and Danish "fishermen" smuggled ninety-five percent of Danish Jews to safety in Sweden.

Dehumanization should be opposed openly whenever it shows its ugly face. Genocidal societies lack constitutional protection for countervailing speech, and should be treated differently than democracies. Hate radio stations should be shut down, and hate propaganda banned. Although restrictions on free speech are not necessary in a healthy polity, even in democracies hate speech should be actively exposed and publicly opposed. Direct incitements to genocide should be outlawed. Incitement to genocide is not protected speech. Hate crimes and atrocities should be promptly punished. Impunity breeds contempt for law, and emboldens genocidists, who can literally get away with murder.

Organizations that commit acts of genocide should be banned, and membership in them made a crime. Freedom of association in a democratic society should not be misconstrued as protecting membership in criminal organizations. At Nuremberg, membership in the SS was itself prosecuted. Similarly the *Interahamwe* and other genocidal hate groups should be outlawed, and their members arrested and tried for conspiracy to commit genocide. The UN should impose arms embargoes on governments or militias that commit genocide. Because arms embargoes are difficult to enforce, for Rwanda, the UN established an international commission to investigate and document violations of the arms embargo. The UN may also require member states to freeze the assets of persons who organize and finance genocidal groups.

Polarization can be fought by providing financial and technical aid to the moderate center. It may mean security protection for moderate leaders, or assistance to human rights groups. Assets of extremists may be seized, and visas for international travel denied to them. Coups d'état by extremists should be immediately opposed by targeted international sanctions on their leaders.

Preparation: Identification of victims considerably speeds genocide. When ID cards identify victims' ethnic or religious group, or when victims are forced to wear yellow stars, the killing is made efficient. As soon as such symbolic markers are imposed, a Genocide Watch should be declared and diplomatic pressure should demand their abolition and impose targeted sanctions on regime leaders. When death lists are drawn up, the international community should recognize that genocide is imminent, and mobilize for armed intervention. Those identified should be given asylum, and assistance in fleeing their persecutors. Had the U.S. or Britain in Palestine accepted all Jewish immigrants, millions of lives might have been saved from the Holocaust.

Extermination whether carried out by governments or by patterned mob violence, can only be stopped by force. Armed intervention must be rapid and overwhelming. Safe areas should be established with real military protection. An intervention force without robust rules of engagement, such as UNAMIR in Rwanda in April, 1994 or UNPROFOR in Bosnia, is worse than useless because it gives genocide victims false hope of security in churches or unsafe "safe areas", delaying their organization for self-defense. In bipolar societies, separation into self-defense zones is the best protection for both groups, particularly if international troops create a buffer zone between them.

Experience with UN peacekeeping has shown that humanitarian intervention should be carried out by a multilateral force authorized by the UN, but led by UN members, rather than by the UN itself. The Military Staff Committee envisioned in Article 47 of the UN Charter has never been organized, and the UN does not have a standing army. The strongest member states must therefore shoulder this responsibility in conjunction with other UN members. The U.S. is now promoting the organization of an African Crisis Response Initiative composed of African military units coordinated and trained by the U.S., Europeans, and other powers. Regional forces such as those of NATO, ECOWAS, or the EU, or mandated by the African Union or Organization of American States may also effectively intervene if given strong support by major military powers.

Denial, the final stage of genocide is best overcome by public trials and truth commissions, followed by years of education about the facts of the genocide, particularly for the children of the group or nation that committed the crime. The black hole of forgetting is the negative force that results in future genocides. When Adolf Hitler was asked if his planned invasion of Poland was a violation of international law, he scoffed, "Who ever heard of the extermination of the Armenians?" Impunity—literally getting away with murder—is the weakest link in the chains that restrain genocide. In Rwanda, Hutus were never arrested and brought to trial for massacres of Tutsis that began years before the April, 1994 genocide. In Burundi, Tutsi youth gangs have never been tried for killing Hutus. Burundi judges are nearly all Tutsis, as are the army and police. They seldom, if ever, convict their own.

Social order abhors a legal vacuum. When courts do not dispense justice the victims have no recourse but revenge. In societies with histories of ethnic violence, the cycle of killing will eventually spiral downward into the vortex of genocide. In such societies, the international community should fill the legal vacuum by creating tribunals to prosecute and try genocide. That has been done for the former Yugoslavia and Rwanda and will soon be done for Cambodia. We finally have the International Criminal Court (ICC) that will have world-wide jurisdiction to try genocide, war crimes, and crimes against humanity. But the ICC still has no jurisdiction over genocide committed in nations that contain over half of the world's population because their nations have not become parties to the Rome Treaty of the ICC. The Court must be supported by effective institutions to arrest and imprison those indicted and convicted by the Court. Only such a permanent court will provide a deterrent to those planning future genocides.

The strongest antidote to genocide is justice.

Source: Gregory H. Stanton. Available online at www.genocidewatch.org/images/8StagesBriefingpaper.pdf. Used by permission.

6. Geneva Convention Relating to Prisoners of War (1929)

The following document details the treatment of prisoners of war as outlined at the 1929 Geneva Convention in Switzerland. The Geneva Conventions, referring to a total of four treaties and three protocols, are an important example of international diplomacy, outlining humane treatment of civilians, and prisoners of war as well as the sick and wounded. Though amended in 1949, the Convention relative to the Treatment of Prisoners of War holds the detaining power responsible for the safety, health, and hygiene of captured soldiers. It also allows soldiers to maintain many of their possessions as well as to contact their family, and if need be, their government. Following the conclusion of a conflict, arrangements for the return of POWs are to be made.

Recognizing that, in the extreme event of a war, it will be the duty of every Power, to mitigate as far as possible, the inevitable rigours thereof and to alleviate the condition of prisoners of war;

Being desirous of developing the principles which have inspired the international conventions of The Hague, in particular the Convention concerning the Laws and Customs of War and the Regulations thereunto annexed,

Have resolved to conclude a Convention for that purpose and have appointed as their Plenipotentiaries:

(Here follow the names of Plenipotentiaries)

Who, having communicated their full powers, found in good and due form, have agreed is follows.

Article 1. The present Convention shall apply without prejudice to the stipulations of Part VII:

(1) To all persons referred to in Articles 1, 2, and 3 of the Regulations annexed to the Hague Convention
    (IV) of 18 October 1907, concerning the Laws and Customs of War on Land, who are captured by the enemy.

(2) To all persons belonging to the armed forces of belligerents who are captured by the enemy in the course of operations of maritime or aerial war, subject to such exceptions (derogations) as the conditions of such capture render inevitable. Nevertheless these exceptions shall not infringe the fundamental principles of the present Convention; they shall cease from the moment when the captured persons shall have reached a prisoners of war camp.

Art. 2. Prisoners of war are in the power of the hostile Government, but not of the individuals or formation which captured them.

They shall at all times be humanely treated and protected, particularly against acts of violence, from insults and from public curiosity.

Measures of reprisal against them are forbidden.

Art. 3. Prisoners of war are entitled to respect for their persons and honour. Women shall be treated with all consideration due to their sex.

Prisoners retain their full civil capacity.

Art. 4. The detaining Power is required to provide for the maintenance of prisoners of war in its charge.

Differences of treatment between prisoners are permissible only if such differences are based on the military rank, the state of physical or mental health, the professional abilities, or the sex of those who benefit from them.

Art. 5. Every prisoner of war is required to declare, if he is interrogated on the subject, his true names and rank, or his regimental number.

If he infringes this rule, he exposes himself to a restriction of the privileges accorded to prisoners of his category.

No pressure shall be exercised on prisoners to obtain information regarding the situation in their armed forces or their country. Prisoners who refuse to reply may not be threatened, insulted, or exposed to unpleasantness or disadvantages of any kind whatsoever.

If, by reason of his physical or mental condition, a prisoner is incapable of stating his identity, he shall be handed over to the Medical Service.

Art. 6. All personal effects and articles in personal use—except arms, horses, military equipment and military papers—shall remain in the possession of prisoners of war, as well as their metal helmets and gas-masks.

Sums of money carried by prisoners may only be taken from them on the order of an officer and after the amount has been recorded. A receipt shall be given for them. Sums thus impounded shall be placed to the account of each prisoner.

Their identity tokens, badges of rank, decorations and articles of value may not be taken from prisoners.

Art. 7. As soon as possible after their capture, prisoners of war shall be evacuated to depots sufficiently removed from the fighting zone for them to be out of danger.

Only prisoners who, by reason of their wounds or maladies, would run greater risks by being evacuated than by remaining may be kept temporarily in a dangerous zone.

Prisoners shall not be unnecessarily exposed to danger while awaiting evacuation from a fighting zone.

The evacuation of prisoners on foot shall in normal circumstances be effected by stages of not more than 20 kilometres per day, unless the necessity for reaching water and food depôts requires longer stages.

Art. 8. Belligerents are required to notify each other of all captures of prisoners as soon as possible, through the intermediary of the Information Bureaux organised in accordance with Article 77. They are likewise required to inform each other of the official addresses to which letter from the prisoners' families may be addressed to the prisoners of war.

As soon as possible, every prisoner shall be enabled to correspond personally with his family, in accordance with the conditions prescribed in Article 36 and the following Articles.

As regards prisoners captured at sea, the provisions of the present article shall be observed as soon as possible after arrival in port.

Art. 9. Prisoners of war may be interned in a town, fortress or other place, and may be required not to go beyond certain fixed limits. They may also be interned in fenced camps; they shall not be confined or imprisoned except as a measure indispensable for safety or health, and only so long as circumstances exist which necessitate such a measure.

Prisoners captured in districts which are unhealthy or whose climate is deleterious to persons coming from temperate climates shall be removed as soon as possible to a more favourable climate.

Belligerents shall as far as possible avoid bringing together in the same camp prisoners of different races or nationalities.

No prisoner may at any time be sent to an area where he would be exposed to the fire of the fighting zone, or be employed to render by his presence certain points or areas immune from bombardment.

Art. 10. Prisoners of war shall be lodged in buildings or huts which afford all possible safeguards as regards hygiene and salubrity.

The premises must be entirely free from damp, and adequately heated and lighted. All precautions shall be taken against the danger of fire.

As regards dormitories, their total area, minimum cubic air space, fittings and bedding material, the conditions shall be the same as for the depot troops of the detaining Power.

Art. 11. The food ration of prisoners of war shall be equivalent in quantity and quality to that of the depot troops.

Prisoners shall also be afforded the means of preparing for themselves such additional articles of food as they may possess.

Sufficient drinking water shall be supplied to them. The use of tobacco shall be authorized. Prisoners may be employed in the kitchens.

All collective disciplinary measures affecting food are prohibited.

Art. 12. Clothing, underwear and footwear shall be supplied to prisoners of war by the detaining Power. The regular replacement and repair of such articles shall be assured. Workers shall also receive working kit wherever the nature of the work requires it.

In all camps, canteens shall be installed at which prisoners shall be able to procure, at the local market price, food commodities and ordinary articles.

The profits accruing to the administrations of the camps from the canteens shall be utilised for the benefit of the prisoners.

Art. 13. Belligerents shall be required to take all necessary hygienic measures to ensure the cleanliness and salubrity of camps and to prevent epidemics.

Prisoners of war shall have for their use, day and night, conveniences which conform to the rules of hygiene and are maintained in a constant state of cleanliness.

In addition and without prejudice to the provision as far as possible of baths and shower-baths in the camps, the prisoners shall be provided with a sufficient quantity of water for their bodily cleanliness.

They shall have facilities for engaging in physical exercises and obtaining the benefit of being out of doors.

Art. 14. Each camp shall possess an infirmary, where prisoners of war shall receive attention of any kind of which they may be in need. If necessary, isolation establishments shall be reserved for patients suffering from infectious and contagious diseases.

The expenses of treatment, including those of temporary remedial apparatus, shall be borne by the detaining Power.

Belligerents shall be required to issue, on demand, to any prisoner treated, and official statement indicating the nature and duration of his illness and of the treatment received.

It shall be permissible for belligerents mutually to authorize each other, by means of special agreements, to retain in the camps doctors and medical orderlies for the purpose of caring for their prisoner compatriots.

Prisoners who have contracted a serious malady, or whose condition necessitates important surgical treatment, shall be admitted, at the expense of the detaining Power, to any military or civil institution qualified to treat them.

Art. 15. Medical inspections of prisoners of war shall be arranged at least once a month. Their object shall be the supervision of the general state of health and cleanliness, and the detection of infectious and contagious diseases., particularly tuberculosis and venereal complaints.

Art. 16. Prisoners of war shall be permitted complete freedom in the performance of their religious duties, including attendance at the services of their faith, on the sole condition that they comply with the routine and police regulations prescribed by the military authorities.

Ministers of religion, who are prisoners of war, whatever may be their denomination, shall be allowed freely to minister to their co-religionists.

Art. 17. belligerents shall encourage as much as possible the organization of intellectual and sporting pursuits by the prisoners of war.

Art. 18. Each prisoners of war camp shall be placed under the authority of a responsible officer.

In addition to external marks of respect required by the regulations in force in their own armed forces with regard to their nationals, prisoners of war shall be required to salute all officers of the detaining Power.

Officer prisoners of war shall be required to salute only officers of that Power who are their superiors or equals in rank.

Art. 19. The wearing of badges of rank and decorations shall be permitted.

Art. 20. Regulations, orders, announcements and publications of any kind shall be communicated to prisoners of war in a language which they understand. The same principle shall be applied to questions.

Art. 21. At the commencement of hostilities, belligerents shall be required reciprocally to inform each other of the titles and ranks in use in their respective armed forces, with the view of ensuring equality of treatment between the corresponding ranks of officers and persons of equivalent status.

Officers and persons of equivalent status who are prisoners of war shall be treated with due regard to their rank and age.

Art. 22. In order to ensure the service of officers' camps, soldier prisoners of war of the same armed forces, and as far as possible speaking the same language, shall be detached for service therein in sufficient number, having regard to the rank of the officers and persons of equivalent status.

Officers and persons of equivalent status shall procure their food and clothing from the pay to be paid to them by the detaining Power. The management of a mess by officers themselves shall be facilitated in every way.

Art. 23. Subject to any special arrangements made between the belligerent Powers, and particularly those contemplated in Article 24, officers and persons of equivalent status who are prisoners of war shall receive from the detaining Power the same pay as officers of corresponding rank in the armed forces of that Power, provided, however, that such pay does not exceed that to which they are entitled in the armed forces of the country in whose service they have been. This pay shall be paid to them in full, once a month if possible, and no deduction therefrom shall be made for expenditure devolving upon the detaining Power, even if such expenditure is incurred on their behalf.

An agreement between the belligerents shall prescribe the rate of exchange applicable to this payment; in default of such agreement, the rate of exchange adopted shall be that in force at the moment of the commencement of hostilities.

All advances made to prisoners of war by way of pay shall be reimbursed, at the end of hostilities, by the Power in whose service they were.

Art. 24. At the commencement of hostilities, belligerents shall determine by common accord the maximum amount of cash which prisoners of war of various ranks and categories shall be permitted to retain in their possession. Any excess withdrawn or withheld from a prisoner, and any deposit of money effected by him, shall be carried to his account, and may not be converted into another currency without his consent.

The credit balances of their accounts shall be paid to the prisoners of war at the end of their captivity.

During the continuance of the latter, facilities shall be accorded to them for the transfer of these amounts, wholly or in part, to banks or private individuals in their country of origin.

Art. 25. Unless the course of military operations demands it, sick and wounded prisoners of war shall not be transferred if their recovery might be prejudiced by the journey.

Art. 26. In the event of transfer, prisoners of war shall be officially informed in advance of their new destination; they shall be authorized to take with them their personal effects, their correspondence and parcels which have arrived for them.

All necessary arrangements shall be made so that correspondence and parcels addressed to their former camp shall be sent on to them without delay.

The sums credited to the account of transferred prisoners shall be transmitted to the competent authority of their new place of residence.

Expenses incurred by the transfers shall be borne by the detaining Power.

Art. 27. Belligerents may employ as workmen prisoners of war who are physically fit, other than officers and persons of equivalent statue, according to their rink and their ability.

Nevertheless, if officers or persons of equivalent status ask for suitable work, this shall be found for them as far as possible.

Non-commissioned officers who are prisoners of war may be compelled to undertake only supervisory work, unless they expressly request remunerative occupation.

During the whole period of captivity, belligerents are required to admit prisoners of war who are victims of accidents at work to the benefit of provisions applicable to workmen of the same category under the legislation of the detaining Power. As regards prisoners of war to whom these legal provisions could not be applied by reason of the legislation of that Power, the latter undertakes to recommend to its legislative body all proper measures for the equitable compensation of the victims.

Art. 28. The detaining Power shall assume entire responsibility for the maintenance, care, treatment and the payment of the wages of prisoners of war working for private individuals.

Art. 29. No prisoner of war may be employed on work for which he is physically unsuited.

Art. 30. The duration of the daily work of prisoners of war, including the time of the journey to and from work, shall not be excessive and shall in no case exceed that permitted for civil workers of the locality employed on the same work. Each prisoner shall be allowed a rest of twenty-four consecutive hours each week, preferably on Sunday.

Art. 31. Work done by prisoners of war shall have no direct connection with the operations of the war. In particular, it is forbidden to employ prisoners in the manufacture or transport of arms or munitions of any kind, or on the transport of material destined for combatant units.

In the event of violation of the provisions of the preceding paragraph, prisoners are at liberty, after performing or commencing to perform the order, to have their complaints presented through the intermediary of the prisoners' representatives whose functions are described in Articles 43 and 44, or, in the absence of a prisoners' representative, through the intermediary of the representatives of the protecting Power.

Art. 32. It is forbidden to employ prisoners of war on unhealthy or dangerous work. Conditions of work shall not be rendered more arduous by disciplinary measures.

Art. 33. Conditions governing labour detachments shall be similar to those of prisoners-of-war camps, particularly as concerns hygienic conditions, food, care in case of accidents or sickness, correspondence, and the reception of parcels.

Every labour detachment shall be attached to a prisoners' camp. The commander of this camp shall be responsible for the observance in the labour detachment of the provisions of the present Convention.

Art. 34. Prisoners of war shall not receive pay for work in connection with the administration, internal arrangement and maintenance of camps.

Prisoners employed on other work shall be entitled to a rate of pay, to be fixed by agreements between the belligerents.

These agreements shall also specify the portion which may be retained by the camp administration, the amount which shall belong to the prisoner of war and the manner in which this amount shall be placed at his disposal during the period of his captivity.

Pending the conclusion of the said agreements, remuneration of the work of prisoners shall be fixed according to the following standards:

(a) Work done for the State shall be paid for according to the rates in force for soldiers of the national forces doing the same work, or, if no such rates exist, according to a tariff corresponding to the work executed.

(b) When the work is done for other public administrations or for private individuals, the conditions shall be settled in agreement with the military authorities.

The pay which remains to the credit of a prisoner shall be remitted to him on the termination of his captivity. In case of death, it shall be remitted through the diplomatic channel to the heirs of the deceased.

Art. 35. On the commencement of hostilities, belligerents shall publish the measures prescribed for the execution of the provisions of the present section.

Art. 36. Each of the belligerents shall fix periodically the number of letters and postcards which prisoners of war of different categories shall be permitted to send per month, and shall notify that number to the other belligerent. These letters and cards shall be sent by post by the shortest route. They may not be delayed or withheld for disciplinary motives.

Not later than one week after his arrival in camp, and similarly in case of sickness, each prisoner shall be enabled to send a postcard to his family informing them of his capture and the state of his health. The said postcards shall be forwarded as quickly as possible and shall not be delayed in any manner.

As a general rule, the correspondence of prisoners shall be written in their native language. Belligerents may authorize correspondence in other languages.

Art. 37. Prisoners of war shall be authorized to receive individually postal parcels containing foodstuffs and other articles intended for consumption or clothing. The parcels shall be delivered to the addressees and a receipt given.

Art. 38. Letters and remittances of money or valuables, as well as postal parcels addressed to prisoners of war, or despatched by them, either directly or through the intermediary of the information bureaux mentioned in Article, shall be exempt from all postal charges in the countries of origin and destination and in the countries through which they pass.

Presents and relief in kind intended for prisoners of war shall also be exempt from all import or other duties, as well as any charges for carriage on railways operated by the State.

Prisoners may, in cases of recognized urgency, be authorized to send telegrams on payment of the usual charges.

Art. 39. Prisoners of war shall be permitted to receive individually consignments of books which may be subject to censorship.

Representatives of the protecting Powers and of duly recognized and authorized relief societies may send works and collections of books to the libraries of prisoners, camps. The transmission of such consignments to libraries may not be delayed under pretext of difficulties of censorship.

Art. 40. The censoring of correspondence shall be accomplished as quickly as possible. The examination of postal parcels shall, moreover, be effected under such conditions as will ensure the preservation of any foodstuffs which they may contain, and, if possible, be done in the presence of the addressee or of a representative duly recognized by him.

Any prohibition of correspondence ordered by the belligerents, for military or political reasons, shall only be of a temporary character and shall also be for as brief a time as possible.

Art. 41. Belligerents shall accord all facilities for the transmission of documents destined for prisoners of war or signed by them, in particular powers of attorney and wills.

They shall take the necessary measures to secure, in case of need, the legalisation of signatures of prisoners.

Art. 42. Prisoners of war shall have the right to bring to the notice of the military authorities, in whose hands they are, their petitions concerning the conditions of captivity to which they are subjected.

They shall also have the right to communicate with the representatives of the protecting Powers in order to draw their attention to the points on which they have complaints to make with regard to the conditions of captivity.

Such petitions and complaints shall be transmitted immediately.

Even though they are found to be groundless, they shall not give rise to any punishment.

Art. 43. In any locality where there may be prisoners of war, they shall be authorized to appoint representatives to represent them before the military authorities and the protecting Powers.

Such appointments shall be subject to the approval of the military authorities.

The prisoners' representatives shall be charged with the reception and distribution of collective consignments. Similarly, in the event of the prisoners deciding to organize amongst themselves a system of mutual aid, such organization shall be one of the functions of the prisoners" representatives. On the other hand, the latter may offer their services to prisoners to facilitate their relations with the relief societies mentioned in Article 78.

In camps of officers and persons of equivalent status the senior officer prisoner of the highest rank shall be recognized as intermediary between the camp authorities and the officers and similar persons who are prisoners, for this purpose he shall have the power to appoint an officer prisoner to assist him as interpreter in the course of conferences with the authorities of the camp.

Art. 44. When the prisoners representatives are employed as workmen, their work as representatives of the prisoners of war shall be reckoned in the compulsory period of labour.

All facilities shall be accorded to the prisoners' representatives for their correspondence with the military authorities and the protecting Power. Such correspondence shall not be subject to any limitation.

No prisoners' representative may be transferred without his having been allowed the time necessary to acquaint his successors with the current business.

Art. 45. Prisoners of war shall be subject to the laws, regulations and orders in force in the armed forces of the detaining Power.

Any act of insubordination shall render them liable to the measures prescribed by such laws, regulations, and orders, except as otherwise provided in this Chapter.

Art. 46. Prisoners of war shall not be subjected by the military authorities or the tribunals of the detaining Power to penalties other than those which are prescribed for similar acts by members of the national forces.

Officers, non-commissioned officers or private soldiers, prisoners of war, undergoing disciplinary punishment shall not be subjected to treatment less favourable than that prescribed, as regards the same punishment, for similar ranks in the armed forces of the detaining Power.

All forms of corporal punishment, confinement in premises not lighted by daylight and, in general, all forms of cruelty whatsoever are prohibited.

Collective penalties for individual acts are also prohibited.

Art. 47. A statement of the facts in cases of acts constituting a breach of discipline, and particularly an attempt to escape, shall be drawn up in writing without delay. The period during which prisoners of war of whatever rank are detained in custody (pending the investigation of such offences) shall be reduced to a strict minimum.

The judicial proceedings against a prisoner of war shall be conducted as quickly as circumstances will allow. The period during which prisoners shall be detained in custody shall be as short as possible.

In all cases the period during which a prisoner is under arrest (awaiting punishment or trial) shall be deducted from the sentence, whether disciplinary or judicial, provided such deduction is permitted in the case of members of the national forces.

Art. 48. After undergoing the judicial or disciplinary punishment which has been inflicted on them, prisoners of war shall not be treated differently from other prisoners.

Nevertheless, prisoners who have been punished as the result of an attempt to escape may be subjected to a special régime of surveillance, but this shall not involve the suppression of any of the safeguards accorded to prisoners by the present Convention.

Art. 49. No prisoner of war may be deprived of his rank by the detaining Power.

Prisoners on whom disciplinary punishment is inflicted shall not be deprived of the privileges attaching to their rank. In particular, officers and persons of equivalent status who suffer penalties entailing deprivation of liberty shall not be placed in the same premises as non-commissioned officers or private soldiers undergoing punishment.

Art. 50. Escaped prisoners of war who are re-captured before they have been able to rejoin their own armed forces or to leave the territory occupied by the armed forces which captured them shall be liable only to disciplinary punishment.

Prisoners who, after succeeding in rejoining their armed forces or in leaving the territory occupied by the armed forces which captured them, are again taken prisoner shall not be liable to any punishment for their previous escape.

Art. 51. Attempted escape, even if it is nut a first offence, shall not be considered as an aggravation of the offence in the event of the prisoner of war being brought before the courts for crimes or offences against persons or property committed in the course of such attempt.

After an attempted or successful escape, the comrades of the escaped person who aided the escape shall incur only disciplinary punishment therefor.

Art. 52. Belligerents shall ensure that the competent authorities exercize the greatest leniency in considering the question whether an offence committed by a prisoner of war should be punished by disciplinary or by judicial measures.

This provision shall be observed in particular in appraising facts in connexion with escape or attempted escape.

A prisoner shall not be punished more than once for the same act or on the same charge.

Art. 53. No prisoner who has been awarded any disciplinary punishment for an offence and who fulfils the conditions laid down for repatriation shall be retained on the ground that he has not undergone his punishment.

Prisoners qualified for repatriation against whom any prosecution for a criminal offence has been brought may be excluded from repatriation until the termination of the proceedings and until fulfilment of their sentence, if any; prisoners already serving a sentence of imprisonment may be retained until the expiry of the sentence.

Belligerents shall communicate to each other lists of those who cannot be repatriated for the reasons indicated in the preceding paragraph.

Art. 54. Imprisonment is the most severe disciplinary punishment which may be inflicted on a prisoner of war.

The duration of any single punishment shall not exceed thirty days.

This maximum of thirty days shall, moreover, not be exceeded in the event of there being several acts for which the prisoner is answerable to discipline at the time when his case is disposed of, whether such acts are connected or not.

Where, during the course or after the termination of a period of imprisonment, a prisoner is sentenced to a fresh disciplinary penalty, a period of at least three days shall intervene between each of the periods of imprisonment, if one of such periods is of ten days or over.

Art. 55. Subject to the provisions of the last paragraph of Article 11 javascript: open Link ('http://www.icrcorg/—c125672200286a21.nsf/9ac284404d38ed2bc1256311002afd89/8e9c103689020e3bc12563cd00518ded&Name=CN%3DGV ALNBD1%2FO%3DICRC');, the restrictions in regard to food permitted in the armed forces of the detaining Power may be applied, as an additional penalty, to prisoners of war undergoing disciplinary punishment.

Such restrictions shall, however, only be ordered if the state of the prisoner's health permits.

Art. 56. In no case shall prisoners of war be transferred to penitentiary establishments (prisoners, penitentiaries, convict establishments, etc.) in order to undergo disciplinary sentence there.

Establishments in which disciplinary sentences are undergone shall conform to the requirements of hygiene.

Facilities shall be afforded to prisoners undergoing sentence to keep themselves in a state of cleanliness.

Every day, such prisoners shall have facilities for taking exercise or for remaining out of doors for at least two hours.

Art. 57. Prisoners of war undergoing disciplinary punishment shall be permitted to read and write and to send and receive letters.

On the other hand, it shall be permissible not to deliver parcels and remittances of money to the addressees until the expiration of the sentence. If the undelivered parcels contain perishable foodstuffs, these shall be handed over to the infirmary or to the camp kitchen.

Art. 58. Prisoners of war undergoing disciplinary punishment shall be permitted, on their request, to present themselves for daily medical inspection. They shall receive such attention as the medical officers may consider necessary, and, if need be, shall be evacuated to the camp infirmary or to hospital.

Art. 59. Without prejudice to the competency of the courts and the superior military authorities, disciplinary sentences may only be awarded by an officer vested with disciplinary powers in his capacity as commander of the camp or detachment, or by the responsible officer acting as his substitute.

Art. 60. At the commencement of a judicial hearing against a prisoner of war, the detaining Power shall notify the representative of the protecting Power as soon as possible, and in any case before the date fixed for the opening of the hearing.

The said notification shall contain the following particulars:

(a) Civil status and rank of the prisoner.
(b) Place of residence or detention.
(c) Statement of the charge or charges, and of the legal provisions applicable.

If it is not possible in this notification to indicate particulars of the court which will try the case, the date of the opening of the hearing and the place where it will take place, these particulars shall be furnished to the representative of the protecting Power at a later date, but as soon as possible and in any case at least three weeks before the opening of the hearing.

Art. 61. No prisoner of war shall be sentenced without being given the opportunity to defend himself.

No prisoner shall be compelled to admit that he is guilty of the offence of which he is accused.

Art. 62. The prisoner of war shall have the right to be assisted by a qualified. advocate of his own choice and, if necessary, to have recourse to the offices of a competent interpreter. He shall be informed of his right by the detaining Power in good time before the hearing.

Failing a choice on the part of the prisoner, the protecting Power may procure an advocate for him. The detaining Power shall, on the request of the protecting Power, furnish to the latter a list of persons qualified to conduct the defence.

The representatives of the protecting Power shall have the right to attend the hearing of the case.

The only exception to this rule is where the hearing has to be kept secret in the interests of the safety of the State. The detaining Power would then notify the protecting Power accordingly.

Art. 63. A sentence shall only be pronounced on a prisoner of war by the same tribunals and in accordance with the same procedure as in the case of persons belonging to the armed forces of the detaining Power.

Art. 64. Every prisoner of war shall have the right of appeal against any sentence against him in the same manner as persons belonging to the armed forces of the detaining Power.

Art. 65. Sentences pronounced against prisoners of war shall be communicated immediately to the protecting Power.

Art. 66. If sentence of death is passed on a prisoner of war, a communication setting forth in detail the nature and the circumstances of the offence shall be addressed as soon as possible to the representative of the protecting Power for transmission to the Power in whose armed forces the prisoner served.

The sentence shall not be carried out before the expiration of a period of at least three months from the date of the receipt of this communication by the protecting Power.

Art. 67. No prisoner of war may be deprived of the benefit of the provisions of Article 42 of the present Convention as the result of a judgment or otherwise.

Art. 68. Belligerents shall be required to send back to their own country, without regard to rank or numbers, after rendering them in a fit condition for transport, prisoners of war who are seriously ill or seriously wounded.

Agreements between the belligerents shall therefore determine, as soon as possible, the forms of disablement or sickness requiring direct repatriation and cases which may necessitate accommodation in a neutral country. Pending the conclusion of such agreements, the belligerents may refer to the model draft agreement annexed to the present Convention.

Art. 69. On the opening of hostilities, belligerents shall come to an understanding as to the appointment of mixed medical commissions. These commissions shall consist of three members, two of whom shall belong to a neutral country and one appointed by the detaining Power; one of the medical officers of the neutral country shall preside. These mixed medical commissions shall proceed to the examination of sick or wounded prisoners and shall make all appropriate decisions with regard to them.

The decisions of these commissions shall be decided by majority and shall be carried into effect as soon as possible.

Art. 70. In addition to those prisoners of war selected by the medical officer of the camp, the following shall be inspected by the mixed medical Commission mentioned in Article 69, with a view to their direct repatriation or accommodation in a neutral country:

(a) Prisoners who make a direct request to that effect to the medical officer of the camp;
(b) Prisoners presented by the prisoners' representatives mentioned in Article 43, the latter acting on their own initiative or on the request of the prisoners themselves;
(c) Prisoners nominated by the Power in whose armed forces they served or by a relief society duly recognized and authorized by that Power.

Art. 71. Prisoners of war who meet with accidents at work, unless the injury is self-inflicted, shall have the benefit of the same provisions as regards repatriation or accommodation in a neutral country.

Art. 72. During the continuance of hostilities, and for humanitarian reasons, belligerents may conclude agreements with a view to the direct repatriation or accommodation in a neutral country of prisoners of war in good health who have been in captivity for a long time.

Art. 73. The expenses of repatriation or transport to a neutral country of prisoners of war shall be borne, as from the frontier of the detaining Power, by the Power in whose armed forces such prisoners served.

Art. 74. No repatriated person shall be employed on active military service.

Art. 75. When belligerents conclude an armistice convention, they shall normally cause to be included therein provisions concerning the repatriation of prisoners of war. If it has not been possible to insert in that convention such stipulations, the belligerents shall, nevertheless, enter into communication with each other on the question as soon as possible. In any case, the repatriation of prisoners shall be effected as soon as possible after the conclusion of peace.

Prisoners of war who are subject to criminal proceedings for a crime or offence at common law may, however, be detained until the end of the proceedings, and, if need be, until the expiration of the sentence. The same applies to prisoners convicted for a crime or offence at common law.

By agreement between the belligerents, commissions may be instituted for the purpose of searching for scattered prisoners and ensuring their repatriation.

Art. 76. The wills of prisoners of war shall be received and drawn up under the same conditions as for soldiers of the national armed forces.

The same rules shall be followed as regards the documents relative to the certification of the death.

The belligerents shall ensure that prisoners of war who have died in captivity are honourably buried, and that the graves bear the necessary indications and are treated with respect and suitably maintained.

Art. 77. At the commencement of hostilities, each of the belligerent Powers and the neutral Powers who have belligerents in their care, shall institute an official bureau to give information about the prisoners of war in their territory.

Each of the belligerent Powers shall inform its Information Bureau as soon as possible of all captures of prisoners effected by its armed forces, furnishing them with all particulars of identity at its disposal to enable the families concerned to be quickly notified, and stating the official addresses to which families may write to the prisoners.

The Information Bureau shall transmit all such information immediately to the Powers concerned, on the one hand through the intermediary of the protecting Powers, and on the other through the Central Agency contemplated in Article 79.

The Information Bureau, being charged with replying to all enquiries relative to prisoners of war, shall receive from the various services concerned all particulars respecting internments and transfers, releases on parole, repatriations, escapes, stays in hospitals, and deaths, together with all other particulars necessary for establishing and keeping up to date an individual record for each prisoner of war.

The Bureau shall note in this record, as far as possible, and subject to the provisions of Article 5, the regimental number, names and surnames, date and place of birth, rank and unit of the prisoner, the surname of the father and name of the mother, the address of the person to be notified in case of accident, wounds, dates and places of capture, of internment, of wounds, of death, together with all other important particulars.

Weekly lists containing all additional particulars capable of facilitating the identification of each prisoner shall be transmitted to the interested Powers.

The individual record of a prisoner of war shall be sent after the conclusion of peace to the Power in whose service he was.

The Information Bureau shall also be required to collect all personal effects, valuables, correspondence, pay-books, identity tokens, etc., which have been left by prisoners of war who have been repatriated or released on parole, or who have escaped or died, and to transmit them to the countries concerned.

Art. 78. Societies for the relief of prisoners of war, regularly constituted in accordance with the laws of their country, and having for their object to serve as intermediaries for charitable purposes, shall receive from the belligerents, for themselves and their duly accredited agents, all facilities for the efficacious performance of their humane task within the limits imposed by military exigencies. Representatives of these societies shall be permitted to distribute relief in the camps and at the halting places of repatriated prisoners under a personal permit issued by the military authority, and on giving an undertaking in writing to comply with all routine and police orders which the said authority shall prescribe.

Art. 79. A Central Agency of information regarding prisoners of war shall be established in a neutral country. The International Red Cross Committee shall, if they consider it necessary, propose to the Powers concerned the organization of such an agency.

This agency shall be charged with the duty of collecting all information regarding prisoners which they may be able to obtain through official or private channels, and the agency shall transmit the information as rapidly as possible to the prisoners' own country or the Power in whose service they have been.

These provisions shall not be interpreted as restricting the humanitarian work of the International Red Cross Committee.

Art. 80. Information Bureaux shall enjoy exemption from fees on postal matter as well as all the exemptions prescribed in Article 38

Art. 81. Persons who follow the armed forces without directly belonging thereto, such as correspondents, newspaper reporters, sutlers, or contractors, who fall into the hands of the enemy, and whom the latter think fit to detain, shall be entitled to be treated as prisoners of war, provided they are in possession of an authorization from the military authorities of the armed forces which they were following.

Art. 82. The provisions of the present Convention shall be respected by the High Contracting Parties in all circumstances.

In time of war if one of the belligerents is not a party to the Convention, its provisions shall, nevertheless, remain binding as between the belligerents who are parties thereto.

Art. 83. The High Contracting Parties reserve to themselves the right to conclude special conventions on all questions relating to prisoners of war concerning which they may consider it desirable to make special provisions.

Prisoners of war shall continue to enjoy the benefits of these agreements until their repatriation has been effected, subject to any provisions expressly to the contrary contained in the above-mentioned agreements or in subsequent agreements, and subject to any more favourable measures by one or the other of the belligerent Powers concerning the prisoners detained by that Power.

In order to ensure the application, on both sides, of the provisions of the present Convention, and to facilitate the conclusion of the special conventions mentioned above, the belligerents may, at the commencement of hostilities, authorize meetings of representatives of the respective authorities charged with the administration of prisoners of war.

Art. 84. The text of the present Convention and of the special conventions mentioned in the preceding Article shall be posted, whenever possible, in the native language of the prisoners of war, in places where it may be consulted by all the prisoners.

The text of these conventions shall be communicated, on their request, to prisoners who are unable to inform themselves of the text posted.

Art. 85. The High Contracting Parties shall communicate to each other, through the intermediary of the Swiss Federal Council, the official translations of the present Convention, together with such laws and regulations as they may adopt to ensure the application of the present Convention.

Art. 86. The High Contracting Parties recognize that a guarantee of the regular application of the present Convention will be found in the possibility of collaboration between the protecting Powers charged with the protection of the interests of the belligerents; in this connexion, the protecting Powers may, apart from their diplomatic personnel, appoint delegates from among their own nationals or the nationals of other neutral Powers. The appointment of these delegates shall be subject to the approval of the belligerent with whom they are to carry out their mission.

The representatives of the protecting Power or their recognized delegates shall be authorized to proceed to any place, without exception, where prisoners of war are interned. They shall have access to all premises occupied by prisoners and may hold conversation with prisoners, as a general rule without witnesses, either personally or through the intermediary of interpreters.

Belligerents shall facilitate as much as possible the task of the representatives or recognized delegates of the protecting Power. The military authorities shall be informed of their visits.

Belligerents may mutually agree to allow persons of the prisoners own nationality to participate in the tours of inspection.

Art. 87. In the event of dispute between the belligerents regarding the application of the provisions of the present Convention, the protecting Powers shall, as far as possible, lend their good offices with the object of settling the dispute.

To this end, each of the protecting Powers may, for instance, propose to the belligerents concerned that a conference of representatives of the latter should be held, on suitably chosen neutral territory. The belligerents shall be required to give effect to proposals made to them with this object. The protecting Power may, if necessary, submit fur the approval of the Powers in dispute the name of a person belonging to a neutral Power or nominated by the International Red Cross Committee, who shall be invited to take part in this conference.

Art. 88. The foregoing provisions do not constitute any obstacle to the humanitarian work which the International Red Cross Committee may perform for the protection of prisoners of war with the consent of the belligerents concerned.

Art. 89. In the relations between the Powers who are bound either by The Hague Convention concerning the Laws and Customs of War on Land of 29 July 1899, or that of 18 October 1907, and are parties to the present Convention, the latter shall be complementary to Chapter 2 of the Regulations annexed to the above-mentioned Conventions of The Hague.

Art. 90. The present Convention, which shall bear this day's date, may be signed up to 1 February 1930, on behalf of any of the countries represented at the Conference which opened at Geneva on 1 July 1929.

Art. 91. The present Convention shall be ratified as soon as possible.

The ratifications shall be deposited at Berne.

In respect of the deposit of each instrument of ratification, a 'procès-verbal' shall be drawn up, and copy thereof, certified correct, shall be sent by the Swiss Federal Council to the Governments of all the countries on whose behalf the Convention has been signed or whose accession has been notified.

Art. 92. The present Convention shall enter into force six months after at least two instruments of ratification have been deposited.

Thereafter it shall enter into force for each High Contracting Party six months after the deposit of its instrument of ratification.

Art. 93. As from the date of its entry into force, the present Convention shall be open to accession notified in respect of any country on whose behalf this Convention has not been signed.

Art. 94. Accessions shall be notified in writing to the Swiss Federal Council and shall take Effect six months after the date on which they have been received.

The Swiss Federal Council shall notify the accessions to the Governments of all the countries on whose behalf the Convention has been signed or whose accession has been notified.

Art. 95. A state of war shall give immediate effect to ratifications deposited-and to accessions notified by the belligerent Powers before or after the commencement of hostilities. The communication of ratifications or accessions received from Powers in a state of war shall be effected by the Swiss Federal Council by the quickest method.

Art. 96. Each of the High Contracting Parties shall have the right to denounce the present Convention. The denunciation shall only take effect one year after notification thereof has been made in writing to the Swiss Federal Council. The latter shall communicate this notification to the Governments of ill the High Contracting Parties.

The denunciation shall only be valid in respect of the High Contracting Party which has made notification thereof.

Such denunciation shall, moreover, not take effect during a war in which the denouncing Power is involved. In this case, the present Convention shall continue binding, beyond the period of one year, until the conclusion of peace and, in any case, until operations of repatriation shall have terminated.

Art. 97. A copy of the present Convention, certified to be correct, shall be deposited by the Swiss Federal Council in the archives of the League of Nations. Similarly, ratifications, accessions and denunciations notified to the Swiss Federal Council shall be communicated by them to the League of Nations.

In faith whereof the above-mentioned Plenipotentiaries have signed the present Convention.

Done at Geneva the twenty-seventh July, one thousand nine hundred and twenty-nine, in a single copy, which shall remain deposited in the archives of the Swiss Confederation, and of which copies, certified correct, shall be transmitted to the Governments of all the countries invited to the Conference.

Annex

I. Guiding Principles for Direct Repatriation or Accommodation in a Neutral Country

A. 'Guiding Principles for Direct Repatriation'

The following shall be repatriated directly:

1. Sick and wounded whose recovery within one year is not probable according to medical prognosis, whose condition requires treatment, and whose intellectual or bodily powers appear to have undergone a considerable diminution.
2. Incurable sick and wounded whose intellectual or bodily powers appear to have undergone a considerable diminution.
3. Convalescent sick and wounded, whose intellectual or bodily powers appear to have undergone a considerable diminution.

B. 'Guiding Principles for Accommodation in a Neutral Country.'

The following shall be accommodated in a neutral country:

1. Sick and wounded whose recovery is presumable within the period of one year, which it appears that such recovery would be more certain and more rapid if the sick and wounded were given the benefit of the resources offered by the neutral country than if their captivity, properly so called, were prolonged.
2. Prisoners of war whose intellectual or physical health appears, according to medical opinion, to be seriously threatened by continuance in captivity, while accommodation in a neutral country would probably diminish that risk.

C. 'Guiding Principles for the Repatriation of Prisoners in a Neutral Country.'

Prisoners of war who have been accommodated in a neutral country, and belong to the following categories, shall be repatriated:

1. Those whose state of health appears to be, or likely to become such that they would fall into the categories of those to be repatriated for reasons of health.
2. Those who are convalescent, whose intellectual or physical powers appear to have undergone a considerable diminution.

II. Special Principles for Direct Repatriation or Accommodation in a Neutral Country

A. 'Special Principles for Repatriation'

The following shall be repatriated:

1. All prisoners of war suffering the following effective or functional disabilities as the result of organic injuries: loss of a limb, paralysis, articular or other disabilities, when the defect is at least the loss of a foot or a hand, or the equivalent of the loss of a foot or a hand.
2. All wounded or injured prisoners of war whose condition is such as to render them invalids whose cure within a year cannot be medically foreseen.
3. All sick prisoners whose condition is such as to render them invalids whose cure within a year cannot be medically foreseen.

The following in particular belong to this category:

(a) Progressive tuberculosis of any organ which, according to medical prognosis, cannot be cured or at least considerably improved by treatment in a neutral country;
(b) Non-tubercular affections of the respiratory organs which are presumed to be incurable (in particular, strongly developed pulmonary emphysema, with or without bronchitis, bronchiectasis, serious asthma, gas poisoning, etc.):
(c) Grave chronic affections of the circulatory organs (for example: valvular affections with a tendency to compensatory troubles, relatively gave affections of the myocardium, pericardium or the vessels, in particular, aneurism of the larger vessels which cannot be operated on, etc.);
(d) Grave chronic affections of the digestive organs;
(e) Grave chronic affections of the urinary and sexual organs, in particular, for example: any case of chronic nephritis, confirmed by symptoms, and especially when cardiac and vascular deterioration already exists; the same applies to chronic pyelitis and cystitis, etc.;
(f) Grave chronic maladies of the central and peripheral nervous system; in particular grave neurasthenia and hysteria, any indisputable case of epilepsy, grave Basedow's disease, etc.;
(g) Blindness of both eyes, or of one eye when the vision of the other is less than 1 in spite of the use of corrective glasses. Diminution of visual acuteness in cases where it is impossible to restore it by correction to an acuteness of 1/2 in at least one eye. The other ocular affections falling within the present category (glaucoma, iritis, choroiditis, etc.);
(h) Total bilateral deafness, and total unilateral deafness in cases where the ear which is not completely deaf cannot hear ordinary speaking voice at a distance of one metre;
(i) Any indisputable case of mental affection;
(k) Grave cases of chronic poisoning by metals or other causes (lead poisoning, mercury poisoning, morphinism, cocainism, alcoholism, gas poisoning, etc.);
(l) Chronic affections of the locomotive organs (arthritis deformans, gout, or rheumatism with impairment, which can be ascertained clinically), provided that they are serious;
(m) Malignant growths, if they are not amenable to relatively mild operations without danger to the life of the person operated upon;
(n) All cases of malaria with appreciable organic deterioration (serious chronic enlargement of the liver or spleen, cachexy, etc.);

(o) Grave chronic cutaneous affections, when their nature does not constitute a medical reason for treatment in a neutral country;

(p) Serious avitaminosis (beri-beri, pellagra, chronic scurvy).

B. 'Special Principles for Accommodation in a Neutral Country.'

Prisoners of war shall be accommodated in a neutral country if they suffer from the following affections:

1. All forms of tuberculosis of any organ, if, according to present medical knowledge, they can be cured or their condition considerably improved by methods applicable in a neutral country(altitude, treatment in sanatoria, etc.).

2. All forms necessitating treatment of affections of the respiratory, circulatory, digestive, genito-urinary, or nervous organs, of the organs of the senses, or of the locomotive or cutaneous functions, provided that such forms of affection do not belong to the categories necessitating direct repatriation, or that they are not acute maladies (properly so called) susceptible of complete cure. The affections referred to in this paragraph are such as admit, by the application of methods of treatment available in the neutral country, of really better chances of the patient's recovery than if he were treated in captivity.

    Special consideration should be given to nervous troubles, the effective or determining causes of which are the effects of the war or of captivity, such as psychasthenia of prisoners of war or other analogous cases.

    All duly established cases of this nature must be treated in neutral countries when their gravity or their consitutional character does not render them cases for direct repatriation.

    Cases of psychasthenia of prisoners of war who are not cured after three months' sojourn in a neutral country, or which after that period are not manifestly on the way to complete recovery, shall be repatriated.

3. All cases of wounds or injuries or their consequences which offer better prospects of cure in a neutral country than in captivity, provided that such cases are neither such as justify direct repatriation, nor insignificant cases.

4. All duly established cases of malaria which do not show organic deterioration clinically ascertainable (chronic enlargement of the liver or spleen, cachexy, etc.), if sojourn in a neutral country offers particularly favourable prospects of final cure.

5. All cases of poisoning (in particular by gas, metals, or alkaloids) for which the prospects of cure in a neutral country are especially favourable.

The following are excluded from accommodation in a neutral country:

1. All cases of duly established mental affections.

2. All organic or functional nervous affections which are reputed to be incurable. (These two categories belong to those which entitle direct repatriation).

3. Grave chronic alcoholism.

4. All contagious affections during the period when they are transmissible (acute infectious diseases, primary and secondary (syphilis, trachoma, leprosy, etc.).

III. General Observations

The conditions stated above must, in a general way, be interpreted and applied in as broad a spirit as possible.

This breadth of interpretation must especially be applied in neuropathic or psychopathic cases caused or aggravated by the effects of war or captivity (psychasthenia of prisoners of war), and in cases of tuberculosis in all degrees.

It is obvious that camp doctors and mixed medical commissions may find themselves faced with many cases not mentioned amongst the examples given under Section II above, or with cases that cannot be assimilated to these examples. The above-mentioned examples are only given as typical examples; a similar list of surgical disabilities has not been drawn up because, apart from cases which are indisputable on account of their very nature (amputations), it is difficult to draw up a list of specified types; experience has shown that a list of such specified cases was not without inconvenience in practice.

Cases not conforming exactly with the examples quoted shall be determined in the spirit of the guiding principles given above.

Source: International convention relative to the treatment of prisoners of war. Geneva, July 27, 1929. United States Statutes at Large 47, Stat. 2021.

7. Geneva Convention Protocol II (1977)

This Protocol Additional to the Geneva Conventions of August 12, 1949, and relating to the Protection of Victims of Non-International Armed Conflicts (Protocol II), expands upon Article 3 of the 1949 Geneva Convention. Protocol II, added in 1977, is to be applied in cases of non-international armed conflict. It is not designed to affect national sovereignty, but to protect the liberty, health, and safety of the civilian population threatened by armed conflict. The protocol bans forced relocations as well as the use of starvation as a combat decision. It also awards protection to medical and relief workers in the conflict zone.

Preamble

The High Contracting Parties, Recalling that the humanitarian principles enshrined in Article 3 common to the Geneva Conventions of 12 August 1949, constitute the foundation of respect for the human person in cases of armed conflict not of an international character,

Recalling furthermore that international instruments relating to human rights offer a basic protection to the human person,

Emphasizing the need to ensure a better protection for the victims of those armed conflicts,

Recalling that, in cases not covered by the law in force, the human person remains under the protection of the principles of humanity and the dictates of the public conscience,

Have agreed on the following:

Part I. Scope of this Protocol

Art 1. Material field of application

1. This Protocol, which develops and supplements Article 3 common to the Geneva Conventions of 12 August 1949 without modifying its existing conditions of application, shall apply to all armed conflicts which are not covered by Article 1 of the Protocol Additional to the Geneva Conventions of 12 August 1949, and relating to the Protection of Victims of International Armed Conflicts (Protocol I) and which take place in the territory of a High Contracting Party between its armed forces and dissident armed forces or other organized armed groups which, under responsible command, exercise such control over a part of its territory as to enable them to carry out sustained and concerted military operations and to implement this Protocol.

2. This Protocol shall not apply to situations of internal disturbances and tensions, such as riots, isolated and sporadic acts of violence and other acts of a similar nature, as not being armed conflicts.

Art 2. Personal field of application

1. This Protocol shall be applied without any adverse distinction founded on race, colour, sex, language, religion or belief, political or other opinion, national or social origin, wealth, birth or other status, or on any other similar criteria (hereinafter referred to as "adverse distinction") to all persons affected by an armed conflict as defined in Article 1.

2. At the end of the armed conflict, all the persons who have been deprived of their liberty or whose liberty has been restricted for reasons related to such conflict, as well as those deprived of their liberty or whose liberty is restricted after the conflict for the same reasons, shall enjoy the protection of Articles 5 and 6 until the end of such deprivation or restriction of liberty.

Art 3. Non-intervention

1. Nothing in this Protocol shall be invoked for the purpose of affecting the sovereignty of a State or the responsibility of the government, by all legitimate means, to maintain or re-establish law and order in the State or to defend the national unity and territorial integrity of the State.

2. Nothing in this Protocol shall be invoked as a justification for intervening, directly or indirectly, for any reason whatever, in the armed conflict or in the internal or external affairs of the High Contracting Party in the territory of which that conflict occurs.

Part II. Humane Treatment
Art 4 Fundamental guarantees

1. All persons who do not take a direct part or who have ceased to take part in hostilities, whether or not their liberty has been restricted, are entitled to respect for their person, honour and convictions and religious practices. They shall in all circumstances be treated humanely, without any adverse distinction. It is prohibited to order that there shall be no survivors.

2. Without prejudice to the generality of the foregoing, the following acts against the persons referred to in paragraph I are and shall remain prohibited at any time and in any place whatsoever:

   (a) violence to the life, health and physical or mental well-being of persons, in particular murder as well as cruel treatment such as torture, mutilation or any form of corporal punishment;
   (b) collective punishments;
   (c) taking of hostages;
   (d) acts of terrorism;
   (e) outrages upon personal dignity, in particular humiliating and degrading treatment, rape, enforced prostitution and any form or indecent assault;
   (f) slavery and the slave trade in all their forms;
   (g) pillage;
   (h) threats to commit any or the foregoing acts.

3. Children shall be provided with the care and aid they require, and in particular:

   (a) they shall receive an education, including religious and moral education, in keeping with the wishes of their parents, or in the absence of parents, of those responsible for their care;
   (b) all appropriate steps shall be taken to facilitate the reunion of families temporarily separated;
   (c) children who have not attained the age of fifteen years shall neither be recruited in the armed forces or groups nor allowed to take part in hostilities;
   (d) the special protection provided by this Article to children who have not attained the age of fifteen years shall remain applicable to them if they take a direct part in hostilities despite the provisions of subparagraph (c) and are captured;
   (e) measures shall be taken, if necessary, and whenever possible with the consent of their parents or persons who by law or custom are primarily responsible for their care, to remove children temporarily from the area in which hostilities are taking place to a safer area within the country and ensure that they are accompanied by persons responsible for their safety and well-being.

Art 5. Persons whose liberty has been restricted

1. In addition to the provisions of Article 4 the following provisions shall be respected as a minimum with regard to persons deprived of their liberty for reasons related to the armed conflict, whether they are interned or detained;

(a) the wounded and the sick shall be treated in accordance with Article 7;

(b) the persons referred to in this paragraph shall, to the same extent as the local civilian population, be provided with food and drinking water and be afforded safeguards as regards health and hygiene and protection against the rigours of the climate and the dangers of the armed conflict;

(c) they shall be allowed to receive individual or collective relief;

(d) they shall be allowed to practise their religion and, if requested and appropriate, to receive spiritual assistance from persons, such as chaplains, performing religious functions;

(e) they shall, if made to work, have the benefit of working conditions and safeguards similar to those enjoyed by the local civilian population.

2. Those who are responsible for the internment or detention of the persons referred to in paragraph 1 shall also, within the limits of their capabilities, respect the following provisions relating to such persons:

(a) except when men and women of a family are accommodated together, women shall be held in quarters separated from those of men and shall be under the immediate supervision of women;

(b) they shall be allowed to send and receive letters and cards, the number of which may be limited by competent authority if it deems necessary;

(c) places of internment and detention shall not be located close to the combat zone. The persons referred to in paragraph 1 shall be evacuated when the places where they are interned or detained become particularly exposed to danger arising out of the armed conflict, if their evacuation can be carried out under adequate conditions of safety;

(d) they shall have the benefit of medical examinations;

(e) their physical or mental health and integrity shall not be endangered by any unjustified act or omission. Accordingly, it is prohibited to subject the persons described in this Article to any medical procedure which is not indicated by the state of health of the person concerned, and which is not consistent with the generally accepted medical standards applied to free persons under similar medical circumstances.

3. Persons who are not covered by paragraph 1 but whose liberty has been restricted in any way whatsoever for reasons related to the armed conflict shall be treated humanely in accordance with Article 4 and with paragraphs 1 (a), (c) and (d), and 2 (b) of this Article.

4. If it is decided to release persons deprived of their liberty, necessary measures to ensure their safety shall be taken by those so deciding.

Art 6. Penal prosecutions

1. This Article applies to the prosecution and punishment of criminal offences related to the armed conflict.

2. No sentence shall be passed and no penalty shall be executed on a person found guilty of an offence except pursuant to a conviction pronounced by a court offering the essential guarantees of independence and impartiality.

In particular:

(a) the procedure shall provide for an accused to be informed without delay of the particulars of the offence alleged against him and shall afford the accused before and during his trial all necessary rights and means of defence;

(b) no one shall be convicted of an offence except on the basis of individual penal responsibility;

(c) no one shall be held guilty of any criminal offence on account of any act or omission which did not constitute a criminal offence, under the law, at the time when it was committed; nor shall a heavier penalty be imposed than that which was applicable at the time when the criminal offence was committed; if, after the commission of the offence, provision is made by law for the imposition of a lighter penalty, the offender shall benefit thereby;

(d) anyone charged with an offence is presumed innocent until proved guilty according to law;

(e) anyone charged with an offence shall have the right to be tried in his presence;

(f) no one shall be compelled to testify against himself or to confess guilt.

3. A convicted person shall be advised on conviction of his judicial and other remedies and of the time-limits within which they may be exercised.

4. The death penalty shall not be pronounced on persons who were under the age of eighteen years at the time of the offence and shall not be carried out on pregnant women or mothers of young children.

5. At the end of hostilities, the authorities in power shall endeavour to grant the broadest possible amnesty to persons who have participated in the armed conflict, or those deprived of their liberty for reasons related to the armed conflict, whether they are interned or detained.

Part III. Wounded, Sick and Shipwrecked

Art 7. Protection and care

1. All the wounded, sick and shipwrecked, whether or not they have taken part in the armed conflict, shall be respected and protected.

2. In all circumstances they shall be treated humanely and shall receive to the fullest extent practicable and with the least possible delay, the medical care and attention required by their condition. There shall be no distinction among them founded on any grounds other than medical ones.

Art 8. Search

Whenever circumstances permit and particularly after an engagement, all possible measures shall be taken, without delay, to search for and collect the wounded, sick and shipwrecked, to protect them against pillage and ill-treatment, to ensure their adequate care, and to search for the dead, prevent their being despoiled, and decently dispose of them.

Art 9. Protection of medical and religious personnel

1. Medical and religious personnel shall be respected and protected and shall be granted all available help for the performance of their duties. They shall not be compelled to carry out tasks which are not compatible with their humanitarian mission.

2. In the performance of their duties medical personnel may not be required to give priority to any person except on medical grounds.

Art 10. General protection of medical duties

1. Under no circumstances shall any person be punished for having carried out medical activities compatible with medical ethics, regardless of the person benefiting therefrom.

2. Persons engaged in medical activities shall neither be compelled to perform acts or to carry out work contrary to, nor be compelled to refrain from acts required by, the rules of medical ethics or other rules designed for the benefit of the wounded and sick, or this Protocol.

3. The professional obligations of persons engaged in medical activities regarding information which they may acquire concerning the wounded and sick under their care shall, subject to national law, be respected.

4. Subject to national law, no person engaged in medical activities may be penalized in any way for refusing or failing to give information concerning the wounded and sick who are, or who have been, under his care.

Art 11. Protection of medical units and transports

1. Medical units and transports shall be respected and protected at all times and shall not be the object of attack.

2. The protection to which medical units and transports are entitled shall not cease unless they are used to commit hostile acts, outside their humanitarian function. Protection may, however, cease only after a warning

has been given, setting, whenever appropriate, a reasonable time-limit, and after such warning has remained unheeded.

Art 12. The distinctive emblem

Under the direction of the competent authority concerned, the distinctive emblem of the red cross, red crescent or red lion and sun on a white ground shall be displayed by medical and religious personnel and medical units, and on medical transports. It shall be respected in all circumstances. It shall not be used improperly.

Part IV. Civilian Population

Art 13. Protection of the civilian population

1. The civilian population and individual civilians shall enjoy general protection against the dangers arising from military operations. To give effect to this protection, the following rules shall be observed in all circumstances.
2. The civilian population as such, as well as individual civilians, shall not be the object of attack. Acts or threats of violence the primary purpose of which is to spread terror among the civilian population are prohibited.
3. Civilians shall enjoy the protection afforded by this part, unless and for such time as they take a direct part in hostilities.

Art 14. Protection of objects indispensable to the survival of the civilian population

Starvation of civilians as a method of combat is prohibited. It is therefore prohibited to attack, destroy, remove or render useless for that purpose, objects indispensable to the survival of the civilian population such as food-stuffs, agricultural areas for the production of food-stuffs, crops, livestock, drinking water installations and supplies and irrigation works.

Art 15. Protection of works and installations containing dangerous forces

Works or installations containing dangerous forces, namely dams, dykes and nuclear electrical generating stations, shall not be made the object of attack, even where these objects are military objectives, if such attack may cause the release of dangerous forces and consequent severe losses among the civilian population.

Art 16. Protection of cultural objects and of places of worship

Without prejudice to the provisions of the Hague Convention for the Protection of Cultural Property in the Event of Armed Conflict of 14 May 1954, it is prohibited to commit any acts of hostility directed against historic monuments, works of art or places of worship which constitute the cultural or spiritual heritage of peoples, and to use them in support of the military effort.

Art 17. Prohibition of forced movement of civilians

1. The displacement of the civilian population shall not be ordered for reasons related to the conflict unless the security of the civilians involved or imperative military reasons so demand. Should such displacements have to be carried out, all possible measures shall be taken in order that the civilian population may be received under satisfactory conditions of shelter, hygiene, health, safety and nutrition.
2. Civilians shall not be compelled to leave their own territory for reasons connected with the conflict.

Art 18. Relief societies and relief actions

1. Relief societies located in the territory of the High Contracting Party, such as Red Cross (Red Crescent, Red Lion and Sun) organizations may offer their services for the performance of their traditional functions in relation to the victims of the armed conflict. The civilian population may, even on its own initiative, offer to collect and care for the wounded, sick and shipwrecked.
2. If the civilian population is suffering undue hardship owing to a lack of the supplies essential for its survival, such as food-stuffs and medical supplies, relief actions for the civilian population which are of an exclusively humanitarian and impartial nature and which are conducted without any adverse distinction shall be undertaken subject to the consent of the High Contracting Party concerned.

Part V. Final Provisions

Art 19. Dissemination

This Protocol shall be disseminated as widely as possible.

Art 20. Signature

This Protocol shall be open for signature by the Parties to the Conventions six months after the signing of the Final Act and will remain open for a period of twelve months.

Art 21. Ratification

This Protocol shall be ratified as soon as possible. The instruments of ratification shall be deposited with the Swiss Federal Council, depositary of the Conventions.

Art 22. Accession

This Protocol shall be open for accession by any Party to the Conventions which has not signed it. The instruments of accession shall be deposited with the depositary.

Art 23. Entry into force

1. This Protocol shall enter into force six months after two instruments of ratification or accession have been deposited.
2. For each Party to the Conventions thereafter ratifying or acceding to this Protocol, it shall enter into force six months after the deposit by such Party of its instrument of ratification or accession.

Art 24. Amendment

1. Any High Contracting Party may propose amendments to this Protocol. The text of any proposed amendment shall be communicated to the depositary which shall decide, after consultation with all the High Contracting Parties and the International Committee of the Red Cross, whether a conference should be convened to consider the proposed amendment.
2. The depositary shall invite to that conference all the High Contracting Parties as well as the Parties to the Conventions, whether or not they are signatories of this Protocol.

Art 25. Denunciation

1. In case a High Contracting Party should denounce this Protocol, the denunciation shall only take effect six months after receipt of the instrument of denunciation. If, however, on the expiry of six months, the denouncing Party is engaged in the situation referred to in Article 1, the denunciation shall not take effect before the end of the armed conflict. Persons who have been deprived of liberty, or whose liberty has been restricted, for reasons related to the conflict shall nevertheless continue to benefit from the provisions of this Protocol until their final release.
2. The denunciation shall be notified in writing to the depositary, which shall transmit it to all the High Contracting Parties.

Art 26. Notifications

The depositary shall inform the High Contracting Parties as well as the Parties to the Conventions, whether or not they are signatories of this Protocol, of:

(a) signatures affixed to this Protocol and the deposit of instruments of ratification and accession under Articles 21 and 22;
(b) the date of entry into force of this Protocol under Article 23; and
(c) communications and declarations received under Article 24.

Art 27. Registration

1. After its entry into force, this Protocol shall be transmitted by the depositary to the Secretariat of the United Nations for registration and publication, in accordance with Article 102 of the Charter of the United Nations.

2. The depositary shall also inform the Secretariat of the United Nations of all ratifications, accessions and denunciations received by it with respect to this Protocol.

Art 28.—Authentic texts

The original of this Protocol, of which the Arabic, Chinese, English, French, Russian and Spanish texts are equally authentic, shall be deposited with the depositary, which shall transmit certified true copies thereof to all the Parties to the Conventions.

Source: Protocols additional to the Geneva Conventions of 12 August 1949, International Committee of the Red Cross, Geneva, 1977. Available online at http://www.icrc.org/ihl.nsf/INTRO/475?OpenDocument

8. Genocide Convention Implementation Act of 1987 (1988)

Approved November 4, 1988, the Genocide Convention Implementation Act of 1987 is a U.S. law which implements the International Convention on the Prevention and Punishment of Genocide. This law relates to genocide committed by U.S. citizens as well as genocide committed in the United States. It defines genocide, also defining terms used within this definition, and provides guidelines for the punishment of genocide offenses, which range from imprisonment for life and $1,000,000 to five years in prison or a fine of $500,000.

An Act

To implement the International Convention on the Prevention and Punishment of Genocide

Be it enacted by the Senate and House of Representative of the United States of America in Congress assembled,

Section 1. Short Title

This Act may be cited at the "Genocide Convention Implementation Act of 1987(The Proxmire Act)".

Sec. 2 Title 18 Amendments

(a) In General-Part 1 of title 18, United States Code, is amended by inserting after Chapter 50 the following:

Chapter 50A-Genocide

sec

1091 Genocide

1092 Exclusive remedies

1093 Definitions

1091. Genocide

(a) Basic Offense-Whoever, whether in time of peace or in time of war, in a circumstance described in subsection (d) and with the specific intent to destroy, in whole or substantial part, a national, ethnic, racial, or relgious group as such—

   (1) kills members of that group;
   (2) causes serious bodily injury to members of that group;
   (3) causes the permanent impairment of the mental faculties of members of the group through drugs, torture, or similar techniques;
   (4) subjects the group to conditions of life that are intended to cause the physical destruction of the group in whole or in part;
   (5) imposes measures intended to prevent births within the group; or
   (6) transfers by force children of the group to another group; or attempts to do so, shall be punished as provided in subsection (b).

(b) Punishment for Basic Offense—The punishment for an offense under subsection (a) is

   (1) in the case of an offense under subsection (a)(1), a fine of not more that $1,000,000 and imprisonment for life; and
   (2) a fine of not more than $1,000,000 or imprisonment for not more than twenty years, or both, in any other case.

(c) Incitement Offense—Whoever in a circumstance described in subsection (d) directly and publicly incites another to violate subsection (a) shall be fined not more than $500,000 or imprisoned not more than five years, or both.

(d) Required Circumstance for Offenses—The circumstance referred to in subsections (a) and (c) is that—

(1) the offense is committed within the United States; or

(2) the alleged offender is a national of the United States (as defined in section 101 of the Immigration and Nationality Act(8 U.S.C.1101)).

(e) Nonapplicability of Certain Limitations—Notwithstanding section 3282 of this title, in the case of an offense under subsection (a)(1), an indictment may be found, or information instituted, at any time without limitation.

1092. Exclusive remedies

Nothing in this chapter shall be construed as precluding the application of State or local laws to the conduct proscribed by this chapter, nor shall anything in this chapter be construed as creating any substantive or procedural right enforecable by law by any party in any proceeding.

1093. Definitons

As used in this chapter—

(1) the term 'children' means the plural and means individuals who have not yet attained the age of eighteen years;

(2) the term 'ethnic group' means a set of individuals whose identity as such is distinctive in terms of common cultural traditions or heritage;

(3) the term 'incites' means urges another to engage imminently in conduct in circumstances under which there is a substantial likelihood of imminently causing such conduct;

(4) the term 'members' means the plural;

(5) the term 'national group' means a set of individuals whose identity is distinctive in terms of nationality or national origins;

(6) the term 'racial group' means a set of individuals whose identity is distinctive in terms of physical characteristics or biological descent;

(7) the term 'religious group' means a set of individuals whose identity is distinctive in terms of common religious creed, beliefs, doctrines, practices, or rituals; and

(8) the term 'substantial part' means a part of a group of such numerical significance that the destruction or loss of the part would cause the destruction of the group as a viable entity within the nation of which such group is a part.

(b) Clerical Amendment—The table of chapters at the beginning of part 1 of title 18, United States Code, is amended by inserting after relating to chapter 50 the following new item:

50A Genocide 1091
Approved November 4, 1988.

Source: Public Law 100–606-Nov. 4, 1988. 102 STAT.3045.

Bibliography

Abdel-Malek, Anouar. *Egypt: Military Society, the Army Regime, the Left, and Social Change under Nasser.* New York: Random House, 1968.

Akcam, Taner. *The Young Turks' Crime against Humanity: The Armenian Genocide and Ethnic Cleansing in the Ottoman Empire.* Princeton, NJ: Princeton University Press, 2012.

Anderson, Thomas. *Matanza: El Salvador's Communist Revolt of 1932.* Lincoln: University of Nebraska Press, 1971.

Ansari, Ali. *A History of Modern Iran since 1921: The Pahlavis and After.* Boston: Longman, 2003.

Applebaum, Anne. *Gulag: A History.* New York: Broadway Books, 2003.

Arditti, Rita. *Searching for Life: The Grandmothers of the Plaza de Mayo and the Disappeared Children of Argentina.* Berkeley: University of California Press, 1999.

Australian Government. *Bringing Them Home: Report of the National Inquiry into the Separation of Aboriginal and Torres Strait Islander Children from Their Families.* Sydney: Human Rights and Equal Opportunity Commission, 1997.

Autesserre, Séverine. *The Trouble with the Congo: Local Violence and the Failure of International Peacekeeping.* Cambridge, UK: Cambridge University Press, 2010.

Avirgan, Toni, and Martha Honey. *War in Uganda: The Legacy of Idi Amin.* Westport, CT: L. Hill, 1982.

Axe, David, and Tim Hamilton. *Army of God: Joseph Kony's War in Central Africa.* New York: PublicAffaris, 2013.

Bachman, David. *Bureaucracy, Economy, and Leadership in China: The Institutional Origins of the Great Leap Forward.* New York: Cambridge University Press, 1991.

Barnett, Michael. *Eyewitness to a Genocide: The United Nations and Rwanda.* Ithaca, NY: Cornell University Press, 2002.

Bass, Gary Jonathan. *Stay the Hand of Vengeance: The Politics of War Crimes Tribunals.* Princeton: Princeton University Press, 2001.

Bassiouni, M. Cherif. *Crimes against Humanity in International Criminal Law.* 2nd Rev. ed. Boston: Kluwer Law International, 1999.

Bassiouni, M. Cherif, ed. *International Criminal Law.* Ardsley, NY: Transnational Publishers, 1999, 3 vols.

Bassiouni, M. Cherif, and Peter Manikas. *The Law of the International Criminal Tribunal for the Former Yugoslavia.* Irvington-on-Hudson, NY: Transnational Publishers, 1996.

Bateman, Robert L., III. *No Gun Ri: A Military History of the Korean War Incident.* Mechanicsburg, PA: Stackpole Books, 2002.

Bauer, Yehuda. *A History of the Holocaust.* Rev. ed. New York: Franklin Watts, 2001.

Beattie, Kirk J. *Egypt during the Sadat Years.* New York: Palgrave, 2000.

Becker, Jasper. *Hungry Ghosts: Mao's Secret Famine.* New York: The Free Press, 1996.

Belknap, Michael R. *The Vietnam War on Trial: The My Lai Massacre and the Court-Martial of Lieutenant Calley.* Lawrence: University Press of Kansas, 2002.

Bell-Fialkoff, Andrew. *Ethnic Cleansing.* Sydney, Australia: Palgrave Macmillan, 1999.

Berkhoff, Karel C. *Harvest of Despair: Life and Death in Ukraine under Nazi Rule.* Cambridge, MA: Belknap Press of Harvard University Press, 2004.

Blair, Clay. *The Forgotten War: America in Korea 1950–1953.* New York: Times Books, 1987.

Boas, Morten, and Kevin C. Dunn. *African Guerrillas: Raging against the Machine.* Boulder, CO: Lynne Rienner, 2007.

Boot, Max. *The Savage Wars of Peace: Small Wars and the Rise of American Power.* New York: Perseus, 2002.

Bortolotti, Dan. *Hope in Hell: Inside the World of Doctors Without Borders.* New York: Firefly Books, 2010.

Bose, Sarmila. *Dead Reckoning: Memories of the 1971 Bangladesh War.* New York: Columbia University Press, 2011.

Bothe, M., K.J. Partsch, and W.A. Solf. *New Rules for Victims of Armed Conflicts.* The Hague: Martinus Nijhoff Publishers, 1982.

Boutros-Ghali, Boutros. *An Agenda for Peace: Preventive Diplomacy, Peacemaking and Peace-Keeping.* New York: United Nations, 1992.

Bouvard, Marguerite Guzmán. *Revolutionizing Motherhood: The Mothers of the Plaza de Mayo.* Wilmington, DE: Scholarly Resources, 1994.

Brackman, Arnold C. *The Other Nuremberg: The Untold Story of the Tokyo War Crimes Trials.* New York: Morrow, 1987.

Bradley, J.F.N. *Lidice: Sacrificial Village.* New York: Ballantine Books, 1972.

Brand, Emanuel. "Nazi Criminals on Trial in the Soviet Union." *Yad Vashem Bulletin* Vol. 19 (1966): 36–44.

Braun, Herbert. *Our Guerrillas, Our Sidewalks: A Journey into the Violence in Colombia.* Lanham, MD: Rowman & Littlefield Publishers, 2003.

Brecher, Jeremy, Jill Cutler, and Bendan Smith. *In the Name of Democracy: American War Crimes in Iraq and Beyond.* New York: Metropolitan Books, 2005.

Brown, D. Alexander. *Bury My Heart at Wounded Knee: An Indian History of the American West.* New York: Holt, Rinehart & Winston, 1973.

Brown, Michael, Gary Freeman and Kay Miller. *Passing-By: The United States and Genocide in Burundi, 1972.* New York: The Carnegie Endowment for International Peace, 1973.

Buckley, Tom. *Violent Neighbors: El Salvador, Central America and the United States.* New York: Times Books, 1984.

Burr, J. Millard, and Robert O. Collins. *Darfur: The Long Road to Disaster.* Princeton: Markus Weiner, 2006.

Buruma, Ian. *Wages of Guilt: Memories of War in Germany and Japan.* New York: Farrar, Straus, and Giroux, 1994.

Bwengye, Francis Aloysius Wazarwahi. *The Agony of Uganda, from Idi Amin to Obote: Repressive Rule and Bloodshed: Causes, Effects, and the Cure.* New York: Regency Press, 1985.

Campbell, Bruce B. and Arthur D. Brenner, eds. *Death Squads in Global Perspective: Murder with Deniability.* New York: St. Martin's Press, 2000.

Carey, Peter. *East Timor at the Crossroads: The Forging of a Nation.* New York: Continuum, 1995.

Cave, Alfred A. "Abuse of Power: Andrew Jackson and the Indian removal Act of 1830." *Historian* Vol. 65 (Winter 2003): 1130–1153.

Chaliand, Gerard. *A People without a Country: The Kurds and Kurdistan.* London: Olive Branch Press, 1993.

Chalk, Frank, and Kurt Jonassohn. *The History and Sociology of Genocide: Analyses and Case Studies.* New Haven, CT: Yale University Press, 1990.

Chan, Alfred L. *Mao's Crusade: Politics and Policy Implementation in China Great Leap Forward.* New York: Oxford University Press, 2001.

Charny, Israel W. *How Can We Commit the Unthinkable? Genocide: The Human Cancer.* Boulder, CO: Westview Press, 1982.

Cheadle, Don, and John Prendergast. *The Enough Moment: Fighting to End Africa's Worst Human Rights Crimes.* New York: Three Rivers Press, 2010.

Cheadle, Don, and John Prendergast. *Not on Our Watch: The Mission to End Genocide in Darfur and Beyond.* New York: Hyperion, 2007.

Chickering, Roger, and Stig Förster, eds., *Great War, Total War: Combat and Mobilization on the Western Front, 1914–1918,* 2000.

Chinnock, Frank W. *Nagasaki: The Forgotten Bomb.* New York: World Publishing, 1969.

Chirot, Daniel. *Modern Tyrants: The Power and Prevalence of Evil in Our Age.* Princeton, NJ: Princeton University Press, 1994.

Choudhury, G.W. *The Last Days of United Pakistan.* Oxford, UK: Oxford University Press, 1994.

Churchill, Ward. *A Little Matter of Genocide: Holocaust and Denial in the Americas, 1492 to the Present.* San Francisco, CA: City Lights Books, 1997.

Clark, Ann Marie. *Diplomacy of Conscience: Amnesty International and Changing Human Rights Norms.* Princeton: Princeton University Press, 2001.

Conquest, Robert. *The Harvest of Sorrow: Soviet Collectivization and the Terror-Famine.* New York: Oxford University Press, 1987.

Conquest, Robert. *Reflections on a Ravaged Century.* New York: W.W. Norton, 2000.

Conquest, Robert. *Stalin: Breaker of Nations.* New York: Penguin, 1991.

Constable, Pamela, and Arturo Valenzuela. *A Nation of Enemies: Chile Under Pinochet.* New York: W.W. Norton and Company, 1993.

Cook, Sherburne F. *The Conflict Between the California Indian and White Civilization.* Berkeley: University of California Press, 1976.

Cook, Susan E., ed. *Genocide in Cambodia and Rwanda: New Perspectives.* New Brunswick, NJ: Transaction Publishers, 2006.

Costo, Rupert, and Jeannette Henry Costo, eds. *The Missions of California: A Legacy of Genocide.* San Francisco: Indian Historian Press, 1987.

Crabtree, John, and Jim Thomas, eds. *Fujimori's Peru: The Political Economy.* London: Institute of Latin American Studies, 1998.

Crampton, R.J. *A Concise History of Bulgaria.* New York: Cambridge University, 1997.

Crane, Conrad C. *Bombs, Cities, and Civilians: American Airpower Strategy in World War II.* Lawrence: University Press of Kansas, 1993.

Cribb, Robert, and Colin Brown. *Modern Indonesia: A History since 1945.* London: Longman, 1995.

Crosby, Alfred W., Jr. *The Columbian Exchange: Biological and Cultural Consequences of 1492.* Westport, CT: Greenwood Press, 1972.

Cryer, Robert, Hakan Friman, Darryl Robinson, and Elizabeth Wilmhurst. *An Introduction to International Criminal Law and Procedure.* Cambridge, UK: Cambridge University Press, 2007.

Dadrian, Vahakn N. *The History of the Armenian Genocide: Ethnic Conflict from the Balkans to Anatolia to the Caucasus.* Oxford: Berghahn Books, 1995.

Dallaire, Roméo. *Shake Hands with the Devil: The Failure of Humanity in Rwanda.* Toronto: Random House, Canada, 2004.

Dam, Nikolaos van. *The Struggle for Power in Syria: Politics and Society under Asad and the Ba'ath Party.* New York: I.B. Tauris, 1996.

Daubier, Jean. *A History of the Chinese Cultural Revolution.* Translated by Richard Seaver. New York: Vintage, 1974.

Davidson, Phillip B. *Vietnam at War: The History, 1945–1975.* Novato, CA: Presidio, 1988.

Davies, R.W. *The Soviet Collective Farm, 1929–1930.* Cambridge, MA: Harvard University Press, 1980.

Dawson, Greg. *Judgment Before Nuremberg: The Holocaust in the Ukraine and the First Nazi War Crimes Trial.* New York: Pegasus, 2012.

De Silva, Chandra Richard. *Sri Lanka: A History.* 2nd ed. New Delhi: Vikas, 1997.

Deng, Francis Mading. *War of Visions: Conflict of Identities in the Sudan.* Washington, DC: Brookings Institution Press, 1995.

Desmond, Cosmas. *Persecution East and West: Human Rights, Political Prisoners, and Amnesty.* New York: Penguin Books, 1983.

Domenach, Jean-Luc. *The Origins of the Great Leap Forward: The Case of One Chinese Province.* Translated by A.M. Berrett. Boulder, CO: Westview, 1995.

Donnelly, Jack. *Universal Human Rights in Theory and Practice.* 2nd ed. Ithaca, NY: Cornell University Press, 2002.

Dowd, Gregory Evans. *A Spirited Resistance: The North American Indian Struggle for Unity, 1745–1815.* Baltimore: Johns Hopkins University Press, 1992.

Drake, Paul, and Iván Jaksic, eds. *The Struggle for Democracy in Chile, 1982–1990.* Lincoln: University of Nebraska Press, 1991.

Dresch, Paul. *A History of Modern Yemen.* Cambridge, UK: Cambridge University Press, 2008.

Dreyer, Edward L. *China at War, 1901–1949.* New York: Longman, 1995.

Dudley, Steven. *Murder and Guerrilla Politics in Colombia.* London: Routledge Press, 2006.

Dupree, Louis. *Afghanistan.* Princeton, NJ: Princeton University Press, 1980.

Dziewanowski, M.K. *A History of Soviet Russia.* Englewood Cliffs, NJ: Prentice-Hall, 1979.

Edgerton, Robert. *The Troubled Heart of Africa: A History of the Congo.* New York, St. Martin's Press, 2002.

Edoin, Hoito. *The Night Tokyo Burned.* New York: St. Martin's Press, 1987.

Ehle, John. *Trail of Tears: The Rise and Fall of the Cherokee.* New York: Anchor, 1988.

El-Khazen, Farid. *The Breakdown of the State in Lebanon, 1967–1976.* Cambridge, MA: Harvard University Press, 2000.

Facing History and Ourselves. *Decision-Making in Times of Injustice.* Brookline, MA: Facing History and Ourselves National Foundation, 2009.

Falk, Stanley Lawrence. *Bataan: The March of Death.* New York: Norton, 1962.

Falola, Toyin. *The History of Nigeria.* Westport, CT: Greenwood, 1999.

Farmer, Sarah B. *Martyred Village: Commemorating the 1944 Massacre at Oradour-sur-Glane.* Berkeley: University of California Press, 1999.

Fasulo, Linda. *An Insider's Guide to the UN.* New Haven, CT: Yale University Press, 2003.

Fatton, Robert. *Haiti's Predatory Republic: The Unending Transition to Democracy.* Boulder, CO: Lynne Rienner, 2002.

Fawthrop, Tom, and Helen Jarvis. *Getting Away with Genocide? Elusive Justice and the Khmer Rouge Tribunal.* London and Ann Arbor, MI: Pluto Press, 2004.

Fein, Helen. *Genocide: A Sociological Perspective.* London: Sage Publications, 1993.

Ferencz, Benjamin B. *An International Criminal Court: A Step toward World Peace.* New York: Oceana Publications, 1980, 2 vols.

Ferguson, Niall. *The Pity of War: Explaining World War I.* New York: Basic Books, 1999.

Fergusson, James. *The World's Most Dangerous Place: Inside the Outlaw State of Somalia.* New York: Da Capo Press, 2013.

Fernandes, Clinton. *The Independence of East Timor: Multi-Dimensional Perspectives—Occupation, Resistance, and International Political Activism.* Eastbourne, UK: Sussex Academic Press, 2011.

Fink, Christina. *Living Silence: Burma under Military Rule.* Bangkok: White Lotus, 2001.

Fisher, Jo. *Mothers of the Disappeared.* Boston: South End Press, 1989.

Fisk, Robert. *Pity the Nation: Lebanon at War.* Oxford: Oxford University Press, 2001.

Flint, Julie, and Alex de Waal. *Darfur: A Short History of a Long War.* London: Zed Books, 2006.

Fogel, Joshua. *The Nanjing Massacre in History and Historiography.* Berkeley: University of California Press, 2000.

Foster, S.G., and Bain Attwood. *Frontier Conflict: The Australian Experience.* Canberra: National Museum of Australia, 2003.

Frederick, Sharon. *Rape: Weapon of Terror.* River Edge, NJ: Global, 2001.

Freeman, Mark. *Truth Commissions and Procedural Fairness.* Cambridge, UK: Cambridge University Press, 2006.

Garlinski, Jozef. *Poland in the Second World War.* New York: Hippocrene Books, 1985.

Ginzburgs, George. "Laws of War and War Crimes on the Russian Front during World War II: The Soviet View." *Soviet Studies* Vol. XI, no. 3 (1960): 253–285.

Giorgis, Dawit Wolde. *Red Tears: War, Famine, and Revolutions in Ethiopia.* Trenton, NJ: Red Sea Press, 1989.

Gold, Hal. *Unit 731 Testimony: Japan's Wartime Human Experimentation Program.* Boston, Charles Tuttle, 1996.

Goodson, Larry P. *Afghanistan's Endless War: State Failure, Regional Politics, and the Rise of the Taliban.* Seattle: University of Washington Press, 2001.

Graham, Helen. *The Spanish Republic at War, 1936–1939.* New York: Cambridge University Press, 2002.

Grillo, Ioan. *Narco: The Bloody Rise of Mexican Drug Cartels.* 2nd ed. London: Bloomsbury Publishing, 2012.

Gross, Jan Tomasz, *Revolution from Abroad: The Soviet Conquest of Poland's Western Ukraine and Western Belorussia.* Princeton: Princeton University Press, 1988.

Gupta, Vijay. *Obote: Second Liberation.* New Delhi: Vikus, 1983.

Gurr, Ted Robert. *Minorities at Risk: A Global View of Ethnopolitical Conflicts.* Washington, DC: U.S. Institute of Peace Press, 1993.

Gutman, Israel, ed. *Encyclopedia of the Holocaust.* 4 vols. New York: Macmillan, 1990.

Gutman, Roy, ed. *Crimes of War: What the Public Should Know.* New York: W.W. Norton & Company, 1999.

Hagan, John. *Justice in the Balkans: Prosecuting War Crimes in the Hague Tribunal.* Chicago, IL: University of Chicago Press, 2003.

Hamilton, Rebecca. *Fighting for Darfur: Public Action and the Struggle to Stop Genocide.* London: Palgrave Macmillan, 2011.

Hanf, Theodor. *Coexistence in Wartime Lebanon: Decline of a State and Rise of a Nation.* London: Centre for Lebanese Studies and Tauris, 1993.

Hanley, Charles J., Sang-hun Chol, and Martha Mendoza. *The Bridge at No Gun Ri: A Hidden Nightmare from the Korean War.* New York: Henry Holt, 2001.

Hanlon, Joseph. *Mozambique: The Revolution under Fire.* London: Zed, 1984.

Harrington, Joanna, ed. *Bringing Power to Justice?: The Prospects of the International Criminal Court.* Montreal, Canada: McGill-Queen University Press, 2006.

Harris, Robert, and Jeremy Paxman. *A Higher Form of Killing.* New York: Hill and Wang, 1982.

Harris, Sheldon H. *Factories of Death: Japanese Biological Warfare 1932–1945 and the American Cover Up.* New York: Routledge, 1994.

Hart, Peter. *At the Sharp End: From Le Paradis to Kohima.* Barnsley, UK: L. Cooper, Pen and Sword Books, 1998.

Hastings, Max. *The Korean War.* New York: Simon & Schuster, 1987.

Hauner, Milan. *The Soviet War in Afghanistan: Patterns of Russian Imperialism.* Lanham, MD: University Press of America, 1991.

Hawkins, Darren G. *International Human Rights and Authoritarian Rule in Chile.* Lincoln: University of Nebraska Press, 2002.

Hayner, Priscilla B. *Unspeakable Truths: Confronting State Terror and Atrocity.* New York. Routledge, 2000.

Hayward, Anthony. *In the Name of Justice: The Television Reporting of John Pilger.* London: Bloomsbury, 2002.

Herf, Jeffrey. *The Jewish Enemy: Nazi Propaganda during World War II and the Holocaust.* Cambridge, MA: Belknap Press, 2006.

Hernon, Ian. *Britain's Forgotten Wars: Colonial Campaigns of the 19th Century.* Stroud, Gloucestershire, UK: The History Press, 2003.

Hodges, Donald Clark. *Argentina's "Dirty War": An Intellectual Biography.* Austin: University of Texas Press, 1991.

Honda, Katsuichi. *The Nanjing Massacre: A Japanese Journalist Confronts Japan's National Shame.* Edited by Frank Gibney. Armonk, NY: M.E. Sharpe, 1999.

Hondros, John Lewis. *Occupation and Resistance: The Greek Agony, 1941–1949.* New York: Pella Books, 1983.

Horne, John, and Alan Kramer. *German Atrocities, 1914: A History of Denial.* New Haven, CT: Yale University Press, 2001.

Horsman, Reginald. *Race and Manifest Destiny: The Origins of American Racial Anglo-Saxonism.* Cambridge, MA: Harvard University Press, 1981.

Hosoya, Chihiro, ed. *The Tokyo War Crimes Trials: An International Symposium.* Tokyo: Kodansha, 1986.

Hovespian, Nubar, ed. *The War on Lebanon: A Reader.* Northampton, MA: Olive Branch, 2008.

Huband, Mark. *The Liberian Civil War.* London: Frank Cass, 1998.

Human Rights Watch. *War without Quarter: Colombia and International Humanitarian Law.* New York: Human Rights Watch, 1998.

Ingham, Kenneth. *Obote: A Political Biography.* New York: Routledge, 1994.

Irving, David. *The Destruction of Dresden.* New York: Ballantine, 1965.

Isaacman, Allen, and Barbara Isaacman. *Mozambique: From Colonialism to Revolution, 1900–1982.* Boulder, CO: Westview, 1983.

Ishikawa, Eisei. *Hiroshima and Nagasaki: The Physical, Medical, and Social Effects of the Atomic Bombings.* Translated by David L. Swain. New York: Basic Books, 1981.

Jacobs, Steven Leonard. *Lemkin on Genocide.* Lanham: Lexington Books, 2012.

James, Lawrence. *Raj: The Making and Unmaking of British India.* New York: St. Martin's Griffin, 1997.

Jennings, Francis. *The Invasion of America: Indians, Colonialism, and the Cant of Conquest.* New York: W.W. Norton & Company, 1976.

Johansen, Bruce E. *Shapers of the Great Debate on Native Americans: Land, Spirit, Power.* Westport, CT: Greenwood Press, 2000.

Johnson, Douglas H. *The Root Causes of Sudan's Civil Wars.* Bloomington: Indiana University Press, 2003.

Jones, Owen Bennett. *Pakistan: Eye of the Storm.* New Haven, CT: Yale University Press, 2002.

Josephy, Alvin M., Jr. *The Civil War in the American West.* New York: Knopf, 1991.

Journalists of Reuters. *The Israeli-Palestinian Conflict: Crisis in the Middle East.* New York: Reuters/Prentice Hall, 2002.

Kargbo, Michael. *British Foreign Policy Conflict in Sierra Leone, 1991–2001.* New York: Peter Lang, 2006.

Karnow, Stanley. *Vietnam: A History.* Rev. ed. New York: Penguin Books, 1991.

Kassem, Maye. *Egyptian Politics: The Dynamics of Authoritarian Rule.* Boulder, CO: Lynne Rienner, 2004.

Kei, Ushimura. *Beyond the "Judgment of Civilization": The Intellectual Legacy of the Japanese War Crimes Trials, 1946–1949.* Translated by Steven J. Ericson. Tokyo: International House of Japan, 2003.

Kennedy, Paul. *The Parliament of Man: The Past, Present, and Future of the United Nations.* New York: Vintage, 2007.

Khevniuk, Oleg. *History of the Gulag.* New Haven, CT: Yale University Press, 2003.

Kiernan, Ben. *Blood and Soil: A World History of Genocide and Extermination from Sparta to Darfur.* New Haven, CT: Yale University Press, 2007.

Kiernan, Ben. *The Pol Pot Regime: Race, Power, and Genocide in Cambodia under the Khmer Rouge, 1975–79.* 2nd ed. New Haven, CT: Yale University Press, 2002.

Kinealy, Christine. *A Death-Dealing Famine: The Great Hunger in Ireland.* Chicago: Pluto Press, 1997.

Kippenberg, Juliane. *Soldiers Who Rape, Commanders Who Condone: Sexual Violence and Military Reform in the Democratic Republic of Congo.* New York, NY: Human Rights Watch, 2009.

Kirk, Robin. *More Terrible than Death: Massacres, Drugs and America's War in Colombia.* New York: PublicAffairs Books, 2004.

Kissi, Edward. *Revolution and Genocide in Ethiopia and Cambodia.* Lanham, MD: Lexington Books, 2006.

Kladov, Ignatik Fedorovich. *The People's Verdict: A Full Report of the Proceedings at the Krasnodar and Kharkov German Atrocity Trials.* London: Hutchinson & Co., 1944.

Klier, John D., and Shlomo Lambroza. *Pogroms: Anti-Jewish Violence in Modern Russian History.* Cambridge, UK: Cambridge University Press, 1992.

Knight, Amy. *Beria: Stalin's First Lieutenant.* Princeton, NJ: Princeton University Press, 1993.

Kochavi, Arieh. *Prelude to Nuremberg: Allied War Crimes Policy and the Question of Punishment.* Chapel Hill: University of North Carolina Press, 1998.

Kressel, Neil Jeffrey. *Mass Hate: The Global Rise of Genocide and Terror.* New York: Plenum Press, 1996.

Kulah, Arthur F. *Liberia Will Rise Again: Reflections on the Liberian Civil Crisis.* Nashville: Abingdon Press, 1999.

Kuper, Leo. *Genocide: Its Political Use in the Twentieth Century.* New Haven, CT: Yale University Press, 1983.

Kuper, Leo. *The Prevention of Genocide.* New Haven, CT: Yale University Press, 1985.

Lael, Richard L. *The Yamashita Precedent: War Crimes and Command Responsibility.* Wilmington, DE: Scholarly Resources Inc., 1982.

Lamb, Richard. *War in Italy, 1943–1945: A Brutal Story.* New York: Da Capo Press, 1996.

Laqueur, Walter, and Barry Rubin, eds. *The Israel-Arab Reader: A Documentary History of the Middle East Conflict.* London: Penguin Books, 2001.

LeBor, Adam. *"Complicity with Evil": The United Nations in the Age of Modern Genocide.* New Haven, CT: Yale University Press, 2008.

Lemarchand, René, ed. *Forgotten Genocides: Oblivion, Denial and Memory.* Philadelphia: University of Pennsylvania Press, 2011.

Lemkin, Raphael. *Axis Rule in Occupied Europe: Laws of Occupation, Analysis of Government, Proposals for Redress.* New Haven, CT: The Lawbook Exchange, 2008.

Levie, Howard. *The Law of Non-International Armed Conflict: Protocol II to the 1949 Geneva Convention.* The Hague: Martinus Nijhoff Publishers, 1987.

Lewis, David. *Bangladesh: Politics, Economy and Civil Society.* Cambridge, UK: Cambridge University Press, 2011.

Li, Fei Fei, Robert Sabella, and David Liu, eds. *Nanking: Memory and Healing.* Armonk, NY: M.E. Sharpe, 2002.

Linn, Brian M. *The Philippine War.* Lawrence: University Press of Kansas, 2002.

Lord Russell of Liverpool. *The Knights of Bushido: A History of Japanese War Crimes during World War II.* New York: Skyhorse Publishing, 2008.

Lotnik, Waldemar. *Nine Lives: Ethnic Conflict in the Polish-Ukrainian Borderlands.* London: Serif, 1999.

Lowe, Vaughan, and Malgosia Fitzmaurice, eds. *Fifty Years of the International Court of Justice: Essays in Honor of Sir Robert Jennings.* New York: Cambridge University Press, 1996.

Lukas, Richard C. *Forgotten Holocaust: The Poles under German Occupation, 1939–1944.* Lexington, KY: University Press of Kentucky, 1986.

MacFarquhar, Roderick. *The Great Leap Forward, 1958–1960. The Origins of the Cultural Revolution.* Vol. 2. New York: Columbia University Press, 1983.

Mackintosh-Smith, Martin. *Yemen: The Unknown Arabia.* Woodstock, NY: Overlook, 2001.

Maga, Timothy. *Judgement at Tokyo.* Lexington: University Press of Kentucky, 2001.

Maguire, Peter. *Facing Death in Cambodia.* New York: Columbia University Press, 2005.

Mahmud, Ushari Ahmed, and Suleyman Ali Baldo. *Human Rights Violations in the Sudan, 1987: Al Diein Massacre, Slavery in the Sudan.* Khartoum: Khartoum University Press, 1987.

Maley, William. *The Afghanistan Wars.* New York: Palgrave Macmillan, 2002.

Malvern, Linda. *Conspiracy to Murder: The Rwanda Genocide.* Rev. ed. London: Verso, 2006.

Mann, Michael. *The Dark Side of Democracy: Explaining Ethnic Cleansing.* Cambridge, UK: Cambridge University Press, 2004.

Maoz, Moshe, and Avner Yaniv, eds. *Syria under Assad: Domestic Constraints and Regional Risks.* London: Croom Helm, 1987.

Marrus, Michael R., ed. *The Nazi Holocaust: Historical Articles on the Destruction of European Jews.* 9 vols. Westport, CT: Meckler, 1989.

Masterson, Daniel. *The History of Peru.* Santa Barbara, CA: Greenwood, 2009.

Masterson, Daniel. *Militarism and Politics in Latin America: Peru from Sanchez Cerro to "Sendero Luminoso."* Westport, CT: Greenwood, 1991.

Mazower, Mark. *Hitler's Empire: How the Nazis Ruled Europe.* Penguin Press: New York, 2008.

Mazower, Mark. *Inside Hitler's Greece. The Experience of Occupation 1941–1944.* New Haven and New York: Yale University Press, 1993.

McDowall, David. *A Modern History of the Kurds.* New York: I. B. Tauris, 2004.

McKissick, Patricia C. *History of Haiti.* Maryknoll, NY: Henry Holt, 1998.

Medvedev, Roy A. *Let History Judge: The Origins and Consequences of Stalinism.* New York: Columbia University Press, 1989.

Meisler, Stanley. *Kofi Annan: A Man of Peace in a World of War.* New York: Wiley, 2008.

Melson, Robert. *Revolution and Genocide: On the Origins of the Armenian Genocide and the Holocaust.* Chicago: University of Chicago Press, 1992.

Menjívar, Cecilia, and Néstor Rodríguez. *When States Kill: Latin America, the U.S., and Technologies of Terror.* Austin: University of Texas Press, 2005.

Menkhaus, Kenneth. *Somalia: State Collapse and the Threat of Terrorism.* Oxford, UK: Oxford University Press, 2004.

Mertus, Julie. *The United Nations and Human Rights: A Guide for a New Era.* New York: Routledge, 2005.

Meyer, Michael C., William L. Sherman, and Susan M. Deeds. *The Course of Mexican History.* 7th ed. New York: Oxford University Press, 2003.

Middlebrook, Martin. *The Battle of Hamburg.* New York: Charles Scribner's Sons, 1981.

Middleton, John, ed. *Encyclopedia of Africa South of the Sahara.* New York: Charles Scribner's Sons, 1997.

Miller, Marc S., ed. *State of the Peoples: A Global Human Rights Report on Societies in Danger.* Boston, MA: Beacon Press, 1993.

Miller, Stuart Creighton. *"Benevolent Assimilation": The American Conquest of the Philippines, 1899–1903.* New Haven CT: Yale University Press, 1982.

Millett, Allan R. *Their War in Korea: American, Asian, and European Combatants and Civilians, 1945–1953.* Princeton, NJ: Princeton University Press, 2002.

Milliss. Roger. *Waterloo Creek: The Australia Day Massacre of 1838, George Gipps and the British Conquest of New South Wales.* McPhee Gribble: Melbourne, 1992.

Minnear, Richard H. *Victors' Justice: The Tokyo War Crimes Trial.* Princeton, NJ: Princeton University Press, 1971.

Morley, David. *Healing Our World: Inside Doctors Without Borders.* Markham, Canada: Fitzhenry and Whiteside, 2008.

Morris, Benny. *Righteous Victims: A History of the Zionist-Arab Conflict, 1881–2001.* New York: Vintage Books, 2001.

Morsink, Johannes. *The Universal Declaration of Human Rights: Origins, Drafting, and Intent.* Philadelphia: University of Philadelphia Press, 2000.

Myint-U, Thant. *The River of Lost Footsteps—Histories of Burma.* New York: Farrar, Straus and Giroux, 2006.

Naimark, Norman M. *Fires of Hatred: Ethnic Cleansing in Twentieth-Century Europe.* Cambridge, MA.: Harvard University Press, 2002.

Narayanan, V.N. *Tryst with Terror: Punjab's Turbulent Decade.* Columbia, MO: South Asia Books, 1996.

Nayar, Kuldip. *Tragedy of Punjab: Operation Bluestar and After.* New Delhi: Vision Books, 1984.

Newell, Sasha. *The Modernity Bluff: Crime, Consumption, and Citizenship in Côte d'Ivoire.* Chicago: The University of Chicago Press, 2012.

Nobile, Philip. *Judgment at the Smithsonian: The Bombing of Hiroshima and Nagasaki.* New York: Marlowe and Company, 1995.

Norton, Jack. *Genocide in Northwestern California: When Our Worlds Cried.* San Francisco, CA: The Indian Historian Press, 1979.

Nubin, Walter. *Sri Lanka: Current Issues and Historical Background.* Bloomington: Indiana University Press, 2004.

Nzongola-Ntalaja, Georges. *The Congo: From Leopold to Kabila: A People's History.* London: Zed Books, 2002.

O Grada, Cormac. *The Great Irish Famine.* New York: Cambridge University Press, 1995.

O'Reilly, Charles T. *Forgotten Battles: Italy's War of Liberation, 1943–1945.* Lanham, MD: Lexington Books, 2001.

Olson, James S., and Randy Roberts. *My Lai: A Brief History with Documents.* New York: Bedford/St. Martin's, 1998.

Palmer, David Scott, ed. *Shining Path of Peru.* 2nd ed. New York: St. Martin's, 1994.

Paul, Allen. *Katyń: The Untold Story of Stalin's Massacre.* New York: Scribner's, 1991.

Pavlowitch, Stevan K. *Hitler's New Disorder: The Second World War in Yugoslavia.* New York: Columbia University Press, 2008.

Pettifer, James. *The Kosova Liberation Army: Underground War to Balkan Insurgency, 1948–2001.* New York: Columbia University Press, 2012.

Piccigallo, P.R. *The Japanese on Trial: Allied War Crimes Operations in the Far East 1945–1951.* Austin: University of Texas Press, 1979.

Pohl, J. Otto. *Ethnic Cleansing in the USSR, 1937–1949.* Westport, CT: Greenwood, 1999.

Poniatowska, Elena. *Massacre in Mexico.* Translated by Helen R. Lane. New York: Viking Press, 1975.

Power, Jonathan. *Amnesty International, the Human Rights Story.* New York: Pergamon Press, 1981.

Power, Samantha. *"A Problem from Hell": America and the Age of Genocide.* New York: Harper Perennial, 2007.

Price, Richard M. *The Chemical Weapons Taboo.* Ithaca, NY: Cornell University Press, 1997.

Pritchard, R. John, and Sonia M. Zaide, eds. *The Tokyo War Crimes Trial: The Complete Transcripts of the Proceedings of the International Military Tribunal for the Far East in Twenty Two Volumes.* New York: Garland, 1981.

Proxmire, William. *Report from Wasteland: America's Military-Industrial Complex.* Westport, CT: Praeger, 1970.

Prunier, Gerard. *Darfur: The Ambiguous Genocide.* Ithaca, NY: Cornell Univeristy Press, 2005.

Prunier, Gérard. *The Rwanda Crisis, 1959–1994: History of a Genocide.* Kampala: Fountain Publishers, 1995.

Qumsiyeh, Mazin B. *Sharing the Land of Canaan: Human Rights and the Israeli-Palestinian Struggle.* London: Pluto, 2004.

Rabil, Robert. *Embattled Neighbors: Syria, Israel, and Lebanon.* Boulder, CO: Lynne Rienner, 2003.

Ramos-Horta, José Manuel. *Funu: The Unfinished Saga of East Timor.* Trenton, NJ: Red Sea Press, 1986.

Reid, Anna. *Borderland: A Journey through the History of Ukraine.* New York: Basic Books, 2000.

Ricklefs, Merle Calvin. *A History of Modern Indonesia since c. 1200.* Stanford, CA: Stanford University Press, 2001.

Rittner, Carol. *Genocide in Rwanda: Complicity of the Churches.* St. Paul, MN: Paragon House, 2004.

Roach, Steven. *Politicizing the International Criminal Court: The Convergence of Politics, Ethics, and Law.* Lanham, MD: Rowman and Littlefield Publishers, Inc., 2006.

Roberts, Adam, and Richard Guelff. *Documents on the Laws of War.* Oxford: Oxford University Press, 2000.

Robinson, Geoffrey. *The Dark Side of Paradise: Political Violence in Bali.* Ithaca, NY: Cornell University Press, 1995.

Robinson, Thomas, ed. *The Cultural Revolution in China.* Berkeley: University of California Press, 1971.

Rock, David. *Authoritarian Argentina.* Berkeley: University of California Press, 1993.

Ronayne, Peter. *Never Again? The United States and the Prevention and Punishment of Genocide since the Holocaust.* Lanham, MD: Rowman & Littlefield Publishers, 2001.

Rosenne, Shabtai. *The World Court: What It Is and How It Works.* 5th ed. Dordrecht, The Netherlands: Martinus Nijhoff Publishers, 1995.

Ross, Robert. *A Concise History of South Africa.* 2nd ed. Cambridge, UK: Cambridge University Press, 2009.

Rotberg, Robert, and Dennis Thompson. *Truth v. Justice: The Morality of Truth Commissions.* Princeton, NJ: Princeton University Press, 2000.

Rummel, R. J. *Death by Government.* Piscataway, NJ: Transaction Publishers, 1997.

Rummel, R. J. *Democide: Nazi Genocide and Mass Murder.* Piscataway, NJ: Transaction Publishers, 1991.

Sachs, Susan, "Exiled Relative Issues Challenge to Syria's Heir to Power." *The New York Times,* June 13, 2000.

Salisbury, Harrison E. *The New Emperors: China in the Era of Mao and Deng.* Boston: Little, Brown, 1993.

Sarkar, Sumit. *Modern India, 1885–1947.* New York: St. Martin's Press, 1989.

Schabas, William A. *An Introduction to the International Criminal Court.* 2nd ed. Cambridge: Camridge University Press, 2004.

Schabas, William A. *Genocide in International Law: The Crime of Crimes.* Cambridge, UK: Cambridge University Press, 2000.

Schaffer, David. *The Iran-Iraq War.* San Diego, CA: Lucent Books, 2003.

Schendel, Willem van. *A History of Bangladesh.* Cambridge, UK: Cambridge University Press, 2009.

Scherrer, P. Christian. *Genocide and Crisis in Central Africa: Conflict Roots, Mass Violence, and Regional War.* Westport, CT: Praeger, 2002.

Schoenhals, Michael, ed. *China's Cultural Revolution, 1966–1969: Not a Dinner Party.* Armonk, NY: M.E. Sharpe, 1996.

Schrier, Arnold. *Ireland and the American Emigration, 1850–1900.* Chester Springs, PA: Dufour Editions, 1997.

Schucking, Walther. *The International Union of the Hague Conferences.* Oxford, UK: Clarendon Press, 1918.

Schulz, William F, ed. *The Phenomenon of Torture: Readings and Commentary.* Philadelphia: University of Pennsylvania Press, 2007.

Schwab, Peter. *Designing West Africa: Prelude to 21st-Century Calamity.* New York: Palgrave, 2004.

Segev, Tom. *One Palestine, Complete: Jews and Arabs under the British Mandate.* New York: Owl Books, 2001.

Sewall, Saray, and Carl Kaysen. *The United States and the International Criminal Court.* Lanham, MD: Rowman and Littlefield Publishers, Inc., 2000.

Shadid, Anthony. *Night Draws Near: Iraq's People in the Shadow of America's War.* New York: Henry Holt and Company, 2005.

Sherman, John. *War Stories: A Memoir of Nigeria and Biafra.* Indianapolis, IN: Mesa Verde Press, 2002.

Shillony, Ben-Ami. *Politics and Culture in War-Time Japan.* Oxford, UK: Clarendon, 1981.

Simons, Geoff. *Libya and the West: From Independence to Lockerbie.* London: I. B. Tauris, 2004.

Sisson, Richard, and Leo Rose. *War and Secession: Pakistan, India, and the Creation of Bangladesh.* Berkeley: University of California Press, 1990.

Sluka, Jeffrey A., ed. *Death Squad: Anthropology of State Terror.* Philadelphia: University of Pennsylvania Press, 2000.

Solzhenitsyn, Aleksandr. *The Gulag Archipelago, 1918–1956: An Experiment in Literary Investigation.* 3 vols. New York: Harper and Row, 1974–1978.

Soyinka, Wole. *The Open Sore of a Continent: A Personal Narrative of the Nigerian Crisis.* New York: Oxford University Press, 1996.

Spiers, Edward. *Chemical Warfare.* Urbana: University of Illinois Press, 1986.

Spooner, Mary Helen. *Soldiers in a Narrow Land: The Pinochet Regime in Chile.* Berkeley: University of California Press, 1994.

Sriram, Chandra Lekha, Olga Martin-Ortega, and Johanna Herman. *War, Conflict and Human Rights: Theory and Practice.* New York: Routledge, 2010.

Stanley, William D. *The Protection Racket State: Elite Politics, Military Extortion, and Civil War in El Salvador.* Philadelphia: Temple University Press, 1996.

Stannard, David E. *American Holocaust: The Conquest of the New World.* New York: Oxford University Press, 1993.

Straus, Scott. *The Order of Genocide: Race, Power, and War in Rwanda.* Ithaca, NY: Cornell University Press, 2008.

Taylor, Frederick. *Dresden: Tuesday, February 13, 1945.* New York: HarperCollins, 2004.

Taylor, John G. *Indonesia's Forgotten War: The Hidden History of East Timor.* London: Zed, 1991.

Taylor, S. J. *Stalin's Apologist: Walter Duranty: The New York Times' Man in Moscow.* New York: Oxford University Press, 1990.

Taylor, Telford. *The Anatomy of the Nuremberg Trials.* New York: Alfred A. Knopf, 1992.

Tessler, Mark. *A History of the Israeli-Palestinian Conflict.* Bloomington: Indiana University Press, 1994.

Thornton, Russell. *American Indian Holocaust and Survival: A Population History since 1492.* Norman: University of Oklahoma Press, 1987.

Titley, Brian. *Dark Age: The Political Odyssey of Emperor Bokassa.* Montreal: McGill-Queen's University Press, 1997.

Toland, John. *The Rising Sun: The Decline and Fall of the Japanese Empire, 1936–1945.* New York: Random House, 1970.

Tolley, Howard, Jr. *The U.N. Commission on Human Rights.* Boulder, CO: Westview Press, 1987.

Trask, David F. *The War with Spain in 1898.* Lincoln: University of Nebraska Press, 1996.

Tripp, Charles. *A History of Iraq.* Cambridge, UK: Cambridge University Press, 2000.

Tripp, Charles, and Roger Owen. *Egypt under Mubarak.* London: Routledge, 1990.

Tucker, Robert C. *Stalin in Power: The Revolution from Above, 1928–1941.* New York: Norton, 1990.

Turnbull, Clive. *Black War: The Extermination of the Tasmanian Aborigines.* Melbourne: Cheshire-Lansdowne Press, 1965.

United Nations. *Atrocities and International Accountability: Beyond Transitional Justice.* New York: United Nations, 2008.

United Nations War Crimes Commission. *History of the United Nations War Crimes Commission.* London: His Majesty's Stationary Office, 1948.

United Nations War Crimes Commission. *Law-Reports of Trials of War Criminals.* Vol. VIII, Case No. 43. London: HMSO, 1948.

United States Commission on the Ukraine Famine. Report to Congress. Washington, DC: U.S. Government Printing Office, 1988.

Utley, Robert M. *Frontier Regulars: The United States and the American Indian, 1866–1891.* New York: Macmillan, 1973.

Utley, Robert Marshall. *The Indian Frontier of the American West, 1846–1890.* Albuquerque: University of New Mexico Press, 1984.

Uzokwe, Alfred Obiora. *Surviving in Biafra: The Story of the Nigerian Civil War.* New York: Writer's Advantage, 2003.

Vargas Llosa, Alvaro. *The Madness of Things Peruvian: Democracy under Siege.* New Brunswick, NJ: Transaction Publishers, 1994.

Vickers, Miranda. *The Albanians: A Modern History.* London: Tauris, 1999.

Wallace, Anthony C. *The Long, Bitter Trail: Andrew Jackson and the Indians.* New York: Hill and Wang, 1993.

Webster, Charles, and Noble Frankland. *The Strategic Air Offensive against Germany.* 4 vols. London: Her Majesty's Stationery Office, 1961.

Weiss, Thomas G., David P. Forsythe, and Roger A. Coate. *The United Nations and Changing World Politics.* Westport, CT: Westview Press, 2004.

Werrell, Kenneth P. *Blankets of Fire: U.S. Bombers over Japan during World War II.* Washington, DC: Smithsonian Institution Press, 1996.

White, Christopher M. *The History of El Salvador.* Westport, CT: Greenwood Press, 2009.

Williams, Peter, and David Wallace. *Unit 731: Japan's Secret Biological Warfare in World War II.* New York: Free Press, 1989.

Willis, James F. *Prologue to Nuremberg: The Politics and Diplomacy of Punishing War Criminals of the First World War.* Westport, CT: Greenwood, 1982.

Wolpert, Stanley. *A New History of India.* Oxford: Oxford University Press, 2004.

Woodham Smith, Cecil Blanche Fitz Gerald. *The Great Hunger: Ireland, 1845–1849.* London: Penguin, 1991.

Wright, John. *Libya: A Modern History.* Baltimore: Johns Hopkins University Press, 1981.

Wynbrandt, James. *A Brief History of Saudi Arabia.* New York: Checkman, 2004.

Wynia, Gary W. *Argentina: Illusions and Realities.* 2nd ed. New York: Holmes & Meier, 1992.

Yamamoto, Masahiro. *Nanking: Anatomy of an Atrocity.* Westport, CT: Praeger, 2000.

Yglesias, Jose. *The Franco Years.* Indianapolis: Bobbs-Merrill, 1977.

Yuma Totani. *The Tokyo War Crimes Trial: The Pursuit of Justice in the Wake of World War II.* Cambridge, MA: Harvard University Asia Center, 2009.

Zaheer, Hasan. *The Separation of East Pakistan: The Rise and Realization of Bengali Muslim Nationalism.* Oxford, UK: Oxford University Press, 1994.

Zawodny, Janusz. *Death in the Forest: The Story of the Katyn Forest Massacre.* 4th ed. Notre Dame, IN: University of Notre Dame Press, 1980.

Zuckerman, Larry. *The Rape of Belgium: The Untold Story of World War I.* New York: New York University Press, 2004.

Zuhur, Sherifa. *Saudi Arabia: Islamic Threat, Political Reform and the Global War on Terror.* Carlisle Barracks, PA: Strategic Studies Institute, 2005.

Zürcher, Erik J. *Turkey: A Modern History.* London and New York: I. B. Taurus, 1993.

Contributors

Ewen Allison
Partner
Capital Area Law Group

Alan Allport
Department of History
Syracuse University, NY

Ralph Martin Baker
Historian

Dr. Gregg Barak
Professor of criminology and criminal justice at Eastern
    Michigan University
Eastern Michigan University

Dr. Paul R. Bartrop
Professor of History
Director of the Center for Judaic, Holocaust, and Genocide
    Studies
Florida Gulf Coast University

Dr. Jeffrey D. Bass
Professor
Baylor University

Robert L. Bateman
Adjunct Professor

Center for Security Studies
Georgetown University

Frank Beyersdorf
Instructor
Freie Universitat Berlin, Germany

Amy Hackney Blackwell
Independent Scholar

Dr. Arthur W. Blaser
Professor of Political Science
Chapman University

Gilles Boué
Independent Scholar
Paris, France

Dr. Wayne Bowen
Professor
Southeast Missouri State University

Sara E. Brown
Strassler Center for Holocaust and Genocide Studies
Clark University

Sonya Brown
Griffith University, Australia

Dr. Henry Carey
Associate Professor of Political Science
Georgia State University

Dr. Alton Carroll
Assistant Professor
Northern Virginia Community College

Bob Couttie
Independent Scholar

Conrad C. Crane
Chief of Historical Services
Army Heritage and Education Center
Carlisle Barracks
U.S. Army War College

Dr. Robert Cribb
Professor
Australian National University

Elizabeth F. Defeis
Professor of Law
Seton Hall University

Dr. Bruce J. DeHart
Professor of History
University of North Carolina, Pembroke

Dr. Gregory J. Dehler
Instructor
Front Range Community College, Colorado

Margaret Detraz
Independent Scholar

Benjamin C. Dubberly
Independent Scholar

William J. Fenrick
Adjunct Professor
Dalhousie University School of Law, Canada

Arthur T. Frame
Professor
U.S. Army Command and General Staff College

Dr. James W. Frusetta
Assistant Professor
Hampden Sydney College

Wendy Jo Gertjejanssen
University of Minnesota

Dr. R. Matthew Gildner
Assistant Professor of History
Washington and Lee University

Dr. Maia Carter Hallward
Assistant Professor of Political Science
Kennesaw State University

Glen Anthony Harris
Department of History
University of North Carolina, Wilmington

Glenn E. Helm
Director
Navy Department Library

Dr. Laura J. Hilton
Associate Professor and Chair
Department of History
Muskingum University

Dr. Jesse Hingson
Assistant Professor of History
Jacksonville University

Dr. Robert K. Hitchcock
Professor and Chair
Department of Anthropology
Michigan State University

Dr. Larry Hufford
Professor
St. Mary's University

Arnold R. Isaacs
Journalist

Dr. Obiwu Iwuanyanwu
Assistant Professor
Central State University

Jerry Keenan
Historian

Dr. David L. Kenley
Associate Professor of History
Elizabethtown College

Dr. Gary Kerley
Historian

Dr. Jinwung Kim
Professor of History
Kyungpook National University, South Korea

Dr. C. Richard King
Professor & Chair
Comparative Ethnic Studies
Washington State University

Dr. Arne Kislenko
Associate Professor of History
Ryerson University, Canada

Dr. Edward Kissi
Associate Professor
University of South Florida

Dr. Bohdan Klid
Assistant Director of the Canadian Institute of Ukrainian
    Studies
University of Alberta

Dr. Srikanth Kondapalli
Professor of East Asian Studies
Jawaharlal Nehru University, India

Dr. Ken Kotani
Lecturer
National Institute for Defense Studies, Japan

Matthew J. Krogman
Independent Scholar

Dr. Fumitaka Kurosawa
Professor
Tokyo Women's Christian University

Robert S. La Forte
Independent Scholar

Debbie Law Yuk-fun
Shue Yan University, Hong Kong

Dr. Daniel Lewis
Professor of History and Associate Dean
California Polytechnic State University California, Pomona

Dr. Peter Lieb
Senior Lecturer
Department of War Studies
Royal Military Academy, Sandhurst, United Kingdom

Dr. Kerstin von Lingen
Lecturer
University of Heidelberg, Germany

James E. Mace
Independent Scholar

Philip J. MacFarlane
Independent Scholar

Robert W. Malick
Adjunct Professor of History
Harrisburg Area Community College

Dr. Eric Markusen
Research Director
Danish Center for Holocaust and Genocide Studies
Professor of Sociology
Southwest Minnesota State University

Jim Mellen
Independent Scholar

Abraham O. Mendoza
Independent Scholar

Dr. Alexander Mikaberidze
Assistant Professor
Department of History and Social Sciences
Louisiana State University, Shreveport

Dr. John Morello
Senior Professor
DeVry University

Dr. Jerry D. Morelock
Editor-in-Chief
Armchair General Magazine

Dr. Justin D. Murphy
Brand Professor of History, Dean of the School of
    Humanities
Howard Payne University, Brownwood, Texas

Dr. Caryn E. Neumann
Visiting Assistant Professor of History
Miami University, Ohio

Charlene T. Overturf
Armstrong Atlantic State University

Dr. Jim Piecuch
Associate Professor of History
Kennesaw State University, Georgia

Dr. Paul G. Pierpaoli Jr.
Fellow
Military History, ABC-CLIO, Inc.

Dr. J. Otto Pohl
Lecturer
Department of History
University of Ghana

Dr. Alexander V. Prusin
Associate Professor of History
New Mexico Tech

Elizabeth Pugliese
Independent Scholar

Dr. Priscilla Roberts
Associate Professor of History, School of
    Humanities
Honorary Director, Centre of American
    Studies
University of Hong Kong

Robyn Rodriguez
Ohio State University

Dr. Ralph Rotte
University Professor of Economics
Aachen University, Germany

Dr. Joshua Rubenstein
Associate of the Davis Center for Russian and Eurasian
    Studies
Harvard University

Dr. Estela Schindel
Research Assistant
Rupert Karl University of Heidelberg, Germany

Dr. Daniel Marc Segesser
Lecturer
University of Bern, Switzerland

Terry Shoptaugh
Professor of History and
    American Studies
Minnesota State University, Moorhead

Charles R. Shrader
Historian

Dr. Roger W. Smith
Professor Emeritus of Government
College of William and Mary

T. Jason Soderstrum
Iowa State University

Phillip M. Sozansky
Instructor, American History
Cedar Park Middle School

Dr. Gregory H. Stanton
Professor in Genocide Studies
    and Prevention
School for Conflict Analysis and
    Resolution
George Mason University

Dr. Colin Tatz
Director
Australian Institute for Holocaust and Genocide
    Studies

Dr. Henry C. Theriault
Professor and Chair of the Philosophy
    Department
Worcester State University

Dr. John P. Thorp
Independent Scholar

Pascal Trees
University of Bonn, Germany

Dr. Spencer C. Tucker
Senior Fellow
Military History, ABC-CLIO, Inc.

Dr. Mark E. Van Rhyn
History Instructor
Louisiana School for Math, Science, and the Arts

Roderick S. Vosburgh
Professor of History
La Salle University

Tim J. Watts
Humanities Librarian
Collection Management

Hale Library
Kansas State University

Duane L. Wesolick
Adjunct professor
Southwestern Community College, North
    Carolina.

Dr. James F. Willis
Department of History and Political Science
Southern Arkansas University

Glossary

Aktion *Aktion* can be best understood as a term used predominantly by the SS (*Schutzstaffel* or "security police") and their allies to describe the nonmilitary campaign of roundups and deportations of Jews and other "undesirables" in the eastern territories under German occupation. The two most significant of these *aktionen* were (1) *Aktion Reinhard*, after the assassination of RHSA (*Reichssicherheitshauptamt*, "Reich Security Main Office") chief Reinhard Heydrich on May 27, 1942, in Prague, Czechoslovakia, whose purpose was to murder all the Jews in the five districts of the *Generalgouvernement* (general government) encompassing Krakow, Warsaw, Radom, Lublin, and Galicia, and later expanded to include all Jews deported to occupied Poland; and (2) *Aktion 1005*, which was developed in the summer of 1942 to obliterate all traces of the Nazi *Endlösung* (final solution) by the use of slave laborers, including Jews who were subsequently murdered, to both exhume and burn the bodies of the Nazis' victims. Nearly 400 anti-Jewish *aktionen* took place between November 1939 and October 1944.

Arabism Arabism refers to the concept held by some Arabs that Arabic culture, religion, language, dress, and societal norms are superior to any others. Arabism has existed to one extent or another for centuries, but only a relatively small minority of Arabs subscribe to this way of thinking. Arabism developed mainly as a reaction to colonial subjugation of Arab populations, especially in the Middle East. More recently, Arabism has been a significant contributing factor to the Darfur Genocide in the western region of Sudan. Years prior to the Darfur Genocide, the Arab-dominated Sudanese government had systematically oppressed and discriminated against Sudan's non-Arab, black indigenous population. Blacks in Darfur were routinely marginalized as subhumans, and frequently referred to as slaves or dogs. This government-sanctioned oppression tended to encourage Arabs within Sudan to treat black Africans with disdain. Clearly, many of Sudan's Arabs believed that their cultural and societal norms were superior to those of the black Sudanese population. In February 2003, several non-Arab rebel groups rose up in revolt against the Sudanese government. This triggered a brutal war of reprisal on the part of the Sudanese government, the Janjaweed (an Arab militia force), and other allied groups that soon became a campaign of genocide against the Darfuri people.

Aryan Term taken from Sanskrit that initially referred to a nobleman, or gentleman, in portions of India. By the 1920s, German Nazis, including Adolf Hitler, began to employ the term when referring to the "master race," the allegedly pure Germanic/Nordic race of people who were supposed to be racially, physically, and intellectually above "lesser" peoples. This was part of the Nazis' larger and deeply flawed theories involving "racial hygiene" and race. The Aryan ideal was a Nordic type—tall, with blond hair and blue eyes. Ironically, many Nazi leaders, including Hitler, did not fit this set of physical characteristics.

Beneath the "master race" were various Indo-European-speaking peoples, who were deemed "partly Aryan" because they had mixed or intermarried with "inferior" races. Jews, along with blacks, Roma (Gypsies), Indians, and other peoples from the subcontinent and Asia, were not considered Aryans and were thus undesirables. The concept of the Aryan race helped drive and rationalize the Holocaust against Jews and other minorities.

Asocials *Asocials* was the general Nazi term for those persons declared outside the community of the *Volk*, the latter of which was used to indicate a highly mystical understanding of membership. Asocials included criminals, prostitutes, drug addicts, juvenile delinquents, homosexuals, vagrants, and the Roma peoples. The Nazi orientation toward such persons was that their behaviors were genetically and racially determined and, therefore, beyond correction. Once inside the concentration and death camps, asocials were forced to wear black triangles on their clothing, whereas pink triangles designated homosexuals and brown triangles designated Romas.

Assimilation Assimilation is the process whereby members of an ethnic group replace their cultural practices with those of the dominant culture in a society. When this conversion is imposed upon an entire group of people by the state, it is often referred to as "cultural genocide" because while members of the group being assimilated might not be systematically killed, their culture is often effectively destroyed. Assimilation policies are often a common precursor of genocide because they can be used by the perpetrators in the initial stages as a way to delegitimize or dehumanize the victims by portraying them as "nonhumans" from a "backward" culture in need of reintegration into society. This can also be used later on during the genocide as a way for the perpetrators to "justify" the use of increased brutality against their victims if assimilation is seen as an ineffective method for achieving their goals.

Atrocities The term "atrocities" refers to appalling acts that are extremely brutal or cruel in nature. Within the context of genocide, "atrocities" refer to acts of extreme violence or cruelty typically carried out against civilians, though atrocities can also be committed against military forces on either side. Examples of atrocities that tend to occur during genocide include murder, massacres, torture, rape, starvation, extreme deprivation, forced marches, enslavement, brutal violence, and systematic extermination.

Awlad Al-Beled This Arabic term literally means "children of the country." A self-given sobriquet of the riverine Arabs living in Sudan, it denotes that they are "the true Sudanese" within Sudan. It is a term, then, that separates them from, for example, the black Africans of Darfur, who are not considered to be "true Sudanese" by the riverine Arabs.

BAKIN BAKIN, an Indonesian acronym for the State Intelligence Coordination Body (*Badan Koordinasi Intelijen Negara*), was established by Suharto's presidential decree on May 27, 1967. It stood at the pinnacle of the Indonesian intelligence community and was a vital pillar of Suharto's power along with the Operations Command for the Restoration of Security and Order (KOPKAMTIB) and the covert intelligence organization Special Operations (OPSUS). It targeted domestic opposition groups and also conducted various overseas intelligence operations. BAKIN was not part of any government department but reported directly to the president. It received funds officially through the state secretariat and unofficially through offline funding. Its duties included the coordination of Indonesian intelligence activities in respect of the reopening of China's embassy in Jakarta, the supervision of army, navy, and air force attachés who collected intelligence overseas, and the conduct of intelligence liaison with foreign states. It also screened government employees who required security clearances and organized physical security arrangements for Indonesian dignitaries traveling abroad.

Black Africans Black Africans is a term used to describe non-Arab people living in the Darfur region of Sudan. It has taken on a pejorative meaning in Sudan because the Arab-dominated Sudanese government, along with the Janjaweed (an Arab militia force), view themselves as culturally, socially, and religiously superior to black Africans. In 2003, several non-Arab rebel groups rose up in revolt against the Sudanese government. This triggered a brutal war of reprisal on the part of the Sudanese government, the Janjaweed, and other allied groups that soon became a campaign of genocide against the Darfuri people.

Blue Scarf The Khmer Rouge leadership of Communist Kampuchea (1975–1979) reportedly issued a blue scarf to each cadre member from the country's Eastern Zone who they forcibly relocated to the northwest province of Pursat. The blue scarf marked them—and ostracized them—as "impure Khmers" who were destined to be murdered.

Bystander   A bystander is an individual, group, or even an entire country that is present at or aware of a potentially genocidal event, but chooses not to get involved. During a genocide, bystanders are aware of atrocities being committed and yet, for a variety of reasons, decide to not intervene.

Chap teuv   *Chap teuv* is the Cambodian phrase for "taken away, never to be seen again." In the context of the Khmer Rouge–perpetrated genocide (1975–1979), it referred to those individuals who disappeared abruptly, were taken somewhere—for no apparent reason—by the Khmer Rouge, and were never to return. Such disappearances served the purpose of instilling chilling fear in people of not following the exact orders they were given by the Khmer Rouge /or doing something "wrong" or "incorrectly."

"Clearing the Bush"   "Clearing the Bush" is a euphemistic term for the mass killing of Tutsis at the order of the Hutu-dominated government in Rwanda. It is believed that the term was first employed in late 1963. During December of that year, a few hundred well-armed Tutsi guerillas infiltrated southern Rwanda from neighboring Burundi. They managed to advance within 12 miles from the capital city of Kigali, but were turned back by Rwandan army forces. To prevent further such incidents, and to punish Tutsis living in Rwanda, the Rwandan government issued an order to "clear the bush," meaning that government-backed forces would eliminate subversive and opposition elements in the country. It is estimated that by the end of December, some 14,000 Tutsis had been killed in the southern province of Gikongoro. This set the stage for further violence, which culminated in the 1994 Rwanda Genocide.

Concentration Camp   A concentration camp is a secure compound run by the state where people, usually ethnic or religious minorities, political prisoners, or prisoners of war, are held and forced to endure brutal conditions. Most concentration camps serve as detention facilities, labor camps, or exterminations centers, though most usually function as a combination of all three. While concentration camps are usually associated with the Holocaust, they are a common feature of genocide because they provide a way to detain a large group of victims who can then be used as labor or be easily disposed of in large numbers.

Crimes against Humanity   A crime against humanity is an instance when an atrocity is committed against civilians on a large scale during wartime. This can take the form of massacres, forced marches, deportations, mass starvation and deprivation, torture, and rape, among other things. Prior to the coining of the term "genocide" by Raphael Lemkin in 1944, the kinds of acts now considered to be genocide fell under the category of crimes against humanity. However, Lemkin and others felt that crimes against humanity did not sufficiently account for atrocities carried out with the intention of destroying entire ethnic groups as well as the fact that such events could occur during peacetime. Thus, while crimes against humanity do occur during genocide, the two terms are not equivalent.

Death Squads   A "death squad" is a team of assassins contracted to carry out politically motivated killings and forcible disappearances. Although civilians can use death squads, they are most often associated with government efforts to eliminate political opponents, and they are usually comprised of active or former members of government security forces (elite army or police squadrons specially trained in terror tactics). Hiding such violence behind the term "death squads" allows the government to deny its own involvement in the repression. During Guatemala's armed conflict, most of the death squads were controlled by military intelligence, although they had names like "Secret Anti-Communist Army" and "Jaguars for Justice." The Guatemalan Army kept careful records of its death squad activity, and some of these records have recently come to light, including one internal military log that documents the fate of 183 disappeared people, and which human rights groups have dubbed the "Death Squad Dossier."

Democratic Kampuchea   Immediately upon its takeover of Cambodia in 1975, the revolutionary Communist Khmer Rouge renamed the country Democratic Kampuchea. The use of the word "democratic" was both ironic and cynical, as there was nothing democratic about the ironclad, totalitarian state that eventually became infamous for its genocidal policies and "killing fields."

Displacement   Displacement is when an individual or group is forced to leave their home and move to another location. In the context of genocide, displacement generally occurs when members of an ethnic group are forced by the state to leave their homes or the land that their people have traditionally occupied and move to another location. Though displacement can also occur when the violence reaches areas where members of the group being persecuted live, leaving them no choice but to flee. In most cases, victims are forced to move to a state-designated location, often enduring long, brutal marches along the way. Policies of displacement are used during genocide in order to free up land that can be settled by members of the same ethnic group as the perpetrators as well as to make it easier to carry out their policies of extermination. Displacement is especially common in cultural genocide since when a group is forced to leave their traditional homeland, much of their culture and traditions are left there to fade into the past.

Dohuk Fort Dohuk Fort is located in the north of contemporary Kurdish-controlled Iraq. The fort itself, an enormous concrete structure modeled after a 1970s Soviet-style fortification that included a prison facility, was intended to intimidate the local population as much as send a warning to hostile neighbors. On its roof, Saddam Hussein's regime installed antiaircraft batteries to increase his army's ability to defend itself against potential air assaults. The Baathist regime used the fort as a holding compound and transit station for thousands of Kurds eventually murdered by Hussein's forces during the waves of the al-Anfal genocide campaign. As in other detention sites such as Topzawa, men, women, children, and the elderly were segregated and then brutally interrogated. Physical and emotional torture was systematically applied, food and water withheld, and nearly all men who arrived in Dohuk Fort disappeared and were later found dead in ditches and shallow graves. Many had been shot dead in mass executions.

Eastern Zone An area in Kampuchea (Cambodia) where Communist dictator Pol Pot looked askance at the relative autonomy of the people residing there and sent in Khmer Rouge troops in May 1978 to "purify" the zone. The "purification" resulted in massacres of the Khmer Rouge's own cadre members, a much more brutal work schedule for those who were allowed to live and remain in the area, and the deportation of tens of thousands to provinces in the northwest.

Eliticide The systematic killing of political and religious leaders, intellectuals, professionals, and other individuals of stature in a particular group or locale. The term is a mixture of French (*élite*, meaning the "chosen" or "select") and Latin (*caedere*, meaning to "cut" or "kill"). Eliticide often commences at the beginning of a genocide. It is intended to neutralize individuals who are most likely to attempt resistance and to instill confusion, panic, and a sense of loss among the group being targeted. Eliticide was employed before and during the Armenian Genocide (1915–1923), the Cambodian Genocide (1975–1979), and most recently during the ethnic cleansing in the former Yugoslavia in the 1990s. As Serbs targeted Muslims for ethnic cleansing, Serbian troops would locate local Serbs who would single out

the educated and elite Muslims in a given village or town. They would then be rounded up and shot.

Famine A famine is when food becomes extremely scarce which usually results in widespread hunger and sometimes death. While famines tend to occur during genocide, this is not always intentional as famines can be caused by drought or other unfavorable weather conditions as well as poor farming practices. However, famines are sometimes intentionally induced during genocide in order to weaken and torture victims, pacify resistance, or exterminate entire populations through starvation.

Gacaca Law Gacaca Law is a traditional, indigenous justice system instituted in March 2001 in Rwanda to deal with the many thousands of Rwandans accused of having participated in the 1994 Rwandan Genocide. By that time, it is estimated that as many as 120,000 Rwandans suspected of genocidal crimes were incarcerated in prisons and jails awaiting trial. The slowness of the Rwandan justice system meant that it would require nearly 100 years to try all of the suspects. Thus, the Rwandan government decided to establish Gacaca Law, which is based on communal law that had its antecedents in the precolonial era. In addition to giving the Rwandan people themselves more involvement in prosecuting crimes related to the genocide, the system promotes national healing and forgiveness. The establishment of the Gacaca Law has helped reduce the backlog of genocide-related criminal cases.

Gacacas are organized at the village or communal level and may try any genocide suspect except for those who are accused of having planned or supervised the mass killings or those accused of rape. Those individuals are tried in regular Rwandan courts or in the International Criminal Tribunal for Rwanda. Most of the suspects are tried in the same locale in which their alleged crimes were committed. All villagers and victims are given the opportunity to speak or testify at the proceedings. The judges, along with other court personnel, number about 250,000 nationwide, and they have all received at least some training in criminal and court-room procedures. The first cases were not adjudicated until March 2005. Since then, about 20 percent of the defendants have been acquitted. The rest were either found guilty or were released because of lack of evidence or some other procedural error. The Gacaca legal system also permits defendants to confess to their crimes and ask for sincere forgiveness. Those who do so are given more lenient sentences, sometimes as much as half of the prescribed penalty.

Genocide Genocide is the "deliberate and systematic destruction, in whole or in part, of an ethnic, racial, religious, or national group" as defined by the 1948 United Nations Convention on the Prevention and Punishment of the Crime of Genocide. Critics of the term differ on what exactly constitutes "part" of a group, making this a contentious definition.

Hollerith Machine Electric machine that employed punch cards to tabulate and compile statistics and other information. Pioneered by the U.S.-based International Business Machines (IBM) Company, the Hollerith machine was named for the German Hollerith Machine Company, which manufactured the machines in Germany during 1922–1945. The punch cards that were fed into the machines were made of stiff paper that had hundreds of small holes in each one; the number and position of the holes were read by the machine and represented specific digital information. The cards themselves were made by IBM and were sold to the Hollerith Company. It is estimated that IBM supplied as many as 1 billion punch cards per year to the Germans. The machines, which were precursors to modern computers, were used to tabulate German census figures and a wide variety of other government statistics. Some were used to track Jews and others. The Hollerith machine thus played an important role in Nazi racial policies and the Holocaust.

Inyenzi *Inyenzi* is a Kinyarwanda (Rwandan) word that translates as "cockroaches." In the early 1960s, after the Hutus overthrew the Tutsi monarchy and established Hutu-dominated rule in Rwanda, exiled Tutsis who called themselves *inyenzi* because of their stealth and resilience launched many raids into Rwanda. Beginning in 1990, with the full flowering of the Hutu Power Movement and the advent of the Rwandan Civil War, Hutus began referring to all Tutsis residing in Rwanda as *inyenzi*. This was a demeaning and derogatory term that was intended to dehumanize and humiliate Tutsis. Pro-Hutu propaganda radio, television, and newspapers employed the term frequently, and when the Rwandan Genocide began in 1994, many Hutus called for the extermination of the Tutsis, just as one would exterminate cockroaches.

Jash The Jash forces, officially known as the *Fursan Salah al-Din* (Knights of Saladin), were Kurdish tribal militias that collaborated with the Iraqi regime. They frequently engaged in fierce skirmishes with tribal competitors or nationalists allied with Mullah Mustafa (Mustafa al-Barzani). The term Jash itself is intended to be derogatory and translates as "small donkey." It referred to a Kurdish collaborator who accepted payments from the central government in exchange for targeting rival Kurdish units.

By the mid-1980s, estimates suggested that more than 150,000 Kurdish men had signed up to serve in the Fursan units, mostly to avoid military service in the deadly Iran-Iraq War. Often, Fursan militias consisted of poorly trained and underequipped units that served the Iraqi regime by managing basic security duties. They checked transit papers at road blocks and kept an eye on local villages. Members of the Kurdistan Democratic Party and the Patriotic Union of Kurdistan accused each other as serving as Jash forces under Saddam Hussein at different times.

Machete Genocide General term used to describe the 1994 Rwandan Genocide. It was known as the Machete Genocide because a great number of the Tutsis who were murdered by the Hutus died from blows and cuts from machetes. A machete is a large knife shaped like a cleaver (12 to 21 inches in length) that is typically used to cut through undergrowth or harvest certain crops, especially sugarcane. The Hutus used the machete as a symbol of their power; in 1992, a pro-Hutu newspaper ran a photo of a machete with the message: "What Shall We Do to Complete the Social Revolution of 1959?"

Mandi Laut Indonesian; literally "gone for a swim." A euphemism used by Indonesian soldiers to refer to those East Timorese who "disappeared" (mid-1970s into the 1980s). More specifically, the term referred to those people who had been taken prisoner and were flown by helicopter out to sea and then dumped with weights bound to their legs and feet to die a watery death.

Massacre A massacre is when a large number of people, typically unarmed or unresisting, are brutally killed. Massacres are a common occurrence during genocide since they are one of the most effective ways for the perpetrators to carry out their goal of annihilating an entire or a large part of an ethnic population. Massacres can also fall under the category of crimes against humanity if the intent of the perpetrator is not the destruction of an ethnic group.

Mischlinge German, literally "hybrid" but understood in the Nazi context to mean something like "mongrel," "half-breed," or "mixed breed."

Once the Nazis were in power, the Nazi agenda during the Third Reich would, ultimately, evolve to the extermination of the Jews. The initial step was that of definition, and the infamous Nuremberg Laws of 1935 was the legal attempt to clarify who was, in fact, a Jew, who was not (a so-called Aryan), and who fell in-between, in line with the Nazi obsession with "racial purity." Thus, persons with four Jewish grandparents were "full Jews." Persons with three Jewish grandparents were "three-quarter Jews." Persons with two Jewish grandparents were considered Mischlinge of the First Degree, provided they were not identified with the Jewish religion and not married to Jewish spouses; and persons with only one Jewish grandparent were Mischlinge of the Second Degree. In 1935, such persons in the latter two categories were said to number anywhere between 100,000 and 350,000. Mischlinge were not permitted to join the SS, nor were they permitted to advance in the officer ranks of the Wehrmacht (Germany's military). For the most part, Mischlinge of the First Degree were classified as Jews; those of the Second Degree were absorbed into German society, albeit with restrictions and discriminations.

Mogadishu Line   The Mogadishu Line was a metaphoric term coined by General Sir Michael Rose, commander of the United Nations Protection Force for Bosnia, to describe the situation whereby UN peacekeepers become directly involved in a local conflict, as was the case in Somalia in the early 1990s, between government military and rebel forces. Violation of this "line" is thus at the heart of the United Nations' perception of its own military role as "observers," "neutrals," or "peacekeepers," whose task is to intervene only in cases of uprising, armed conflict, or genocide. The most tragic expression, however, of its own failure to "cross this line" is the case of Rwanda in the early 1990s where Lieutenant General Roméo Dallaire's, commander of the United Nations Assistance Mission for Rwanda (UNAMIR), request submitted to UN Headquarters for an additional 5,000 troops to prevent what he truly believed would become a genocide was denied for internal political and bureaucratic reasons. Ultimately, between 500,000 and 1 million Tutsis and moderate Hutus were slain in 100 days between April and July 1994.

Mustard Gas   Mustard gas is a chemical warfare agent first used by the German Army during the Battle of Passchendaele in 1917 and employed by both sides of World War I thereafter. The gas is a colorless, oily compound of carbon, hydrogen, sulfur, and chlorine, and was dispersed by spraying from tanks and aircraft or loaded into the payload of artillery and bombs. Mustard gas destroys the mucous membrane of the bronchial tubes, causes blistering of the skin and lungs, and temporary blindness. The Geneva Protocol formally outlawed the use of mustard gas in 1925, but it was most recently used by Iraq against Kurdish rebels in 1988. The improvement of gas mask defenses, the inability to control its direction after dispersing, the fear of its use in retaliation on unprepared civilians, and its general ineffectiveness in causing death ended the military viability of mustard gas prior to 1925.

Nationalism   Nationalism is a sense of loyalty or devotion to one's nation, especially above all other nations, groups, or one's own individual interests. Nationalist feelings can play an important role in initiating genocide as states will often use them as a rallying point in order to "justify" reeducation policies as well as the expulsion or elimination of an ethnic group that is seen as a threat to national cohesion within a state.

"Ordinary Men"   The phrase "ordinary men" is taken from the title of Christopher Browning's 1992 book *Ordinary Men: Reserve Police Battalion 101 and the Final Solution in Poland* and refers specifically to the very ordinariness of the 500 middle-aged, lower- and lower-middle class family men from Hamburg, Germany, drafted into Reserve Police Battalion 101 (the so-called Order Police) and who were active in murdering the 1,800 Jews of Josefow, Poland, and the surrounding area in July 1942 and beyond. Estimates of their overall involvement in such death-related activities run as high as 38,000, with commensurate transportation responsibilities in the hundreds of thousands. Why did the majority of these nonmilitary combatants engage in this genocidal behavior when others in their unit, perhaps 10 to 20 percent, did not (and did not suffer punishments because of their refusal) remains, even today, deeply troubling and deeply disturbing. Although Browning presents a variety of hypotheses regarding the motivation behind their behavior—wartime brutalization, racism, segmentation and routinization of task, special selection of perpetrators, careerism, obedience to authority and orders, deference to that same authority, ideological indoctrination, conformity, quasi-military status, and a sense of elitism (perhaps for many for the first time)—he also asserts, reasonably, that no one explanation provides either the answer or the key insight. That the men themselves, after being interviewed (more than 400 interviews were conducted), could not themselves explain their own behavior remains equally troubling and reveals quite starkly how little we continue to understand about the psychological totality and capacity of the human person to engage in horrific behaviors and to rationalize such activity.

Peace Patrols In November 1905, the incoming governor Friedrich von Lindequist introduced a new strategy to deal with the threat posed to the German settler by Herero communities still hiding out in the expansive bushlands of central Namibia. He tasked the Rhenish and Catholic missions with the pacification and collection of the Herero. Groups of Herero prisoners, who were considered to be loyal to the mission, did the actual work. There were typically 10 men to a group. They were issued guns and enough food to last them for a few weeks. Their most potent weapon, however, was a letter from the governor offering peace and food if the Herero communities were to surrender and report themselves at the strategically placed collection points, placed at former mission stations. Because they were ostensibly doing the work of peace, the missionaries dubbed the groups of loyal Hereros working for the mission, the Peace Patrols. From the missionary collection points more than 12,000 Herero people who surrendered to the Peace Patrols were eventually ushered into concentration camps.

Porrajmos *Porrajmos* is the Romani term for the experience of the Sinti, Roma, and Lalleri (colloquial terms for "Gypsies") people under the Nazis. The Roma and Sinti were targeted for extermination by the Nazis and perished in the tens of thousands as a result of mass murder and horrific treatment in concentration camps and death camps. A quarter of a million Gypsies were killed, and proportionately they suffered losses greater than any other group of victims except the Jews.

Racial Hygiene Designation introduced and developed in 1894 by German physician Alfred Ploetz (1860–1940) and adopted by many others in the early part of the 20th century. Racial hygiene was a concept that had at its base the notion of eugenics, the branch of science dealing with the production of genetically superior human beings through improvements in their inherited qualities. Some translated this into proposals calling for the compulsory sterilization of physically and psychologically "inferior" humans; others called for additional measures designed to control the breeding of those with criminal tendencies, with incurable diseases (or even those that were curable but perceived as an aberration, such as venereal disease), or with social abnormalities such as chronic alcoholism or mental illness. The fear of degeneration of the German "race" should such "maladies" go unchecked became a crucial element of Nazi ideology, and was attractive to the racial thinking that dominated the National Socialist worldview, to such a degree that sterilization and, later, compulsory euthanasia became state policy for the purpose of ensuring the health and virility of the German people in the future.

Rassenkampf *Rassenkampf* (German for "racial fight" or "racial struggle") is the Nazi conception that all human life constituted an ongoing confrontation for supremacy between competing races of people. In the Nazi understanding, this struggle was both typified by and expressed at its most extreme by a conflict between the "Aryan race" and the Jewish "race"—a conflict forced, the Nazis asserted continually, by the Jews for the purpose of subverting what the Nazis considered to be a perfect world order in which the Aryans should (by virtue of their superiority) rightly predominate. According to Nazi beliefs, the *rassenkampf* was relentless and had to be fought until the death of one of the two parties. Resolution of the struggle, in the Nazi worldview, would see either an ideal future for the world under the unchallenged rule of the Aryans or a hopeless future dominated by the forces of darkness unleashed by the so-called satanic Jew. For the Nazis, the race struggle, of necessity, had to be genocidal in scope; neither compromise nor mercy would ever be possible if the required victory was to be achieved.

Rassenschande *Rassenschande* (German for "race shame" or "racial defilement") referred to any act of a sexual nature between a Jew and a non-Jew (in the Nazi conception, an "Aryan"), even those who were intermarried. Under the Nuremberg Laws of 1935, various relationships between Jews and non-Jews were proscribed, and sexual relations were banned. It was the Nazis' understanding of such that it would pollute, and thereby weaken, the "purity" of the Aryan race, especially if children resulted from the sexual liaison. This ruling also applied to sexual contact between German Aryans and Slavs. By February 1944, such sexual contact was made a capital offense.

Rasseverrat The term *rasseverrat* (German for "racial treason") was used earlier than *rassenschande* by the Nazis, but with the same meaning: the perceived illicit sexual relationship between Jews and German "Aryans." Such "bedroom legislation" on the part of the Nazis, as reflected in the Nuremberg Laws of September 1935, is a clear indicator of how seriously the Nazis perceived the racial construct of "the Jews" as the enemy of the Third Reich.

Refoulement *Refoulement* (French for "forcing back") was a policy that refers to the return of a person to a country or territory that he or she has left due to the fear of being harmed in some grievous manner and where he or she may be at risk of being persecuted upon return. *Refoulement* is a violation of the principle of non-refoulement and thus constitutes an infraction or breach of customary international law and refugee law.

Righteous among the Nations　The term used to designate those non-Jews who risked their lives, and at times the lives of their families, to save Jews during the Holocaust. The term is taken from the *Talmud:* "The righteous of all nations have a share in the world to come." Since the early 1960s, Yad Vashem, Israel's Holocaust Memorial Authority in Jerusalem, has honored such persons by the planting of a tree with a plaque, the casting of a medal, and the presentation of a certificate. The criteria by which such persons can be so honored are based on the following: (1) actual incident of rescue, (2) carried out at personal risk, and (3) no gain or benefit, financial or other, received. As of 2014, more than 25,000 such individuals have been so honored.

Rubanda Nyanwinshi　*Rubanda Nyanwinshi* is a Kinyarwanda phrase, which came to be understood colloquially in pregenocide Rwanda as a political philosophy of sorts that meant "the Hutu majority." Following the so-called social revolution of 1959 (in which the Hutu majority revolted against, overthrew the Tutsi monarchy and carried out massacres of Tutsis, precipitating a mass exodus of Tutsis into exile), adherence to this "philosophy" resulted in a situation that circumvented the fundamental tenets of democracy. That is, from that point forward, Tutsis were treated as second-class citizens by the government, schools, and fellow citizens who were Hutus.

Sarin Nerve Gas　Sarin nerve gas is classified as extremely toxic. Once exposed to Sarin, a victim develops difficulty breathing, and suffers nausea and vomiting. The person then loses control over all bodily functions and frequently experiences uncontrollable shaking and twitching before suffocating in convulsive spasms. Soil samples obtained by international human rights organizations and records revealed during Saddam Hussein's trial indicated that planes and helicopters of the Iraqi military dropped a combination of nerve gas agents such as Sarin, Tabun, VX, and mustard gas on unsuspecting communities in Iraq (and Iran). During the 1988 al-Anfal campaigns, the Kurdish area of Halabja was targeted for several days with chemical cluster bombs, causing 5,000 Kurdish civilians to be severely injured and about 7,000 to perish in agony. Several U.S., European, and Asian companies provided the Baathist regime with both the technical know-how and materials to produce these chemical weapons. Survivors of the gas attacks as well as their offspring suffer from increased rates of cancers and other serious illnesses today.

Schreibtischtater　The term *schreibtischtater* (in German; colloquially "desk murderer") has been used by some historians and commentators in recent times to refer to those bureaucrats, primarily in the Berlin offices of the SS, who maintained the paper flow of documents with regard to the Nazis' mass murder of European Jewry. Such documents would have information related to personnel and resource allocations, contracts, transportation schedules, and so on. Such persons, however, were never instrumentally involved in the actual execution or extermination process themselves, never experienced the events, and, more often than not, never even visited the sites of the various killing centers.

Shoah　*Shoah* is a Hebrew word used to describe the mass murder of several million Jews by the Nazis and their allies during the 1930s and 1940s. It is a synonym for the Holocaust. *Shoah* may be translated as "devastation," "destruction," or "catastrophe." In recent years, an increasing number of scholars, Holocaust researchers, and Jews themselves have begun to eschew the use of the term Holocaust, and have been substituting it with the word *Shoah*. One of the problems with the term "Holocaust" is that it was a label given to the genocide of the Jews largely by non-Jews. The other problem with the term is that it is derived from the Old Testament (the Torah) concept of offering a complete and consumable burnt offering to God for the expiation of sins. The Holocaust was certainly not an offering to God, so scholars and others sought a better descriptor for the genocide of the Jews. The word *Shoah* can be found in the Book of Isaiah (10:3), and in that context refers to the day of reckoning that will precede the final judgment of the Israelites. Although *Shoah* is perhaps closer than the word Holocaust in describing the Nazi-inspired genocide of European Jews, it too does not fully describe the events of the 1930s and 1940s, which were not set into motion by God, but rather by evil-minded human beings. The term *Shoah* was first used in print in 1940, and it was popularized in 1985, when French filmmaker Claude Lanzmann released a 10-hour documentary film by the same name that examined the events of the Holocaust and its aftereffects through a series of interviews with witnesses and survivors.

Sjambok　The *sjambok* was a heavy whip traditionally made of hippopotamus (or occasionally rhinoceros or giraffe) hide, though modern versions are typically of plastic. The word is also a verb for beating someone or something with a sjambok. The sjambok is not plaited from multiple thongs but consists of a single, tapering leather strip rolled lengthwise into the form of a stout but flexible rod, approximately three to five feet in length and attached to a handle. It is not cracked like a bullwhip but is swung like a stick to strike its target and therefore requires little expertise to use. The sjambok has many uses, particularly driving cattle and killing snakes, but it has been used most notoriously by whites in southern Africa to coerce obedience and labor from blacks and to mete out punishment.

Sniper Alley   Sniper Alley is the nickname given to a stretch of road in Sarajevo, the capital city of Bosnia-Herzegovina, during the Bosnian War of 1992–1995. In reality, it is one long arterial road that officially undergoes a name change as it gets closer to the city, from Bulevar Mese Selimovica to Zmaj od Bosne, just prior to entering the central business district where once more it changes to the Oblala Kulina Bana. "Sniper Alley" is thus the major approach road from Sarajevo's western industrial suburbs to the city center. During the Siege of Sarajevo, long sections of the road were an easy target for Bosnian Serb snipers in the hills surrounding the city, which resulted in hundreds being killed as they attempted to traverse the vulnerable sections of the road/city. As one of the primary "no-go" areas leading to downtown, Sniper Alley was a road on which drivers were strongly discouraged to travel. If a journey absolutely had to be made, drivers were encouraged to speed, dodge, weave, and do anything else they could do to avoid being hit by gunfire. It was most certainly not a place for pedestrians, even though many found no alternative but to use the thoroughfare in going about their daily business. Sniper Alley became symbolic of the Siege of Sarajevo, littered with burnt-out and shot-out wrecks of motor vehicles and with makeshift barriers of all kinds from which pedestrians would run from one to another seeking cover. There are proposals that Sniper Alley will at some time in the future undergo a beautification process that will restore its dignity as a major thoroughfare while paying respect to all those who lost their lives along its precincts during the siege.

Somalia Factor   On October 3, 1993, while engaged in an attempt to track down members of Mohammed Farah Aidieed's militia who had killed 24 Pakistani UN peacekeepers who were deployed in Somalia in an attempt to keep the peace, U.S. Army Rangers and Delta special forces were ambushed by the militia. Eighteen U.S. soldiers were killed, 73 were wounded, and the pilot of a Black Hawk helicopter was kidnapped. Newscasts around the world showed the members of the militia dragging the naked, dead body of a U.S. Ranger through the streets of Mogadishu. Both the attack and the brutal aftermath caused such great consternation among U.S. citizens and politicians that it impacted future U.S. foreign policy decisions. More specifically, U.S. foreign policymakers became extremely tentative about deploying any U.S. troops in violent conflicts far from home in which the United States ostensibly had little to no real "interests." Ultimately, due in large part to this "Somalia factor," U.S. president Bill Clinton and his administration consciously decided not to attempt to prevent, let alone attempt to halt, the 1994 Rwandan genocide that took the lives of between 500,000 and 1 million Tutsis and moderate Hutus in 100 days during April, May, June, and July 1994.

Tetum   Tetum, an Austronesian language that is indigenous to East Timor, has two major variants: Tetum-Prasa (market Tetum), also known as Tetum-Dili (after the capital, Dili); and Tetum-Terik, which is also understood in Indonesian West Timor. Indonesia banned the use of Portuguese in liturgical services a few years after the invasion. However, instead of using Indonesian in church services, the local Catholic Church replaced Portuguese with Tetum, which became more widely used. Since independence, Tetum has been designated as East Timor's national language. Liturgical Tetum is widely understood today but more informal versions are used in everyday conversations in much of the territory.

Timor Gap   The Timor Gap is the seabed area between Australia and East Timor. The "gap" refers to the seabed area not covered by the 1972 Seabed Agreement between Australia and Indonesia, which delineated their maritime boundary based on a natural prolongation of the continental shelf. This had set the boundary much closer to Indonesia than to Australia, giving Australia the lion's share of any resources. Portugal had not been a party to these negotiations. It preferred to wait, knowing that the negotiating texts of the United Nations Third Conference on the Law of the Sea were moving away from the continental shelf principle. The maritime boundary was therefore incomplete, resulting in what was known as the Timor Gap. In December 1989, Australia and Indonesia signed the Timor Gap Treaty in order to exploit East Timor's energy resources. The treaty provided a framework for petroleum and gas exploration in the maritime zone between Australia and East Timor and for the division of any resulting royalties between Australia and Indonesia. When Indonesia withdrew from East Timor in October 1999, the transitional administration in East Timor renegotiated the terms of the treaty with Australia.

Topzawa The army base of Topzawa became a detention facility during the al-Anfal Campaign of the late 1980s near the city of Kirkuk, Iraq. Upon arrival by truck from their remote villages, hungry, dehydrated, and injured prisoners were forced to assemble in the sprawling parade area of the base. Adult males and boys who stood accused of treason for having cooperated with Kurdish fighters faced particularly brutal treatment. Separated from other prisoners, they were forced into overcrowded and filthy cells. Most men received little water and food, and experienced vicious torture before their executions. Women and children also endured hideous conditions. They only occasionally received food and security guards randomly separated children from their mothers. The bodies of these infants and small children ended up in a pit outside the base. Iraqi soldiers frequently forced women to witness the daily torture of their male relatives, many of whom did not survive. On average, Iraqi forces held between 4,000 and 5,000 people at Topzawa during the height of the Kurdish Genocide.

Urbicide Term used to describe the deliberate destruction of a city or urban environment, particularly during a war. Urbicide is derived from Latin (*urbs* [city] and *caedere* [cut or kill]). The term was first employed in the 1960s by critics of urban renewal and restructuring in the United States. Certainly the deliberate bombing of European and Japanese cities during World War II can be categorized as urbicide, but the word took on a somewhat different meaning during the war in Bosnia during the 1990s.

Vernichtung The German term *vernichtung* (extermination) was used in various ways to describe Nazi actions, primarily against Jews: *vernichtung durch arbeit* (destruction through work), *vernichtungsanstalt* (extermination facility), *vernichtungskommando* (extermination or death squads), and *vernichtungslager* (death camp).

Vernichtungslager *Vernichtungslager* was the German term for the death camps, primarily in occupied Poland, wherein the majority of Europe's Jews (and others such as the Roma) were murdered by the Nazis and their collaborators during World War II via gassings (the use of the insecticide Zyklon-B), beatings, torture, starvation, and other forms of brutalization, all as part of the "Final Solution to the Jewish Problem." The main centers of death were Auschwitz-Birkenau (where 1.5 million Jews were murdered), Belzec (600,000 Jews), Chelmno (320,000 Jews), Majdanek (360,000 Jews), Sobibor (250,000 Jews), and Treblinka (870,000 Jews). Overall, it is estimated that more than 3.5 million Jews were murdered in these locations, many upon their immediate arrival, others only after nearly (and in many cases, literally) being worked to death, and still others as the result of diseases such as typhus and dysentery.

Volk The concept of *Volk* (German for "the people") constitutes the almost mystical understanding of the Nazis (and others) of the ties that bound the German people as a separate and distinct entity from others, best expressed by the German expression *Blut und Boden* (blood and soil), but equally reflecting a sense of both racial purity (Aryanization) and a uniquely distinctive Germanic culture. The term *Volk*, itself, first surfaced in the 19th century among German romantics as a self-description of the nation-state as an organic living entity. Once adapted, it was able to provide an ideological foundation for the Nazi-inspired and Nazi-driven "Final Solution," and, thus, the elimination of those "undesirables" who could never be part of the German people.

War Crimes A war crime is a violation of the laws governing conduct during war, entailing individual criminal responsibility under international law. Both genocide and crimes against humanity fall under the category of war crimes as they include acts that are flagrant violations of international law, with the crime of genocide being the most severe.

White Arm Bands In Bosnia in the mid-1990s, Serb paramilitary forces forced Muslims to wear white arm bands in order to distinguish them from their neighbors. It was a method, much like the badges the Nazis forced the Jews to wear, of singling the Muslims out, as well as being a way of humiliating them. The practice varied from place to place and was employed at different times in different locations.

Wilde-KZ Abbreviation for the longer German term *Wilde-Konzentrationslager*, alluding to unauthorized places of incarceration established in Germany by local Nazis in the earliest stages of the Third Reich. These camps frequently operated without any apparent system or direction. There was little in the way of planning or procedure. Often, the very location of these places was impromptu. For example, Dachau was a former gunpowder factory, Oranienburg was originally a brewery (and later a foundry), and Borgermoor and Esterwegen were initially simply rows of barracks set down on open expanses of marshy heathland. Elsewhere, prisoners had to build their own habitations and begin their camp life living in tents. The *Wilde-KZ* were rapidly established, highly improvised affairs. Little regard was paid to administration, discipline, or utilization. Some were run by SS officers; many were staffed by SA men, often locals, who knew or were known by those they were guarding. The essential function of these camps was to gag political opposition to the new Nazi government of Germany (which was appointed to office on January 30, 1933), and generally to intimidate the wider population through the camps' reputation for arbitrary brutality. Only with a more coordinated approach to political incarceration, through the establishment of the Inspectorate of Concentration Camps in mid-1934 under Theodor Eicke, did the *Wilde-KZ* give way to a unified form of administration, discipline, and ethos. Most of the *Wilde-KZs* had closed down by the spring of 1934.

Year Zero In 1975, following the Khmer Rouge's overthrow of the Cambodian government, Pol Pot, the leader of the Khmer Rouge, declared that Kampuchea (the new name the Khmer Rouge gave Cambodia) marked the "Year Zero," signaling that more than 2,000 years of Cambodian history had come to an end. Wanting to create a totally new Cambodia (one that was agrarian, totally self-sufficient, and adhered to the dictates of the Communist Party of Kampuchea), Pol Pot and his cronies set out to totally destroy Cambodia's past by wiping out its cities; destroying all aspects of religious life (which included the mass murder of Buddhist monks); disassembling families; forcing all its people to work with their hands (mostly in the fields to raise food); and killing off those who were suspected of being intellectuals, educated, or tied in any way to the leadership of the fallen Cambodian regime. Eventually, the Khmer Rouge leadership began turning on its own members, carrying out vicious, large-scale, and deadly purges.

Zurug *Zurug* is a highly derogatory and offensive term used by Arabs in Sudan in reference to non-Arab, indigenous black individuals, particularly in the western region of Sudan. The word is derived from Arabic and translates very roughly as "dark." The term is an integral part of the concept of Arabism in Sudan. Arabism refers to the concept held by some Arabs that Arabic culture, religion, language, dress, and societal norms are superior to any others. Arabism has existed to one extent or another for centuries, but only a relatively small minority of Arabs subscribe to this way of thinking. Arabism developed mainly as a reaction to colonial subjugation of Arab populations, especially in the Middle East. More recently, Arabism has been a significant contributing factor to the ongoing Darfur Genocide in Darfur region of Sudan, which commenced in earnest in 2003.

Zyklon-B Zyklon-B was a pesticide used in the gas chambers of various Nazi concentration camps to kill Jews during the Holocaust. A commercial form of hydrocyanic acid, it was manufactured by the German firm Degesch for use as a disinfectant and pesticide. Zyklon-B was brought to Auschwitz for those purposes in 1941 but was soon being used to kill the prisoners of the camp. Zyklon-B was pumped into the gas chambers through vents in the ceiling and entered the body through the mouth, respiratory organs, or pores of the skin, and killed most of its victims immediately.

Index

Note: Page numbers followed by an *f* indicate figures.

About the Editors

Paul R. Bartrop, PhD, one of the world's leading scholars of the Holocaust and genocide, is professor of history and director of the Center for Judaic, Holocaust, and Genocide Studies at Florida Gulf Coast University, Fort Myers. He received his BA and MA from La Trobe University and his PhD from Monash University, both located in Melbourne, Australia. He was the 2011–2012 Ida E. King Distinguished Visiting Professor of Holocaust and Genocide Studies at Richard Stockton College, New Jersey. Prior to this appointment, he was head of the Department of History at Bialik College, Melbourne, Victoria, Australia, between 2003 and 2011, teaching a range of subjects in history, Jewish studies, international studies, and comparative genocide studies. He is a past president of the Australian Association of Jewish Studies, and is currently vice president of the Midwest Jewish Studies Association. Among his published works is *Fifty Key Thinkers on the Holocaust and Genocide* (2010), *The Genocide Studies Reader* (2009); *A Dictionary of Genocide* (2 vols.) (2008); *Teaching about the Holocaust: Essays by University and College Educators* (2004); *Surviving the Camps: Unity in Adversity during the Holocaust* (2000); *False Havens: The British Empire and the Holocaust* (1995); *Australia and the Holocaust, 1933–1945* (1994); and *A Biographical Encyclopedia of Contemporary Genocide: Portraits of Evil and Good* (ABC-CLIO, 2012).

Steven Leonard Jacobs, DHL, holds the Aaron Aronov Endowed Chair of Judaic Studies at the University of Alabama, Tuscaloosa, Alabama, where he is also an associate professor in the Department of Religious Studies. He received his BA from Penn State University, and his BHL, MAHL, DHL, and DD from the Hebrew Union College-Jewish Institute of Religion. Among his publications are *Lemkin on Genocide* (2013); *Confronting Genocide: Judaism, Christianity and Islam* (2011); *Fifty Key Thinkers on the Holocaust and Genocide* (2010); *Teaching about the Holocaust: Essays by University and College Educators* (2004); *In Search of Yesterday: The Holocaust and the Quest for Meaning* (2006); *Dismantling the Big Lie: The Protocols of the Elders of Zion* (2003); *Pioneers of Genocide Studies* (1999); *The Encyclopedia of Genocide* (1999); *Rethinking Jewish Faith: The Child of a Survivor Responds* (1994); and *Raphael Lemkin's Thoughts on Nazi Genocide: Not Guilty?* (1992). He is also a major contributor to the *Dictionary of Genocide* (2008), as well as associate editor of *The Journal for the Study of Antisemitism*.